452 #174

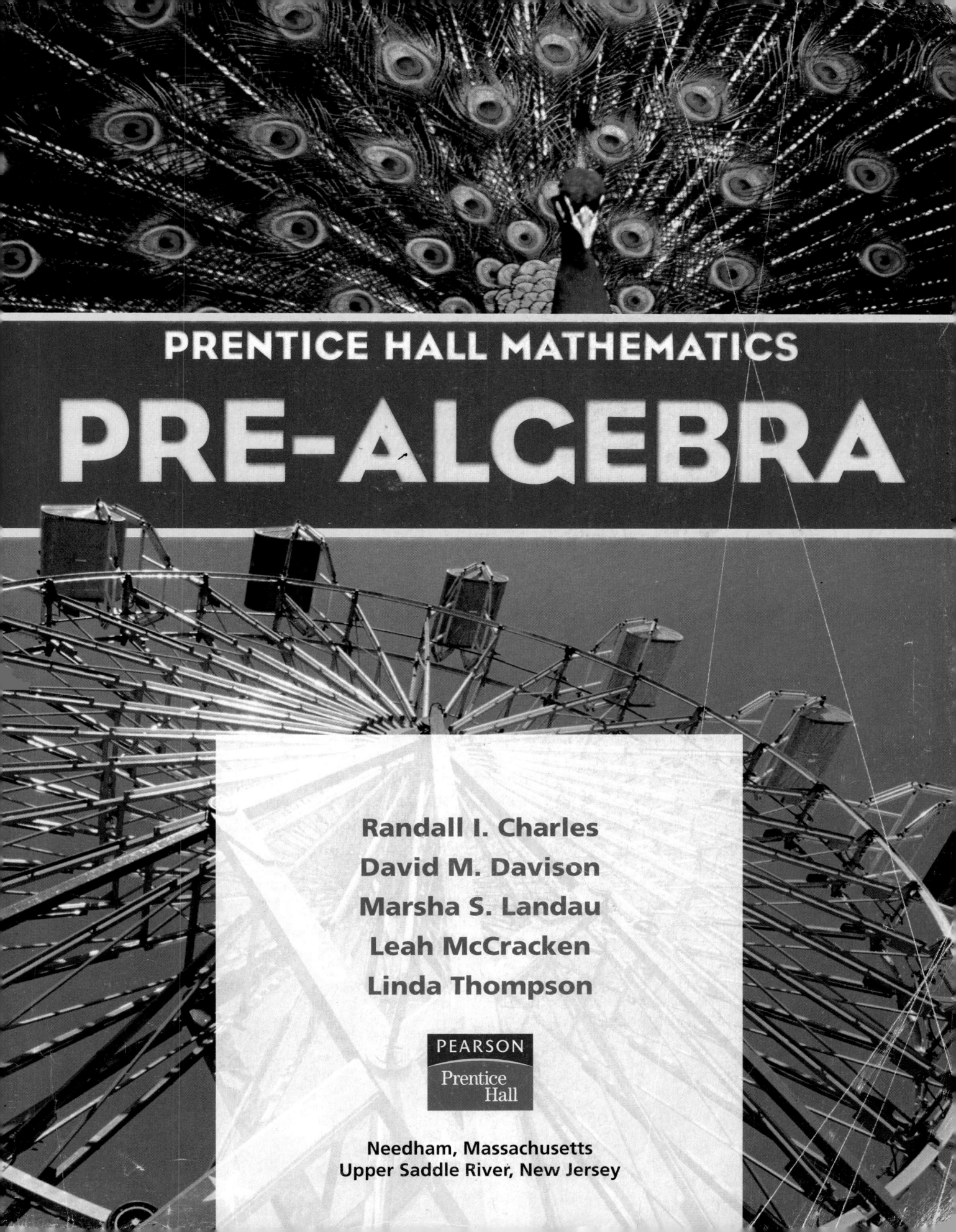

PRENTICE HALL MATHEMATICS

PRE-ALGEBRA

Randall I. Charles

David M. Davison

Marsha S. Landau

Leah McCracken

Linda Thompson

PEARSON

Prentice Hall

Needham, Massachusetts
Upper Saddle River, New Jersey

Authors

Randall I. Charles, Ph.D., is Professor Emeritus in the Department of Mathematics and Computer Science at San Jose State University, San Jose, California. He began his career as a high school mathematics teacher, and he was a mathematics supervisor for five years. Dr. Charles has been a member of several NCTM committees and is the former Vice President of the National Council of Supervisors of Mathematics. Much of his writing and research has been in the area of problem solving. He has authored more than 75 mathematics textbooks for kindergarten through college.

David M. Davison, Ph.D., is a Professor of Mathematics Education at Montana State University in Billings, Montana. One of Dr. Davison's areas of special focus is the integration of mathematics with other disciplines, especially science. He is also the author of a book and several articles on integrating mathematics and science and teaching mathematics to Native Americans.

Marsha Landau, Ph.D., is a mathematics education specialist from Evanston, Illinois. Dr. Landau works with teachers and students in grades K–9 to support mathematics learning, and is particularly active with individual students talented in mathematics.

Leah McCracken has more than 30 years experience in mathematics classrooms, Grade 5 through college. She currently works with students, teachers, and school leaders across the country, especially in the area of integrating technology into the curriculum. Ms. McCracken is a past recipient of the Montana Mathematics Teacher of the Year award as well as the Presidential Award for Excellence in Mathematics Teaching.

Linda Thompson is a mathematics consultant from Warrenton, Oregon. Ms. Thompson, who is listed in *Who's Who's in American Education*, is a contributing author of elementary and secondary mathematics textbooks, as well as numerous articles on mathematics education.

ISBN 0-13-068608-5

2 3 4 5 6 7 8 9 10   07 06 05 04 03

Reviewers

Chandler Cox
White Knoll Middle School
West Columbia, South Carolina

Fred Ferguson
Yough High School
Herminie, Pennsylvania

Nancy Hughes
Indian Hills Middle School
Shawnee Mission, Kansas

Dorothy (Dot) Johnson-Manning
Siwell Road Middle School
Jackson, Mississippi

Ellice P. Martin, Ed.D.
Lanier County Middle School
Lakeland, Georgia

Desireé Marcelin McNeal
Susan Miller Dorsey High School
Los Angeles, California

Consultants

Reading Consultant

Bonnie B. Armbruster, Ph.D.
Department of Curriculum and Instruction
University of Illinois at Champaign-Urbana
Champaign, Illinois

Content Consultants

Courtney Lewis
Mathematics
Prentice Hall Senior National Consultant
Baltimore, Maryland

Kimberly Margel
Mathematics
Prentice Hall National Consultant
Scottsdale, Arizona

Deana Cerroni
Mathematics
Prentice Hall National Consultant
Las Vegas, Nevada

Sandra Mosteller
Mathematics
Prentice Hall National Consultant
Anderson, South Carolina

Rita Corbett
Mathematics
Prentice Hall Consultant
Elgin, Illinois

Addie Martin
Mathematics
Prentice Hall Consultant
Upper Marlboro, Maryland

Charlotte Samuels
Mathematics
Prentice Hall Consultant
Lafayette Hill, Pennsylvania

Cathy Davies
Mathematics
Prentice Hall Consultant
Laguna Niguel, California

Rose Primiani
Mathematics
Prentice Hall Consultant
Brick, New Jersey

Margaret Thomas
Mathematics
Prentice Hall Consultant
Indianapolis, Indiana

Sally Marsh
Mathematics
Prentice Hall Consultant
Baltimore, Maryland

Loretta Rector
Mathematics
Prentice Hall Consultant
Foresthill, California

Contents in Brief

Algebraic Expressions and Integers

Solving One-Step Equations and Inequalities

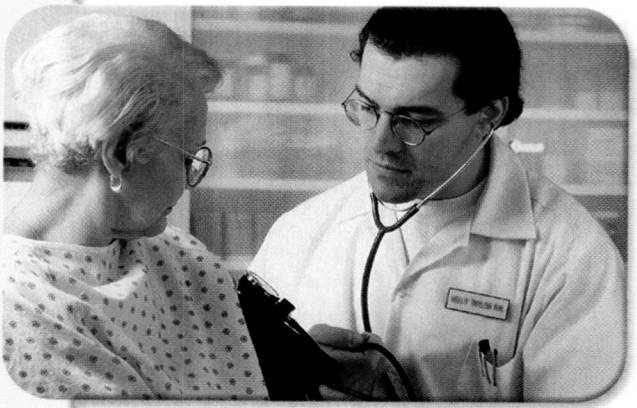

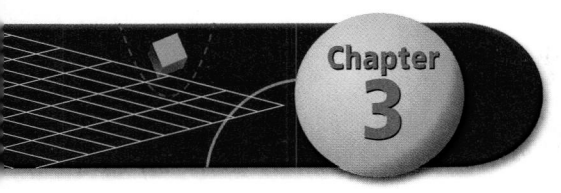

Chapter 3

Decimals and Equations

Chapter 4

Factors, Fractions, and Exponents

Student Support

Operations With Fractions

Chapter 6

Ratios, Proportions, and Percents

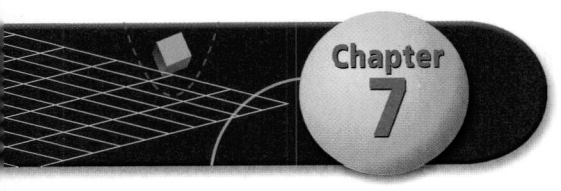

Chapter 7

Solving Equations and Inequalities

Chapter 8

Linear Functions and Graphing

Chapter 9

Spatial Thinking

Student Support

 Instant Check System

Comprehensive Test Prep

Reading Math

 Writing in Math

Real-World Problem Solving

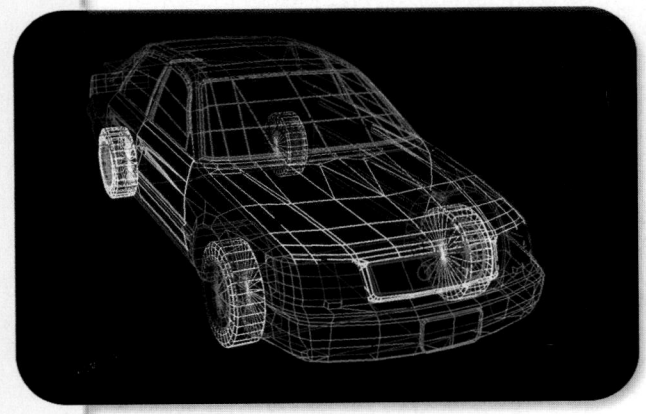

Chapter 10

Area and Volume

Chapter 11

Right Triangles in Algebra

Student Support

 Instant Check System

Diagnosing Readiness, 578

Check Skills You'll Need, 580, 584, 592, 598, 602, 608, 614

Check Understanding, 580, 581, 585, 586, 593, 594, 599, 603, 604, 609, 610, 615, 616

Checkpoint Quiz, 596, 612

Comprehensive Test Prep

Daily Test Prep, 583, 589, 596, 601, 606, 612, 618

Test-Taking Tip, 598

Test-Taking Strategies, 620

Cumulative Test Prep, 625

Reading Math

Reading Math, 580, 593, 594, 609, 616, 617

Reading for Problem Solving, 619

Understanding Vocabulary, 621

Reading Comprehension, 612, 625

 Writing in Math

Daily Writing Practice, 582, 588, 596, 605, 606, 611, 617, 624

Writing to Justify, 597

 Real-World Problem Solving

Strategy: Write a Proportion, 598–601
Lifeguarding, 581
Math at Work, 589
Surveying, 598
Ramps, 610
. . . and more!

Chapter 12

Data Analysis and Probability

Student Support

 Instant Check System

Diagnosing Readiness, 628

Check Skills You'll Need, 630, 635, 642, 649, 654, 659, 665, 669, 674

Check Understanding, 631, 636, 637, 642, 643, 644, 649, 650, 651, 655, 656, 659, 660, 661, 665, 666, 669, 670, 675

Checkpoint Quiz, 653, 672

 **Comprehensive Test Prep**

Daily Test Prep, 633, 639, 647, 653, 658, 663, 668, 671, 677

Test-Taking Tip, 650

Test-Taking Strategies, 678

Cumulative Test Prep, 683

 Reading Math

Reading Math, 631, 646

Reading for Problem Solving, 648

Understanding Vocabulary, 679

Writing in Math

Daily Writing Practice, 633, 638, 646, 652, 657, 663, 668, 671, 677, 682

Real-World Problem Solving

Strategy: Simulate the Problem, 674–677
Surveys, 631
Biology, 636
Population, 642
Math at Work, 663
. . . and more!

Nonlinear Functions and Polynomials

Connect Your Learning
Through Problem Solving, Activities, and the Web

Applications: Real-World Applications

And Over 100 More Topics!
See Real-World Applications in the Index, Page 879

Applications: Math at Work

Applications: Interdisciplinary Connections

Problem-Solving Strategies

The Problem-Solving Lessons included in Prentice Hall *Pre-Algebra* progress in depth and sophistication throughout the course. You will learn to combine and compare strategies to solve problems. Throughout the text, a greater focus on the strategy "Write an Equation" helps prepare you for success in algebra.

The Problem-Solving Lessons in each chapter of Prentice Hall Mathematics progress in depth and sophistication within a course and from course to course.

Take It to the Net

Throughout this book you will find links to the Prentice Hall Web site. Use the Web Code provided with each link to gain direct access to online material.

Here's how to **Take It to the NET**:
- Go to **PHSchool.com**.
- Enter the Web Code.
- Click Go!

For a complete list of online features, use Web Code adk-0099

Lesson Quiz Web Codes

There is an online quiz for each lesson. Access these quizzes with Web Codes ada-0101 through ada-1308 for Lesson 1-1 through Lesson 13-8. *See page 22.*

115 Lesson Quizzes
Web Code format: ada-   04
= Chapter 2   04 = Lesson 4

Chapter Resource Web Codes

Chapter	Vocabulary Quizzes *See page 57.*	Chapter Tests *See page 60.*	Dorling Kindersley Real-World Snapshots *See pages 62–63.*	Chapter Projects
1	adj-0151	ada-0152	ade-0153	add-0161
2	adj-0251	ada-0252	ade-0253	add-0261
3	adj-0351	ada-0352	ade-0353	add-0361
4	adj-0451	ada-0452	ade-0453	add-0461
5	adj-0551	ada-0552	ade-0553	add-0561
6	adj-0651	ada-0652	ade-0653	add-0661
7	adj-0751	ada-0752	ade-0753	add-0761
8	adj-0851	ada-0852	ade-0853	add-0861
9	adj-0951	ada-0952	ade-0953	add-0961
10	adj-1051	ada-1052	ade-1053	add-1061
11	adj-1151	ada-1152	ade-1153	add-1161
12	adj-1251	ada-1252	ade-1253	add-1261
13	adj-1351	ada-1352	ade-1353	add-1361
End-of-Course		ada-1154		

Additional Resource Web Codes

Data Updates Use Web Code adg-2041 to get up-to-date government data for use in examples and exercises. *See page 95.*

Math at Work For information about each Math at Work feature, use Web Code adb-2031. *See page 29.*

TEXT Complete student textbok available online. Includes interactivities and videos.

Using Your Book for Success

Welcome to Prentice Hall *Pre-Algebra*. There are many features built into the daily lessons of this text that will help you learn the important skills and concepts you will need to be successful in this course. Look through the following pages for some study tips that you will find useful as you complete each lesson.

Instant Check System™
An *Instant Check System™*, built into the text and marked with a ✓, allows you to check your understanding of skills before moving on to the next topic.

✓ Diagnosing Readiness
Complete the *Diagnosing Readiness* exercises to see what topics you may need to review before you begin the chapter.

✓ Check Skills You'll Need
Complete the *Check Skills You'll Need* exercises to make sure you have the skills needed to successfully learn the concepts in the lesson.

✓ Check Understanding
Every lesson includes numerous *Examples,* each followed by a *Check Understanding* question that you can do on your own to see if you understand the skill being introduced. Check your progress with the answers at the back of the book.

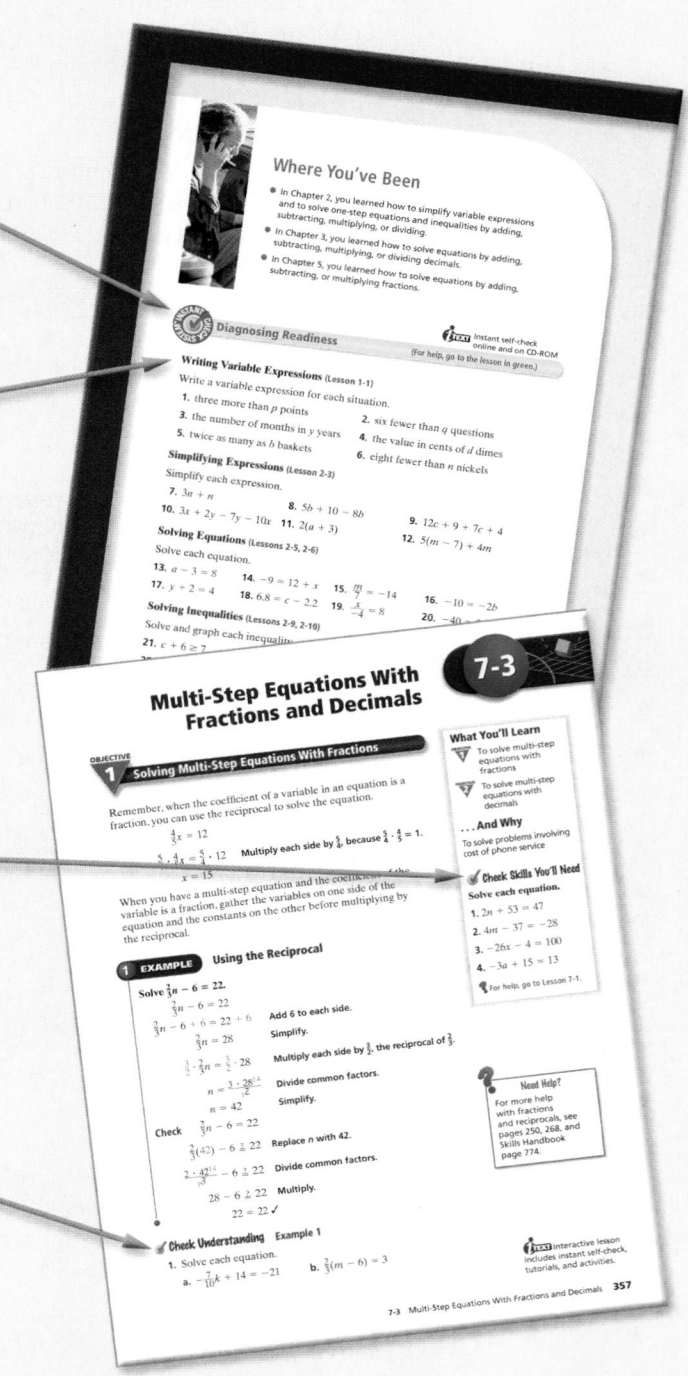

Need Help?

Need Help? notes provide a quick review of a concept you need to understand the topic being presented. Look for the green labels throughout your book to tell you where to "Go" for help.

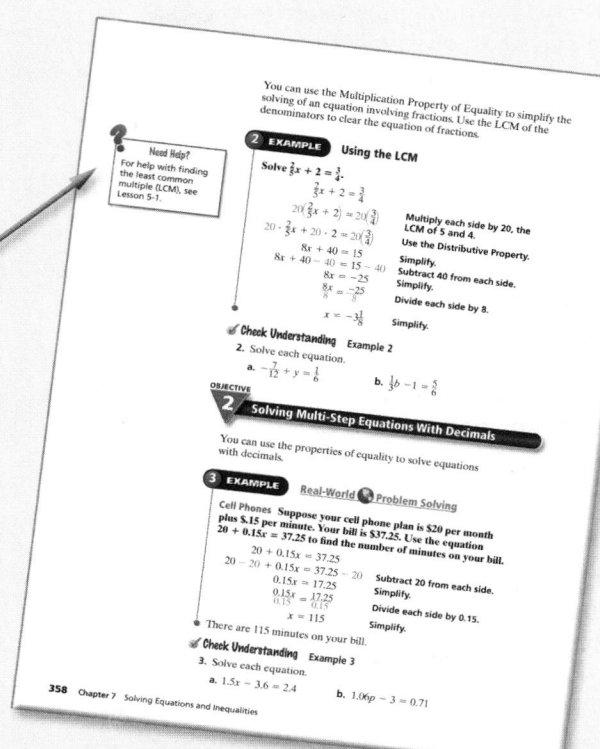

More Than One Way

The *More Than One Way* feature shows you two different methods to solve a problem. By analyzing each student's method, you can think critically about the solution and then choose a method you would use to solve a similar problem.

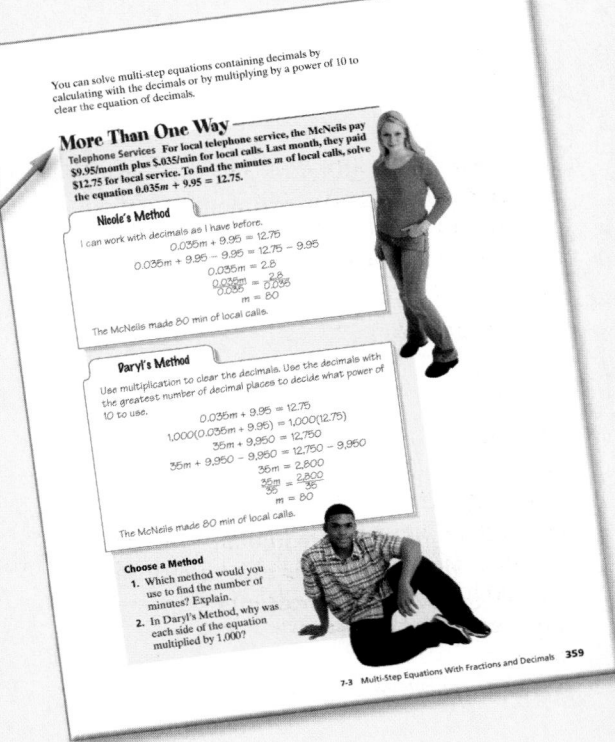

Exercise Sets

Exercises
There are numerous *Exercises* in each lesson that give you the practice you need to master the concepts in the lesson. Each practice set includes the following sections.

A: Practice by Example
The *A: Practice by Example* exercises refer you back to the Examples in the lesson, in case you need help with completing these exercises.

B: Apply Your Skills
The *B: Apply Your Skills* exercises combine skills from earlier lessons to offer you richer skill exercises and multi-step application problems.

C: Challenge
The *C: Challenge* exercises give you an opportunity to solve problems that extend and stretch your thinking.

Test Prep
Test Prep exercises give you daily practice with all the types of test question formats that you will encounter on state and national tests.

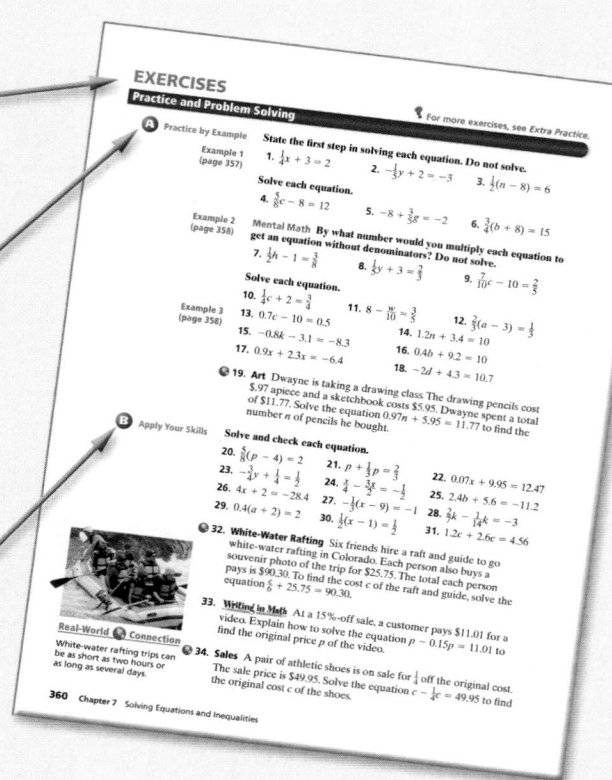

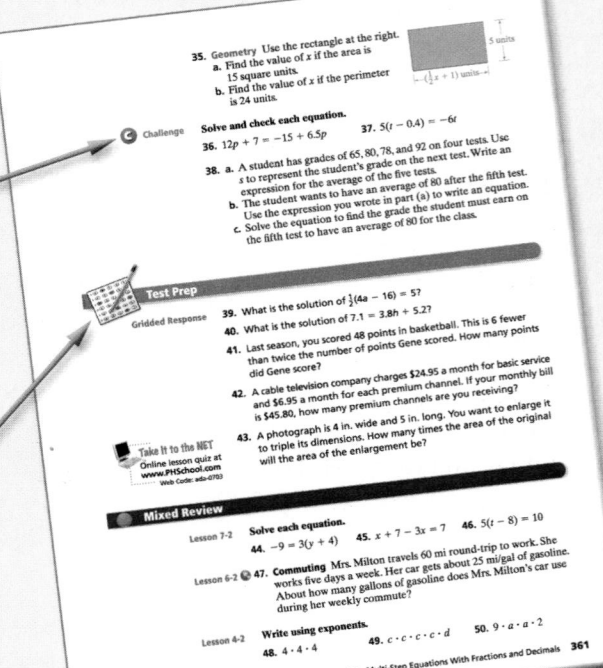

Preparing for Tests

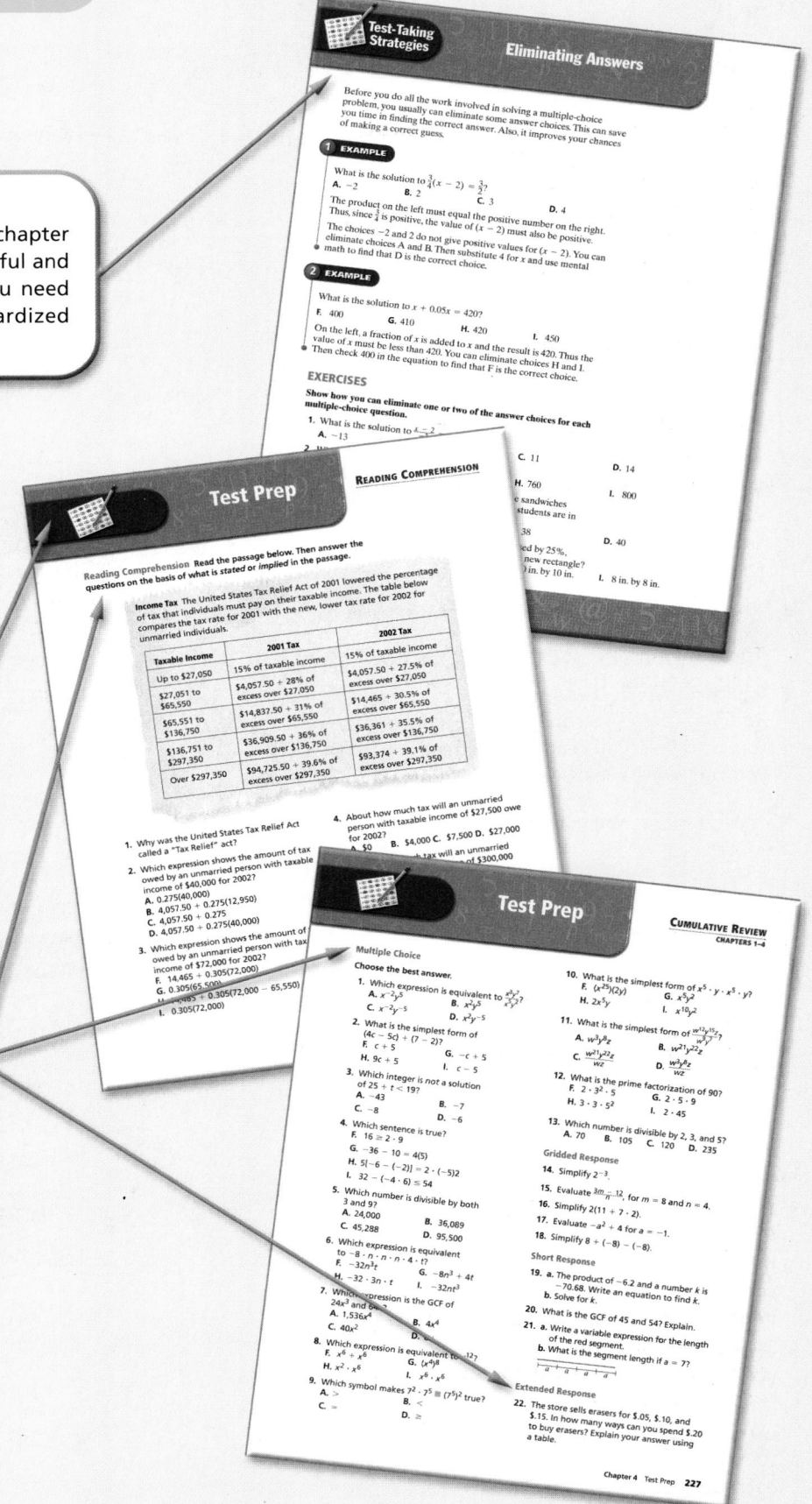

Test-Taking Strategies
Test-Taking Strategies in every chapter teach you strategies to be successful and give you practice in the skills you need to pass state tests and standardized national exams.

Test Prep
In addition to the exercises in every lesson, the *Test Prep* pages in every chapter give you more opportunities to prepare for the tests you will have to take.

Test Item Formats
The *Test Prep* exercises in your book give you the practice you need to answer all types of test questions.
- *Multiple Choice*
- *Gridded Response*
- *Short Response* (scored with a rubric)
- *Extended Response* (scored with a rubric)
- *Reading Comprehension*

Reading and Writing to Learn

Your *Pre-Algebra* text provides even more ways for you to develop your ability to read and write mathematically so that you are successful in this course and on state tests.

New Vocabulary
New Vocabulary is listed for each lesson so you can pre-read the text. As each term is introduced, it is highlighted in yellow.

Reading Math hints
These *hints* help you to use mathematical notation correctly, understand vocabulary, and translate symbols into everyday English so you can talk about what you've learned.

Reading Math lessons
Reading Math lessons focus on a variety of topics to help you read more effectively, so that you can write, speak, and think mathematically.

Writing in Math lessons
Writing in Math lessons help you to write more effectively about the mathematics you are learning.

For more help:

- **Reading Math exercises**
  Reading Math exercises in the Chapter Review help you to understand and correctly use the vocabulary presented in the chapter.

- **English/Spanish Illustrated Glossary**
  While you are learning, use this handy reference that contains a written explanation and an illustrated example to help you understand and remember. each term.

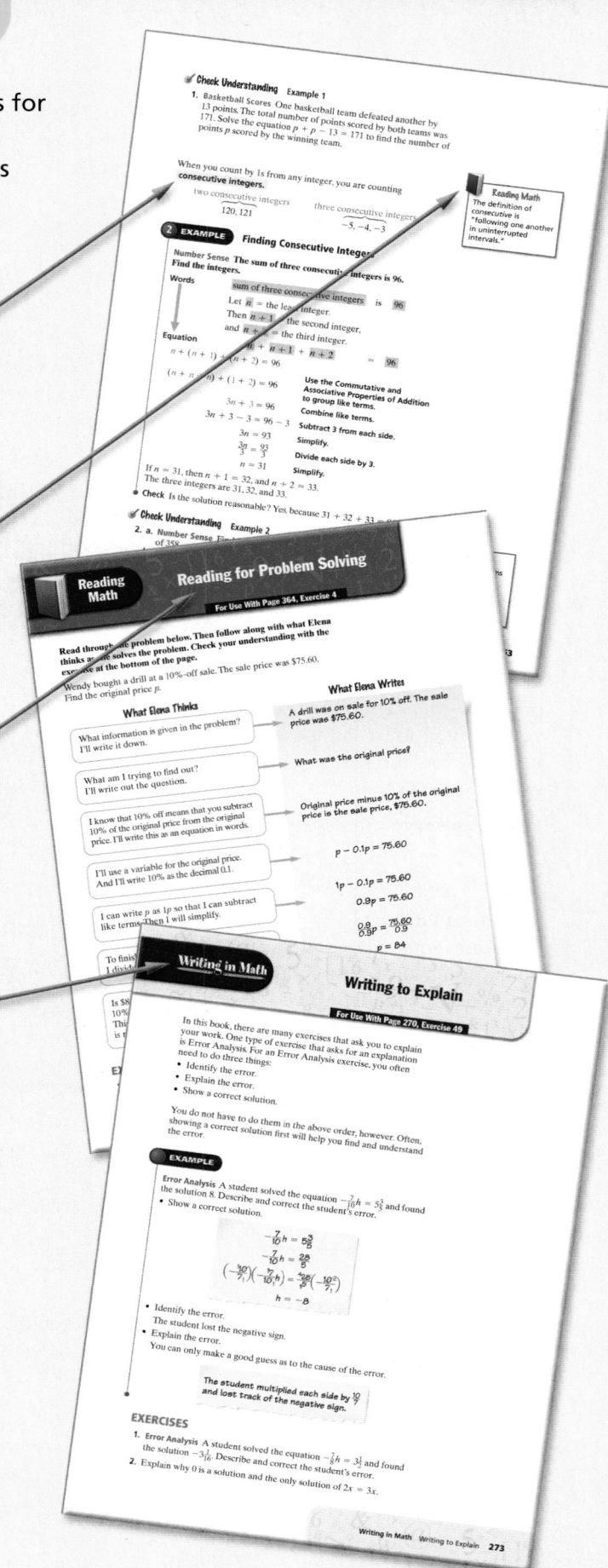

Dorling Kindersley (DK) Real-World Snapshots

 Dorling Kindersley (DK) is an international publishing company that specializes in the creation of high-quality, illustrated information books for children and adults. DK is part of the Pearson family of companies.

Real-World Snapshots
The *Real-World Snapshots* feature applies the exciting and unique graphic presentation style found in Dorling Kindersley books to show you how mathematics is used in real life.

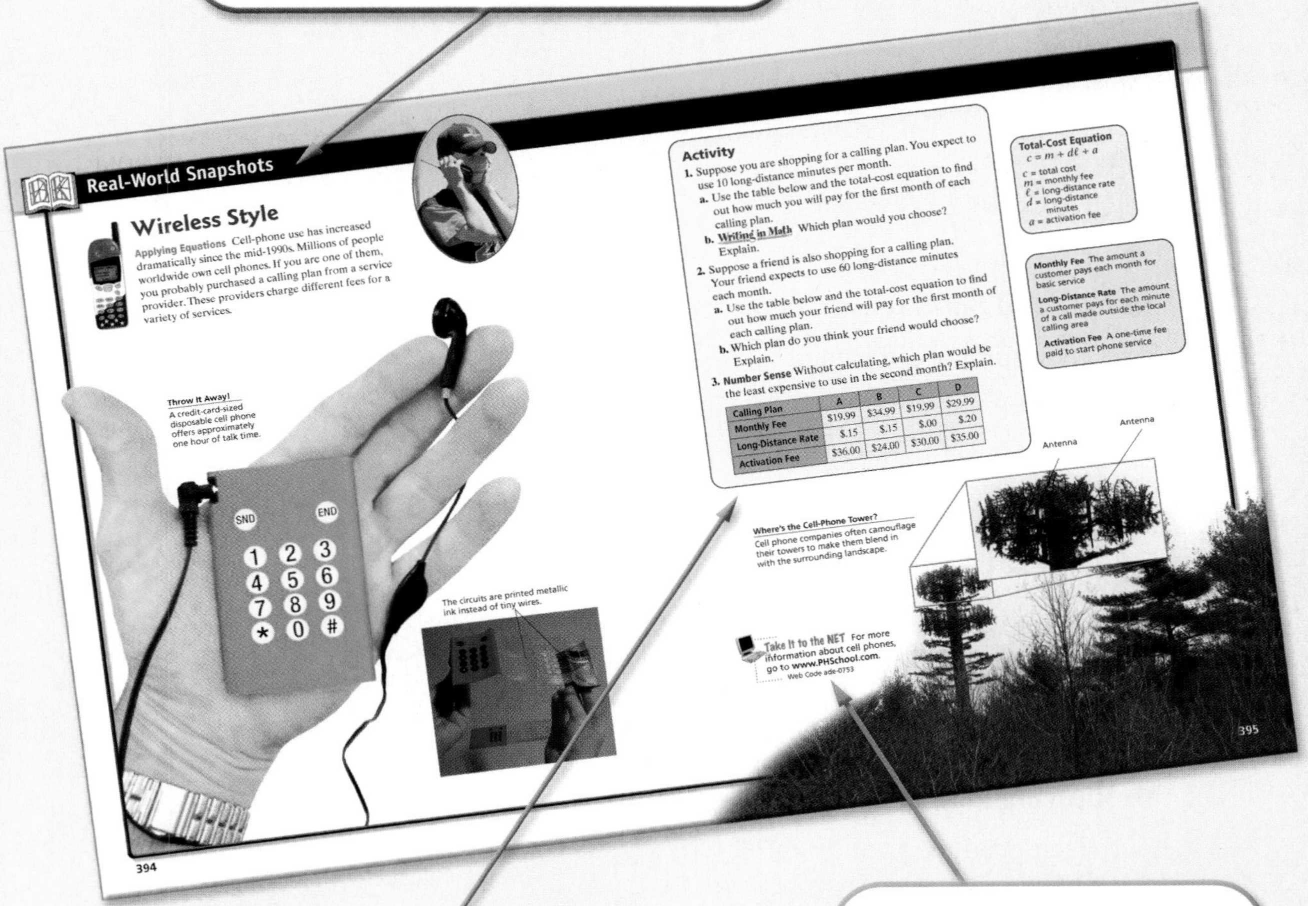

Real-World Snapshots

Wireless Style

Applying Equations Cell-phone use has increased dramatically since the mid-1990s. Millions of people worldwide own cell phones. If you are one of them, you probably purchased a calling plan from a service provider. These providers charge different fees for a variety of services.

Throw It Away!
A credit-card-sized disposable cell phone offers approximately one hour of talk time.

The circuits are printed metallic ink instead of tiny wires.

Activity
1. Suppose you are shopping for a calling plan. You expect to use 10 long-distance minutes per month.
   a. Use the table below and the total-cost equation to find out how much you will pay for the first month of each calling plan.
   b. **Writing in Math** Which plan would you choose? Explain.
2. Suppose a friend is also shopping for a calling plan. Your friend expects to use 60 long-distance minutes each month.
   a. Use the table below and the total-cost equation to find out how much your friend will pay for the first month of each calling plan.
   b. Which plan do you think your friend would choose? Explain.
3. **Number Sense** Without calculating, which plan would be the least expensive to use in the second month? Explain.

Calling Plan	A	B	C	D
Monthly Fee	$19.99	$34.99	$19.99	$29.99
Long-Distance Rate	$.15	$.15	$.00	$.20
Activation Fee	$36.00	$24.00	$30.00	$35.00

Total-Cost Equation
$c = m + d\ell + a$

c = total cost
m = monthly fee
ℓ = long-distance minutes
d = long-distance rate
a = activation fee

Monthly Fee The amount a customer pays each month for basic service

Long-Distance Rate The amount a customer pays for each minute of a call made outside the local calling area

Activation Fee A one-time fee paid to start phone service

Where's the Cell-Phone Tower?
Cell phone companies often camouflage their towers to make them blend in with the surrounding landscape.

Antenna   Antenna

Take It to the NET For more information about cell phones, go to **www.PHschool.com**. Web Code ade-0753

394

395

Activities
Using data from these pages and data that you gather, complete the hands-on *Activities* to apply the mathematics you are learning in real-world situations.

Take It to the Net
Enter the Web Code for online information you can use to learn more about the topic of the feature.

Where You've Been

In previous courses you learned:

- How to evaluate expressions using the order of operations.
- How to add, subtract, multiply, and divide whole numbers.
- How to compare whole numbers.
- How to relate numbers to points on a number line.

 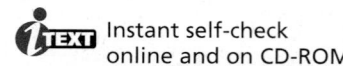 Instant self-check online and on CD-ROM

Diagnosing Readiness

(For help, go to the Skills Handbook.)

Adding and Subtracting Whole Numbers (Previous Course)

Find each sum or difference.

1. $7 - 6$ **2.** $9 + 2$ **3.** $15 - 4$ **4.** $11 + 8$

5. $20 - 7$ **6.** $32 + 8$ **7.** $32 - 15$ **8.** $26 + 17$

9. $67 + 109$ **10.** $82 - 54$ **11.** $44 + 122$ **12.** $91 - 16$

Comparing Whole Numbers (Skills Handbook, p. 757)

Compare. Use $>$, $<$, or $=$ to complete each statement.

13. $5 \blacksquare 2$ **14.** $1 \blacksquare 0$ **15.** $14 \blacksquare 17$

16. $6 + 12 \blacksquare 7 + 13$ **17.** $10 - 2 \blacksquare 27 - 18$ **18.** $4 \times 7 \blacksquare 2 \times 14$

Multiplying and Dividing Whole Numbers (Skills Handbook, pp. 759, 760)

Find each product or quotient.

19. $36 \div 3$ **20.** 10×3 **21.** $7(4)$ **22.** $25 \div 5$

23. $12 \cdot 8$ **24.** $7\overline{)35}$ **25.** $20 \cdot 10$ **26.** $9\overline{)720}$

27. $124 \div 4$ **28.** $12\overline{)156}$ **29.** $4 \cdot 12 \cdot 10$ **30.** $132 \div 11$

Reading Numbers on a Number Line (Skills Handbook, p. 757)

What is the distance of each point from zero on the number line?

31. A **32.** B

33. C **34.** D

Algebraic Expressions and Integers

Key Vocabulary

- absolute value (p. 19)
- conjecture (p. 35)
- coordinate plane (p. 50)
- counterexample (p. 37)
- evaluate (p. 14)
- inductive reasoning (p. 35)
- integers (p. 19)
- opposites (p. 19)
- order of operations (p. 8)
- ordered pair (p. 50)
- origin (p. 50)
- quadrants (p. 50)
- variable (p. 4)
- variable expression (p. 4)
- x-axis (p. 50)
- x-coordinate (p. 50)
- y-axis (p. 50)
- y-coordinate (p. 50)

Where You're Going

In this chapter, you will learn how to

- Use variables and variable expressions.
- Perform operations with integers.
- Graph points in the coordinate plane.
- Solve a problem by looking for a pattern.

Real-World Snapshots Applying what you learn, on pages 62–63 you will solve problems about sunken ships.

Variables and Expressions

What You'll Learn

OBJECTIVE 1 To identify variables, numerical expressions, and variable expressions

OBJECTIVE 2 To write variable expressions for word phrases

...And Why

To use the language of algebra to model real-world problems

Check Skills You'll Need

Complete each equation.

1. 1 week = ■ days

2. 1 foot = ■ inches

3. 1 nickel = ■ cents

4. 1 gallon = ■ quarts

5. 1 yard = ■ feet

 For help, go to Table 1, p. 776.

New Vocabulary

- variable
- variable expression

OBJECTIVE

1 Identifying Numerical and Variable Expressions

Gas Mileage How many miles can you drive on ten gallons of gas? The answer depends on the type of vehicle you drive. The table shows some typical data.

Vehicle Type	Miles	Gallons	Miles per Gallon
Subcompact	330	10	$330 \div 10$
Compact	300	10	$300 \div 10$
Mid-size sedan	245	10	$245 \div 10$
Sport utility vehicle	175	10	$175 \div 10$
Pickup truck	160	10	$160 \div 10$

The last column gives a *numerical expression* for each vehicle's miles per gallon.

If you don't know the number of miles, you can use a *variable* to stand for the number. Then you can write a *variable expression* for miles per gallon.

variable → m ← miles on 10 gallons

variable expression → $m \div 10$ ← miles per gallon

A **variable** is a letter that stands for a number.
A **variable expression** is a mathematical phrase that uses variables, numerals, and operation symbols.

1 EXAMPLE Identifying Expressions

Identify each expression as a *numerical expression* or a *variable expression*. For a variable expression, name the variable.

a. $5 - 5$
   numerical expression

b. $c - 5$
   Variable expression; c is the variable.

TEXT Interactive lesson includes instant self-check, tutorials, and activities.

✓ Check Understanding   Example 1

1. Identify each expression as a *numerical expression* or a *variable expression*. For a variable expression, name the variable.

   a. $8 \div x$ **b.** 100×6 **c.** $d + 43 - 9$

2 ▶ Writing Variable Expressions

You can translate word phrases into variable expressions.

Word Phrase	Variable Expression
Nine more than a number y	$y + 9$
4 less than a number n	$n - 4$
A number z times three	$z \cdot 3$ or $3z$ or $3(z)$
A number a divided by 12	$a \div 12$ or $\frac{a}{12}$
5 times the quantity 4 plus a number c	$5 \cdot (4 + c)$ or $5(4 + c)$

Writing in Math

You can translate many words for operations into operation symbols.

total	$+$
more than	$+$
increased by	$+$
difference	$-$
fewer than	$-$
less than	$-$
decreased by	$-$
product	$\times$ or $\cdot$ or ( )
times	$\times$ or $\cdot$ or ( )
quotient	$\div$ or —
divided by	$\div$ or —

2 EXAMPLE   Real-World ● Problem Solving

Science The fastest dinosaur may have been *Ornithomimus,* which could run about 60 ft in a second. Write a variable expression for the distance Ornithomimus could run in a given time.

Words   60   times   number of seconds

Let s = number of seconds.

Expression   60   · s

The variable expression $60 \cdot s$, or $60s$, describes the distance in feet Ornithomimus could run in s seconds.

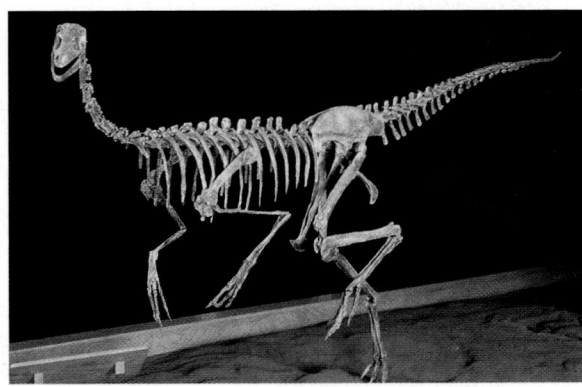

Real-World ● Connection

Ornithomimus was an ostrich-like oviraptor about 7 ft tall. Its long tail acted as a counterbalance and as a stabilizer during fast turns.

✓ Check Understanding   Example 2

2. **a.** Bagels cost $.50 each. Write a variable expression for the cost of b bagels.
   b. **Measurement** Write a variable expression for the number of hours in m minutes.

EXERCISES

For more exercises, see *Extra Practice*.

Practice and Problem Solving

 Practice by Example

Example 1
(page 4)

Identify each expression as a *numerical expression* or a *variable expression*. For a variable expression, name the variable.

1. $b + 6$ **2.** $80 \div 8$ **3.** $14 - n$

4. 14×14 **5.** $100x$ **6.** $8 + 8 + 8 + 8$

Example 2
(page 5)

Write a variable expression for each word phrase.

7. 16 more than m **8.** 6 divided by z

9. the product of c and 3 **10.** 2 less than p

11. b times 3 **12.** 4 fewer than j

13. n divided by 3 **14.** 3 divided by n

15. x less than 2 **16.** 8 less than z

Write a numerical or variable expression for each quantity.

17. two dozen eggs **18.** d dozen eggs

19. the value in cents of 7 nickels **20.** the value in cents of n nickels

21. number of quarts in 3 gallons **22.** number of quarts in g gallons

 **Apply Your Skills**

Identify each expression as a *numerical expression* or a *variable expression*. For a variable expression, name the variable.

23. $d + 53$ **24.** $12 - 7$ **25.** $\frac{g}{9}$ **26.** $4(5)$

Measurement Write an expression for each quantity.

27. the number of days in 4 weeks

28. the number of days in w weeks

29. number of pounds in 160 ounces

30. number of pounds in z ounces

31. the number of feet in 100 inches

32. the number of feet in i inches

33. Mia has $20 less than Brandi. Brandi has d dollars. Write a variable expression for the amount of money Mia has.

Use the calorie chart at the left for Exercises 34 and 35.

34. Write a variable expression for the number of calories in e eggs and one slice of bread.

35. Write a variable expression for the number of calories in a fruit salad made from a apples and b bananas.

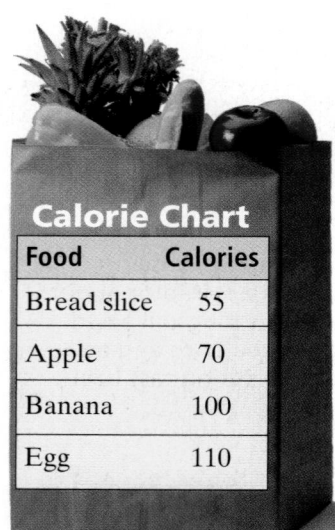

Calorie Chart

Food	Calories
Bread slice	55
Apple	70
Banana	100
Egg	110

6 Chapter 1 Algebraic Expressions and Integers

Modeling In each model, the red line represents a variable expression. Match each model with its expression.

A. $\frac{x}{4}$ **B.** $4 + x$ **C.** $4x$ **D.** $x - 4$

36.

37.

38.

39.

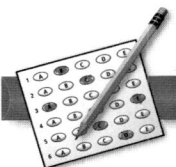 **Challenge**

40. Writing in Math How are numerical expressions and variable expressions similar? How are they different?

41. Error Analysis A student wrote the variable expression $n - 5$ for the word phrase *n less than five*. Explain the student's error.

Test Prep

Multiple Choice

A hot-air balloon is at an altitude of m meters. In Exercises 42–44, which expression matches the given word phrase?

42. the balloon's new altitude after rising 34 meters
 A. $m - 34$ **B.** $m + 34$ **C.** $3m$ **D.** $34m$

43. the balloon's new altitude after falling 2,000 meters
 F. $m + 2{,}000$ **G.** $2{,}000 - m$ **H.** $2{,}000m$ **I.** $m - 2{,}000$

44. the balloon's new altitude after tripling its altitude
 A. $m - 34$ **B.** $m + 34$ **C.** $3m$ **D.** $34m$

Take It to the NET
Online lesson quiz at
www.PHSchool.com
Web Code: ada-0101

45. Pam is 15 years old. Which expression gives Pam's age p years ago?
 F. $p - 15$ **G.** $p + 15$ **H.** $15 - p$ **I.** $\frac{p}{15}$

Mixed Review

Previous Course

Compute.

46. $105 + 25 + 95$ **47.** $3 \times 6 \times 4$ **48.** $8 + 1 - 1$

49. $648 - 573$ **50.** $169 \div 13$ **51.** $22{,}534 - 12{,}971$

52. Purchasing A customer buys orange juice for $.95 and two apples for $.55 each. She gives the cashier a five-dollar bill. How much change should the cashier give the customer?

53. a. Recall the *counting numbers*, 1, 2, 3, 4, . . . Of the first 1,000 counting numbers, how many end in 1, 3, 5, 7, or 9?
 b. How many end in 2, 4, 6, or 8?

The Order of Operations

What You'll Learn

OBJECTIVE
1 To use the order of operations

OBJECTIVE
2 To use grouping symbols

. . . And Why

To find the value of an expression with more than one operation

 Check Skills You'll Need

Find each quotient.

1. $164 \div 2$ **2.** $344 \div 8$

3. $284 \div 4$ **4.** $133 \div 7$

5. $182 \div 13$ **6.** $650 \div 25$

 For help, go to Skills Handbook, p. 760.

New Vocabulary

• order of operations

OBJECTIVE

1 Using the Order of Operations

Investigation

Experimenting With Order

In most languages, the meaning of words depends on their order. For example, "sign the check" is not the same as "check the sign."

Similarly, order is important in the language of mathematics.

1. **Mental Math** Find the value of the expression $3 + 5 \times 2$.

2. **Analyze** What answer do you get to Question 1 if you multiply before adding? If you add before multiplying?

3. **Reasoning** How does the order in which you do the operations affect your answer?

The order in which you perform operations can affect the value of an expression. To avoid confusion, mathematicians have agreed on an **order of operations.** Multiply and divide first. Then add and subtract.

To *simplify* a numerical expression, you use the order of operations and replace the expression with the simplest name for its value.

1 EXAMPLE **Simplifying Expressions**

Simplify $4 + 15 \div 3$.

$$4 + 15 \div 3$$
$$4 + 5 \qquad \text{First divide.}$$
$$9 \qquad \text{Then add.}$$

Check Understanding Example 1

1. Simplify each expression.

   a. $2 + 5 \times 3$ **b.** $12 \div 3 - 1$ **c.** $10 - 1 \cdot 7$

When operations have the same rank in the order of operations, do them from left to right.

TEXT Interactive lesson includes instant self-check, tutorials, and activities.

2 EXAMPLE Using the Order of Operations

Simplify $3 \cdot 5 - 8 \div 4 + 6$.

$3 \cdot 5 - 8 \div 4 + 6$

$15 \quad - \quad 2 \quad + \quad 6$ **Multiply and divide from left to right.**

$13 + 6$ **Add and subtract from left to right.**

19 **Add.**

✓ Check Understanding Example 2

2. Simplify each expression.

a. $4 - 1 \cdot 2 + 6 \div 3$ **b.** $5 + 6 \cdot 4 \div 3 - 1$

Calculator Hint

Many calculators use the order of operations. To test yours, enter $10 - 4 \div 2$. If the answer is 8, then your calculator uses the order of operations.

If the answer is 3, then your calculator does not use the order of operations.

OBJECTIVE

2 Using Grouping Symbols

Grouping symbols, such as parentheses, ( ), and brackets, [ ], indicate order. A fraction bar also is a grouping symbol, since $\frac{4 + 2}{3} = (4 + 2) \div 3$. Always work inside grouping symbols first.

Key Concepts Order of Operations

1. Work inside grouping symbols.

2. Multiply and divide in order from left to right.

3. Add and subtract in order from left to right.

3 EXAMPLE Simplifying With Grouping Symbols

Simplify $10 \div [9 - (2 \cdot 2)]$.

$10 \div [9 - (2 \cdot 2)]$

$10 \div [9 \quad - \quad 4]$ **Multiply within parentheses.**

$10 \quad \div \quad 5$ **Subtract within brackets.**

2 **Divide.**

Reading Math

For help with reading an Example, see page 13.

✓ Check Understanding Example 3

3. Simplify each expression.

a. $2[(13 - 4) \div 3]$ **b.** $1 + \frac{10 - 2}{4}$

You can use the order of operations to find the area of an irregular figure by more than one method.

More Than One Way

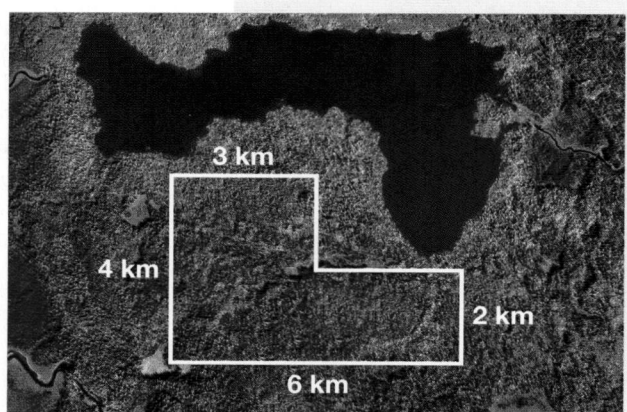

Urban Planning Some urban planners specialize in planning entire new towns. These towns are designed for livability, with plenty of open space. The sketch shows the dimensions for a new town called Panorama. Find Panorama's area.

Kevin's Method

Divide the figure into rectangles. Then add their areas.

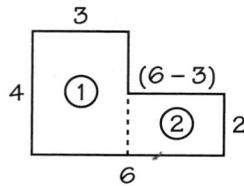

$$\text{Area} = \text{Area}\,①\,+\,\text{Area}\,②$$
$$= 4 \cdot 3 + (6 - 3) \cdot 2$$
$$= 4 \cdot 3 + 3 \cdot 2$$
$$= 12 + 6$$
$$= 18$$

Panorama's area is 18 km².

Tina's Method

Visualize attaching a small rectangle to complete a large rectangle. Then subtract the small area from the large area.

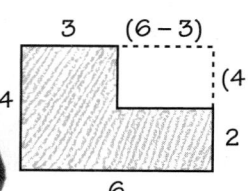

$$\text{Area} = \begin{array}{c} \text{Area of large} \\ \text{rectangle} \end{array} - \begin{array}{c} \text{Area of small} \\ \text{rectangle} \end{array}$$
$$= 6 \cdot 4 - (6 - 3) \cdot (4 - 2)$$
$$= 6 \cdot 4 - 3 \cdot 2$$
$$= 24 - 6$$
$$= 18$$

Panorama's area is 18 km².

Choose a Method

1. Which method would you use to find the town's area? Explain.
2. Can you think of another way to solve the problem? Explain.

EXERCISES

For more exercises, see *Extra Practice*.

Practice and Problem Solving

A **Practice by Example**

Examples 1 and 2
(pages 8 and 9)

Simplify each expression.

1. $3 + 6 \times 4$

2. $35 \div 7 - 2$

3. $8 - 2 \cdot 3$

4. $6 - 6 \div 3$

5. $21 - 13 + 8$

6. $6 \cdot 2 + 4$

7. $12 - 8 \div 2 + 3$

8. $21 \div 7 + 14 \times 2$

9. $2 \cdot 2 + 0 \cdot 4$

10. $4(4) - 2(5)$

11. $2 + 3 \cdot 24 \div 6$

12. $4 \div 4 \cdot 4 + 4 - 4$

Example 3
(page 9)

13. $7 + 3 \cdot (8 \div 4)$

14. $2(15 - 9) \cdot 9$

15. $[2 + (6 \cdot 8)] - 1$

16. $2(6) + \dfrac{7 + 8}{3}$

17. $3(7 + 4)$

18. $12 \div (3 - 2) + 1$

19. $6 + \dfrac{6 + 2}{4}$

20. $\dfrac{21 + 15}{3 + 6}$

21. $(21 + 3) \div 4 \div 2$

B **Apply Your Skills**

22. Error Analysis A student found the value of the expression $30 \div 6 - 1$ to be 6. Explain the student's error.

23. Writing in Math Why do we need to agree on an order of operations?

Simplify each expression.

24. $(56 - 5) \div 17$

25. $60 \div 4 + 9$

26. $2[8 + (5 - 3)] - 8$

27. $12 \div 3 \times 4$

28. $36 - 27 \div 9 \div 1$

29. $6(4 + 1) - 5$

30. $14 + 5 \times 2$

31. $440 \div (2 + 18)$

32. $16 \div 8 \times 2$

Compare. Use >, <, or = to complete each statement.

33. $15 \cdot 3 - 2 \ \blacksquare \ 15 \cdot (3 - 2)$

34. $18 - 6 \div 3 \ \blacksquare \ (18 - 6) \div 3$

35. $8 + 12 \div 4 \ \blacksquare \ (8 + 12) \div 4$

36. $22 - 7 \cdot 2 \ \blacksquare \ (22 - 7) \cdot 2$

37. $12 \div 3 + 9 \cdot 4 \ \blacksquare \ 12 \div (3 + 9) \cdot 4$

38. $(19 - 15) \div (3 + 1) \ \blacksquare \ 19 - 15 \div 3 + 1$

Insert grouping symbols to make each number sentence true.

39. $7 + 4 \cdot 6 = 66$

40. $7 \cdot 8 - 6 + 3 = 17$

41. $3 + 8 - 2 \cdot 5 = 45$

42. $6 \cdot 3 + 9 - 4 = 23$

Write a numerical expression for each phrase. Then simplify.

43. five added to the product of four and nine

44. twenty-one minus the sum of fifteen and five

45. seventeen minus the quotient of twenty-five and five

46. On the Job A part-time employee worked 4 hours on Monday and 7 hours each day for the next 3 days. Write and simplify an expression that shows the total number of hours worked.

C Challenge **Write two expressions you could use to find the area of each shaded figure. Find the area.**

47.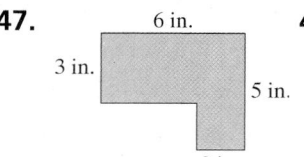
6 in.
3 in.
5 in.
2 in.

48.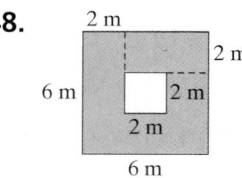
2 m
2 m
6 m
2 m
2 m
6 m

49.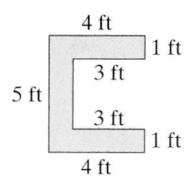
4 ft
1 ft
3 ft
5 ft
3 ft
1 ft
4 ft

50. Open-Ended Write a word problem for the numerical expression $3(4 + 3) + 2$. Then simplify the expression.

51. Number Sense Use the digits 1–9 in order. Insert operation signs and grouping symbols to get a value of 100.

Test Prep

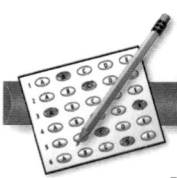

Multiple Choice

52. Which expression has a value of 18?
  A. $3 \cdot 2 + 4$
  B. $(18 - 10) \div 4 + 15$
  C. $4 \cdot 2 + 3 - 2$
  D. $27 - 13 \cdot 2 + 17(6 - 5)$

53. Which expression gives the area of the garden?
  F. $4(2 + 5) + 5 \cdot 5$
  G. $(2 + 5 + 2) \cdot (2 + 5 + 2) - 4(2 \cdot 2)$
  H. $(2 + 5 + 2) - (2 \cdot 2)$
  I. $4(2 \cdot 2) + 4(5 \cdot 2) + 5 \cdot 5$

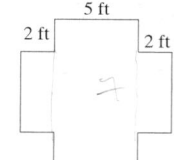
5 ft
2 ft
2 ft

 Test-Taking Tip
You should consider all answer choices before deciding on the appropriate one.

54. Which set of grouping symbols makes the equation true? $2 \cdot 3 + 5 - 2 \cdot 2 = 12$
  A. $(2 \cdot 3) + 5 - (2 \cdot 2)$
  B. $2 \cdot [3 + (5 - 2)] \cdot 2$
  C. $2 \cdot [3 + (5 - 2 \cdot 2)]$
  D. $2 \cdot (3 + 5) - 2 \cdot 2$

55. What is the value of $8 \cdot 5 - 3(24 \div 6)$?
  F. 28
  G. 64
  H. 111
  I. 148

Take It to the NET
Online lesson quiz at
www.PHSchool.com
Web Code: ada-0102

Mixed Review

Lesson 1-1

Write a variable expression for each word phrase.

56. the product of a number n and 8

57. k divided by 20

58. six less than a number h

59. the value, in cents, of d dimes

60. A telephone call costs c cents per minute. Write a variable expression for the cost of a 15-minute call.

The description below explains how to read an example. Read the description. Study the Example. Then do the exercises at the bottom of the page to check your understanding.

Before an example, there usually is information that will help you understand what the example is teaching. For Example 3 on page 9, the paragraph before the Key Concepts box describes grouping symbols and how to work with them.

The Key Concepts box shows you that your work with grouping symbols occurs first in the order of operations:

1. Work inside grouping symbols.

2. Multiply and divide in order from left to right.

3. Add and subtract in order from left to right.

Examples show you how to use the concepts taught in the lesson. In an example, the steps are on the left and the explanations are in **bold** on the right. As you read an example, make sure you understand each step and its explanation.

EXAMPLE **Simplifying With Grouping Symbols**

Simplify $10 \div [9 - (2 \cdot 2)]$.

$10 \div [9 - (2 \cdot 2)]$

$10 \div [9 - 4]$ **Multiply within parentheses.**

$10 \div 5$ **Subtract within brackets.**

2 **Divide.**

Read the problem and locate the grouping symbols.

The red lines show the work inside the innermost grouping symbols.

The text in bold explains the step.

Make mental math checks while you read:
$2 \cdot 2 = 4 \checkmark$
$9 - 4 = 5 \checkmark$
$10 \div 5 = 2 \checkmark$

✓ **Check Understanding** appears after each Example. It provides exercises like the following to let you instantly check how well you understand what is being taught in the Example.

EXERCISES

Simplify each expression.

1. $2[(13 - 4) \div 3]$

2. $1 + \frac{10 - 2}{4}$

3. $3[(8 + 4) \div 6]$

4. $\frac{6 + 9}{3} - 2$

5. $4 \cdot [3 + (2 \cdot 3)]$

6. $16 \div (8 - 4) - 2$

Evaluating Expressions

What You'll Learn

OBJECTIVE 1 To evaluate variable expressions

OBJECTIVE 2 To solve problems by evaluating expressions

. . . And Why

To solve real-world problems involving packaging and shopping

 Check Skills You'll Need

Simplify each expression.

1. $6(9 + 1)$

2. $17 - 2 + 3$

3. $9 + 8 \cdot 2 + 4$

4. $[3(5) + 1] \cdot 2$

 For help, go to Lesson 1-2.

New Vocabulary

• evaluate

OBJECTIVE

1 Evaluating Variable Expressions

To **evaluate** a variable expression, you first replace each variable with a number. Then, you use the order of operations to simplify.

1 EXAMPLE Evaluating a Variable Expression

Evaluate $4y - 15$ for $y = 9$.

$$4y - 15 = 4(9) - 15 \quad \text{Replace } y \text{ with 9.}$$
$$= 36 - 15 \quad \text{Multiply.}$$
$$= 21 \quad \text{Subtract.}$$

✔ Check Understanding Example 1

1. Evaluate each expression.

   a. $63 - 5x$, for $x = 7$ **b.** $4(t + 3) + 1$, for $t = 8$

Sometimes expressions have more than one variable.

2 EXAMPLE Replacing More Than One Variable

Evaluate $3ab + \dfrac{c}{2}$ for $a = 2$, $b = 5$, and $c = 10$.

$$3ab + \frac{c}{2} = 3 \cdot 2 \cdot 5 + \frac{10}{2} \quad \text{Replace the variables.}$$
$$= 3 \cdot 2 \cdot 5 + 5 \quad \text{Work within grouping symbols.}$$
$$= 6 \cdot 5 + 5 \quad \text{Multiply from left to right.}$$
$$= 30 + 5 \quad \text{Multiply.}$$
$$= 35 \quad \text{Add.}$$

✔ Check Understanding Example 2

2. Evaluate each expression.

   a. $6(g + h)$, for $g = 8$ and $h = 7$
   b. $2xy - z$, for $x = 4$, $y = 3$, and $z = 1$
   c. $\dfrac{r + s}{2}$, for $r = 13$ and $s = 11$

 TEXT Interactive lesson includes instant self-check, tutorials, and activities.

OBJECTIVE

2 Solving Problems by Evaluating Expressions

You can write and evaluate variable expressions to solve problems.

3 EXAMPLE Real-World  Problem Solving

Purchasing Energy drinks come in cases of 24 bottles.
a. Write a variable expression for the number of cases a store should order to get *b* bottles of energy drinks.
b. Evaluate the expression for 120 bottles.

a. *b* bottles

$\dfrac{b}{24}$

b. 120 bottles

$\dfrac{b}{24} = \dfrac{120}{24}$ Evaluate for *b* = 120.

$= 5$ Divide.

● The store should order five cases to get 120 bottles.

✓ Check Understanding Example 3

3. The store in Example 3 pays $29 for each case of energy drinks. Write a variable expression for the cost of *c* cases. Evaluate the expression to find the cost of five cases.

Real-World Connection

In a case, bottles are often arranged in 4 rows of 6 (or 6 rows of 4).

4 EXAMPLE Real-World Problem Solving

Online Shopping An online music store charges $14 for each CD. Shipping costs $6 per order. Write a variable expression for the cost of ordering CDs. Find the cost of ordering four CDs.

Words $14   for each   CD   plus $6 shipping

Let *n* = number of CDs.

Expression   14   ·   *n*   +   6

Evaluate the expression for *n* = 4.

$14 \cdot n + 6 = 14 \cdot 4 + 6$ **Replace *n* with 4.**

$= 56 + 6$ **Multiply.**

$= 62$ **Add.**

● It costs $62 to order four CDs.

Reading Math

In Example 4, the phrase *for each* implies multiplication. So *$14 for each CD* means "$14 times the number of CDs."

✓ Check Understanding Example 4

4. Evaluate the expression in Example 4 to find the cost of ordering seven CDs.

EXERCISES

💡 For more exercises, see *Extra Practice*.

Practice and Problem Solving

A Practice by Example

Example 1
(page 14)

Evaluate each expression.

1. $7b$, for $b = 5$ **2.** $5 - c$, for $c = 3$ **3.** $x \div 8$, for $x = 40$

4. $3n + 2$, for $n = 7$ **5.** $41 - 4h$, for $h = 10$ **6.** $5a + 7$, for $a = 20$

Example 2
(page 14)

Evaluate each expression for $x = 2$, $y = 3$, and $z = 10$.

7. xyz **8.** $8y \div x$ **9.** $\frac{z}{5} + 2$ **10.** $4y - x$

11. $2z + xy$ **12.** $\frac{9 + y}{x}$ **13.** $4xy - z$ **14.** $5(y + z)$

Examples 3 and 4
(page 15)

🌐 **15. Word Processing** An office assistant types 55 words per minute.
   a. Write a variable expression for the number of words the office assistant types in m minutes.
   b. Evaluate the expression for 20 minutes.

🌐 **16. Online Purchasing** An online video store charges $24 for each DVD. Shipping costs $4 per order.
   a. Write a variable expression for the cost of ordering DVDs.
   b. Find the cost of ordering 3 DVDs.

B Apply Your Skills

Evaluate each expression.

17. $2a + 5$, for $a = 5$ **18.** $105z$, for $z = 7$

19. $6 \div a + 8$, for $a = 2$ **20.** $19 - (a - 4)$, for $a = 8$

21. $13ab$, for $a = 1$ and $b = 7$ **22.** $16 - 4mn$, for $m = 0$ and $n = 3$

23. $j(5 + k)$, for $j = 11$ and $k = 4$ **24.** rst, for $r = 5$, $s = 5$, and $t = 5$

25. $\frac{150}{z + y}$, for $y = 25$ and $z = 50$ **26.** $\frac{x - y}{4}$, for $x = 52$ and $y = 12$

Real-World 🌐 Connection

By *porpoising* (jumping clear of the water), dolphins can travel as fast as 26 km/h.

🌐 **27. Marine Biology** Write an expression for the number of kilometers a dolphin travels in d hours swimming at 8 km/h. Then find the number of kilometers the dolphin travels in 3 hours.

28. Data Analysis Use the chart to find how many calories a 100-lb person uses in an hour of moderate walking.
   a. Write an expression for the number of calories a 100-lb person uses in moderate walking for w hours.
   b. Evaluate the expression to find the number of calories a 100-lb person uses in moderate walking for 2 hours.

Calories per Hour Used by a 100-lb Walker

Type of Walking	Calories
Slow	110
Moderate	153
Brisk	175
Racing	295

Source: www.nutristrategy.com

29. Error Analysis Your friend evaluates $(10 - k) \div 5$ for $k = 5$, and gets 9 for an answer. Explain your friend's error.

30. Evaluate $4a - b + \frac{b}{2}$, for $a = 3$ and $b = 4$.

31. A fitness club requires a $100 initiation fee and dues of $25 each month. Write an expression for the cost of membership for n months. Then find the cost of membership for one year.

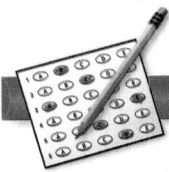 **Challenge**

32. A carnival charges $5 for admission plus $2 per ride.
  a. Write an expression for the cost of admission plus r rides.
  b. Find the cost of admission plus six rides.
  c. How many rides can you afford if you have $15 to spend?

33. **Writing in Math** Write a word problem that could be solved by evaluating the expression $3x - 5$ for $x = 5$.

Test Prep

Multiple Choice

In Exercises 34–37, use the following fact to answer the questions: Every minute, about 145 babies are born in the world.

34. Which expression shows how many babies are born in the world in m minutes?
  A. $60m$
  B. $145m + 60$
  C. $60m + 145$
  D. $145m$

35. How many babies are born in the world in 6 minutes?
  F. 360 babies
  G. 505 babies
  H. 870 babies
  I. 930 babies

36. How many babies are born in the world in one day?
  A. 3,480 babies
  B. 86,400 babies
  C. 104,400 babies
  D. 208,800 babies

Take It to the NET
Online lesson quiz at
www.PHSchool.com
Web Code: ada-0103

37. How many babies are born in the world in one week?
  F. 1,461,600 babies
  G. 522,000 babies
  H. 60,900 babies
  I. 10,080 babies

Mixed Review

Lesson 1-2

Simplify each expression.

38. $(60 - 6) \div 9$ **39.** $80 \div 2 + 13$ **40.** $5 \div 5 \cdot 5 - 5$

Lesson 1-1

Write a variable expression for each word phrase.

41. t fewer than 19   **42.** d divided by 20   **43.** the sum of 8 and n

Previous Course

44. **Error Analysis** Valerie has test grades of 96, 82, 78, and 76. Using a calculator, she found her average grade to be 275. Is Valerie's answer reasonable? Explain Valerie's error.

1-4 Integers and Absolute Value

What You'll Learn

 OBJECTIVE 1 To represent, graph, and order integers

 OBJECTIVE 2 To find opposites and absolute values

. . . And Why

To represent real-world quantities that are less than zero, such as cold temperatures

✓ Check Skills You'll Need

Write an integer for each situation.

1. lose $7

2. find $9

3. 8 steps forward

4. 3 yards gained

5. 5 floors down

❓ For help, go to Skills Handbook, p. 775.

New Vocabulary

• opposites
• integers
• absolute value

OBJECTIVE

1 Comparing Integers

Antifreeze is mixed with the water in a car's radiator to prevent the water from freezing. Pure water freezes at about 32 degrees Fahrenheit (°F) *above* zero. A mixture of equal parts water and antifreeze freezes at about 32 degrees *below* zero.

Freezing Points

Substance	Freezing Temperature (°F)
Water	32
Antifreeze and water	−32
Seawater	28
Gasoline	−36

You can write 32 degrees above zero as +32°F or 32°F. You can write 32 degrees below zero as −32°F. Read the numbers 32 and −32 as "*positive* 32" and "*negative* 32," respectively.

1 EXAMPLE **Representing Negative Numbers**

Temperature **Write a number to represent the temperature shown by the thermometer.**

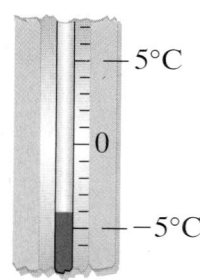

The temperature of the liquid in the thermometer is 4 degrees Celsius below zero, or −4°C.

✓ Check Understanding Example 1

1. Temperature Seawater freezes at about 28°F, or about 2 degrees Celsius below zero. Write a number to represent the Celsius temperature.

You can graph positive and negative numbers on a number line. A number line helps you compare numbers and arrange them in order.

Numbers increase in value from left to right.

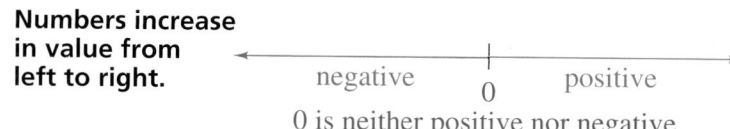

0 is neither positive nor negative.

🅘 **TEXT** Interactive lesson includes instant self-check, tutorials, and activities.

2 EXAMPLE · Graphing on a Number Line

Graph −1, 4, and −5 on a number line. Order the numbers from least to greatest.

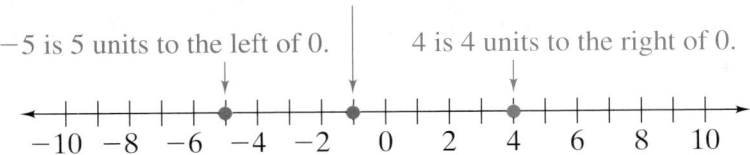

−1 is 1 unit to the left of 0.

−5 is 5 units to the left of 0.

4 is 4 units to the right of 0.

● The numbers from least to greatest are −5, −1, and 4.

✓ Check Understanding   Example 2

2. Graph 0, 2, and −6 on a number line. Order the numbers from least to greatest.

OBJECTIVE
2 ▸ Finding Absolute Value

Numbers that are the same distance from zero on a number line but in opposite directions are called **opposites.**

|← 4 units →|← 4 units →| −4 and 4
−5 −4 −3 −2 −1 0 1 2 3 4 5   are opposites.

Integers are the whole numbers and their opposites. A number's distance from zero on the number line is called its **absolute value.** You write *the absolute value of 3* as |3|.

> **Need Help?**
> Recall: The whole numbers, 0, 1, 2, 3, 4, . . . , are the counting numbers and zero.

3 EXAMPLE · Finding Absolute Value

Use a number line to find |−3| and |3|.

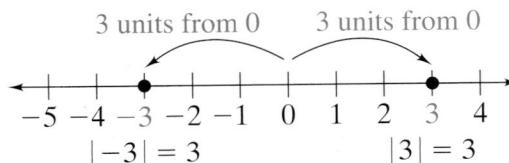

3 units from 0   3 units from 0

−5 −4 −3 −2 −1 0 1 2 3 4

|−3| = 3 |3| = 3

✓ Check Understanding   Example 3

3. Write |−10| in words. Then find |−10|.

EXERCISES

For more exercises, see *Extra Practice*.

Practice and Problem Solving

A Practice by Example

Write a number to represent each quantity.

Example 1
(page 18)

1. a profit of $250   **2.** 18°C below zero   **3.** 45 s before launch

4. a deposit of $110   **5.** a debt of $50   **6.** win by 7 points

7. 300 ft below sea level   **8.** a loss of 8 yd   **9.** an elevation of 3,400 ft

Example 2
(page 19)

Write the number represented by each point on the number line.

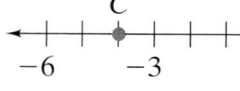 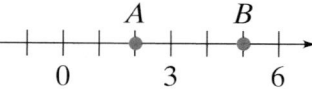

10. A **11.** B **12.** C

Graph each set of numbers on a number line. Then order the numbers from least to greatest.

13. $-2, 8, -9$ **14.** $-3, -12, -9$ **15.** $0, 6, -6$

Example 3
(page 19)

Use a number line to find the absolute values of the integers in each pair.

16. $1, -1$ **17.** $-2, 2$ **18.** $-8, 8$ **19.** $-7, 7$ **20.** $6, -6$ **21.** $-4, 4$

Simplify each expression.

22. $|18|$ **23.** the absolute value of -9

24. $|-3|$ **25.** the absolute value of 6

26. $|-7|$ **27.** the absolute value of -2

B Apply Your Skills

Open-Ended Describe a quantity each integer could represent.

28. $-1,000$ **29.** 28 **30.** -126

Write the integer represented by each point.

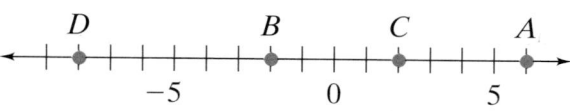

31. A **32.** B **33.** C **34.** D

Simplify each expression.

35. $|0|$ **36.** $|-1,000|$ **37.** $-|-13|$

38. $|-56|$ **39.** $-|-23|$ **40.** $-|12|$

Compare. Use >, <, or = to complete each statement.

41. $-8 \blacksquare 0$ **42.** $4 \blacksquare -25$ **43.** $-9 \blacksquare -2$

44. $|-1| \blacksquare |50|$ **45.** $|-6| \blacksquare |-12|$ **46.** $|10| \blacksquare |-10|$

Write an expression to represent each quantity.

47. 10 times your height h in inches

48. a loss of $\frac{1}{3}$ of an investment of d dollars

49. n degrees Fahrenheit above $r°$F room temperature

Read the passage below before doing Exercises 50 and 51.

Finding Famous Ships

Scientist-explorer Robert D. Ballard led the expeditions that found two famous ships deep in the North Atlantic Ocean.

In 1912, the luxury passenger liner *Titanic* struck an iceberg. It came to rest 12,500 ft below sea level. *Titanic* was 882 ft long and 92 ft wide.

In 1941, the mighty warship *Bismarck* sank in battle. *Bismarck* was 823 ft long and 118 ft wide.

Star Hercules, only 269 ft long, towed the underwater camera sled that found *Bismarck* under 15,617 ft of water.

50. Write integers that represent the positions of *Titanic* and *Bismarck*.

51. A friend says that *Bismarck*'s resting place is higher than *Titanic*'s, since 15,617 is higher than 12,500. Explain your friend's error.

Complete each sentence with a word that makes it true.

52. An integer is negative, positive, or   ? .

53. All   ?   integers are less than zero.

54. The opposite of a   ?   number is negative.

55. The absolute value of an integer is never   ? .

 **Challenge**

Open-Ended Name two consecutive integers between the given integers.

56. $-6, 2$ **57.** $0, -4$ **58.** $-8, -12$

59. a. Data Analysis Use a number line to graph the temperatures in the chart at the left. Label each temperature with the name of the state where it was recorded.
   b. Which state recorded the lowest temperature?

60. Writing in Math How can you use integers to describe elevations above and below sea level?

61. Reasoning Explain why $|x + y|$ and $|x| + |y|$ are not the same. Give examples to show that $|x + y| = |x| + |y|$ for some values of x and y, and that $|x + y| \neq |x| + |y|$ for other values of x and y.

Record Low Temperatures for Three States

State	Temperature (°C)
California	-45
Nevada	-50
Georgia	-17

Source: *The World Almanac*

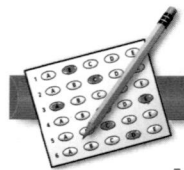

Multiple Choice

62. Which list shows the values in order from least to greatest?
  A. 0, 3, −17, −25   **B.** −25, −17, 0, 3
  C. 0, −17, −25, 3   **D.** −25, 0, 3, −27

63. Which expression has the value −90?
  F. $|-90|$ **G.** 90   **H.** $|90|$ **I.** $-|90|$

64. Which list shows the values in order from least to greatest?
  A. $|-6|, 6, |-3|, 3$ **B.** $-6, -|-3|, 3, |-6|$
  C. $|-6|, |-3|, |3|, |6|$ **D.** $-3, -|-6|, -|3|, 6$

65. Which two integers are between −5 and 2?
  F. −4, 1   **G.** −3, 3   **H.** −6, 1   **I.** 0, 4

Take It to the NET
Online lesson quiz at
www.PHSchool.com
Web Code: ada-0104

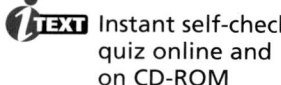
Mixed Review

Lesson 1-3

Evaluate each expression.

66. $p - 5$, for $p = 19$ **67.** $3d + 3$, for $d = 7$ **68.** $55y$, for $y = 8$

Lesson 1-2

Compare. Use >, <, or = to complete each statement.

69. $5 + 10 \div 5 \blacksquare (5 + 10) \div 5$

70. $(9 - 6) \div (2 + 1) \blacksquare 9 - 6 \div 2 + 1$

Lesson 1-1

71. Suppose you have c CDs. Your friend has 6 more CDs than you do. Write an expression for the number of CDs your friend has.

✓ Checkpoint Quiz 1   Lessons 1-1 through 1-4

TEXT Instant self-check quiz online and on CD-ROM

Write a variable expression for each word phrase.

  1. 23 more than f **2.** g divided by 34   **3.** product of 9 and p

Simplify each expression.

  4. $17 + 16 - 13$ **5.** $70 \div [5(3 + 4)]$ **6.** $9 \times 6 \div 3 + 1$

Evaluate each expression for $x = 4$, $y = 6$, and $z = 12$.

  7. $2x - 8$ **8.** $3(z + y)$ **9.** $4y - z + \frac{z}{x}$

🌐 **10. Temperature** On Monday the average temperature was −10°F. On Tuesday it was −15°F. On Wednesday it was −13°F. On Thursday it was 0°F.
  a. Graph the temperatures on a number line.
  b. Write the days in order from coldest to warmest.

You can use models, such as colored tiles, to represent integers.
Use a yellow tile ▢ to represent a positive integer.
Use a red tile ■ to represent a negative integer.

1 EXAMPLE

Use models to represent the integers 3, −1, and −4.

▢▢▢ 3   ■ −1   ■■■■ −4

An equal number of yellow tiles and red tiles combine to make zero.

These tiles make a zero pair. ⟶ ▢■ represents zero, or ▢ + ■ = 0.

You can remove zero pairs in sets of mixed tiles.

2 EXAMPLE

Write the integer that is represented by ■■■■■▢▢.

**Group the zero pairs.
Then remove them.**

■■■ −3   **Write the integer that the
remaining tiles represent.**

EXERCISES

Use tiles to model each integer.

1. −3   **2.** 5   **3.** −2   **4.** 7

5. 0   **6.** −6   **7.** 2   **8.** −8

Write an integer for each model.

9. ▢▢

10. ■■■■■

11. ■■

12. ▢▢▢▢▢▢

13. ■■▢▢ ▢▢■■

14. ■■▢▢■▢ ▢

15. ▢■▢▢▢▢ ▢▢■■

16. ■■▢▢▢■■

1-5 Adding Integers

What You'll Learn

OBJECTIVE 1 To use models to add integers

OBJECTIVE 2 To use rules to add integers

. . . And Why

To use integers to solve real-world problems in sports and Earth science

Check Skills You'll Need

Compare. Use >, <, or = to complete each statement.

1. $-6 \blacksquare -3$

2. $2 \blacksquare -15$

3. $-5 \blacksquare |5|$

4. $|10| \blacksquare |-10|$

5. $|9| \blacksquare |-2|$

6. $|-8| \blacksquare |0|$

For help, go to Lesson 1-4.

OBJECTIVE

1 Using Models to Add Integers

If a car goes forward 20 ft and then backs up 20 ft, it ends where it started. Using opposite integers, you can represent this situation as $20 + (-20) = 0$.

When you add opposites, the sum is zero. So, opposites are also called *additive inverses*.

Key Concepts   **Addition of Opposites**

The sum of an integer and its opposite is zero.

Arithmetic	Algebra
$1 + (-1) = 0$	$x + (-x) = 0$
$-1 + 1 = 0$	$-x + x = 0$

You can use tiles to add integers. One positive tile and one negative tile combine to make a zero pair, since $\square + \blacksquare = 0$.

To add integers using tiles, combine tiles and remove the zero pairs.

1 EXAMPLE   Using Tiles to Add Integers

Modeling Use tiles to find $2 + (-5)$.

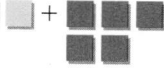

$2 + (-5)$ Model the sum.

-3 Group and remove zero pairs. There are three negative tiles left.

• $2 + (-5) = -3$

Check Understanding   Example 1

1. Use tiles to find each sum.

   a. $-1 + 4$ **b.** $7 + (-3)$ **c.** $-2 + (-2)$

iTEXT Interactive lesson includes instant self-check, tutorials, and activities.

A number line provides another model that you can use to add integers, as shown in Example 2.

2 EXAMPLE Using a Number Line

Football On two plays, a football team first loses 8 yd and then gains 3 yd. Find $-8 + 3$ to find the result of the two plays.

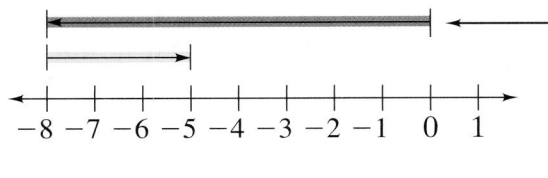

Start at 0. To represent -8, move left 8 units. To add positive 3, move right 3 units to -5.

$$-8 + 3 = -5$$

● The result of the two plays is a loss of 5 yd.

✓ **Check Understanding** Example 2

2. Use a number line to find each sum.

   a. $2 + (-6)$ **b.** $-4 + 9$ **c.** $-5 + (-1)$

OBJECTIVE

2 **Using Rules to Add Integers**

You can also use rules to find the sum of two integers.

Key Concepts Adding Integers

Same Sign The sum of two positive integers is positive. The sum of two negative integers is negative.

Different Signs To add two integers with different signs, find the difference of their absolute values. The sum has the sign of the integer with the greater absolute value.

3 EXAMPLE Applying Rules to Add Integers

Find each sum.

a. $-12 + (-31)$

   $-12 + (-31) = -43$ Since both integers are negative, the sum is negative.

b. $7 + (-18)$

   $|-18| - |7| = 18 - 7$ Find the difference of the absolute values.

   $\qquad\quad = 11$ Simplify.

   $7 + (-18) = -11$ Since -18 has the greater absolute value, the sum is negative.

3. Find each sum.

   a. $-22 + (-16)$ **b.** $60 + (-13)$ **c.** $-125 + 35$

4 **EXAMPLE**   Real-World  Problem Solving

Earth Science The earthquake monitor in Hockley, Texas, is located in a salt mine at an elevation of -416 m. The elevation of the monitor in Albuquerque, New Mexico, is 2,156 m higher than the one in Hockley. Find the elevation of the monitor in Albuquerque.

$-416 + 2,156$	Write an expression.
$\lvert 2,156 \rvert - \lvert -416 \rvert = 2,156 - 416$	Find the difference of the absolute values.
$= 1,740$	Simplify.
$-416 + 2,156 = 1,740$	Since 2,156 has the greater absolute value, the sum is positive.

Real-World Connection

A worldwide network of monitors keeps track of earthquake activity. Here technicians check the monitor in Albuquerque.

● The elevation of the monitor in Albuquerque is 1,740 m.

✓ **Check Understanding**   Example 4

4. The elevation of a monitor in Piñon Flat, California, is 1,696 m higher than the monitor in Hockley, Texas. Find the elevation of the monitor in Piñon Flat.

To add several integers, use the order of operations.

5 **EXAMPLE**   Using the Order of Operations

Find $-12 + (-6) + 15 + (-2)$.

$-12 + (-6) + 15 + (-2)$	Add from left to right.
$-18 \quad + \quad 15 + (-2)$	The sum of two negative integers is negative.
$-3 \quad + \quad (-2)$	$\lvert -18 \rvert - \lvert 15 \rvert = 3.$ Since -18 has the greater absolute value, the sum is negative.
-5	The sum of two negative integers is negative.

● $-12 + (-6) + 15 + (-2) = -5$

✓ **Check Understanding**   Example 5

5. Find each sum.

   a. $1 + (-3) + 2 + (-10)$ **b.** $-250 + 200 + (-100) + 220$

EXERCISES

❓ For more exercises, see *Extra Practice*.

Practice and Problem Solving

A Practice by Example

Examples 1 and 2
(pages 24 and 25)

Modeling Write an expression for each model. Find the sum.

1.

2.

3.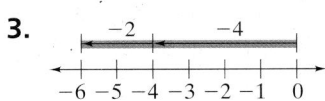

4.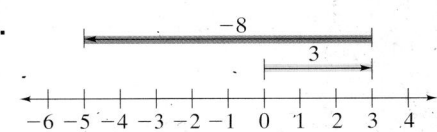

Draw a model and find each sum.

5. $2 + (-5)$ 6. $-5 + 2$ 7. $5 + (-2)$ 8. $-5 + (-2)$

9. $-6 + 1$ 10. $-3 + (-6)$ 11. $-3 + 2$ 12. $-3 + 4$

Example 3
(page 25)

Find each sum.

13. $14 + (-11)$ 14. $0 + (-9)$ 15. $-6 + (-7)$

16. $-18 + 4$ 17. $-40 + 93$ 18. $-26 + (-39)$

19. $450 + (-350)$ 20. $100 + (-100)$ 21. $235 + (-420)$

Example 4 🌐
(page 26)

22. **Geography** The highest peak at Mount Ellsworth in Montana is 3,275 m lower than the highest peak of Mount Kilimanjaro in Kenya, at 5,895 m. Find the elevation of the highest peak at Mount Ellsworth.

Example 5
(page 26)

Find each sum.

23. $19 + (-9) + 45 + (-32)$ 24. $-3 + 2 + (-7) + 7 + 13$

25. $-94 + 68 + (-22) + (-13)$ 26. $-20 + (-89) + 112 + 9$

B Apply Your Skills

Reasoning Without adding, tell whether each sum is positive, negative, or zero. Explain how you found your answer.

27. $-4 + (-10)$ 28. $11 + (-3)$ 29. $6 + (-6)$

Mental Math Find each sum.

30. $-5 + 20$ 31. $9 + (-9)$ 32. $-4 + (-2) + (-2)$

33. $10 + (-3)$ 34. $-5 + 5 + 16$ 35. $-120 + 100 + (-20)$

Compare. Use >, <, or = to complete each statement.

36. $-6 + 1$ ▇ $5 + 1$ 37. $0 + 3$ ▇ $-2 + 0$

38. $10 + (-2)$ ▇ $-4 + 12$ 39. $-1 + 1$ ▇ $-2 + 0$

40. $49 + (-21)$ ▇ $|-18|$ 41. $|-20| + (-7)$ ▇ $-11 + (-11)$

Evaluate each expression for $n = -15$.

42. $n + (-7) - n$　　　**43.** $15 + n + (-8)$　　　**44.** $n + (-15) + n$

Write a numerical expression for each of the following. Then find the sum.

45. You borrow $20, and then pay back $18.

46. You save $200, and then spend $75.

47. A man deposits $120, and then writes a check for $25.

48. A submarine at 35 ft below sea level moves up 10 ft.

Use the order of operations to find each sum.

49. $4 + (-6) + 3$　　　　　　　　**50.** $-1 + 1 + (-3)$

51. $-72 + 36 + (-6) + (-18)$

52. Football A football team gained 4 yd, lost 2 yd, gained 11 yd, lost 8 yd, and then lost 9 yd. Find the net gain or loss.

53. Finance Maria had $123. She spent $35, loaned $20 to a friend, and received her $90 paycheck. How much does she have now?

54. Error Analysis A friend says that the value of $-17 + 5$ is -22. Explain how your friend may have made this error.

55. Writing in Math A friend is having trouble finding the sum of -84 and 28. What explanation would you give to help your friend?

C Challenge　　**Reasoning** For Exercises 56–59, use the number line and tell whether the value of each expression is positive or negative.

a　　　　　b　0　　　　c

56. $a + b$　　　**57.** $b + c$　　　**58.** $a + a$　　　**59.** $|a + b + c|$

Test Prep

Multiple Choice　　**60.** The temperature starts at $-10°$F, drops $2°$, drops $5°$, and rises $1°$. Which expression gives the current temperature?

　　A. $(-10) + 2 + 5 + 1$　　　**B.** $-10 + (-2) + (-5) + 1$
　　C. $10 + 2 + 5 + (-1)$　　　**D.** $10 + 2 + 5 + 1$

61. A stock price starts at $6, rises $3, falls $1, and falls $1 again. What is the current price of the stock?

　　F. $1　　　**G.** $5　　　**H.** $7　　　**I.** $11

62. Which statement shows an example of additive inverses?

　　A. $xy = yx$　　　**B.** $x[y + (-y)] = x(0)$
　　C. $x + y = y + x$　　　**D.** $x\left(\dfrac{y}{y}\right) = x(1)$

63. Refer to the map at the right. The lowest temperature recorded in South America is 54 degrees higher than the lowest temperature recorded in North America. What is the lowest temperature recorded in South America?

F. −135°F   **G.** −27°F

H. −17°F   **I.** −138°F

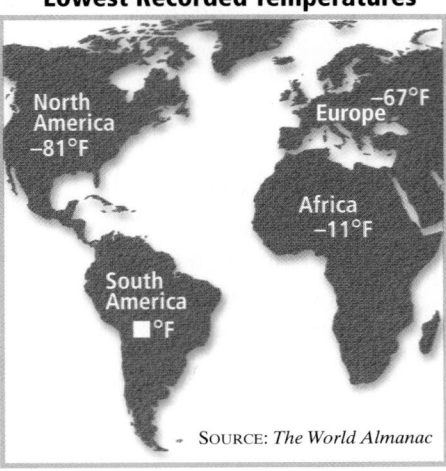

Lowest Recorded Temperatures

North America −81°F

Europe −67°F

Africa −11°F

South America ■°F

SOURCE: *The World Almanac*

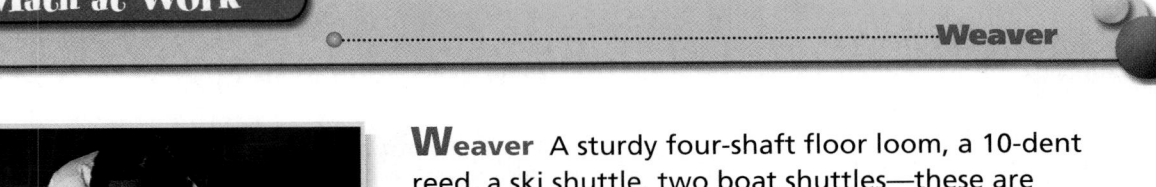

Mixed Review

Lesson 1-4   **Compare. Use >, <, or = to complete each statement.**

64. −90 ■ −6   **65.** −2 ■ −7   **66.** |−15| ■ −15

67. 0 ■ −8   **68.** −45 ■ −44   **69.** 100 ■ |−101|

70. Write a numerical expression for the phrase *one hundred thirty added to the difference of one hundred sixteen and eight.* Then simplify the expression.

Lesson 1-3 🌐 **71. Repairs** A repair center charges a $25 flat fee plus $10 per hour for labor. Write an expression for the cost of a repair that takes *n* hours. Then evaluate the expression to find the cost of an oven repair that takes 3 hours.

Math at Work

Weaver

Weaver A sturdy four-shaft floor loom, a 10-dent reed, a ski shuttle, two boat shuttles—these are some of the tools and terms of the ancient craft of weaving. Weavers use yarn, ribbon, and thread. They design and make colorful, unique items such as rugs, tapestries, and handbags. Like a pattern in algebra, each design has rules that must be followed for the desired result.

Take It to the NET For more information about weavers, go to **www.PHSchool.com**.
Web Code: adb-2031

Subtracting Integers

What You'll Learn

OBJECTIVE 1 To use models to subtract integers

OBJECTIVE 2 To use a rule to subtract integers

. . . And Why

To use integers to solve real-world problems involving weather

✓ Check Skills You'll Need

Find each sum.

1. $8 + (-9)$

2. $-11 + (-18)$

3. $-4 + (-6)$

4. $14 + (-3)$

5. $6 + (-6)$

6. $-13 + (-10)$

💡 For help, go to Lesson 1-5.

OBJECTIVE

1 Using Models to Subtract Integers

You can use tiles to help you understand subtraction of integers.

1 EXAMPLE Using Tiles to Subtract Integers

Find $-6 - (-2)$.

 Start with 6 negative tiles.

 Take away 2 negative tiles.
There are 4 negative tiles left.

• $-6 - (-2) = -4$

✓ Check Understanding Example 1

1. Use tiles to find each difference.

a. $-7 - (-2)$ **b.** $-4 - (-3)$ **c.** $-8 - (-5)$

You can use zero pairs to subtract an integer from a smaller integer.

2 EXAMPLE Using Zero Pairs to Subtract Integers

Find $3 - 5$.

 Start with 3 positive tiles.

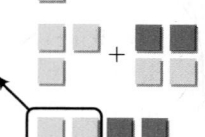 There are not enough positive tiles to take away 5. Add 2 zero pairs.

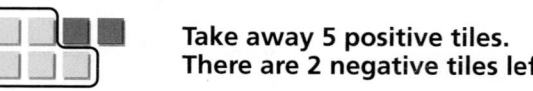 Take away 5 positive tiles.
There are 2 negative tiles left.

• $3 - 5 = -2$

✓ Check Understanding Example 2

2. Use tiles to find each difference.

a. $4 - 8$ **b.** $-1 - 5$ **c.** $-2 - (-7)$

iTEXT Interactive lesson includes instant self-check, tutorials, and activities.

You can use models to show the relationship between adding and subtracting integers.

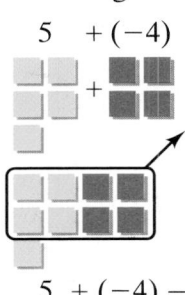

5 + (−4)

5 + (−4) = 1

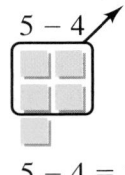

5 − 4

5 − 4 = 1

Both 5 + (−4) and 5 − 4 equal 1. So, 5 + (−4) = 5 − 4.

The models suggest the following rule for subtracting integers.

> **Key Concepts**   **Subtracting Integers**
>
> To subtract an integer, add its opposite.
>
> | Arithmetic | Algebra |
> |---|---|
> | $2 - 5 = 2 + (-5) = -3$ | $a - b = a + (-b)$ |
> | $2 - (-5) = 2 + 5 = 7$ | $a - (-b) = a + b$ |

3 EXAMPLE **Real-World** ● **Problem Solving**

Weather **In January, 1916, the temperature in Browning, Montana, dropped 100 degrees overnight. The initial temperature was 44°F. What was the final temperature?**

$44 - 100$ Write an expression.

$44 - 100 = 44 + (-100)$ To subtract 100, add its opposite.

$\qquad\quad = -56$ Simplify.

● The final temperature was −56°F.

✓ **Check Understanding** Example 3

3. Find each difference.

    a. $32 - (-3)$ **b.** $-40 - 66$ **c.** $2 - 48$

    d. The lowest temperature ever recorded on the moon was about −170°C. The lowest temperature ever recorded in Antarctica was −89°C. Find the difference in the temperatures.

Real-World ● **Connection**

The lowest temperature ever recorded on Earth was −129°F (−89°C) in Vostok, Antarctica. Scientists there are taking ice-core samples to depths of −3,600 m.

EXERCISES

❓ For more exercises, see *Extra Practice*.

Practice and Problem Solving

Ⓐ Practice by Example

Examples 1 and 2
(page 30)

Write a number sentence for each model.

1. 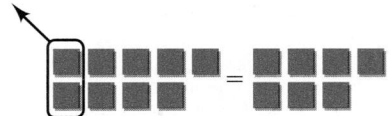   2.

Modeling Use tiles to help you find each difference.

3. $-7 + (-3)$ 4. $-15 - (-7)$ 5. $-5 - (-6)$

6. $-9 - (-7)$ 7. $-7 - (-9)$ 8. $-16 - (-9)$

9. $-8 - (-3)$ 10. $-1 - (-3)$ 11. $10 - (-5)$

12. $9 - (-8)$ 13. $-14 - (-8)$ 14. $-7 - (-7)$

15. $2 - 3$ 16. $-2 - 3$ 17. $-10 - 2$

Example 3
(page 31)

Write each difference as a sum. Then simplify.

18. $6 - 2$ 19. $6 - (-2)$ 20. $-6 - 2$ 21. $2 - 6$

22. $2 - (-6)$ 23. $-2 - 6$ 24. $5 - 11$ 25. $75 - (-25)$

26. $22 - (-7)$ 27. $87 - (-9)$ 28. $35 - 15$ 29. $100 - (-91)$

🌐 30. **Account Balances** Terry has $43 in a checking account. If Terry writes a check for $62, what is the new account balance?

🌐 31. **Scores** Suppose you have a score of 35 in a game. You get a 50-point penalty. What is your new score?

Ⓑ Apply Your Skills

Find each difference.

32. $-49 - 75$ 33. $-65 - 15$ 34. $16 - (-3)$

35. $120 - (-50)$ 36. $989 - 76$ 37. $-35 - 25$

38. $-92 - (-9)$ 39. $-81 - (-13)$ 40. $36 - 88$

Simplify.

41. $-90 - (-80) - 20$ 42. $810 - 30 - (-70)$

43. $23 - (-15) - 28$ 44. $-17 + 25 - (-58)$

Open-Ended Use positive and negative integers to write two different subtraction number sentences for each difference.

SAMPLE   ■ − ■ = −5 $17 - 22 = -5$
                        $-20 - (-15) = -5$

45. ■ − ■ = 0   46. ■ − ■ = 10   47. ■ − ■ = −6

48. ■ − ■ = −15   49. ■ − ■ = $|-3|$ 50. ■ − ■ = $|11|$

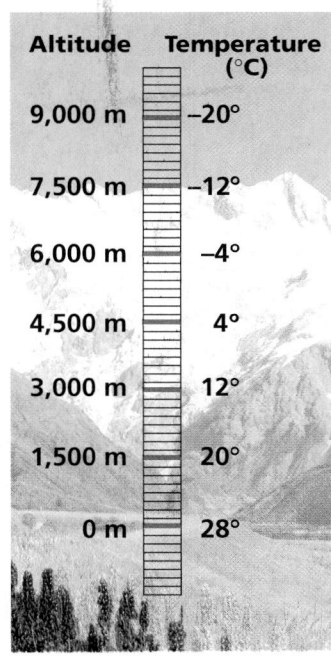

Altitude	Temperature (°C)
9,000 m	−20°
7,500 m	−12°
6,000 m	−4°
4,500 m	4°
3,000 m	12°
1,500 m	20°
0 m	28°

Meteorology The graph at the left shows how temperature changes with altitude. Use this graph for Exercises 51–53.

51. As the altitude increases, what happens to the temperature?

52. What is the change in temperature from 1,500 m to 6,000 m?

53. What is the change in temperature for every 1,500-m increase in altitude?

Mental Math Simplify each expression.

54. $-6 - (-8)$
55. $-45 - 15$
56. $-7 - (-7) + (-7)$

57. $100 - (-50)$
58. $20 - (-10) - 20$
59. $-11 + 22 - (-55)$

60. $3 - (-3) + 6$
61. $-32 + 2 + (-10)$
62. $-87 + (-3) + 90$

63. $6 - (-6) + 6$
64. $0 + (-15) - 15$
65. $-13 - 17 + 10$

Write a numerical expression for each phrase. Then simplify and answer the question.

66. You are $2 in debt. You borrow $4 more. What is the total amount of your debt?

67. An airplane takes off, climbs 3,000 ft, and then descends 600 ft. What is the airplane's current height?

68. From 0°F, the temperature increases 15 degrees and then drops 25 degrees. What is the current temperature?

C Challenge

Estimation Round each number. Then estimate the sum or difference.

SAMPLE $-2,216 - 488 \approx -2,200 - 500 = -2,700$

69. $-41 - (-86)$
70. $-227 - 49$
71. $-398 - 67$

72. $-86 - 22$
73. $288 - 59$
74. $63 - (-21)$

75. a. **Writing in Math** A thermometer is like a vertical number line. Use the one at the right to write a subtraction problem.
b. Write and simplify a numerical expression for your problem.

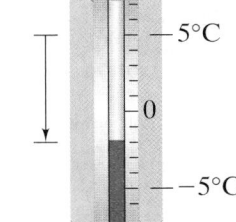
5°C
0
−5°C

76. a. **Patterns** Copy and complete. The first one is done for you.
$8 - (-4) = 12$
$12 - (-4) = \blacksquare$
$16 - (-4) = \blacksquare$
$20 - (-4) = \blacksquare$
$24 - (-4) = \blacksquare$
b. If you begin at 8 and subtract −4 five times, the result is $\blacksquare$.
c. Begin at 0 and subtract −4 six times. What is the result?

77. **Reasoning** For what values of a is each statement true? Give an example, if possible.
a. $|a - 5| = |a| - 5$ **b.** $|a - 5| > |a| - 5$ **c.** $|a - 5| < |a| - 5$

In each number square, the rows, columns, and diagonals have the same sum. Copy and complete each number square.

78.

5	−9	▦
▦	−1	▦
−3	▦	−7

sum = ▦

79.

−2	▦	▦
−9	−5	▦
−4	▦	▦

sum = ▦

80.

▦	−5	▦	6
▦	4	3	▦
2	0	▦	5
−3	▦	▦	−6

sum = ▦

81.

−6	4	5	−9
2	▦	−1	−3
−5	1	▦	0
▦	−7	−8	▦

sum = ▦

Test Prep

Multiple Choice

82. Three of the four expressions have the same value. Which one has a different value?
  A. $6 + (−4)$ **B.** $6 − 4$ **C.** $|4 − 6|$ **D.** $−6 − 4$

83. Suppose you have a score of 25 in a game. You get a penalty that lowers your score by 60 points. What is your new score?
  F. $−85$ **G.** $−40$ **H.** $−35$ **I.** 15

84. How many degrees warmer is a temperature of 20°C than a temperature of −7°C?
  A. $−27°C$ **B.** $−13°C$ **C.** $13°C$ **D.** $27°C$

85. What is the value of $−23 + −(−15) + |−17| + (−35)$?
  F. $−56$ **G.** $−26$ **H.** $|−26|$ **I.** 56

Take It to the NET
Online lesson quiz at
www.PHSchool.com
Web Code: ada-0106

Mixed Review

Lesson 1-5   **Find each sum.**

86. $−17 + 12$ **87.** $−8 + 15$ **88.** $−9 + (−4) + 7$

Lesson 1-4   **Open-Ended** **Complete each statement with an integer.**

89. $−5 > $ ▦   **90.** ▦ < 6 **91.** $|−1| > $ ▦   **92.** $|▦| < 8$

Lesson 1-1   **93.** Write an expression for the phrase *one hundred plus the product of six and nine*. Simplify the expression.

Inductive Reasoning

OBJECTIVE
1 **Writing Rules for Patterns**

Inductive reasoning is making conclusions based on patterns you observe. A conclusion you reach by inductive reasoning is a **conjecture**.

1 EXAMPLE **Reasoning Inductively**

Visual Patterns Use inductive reasoning. Make a conjecture about the next figure in the pattern. Then draw the figure.

 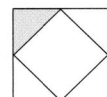 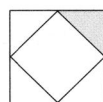

Observation: The shaded triangle is rotating clockwise around the square.

Conjecture: The next figure will have a shaded triangle in the bottom-right corner.

✓**Check Understanding** Example 1

1. Make a conjecture about the next figure in the pattern at the right. Then draw the figure.

For a number pattern, a conjecture can be a rule that explains how to make the pattern.

2 EXAMPLE **Writing Rules for Patterns**

Number Patterns Write a rule for each number pattern.

a. 30, 25, 20, 15, . . . Start with 30 and subtract 5 repeatedly.

b. 2, −2, 2, −2, . . . Alternate 2 and its opposite.

c. 1, 3, 4, 12, 13, . . . Start with 1. Alternate multiplying by 3 and adding 1.

✓**Check Understanding** Example 2

2. Write a rule for each pattern.

   a. 4, 9, 14, 19, . . .   b. 3, 9, 27, 81, . . .   c. 1, 1, 2, 3, 5, 8, . . .

What You'll Learn

OBJECTIVE
1 To write rules for patterns

OBJECTIVE
2 To make predictions and test conjectures

. . . And Why

To use inductive reasoning in finding patterns and in making conjectures about economic data

✓ Check Skills You'll Need

Find each difference.

1. −3 − 4   2. −7 − 4

3. −11 − 4   4. −15 − 4

🔎 For help, go to Lesson 1-6.

New Vocabulary

- inductive reasoning
- conjecture
- counterexample

Reading Math
The three dots in a pattern tell you that the pattern continues.

iTEXT Interactive lesson includes instant self-check, tutorials, and activities.

3 EXAMPLE Extending a Pattern

Number Patterns Write a rule for the number pattern
640, 320, 160, 80, . . . Find the next two numbers in the pattern.

640,   320,   160,   80
     $\div 2$ $\div 2$ $\div 2$

The first number is 640. The next numbers are found by dividing by 2.

The rule is *Start with 640 and divide by 2.* The next two numbers
in the pattern are 80 ÷ 2 = 40 and 40 ÷ 2 = 20.

✔ Check Understanding Example 3

3. Write a rule for the pattern 1, 3, 5, 7, . . . Find the next two
numbers in the pattern.

OBJECTIVE

2 Predictions and Counterexamples

With sufficient information, you can make predictions based on
reasonable conjectures. Such predictions will probably—but not
necessarily—turn out to be accurate.

4 EXAMPLE Real-World 🌐 Problem Solving

Statistics See the graph below. Is a conjecture that average hourly
earnings in the year 2005 will be about $15.75 reasonable?

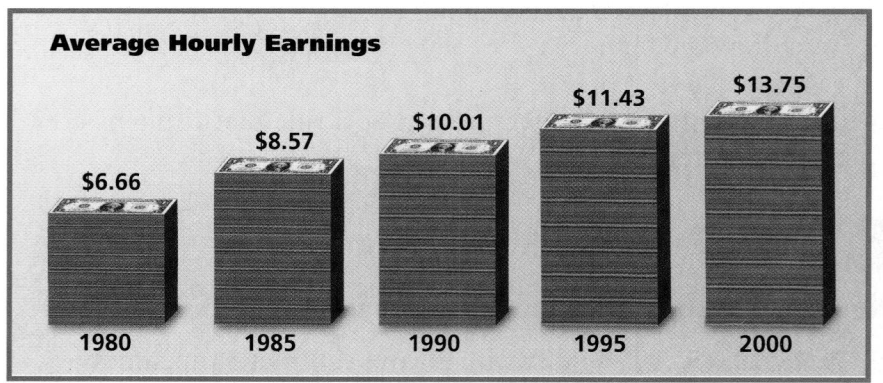

Average Hourly Earnings

$6.66 — 1980
$8.57 — 1985
$10.01 — 1990
$11.43 — 1995
$13.75 — 2000

Average hourly earnings appear to increase by $1.50 to $2.50
every five years. The conjecture of $15.75 in 2005 is reasonable,
since it is about $2.00 more than the earnings for 2000.

✔ Check Understanding Example 4

4. You toss a coin four times, and it comes up heads each time. Is
the conjecture *The coin will come up heads on every toss*
reasonable? Explain.

An example that proves a statement false is a **counterexample.** You need only one counterexample to prove that a conjecture is incorrect.

5 EXAMPLE **Analyzing Conjectures**

Inductive Reasoning Is each conjecture correct or incorrect? If it is incorrect, give a counterexample.

a. **Every four-sided figure is a rectangle.**
   The conjecture is incorrect. The figure below has four sides, but it is not a rectangle.

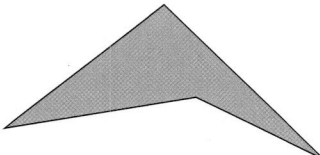

b. **The absolute value of any integer is positive.**
   The conjecture is incorrect. The absolute value of zero is zero, which is neither positive nor negative.

c. **The next figure in the pattern below has 15 dots.**

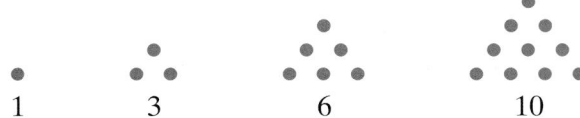

1   3   6   10

The conjecture is correct. The diagram below shows the next figure in the pattern.

Check Understanding Example 5

5. Is each conjecture correct or incorrect? If it is incorrect, give a counterexample.

   a. The last digit of the product of 5 and a whole number is either 0 or 5.
   b. A number and its absolute value are always opposites.
   c. The next figure in the pattern has 25 dots.

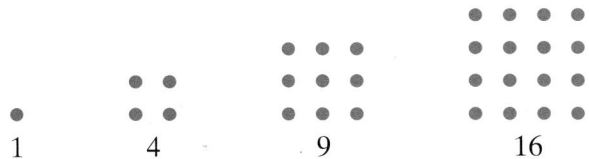

1   4   9   16

EXERCISES

 For more exercises, see *Extra Practice.*

Practice and Problem Solving

A Practice by Example

Example 1
(page 35)

Visual Patterns **Describe the next figure in each pattern. Then draw the figure.**

1.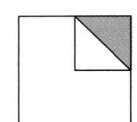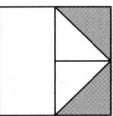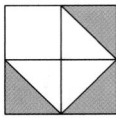

2.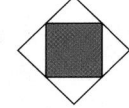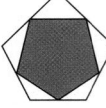

Examples 2 and 3
(pages 35 and 36)

Write a rule for each pattern. Then find the next two numbers in each pattern.

3. $100, 85, 70, 55, \ldots$ 4. $5, 20, 80, 320, \ldots$ 5. $2, 7, 12, 17, \ldots$

6. $-10, -4, 2, 8, \ldots$ 7. $1, 4, 7, 10, \ldots$ 8. $1, 2, 5, 6, 9, \ldots$

Example 4
(page 36)

9. Mario caught a cold on each of his last three visits with his cousin. Is it reasonable for Mario to conclude that his catching a cold is the result of visiting his cousin? Explain.

Example 5
(page 37)

Is each conjecture correct or incorrect? If it is incorrect, give a counterexample.

10. All birds can fly.

11. Every square is a rectangle.

12. The product of two numbers is never less than either of the numbers.

B Apply Your Skills

Visual Patterns **Describe the next figure in each pattern. Then draw the figure.**

13.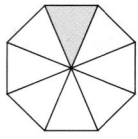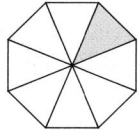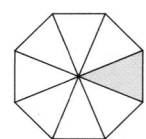

14.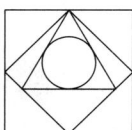

Write a rule for each pattern. Then find the next three numbers in each pattern.

15. $1, 1.5, 2, 2.5, 3, \ldots$ 16. $-1, 1, -2, 2, -3, 3, \ldots$ 17. $6, 4, 2, 0, \ldots$

Reasoning Is each conjecture correct? If incorrect, give a counterexample.

18. Every clover has three leaves.

19. The sum of two numbers is always greater than either of the two numbers.

20. A whole number is divisible by 3 if the sum of its digits is divisible by 3.

C Challenge

Write a rule for each pattern. Then find the next three numbers.

21. $1, 4, 10, 22, 46, 94, \ldots$

22. $1, -2, 4, -5, 7, -8, \ldots$

23. a. Writing in Math Use the graph at the right. Write a conjecture about the unemployment rate in 2001. Justify your reasoning.
b. How could you test your conjecture?

U.S. Unemployment Rate

Test Prep

Multiple Choice

24. What are the next three numbers in this pattern? 11, 22, 12, 23, . . .
A. 13, 23, 14   **B.** 13, 24, 15   **C.** 13, 24, 14   **D.** 32, 43, 33

25. Which best describes the rule for this pattern?
1, −12, 12, −1, . . .
F. subtract 24, then add 13   **G.** subtract 13, then add 24
H. subtract −24, then add 13   **I.** subtract −13, then add 24

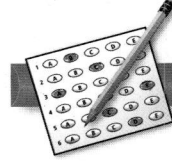

Take It to the NET
Online lesson quiz at
www.PHSchool.com
Web Code: ada-0107

26. Which letter continues this pattern of letters in the alphabet?
B, E, I, N, ▨
A. R   **B.** S   **C.** T   **D.** U

Mixed Review

Lesson 1-6

Find each difference.

27. $1 - 8$

28. $-4 - (-9)$

29. $86 - (-17)$

Lessons 1-3, 1-5

Evaluate each expression for $x = -1$ and $y = -3$.

30. $x + y$

31. $y + x + 2$

32. $24 + x + y$

Lesson 1-3 33. Science The water in a stream flows at the rate of 1,500 gal/h. Write a variable expression for the amount of water that flows in n hours. Evaluate your expression for $n = 24$.

1-8 Problem Solving

Look for a Pattern

OBJECTIVE
1 Finding Number Patterns

What You'll Learn

OBJECTIVE 1 To find number patterns

. . . And Why

To use patterns to solve real-world problems involving communication

✓ Check Skills You'll Need

Write a rule for each pattern. Find the next three numbers.

1. 8, 11, 14, 17, . . .

2. 1, 5, 4, 8, 7, . . .

3. 3, 5, 10, 12, 24, . . .

4. 1, 4, 7, 10, . . .

📖 For help, go to Lesson 1-7.

Math Strategies in Action
What do songs on the radio, computer code, and your body's DNA have in common?

All are based on patterns. Radio uses patterns of electromagnetic waves. Computer code consists of patterns of numbers. Your DNA is made up of molecules that repeat in special patterns.

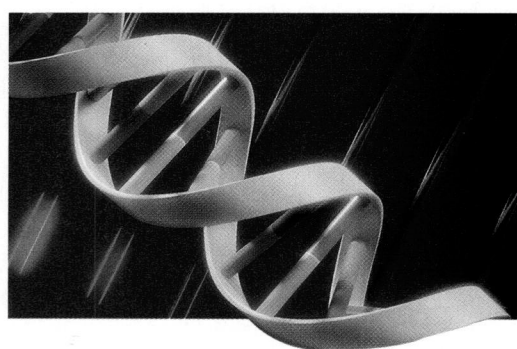

You can solve many types of problems by finding and using patterns. Making predictions from patterns is a form of inductive reasoning.

1 EXAMPLE   Real-World 🌐 Problem Solving

Information News spreads quickly at Riverdell High. Each student who hears a story repeats it 15 minutes later to two students who have not yet heard it, and then tells no one else.

Suppose one student hears some news at 8:00 A.M. How many students will know the news at 9:00 A.M.?

Read and Understand

1. How many students does each student tell?

2. How long does the news take to reach the second and third students?

Plan and Solve

Make a table to organize the numbers. Then look for a pattern.

3. How many *new* students will hear the news at 8:15 A.M.?

4. How many 15-minute periods are there between 8:00 A.M. and 9:00 A.M.?

📱 **TEXT** Interactive lesson includes instant self-check, tutorials, and activities.

The pattern is to add the number of new students to the number who already know.

$$1 + 2 = 3 \quad \text{the number who know at 8:15}$$
(One student talks to 2.)

$$3 + 4 = 7 \quad \text{the number who know at 8:30}$$
(Two students talk to 4.)

Make a table and extend the pattern to 9:00.

Time	8:00	8:15	8:30	8:45	9:00
Number of new students told	1	2	4	8	16
Number of students who know	1	1 + 2 = 3	3 + 4 = 7	7 + 8 = 15	15 + 16 = 31

By 9:00 A.M., 31 students will know the news.

Look Back and Check

One way to check a solution is to solve the problem by another method. You can use a *tree diagram* to show the pattern visually.

Time	New Students	Students Who Know
8:00	1	1
8:15	2	3
8:30	4	7
8:45	8	15
9:00	16	31

5. Describe two ways to find the number of students who will know the news at 9:15 A.M.

6. Suppose you want to continue the pattern beyond 9:15. Which would work better, a table or a tree diagram? Explain.

7. There are 251 students at Riverdell High. By what time will every student know the news?

✓ Check Understanding

8. Suppose each student who hears the story repeats it in 10 minutes. How many students will know the news at 9:00 A.M.?

EXERCISES

For more exercises, see *Extra Practice*.

Practice and Problem Solving

A Practice by Example

Example 1
(page 40)

Look for a Pattern to help you solve each problem.

1. Data Analysis Caroline is training for a swim meet. The graph shows the number of laps per day she swims each week. If she stays with this training pattern, how many laps per day will Caroline swim in week 8?

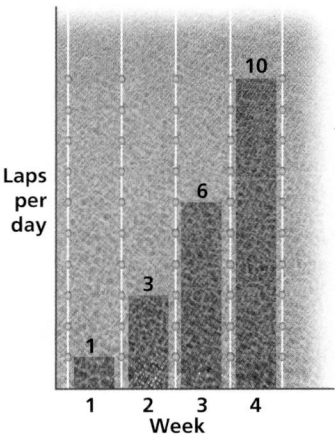

2. Students are to march in a parade. There will be one first grader, two second graders, three third graders, and so on, through the twelfth grade. How many students will march in the parade?

 3. Savings Suppose that every day you save twice as many pennies as you saved the day before. You start by saving one penny on January 1. How much money will you have in all on January 10?

4. An old clock started to lose one minute each day. It was too fragile to fix, but too beloved to stop. How slow was the clock after one year of this? After two years?

B Apply Your Skills

Solve using any strategy.

Strategies

- Account for All Possibilities
- Draw a Diagram
- Look for a Pattern
- Make a Model
- Make a Table
- Simplify the Problem
- Simulate the Problem
- Solve by Graphing
- Try, Test, Revise
- Use Multiple Strategies
- Work Backward
- Write an Equation
- Write a Proportion

5. Geometry You can cut a pizza into two pieces with one straight cut. With two cuts you can get four pieces. Three cuts give a maximum of seven pieces. What is the maximum number of pieces with four cuts? With five cuts?

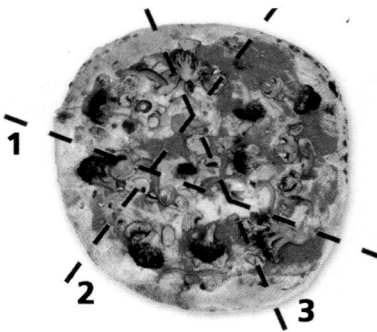

6. a. Number Sense Complete. Then look for a pattern.

$2 \cdot 2 = $ ▪	$3 \cdot 3 = $ ▪
$1 \cdot 3 = $ ▪	$2 \cdot 4 = $ ▪
Difference = ▪	Difference = ▪
$4 \cdot 4 = $ ▪	$5 \cdot 5 = $ ▪
$3 \cdot 5 = $ ▪	$4 \cdot 6 = $ ▪
Difference = ▪	Difference = ▪

b. Which is greater, $10 \cdot 12$ or $11 \cdot 11$? What is the difference?

c. Reasoning Suppose you know that $47 \cdot 47 = 2,209$. Use this to find $46 \cdot 48$.

d. Suppose you know that $64 \cdot 66 = 4,224$. Use this to find $65 \cdot 65$.

7. For a buffet dinner, a restaurant charges $10 for one person, $20 for two, $29 for three, $37 for four, $44 for five, and so on.
  a. How much does a buffet dinner for 8 cost? How much does a group of 8 save by eating together rather than separately?
  b. The buffet costs the restaurant $6 per person. How large a group can the restaurant serve without losing money?

 **Challenge** **8.** A woman jogging at 6 mi/h passes a man biking in the opposite direction at 12 mi/h. If they maintain their speeds, how far from each other will they be 10 minutes after passing?

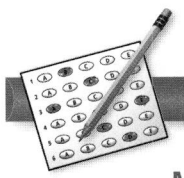

Test Prep

Multiple Choice

9. One edition of *Alice's Adventures in Wonderland* has 352 pages. How many 4s were used in its page numbers?
  A. 38   **B.** 52   **C.** 75   **D.** 88

10. Jayne has 3 quarters, 2 dimes, a nickel, and 2 pennies in her pocket. How many different amounts of money can she make using three of these coins?
  F. 24   **G.** 20   **H.** 17   **I.** 14

11. Assuming one yeast cell "buds" into two cells (the original cell and one new cell) at a rate of once every hour, how many yeast cells will be present from one yeast cell after 8 hours?
  A. 128   **B.** 256   **C.** 512   **D.** 1,024

Take It to the NET
Online lesson quiz at
www.PHSchool.com
Web Code: ada-0108

Mixed Review

Lesson 1-7 **Visual Patterns** Describe the next figure in each pattern. Then draw the figure.

12.

13.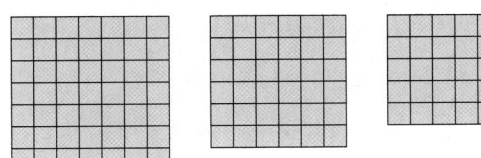

Lesson 1-5 **14. Weather** At midnight, the temperature was $-5°$F. By dawn, the temperature had risen $14°$. What was the temperature at dawn?

Lesson 1-3 Evaluate each expression for $m = 1$ and $n = 4$.

15. $4m - n$ **16.** $mn + 13$ **17.** $4(n + 2) + m$

1-9 Multiplying and Dividing Integers

What You'll Learn

OBJECTIVE 1 To multiply integers using repeated addition, patterns, and rules

OBJECTIVE 2 To divide integers using rules

. . . And Why

To solve real-world problems involving deep-sea exploration and currency

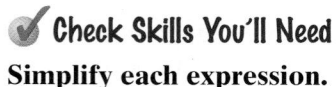
Check Skills You'll Need

Simplify each expression.

1. $5 \cdot 4$ **2.** $3 \cdot 8$

3. $5 \cdot 5$ **4.** $14 \cdot 2$

5. $6 \cdot 5$ **6.** $20 \cdot 7$

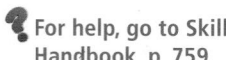 For help, go to Skills Handbook, p. 759.

  **Investigation**

Preparing to Multiply Integers

1. Copy and complete the table. The first row is done for you.

Multiplication	Repeated Addition	Sum
$3 \cdot (-5)$	$-5 + (-5) + (-5)$	-15
$5 \cdot (-4)$	▪	▪
$2 \cdot (-8)$	▪	▪
$4 \cdot (-10)$	▪	▪

2. What do you notice about the signs of the sums?

3. Inductive Reasoning What does the pattern suggest about the product of a positive integer and a negative integer?

You can think of multiplication as repeated addition.

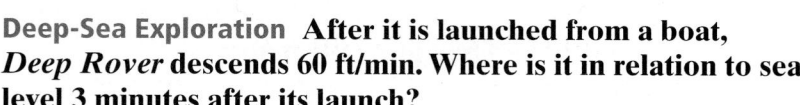 **1 EXAMPLE** **Real-World Problem Solving**

Deep-Sea Exploration **After it is launched from a boat,** *Deep Rover* **descends 60 ft/min. Where is it in relation to sea level 3 minutes after its launch?**

Use a number line to show repeated addition.

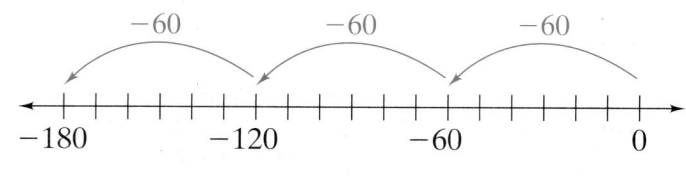

$3(-60) = (-60) + (-60) + (-60) = -180$

● *Deep Rover* is at -180 feet, or 180 feet below sea level.

Real-World Connection

Scientists explore the deep waters of the Pacific Ocean in *Deep Rover*, a submersible designed for research.

iTEXT Interactive lesson includes instant self-check, tutorials, and activities.

Check Understanding Example 1

1. Simplify each product.

a. $2(-6)$ **b.** $4(-3)$ **c.** $7(-2)$

You can use patterns to simplify the product of a negative number and a positive number, or the product of two negative numbers.

2 EXAMPLE Using Patterns to Multiply Integers

Patterns Use a pattern to find each product.

a. $-2(5)$

$2(5) = 10$ **Start with products you know.**

$1(5) = 5$

$0(5) = 0$

$-1(5) = -5$ **Continue the pattern.**

$-2(5) = -10$

b. $-2(-5)$

$2(-5) = -10$

$1(-5) = -5$

$0(-5) = 0$

$-1(-5) = 5$

$-2(-5) = 10$

Writing in Math	
Symbols for multiplication:	
×	-2×2
·	$-2 \cdot 2$
( )	$-2(3)$
*	$-2 * 3$

✓ **Check Understanding** Example 2

2. Patterns Use a pattern to simplify $-3(-4)$.

By inductive reasoning, the patterns from Example 2 suggest rules for multiplying integers.

Key Concepts   Multiplying Integers

The product of two integers with the same sign is positive.
The product of two integers with different signs is negative.
The product of zero and any integer is zero.

Examples

$3(4) = 12$ $3(-4) = -12$

$-3(-4) = 12$ $-3(4) = -12$

$3(0) = 0$ $-4(0) = 0$

3 EXAMPLE Using Rules to Multiply Integers

Multiply $-3 \cdot 5(-4)$.

$-3 \cdot 5(-4) = -15(-4)$ **Multiply from left to right. The product of a negative integer and a positive integer is negative.**

$= 60$ **Multiply. The product of two negative integers is positive.**

✓ **Check Understanding** Example 3

3. Simplify each product.

a. $-4 \cdot 8(-2)$ **b.** $6(-3)(5)$ **c.** $-7 \cdot (-14) \cdot 0$

OBJECTIVE

2 Dividing Integers

The rules for dividing integers are similar to those for multiplying.

Key Concepts **Dividing Integers**

The quotient of two integers with the same sign is positive.
The quotient of two integers with different signs is negative.
Remember that division by zero is undefined.

Examples

$$12 \div 3 = 4 \qquad 12 \div (-3) = -4$$
$$-12 \div (-3) = 4 \qquad -12 \div 3 = -4$$

4 EXAMPLE Real-World Problem Solving

Currency **Find the average of the differences in the values of a Canadian dollar and a U.S. dollar for 1994–1998.**

Value of Dollars (U.S. Cents)

Year	Canadian Dollar	U.S. Dollar	Difference
1994	73	100	−27
1995	73	100	−27
1996	74	100	−26
1997	72	100	−28
1998	68	100	−32

SOURCES: Bank of Canada; *The World Almanac*

$$\frac{-27 + (-27) + (-26) + (-28) + (-32)}{5}$$ Write an expression for the average.

$$= \frac{-140}{5}$$ Use the order of operations. The fraction bar acts as a grouping symbol.

$$= -28$$ The quotient of a negative integer and a positive integer is negative.

For 1994–1998, the average difference was −28¢. The Canadian dollar was worth an average of 28¢ less than the U.S. dollar.

✓ Check Understanding Example 4

4. Simplify each quotient.

 a. $-32 \div 8$ **b.** $-48 \div (-6)$ **c.** $-56 \div (-4)$
 d. Find the average of 4, −3, −5, 2, and −8.

EXERCISES

❓ For more exercises, see *Extra Practice*.

Practice and Problem Solving

Ⓐ Practice by Example

Example 1
(page 44)

1. Write a number sentence for the product shown on the number line.

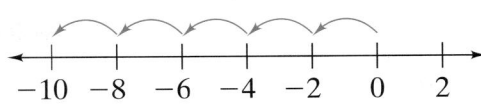

Write each sum as a product. Simplify the product.

2. $(-9) + (-9) + (-9) + (-9)$

3. $(-5) + (-5) + (-5) + (-5) + (-5)$

🌐 **4. Weather** The temperature dropped 5 degrees each hour for 7 h. Use an integer to represent the total change in temperature.

Simplify each product.

5. $3(-3)$	**6.** $4(-11)$	**7.** $3(-8)$
8. $5(-10)$	**9.** $6(-3)$	**10.** $2(-15)$
11. $9(-9)$	**12.** $3(-24)$	**13.** $8(-6)$

Examples 2 and 3
(page 45)

14. $-5(-3)$	**15.** $-6 \cdot 10$	**16.** $-10 \cdot 0$
17. $-9(-8)(-5)$	**18.** $0(-12) \cdot 4$	**19.** $8 \cdot 3(-4)$

Example 4
(page 46)

Find each quotient.

20. $24 \div (-24)$	**21.** $18 \div (-1)$	**22.** $-120 \div 12$
23. $56 \div (-8)$	**24.** $-72 \div 12$	**25.** $-100 \div (-10)$
26. $-38 \div (-2)$	**27.** $-72 \div 6$	**28.** $-33 \div 11$

For each group, find the average.

29. temperatures: $-9°C, -12°C, 9°C, 4°C, -2°C$

30. football yardage: 10 yd, -5 yd, 7 yd, 9 yd, -11 yd

31. golf scores: $-3, 4, 2, 1, -4, -1, 3, -2$

32. bank balances: $325, -\$150, \$130, \$200, -\$45$

Ⓑ Apply Your Skills

Mental Math **Without computing, tell whether each product or quotient is *positive* or *negative*. Explain your reasoning.**

33. $-6(-20)$ **34.** $7(-83)$ **35.** $39 \div (-3)$ **36.** $-3(8)(-24)$

Name the point on the number line that is the graph of each product.

```
   D   F   C         A       B       E
 ┼─┼─┼─●─┼─●─┼─●─┼─┼─┼─●─┼─┼─┼─●─┼─┼─●─┼─┼
  -8  -6  -4  -2   0   2   4   6   8
```

37. $-2 \cdot 0$ **38.** $4(-2)$ **39.** $2(-2)$ **40.** $|-2| \cdot |-2|$

Use repeated addition, patterns, or rules to simplify each product or quotient.

41. $225 \div (-15)$ **42.** $|-2| \cdot (-7)$ **43.** $-59(-79)$

44. $243(-88)$ **45.** $-200 \div -25$ **46.** $-18(-12)$

47. $38(-2)$ **48.** $1,000 \div (-50)$ **49.** $24(-16)(-32)$

50. Investing The price of one share of a stock fell $3 each day for 12 days.
  a. Write an integer to represent the total change in price of a share of the stock.
  b. The original stock price was $76 per share. What was the price after the drop?

Compare. Use >, <, or = to complete each statement.

51. $(-9)(-6) \blacksquare 8(-10)$ **52.** $5(-2) \blacksquare (-6)(-1)$

53. $-10 \div (-2) \blacksquare 25 \div (-5)$ **54.** $-|-28| \div 7 \blacksquare -28 \div (-7)$

55. $|-25| \div |-5| \blacksquare |-25 \div (-5)|$ **56.** $-(-15 \div 5) \blacksquare -100 \div (-20)$

Number Sense Use integer rules and other math facts to answer each question.

57. What integer and -8 have the product -96?

58. What integer and 9 have the product -135?

59. What integer and -3 have the quotient 9?

60. What two integers have a sum of negative ten and a product of negative seventy-five?

C Challenge   **Open-Ended** Simplify each pair of expressions. Then write an integer that is between the values of the expressions.

61. $-2 \cdot (-2)$ and $2 \cdot 4$ **62.** $10 + (-7)$ and $10 \div (-5)$

63. $50 + (-48)$ and $80 \div (-20)$ **64.** $121 \div (-11)$ and $|-7| - |7|$

65. a. Inductive Reasoning Will the sign be positive or negative for the product of three negative integers? Of four negative integers? Of five negative integers?
  b. Writing in Math Use inductive reasoning to write a rule for the sign of the product of more than two negative integers.

66. Reasoning If a and b are positive integers, and x and y are negative integers, what is the sign of $\frac{a + b}{x + y}$? Explain.

67. Investing Jerry owns 20 shares of stock valued at $23 each. One day, the price of the stock rose $2. It fell $1 on each of the next three days. The stock price rose $4 on the next day. What was the average daily gain or loss for a share of the stock over this time period? What was the total value of Jerry's stock at the end of this time period?

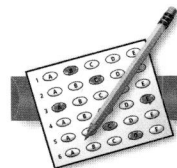
Multiple Choice

68. A scuba diver descended to a depth of 50 feet in 25 seconds. Which integer indicates the average number of feet per second the diver traveled?

A. -50 **B.** -25 **C.** -2 **D.** -1

69. Which of the following is the simplest form of $\frac{-1,225}{35}$?

F. -35 **G.** -25 **H.** -25 **I.** 35

In Exercises 70 and 71, what is the average for each group of data?

70. bank balances: $200, $-85, $120, $200, $280

A. $97   **B.** $119   **C.** $143   **D.** $177

71. feet above and below sea level:

     135 ft, -56 ft, 92 ft, -29 ft, -88 ft, -60 ft

F. -31 ft   **G.** -1 ft   **H.** 19 ft   **I.** 76 ft

Take It to the NET
Online lesson quiz at
www.PHSchool.com
Web Code: ada-0109

Mixed Review

Lesson 1-8

72. Reasoning How many whole numbers from 10 to 200 have exactly two identical digits?

Lessons 1-5 and 1-6

Compare. Use $>$, $<$, or $=$ to complete each statement.

73. $-3 + (-8)$ ▉ $12 - (-6)$

74. $-9 + 13$ ▉ $24 - 30$

75. $|-6| - |12|$ ▉ $-8 + |-12|$

Lesson 1-1

Write a variable expression for each word phrase.

76. 50 decreased by a number n **77.** the product of y and 60

78. the sum of x and y **79.** the quotient of d divided by 5

✓ **Checkpoint Quiz 2**   **Lessons 1-5 through 1-9**

 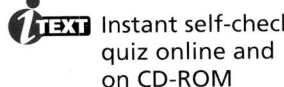 Instant self-check quiz online and on CD-ROM

Simplify each expression.

1. $3 + (-11)$ **2.** $12 - (-8)$ **3.** $-9 \cdot 5$

4. $-64 \div (-8)$ **5.** $|3| \cdot 8 \div (-2)$ **6.** $-8(-3)(3)$

Open-Ended Use integers to complete each equation.

7. ▉ $+$ ▉ $= -7$ **8.** ▉ $- (-20) =$ ▉   **9.** ▉ $\cdot$ ▉ $= -40$

Patterns Find the next three numbers in each pattern.

10. $-7, -2, 3, 8, \ldots$ **11.** $1, 3, 9, 27, \ldots$

The Coordinate Plane

What You'll Learn

OBJECTIVE 1 To name coordinates and quadrants in the coordinate plane

OBJECTIVE 2 To graph points in the coordinate plane

. . . And Why

To solve real-world problems involving geography

✔ **Check Skills You'll Need**

Graph the numbers on a number line.

1. $-2, 1, -5$

2. $0, 2, -4$

3. $-3, 3, -2$

4. $-1, -5, -8$

? For help, go to Lesson 1-4.

New Vocabulary

- **coordinate plane**
- **x-axis**
- **y-axis**
- **quadrants**
- **origin**
- **ordered pair**
- **x-coordinate**
- **y-coordinate**

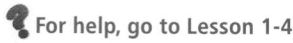

OBJECTIVE

1 Naming Coordinates and Quadrants

A **coordinate plane** is formed by the intersection of two number lines. The horizontal number line is called the **x-axis** and the vertical number line is called the **y-axis**.

The *x*- and *y*-axes divide the coordinate plane into four **quadrants**.

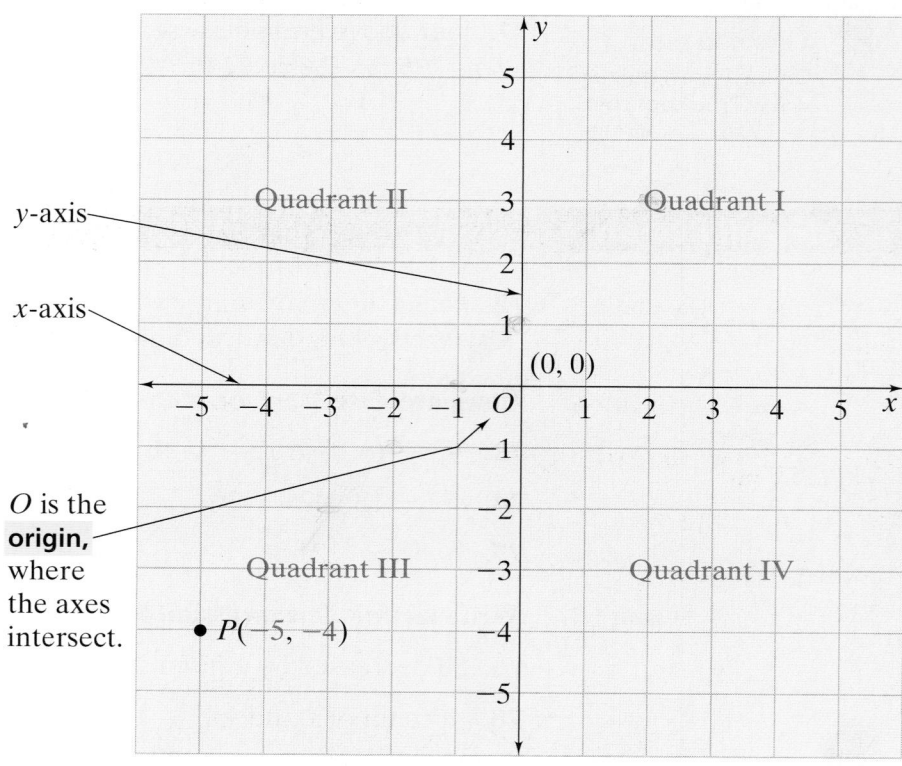

An **ordered pair** gives the coordinates and location of a point. The ordered pair $(-5, -4)$ identifies point P in Quadrant III above.

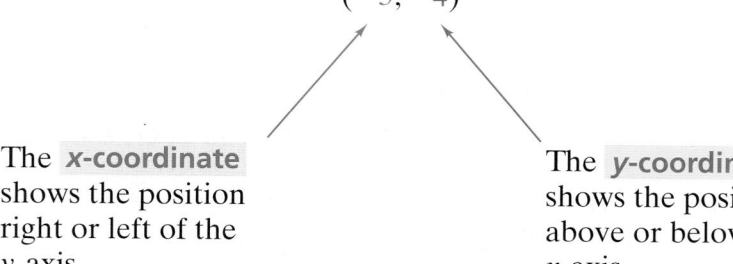

$(-5, -4)$

The **x-coordinate** shows the position right or left of the *y*-axis.

The **y-coordinate** shows the position above or below the *x*-axis.

1 EXAMPLE Naming Coordinates and Quadrants

Write the coordinates of point *A*. In which quadrant is point *A* located?

Point *A* is located 2 units to the left of the *y*-axis. So the *x*-coordinate is -2. The point is 1 unit above the *x*-axis. So the *y*-coordinate is 1.

The coordinates of point *A* are $(-2, 1)$. Point *A* is located in Quadrant II.

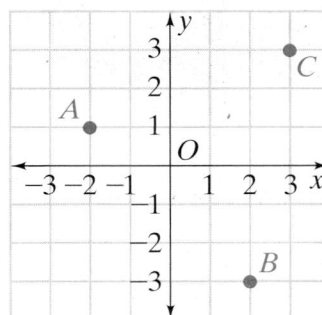

✓ Check Understanding Example 1

1. **a.** Use the graph in Example 1. Write the coordinates of *B* and *C*.
   b. Identify the quadrants in which *B* and *C* are located.

OBJECTIVE

2 Graphing Points

To graph a point $A(x, y)$ in a coordinate plane, you graph the ordered pair (x, y).

2 EXAMPLE Graphing Points

Graph point $R(3, -5)$.

Step 1
Start at the origin.

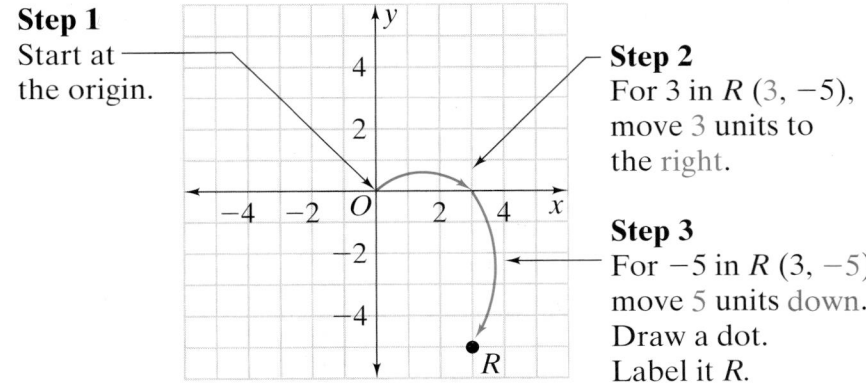

Step 2
For 3 in $R(3, -5)$, move 3 units to the right.

Step 3
For -5 in $R(3, -5)$, move 5 units down. Draw a dot. Label it *R*.

✓ Check Understanding Example 2

2. **a.** Graph these points on one coordinate plane: $K(3, 1)$, $L(-2, 1)$, and $M(-2, -4)$.
   b. **Geometry** Draw lines to connect points *K*, *L*, and *M*. Describe the figure that results.

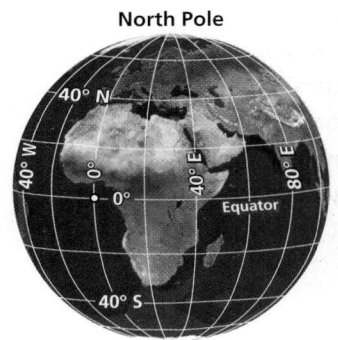

North Pole

South Pole

Real-World 🌐 Connection

Latitude and longitude are measurements in a coordinate system that locates every point on Earth's surface.

🔎 For more exercises, see *Extra Practice*.

Practice and Problem Solving

Ⓐ Practice by Example

Example 1
(page 51)

In which quadrant does each point lie?

1. *J*
2. *V*
3. *M*
4. *K*
5. *P*
6. *Q*

Write the coordinates of each point.

7. *T*
8. *G*
9. *R*
10. *Q*
11. *P*
12. *M*

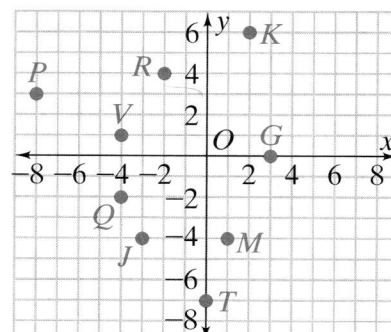

Example 2
(page 51)

Draw a coordinate plane. Then graph each point.

13. $A(-1, 3)$
14. $B(-4, -1)$
15. $C(2, 5)$
16. $D(2, -2)$
17. $E(0, 6)$
18. $F(-3, 2)$
19. $G(6, 0)$
20. $H(1, 7)$
21. $K(5, -6)$
22. $L(0, 0)$
23. $M(-5, -2)$
24. $N(7, 0)$
25. $P(-1, -3)$
26. $Q(1, 1)$
27. $R(0, -4)$
28. $S(-3, 4)$

Ⓑ Apply Your Skills

29. What ordered pair names the origin?

Name the point with the given coordinates.

30. $(3, 2)$
31. $(0, -5)$
32. $(2, 3)$
33. $(-2, -3)$

Write the coordinates of each point.

34. *A*
35. *B*
36. *C*
37. *D*

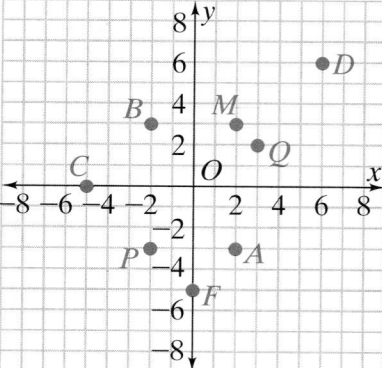

Mental Math Write the coordinates of each point.

38. the point 5 units to the left of the *y*-axis and 2 units below the *x*-axis

39. the point on the *y*-axis 4 units below the *x*-axis

40. the point on the *x*-axis 3 units to the right of the origin

Mental Math In which quadrant does $P(x, y)$ lie?

41. *x* is positive, *y* is negative.
42. *x* is positive, *y* is positive.
43. *x* is negative, *y* is positive.
44. *x* is negative, *y* is negative.

In which quadrant or on which axis does each point lie?

45. $V(13, 25)$

46. $W(x, y)$ if $x = 0, y > 0$

47. $X(-17, -2)$

48. $Z(x, y)$ if $x > 0, y < 0$

49. $B(0, |-2|)$

50. $R(x, y)$ if $x < 0, y > 0$

Geometry Graph and connect the points in the order given. Connect the last point to the first. Name the figure.

51. $(-4, 1), (1, 1), (-3, -1)$

52. $(2, 2), (2, -1), (-5, -1), (-5, 2)$

53. $(-1, 2), (1, 5), (7, 5), (5, 2)$

54. $(2, -4), (7, -1), (4, 4), (-1, 1)$

Geometry *PQRS* is a square. Find the coordinates of *S*.

55. $P(-5, 0), Q(0, 5), R(5, 0), S(\blacksquare, \blacksquare)$

56. $P(-1, 3), Q(4, 3), R(4, -2), S(\blacksquare, \blacksquare)$

🌐 **Geography** On a map, coordinates are given in degrees of longitude and latitude. Use the map below for Exercises 57–60.

SAMPLE
Little Rock, Arkansas:
Longitude:
    about 92° W
Latitude:
    about 34° N

57. Find the longitude and latitude of Jackson, Mississippi.

58. Find the longitude and latitude of Topeka, Kansas.

59. What city is located near 85° W, 38° N?

60. What city is located near 106° W, 35° N?

Geometry Use one coordinate plane for Exercises 61–63.

61. Graph the points $(-2, 1), (-2, 3), (1, 3),$ and $(1, 1)$. Connect them in the order given. Connect the last point to the first.

62. Change the coordinates of Exercise 61 as described below. Graph and connect the points for each new set of coordinates. Use a different color for each set.
    a. Multiply each *x*-coordinate by -1.
    b. Multiply each *y*-coordinate by -1.
    c. Multiply each coordinate by -1.
    d. Multiply each coordinate by 2.

63. **Writing in Math** Compare each figure in Exercise 62 to the figure in Exercise 61. Write a short paragraph describing your results.

64. Open-Ended Draw a dot-to-dot picture on a coordinate grid. Write the coordinates of the points in order. Exchange coordinates with a classmate and draw the other's picture.

65. Reasoning Assume that $a \neq b$. Do (a, b) and (b, a) describe the same point? Explain.

66. Write the coordinates of four points in the coordinate plane that are 3 units from the origin. Graph the points.

Test Prep

Multiple Choice

67. $P(a, b)$ is in Quadrant III. Which word pair makes the following sentence true?

The value of a must be __?__ and the value of b must be __?__

A. positive; positive   B. positive; negative
C. negative; positive   D. negative; negative

68. $C(x, y)$ is in Quadrant IV. Which ordered pair could be the coordinates of C?

F. $(-3, -7)$ G. $(0, 2)$ H. $(-8, 0)$ I. $(5, -6)$

69. To graph point R, start at the origin, move 10 units to the right, 4 units down, and 6 units to the left. What are the coordinates of point R?

A. $(4, -4)$ B. $(10, 2)$ C. $(6, 10)$ D. $(-4, -6)$

70. $P(a, b)$ is located on the x-axis. Which statement is true for all nonzero values of a and b?

F. $a > b$ G. $b > a$ H. $|a| > b$ I. $|b| > a$

71. $T(a, b)$ is located in Quadrant II. Which statement is *never* true?

A. $a > b$ B. $b > a$ C. $|a| > b$ D. $|b| > a$

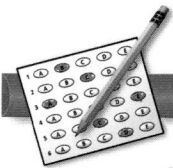

Take It to the NET
Online lesson quiz at
www.PHSchool.com
Web Code: ada-0110

Mixed Review

Lesson 1-9   **Find each product or quotient.**

72. $-11 \cdot 11$ **73.** $-432 \div 48$ **74.** $\dfrac{0}{-56}$

Lesson 1-5 🌐 **75. Submarines** A submarine at sea level dives 800 ft and then another 125 ft. Find the submarine's final depth.

Lesson 1-4   **Write the value of each expression.**

76. $|-8|$ **77.** $-|-95|$ **78.** the opposite of 12

79. $|16| + 4$ **80.** $|-6| - 2$ **81.** the opposite of -3

Technology

Graphing Ordered Pairs

For Use With Lesson 1-10

You can use a graphing calculator to display ordered pairs on a coordinate plane.

EXAMPLE

Graph these ordered pairs: $(-6, 2), (-5, 6), (-4, -1), (-3, -5),$ $(-2, 4), (0, 9), (1, 5), (2, -4), (2, 0), (3, 6), (5, 2), (7, -5), (8, 4)$

Step 1 Enter the ordered pairs into list L_1 for the x-coordinates and list L_2 for the y-coordinates.

Press LIST . To clear old entries in L_1, select **L₁**

and press CLEAR ENTER . (Clear old entries in other columns in a similar way.) Enter all the x-coordinates into list L_1. Enter all y-coordinates into list L_2. Check L_1 and L_2 to make sure the coordinates align as they should.

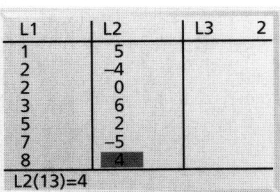

Step 2 In **PLOT,** enter 1 and select **On.** Select the Type as shown below, and check that Xlist and Ylist show L_1 and L_2, respectively.

Step 3 Press GRAPH

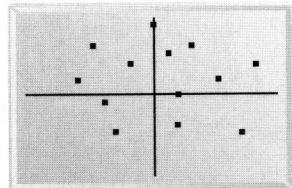

EXERCISES

Graph each group of ordered pairs.

1. $(-5, -1), (-2, 4), (-1, 3), (0, 4), (1, 6), (3, 0), (4, 2), (5, -3)$

2. $(-5, 7), (4, 6), (9, 2), (-2, -8), (0, 3), (-3, -1), (-6, 1), (5, 5),$ $(1, -6), (-1, -3), (3, -2), (-4, 9), (-8, 4), (2, -5), (6, 0), (7, -4)$

Graph the ordered pairs. Adjust the window settings to see all the points.

3. $(5, 2), (6, 5), (8, 1), (11, 3), (12, 8), (14, 10), (15, 6), (17, 2)$

4. $(-10, -5), (-8, -9), (-6, 2), (-5, 8), (7, -3), (9, -6), (10, 4), (12, 9)$

Graph the ordered pairs. Describe the pattern you see.

5. $(7, 3), (-3, -2), (1, 0), (-5, -3), (9, 4), (3, 1), (5, 2), (-7, -4)$

6. $(0, -5), (-2, -3), (4, -5), (0, -1), (2, -3), (-4, -5)$

Some tests require you to enter a number answer on a grid. You must find the answer and also show it in a form that you can fit on the grid. For example, you can enter an improper fraction on the grid, but not a mixed number.

1 EXAMPLE

What is the sum of -0.5 and 2?

$$-0.5 + 2 = 1.5, \frac{3}{2}, \text{ or } 1\frac{1}{2}.$$

For the grid, you can use 1.5 or $\frac{3}{2}$, but not $1\frac{1}{2}$. You write the answer in the spaces at the top of the grid and fill in the corresponding bubbles below.

● The grids at the right are correct for 1.5 and $\frac{3}{2}$, respectively.

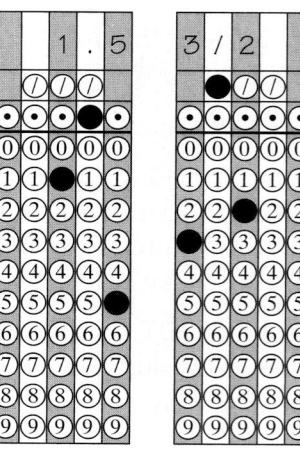

Here are things to remember as you grid your responses:
• You must begin in the left column OR end in the right column.
• You cannot have blanks in the middle of a response.
• Always write a mixed number as an improper fraction.
• You do not have to simplify fractions.

2 EXAMPLE

The surface of a lake is 29.8 ft below sea level. What is the elevation in feet of a hilltop that is 350 ft above the surface of the lake?

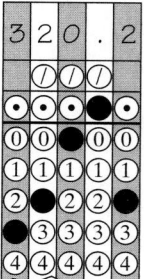

$(-29.8) + 350$	**Write an expression.**
$\|350\| - \|-29.8\|$	**Find the difference of the absolute values.**
320.2	**Simplify. Since 350 has the greater absolute value, the sum is positive.**

The hilltop is 320.2 feet above sea level. Enter 320.2 on the grid as shown. You do not enter the units.

EXERCISES

Write what you would grid for each answer.

1. Simplify $12 \div [12 - (4 \cdot 2)]$.

2. What is the next number in the pattern 0.4, 0.8, 1.3, 1.9, 2.6, . . . ?

3. What is the next number in the pattern $0, \frac{1}{2}, 1, 1\frac{1}{2}, 2, . . .$?

Chapter Review

Vocabulary

absolute value (p. 19)	**integers** (p. 19)	**variable** (p. 4)
conjecture (p. 35)	**opposites** (p. 19)	**variable expression** (p. 4)
coordinate plane (p. 50)	**order of operations** (p. 8)	**x-axis** (p. 50)
counterexample (p. 37)	**ordered pair** (p. 50)	**x-coordinate** (p. 50)
evaluate (p. 14)	**origin** (p. 50)	**y-axis** (p. 50)
inductive reasoning (p. 35)	**quadrants** (p. 50)	**y-coordinate** (p. 50)

Reading Math
Understanding Vocabulary

Take It to the NET
Online vocabulary quiz at **www.PHSchool.com**
Web Code: adj-0151

Choose the vocabulary term that correctly completes the sentence.

1. The ordered pair $(0, 0)$ represents the location of the ? .

2. A letter that stands for a number in an expression is a(n) ? .

3. The vertical axis in the coordinate plane is known as the ? .

4. The coordinate plane is divided into four ? .

5. All whole numbers and their opposites are ? .

6. In the ordered pair $(-5, 2)$, the number -5 is the ? .

7. The distance that a number is from zero on a number line is the ? of the number.

Skills and Concepts

1-1 Objectives

▼ To identify variables, numerical expressions, and variable expressions (p. 4)

▼ To write variable expressions for word phrases (p. 5)

A **variable** is a letter that stands for a number. A **variable expression** uses variables, numerals, and operation symbols.

Write a variable expression for each word phrase.

8. twenty-five less than x

9. the product of n and 3

10. ten decreased by t

11. a number x divided by 4

12. a number n increased by 5

13. two more than y

1-2 Objectives

▼ To use the order of operations (p. 8)

▼ To use grouping symbols (p. 9)

To simplify a numerical expression, follow the **order of operations.**

1. Work inside grouping symbols.

2. Multiply and divide in order from left to right.

3. Add and subtract in order from left to right.

Simplify each expression.

14. $3 \cdot 7 + 6 \div 2$

15. $(4 + 8) \div 2 \cdot 2$

16. $9 \cdot 5 - 4(12 \div 6)$

1-3 Objectives

▼ To evaluate variable expressions (p. 14)

▼ To solve real-world problems involving packaging and shopping (p. 15)

To **evaluate** a variable expression, substitute a number for each variable. Use the order of operations to simplify.

Evaluate each expression.

17. $3x + 4$, for $x = 5$

18. $15 + 10 \div n$, for $n = 5$

19. $(y - 6)2$, for $y = 16$

20. $4(4 + m)$, for $m = 6$

21. $15t \cdot 10$, for $t = 3$

22. $z + [15 - (z - 1)]$, for $z = 4$

1-4 Objectives

▼ To represent, graph, and order integers (p. 18)

▼ To find opposites and absolute values (p. 19)

Integers are the set of whole numbers and their **opposites**. The **absolute value** of an integer is its distance from zero on a number line. On a number line, the integer farther to the right is the greater integer.

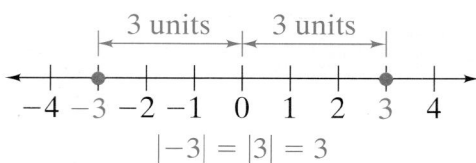

Simplify each expression.

23. the opposite of 17

24. $|-1{,}000|$

25. the absolute value of negative 9

26. the opposite of the absolute value of 12

Compare. Use >, <, or = to complete each statement.

27. $-7 \ \blacksquare \ -9$ **28.** $0 \ \blacksquare \ -3$ **29.** $-6 \ \blacksquare \ 2$ **30.** $|-5| \ \blacksquare \ |5|$

🌐 **31. Water Slides** A slide at a water park is 30 ft high. What integer represents your change in elevation when you go down the slide?

1-5 and 1-6 Objectives

▼ To use models to add integers (p. 24)

▼ To use rules to add integers (p. 25)

▼ To use models to subtract integers (p. 30)

▼ To use a rule to subtract integers (p. 31)

To add integers with the *same* sign, add their absolute values. The sum has the same sign. To add integers with *different* signs, find the difference of their absolute values. The sum has the sign of the integer with the greater absolute value. To subtract an integer, add its opposite.

Simplify each expression.

32. $8 + (-15)$ **33.** $-9 + 21$ **34.** $9 - (-5)$

35. $14 + (-9) + (-20)$ **36.** $-62 + (+59) - 24$

37. $-7 - 4$ **38.** $-4 + 12 + (-3) + (-6)$

🌐 **39. Wildlife** An eagle leaves her nest on the side of a cliff. She soars upward 60 ft and then dives 80 ft. What is her change in elevation after leaving the nest?

1-7 Objectives

▼ To write rules for patterns (p. 35)

▼ To make predictions and test conjectures (p. 36)

Inductive reasoning is making conclusions based on patterns you observe. A conclusion reached by inductive reasoning is a **conjecture.**

Write a rule for each pattern. Find the next three numbers in the pattern.

40. $0, 6, 12, 18, \ldots$ **41.** $-18, -9, 0, 9, \ldots$ **42.** $\frac{1}{2}, 1, 1\frac{1}{2}, 2, \ldots$

1-8 Objectives

▼ To find number patterns using rules (p. 40)

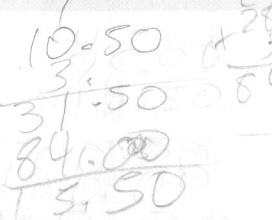

You can use patterns to solve problems.

43. Suppose you plan to save $12 per week. You have already saved $7.50. In how many weeks will you have saved at least $100?

44. A four-line classified ad costs $28 for a week. Each additional line costs $10.50. What is the weekly cost of a 12-line ad?

1-9 Objectives

▼ To multiply integers using repeated addition, patterns, and rules (p. 44)

▼ To divide integers using rules (p. 46)

To multiply or divide integers, multiply or divide the absolute values of the integers. If the integers have the same sign, the product or quotient is positive. If the integers have different signs, the product or quotient is negative.

Multiply or divide.

45. $7(-6)$ **46.** $250 \div (-50)$ **47.** $(-9)(-8)$

48. $-56 \div (-8)$ **49.** $-120 \div 40$ **50.** $-15(11)$

51. $\frac{-64}{8}$ **52.** $(-5)(-7)$ **53.** $(-6)(-17)$

1-10 Objectives

▼ To name coordinates and quadrants in the coordinate plane (p. 50)

▼ To graph points in the coordinate plane (p. 51)

A **coordinate plane** is formed by the intersection of two number lines. The **x-axis** and the **y-axis** divide the coordinate plane into four **quadrants.** An **ordered pair** gives the coordinates of a point. The **x-coordinate** shows the position right or left of the y-axis. The **y-coordinate** shows the position above or below the x-axis.

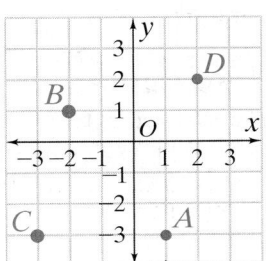

Write the coordinates of each point.

54. A **55.** B **56.** C **57.** D

Chapter Test

 **Take It to the NET**
Online chapter test at
www.PHSchool.com
Web Code: ada-0152

Write an expression for each phrase.

1. a number n increased by nineteen

2. ten less than negative three

3. the product of x and negative five

4. 5 more than the opposite of y

Evaluate each expression for the given values of the variables.

5. $3a + 5$, for $a = -5$

6. $5m + 9 + 7n$, for $m = 8$ and $n = 1$

7. $3|x - y| + x$, for $x = 1$ and $y = 8$

8. $20 - 2(a - b)$, for $a = 3$ and $b = 2$

Simplify each expression.

9. $|-5|$ 10. opposite of -9

11. opposite of 7   12. $|15|$

Use $>$, $<$, or $=$ to complete each sentence.

13. $-6 \blacksquare -5$ 14. $8 \blacksquare -10$

15. $-3 \blacksquare 3$ 16. $0 \blacksquare -7$

Simplify each expression.

17. $15 + (-7)$ 18. $-8 + (-12)$

19. $-9(-7)$ 20. $54 \div (-6)$

21. $-6 \cdot 48$ 22. $\frac{-56}{-7}$

23. $119 \div (-24)$ 24. $-47 + (-21)$

25. $-83 + 17$ 26. $5(-12)(-3)(-1)$

27. $2 \cdot |14 - (-9)|$ 28. $8 \cdot 6 \div (2 + 1)$

29. $4 + 7 \cdot 2 + 8$ 30. $16 \div 2 \cdot (5 + 3)$

In which quadrant or on which axis does each point lie?

31. $(-5, 7)$ 32. $(0, -4)$ 33. $(-8, -6)$

Write the coordinates of each point.

34. F

35. G

36. H

37. J

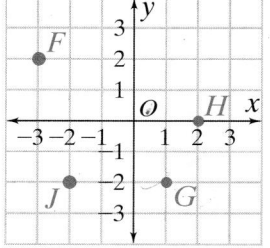

38. A shirt costs \$15 and jeans cost \$25.
   a. Write an expression for the cost of j jeans and s shirts.
   b. Evaluate the expression to find the cost of three pairs of jeans and five shirts.
   c. How many pairs of jeans can you buy for \$60?

39. Which statement is *always* true?
   A. The absolute value of an integer is equal to the opposite of the integer.
   B. The absolute value of an integer is greater than zero.
   C. An integer is greater than its opposite.
   D. A positive integer is greater than a negative integer.

40. A submarine was 250 m below sea level. It rose 75 m. Use an integer to describe the new depth of the submarine.

41. Write a rule for the pattern below. Find the next three numbers in the pattern.
   $100, 90, 85, 75, 70, 60, \ldots$

42. You are in an elevator on the seventh floor. You go down 4 floors and then up 8 floors. Then you go down 3 floors and up 9 floors. The elevator goes down again 2 floors, and you get off. According to the pattern, on which floor are you now?

43. **Writing in Math** Describe how to order the integers $2, -6, 9, 0$, and -13 from least to greatest.

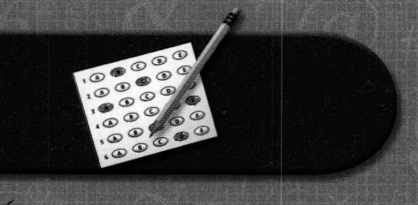
Reading Comprehension Read each passage below. Then answer the questions on the basis of what is *stated* or *implied* in the passage.

> **Numbers in Nature** Numbers appear everywhere in the patterns of nature. For example, the numbers of petals on flowers form patterns. Find some flowers and count their petals. You will find, with few exceptions, the number of petals to be one of 3, 5, 8, 13, 21, 34, and so forth. Also, although all snowflakes are different, each one has 6-fold symmetry. Put 20 pennies on a table and push them as close together as you can. Notice that all the pennies in the middle are surrounded by 6 others. This is an example of 6-fold symmetry.

1. What is true about the pattern for numbers of petals on flowers?
   A. The numbers are all odd.
   B. The increases from one to the next are always the same.
   C. The increases from one to the next suggest a pattern you've seen before.
   D. The number of petals on any flower has to be a number in the pattern.

2. Describe the pattern for the numbers of petals in flowers.

3. What number would follow 34 in the pattern for the numbers of petals on flowers?
   F. 4th   **G.** 35   **H.** 55   **I.** 68

4. What do patterns in snowflakes and pennies pushed close together have in common?

> **Wings or Wheels?** The Arctic tern, a small sea bird, is the animal that migrates the longest distance each year. It can fly from a latitude of 84°N in the Arctic to 78°S in the Antarctic, and back. For some terns, this journey may be about 25,000 mi, which is about the distance around Earth at the equator. By contrast, the average number of miles a vehicle in the United States travels each year is about 14,000. Some Arctic terns live 25 years, which means they pile up an impressive number of miles traveled in a lifetime.

5. About how far does an Arctic tern fly in one migration south?
   A. 162 mi   **B.** 14,000 mi
   C. 12,500 mi   **D.** 25,000 mi

6. On average, how far does a vehicle in the United States travel each year?
   F. 14,000 mi   **G.** 14,000 km
   H. 25,000 mi   **I.** 25,000 km

7. Which travels farther in a year, an Arctic tern in its annual migration or a vehicle that's driven the average number of miles? About how much farther?

8. About how far could an Arctic tern fly in its migrations over 25 years? Justify your answer.

Locating Sunken Ships

Applying Integers Marine archeologists are scientists who study sunken ships. They use scanning devices to locate objects on the ocean floor. When they find a "hot spot," divers take a closer look. If they find a sunken ship, the divers take underwater photographs and record the ship's latitude and longitude, identifying a specific point on Earth's surface.

Ancient World
This globe includes latitude (lines that run east–west) and longitude (lines that run north–south) rings.

Activity

Which part of Earth's coordinate globe corresponds to the indicated part of a coordinate plane?

1. the *x*-axis   **2.** the *y*-axis   **3.** the origin

Write and simplify an expression to show how the depth of a submersible robot changes.

4. from the *Edmund Fitzgerald* to the *Andrea Doria*

5. from the *Titanic* to the *Atocha*

6. from the water's surface to the *Atocha*

7. Estimation About how many times the depth of the *Atocha* is the depth of the *Andrea Doria*? Write an equation to model this relationship.

8. Research Pick one of the ships discussed here or another sunken ship. What factors led to its sinking? Explain.

Prime Meridian
0° Longitude

Titanic
41° N 49° W
−12,600 ft

Edmund Fitzgerald
47° N 85° W
−530 ft

Equator
0° Latitude

Atocha
24° N 82° W
−55 ft

Andrea Doria
40° N 69° W
−240 ft

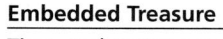

Embedded Treasure
Time and water pressure pushed these coins into a piece of wood.

Sunken World

Scientists explore shipwrecks in submersible vehicles such as Alvin (above) when the ship is too deep for scuba gear (worn by the diver).

Take It to the NET For more information about sunken ships, go to **www.PHSchool.com**.
Web Code: ade-0153

Where You've Been

In Chapter 1, you learned:

● How to apply the order of operations to evaluate numerical expressions.

● How to evaluate expressions with variables.

● How to add, subtract, multiply, and divide integers.

TEXT Instant self-check online and on CD-ROM

Diagnosing Readiness (For help, go to the lesson in green.)

Related Equations (Previous Course)

Complete the related equations.

1. $20 - \blacksquare = 9$ $9 + \blacksquare = 20$ **2.** $-2 + \blacksquare = 3$ $3 - \blacksquare = -2$

3. $20 - \blacksquare = 23$ $23 + \blacksquare = 20$ **4.** $\blacksquare + 12 = -7$ $-7 - \blacksquare = 12$

5. $3 \cdot \blacksquare = 75$ $75 \div \blacksquare = 3$ **6.** $72 \div \blacksquare = 12$ $12 \cdot \blacksquare = 72$

7. $-36 \div \blacksquare = -6$ $-6 \cdot \blacksquare = -36$ **8.** $\blacksquare \cdot (-10) = -70$ $-70 \div \blacksquare = -10$

Comparing Numbers (Lessons 1-5, 1-6, and 1-9)

Compare. Use $>$, $<$, or $=$ to complete each statement.

9. $6 \ \blacksquare \ 16$

10. $5 \ \blacksquare \ -5$

11. $-52 \ \blacksquare \ -21$

12. $0 \ \blacksquare \ -8$

13. $-7 \ \blacksquare \ 3$

14. $12 + 3 \ \blacksquare \ 19 - 4$

15. $-2 \cdot 6 \ \blacksquare \ 4 \cdot (-3)$

16. $27 \div 9 \ \blacksquare \ 6 \cdot 2$

17. $18 - 27 \ \blacksquare \ -34 + 12$

18. $8(-5) \ \blacksquare \ 100 - 65$

19. $6 \div (10 - 8) \ \blacksquare \ 1 + 5$

20. $3(-2)(-4) \ \blacksquare \ 4(-3)(2)$

Order of Operations With Integers (Lesson 1-2)

Simplify each expression.

21. $5 \cdot 2 + 5 \cdot 3$

22. $7(6 - 2)$

23. $10 \cdot 3 - 5 \cdot 3$

24. $-(34 + 76)$

25. $4(6) + 4(3)$

26. $-4(12 - 16)$

27. $7(8) - 10(8)$

28. $11 \cdot 9 - 6 \cdot 9$

29. $-2 \cdot 3 - 2 \cdot 7$

30. $6 \cdot (-9) - 3(-9)$

31. $-5(3) - (-5)(2)$

32. $(72 - 81)(5)$

Solving One-Step Equations and Inequalities

Where You're Going

In this chapter, you will learn how to

● Use the Distributive Property.

● Write and solve equations.

● Write, solve, and graph inequalities.

● Solve a problem by Try, Test, Revise.

Real-World Snapshots Applying what you learn, on pages 122–123 you will solve problems about a school fair.

Key Vocabulary

- coefficient (p. 76)
- constant (p. 76)
- deductive reasoning (p. 77)
- equation (p. 80)
- inequality (p. 102)
- inverse operations (p. 86)
- like terms (p. 76)
- open sentence (p. 80)
- simplify a variable expression (p. 76)
- solution of an equation (p. 81)
- solution of an inequality (p. 102)
- term (p. 76)

2-1

Properties of Numbers

What You'll Learn

OBJECTIVE 1 To identify properties of addition and multiplication

OBJECTIVE 2 To use properties to solve problems

. . . And Why

To solve real-world problems involving purchases

 Check Skills You'll Need

Simplify.

1. $-18 + (-7)$

2. $32 - (-3)$

3. $(-13) + 6$

4. $2 - 48$

For help, go to Lesson 1-6.

New Vocabulary

- **Commutative Properties**
- **Associative Properties**
- **additive identity**
- **multiplicative identity**
- **Identity Properties**

The sum of 6 and 4 is the same as the sum of 4 and 6. Similarly, the product of 9 and 5 is the same as the product of 5 and 9. These suggest the following properties.

Key Concepts — Commutative Properties of Addition and Multiplication

Changing the order of the values you are adding or multiplying does not change the sum or product.

Arithmetic	Algebra
$6 + 4 = 4 + 6$	$a + b = b + a$
$9 \cdot 5 = 5 \cdot 9$	$a \cdot b = b \cdot a$

You can also change the grouping of the values before you add or multiply them.

Key Concepts — Associative Properties of Addition and Multiplication

Changing the grouping of the values you are adding or multiplying does not change the sum or product.

Arithmetic	Algebra
$(2 + 7) + 3 = 2 + (7 + 3)$	$(a + b) + c = a + (b + c)$
$(9 \cdot 4)5 = 9(4 \cdot 5)$	$(ab)c = a(bc)$

1 EXAMPLE — Real-World Problem Solving

Golf Carlos rented a set of golf clubs for $7 and a golf cart for $12. He paid a greens fee of $23. Find his total cost.

You can use the Associative Property of Addition to find the total cost in two different ways.

$(7 + 12) + 23 = 19 + 23 = 42$ **Add 7 and 12 first.**
$7 + (12 + 23) =\ 7 + 35 = 42$ **Add 12 and 23 first.**

Carlos's total cost was $42.

TEXT Interactive lesson includes instant self-check, tutorials, and activities.

✓ Check Understanding Example 1

1. You spend $6 for dinner, $8 for a movie, and $4 for popcorn. Find your total cost. Explain which property or properties you used.

When you add a number and 0, the sum equals the original number. The **additive identity** is 0. When you multiply a number and 1, the product equals the original number. The **multiplicative identity** is 1.

Key Concepts **Identity Properties of Addition and Multiplication**

The sum of any number and zero is the original number. The product of any number and 1 is the original number.

Arithmetic	Algebra
$12 + 0 = 12$; $10 \cdot 1 = 10$	$a + 0 = a$; $a \cdot 1 = a$

---

2 EXAMPLE Identifying Properties

Name each property shown.

a. $5 \cdot 7 = 7 \cdot 5$ Commutative Property of Multiplication

b. $c \cdot 1 = c$ Identity Property of Multiplication

c. $7 + a = a + 7$ Commutative Property of Addition

d. $5(xy) = (5x)y$ Associative Property of Multiplication

✓ Check Understanding Example 2

2. Name each property shown.

   a. $3 + 6 = 6 + 3$ **b.** $8 = 1 \cdot 8$ **c.** $(3z)m = 3(zm)$

OBJECTIVE

2 Using Properties

You can use properties and mental math to help you find sums.

3 EXAMPLE Using Mental Math With Addition

Use mental math to simplify $(81 + 6) + 9$.

$(81 + 6) + 9$

$= (6 + 81) + 9$ **Use the Commutative Property of Addition.**

$= 6 + (81 + 9)$ **Use the Associative Property of Addition.**

$= 6 + 90$ **Add within parentheses.**

$= 96$ **Add.**

Test-Taking Tip
Look for combinations that equal 10 or a multiple of 10, since they are easier to use in calculating mentally.

✓ **Check Understanding**   Example 3

3. Use mental math to simplify each expression.

    a. $6 + 7 + 14$ **b.** $8 + 0 + 2 + (-7)$
    c. $5 + 12 + 18 + 5$ **d.** $19 + (-30) + 21$

 **EXAMPLE**   <u>Real-World</u> 🌐 **Problem Solving**

School Supplies **Suppose you buy the school supplies shown at the left. Use mental math to find the cost of the supplies.**

$$1.65 + 0.85 + 0.35$$

$= 0.85 + 1.65 + 0.35$	**Use the Commutative Property of Addition.**
$= 0.85 + (1.65 + 0.35)$	**Use the Associative Property of Addition.**
$= 0.85 + 2.00$	**Add within parentheses.**
$= 2.85$	**Add.**

● The cost of the school supplies is $2.85.

$.85

$.35

$1.65

Need Help?
For help with adding decimals, see Skills Handbook, page 764.

✓ **Check Understanding**   Example 4

4. Use the supermarket receipt and mental math to find the cost of the groceries.

```
      SOUTH STREET
         MARKET


DATE 08.03.03    THU
1 GALLON MILK   $2.30
BREAD           $1.80
APPLES          $2.20
```

You can also use mental math to help you find products.

 **EXAMPLE**   **Using Mental Math With Multiplication**

Use mental math to simplify $(4 \cdot 9) \cdot 5$.

$(4 \cdot 9) \cdot 5 = (9 \cdot 4) \cdot 5$	**Use the Commutative Property of Multiplication.**
$= 9 \cdot (4 \cdot 5)$	**Use the Associative Property of Multiplication.**
$= 9 \cdot 20$	**Multiply within parentheses.**
$= 180$	**Multiply.**

✓ **Check Understanding**   Example 5

5. Use mental math to simplify each expression.

    a. $25 \cdot (3 \cdot 4)$ **b.** $3 \cdot 1 \cdot -5 \cdot 8$
    c. $2(-8)(-15)$ **d.** $5 \cdot 9 \cdot 6 \cdot (-2) \cdot (-1)$

EXERCISES

For more exercises, see *Extra Practice*.

Practice and Problem Solving

A Practice by Example

Example 1
(page 66)

Use the Associative Property to write two different expressions that you could use to find each sum.

1. Add 1, 3, and 25.

2. Add 5, 91, and 11.

3. Travel On a road trip, your family spends $120 for gas, $15 for bottled water, and $80 for food. Find your family's total cost. Explain which property or properties you used.

Example 2
(page 67)

Name each property shown.

4. $7 + 6 = 6 + 7$

5. $0 + 8 = 8$

6. $(6 \cdot 15)2 = 6(15 \cdot 2)$

7. $(12r)s = 12(rs)$

8. $999 \cdot 1 = 999$

9. $ab = ba$

Example 3
(page 67)

Mental Math Use mental math to simplify each expression.

10. $(5 + 23) + 65$

11. $(3 + 62) + 7$

12. $9 + (14 + 1)$

13. $-8 + 35 + 15$

14. $31 + 0 + (-2)$

15. $15 + 13 + (-25)$

Example 4
(page 68)

16. $(0.50 + 34) + 3.50$

17. $(4.55 + 27) + 5.45$

18. $1.50 + (3.17 + 6.50)$

19. $-0.25 + 4.88 + 3.25$

20. $7.02 + 3.40 + 1.98$

21. $8.39 + (-2.00) + 1.61$

$15.20

$7.65

$1.35

22. Gardening Lance has purchased some supplies to start his new garden. Use the prices shown at the left and mental math to find the cost of the supplies.

Example 5
(page 68)

Mental Math Use mental math to simplify each expression.

23. $6 \cdot 3 \cdot 5$

24. $5 \cdot 7 \cdot (-2)$

25. $25 \cdot 4 \cdot 8$

26. $8 \cdot 4 \cdot (-10)$

B Apply Your Skills

Name each property shown.

27. $8(3 \cdot 2) = (8 \cdot 3)2$

28. $5 + 8 = 8 + 5$

29. $(6x)y = 6(xy)$

30. $6 \cdot 1 = 6$

31. $999 + 0 = 999$

32. $a \cdot 1 = 1 \cdot a$

Simplify each expression.

33. $25 + 157 + (-75)$

34. $140 + 17 + (-60)$

35. $5 \cdot 50 \cdot 20 \cdot (-2)$

36. $125 + 18 + 75 + 162$

37. Mental Math Loryn is flying roundtrip from Dallas, Texas, to Minneapolis, Minnesota. The fare for her ticket is $308. Each airport charges a $16 airport fee. There is also a tax of $12 on the fare. What is the total cost of Loryn's ticket?

38. Writing in Math Which two numbers would you combine first to simplify $3 + 6 + 27$? Explain.

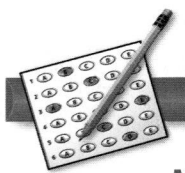

Mental Math Evaluate each expression.

39. $x(y \cdot z)$, for $x = 4, y = 27$, and $z = 5$

40. $t(u)(-v)$, for $t = 3, u = 20$, and $v = 8$

41. $a + b + c$, for $a = 14, b = 252$, and $c = 26$

42. $d(v)(d)$, for $d = 5$ and $v = 24$

43. Reasoning Can you use $4 + 2 = 6$ as your first step in simplifying $3 \cdot 4 + 2 \div (-2)$? Explain.

Test Prep

Multiple Choice

44. Which equation shows the Associative Property of Addition?
 A. $8 + 6 + 7 = 8 + 7 + 6$ **B.** $(10 + 5) + 15 = 10 + (5 + 15)$
 C. $9 + 0 + (-1) = 9 + (-1)$ **D.** $(-2) \cdot 1 \cdot 9 = (-2) \cdot 9$

Reading Comprehension

Read the passage below before doing Exercises 45 and 46.

A Fair Fare in Alaska

Railroads are a popular means of transportation in Alaska. One scenic train route travels 356 miles from Anchorage to Fairbanks. It includes a stop in Denali Park, where you can see the tallest mountain in the United States, Mount McKinley. A one-way fare for the 12-hour trip is $154 in the summer and $120 in the spring and fall. A one-way fare for the 7.5-hour trip from Anchorage to Denali Park is $102 in the summer, and $84 in the spring and fall. Children's fares are half the fares for adults.

45. Two adults and two children plan to travel round trip from Anchorage to Fairbanks. How much will the trip cost in the summer?
 F. $360 **G.** $462 **H.** $720 **I.** $924

Take It to the NET
Online lesson quiz at
www.PHSchool.com
Web Code: ada-0201

46. Three adults and two children plan to travel round trip from Anchorage to Denali Park. How much will the trip cost in the fall?
 A. $672 **B.** $504 **C.** $336 **D.** $252

Mixed Review

Lesson 1-10 **In which quadrant does the graph of each ordered pair lie?**

47. $(-6, -3)$ **48.** $(8, -1)$ **49.** $(-4, 17)$ **50.** $(-1, 4)$

Lesson 1-9 **51. Recreation** Lin worked 4 hours per day for 3 days to build a model bridge. How many hours did she spend on the project?

Lesson 1-2 **Simplify each expression.**

52. $3 \cdot 5 + 3 \cdot 15$ **53.** $4 \cdot 7 + 4 \cdot 11$ **54.** $5 \cdot 22 - 5 \cdot 2$

The Distributive Property

OBJECTIVE

1 Numerical Expressions

vestigation

Exploring the Distributive Property

You can find the total area of two rectangles by two methods.

1. **Method 1:** Find the area of each rectangle. Then find the sum of the areas.

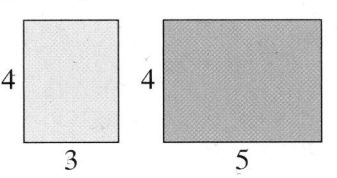

2. **Method 2:** Combine the two rectangles into one large rectangle. Find its length. Find its width. Then find its area.

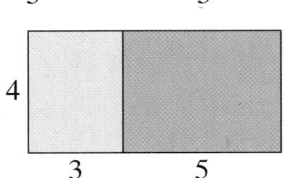

3. On a piece of paper, draw two rectangles with the same width, and lengths different from those above. Label the dimensions. Repeat Method 1 and Method 2 with your pair of rectangles. What do you notice about your results?

✔ **Check Skills You'll Need**

Simplify each expression.

1. $3 \cdot 7 - 9$

2. $(9 - 5)6$

3. $8 + 2 \cdot 6$

4. $2(6 - 3)$

5. $4 \cdot 5 - 4 \cdot 3$

6. $3 \cdot 2 - 1 \cdot 2$

❓ For help, go to Lesson 1-2.

New Vocabulary

• Distributive Property

The Investigation above shows different ways to find the sum of the areas of two rectangles. It suggests the *Distributive Property*, which combines multiplication with addition and subtraction.

Key Concepts | **Distributive Property**

To multiply a sum or difference, multiply each number within the parentheses by the number outside the parentheses.

Arithmetic	Algebra
$3(2 + 6) = 3(2) + 3(6)$	$a(b + c) = ab + ac$
$(2 + 6)3 = 2(3) + 6(3)$	$(b + c)a = ba + ca$
$6(7 - 4) = 6(7) - 6(4)$	$a(b - c) = ab - ac$
$(7 - 4)6 = 7(6) - 4(6)$	$(b - c)a = ba - ca$

 **TEXT** Interactive lesson includes instant self-check, tutorials, and activities.

You can use the Distributive Property to multiply mentally.

1 EXAMPLE **Using the Distributive Property I**

Use the Distributive Property to find 20(102) mentally.

$$20(102) = 20(100 + 2)$$ **Write 102 as (100 + 2).**

$$20(100 + 2) = 20 \cdot 100 + 20 \cdot 2$$ **Use the Distributive Property.**

$$= 2{,}000 + 40$$ **Multiply.**

$$= 2{,}040$$ **Add.**

✓ Check Understanding   Example 1

1. Find each product mentally.

    a. $(53)50$ **b.** $30 \cdot 104$ **c.** $9 \cdot 199$

2 EXAMPLE   <u>Real-World</u> 🌐 <u>Problem Solving</u>

Fundraising **At the Parent-Teacher Association (PTA) Pancake Breakfast, the PTA served 397 people 4 pancakes each. How many pancakes did the PTA serve?**

$$(397)4 = (400 - 3)4$$ **Write 397 as (400 − 3).**

$$= 400 \cdot 4 - 3 \cdot 4$$ **Use the Distributive Property.**

$$= 1{,}600 - 12$$ **Multiply.**

$$= 1{,}588$$ **Subtract.**

The PTA served 1,588 pancakes.

✓ Check Understanding   Example 2

2. Your club sold calendars for $7. Club members sold 204 calendars. How much money did they raise?

3 EXAMPLE **Using the Distributive Property II**

Simplify 8(15) − 8(5).

$$8(15) - 8(5) = 8(15 - 5)$$ **Use the Distributive Property.**

$$= 8(10)$$ **Subtract within parentheses.**

$$= 80$$ **Multiply.**

✓ Check Understanding   Example 3

3. Simplify each expression.

    a. $7(21) + 7(9)$ **b.** $12(52) - 12(62)$ **c.** $(16)7 - (11)7$

2 Variable Expressions

You can use algebra tiles to model the Distributive Property with variable expressions.

4 EXAMPLE Using Tiles to Multiply

Use algebra tiles to multiply $3(2x + 5)$.

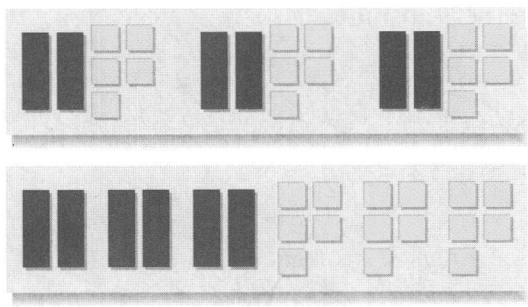

Model three groups of $2x + 5$.

Group like tiles.

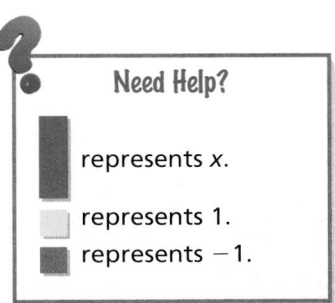

Need Help?

▮ represents x.

☐ represents 1.

▪ represents -1.

● So, $3(2x + 5) = 6x + 15$.

✓ Check Understanding Example 4

4. Use algebra tiles to multiply.

   a. $4(2x - 3)$ **b.** $3(x + 4)$ **c.** $(3x + 1)2$

In Example 4, notice that 3 multiplies both $2x$ and 5.
That is, $3(2x + 5) = 3(2x) + 3(5)$.

5 EXAMPLE Using the Distributive Property III

Multiply.

a. $-5(4x - 3)$

$-5(4x - 3) = -5(4x) - (-5)(3)$ **Use the Distributive Property.**

$ = -20x - (-15)$ **Multiply.**

$ = -20x + 15$ **Simplify.**

b. $(2x + 5)7$

$(2x + 5)7 = (2x)7 + (5)7$ **Use the Distributive Property.**

$ = 14x + 35$ **Multiply.**

Reading Math

When you distribute papers in class, you give some to each classmate. Similarly, when you distribute a number over a sum or difference, you multiply each value within the parentheses by that number.

✓ Check Understanding Example 5

5. Multiply.

   a. $2(7 - 3d)$ **b.** $(6m + 1)(3)$ **c.** $-3(5t - 2)$

EXERCISES

For more exercises, see *Extra Practice*.

Practice and Problem Solving

A Practice by Example

Examples 1 and 2
(page 72)

Mental Math **Use the Distributive Property to simplify.**

1. 6(23)   **2.** 5(18)   **3.** 7(48)   **4.** 13(101)

5. (104)(9)   **6.** 6(52)   **7.** 8(98)   **8.** (208)4

9. Ticket Sales A theater sold out its evening performances four nights in a row. The theater has 294 seats. How many people attended the theater in the four nights?

Example 3
(page 72)

Simplify each expression.

10. 7(3) + 7(5)   **11.** 2(9) − 3(9)   **12.** 6(4) + 6(8)

13. 9(3) − 2(3)   **14.** (12)27 − (12)24   **15.** (3)5 + (27)5

Example 4
(page 73)

Write an expression using parentheses for each model. Then multiply.

16.

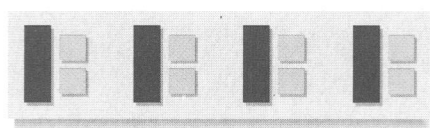

17.

Multiply. Use algebra tiles as needed.

18. $2(t - 5)$ **19.** $(v - 3)4$ **20.** $3(2h - 1)$ **21.** $-2(7z + 3)$

Example 5
(page 73)

Multiply.

22. $7(b - 3)$ **23.** $12(a + 3)$ **24.** $(2 + 3d)5$ **25.** $-5(m + 6)$

26. $3(5 - 3w)$ **27.** $-7(t - 4)$ **28.** $4(b + 5)$ **29.** $(y - 6)2$

B Apply Your Skills

Mental Math **Use the Distributive Property to simplify.**

30. 5(1,005)   **31.** $(8) \cdot 11 + (-13) \cdot 11$

32. $13 \cdot (-3) + 7 \cdot (-3)$ **33.** $-32 \cdot 6 + 29 \cdot 6$

34. $4 \cdot 19 - 4 \cdot (11)$ **35.** $(-8) \cdot 10 + 3 \cdot (-8)$

Mental Math **Solve using mental math.**

36. Every day, Lila eats a bowl of cereal that has 193 calories. What is the total number of calories from cereal that Lila eats in a week?

37. The trip from Roberto's house to his aunt's house is 896 miles. How long is the round trip?

Use the Distributive Property to multiply.

38. $-3(2t + 6)$ **39.** $-7(-3n + 2)$ **40.** $(4 - t)(-7)$

41. $-5(-m + 6)$ **42.** $-8(6 - c)$ **43.** $(5y + 8)(-3)$

44.  **Writing in Math** Explain how to use the Distributive Property to multiply $6(3r + 4s)$.

45. **Error Analysis** Suppose your friend wrote $7(2m + t) = 14m + t$. What error did your friend make?

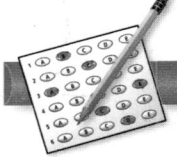 **Challenge**

Mental Math Use the Distributive Property to simplify.

46. $(-4)(70) + (-4)(-90)$ **47.** $3(9) - 3(5) + 3(6)$

Name each property shown.

48. $m[t + (-t)] = mt + m(-t)$ **49.** $m[t + (-t)] = m(-t + t)$

50. $m[t + (-t)] = [t + (-t)]m$ **51.** $m + [t + (-t)] = (m + t) + (-t)$

Test Prep

Multiple Choice

52. According to the map, if you drive from Atlanta to Los Angeles (L.A.) and back, how many miles would you travel?
A. 7,776 mi   **B.** 3,888 mi
C. 1,944 mi   **D.** 1,888 mi

53. Which equation correctly illustrates the Distributive Property?
F. $18(100 + 4) = (18 \cdot 100) + 4$
G. $18(100 + 4) = (18 + 100) \cdot (18 + 4)$
H. $18(100 + 4) = (18 + 100) \cdot 4$
I. $18(100 + 4) = (18 \cdot 100) + (18 \cdot 4)$

54. You rent three videos for $2.95 each. What do you pay?
A. $6.95   **B.** $8.85   **C.** $9.00   **D.** $9.15

Take It to the NET
Online lesson quiz at
www.PHSchool.com
Web Code: ada-0202

Mixed Review

Lesson 2-1

Name the property shown.

55. $3(6 \cdot 2) = 3(2 \cdot 6)$ **56.** $8 = 8 + 0$ **57.** $4(8 \cdot 3) = (4 \cdot 8)3$

Lessons 1-5 and 1-6

58. You have $120 in your checking account. In one month, you deposit $30, write a check for $21, withdraw $20, and deposit $45. Find your balance at the end of the month.

Lesson 1-3

Evaluate each expression.

59. $7 - m$, for $m = 6$ **60.** $6t + 1$, for $t = -2$ **61.** $c \div 3 - 5$, for $c = 6$

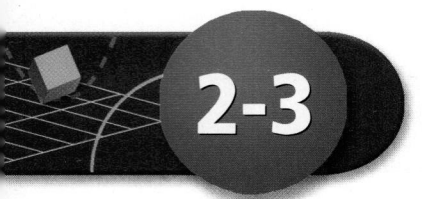
Simplifying Variable Expressions

What You'll Learn

OBJECTIVE 1 To identify parts of a variable expression

OBJECTIVE 2 To simplify expressions

. . . And Why

To extend addition and subtraction skills to include variables

 Check Skills You'll Need

Simplify each expression.

1. $5(b + 4)$

2. $-3(2x + 5)$

3. $4(-8 - 3q)$

4. $-6(2b - 7)$

 For help, go to Lesson 2-2.

New Vocabulary

- term
- constant
- like terms
- coefficient
- simplify a variable expression
- deductive reasoning

OBJECTIVE

1 Identifying Parts of a Variable Expression

The diagram shows the possible parts of a variable expression.

A **term** is a number or the product of a number and variable(s).

$$7a + 4a + 3b - 6$$

A **constant** is a term that has no variable.

Like terms have identical variables.

A **coefficient** is a number that multiplies a variable.

When you have a variable expression that includes subtraction, you can rewrite the expression using only addition. This will help you find the coefficient(s) and constant(s).

$$5x - 3y + z - 2$$
$$= 5x + (-3y) + z + (-2) \quad \text{Rewrite subtraction as adding opposites.}$$
$$= 5x + (-3y) + 1z + (-2) \quad \text{Identity Property of Multiplication}$$

Rewriting the expression using addition shows that the coefficients are 5, -3, and 1. The constant is -2. Notice that the sign between terms in the original expression determines whether a coefficient or constant is positive or negative.

1 EXAMPLE Identifying Parts of an Expression

Name the coefficients, the like terms, and the constants in $3m - 2n + n - 4$.

Coefficients: 3, -2, 1   Like terms: $-2n$ and n Constant: -4

 Check Understanding Example 1

1. Name the coefficients, the like terms, and the constants.

a. $6 + 2s + 4s$ **b.** $-4x$ **c.** $9m + 2r - 2m + r$

OBJECTIVE

2 Simplifying Variable Expressions

You **simplify a variable expression** by replacing it with an equivalent expression that has as few terms as possible. Algebra tiles can help you model this process.

TEXT Interactive lesson includes instant self-check, tutorials, and activities.

2 EXAMPLE Using Tiles to Simplify

Simplify $2x + 4 + 3x$.

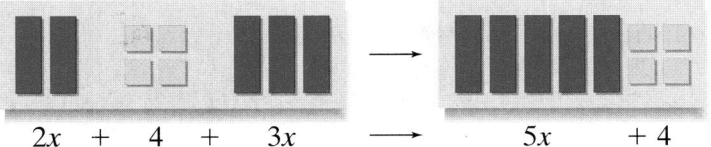

$$2x \quad + \quad 4 \quad + \quad 3x \quad \longrightarrow \quad 5x \quad + 4$$

✓ Check Understanding Example 2

2. Use tiles to simplify $3a + 2 + 4a - 1$.

You can also use the Distributive Property to combine like terms.

3 EXAMPLE Combining Like Terms

Simplify $5y + y$.

$5y + y = 5y + 1y$	**Use the Identity Property of Multiplication.**
$= (5 + 1)y$	**Use the Distributive Property.**
$= 6y$	**Simplify.**

✓ Check Understanding Example 3

3. Simplify each expression.

    a. $3b - b$ **b.** $-4m - 9m$ **c.** $p + 6p - 4p$

Deductive reasoning is the process of reasoning logically from given facts to a conclusion. As you use properties, rules, and definitions to justify the steps in a problem, you are using deductive reasoning.

4 EXAMPLE Using Deductive Reasoning

Simplify $4g + 3(3 + g)$. Justify each step.

$4g + 3(3 + g) = 4g + 9 + 3g$	**Use the Distributive Property.**
$= 4g + 3g + 9$	**Use the Commutative Property of Addition.**
$= (4 + 3)g + 9$	**Use the Distributive Property to combine like terms.**
$= 7g + 9$	**Simplify.**

✓ Check Understanding Example 4

4. Simplify each expression. Justify each step.

    a. $6y + 4m - 7y + m$ **b.** $4x + 3 - 2(5 + x)$

EXERCISES

For more exercises, see *Extra Practice*.

Practice and Problem Solving

A Practice by Example

Name the coefficients, the like terms, and the constants.

Example 1
(page 76)

1. $3x + 5y - 3$

2. $2x - 7$

3. $4x - 7x + 3x$

4. $6xy - 5xy$

5. $-3x$

6. $a + 2a + 3a - 4a$

Example 2
(page 77)

Use tiles to simplify each expression.

7. $x + 2 + 3x + 5 + x + 3 + 2x$

8. $2x + 1 + x - 4 + 4x + 1$

9. $x + 2 + 3x$

10. $2x + 1 + 6x - 4$

Example 3
(page 77)

Simplify each expression.

11. $12a + a$

12. $5a + 8a$

13. $-2b + b$

14. $7w - w$

15. $2r + 5 + 6r$

16. $4a + 3 + 5a$

Example 4
(page 77)

Simplify each expression. Justify each step.

17. $2g + 3(g + 5)$

18. $-3z + 8(z + y)$

19. $4m + 3d - 5m + d$

20. $t - 3 + 2(t + 2)$

B Apply Your Skills

Simplify each expression.

21. $8z + 8y + 3z$

22. $t + 3t + 2t + 4$

23. $18 + 6(9k - 13)$

24. $r + 3 + 6r + r$

25. $-4(a + 3) + a$

26. $4m + 3 - 5m + m$

27. $3(g + 5) + 2g$

28. $2b - 6 + 3b + b$

29. $-5 + 3x + 3 + 2$

30. $4(w + 2x) + 9(-4w)$

31. $3(2n + 4) - 2(3n + 6)$

32. Pet Supplies Juan bought supplies for his new gecko. He bought four plants for p dollars each. He also bought a 10-gallon tank for $10 and a water dish for $3. Write an expression Juan could use to find the total cost of the supplies.

33. Error Analysis Your friend simplified $x + y + xy$ to $2xy$. What error did your friend make?

34. Open-Ended Use the variables r and s to write a variable expression. Evaluate your expression for $r = 2$ and $s = -5$.

35. Writing in Math The expression $10bc$ has two variables. Explain why $10bc$ is not two terms.

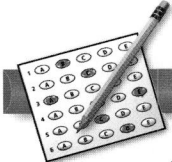
C **Challenge**

Simplify each expression. Justify each step.

36. $12 - 4(-8v + 17)$ **37.** $6(2x + y) + 2y - 12x$

38. $(2t + 4)3 + 6(-5t) - (-8)$ **39.** $-12(5x) + 3(-7x) - x$

40. $w + 3w + 4(5 + w - 3w)$ **41.** $18u - 6(9k + 7 - 10u) + 4k$

Test Prep

Multiple Choice

42. Which expression has exactly two like terms?
   A. $3t + 1 - t$ **B.** $7 + 2m$ **C.** $8q + 3p$ **D.** $6r + r - 9r$

43. Which expression simplifies to $3x + 4z + 6$?
   F. $3(x + 6) + 4z$ **G.** $7(x + z) + 6$
   H. $7z + 3(x + 2) - 3z$ **I.** $3 + x + 4 + z + 6$

44. Jaleesa bought three folders for b cents each and two report covers for c cents each. She also bought a binder for $1.89. Which expression could Jaleesa use to find the total cost?
   A. $b + c + 189$ **B.** $3b + 189$
   C. $3b + 2c + 189$ **D.** $189 - 2b - 3c$

Take It to the NET
Online lesson quiz at
www.PHSchool.com
Web Code: ada-0203

Mixed Review

Lesson 2-2 **Mental Math Use the Distributive Property to find each product.**

45. $8(102)$ **46.** $54 \cdot 6$ **47.** $19(30)$ **48.** $(41)(9)$

Lesson 1-8 **49. Rock Climbing** A pair of rock climbers start up a 1,000-ft cliff. After one hour, they have gone up 160 ft. After two hours, they have gone up 320 ft. If they continue at this rate, how far up will they have gone after five hours?

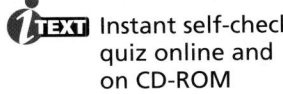
✓ Checkpoint Quiz 1 Lessons 2-1 through 2-3

TEXT Instant self-check quiz online and on CD-ROM

Name each property shown.

1. $3 \cdot (-6) = -6 \cdot 3$ **2.** $(3a)b = 3(ab)$

3. $17 \cdot 1 = 17$ **4.** $6 + 0 = 0 + 6$

5. $(3 + 2)(4) = (4)(3 + 2)$ **6.** $4(3 - 2) = 4(3) - 4(2)$

Simplify each expression.

7. $3(a + 2a)$ **8.** $9y - 3y + 12y$ **9.** $7(2w) + 2(w - 3)$

2-4 Variables and Equations

What You'll Learn

 OBJECTIVE 1 To classify types of equations

 OBJECTIVE 2 To check equations using substitution

. . . And Why

To check solutions of real-world equations involving weights

 **Check Skills You'll Need**

Write a variable expression for each phrase.

1. the sum of x and 46

2. four less than g

3. t decreased by five

4. the quotient of z and 26

🔎 For help, go to Lesson 1-1.

New Vocabulary

- equation
- open sentence
- solution of an equation

Writing in Math

The verb *is* between two quantities suggests writing the equal sign.

ⓘ **TEXT** Interactive lesson includes instant self-check, tutorials, and activities.

OBJECTIVE

1 Classifying Types of Equations

An **equation** is a mathematical sentence with an equal sign. Here are three of the ways you will see equations in this book.

$9 + 2 = 11$	a numerical expression equal to a numerical expression
$x + 7 = 37$	a variable expression equal to a numerical expression
$a + (-3) = 2a + 5$	a variable expression equal to a variable expression

An equation with a numerical expression equal to another numerical expression is either *true* or *false*. An equation with one or more variables is an **open sentence**.

1 EXAMPLE Classifying Equations

State whether each equation is *true, false,* or an *open sentence*.

a. 6 + 12 = 18   true, because $18 = 18$

b. 6 = 4 + 3   false, because $6 \neq 7$

c. 6y = −3 + 5y   an open sentence, because there is a variable

✔ **Check Understanding**   Example 1

1. State whether each equation is *true, false,* or an *open sentence*. Explain.

    a. $9 - 7 = 3$ **b.** $8 + x = 2$ **c.** $4 \cdot 5 = 20$

You can write a mathematical word sentence as an equation.

2 EXAMPLE Writing an Equation

Write an equation for
Nine times the opposite of five is forty-five.
State whether the equation is *true, false,* or an *open sentence*.

Words	nine	times	the opposite of five	is	forty-five
⬇	9	times	−5	is	45
Equation	9	·	(−5)	=	45

● The equation is false. $9 \cdot (-5) = -45$, and $-45 \neq 45$.

✅ **Check Understanding**   Example 2

2. Write an equation for *Twenty minus x is three.*
Is the equation true, false, or an open sentence? Explain.

OBJECTIVE

2   Checking Equations Using Substitution

A **solution of an equation** is a value for a variable that makes an equation true. You substitute a number for a variable to determine whether the number is a solution of the equation.

3 EXAMPLE   **Substituting to Check**

Is 30 a solution of the equation $170 + x = 200$?

$$170 + x = 200$$
$$170 + 30 \overset{?}{=} 200 \quad \textbf{Substitute 30 for } x.$$
$$200 = 200$$

● Yes, 30 is a solution of the equation.

> **Reading Math**
>
> ≠ shows that two values are not equal.
> $\overset{?}{=}$ asks whether two values are equal.

✅ **Check Understanding**   Example 3

3. Is the given number a solution of the equation?

   a. $8 + t = 2t; 1$ **b.** $9 - m = 3; 6$

4 EXAMPLE   **Real-World 🌐 Problem Solving**

Scuba Diving A diver's equipment weighs 35 lb. The diver plus the equipment weighs 165 lb. Can the diver's weight be 200 lb?

Words	weight of diver	plus	weight of equipment	is	165 lb

Let d = weight of diver.

Equation	d	+	35	=	165

$$d + 35 = 165$$
$$200 + 35 \overset{?}{=} 165 \quad \textbf{Substitute 200 for the variable.}$$
$$235 \neq 165$$

● No, the diver's weight cannot be 200 lb.

Real-World 🌐 Connection

A scuba tank can hold 63 ft^3 of compressed air. It weighs 29 lb when full.

✅ **Check Understanding**   Example 4

4. A tent weighs 6 lb. Your backpack and the tent together weigh 33 lb. Use an equation to find whether the backpack weighs 27 lb.

EXERCISES

❓ For more exercises, see *Extra Practice*.

Practice and Problem Solving

(A) Practice by Example
Example 1
(page 80)

State whether each equation is *true, false,* or an *open sentence.* Explain.

1. $5 + 9 = 14$ **2.** $4x - 8 = 25$ **3.** $15 = 3 \cdot 5$

4. $x - 10 = 22 - x$ **5.** $6 + 1 = 5 + 3$ **6.** $4c - 12 = 20$

7. $20 = 2 \cdot 10$ **8.** $20 + 3x = 42$ **9.** $3 \cdot 9 = 30$

Example 2
(page 80)

Write an equation for each sentence. State whether the equation is *true, false,* or an *open sentence.* Explain.

10. Four times the opposite of five equals negative twenty.

11. Twenty-five equals a number v plus fifteen.

Example 3
(page 81)

Is the given number a solution of the equation?

12. $c + 5 = 3; -2$ **13.** $24 = c + 29; -2$ **14.** $4 + d = 6; 2$

15. $20 - c = 12; 8$ **16.** $8 = a + 3; 10$ **17.** $3 + 2t = 7; 4$

18. $3 = 12 - a; 6$ **19.** $2m = m + 6; 4$ **20.** $5q - 1 = -1; 0$

Example 4
(page 81)

Write an equation. Is the given value a solution?

21. Weight A veterinarian weighs 140 lb. When she steps on a scale while holding a dog, the scale shows 192 lb. Let d represent the weight of the dog. Does the dog weigh 52 lb?

22. Income A family's expenses are $1,200. One parent makes $850. Must the other earn $400 for both incomes to equal expenses?

(B) Apply Your Skills

Determine whether each statement is true or false. Explain.

23. An equation can be false.

24. $3w - 7$ is an open sentence.

25. An open sentence must contain a variable.

26. Some open sentences are true for all variable values.

State whether each equation is *true, false,* or an *open sentence.* Explain.

27. $18 = -3(-6)$ **28.** $-24(-2) = 18(4 + 2)$

29. $-9 + x = 50 \div 10 + 3$ **30.** $-2(3 - 8) = 2[-3 - (-8)]$

31. $6[-3 - (-5)] = 2(-4 + 10)$ **32.** $4[2 + (-6)] = 2[x - (-12)]$

Write an equation for each sentence. State whether each equation is *true, false,* or an *open sentence.* Explain.

33. The product of negative twenty and nine is negative eleven.

34. The sum of fifteen and a number n is fifty.

35. Forty-eight divided by twelve equals three.

36. Writing in Math Equations can be true or false. Can an expression be true or false? Explain.

Is the given number a solution of the equation? Explain.

37. $\frac{c}{2} - 8 = 3(-3); -2$ **38.** $14 = 28 \div x; 14$

39. $-x - 5 = 6; 1$ **40.** $3b \div 18 = 2; 12$

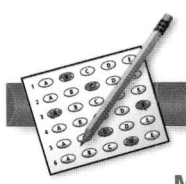 **Challenge** 🌐 **Language Arts** Some word sentences are similar to equations. Exercises 41–43 are about word sentences.

41. The sentence *Abraham Lincoln was an American president* is true. Write two other true sentences.

42. The sentence *Eleanor Roosevelt was an American president* is false. Write two other false sentences.

43. The sentence *He is a professional baseball player* is open. It is not clear to whom the word *he* refers. Write two other open sentences.

Test Prep

Multiple Choice

44. Which equation is false?
  A. $3 + (-7) = 10$ **B.** $6 \div 2 = 3$
  C. $8 \cdot 2 - 15 = 1$ **D.** $7w = 3w + 12$

45. Together Mike and Amy weigh 350 pounds. Amy weighs 150 pounds and Mike weighs m pounds. Which equation represents this situation?
  F. $m + 350 = 150$ **G.** $m = 350 + 200$
  H. $m - 200 = 150$ **I.** $m = 350 - 150$

46. A recipe calls for 4 c of flour. You have 20 c of flour. Let r represent the flour you have left after making the recipe. Which equation represents this situation?
  A. $r - 20 = 4$ **B.** $20 - 4 = r$ **C.** $r - 4 = 16$ **D.** $r - 4 = 20$

Take It to the NET
Online lesson quiz at
www.PHSchool.com
Web Code: ada-0204

Mixed Review

Lesson 2-3 **Simplify each expression.**

47. $6m + 7 - 2m$ **48.** $-8t + 4t - 19$ **49.** $3w + 5k - 4w + k$

Lesson 1-8 🌐 **50. Marathon Training** Larissa ran 15 mi per week before she decided to train for a marathon. The first week of training she ran 17 mi. The second week she ran 19 mi. If she continued her pattern, how far did she run the fifth week?

Lesson 1-3 **Evaluate each expression for $a = 3$ and $b = 2$.**

51. $a - b + 15$ **52.** $(3b - 2a) \div 4$ **53.** $3(b + 2) - 4$

You can model an equation using algebra tiles. Use a green rectangular tile to represent the variable. Here are two examples.

Equation 1

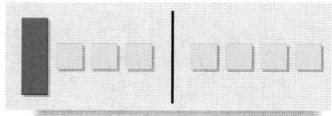

$$x + 3 = 4$$

Equation 2

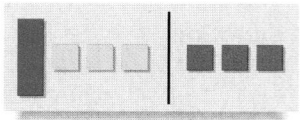

$$x + 3 = -3$$

Model each equation.

1. $x + 3 = 5$ 2. $z + 2 = -6$ 3. $y + 1 = 4$

4. $-3 = a - 4$ 5. $2b + 2 = 8$ 6. $3 + 3x = -6$

To solve an equation, get the variable alone on one side of the equal sign. To do this, remove the same number of tiles from each side.

Here's how to solve $x + 3 = 7$.

Model the equation.

Solve by removing 3 tiles from each side.

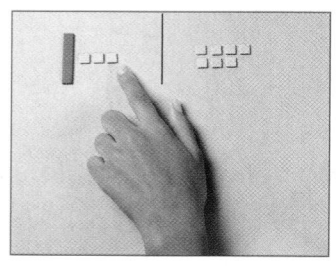
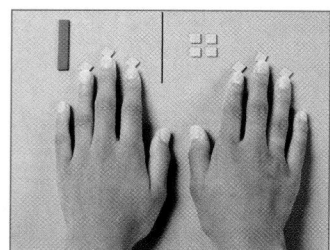
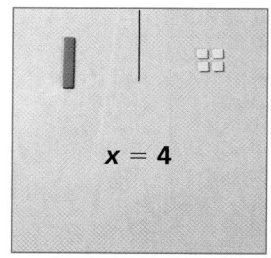

$x = 4$

Check $x + 3 = 7$

$4 + 3 \stackrel{?}{=} 7$ **Replace x with 4.**

$7 = 7$ ✔

Model and solve each equation. Check your result.

7. $x + 3 = 6$ 8. $m + 2 = 8$ 9. $1 = 1 + d$

10. $-4 + y = -7$ 11. $-1 + p = -5$ 12. $w - 2 = -3$

Modeling   Write and solve the equation for each model.

13.
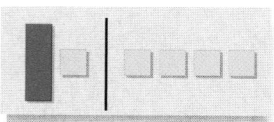

14.
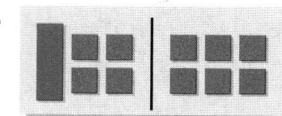

15.
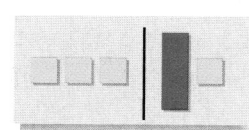

Sometimes you cannot remove the same number of tiles from each side. You may need to add tiles to create zero pairs. Here's how to solve $x + 2 = -4$.

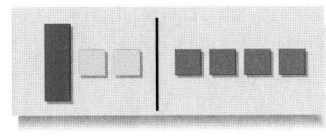 **Model the equation.**

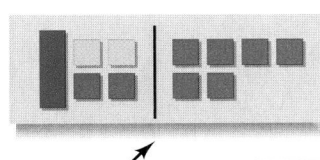 **Add −2 to each side.**

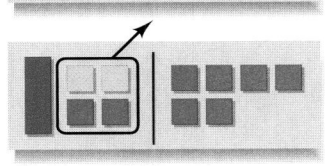 **Remove zero pairs.**

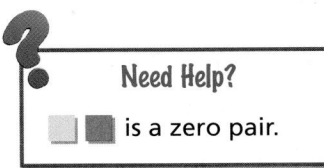

Need Help?

is a zero pair.

 $x = -6$

Check $x + 2 = -4$

$-6 + 2 \stackrel{?}{=} -4$ **Replace x with −6.**

$-4 = -4$ ✔

Model and solve each equation. Check your result.

16. $y + 2 = -2$ **17.** $x + 5 = 2$ **18.** $n + 7 = 1$

19. $-1 = k + 3$ **20.** $x - 4 = 5$ **21.** $2 = z - 3$

Modeling Write and solve the equation for each model.

22. 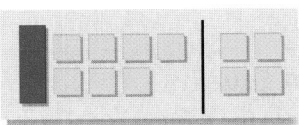   **23.** 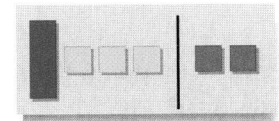   **24.**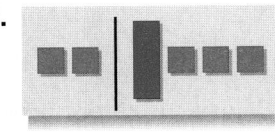

25. Open-Ended Write two different equations that have the solution modeled at the right.

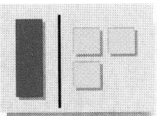

26. Number Sense Give an example of an equation model that has the same color unit squares on each side but still requires zero pairs to solve. Explain why zero pairs are needed.

Solving Equations by Adding or Subtracting

OBJECTIVE

1 Using Subtraction to Solve Equations

What You'll Learn

OBJECTIVE

1 To solve one-step equations using subtraction

OBJECTIVE

2 To solve one-step equations using addition

. . . And Why

To solve real-world problems involving health

 Check Skills You'll Need

Simplify each expression.

1. $3 + 4 - 4$

2. $7 + 9 - 7$

3. $8 - 2 + 2$

4. $6 + 2 - 2$

🔎 For help, go to Lesson 2-1.

New Vocabulary

• inverse operations

Solving an equation is like keeping a barbell balanced. If you add weight to or subtract weight from one side of the bar, you must do the same on the other side.

 Subtract 5 lb from each side.

As you can see in the photos, you keep the barbell balanced when you remove the same weight from each side.

In previous math courses, you used related equations like $3 + 5 = 8$ and $8 - 3 = 5$. These equations show that addition and subtraction undo each other.

When you solve an equation, your goal is to get the variable alone on one side of the equation. The value on the other side tells you the solution of the original equation. You use **inverse operations,** which undo each other, to get the variable alone.

Key Concepts **Subtraction Property of Equality**

You can subtract the same number from each side of an equation.

Arithmetic	Algebra
$10 = 2(5)$	If $a = b$,
$10 - 5 = 2(5) - 5$	then $a - c = b - c$.

ℹ️ **TEXT** Interactive lesson includes instant self-check, tutorials, and activities.

After you solve an equation, use your result in the original equation (as shown in Example 1) to check that your solution is correct.

1 EXAMPLE   Subtracting to Solve an Equation

Solve $x + 6 = 4$.

Method 1

$$x + 6 = 4$$
$$x + 6 - 6 = 4 - 6 \qquad \text{Subtract 6 from each side.}$$
$$x = -2 \qquad \text{Simplify.}$$

Method 2

$$x + 6 = \quad 4$$
$$\underline{\quad -6 \qquad -6}$$
$$x = \quad -2$$

Check
$$x + 6 = 4$$
$$-2 + 6 \stackrel{?}{=} 4 \qquad \text{Replace } x \text{ with } -2.$$
$$4 = 4 \checkmark$$

✓ Check Understanding   Example 1

1. Solve each equation.

a. $x + 8 = 3$ **b.** $5 = d + 1$ **c.** $c + (-4) = -5$

You can write and solve equations describing real-world situations. To help check, decide whether your solution is correct using the original problem.

2 EXAMPLE   Real-World  Problem Solving

Health Fred's target heart rate is 130 beats/min. This is 58 beats/min more than his resting heart rate. Find his resting heart rate.

Words target rate is 58 more than resting rate

Let r = resting heart rate.

Equation 130 = 58 + r

$$130 = 58 + r$$
$$130 = r + 58 \qquad \text{Use the Commutative Property of Addition.}$$
$$130 - 58 = r + 58 - 58 \qquad \text{Subtract 58 from each side.}$$
$$72 = r \qquad \text{Simplify.}$$

Fred's resting heart rate is 72 beats per minute.

Check The resting heart rate plus 58 beats per minute should be 130 beats per minute.
$$72 + 58 = 130 \checkmark$$

Real-World ⊕ Connection

Here is one method for estimating your target heart-rate range: Begin by subtracting your age from 220. Then multiply the result by 0.6 and 0.8 to find the lower and upper limits of your heart-rate range.

✓ Check Understanding   Example 2

2. Cora measures her heart rate at 123 beats per minute. This is 55 beats per minute more than her resting heart rate r. Write and solve an equation to find Cora's resting heart rate.

When you solve an equation involving subtraction, *add* the same number to each side of the equation.

Key Concepts | **Addition Property of Equality**

You can add the same number to each side of an equation.

Arithmetic	Algebra
$8 = 2(4)$	If $a = b$,
$8 + 3 = 2(4) + 3$	then $a + c = b + c$.

3 **EXAMPLE** **Adding to Solve an Equation**

Solve $b - 12 = -49$.

$$b - 12 = -49$$
$$b - 12 + 12 = -49 + 12 \quad \textbf{Add 12 to each side.}$$
$$b = -37 \quad \textbf{Simplify.}$$

✔ **Check Understanding** **Example 3**

3. Solve each equation.

a. $y - 5 = 8$ **b.** $p - 30 = 42$ **c.** $98 = x - 14$

4 **EXAMPLE** **Real-World** **Problem Solving**

Purchasing **Your friend's VCR cost $328 less than her TV. Her VCR cost $179. How much did her TV cost?**

Words   cost of VCR   was $328   less than   cost of TV

Let t = the cost of the TV.

Equation   179   = t −   328

$$179 = t - 328$$
$$179 + 328 = t - 328 + 328 \quad \textbf{Add 328 to each side.}$$
$$507 = t \quad \textbf{Simplify.}$$

Your friend's TV cost $507.

✔ **Check Understanding** **Example 4**

4. A softcover book costs $17 less than its hardcover edition. The softcover costs $5. Write and solve an equation to find the cost h of the hardcover book.

Writing in Math

When you go from words to an equation, the order of the math symbols may be different from the order of the words:

- ten fewer than n → $n - 10$
- eight less than r → $r - 8$
- n times 5 → $5n$

EXERCISES

For more exercises, see *Extra Practice*.

Practice and Problem Solving

 Practice by Example

Solve each equation.

Example 1
(page 87)

1. $a + 8 = 12$ **2.** $t + (-3) = 8$ **3.** $3 = n + 4$

4. $d + (-4) = -7$ **5.** $c + 9 = 37$ **6.** $q + (-10) = -25$

7. $b + 24 = 19$ **8.** $65 = n + 24$ **9.** $40 = w + (-5)$

Example 2
(page 87)

10. Astronomy The average distance from the sun to Jupiter is 778 million km. This distance is 550 million km greater than the average distance from the sun to Mars. Write and solve an equation to find the average distance d that Mars is from the sun.

Reading Math
For help with reading and solving Exercise 11, see page 91.

11. Physics The speed of sound through steel is 5,200 meters per second (m/s). This is 2,520 m/s faster than the speed of sound through silver. Write and solve an equation to find the speed s of sound through silver.

Example 3
(page 88)

Solve each equation.

12. $d - 4 = -7$ **13.** $c - 34 = 20$ **14.** $a - 4 = -18$

15. $r - 3 = 8$ **16.** $z - 100 = 100$ **17.** $5 = d - 1$

18. $40 = g - 20$ **19.** $34 = c - 19$ **20.** $-54 = q - 9$

Example 4
(page 88)

21. Astronomy Venus's average distance from the sun is 108 million km. This distance is 42 million km less than the average distance from the sun to Earth. Write and solve an equation to find Earth's average distance d from the sun.

22. Languages In 1996, 487 million people across the world spoke English. This was 512 million people fewer than the number who spoke Mandarin Chinese. Write and solve an equation to find the number of people n who spoke Mandarin Chinese.

B **Apply Your Skills**

Copy and complete the steps for solving each equation.

23. $35 + b = -90$
    $35 - \blacksquare + b = -90 - \blacksquare$
    $b = \blacksquare$

24. $y - 86 = -322$
    $y - 86 + \blacksquare = -322 + \blacksquare$
    $y = \blacksquare$

Solve each equation.

25. $54 + x = 98$ **26.** $e - 43 = -45$ **27.** $47 = 7 + y$

28. $450 = a - 325$ **29.** $h + 35 = 15$ **30.** $298 + n = 294$

31. $x - 366 = -415$ **32.** $89 + y = 112$ **33.** $-27 = w - 14$

34. Open-Ended Write a word problem that can be solved using the equation $x + 15 = 18$.

35. This year, the Tigers won six more games than the Panthers. What other fact would you need to know in order to use the equation $p + 6 = 22$ to find the number of games, p, that the Panthers won?

Mental Math Use mental math to solve each equation.

36. $b + 15 = -5$ **37.** $130 = 30 + s$ **38.** $x + 800 = 500$

39. Error Analysis A student solved the equation $x - 6 = -6$. His solution was -12. What error did the student make?

40. Writing in Math To solve $x + 25 = -22$, one student subtracted 25 from each side. Another student added -25 to each side. Will both methods work? Explain.

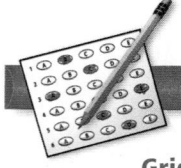 **Challenge** **Solve each equation.**

41. $-45 = x + (-3) + 50$ **42.** $-215 + e + (-43) = -145$

43. $n - 29 - 16 = 246$ **44.** $34 + p + 112 = 78 - 7$

45. $183 + k - 20 = -15$ **46.** $328 = z - 31 + 219$

 **Test Prep**

Gridded Response Solve the equation given by each sentence.

47. Negative six plus y equals eighteen.

48. Twelve equals 23 subtracted from n.

49. Negative five equals x minus eight.

50. The number a plus 5 is 18.

51. Negative 8 plus y equals 13.

52. Seventeen is y less than 32.

Take It to the NET
Online lesson quiz at
www.PHSchool.com
Web Code: ada-0205

Mixed Review

Lesson 2-4 State whether each equation is *true, false,* or an *open sentence.* Explain.

53. $x + 2 = 4$ **54.** $4 = 6 - 2$ **55.** $5 - 3 = 7 - 4$

Lesson 1-8 **56. Patterns** Deric studied 30 min for his first math test. He studied 45 min for the second test, and 60 min for the third test. If he continues this pattern, how long will he study for the fifth test?

Lesson 1-3 **Evaluate.**

57. $6n$, for $n = 8$ **58.** $\frac{k}{20}$, for $k = 140$ **59.** $50x$, for $x = 8$

Read the exercise below and then follow along with what Tom thinks and writes. Check your understanding by solving the exercise at the bottom of the page.

Physics The speed of sound through steel is 5,200 meters per second (m/s). This is 2,520 m/s faster than the speed of sound through silver. Write and solve an equation to find the speed s of sound through silver.

What Tom Thinks

I'll read the problem and write down the important information.

Where to start? Well, it's always helpful to look for a relationship in the problem.

The speed is greater through steel. I will either have to subtract from the speed through steel to get the speed through silver, or add to the speed through silver to get the speed through steel. I'll add.

Since I know the speed through steel, I have to name only one variable.

Now I can write the equation.

I can solve the equation by using the Subtraction Property of Equality.

I have to state what was asked for in the problem.

What Tom Writes

Speed of sound through steel = 5,200 m/s. The speed through steel is 2,520 m/s faster than the speed through silver.

The speed through steel is 2,520 m/s faster than the speed through silver.

Steel speed = silver speed + 2,520

Let s = speed of sound through silver.

$$5,200 = s + 2,520$$

$$5,200 - 2,520 = s + 2,520 - 2,520$$
$$2,680 = s$$

The speed of sound through silver is 2,680 m/s.

EXERCISE

1. Pamela can run the 300-m hurdles in 52.3 s. Elaine takes 2.8 s more than Pamela to make the same run. How long does it take Elaine to run the 300-m hurdles?

Solving Equations by Multiplying or Dividing

OBJECTIVE

1 Using Division to Solve Equations

Division and multiplication are inverse operations. You can solve an equation that involves multiplication by using the Division Property of Equality.

Key Concepts   **Division Property of Equality**

If you divide each side of an equation by the same nonzero number, the two sides remain equal.

Arithmetic	Algebra
$6 = 3(2)$	If $a = b$ and $c \neq 0$,
$\frac{6}{3} = \frac{3(2)}{3}$	then $\frac{a}{c} = \frac{b}{c}$.

1 **EXAMPLE**   **Real-World** 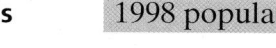 **Problem Solving**

Statistics **The United States population in 1998 was twice the population in 1943. Find the 1943 population in millions.**

Words	1998 population	was	twice	1943 population

Let p = population in 1943.

Equation   270   =   2 · p

$$270 = 2p$$

$$\frac{270}{2} = \frac{2p}{2} \quad \text{Divide each side by 2.}$$

$$135 = p \quad \text{Simplify.}$$

The United States population in 1943 was 135 million people.

Check Is the answer reasonable? Twice the 1943 population should be the 1998 population. Since $135 \cdot 2 = 270$, the answer is reasonable.

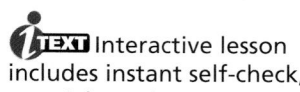

270 million

? million

1943   1998

U.S. Population Growth

✓ **Check Understanding** **Example 1**

1. Solve each equation.

a. $4x = 84$ **b.** $91 = 7y$ **c.** $12w = 108$

2 EXAMPLE Dividing to Solve an Equation

Solve $5r = -20$.

$$5r = -20$$
$$\frac{5r}{5} = \frac{-20}{5} \quad \textbf{Divide each side by 5.}$$
$$r = -4 \quad \textbf{Simplify.}$$

Check
$$5r = -20$$
$$5 \cdot (-4) \stackrel{?}{=} -20 \quad \textbf{Replace } r \textbf{ with } -4.$$
$$-20 = -20 \; ✔$$

✔ **Check Understanding** Example 2

2. Solve each equation.

a. $-3b = 24$ **b.** $96 = -8n$ **c.** $-4d = -56$

OBJECTIVE

2 Using Multiplication to Solve Equations

When you multiply each side of an equation by the same number, the two sides remain equal.

> ### Key Concepts Multiplication Property of Equality
>
> You can multiply each side of an equation by the same number.
>
> | **Arithmetic** | **Algebra** |
> |---|---|
> | $12 = 3(4)$ | If $a = b$, |
> | $12 \cdot 2 = 3(4) \cdot 2$ | then $ac = bc$. |

3 EXAMPLE Multiplying to Solve an Equation

Solve $\frac{x}{-9} = -3$.

$$\frac{x}{-9} = -3$$
$$-9\left(\frac{x}{-9}\right) = -9(-3) \quad \textbf{Multiply each side by } -9.$$
$$x = 27 \quad \textbf{Simplify.}$$

Reading Math

Read the equation $\frac{x}{-9} = -3$ as "x divided by negative nine equals negative three."

✔ **Check Understanding** Example 3

3. Solve each equation.

a. $\frac{r}{-5} = 10$ **b.** $\frac{s}{6} = 54$ **c.** $-30 = \frac{t}{20}$

EXERCISES

For more exercises, see *Extra Practice*.

Practice and Problem Solving

A Practice by Example

Examples 1 and 2
(pages 92 and 93)

Solve each equation.

1. $6x = 96$ **2.** $108 = 9x$ **3.** $8y = 112$

4. $45 = 9a$ **5.** $5w = 95$ **6.** $15c = 90$

7. $125 = 25d$ **8.** $180 = 45s$ **9.** $20b = 2{,}000$

10. $8x = -48$ **11.** $4a = 28$ **12.** $-60 = 12m$

13. $-2b = 30$ **14.** $-10d = 100$ **15.** $162 = -18t$

16. $-75 = -15x$ **17.** $-5x = -115$ **18.** $-60y = -360$

19. Earnings Carol earns \$8/h. How many hours must she work to earn \$288?

20. Savings Raul saves \$15 each month. At this rate, how many months will he take to save \$135?

Example 3
(page 93)

Solve each equation.

21. $6 = \frac{a}{7}$ **22.** $\frac{w}{12} = 2$ **23.** $\frac{n}{15} = 7$ **24.** $\frac{b}{-6} = 20$

25. $-2 = \frac{d}{8}$ **26.** $\frac{v}{3} = -4$ **27.** $-\frac{m}{20} = -2$ **28.** $\frac{r}{-5} = -4$

B Apply Your Skills

Solve each equation.

29. $39 = c \cdot 3$ **30.** $25x = -125$ **31.** $\frac{v}{3} = 14$ **32.** $\frac{m}{-4} = 13$

33. $-50 = \frac{n}{-6}$ **34.** $72 = 8n$ **35.** $22p = 110$ **36.** $\frac{r}{-9} = -18$

37. Reasoning You can divide each side of an equation by the same nonzero value. Explain what would result from the equation $4 \cdot 0 = 5 \cdot 0$ if you could divide each side by zero, and if $\frac{0}{0} = 1$.

Mental Math Is -3 a solution of each equation? Explain.

38. $\frac{b}{-3} = 1$ **39.** $\frac{-18}{k} = -6$ **40.** $3t = 9$

Write an equation for each sentence. Solve the equation.

41. The product of negative twenty and y is one hundred.

42. The value n divided by ten is one hundred.

43. Seven multiplied by k is negative one hundred and sixty-eight.

44. Buildings One of the world's tallest office buildings is in Malaysia. The building has 88 stories. The height of the 88 stories is 1,232 ft. What is the height of one story?

U.S. School Enrollment

Grades	Millions of Students
Kindergarten	▪
1–8	32
9–12	16

SOURCE: U.S. Census Bureau.
Go to **www.PHSchool.com** for a
data update. Web Code: adg-2041

45. Use the table at the left. The number of students in grades 1–8 is four times the number of students in kindergarten. Write and solve an equation to find the number of students s in kindergarten.

46. **Writing in Math** How are the procedures to solve $3x = 9$ and $x + 3 = 9$ alike? How are they different?

47. **Open-Ended** Write a question that can be solved using the equation $5x = 45$.

Mental Math Solve each equation.

48. $75m = -7,500$ **49.** $\frac{v}{-50} = 300$ **50.** $3,823 = \frac{s}{100}$

C **Challenge**

For what values of x is each equation true?

51. $|x| = 7$ **52.** $-3|x| = -9$ **53.** $\frac{|x|}{3} = 2$

54. $x - a = b$ **55.** $a + x = b$ **56.** $ax = b$

Multiple Choice

In Exercises 57–60, which equation matches the given sentence?

57. Negative six multiplied by q equals one hundred eight.
  A. $-6 + q = 108$ **B.** $-6q = 108$
  C. $108q = -6$ **D.** $q = -6 + 108$

58. Thirteen equals the quotient of x divided by three.
  F. $13 = \frac{x}{3}$ **G.** $\frac{x}{13}$ **H.** $13 = 3x$ **I.** $\frac{13}{3} = x$

59. Forty-two is the product of some number and 6.
  A. $6(42) = x$ **B.** $\frac{6}{x} = 42$ **C.** $\frac{x}{42} = 6$ **D.** $42 = 6x$

60. Some number divided by eight equals four.
  F. $\frac{8}{x} = 4$ **G.** $\frac{8}{4} = x$ **H.** $\frac{x}{8} = 4$ **I.** $\frac{4}{8} = x$

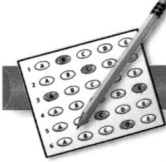

Take It to the NET
Online lesson quiz at
www.PHSchool.com
Web Code: ada-0206

Lesson 2-5   **Solve each equation.**

61. $-4 = a + 7$ **62.** $n - 5 = 12$ **63.** $t - (-4) = -15$ **64.** $y + 10 = 12$

Lesson 1-5 **65.** **Hiking** Suppose you start hiking from a point 92 ft below sea level and break for lunch on a hilltop that is 1,673 ft above sea level. What is your change in elevation?

Lesson 1-1   **Write a variable expression for each phrase.**

66. three less than a **67.** 7 times a number n

2-7 Problem Solving

Try, Test, Revise

What You'll Learn

OBJECTIVE 1
To solve a problem using the Try, Test, Revise strategy

. . . And Why

To solve real-world problems involving money

✓ Check Skills You'll Need

Simplify.

1. $158 + 20$

2. $158 + 30$

3. $158 + 25$

4. $158 + 22$

5. In Exercises 1–4, which result came closest to 181?

❓ For help, go to Lesson 1-5.

OBJECTIVE

1 Try, Test, Revise

Math Strategies in Action Did you know that meteorologists use weather balloons to collect data? They use the temperature, humidity, and other data in mathematical models to bring you the daily weather forecast. As more data become available—from weather balloons and satellites, for example— the models, and therefore the weather reports, become more accurate.

Similarly, in math problems, you can make an initial conjecture. You can test your conjecture. If it is not the right answer, you can use what you learn from your first conjecture to make a better, second conjecture.

Real-World 🌐 Connection

Each day, weather balloons make more than 1,000 measurements of conditions in the upper atmosphere around the world.

1 EXAMPLE Real-World 🌐 Problem Solving

Ticket Sales The theater club at school put on a play. For one performance, the club sold 133 tickets and raised $471. Tickets cost $4 for adults and $3 for students. How many student tickets and how many adult tickets did the club sell?

Read and Understand

Look at the given information to make an informed conjecture.

1. How much does each type of ticket cost?

2. How many tickets did the club sell for the performance?

3. How much money did the club raise from ticket sales for this performance?

Plan and Solve

Make a conjecture, and then test it. Use what you learn from your conjecture to make a better, second conjecture.

🅣🅔🅧🅣 Interactive lesson includes instant self-check, tutorials, and activities.

4. When you make a conjecture for how many adult tickets were sold, how can you use your conjecture to find how many student tickets could have been sold?

5. By what number do you multiply your conjecture of adult tickets sold to find how much money was made on adult tickets?

You can organize conjectures in a table. As a first conjecture, try making about half the tickets adult tickets.

Adult Tickets	Student Tickets	Total Money (in dollars)	
60	$133 - 60 = 73$	$60(4) + 73(3) = 240 + 219$ $= 459$	**The total is too low. Increase the number of adult tickets.**
80	$133 - 80 = 53$	$80(4) + 53(3) = 320 + 159$ $= 479$	**The total is too high. Decrease the number of adult tickets.**
70	$133 - 70 = 63$	$70(4) + 63(3) = 280 + 189$ $= 469$	**The total is very close. Increase the number of adult tickets.**
72	$133 - 72 = 61$	$72(4) + 61(3) = 288 + 183$ $= 471$	**The total is correct.**

There were 72 adult tickets and 61 student tickets sold.

Look Back and Check

Is it possible to solve the problem in another way? Consider using logical reasoning.

- The less expensive ticket is $3. So the theater club would get $133 \cdot \$3 = \$399$ if all the tickets sold were student tickets.
- $\$471 - \$399 = \$72$. The theater club actually raised $72 more than if they had sold only student tickets.
- Since adult tickets are $1 more than student tickets, there must have been 72 adult tickets sold.
- $133 - 72 = 61$. There were 61 student tickets sold.
- Since $72 \cdot 4 + 61 \cdot 3 = 471$, the solution 72 adult tickets and 61 student tickets is correct.

✔ Check Understanding

6. Suppose the club sold the same number of tickets, but raised $452. How many tickets of each type did the theater club sell?

EXERCISES

For more exercises, see *Extra Practice*.

Practice and Problem Solving

A Practice by Example

Example 1
(page 96)

Use the *Try, Test, Revise* strategy to solve each problem.

 1. Coin Collections Bonnie has 16 coins in her pocket worth $1.50. What are two different combinations of coins she could have in her pocket?

2. Currency A cashier's drawer has some $5 bills, some $10 bills, and some $20 bills. There are 15 bills worth a total of $185. How many $5 bills, $10 bills, and $20 bills are there?

3. The Smiths have two children. The sum of their ages is 23. The product of their ages is 132. How old are the children?

4. The sum of Mr. and Mrs. Bergen's ages is 100. The difference between their ages is 10. How old are Mr. and Mrs. Bergen?

B Apply Your Skills

Solve using any strategy.

5. Geometry A rectangular vegetable garden has a length of 5 ft and a width of 8 ft. The length is increased by 2 ft. By how many square feet does the area increase?

6. Trains leave New York for Boston every 40 min. The first train leaves at 5:20 A.M. What departure time is closest to 12:55 P.M.?

7. Lovell is 16 years old. Lovell's age is the same as Rafi's age divided by three. How old is Rafi?

8. Number Theory A number multiplied by itself and then by itself again gives −1,000. What is the number?

9. Coin Collections In a group of quarters and nickels, there are four more nickels than quarters. How many nickels and quarters are there if the coins are worth $2.30?

10. The sum of the page numbers on two facing pages is 245. The product of the numbers is 15,006. What are the page numbers?

11. Shopping A student bought some compact discs for $12 each and some books for $5 each. She spent $39 in all on five items. How many of each item did she buy?

12. Relay Races Two runners ran as a team in a 5,000-m relay race. The first runner ran 500 m farther than the second runner. How many meters did each run?

C Challenge

13. Savings Ron puts three pennies in a jar. His father offers to triple the total amount of money in Ron's jar at the end of each day. How much is in the jar at the end of one week?

14. Biology A certain bacteria doubles the number of its cells every 20 min. A scientist puts 50 cells in a culture dish. How many cells will be in the culture dish after 2 h?

Strategies

- Account for All Possibilities
- Draw a Diagram
- Look for a Pattern
- Make a Model
- Make a Table
- Simplify the Problem
- Simulate the Problem
- Solve by Graphing
- Try, Test, Revise
- Use Multiple Strategies
- Work Backward
- Write an Equation
- Write a Proportion

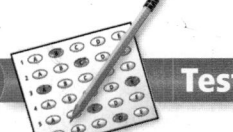
Multiple Choice

15. A photograph is 6 in. × 4 in. If you make a copy of the photograph with double the length and width, what is the area of the copy?
A. 96 in.^{2} **B.** 48 in.^{2} **C.** 24 in.^{2} **D.** 20 in.^{2}

16. Cara's age is 4 times Laura's age. If Cara is 16, how old is Laura?
F. 4 years   **G.** 12 years   **H.** 20 years   **I.** 64 years

17. On a recent test, the lowest score was one fourth the highest score. If the lowest score was 25, how much higher was the highest score?
A. 4   **B.** 25   **C.** 75   **D.** 100

Take It to the NET
Online lesson quiz at
www.PHSchool.com
Web Code: ada-0207

Mixed Review

Lesson 2-6

 **Algebra**   **Solve each equation.**

18. $\frac{m}{4} = 52$ **19.** $3x = -18$ **20.** $63 = \frac{t}{-3}$ **21.** $-32 = -16y$

Lessons 2-1 and 2-2

Identify each property shown.

22. $8 + (6 + 17) = (8 + 6) + 17$ **23.** $1{,}879 \cdot 1 = 1{,}879$

24. $8(5 - 3) = 8(5) - 8(3)$ **25.** $-1 + 7 - 3 = -1 - 3 + 7$

Lesson 1-9 **26.** **Weather** The sound of thunder travels about one mile in five seconds. Suppose a bolt of lightning strikes 3 mi away. How long does it take for the sound of the thunder to reach you?

Math at Work 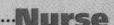 Nurse

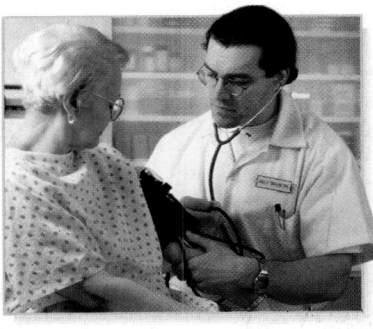

Anyone who has been in a hospital knows that nurses are patients' principal caregivers. Nurses dispense medication, monitor patients' progress, and tend to patients' daily medical needs.

Mathematics is important in a nurse's duties. Nurses compare a patient's blood pressure reading against established norms and make a conclusion about the result. They also solve math problems when they convert one unit of measure of medication to another, and then calculate the total amount of various medications needed for a patient in their care.

 Take It to the NET For more information about nurses, go to **www.PHSchool.com**.
Web Code: adb-2031

Data and Graphs

For Use With Lesson 2-8

Sometimes a graph will help you analyze data. You can use a spreadsheet program to create different types of graphs. First, enter the data in a spreadsheet. Then use a graphing tool to draw an appropriate graph.

1 EXAMPLE

The spreadsheet gives the voting-age populations in thousands for two states. Graph the data in the spreadsheet.

	A	B	C
1	Year	Arizona	Georgia
2	1992	2,812	5,006
3	1994	2,923	5,159
4	1996	3,245	5,420
5	1998	3,405	5,620
6	2000	3,764	6,017

Row 3 contains voting-age populations of both states in 1994.

Cell B3 contains the voting-age population of Arizona in 1994.

Column B contains the voting-age population of Arizona.

Choose an appropriate type of graph from your spreadsheet program. Line graphs are often useful to display changes in data over a period of time. Since the data show changes over time for two states, use a double line graph.

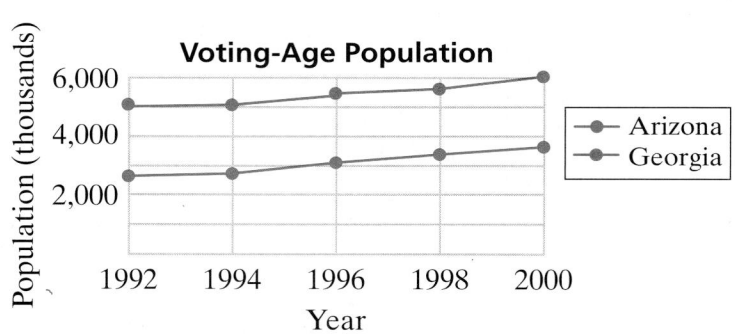

1. Use a spreadsheet to graph the data below.

Average Prices Farmers Received

Year	1990	1991	1992	1993	1994	1995	1996	1997
Price for Turkey (¢/lb)	39.4	38.4	37.7	39.0	40.4	41.6	43.3	39.9
Price for Chicken (¢/lb)	32.6	30.8	31.8	34.0	35.0	34.4	38.1	37.7

SOURCE: U.S. Department of Agriculture.
Go to **www.PHSchool.com** for a data update.
Web Code: adg-2041

The spreadsheet gives population data (in thousands) for five states. Graph the data in the spreadsheet.

	A	B	C
1		Age 25 to 34	Age 75 to 84
2	California	5,285	1,229
3	Florida	1,968	958
4	Illinois	1,764	517
5	New York	2,767	825
6	Texas	2,882	638

Bar graphs are often useful in comparing amounts. Since the data in the spreadsheet show populations for two age ranges, use a double bar graph.

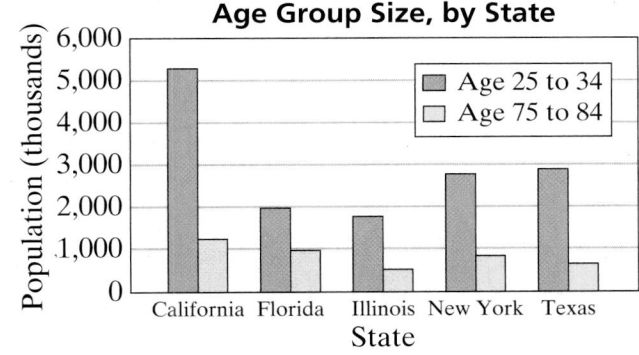

2. a. Use a spreadsheet to make a double bar graph of the postage rate data below.

Postage Rates

Sent from the United States to	First Class 1-oz Letter (¢)	Postcard (¢)
United States	37	23
Canada	60	50
Mexico	60	50
All other countries	80	70

SOURCE: U.S. Postal Service. Go to **www.PHSchool.com** for a data update. Web Code: adg-2041

b. Data Analysis Use the graph you made in part (a). Which bar is tallest? Explain.

3. Writing in Math Explain when you would use a line graph and when you would use a bar graph to display a data set.

Inequalities and Their Graphs

✔ **Check Skills You'll Need**

Graph each set of numbers on a number line. Order the numbers from least to greatest.

1. $-3, 7, -9$

2. $-2, -10, -8$

3. $0, 3, -5$

4. $3, -6, 10$

❓ For help, go to Lesson 1-4.

OBJECTIVE

1 **Graphing Inequalities**

An **inequality** is a mathematical sentence that contains $>, <, \geq, \leq$, or $\neq$. Some inequalities contain a variable. Any number that makes an inequality true is a **solution of the inequality.** For example, -4 is a solution of $y \geq -5$ because $-4 \geq -5$.

You can graph the solutions of an inequality on a number line.

1 EXAMPLE **Graphing Solutions of Inequalities**

Graph the solutions of each inequality on a number line.

a. $y < 3$

An open dot shows that 3 is *not* a solution.

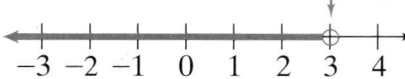

Shade all the points to the left of 3.

b. $x > -1$

An open dot shows that -1 is *not* a solution.

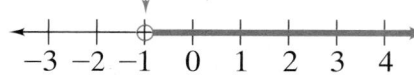

Shade all the points to the right of -1.

c. $a \leq -2$

A closed dot shows that -2 *is* a solution.

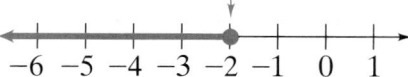

Shade all the points to the left of -2.

d. $-6 \leq g$

A closed dot shows that -6 *is* a solution.

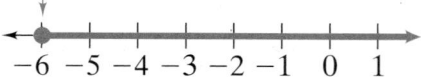

Shade all the points to the right of -6.

✔ **Check Understanding** Example 1

1. Graph the solutions of each inequality.
   a. $z < -2$ **b.** $4 > t$ **c.** $a \geq -5$ **d.** $2 \geq c$

iTEXT Interactive lesson includes instant self-check, tutorials, and activities.

2 Writing Inequalities

You can write an inequality for a graph.

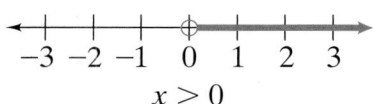

2 EXAMPLE Writing Inequalities to Describe Graphs

Write the inequality shown in each graph.

a.
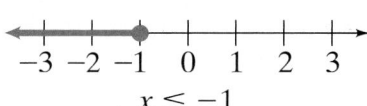

-3 -2 -1 0 1 2 3

$x > 0$

b.

-3 -2 -1 0 1 2 3

$x \leq -1$

> **Reading Math**
>
> Read > as "is greater than."
>
> Read < as "is less than."
>
> Read ≥ as "is greater than or equal to."
>
> Read ≤ as "is less than or equal to."

✓ **Check Understanding**   Example 2

2. Write an inequality for the graph below.

-3 -2 -1 0 1 2 3 4 5

You can write an inequality to describe a real-world situation. Keep in mind that *at most* means "no more than," and hence, "less than or equal to." *At least* means "no less than," and hence, "greater than or equal to."

3 EXAMPLE Real-World  Problem Solving

Nutrition Food can be labeled *low sodium* only if it meets the requirement established by the federal government. Use the table to write an inequality for this requirement.

Label	Definition
Sodium-free food	Less than 5 mg per serving
Very low sodium food	At most 35 mg per serving
Low-sodium food	At most 140 mg per serving

Words | a serving of low-sodium food | has at most | 140 mg sodium |

Let s = number of milligrams of sodium in a serving of low-sodium food.

Inequality | s | $\leq$ | 140 |

✓ **Check Understanding**   Example 3

3. Use the table in Example 3. A certain food is labeled *sodium free*. Write an inequality for *n*, the number of milligrams of sodium in a serving of this sodium-free food.

EXERCISES

Practice and Problem Solving

A Practice by Example

Example 1
(page 102)

Graph the solutions of each inequality on a number line.

1. $x < 7$ **2.** $y > 2$ **3.** $a < 3$ **4.** $c < 1$

5. $-3 < z$ **6.** $x > 1$ **7.** $m \leq -4$ **8.** $b \geq 6$

9. $4 \leq p$ **10.** $a \geq -2$ **11.** $j \geq -1$ **12.** $-5 < w$

Example 2
(page 103)

Write an inequality for each graph.

13.

14.

15.

16.

Example 3
(page 103)

Write an inequality for each situation. Use the variable given.

17. Let t be truck weight in tons. **18.** Let s be speed in mi/h.

B Apply Your Skills

Write an inequality for each sentence. Graph the solutions of each inequality on a number line.

19. x is less than 5. **20.** y is greater than -3.

21. A number c is at least 12. **22.** r is not greater than five.

23. The total t is greater than 7. **24.** p is not more than 30.

25. b is less than or equal to 8. **26.** A number n is positive.

27. Reasoning Explain how you know whether the endpoint of the graph of an inequality should be a closed dot or an open dot.

28. The sign at the amusement park (left) tells you how tall you must be to ride. Write an inequality for this situation. Let h be height in feet.

Real-World Connection

Amusement parks make rules for safety.

Write an inequality for each graph.

29. 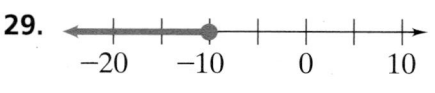 **30.**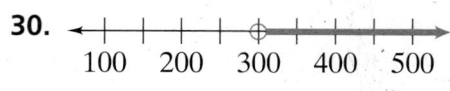

31. 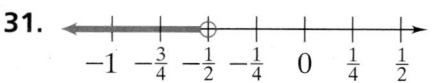 **32.**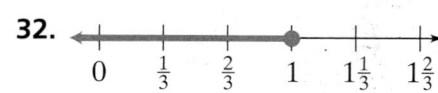

33. Reasoning Explain why graphing the solutions of an inequality is more efficient than listing all the solutions of the inequality.

34. Writing in Math Describe a situation that you could represent with an inequality. Then write the inequality.

35. Movie Tickets Write an inequality to describe this situation. A student pays for three movie tickets with a twenty-dollar bill and gets change back. Let t be the cost of a movie ticket.

36. Nutrition High-fiber foods have at least 5 g of fiber per serving. Write an inequality to represent this situation. Let f be the number of grams of fiber per serving of high-fiber food.

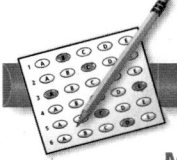 **Challenge**

37. Compare. Use $>$ or $<$ to complete each statement.
a. If $a < b$, then b ▪ a.
b. If $x > y$ and $y > z$, then x ▪ z.

38. Number Sense No more than 50 students walked in a walkathon. Let s be the number of students. Determine which numbers are reasonable values for s: 40, $45\frac{1}{2}$, 50, and 55.

Test Prep

Multiple Choice

39. Which inequality best represents the following sentence? A number t is greater than or equal to -8.
A. $-8 \leq t$ **B.** $t > -8$ **C.** $t \leq -8$ **D.** $-8 \geq t$

40. Which graph matches the inequality $x < -4$?

F.
$-5\ -4\ -3\ -2\ -1\ \ 0$

G.
$-5\ -4\ -3\ -2\ -1\ \ 0$

H.
$-5\ -4\ -3\ -2\ -1\ \ 0$

I.
$-5\ -4\ -3\ -2\ -1\ \ 0$

41. A game-board designer has to design a board that is at least 5 feet wide. Let w be the width of the board. Which inequality describes this situation?
A. $w < 5$ **B.** $w > 5$ **C.** $w \leq 5$ **D.** $w \geq 5$

Take It to the NET
Online lesson quiz at
www.PHSchool.com
Web Code: ada-0208

Mixed Review

Lessons 2-5 and 2-6 **Solve each equation.**

42. $x - 5 = 29$ **43.** $7y = 35$ **44.** $t \div 12 = 6$

Lesson 2-3 **Simplify each expression.**

45. $6 - 5s + 4s + 3$ **46.** $n + (n + 2) + (n + 4)$

Lesson 1-1 **47.** Write a variable expression for the number of weeks in y years.

2-9

Solving One-Step Inequalities by Adding or Subtracting

What You'll Learn

OBJECTIVE 1 To solve one-step inequalities using subtraction

OBJECTIVE 2 To solve one-step inequalities using addition

... And Why

To solve real-world problems involving computer memory

 Check Skills You'll Need

Solve each equation.

1. $m + 7 = 5$

2. $k - 8 = 11$

3. $12 + h = 21$

4. $6 = n - 23$

For help, go to Lesson 2-5.

Solving an inequality is similar to solving an equation. You want to get the variable alone on one side of the inequality.

You can see from the number line that if you subtract 2 from each side of the inequality $-1 < 2$, the resulting inequality $-3 < 0$ is still true.

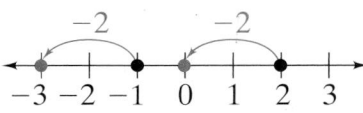

Key Concepts	Subtraction Property of Inequality

You can subtract the same number from each side of an inequality.

Arithmetic	Algebra
$7 > 4$, so $7 - 3 > 4 - 3$	If $a > b$, then $a - c > b - c$.
$6 < 9$, so $6 - 2 < 9 - 2$	If $a < b$, then $a - c < b - c$.

1 EXAMPLE Subtracting to Solve an Inequality

Solve each inequality. Graph the solutions.

a. $n + 8 \geq 19$

$$n + 8 \geq 19$$
$$n + 8 - 8 \geq 19 - 8 \quad \text{Subtract 8 from each side.}$$
$$n \geq 11 \quad \text{Simplify.}$$

<---+---+---+---+---+---+---●---+--->
0   2   4   6   8   10 12

b. $-26 > y + 14$

$$-26 > y + 14$$
$$-26 - 14 > y + 14 - 14 \quad \text{Subtract 14 from each side.}$$
$$-40 > y \text{ or } y < -40 \quad \text{Simplify.}$$

<---+---○---+---+---+---+---+--->
  -50 -40 -30 -20 -10 0   10

✓ **Check Understanding** Example 1

1. Solve each inequality. Graph the solutions.

    a. $m + 3 > 6$ **b.** $8 + t < 15$ **c.** $-3 \leq x + 7$

TEXT Interactive lesson includes instant self-check, tutorials, and activities.

2 EXAMPLE <u>Real-World  Problem Solving</u>

Computers Nearly 32 megabytes (MB) of memory are available for running your computer. If its basic systems require 12 MB, how much memory is available for other programs?

Words	memory for basic systems	plus	memory for other programs	is less than	total memory

Let m = memory available for other programs.

Inequality	12	+	m	<	32

$$12 + m < 32$$
$$12 - 12 + m < 32 - 12 \quad \text{Subtract 12 from each side.}$$
$$m < 20 \quad \text{Simplify.}$$

● Less than 20 MB of memory is available for other programs.

Real-World  Connection

You can increase the memory of a computer by adding more memory chips. These chips have extra memory in multiples of 8 megabytes.

✓ **Check Understanding** Example 2

2. An airline lets you check up to 65 lb of luggage. One suitcase weighs 37 lb. How much can another suitcase weigh?

OBJECTIVE

2 Using Addition to Solve Inequalities

To solve an inequality involving subtraction, use addition.

Key Concepts **Addition Property of Inequality**

You can add the same number to each side of an inequality.

Arithmetic	**Algebra**
$7 > 3$, so $7 + 4 > 3 + 4$	If $a > b$, then $a + c > b + c$.
$2 < 5$, so $2 + 6 < 5 + 6$	If $a < b$, then $a + c < b + c$.

---

3 EXAMPLE **Adding to Solve an Inequality**

Solve $n - 15 < 3$.

$$n - 15 < 3$$
$$n - 15 + 15 < 3 + 15 \quad \text{Add 15 to each side.}$$
$$n < 18 \quad \text{Simplify.}$$

Test-Taking Tip

To check that $n < 18$ is a solution of $n - 15 < 3$, use related equations $n = 18$ and $n - 15 = 3$. Substitute 18 into $n - 15 = 3$ and get $18 - 15 = 3$. The result suggests that you solved correctly.

✓ **Check Understanding** Example 3

3. Solve each inequality.

a. $m - 13 > 29$ **b.** $v - 4 \leq 7$ **c.** $t - 5 \geq 11$

EXERCISES

Practice and Problem Solving

For more exercises, see *Extra Practice*.

A Practice by Example

Example 1
(page 106)

Solve each inequality. Graph the solutions.

1. $w + 5 < 12$ **2.** $2 > 9 + a$ **3.** $x + 6 \geq 7$ **4.** $2 + m \leq 2$

5. $18 \leq 20 + w$ **6.** $-7 < 5 + x$ **7.** $30 \geq t + 45$ **8.** $p + 22 \geq -10$

Example 2
(page 107)

9. Transportation The total weight limit for a truck is 100,000 lb. The truck weighs 36,000 lb empty. What is the most that the truck's load can weigh?

10. Budgeting You are saving to buy a bicycle that will cost at least $120. Your parents give you $45 toward the bicycle. How much money will you have to save?

Example 3
(page 107)

Solve each inequality.

11. $x - 5 \geq 6$ **12.** $n - 12 \leq 3$ **13.** $r - 4 \leq 3$

14. $x - 7 < 15$ **15.** $c - 9 > 5$ **16.** $h - 10 \geq 6$

17. $w - 8 < 3$ **18.** $12 \geq y - 5$ **19.** $4 \geq y - 4$

B Apply Your Skills

What do you do to the first inequality to get the second inequality?

20. $x + 8 \leq 11; x \leq 3$ **21.** $x - 3 > 9; x > 12$

Solve each inequality. Graph the solutions.

22. $x - 8 > -2$ **23.** $6 < y + 19$ **24.** $3 \leq y - 5$

25. $-8 \geq k - 3$ **26.** $-3 + y > 4$ **27.** $a - 0.5 < 2.5$

28. $7 + r > 11$ **29.** $9 < b + 4$ **30.** $u - 3 \geq 9$

Write an inequality for each sentence. Then solve the inequality.

31. Thirteen plus a number n is greater than fifteen.

32. The sum of a number w and 3 is less than or equal to ten.

33. Shopping Jim has $87. He spends $6 for socks and at least $32 for shoes. How much does he have left to spend for shirts?

34. A store's dressing room has a limit of 10 garments per customer. If Carol has at least 3 garments below the limit, how many garments does she have in her dressing room?

C Challenge

Reasoning Justify each step.

35. $4 + a + 3 > 16$
$4 + 3 + a > 16$
$7 + a > 16$
$7 - 7 + a > 16 - 7$
$a > 9$

36. $m - 2(8 - 5) \leq -9$
$m - 2(3) \leq -9$
$m - 6 \leq -9$
$m - 6 + 6 \leq -9 + 6$
$m \leq -3$

37. Writing in Math Which of the inequalities $m > -2$, $m < -2$, $-2 < m$, and $-2 > m$ are solutions to $m + 4 > 2$? Explain.

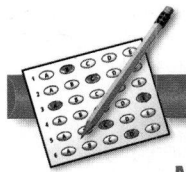

Test Prep

Multiple Choice

38. If x and y are positive and $x > y$, which is true?

A. $x > \dfrac{x + y}{2}$ **B.** $y > \dfrac{x + y}{2}$ **C.** $x = \dfrac{x + y}{2}$ **D.** $x < \dfrac{x + y}{2}$

For Exercises 39 and 40, use the table at the left. Assume that your computer's basic systems use at least 12 MB of memory.

Computer Memory

Application	Memory Requirement
Word processor	11 MB
Spreadsheet	5 MB
Web browser	9 MB
E-mail	4 MB

39. You want to have your e-mail active while you work on a paper with your word processor. How much memory must your computer have?

F. at most 12 MB **G.** at least 15 MB
H. at least 27 MB **I.** at most 32 MB

40. If you search the Web for data at the same time that you have your e-mail active, how much memory must your computer have?

A. at most 41 MB **B.** at least 25 MB
C. at most 20 MB **D.** at least 15 MB

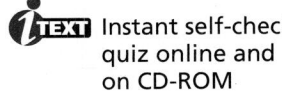

Take It to the NET
Online lesson quiz at
www.PHSchool.com
Web Code: ada-0209

Mixed Review

Lesson 2-8   **Graph the solutions of each inequality.**

41. $x < 2$ **42.** $x \geq -5$ **43.** $y \leq 4$ **44.** $m > 0$

Lesson 2-3   **Simplify each expression.**

45. $4x + 6 - 2x + 6$ **46.** $-4 - 5t + t - 10$

Lesson 1-4   **47.** Write an integer to represent a debt of $35.

✓ Checkpoint Quiz 2   Lessons 2-4 through 2-9

ⓘTEXT Instant self-check quiz online and on CD-ROM

State whether the equation is *true*, *false*, or an *open sentence*. Explain.

1. $4 + 15 = 27 - 8$ **2.** $-30 = 9w$ **3.** $|9 - 10| = 8 - 9$

Solve each equation or inequality.

4. $y - 3 = -7$ **5.** $x + 4 = 8$ **6.** $7t = 42$ **7.** $m \div 8 = -4$

8. $-90 = 10f$ **9.** $9 \leq 3 + a$ **10.** $r - 12 < 7$ **11.** $m + 15 > -4$

12. You have some quarters, dimes, and pennies—eight coins worth $.77 altogether. How many of each type of coin do you have?

2-10 Solving One-Step Inequalities by Multiplying or Dividing

What You'll Learn

OBJECTIVE 1

To solve one-step inequalities using division

OBJECTIVE 2

To solve one-step inequalities using multiplication

. . . And Why

To solve real-world problems involving weight limits

✔ Check Skills You'll Need

Solve each equation.

1. $6x = 24$

2. $63 = -7v$

3. $\frac{x}{-2} = 10$

4. $\frac{t}{6} = 48$

For help, go to Lesson 2-6.

OBJECTIVE 1 | **Solving Inequalities Using Division**

vestigation

Solving Inequalities

Explore what happens when you divide each side of an inequality by a number.

1. Simplify each expression at the right. Replace each ■ with > or <.

$$6 \div 3 \ \blacksquare\ 12 \div 3$$
$$6 \div 2 \ \blacksquare\ 12 \div 2$$
$$6 \div 1 \ \blacksquare\ 12 \div 1$$
$$6 \div (-1) \ \blacksquare\ 12 \div (-1)$$
$$6 \div (-2) \ \blacksquare\ 12 \div (-2)$$
$$6 \div (-3) \ \blacksquare\ 12 \div (-3)$$

2. Patterns Does the direction of the inequality symbol stay the same as you divide each side of an inequality by the given numbers? Explain your reasoning.

You can solve an inequality that involves multiplication by dividing each side of the inequality by a nonzero number.

Key Concepts | **Division Properties of Inequality**

If you divide each side of an inequality by a positive number, you leave the inequality symbol unchanged.

Arithmetic	**Algebra**
$3 < 6$, so $\frac{3}{3} < \frac{6}{3}$	If $a < b$ and c is positive, then $\frac{a}{c} < \frac{b}{c}$.
$8 > 2$, so $\frac{8}{2} > \frac{2}{2}$	If $a > b$ and c is positive, then $\frac{a}{c} > \frac{b}{c}$.

If you divide each side of an inequality by a negative number, *you reverse the inequality symbol.*

Arithmetic	**Algebra**
$6 < 12$, so $\frac{6}{-3} > \frac{12}{-3}$	If $a < b$ and c is negative, then $\frac{a}{c} > \frac{b}{c}$.
$16 > 8$, so $\frac{16}{-4} < \frac{8}{-4}$	If $a > b$ and c is negative, then $\frac{a}{c} < \frac{b}{c}$.

ⓘ TEXT Interactive lesson includes instant self-check, tutorials, and activities.

1 **EXAMPLE** **Real-World** **Problem Solving**

Engineering An elevator can carry up to 2,500 lb. Suppose the weight of an average adult is 150 lb. At most how many average-sized adults can safely ride the elevator at the same time?

Words | the number of adults | times | 150 lb | is less than or equal to | 2,500 lb

Let x = the number of adults.

Inequality | x | · | 150 lb | $\leq$ | 2,500

$150x \leq 2,500$

$\dfrac{150x}{150} \leq \dfrac{2,500}{150}$ **Divide each side by 150.**

$x \leq 16.\overline{6}$ **Simplify. Round the answer down to find a whole number of people.**

At most 16 average adults can safely ride the elevator at one time.

Check Is the answer reasonable? The total weight of 16 average adults is 16(150) = 2,400 lb. This is less than 2,500 lb but so close that another adult could not ride. The answer is reasonable.

Real-World **Connection**

Express elevators can travel as fast as 1,800 ft/min.

STATE INSPECTION CERTIFICATE
Department of Public Safety
Certificate for Use of Elevator

LOCATION: 221 Pat Street
SPEED: 150 ft. per min.
CAPACITY: 2,500 lb.
ISSUED ON: 08/06/03
EXPIRES: 08/06/04

✓ **Check Understanding** **Example 1**

1. Solve each inequality.

a. $4x > 40$ **b.** $-21 > 3m$ **c.** $36 > -9t$

OBJECTIVE

2 **Solving Inequalities Using Multiplication**

You can solve inequalities that involve division.

Key Concepts   **Multiplication Properties of Inequality**

If you multiply each side of an inequality by a positive number, you leave the inequality symbol unchanged.

Arithmetic   **Algebra**

3 < 4, so 3(5) < 4(5)   If $a < b$ and c is positive, then $ac < bc$.

7 > 2, so 7(6) > 2(6)   If $a > b$ and c is positive, then $ac > bc$.

If you multiply each side of an inequality by a negative number, *you reverse the inequality symbol.*

Arithmetic   **Algebra**

6 < 9, so 6(-2) > 9(-2)   If $a < b$ and c is negative, then $ac > bc$.

7 > 5, so 7(-3) < 5(-3)   If $a > b$ and c is negative, then $ac < bc$.

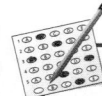

You can check whether the inequality symbol in your solution is correct. For example, for the inequality $\frac{t}{-4} \geq 7$, choose a number that is less than -28, such as -32. Substitute -32 into the original inequality. Since $\frac{-32}{-4} = 8$ and 8 is greater than 7, the inequality symbol in the solution is correct.

2 **EXAMPLE** **Multiplying to Solve an Inequality**

Solve $\frac{t}{-4} \geq 7$.

$$\frac{t}{-4} \geq 7$$

$$-4\left(\frac{t}{-4}\right) \leq -4(7)$$ **Multiply each side by -4 and reverse the inequality symbol.**

$$t \leq -28$$ **Simplify.**

✓ **Check Understanding** **Example 2**

2. Solve each inequality.

   a. $\frac{m}{4} \geq 2$ **b.** $\frac{t}{-3} < 7$ **c.** $5 < \frac{r}{7}$

More Than One Way

Solve $-3x < 12$.

Roberto's Method

Divide each side by -3 and reverse the direction of the inequality symbol.

$$-3x < 12$$
$$\frac{-3x}{-3} > \frac{12}{-3}$$
$$x > -4$$

Michelle's Method

Rewrite the inequality so the coefficient of the variable is positive.

$$-3x < 12$$
$$-3x + 3x < 12 + 3x$$
$$0 < 12 + 3x$$
$$0 - 12 < 3x + 12 - 12$$
$$-12 < 3x$$
$$\frac{-12}{3} < \frac{3x}{3}$$
$$-4 < x, \text{ or } x > -4$$

Choose a Method

1. Which method would you use to solve this inequality? Explain.

2. Solve $18 < -6x$ using Roberto's Method or Michelle's Method.

EXERCISES

For more exercises, see *Extra Practice*.

Practice and Problem Solving

A Practice by Example

Example 1
(page 111)

Solve each inequality.

1. $3t > 21$ **2.** $-2x < 14$ **3.** $8 > -4x$ **4.** $6m > 24$

5. $9x \leq 27$ **6.** $18 < -2m$ **7.** $64 \leq -8k$ **8.** $7m > 28$

9. $3x < 21$ **10.** $81 > -9y$ **11.** $5f \geq -15$ **12.** $-3x < 0$

13. Earnings Paul earns $9 per hour. How many hours must Paul work to earn at least $645?

Example 2
(page 112)

Solve each inequality.

14. $\frac{x}{-6} > 3$ **15.** $\frac{m}{6} \leq -18$ **16.** $\frac{x}{3} \geq 5$ **17.** $\frac{y}{4} > 3$

18. $\frac{r}{-4} > 2$ **19.** $6 > \frac{q}{-3}$ **20.** $20 < \frac{v}{6}$ **21.** $\frac{b}{4} \geq 3$

22. $\frac{v}{-5} < 9$ **23.** $\frac{x}{4} \leq 12$ **24.** $\frac{x}{-3} < 0$ **25.** $8 > \frac{h}{10}$

B Apply Your Skills

What happens to the inequality symbol when you do the following to each side of an inequality?

26. subtract a negative number   **27.** multiply by a positive number

28. divide by a negative number   **29.** multiply by a negative number

Solve each inequality.

30. $-4x < -16$ **31.** $-r \geq 21$ **32.** $\frac{1}{2}x \geq -3$ **33.** $\frac{b}{3} \geq -31$

34. $-3 \geq \frac{g}{-7}$ **35.** $3 > \frac{b}{-6}$ **36.** $4x > -8$ **37.** $-6x \leq -24$

38. Budgeting Marnie pays $.06 per kilowatt-hour for electricity. She has budgeted $72 for her electricity. What is the greatest number of kilowatt-hours Marnie can use and stay within her budget?

39. Error Analysis Your friend solved $3x > -12$ as shown at the left. What error did your friend make? $x < -4$

$$3x > -12$$
$$\frac{3x}{3} < \frac{-12}{3}$$
$$x < -4$$

Write an inequality for each sentence. Then solve the inequality.

40. The product of negative two and a number a is greater than ten.

41. A number t multiplied by seven is less than or equal to 21.

42. A number b divided by 4 is greater than or equal to 3.

43. The quotient of a number v divided by -5 is less than 9.

44. Reasoning The rules for multiplying and dividing both sides of an inequality do not mention zero. Discuss why.

Writing in Math

For help with writing an explanation for Exercise 45, see page 115.

45. Writing in Math Explain how solving $-4t < 32$ is different from solving $4t < -32$.

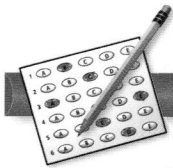

C Challenge   **Reasoning** Justify each step.

46. $2g \geq -18$
$\dfrac{2g}{2} \geq \dfrac{-18}{2}$
$g \geq -9$

47. $-7m \leq -28$
$\dfrac{-7m}{-7} \geq \dfrac{-28}{-7}$
$m \geq 4$

48. $\dfrac{a}{3} > 12$
$\left(\dfrac{a}{3}\right)(3) > 12(3)$
$a > 36$

49. Open-Ended Write a problem that you would solve using the inequality $5m \leq 15$.

50. Day Care In Georgia, for every 18 four-year-old children in day care there must be at least one teacher. At one day-care center, 56 four-year-olds are signed up for next year. At least how many teachers must the center have to teach four-year-olds next year?

Test Prep

Multiple Choice

51. What is done to $\frac{1}{3}x \leq 18$ to get $x \leq 54$?
   A. Multiply each side by 3.   **B.** Divide each side by 3.
   C. Multiply each side by $\frac{1}{3}$.   **D.** Multiply each side by $3x$.

52. Which number is a solution of $-2x \leq -4$?
   F. -2 **G.** 0   **H.** 1   **I.** 10

53. Which inequality has the same solutions as $\frac{a}{4} < -20$?
   A. $4d > 80$ **B.** $\frac{m}{-4} < -40$ **C.** $-2r < -40$ **D.** $\frac{z}{-2} > 40$

54. Which inequality best represents the following sentence?
   A number x divided by 7 is greater than -13.
   F. $\frac{7}{x} > -13$ **G.** $\frac{x}{7} > -13$ **H.** $\frac{7}{x} < -13$ **I.** $\frac{x}{7} < -13$

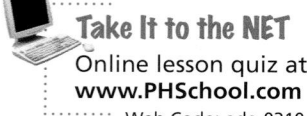

Take It to the NET
Online lesson quiz at
www.PHSchool.com
Web Code: ada-0210

Mixed Review

Lesson 2-9   **Solve each inequality.**

55. $6 + t > 17$ **56.** $m - 4 \leq 6$

57. $-9 \geq r + 5$ **58.** $11 > v - 12$

Lessons 2-1 and 2-2   **Name each property shown.**

59. $-12(100 - 3) = -12(100) - (-12)(3)$

60. $102 + 34 + 98 = 102 + 98 + 34$

61. $(80 + 321) + 109 = 80 + (321 + 109)$

Lesson 1-6 **62. Weather** The high temperature one day in January was $34°F$, and the low temperature was $27°F$. What was the difference between the high and the low temperatures that day?

Sometimes you are asked to compare two or more quantities, methods, or concepts. When you are writing to compare two methods, it is important to explain the similarities and differences.

Writing in Math Explain how solving $-4t < 32$ is different from solving $4t < -32$.

Here is one student's response.

Since the question is to explain how solving the inequalities is different, I will solve each one separately to see what I do differently. Then I will explain the difference.

The first inequality:

$-4t < 32$

$\dfrac{-4t}{-4} < \dfrac{32}{-4}$ **Divide each side of the inequality by -4.**

$t > -8$ **When you divide by a negative number on each side of an inequality, you reverse the inequality symbol.**

The second inequality:

$4t < -32$

$\dfrac{4t}{4} < \dfrac{-32}{4}$ **Divide each side of the inequality by 4.**

$t < -8$ **When you divide by a positive number on each side of an inequality, you keep the inequality symbol as is.**

Now I can explain what is different.

> To solve $-4t < 32$, you divide each side by -4, a negative number. You have to reverse the direction of the inequality symbol.
>
> To solve $4t < 32$, you divide each side by 4, a positive number. You leave the direction of the inequality symbol unchanged.

EXERCISES

1. Explain how solving $\dfrac{x}{3} > -6$ is different from solving $\dfrac{x}{-3} > 6$.

2. Explain how finding the value of $4 \cdot 2 + 5$ is different from finding the value of $4(2 + 5)$.

Test-Taking Strategies

Writing Short Responses

Short-response questions are often worth 2 points. To get full credit you need to give the correct answer and either give a good explanation, justify your thinking, or show your work.

EXAMPLE

Jenna had a coupon for $15 off the price of a graphing calculator. She used it to buy a calculator for $89 before tax. **(a)** Write an equation to find the original price. **(b)** Solve your equation.

Here is a *scoring rubric* to help assess different types of answers.

Scoring Rubric

[2] The original price of the calculator is correct. The equation and the solution are correct with all work shown.

[1] The original price is correct, but no work is shown, OR the original price is incorrect but the work shown has minimal errors.

Here are three responses with the points each received.

2 points	1 point	0 points
x is the original price. $x - 15 = 89$ $x - 15 + 15 = 89 + 15$ $x = 104$ The original price was $104.	x is the original price. $x + 15 = 89$ $x + 15 - 15 = 89 - 15$ $x = 74$ The original price was $74.	The original price was $74.

EXERCISES

Use the scoring rubric to explain the score given for each response.

1. the 2-point response   **2.** the 1-point response   **3.** the 0-point response

Write and solve an equation to solve each problem. Then score your answer using the scoring rubric above.

4. Your grandfather gives you a share of stock that it is currently worth $62. He tells you that it has increased in value by $17 since he purchased it. How much did he pay for the stock?

5. The height of a multistory building is 135 ft. It has 15 stories. What is the height of each story?

Chapter Review

Vocabulary

Reading Math
Understanding Vocabulary

For each definition given on the left, write the letter of the word or phrase being defined.

1. a value that makes an equation true

2. a term that has no variable

3. a number or the product of a number and variable(s)

4. the number that multiplies a variable

5. the number zero

6. terms with identical variables

7. an equation with one or more variables

8. a mathematical sentence with an equal sign

9. the number one

10. a mathematical sentence with $>, <, \geq, \leq,$ or $\neq$

a. coefficient

b. constant

c. additive identity

d. solution of an equation

e. term

f. equation

g. multiplicative identity

h. like terms

i. inequality

j. open sentence

Take It to the NET
Online vocabulary quiz at **www.PHSchool.com**
Web Code: adj-0251

Skills and Concepts

2-1 Objectives

▼ To identify properties of addition and multiplication (p. 66)

▼ To use properties to solve problems (p. 67)

Use the **Commutative Property** to change order. Use the **Associative Property** to change grouping. Adding zero to an expression does not change its value. Multiplying an expression by 1 does not change its value.

Simplify each expression. Justify each step.

11. $58 + 16 + 2 + 4$ **12.** $4 \cdot 7 \cdot 25 \cdot 1$ **13.** $125 + 347 + 75$

14. $(20 \cdot 65) \cdot 5$ **15.** $10 \cdot 15 \cdot 2$ **16.** $37 + 0 + (5 + 63)$

Use the **Distributive Property** to multiply a number outside parentheses by each term of a sum or difference.

Mental Math Use the Distributive Property to simplify.

17. $9(96)$ **18.** $8(62)$ **19.** $(43)(9)$

Use the Distributive Property to multiply.

20. $4(w + 9)$ **21.** $(2 + 4a)12$ **22.** $-7(6 + 2m)$

23. Explain why $5x + 15 = 5(x + 3)$.

To **simplify** a variable expression, replace it with an equivalent expression with as few terms as possible.

Simplify each expression.

24. $8a + 7 - 11a$ **25.** $3(w + 3) + 4w$

26. $6 + x - 4x + 3$ **27.** $19 - 4(5n + 1) - 4n$

28. $10 + 7k - 2(3k + 5)$ **29.** $-7(2r - 1) + 3(8 - r)$

30. Explain how to determine whether terms are like terms.

You can write an **equation** to model a situation. An equation with numerical expressions is true or false. An equation with at least one variable is an **open sentence**. A **solution** of an open-sentence equation is a value of a variable that makes the equation true.

Write an equation for each sentence. Is each equation *true, false,* or an *open sentence*?

31. Thirty-two plus five equals the product of six and six.

32. A number t divided by seventeen equals the opposite of three.

33. The product of four and twenty equals eighty.

34. Culture The admission price to an art museum increased by $1.75 to $6.50. Let p be the original admission price. Write an equation to model the situation.

2-5 and 2-6 Objectives

▼ To solve one-step equations using subtraction (p. 86)

▼ To solve one-step equations using addition (p. 88)

▼ To solve one-step equations using division (p. 92)

▼ To solve one-step equations using multiplication (p. 93)

To solve an equation, use an **inverse operation** and the **properties of equality** to get the variable alone on one side of the equation.

Solve each equation.

35. $6 + y = 17$ **36.** $-2 = a - 10$ **37.** $3x = -15$

38. $\frac{m}{9} = 3$ **39.** $\frac{w}{4} = 32$ **40.** $40 = -5b$

2-7 Objectives

▼ To solve a problem using the Try, Test, Revise strategy (p. 96)

You can solve some problems by trying an answer. Use each incorrect conjecture to make a better conjecture.

41. School Supplies Marcella and Danilo went to a bookstore. Marcella bought 2 notebooks and 3 pens for $14.50. Danilo bought 1 notebook and 2 pens for $7.50. How much does 1 notebook cost?

2-8 Objectives

▼ To graph inequalities (p. 102)

▼ To write inequalities (p. 103)

To graph an **inequality,** use a number line. Use an open dot for $>$ and $<$. Use a closed dot for $\geq$ and $\leq$.

Graph the solutions of each inequality.

42. $m > 5$ **43.** $t \geq -2$ **44.** $0 < r$ **45.** $w \leq 6$

Write an inequality for each sentence.

46. The temperature t is less than zero degrees.

47. The height h is greater than twelve feet.

2-9 and 2-10 Objectives

▼ To solve one-step inequalities using subtraction (p. 106)

▼ To solve one-step inequalities using addition (p. 107)

▼ To solve one-step inequalities using division (p. 110)

▼ To solve one-step inequalities using multiplication (p. 111)

To solve a one-step inequality, use inverse operations and the **properties of inequality** to get the variable alone on one side of the inequality. When multiplying or dividing each side of an inequality by a negative number, *reverse* the direction of the inequality symbol.

Solve each inequality.

48. $n - 4 > 10$ **49.** $-5 \leq k - 7$ **50.** $6s \leq 18$

51. $\frac{m}{3} < -2$ **52.** $-d > 14$ **53.** $\frac{c}{-4} \geq -9$

Take It to the NET
Online chapter test at
www.PHSchool.com
Web Code: ada-0252

Is each equation *true, false,* **or an** *open sentence?* **Explain.**

1. $24 = 3(-8)$

2. $5x + 28 = 153$

3. $18(-7 \div 7) = (-2)(9)$

4. $-6 + 15 = (120 \div 20) - (5 - 8)$

Simplify. Use the Commutative and the Associative Properties.

5. $50 \cdot 38 \cdot 2$

6. $45 + 62 + 55$

7. $2 \cdot 27 \cdot 5$

8. $99 + (-7) + 101$

9. **Open-Ended** Write a number sentence that illustrates the Associative Property of Addition.

Simplify each expression.

10. $2(x + y) - 2y$

11. $5a + 2b + 3a + 7b$

12. $3(2r - 5) + 8(r + 2)$

13. $(-2c + 3d)(-5) + 3(-2c) - (-8d)$

Solve each equation.

14. $k - 23 = 17$

15. $\frac{t}{-5} = 15$

16. $y \div 12 = -3$

17. $7w = -217$

18. $-9 + a = 11$

19. $n - 2 = 13$

20. $120 = 38 + p$

21. $w \cdot (-2) = 14$

22. $r + 6 = 30$

23. $m - 7 = -3$

24. $9t = 18$

25. $-3f = -42$

26. $5 = \frac{s}{-7}$

27. $\frac{h}{12} = 12$

For Exercises 28 and 29, write and solve an equation.

28. **Fencing** Thirty-six sections of fencing, all the same length, are joined to form a fence 180 m long. How long is each section of fencing?

29. Brian bought a used bike for $25 less than its original price. He paid a total of $88 for the bike. What was the original price of the bike?

30. **Writing in Math** How are the rules for solving inequalities similar to those for solving equations? How are they different?

Write an inequality for each situation. Graph the solutions.

31. The total t is greater than 5.

32. The perimeter p is less than 64.

33. The number of passengers p on the bus is no more than 45.

34. The number of students s that ran in the road race was not less than 55.

35. The number of questions q answered correctly is at most 49.

Solve each inequality.

36. $5 \le x + 1$

37. $\frac{a}{3} > 4$

38. $y + 6 < 9$

39. $-2n \le 10$

40. $3b \ge 3$

41. $\frac{p}{-2} < -5$

42. $r + 8 > 12$

43. $j - 7 \le 24$

44. $h - 5 \ge -16$

45. $8 + b < -3$

46. $3k \le -27$

47. $\frac{h}{4} > 16$

48. $9 < \frac{a}{6}$

49. $-7z < 21$

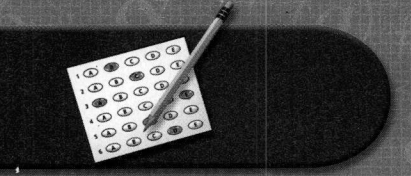

Test Prep

Multiple Choice

Choose the best answer.

1. You make $8.00 per hour. Each week you work *n* hours. Which expression describes your weekly pay?

   A. $\frac{n}{8}$ **B.** $8 - n$ **C.** $n + 8$ **D.** $8n$

2. Which equation shows the Associative Property of Addition?
   F. $9 + 7 + 8 = 9 + 8 + 7$
   G. $(8 + 3) + 13 = 8 + (3 + 13)$
   H. $12 + (-4) + 0 = 12 + (-4)$
   I. $19 \cdot (-3) \cdot 1 = 19 \cdot (-3)$

3. Mara ordered 5 bags of seed for $7 each and 3 wildflower seed kits for $9 each. She also paid a $13 shipping fee. Which expression shows the total cost?
   A. $5 + 7 + 3 + 9 + 13$
   B. $(5 \cdot 7) + (3 \cdot 9) + 13$
   C. $(5 + 3)16 + 13$
   D. $(5 \cdot 7 + 13) + (3 \cdot 9 + 13)$

4. What is the solution of $r + 43 = -45$?
   F. -88 **G.** -2 **H.** 2 **I.** 88

5. What is the value of $5(n + m)$ for $n = 12$ and $m = 6$?
   A. 30 **B.** 66 **C.** 90 **D.** 810

6. Which integer is *not* a solution of $p + 12 < 16$?
   F. 4 **G.** 3 **H.** -4 **I.** -28

7. Which numbers are in order from least to greatest?
   A. $4, 2, -2, -4$ **B.** $|-3|, |-4|, -5, 6$
   C. $-7, 1, 4, |-12|$ **D.** $-3, 4, -5, 6, -7$

8. What is the value of $-23 + (-12)$?
   F. 35 **G.** 11 **H.** -11 **I.** -35

9. Which symbol makes the statement true?
   $11 - (-4) \blacksquare -6 - 12$
   A. $>$ **B.** $<$ **C.** $=$ **D.** $\leq$

10. Which product equals $3t - 12$?
    F. $4(t - 3)$ **G.** $3(t - 4)$
    H. $(4 - t)3$ **I.** $(3 - t)4$

11. Which equation is an open sentence?
    A. $8(8 \div 2) = 32$ **B.** $18 = (2 \cdot 7) + 6$
    C. $5x = 3 + 2x$ **D.** $15 - 1 = 52 \div 4$

12. What is the value of $-(2 \cdot 7) + 6 \cdot 2$?
    F. 26 **G.** -2 **H.** -16 **I.** -26

Short Response

Simplify each expression. Show your work.

13. $3c - 4c + 1$

14. $6(t + 7) + t$

15. $-5(n + 9) - n$

16. $8 - 4(s + 2) - s$

Solve each inequality. Show your work.

17. $24 > b + 17$

18. $x - 9 < -14$

19. $\frac{r}{13} \geq 3$

20. $-4s \geq -56$

21. **a.** How are the rules for solving inequalities with addition and subtraction similar to those for solving inequalities with multiplication and division?
    b. In part (a), how are they different?

22. Simplify $25 \cdot 7 \cdot 4$. Explain how you can use the Commutative and Associative Properties to multiply mentally.

For Exercises 23 and 24, (a) write an expression for total cost and (b) simplify the expression.

23. Lana bought juice for $3.25 and some fruit for $5.25. She also bought five beach passes for *x* dollars each.

24. Chung bought 6 brushes for *b* dollars each, 2 paint tubes for *p* dollars each, 5 more brushes later in the day, and paper for $12.

Gridded Response

Simplify each expression.

25. $7(58)$ 26. $6(92)$ 27. $5(1,002)$

Solve each equation.

28. $b - 7 = 21$

29. $18 + n = 37$

30. $\frac{c}{7} = 8$

31. $-9r = 108$

A Profitable Fair

Applying Equations Many schools hold fairs and other events to raise money for extracurricular activities. To make a profit, you must begin with an idea of what your expenses and your income will be. At your school fair, your student council will rent school tables and sell tickets, hot dogs, and juice. The student council makes plans for this year's fair based on last year's fair.

Activity

Copy the chart. Write and solve equations to fill in the blanks.

1. Find the profit P from renting yard-sale tables.

   > Profit = Income − Cost

Treasurer's Chart

Item	Last Year	This Year	Income	Profit
Tables (yard sale)	45 tables	▦	$35/table = ▦	▦
Tickets	320 sold	▦	▦	$800
Hot dogs (and buns)	200 sold	▦	▦	$280
Juice boxes	200 sold	▦	▦	$100
Total	N/A	N/A	▦	▦

2. Suppose you make the tickets. Find the price T to charge for each ticket to make the planned profit.

3. You calculate that you will have to pay an average of $.35 per hot dog, bun, and toppings. How much will this cost in all?

4. Juice boxes cost you $.25 each. How much will they cost in all?

5. How much, h, should you charge for each hot dog?

6. How much, j, should you charge for each juice box?

7. You could sell a hot dog and juice box only as a combination. If you do, how much, c, should you charge for each "combo"?

8. **Open-Ended** How could you improve the Treasurer's Chart?

Clean Machines
Some schools use donated supplies for their fundraising car washes.

A Little Goes a Long Way

Middle-school students in Maynard, Massachusetts, are collecting 1 million pennies as their school fundraiser.

Painting Faces

Kids of all ages love having their faces painted! But be warned: Small children can't sit still for long, so know what you're going to paint before you begin.

FACE
AINTI

Take It to the NET For more information about school fairs, go to **www.PHSchool.com**. Web Code: ade-0253

Where You've Been

- In Chapter 1, you learned how to add, subtract, multiply, and divide integers.

- In Chapter 2, you solved equations by adding or subtracting.

- In Chapter 2, you also solved equations by multiplying or dividing.

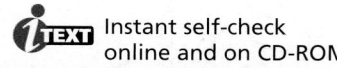

Diagnosing Readiness

Instant self-check online and on CD-ROM

(For help, go to the Skills Handbook.)

Rounding Numbers (Skills Handbook, p. 758)

Round each number to the nearest ten.

1. 37   **2.** 9   **3.** 2   **4.** 602   **5.** 834   **6.** 6,009

Comparing and Ordering Decimals (Skills Handbook, p. 762)

Compare. Use $>$, $<$, or $=$ to complete each statement.

7. 0.96 ▮ 1.32   **8.** 7.641 ▮ 7.593   **9.** 6.3 ▮ 6.38

10. 5.001 ▮ 5.02   **11.** -9.871 ▮ -10.3 **12.** -27.619 ▮ -27.7

Order each group of decimals from least to greatest.

13. 8.35, 8.349, 8.351, 9.25   **14.** 0.02, 0.017, 0.201, 0.0201

15. $-1.4, -1.04, -1.401, -14.1$ **16.** $-2.3, -3.2, -3.19, -2.8$

Operations With Decimals (Skills Handbook, pp. 764, 765, and 769)

Simplify.

17. $3.4 + 8.09$ **18.** $8 - 4.93$ **19.** $0.59 + 3.06$ **20.** $2.19 - 0.984$

21. $(1.001)(6.7)$ **22.** $40.02 \div 5.8$ **23.** $10.4 \cdot 5.3$ **24.** $\dfrac{77.38}{7.3}$

Multiplying and Dividing by Powers of 10 (Skills Handbook, p. 768)

Simplify.

25. $9.87 \cdot 10$ **26.** $5.32 \cdot 100$ **27.** $0.3 \cdot 1,000$ **28.** $15,407 \cdot 10,000$

29. $0.8 \div 10$ **30.** $8.42 \div 100$ **31.** $16.1 \div 1,000$ **32.** $12.09 \div 10,000$

Decimals and Equations

Key Vocabulary

- compatible numbers (p. 133)
- formula (p. 143)
- mean (p. 137)
- measures of central tendency (p. 137)
- median (p. 137)
- mode (p. 137)
- outlier (p. 138)
- perimeter (p. 144)

Where You're Going

In this chapter, you will learn how to

- Estimate with decimals.
- Solve equations with decimals.
- Convert metric units of measure.
- Solve a problem by simplifying the problem.

Real-World Snapshots Applying what you learn, on pages 174–175 you will solve problems about price comparisons.

Writing and Comparing Decimals

Each digit in a decimal has both a place and a value. The value of any place is one-tenth the value of the place to its left. A place-value chart like the one at the right can help you read and write decimals.

ones	.	tenths	hundredths	thousandths	ten thousandths
0	.	4	2	6	

1 EXAMPLE

a. Express 0.426 using words.

The last digit, 6, is in the thousandths place. So, 0.426 ends with the word *thousandths*.

0.426 is four hundred twenty-six thousandths.

b. Write *two and three hundredths* as a decimal.

And represents the decimal point. The hundredths place is the second place to the right of the decimal point.

Two and three hundredths is 2.03.

You can use decimal squares to model and compare decimals.

2 EXAMPLE

a. Model 0.6.

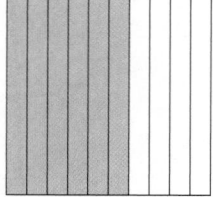

b. Model 0.58.

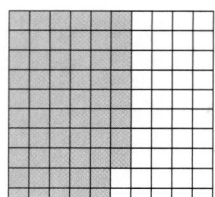

c. Model 1.05.

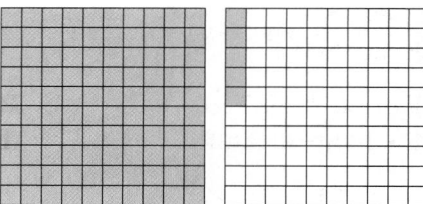

d. Compare 0.6 and 0.58. The models show that 0.6 > 0.58.

EXERCISES

Express each decimal using words.

1. 0.23 **2.** 0.624 **3.** 3.081 **4.** 58.36

Write each as a decimal.

5. three and two tenths **6.** five and forty-one hundredths **7.** fourteen ten-thousandths

Model and compare each pair of decimals.

8. 0.2 and 0.12 **9.** 0.89 and 0.9 **10.** 0.53 and 0.5 **11.** 1.35 and 1.4

Rounding and Estimating

OBJECTIVE

1 Rounding Decimals

Estimating in the Real World

Some real-world problems require only an estimate for an answer. Others require an exact answer. Decide whether each situation needs an estimate or an exact answer. Explain your reasoning.

1. a headline noting the number of people living in China

2. the amount of money a baby sitter charges per hour

3. the width of a window screen

4. the distance from Earth to the moon

5. the hours at soccer practice in one month

6. the number of tickets to sell for a play

You can round decimal numbers when you don't need exact values.

1 EXAMPLE **Rounding Decimals**

a. Round 4.2683 to the nearest tenth.

┌── tenths place
4.2683
└── 5 or greater
┌── Round up to 3.
4.3

b. Round 4.2683 to the nearest one.

┌── ones place
4.2683
└── less than 5
┌── Do not change.
4

✔ **Check Understanding** Example 1

1. Identify the underlined place. Then round each number to that place.

   a. 38.<u>4</u>1
   b. <u>0</u>.7772
   c. 7,098.<u>5</u>6
   d. 274.94<u>3</u>4
   e. 5.<u>0</u>25
   f. 9.8<u>5</u>1

What You'll Learn

OBJECTIVE 1 To round decimals

OBJECTIVE 2 To estimate sums and differences

. . . And Why

To understand and apply appropriate estimation strategies in real-world situations such as grocery shopping

✔ **Check Skills You'll Need**

Use the number 27.3865. Write the value of the given digit.

1. 2   **2.** 3

3. 8   **4.** 6

For help, go to Skills Handbook, p. 761 .

TEXT Interactive lesson includes instant self-check, tutorials, and activities.

You can estimate a result before you calculate. Then, if your answer is close to your estimate, you know that it probably is correct.

Write $126   ≈ $130

Read $126 is approximately equal to $130.

One way to estimate is to round all numbers to the same place.

2 EXAMPLE   **Rounding to Estimate**

Estimate to find whether each answer is reasonable.

a. Calculation   Estimate   **b. Calculation   Estimate**

$$
\begin{array}{rcr}
\$135.95 & \approx & \$140 \\
\$15.90 & \approx & \$20 \\
+\ \$24.05 & \approx & +\ \$20 \\
\hline
\$275.90 & & \$180
\end{array}
\qquad
\begin{array}{rcr}
464.90 & \approx & 460 \\
-\ 125.73 & \approx & -\ 130 \\
\hline
339.17 & & 330
\end{array}
$$

The answer is not close to the estimate. It is *not* reasonable.

The answer is close to the estimate. It is reasonable.

✔ **Check Understanding**   Example 2

   2. Estimate by rounding.

      a. $355.302 + 204.889$ **b.** $453.56 - 230.07$

A *front-end estimate* is often closer to the exact sum than an estimate you find by rounding. First add the front-end digits. Round to estimate the sum of the remaining digits. Then combine estimates.

3 EXAMPLE   **Real-World** 🌐 **Problem Solving**

Grocery Shopping Carrots cost $2.71, peppers cost $1.73, and broccoli costs $1.10. Estimate the total cost of the vegetables.

$1.73

$1.10

$2.71

$$
\begin{array}{l}
\text{Add the} \\
\text{front-end digits.} \longrightarrow
\end{array}
\quad
\begin{array}{r}
2.71 \longrightarrow \\
1.73 \longrightarrow \\
+\ 1.10 \longrightarrow \\
\hline
4 \qquad +
\end{array}
\quad
\left.
\begin{array}{r}
.70 \\
.70 \\
+\ .10 \\
\hline
1.50
\end{array}
\right\}
\begin{array}{l}
\textbf{Estimate by} \\
\textbf{rounding.}
\end{array}
$$

$$4 + 1.50 = 5.50$$

The total cost is about $5.50.

✔ **Check Understanding**   Example 3

   3. Estimate using front-end estimation.

      a. $6.75 + 2.2 + 9.58$ **b.** $1.07 + $2.49 + $7.40

You can also use *clustering* to estimate the sum of several numbers that are all close to the same value.

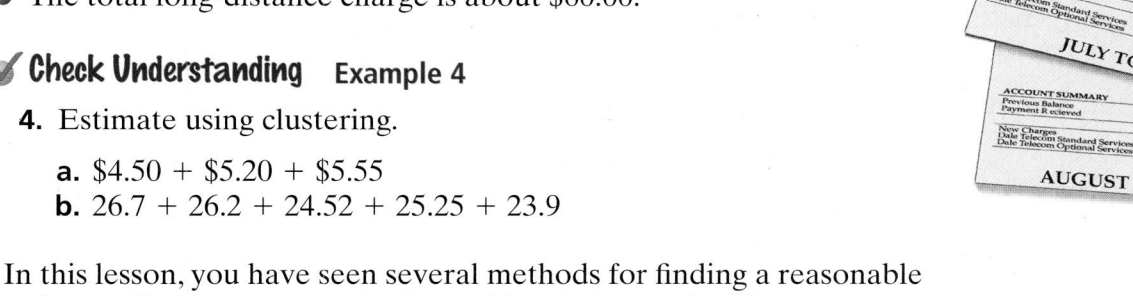

4 EXAMPLE   <u>Real-World</u> Problem Solving

Telephone Service Estimate the total long-distance charge for the months of May, June, July, and August shown at the right.

four months
↓
The values cluster around $15. ⟶ $15 \cdot 4 = 60$

● The total long-distance charge is about $60.00.

✓ **Check Understanding**   Example 4

4. Estimate using clustering.

   a. $4.50 + $5.20 + $5.55
   b. 26.7 + 26.2 + 24.52 + 25.25 + 23.9

In this lesson, you have seen several methods for finding a reasonable estimate. Here are two methods used for the same situation.

More Than One Way

Estimate the total cost of four items priced at $4.39, $3.75, $4.96, and $2.40.

Nicole's Method

Round each price to the nearest dollar. Then add.
$4.39 + $3.75 + $4.96 + $2.40
$4   + $4   + $5   + $2   = $15

Eric's Method

Use front-end estimation.

$4.39	⟶	$.40
3.75	⟶	.80
4.96	⟶	1.00
+ 2.40	⟶	+ .40
$13	+	$2.60 = $15.60

Choose a Method

1. Which method would you use to estimate the cost of the items? Explain.

2. Find the exact cost. Which estimate is nearer the exact cost?

EXERCISES

For more exercises, see *Extra Practice*.

Practice and Problem Solving

A Practice by Example
Example 1
(page 127)

Identify the underlined place. Then round each number to that place.

1. 27.3<u>8</u>56   **2.** 0.91<u>2</u>2   **3.** 1,04<u>5</u>.98   **4.** 74.<u>8</u>79

Round to the underlined place.

5. 345.<u>6</u>78   **6.** 3.1<u>4</u>159   **7.** 21<u>4</u>.76   **8.** 2.94<u>3</u>7

Example 2
(page 128)

Estimate by rounding.

9. $37.99 − $27.32   **10.** 1.58 + 17.0244   **11.** 172.98 − 128.301

12. $4.89 + $3.87   **13.** $16.81 + $11.49   **14.** $565 − $225

Example 3
(page 128)

Estimate using front-end estimation.

15. $6.04 + $3.45 + $4.43   **16.** $5.92 + $4.07

17. 9.89 + 2.43 + 8.37   **18.** 14.39 + 79.12

19. Fitness Kim ran 2.76 miles on Monday, 2.34 miles on Tuesday, and 1.97 miles on Wednesday. Use front-end estimation to estimate the total distance Kim ran.

Example 4
(page 129)

Estimate using clustering.

20. 44.87 + 42.712 + 43.5   **21.** $9.50 + $8.45 + $9.08

22. $21.37 + $22.99 + $22.15   **23.** 15.4 + 16 + 15.9 + 16.25 + 15.7

24. Pets Rico's dog has a litter of four puppies. The puppies weigh 2.33 lb, 2.70 lb, 2.27 lb, and 2.64 lb. Use clustering to estimate the total weight of the puppies.

B Apply Your Skills

Estimate. Use a method of your choice.

25. 8.974 + 2.154   **26.** 102.44 + 48.35   **27.** 600 − 209.52

28. $38.59 + $15.28   **29.** $50.00 − $28.89   **30.** $412.44 + $72.23

31. 800 + 810.5 + 807.3 + 791.1   **32.** (54.23 + 56.12) + (57.98 + 55.55)

Lake Erie

Lake Superior

33. Geography Lake Superior, the largest of the Great Lakes, has an area of about 31,760 mi². Lake Erie, the smallest of the Great Lakes, has an area of about 9,920 mi². About how much larger is Lake Superior than Lake Erie?

Estimate. State the method you used.

34. $8.99 + $8.01   **35.** 2.3 + 2.3 + 4.56   **36.** $89.90 − $49.29

37. 102.54 − 74.75   **38.** 20.55 − 1.48   **39.** 78.87 + 11.49

40. Weather Mobile, Alabama, has an average annual rainfall of 63.96 in. The average annual rainfall in San Francisco, California, is 19.70 in. About how much more rain falls each year in Mobile than in San Francisco?

C Challenge

41. Open-Ended Describe a situation in which a rounded answer is appropriate. Describe one in which an exact answer is necessary.

42. Writing in Math You have $11.50 to buy two presents. You find one item that costs $7.43. Another item costs $4.41. What estimation strategy will help you decide whether you have enough money to buy both? Explain.

43. Error Analysis You used a calculator to find 383.8 − 21.9. Your estimate was 360, but your display reads 164.8. How could you have gotten 164.8 on your calculator?

Test Prep

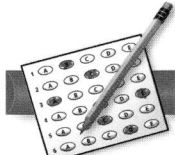

Multiple Choice

44. Which phrase best completes the statement?
The sum of $12.75 and $7.65 is _?_ .
A. less than $20.00   **B.** greater than $20.00
C. an integer   **D.** greater than $25.00

Take It to the NET
Online lesson quiz at
www.PHSchool.com
Web Code: ada-0301

45. When you estimate 320.18 + 46 + 8.68 by rounding to tens, what value do you get?
F 370   **G.** 374.9   **H.** 375   **I.** 380

Short Response

46. In 2000, the population of the state of Georgia was about 8.19 million. In 1950, the population was about 3.44 million.
a. About how much greater was Georgia's population in 2000 than in 1950?
b. Explain how you found your answer for part (a).

Mixed Review

Lesson 2-10   **Solve each inequality.**

47. $9x \le 27$ **48.** $4x < 16$ **49.** $-3y \le 0$ **50.** $-6k > -24$

Lesson 2-7   **51. Collections** Ming's model vehicle collection contains 4-wheeled trucks and 2-wheeled bikes. She owns an even number of vehicles, and they have 26 wheels in all. If Ming has a little more than twice as many bikes as trucks, how many of each does she own?

Lesson 1-9   **Simplify.**

52. $(-2)(-2)$ **53.** $4(-3)$ **54.** $-8 \div 2$ **55.** $6(-5)$

3-2

Estimating Decimal Products and Quotients

What You'll Learn

 OBJECTIVE 1 To estimate products

 OBJECTIVE 2 To estimate quotients

...And Why

To determine the reasonableness of answers to real-world problems involving mass

✓ **Check Skills You'll Need**

Round to the nearest one.

1. 145.89 **2.** 199.27

3. 101.06 **4.** 28.45

❓ For help, go to Lesson 3-1.

New Vocabulary

• compatible numbers

OBJECTIVE

1 Estimating Products

You can use mental math to estimate products and quotients. It is a good idea to estimate answers to check your calculations.

1 EXAMPLE Estimating the Product

Estimate 7.65 · 3.2.

| $7.65 \approx 8$ | $3.2 \approx 3$ | Round to the nearest one. |
| $8 \cdot 3 = 24$ | | Multiply. |

$7.65 \cdot 3.2 \approx 24$

✓ **Check Understanding** Example 1

1. Estimate each product.

a. $4.72 \cdot 1.8$ **b.** $17.02 \cdot 3.78$ **c.** $8.25 \cdot 19.8$

2 EXAMPLE Real-World 🌐 Problem Solving

Quilting Arlene bought 6 yd of fabric to make this Lone Star quilt. The fabric cost $6.75/yd. The sales clerk charged Arlene $45.90 before tax. Did the clerk make a mistake? Explain.

$6.75 \approx 7$ Round to the nearest dollar.

$7 \cdot 6 = 42$ Multiply 7 times 6, the number of yards of fabric.

The sales clerk made a mistake. Since $6.75 < 7$, the actual cost should be less than the estimate. The clerk should have charged Arlene less than $42.00 before tax.

✓ **Check Understanding** Example 2

2. Photography You buy 8 rolls of film for your camera. Each roll costs $4.79. Estimate the cost of the film before tax.

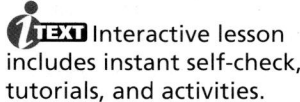 Interactive lesson includes instant self-check, tutorials, and activities.

2 Estimating Quotients

When dividing, remember these names for the parts of a division sentence.

dividend

$6 \div 3 = 2$ ← quotient

divisor

When dividing, you can use *compatible numbers* to estimate quotients. **Compatible numbers** are numbers that are easy to divide mentally. When you estimate a quotient, first round the divisor, and then round the dividend to a compatible number.

3 EXAMPLE Real-World Problem Solving

Measurement A bowling ball has a mass of 5.61 kg. Each bowling pin has a mass of 1.57 kg. How many bowling pins are about equal to the bowling ball in mass? Estimate 5.61 ÷ 1.57.

$1.57 \approx 2$ **Round the divisor.**

$5.61 \approx 6$ **Round the dividend to a multiple of 2 that is close to 5.61.**

$6 \div 2 = 3$ **Divide.**

The mass of three bowling pins is about equal to that of the bowling ball.

Check Understanding Example 3

3. Estimate each quotient.

a. $38.9 \div 1.79$ **b.** $11.95 \div 2.1$ **c.** $82.52 \div 4.25$

5.61 kg

1.57 kg

Real-World Connection

The masses of ten-pin bowling balls range from 3.63 kg to 7.26 kg.

You can estimate to determine the reasonableness of results.

4 EXAMPLE Estimating to Determine Reasonableness

Number Sense Is 2.15 a reasonable quotient for 17.931 ÷ 8.34?

$8.34 \approx 8$ **Round the divisor.**

$17.931 \approx 16$ **Round the dividend to a multiple of 8 that is close to 17.931.**

$16 \div 8 = 2$ **Divide.**

Since 2.15 is close to the estimate 2, it is reasonable.

Check Understanding Example 4

4. Use estimation. Is each quotient reasonable? Explain.

a. $1.564 \div 2.3 = 0.68$ **b.** $26.0454 \div 4.98 = 52.3$

Test-Taking Tip

You can sometimes use estimation to eliminate answer choices on a multiple choice test.

What is 8.19 ÷ 2.1?

A. 39   **B.** 4.1

C. 3.9   **D.** 0.41

If you estimate $8 \div 2 \approx 4$, then you know you can eliminate choices A and D.

EXERCISES

For more exercises, see *Extra Practice*.

Practice and Problem Solving

A Practice by Example

Example 1
(page 132)

Estimate each product.

1. $4.56 \cdot 7.02$ **2.** $11.15 \cdot 4.44$ **3.** $6.3 \cdot 9.2$

4. $24.5 \cdot 4.2$ **5.** $3.29 \cdot 58$ **6.** $0.08 \cdot 40.05$

Example 2
(page 132)

Estimate the cost of each purchase.

7. Food Tom bought 6 hamburgers for $2.89 each.

8. Sports Equipment The athletic director bought 5 soccer balls for $12.29 each.

Example 3
(page 133)

Estimate each quotient using compatible numbers.

9. $3.9 \div 2.1$ **10.** $3.86 \div 1.95$ **11.** $19.56 \div 0.71$

12. $\$585 \div 11.75$ **13.** $18.2 \div 3.4$ **14.** $57.1 \div 7.2$

15. Unit Pricing Marshall buys a sack of peaches for $5.98. If the peaches weigh 2.77 pounds, about what price per pound did Marshall pay?

Example 4
(page 133)

Use estimation. Is each quotient reasonable? Explain.

16. $102.6 \div 22.5 = 45.6$ **17.** $\$32.40 \div 4.80 = \$67.50$

18. Number Sense Explain how you would find a reasonable estimate for $14.90 \div 4.56$.

B Apply Your Skills

Estimate each product or quotient.

19. $193.7 \cdot 1.78$ **20.** $7.95 \div 2.1$ **21.** $9.392 \div 2.9$

22. $876.66 \cdot 39.64$ **23.** $\$75.45 \div 12.48$ **24.** $16.33 \cdot 3.5$

Data Analysis Use the table below for Exercises 25–27.

Hospital Staff Wages (40-h week)

Occupation	Dallas, TX	Washington, DC
Physical Therapist	$733.20	$655.20
Pharmacist	$793.60	$851.60
Nurse	$606.80	$714.80

SOURCE: *The American Almanac of Jobs and Salaries*

Reading Math
For help with reading and solving Exercise 27, see page 136.

25. Estimate the hourly wage for each staff position.

26. Estimate the yearly (52 weeks) salary for each staff position.

27. How much more per hour does a physical therapist in Dallas, Texas, make than a physical therapist in Washington, D.C.?

Use estimation. Is each product or quotient reasonable? Explain.

28. $-46.82(-1.5) = 702.3$

29. $-71.5071 \div (-11.9) = 6.009$

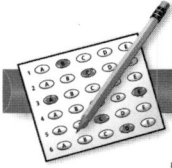 **30. Gas Mileage** Shari is planning a 450-mi car trip. Her car can travel about 39 mi on a gallon of gasoline. Gasoline costs $1.89/gal. About how much will the gas cost for her trip?

C Challenge **Estimate each quotient.**

31. $-483.09 \div 7.29$

32. $-362,400 \div (-4.2)$

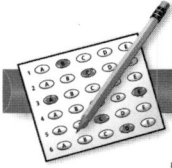 **33. Health** Humans breathe about 15 breaths in a minute. The average breath at rest contains 0.76 liter of air. About how many liters of air will you breathe while at rest for 25 minutes?

34. Writing in Math You estimate $21.2 \div 3.75$ to be 5. Your friend estimates the quotient to be 7. Explain how the two estimates can be different and yet both be reasonable.

Test Prep

Multiple Choice

35. Greta ran the 400-m dash in 49.07 s. If Greta ran at a constant rate, how many meters did she run in one second?
A. between 8 m and 9 m
B. between 9 m and 10 m
C. between 10 m and 11 m
D. between 11 m and 12 m

36. A shrew, the world's smallest mammal, has a heart rate of 790 beats per minute. About how many times does a shrew's heart beat in 5 minutes?
F. 3,500
G. 4,000
H. 4,500
I. 4,790

Short Response

37. Two people estimate the product $1.99 · 8.5.
a. Will they necessarily get the same estimate?
b. Explain your answer.

Take It to the NET
Online lesson quiz at
www.PHSchool.com
Web Code:ada-0302

38. You review your sales slip after buying 4 CDs that cost $14.95 each. Before tax, the total was $77.80. Is this total correct? Explain.

Mixed Review

Lesson 3-1 **Estimate each sum or difference.**

39. $2.99 + $6.01

40. $25.90 − $5.79

41. $12.3 + 12.3 + 14.56$

42. $1,242.24 − 24.05$

43. $18.95 − 7.48$

44. $7.47 − $5.50

Lesson 1-10 **In which quadrant or on which axis of a coordinate plane does each point lie?**

45. $(2, 4)$

46. $(-5, 0)$

47. $(8, -6)$

48. $(0, 8)$

49. $(-5, -3)$

Lesson 1-8 **50. Travel** A bus trip from Sacramento to Los Angeles takes 7 h 40 min. You depart at 11:40 A.M. At what time will you arrive in Los Angeles?

Read the exercise below and then read how the needed data are found in the table. Follow along as the problem is solved. Check your understanding by solving the exercise at the bottom of the page.

Use the table. How much more per hour does a physical therapist in Dallas, Texas, make than a physical therapist in Washington, D.C.?

The title of the table tells you that the table entries are wages for a 40-h week.

Occupations: Look down for physical therapist.

Cities: Look across for Dallas and Washington.

The table tells you that in a 40-h week:
A physical therapist in Dallas makes $733.20.
A physical therapist in Washington makes $655.20.

Hospital Staff Wages (40-h week)

Occupation	Dallas, TX	Washington, DC
Physical Therapist	$733.20	$655.20
Pharmacist	$793.60	$851.60
Nurse	$606.80	$714.80

SOURCE: *The American Almanac of Jobs and Salaries*

Estimate:

A Dallas physical therapist makes
about $730 − $650 = $80 more in a 40-h week.

That's about $80 ÷ 40 = $2 more per hour.

Calculate — Method 1

733.20 − 655.20 = 78.00   **Subtract to find the difference in weekly wages.**

78.00 ÷ 40 = 1.95   **Divide to find the difference in hourly wages.**

Calculate — Method 2

733.20 ÷ 40 = 18.33   **Divide to find the Dallas hourly wage.**

655.20 ÷ 40 = 16.38   **Divide to find the Washington hourly wage.**

18.33 − 16.38 = 1.95   **Subtract to find the difference in hourly wages.**

A Dallas physical therapist makes $1.95/h more than one in Washington.

This is close to the estimate of $2/h.

EXERCISES

1. How much less per hour does a nurse in Dallas make than a nurse in Washington?

2. How much more per hour does a pharmacist in Dallas make than a nurse in Dallas?

Mean, Median, and Mode

OBJECTIVE
1 Finding Mean, Median, and Mode

Mean, *median*, and *mode* are **measures of central tendency** of a collection of data. Consider the data 2, 3, 4, 5, 8, 8, and 12.

The **mean** is the sum of the data values divided by the number of data values.

$$\text{mean} = \frac{2 + 3 + 4 + 5 + 8 + 8 + 12}{7}$$
$$= \frac{42}{7}$$
$$\text{mean} = 6$$

The **median** is the middle number when data values are written in order and there is an odd number of data values. For an even number of data values, the median is the mean of the two middle numbers.

$$2 \quad 3 \quad 4 \quad \underset{\underset{\text{median}}{\uparrow}}{5} \quad 8 \quad 8 \quad 12$$

The **mode** is the data item that occurs most often. There can be one mode, more than one mode, or no mode.

$$2 \quad 3 \quad 4 \quad 5 \quad \underbrace{8 \quad 8}_{\text{mode}} \quad 12$$

1 EXAMPLE Real-World  Problem Solving

Fundraising Six elementary students are participating in a one-week Readathon to raise money for a good cause. Use the graph. Find the (a) mean, (b) median, and (c) mode.

a. Mean: $\dfrac{\text{sum of data values}}{\text{number of data values}}$

$$= \frac{40 + 45 + 48 + 50 + 50 + 59}{6}$$

$$= \frac{292}{6}$$

$$= 48.666\ldots$$

Rounded to the nearest tenth, the mean is 48.7.

b. Median: 40   45   48   50   50   59   **Write the data in order.**

$\dfrac{48 + 50}{2} = 49$ **Find the mean of the two middle numbers.**

The median is 49.

c. Mode: Find the data value that occurs most often.
The mode is 50.

What You'll Learn

OBJECTIVE 1 To find mean, median, and mode of a set of data

OBJECTIVE 2 To choose the best measure of central tendency

. . . And Why

To solve real-world problems involving consumer issues

✓ Check Skills You'll Need

Write the numbers from least to greatest.

1. 8, 6, 4, 9, 3, 5, 6

2. 72, 68, 69, 71, 72

3. 112, 101, 98, 120, 101

4. 3.74, 3, 3.7, 3.3, 37

❓ For help, go to Skills Handbook, p. 757.

New Vocabulary

• measures of central tendency
• mean   • median
• mode   • outlier

ⓘ **TEXT** Interactive lesson includes instant self-check, tutorials, and activities.

✓ **Check Understanding** Example 1

1. Find the mean, median, and mode: 2.3 4.3 3.2 2.9 2.7 2.3

2 **EXAMPLE** **Identifying Modes**

How many modes, if any, does each have?

a. $1.50 $2.00 $2.25 $2.40 $3.50 $4.00
No values are the same, so there is no mode.

b. 2 3 6 <u>8</u> <u>8</u> 10 11 12 <u>14</u> <u>14</u> 18 20
Both 8 and 14 appear the same number of times, and most often.
There are two modes.

c. grape, grape, banana, nectarine, <u>strawberry</u>, <u>strawberry</u>, <u>strawberry</u>, orange, watermelon
Strawberry appears most often. There is one mode.

✓ **Check Understanding** Example 2

2. Find the number of modes.

   a. 11 9 7 7 8 8 13 11   **b.** 38.5 55.4 45.3 38.5 68.4

An **outlier** is a data value that is much greater or less than the other data values. An outlier can affect the mean of a group of data.

3 **EXAMPLE** **Real-World** 🌐 **Problem Solving**

Geography Use the map of Central America at the left.

a. Which data value is an outlier?
The data value for Honduras, 6,500 mi², is an outlier. It is an outlier because it is 1,500 mi² away from the closest data value.

b. How does the outlier affect the mean?

$\dfrac{21,700}{7} = 3,100$ **Find the mean with the outlier.**

$\dfrac{15,200}{6} \approx 2,500$ **Find the mean without the outlier.**

$3,100 - 2,500 = 600$

The outlier raises the mean by about 600 mi².

✓ **Check Understanding** Example 3

3. Find an outlier in each group of data below and tell how it affects the mean. Round to the nearest tenth.

   a. 9 10 12 13 8 9 31 9   **b.** 1 17.5 18 19.5 16 17.5

Approximate Land Areas That Can Be Farmed in Central American Countries

Guatemala 5,000 mi²
Belize 200 mi²
Honduras 6,500 mi²
Nicaragua 4,500 mi²
El Salvador 2,200 mi²
Costa Rica 1,200 mi²
Panama 2,100 mi²

SOURCE: *The New York Times Almanac*

2 Choosing the Best Measure

One measure of central tendency may be better than another to describe data. For example, consider the eight hourly wage rates shown at the right. Here are the measures of central tendency.

Employees' Hourly Wages	
$5.50	$6.20
$5.50	$6.30
$5.50	$8.00
$6.00	$17.00

Mode: $5.50
Mean: $7.50
Median: $6.10

The mode is the lowest wage listed. So the mode does not describe the data well.

The mean is above the hourly wage of all but two workers. The mean is influenced by the outlier, $17.

The median is the best measure of central tendency here since it is not influenced by the size of the outlier.

4 EXAMPLE   Identifying the Best Measure

Which measure of central tendency best describes each situation? Explain.

a. the favorite movies of students in the eighth grade

Mode; since the data are not numerical, the mode is the appropriate measure. When determining the most frequently chosen item, or when the data are not numerical, use the mode.

b. the daily high temperatures during a week in July

Mean; since daily high temperatures in July are not likely to have an outlier, mean is the appropriate measure. When the data have no outliers, use the mean.

c. the distances students in your class travel to school

Median; since one student may live much farther from school than the majority of students, the median is the appropriate measure. When an outlier may significantly influence the mean, use the median.

Reading Math
To help you recall that *median* means "middle number," think of the green, grassy median strip in the middle of a divided highway.

✓ Check Understanding   Example 4

4. a. Comparison Shopping Toshio found the following prices for sport shirts:
$20, $26, $27, $28, $21, $42, $18, and $20.
Find the mean, median, and mode for the shirt prices.

b. Reasoning Which measure of central tendency best describes the data? Justify your reasoning.

EXERCISES

For more exercises, see *Extra Practice*.

Practice and Problem Solving

A **Practice by Example**
Example 1
(page 137)

Find the mean, median, and mode of each group of data. If an answer is not a whole number, round to the nearest tenth.

1. 47 56 57 63 89 44 56

2. 4 5 2 3 2 3 3 3 1 1 3

3. 1 2 4 5 5 6 9

4. 2.8 3.6 3.8 4.1 2.8 3.7 4.3

5. Fitness Mia's workouts lasted 1.0 h, 1.5 h, 2.25 h, 1.5 h, 2.4 h, and 2.1 h. Find the mean, median, and mode of these times. If the answer is not an integer, round to the nearest tenth.

Example 2
(page 138)

How many modes, if any, does each group of data have?

6. 31 44 44 31 38

7. 4.3 4.9 4.9 5.2

8. 64 68 64 65 68 65 72 61

9. Bob, Ana, Ron, Bob, Kay

Example 3
(page 138)

Find the outlier in each group of data and tell how it affects the mean.

10. 37 4 7 3 11 9 13 5

11. 126 123 115 125 123

12. Grades Rita's quiz scores are 72, 96, 74, 80, and 79. Find the outlier and tell how it affects Rita's mean quiz score.

Example 4
(page 139)

Which measure of central tendency best describes each situation? Explain.

13. numbers of apples in 2-lb bags

14. favorite brands of jeans of 14-year-olds

15. ages of students in a fifth-grade classroom

Which measure of central tendency best describes each group of data? Explain.

16. minutes on the Internet
50 63 59 85 367 48

17. heights of students in inches
51 45 47 48 50 50 50 52

B **Apply Your Skills**

For Exercises 18–22, find mean, median, and mode. Which measure of central tendency best describes each group of data? Explain.

18. 3,456 560 435 456

19. 5.6 6.8 1.2 6.5 7.9 6.5

20. 33 76 86 92 86

21. 8 2 4 9 16

22. resting heart rate in beats per minute: 79 72 80 81 40 72

Which measure of central tendency best describes each situation? Explain.

23. shoe colors in a classroom

24. widths of computer screens at a bank

25. numbers of pets owned by classmates

 **Challenge**

Fat and Calorie Content
(per 2-tablespoon serving)

Seed or Nut	Fat (g)	Calories
Peanut	8.9	104
Pecan	9.1	90
Pistachio	7.9	92
Pumpkin	7.9	93
Sunflower	8.9	102
Walnut	7.7	80

For Exercises 26–28, use the table at the left. Round answers to the nearest tenth.

26. **Data Analysis** You make a mixture using the same amount of each kind of seed and nut.
   a. What is the mean number of grams of fat in a 2-tablespoon serving of the mixture?
   b. What is the mean number of calories in a 2-tablespoon serving of the mixture?

27. **Writing in Math** Describe two mixtures that each use a total of 8 tablespoons. Do the two parts of Exercise 26 for your mixtures.

🌐 28. **Nutrition** A mixture of equal amounts of pumpkin seeds, sunflower seeds, and pistachios contains 12 tablespoons in all. How many grams of fat and how many calories does the mixture have?

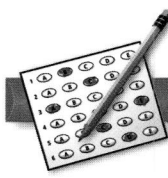

Test Prep

Multiple Choice

29. The average cost of a meal at the Grand Plaza is $20. Which one of the following statements *cannot* be true?
   A. The cost of four meals is greater than $20.
   B. Some meals cost less than $10.
   C. Each meal costs exactly $20.
   D. Each meal costs more than $20.

Take It to the NET
Online lesson quiz at
www.PHSchool.com
Web Code: ada-0303

30. Kayla's first three quiz scores are 90, 85, and 88. Which score on her next quiz will raise Kayla's mean quiz score to 90?
   F. 97   **G.** 95   **H.** 92   **I.** 90

31. Ten out of 20 students score a perfect 100 on a math test. Which of the following describes the score of 100 for the 20 students?
   A. mean   **B.** median   **C.** mode   **D.** outlier

Short Response

32. In a neighborhood with 46 homes, two are more than 6,000 ft² in area, and the rest are less than 2,500 ft² in area.
   a. Would the mean or the median provide a better measure of the typical home size?
   b. Explain your reasoning.

Mixed Review

Lesson 3-2   **Estimate each product or quotient.**

33. $9.01 ÷ $1.42   34. 7.5 · 89.1   35. 12.6 · $2.99

Lesson 2-7 🌐 36. **Retail Sales** Karen sells children's hats for $4 and adults' hats for $7. On Saturday, she sold 120 hats, and she collected $720. How many adults' hats did she sell?

Lesson 2-3   **Simplify each expression.**

37. $6x + 8 + 2$ 38. $5z + 4x + 3z$ 39. $x - 4t + 2t + 5$

3-3 Mean, Median, and Mode   **141**

Technology

Mean and Median on a Graphing Calculator

For Use With Lesson 3-3

You can use a graphing calculator to find means and medians.

EXAMPLE

Find (a) the mean and (b) the median number of acres in Ohio zoos.

Zoos in Ohio

Zoo	Number of Acres	Number of Species
Cincinnati Zoo	70	712
Cleveland Metroparks Zoo	165	599
Columbus Zoo	90	650
Toledo Zoological Gardens	62	633

SOURCE: *The World Almanac*

a. Use the mean function. In **STAT,** select **MATH** and **mean**, then ENTER. Enter the data between braces { } using commas. Press ENTER to find the mean.

```
mean( {70, 165, 90,
62} )
              96.75
■
```

The mean is about 97 acres.

b. Use the median function. In **STAT,** select **MATH** and **median**, then ENTER. Enter the data between braces { } using commas. Press ENTER to find the mean.

```
median( {70, 165, 90,
62} )
                  80
■
```

The median is 80 acres.

EXERCISES

Use a calculator to find the mean and median.

1. number of species in Ohio zoos

2. 85°F, 79°F, 80°F, 75°F, 82°F

3. $3.75, $4.50, $9.25, $4.70, $5.90

4. 100, 95, 82, 102, 78, 76

5.

Miles of Atlantic Coastline by State

State	DE	FL	GA	ME	MD	MA	NH	NJ	NY	NC	RI	SC	VA
Miles	28	580	100	228	31	192	13	130	127	301	40	187	112

SOURCE: National Oceanic and Atmospheric Administration, U.S. Dept. of Commerce

6. Investigate entering the data in a list, L_1, and then using L_1 as the data list in parts (a) and (b) of the Example.

Using Formulas

1 Substituting Into Formulas

A **formula** is an equation that shows a relationship between quantities that are represented by variables.

An important formula in math and science is $d = rt$, where d is the distance, r is the rate, or speed, and t is the time spent traveling.

1 EXAMPLE Real-World 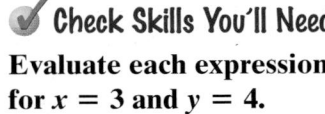 Problem Solving

Travel Suppose you travel 162 miles in 3 hours. Use the formula $d = rt$ to find your average speed.

$d = rt$	Write the formula.
$162 = (r)(3)$	Substitute 162 for d and 3 for t.
$\dfrac{162}{3} = \dfrac{3r}{3}$	Divide each side by 3.
$54 = r$	Simplify.

● Your average speed is 54 mi/h.

✓ Check Understanding Example 1

1. Use the formula $d = rt$. Find d, r, or t.

   a. $d = 273$ mi, $t = 9.75$ h   **b.** $d = 540.75$ in., $r = 10.5$ in./yr

2 EXAMPLE Real-World  Problem Solving

Insects You can estimate the temperature outside using the chirps of a cricket. Use the formula $F = \frac{n}{4} + 37$, where n is the number of times a cricket chirps in one minute, and F is the temperature in degrees Fahrenheit. Estimate the temperature when a cricket chirps 100 times in a minute.

$F = \dfrac{n}{4} + 37$	Write the formula.
$F = \dfrac{100}{4} + 37$	Replace n with 100.
$F = 25 + 37$	Divide.
$F = 62$	Add.

● The temperature is about 62°F.

What You'll Learn

 OBJECTIVE 1 To substitute into formulas

 OBJECTIVE 2 To use the formula for the perimeter of a rectangle

. . . And Why

To use formulas to solve real-world problems involving distances, temperatures, and perimeters

✓ Check Skills You'll Need

Evaluate each expression for $x = 3$ and $y = 4$.

1. $2x + 2y$ **2.** $2x + y$

3. $2(x + y)$ **4.** $\dfrac{x + y}{2}$

❓ For help, go to Lesson 1-3.

New Vocabulary

● formula
● perimeter

📱 **TEXT** Interactive lesson includes instant self-check, tutorials, and activities.

✓ **Check Understanding** Example 2

2. Use the formula $F = \frac{n}{4} + 37$ to estimate the temperature in degrees Fahrenheit for each situation.

    a. 96 chirps/min   **b.** 88 chirps/min   **c.** 66 chirps/min

OBJECTIVE

2 **Using a Perimeter Formula**

The **perimeter** of a figure is the distance around the figure. You can find the perimeter of a rectangle by adding the lengths of the four sides, or by using the formula $P = 2\ell + 2w$, where ℓ is the length and w is the width. For rectangles, it does not matter which dimension you choose to be the length or the width.

3 **EXAMPLE** **Finding Perimeter**

Reading Math
Think of *peRIMeter* as the distance around the "rim" of a figure.

Measurement Find the perimeter of the room. Use the formula for the perimeter of a rectangle, $P = 2\ell + 2w$.

12.5 ft

18.5 ft

$P = 2\ell + 2w$	**Write the formula.**
$P = 2(18.5) + 2(12.5)$	**Replace ℓ with 18.5 and w with 12.5.**
$P = 37 + 25$	**Multiply.**
$P = 62$	**Add.**

● The perimeter of the room is 62 ft.

✓ **Check Understanding** Example 3

3. Find the perimeter of each rectangle.

    a.

    27.3 cm

    16.8 cm

    b.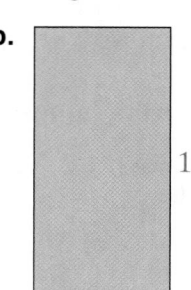

    17.4 in.

    8.6 in.

EXERCISES

For more exercises, see Extra Practice.

Practice and Problem Solving

A Practice by Example

Example 1
(page 143)

Use the formula $d = rt$. Find d, r, or t.

1. $r = 38.5$ m/h, $t = 12.5$ h   **2.** $d = 2,730$ mi, $t = 9.75$ h

3. $d = 596.39$ cm, $r = 2.3$ cm/s   **4.** $d = 10.2$ ft, $r = 0.5$ ft/h

Example 2
(page 143)

Use the formula $F = \frac{n}{4} + 37$ to estimate each temperature.

5. 120 chirps/min   **6.** 80 chirps/min

7. 92 chirps/min   **8.** 64 chirps/min

Example 3
(page 144)

Use the formula $P = 2\ell + 2w$. Find the perimeter of each rectangle.

9.

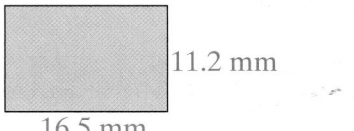
11.2 mm
16.5 mm

10.

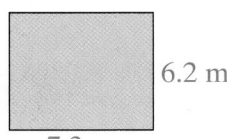
6.2 m
7.3 m

B Apply Your Skills

Given that C is the temperature in degrees Celsius, use the formula $F = 1.8C + 32$ to find each temperature F in degrees Fahrenheit.

11. $C = 58$ **12.** $C = -4$ **13.** $C = 72$ **14.** $C = 56$ **15.** $C = -89$

16. a. Estimation You can *estimate* a temperature in degrees Fahrenheit using the formula $F = 2 \cdot C + 30$, where C is the temperature in degrees Celsius (°C). What is the approximate temperature in degrees Fahrenheit when it is 3°C? 5°C? 25°C?

b. Writing in Math Is this formula better for estimating higher temperatures or lower temperatures? Explain.

Geometry Use the formula $P = 2\ell + 2w$. Find the perimeter of each rectangle. Then use the formula $A = \ell w$ to find each area.

17.

3.5 m
7 m

18.

11.2 cm
25.8 cm

C Challenge

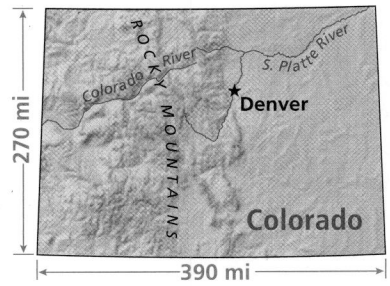

19. The top surface of a world-record rectangular strawberry shortcake was 175.33 ft long and 48 in. wide. Use the formula for perimeter. Find the approximate perimeter of the cake.

20. Find the approximate area of the top of the cake in Exercise 19.

21. The state of Colorado is nearly rectangular in shape. Use the formula for area. Find the approximate area of Colorado.

22. Use the formula for perimeter. Find the approximate perimeter of Colorado.

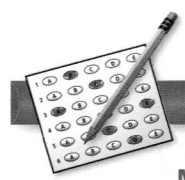

Multiple Choice

23. What is the perimeter of a rectangle that measures 32 cm by 11 cm?
    A. 352 cm   **B.** 86 cm   **C.** 54 cm   **D.** 43 cm

24. Suppose you travel 320 mi in 5 h. What is your average speed?
    F. 58 mi/h   **G.** 60 mi/h   **H.** 64 mi/h   **I.** 75 mi/h

25. A giant tortoise travels about 0.17 mi/h on land. If a tortoise travels at a constant speed, how far can it travel in 2.5 h?
    A. 0.0425 mi   **B.** 0.267 mi   **C.** 0.425 mi   **D.** 4.25 mi

Short Response

Take It to the NET
Online lesson quiz at
www.PHSchool.com
Web Code: ada-0304

26. A rectangular yard has width w and length ℓ. **(a)** What is a formula for its perimeter, P? **(b)** Find P when w is 16.4 m and ℓ is 28.2 m.

27. The pronghorn antelope can run 0.73 mi/min. **(a)** At this speed, how far can this animal travel in 30 seconds? **(b)** In 1.5 minutes?

Mixed Review

Lesson 3-3

Find the mean, median, and mode. Round to the nearest whole number where necessary. Which measure of central tendency best describes the data?

28. minutes of homework
    8 125 154 120 105 125

29. milliliters per container
    250 250 355 355 375 250

Lesson 2-5 **Solve each equation.**

30. $c + 8 = 41$ **31.** $b + 32 = 19$ **32.** $98 = n + 42$

Lesson 1-7

33. Patterns Which equation, $n = 2t$ or $t = n \cdot 2$, describes the relationship between the variables in the table? Explain.

n	14	16	18	20
t	7	8	9	10

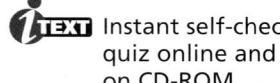
Checkpoint Quiz 1   **Lessons 3-1 through 3-4**

TEXT Instant self-check quiz online and on CD-ROM

Round each number to the underlined place value.

1. 15.6<u>5</u>71   **2.** 0.89<u>1</u>4   **3.** 7,02<u>2</u>.56   **4.** 345.<u>6</u>78

Estimate.

5. $3.7 \cdot 8.06$ **6.** $17.25 + 6.66$ **7.** $8.7 - 9.6$ **8.** $11.7 \div 1.8$

Find the mean, median, and mode.

9. 47, 56, 58, 63   **10.** 1, 4, 1, 3, 1, 2, 3, 2, 1, 2

11. Jennifer drives at an average speed of 54 mi/h. At this rate, how long does it take Jennifer to drive 459 miles?

Technology

Formulas in a Spreadsheet

For Use With Lesson 3-4

You can use a computer spreadsheet to evaluate formulas. Look at the spreadsheet below. In the spreadsheet, the algebraic formula $d = rt$ is evaluated for $r = 50$ mi/h and $t = 3$ h.

The spreadsheet formula "=A2*B2" is used in cell C2 to calculate $d = rt$. The spreadsheet formula means that the value in cell C2 equals the value in cell A2 times the value in cell B2.

	A	B	C
1	r	t	d
2	50	3	150

In spreadsheet formulas the asterisk symbol * means multiply. The slash symbol / means divide.

EXAMPLE

Use a spreadsheet and the formula $P = 2L + 2W$ to find the perimeter P of a rectangle. Evaluate the formula for a length L of 7.8 in. and a width W of 2.6 in.

	A	B	C
1	L	W	P
2	7.8	2.6	20.8

⟵ **Use the spreadsheet formula "=2*A2+2*B2."**

● The perimeter is about 21 in.

EXERCISES

Use a spreadsheet to find each perimeter.

1. $L = 5.6$ in., $W = 7.9$ in.
2. $L = 12.7$ in., $W = 15.6$ in.
3. $L = 0.2$ in., $W = 1.3$ in.

Use a spreadsheet to evaluate the formula $t = d \div r$ for the given values of d and r.

4. $d = 250$ mi, $r = 5$ mi/h
5. $d = 1,400$ mi, $r = 50$ mi/h
6. $d = 4,500$ mi, $r = 250$ mi/h

Write a spreadsheet formula for each algebraic formula.

7. to find A, using $A = 0.5bh$
8. to find P, using $P = 4a$
9. to find y, using $y = mx + b$

10. a. Open-Ended Use a spreadsheet to evaluate the formula $A = \ell w$. How does the value of A change as you double the value of ℓ while keeping w unchanged?
b. How does the value of A change as you double the values of both ℓ and w?

3-5

Solving Equations by Adding or Subtracting Decimals

What You'll Learn

OBJECTIVE 1 To solve one-step decimal equations involving addition

OBJECTIVE 2 To solve one-step decimal equations involving subtraction

. . . And Why

To solve real-world problems involving astronomy and money management

✓ **Check Skills You'll Need**

Simplify.

1. $2.8 + 7.06$

2. $0.65 + 1.8$

3. $4.52 - 2.48$

4. $3.7 - 0.62$

❓ For help, go to Skills Handbook, p. 764.

OBJECTIVE

1 Using Subtraction to Solve Equations

In Lesson 2-5, you used the Subtraction Property of Equality to solve equations involving integers. You can also use this property to solve equations with decimals. Remember to subtract the same number from each side of the equation.

1 EXAMPLE Subtracting to Solve an Equation

Solve $n + 4.5 = -9.7$.

$$n + 4.5 = -9.7$$
$$n + 4.5 - 4.5 = -9.7 - 4.5 \qquad \text{Subtract 4.5 from each side.}$$
$$n = -14.2 \qquad \text{Simplify.}$$

Check $\quad n + 4.5 = -9.7$
$$-14.2 + 4.5 \overset{?}{=} -9.7 \qquad \text{Replace } n \text{ with } -14.2.$$
$$-9.7 = -9.7 ✔$$

✓ **Check Understanding** Example 1

1. Solve each equation.

a. $x + 4.9 = 18.8$ **b.** $14.73 = -24.23 + b$

2 EXAMPLE Real-World 🌐 Problem Solving

Astronomy A communications satellite is circling Earth. Use the diagram below to find the approximate distance from the satellite to the moon.

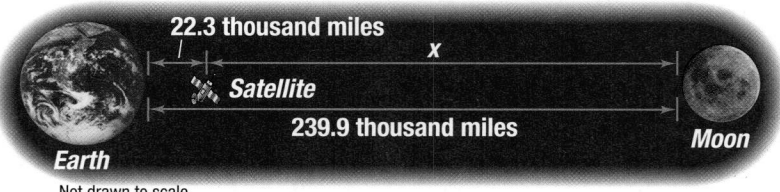

22.3 thousand miles
x
Satellite
239.9 thousand miles
Earth
Moon
Not drawn to scale

$$22.3 + x = 239.9$$
$$22.3 + x - 22.3 = 239.9 - 22.3 \qquad \text{Subtract 22.3 from each side.}$$
$$x = 217.6 \qquad \text{Simplify.}$$
$$x \approx 218 \qquad \text{Round to the nearest one.}$$

The approximate distance from the satellite to the moon is 218 thousand miles.

📱 **TEXT** Interactive lesson includes instant self-check, tutorials, and activities.

✓ Check Understanding Example 2

2. **Analyzing Markup** A store's cost plus markup is the price you pay for an item. Suppose a pair of shoes costs a store $35.48. You pay $70. Write and solve an equation to find the store's markup.

OBJECTIVE

2 Using Addition to Solve Equations

You can also use the Addition Property of Equality to solve an equation involving decimals. Remember to add the same number to each side of the equation.

3 EXAMPLE   Adding to Solve an Equation

Solve $k - 14.4 = -18.39$.

$$k - 14.4 = -18.39$$
$$k - 14.4 + 14.4 = -18.39 + 14.4 \quad \textbf{Add 14.4 to each side.}$$
$$k = -3.99 \quad \textbf{Simplify.}$$

Need Help?

For help with adding and subtracting decimals, see Skills Handbook, page 764.

✓ Check Understanding Example 3

3. Solve each equation.

   a. $n - 5.85 = 15.25$ **b.** $-10 = c - 2.6$

4 EXAMPLE   Real-World 🌐 Problem Solving

Personal Finance **Danzel wrote a check for $76.85. His new account balance is $235.00. What was his previous balance?**

Words   previous balance   minus   check   is   new balance

Let p = previous balance.

Equation p −   76.85   =   235

$$p - 76.85 = 235$$
$$p - 76.85 + 76.85 = 235 + 76.85 \quad \textbf{Add 76.85 to each side.}$$
$$p = 311.85 \quad \textbf{Simplify.}$$

Danzel's previous balance was $311.85.

✓ Check Understanding Example 4

4. **Shopping** You spent $14.95 for a new shirt. You now have $12.48. Write and solve an equation to find how much money you had before you bought the shirt.

EXERCISES

For more exercises, see *Extra Practice.*

Practice and Problem Solving

A Practice by Example

Examples 1 and 2
(page 148)

Solve each equation.

1. $c + 9 = 3.7$ **2.** $b + 7.6 = 23$ **3.** $43.6 = n + 17.5$

4. $6.35 + b = 9.89$ **5.** $12.13 = n + 1.4$ **6.** $x + 0.35 = 9.15$

7. Astronomy The planet Mars takes 599.01 days longer than Mercury to orbit the sun. In all, the Mars orbit takes 686.98 days. Write and solve an equation to find how long it takes Mercury to orbit the sun.

8. Car Sales Julia trades in her small car for a large pickup truck that weighs 1,855.3 lb more than the car. If the truck weighs 4,360.3 lb, what is the weight of the car?

Examples 3 and 4
(page 149)

Solve each equation.

9. $d - 4.9 = 18.8$ **10.** $c - 19.2 = 24$ **11.** $-2.5 = q - 1.7$

12. $-5.6 = y - 8$ **13.** $4.3 = g - 1$ **14.** $a - 108.8 = -203$

15. Personal Finance You spent $13.50 for movie tickets. You now have $26.50. Write and solve an equation to find out how much money you had before buying the tickets.

16. Rachel wrote a check for $161.15. Her new account balance is $423.28. What was her previous account balance?

B Apply Your Skills

Complete the steps for each equation. Justify each step.

17. $x + 1.2 = 15$
$x + 1.2 - \blacksquare = 15 - \blacksquare$
$x = \blacksquare$

18. $y - 3.33 = 12.42$
$y - 3.33 + \blacksquare = 12.42 + \blacksquare$
$y = \blacksquare$

19. Running Michael Johnson's world record in the 200-m sprint is 19.32 s. His 400-m world record is 23.86 s slower than his 200-m record. Write and solve an equation to find Johnson's 400-m record.

20. Biology A hare travels about 17.83 mi/h faster on land than a giant tortoise. A hare can hop at about 18 mi/h. Write and solve an equation to find how fast a giant tortoise can travel on land.

Solve each equation.

21. $4.035 = a - 3.25$ **22.** $h - (-1.5) = 1.5$ **23.** $e + (-7.8) = -6.7$

24. $r - 0.832 = 8.67$ **25.** $b - (-1.5) = -9$ **26.** $-32 = x + (-8.05)$

Real-World Connection

Giant tortoises can weigh up to 500 lb.

Mental Math Use mental math to solve each equation.

27. $1.60 = 0.40 + s$ **28.** $x + 8.8 = 9.9$ **29.** $5.5 = x - 5.5$

$$x - 1.6 = -6$$
$$x - 1.6 + 1.6 = -6 - 1.6$$
$$x = -7.6$$

30. Error Analysis A student solved an equation as shown at the left. Explain the student's error.

31. Writing in Math Explain how you would use the Addition (not Subtraction) Property of Equality to solve $x + 1.8 = -4.7$.

 **Challenge**

Solve each equation.

32. $143.587 + x - 22.96 = 156.4$ **33.** $-924.87 - 1{,}237 + b = 86.125$

34. Reasoning Without solving, tell how the solutions of the equations $x + 14 = 15$, $x + 1.4 = 1.5$, and $x + 0.14 = 0.15$ compare. Explain.

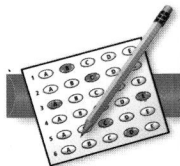

Test Prep

Multiple Choice **35.** Which statement describes how to solve $x + 0.042 = 0.826$?
   A. Add 0.042 to each side.   **B.** Subtract 0.042 from each side.
   C. Add 0.826 to each side.   **D.** Subtract 0.826 from each side.

Reading Comprehension Read the cartoon below before doing Exercises 36 and 37.

SOURCE: ©1993 United Features Syndicate, Inc.

36. How much money does the clerk owe Dilbert?

37. Dilbert does not want any pennies. What other amount of money could Dilbert have given the cashier? Justify your answer.

Take It to the NET
Online lesson quiz at
www.PHSchool.com
Web Code: ada-0305

Mixed Review

Lesson 3-4   **Use the formula $A = \ell w$. Find A.**

38. $\ell = 23.4$ in., $w = 15.8$ in.   **39.** $\ell = 5.5$ cm, $w = 7$ cm

Lesson 2-6   **Solve each equation.**

40. $6a = 24$ **41.** $-2b = 60$ **42.** $-81 = 9a$

Lesson 2-2   **43.** A large juice costs \$.83. A small juice costs \$.57. Ida buys one juice each school day. If Ida buys small juices instead of large juices, how much money will she save each week?

3-6

Solving Equations by Multiplying or Dividing Decimals

What You'll Learn

OBJECTIVE 1
To solve one-step decimal equations involving multiplication

OBJECTIVE 2
To solve one-step decimal equations involving division

. . . And Why

To solve real-world problems in oil production

 Check Skills You'll Need

Find each product.

1. 2.6(4.5)

2. 3.2(0.15)

3. 11.03(0.6)

4. 8.003(0.6)

For help, go to Skills Handbook, p. 765.

OBJECTIVE

1 Using Division to Solve Equations

In Lesson 2-6, you used the Division Property of Equality to solve equations involving integers. You can also use this property to solve equations with decimals. Remember to divide each side of the equation by the same nonzero number.

1 EXAMPLE Dividing to Solve an Equation

Solve $0.9r = -5.4$.

$$0.9r = -5.4$$

$$\frac{0.9r}{0.9} = \frac{-5.4}{0.9} \qquad \text{Divide each side by 0.9.}$$

$$r = -6 \qquad \text{Simplify.}$$

Check
$$0.9r = -5.4$$
$$0.9(-6) \stackrel{?}{=} -5.4 \qquad \text{Replace } r \text{ with } -6.$$
$$-5.4 = -5.4 \checkmark$$

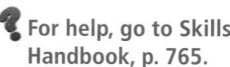 **Check Understanding** Example 1

1. Solve each equation.

a. $0.8x = -1.6$ **b.** $1.15 = 2.3x$ **c.** $-81.81 = -0.9n$

2 EXAMPLE Real-World Problem Solving

Petroleum An oil field produces an average of 16.8 thousand barrels of crude oil per day. About how many days will it take to produce 200 thousand barrels?

Words	daily barrel production	times	number of days	equals	200 thousand barrels

Let d = number of days.

Equation $\qquad 16.8 \qquad \cdot \qquad d \qquad = \qquad 200$

$$16.8d = 200$$

$$\frac{16.8d}{16.8} = \frac{200}{16.8} \qquad \text{Divide each side by 16.8.}$$

$$d = 11.904\ldots \qquad \text{Simplify.}$$

$$d \approx 12 \qquad \text{Round to the nearest whole number.}$$

It will take about 12 days to produce 200 thousand barrels.

Need Help?

For help with dividing decimals, see Skills Handbook, page 769.

iTEXT Interactive lesson includes instant self-check, tutorials, and activities.

2. **Postage** You paid $7.70 to mail a package that weighed 5.5 lb. Write and solve an equation to find the cost per pound.

2 Using Multiplication to Solve Equations

To solve an equation involving division, multiply each side by the same nonzero number.

3 EXAMPLE Multiplying to Solve an Equation

Solve $\frac{m}{-7.2} = -12.5$.

$$\frac{m}{-7.2} = -12.5$$

$$\frac{m}{-7.2}(-7.2) = -12.5(-7.2) \qquad \text{Multiply each side by } -7.2.$$

$$m = 90 \qquad \text{Simplify.}$$

✓ **Check Understanding** Example 3

3. Solve each equation.

a. $\frac{r}{-6.0} = 0.5$ b. $\frac{s}{2.5} = 5$ c. $-80 = \frac{t}{4.5}$

4 EXAMPLE Real-World 🌐 Problem Solving

Batting Averages The 1923 baseball season was one of Babe Ruth's best. He was at bat 522 times and had a batting average of 0.393, rounded to the nearest thousandth. The batting average formula is $a = \frac{h}{n}$, where a is the batting average, h is the number of hits, and n is the number of times at bat. Use the formula to find the number of hits Babe Ruth made.

$$a = \frac{h}{n}$$

$$0.393 = \frac{h}{522} \qquad \text{Replace } a \text{ with 0.393 and } n \text{ with 522.}$$

$$(0.393)(522) = \frac{h}{522}(522) \qquad \text{Multiply each side by 522.}$$

$$h = 205.146 \qquad \text{Simplify.}$$

$$h \approx 205 \qquad \text{Since } h \text{ (hits) represents an integer, round to the nearest integer.}$$

Babe Ruth made 205 hits.

✓ **Check Understanding** Example 4

4. Suppose your batting average is 0.222. You have batted 54 times. How many hits do you have?

Real-World 🌐 Connection

During his professional career, Babe Ruth was at bat 8,399 times and had a batting average of 0.342.

EXERCISES

For more exercises, see *Extra Practice*.

Practice and Problem Solving

A Practice by Example

**Examples 1 and 2
(page 152)**

Solve each equation.

1. $0.8s = -6.4$ **2.** $0.8x = 0.48$ **3.** $-0.5y = -0.73$

4. $2x = -4.88$ **5.** $-0.3y = 7.53$ **6.** $2.21 = 1.7w$

7. $1.92 = 1.6s$ **8.** $3.2n = 27.52$ **9.** $0.7x = 2.8$

10. Manufacturing A factory produces an average of seven thousand televisions per day. About how many days will it take to produce 63.5 thousand televisions?

11. Postage You paid $5.30 to mail a package that weighed 2.5 lb. Write and solve an equation to find the mailing cost per pound.

**Examples 3 and 4
(page 153)**

Solve each equation.

12. $\frac{n}{2.3} = -4.8$ **13.** $0.97 = \frac{c}{-2}$ **14.** $\frac{h}{7} = -8$

15. $\frac{n}{1.7} = 0.22$ **16.** $\frac{k}{2.01} = 0.04$ **17.** $120 = \frac{v}{3.8}$

18. $9 = \frac{a}{1.5}$ **19.** $\frac{m}{7.08} = -100$ **20.** $-200 = \frac{f}{4}$

21. Batting Averages During the 1954 baseball season with the New York Yankees, Yogi Berra was at bat 584 times and had a batting average of 0.307. Use the batting-average formula in Example 4 to find the number of hits Berra made.

B Apply Your Skills

Solve each equation.

22. $6.4x = 0.2816$ **23.** $-5.1z = -11.73$

24. $0.004m = 0.12$ **25.** $4.5 = m \div (-3.3)$

26. $-33.04 = \frac{z}{-0.03}$ **27.** $-0.45 = x \div 12$

28. a. Error Analysis Harry found 324.8 as a solution for the equation $4x = 81.2$. What was Harry's error?

   b. Estimation How could Harry have used estimation to check whether his answer was reasonable?

Write an equation for each sentence. Solve for the variable.

29. The product of a number n and -7.3 is 30.66.

30. The quotient of a number n divided by -4.5 equals 200.6.

31. A number n divided by -2.35 equals 400.9.

32. a. Batting Averages Your batting average is 0.244, and you have been at bat 82 times. How many hits do you have?

   b. Writing in Math Why is it necessary to round your answer in part (a) to the nearest integer?

154 Chapter 3 Decimals and Equations

33. Utilities Jan pays $.08 per kilowatt-hour for electricity. Her electric bill is $59.22. Write and solve an equation to find how many kilowatt-hours of electricity Jan used.

34. Number Sense The weight of a record-setting onion was 12.25 lb. An average-sized onion weighs 0.5 lb. About how many average-sized onions have a total weight equal to the record-setting onion?

C Challenge

35. Measurement If you know a length ℓ in meters, you can multiply the length by 3.28 to find the length in feet f.
   a. Write an equation to model this situation.
   b. A tree is 7.5 m tall. Use your equation to find this height in feet.
   c. A bookshelf is 6 ft tall. What is this height in meters?
   d. A room is 12 ft long and 15 ft wide. Use your equation and the formula for the area of a rectangle to find the area of the room in square meters. Round to the nearest tenth.

36. Reasoning Find values for x and y that satisfy $xy = 0.42$ and $x + y = 1.3$.

37. Batting Averages About how many hits did Babe Ruth have during his professional career? (*Hint*: See page 153.)

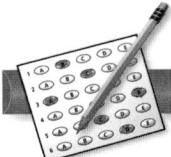

Test Prep

Multiple Choice

38. A group of friends goes out for dinner. The bill is $36.81. If they share the cost equally and each person's share is about $7.35, how many people are in the group?
   A. 4   **B.** 5   **C.** 6   **D.** 7

Take It to the NET
Online lesson quiz at
www.PHSchool.com
Web Code: ada-0306

39. Which equation has 3.2 as its solution?
   F. $20x = 6.4$ **G.** $6.4 = 2x$ **H.** $\frac{x}{2} = 6.4$ **I.** $\frac{x}{6.4} = 2$

Short Response

40. A barber gave enough haircuts in one day to earn $337.50. Each haircut cost $12.50.   **(a)** How many haircuts did the barber give that day?   **(b)** Estimate the amount of money the barber can make in a week.

Mixed Review

Lesson 3-5

Solve each equation.

41. $c + 9 = 3.7$ **42.** $-5.6 = y - 8$ **43.** $4.035 = a - 3.25$

Lesson 2-4

Is the given number a solution of the equation? Show why.

44. $20 - c = 12; c = 8$ **45.** $8 = 2a + 3; a = 0$

Lesson 1-7

46. a. Patterns Multiply $99 \cdot 24, 99 \cdot 25$, and $99 \cdot 26$.
   b. Describe the pattern you found in part (a).
   c. Use the pattern to evaluate $99 \cdot 27$.

3-7

Using the Metric System

What You'll Learn

OBJECTIVE 1
To identify appropriate metric measures

OBJECTIVE 2
To convert metric units

. . . And Why

To solve real-world problems involving metric measures

✓ Check Skills You'll Need

Find each product or quotient.

1. 5×100

2. $14.06 \div 1{,}000$

3. 0.294×10

4. $0.9 \div 100$

For help, go to Skillls Handbook, p. 768.

OBJECTIVE

1 **Identifying Appropriate Metric Measures**

Knowing the approximate size of each metric unit of measure will allow you to choose an appropriate unit.

Key Concepts — Metric Units of Measurement

	Unit	Reference Example
Length	millimeter (mm)	about the thickness of a dime
	centimeter (cm)	about the width of a thumbnail
	meter (m)	about the distance from a doorknob to the floor
	kilometer (km)	a little more than one half mile
Capacity	milliliter (mL)	about 5 drops of water
	liter (L)	a little more than a quart of milk
Mass	milligram (mg)	about the mass of a speck of sawdust
	gram(g)	about the mass of a paper clip
	kilogram (kg)	about one half the mass of this math book

---

1 EXAMPLE **Choosing an Appropriate Unit**

Choose an appropriate metric unit. Explain your choice.

a. height of a classroom chalkboard

Meter; the height of a chalkboard is about twice the distance from the floor to a doorknob.

b. mass of a backpack filled with books

Kilogram; the mass of a backpack filled with books is many times the mass of this textbook.

c. capacity of a birdbath

Liter; several quart bottles of water would fill a birdbath.

✓ Check Understanding Example 1

1. Choose an appropriate metric unit. Explain your choice.

    a. length of a broom   **b.** the mass of an energy bar

    c. mass of a horse   **d.** capacity of a car's gas tank

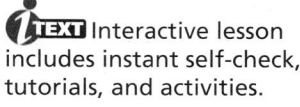
Interactive lesson includes instant self-check, tutorials, and activities.

Estimating With Metric Units

Estimation Choose a reasonable estimate. Explain your choice.

a. capacity of a juice box: 200 mL or 200 L

200 mL; the juice box holds less than a quart of milk.

b. length of a new pencil: 15 cm or 15 m

15 cm; the length of a pencil would be about 15 widths of a thumbnail.

c. mass of a small tube of toothpaste: 100 g or 100 kg

100 g; the mass is about the same as a box of paper clips.

✔ **Check Understanding** Example 2

2. Choose a reasonable estimate. Explain your choice.

a. distance between two cities: 50 mm or 50 km
b. amount of liquid that an eyedropper holds: 10 mL or 10 L

OBJECTIVE

2 **Converting Metric Units**

The metric system uses a decimal system to relate different units to each other. Look at the metric-units chart below. The units highlighted in yellow are the units most often used. From left to right, each unit is 10 times the size of the unit before it.

	milli-	centi-	deci-	UNIT	deka-	hecto-	kilo-
Length	millimeter (mm)	centimeter (cm)	decimeter (dm)	meter (m)	dekameter (dam)	hectometer (hm)	kilometer (km)
Capacity	milliliter (mL)	centiliter (cL)	deciliter (dL)	liter (L)	dekaliter (daL)	hectoliter (hL)	kiloliter (kL)
Mass	milligram (mg)	centigram (cg)	decigram (dg)	gram (g)	dekagram (dag)	hectogram (hg)	kilogram (kg)

You can convert from one unit to another by multiplying or dividing by 10; 100; 1,000; and so on.

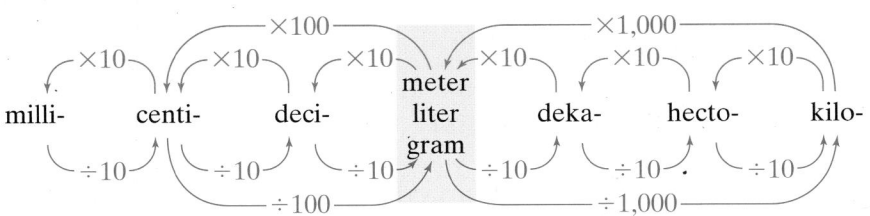

Reading Math

The prefixes, such as *milli, centi,* and *deci,* denote the relative sizes of the units.

To convert from one unit to another in the metric system, find the relationship between the two units.

Remember:

- Multiply if you are going from a larger unit to a smaller unit since there will be more of the smaller units.
- Divide if you are going from a smaller unit to a larger unit since there will be fewer of the larger units.

Need Help?

For help with multiplying and dividing decimals by powers of ten, see Skills Handbook, page 768.

3 EXAMPLE **Converting Between Metric Units**

Mental Math **Complete each statement.**

a. 4.35 L = ▧ mL

$4.35 \cdot 1{,}000 = 4{,}350$

To convert liters to milliliters, multiply by 1,000.

$4.35 \text{ L} = 4{,}350 \text{ mL}$

b. 914 cm = ▧ m

$914 \div 100 = 9.14$

To convert centimeters to meters, divide by 100.

$914 \text{ cm} = 9.14 \text{ m}$

✓ **Check Understanding**   Example 3

3. Complete each statement.

   a. 35 mL = ▧ L   b. ▧ g = 250 kg   c. ▧ cm = 60 m

Real-World 🌎 Connection

The ancient city of Machu Picchu (c. 1450–1550) is located in Peru's Andes Mountains. It is one of the few major pre-Columbian sites found nearly intact.

4 EXAMPLE **Real-World 🌎 Problem Solving**

Geography The ancient Incan city of Machu Picchu is located in Peru. Its altitude is about 2,300 m above sea level. What is Machu Picchu's altitude in kilometers?

Words	altitude in meters	÷	meters per kilometer	=	altitude in kilometers
Equation	2,300	÷	1,000	=	2.3

● Machu Picchu is about 2.3 km above sea level.

✓ **Check Understanding**   Example 4

4. a. The record for the highest a kite has flown is 3.8 km. Find the height of the kite in meters.
   b. **Number Sense** You have a recipe that requires 0.25 L of milk. Your measuring cup is marked only in milliliters. How many milliliters of milk do you need?

EXERCISES

For more exercises, see *Extra Practice*.

Practice and Problem Solving

 Practice by Example

Example 1
(page 156)

Match each quantity with an appropriate metric unit. Explain your choice.

1. length of your thumb
2. mass of a book
3. length of a soccer field
4. amount of water in a fishbowl
5. mass of an eraser
6. amount of fluid in a straw

   A. gram
   B. meter
   C. centimeter
   D. milliliter
   E. liter
   F. kilogram

Example 2
(page 157)

Choose a reasonable estimate. Explain your choice.

7. the mass of a small dog: 5 g or 5 kg
8. amount of liquid you should drink daily: 2,000 mL or 2,000 L
9. the mass of a box of cereal: 350 mg or 350 g

Example 3
(page 158)

Mental Math Complete each statement.

10. $54 \text{ m} = \blacksquare \text{ cm}$
11. $\blacksquare \text{ L} = 234 \text{ mL}$
12. $12 \text{ g} = \blacksquare \text{ kg}$
13. $\blacksquare \text{ m} = 3.01 \text{ km}$
14. $0.25 \text{ m} = \blacksquare \text{ cm}$
15. $\blacksquare \text{ mL} = 7.3 \text{ L}$
16. $595 \text{ g} = \blacksquare \text{ kg}$
17. $35 \text{ m} = \blacksquare \text{ km}$
18. $\blacksquare \text{ mg} = 0.27 \text{ g}$

Example 4
(page 158)

19. **Geography** The shortest street in the world is Elgin Street, in Bacup, England. It is 518 cm long. How many meters long is it?

20. **Biology** A shrew, the mammal with the fastest metabolism, has a mass of only 0.004 kg. What is its mass in grams?

B Apply Your Skills

Choose an appropriate metric unit of measure. Explain your choice.

21. mass of a banana
22. depth of Lake Michigan
23. length of a small calculator
24. mass of a car
25. width of a highway
26. quantity of water in a spoon

27. **Error Analysis** One of the world's largest pearls had a mass of 6,392 g. Camille wrote in her report that the pearl had a mass of 6,392,000 kg. What was her error?

28. **Model Trains** The world's longest model train has 650 cars and is 0.695 km long. How many meters long is the train?

Write the metric unit that makes each statement true.

29. $9.03 \text{ m} = 9,030 \blacksquare$
30. $890 \text{ cm} = 8.9 \blacksquare$
31. $130,000 \blacksquare = 1.3 \text{ km}$

Real-World 🌐 Connection

A hydroelectric power plant at Niagara Falls can produce 2,100,000 kilowatts of electricity.

🌐 **32. Earth Science** The flow of water over Niagara Falls averages 6,008,835,000 mL/s.
   a. On the average, about how many liters of water flow over Niagara Falls each second?
   b. About how many liters flow over the falls in a minute?

Estimation Choose a reasonable estimate. Explain your choice.

33. the width of a sidewalk: 150 cm or 150 m

34. the length of 24 city blocks: 2 m or 2 km

35. the mass of a thumbtack: 1 mg or 1 g

Mental Math Complete each statement.

36. 90,050 mL = ▓ L   **37.** ▓ m = 875 cm   **38.** 620 m = ▓ km

39. 9,120 mg = ▓ g   **40.** 900 km = ▓ m   **41.** 5 g = ▓ kg

42. ▓ cm = 13 km   **43.** 301 kg = ▓ mg   **44.** ▓ km = 562,300 cm

🌐 **45. Nutrition** A world-record grapefruit had a mass of 3,068 g. What was its mass in kilograms?

🌐 **46. Zoology** A hippopotamus is so large that it has a stomach 304.8 cm long, yet it is agile enough to outrun a human. How long is the stomach of a hippopotamus in meters?

Number Sense Match each measurement with its equivalent measurement from the table.

47. 0.015 km   **48.** 1,500 cm   **49.** 150,000 mg

50. 0.15 L   **51.** 15 L   **52.** 1,500 g

A. 15,000 mL	**B.** 150 cm	**C.** 150 g
D. 1.5 kg	**E.** 15 m	**F.** 150 mL
G. 150 kg	**H.** 0.15 mL	**I.** 1,500 mm

🌐 **53. Marine Biology** The blue whale is the largest of all known animals. The largest known blue whale measured 33.58 meters in length.
   a. How many millimeters long was this whale?
   b. How many kilometers long was this whale?

ⓒ Challenge 🌐 **54. Writing in Math** The prefix kilo- means "one thousand," and the prefix milli- means "one thousandth." What do the prefixes tell you about kilometer and kilogram, and milliliter and milligram?

🌐 **55. Physical Fitness** You walk about 3 mi/h.
   a. Approximately how many kilometers can you walk in an hour?
   b. How many meters can you walk in an hour?

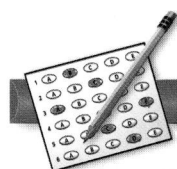
Gridded Reponse

56. The albatross has a wingspan of 3,350 mm, the largest wingspan of any bird. What is the wingspan of an albatross in meters?

57. What part of a second is a millisecond?

58. A worm is about 143 mm long. What is the length of the worm in meters?

59. A pitcher threw a baseball 95 mi/h at a baseball game. Rounded to the nearest tenth, how many feet per second is this?

60. Sean tries to drink $2\frac{1}{2}$ qt of water every day. How many gallons does he average in a week?

Take It to the NET
Online lesson quiz at
www.PHSchool.com
Web Code: ada-0307

Mixed Review

Lesson 3-6 🌐 **61. Knot Tying** Clinton Bailey, Sr., holds the record for knot tying. He tied six different rope knots in 8.1 s. Write and solve an equation to find his average time per knot.

Lesson 3-2 **Estimate each product or quotient.**

62. $28.134 \div 3.75$ **63.** $8.517 \cdot 9.82$ **64.** $101.49 \div 9.51$

Lessons 2-9 and 2-10 **Solve each inequality.**

65. $a - 5 \geq 16$ **66.** $n + 8 < -7$ **67.** $-3r \leq 21$

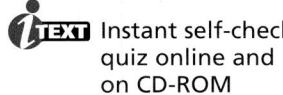
Checkpoint Quiz 2   **Lessons 3-5 through 3-7**

TEXT Instant self-check quiz online and on CD-ROM

Solve each equation.

1. $0.5m = 0.125$ **2.** $d \div 0.3 = 28.5$ **3.** $y - 135.43 = -5.43$

4. $12.2 = 4x$ **5.** $29.25 = 4.5w$ **6.** $k + 870.9 = 1,000.5$

Choose the most reasonable estimate. Explain your choice.

7. height of a standard house window: 1.5 cm or 1.5 m

8. capacity of a shampoo bottle: 500 mL or 500 L

Complete each statement.

9. 95 mL = ■ L   **10.** ■ cm = 76.5 km

11. ■ km = 675 m   **12.** 7.1 kg = ■ g

🌐 **13. Horses** The world's smallest horse had a mass of only 9.1 kg. What was the mass of the horse in grams?

Precision and Significant Digits

The pin at the right measures about 5 cm. A more precise measurement is 4.5 cm. An even more precise measurement is 46 mm. The smaller the units on the scale of a measuring instrument, the more precise the measurement is.

1 EXAMPLE

Choose the more precise measurement.

a. 5 g or 8 mg
Since a milligram is a smaller unit of measure than a gram, 8 mg is more precise than 5 g.

b. 2.72 m or 3.5 m
A hundredth of a meter is a smaller unit of measure than a tenth of a meter. So 2.72 m is more precise than 3.5 m.

A calculation will be only as precise as the least precise measurement used in the calculation. So, round your results to match the precision of the least precise measurement.

2 EXAMPLE

Add the lengths 6.31 m, 5.447 m, and 2.8 m.

$6.31 + 5.447 + 2.8 = 14.557$

Rounded to tenths ≈ 14.6 m

The least precise measurement is 2.8 m. Round the sum to the nearest tenth of a meter.

Digits that represent an actual measurement are *significant digits*. Nonzero digits (1–9) are always significant. The rules below will help you decide whether a zero is a significant digit.

Type of Number	Which Zeros Are Significant	Example
decimal numbers between 0 and 1	Zeros to the left of *all* the nonzero digits are not significant. All other zeros are significant.	significant digits 0.006040 not significant digits
positive integers	Zeros to the right of *all* the nonzero digits are not significant (unless specifically known to be). Zeros between nonzero digits are significant.	significant digits 203,400 not significant digits
noninteger decimal numbers greater than 1	All zeros are significant.	significant digits 350.07050

How many significant digits are in 0.0504 m?

The 5 and the 4 are significant. The zero between them is significant. The other zeros are not significant. There are three significant digits.

When you multiply or divide measurements, round your answer to match the least number of significant digits in the problem.

A plot for a new house measures 152.6 m by 121 m. What is the area of the plot? Use significant digits.

┌──── **3 significant digits**

$152.6 \cdot 121 = 18,464.6$ ←──── **Multiply.**

└──── **4 significant digits**

The area is 18,500 m². ←──── **Round the area to 3 significant digits.**

EXERCISES

Choose the more precise measurement.

1. 3 m or 5.2 m **2.** 8 mL or 9.5 L **3.** 1.89 km or 8.7 cm **4.** 1.9 kg or 1.87 kg

5. Error Analysis Your friend says that 4.35 km is more precise than 5.2 cm because a hundredths unit is a smaller unit than a tenths unit. What mistake did your friend make?

Find each sum or difference. Round to the place value of the less precise measurement.

6. 5.6 g + 8 g **7.** 8.35 kg + 6.2 kg **8.** 8.2 km − 1.75 km **9.** 9 cm − 2.3 cm

Determine the number of significant digits in each measurement.

10. 0.069 m **11.** 100.5 L **12.** 3,400 kL **13.** 5.2100 km

Find each product or quotient. Use significant digits.

14. 1,234 in. · 31 in. **15.** 0.0702 ft · 227 ft **16.** 16,250 m ÷ 14.5 s **17.** 132.5 cm · 43.2 cm

3-8 Problem Solving

Simplify the Problem

What You'll Learn

OBJECTIVE 1
To solve complex problems by first solving simpler cases

. . . And Why

To solve real-world problems involving motion

✔ Check Skills You'll Need

Write a rule for each number pattern. Find the next three numbers in the pattern.

1. 0, 6, 12, 18, . . .

2. −18, −9, 0, 9, . . .

3. 0, 2, 1, 3, 2, 4, 3, . . .

4. 7, 6, 8, 7, 9, 8, 10, . . .

💬 For help, go to Lesson 1-7.

Math Strategies in Action
Scientists often encounter problems that are very complicated. When they work to develop a new vaccine or develop a new method to fight disease, they usually work on smaller or simpler pieces of the problem first. Sometimes when you solve a problem, it helps to solve other problems that have similar conditions. Here is a well-known problem that shows you how to use this strategy.

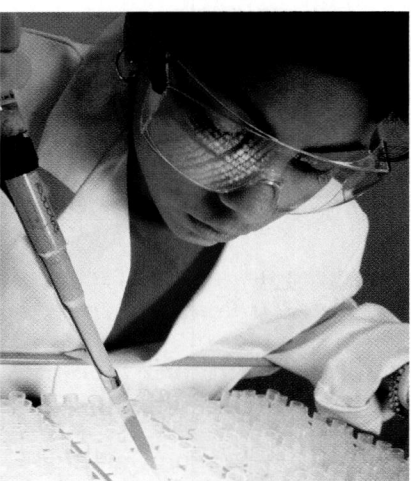

1 EXAMPLE   Real-World 🌐 Problem Solving

A snail is trying to escape from a well 10 ft deep. The snail can climb 2 ft each day, but each night it slides back 1 ft. How many days will the snail take to climb out of the well?

Read and Understand

A snail needs to climb 10 ft to escape from a well. It can climb 2 ft per day. At night the snail slides back 1 ft.

1. How far up the well will the snail be after the first day and the first night?

2. How far up the well will the snail be after the second day?

3. How far up the well will the snail be after the second day and the second night?

Plan and Solve

At first you might think that the snail progresses 1 ft each day and will therefore take 10 days to escape. This answer is wrong, however, because it leaves out an important part of the problem.

Try to solve a simpler problem. Change the problem to a simpler one based on a 3-ft well, and then try a 4-ft well to see if there is a pattern.

Time	3-ft Well	4-ft Well
Day 1	Up 2 ft from bottom	Up 2 ft from bottom
Night 1	Up 1 ft from bottom	Up 1 ft from bottom
Day 2	Up 3 ft from bottom; OUT!	Up 3 ft from bottom
Night 2		Up 2 ft from bottom
Day 3		Up 4 ft from bottom; OUT!

4. Using the information from the simpler 3-ft-well and 4-ft-well problems, describe the pattern.

5. How many days will the snail take to escape from the 10-ft well?

Look Back and Check

You can check your answer by drawing a diagram.

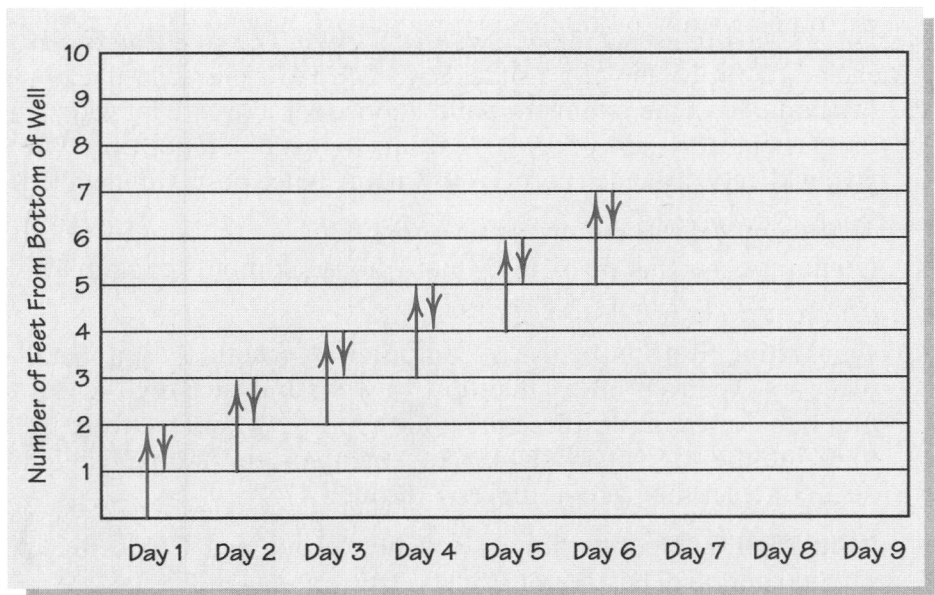

Check Understanding

6. Copy and complete the diagram to check your answer.

EXERCISES

For more exercises, see *Extra Practice*.

Practice and Problem Solving

A Practice by Example

Example 1
(page 164)

Solve by simplifying each problem.

1. You decide to number the 58 pages in your journal from 1 to 58. How many digits do you have to write?

2. **Sports** In a tennis tournament, each athlete plays one match against each of the other athletes. There are 12 athletes scheduled to play in the tournament. How many matches will be played?

3. **Geometry** What is the total number of triangles in the figure at the right?

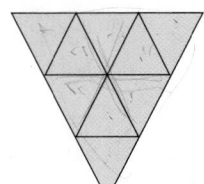

B Apply Your Skills

Solve using any strategy.

4. The school store buys pencils for $.20 each. It sells the pencils for $.25 each. How much profit does the store make if it sells five dozen pencils?

Strategies

- Account for All Possibilities
- Draw a Diagram
- Look for a Pattern
- Make a Model
- Make a Table
- Simplify the Problem
- Simulate the Problem
- Solve by Graphing
- Try, Test, Revise
- Use Multiple Strategies
- Work Backward
- Write an Equation
- Write a Proportion

5. **Construction** To accommodate a wheelchair, a builder installed countertops that are 0.75 ft lower than the original ones. The new countertops are 2.5 ft high. How high were the original countertops?

6. What is the total number of squares in the figure at the right?

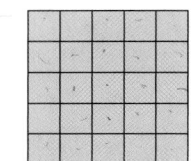

7. There are 10 girls and 8 boys at a party. A cartoonist wants to sketch a picture of each boy with each girl. How many sketches are required?

8. **Fencing** A rancher wants to build a fence for a square lot with dimensions of 50 yd by 50 yd. He wants to install a fence post every 5 yd with a post at each corner. How many fence posts will he need?

9. **Writing in Math** The houses on your street are numbered 1 to 120. No numbers are skipped. How many house numbers contain at least one 5? Explain your strategy.

C Challenge

10. **Typesetting** Before the use of computers, typesetters used metal pieces of type to print each letter in a word and each digit in a number. For example, three pieces of type—1, 4, and 8—were used to create the page number 148. How many pieces of type would be needed to set the page numbers 1 through 476?

11. **Population** The population of Rancho Cucamonga, California, is 117,000 people. The area of Rancho Cucamonga is 37.8 mi^2. Find the population density—the number of people per square mile. Show your work.

12. You are hiking with three friends. You pass a group of six hikers going the other way. Each person in one group greets each person in the other group. How many greetings are there? Explain.

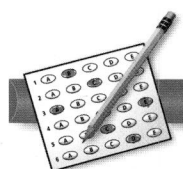

Test Prep

Multiple Choice

What is the solution of each equation?

13. $x - 8 = -4.8$

A. -12.8 **B.** -3.2 **C.** 3.2 **D.** 12.8

Take It to the NET
Online lesson quiz at
www.PHSchool.com
Web Code: ada-0308

14. $8 + c = -2.3$

F. -10.3 **G.** -5.7 **H.** 5.7 **I.** 10.3

15. $7.53 = -0.3y$

A. 25.1 **B.** 2.26 **C.** -2.26 **D.** -25.1

Short Response

16. A corral is ringed by 60 ft of fencing with posts every 4 ft. How many fence posts are there? Show your work.

Mixed Review

Lesson 3-7   **Measurement**   **Complete each statement.**

17. $27 \text{ cm} = \blacksquare \text{ m}$ **18.** $5{,}200 \text{ km} = \blacksquare \text{ m}$ **19.** $2{,}000 \text{ mg} = \blacksquare \text{ g}$

20. $0.5 \text{ L} = \blacksquare \text{ mL}$ **21.** $3 \text{ m} = \blacksquare \text{ cm}$ **22.** $6 \text{ kg} = \blacksquare \text{ mg}$

Lesson 3-3   **23. Test Scores**   Your test scores so far this semester are 100, 90, 82, 96, and 78. You have one more 100-point test to take. After you complete the last test, what is your highest possible average?

Lesson 3-1   **Estimate using front-end estimation.**

24. $\$9.54 + \$1.25$ **25.** $\$6.72 + \$5.28$ **26.** $\$12.19 + \$5.66$

Math at Work

Woodworker

Woodworkers cut, shape, assemble, and finish wood to create tables, chairs, and other types of furniture. To create these items, woodworkers must plan and carry out many individual steps in sequence.

Machines used in professional woodworking shops cut and shape wood with great precision. The most sophisticated machines are controlled by computer programs. Woodworkers can enhance their skills by taking mathematics and computer courses that develop their ability to think three-dimensionally.

Take It to the NET   For more information about woodworkers, go to **www.PHSchool.com**.
Web Code: adb-2031

An extended-response question can be worth as many as four points. It often has multiple parts. To get full credit, you need to answer each part and show all of your work or justify your thinking.

EXAMPLE

To get a 90 for this grading period, Jerilyn needs a test average of 94.5. She had a 93.2 average on her first three tests and scored 97 on the fourth test. **(a)** Explain in words how to find the next score she needs. **(b)** Write an equation to find the fifth test score. **(c)** Solve your equation.

Here are three responses with the points each received.

4 points	3 points	1 point
There are 5 tests. For a test average of 94.5, the sum of the test scores must be 5 times 94.5, or 472.5 points.	There are 5 tests. For a test average of 94.5, the sum of the test scores must be 5 times 94.5, or 472.5 points.	Let g = grade on fifth test. $93.2 + 97 + g = 90$ $190.2 + g = 90$ $g = 90 - 190.2$ $g = 100.2$
Let g = grade on fifth test. $3(93.2) + 97 + g = 472.5$ $376.6 + g = 472.5$ $g = 472.5 - 376.6$ $g = 95.9$ Jerilyn must score 95.9 or higher on her fifth test.	Let g = grade on fifth test. $3(93.2) + 97 + g = 472.5$ $276.9 + 97 + g = 472.5$ $373.9 + g = 472.5$ $g = 472.5 - 373.9$ $g = 98.6$ Jerilyn must score 98.6.	

The 4-point response shows the work and gives a written answer to the problem. Note that it identifies the variable before writing the equation. The 3-point response contains a computational error, but the student completed all parts. The 1-point response shows an incorrect equation, and it does not explain the process.

EXERCISES

Use the Example above to do each exercise.

1. **Error Analysis** What is the error in the 3-point response?

2. Write a possible 2-point response for the problem. Explain why it is worth 2 points.

Chapter Review

Vocabulary

compatible numbers (p. 133)	mean (p. 137)	median (p. 137)	outlier (p. 138)
formula (p. 143)	measures of central tendency (p. 137)	mode (p. 137)	perimeter (p. 144)

Reading Math
Understanding Vocabulary

Choose the vocabulary word that completes each sentence.

1. The sum of a group of data items divided by the number of data items is the ? .

2. Numbers that are easy to divide are called ? .

3. The data item that occurs most often in a group is the ? .

4. A data item that is much greater or much less than the rest of the data items in a group is a(n) ? .

5. When an odd number of data items are written in order, the middle item is the ? .

6. An equation that shows a relationship between quantities that are represented by variables is a(n) ? .

7. Numbers that describe groups of data items are called ? .

8. The distance around a figure is the ? .

Take It to the NET
Online vocabulary quiz
at **www.PHSchool.com**
Web Code: adj-0351

Skills and Concepts

3-1 Objectives

▼ To round decimals (p. 127)

▼ To estimate sums and differences (p. 128)

You can estimate the sum of decimals by rounding, front-end estimating, or clustering.

You can estimate the difference of decimals by rounding.

Estimate each sum or difference. State which method you used.

9. $3.14 + 6.952$

10. $10.2538 - 6.095$

11. $14.451 + 9.736$

12. $14.27 - 4.268$

13. $20.681 + 19.39 + 20.56$

14. $12.814 - 6.3791$

15. $9.0426 + 2.7182$

16. $21.9384 - 15.639$

17. $6.257 + 6.129 + 6.34$

18. $19.83 - 14.268$

19. Explain when you would use each estimation method named above to estimate a sum of decimals. Use examples.

20. **Weather** Last year Lake Jones rose to 672.42 feet during the spring floods. This year Lake Jones rose to 711.36 feet. About how much higher did the lake rise this year?

3-2 Objectives

▼ To estimate products (p. 132)

▼ To estimate quotients (p. 133)

You can estimate a product by rounding. You can estimate a quotient of two decimals by using **compatible numbers.**

Estimate each product or quotient.

21. 8.15(6.04)   **22.** 19.28 ÷ 5.439   **23.** 1.9 · 4.92

24. 25.1 ÷ 4.87   **25.** 12.497 · 0.894   **26.** 59.3581 ÷ 11.5304

27. 3.59(−2.3291)   **28.** −17.45 ÷ 3.059   **29.** (−2.0936)(−5.6892)

3-3 Objectives

▼ To find mean, median, and mode of a set of data (p. 137)

▼ To choose the best measure of central tendency (p. 139)

You can use a **measure of central tendency** to describe a collection of data. The **mean** is the sum of the data items divided by the number of data items. The **median** is the middle value or the mean of the two middle values when the data are written in order. The **mode** is the data item that occurs most often. An **outlier** is a data item that is much greater or much less than the rest of the data items.

Find the mean, median, and mode. When an answer is not an integer, round to the nearest tenth. Identify any outliers.

30. 2, 3, 6, 2, 8, 9, 5, 10, 4, 5   **31.** 16.1, 16.3, 15.9, 16.2, 16.3, 16.3, 15.8

32. 32, 35, 31, 57, 33, 30, 34   **33.** 0.1, 7.9, 0.2, 0.3, 0.1, 0.2, 0.1, 0.1, 0.3

Which measure of central tendency best describes each situation? Explain.

34. the favorite radio stations of teenagers in your neighborhood

35. the numbers of videos owned by students in your class

36. the prices of 8-oz containers of yogurt at six local grocery stores

3-4 Objectives

▼ To substitute into formulas (p. 143)

▼ To use the formula for the perimeter of a rectangle (p. 144)

A **formula** is an equation that shows a relationship between quantities that are represented by variables. You can use formulas to find such things as **perimeter,** area, and distance.

Evaluate each formula for the values given.

37. distance: $d = rt$
when $r = 35$ mi/h and
$t = 2$ h

38. area of a rectangle: $A = \ell w$
when $\ell = 16$ mm and
$w = 24$ mm

39. Circumference: $C = 2\pi r$
when $r = 6$ in. Use 3.14 for π.

40. perimeter of a square: $P = 4s$
when $s = 13$ cm

To solve a one-step equation, use an inverse operation and a property of equality to get the variable alone on one side of the equation.

Solve each equation.

41. $n + 3.8 = 10.9$ **42.** $y - 6.72 = 2.53$ **43.** $h + 0.67 = -1.34$

44. $t - 2.7 = 23.5$ **45.** $12.9 + x = 3.8$ **46.** $5.7 = b - 4.9$

47. $6.3m = 15.75$ **48.** $a \div 4.9 = 8.33$ **49.** $v \cdot 7.1 = 80.23$

50. $c \div 12.5 = 77.5$ **51.** $-5.7z = 110.58$ **52.** $d \div 4.75 = -38.95$

53. Finance On Monday a stock is worth $3.20 per share. By Friday the stock is worth $2.64 per share.
   a. Write an equation to model the change in price.
   b. Solve the equation to find the amount by which the price changed.

The **metric system** of measurement uses a decimal system to relate units to one another. To measure, you must choose an appropriate unit of measure.

Choose an appropriate metric unit of measure. Explain each choice.

54. height of a building   **55.** mass of a bicycle   **56.** amount of milk in a glass

Mental Math **Complete each statement.**

57. $0.85 \, m = \blacksquare \, cm$ **58.** $160 \, mL = \blacksquare \, L$ **59.** $2.3 \, m = \blacksquare \, cm$

60. $1.6 \, kg = \blacksquare \, g$ **61.** $0.62 \, L = \blacksquare \, mL$ **62.** $80 \, g = \blacksquare \, kg$

63. Explain why centimeters would be an inappropriate unit to measure the height of a mature oak tree.

When a problem is complicated, you can solve related simpler problems to better understand the problem.

64. Reasoning A school's lockers are numbered 1 to 100. One hundred students enter the school one at a time. The first student opens the lockers. The second student closes the even-numbered lockers. The third student either closes or opens every third locker. The remaining students continue the pattern. After all the students have passed the lockers, which lockers are open?

Chapter Test

 **Take It to the NET**
Online chapter test at
www.PHSchool.com
Web Code: ada-0352

Estimate each value.

1. $6.43 - 4.079$

2. $2.06 + 3.91$

3. $5.97 - 1.674$

4. $6.025 + 0.35$

5. $8.54 + 2.3$

6. $6.25 \cdot 9.87$

7. $12.89 \div 3.04$

8. $1.76 \cdot 3.93$

9. $4.96 \div 2.49$

10. $3.2 \cdot 14.69$

Find the mean, median, and mode. When an answer is not an integer, round to the nearest tenth. Identify any outliers.

11. $11, 12, 9, 13, 10, 12, 11, 14, 12$

12. $5.3, 5.6, 5.2, 5.0, 5.4, 5.6, 5.1, 5.0$

13. $10.6, 9.8, 11.6, 29.1, 3.4, 11.4, 12.7$

14. $8.7, 8.5, 8.7, 8.5, 8.6, 8.5, 8.7, 8.6$

Evaluate each formula for the given values.

15. area of a rectangle: $A = \ell w$
when $\ell = 3.8$ in. and $w = 1.5$ in.

16. perimeter of a square: $P = 4s$
when $s = 4.7$ cm

17. perimeter of a rectangle: $P = 2\ell + 2w$
when $\ell = 2.9$ m and $w = 6.05$ m

Solve each equation.

18. $x + 7.8 = 12.5$

19. $n - 5.9 = 0.5$

20. $4.1 + c = -1.2$

21. $d - 6.3 = 11$

22. $-9.7 + h = 10.3$

23. $m \div 2.7 = 14.58$

24. $h \cdot 4.7 = 30.55$

25. $b \div (-7.8) = -79.56$

26. $-3.4t = 30.94$

Write an appropriate metric unit of measure for each quantity.

27. the height of a truck

28. the capacity of a standard shampoo bottle

29. the mass of a pineapple

30. the width of a paperback book

Complete.

31. $4.5 \text{ m} = \blacksquare \text{ cm}$

32. $68 \text{ mL} = \blacksquare \text{ L}$

33. $90 \text{ kg} = \blacksquare \text{ g}$

34. $6,700 \text{ cm} = \blacksquare \text{ m}$

35. $4 \text{ L} = \blacksquare \text{ mL}$

36. $50.2 \text{ g} = \blacksquare \text{ kg}$

For Exercises 37 and 38, write an equation, and then solve.

37. Shopping You spend $6.50 on a pair of gloves. You now have $7.00. How much money did you have originally?

38. Reptiles The fastest speed recorded for a reptile on land is 9.7 m/s for a spiny-tailed iguana. At this rate, how long would it take this iguana to travel 116.4 m?

39. Geography Madrid and Barcelona are cities in Spain. The distance between them is 636,000 m. What is this in kilometers?

40. You have an 18-ft metal pipe. How many cuts must you make to cut the pipe into 2-ft-long pieces?

41. Data Analysis Which measure of central tendency best describes the weights of the dogs in one neighborhood?

15 lb, 20 lb, 18 lb, 27 lb, 15 lb, 70 lb

A. mean

B. median

C. mode

D. all of the above

42. Writing in Math Explain how the outlier in the data set affects the mean.

$3, 2, 6, 3, 5, 4, 15, 4, 3$

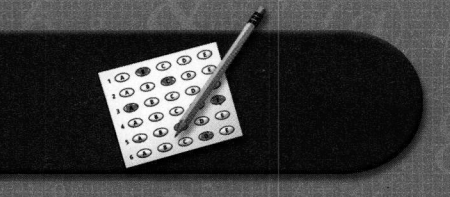

Reading Comprehension Read the passages below. Then answer the questions on the basis of what is stated or implied in each passage.

> **Milk and Calcium** Doctors and dieticians agree that calcium is an important part of good nutrition as calcium helps to build and maintain strong bones. The recommended daily intake of calcium for adults is 1,000 mg. The National Academy of Sciences recommends that people from 9 to 18 years of age get at least 1,300 mg of calcium per day. Milk, perhaps the best-known source for calcium, has 300 mg of calcium per cup.

1. Which is true about n, the number of milligrams of calcium recommended daily for an adult?
   A. $n > 1,000$ B. $n < 1,000$
   C. $n = 1,000$ D. $n = 10,000$

2. Which is true about c, the number of milligrams of calcium recommended daily for people ages 9 to 18?
   F. $c = 1,000$ G. $c > 1,300$
   H. $c < 1,300$ I. $c \geq 1,300$

3. How many more milligrams of calcium per day does a young person need than an adult?
   A. 300 mg   B. 1,000 mg
   C. 1,300 mg   D. 10,000 mg

4. How many full cups of milk does 14-year-old Janet have to drink if she is going to get her daily-recommended amount of calcium from milk?

> **Other Sources of Calcium** Although one slice of cheese pizza supplies 220 milligrams of calcium, dairy products are not the only source of calcium. For example, $\frac{3}{4}$ cup of a certain brand of cereal supplies 330 mg of calcium, 1 cup of broccoli supplies 90 mg of calcium, and 3 oz of canned salmon with bones supplies 180 mg of calcium. You can get 300 mg from one cup of calcium-fortified orange juice. However, it is important to know that exercising can do as much to help you build strong bones as calcium in your diet.

5. Which of these foods has the most calcium per portion?
   F. cheese pizza   G. cereal
   H. broccoli   I. salmon

6. How many cups of broccoli give you 45 mg of calcium?
   A. 0.25 cup   B. 0.5 cup
   C. 1 cup   D. 2 cups

7. How many cups of orange juice would supply exactly 1,000 mg of calcium?

8. How else can you build strong bones besides getting enough calcium from food?

9. From the items in the passage, plan what you could eat that would give you exactly 1,300 mg of calcium in a day. Make a list to show your one-day diet.

Real-World Snapshots

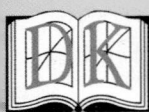

What's $10 Worth?

Applying Decimals If you shop with an older adult, you may have heard the statement, "Ten dollars isn't worth what it used to be!" Of course, $10 is always worth ten $1 bills, or 40 quarters, or 100 dimes. That doesn't change. What does change is the price of items. For example, a stamp for a letter cost $.03 back in 1950. The 2002 cost of a stamp, $.37, is more than twelve times that price. Back in 1950, you could buy 333 first-class stamps with a $10 bill. Today, that same $10 bill will get you only 27 stamps!

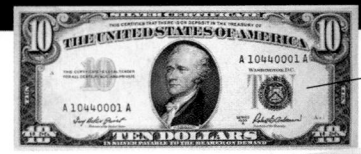

A $10 bill in 1950 looked like this.

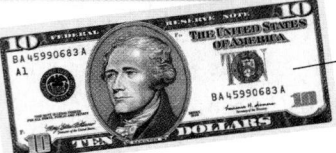

A $10 bill today looks like this.

$10 Bills

Federal Reserve Notes began circulating in 1913. The design remained virtually unchanged until May 2000.

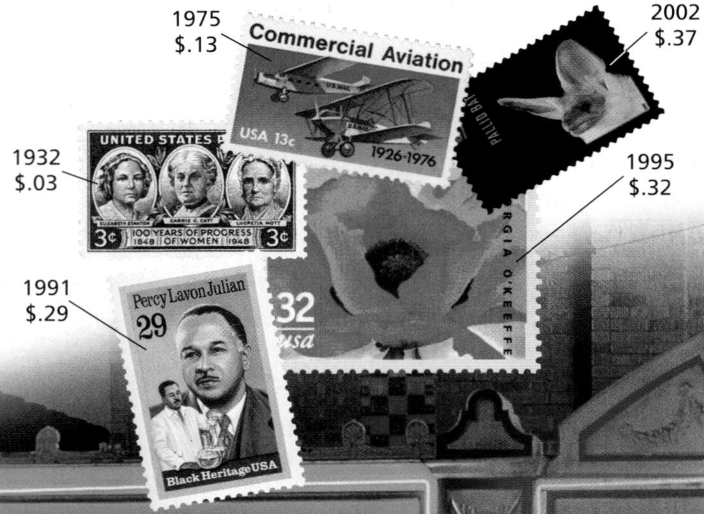

1975 $.13
Commercial Aviation
2002 $.37
1932 $.03
1995 $.32
1991 $.29
Percy Lavon Julian

Averages — Then and Now

Item	1950	2002
New home	$9,422	$169,000
Weekly income	$29	$572
Washing machine	$64.95	$379

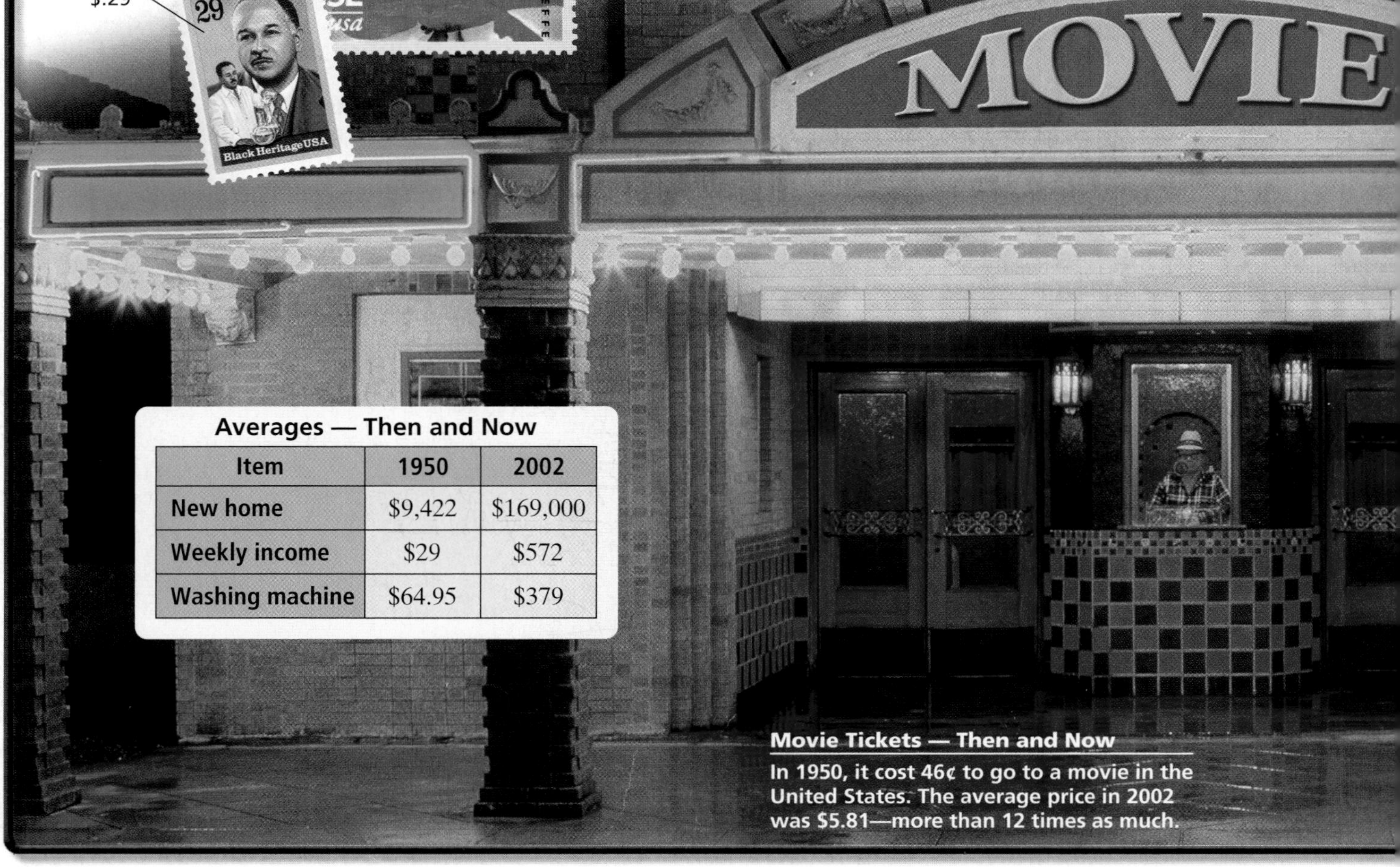

MOVIE

Movie Tickets — Then and Now

In 1950, it cost 46¢ to go to a movie in the United States. The average price in 2002 was $5.81—more than 12 times as much.

Full Service

In the 1950s, gas-station attendants pumped your gas, checked your oil, and washed your windshield. Mechanics were ready to help if something was wrong with your car.

Activity

Suppose you have a $10 bill.

1. How many pounds of steak could you buy in 1950? In 2002?

2. **a.** How many gallons of gas could you buy in 1950?
   b. How much would that same gas have cost you in 2002?

3. Compare the prices of milk.
   a. What fraction of the 2002 price is the 1950 price?
   b. How many times the 1950 price is the 2002 price?

4. Suppose you earn the average weekly income and you buy the items on the shopping list.
   a. What is your total cost in 1950? In 2002?
   b. What part of your weekly income is this in 1950? In 2002?
   c. **Writing in Math** In which year is the average worker better off, 1950 or 2002? Explain.

Shopping List

2 loaves bread
1 lb coffee
2 gal milk
1 dozen muffins
2 bars soap
1 lb steak
3 cans tuna

Prices of Common Items

Item	Cost in 1950	Cost in 2002
Bread (1 loaf)	$.18	$1.49
Coffee (1 lb)	$.93	$3.29
Cookies (12-oz package)	$.39	$2.59
Gas (1 gal)	$.20	$1.35
Milk (1 gal)	$.92	$3.05
Muffins (6)	$.24	$2.89
Soap (2 bars)	$.29	$1.79
Steak (1 lb)	$.77	$3.89
Tuna (1 large can)	$.25	$1.39

Take It to the NET For more information about the 1950s, go to **www.PHSchool.com**.
Web Code: ade-0353

175

Where You've Been

- In Chapter 1, you learned how to add, subtract, multiply, and divide integers.

- In Chapter 2, you solved equations by adding, subtracting, multiplying, and dividing.

- In Chapter 3, you estimated solutions and solved equations with decimals.

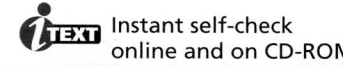
Instant self-check
online and on CD-ROM

 **Diagnosing Readiness**

(For help, go to the lesson in green.)

Multiplying Three or More Factors (Lesson 1-9)

Find each product.

1. $12 \cdot 12 \cdot 12$ **2.** $(-4)(-4)(-4)$ **3.** $9 \cdot 9 \cdot 9 \cdot 9$

4. $5 \cdot 5 \cdot 5 \cdot 5 \cdot 5 \cdot 5$ **5.** $8 \cdot 8 \cdot 8$ **6.** $(-2)(-2)(-2)(-2)(-2)(-2)$

Recalling Multiplication Facts (Previous Course)

Write two numbers that, when multiplied, result in each product.

7. 12   **8.** 45   **9.** 18   **10.** 63   **11.** 24

12. 50   **13.** 32   **14.** 81   **15.** 54   **16.** 60

17. 28   **18.** 56   **19.** 44   **20.** 36   **21.** 72

Dividing Whole Numbers (Skills Handbook, p. 760)

Find each quotient.

22. $720 \div 8$ **23.** $7{,}200 \div 8$ **24.** $6\overline{)132}$

25. $3\overline{)147}$ **26.** $\frac{189}{9}$ **27.** $\frac{450}{10}$

28. $424 \div 2$ **29.** $700 \div 5$ **30.** $92 \div 4$

31. $5\overline{)135}$ **32.** $\frac{273}{3}$ **33.** $10\overline{)1{,}300}$

Factors, Fractions, and Exponents

Where You're Going

In this chapter, you will learn how to

- Simplify expressions with exponents.
- Simplify fractions.
- Write and calculate in scientific notation.
- Solve problems by accounting for all possibilities.

 **Real-World Snapshots** Applying what you learn, on pages 228–229 you will solve problems about cicada emergence cycles.

4-1   Divisibility and Factors

OBJECTIVE

1   Using Divisibility Tests

What You'll Learn

OBJECTIVE

1   To use divisibility tests

OBJECTIVE

2   To find factors

. . . And Why

To solve real-world problems involving arrangements

✔ Check Skills You'll Need

Find each quotient.

1. 480 ÷ 3   **2.** 365 ÷ 5

3. 459 ÷ 9   **4.** 288 ÷ 6

5. $\frac{354}{2}$ **6.** $\frac{354}{3}$

❓ For help, go to Skills Handbook, p. 760.

New Vocabulary

- divisible
- factor

One integer is **divisible** by another if the remainder is 0 when you divide. Because 18 ÷ 3 = 6, 18 is divisible by 3. You can test for divisibility using mental math.

> **Key Concepts**   **Divisibility Rules for 2, 5, and 10**
>
> An integer is divisible by
> - 2 if it ends in 0, 2, 4, 6, or 8.
> - 5 if it ends in 0 or 5.
> - 10 if it ends in 0.
>
> *Even* numbers end in 0, 2, 4, 6, or 8 and are divisible by 2.
> *Odd* numbers end in 1, 3, 5, 7, or 9 and are not divisible by 2.

1 EXAMPLE   **Divisibility by 2, 5, and 10**

Is the first number divisible by the second? Explain.

a. 567 by 2   No; 567 does not end in 0, 2, 4, 6, or 8.

b. 1,015 by 5   Yes; 1,015 ends in 5.

c. 111,120 by 10   Yes; 111,120 ends in 0.

✔ Check Understanding   Example 1

1. Is the first number divisible by the second? Explain.

   a. 160 by 5   **b.** 56 by 10   **c.** 53 by 2   **d.** 1,118 by 2

To see a pattern for divisibility by 3 and 9, compare the answers to the questions asked in this table.

Number	Sum of digits	Is the sum divisible by 3?	Is the sum divisible by 9?	Is the number divisible by 3?	Is the number divisible by 9?
282	2 + 8 + 2 = 12	Yes	No	Yes	No
468	4 + 6 + 8 = 18	Yes	Yes	Yes	Yes
215	2 + 1 + 5 = 8	No	No	No	No
1,017	1 + 0 + 1 + 7 = 9	Yes	Yes	Yes	Yes

ⓘ**TEXT** Interactive lesson includes instant self-check, tutorials, and activities.

The pattern in the table suggests the following rules for divisibility by 3 and 9.

> **Key Concepts** **Divisibility Rules for 3 and 9**
>
> An integer is divisible by
> - 3 if the sum of its digits is divisible by 3.
> - 9 if the sum of its digits is divisible by 9.

2 EXAMPLE **Divisibility by 3 and 9**

Is the first number divisible by the second? Explain.

a. 567 by 3   Yes; $5 + 6 + 7 = 18$. 18 is divisible by 3.

b. 1,015 by 9   No; $1 + 0 + 1 + 5 = 7$. 7 is not divisible by 9.

✓ **Check Understanding** **Example 2**

2. Is the first number divisible by the second? Explain.

   a. 64 by 9   **b.** 472 by 3   **c.** 174 by 3   **d.** 43,542 by 9

OBJECTIVE

2 Finding Factors

You can form the three rectangles at the right with 12 squares. Each rectangle has an area of 12 square units. Their dimensions, 1, 2, 3, 4, 6, and 12, are the *factors* of 12. One integer is a **factor** of another nonzero integer if it divides that integer with remainder zero.

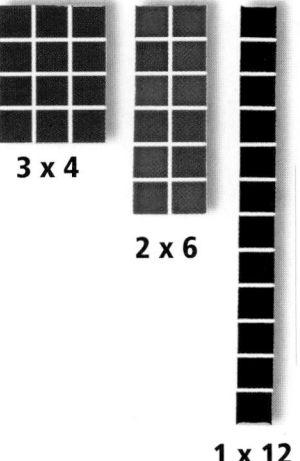

3 x 4

2 x 6

1 x 12

3 EXAMPLE **Real-World** 🌎 **Problem Solving**

Concerts There are 20 students singing at a school concert. Each row of singers must have the same number of students. If there are at least 5 students in each row, what are all the possible arrangements?

   $1 \cdot 20$, $2 \cdot 10$, $4 \cdot 5$ Find the factors of 20.

There can be 1 row of 20 students, 2 rows of 10 students, or 4 rows of 5 students.

✓ **Check Understanding** **Example 3**

3. List the positive factors of each integer.

   a. 10   **b.** 21   **c.** 24   **d.** 31
   e. What are the possible arrangements for Example 3 if there are 36 students singing at the concert?

EXERCISES

For more exercises, see *Extra Practice*.

Practice and Problem Solving

A Practice by Example

Example 1
(page 178)

Example 2
(page 179)

Is the first number divisible by the second? Explain.

1. 20 by 10   **2.** 37 by 2   **3.** 45 by 5   **4.** 240 by 2
5. 60 by 5   **6.** 123 by 2   **7.** 1,468 by 2   **8.** 2,005 by 10
9. 78 by 9   **10.** 69 by 3   **11.** 108 by 9   **12.** 258 by 3
13. 3,694 by 9   **14.** 5,751 by 9   **15.** 123 by 3   **16.** 456 by 3

Example 3
(page 179)

List the positive factors of each integer.

17. 4   **18.** 8   **19.** 23   **20.** 75

21. Drill Team There are 32 students in the school drill team performance. Each row of team members must have the same number of students. If there are at least 8 students in each row, what are all the possible arrangements?

B Apply Your Skills

State whether each number is divisible by 2, 3, 5, 9, 10, or none. Explain. Some numbers may have more than one divisor.

22. 111   **23.** 131   **24.** 288   **25.** 300
26. 52   **27.** 891   **28.** 4,805   **29.** 437,684

30. a. Which of the following numbers are divisible by both 2 and 3?
     10   66   898   4,710   975
b. Which of the numbers above are divisible by 6?
c. Using your results, write a divisibility rule for 6.

Show all possible ways that each integer can be written as the product of two positive factors.

31. 25   **32.** 28   **33.** 32   **34.** 35
35. 37   **36.** 50   **37.** 53   **38.** 72

Write the missing digit to make each number divisible by 9.

39. 22■,034   **40.** 3■,817   **41.** 2,03■,371   **42.** 1■,111

43. Writing in Math If a number is divisible by 9, is it also divisible by 3? Explain how you reached your conclusion.

44. Reasoning John made oatmeal cookies for a class bake sale. The cookies need to be distributed equally on 2 or more plates. If each plate gets at least 7 cookies, what are the possible combinations for the totals below?
a. 42 cookies   **b.** 56 cookies
c. 60 cookies   **d.** 144 cookies

45. a. Copy and complete the table.

Number	Last two digits	Are last two digits divisible by 4?	Is the number divisible by 4?
136	36	Yes	Yes
1,268	68	Yes	Yes
314	14	No	No
1,078	■	■	■
696	■	■	■

b. Reasoning Write a divisibility rule for 4.

Open-Ended Write three numbers greater than 20 that match each description.

46. Divisible by 5, but not divisible by 10

47. Divisible by 3, but not divisible by 5, 9, or 10

48. Divisible by 2, 3, 5, and 10, but not divisible by 9

49. Reasoning If a is divisible by 2, what can you conclude about $a + 1$? Justify your answer.

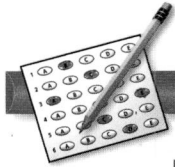

Test Prep

Multiple Choice

50. Which list shows all the positive factors of 15?
 A. 1, 15 **B.** 1, 3, 15 **C.** 1, 5, 15 **D.** 1, 3, 5, 15

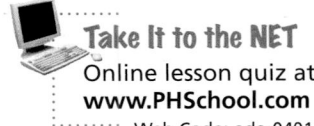
Take It to the NET
Online lesson quiz at
www.PHSchool.com
Web Code: ada-0401

51. Which list shows all the positive factors of 17?
 F. 1, 17 **G.** 1, 7, 17 **H.** 1, 2, 7, 17 **I.** 1, 2, 8, 17

52. Which number is NOT a factor of 438?
 A. 2 **B.** 3 **C.** 5 **D.** 6

Short Response

53. a. What three positive numbers less than 100 are divisible by 2, 3, and 5?
 b. Justify your answer.

Mixed Review

Lesson 3-7   **Complete each statement.**

54. 24 ■ = 24,000 mg   **55.** 18.2 km = 1,820,000 ■

Lesson 2-9   **56. Grocery Shopping** You have $5 to spend at the grocery store. You need $2.89 for a gallon of milk. Write and solve an inequality to show how much money m you can spend on a box of cereal.

Lesson 1-3   **Evaluate.**

57. $3y + 3$, for $y = 8$ **58.** $4(2 + a)$, for $a = 10$

4-2 Exponents

What You'll Learn

OBJECTIVE 1
To use exponents

OBJECTIVE 2
To use the order of operations with exponents

...And Why

To solve real-world problems involving magnification

 Check Skills You'll Need

Find each product.

1. $3 \cdot 3 \cdot 3 \cdot 3$

2. $-12 \cdot (-12)$

3. $(-4)(-4)(-4)$

4. $10 \cdot 10 \cdot 10 \cdot 10$

 For help, go to Lesson 1-9.

New Vocabulary

- exponents
- power
- base

OBJECTIVE

1 Using Exponents

You can use **exponents** to show repeated multiplication.

$$\text{base} \rightarrow 2\overset{\text{exponent}}{\underset{\text{power}}{6}} = \underbrace{2 \cdot 2 \cdot 2 \cdot 2 \cdot 2 \cdot 2}_{\text{The base 2 is used as a factor 6 times.}} = 64 \leftarrow \text{the value of the expression}$$

A **power** has two parts, a **base** and an exponent. The expression 2^6 is read as "two to the sixth power."

Power	Verbal Expression	Value
12^1	*Twelve to the first power*	12
6^2	*Six to the second power, or six squared*	$6 \cdot 6 = 36$
$(0.2)^3$	*Two tenths to the third power, or two tenths cubed*	$(0.2)(0.2)(0.2) = 0.008$
-7^4	*The opposite of the quantity seven to the fourth power*	$-(7 \cdot 7 \cdot 7 \cdot 7) = -2,401$
$(-8)^5$	*Negative eight to the fifth power*	$(-8)(-8)(-8)(-8)(-8) = -32,768$

1 EXAMPLE   Using an Exponent

Write the expression using an exponent.

a. $(-5)(-5)(-5)$

$(-5)^3$ Include the negative sign within parentheses.

b. $-2 \cdot a \cdot b \cdot a \cdot a$

$-2 \cdot a \cdot a \cdot a \cdot b$ Rewrite the expression using the Commutative and Associative Properties.

$-2a^3b$ Write $a \cdot a \cdot a$ using exponents.

 **Check Understanding**   Example 1

1. Write using exponents.

a. $6 \cdot 6 \cdot 6$ **b.** $4 \cdot y \cdot x \cdot y$ **c.** $(-3)(-3)(-3)(-3)$

TEXT Interactive lesson includes instant self-check, tutorials, and activities.

182   Chapter 4   Factors, Fractions, and Exponents

2 EXAMPLE <u>Real-World</u> Problem Solving

Science A microscope can magnify a specimen 10^3 times. How many times is that?

$$10^3 = 10 \cdot 10 \cdot 10 \qquad \text{The exponent indicates that the base 10 is used as a factor 3 times.}$$
$$= 1{,}000 \qquad \text{Multiply.}$$

The microscope can magnify the specimen 1,000 times.

✓ Check Understanding   Example 2

2. a. Simplify 7^2.   **b.** Evaluate $-a^4$ and $(-a)^4$, for $a = 2$.

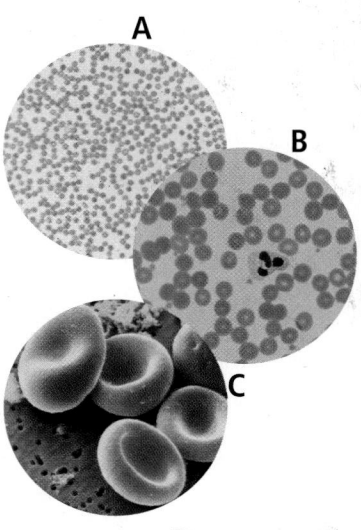

OBJECTIVE

2 Using the Order of Operations With Exponents

You can extend the order of operations to include exponents.

<u>Real-World</u> **Connection**

Human blood cells are shown here magnified (A) 10^2 times, (B) 10^3 times, and (C) 10^4 times.

Key Concepts   **Order of Operations**

1. Work inside grouping symbols.
2. Simplify any terms with exponents.
3. Multiply and divide in order from left to right.
4. Add and subtract in order from left to right.

---

3 EXAMPLE   Using the Order of Operations

a. Simplify $4(3 + 2)^2$.

$$4(3 + 2)^2 = 4(5)^2 \qquad \text{Work within parentheses first.}$$
$$= 4 \cdot 25 \qquad \text{Simplify } 5^2.$$
$$= 100 \qquad \text{Multiply.}$$

b. Evaluate $-2x^3 + 4y$, for $x = -2$ and $y = 3$.

$$-2x^3 + 4y = -2(-2)^3 + 4(3) \qquad \text{Replace } x \text{ with } -2 \text{ and } y \text{ with 3.}$$
$$= -2(-8) + 4(3) \qquad \text{Simplify } (-2)^3.$$
$$= 16 + 12 \qquad \text{Multiply from left to right.}$$
$$= 28 \qquad \text{Add.}$$

Reading Math

The expression $4(3 + 2)^2$ is read as "four times the square of the quantity three plus two."

✓ Check Understanding   Example 3

3. a. Simplify $2 \cdot 5^2 + 4 \cdot (-3)^3$.
   b. Evaluate $3a^2 + 6$, for $a = -5$.

EXERCISES

For more exercises, see *Extra Practice*.

Practice and Problem Solving

A Practice by Example

Example 1
(page 182)

Write using exponents.

1. $8 \cdot 8 \cdot 8$ 2. $r \cdot r \cdot r \cdot r \cdot s \cdot s$ 3. $-7 \cdot a \cdot a \cdot b$

4. $5 \cdot 5 \cdot a \cdot a$ 5. $9 \cdot 9 \cdot 9 \cdot 9 \cdot 9$ 6. $(-5)(-5)(-5)(-5)$

Example 2
(page 183)

Simplify.

7. 10^4 8. 4^3 9. 2^6 10. $(-4)^3$ 11. -4^3 12. $(-6)^3$

13. **Science** An electron microscope can magnify a specimen about 10^6 times. How many times is that?

Example 3
(page 183)

Simplify.

14. $3(4 + 2)^2$ 15. $49 - (4 \cdot 2)^2$ 16. $-3^2 + 5 \cdot 2^3$

17. $2(9 - 4)^2$ 18. $25 - (3 \cdot 2)^2$ 19. $2 \cdot (-2)^4 + 10^1$

Evaluate.

20. $3a^2 - 2$, for $a = 5$ 21. $c^3 + 4$, for $c = -6$

22. $-4y^2 + y^3$, for $y = 3$ 23. $2m^2 + n$, for $m = -3$ and $n = 4$

B Apply Your Skills

Write using exponents.

24. $-5 \cdot x \cdot x \cdot 3 \cdot y$ 25. d cubed   26. $-2 \cdot a \cdot (-4) \cdot b \cdot b$

27. **Error Analysis** A student gives ab^3 as an answer when asked to write the expression $ab \cdot ab \cdot ab$ using exponents. What is the student's error?

Simplify.

28. -1^8 and $(-1)^8$ 29. -2^4 and $(-2)^4$ 30. $15 + (4 + 6)^2 \div 5$

31. $(-4)(-6)^2 (2)$ 32. $(4 + 8)^2 \div 4^2$ 33. $(12 - 3)^2 \div (2^2 - 1^2)$

Evaluate each expression.

34. $-6m^2$, for $m = 2$ 35. $5k^2$, for $k = 1.2$

36. $8 - x^3$, for $x = -2$ 37. $3(2m + 5)^2$, for $m = 2$

38. $4(2y - 3)^2$, for $y = 5$ 39. $y^2 + 2y + 5$, for $y = -6$

n	$4n$	4^n	n^4
1			
2			
3			
4			

40. **a.** Copy and complete the table at the left.
    b. For what value(s) of n is each sentence true?

   $4^n = n^4$ $4^n < n^4$ $4^n > n^4$

41. **Reasoning** Does $-a^2 = (-a)^2$ for any values of a? Explain.

42. **Mental Math** Given that $2^{10} = 1{,}024$, find 2^{11} mentally.

43. Read the word phrase that follows:

the square of *a*, increased by the sum of twice *a* and 3.
  a. Write a variable expression for the word phrase.
  b. Evaluate the expression for $a = 7$.

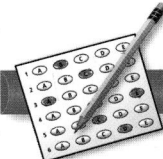

C Challenge

Edge length $s = 3$ in.
Area of Face $= s^2$
$= 9$ in.^{2}
Volume $= s^3$
$= 27$ in.^{3}

Geometry Exercises 44–48 involve cubes made from smaller cubes, like the one at the left. Suppose such a cube has edges of length 5 cm.

44. What is the area of a face?   **45.** What is the volume?

What is the length of an edge of a cube that has the following measurement?

46. face area of 64 in.^{2} **47.** a volume of 64 in.^{3}

48. Language Arts Why do you think *squared* and *cubed* are used to indicate the second power and the third power?

49. Reasoning Describe all pairs of values of x and y for which $5x^2y = 5xy^2$. Justify your answer.

50. Writing in Math   Evaluate $(-1)^m$ for $m = 2, 4,$ and 6. Then evaluate $(-1)^m$ for $m = 1, 3,$ and 5. Write a conjecture about the sign of an even power of a negative number. Then write a conjecture about the sign of an odd power of a negative number.

Test Prep

Multiple Choice

51. What is the value of $(0.5)^2$?
  A. 0.1   **B.** 0.25   **C.** 1.0   **D.** 25

Take It to the NET
Online lesson quiz at
www.PHSchool.com
Web Code: ada-0402

52. What is the value of xy^2 for $x = 3$ and $y = 4$?
  F. 12   **G.** 24   **H.** 36   **I.** 48

53. Which expression equals 1?
  A. -1^2 **B.** $(-1)^3$ **C.** $-(-1)^2$ **D.** $|-1|^3$

Short Response

54. Is $a^3 \geq a$ for all integer values of *a*? Explain and give an example.

Mixed Review

Lesson 4-1

State whether each number is divisible by 2, 3, 5, 9, 10, or none.

55. 36   **56.** 135   **57.** 171   **58.** 190

59. 253   **60.** 123   **61.** 117   **62.** 30

Lesson 3-3

63. a. Sara's grades are 79, 82, 75, 86, and 93. What is the mean?
   b. What is the median?

Lesson 2-3

Simplify each expression.

64. $3x - 2y + x$ **65.** $w + 8 - 4w - 15$ **66.** $9a + 2(a - 5) + 3$

4-3

Prime Factorization and Greatest Common Factor

What You'll Learn

 OBJECTIVE 1 To find the prime factorization of a number

 OBJECTIVE 2 To find the greatest common factor (GCF) of two or more numbers

. . . And Why

To solve real-world problems involving organization

✔ Check Skills You'll Need

List the positive factors of each number.

1. 15 **2.** 35 **3.** 7

4. 20 **5.** 100 **6.** 121

🔎 For help, go to Lesson 4-1.

New Vocabulary

• prime number
• composite number
• prime factorization
• greatest common factor (GCF)

Investigation

Exploring Prime Numbers

The diagram shows the only rectangle you can make with integer side lengths and an area of 5 square units. Work with a partner. Find the number of rectangles you can make with each number of unit squares: 2, 3, 4, 5, 6, 7, 8, 9, and 10.

1. For which numbers of squares is only one rectangle possible?

2. For which numbers of squares is more than one rectangle possible?

3. List the dimensions of the rectangles you can make with each of the following numbers of unit squares: 13, 15, 17, 19, and 21.

A **prime number** is an integer greater than 1 with exactly two positive factors, 1 and the number itself. The numbers 2, 3, 5, and 7 are prime numbers.

A **composite number** is an integer greater than 1 with more than two positive factors. The numbers 4, 6, 8, 9, and 10 are composite numbers. The number 1 is neither prime nor composite.

1 EXAMPLE **Prime or Composite?**

State whether each number is *prime* or *composite*. Explain.

a. 23 Prime; it has only two factors, 1 and 23.

b. 129 Composite; it has more than two factors, 1, 3, 43, and 129.

✔ Check Understanding Example 1

1. Which numbers from 10 to 20 are prime? Which are composite?

🖥 **TEXT** Interactive lesson includes instant self-check, tutorials, and activities.

Writing a composite number as a product of its prime factors shows the **prime factorization** of the number. You can use a *factor tree* to find prime factorizations. Write the final factors in increasing order from left to right. Use exponents to indicate repeated factors.

Test-Taking Tip

To check whether a number is prime, look for prime factors in order, starting with 2. When you get to a prime whose square is greater than the original number, you can stop. For 23, check 2 and 3. Then stop at 5, since $5^2 > 23$. Since 2, 3, and 5 are not factors of 23, 23 is prime.

2 EXAMPLE   **Writing the Prime Factorization**

Use a factor tree to write the prime factorization of 825.

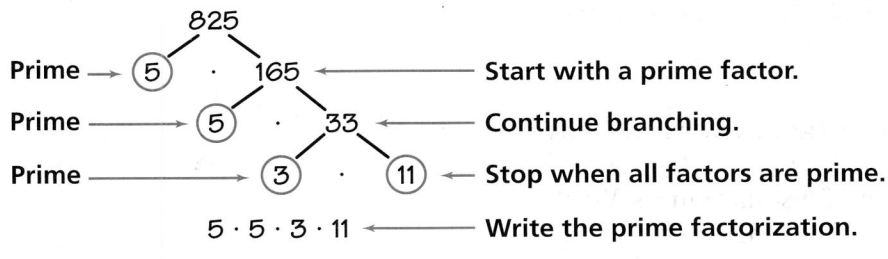

Prime → ⑤ · 165 ←——— **Start with a prime factor.**

Prime ——→ ⑤ · 33 ←——— **Continue branching.**

Prime ————→ ③ · ⑪ ←— **Stop when all factors are prime.**

5 · 5 · 3 · 11 ←——— **Write the prime factorization.**

● $825 = 3 \cdot 5^2 \cdot 11$ **Use exponents to write the prime factorization.**

✓ **Check Understanding** **Example 2**

2. Write the prime factorization of each number.

a. 72   **b.** 121   **c.** 225   **d.** 236

OBJECTIVE

2 **Finding the Greatest Common Factor**

Factors that are the same for two or more numbers or expressions are *common factors*. The greatest of these common factors is called the **greatest common factor (GCF).** You can use prime factorization to find the GCF of two or more numbers or expressions. If there are no prime factors and variable factors in common, the GCF is 1.

3 EXAMPLE   **Finding the GCF**

Find the GCF of each pair of numbers or expressions.

a. 40 and 60   **b.** $6a^3b$ and $4a^2b$

$40 = 2^3 \cdot 5$ **Write the prime** $6a^3b = 2 \cdot 3 \cdot a^3 \cdot b$
$60 = 2^2 \cdot 3 \cdot 5$ **factorizations.** $4a^2b = 2 \cdot 2 \cdot a^2 \cdot b$

Find the common factors. Use the lesser power of the common factors.

GCF $= 2^2 \cdot 5$ GCF $= 2 \cdot a^2 \cdot b$
   $= 20$ $= 2a^2b$

The GCF of 40 and 60 is 20.   The GCF of $6a^3b$ and $4a^2b$ is $2a^2b$.

3. Use prime factorizations to find each GCF.

    a. 8, 20   **b.** 12, 87   **c.** $12r^3, 8r$ **d.** $15m^2n, 45m$

You can find the GCF of two or more numbers or expressions by listing factors or by using prime factorizations.

More Than One Way

A parade organizer wants each of three marching bands to have the same number of band members in each row. The bands have 48, 32, and 56 band members. What is the greatest number of band members possible for each row?

Jasmine's Method

List the factors of each number. Then find the greatest factor the numbers have in common.

    48: 1, 2, 3, 4, 6, (8), 12, 16, 24, 48

    32: 1, 2, 4, (8), 16, 32

    56: 1, 2, 4, 7, (8), 14, 28, 56

The GCF of 48, 32, and 56 is 8. The greatest possible number of band members in each row is 8.

Daryl's Method

Find the prime factorization of each number. Then find the least power of all common prime factors.

    48: $2^4 \cdot 3$

    32: 2^5

    56: $2^3 \cdot 7$

The GCF of 48, 32, and 56 is 2^3, or 8. The greatest possible number of band members in each row is 8.

Choose a Method

1. Which method do you prefer to find the GCF? Explain why.

2. Which method would you use to find the GCF of 4, 8, and 24? Of 54, 27, and 36? Explain why.

EXERCISES

❓ For more exercises, see *Extra Practice*.

Practice and Problem Solving

A Practice by Example

Example 1
(page 186)

State whether each number is prime or composite. Explain.

1. 27   **2.** 19   **3.** 31   **4.** 38

5. 45   **6.** 53   **7.** 87   **8.** 93

Example 2
(page 187)

Write the prime factorization of each number.

9. 8   **10.** 49   **11.** 34   **12.** 42

13. 360   **14.** 115   **15.** 186   **16.** 621

Example 3
(page 187)

Use prime factorization to find each GCF.

17. $10, 45$ **18.** $14, 21$ **19.** $25, 100$ **20.** $57, 84$

21. $14c^2, 35c$ **22.** $3y^2, 24y^3$ **23.** $18c^3, 24c^3$ **24.** $6m^3n, 8mn^2$

B Apply Your Skills

Is each number prime, composite, or neither? For each composite number, write the prime factorization.

25. 17   **26.** 1   **27.** 49   **28.** 522

🌐 **29. Organization** A math teacher and a science teacher combine their first-period classes for a group activity. The math class has 24 students and the science class has 16 students. The teachers need to divide the students into groups of the same size. Each group must have the same number of math students. Find the greatest number of groups possible.

Find each GCF.

30. $6, 8, 12$ **31.** $42, 65$ **32.** $54, 144$ **33.** $8, 16, 20$

34. $12, 18, 21$ **35.** $143, 169$ **36.** z, z^2 **37.** $180a^2, 210a$

38. x^2y, xy^2 **39.** a^3b, a^2b^2 **40.** c^3df^2, c^2d^2f **41.** a^2b, b^2c, ac^2

42. Reasoning Find the integers that fit the following conditions:
- They are between 44 and 53.
- The sums of their digits are prime.
- They have more than three factors.

43. Open-Ended The GCF of 36 and x is 6. What are two possible values for x?

🌐 **44. Seating Arrangements** Organizers for a high school graduation have set up chairs in two sections. They put 126 chairs for graduates in the front section and 588 chairs for guests in the back section. If all rows have the same number of chairs, what is the greatest number of chairs possible for a row?

C Challenge

Is each number prime, composite, or neither? For each composite number, write the prime factorization.

45. 253   **46.** 1,575   **47.** 1,003   **48.** 283

Two numbers are *relatively prime* if their GCF is 1. Are the numbers in each pair below relatively prime? Explain.

SAMPLE   8, 17   Yes, 8 and 17 are relatively prime. The GCF is 1.
            7, 35   No, 7 and 35 are not relatively prime. The GCF is 7.

49. 3, 20   **50.** 9, 42   **51.** 13, 52   **52.** 24, 47

53. 52, 65   **54.** 63, 74   **55.** 15, 22   **56.** 42, 72

57. <u>Writing in Math</u> Explain how to find the prime factorization of 50.

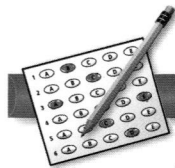

Test Prep

Multiple Choice

In Exercises 58 and 59, what is the GCF of each given pair?

58. $27x^2y^3$ and $46x^2y$
    A. $3x^2y$ **B.** x^2y^2 **C.** x^2y **D.** $9x^2y$

59. $25b^2c$ and $42bc$
    F. bc^2 **G.** bc **H.** b^2c **I.** b^2c^2

Take It to the NET
Online lesson quiz at
www.PHSchool.com
Web Code: ada-0403

60. For which pair is the GCF 12?
    A. 3, 4   **B.** $24x^2$, 36y   **C.** 12xy, 24y   **D.** 3x, 12x

61. Simon is covering a wall with equal-sized tiles that cannot be cut into smaller pieces. The wall is 66 inches high by 72 inches wide. What is the area of the largest square tile that Simon can use?
    F. 9 in.^{2} **G.** 16 in.^{2} **H.** 36 in.^{2} **I.** 64 in.^{2}

Extended Response

62. a. Is the product of two prime numbers also prime?
      b. Justify your answer.   **c.** Give an example.

Mixed Review

Lesson 4-2

Evaluate for $x = 2$ and $y = 5$.

63. x^2y **64.** xy^2 **65.** $x^2 + y^2$ **66.** $x^4 - y$

Lesson 3-6

Solve each equation.

67. $3x = 5.4$ **68.** $-0.5a = 4.35$

69. $4.32 = 1.6y$ **70.** $-8m = -74.4$

Lesson 2-7 🌐 **71. Bookstore** A store manager ordered three times as many books as magazines. She ordered a total of 108 books and magazines. How many books did she order?

190 Chapter 4   Factors, Fractions, and Exponents

Venn Diagrams

In a *Venn diagram* you use circles to represent collections of objects. The *intersection,* or overlap, of two circles indicates what is common to both collections.

1 EXAMPLE

School coaches plan to send notices to all students playing fall or winter sports. How many notices do they need to send?

Students in Sports

Season	Students
Fall	155
Winter	79
Both fall and winter	28

number who played only a fall sport
155 − 28 = 127

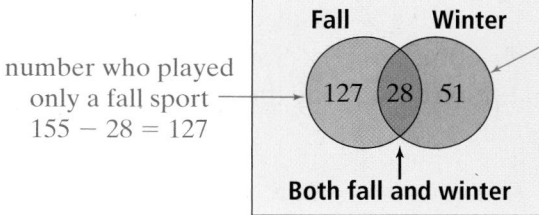

number who played only a winter sport
79 − 28 = 51

Add all three numbers to find the number of notices needed.

127 + 28 + 51 = 206

Both fall and winter

● The coaches need to send 206 notices.

You can use a Venn diagram to find the GCF of two numbers.

2 EXAMPLE

Find the GCF of 30 and 84.

Include the common prime factors of 30 and 84 in the intersection.

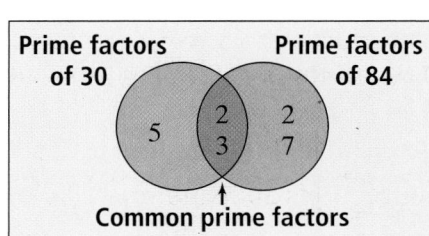

Common prime factors

The GCF is the product of the factors in the intersection.

● The GCF is 2 · 3, or 6.

EXERCISES

1. In a class of 38 students, 32 are wearing jeans, 21 are wearing T-shirts, and 15 are wearing both. How many students are wearing jeans and something other than a T-shirt?

Draw a Venn diagram to find the GCF of each pair of numbers.

2. 24, 56   **3.** 35, 49   **4.** 36, 84   **5.** 72, 108

Simplifying Fractions

What You'll Learn

OBJECTIVE 1 To find equivalent fractions

OBJECTIVE 2 To write fractions in simplest form

...And Why

To solve real-world problems involving statistics

 **Check Skills You'll Need**

Find each GCF.

1. 14, 21   **2.** 48, 60

3. $5mn, 15m^2n$

4. $63r^2, 48s^3$

For help, go to Lesson 4-3.

New Vocabulary

• equivalent fractions
• simplest form

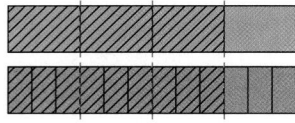

OBJECTIVE 1 Finding Equivalent Fractions

Each fraction model below represents one whole. The blue model is divided into four equal parts. The orange model is divided into twelve equal parts.

$\frac{3}{4}$ of the model is shaded.

$\frac{9}{12}$ of the model is shaded.

$$\frac{3}{4} = \frac{3 \cdot 3}{4 \cdot 3} = \frac{9}{12}$$

The fraction models show that $\frac{3}{4} = \frac{9}{12}$. The fractions $\frac{3}{4}$ and $\frac{9}{12}$ are **equivalent fractions** because they describe the same part of a whole.

You can find equivalent fractions by multiplying or dividing the numerator and denominator by the same nonzero factor.

1 EXAMPLE **Finding an Equivalent Fraction**

Find two fractions equivalent to $\frac{4}{12}$.

a. $\frac{4}{12} = \frac{4 \cdot 3}{12 \cdot 3}$

$= \frac{12}{36}$

b. $\frac{4}{12} = \frac{4 \div 4}{12 \div 4}$

$= \frac{1}{3}$

The fractions $\frac{12}{36}$ and $\frac{1}{3}$ are both equivalent to $\frac{4}{12}$.

✓ **Check Understanding** Example 1

1. Find two fractions equivalent to each fraction.

a. $\frac{5}{15}$ **b.** $\frac{10}{12}$ **c.** $\frac{14}{20}$

OBJECTIVE 2 Writing Fractions in Simplest Form

A fraction is in **simplest form** when the numerator and the denominator have no common factors other than 1. You can use the GCF to write a fraction in simplest form.

Reading Math

Most fraction names are made by adding *th* or *ths* to the denominator. You read $\frac{1}{4}$ as "one fourth," $\frac{2}{5}$ as "two fifths," and $\frac{8}{10}$ as "eight tenths." Halves and thirds are two exceptions.

 TEXT Interactive lesson includes instant self-check, tutorials, and activities.

2 EXAMPLE — Real-World  Problem Solving

Statistics You survey your friends about their favorite sandwich and find that 8 out of 12, or $\frac{8}{12}$, prefer peanut butter. Write this fraction in simplest form.

The GCF of 8 and 12 is 4.

$$\frac{8}{12} = \frac{8 \div 4}{12 \div 4}$$ **Divide the numerator and denominator by the GCF, 4.**

$$= \frac{2}{3}$$ **Simplify.**

● The favorite sandwich of $\frac{2}{3}$ of your friends is peanut butter.

Real-World Connection

The average American child will eat 1,500 peanut butter and jelly sandwiches by the time she or he graduates from high school.

✓ Check Understanding   Example 2

2. Write each fraction in simplest form.

   a. $\frac{6}{8}$ **b.** $\frac{9}{12}$ **c.** $\frac{28}{35}$

You can often simplify a fraction that contains a variable. In this book, you may assume that no expression for a denominator equals zero.

3 EXAMPLE   Simplifying a Fraction

Write in simplest form.

a. $\frac{y}{xy}$

$$\frac{y}{xy} = \frac{y^1}{xy_1}$$ **Divide the numerator and denominator by the common factor, y.**

$$= \frac{1}{x}$$ **Simplify.**

b. $\frac{3ab^2}{12ac}$

$$\frac{3ab^2}{12ac} = \frac{3 \cdot a \cdot b \cdot b}{2 \cdot 2 \cdot 3 \cdot a \cdot c}$$ **Write as a product of prime factors.**

$$= \frac{3^1 \cdot a^1 \cdot b \cdot b}{2 \cdot 2 \cdot {}_1 3 \cdot {}_1 a \cdot c}$$ **Divide the numerator and denominator by the common factors.**

$$= \frac{b \cdot b}{2 \cdot 2 \cdot c}$$ **Simplify.**

$$= \frac{b \cdot b}{4 \cdot c}$$

$$= \frac{b^2}{4c}$$

Test-Taking Tip

You will see the directions *write in lowest terms* on some tests. This is another way of saying "write in simplest form."

✓ Check Understanding   Example 3

3. Write in simplest form.

   a. $\frac{b}{abc}$ **b.** $\frac{2mn}{6m}$ **c.** $\frac{24x^2y}{8xy}$

EXERCISES

? **For more exercises, see** *Extra Practice.*

Practice and Problem Solving

A **Practice by Example**

Example 1 (page 192)

Find two fractions equivalent to each fraction.

1. $\frac{2}{8}$ **2.** $\frac{8}{10}$ **3.** $\frac{3}{9}$ **4.** $\frac{8}{36}$ **5.** $\frac{6}{18}$ **6.** $\frac{20}{22}$

Example 2 (page 193)

Write each fraction in simplest form.

7. $\frac{3}{9}$ **8.** $\frac{4}{10}$ **9.** $\frac{12}{48}$ **10.** $\frac{2}{10}$ **11.** $\frac{4}{12}$ **12.** $\frac{6}{15}$

13. Health Doctors suggest that most people need about 8 h of sleep each night to stay healthy. What fraction of the day is this? Write your answer in simplest form.

Example 3 (page 193)

Write in simplest form.

14. $\frac{2x}{3x}$ **15.** $\frac{4km^2}{12k}$ **16.** $\frac{b}{bc}$ **17.** $\frac{24x}{16}$

18. $\frac{8pr}{12p}$ **19.** $\frac{14a^2}{24a}$ **20.** $\frac{4bc}{16b}$ **21.** $\frac{40ab^2}{5ab}$

B **Apply Your Skills**

Find two fractions equivalent to each fraction.

22. $\frac{4}{8}$ **23.** $\frac{4}{10}$ **24.** $\frac{5}{20}$ **25.** $\frac{10}{16}$ **26.** $\frac{18}{20}$ **27.** $\frac{25}{100}$

Write in simplest form.

28. $\frac{8}{14}$ **29.** $\frac{18}{32}$ **30.** $\frac{20}{30}$ **31.** $\frac{12}{16}$

32. $\frac{15^3}{15^2}$ **33.** $\frac{56pq}{7pq}$ **34.** $\frac{5c^2d}{15c}$ **35.** $\frac{4r^3st}{36st^2}$

36. $\frac{5t}{10t^2}$ **37.** $\frac{x^2y}{3yz}$ **38.** $\frac{12gh}{8g^2h^2}$ **39.** $\frac{6m^2n^2}{9mn^2}$

> **Reading Math**
> For help with reading and solving Exercise 40, see page 196.

40. Error Analysis A student claims $\frac{65}{91}$ is in simplest form. Do you agree? Explain.

41. Open-Ended Write two fractions whose simplest form is $\frac{3x}{5}$.

42. Writing in Math Does $\frac{1}{2}$ of one pizza represent the same amount as $\frac{1}{2}$ of another pizza? Justify your answer.

C **Challenge**

PC and On-Line Households in the U.S. (millions)

Households	1997	1998
Total households	100	101
Households with PCs	44	48
Households with Internet access	21	27

Source: *The Wall Street Journal Almanac 1999*

Data Analysis The table shows the number of personal computers (PCs) and households with Internet access in the United States. For Exercises 43–45, write each fraction in simplest form.

43. In 1997, what fraction of U.S. households had PCs?

44. In 1997, what fraction of U.S. households with PCs had Internet access? (Assume that a household with Internet access had a PC.)

45. a. In 1998, what fraction of U.S. households with PCs had Internet access? (*Hint:* See Exercise 44.)
  b. Was the fraction greater in 1997 or 1998? Explain.

46. Write the numerator and denominator of $\frac{24}{32}$ as products of prime factors. Then use the prime factors to write $\frac{24}{32}$ in simplest form.

Test Prep

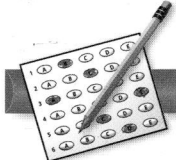

Multiple Choice

47. Which fraction is equivalent to $\frac{15}{30}$?

    A. $\frac{2}{4}$ **B.** $\frac{3}{5}$ **C.** $\frac{3}{4}$ **D.** $\frac{5}{6}$

Take It to the NET
Online lesson quiz at
www.PHSchool.com
Web Code: ada-0404

48. What is the simplest form for $\frac{14}{42}$?

    F. $\frac{1}{3}$ **G.** $\frac{7}{21}$ **H.** $\frac{2}{6}$ **I.** $\frac{2}{3}$

49. What is the simplest form for $\frac{6m}{15m}$?

    A. $\frac{2m}{15m}$ **B.** $\frac{3m}{5m}$ **C.** $\frac{3}{5}$ **D.** $\frac{2}{5}$

Short Response

50. a. Is $\frac{ab}{5}$ equivalent to $\frac{15a^2b}{75a}$?   **b.** Justify your answer.

Mixed Review

Lesson 4-3

Find the GCF for each pair.

51. $10, 12$ **52.** $28, 60$ **53.** $14a, 21a$ **54.** $24x^2, 40x^3$

Lesson 3-5

Solve each equation.

55. $y + 3.23 = 5.85$ **56.** $b - 2.13 = 9.9$ **57.** $12.8 + z = 6.47$

Lesson 3-2 **58. Oil Spills** A damaged oil tanker spilled 34.7 million gallons of crude oil over 4 days. On the average, about how many gallons did the tanker spill each day?

Checkpoint Quiz 1   **Lessons 4-1 through 4-4**

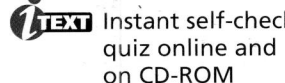 Instant self-check quiz online and on CD-ROM

State whether each number is divisible by 2, 3, 5, 9, 10, or none.

    1. 30 **2.** 54 **3.** 48 **4.** 161 **5.** $2,583$

Evaluate each expression.

    6. x^2, for $x = 8$ **7.** a^3, for $a = 5$ **8.** $-2z^2$, for $z = -3$

Write in simplest form.

    9. $\frac{8}{16}$ **10.** $\frac{14}{21}$ **11.** $\frac{16}{28}$ **12.** $\frac{3a}{12a}$ **13.** $\frac{2xy}{x}$

14. Open-Ended Write two expressions whose GCF is $5a^2$.

Read the exercise below and then follow along with what Tina thinks and writes. Check your understanding by solving the exercises at the bottom of the page.

Error Analysis A student claims $\frac{65}{91}$ is in simplest form. Do you agree? Explain.

What Tina Thinks and Writes

Do I agree?

The wording of the problem suggests that the student is wrong. I'll write:

No.

Now I have to "Explain."

What does simplest form mean for a fraction?

The numerator and denominator can have no common factor other than 1.

65 ends in 5, so 65 has 5 as a factor. Is 5 also a factor of 91?

No! 91 does not end in 5. 5 is not a factor of 91.

Are there other possibilities for common factors?

Since 5 is a factor of 65. There has to be another factor. 65 = 5 · 13

Is 13 a factor of 91?

91 = 7 · 13. A ha! I'll finish:

No.

$$\frac{65}{91} = \frac{5 \cdot \overset{1}{\cancel{13}}}{7 \cdot \underset{1}{\cancel{13}}} = \frac{5}{7}$$

$\frac{5}{7}$ is the simplest form for the fraction.

I'm done!

EXERCISES

Use what you know about factors to decide whether each fraction is in simplest form. If not, simplify.

1. $\frac{17}{51}$ **2.** $\frac{39}{91}$ **3.** $\frac{51}{57}$ **4.** $\frac{57}{76}$ **5.** $\frac{57}{87}$

Account for All Possibilities

OBJECTIVE 1

Account for All Possibilities

Math Strategies in Action Have you ever lost something that you just couldn't find anywhere? Don't you usually discover that you didn't check *every* place you could, even when you thought you had?

"Has anyone seen the remote?"

Even for a situation like losing a TV remote control, making a list of places to search might help.

In some problems, you need to count the possibilities. To solve these problems, you need to be sure that you have found every possibility. Organized lists and diagrams help you keep track of the possibilities as you find them.

1 EXAMPLE   Real-World Problem Solving

Photography Mandy, Jim, Keisha, Darren, Lin, Chris, and Jen are friends. They want to take pictures of themselves with two people in each picture. How many pictures do they need to take?

Read and Understand

1. What do you need to find?

2. How many people are there in all?

3. How many people will be in each photograph?

What You'll Learn

OBJECTIVE 1 To find all possibilities when you solve a problem

. . . And Why

To solve real-world problems involving photography

✓ Check Skills You'll Need

Compare.
Use > or < to complete each statement.

1. $3 \blacksquare 0$

2. $-16 \blacksquare -25$

3. $0 \blacksquare 1$

4. $-30 \blacksquare -20$

❓ For help, go to Skills Handbook, p. 775.

---

i TEXT Interactive lesson includes instant self-check, tutorials, and activities.

Plan and Solve

To make sure that you account for every pair of friends, make an organized list.

First pair Mandy with each of her six friends. Next, pair Jim with each of the five friends left. Since Mandy and Jim have already been paired, you don't need to count them again.

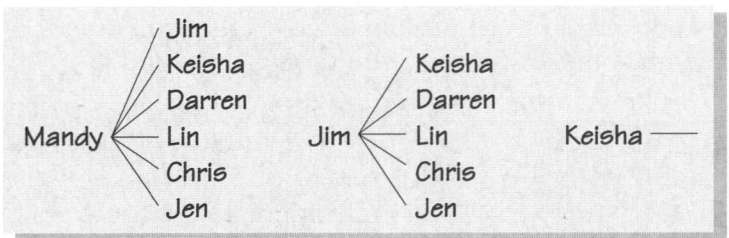

4. Copy and complete the list of paired friends.

5. What pattern do you see?

6. How many pictures do they need to take?

Look Back and Check

Another way to solve this problem is to use a diagram. Draw line segments to show all possible pairs of friends.

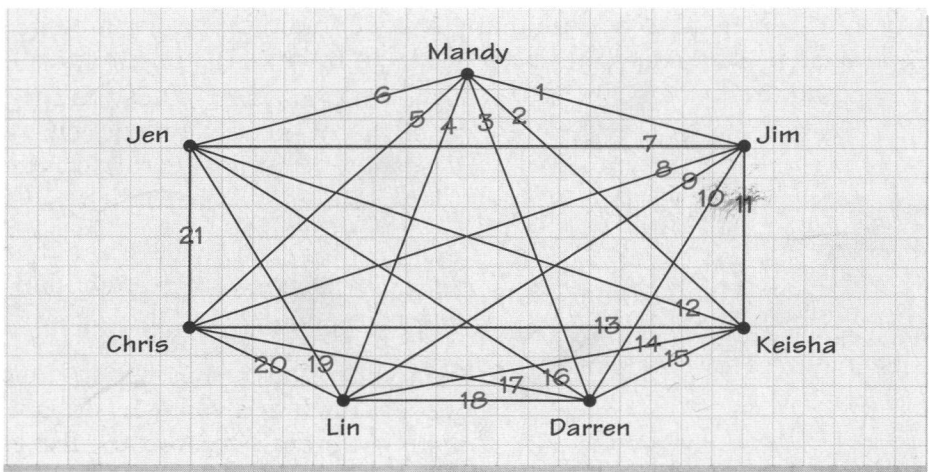

There are 21 line segments. This shows there are 21 pairs of friends.

✔ Check Understanding

7. Suppose Mandy and nine friends pair up for pictures. Use the pattern suggested above and find how many pictures there will be.

EXERCISES

For more exercises, see *Extra Practice*.

Practice and Problem Solving

A Practice by Example

Example 1
(page 197)

Solve each problem by accounting for all possibilities.

1. A sandwich shop serves turkey, ham, tuna, chicken, and egg salad sandwiches. You can have any sandwich using white, wheat, or rye bread. Suppose you eat there every day. For how many days can you order a sandwich that is different from any you have ordered before? The start of an organized list is shown above. Copy and complete the list to solve the problem.

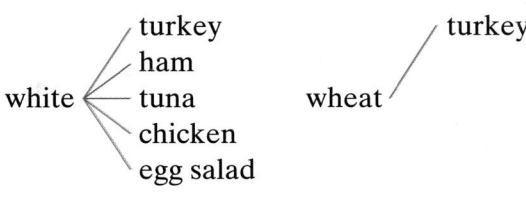

white — turkey, ham, tuna, chicken, egg salad   wheat — turkey

Strategies

- Account for All Possibilities
- Draw a Diagram
- Look for a Pattern
- Make a Model
- Make a Table
- Simplify the Problem
- Simulate the Problem
- Solve by Graphing
- Try, Test, Revise
- Use Multiple Strategies
- Work Backward
- Write an Equation
- Write a Proportion

2. You throw three darts at the board shown at the right. If each dart hits the board, what possible point totals can you score?

3. You have pepperoni, mushrooms, onions, and green peppers. How many different pizzas can you make by using one, two, three, or four of the toppings?

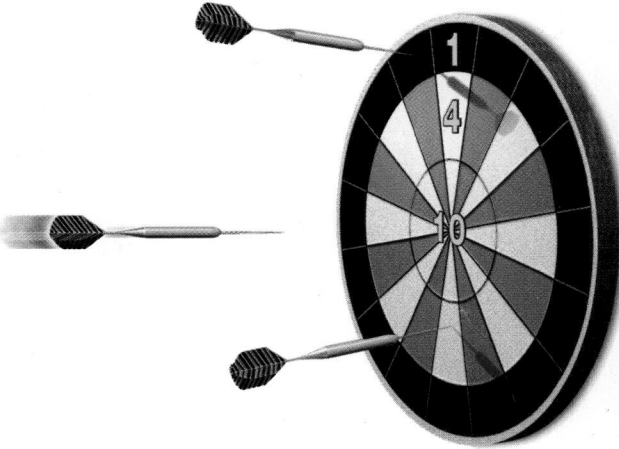

A dart landing on the board scores 1, 4, or 10 points.

4. Elections Four candidates run for president of the student council. Three other candidates run for vice-president. In how many different ways can the two offices be filled?

B Apply Your Skills

5. Patterns Eight people are at a party. Everyone shakes hands once with everyone else. How many handshakes are there altogether?   7 + 6 + 5 + 4 + 3 + 2 + 1

6. Geometry You have 24 feet of fence to make a rectangular garden. Each side will measure a whole number of feet. How many different-sized rectangular gardens can you make?

Solve using any strategy.

7. Patterns The bottom row of a stack of blocks contains 11 blocks. The row above it contains 9 blocks. The next higher row contains 7 blocks. The rows continue in this pattern, and the top row contains a single block. How many blocks does the stack contain in all?

 **Challenge** **8. Routes** Copy the diagram at the left. Using the paths shown, Jill can walk to Trisha's house in many different ways. Draw each route that is four blocks long. How can you be sure that you have found all possible routes?

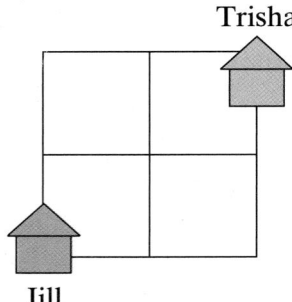

Trisha

Jill

9. Seating Arrangements Ana, Brian, Carla, David, and Eric are friends. They go to a movie, but cannot find five seats together. They have to split up into a group of three and a group of two. How many different ways can the friends organize themselves into these two groups?

10. You have one penny, one nickel, one dime, and one quarter. How many different amounts of money can you make using one or more of these coins?

11. Softball There are seven softball teams in a league. Each team plays each of the other teams twice. What is the total number of games played?

12. Geometry How many different rectangles are there with an area of 36 cm² if the side lengths of each, in centimeters, are whole numbers?

Test Prep

Multiple Choice

13. Which list shows all the positive factors of 32?
  A. 1, 2, 3, 8, 16, 32   **B.** 1, 2, 4, 8, 16, 32
  C. 1, 2, 3, 4, 8, 16, 32   **D.** 1, 2, 4, 6, 8, 16, 32

14. What is the value of $(0.3)^2$?
  F. 0.6   **G.** 0.9   **H.** 0.06   **I.** 0.09

15. What is the GCF of $24x^2y^3$ and $32x^3y$?
  A. $4xy$ **B.** $4x^2y$ **C.** $8xy$ **D.** $8x^2y$

Take It to the NET
Online lesson quiz at
www.PHSchool.com
Web Code: ada-0405

16. Which fraction is the simplest form of $\frac{45}{60}$?
  F. $\frac{2}{3}$ **G.** $\frac{3}{4}$ **H.** $\frac{15}{20}$ **I.** $\frac{5}{6}$

Mixed Review

Lesson 4-4 **Write in simplest form.**

17. $\frac{6}{12}$ **18.** $\frac{10}{40}$ **19.** $\frac{6a^2}{15}$ **20.** $\frac{14a^3}{28a^2}$

Lesson 1-7 **Write a rule for each pattern.**

21. $10, 20, 30, \ldots$ **22.** $8, 5, 2, -1, \ldots$ **23.** $2, 6, 18, 54, \ldots$

Lesson 1-2 **24.** Elki has read the first 60 pages of a book. When he has read 35 more pages, he will have read half the book. How many pages are in the book?

Rational Numbers

OBJECTIVE 1 — Identifying and Graphing Rational Numbers

A **rational number** is any number you can write as a quotient $\frac{a}{b}$ of two integers, where b is not zero. The diagram below shows relationships among rational numbers.

Notice that all integers are rational numbers. This is true because you can write any integer a as $\frac{a}{1}$.

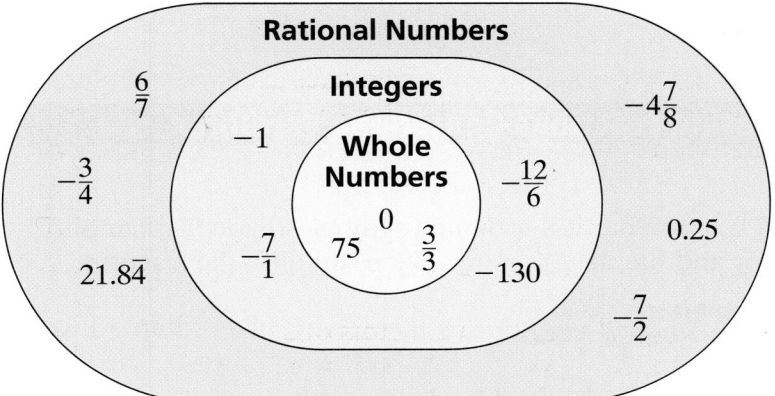

Here are three ways you can write a negative rational number.

$$-\frac{7}{9} = \frac{-7}{9} = \frac{7}{-9}$$

For each rational number, there is an unlimited number of equivalent fractions.

1 EXAMPLE   Writing Equivalent Fractions

Write two lists of fractions equivalent to $\frac{1}{2}$.

$\frac{1}{2} = \frac{2}{4} = \frac{3}{6} = \cdots$ **Numerators and denominators are positive.**

$\frac{1}{2} = \frac{-1}{-2} = \frac{-2}{-4} = \cdots$ **Numerators and denominators are negative.**

✔ Check Understanding   Example 1

1. Write three fractions equivalent to each fraction.

   a. $\frac{1}{3}$ **b.** $-\frac{4}{5}$ **c.** $\frac{5}{8}$ **d.** $-\frac{1}{2}$

What You'll Learn

OBJECTIVE 1 To identify and graph rational numbers

OBJECTIVE 2 To evaluate fractions containing variables

. . . And Why

To solve real-world problems involving rates

✔ Check Skills You'll Need

Write in simplest form.

1. $\frac{2}{10}$ **2.** $\frac{14}{21}$

3. $\frac{28}{35}$ **4.** $\frac{6}{8}$

 For help, go to Lesson 4-4.

New Vocabulary

- rational number

Need Help?

The quotient of two integers with the same sign is positive.

iTEXT Interactive lesson includes instant self-check, tutorials, and activities.

You can graph rational numbers on a number line.

2 EXAMPLE **Graphing a Rational Number**

Graph each rational number on a number line.

a. $\frac{1}{2}$ b. $-\frac{8}{10}$ c. 1   d. -0.2

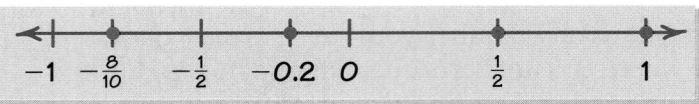

✓ Check Understanding Example 2

2. Graph each rational number on a number line.

   a. $-\frac{1}{2}$ b. $-\frac{4}{10}$ c. -2 d. 0.9

OBJECTIVE

2 Evaluating Fractions Containing Variables

Recall that a fraction bar is a grouping symbol, so you first simplify the numerator and the denominator. Then, simplify the fraction.

Simplify the **numerator.** ⟶ $\dfrac{1+9+2}{2-5} = \dfrac{12}{-3} = -4$ ←simplest form
Simplify the **denominator.** ⟶

To simplify a fraction with variables, first substitute for the variables.

3 EXAMPLE **Real-World 🌐 Problem Solving**

Science The speed of a car changes from 37 ft/s to 102 ft/s in five seconds. What is its acceleration in feet per second per second (ft/s^2)? Use the formula $a = \dfrac{f - i}{t}$ where a is acceleration, f is final speed, i is initial speed, and t is time.

$a = \dfrac{f - i}{t}$ Use the acceleration formula.

$= \dfrac{102 - 37}{5}$ Substitute for the variables.

$= \dfrac{65}{5}$ Subtract.

$= 13$ Write in simplest form.

• The car's acceleration is 13 ft/s².

✓ Check Understanding Example 3

3. Evaluate for $a = 6$ and $b = -5$. Write in simplest form.

   a. $\dfrac{a + b}{-3}$ b. $\dfrac{7 - b}{3a}$ c. $\dfrac{a + 9}{b}$

EXERCISES

🕯 For more exercises, see *Extra Practice.*

Practice and Problem Solving

Ⓐ Practice by Example

Example 1
(page 201)

Show the next three fractions equivalent to $\frac{1}{2}$ in each list.

1. $\frac{1}{2}, \frac{2}{4}, \frac{3}{6}, \cdots$
2. $\frac{1}{2}, \frac{-1}{-2}, \frac{-3}{-6}, \cdots$

Write three fractions equivalent to each fraction.

3. $\frac{1}{6}$ **4.** $\frac{3}{5}$ **5.** $-\frac{5}{9}$ **6.** $-\frac{4}{4}$ **7.** $-\frac{2}{3}$ **8.** $\frac{4}{7}$

Example 2
(page 202)

Graph each rational number on a number line.

9. $\frac{1}{10}$ **10.** $-\frac{3}{5}$ **11.** 2 **12.** -0.3 **13.** -0.75 **14.** $\frac{2}{3}$

Example 3
(page 202)

Evaluate for $a = -4$ and $b = -6$. Write in simplest form.

15. $\frac{a}{b}$ **16.** $\frac{a+9}{b}$ **17.** $\frac{b+a}{3a}$ **18.** $\frac{2a+b}{20}$ **19.** $\frac{b+7}{2a}$ **20.** $\frac{b-a}{3b}$

🌐 **21. Boat Races** The speed of a racing boat changes from 0 ft/s to 264 ft/s in six seconds. What is the acceleration of the boat in ft/s²? Use the acceleration formula given in Example 3.

Ⓑ Apply Your Skills

Write three fractions equivalent to each fraction.

22. $\frac{2}{8}$ **23.** $-\frac{2}{5}$ **24.** $\frac{4}{12}$ **25.** $-\frac{12}{27}$ **26.** $\frac{7}{11}$ **27.** $-\frac{5}{13}$

Write a rational number that is between each pair of numbers.

28. $0, -1$ **29.** $0.9, 1.1$ **30.** $\frac{-1}{5}, \frac{-4}{5}$

Evaluate. Write in simplest form.

31. $\frac{y}{-x}$, for $x = 5$ and $y = -4$ **32.** $\frac{-2y}{x^2}$, for $x = 9$ and $y = 3$

33. $\frac{m}{n}$, for $m = -2$ and $n = 8$ **34.** $\frac{m-n}{-12}$, for $m = -3$ and $n = 6$

35. $\frac{6b-16}{3c}$, for $b = 8$ and $c = 12$ **36.** $\frac{3m-11}{n}$, for $m = 7$ and $n = 14$

37. Which of the following rational numbers are equivalent to $-\frac{4}{5}$?
$\frac{4}{-5}, \frac{-12}{15}, -\frac{16}{20}, \frac{-4}{-5}$

38. a. Open-Ended Write two rational numbers between 0 and $\frac{1}{2}$.
   b. How many other rational numbers are between 0 and $\frac{1}{2}$? Explain.

39. Reasoning What are three fractions equivalent to $\frac{a}{b}$? Explain.

🌐 **40. Science** The formula $s = \frac{1{,}600}{d^2}$ gives the strength s of a radio signal at a distance d miles from the transmitter. What is the strength at 5 mi? Write your answer in simplest form.

41. Writing in Math Explain why a whole number is an integer and an integer is a rational number.

42. If the *Thrust SSC* (see page 202) can go from 0 ft/s to 1,119 ft/s in 30 s, what is its acceleration in feet per second per second?

C Challenge

Write the opposite and the absolute value of each number.

SAMPLE Find the opposite and the absolute value of $-\frac{3}{5}$.

Opposite:

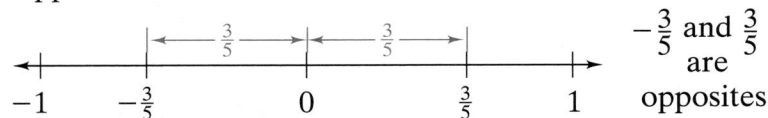

$-\frac{3}{5}$ and $\frac{3}{5}$ are opposites.

Absolute value:

$|-\frac{3}{5}| = \frac{3}{5}$

43. $\frac{2}{3}$ **44.** $-\frac{5}{6}$ **45.** $\frac{-4}{5}$ **46.** $\frac{2}{-7}$ **47.** $\frac{-3}{-5}$ **48.** $-\frac{a}{b}$

Reasoning Tell whether each statement is true for all positive integers a and b. If the statement is not always true, give a counterexample.

49. $\frac{a^2}{b} > \frac{a}{b}$ **50.** $\frac{3a}{3b} = \frac{a}{b}$ **51.** $\frac{a^2}{b^2} > \frac{a}{b}$

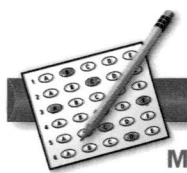

Test Prep

Multiple Choice

52. Which three fractions are equivalent to $\frac{3}{4}$?

A. $\frac{6}{8}, \frac{9}{16}, \frac{-6}{-8}$ **B.** $\frac{-3}{-4}, \frac{12}{16}, \frac{15}{20}$ **C.** $\frac{6}{8}, \frac{-3}{-4}, \frac{9}{12}$ **D.** $\frac{15}{20}, \frac{12}{16}, \frac{-6}{8}$

Take It to the NET
Online lesson quiz at
www.PHSchool.com
Web Code: ada-0406

53. What is the simplest form of $\frac{y(xy - 7)}{10}$ when $x = 6$ and $y = 2$?

F. 3 **G.** $\frac{30}{10}$ **H.** 1 **I.** $\frac{10}{10}$

54. Which pair of numbers is between -3 and -2?

A. $-2\frac{1}{2}, -2\frac{1}{3}$ **B.** $-3\frac{1}{2}, -3\frac{1}{3}$ **C.** $-2, -\pi$ **D.** $-2\frac{1}{2}, -3$

Short Response

55. Is $\frac{a^2}{b^2} > \frac{a}{b}$ true for all negative integers a and b? Explain.

Mixed Review

Lesson 4-5

56. **Patterns** Lucia has 4 pairs of slacks, 5 shirts, and 2 sweaters. How many different three-piece outfits can she make?

Lesson 1-9

Multiply or divide.

57. $-7 \cdot 4$ **58.** $19(-5)$ **59.** $-124 \div (-4)$ **60.** $-204 \div 6$

Lesson 1-4

Write the integer represented by each point on the number line.

61. A **62.** B

63. C **64.** D

Exponents and Multiplication

OBJECTIVE

1 Multiplying Powers With the Same Base

In Lesson 4-2, you learned how to use exponents to indicate repeated multiplication. What happens when you multiply two powers with the same base, such as 7^2 and 7^3?

$$7^2 \cdot 7^3 = (7 \cdot 7) \cdot (7 \cdot 7 \cdot 7) = 7^5$$

Notice that $7^2 \cdot 7^3 = 7^5 = 7^{2+3}$. In general, when you multiply powers with the same base, you can add the exponents.

Key Concepts   **Multiplying Powers With the Same Base**

To multiply numbers or variables with the same base, add the exponents.

Arithmetic	Algebra
$2^3 \cdot 2^4 = 2^{3+4} = 2^7$	$a^m \cdot a^n = a^{m+n}$, for positive integers m and n.

You *simplify* an expression by doing as many of the indicated operations as possible.

1 EXAMPLE   Multiplying Powers

Simplify each expression.

a. $3 \cdot 3^3$

$3^1 \cdot 3^3 = 3^{1+3}$ **Add the exponents of powers with the same base.**

$= 3^4$

$= 81$ **Simplify.**

b. $a^5 \cdot a \cdot b^2$

$a^5 \cdot a^1 \cdot b^2 = a^{5+1}b^2$ **Add the exponents of powers with the same base.**

$= a^6b^2$ **Simplify.**

✓ **Check Understanding**   Example 1

1. Simplify each expression.

a. $2^2 \cdot 2^3$ **b.** $m^5 \cdot m^7$ **c.** $x^2 \cdot x^3 \cdot y \cdot y^4$

What You'll Learn

OBJECTIVE 1 To multiply powers with the same base

OBJECTIVE 2 To find a power of a power

...And Why

To learn the rules for operating with exponents

✓ **Check Skills You'll Need**

Write using exponents.

1. $k \cdot k \cdot k \cdot k$

2. $m \cdot n \cdot m \cdot n$

3. $2 \cdot 2 \cdot 2 \cdot 2$

4. $5 \cdot 5 \cdot 5$

🔍 For help, go to Lesson 4-2.

Need Help?

Recall that $3 = 3^1$ and $a = a^1$ because a base with exponent 1 is equal to the base itself.

---

iTEXT Interactive lesson includes instant self-check, tutorials, and activities.

2 EXAMPLE   **Using the Commutative Property**

Simplify $-2x^2 \cdot 3x^5$.

$-2x^2 \cdot 3x^5 = -2 \cdot 3 \cdot x^2 \cdot x^5$ Use the Commutative Property of Multiplication.

$\qquad = -6x^{2+5}$ Add the exponents.

$\qquad = -6x^7$ Simplify.

☑ **Check Understanding**   Example 2

2. Simplify each expression.

a. $6a^3 \cdot 3a$ **b.** $-5c^2 \cdot -3c^7$ **c.** $4x^2 \cdot 3x^4$

Test-Taking Tip

When in doubt, write it out! If you are unsure about the rules for multiplying powers, write the powers out. For instance, write $x^2 \cdot x^5$ as $(x \cdot x) \cdot (x \cdot x \cdot x \cdot x \cdot x)$. This simplifies to x^7.

OBJECTIVE

2   Finding a Power of a Power

You can find the power of a power by using the rule of Multiplying Powers With the Same Base.

$(7^2)^3 = (7^2) \cdot (7^2) \cdot (7^2)$ Use 7^2 as a base 3 times.

$\qquad = 7^{2+2+2}$ When multiplying powers with the same base, add the exponents.

$\qquad = 7^6$ Simplify.

Notice that $(7^2)^3 = 7^6 = 7^{2 \cdot 3}$. You can raise a power to a power by multiplying the exponents.

Key Concepts   **Finding a Power of a Power**

To find a power of a power, multiply the exponents.

Arithmetic	Algebra
$(2^3)^4 = 2^{3 \cdot 4} = 2^{12}$	$(a^m)^n = a^{m \cdot n}$, for positive integers m and n.

Reading Math

You read $(3^2)^3$ as "three squared to the third power." You read $(a^6)^2$ as "a to the sixth power squared."

3 EXAMPLE   **Simplifying Powers of Powers**

Simplify each expression.

a. $(3^2)^3$ **b.** $(a^6)^2$

$(3^2)^3 = (3)^{2 \cdot 3}$ ← Multiply the exponents. → $(a^6)^2 = a^{6 \cdot 2}$

$\qquad = (3)^6$ ← Simplify the exponent. → $\qquad = a^{12}$

$\qquad = 729$ ← Simplify.

☑ **Check Understanding**   Example 3

3. Simplify each expression.

a. $(2^4)^2$ **b.** $(c^5)^4$ **c.** $(m^3)^2$

EXERCISES

For more exercises, see *Extra Practice*.

Practice and Problem Solving

A Practice by Example

Simplify each expression.

Example 1
(page 205)

1. $4^2 \cdot 4$

2. $a^2 \cdot a^5$

3. $x^4 \cdot y \cdot x^5 \cdot y$

4. $10^2 \cdot 10^5$

5. $2^2 \cdot 2^5$

6. $x^4 \cdot x^4$

7. $m^{50} \cdot m^2$

8. $(3)^2 \cdot (2)^3 \cdot 2 \cdot 3$

9. $x \cdot y \cdot y \cdot x^5 \cdot y^3$

Example 2
(page 206)

10. $7b^3 \cdot 4b^4$

11. $-9c^2 \cdot -2c^8$

12. $5x^3 \cdot 2x^6$

13. $4y^7 \cdot 6y^4$

14. $-2a^2 \cdot -2a^2$

15. $9b^2 \cdot -4b^2$

16. $-7x^6 \cdot -5x^8$

17. $-5d^5 \cdot 6d^2$

18. $4b^4 \cdot 12b^7$

Example 3
(page 206)

19. $(10^3)^2$

20. $(x^3)^4$

21. $(m^6)^4$

22. $(2^2)^3$

23. $(3^2)^4$

24. $(c^2)^8$

25. $(x^5)^7$

26. $(0^5)^8$

27. $(g^8)^{12}$

B Apply Your Skills

Complete each equation.

28. $8^2 \cdot 8^{\blacksquare} = 8^9$

29. $c^{\blacksquare} \cdot c^4 = c^{11}$

30. $(9^{\blacksquare})^4 = 9^{16}$

31. $5^6 \cdot 5^{\blacksquare} = 5^{14}$

32. $x^{\blacksquare} \cdot x^{12} = x^{15}$

33. $(a^{\blacksquare})^9 = a^{27}$

Compare. Use >, <, or = to complete each statement.

34. $25^2 \ \blacksquare \ (5^2)^2$

35. $(2^7)^7 \ \blacksquare \ (2^{25})^2$

36. $(4^3 \cdot 4^2)^3 \ \blacksquare \ 4^9$

37. Open-Ended A megabyte is 2^{20} bytes. Use exponents to write 2^{20} in four different ways.

38. Writing in Math Explain why $x^8 \cdot x^2$ has the same value as $x^5 \cdot x^5$.

39. Error Analysis Marcos thinks that $x^4 + x^4$ simplifies to $2x^4$. Doug thinks that $x^4 + x^4$ simplifies to x^8. Which result is correct? Explain.

C Challenge

40. Reasoning Does $-(2^3)^2$ have the same value as $(-2^3)^2$? Justify your answer.

41. Reasoning Which of 2^{30} or 2^{16} is twice the value of 2^{15}? Explain.

Geometry **Find the area of each rectangle.**

42.

$3x^2$

x

43.

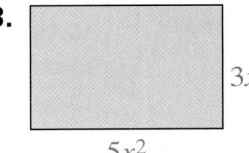

$3x$

$5x^2$

44.

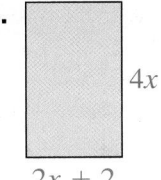

$4x$

$2x + 2$

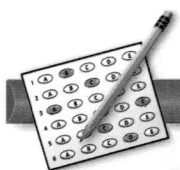

Test Prep

Multiple Choice

45. $(x^2)(y^5)(x) = \underline{\ ?\ }$

A. x^2y B. x^2y^5 C. x^3y^5 D. x^7y

Take It to the NET
Online lesson quiz at
www.PHSchool.com
Web Code: ada-0407

46. What is the simplest form for $a^{10} \cdot a \cdot a^2$?

F. $a^{10} \cdot a^3$ G. a^{12} H. a^{13} I. a^{20}

47. $(9^5)^5 = \underline{\ ?\ }$

A. 9^1 B. 9^{10} C. 9^{25} D. 9^{55}

Short Response

48. a. Find four expressions equivalent to 2^{13}.

     b. Explain why each is equivalent to 2^{13} for part (a).

Mixed Review

Lesson 4-6 **Evaluate. Write in simplest form.**

49. $\dfrac{mn}{m-6}$, for $m = 4$ and $n = 2$

50. $\dfrac{g + gh}{h - g}$, for $g = -3$ and $h = -5$

Lesson 2-8 **Graph the solutions of each inequality on a number line.**

51. $x < -3$ **52.** $a > 0$ **53.** $y \le -4$ **54.** $b > -2$

Lesson 1-2  **55. Party Planning** The Scotts are getting ready for a barbeque. They buy 8 lb of hamburger at $1.50/lb and 10 lb of chicken at $1.25/lb. Write and simplify an expression that shows the total cost.

Math at Work

Geophysicist

A **geophysicist** studies Earth's surface, including the history of Earth's crust and rock formations. Geophysicists search for oil, natural gas, minerals, and underground water. They also work to solve environmental problems. They study what makes up Earth's interior, as well as its magnetic, electrical, and gravitational forces. They often study earthquakes and volcanoes.

Geophysicists use physics and mathematics in their studies. Much of their work involves measurement. They use instruments to track sound waves, gravity, energy waves, and magnetic fields. Exponents appear in the data that geophysicists gather because they often work with very large numbers.

Take It to the NET For more information about geophysicists, go to **www.PHSchool.com**.
Web Code: adb-2031

Evaluating Expressions With Graphing Calculators

For Use With Lesson 4-7

You can use a graphing calculator to evaluate an expression.

1 EXAMPLE

Use a graphing calculator to evaluate $-4x^2 + x - 2$ for $x = 6$.

Step 1 First store the value 6 to the variable x.
Press 6 $\boxed{\text{STO}\blacktriangleright}$ $\boxed{x}$ $\boxed{\text{ENTER}}$.

Step 2 Enter $-4x^2 + x - 2$. Press $\boxed{\text{ENTER}}$.

```
6→X
                          6
-4X²+X-2
                      -140
■
```

To evaluate the expression in Example 1 for another value of x, start by storing that value to x. Press **ENTRY** *twice* to recall the expression $-4x^2 + x - 2$ from memory. Then press $\boxed{\text{ENTER}}$ again. Repeat to evaluate the expression for another value of x.

2 EXAMPLE

Use a graphing calculator to evaluate $3c^3 + 5d - 6$ for $c = -2$ and $d = 7$.

You can evaluate an expression with more than one variable by following Step 1 twice to store the value of each variable separately. Then follow the directions in Step 2 to enter and evaluate the expression.

```
-2→C
                         -2
7→D
                          7
3C^3+5D-6
                          5
■
```

To evaluate the expression for other values of the variables, first store the new values. Press **ENTRY** until the expression appears on the calculator screen. Then press $\boxed{\text{ENTER}}$ again to evaluate the expression.

EXERCISES

Use a graphing calculator. Evaluate each expression for the given values of the variable(s). Round to the nearest hundredth where necessary.

1. $x^2 - 3x + 8$
   a. $x = 2$ **b.** $x = -3$ **c.** $x = 4.2$

2. $y^6 + y$
   a. $y = -5$ **b.** $y = 3$ **c.** $y = 1.5$

3. $-4c^2 + 34b - 42$
   a. $c = -12; b = 3$ **b.** $c = 2; b = 4$ **c.** $c = 5.1; b = 4$

4. Evaluate $6x^3 - 2x$ for whole number values of x from 1 to 10.

4-8 Exponents and Division

What You'll Learn

OBJECTIVE 1 To divide expressions containing exponents

OBJECTIVE 2 To simplify expressions with integer exponents

. . . And Why

To solve real-world problems involving science

 Check Skills You'll Need

Write in simplest form.

1. $\dfrac{x^2}{x}$

2. $\dfrac{y}{y^2}$

3. $\dfrac{6xy}{9y}$

4. $\dfrac{4ab^2}{16b}$

 For help, go to Lesson 4-4.

OBJECTIVE

1 Dividing Expressions Containing Exponents

In Lesson 4-7, you learned that you add exponents to multiply powers with the same base. To divide powers with the same base, you subtract exponents. Here's why.

$$\frac{7^8}{7^3} = \frac{7 \cdot 7 \cdot 7 \cdot 7 \cdot 7 \cdot 7 \cdot 7 \cdot 7}{7 \cdot 7 \cdot 7}$$ **Expand the numerator and denominator.**

$$= \frac{7^1 \cdot 7^1 \cdot 7^1 \cdot 7 \cdot 7 \cdot 7 \cdot 7 \cdot 7}{_1 7 \cdot _1 7 \cdot _1 7}$$ **Divide common factors.**

$$= 7^5$$

Notice that $\dfrac{7^8}{7^3} = 7^5 = 7^{8-3}$. This suggests the following rule.

Key Concepts — Dividing Powers With the Same Base

To divide numbers or variables *with the same nonzero base*, subtract the exponents.

Arithmetic

$$\frac{4^5}{4^2} = 4^{5-2} = 4^3$$

Algebra

$$\frac{a^m}{a^n} = a^{m-n}, \text{ for } a \neq 0 \text{ and positive integers } m \text{ and } n.$$

---

1 EXAMPLE Dividing a Power by a Power

Simplify each expression.

a. $\dfrac{3^8}{3^5}$

b. $\dfrac{a^4}{a^2}$

$\dfrac{3^8}{3^5} = 3^{8-5}$ ⟵ **Subtract the exponents.** ⟶ $\dfrac{a^4}{a^2} = a^{4-2}$

$= 3^3$ ⟵ **Simplify the exponent.** ⟶ $= a^2$

$= 27$ ⟵ **Simplify.**

✓ Check Understanding Example 1

1. Simplify each expression.

a. $\dfrac{10^7}{10^4}$

b. $\dfrac{x^{25}}{x^{18}}$

c. $\dfrac{12m^5}{3m}$

TEXT Interactive lesson includes instant self-check, tutorials, and activities.

2 Simplifying Expressions With Integer Exponents

What happens when you divide powers with the same base and get zero as an exponent? Consider $\frac{3^4}{3^4}$.

$$\frac{3^4}{3^4} = 3^{4-4} = 3^0 \qquad \frac{3^4}{3^4} = \frac{3^1 \cdot 3^1 \cdot 3^1 \cdot 3^1}{3^1 \cdot 3^1 \cdot 3^1 \cdot 3^1} = \frac{1}{1} = 1$$

Notice that $\frac{3^4}{3^4} = 3^0$ and $\frac{3^4}{3^4} = 1$. This suggests the following rule.

Key Concepts | **Zero as an Exponent**

Arithmetic	Algebra
$3^0 = 1$	$a^0 = 1$, for $a \neq 0$.

2 EXAMPLE Simplifying When Zero Is an Exponent

Simplify each expression.

a. $\dfrac{(-8)^2}{(-8)^2}$

$\dfrac{(-8)^2}{(-8)^2} = (-8)^{2-2}$ **Subtract the exponents.**

$= (-8)^0$ **Simplify.**

$= 1$

b. $\dfrac{6b^3}{18b^3}$

$\dfrac{6b^3}{18b^3} = \frac{1}{3}b^0$ **Subtract the exponents. Simplify $\frac{6}{18}$.**

$= \frac{1}{3} \cdot 1$ **Simplify b^0.**

$= \frac{1}{3}$ **Multiply.**

✔ **Check Understanding** Example 2

2. Simplify each expression.

a. 43^0 **b.** $\dfrac{5^2 x^6}{5x^6}$ **c.** $\dfrac{x^5 y^6}{x^5 y^3}$ **d.** $5x^0$

What happens when you divide powers with the same base and get a negative exponent? Consider $\frac{3^2}{3^4}$.

$$\frac{3^2}{3^4} = 3^{2-4} = 3^{-2} \qquad \frac{3^2}{3^4} = \frac{3^1 \cdot 3^1}{3^1 \cdot 3^1 \cdot 3 \cdot 3} = \frac{1}{3^2}$$

These results suggest the rule at the top of page 212.

Key Concepts   **Negative Exponents**

Arithmetic	**Algebra**
$3^{-2} = \dfrac{1}{3^2}$	$a^{-n} = \dfrac{1}{a^n}$, for $a \neq 0$.

Real-World 🌐 Connection

Hummingbirds may range from 0.0022 kg to 0.02 kg in mass.

A hummingbird has a mass of about 10^{-2} kg, or $\dfrac{1}{10^2}$ kg. To simplify 10^{-2}, you write $\dfrac{1}{100}$ or 0.01. So the hummingbird has a mass of 0.01 kg. To simplify an expression such as x^{-2}, you write it as $\dfrac{1}{x^2}$, using no negative exponents.

3 EXAMPLE   **Using Positive Exponents**

Simplify each expression.

a. $\dfrac{5^6}{5^8}$ b. $\dfrac{m^2}{m^5}$

$\dfrac{5^6}{5^8} = 5^{6-8}$ ←— **Subtract the exponents.** —→ $\dfrac{m^2}{m^5} = m^{2-5}$

$= 5^{-2}$ $= m^{-3}$

$= \dfrac{1}{5^2}$ ←— **Write with a positive exponent.** —→ $= \dfrac{1}{m^3}$

$= \dfrac{1}{25}$ ←— **Simplify.**

✓ **Check Understanding**   Example 3

3. Simplify each expression.

a. $\dfrac{4^5}{4^7}$ b. $\dfrac{a^4}{a^6}$ c. $\dfrac{3y^8}{9y^{12}}$

You can also write an expression such as $\dfrac{1}{x^2}$ so that there is no fraction bar.

4 EXAMPLE   **Using Negative Exponents**

Write $\dfrac{x^2 y^3}{x^3 y}$ without a fraction bar.

$\dfrac{x^2 y^3}{x^3 y} = x^{2-3} y^{3-1}$ **Use the Rule for Dividing Powers With the Same Base.**

$= x^{-1} y^2$ **Subtract the exponents.**

✓ **Check Understanding**   Example 4

4. Write each expression without a fraction bar.

a. $\dfrac{b^3}{b^9}$ b. $\dfrac{m^3 n^2}{m^6 n^8}$ c. $\dfrac{x y^5}{x^5 y^3}$

EXERCISES

For more exercises, see *Extra Practice*.

Practice and Problem Solving

 **Practice by Example**

Example 1
(page 210)

Simplify each expression.

1. $\dfrac{2^5}{2^2}$
2. $\dfrac{h^6}{h^2}$
3. $\dfrac{10y^7}{6y^2}$
4. $\dfrac{10b^8}{2b^6}$

5. $\dfrac{6^2}{6^1}$
6. $\dfrac{11^5}{11^3}$
7. $\dfrac{x^7}{x^3}$
8. $\dfrac{a^{27}}{a^{19}}$

Example 2
(page 211)

9. $\dfrac{18x^{20}}{18x^{20}}$
10. $(-4)^0$
11. $\dfrac{w^8z^{15}}{w^8z^8}$
12. 3^0

13. $\dfrac{b^3c^2}{b^3c}$
14. $\dfrac{(-2)^4}{(-2)^4}$
15. $2b^0$
16. $\dfrac{2y^3}{8y^3}$

Example 3
(page 212)

17. $\dfrac{7^3}{7^5}$
18. $\dfrac{m^2}{m^6}$
19. $\dfrac{4a^3}{20a^6}$
20. $\dfrac{100m^{100}}{200m^{200}}$

21. $\dfrac{b^5}{b^8}$
22. $\dfrac{3m}{15m^3}$
23. $\dfrac{6^7}{6^{11}}$
24. $\dfrac{a^2}{a^7}$

Example 4
(page 212)

Write each expression without a fraction bar.

25. $\dfrac{y^4}{y^7}$
26. $\dfrac{a^2b^4}{a^8b^2}$
27. $\dfrac{m^5n^6}{m^7n^8}$
28. $\dfrac{xy^2}{x^4y^9}$

 **Apply Your Skills**

Complete each equation.

29. $\dfrac{x^6}{x^{\blacksquare}} = x^4$
30. $\dfrac{14x^5}{7x^3} = 2x^{\blacksquare}$
31. $\dfrac{10^5}{10^{\blacksquare}} = 1$

32. $\dfrac{1}{a^3} = a^{\blacksquare}$
33. $\dfrac{y^{\blacksquare}}{y^9} = y^{-4}$
34. $\dfrac{1}{-27} = (-3)^{\blacksquare}$

35. Earthquakes The *magnitude* of an earthquake is a measure of the amount of energy released. An earthquake of magnitude 6 releases about 30 times as much energy as an earthquake of magnitude 5. The magnitude of the 1989 earthquake in Loma Prieta, California, was about 7. The magnitude of the 1933 earthquake in Sanriku, Japan, was about 9. Simplify $\dfrac{30^9}{30^7}$ to find how many times as much energy was released in the Sanriku earthquake.

36. Error Analysis A student wrote that $-5^0 = 1$. What was the student's error?

Real-World Connection

The photo shows damage from the Loma Prieta, California, earthquake of October 17, 1989.

37. Open-Ended Write three different quotients that equal 5^{-7}.

38. Writing in Math Is -3^{-2} positive or negative? Justify your answer.

Write each expression without a fraction bar.

39. $\dfrac{x^3}{x^5}$
40. $\dfrac{a^9b^3}{a^7b^8}$
41. $\dfrac{m^9n^3}{m^2n^{10}}$
42. $\dfrac{b^{14}c^2}{b^9c^{11}}$

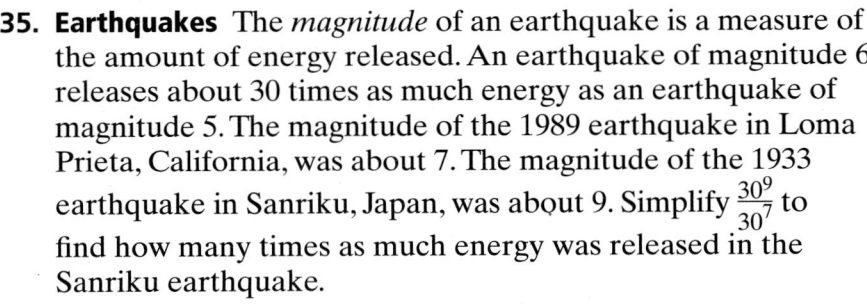 **Challenge**

Simplify each expression.

43. $\dfrac{5x^2}{10x^{-5}}$
44. $\dfrac{5b^{-7}}{5b^{-2}}$
45. $\dfrac{4^2 + 6^2}{2^2}$
46. $\dfrac{r^{-5}}{s^{-2}}$

4-8 Exponents and Division **213**

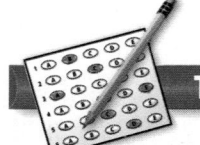

Multiple Choice

47. What is a simpler form of $\frac{x^5 y^4}{x^2 y^9}$?

  A. $\frac{x^5}{y^3}$ **B.** $\frac{y^5}{x^3}$ **C.** $x^3 y^5$ **D.** $\frac{x^3}{y^5}$

Take It to the NET
Online lesson quiz at
www.PHSchool.com
Web Code: ada-0408

48. What is a simpler form of $\frac{12a^{35}}{36a^{50}}$?

  F. $\frac{1^{85}}{3^a}$ **G.** $\frac{1}{3a^{85}}$ **H.** $\frac{1}{3a^{15}}$ **I.** $\frac{1}{3}a^{15}$

49. Which expression is equal to $\frac{42a^6 b^7}{7a^3 b^3}$?

  A. $6a^3 b^{-4}$ **B.** $6a^3 b^4$ **C.** $6a^{-3} b^4$ **D.** $6a^{-3} b^{-4}$

Short Response

50. **a.** Is 5^{-3} a negative number?   **b.** Explain your answer.

Mixed Review

Lesson 4-7   **Simplify each expression.**

51. $5^2 \cdot 5$ **52.** $x^7 \cdot x^2$ **53.** $2a^9 \cdot 8a^7$

Lesson 3-1   **Estimate using front-end estimation.**

54. $5.68 + 3.24$ **55.** $17.86 + 2.321$ **56.** $20.2 + 5.8$

Lesson 2-7   **57.** **Number Sense** The sum of three consecutive integers is 264. What are the three integers?

✓ Checkpoint Quiz 2   Lessons 4-5 through 4-8

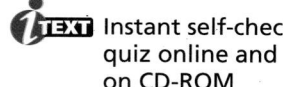 Instant self-check
quiz online and
on CD-ROM

Write three fractions equivalent to each given fraction.

  1. $\frac{3}{12}$ **2.** $\frac{12}{36}$ **3.** $\frac{49}{70}$ **4.** $\frac{18}{28}$ **5.** $\frac{4}{5}$

Evaluate for $a = 4$ and $b = -6$. Write in simplest form.

  6. $\frac{a}{2b}$ **7.** $\frac{b + a}{a}$ **8.** $\frac{a - b}{15}$ **9.** $\frac{b - a}{a^2}$ **10.** $\frac{3a + b}{24}$

Graph the rational numbers below on the same number line.

  11. -0.8○   **12.** $\frac{1}{2}$ **13.** 0.6○   **14.** $-\frac{2}{10}$ **15.** $\frac{9}{10}$

Simplify each expression.

  16. $2^3 \cdot 2^4$ **17.** $(x^5)^{10}$ **18.** $\frac{18a^4}{3a^2}$ **19.** $\frac{x^3}{x^8}$ **20.** $\frac{a^3 b^5}{a^9 b^5}$

21. If 12 of 16 students vote to do a project, what fraction of the students is this? Write the fraction in simplest form.

Scientific Notation

4-9

OBJECTIVE

1 Writing and Evaluating Scientific Notation

vestigation

Exploring Scientific Notation

1. Copy and complete the chart below.

5×10^4	$= 5 \times 10,000$	$= 50,000$
5×10^3	$= 5 \times 1,000$	$= \blacksquare$
5×10^2	$= 5 \times \blacksquare$	$= \blacksquare$
5×10^1	$= 5 \times \blacksquare$	$= \blacksquare$
5×10^0	$= 5 \times \blacksquare$	$= \blacksquare$
$5 \times 10^{-1} = 5 \times \frac{1}{10}$	$= 5 \times 0.1$	$= 0.5$
$5 \times 10^{-2} = 5 \times \blacksquare$	$= 5 \times 0.01$	$= 0.05$
$5 \times 10^{-3} = 5 \times \blacksquare$	$= 5 \times \blacksquare$	$= 0.005$
$5 \times 10^{-4} = 5 \times \blacksquare$	$= 5 \times \blacksquare$	$= \blacksquare$

2. Patterns Describe any related patterns that you see in your chart.

3. a. Based on the patterns you see, simplify 5×10^7.
b. Simplify 5×10^{-6}.

What You'll Learn

OBJECTIVE
1 To write and evaluate numbers in scientific notation

OBJECTIVE
2 To calculate with scientific notation

. . . And Why

To solve real-world problems involving weight and mass

 Check Skills You'll Need

Write each expression with a single exponent.

1. $10^3 \cdot 10^5$

2. $10^7 \cdot 10^9$

3. $10^5 \cdot 10^{-3}$

4. $10^{-6} \cdot 10^3$

For help, go to Lesson 4-7.

New Vocabulary
• scientific notation
• standard notation

Scientific notation provides a way to write numbers using powers of 10. You write a number in scientific notation as the product of two factors.

Second factor is a power of 10.

$$7,500,000,000,000 = 7.5 \times 10^{12}$$

First factor is greater than or equal to 1, but less than 10.

Scientific notation lets you know the size of a number without having to count digits. For example, if the exponent of 10 is 6, the number is in the millions. If the exponent is 9, the number is in the billions.

 Need Help?

For help with multiplying by powers of ten, see Skills Handbook, page 768.

TEXT Interactive lesson includes instant self-check, tutorials, and activities.

1 EXAMPLE Real-World 🌐 Problem Solving

About 4,200,000 people visit the Statue of Liberty every year. Write this number in scientific notation.

4,200,000 6 places	Move the decimal point to get a decimal greater than 1 but less than 10.
4.2	Drop the zeros after the 2.
4.2×10^6	You moved the decimal point **6** places. The number is large. Use 6 as the exponent of 10.

✓ **Check Understanding** Example 1

1. Write each number in scientific notation.

   a. 54,500,000   b. 723,000   c. 602,000,000,000

In scientific notation, you use a negative exponent to write a number between 0 and 1.

2 EXAMPLE Writing in Scientific Notation

Write 0.000079 in scientific notation.

0.000079 5 places	Move the decimal point to get a decimal greater than 1 but less than 10.
7.9	Drop the zeros before the 7.
7.9×10^{-5}	You moved the decimal point **5** places. The number is small. Use −5 as the exponent of 10.

✓ **Check Understanding** Example 2

2. Write each number in scientific notation.

   a. 0.00021   b. 0.00000005   c. 0.0000000000803

You can change expressions from scientific notation to **standard notation** by simplifying the product of the two factors.

3 EXAMPLE Writing in Standard Notation

Write each number in standard notation.

a. 8.9×10^5 b. 2.71×10^{-6}

8.90000	Write zeros while moving the decimal point.	000002.71
890,000	Rewrite in standard notation.	0.00000271

3. Write each number in standard notation.

    a. 3.21×10^7 **b.** 5.9×10^{-8} **c.** 1.006×10^{10}

For a number to be in scientific notation, the digit in front of the decimal must be 1 or between 1 and 10.

4 EXAMPLE   **Changing to Scientific Notation**

Write each number in scientific notation.

a. 0.37×10^{10}

$$0.37 \times 10^{10} = 3.7 \times 10^{-1} \times 10^{10} \quad \text{Write 0.37 as } 3.7 \times 10^{-1}.$$
$$= 3.7 \times 10^{9} \quad \text{Add the exponents.}$$

b. 453.1×10^{8}

$$453.1 \times 10^{8} = 4.531 \times 10^{2} \times 10^{8} \quad \text{Write 453.1 as } 4.531 \times 10^{2}.$$
$$= 4.531 \times 10^{10} \quad \text{Add the exponents.}$$

✓ **Check Understanding** Example 4

4. Write each number in scientific notation.

    a. 16×10^5 **b.** 0.203×10^6 **c.** $7,243 \times 10^{12}$

You can compare and order numbers using scientific notation. First compare the powers of 10, and then compare the decimals.

5 EXAMPLE   **Comparing and Ordering Numbers**

Order 0.064×10^8, 312×10^2, and 0.58×10^7 from least to greatest.

Write each number in scientific notation.

0.064×10^8 312×10^2 0.58×10^7
      ↓   ↓   ↓
6.4×10^6 3.12×10^4 5.8×10^6

Order the powers of 10. Arrange the decimals with the same power of 10 in order.

3.12×10^4 5.8×10^6 6.4×10^6

Write the original numbers in order.

   $312 \times 10^2, 0.58 \times 10^7, 0.064 \times 10^8$

✓ **Check Understanding** Example 5

5. Order from least to greatest.

    a. $526 \times 10^7, 18.3 \times 10^6, 0.098 \times 10^9$
    b. $8 \times 10^{-9}, 14.7 \times 10^{-7}, 0.22 \times 10^{-10}$

2 Calculating With Scientific Notation

You can multiply numbers in scientific notation using the rule for Multiplying Powers with the Same Base.

6 EXAMPLE Multiplying With Scientific Notation

Multiply 3×10^{-7} and 9×10^3. Express the result in scientific notation.

$(3 \times 10^{-7})(9 \times 10^3) = 3 \times 9 \times 10^{-7} \times 10^3$	Use the Commutative Property of Multiplication.
$= 27 \times 10^{-7} \times 10^3$	Multiply 3 and 9.
$= 27 \times 10^{-4}$	Add the exponents.
$= 2.7 \times 10^1 \times 10^{-4}$	Write 27 as 2.7×10^1.
$= 2.7 \times 10^{-3}$	Add the exponents.

✓ **Check Understanding** Example 6

6. Multiply. Express each result in scientific notation.

　a. $(4 \times 10^4)(6 \times 10^6)$　　**b.** $(7.1 \times 10^{-8})(8 \times 10^4)$

7 EXAMPLE Real-World Problem Solving

Measurement The Great Pyramid of Giza in Egypt contains about 2.3×10^6 blocks of stone. On the average, each block of stone weighs about 5×10^3 lb. About how many pounds of stone does the Great Pyramid contain?

$(2.3 \times 10^6)(5 \times 10^3)$	Multiply number of blocks by weight of each.
$= 2.3 \times 5 \times 10^6 \times 10^3$	Use the Commutative Property of Multiplication.
$= 11.5 \times 10^6 \times 10^3$	Multiply 2.3 and 5.
$= 11.5 \times 10^9$	Add the exponents.
$= 1.15 \times 10^1 \times 10^9$	Write 11.5 as 1.15×10^1.
$= 1.15 \times 10^{10}$	Add the exponents.

The Great Pyramid contains about 1.15×10^{10} lb of stone.

✓ **Check Understanding** Example 7

7. **Chemistry** A hydrogen atom has a mass of 1.67×10^{-27} kg. What is the mass of 6×10^3 hydrogen atoms? Express the result in scientific notation.

Real-World Connection

In ancient times, the Great Pyramid of Giza was plundered inside and out. Outside, most of the casing of smooth, white limestone was removed. The height of the pyramid is now about 30 ft less than the original height.

EXERCISES

For more exercises, see *Extra Practice*.

Practice and Problem Solving

A Practice by Example

Examples 1 and 2
(page 216)

In Exercises 1–7, write each number in scientific notation.

1. 8,900,000,000
2. 555,900,000
3. 0.000631
4. 0.000006
5. 0.209
6. 0.00409
7. **Solar System** Pluto is about 5 billion km from the sun.

Example 3
(page 216)

Write each number in standard notation.

8. 5.94×10^7
9. 2.104×10^{-8}
10. 1.2×10^5
11. 7.2×10^{-4}
12. 2.75×10^8
13. 6.0502×10^{-3}

Example 4
(page 217)

Write each number in scientific notation.

14. 0.09×10^{12}
15. 0.72×10^{-4}
16. 52.8×10^9
17. $3,508 \times 10^{-7}$

Example 5
(page 217)

Order from least to greatest.

18. $16 \times 10^9, 2.3 \times 10^{12}, 0.065 \times 10^{11}$
19. $253 \times 10^{-9}, 3.7 \times 10^{-8}, 12.9 \times 10^{-7}$
20. $65 \times 10^4, 432 \times 10^3, 2.996 \times 10^4$

Example 6
(page 218)

Multiply. Express each result in scientific notation.

21. $(5 \times 10^6)(6 \times 10^2)$
22. $(4.3 \times 10^3)(2 \times 10^{-8})$
23. $(9 \times 10^{-3})(7 \times 10^8)$
24. $(3 \times 10^2)(2 \times 10^2)$

Example 7
(page 218)

25. **Zoology** An ant weighs about 2×10^{-5} lb. There are about 10^{15} ants on Earth. How many pounds of ants are on Earth?

B Apply Your Skills

In Exercises 26–30, write each number in standard notation.

26. 9×10^2
27. 8.43×10^6
28. 6.02×10^{-7}

29. **Astronomy** One light year is 5.88×10^{12} mi.

30. **Zoology** The most venomous scorpion delivers 9×10^{-6} oz of venom per bite.

Order from least to greatest.

31. $10^9, 10^{-8}, 10^5, 10^{-6}, 10^0$
32. $55.8 \times 10^{-5}, 782 \times 10^{-8}, 9.1 \times 10^{-5}, 1,009 \times 10^2, 0.8 \times 10^{-4}$

33. **Writing in Math** Explain how to write each number in scientific notation.
    a. 0.00043
    b. 523.4×10^5

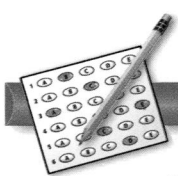

C Challenge   **Solve. Write each result in scientific notation.**

🌐 **34. Statistics** The population density of India is about 8.33×10^2 people per square mile. The area of India is 1.2×10^6 mi^2. What is the approximate population of India?

🌐 **35. Health Care** In the year 2005, the population of the United States is expected to be about 296 million. Health expenditures will be about $7,350 per person. In total, about how much will the United States spend on health care in 2005?

Test Prep

Multiple Choice   **36.** What is 55,000 in scientific notation?
    A. 5.5×10^{-4} **B.** 55×10^3 **C.** 0.55×10^4 **D.** 5.5×10^4

37. What is 2×10^{-4} in standard notation?
    F. 8,000   **G.** 0.0008   **H.** 0.0002   **I.** 2,000

Reading Comprehension   Read the passage before doing Exercises 38 and 39.

One Giant Leap

On July 20, 1969, Neil Armstrong and Edwin "Buzz" Aldrin, Jr., were first to set foot on the moon. With his first step, Armstrong announced over the radio, "That's one small step for a man, one giant leap for mankind."

The moon is about 380,000 km from Earth. The footsteps the astronauts left on the moon will probably be visible for at least 10 million years.

38. What is the distance in meters from Earth to the moon? Use scientific notation.

39. How many 0.5-meter footsteps would it take to walk from Earth to the moon? Use scientific notation.

Take It to the NET
Online lesson quiz at
www.PHSchool.com
Web Code: ada-0409

Mixed Review

Lesson 4-8   **Simplify each expression.**

40. $\dfrac{10^7}{10^9}$ **41.** $\dfrac{x^3 y}{xy}$ **42.** $\dfrac{15b^2}{10b^5}$ **43.** $\dfrac{9m^7}{3m^5 n}$

Lesson 3-4   **Algebra** Use the formula $d = rt$. Find d, r, or t.

44. $r = 46.2$ m/h,   **45.** $d = 4.68$ ft,   **46.** $d = 988$ cm,
    $t = 2.75$ h $t = 5.2$ h $r = 6.5$ cm/s

Lesson 1-8   **47. Patterns** A clock strikes a chime once at one o'clock, twice at two o'clock, and so on. In a twelve-hour period, what is the total number of chimes the clock strikes?

When you enter a number with more digits than a calculator can display, the calculator translates the number into scientific notation. "E11" in the output below means "$\times 10^{11}$."

112,345,678,999 [ENTER] $\longrightarrow$ *1.12345679E11*   **The display shows the number rounded.**

You can use a calculator to calculate with numbers in scientific notation.

1 EXAMPLE

Use a calculator to find
$(9.8 \times 10^5)(4.56 \times 10^4)$.

> 9.8E5*4.56E4
>
>   4.4688E10

Use
EE 5 to enter E5 and
EE 4 to enter E4.

● The product is 4.4688×10^{10}.

2 EXAMPLE

Use a calculator to find
$3.9 \times 10^{-7} + 4.7 \times 10^{-8}$.

> 3.9E-7+4.7E-8
>
>   4.37E-7

Use [(−)] for
negative exponents.

● The sum is 4.37×10^{-7}.

EXERCISES

Use a calculator to simplify. Write each result in scientific notation.

1. $1.5 \times 10^{11} - 2.4 \times 10^8$

2. $6.97 \times 10^5 + 4.8 \times 10^{10}$

3. $(1.02 \times 10^9)(1.98 \times 10^7)$

4. $(5.1 \times 10^3) \div (3.64 \times 10^{10})$

5. $(2.8 \times 10^{13})(3.335 \times 10^{10})$

6. $9.807 \times 10^7 + 7.08 \times 10^{10}$

7. $7.1 \times 10^{-5} - 9.1 \times 10^{-6}$

8. $3.5 \times 10^{-6} + 6.76 \times 10^{-4}$

9. $(2.43 \times 10^{-3})(4.9 \times 10^{-10})$

10. $(1.08 \times 10^4) \div (7.3 \times 10^{-7})$

11. $(5.01 \times 10^{-3})(8.5 \times 10^{-8})$

12. $1.99 \times 10^{-5} - 3.81 \times 10^{-4}$

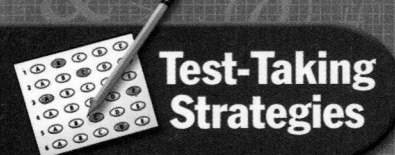
Reading-comprehension questions require that you read and understand information given to you in print in order to use mathematics to solve the problem.

EXAMPLE

Read the passage below. Then answer the questions based on what is stated or implied in the passage.

> **Solar System Masses** The sun is the largest object in our solar system. It contains approximately 98% of the total solar-system mass. The interior of the sun can hold over 1.3 million Earths. The mass of Earth is 5.98×10^{24} kg. The sun is approximately 330,000 times the mass of Earth.

What is the mass of the sun?

You read, "The sun is approximately 330,000 times the mass of Earth."

$$
\begin{aligned}
\text{Mass of sun} &\approx 330{,}000 \times \text{mass of Earth.} \\
M &\approx 330{,}000 \times 5.98 \times 10^{24} \\
&\approx 3.3 \times 10^5 \times 5.98 \times 10^{24} \\
&\approx 19.734 \times 10^{29} \\
&\approx 1.97 \times 10^{30}
\end{aligned}
$$

● The mass of the sun is about 1.97×10^{30} kg.

EXERCISES

Read the passage below. Then answer the questions based on what is stated or implied in the passage.

> **Planet Distances** The diameter of Jupiter is 142,800 km. Saturn is almost as big with a diameter of 120,000 km. Earth, by comparison, has a diameter of only 12,756 km. Jupiter's mass is 318 times the mass of Earth. Saturn's mass is only 95 times the mass of Earth.

1. Put the planets named in the above passage in order from smallest to largest, based on their diameters.

2. The mass of Jupiter is about how many times the mass of Saturn?

3. The diameter of Jupiter is about how many times the diameter of Saturn?

4. What could you conclude about Saturn from this passage?

Chapter Review

Vocabulary

base (p. 182)
composite number (p. 186)
divisible (p. 178)
equivalent fractions (p. 192)
exponents (p. 182)

factor (p. 179)
greatest common
    factor (GCF) (p. 187)
power (p. 182)
prime factorization (p. 187)

prime number (p. 186)
rational number (p. 201)
scientific notation (p. 215)
simplest form (p. 192)
standard notation (p. 216)

Reading Math
Understanding
Vocabulary

Choose the vocabulary term that correctly completes each sentence.

1. One integer is a ___?___ of another integer if it divides that integer with remainder zero.

2. A fraction is in ___?___ when the numerator and denominator have no factors in common other than 1.

3. A number that you can write as the quotient $\frac{a}{b}$ of two integers, where b is not zero, is a ___?___.

4. You can write numbers using powers of 10 in a shorthand way called ___?___.

5. You can show repeated multiplication with ___?___.

6. If a positive integer greater than 1 has exactly two factors, 1 and the integer itself, the integer is a ___?___.

Take It to the NET
Online vocabulary quiz
at **www.PHSchool.com**
Web Code: adj-0451

Skills and Concepts

4-1 Objectives

▼ To use divisibility tests (p. 178)

▼ To find factors (p. 179)

One integer is **divisible** by another if the remainder is zero when you divide. Divisibility tests help you find factors. One integer is a **factor** of another integer if it divides that integer with remainder zero.

List the positive factors of each number.

7. 12   **8.** 30   **9.** 42   **10.** 72   **11.** 111   **12.** 252

4-2 Objectives

▼ To use exponents (p. 182)

▼ To use the order of operations with exponents (p.183)

To simplify an expression that has an **exponent,** remember that the **base** is the number used as a factor. The exponent shows the number of times the base is used as a factor.

Simplify each expression.

13. 2^3

14. $3(10 - 7)^2$

15. $28 + (1 + 5)^2 \cdot 4$

16. -5^2

Evaluate each expression.

17. x^2, for $x = 11$

18. $7m^2 - 5$, for $m = 3$

19. $(2a + 1)^2$, for $a = -4$

20. b^2, for $b = -4$

4-3 Objectives

▼ To find the prime factorization of a number (p. 186)

▼ To find the greatest common factor (GCF) of two or more numbers (p. 187)

A **prime number** is an integer greater than 1 with exactly two positive factors, 1 and itself. An integer greater than 1 with more than two factors is a **composite number**. The **prime factorization** of a composite number is the product of its prime factors.

The **greatest common factor (GCF)** of two or more numbers or expressions is the greatest factor that the numbers or expressions have in common. You can list factors or use prime factorization to find the GCF of two or more numbers or expressions.

Is each number *prime, composite,* or *neither*? For each composite number, write the prime factorization. Use exponents where possible.

21. 13   **22.** 20   **23.** 73   **24.** 110   **25.** 87

Find the GCF.

26. 16, 60

27. 36, 81, 27

28. 15, 17, 30

29. $3x^2y, 9x^2$

30. $8a^2b, 14ab^2$

31. $3cd^4, 12c^3d, 6c^2d^2$

32. Reasoning Why is the GCF of two or more positive integers never greater than the least of the numbers?

4-4 Objectives

▼ To find equivalent fractions (p. 192)

▼ To write fractions in simplest form (p. 192)

Equivalent fractions describe the same part of a whole. A fraction is in **simplest form** when the numerator and the denominator have no common factors other than 1. You can use the GCF of the numerator and denominator to write a fraction in simplest form.

Write in simplest form.

33. $\frac{3}{15}$ **34.** $\frac{10}{20}$ **35.** $\frac{16}{52}$ **36.** $\frac{28}{40}$ **37.** $\frac{21}{33}$ **38.** $\frac{9}{54}$

39. $\frac{xy}{y}$ **40.** $\frac{25m}{5m}$ **41.** $\frac{2y}{8y}$ **42.** $\frac{2c}{5c}$ **43.** $\frac{9x^2}{27x}$ **44.** $\frac{36bc}{9c}$

4-5 Objectives

▼ To find all possibilities when you solve a problem (p. 197)

To account for all possibilities in a word problem, make an organized list or a diagram to keep track of possibilities as you find them.

45. School Mike, Don, Tameka, and Rosa sit in the four desks in the last row of desks. Each day they sit in a different order. How many days can they do this before they repeat a seating pattern?

4-6 Objectives

▼ To identify and graph rational numbers (p. 201)

▼ To evaluate fractions containing variables (p. 202)

A **rational number** is any number you can write as a quotient $\frac{a}{b}$ of two integers, where b is not zero.

Graph the rational numbers below on the same number line.

46. 2   **47.** -0.6 **48.** $-\frac{5}{10}$ **49.** $\frac{2}{10}$

Evaluate each expression for $a = -5$ and $b = -2$. Write in simplest form.

50. $\frac{b}{a}$ **51.** $\frac{a+b}{4b}$ **52.** $\frac{b-a}{a-b}$ **53.** $\frac{b^2}{a}$

4-7 and 4-8 Objectives

▼ To multiply powers with the same base (p. 205)

▼ To find a power of a power (p. 206)

▼ To divide expressions containing exponents (p. 210)

▼ To simplify expressions with integer exponents (p. 211)

To multiply numbers or variables with the same base, add the exponents. To raise a power to a power, multiply the exponents. To divide numbers or variables with the same nonzero base, subtract the exponents.

Simplify each expression.

54. $2^4 \cdot 2^3$ **55.** $7a^4 \cdot 3a^2$ **56.** $b \cdot c^2 \cdot b^6 \cdot c^2$ **57.** $(x^3)^5$

58. $(y^4)^5$ **59.** $\frac{4^8}{4^2}$ **60.** $\frac{b^2}{b^4}$ **61.** $\frac{28xy^7}{32xy^{12}}$

4-9 Objectives

▼ To write and evaluate numbers in scientific notation (p. 215)

▼ To calculate with scientific notation (p. 218)

Scientific notation provides a way to write numbers as the product of two factors, a power of 10 and a decimal greater than or equal to 1, but less than 10. To multiply numbers in scientific notation, multiply the decimals, multiply the powers of ten, and then put the result into scientific notation.

Write each number in scientific notation.

62. 2,000,000   **63.** 458,000,000   **64.** 0.0000007   **65.** 0.0000000059

Write each number in standard notation.

66. 8×10^{11} **67.** 3.2×10^{-6} **68.** 1.119×10^7 **69.** 5×10^{-12}

Order from least to greatest.

70. $3{,}644 \times 10^9, 12 \times 10^{11}, 4.3 \times 10^{10}$

71. $58 \times 10^{-10}, 8 \times 10^{-10}, 716 \times 10^{-10}$

Multiply. Express each result in scientific notation.

72. $(4 \times 10^9)(6 \times 10^6)$ **73.** $(5 \times 10^7)(3.6 \times 10^3)$

Chapter Test

Take It to the NET
Online chapter test at
www.PHSchool.com
Web Code: ada-0452

State whether each number is divisible by 2, 3, 5, 9, or 10.

1. 36   **2.** 100   **3.** 270

4. 84   **5.** 555   **6.** 49

List all the factors of each number.

7. 16   **8.** 30   **9.** 41

10. 23   **11.** 55   **12.** 64

Simplify each expression.

13. 5^3 **14.** $2^0 \cdot 2^3$ **15.** $3^2 + 3^3$

16. $4^2 \cdot 1^3$ **17.** $(-9)^2$ **18.** $(7-6)^4$

19. $-2(3+2)^2$ **20.** $-6^2 + 6$

21. Writing in Math A number written in scientific notation is doubled. Must the exponent of the power of 10 change? Explain.

Evaluate for $a = -2$ and $b = 3$.

22. $(a \cdot b)^2$ **23.** $a^2 b$ **24.** $b^3 \cdot b^0$

25. $(a+b)^5$ **26.** $b^2 - a$ **27.** $2(a^2 + b^3)$

Is each number *prime* or *composite*? For each composite number, write the prime factorization.

28. 24   **29.** 17   **30.** 42

31. 54   **32.** 72   **33.** 100

Find each GCF.

34. 56, 96   **35.** 36, 60   **36.** 14, 25

37. $15x, 24x^2$ **38.** $14a^2 b^3, 21ab^2$

Simplify.

39. $\frac{4}{16}$ **40.** $\frac{44}{52}$ **41.** $\frac{15}{63}$

42. $\frac{a^3}{a^2}$ **43.** $\frac{5b^4}{b}$ **44.** $\frac{8m^4 n^2}{40mn}$

Graph the numbers on the same number line.

45. $\frac{1}{10}$ **46.** -0.3 **47.** $-\frac{1}{2}$ **48.** 1

49. A car manufacturer offers exterior colors of white, blue, red, black, and silver. The manufacturer offers interior colors of black and silver. How many different color combinations are there?

Evaluate for $x = 4$ and $y = -3$. Write in simplest form.

50. $\frac{2y}{x^2}$ **51.** $\frac{xy}{5x}$ **52.** $\frac{(x+y)^3}{x}$

53. $\frac{x+3y}{10}$ **54.** $\frac{y^2 - x}{5}$ **55.** $\frac{x-y}{x+y}$

Simplify each expression.

56. $a^4 \cdot a$ **57.** $(y^3)^6$ **58.** $x^3 \cdot x^6 \cdot y^2$

59. $(a^3)^2$ **60.** $6b^7 \cdot 5b^2$ **61.** $\frac{9^8}{9^2}$

62. $\frac{6a^7}{15a^3}$ **63.** $\frac{b^8}{b^{11}}$ **64.** $\frac{2x^2 y^5}{8x^3 y^5}$

Write each number in scientific notation.

65. 43,000,000   **66.** 6,000,000,000

67. 0.0000032   **68.** 0.00000000099

Write each number in standard notation.

69. 5×10^5 **70.** 3.812×10^{-7}

71. 9.3×10^8 **72.** 1.02×10^{-9}

Order from least to greatest.

73. $3 \times 10^{10}, 742 \times 10^7, 0.006 \times 10^{12}$

74. $85 \times 10^{-7}, 2 \times 10^{-5}, 0.9 \times 10^{-8}$

Multiply. Express each result in scientific notation.

75. $(3 \times 10^{10})(7 \times 10^8)$

76. $(8.3 \times 10^6)(3 \times 10^5)$

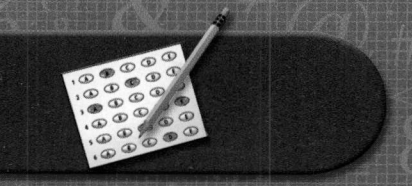

Test Prep

Multiple Choice

Choose the best answer.

1. Which expression is equivalent to $\frac{x^3y^7}{x^5y^2}$?
   A. $x^{-2}y^5$ B. x^2y^5
   C. $x^{-2}y^{-5}$ D. x^2y^{-5}

2. What is the simplest form of $(4c - 5c) + (7 - 2)$?
   F. $c + 5$ G. $-c + 5$
   H. $9c + 5$ I. $c - 5$

3. Which integer is *not* a solution of $25 + t < 19$?
   A. -43 B. -7
   C. -8 D. -6

4. Which sentence is true?
   F. $16 \geq 2 \cdot 9$
   G. $-36 - 10 = 4(5)$
   H. $5[-6 - (-2)] = 2 \cdot (-5)2$
   I. $32 - (-4 \cdot 6) \leq 54$

5. Which number is divisible by both 3 and 9?
   A. 24,000   B. 36,089
   C. 45,288   D. 95,500

6. Which expression is equivalent to $-8 \cdot n \cdot n \cdot n \cdot 4 \cdot t$?
   F. $-32n^3t$ G. $-8n^3 + 4t$
   H. $-32 \cdot 3n \cdot t$ I. $-32nt^3$

7. Which expression is the GCF of $24x^3$ and $64x$?
   A. $1{,}536x^4$ B. $4x^4$
   C. $40x^2$ D. $8x$

8. Which expression is equivalent to x^{12}?
   F. $x^6 + x^6$ G. $(x^4)^8$
   H. $x^2 \cdot x^6$ I. $x^6 \cdot x^6$

9. Which symbol makes $7^2 \cdot 7^5 \;\blacksquare\; (7^5)^2$ true?
   A. $>$ B. $<$
   C. $=$ D. $\geq$

10. What is the simplest form of $x^5 \cdot y \cdot x^5 \cdot y$?
    F. $(x^{25})(2y)$ G. x^5y^2
    H. $2x^5y$ I. $x^{10}y^2$

11. What is the simplest form of $\frac{w^{12}y^{15}z}{w^9y^7}$?
    A. w^3y^8z B. $w^{21}y^{22}z$
    C. $\frac{w^{21}y^{22}z}{wz}$ D. $\frac{w^3y^8z}{wz}$

12. What is the prime factorization of 90?
    F. $2 \cdot 3^2 \cdot 5$ G. $2 \cdot 5 \cdot 9$
    H. $3 \cdot 3 \cdot 5^2$ I. $2 \cdot 45$

13. Which number is divisible by 2, 3, and 5?
    A. 70   B. 105   C. 120   D. 235

Gridded Response

14. Simplify 2^{-3}.

15. Evaluate $\frac{3m - 12}{n}$, for $m = 8$ and $n = 4$.

16. Simplify $2(11 + 7 \cdot 2)$.

17. Evaluate $-a^2 + 4$ for $a = -1$.

18. Simplify $8 + (-8) + (+8)$.

Short Response

19. a. The product of -6.2 and a number k is -70.68. Write an equation to find k.
    b. Solve for k.

20. What is the GCF of 45 and 54? Explain.

21. a. Write a variable expression for the length of the red segment.
    b. What is the segment length if $a = 7$?

Extended Response

22. The store sells erasers for $.05, $.10, and $.15. In how many ways can you spend $.20 to buy erasers? Explain your answer using a table.

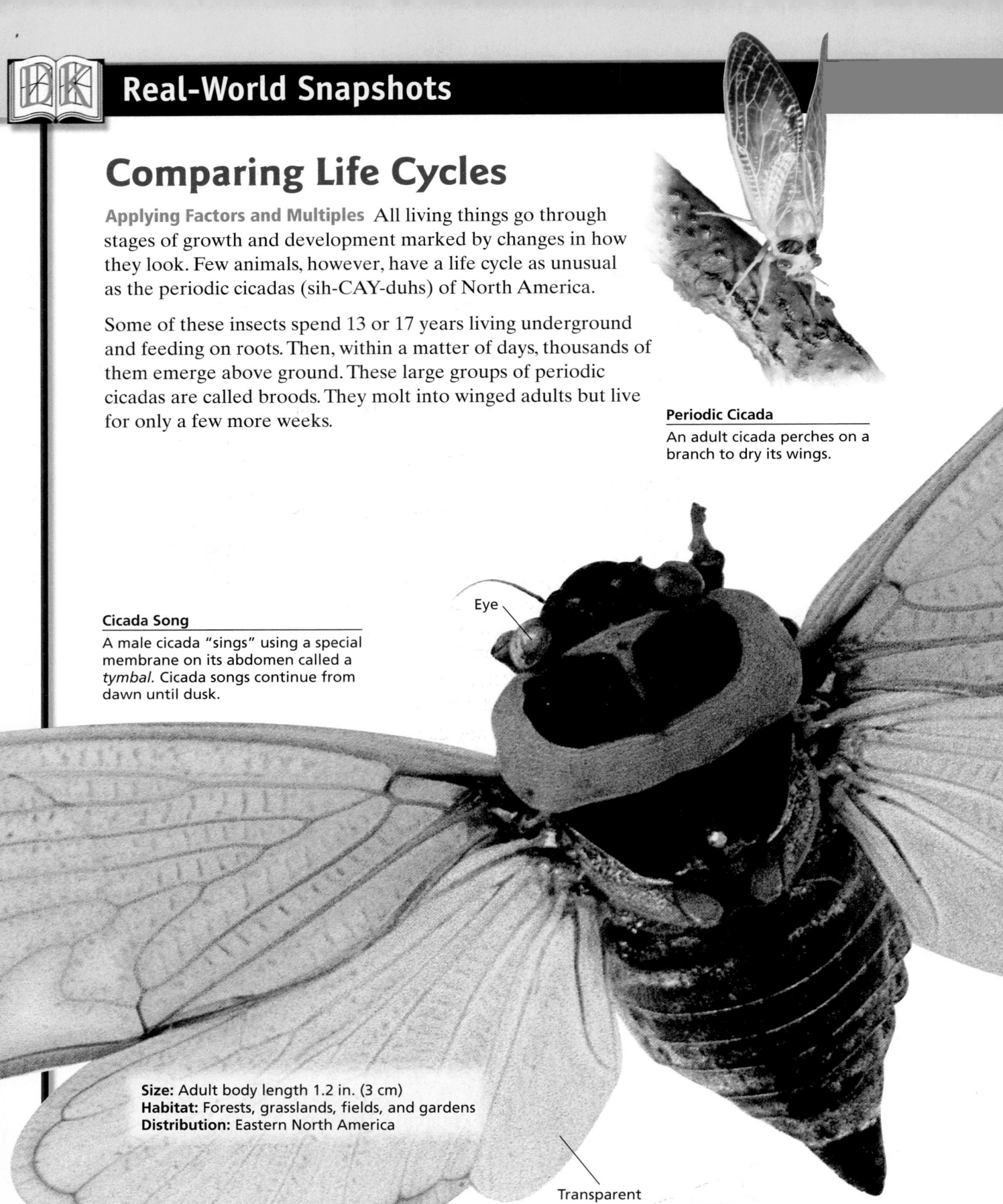

Comparing Life Cycles

Applying Factors and Multiples All living things go through stages of growth and development marked by changes in how they look. Few animals, however, have a life cycle as unusual as the periodic cicadas (sih-CAY-duhs) of North America.

Some of these insects spend 13 or 17 years living underground and feeding on roots. Then, within a matter of days, thousands of them emerge above ground. These large groups of periodic cicadas are called broods. They molt into winged adults but live for only a few more weeks.

Periodic Cicada
An adult cicada perches on a branch to dry its wings.

Cicada Song
A male cicada "sings" using a special membrane on its abdomen called a *tymbal.* Cicada songs continue from dawn until dusk.

Eye

Size: Adult body length 1.2 in. (3 cm)
Habitat: Forests, grasslands, fields, and gardens
Distribution: Eastern North America

Transparent
wings

Activity

Use the information in the tables.

1. **a.** When was the last time brood IV emerged?
  b. When will brood IV emerge next?
  c. How many times will brood IV emerge during this century?

2. How many times did brood XXII emerge during the last century?

3. In 1998, a 17-year brood and a 13-year brood both emerged in Missouri.
  a. How many years will pass before they emerge together again?
  b. What year will it be?
  c. **Reasoning** Suppose these two broods are the only cicadas that emerge in Missouri. Before 1998, how many years had passed without adult cicadas in Missouri? Explain.

4. Brood VII and brood XXII recently emerged in the same year. How many years earlier did they also emerge together?

5. Some cicadas are called "dog-day" cicadas. These cicadas have cycles of 2 to 5 years. Suppose broods of 3-year, 4-year, and 5-year cicadas emerged in 2005. In what year would all three broods next emerge together? Explain.

6. Suppose a 17-year cicada emerges, molts, and dies after 4 weeks. What percent of its life has the cicada spent as an adult?

17-Year Cicadas

Brood	Year Seen
III	1997
IV	1998
VII	2001

13-Year Cicadas

Brood	Year Seen
XIX	1998
XXII	2001
XXIII	2002

Gathering Insects

Students taking a class on entomology collect and study insects.

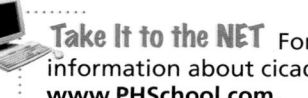

Take It to the NET For more information about cicadas, go to **www.PHSchool.com**.
Web Code: ade-0453

229

Where You've Been

- In Chapter 1, you learned how to add, subtract, multiply, and divide integers.

- In Chapter 2, you solved equations by adding, subtracting, multiplying, and dividing.

- In Chapter 4, you investigated exponents.

Diagnosing Readiness

🅸 TEXT Instant self-check online and on CD-ROM

(For help, go to the lesson in green.)

Solving Equations (Lessons 3-5 and 3-6)

Solve each equation.

1. $x + 1.8 = 3$　　**2.** $n - 41 = 19$　　**3.** $a \div (-3) = 15$　　**4.** $-19 = p + 21$

5. $6t = 9$　　　　**6.** $40 = z - 34$　　**7.** $8d = 64$　　　**8.** $-0.89 = \frac{x}{2}$

Finding the Greatest Common Factor (Lesson 4-3)

Find the GCF of each group of numbers.

9. $3, 15$　　**10.** $16, 20$　　**11.** $12, 36$　　**12.** $11, 30$　　**13.** $30, 40, 210$

14. $45, 80$　　**15.** $27, 72$　　**16.** $15, 121$　　**17.** $30, 500$　　**18.** $14, 28, 84$

Reading and Writing Fractions (Lesson 4-4)

Write two equivalent fractions to describe each model.

19. 　　**20.** 　　**21.**

Writing Fractions and Decimals (Lesson 4-6)

Write each fraction in simplest form.

22. $\frac{10}{12}$　**23.** $\frac{8}{20}$　**24.** $-\frac{32}{16}$　**25.** $\frac{25}{100}$　**26.** $-\frac{120}{125}$　**27.** $\frac{15}{45}$

28. $\frac{-20}{-75}$　**29.** $\frac{16}{124}$　**30.** $-\frac{18}{81}$　**31.** $-\frac{10}{65}$　**32.** $\frac{14}{84}$　**33.** $\frac{55}{77}$

Divide. Write each quotient as a decimal.

34. $27 \div 5$　　**35.** $6 \div 10$　　**36.** $10 \div 16$　　**37.** $9 \div 12$　　**38.** $15 \div 40$

Operations With Fractions

Key Vocabulary

- dimensional analysis (p. 254)
- least common denominator (LCD) (p. 234)
- least common multiple (LCM) (p. 232)
- multiple (p. 232)
- reciprocals (p. 250)
- repeating decimal (p. 238)
- terminating decimal (p. 237)

Where You're Going

In this chapter, you will learn how to

- Perform operations with fractions.
- Solve equations with fractions.
- Find powers of products and quotients.
- Solve problems by working backward.

Real-World Snapshots Applying what you learn, on pages 284–285 you will solve problems about quiltmaking.

5-1

Comparing and Ordering Fractions

What You'll Learn

 OBJECTIVE 1 To find the least common multiple

 OBJECTIVE 2 To compare fractions

. . . And Why

To solve real-world problems involving team records

✔ **Check Skills You'll Need**

Write the prime factorization of each number.

1. 20   **2.** 125   **3.** 45

4. 186   **5.** 621   **6.** 1,575

❓ For help, go to Lesson 4-3.

New Vocabulary

• multiple
• least common multiple (LCM)
• least common denominator (LCD)

OBJECTIVE

1 Finding the Least Common Multiple

A **multiple** of a number is the product of that number and any nonzero whole number.

Multiples of 4: 4, 8, ⑫ 16, 20, ㉔ 28, 32, ㊱, . . .

Multiples of 6: 6, ⑫ 18, ㉔ 30, ㊱ 42, . . .

The numbers 12, 24, and 36 are *common multiples* of 4 and 6. The common multiple 12 is their **least common multiple (LCM)**.

1 EXAMPLE **Real-World** 🌐 **Problem Solving**

Sports Today, both the school baseball and school soccer teams had games. The baseball team plays every 6 days. The soccer team plays every 5 days. When will both teams have games on the same day again?

6, 12, 18, 24, ㉚ 36, . . .   **List the multiples of 6.**

5, 10, 15, 20, 25, ㉚ . . .   **List the multiples of 5.**

• The LCM is 30. In 30 days both teams will have games again.

✔ **Check Understanding** Example 1

1. Find the LCM.

a. 3, 4   **b.** 4, 5   **c.** 3, 4, 5

You can also use prime factorization to find the LCM.

2 EXAMPLE **Using Prime Factorization**

Find the LCM of 12 and 40.

$$\left.\begin{array}{l} 12 = 2^2 \cdot ③ \\ 40 = ㊈ \cdot ⑤ \end{array}\right\} \text{ Write the prime factorizations.}$$

$$\begin{array}{l} \text{LCM} = 2^3 \cdot 3 \cdot 5 \quad \text{ Use the greatest power of each factor.} \\ \quad\quad = 120 \quad\quad\quad\quad \text{ Multiply.} \end{array}$$

• The LCM of 12 and 40 is 120.

ℹ TEXT Interactive lesson includes instant self-check, tutorials, and activities.

✓ Check Understanding   Example 2

2. Use prime factorization to find the LCM.

    a. 6, 16   **b.** 9, 15   **c.** 12, 15, 18

You can find the LCM of a variable expression.

3 EXAMPLE   Finding the LCM of Variable Expressions

Find the LCM of $6a^2$ and $18a^3$.

$$\left.\begin{array}{l} 6a^2 = ②\cdot 3 \cdot a^2 \\ 18a^3 = 2 \cdot ③^2 \cdot ⓐ^3 \end{array}\right\}$$ **Write the prime factorizations.**

$\text{LCM} = 2 \cdot 3^2 \cdot a^3$ **Use the greatest power of each factor.**

$\phantom{\text{LCM}} = 18a^3$ **Multiply.**

● The LCM of $6a^2$ and $18a^3$ is $18a^3$.

✓ Check Understanding   Example 3

3. Find the LCM.

    a. $12x, 15xy$ **b.** $8m^2, 14m^4$ **c.** $25y^2, 15x$

OBJECTIVE

2 Comparing Fractions

You can use a number line to compare fractions.

4 EXAMPLE   Using a Number Line

Graph and compare the fractions in each pair.

a. $\dfrac{9}{11}, \dfrac{6}{11}$ **b.** $-\dfrac{1}{2}, -\dfrac{1}{10}$

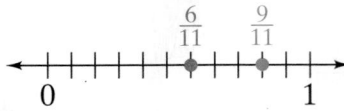   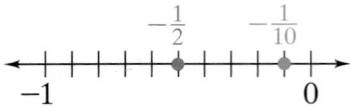

● $\dfrac{9}{11}$ is on the right, so $\dfrac{9}{11} > \dfrac{6}{11}$. $-\dfrac{1}{2}$ is on the left, so $-\dfrac{1}{2} < \dfrac{1}{10}$.

✓ Check Understanding   Example 4

4. Use a number line to compare the fractions in each pair.

    a. $\dfrac{4}{9}, \dfrac{2}{9}$ **b.** $-\dfrac{4}{9}, -\dfrac{2}{9}$ **c.** $-\dfrac{4}{9}, \dfrac{2}{9}$

Reading Math
The LCD is sometimes called the *lowest common denominator.*

When fractions have different denominators, rewrite the fractions with a common denominator. Then compare the numerators. The **least common denominator (LCD)** of two or more fractions is the LCM of the denominators.

5 EXAMPLE   Real-World   Problem Solving

Academic Competitions The math team won $\frac{5}{8}$ of its competitions and the debate team won $\frac{7}{10}$ of its competitions. Which team won the greater fraction of competitions?

Step 1 Find the LCM of 8 and 10.

$8 = 2^3$ and $10 = 2 \cdot 5$
$\text{LCM} = 2^3 \cdot 5 = 40$

Step 2 Write equivalent fractions with a denominator of 40.

$$\frac{5 \cdot 5}{8 \cdot 5} = \frac{25}{40}$$

$$\frac{7 \cdot 4}{10 \cdot 4} = \frac{28}{40}$$

Step 3 Compare the fractions.
$$\frac{25}{40} < \frac{28}{40}, \text{ so } \frac{5}{8} < \frac{7}{10}.$$

● The debate team won the greater fraction of competitions.

Real-World Connection

High school debate teams can have as few as 8 debates and as many as 20 debates in a school year.

✓ **Check Understanding**   Example 5

5. Compare the fractions in each pair.
   a. $\frac{6}{7}, \frac{4}{5}$ b. $\frac{2}{3}, \frac{3}{4}$ c. $-\frac{3}{4}, -\frac{7}{10}$

6 EXAMPLE   Ordering Fractions

Order $\frac{1}{2}, \frac{3}{4},$ and $\frac{2}{5}$ from least to greatest.

$$\left.\begin{array}{l} \frac{1}{2} = \frac{1 \cdot 10}{2 \cdot 10} = \frac{10}{20} \\[2mm] \frac{3}{4} = \frac{3 \cdot 5}{4 \cdot 5} = \frac{15}{20} \\[2mm] \frac{2}{5} = \frac{2 \cdot 4}{5 \cdot 4} = \frac{8}{20} \end{array}\right\}$$ The LCM of 2, 4, and 5 is 20. Use 20 as the common denominator.

$\frac{8}{20} < \frac{10}{20} < \frac{15}{20},$ so $\frac{2}{5} < \frac{1}{2} < \frac{3}{4}.$

✓ **Check Understanding**   Example 6

6. Order from least to greatest.
   a. $\frac{2}{3}, \frac{1}{6}, \frac{7}{12}$ b. $\frac{3}{10}, \frac{1}{5}, \frac{1}{2}, \frac{7}{12}$

EXERCISES

For more exercises, see *Extra Practice*.

Practice and Problem Solving

A Practice by Example

Example 1
(page 232)

Find the LCM of each pair by listing multiples.

1. 10, 45   **2.** 6, 9   **3.** 12, 20   **4.** 5, 9

5. 10, 36   **6.** 7, 12   **7.** 5, 6   **8.** 5, 6, 7

9. Schedules Both the football and volleyball teams have games today. The football team plays every 7 days. The volleyball team plays every 3 days. When will both teams have games on the same day again?

Examples 2 and 3
(page 232 and 233)

Find the LCM.

10. 20, 36   **11.** 15, 27   **12.** 8, 14, 20   **13.** 5, 12, 15

14. $12x, 40y$ **15.** $8x, 25y$ **16.** $2b^2, 6c^3$ **17.** $6a^3, 8a$

Example 4
(page 233)

Graph and compare the fractions in each pair.

18. $\frac{4}{5}, \frac{2}{5}$ **19.** $-\frac{2}{3}, -\frac{1}{3}$ **20.** $\frac{5}{8}, -\frac{5}{8}$ **21.** $\frac{11}{12}, \frac{7}{12}$

Example 5
(page 234)

Compare the fractions in each pair.

22. $\frac{5}{6} \blacksquare \frac{3}{4}$ **23.** $\frac{6}{8} \blacksquare \frac{7}{9}$ **24.** $\frac{1}{6} \blacksquare \frac{1}{8}$ **25.** $-\frac{5}{18} \blacksquare -\frac{1}{3}$

26. Track and Field At the track meet, Maria placed first in $\frac{4}{5}$ of her events and Carla placed first in $\frac{2}{3}$ of her events. Who placed first in the greater fraction of events?

Example 6
(page 234)

Order from least to greatest.

27. $\frac{7}{9}, \frac{3}{9}, \frac{5}{9}$ **28.** $\frac{1}{2}, \frac{1}{3}, \frac{1}{4}$ **29.** $\frac{2}{5}, \frac{2}{3}, \frac{2}{7}$ **30.** $\frac{2}{5}, \frac{3}{8}, \frac{1}{3}, \frac{2}{4}$

B Apply Your Skills

Mental Math Compare. Use >, <, or = to complete each statement.

31. $-\frac{3}{19} \blacksquare \frac{1}{200}$ **32.** $\frac{-1}{-3} \blacksquare \frac{1}{3}$ **33.** $\frac{9}{11} \blacksquare \frac{7}{11}$ **34.** $\frac{-2}{-7} \blacksquare \frac{4}{14}$

35. $\frac{8}{8} \blacksquare \frac{3}{3}$ **36.** $\frac{2}{10} \blacksquare \frac{2}{100}$ **37.** $\frac{2}{5} \blacksquare 3\frac{2}{5}$ **38.** $\frac{-4}{-17} \blacksquare -\frac{5}{2}$

39. Measurement You need $\frac{5}{8}$ yd of fabric for a craft project. You find a piece marked $\frac{2}{3}$ yd. Is the piece long enough? Explain.

40. The manager of Frank's Snack Shop buys hot dogs in packages of 36. He buys hot dog buns in packages of 20. He cannot buy part of a package. What is the least number of packages of each product he can buy to have an equal number of hot dogs and buns?

Find the LCM.

41. 45, 120, 150   **42.** 2, 5, 12, 15   **43.** $12x, 40$ **44.** $7ab, 8a^3b^2, 10a^4$

45. $8x, 18xy$ **46.** $9b^3, 12bc^2$ **47.** $4g^2, 10j^4$ **48.** $2x^3, 5y^2, 15xy^2$

5-1 Comparing and Ordering Fractions **235**

Compare. Use >, <, or = to complete each statement.

49. $\frac{7}{14}$ ▪ $\frac{3}{6}$ 50. $-\frac{7}{9}$ ▪ $-\frac{2}{3}$ 51. $\frac{8}{5}$ ▪ $\frac{3}{2}$ 52. $-\frac{19}{24}$ ▪ $-\frac{5}{6}$

53. $-\frac{3}{8}$ ▪ $-\frac{6}{16}$ 54. $\frac{10}{11}$ ▪ $\frac{4}{5}$ 55. $\frac{1}{2}$ ▪ $\frac{2}{4}$ 56. $-\frac{7}{12}$ ▪ $-\frac{28}{48}$

57. **Writing in Math** Jeremy and Fran want to compare $\frac{5}{8}$ to $\frac{9}{12}$. Jeremy writes equivalent fractions with a denominator of 96. Fran writes equivalent fractions with a denominator of 24. Which method would you prefer? Explain.

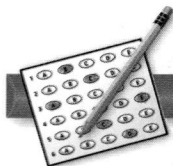 **Challenge**

58. **Geometry** You have tiles that measure 4 in. by 5 in. What is the smallest square region you can cover without cutting or overlapping the tiles? Explain.

59. **Servings** Suppose you and your brother shared two 12-in. pizzas, a mushroom pizza cut into 8 slices and a cheese pizza cut into 6 slices. If you ate 5 slices of the mushroom pizza, and your brother ate 3 slices of the cheese pizza, who ate more pizza?

Test Prep

Take It to the NET
Online lesson quiz at
www.PHSchool.com
Web Code: ada-0501

Multiple Choice

60. What is the LCM of 2, 3, 4, and 5?
   A. 30   **B.** 60   **C.** 90   **D.** 120

61. What is the GCF of $6a^3b$ and $4a^2b$?
   F. a^2b **G.** a^5b^2 **H.** $2a^2b$ **I.** $4a^5b^2$

62. Salt shakers come in boxes of 30 and pepper shakers come in boxes of 24. How many whole boxes of each must you buy to get an equal number of salt and pepper shakers?
   A. 4 salt, 5 pepper   **B.** 5 salt, 4 pepper
   C. 24 salt, 30 pepper   **D.** 30 salt, 24 pepper

Short Response

63. Are the numbers in order from least to greatest: $\frac{5}{8}$, $\frac{7}{16}$, $\frac{11}{20}$? Explain.

Mixed Review

Lesson 4-9   **Write in scientific notation.**

64. 5,000,000   65. 0.001394   66. 8,900,000   67. 0.000005

Lesson 4-3   **Find each GCF.**

68. 24, 42   69. 16, 52   70. $25c, 55c^2$ 71. $90xy, 45x^2$

Lesson 2-5   72. **History** The first modern Olympics took place in 1896 in Athens, Greece. One hundred years later, 197 nations took part in the Olympics in Atlanta, Georgia. This was 184 more nations than at the first Olympics. Solve the equation $x + 184 = 197$ to find the number of nations at the first Olympics.

Fractions and Decimals

OBJECTIVE

1 Writing Fractions as Decimals

You can write a fraction as a decimal by dividing the numerator by the denominator. When the division ends with a remainder of zero, the quotient is called a **terminating decimal.**

$$\frac{5}{8} \text{ or } 5 \div 8 \longrightarrow$$

```
        0.625  ← quotient
    8)5.000
     -4 8
       20
      -16
       40
      -40
        0  ← remainder
```

The division process for $5 \div 8$ ends with a remainder of zero. So 0.625 is a terminating decimal.

1 EXAMPLE Real-World Problem Solving

Consumer Issues A customer at a delicatessen asks for $\frac{3}{4}$ lb of potato salad. The scale reads 0.75. Is the customer getting the amount of potato salad she requested? Explain.

$$\frac{3}{4} = 3 \div 4 = 0.75$$

Since $\frac{3}{4} = 0.75$, the customer is getting the right amount of potato salad.

✓ Check Understanding Example 1

1. Write each fraction or mixed number as a decimal.

   a. $\frac{1}{4}$ **b.** $1\frac{7}{8}$

   c. $3\frac{3}{10}$ **d.** $\frac{3}{5}$

What You'll Learn

OBJECTIVE 1 To write fractions as decimals

OBJECTIVE 2 To write terminating and repeating decimals as fractions

. . . And Why

To solve real-world problems involving buying food

✓ Check Skills You'll Need

Write the decimals in order from least to greatest.

1. 2.41, 0.241, 24.1, 12.4

2. 1.030, 13.03, 1.300, 1.003

3. 0.1, 0.01, −0.1, −0.01

 For help, go to Skills Handbook, p. 762.

New Vocabulary

• terminating decimal
• repeating decimal

TEXT Interactive lesson includes instant self-check, tutorials, and activities.

In a **repeating decimal,** the same block of digits repeats infinitely many times. The block of digits that repeats can be one digit or more than one digit.

2 EXAMPLE   Writing a Repeating Decimal

Calculator Hint
Enter 2 ÷ 3 into your calculator. Then check whether the last digit in the display is 6 or 7 to see how your calculator rounds.

Write each fraction as a decimal. State the block of digits that repeats.

a. $\frac{2}{3}$ b. $\frac{15}{11}$

$2 \div 3 = 0.66666\ldots$ ←—Divide.—→ $15 \div 11 = 1.36363\ldots$

Place a bar over the
$= 0.\overline{6}$ ←— block of digits —→ $= 1.\overline{36}$
that repeats.

$\frac{2}{3} = 0.\overline{6}$; the digit that repeats is 6. $\frac{15}{11} = 1.\overline{36}$; the block of digits that repeats is 36.

✓ Check Understanding   Example 2

2. Write each fraction as a decimal. State whether the decimal is *terminating* or *repeating.* If the decimal repeats, state the block of digits that repeats.

   a. $\frac{7}{9}$ b. $\frac{21}{22}$ c. $\frac{11}{8}$ d. $\frac{8}{11}$

When you compare and order decimals and fractions, it may be helpful to first write the fractions as decimals.

3 EXAMPLE   Ordering Fractions and Decimals

Write the numbers in order, from least to greatest.

$$\frac{1}{4}, -0.2, -\frac{3}{5}, 1.1$$

$1 \div 4 = 0.25$ ⎫
                   ⎬ **Change the fractions to decimals.**
$-3 \div 5 = -0.6$ ⎭

$-0.6 < -0.2 < 0.25 < 1.1$ **Compare the decimals.**

From least to greatest, the numbers are $-\frac{3}{5}, -0.2, \frac{1}{4}$, and 1.1.

✓ Check Understanding   Example 3

3. Order from least to greatest.

   a. $0.2, \frac{4}{5}, \frac{7}{10}, 0.5$ b. $-\frac{1}{8}, -0.75, -\frac{1}{4}, -0.375$

2 Writing Decimals as Fractions

Reading a decimal correctly provides a way to write a fraction.

Decimal	Read	Fraction
0.43	"forty-three hundredths"	$\frac{43}{100}$

If a decimal is greater than 1, you can write it as a mixed number.

4 EXAMPLE   Writing a Decimal as a Fraction

Write 1.12 as a mixed number in simplest form.

$1.12 = 1\frac{12}{100}$ **Keep the whole number 1. Write twelve hundredths as a fraction.**

$= 1\frac{12 \div 4}{100 \div 4}$ **Divide the numerator and denominator of the fraction by the GCF, 4.**

$1.12 = 1\frac{3}{25}$ **Simplify.**

✓ Check Understanding   Example 4

4. Write as a fraction or a mixed number in simplest form.

a. 1.75   **b.** 2.32   **c.** 0.65

You can use algebra to write a repeating decimal as a fraction.

5 EXAMPLE   Writing a Repeating Decimal as a Fraction

Write the repeating decimal $0.\overline{72}$ as a fraction in simplest form.

$n = 0.\overline{72}$ **Let the variable n equal the decimal.**

$100n = 72.\overline{72}$ **Multiply each side by 10^2, or 100.**

$\begin{array}{r} 100n = 72.\overline{72} \\ -n = -0.\overline{72} \\ \hline 99n = 72 \end{array}$ **The Subtraction Property of Equality lets you subtract the same value from each side of the equation.**

$\frac{99n}{99} = \frac{72}{99}$ **Divide each side by 99.**

$n = \frac{72 \div 9}{99 \div 9}$ **Divide the numerator and denominator by the GCF, 9.**

$= \frac{8}{11}$ **Simplify.**

As a fraction in simplest form, $0.\overline{72} = \frac{8}{11}$.

Need Help?
Properties of Equality allow you to change both sides of an equation in the same way.

✓ Check Understanding   Example 5

5. Write each decimal as a fraction in simplest form.

a. $0.\overline{7}$ **b.** $0.\overline{54}$ **c.** $0.\overline{213}$

EXERCISES

For more exercises, see *Extra Practice.*

Practice and Problem Solving

 A Practice by Example

Example 1
(page 237)

Write each fraction or mixed number as a decimal.

1. $\frac{7}{25}$ **2.** $\frac{3}{5}$ **3.** $1\frac{9}{20}$ **4.** $6\frac{1}{4}$

5. Remodeling Randy and Becky measure a carpet. Becky says the carpet's length is $10\frac{5}{16}$ ft. Randy writes "10.3125 ft." Did Randy write the correct measurement? Explain.

Example 2
(page 238)

Write each fraction as a decimal. State whether the decimal is *terminating* or *repeating*. If the decimal repeats, state the block of digits that repeats.

6. $-\frac{5}{8}$ **7.** $-\frac{1}{6}$ **8.** $\frac{2}{9}$ **9.** $\frac{9}{11}$

Example 3
(page 238)

Order from least to greatest.

10. $1.2, \frac{3}{5}, -0.5, \frac{9}{10}$

11. $\frac{1}{2}, \frac{3}{2}, \frac{5}{2}, 0.3$

12. $-\frac{1}{4}, +\frac{1}{8}, -0.75, -0.625$

13. $\frac{3}{2}, \frac{2}{5}, \frac{6}{5}, 0.06$

14. $-\frac{7}{10}, -\frac{8}{10}, -0.77, -0.87$

15. $2.1, \frac{22}{10}, 2.01, \frac{22}{11}$

Examples 4 and 5
(page 239)

Write each decimal as a fraction or a mixed number in simplest form.

16. 2.25 **17.** 3.4 **18.** 0.08 **19.** 7.15

20. 2.48 **21.** 6.37 **22.** 5.36 **23.** 2.55

24. $0.\overline{5}$ **25.** $0.\overline{126}$ **26.** $0.\overline{27}$ **27.** $-0.\overline{3}$

B Apply Your Skills

Mental Math Compare. Use >, <, or = to complete each statement.

28. $\frac{1}{2}$ ■ 1.2 **29.** $\frac{7}{8}$ ■ 0.875 **30.** $\frac{3}{5}$ ■ 0.25 **31.** $\frac{1}{8}$ ■ 0.375

32. Number Sense A carpenter has a bolt with diameter $\frac{5}{32}$ in. Will the bolt fit in a hole made by a drill bit with diameter 0.2 in.? Explain.

Write each fraction or mixed number as a decimal.

33. $5\frac{3}{8}$ **34.** $2\frac{5}{16}$ **35.** $\frac{1}{25}$ **36.** $3\frac{4}{5}$ **37.** $-\frac{31}{100}$ **38.** $\frac{7}{11}$

Write as a fraction or a mixed number in simplest form.

39. 0.35 **40.** 6.8 **41.** -3.9 **42.** $10.\overline{105}$

43. Batting averages are usually expressed as decimals. Sarah got 32 hits in 112 times at bat. Lizzie got 26 hits in 86 times at bat.
   a. Data Analysis Find their batting averages, to the nearest thousandth.
   b. Probability Based on their batting averages, who is more likely to get a hit? Explain.

44. Number Sense Copy and complete this table of some commonly used fractions and decimals. Write the fractions in simplest form.

Fraction	■	■	$\frac{3}{8}$	$\frac{1}{2}$	■	$\frac{3}{4}$	$\frac{7}{8}$
Decimal	0.125	0.25	■	■	0.625	■	■

C Challenge

Write as a fraction or a mixed number in simplest form.

45. $0.0\overline{6}$ **46.** $0.1\overline{83}$ **47.** $0.\overline{272727}$ **48.** $1.1\overline{9}$

49. Writing in Math Is 3.010010001... a repeating decimal? Explain.

50. Number Sense The number of digits that repeat in a repeating decimal is called the *period* of the decimal. The period of $0.\overline{3}$ is 1.
 a. Write $\frac{5}{7}$, $\frac{4}{13}$, and $\frac{7}{15}$ as decimals.
 b. What is the period of each decimal you wrote in part (a)?

51. Reasoning Seth had just finished a division problem on his calculator when the telephone rang. He got distracted. When he looked back at the calculator, all he could see was the display 0.04040404. What might have been the division problem? Explain.

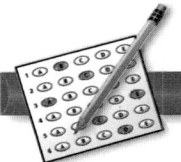

Test Prep

Multiple Choice

Take It to the NET
Online lesson quiz at
www.PHSchool.com
Web Code: ada-0502

Short Response

52. Which decimal is the closest approximation to $\frac{2}{3}$?
 A. 0.230   **B.** 0.233   **C.** 0.600   **D.** 0.667

53. A clerk puts slices of cheese on a scale until it reads 1.625 lb. What is this amount as a mixed number?
 F. $1\frac{1}{6}$ lb   **G.** $1\frac{1}{4}$ lb   **H.** $1\frac{5}{8}$ lb   **I.** $1\frac{6}{25}$ lb

54. Lucia's math teacher asks her to write $\frac{3}{11}$ as a decimal. She enters $3 \div 11$ on her calculator. The calculator displays 0.2727273.   **(a)** Is this the answer Lucia should record?   **(b)** Explain your response.

Mixed Review

Lesson 5-1   **Order the fractions in each group from least to greatest.**

55. $-\frac{1}{3}, \frac{2}{3}, -\frac{5}{6}, \frac{1}{6}$ **56.** $\frac{5}{8}, \frac{3}{8}, \frac{1}{5}, \frac{3}{5}, \frac{1}{8}$ **57.** $-\frac{4}{7}, -\frac{1}{14}, -\frac{3}{14}, -\frac{6}{7}$

Lesson 4-9 🌐 **58. Geography** Lake Mead, located between Arizona and Nevada, has a capacity of 34,850,000,000 m³. Write this number in scientific notation.

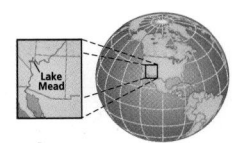

Previous Course   **Change each number to an improper fraction.**

59. $3\frac{2}{3}$ **60.** $1\frac{5}{6}$ **61.** $10\frac{3}{7}$ **62.** $7\frac{5}{8}$ **63.** $4\frac{7}{10}$

Estimating With Fractions and Mixed Numbers

You can round to estimate sums and differences involving fractions and mixed numbers. In one method, you round the fraction or the fraction part of a mixed number to $0, \frac{1}{2}$, or 1.

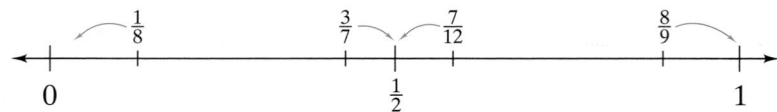

Round to 0 when the numerator is less than half of the denominator.

Round to $\frac{1}{2}$ when the numerator is about half the denominator.

Round to 1 when the numerator and denominator are almost equal.

① EXAMPLE

a. Estimate $\frac{5}{6} + \frac{5}{12}$.

$$\frac{5}{6} \approx 1$$

$$+\frac{5}{12} \approx +\frac{1}{2}$$

$$1\frac{1}{2}$$

← Round each fraction. →

← Add or subtract. →

b. Estimate $\frac{9}{20} - \frac{1}{5}$.

$$\frac{9}{20} \approx \frac{1}{2}$$

$$-\frac{1}{5} \approx -0$$

$$\frac{1}{2}$$

You can get reasonable estimates when multiplying by first rounding to the nearest whole number. For division, use compatible numbers.

② EXAMPLE

a. Estimate $4\frac{1}{8} \cdot 1\frac{9}{10}$.

$$4\frac{1}{8} \cdot 1\frac{9}{10}$$

If the fractional part is greater than $\frac{1}{2}$, round up.

$$4 \cdot 2 = 8 \quad \text{Multiply.}$$

b. Estimate $16\frac{1}{5} \div 2\frac{3}{4}$.

$$16\frac{1}{5} \div 2\frac{3}{4}$$

$2\frac{3}{4}$ rounds to 3. A number compatible with 3 and close to $16\frac{1}{5}$ is 15.

$$15 \div 3 = 5 \quad \text{Divide.}$$

EXERCISES

Estimate the value of each expression.

1. $\frac{2}{3} + \frac{7}{8}$

2. $5\frac{1}{12} - 2\frac{7}{9}$

3. $\frac{1}{5} + 5\frac{5}{8}$

4. $4\frac{11}{24} - \frac{7}{12}$

5. $\frac{11}{12} \cdot 4$

6. $6\frac{8}{9} \div 1\frac{1}{5}$

7. $10\frac{1}{10} \div 4\frac{7}{8}$

8. $2\frac{4}{5} \cdot 5$

Adding and Subtracting Fractions

OBJECTIVE

1 Adding and Subtracting Fractions

estigation

Using Models to Add Fractions

Use the models to answer each question below.

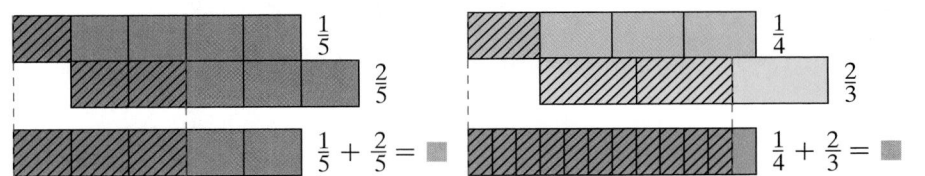

$\frac{1}{5}$

$\frac{2}{5}$

$\frac{1}{5} + \frac{2}{5} = \blacksquare$

$\frac{1}{4}$

$\frac{2}{3}$

$\frac{1}{4} + \frac{2}{3} = \blacksquare$

1. a. Refer to the model for $\frac{1}{5} + \frac{2}{5}$. What fraction does
  $\frac{1}{5} + \frac{2}{5}$ equal?

  b. Reasoning The sum of any two fractions can be written
  as a fraction. Write a conjecture about how to find the
  numerator and denominator of such a sum.

2. a. Refer to the model for $\frac{1}{4} + \frac{2}{3}$. What fraction does
  $\frac{1}{4} + \frac{2}{3}$ equal?

  b. Can you add the numerators to find the sum? Explain.
  c. Can you add the denominators to find the sum? Explain.

In the model for $\frac{1}{5} + \frac{2}{5}$ above, you can see that the sum (or difference)
of fractions with the same denominator is the sum (or difference) of
the numerators. The denominators do not change.

1 EXAMPLE Simplifying With Like Denominators

Find each sum or difference. Simplify if possible.

a. $\frac{1}{8} + \frac{3}{8}$

b. $\frac{9}{x} - \frac{7}{x}$

$\frac{1}{8} + \frac{3}{8} = \frac{1+3}{8}$ Add or subtract
the numerators.

$\frac{9}{x} - \frac{7}{x} = \frac{9-7}{x}$

$= \frac{4}{8} = \frac{1}{2}$ Simplify.

$= \frac{2}{x}$

✔ Check Understanding Example 1

1. Find each sum or difference. Simplify if possible.

  a. $\frac{3}{7} + \frac{1}{7}$ **b.** $\frac{2}{k} + \frac{3}{k}$ **c.** $\frac{7}{10} - \frac{3}{10}$ **d.** $\frac{11}{y} + \left(-\frac{5}{y}\right)$

What You'll Learn

OBJECTIVE 1 To add and subtract
fractions

OBJECTIVE 2 To add and subtract
mixed numbers

... And Why

To solve real-world problems
involving cooking

✔ Check Skills You'll Need

**Find the LCM of each
group of numbers
or expressions.**

1. 4, 8   **2.** 9, 18

3. 2n, 5   **4.** 3, 6, 9

5. 8, 5, 4   **6.** 10, n

❓ For help, go to Lesson 5-1.

ⓘ**TEXT** Interactive lesson
includes instant self-check,
tutorials, and activities.

Before you can add or subtract fractions with unlike denominators, first write the fractions with a common denominator. The method shown here for addition works with subtraction also.

Arithmetic $\quad \frac{2}{3} + \frac{1}{5}$

$$\frac{2}{3} \cdot \frac{5}{5} + \frac{1}{5} \cdot \frac{3}{3}$$

$$\frac{10}{15} + \frac{3}{15}$$

$$\frac{13}{15}$$

Algebra $\quad \frac{a}{b} + \frac{c}{d}$

$$\frac{a}{b} \cdot \frac{d}{d} + \frac{c}{d} \cdot \frac{b}{b}$$

$$\frac{ad}{bd} + \frac{bc}{bd}$$

$$\frac{ad + bc}{bd}$$

2 EXAMPLE Simplifying With Unlike Denominators

Simplify each difference.

a. $\frac{1}{8} - \frac{5}{6}$

$$\frac{1}{8} - \frac{5}{6} = \frac{1 \cdot 6 - 8 \cdot 5}{8 \cdot 6}$$ Rewrite using a common denominator.

$$= \frac{6 - 40}{48}$$ Use the Order of Operations to simplify.

$$= \frac{-34}{48} = -\frac{17}{24}$$ Simplify.

b. $\frac{1}{8} - \frac{5x}{6}$

$$\frac{1}{8} - \frac{5x}{6} = \frac{1 \cdot 6 - 8 \cdot 5x}{8 \cdot 6}$$

$$= \frac{6 - 40x}{48}$$

Need Help?

If either the numerator or denominator is negative, or if the negative sign is in front of the fraction, then the entire fraction is negative. $\frac{-17}{24} = -\frac{17}{24}$

✔ **Check Understanding** Example 2

2. Simplify each sum or difference.

a. $\frac{2}{3} - \frac{1}{5}$ b. $-\frac{7}{8} + \frac{3}{4}$ c. $\frac{3}{7} - \frac{2}{m}$

OBJECTIVE

2 Adding and Subtracting Mixed Numbers

Before you add or subtract mixed numbers, write the mixed numbers as improper fractions.

3 EXAMPLE Real-World Problem Solving

Hiking Suppose you hiked $2\frac{2}{3}$ mi near Mt. Shasta and then another $1\frac{3}{4}$ mi to your campsite. How far did you hike in all?

$$2\frac{2}{3} + 1\frac{3}{4} = \frac{8}{3} + \frac{7}{4}$$ Write mixed numbers as improper fractions.

$$= \frac{8 \cdot 4 + 3 \cdot 7}{3 \cdot 4}$$ Rewrite using a common denominator.

$$= \frac{32 + 21}{12}$$ Use the Order of Operations to simplify.

$$= \frac{53}{12} = 4\frac{5}{12}$$ Write as a mixed number.

You hiked $4\frac{5}{12}$ mi in all.

Real-World Connection

Mt. Shasta, in northern California, is 14,162 ft high. You can hike the Avalanche Gulch route from Bunny Flat for 6 mi and climb 7,000 ft.

3. Find each sum or difference. Simplify if possible.

   a. $5\frac{3}{4} + \frac{7}{8}$ **b.** $5\frac{2}{3} - 3\frac{1}{6}$ **c.** $2\frac{3}{8} + \frac{7}{8}$

   d. A recipe for punch calls for $1\frac{1}{2}$ qt of orange juice, $1\frac{1}{4}$ qt of ginger ale, and $\frac{3}{4}$ qt of cranberry juice. How many quarts of punch will the recipe make?

Need Help?

For help with mixed numbers and improper fractions, see Skills Handbook, page 772.

You can subtract mixed numbers in more than one way.

More Than One Way

You are making banana bread for a bake sale, using the recipe at the right. You have $1\frac{3}{4}$ c of sugar left in a bag of sugar. How much more sugar do you need?

Banana Bread

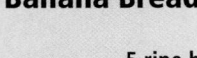

5 ripe bananas	$3\frac{1}{2}$ cups flour
4 eggs	2 tsp baking soda
1 cup shortening	1 tsp salt
$2\frac{1}{2}$ cups sugar	$1\frac{1}{2}$ cups chopped walnuts, optional
3 tsp vanilla	

Tina's Method

You write both mixed numbers as improper fractions.

$$2\frac{1}{2} - 1\frac{3}{4} = \frac{5}{2} - \frac{7}{4}$$
$$= \frac{5 \cdot 4 - 2 \cdot 7}{2 \cdot 4}$$
$$= \frac{20 - 14}{8}$$
$$= \frac{\cancel{6}^{3}}{\cancel{8}_{4}} = \frac{3}{4}$$

You need $\frac{3}{4}$ c more sugar.

Kevin's Method

You write $2\frac{1}{2}$ as $2\frac{2}{4}$, and then rewrite it as $1\frac{6}{4}$ before subtracting.

$$2\frac{1}{2} - 1\frac{3}{4} = 2\frac{2}{4} - 1\frac{3}{4}$$
$$= 1\frac{6}{4} - 1\frac{3}{4}$$
$$= \frac{3}{4}$$

You need $\frac{3}{4}$ c more sugar.

Choose a Method

1. For the problem above, which method do you prefer? Explain.

2. Which method would you use to find $2\frac{4}{7} - 1\frac{9}{14}$? Which method would you use to find $-1\frac{1}{2} - 1\frac{3}{4}$? Explain your choices.

EXERCISES

For more exercises, see *Extra Practice*.

Practice and Problem Solving

A Practice by Example

Example 1
(page 243)

Find each sum or difference. Simplify if possible.

1. $\frac{3}{16} + \frac{7}{16}$
2. $\frac{6}{z} + \left(-\frac{2}{z}\right)$
3. $\frac{15}{q} - \frac{8}{q}$
4. $\frac{5}{11} + \frac{4}{11}$

5. $\frac{11}{12} - \frac{7}{12}$
6. $\frac{7}{8} + \frac{5}{8}$
7. $\frac{3}{10} - \frac{7}{10}$
8. $\frac{2}{x} + \frac{3}{x}$

Example 2
(page 244)

Simplify each sum or difference.

9. $\frac{3}{4} - \frac{2}{3}$
10. $\frac{12}{20} - \frac{1}{4}$
11. $-\frac{3}{10} - \frac{5}{100}$
12. $\frac{6}{x} - \frac{2}{5}$

Example 3
(page 244)

Find each sum or difference. Simplify if possible.

13. $3\frac{3}{4} + 2\frac{1}{4}$
14. $\frac{4}{16} + 1\frac{3}{8}$
15. $10\frac{1}{8} + 3\frac{3}{4}$
16. $3\frac{5}{8} + 2\frac{7}{12}$

17. $1\frac{5}{9} - 1\frac{2}{9}$
18. $5\frac{3}{4} - 2\frac{1}{8}$
19. $1\frac{17}{18} - \frac{7}{9}$
20. $1\frac{7}{8} - 2\frac{3}{4}$

21. **Homework** Kim works on Social Studies homework for $2\frac{2}{5}$ h. Then she works on Math homework for $1\frac{1}{4}$ h. How many hours total does Kim spend doing homework?

B Apply Your Skills

Estimation **Estimate each sum or difference.**

22. $2\frac{1}{3} + 7\frac{1}{8}$
23. $25\frac{5}{18} - 9\frac{11}{17}$
24. $15\frac{3}{4} + 31\frac{1}{2}$
25. $-4\frac{7}{8} + 15\frac{1}{10}$

26. **Writing in Math** Describe why estimating a sum or difference before adding or subtracting is useful.

27. **Crafts** A doll artist cuts a piece of lace $8\frac{5}{8}$ in. long from a piece $10\frac{1}{2}$ in. long. How many inches of lace are left?

Find each sum or difference.

28. $\frac{12}{15} + \frac{1}{2}$
29. $\frac{3}{n} - \frac{3}{10}$
30. $\frac{7}{10} + \frac{2d}{3}$
31. $\frac{5}{6} + \frac{7}{9}$

Mental Math **Find each sum.**

32. $\frac{3}{4} + \frac{3}{8} + \frac{1}{4}$
33. $2\frac{5}{7} + 1\frac{2}{5} + 3\frac{2}{7}$
34. $\frac{2}{7} + \frac{x}{2} + \left(-\frac{2}{7}\right)$

35. **Weather** There were three snowstorms last winter. The storms dropped $3\frac{1}{2}$ in., $6\frac{1}{2}$ in., and $10\frac{3}{4}$ in. of snow. What was the combined snowfall of the three storms?

C Challenge

Use prime factors to find the LCD. Then simplify each expression.

36. $\frac{7}{24} - \frac{15}{90}$
37. $\frac{-5}{66} + \frac{-7}{99}$
38. $\frac{2}{28} + \frac{1}{49}$

39. **Collections** Dora and Paul have a collection of x marbles. Dora has $\frac{x}{3}$ marbles. What fraction of the marbles does Paul have?

Multiple Choice

40. Which sum or difference is greater than 0?

A. $-\frac{7}{8} + \frac{3}{4}$ **B.** $-\frac{7}{8} - \frac{3}{4}$ **C.** $-\frac{7}{8} + \left(-\frac{3}{4}\right)$ **D.** $\frac{7}{8} + \left(-\frac{3}{4}\right)$

41. Sue is fishing. She catches a bass weighing $5\frac{1}{4}$ lb. Then she catches three more weighing $3\frac{1}{2}$ lb, $1\frac{3}{4}$ lb, and 2 lb. She releases the smallest fish. What is the total weight of the fish Sue keeps?

F. $8\frac{3}{4}$ lb **G.** $9\frac{1}{4}$ lb **H.** $10\frac{3}{4}$ lb **I.** $12\frac{1}{2}$ lb

42. Which expression is equal to $\frac{1}{3} + \frac{1}{6}$?

A. $\frac{1}{2} + \frac{2}{4}$ **B.** $\frac{1}{4} + \frac{2}{8}$ **C.** $\frac{1}{5} + \frac{2}{10}$ **D.** $\frac{1}{7} + \frac{2}{14}$

Short Response

43. In 2003, first-class postage in the United States costs 37¢ for 1 oz. Your letter weighs $\frac{3}{4}$ oz. **(a)** Do you need extra postage to include a newspaper clipping that weighs $\frac{3}{8}$ oz? **(b)** Explain.

Take It to the NET
Online lesson quiz at
www.PHSchool.com
Web Code: ada-0503

44. José and Letty plan to ride their bicycles at least eight miles. They ride for $5\frac{3}{8}$ miles and stop for a break. Then they ride for another $2\frac{5}{7}$ miles. **(a)** Do they meet their goal? **(b)** Explain your answer.

Mixed Review

Lesson 5-2 **Order from least to greatest.**

45. $\frac{5}{8}, \frac{4}{7}, \frac{3}{6}$ **46.** $\frac{2}{3}, 0.6, 0.66$ **47.** $\frac{10}{9}, \frac{9}{10}, -\frac{9}{10}, -\frac{10}{9}$

Lesson 4-7 **Simplify each expression.**

48. $x \cdot x^2$ **49.** $(x^3)^4$

Lesson 3-3 **50. Data Analysis** Use the data at the right. Find the mean, median, and mode of the annual salaries. Which statistic would you use to encourage someone to take a job at Company A?

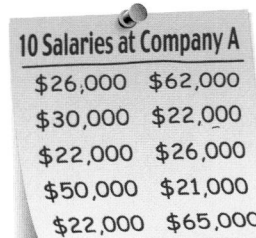

10 Salaries at Company A	
$26,000	$62,000
$30,000	$22,000
$22,000	$26,000
$50,000	$21,000
$22,000	$65,000

✓ Checkpoint Quiz 1 **Lessons 5-1 through 5-3**

 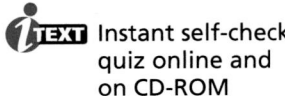 Instant self-check quiz online and on CD-ROM

Compare. Use >, <, or = to complete each statement.

1. $\frac{2}{3}$ ■ $\frac{2}{5}$ **2.** $2\frac{2}{3}$ ■ $2\frac{4}{6}$ **3.** $-\frac{1}{5}$ ■ $-\frac{1}{8}$ **4.** -1.65 ■ $-1\frac{5}{8}$

Write each fraction or mixed number as a decimal and each decimal as a fraction in simplest form.

5. $\frac{51}{100}$ **6.** 0.012 **7.** $1\frac{1}{4}$ **8.** $0.\overline{3}$ **9.** $\frac{5}{6}$ **10.** $0.\overline{51}$

Find each sum or difference. Simplify if possible.

11. $\frac{6}{13} + \frac{5}{13}$ **12.** $\frac{11}{12} - \frac{7}{9}$ **13.** $1\frac{3}{5} + 2\frac{7}{8}$ **14.** $4\frac{1}{7} - 3\frac{10}{21}$

5-4 Multiplying and Dividing Fractions

What You'll Learn

OBJECTIVE 1 To multiply fractions

OBJECTIVE 2 To divide fractions

. . . And Why

To solve real-world problems involving area

✔ Check Skills You'll Need

Write each mixed number as a fraction.

1. $2\frac{1}{3}$ 2. $3\frac{3}{10}$ 3. $1\frac{4}{9}$

4. $4\frac{4}{5}$ 5. $7\frac{7}{8}$ 6. $5\frac{1}{7}$

For help, go to Skills Handbook, p. 772.

New Vocabulary

• reciprocals

OBJECTIVE

1 Multiplying Rational Numbers

Investigation

Modeling Multiplication of Fractions

Use paper folding to find $\frac{2}{3}$ of $\frac{1}{4}$, or $\frac{2}{3} \cdot \frac{1}{4}$.

1. Fold a sheet of paper into fourths as shown. Shade $\frac{1}{4}$ of it.

2. Now unfold the paper and fold it into thirds as shown in the second picture. Shade $\frac{2}{3}$ of it.

3. **a.** Count the small rectangles.
   b. How many did you shade twice?
   c. What fraction of the small rectangles is this?

4. Use your model to complete:
   $\frac{2}{3} \cdot \frac{1}{4} = \dfrac{\blacksquare}{\blacksquare}$

5. **Modeling** Use paper folding and shading to find $\frac{3}{4} \cdot \frac{1}{2}$.

To multiply fractions, first multiply their numerators and multiply their denominators. Then write the result in simplest form.

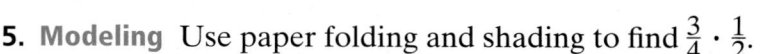 **EXAMPLE** **Multiplying Fractions**

Find $\frac{3}{7} \cdot \frac{4}{5}$. Simplify if possible.

$\frac{3}{7} \cdot \frac{4}{5} = \frac{3 \cdot 4}{7 \cdot 5}$ ⟵ Multiply the numerators.
⟵ Multiply the denominators.

$= \frac{12}{35}$ Simplify.

✔ Check Understanding Example 1

1. Find each product. Simplify if possible.
   a. $\frac{2}{5}\left(\frac{1}{3}\right)$ **b.** $-\frac{5}{6} \cdot \frac{2}{3}$ **c.** $\frac{7}{8} \cdot \frac{5}{9}$ **d.** $-\frac{1}{4}\left(-\frac{3}{8}\right)$

 Interactive lesson includes instant self-check, tutorials, and activities.

When a numerator and a denominator have common factors, you can simplify before multiplying.

2 EXAMPLE **Simplifying Before Multiplying**

a. Find $\frac{9}{15} \cdot \frac{5}{9}$.

$$\frac{9}{15} \cdot \frac{5}{9} = \frac{\cancel{9}^{1}}{3\cancel{15}} \cdot \frac{\cancel{5}^{1}}{\cancel{9}_{1}} \quad \text{Divide the common factors.}$$

$$= \frac{1}{3} \quad \text{Multiply.}$$

b. Find $\frac{y}{4} \cdot \frac{8}{11}$.

$$\frac{y}{4} \cdot \frac{8}{11} = \frac{y}{\cancel{4}_{1}} \cdot \frac{\cancel{8}^{2}}{11} \quad \text{Divide the common factors.}$$

$$= \frac{2y}{11} \quad \text{Multiply.}$$

✓ **Check Understanding** Example 2

2. Find each product. Simplify if possible.

a. $\frac{2}{3} \cdot \frac{6}{7}$ **b.** $-\frac{5}{15} \cdot \frac{21}{25}$ **c.** $\frac{2x}{9} \cdot \frac{3}{4}$

To multiply mixed numbers, first write them as improper fractions. Then simplify before multiplying, if possible.

3 EXAMPLE **Real-World 🌐 Problem Solving**

Geometry Central Park in New York City is a rectangle. It is approximately $2\frac{1}{2}$ mi long and $\frac{1}{2}$ mi wide. What is the area of Central Park?

$$A = 2\frac{1}{2} \cdot \frac{1}{2} \quad \text{Area of a rectangle = length · width.}$$

$$= \frac{5}{2} \cdot \frac{1}{2} \quad \text{Write } 2\frac{1}{2} \text{ as an improper fraction, } \frac{5}{2}.$$

$$= \frac{5}{4} \quad \text{Multiply.}$$

$$= 1\frac{1}{4} \quad \text{Write as a mixed number.}$$

● The area of Central Park is about $1\frac{1}{4}$ mi^2.

✓ **Check Understanding** Example 3

3. Find each product. Simplify if possible.

a. $3\frac{3}{4} \cdot \frac{2}{5}$ **b.** $\frac{2}{3} \cdot 1\frac{2}{7}$ **c.** $\left(-2\frac{5}{6}\right) \cdot 1\frac{3}{5}$

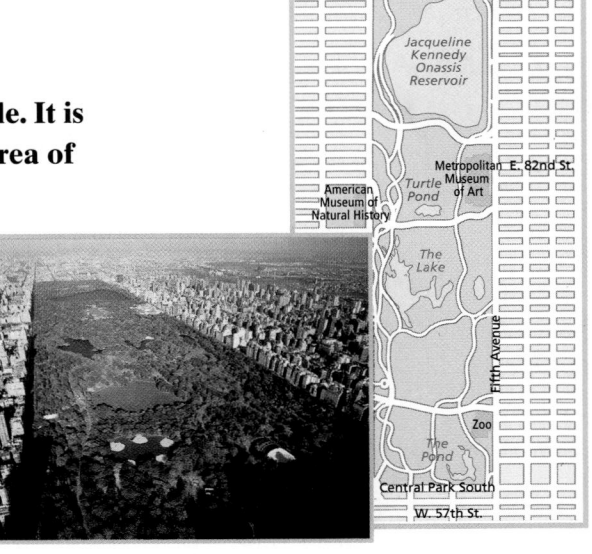

Real-World 🌐 Connection

Central Park is a rectangle. The angle of the photo makes two sides appear to be not parallel.

2 Dividing Rational Numbers

Asking "What is $2 \div \frac{1}{2}$?" is the same as asking "How many halves are in two wholes?" As the oranges show, there are four halves in two wholes.

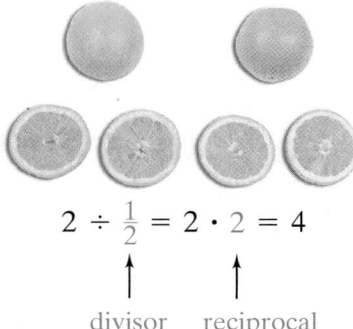

Numbers like $\frac{1}{2}$ and 2 (or $\frac{2}{1}$) are **reciprocals** because their product is 1. To divide fractions, rewrite the division as a related multiplication in which you multiply by the reciprocal of the divisor.

$$2 \div \frac{1}{2} = 2 \cdot 2 = 4$$

↑ divisor   ↑ reciprocal

> **Reading Math**
>
> Reciprocals are also called *multiplicative inverses*.

4 EXAMPLE Dividing Fractions

a. Find $\frac{2}{9} \div \frac{2}{5}$.

$$\frac{2}{9} \div \frac{2}{5} = \frac{2}{9} \cdot \frac{5}{2} \quad \text{Multiply by the reciprocal of the divisor.}$$

$$= \frac{2^1}{9} \cdot \frac{5}{{}_1 2} \quad \text{Divide the common factors.}$$

$$= \frac{5}{9} \quad \text{Simplify.}$$

b. Find $\frac{x}{3} \div \frac{x}{4}$.

$$\frac{x}{3} \div \frac{x}{4} = \frac{x}{3} \cdot \frac{4}{x}$$

$$= \frac{x^1}{3} \cdot \frac{4}{1x}$$

$$= \frac{4}{3} = 1\frac{1}{3}$$

✓ Check Understanding Example 4

4. Find each quotient. Simplify if possible.

    a. $-\frac{1}{4} \div \frac{1}{2}$
    b. $\frac{5a}{8} \div \frac{2}{3}$
    c. $\frac{3b}{7} \div \frac{6}{7}$

To divide mixed numbers, change the mixed numbers to improper fractions before multiplying by the reciprocal of the divisor.

5 EXAMPLE Dividing Mixed Numbers

Find $1\frac{3}{4} \div \left(-2\frac{5}{8}\right)$.

$$1\frac{3}{4} \div \left(-2\frac{5}{8}\right) = \frac{7}{4} \div \left(-\frac{21}{8}\right) \quad \text{Change to improper fractions.}$$

$$= \frac{7}{4} \cdot \left(-\frac{8}{21}\right) \quad \text{Multiply by } -\frac{8}{21}, \text{ the reciprocal of } -\frac{21}{8}.$$

$$= \frac{{}^1 7}{{}_1 4} \cdot -\frac{{}^2 8}{{}_3 21} = -\frac{2}{3} \quad \begin{array}{l}\text{Divide the common factors.} \\ \text{Simplify.}\end{array}$$

✓ Check Understanding Example 5

5. Find each quotient. Simplify if possible.

    a. $1\frac{1}{3} \div \frac{5}{6}$
    b. $-1\frac{3}{5} \div 1\frac{1}{5}$
    c. $12\frac{1}{2} \div 1\frac{2}{3}$

EXERCISES

For more exercises, see *Extra Practice*.

Practice and Problem Solving

A Practice by Example

Examples 1 and 2
(pages 248 and 249)

Find each product. Simplify if possible.

1. $\frac{2}{3} \cdot \frac{1}{5}$ **2.** $-\frac{1}{2}\left(\frac{3}{8}\right)$ **3.** $-\frac{4}{7} \cdot -\frac{3}{5}$ **4.** $\left(-\frac{2}{3}\right)\left(\frac{11}{13}\right)$

5. $\left(-\frac{7}{8}\right)\left(-\frac{4}{5}\right)$ **6.** $\frac{12y}{25} \cdot \frac{5}{6}$ **7.** $\frac{9}{10} \cdot \frac{15x}{3}$ **8.** $\frac{5}{9}\left(\frac{9}{10}\right)$

Example 3
(page 249)

9. $5\frac{7}{8} \cdot \frac{6}{7}$ **10.** $2\frac{3}{4} \cdot 1\frac{1}{5}$ **11.** $-1\frac{2}{5} \cdot 2\frac{2}{7}$ **12.** $-3\frac{2}{5} \cdot -1\frac{2}{3}$

13. Homework Jim spends $\frac{3}{4}$ of an hour on homework. His older sister Gina spends $1\frac{2}{3}$ times as much on her homework as Jim spends on his. How much time does Gina spend doing her homework?

Example 4
(page 250)

Find each quotient. Simplify if possible.

14. $\frac{1}{2} \div \frac{1}{3}$ **15.** $\frac{5}{8} \div \frac{3}{4}$ **16.** $-\frac{3}{4} \div \frac{1}{3}$ **17.** $\frac{11}{12} \div \left(-\frac{7}{8}\right)$

18. $\frac{3}{4} \div \frac{8}{9}$ **19.** $\frac{3}{4} \div \frac{1}{2}$ **20.** $\frac{2t}{5} \div \frac{2}{5}$ **21.** $\frac{1}{x} \div \frac{3}{x}$

Example 5
(page 250)

22. $12\frac{2}{3} \div \frac{3}{4}$ **23.** $1\frac{3}{8} \div 2\frac{1}{16}$ **24.** $-1\frac{7}{9} \div \frac{8}{9}$ **25.** $-3\frac{2}{3} \div \left(-2\frac{4}{9}\right)$

26. $3\frac{1}{2} \div \frac{4}{21}$ **27.** $7\frac{2}{3} \div 1\frac{5}{6}$ **28.** $6\frac{3}{4} \div \frac{9}{10}$ **29.** $1\frac{4}{5} \div \left(-1\frac{1}{2}\right)$

B Apply Your Skills

Find each product. Simplify if possible.

30. $\frac{6x}{7} \cdot \frac{1}{3}$ **31.** $-\frac{2}{3} \cdot \frac{9}{10}$ **32.** $\frac{8}{9} \cdot \frac{15}{28}$ **33.** $-1\frac{1}{4} \cdot 6\frac{2}{3}$

34. $\frac{4}{t} \cdot \frac{3t}{8}$ **35.** $\frac{4a}{9} \cdot \frac{3}{10}$ **36.** $1\frac{3}{5} \cdot \left(-2\frac{1}{2}\right)$ **37.** $\left(-\frac{7}{12}\right)\left(-\frac{5}{6}\right)$

38. Number Sense One granola bar weighs $1\frac{1}{2}$ oz. What is the weight of six granola bars?

Find each quotient. Simplify if possible.

39. $-\frac{1}{2} \div \frac{2}{3}$ **40.** $\frac{10}{13} \div \frac{15}{26}$ **41.** $-\frac{5}{6} \div \frac{4}{9}$ **42.** $\frac{4}{9x} \div \frac{2}{3x}$

43. $\frac{2}{5} \div \frac{15}{16}$ **44.** $-\frac{6n}{7} \div \frac{n}{3}$ **45.** $\frac{2}{9} \div \frac{w}{3}$ **46.** $\frac{3}{8} \div \frac{6}{32}$

Mental Math Simplify each expression.

47. $\frac{1}{2} \cdot \frac{2}{5}$ **48.** $\frac{1}{2} \div \frac{2}{5}$ **49.** $10 \cdot \frac{1}{4}$ **50.** $10 \div \frac{1}{4}$

51. $\frac{5}{8} \cdot \frac{3}{5}$ **52.** $\frac{5}{8} \div \frac{3}{5}$ **53.** $\frac{3}{7} \cdot \frac{12}{21}$ **54.** $\frac{3}{7} \div \frac{12}{21}$

55. Construction A cable television crew has to install cable along a road $1\frac{1}{2}$ mi long. The crew takes a day to install each $\frac{1}{4}$ mi of cable. How many days will the installation take?

56. a. Write an expression for the following: The product of $\frac{1}{2}a$ and 3 is decreased by the quotient $a \div (-4)$.
   b. Evaluate your expression for $a = 3$.

57. A cheetah can run as fast as 64 mi/h. At that speed, how far could a cheetah run in $\frac{1}{16}$ h? $\frac{1}{30}$ h?

58. You are hiking along a trail that is $13\frac{1}{2}$ mi long. You plan to rest every $2\frac{1}{4}$ mi. How many rest stops will you make?

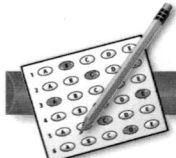 **Challenge**

59. Writing in Math Why must you change mixed numbers to improper fractions before multiplying or dividing them?

60. a. Patterns Find each quotient: $\frac{1}{2} \div 2, \frac{1}{2} \div 3, \frac{1}{2} \div 4$, and $\frac{1}{2} \div 5$.
   b. Explain what happens to the quotients as the divisor increases in value.

61. Reasoning Write a multiplication equation and a division equation that you could use to show the result of cutting four melons into eight equal slices each.

62. Open-Ended Find two fractions greater than $\frac{1}{2}$ with a product less than $\frac{1}{2}$.

Test Prep

Multiple Choice

63. Which quotient does NOT equal 1?
   A. $2\frac{3}{4} \div \frac{11}{4}$ **B.** $\frac{3}{8} \div 0.375$ **C.** $\frac{7}{8} \div \frac{7}{8}$ **D.** $-1\frac{2}{3} \div \left(-\frac{3}{5}\right)$

64. Which expression simplifies to $\frac{x}{3}$?
   F. $\frac{5x}{36}\left(\frac{5}{12}\right)$ **G.** $\frac{x}{6}\left(2\frac{2}{5}\right)$ **H.** $\frac{5x}{36}\left(2\frac{2}{5}\right)$ **I.** $\frac{36}{5x}\left(2\frac{2}{5}\right)$

Short Response

65. a. A family wants to travel 300 miles. They drive at an average speed of 65 mi/h for $3\frac{1}{2}$ hours. Have they driven far enough?
   b. Explain your answer for part (a).

Take It to the NET
Online lesson quiz at
www.PHSchool.com
Web Code: ada-0504

66. Natasha's bedroom floor is $10\frac{1}{2}$ ft by $14\frac{3}{4}$ ft. She buys 160 ft^2 of carpet. Does she have enough carpet to cover the floor? Explain.

Mixed Review

Lesson 5-3

Add or subtract.

67. $\frac{4}{5} + \frac{6}{7}$ **68.** $\frac{10}{13} - \frac{25}{26}$ **69.** $-\frac{3}{10} + \frac{3}{5}$ **70.** $\frac{16}{21} - \frac{5}{7}$

Lesson 4-4

Simplify each fraction.

71. $\frac{10}{12}$ **72.** $\frac{24}{40}$ **73.** $\frac{45}{10}$ **74.** $\frac{12}{50}$ **75.** $\frac{34}{51}$ **76.** $\frac{105}{135}$

Lesson 2-7

77. Hal's age is three times Ida's age. In 8 years Hal will be twice as old as Ida. How old is Hal?

78. Personal Finance You spent $\frac{1}{4}$ of your money on lunch. After lunch, you gave half of what you had left to a friend, and then you spent \$3 on a book. You have \$4.50 left. How much money did you have before lunch?

Using Customary Units of Measurement

OBJECTIVE

1 Identifying Appropriate Units of Measure

Most people in the United States use the *customary system* of measurement.

Customary Units of Measure

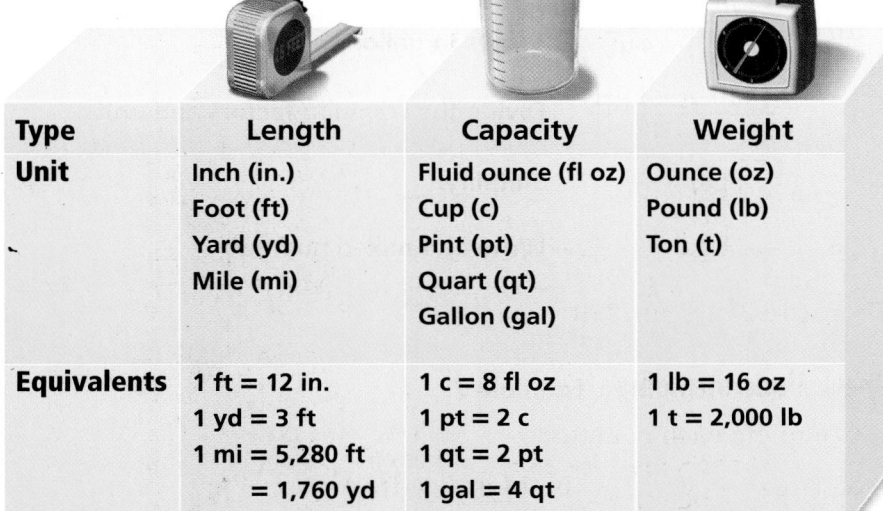

Type	Length	Capacity	Weight
Unit	Inch (in.) Foot (ft) Yard (yd) Mile (mi)	Fluid ounce (fl oz) Cup (c) Pint (pt) Quart (qt) Gallon (gal)	Ounce (oz) Pound (lb) Ton (t)
Equivalents	1 ft = 12 in. 1 yd = 3 ft 1 mi = 5,280 ft = 1,760 yd	1 c = 8 fl oz 1 pt = 2 c 1 qt = 2 pt 1 gal = 4 qt	1 lb = 16 oz 1 t = 2,000 lb

In order to measure an object, you should choose an appropriate unit of measure.

1 EXAMPLE Choosing a Unit of Measure

Choose an appropriate unit of measure. Explain your choice.

a. weight of a truck Measure its weight in tons because a truck is very heavy.

b. length of a hallway rug Measure its length in feet or yards because the length is too great to measure in inches.

✓ **Check Understanding** Example 1

1. Choose an appropriate unit of measure. Explain.

    a. length of a swimming pool **b.** weight of a baby
    c. length of a pencil **d.** capacity of an eyedropper

What You'll Learn

OBJECTIVE
1 To identify appropriate customary units

OBJECTIVE
2 To convert customary units

. . . And Why

To solve real-world problems involving consumer issues

✓ Check Skills You'll Need

Find each product.

1. $4 \cdot \frac{1}{12}$ **2.** $3\frac{1}{4} \cdot \frac{16}{1}$

3. $1\frac{1}{4} \cdot \frac{8}{1}$ **4.** $4\frac{1}{2} \cdot \frac{1}{3}$

❓ For help, go to Lesson 5-4.

New Vocabulary

• dimensional analysis

---

iTEXT Interactive lesson includes instant self-check, tutorials, and activities.

OBJECTIVE

2 Converting Customary Units

> **Test-Taking Tip**
> You can work faster during tests if you memorize common conversions.

You can use *conversion factors* to change from one unit of measure to another in a process called **dimensional analysis**. You use equivalent units to write a conversion factor. For example, $\frac{12 \text{ in.}}{1 \text{ ft}} = 1$, so you can use $\frac{12 \text{ in.}}{1 \text{ ft}}$ to convert from feet to inches.

2 EXAMPLE Using Dimensional Analysis

Use dimensional analysis to convert 10 quarts to gallons.

$$10 \text{ qt} = \frac{10 \text{ qt}}{1} \cdot \frac{1 \text{ gal}}{4 \text{ qt}} \qquad \text{Use a conversion factor that changes quarts to gallons.}$$

$$= \frac{{}^{5}\cancel{10} \text{ qt} \cdot 1 \text{ gal}}{{}_{2}\cancel{4} \text{ qt}} \qquad \text{Divide the common factors and units.}$$

$$= \frac{5}{2} \text{ gal} \qquad \text{Simplify.}$$

$$= 2\frac{1}{2} \text{ gal} \qquad \text{Write as a mixed number.}$$

- There are $2\frac{1}{2}$ gal in 10 qt.

✔ **Check Understanding** Example 2

2. Complete each equation.

    a. 14 oz = ▦ lb   **b.** 14 in. = ▦ ft   **c.** 14 pt = ▦ qt

Converting units can help you make comparisons.

3 EXAMPLE Real-World 🌐 Problem Solving

Consumer Issues At Store A, a $4\frac{1}{4}$-lb bag of cashew nuts costs $15.99. Store B charges the same price for a 76-oz bag of cashews. Which store gives you more for your money?

$$4\frac{1}{4} \text{ lb} = \frac{17}{4} \text{ lb} \cdot \frac{16 \text{ oz}}{1 \text{ lb}} \qquad \text{Use a conversion factor that changes pounds to ounces.}$$

$$= \frac{17}{{}_{1}\cancel{4}} \text{ lb} \cdot \frac{{}^{4}\cancel{16} \text{ oz}}{1 \text{ lb}} \qquad \text{Divide the common factors and units.}$$

$$= 68 \text{ oz} \qquad \text{Multiply.}$$

- Since 76 oz > 68 oz, Store B gives you more for your money.

✔ **Check Understanding** Example 3

3. Complete each equation.

    a. $3\frac{1}{2}$ lb = ▦ oz   **b.** $3\frac{1}{2}$ yd = ▦ ft   **c.** $3\frac{1}{2}$ pt = ▦ c

69. Error Analysis Suzanne claims a quarter-pound hamburger is heavier than a 6-oz hamburger. Explain why she is incorrect.

 **Challenge**

Complete each equation.

70. $2\frac{1}{4}$ yd = $6\frac{3}{4}$ ■

71. 6 qt = $1\frac{1}{2}$ ■

72. 100 lb = $\frac{1}{20}$ ■

73. 6 c = 48 ■

74. $1\frac{1}{2}$ pt = ■ qt

75. $4\frac{1}{4}$ ft = ■ in.

Test Prep

Gridded Response

Complete each equation.

76. 9 lb 2 oz = ■ oz

77. 4 ft = ■ in.

78. 3 yd 2 ft = ■ ft

79. 12 pt = ■ c

80. 8 oz = ■ lb

81. 7 ft = ■ yd

82. $4\frac{1}{2}$ c = ■ pt

83. $1\frac{1}{2}$ gal = ■ qt

84. $2\frac{1}{2}$ yd = ■ in.

Take It to the NET
Online lesson quiz at
www.PHSchool.com
Web Code: ada-0505

Mixed Review

Lesson 5-4

Multiply or divide.

85. $\frac{9}{11} \div 2\frac{7}{11}$

86. $1\frac{5}{7} \cdot 1\frac{1}{2}$

87. $\frac{9}{10} \div \frac{3}{4}$

88. $2\frac{2}{5} \cdot 3\frac{2}{3}$

Lesson 2-3

Simplify each expression.

89. $3x + (-2x) + 3y$

90. $10 - 3t - 4t$

91. $2y - 5y$

Lesson 1-7 **92. Softball** In a single-elimination softball tournament, each team plays until it loses. Eight teams are playing in a single-elimination tournament. How many games must be played?

Math at Work

Technical Artist

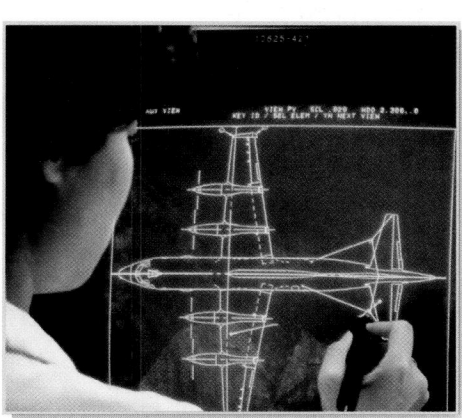

Technical artists prepare the drawings used by manufacturing and construction workers. The drawings give visual guidelines and technical details of products, buildings, and structures. Technical artists specify dimensions and materials to be used in the building process, and state procedures and processes to be followed. Many technical artists use computer-aided design (CAD) systems to prepare plans. Since they draw technical plans to scale, fractions and operations with fractions are an important part of their work.

Take It to the NET For more information about technical artists, go to **www.PHSchool.com**.
Web Code: adb-2031

Greatest Possible Error

Measurement is not exact. To the nearest centimeter, each segment at the right measures 3 cm.

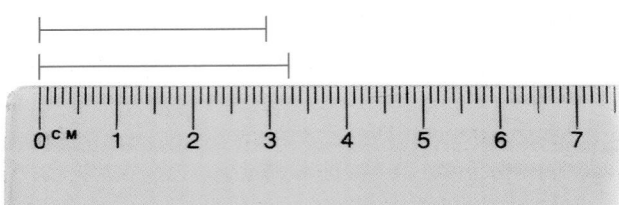

When a measurement is rounded to the nearest centimeter, it can vary from the actual length by as much as one half centimeter. The *greatest possible error* of a measurement is half the unit used for measuring.

EXAMPLE

Find the greatest possible error for each measurement.

a. $1\frac{1}{2}$ in. The measurement is to the nearest $\frac{1}{2}$ in.

Since $\frac{1}{2} \cdot \frac{1}{2} = \frac{1}{4}$, the greatest possible error is $\frac{1}{4}$ in.

b. 15.6 L The measurement is to the nearest tenth of a liter.

Since $\frac{1}{2} \cdot 0.1 = 0.05$, the greatest possible error is 0.05 L.

c. 3.004 mm The measurement is to the nearest 0.001 mm.

Since $\frac{1}{2} \cdot 0.001 = 0.0005$, the greatest possible error is 0.0005 mm.

EXERCISES

Find the greatest possible error for each measurement.

1. 45.98 mg

2. $12\frac{1}{4}$ in.

3. 54.4 cm

4. $1\frac{3}{4}$ c

5. 3 ft

6. 9 g

7. 12.3 L

8. 15.575 mm

9. $24\frac{1}{2}$ yd

10. 512 m

11. $10\frac{1}{8}$ oz

12. $3\frac{1}{16}$ in.

13. Geometry A rectangle measures 12 cm by 10.5 cm. What is the greatest possible error for each measurement?

14. Carpentry A carpenter is cutting a table leg that is $2\frac{1}{4}$ ft long.
  a. What is the greatest possible error?
  b. **Writing in Math** Is the greatest possible error acceptable in this situation? Explain.

Work Backward

OBJECTIVE

1 Work Backward

Math Strategies in Action The Longleat hedge maze in England was designed in 1975. The hedges are so high you can't see over them unless you stand on one of the wooden staircases placed throughout the maze. Once you find the center of the maze in its 1.7 miles of pathways, you have to remember the path you followed and work backward to get out.

Visitors to the Longleat hedge maze often take 90 min to reach the center.

Working backward from known information will sometimes help you solve a problem.

1 EXAMPLE Real-World Problem Solving

Time You are planning to go to a baseball game that starts at 1:00 P.M. You want to arrive half an hour early. Your walk to the train station is about 10 minutes long. The train ride to the city takes $\frac{3}{4}$ of an hour. After you arrive in the city, you will need to walk for about 10 more minutes to get to the stadium. What time should you plan to leave?

Read and Understand

Think about the information you are given.

1. What do you want to find?

2. What is your arrival time?

3. How much time will you spend walking to the train?

4. How much time will you spend on the train?

5. How much time will you spend walking from the train?

What You'll Learn

OBJECTIVE
1   To solve problems by working backward

. . . And Why

To solve real-world problems involving time

✔ **Check Skills You'll Need**

Order the fractions from least to greatest.

1. $\frac{1}{2}, \frac{1}{3}, \frac{1}{4}, \frac{1}{5}, \frac{1}{10}$

2. $\frac{7}{3}, \frac{5}{3}, \frac{13}{3}, \frac{3}{3}$

3. $\frac{3}{7}, \frac{3}{5}, \frac{3}{13}, \frac{3}{3}$

4. $-\frac{3}{7}, -\frac{3}{5}, -\frac{3}{13}, -\frac{3}{3}$

❓ For help, go to Lesson 5-2.

ⓘ TEXT Interactive lesson includes instant self-check, tutorials, and activities.

You know that the series of events must end at 1:00 P.M. Work backward to find when the events must begin.

Move the hands of a clock to find your departure time.

6. Write the starting time for each event.

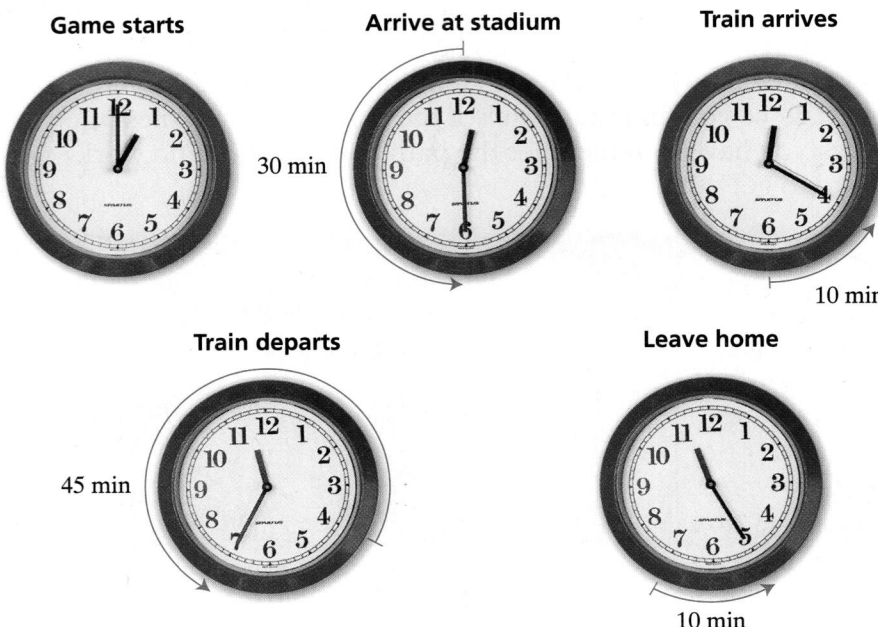

Game starts	Arrive at stadium	Train arrives

30 min

10 min

Train departs	Leave home

45 min

10 min

You should leave home at 11:25 A.M.

Look Back and Check

Check the departure time. Find the total time needed.

10 min + 45 min + 10 min + 30 min = 95 min

Add 95 minutes to your departure time.

$$
\begin{array}{r}
11{:}\ 25 \\
+\ 0{:}\ 95 \\
\hline
11{:}120
\end{array}
$$
    120 min = 2 h

11:120 = 2 hours after 11:00, or 1:00 P.M.

Since the game starts at 1 P.M., your departure time is correct.

✓ Check Understanding

7. Suppose you must be home by 6:00 P.M. If the return trip takes the same amount of time, how long can the game run in order for you to be at home on time?

EXERCISES

For more exercises, see *Extra Practice*.

Practice and Problem Solving

A Practice by Example

Example 1
(page 259)

Work backward to solve each problem.

1. **Lawn Care** Eduardo wants to finish mowing lawns at 3:00 P.M. on Saturday. It takes $1\frac{1}{2}$ h to mow the first lawn and twice as long to mow the lawn next door. The lawn across the street takes $1\frac{1}{2}$ h to mow. Eduardo plans to take a $\frac{1}{2}$-h break between the second and third lawns. What time should he plan to start mowing?

2. **Travel** Siobhan's family is planning a trip to the Grand Canyon. It will take 5 h of driving along with three $\frac{1}{2}$-h stops. They want to arrive at 3:30 P.M. What time should they plan to leave?

3. **Transportation** Korin is going to a movie. The movie begins at 1:00 P.M. She has a 15-minute walk to the bus from her home and a 5-minute walk from the bus to the movie. The bus ride takes 38 min. What is the latest bus she can take to make the movie?

BUS DEPARTURE TIMES

10:10 A.M.	12:05 P.M.
10:30 A.M.	12:15 P.M.
11:00 A.M.	12:25 P.M.
11:35 A.M.	12:40 P.M.

Strategies

- Account for All Possibilities
- Draw a Diagram
- Look for a Pattern
- Make a Model
- Make a Table
- Simplify the Problem
- Simulate the Problem
- Solve by Graphing
- Try, Test, Revise
- Use Multiple Strategies
- Work Backward
- Write an Equation
- Write a Proportion

Solve using any strategy.

4. Pump A can fill 5 identical tanks in 60 min.
   Pump B can fill 3 tanks that same size in 60 min.
   a. How long does it take pump A to fill one tank?
   b. How long does it take pump B to fill one tank?
   c. How long does it take pumps A and B together to fill one tank?

B Apply Your Skills

5. You have two nickels, three dimes, and a quarter. Using at least one of each coin, how many different amounts of money can you make? Explain.

6. **Geometry** Zach's rectangular garden measures 12 ft by 10 ft. He puts a stake in each corner and one every 2 ft along each side. How many stakes are there in all?

7. You spent half of your money at the amusement park and had $15 left. How much money did you have originally?

8. Describe the pattern of the numbers below. Then find the next three numbers in the pattern.
$$\frac{2}{3}, 1\frac{5}{12}, 2\frac{1}{6}, 2\frac{11}{12}, \blacksquare, \blacksquare, \blacksquare, \ldots$$

Reading Math

For help with reading and describing the pattern in Exercise 8, see page 263.

C Challenge

9. **Number Sense** Use the equation at the right. Choose from the numbers 1, 2, 3, 5, and 6, and make four different true equations.

$$\frac{\blacksquare}{\blacksquare} + \frac{\blacksquare}{\blacksquare} = \frac{\blacksquare}{\blacksquare}$$

10. Several freshmen tried out for the school track team.

After Round 1, $\frac{1}{2}$ of the freshmen were eliminated.

After Round 2, $\frac{1}{3}$ of those remaining were eliminated.

After Round 3, $\frac{1}{4}$ of those remaining were eliminated.

After Round 4, $\frac{1}{5}$ of those remaining were eliminated.

After Round 5, $\frac{1}{6}$ of those remaining were eliminated.

The 10 freshmen who remained made it onto the track team. How many freshmen originally tried out?

Test Prep

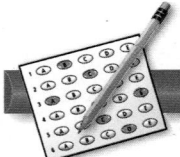

Multiple Choice

11. You spent $\frac{1}{2}$ of your money at the theater and $\frac{1}{4}$ at an arcade. You have $17.50 left. How much money did you have originally?
    A. $70   B. $35   C. $17.50   D. $13.12

Take It to the NET
Online lesson quiz at
www.PHSchool.com
Web Code: ada-0506

12. Angela is twice as old as Brent. Brent is $2\frac{1}{2}$ times as old as Casey. Casey is 5 years old. How old is Angela?
    F. 5 years   G. 10 years   H. 25 years   I. 50 years

13. What is the next number in this pattern?
    $\frac{3}{4}$, $1\frac{1}{2}$, $2\frac{1}{4}$, 3, . . .
    A. $3\frac{1}{4}$ B. $3\frac{1}{2}$ C. $3\frac{3}{4}$ D. 4

Short Response

14. The odometer on Melissa's bike reads 813 miles. When she let Joan borrow the bike last week, it read 799 miles. Joan rode the bike 1 mile to school every day and then back home. **(a)** Did Joan ride the bike anywhere else? **(b)** Explain your answer.

Mixed Review

Lessons 5-4 and 1-9

Simplify each expression.

15. $\frac{1}{3} \div \frac{5}{6}$ 16. $1\frac{2}{3} \div 1\frac{1}{9}$ 17. $\frac{2}{5} \cdot (-20)$

18. $\frac{4}{9} \cdot \frac{5}{12}$ 19. $\frac{3}{4} \div 8$ 20. $-\frac{1}{6} \cdot (-12)$

21. $-8 \cdot 5$ 22. $2 \cdot 3 \cdot (-4) \cdot 5$ 23. $-1(-1)$

24. $-56 \div 8$ 25. $100 \div (-2)$ 26. $-100 \div (-10)$

Lesson 3-2

27. **Estimation** You want to buy three shirts for $15.95 each. Estimate the total cost of the shirts.

Read the problem below. Then follow along with what Greg thinks as he solves the problem. Check your understanding with the exercise at the bottom of the page.

Describe the pattern of the numbers below. Then find the next three numbers in the pattern.

$\frac{2}{3}$, $1\frac{5}{12}$, $2\frac{1}{6}$, $2\frac{11}{12}$, ■, ■, ■, ...

What Greg Thinks

I must find what kind of pattern this is so that I can describe it. I'll check the differences between terms.

The differences are the same, $\frac{3}{4}$. I can describe the pattern.

Now I have to find the next three numbers. A fraction calculator would help, but I'll do it longhand.

First I have to find $2\frac{11}{12} + \frac{3}{4}$.

Next, $3\frac{2}{3} + \frac{3}{4}$.

Finally, $4\frac{5}{12} + \frac{3}{4}$.

I'm done!

What Greg Writes

$1\frac{5}{12} - \frac{2}{3} = \frac{17}{12} - \frac{2}{3} = \frac{17}{12} - \frac{8}{12} = \frac{9}{12}$, or $\frac{3}{4}$

$2\frac{1}{6} - 1\frac{5}{12} = \frac{13}{6} - \frac{17}{12} = \frac{26}{12} - \frac{17}{12} = \frac{9}{12}$, or $\frac{3}{4}$

$2\frac{11}{12} - 2\frac{1}{6} = 2\frac{11}{12} - 2\frac{2}{12} = \frac{9}{12}$, or $\frac{3}{4}$

Start with $\frac{2}{3}$ and add $\frac{3}{4}$ repeatedly.

$2\frac{11}{12} + \frac{3}{4} = 2\frac{11}{12} + \frac{9}{12}$
$= 2\frac{20}{12} = 3\frac{8}{12} = 3\frac{2}{3}$

$3\frac{2}{3} + \frac{3}{4} = \frac{11}{3} + \frac{3}{4}$
$= \frac{44}{12} + \frac{9}{12} = \frac{53}{12} = 4\frac{5}{12}$

$4\frac{5}{12} + \frac{3}{4} = 4\frac{5}{12} + \frac{9}{12}$
$= 4\frac{14}{12} = 5\frac{2}{12} = 5\frac{1}{6}$

The next three numbers are $3\frac{2}{3}$, $4\frac{5}{12}$, and $5\frac{1}{6}$.

EXERCISE

1. Describe the pattern of the numbers below. Then find the next three numbers in the pattern.
   $1\frac{3}{4}$, 3, $4\frac{1}{4}$, $5\frac{1}{2}$, ■, ■, ■, ...

5-7

Solving Equations by Adding or Subtracting Fractions

1 Using Subtraction to Solve Equations

What You'll Learn

 OBJECTIVE 1 To solve equations by subtracting fractions

 OBJECTIVE 2 To solve equations by adding fractions

... And Why

To solve real-world problems involving recycling

✔ **Check Skills You'll Need**

Find each sum or difference.

1. $1\frac{3}{4} - 2\frac{7}{8}$

2. $3\frac{5}{8} + 4\frac{7}{12}$

3. $5\frac{3}{4} - 3\frac{1}{8}$

4. $-4\frac{1}{6} - 3\frac{2}{9}$

📖 For help, go to Lesson 5-3.

You solve equations with fractions the same way you solve equations with integers and decimals, by using inverse operations and the Properties of Equality.

1 EXAMPLE <u>Real-World</u> **Problem Solving**

Recycling In 1999, the average household in the United States recycled about $\frac{1}{4}$ of its solid waste. The Environmental Protection Agency (EPA) has set a goal of recycling about $\frac{1}{3}$ of solid waste. By how much would the average U.S. household need to increase its recycling to meet the EPA goal?

Words | fraction U.S. households recycle | plus | the increase | is | EPA goal |

Let n = the increase.

Equation $\frac{1}{4}$ $+$ n $=$ $\frac{1}{3}$

$$\frac{1}{4} + n = \frac{1}{3}$$

$\frac{1}{4} - \frac{1}{4} + n = \frac{1}{3} - \frac{1}{4}$ **Subtract $\frac{1}{4}$ from each side.**

$n = \frac{4 \cdot 1 - 3 \cdot 1}{3 \cdot 4}$ **Use 3 · 4 as the common denominator.**

$n = \frac{4 - 3}{12}$ **Use the Order of Operations.**

$n = \frac{1}{12}$ **Simplify.**

To meet the EPA goal, the average U.S. household needs to recycle $\frac{1}{12}$ more of its waste.

Check Is the answer reasonable? The present fraction of solid waste that is recycled plus the increase must equal the goal. Since $\frac{1}{4} + \frac{1}{12} = \frac{3}{12} + \frac{1}{12} = \frac{4}{12} = \frac{1}{3}$, the answer is reasonable.

✔ **Check Understanding** **Example 1**

1. Solve and check each equation.

a. $y + \frac{8}{9} = \frac{5}{9}$ b. $\frac{2}{3} = u + \frac{3}{5}$ c. $c + \frac{3}{10} = \frac{11}{15}$

📱 **iTEXT** Interactive lesson includes instant self-check, tutorials, and activities.

2 Using Addition to Solve Equations

You can use addition to solve an equation involving subtraction.

2 EXAMPLE **Adding a Fraction to Solve an Equation**

Solve $n - \frac{3}{4} = -\frac{5}{8}$.

$$n - \frac{3}{4} = -\frac{5}{8}$$

$$n - \frac{3}{4} + \frac{3}{4} = -\frac{5}{8} + \frac{3}{4}$$ Add $\frac{3}{4}$ to each side.

$$n = \frac{-5 \cdot 4 + 8 \cdot 3}{8 \cdot 4}$$ Use $8 \cdot 4$ as the common denominator.

$$n = \frac{-20 + 24}{32}$$ Use the Order of Operations.

$$n = \frac{4^1}{32_8} = \frac{1}{8}$$ Divide the common factors and simplify.

Need Help?
To review the Order of Operations, see page 183.

✔ **Check Understanding** Example 2

2. Solve and check each equation.

   a. $a - \frac{3}{5} = \frac{1}{5}$ **b.** $\frac{6}{7} = x - \frac{2}{7}$

You can use the same methods to solve equations with mixed numbers.

3 EXAMPLE **Using a Mixed Number to Solve an Equation**

Solve $p - 1\frac{3}{5} = 2\frac{1}{4}$.

$$p - 1\frac{3}{5} = 2\frac{1}{4}$$

$$p - 1\frac{3}{5} + 1\frac{3}{5} = 2\frac{1}{4} + 1\frac{3}{5}$$ Add $1\frac{3}{5}$ to each side.

$$p = \frac{9}{4} + \frac{8}{5}$$ Write mixed numbers as improper fractions.

$$p = \frac{9 \cdot 5 + 4 \cdot 8}{4 \cdot 5}$$ Use $4 \cdot 5$ as the common denominator.

$$p = \frac{45 + 32}{20}$$ Use the Order of Operations.

$$p = \frac{77}{20} = 3\frac{17}{20}$$ Simplify. Write as a mixed number.

✔ **Check Understanding** Example 3

3. Solve and check each equation.

   a. $c - 2\frac{1}{6} = 5\frac{1}{4}$ **b.** $3\frac{7}{18} = z + 1\frac{1}{3}$

EXERCISES

? For more exercises, see *Extra Practice*.

Practice and Problem Solving

A **Practice by Example**

Solve and check each equation.

Example 1
(page 264)

1. $b + \frac{4}{5} = \frac{9}{10}$ **2.** $g + \frac{9}{10} = \frac{7}{10}$ **3.** $m + \frac{3}{4} = \frac{1}{4}$

4. $a + \frac{3}{5} = \frac{4}{5}$ **5.** $\frac{5}{16} = c + \frac{3}{16}$ **6.** $t + \frac{1}{4} = \frac{5}{9}$

7. Reading Jarrel's goal is to be half finished with the book he is reading by Friday. By Wednesday he has read $\frac{1}{3}$ of the book. How much more does he need to read to meet his goal?

Example 2
(page 265)

Solve and check each equation.

8. $a - \frac{1}{8} = \frac{5}{8}$ **9.** $t - \frac{2}{3} = \frac{4}{9}$ **10.** $c - \frac{9}{10} = \frac{1}{3}$

11. $\frac{1}{2} = n - \frac{5}{8}$ **12.** $a - \frac{5}{8} = \frac{7}{12}$ **13.** $3 = j - \frac{5}{8}$

Example 3
(page 265)

14. $x + 1\frac{1}{4} = 4\frac{3}{4}$ **15.** $5\frac{1}{4} = w + 2\frac{1}{2}$ **16.** $10\frac{1}{2} = x + 1\frac{1}{2}$

17. $z + 7\frac{5}{9} = 7\frac{5}{9}$ **18.** $c - 2\frac{1}{12} = 3\frac{1}{12}$ **19.** $y + 4\frac{7}{8} = 2$

B **Apply Your Skills**

Number Sense **Without solving each equation, state whether x is *positive*, *negative*, or *zero*. Justify your response.**

20. $x + 2\frac{9}{11} = 2\frac{9}{11}$ **21.** $x + \frac{9}{10} = \frac{1}{2}$ **22.** $x + 4\frac{1}{5} = 5\frac{1}{2}$

23. Growth At the beginning of the school year, Jamie's height was $62\frac{1}{2}$ inches. During the school year she grew $1\frac{3}{4}$ inches, $\frac{1}{8}$ inch more than she grew the previous year.
a. What was Jamie's height at the end of the school year?
b. How tall was Jamie at the start of the previous school year?

Solve and check each equation.

24. $p - 3\frac{2}{3} = 1\frac{1}{3}$ **25.** $1\frac{3}{8} = b + 2\frac{1}{6}$ **26.** $y - 4\frac{7}{8} = \frac{3}{4}$

27. $k + 2\frac{1}{9} = 1\frac{1}{3}$ **28.** $f + 4\frac{5}{12} = 5\frac{3}{8}$ **29.** $g + 8\frac{4}{9} = 3\frac{1}{6}$

30. $h + 2\frac{1}{2} = 5\frac{7}{10}$ **31.** $6\frac{1}{4} = a + \frac{5}{8}$ **32.** $2\frac{1}{16} = d + 5\frac{7}{16}$

Real-World 🌐 **Connection**

The average weight of an Alaskan Coho salmon is about $7\frac{9}{10}$ lb.

33. Seafood A restaurant chef needs $8\frac{1}{2}$ lb of salmon. To get a good price, he buys more than he needs. He ends up with $4\frac{7}{8}$ lb too much. How much salmon did he buy?

34. Carpentry A carpenter used $3\frac{3}{16}$ lb of nails for a job. After the job was over, the remaining nails weighed $1\frac{1}{16}$ lb. How many pounds of nails did the carpenter have at the beginning of the job?

C **Challenge**

Solve and check each equation.

35. $x + \frac{2}{3} - \frac{1}{3} = 3\frac{1}{3}$ **36.** $x - \frac{3}{4} + \frac{1}{6} = 1\frac{5}{12}$ **37.** $x - 2\frac{2}{5} + 3\frac{1}{10} = \frac{3}{5}$

38. <u>Writing in Math</u> Write a problem that you could solve with the equation $x + \frac{1}{2} = 7$. Solve your problem.

39. Environment During a recent wet spell, the water level in Jasper's Pond rose $2\frac{3}{4}$ in. The depth of the pond was then 10 ft 3 in. What was the depth of the water in the pond before the wet spell?

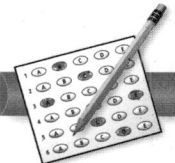

Test Prep

Multiple Choice

40. A tree is $10\frac{1}{2}$ ft tall. Which equation can you use to find the height of the tree before last spring's growth of 8 in.?

  A. $t + \frac{8}{12} = 10\frac{1}{2}$ **B.** $t - \frac{8}{12} = 10\frac{1}{2}$

  C. $t + 10\frac{1}{2} = \frac{8}{12}$ **D.** $t - 10\frac{1}{2} = \frac{8}{12}$

41. What is the value of d in the equation $d + \frac{3}{4} = 4\frac{5}{8}$?

  F. $3\frac{1}{2}$ **G.** $3\frac{7}{8}$ **H.** $4\frac{1}{4}$ **I.** $5\frac{3}{8}$

42. What is the value of c in $1\frac{1}{4} - c = \frac{3}{8}$?

  A. $-1\frac{5}{8}$ **B.** $-\frac{7}{8}$ **C.** $\frac{7}{8}$ **D.** $1\frac{5}{8}$

Extended Response

43. Below is a student's work for solving the equation $x - (-\frac{1}{2}) = 3$.

  a. What is the student's error?
  b. What likely caused the error?
  c. What is the correct value of x?
  d. How did the error affect the value of x?

$$x - (-\tfrac{1}{2}) = 3$$
$$x - (-\tfrac{1}{2}) + \tfrac{1}{2} = 3 + \tfrac{1}{2}$$
$$x = 3\tfrac{1}{2}$$

Take It to the NET
Online lesson quiz at
www.PHSchool.com
Web Code: ada-0507

Mixed Review

Lesson 5-5 **Complete each statement.**

44. $2\frac{2}{3}$ ft = 32 ▨   **45.** $1\frac{1}{2}$ ▨ = 12 fl oz   **46.** 9 pt = $4\frac{1}{2}$ ▨

47. $\frac{1}{2}$ ▨ = $\frac{1}{4}$ qt   **48.** 750 lb = $\frac{3}{8}$ ▨   **49.** $1\frac{2}{3}$ ▨ = 5 ft

Lesson 5-4 **50. a. Jobs** Your job is to paint $\frac{1}{4}$ of the lockers in the school. Your friend agrees to share the job equally with you. What fraction of the lockers will each of you paint?

  b. If the job of painting all of the lockers in the school pays $1,100, how much will you earn?

Lesson 3-6 **Solve each equation.**

51. $3.5t = 8.75$ **52.** $\frac{b}{4} = -38$

53. $y \div 7.5 = -3.75$ **54.** $1.7x = 8.5$

5-8 Solving Equations by Multiplying Fractions

What You'll Learn

OBJECTIVE 1
To solve equations by multiplying fractions

OBJECTIVE 2
To solve equations by multiplying mixed numbers

... And Why

To solve real-world problems involving carpentry

 Check Skills You'll Need

Find each product.

1. $\frac{4}{7} \cdot \frac{5}{8}$

2. $\frac{9}{10} \cdot \left(-\frac{5}{3}\right)$

3. $-1\frac{1}{4} \cdot \left(-\frac{5}{1}\right)$

4. $4\frac{1}{2} \cdot \frac{2}{3}$

 For help, go to Lesson 5-4.

OBJECTIVE 1 — Using Multiplication to Solve Equations

You know how to undo multiplication by dividing each side of an equation by the same number. You can also multiply each side of an equation by the same fraction to undo multiplication.

1 EXAMPLE Multiplying by a Reciprocal

Solve $5a = \frac{1}{7}$.

$$5a = \frac{1}{7}$$

$\frac{1}{5} \cdot (5a) = \frac{1}{5} \cdot \frac{1}{7}$ **Multiply each side by $\frac{1}{5}$, the reciprocal of 5.**

$a = \frac{1}{35}$ **Simplify.**

 Check Understanding Example 1

1. Solve each equation.

   a. $8x = \frac{5}{7}$ **b.** $2y = \frac{7}{9}$ **c.** $3a = \frac{4}{5}$

When a numerator and a denominator have common factors, you can divide the common factors to help you multiply.

2 EXAMPLE Simplifying Before Multiplying

Solve $\frac{4}{5}m = \frac{9}{10}$.

$$\frac{4}{5}m = \frac{9}{10}$$

$\frac{5}{4} \cdot \frac{4}{5}m = \frac{5}{4} \cdot \frac{9}{10}$ **Multiply each side by $\frac{5}{4}$, the reciprocal of $\frac{4}{5}$.**

$m = \frac{\cancel{5}^{1}}{4} \cdot \frac{9}{\cancel{10}_{2}}$ **Divide common factors.**

$m = \frac{9}{8}$ **Simplify.**

$m = 1\frac{1}{8}$ **Write as a mixed number.**

Need Help?

To review reciprocals, see page 250.

 Check Understanding Example 2

2. Solve each equation.

   a. $\frac{2}{9}t = \frac{5}{6}$ **b.** $\frac{3}{4}s = \frac{8}{9}$ **c.** $\frac{5}{4} = \frac{5}{4}d$

TEXT Interactive lesson includes instant self-check, tutorials, and activities.

3 EXAMPLE — Multiplying by the Negative Reciprocal

Solve $-\frac{14}{25}k = \frac{8}{15}$.

$$-\frac{14}{25}k = \frac{8}{15}$$

$$-\frac{25}{14}\left(-\frac{14}{25}k\right) = -\frac{25}{14}\left(\frac{8}{15}\right)$$

Multiply each side by $-\frac{25}{14}$, the reciprocal of $-\frac{14}{25}$.

$$k = -\frac{{}^{5}25 \cdot 8^{4}}{{}^{7}14 \cdot 15_{3}} = -\frac{20}{21}$$

Divide common factors and simplify.

✓ Check Understanding Example 3

3. Solve each equation.

a. $-\frac{6}{7}r = \frac{3}{4}$ **b.** $-\frac{10}{13}b = -\frac{2}{3}$ **c.** $-6n = \frac{3}{7}$

OBJECTIVE

2 Solving Equations With Mixed Numbers

Change mixed numbers to improper fractions before multiplying.

4 EXAMPLE — Real-World 🌐 Problem Solving

Carpentry Your teacher needs a shelf to hold a set of textbooks each $1\frac{5}{8}$ in. wide. How many books will fit on a 26-in.-long shelf?

Words

width of each book	times	the number of books	is	width of bookself

Let n = the number of books.

Equation $1\frac{5}{8}$ · n = 26

$$1\frac{5}{8} \cdot n = 26$$

$$\frac{13}{8}n = 26$$

Write $1\frac{5}{8}$ as $\frac{13}{8}$.

$$\frac{8}{13} \cdot \frac{13}{8}n = \frac{8}{13} \cdot 26$$

Multiply each side by $\frac{8}{13}$, the reciprocal of $\frac{13}{8}$.

$$n = \frac{8 \cdot 26^{2}}{{}_{1}13 \cdot 1} = 16$$

Divide common factors and simplify.

● Your teacher can fit 16 books on the shelf.

✓ Check Understanding Example 4

4. Solve each equation.

a. $3\frac{1}{2}n = 28$ **b.** $-\frac{7}{20} = 1\frac{1}{6}r$ **c.** $-2\frac{3}{4}h = -12\frac{1}{2}$

5-8 Solving Equations by Multiplying Fractions **269**

EXERCISES

❓ For more exercises, see *Extra Practice*.

Practice and Problem Solving

Ⓐ Practice by Example

Examples 1–3
(pages 268 and 269)

Solve each equation.

1. $6p = \frac{5}{8}$ **2.** $5x = \frac{2}{3}$ **3.** $2k = \frac{5}{6}$ **4.** $7z = \frac{3}{8}$

5. $2y = \frac{1}{3}$ **6.** $3b = \frac{4}{7}$ **7.** $7c = \frac{3}{4}$ **8.** $9y = \frac{5}{7}$

9. $\frac{2}{3}d = \frac{5}{8}$ **10.** $\frac{5}{8} = \frac{5}{8}k$ **11.** $\frac{5}{9} = \frac{1}{8}h$ **12.** $\frac{1}{7}x = \frac{4}{7}$

13. $\frac{3}{4}d = \frac{3}{8}$ **14.** $\frac{10}{27} = \frac{5}{9}t$ **15.** $\frac{2}{7}a = \frac{5}{8}$ **16.** $\frac{1}{9}p = \frac{5}{6}$

17. $-\frac{2}{3}t = -2$ **18.** $-5s = \frac{5}{7}$ **19.** $\frac{8}{9} = -6d$ **20.** $\frac{2}{3}x = -8$

Example 4  **21. Construction** A sheet of plywood is $\frac{3}{4}$ in. thick. Write and solve
(page 269) an equation to find how many sheets of plywood are in a stack
9 in. high.

Solve each equation.

22. $3 = 1\frac{1}{2}b$ **23.** $2\frac{1}{2}x = \frac{2}{5}$ **24.** $2\frac{1}{3}m = \frac{7}{12}$ **25.** $-1\frac{6}{7}g = -\frac{13}{15}$

26. $\frac{1}{15} = -1\frac{1}{10}t$ **27.** $2\frac{1}{8}k = 7$ **28.** $1\frac{1}{2}n = 3\frac{4}{9}$ **29.** $-9\frac{1}{3} = -1\frac{1}{4}t$

Ⓑ Apply Your Skills

Real-World 🌐 Connection

A native of China and Japan, kudzu was brought to the United States in 1876. Left alone, it grows over trees, telephone poles, and abandoned houses and cars.

Number Sense **Without solving each equation, state whether x is
positive, *negative*, or *zero*. Justify your response.**

30. $17x = -\frac{11}{30}$ **31.** $\frac{1}{57}x = 2$ **32.** $\frac{4}{13}x = 0$ **33.** $-6\frac{1}{2}x = 0$

🌐 **34. Boat Building** Tomás calculates that he will need 86 hours to build
a boat. He can work on the boat $8\frac{3}{5}$ hours per week. How many
weeks will it take Tomás to build the boat?

🌐 **35. Biology** In ideal conditions, the kudzu plant can grow at least $1\frac{3}{20}$ ft
per week. At this rate, how many weeks would it take a kudzu plant
to grow 23 ft?

Solve each equation.

36. $-\frac{5}{7}x = \frac{9}{10}$ **37.** $\frac{9}{13} = -\frac{6}{11}s$ **38.** $-3b = \frac{2}{3}$

39. $-\frac{12}{13} = -\frac{1}{4}w$ **40.** $3\frac{1}{9}a = \frac{3}{7}$ **41.** $2\frac{3}{4} = -6\frac{3}{5}y$

42. $1\frac{1}{2}m = 1\frac{3}{4}$ **43.** $3\frac{3}{5}p = -4\frac{4}{9}$ **44.** $\frac{1}{8}d = \frac{1}{4}$

45. $\frac{1}{3}y = 2$ **46.** $\frac{3}{7}x = 1$ **47.** $\frac{7}{8}z = 3\frac{1}{2}$

Writing in Math

For help with writing to explain the error in Exercise 49, see page 273.

🌐 **48. Astronomy** The Chandra satellite telescope views X-rays in space.
It orbits as much as 87,000 miles above Earth. This is about $\frac{1}{3}$ of
the distance to the moon. About how far away is the moon?

🌐 **49. Error Analysis** A student solved the equation $-\frac{7}{10}h = 5\frac{3}{5}$ and
found the solution 8. Describe and correct the student's error.

50. Writing in Math Describe how you would solve and check the equation $\frac{2}{3}x = 3$.

C Challenge **Solve each equation.**

51. $-\frac{3}{4}x + \frac{1}{4}x = -6$ **52.** $\frac{5}{8}x - 6\frac{3}{8}x = 1\frac{1}{2}$ **53.** $\frac{-5}{-7}x + \left(-\frac{1}{5}x\right) = -\frac{3}{5}$

54. Reasoning By what would you multiply each side of the equation $ax = 27$ to solve for x? By what would you multiply each side of the equation $\frac{1}{a}x = 27$ to solve for x?

55. Marine Biology A sailfish can swim about $11\frac{1}{3}$ mi in 10 min. About how many miles can a sailfish swim per minute? At that speed, about how many feet does a sailfish swim in one second?

56. Aviation A small airplane coming in for a landing descends $\frac{5}{66}$ mi/min. About how long does it take to descend 4,000 ft? (*Hint:* 1 mi = 5,280 ft)

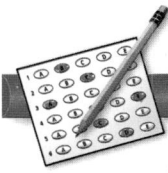

Test Prep

Multiple Choice
57. Which equation has a solution greater than 1?

A. $-5x = \frac{5}{8}$ **B.** $-\frac{5}{8}x = 5$ **C.** $\frac{5}{8}x = 5$ **D.** $5x = \frac{5}{8}$

58. What is the value of h in the equation $2\frac{1}{2} + h = -1\frac{3}{8}$?

F. $-3\frac{7}{8}$ **G.** $-1\frac{1}{8}$ **H.** $1\frac{1}{8}$ **I.** $3\frac{7}{8}$

59. The Jones family uses an average of 1 quart of milk each day. At this rate how many days will it take the family to use $5\frac{1}{2}$ gallons of milk?

A. $19\frac{1}{2}$ **B.** 20 **C.** $21\frac{1}{2}$ **D.** 22

60. A single copy of a book is $2\frac{3}{4}$ in. thick. A shipping box will hold a stack of books up to $16\frac{1}{2}$ in. tall. How many copies of the book can you stack in the box?

F. 6 **G.** 8 **H.** 32 **I.** 45

Reading Comprehension   Read the passage below before doing Exercises 61 and 62.

Paper Recycling on the Rise During the 1990s, recycling in the United States steadily increased. In 1996, people in the United States recycled about nine twentieths of their paper waste. This amounted to 42.3 million tons of paper, or about 295 lb/person. Only one year earlier, Americans recycled just over two fifths of their paper waste, a total of about 32.7 million tons of paper.

Take It to the NET
Online lesson quiz at
www.PHSchool.com
Web Code: ada-0508

61. How much paper waste did Americans produce in 1995?

62. How much paper waste did Americans produce in 1996?

Lesson 5-7 **Solve each equation.**

63. $j + \frac{3}{4} = \frac{7}{8}$ **64.** $\frac{4}{5} = y - \frac{3}{5}$ **65.** $6\frac{1}{2} = m + 2\frac{7}{8}$

Lesson 5-3 **66. Snacks** One bag of popcorn holds $1\frac{5}{8}$ oz. Another holds $1\frac{3}{4}$ oz.
   a. Which bag holds more popcorn?
   b. How much more?
   c. How much popcorn is there in all in both bags?

Lessons 4-7 and 4-8 **Simplify each expression.**

67. $3r \cdot r^4$ **68.** $\frac{6x^3}{2x}$ **69.** $10s^2 \cdot 10s^3$

70. $\frac{20a^5}{4a^2}$ **71.** $x^3 \cdot x^{10}$ **72.** $q^5 \cdot 3q$

✓ **Checkpoint Quiz 2**   **Lessons 5-4 through 5-8**

iTEXT Instant self-check quiz online and on CD-ROM

Multiply or divide.

1. $\frac{2}{3}(21)$ **2.** $\frac{4}{5} \cdot \frac{5}{8}$ **3.** $-\frac{4}{9}\left(\frac{1}{3}\right)$

4. $\frac{2}{5} \div \frac{3}{10}$ **5.** $-\frac{3}{4} \div \frac{3}{8}$ **6.** $8\frac{1}{2} \div \frac{1}{4}$

Complete each statement.

7. ■ t = 4,500 lb   **8.** $2\frac{1}{2}$ yd = ■ in.

9. 24 oz = ■ lb   **10.** ■ mi = 1,760 ft

Solve each equation.

11. $y + \frac{2}{5} = \frac{3}{5}$ **12.** $t - \frac{3}{4} = \frac{7}{8}$ **13.** $x - 4\frac{1}{2} = 6\frac{3}{4}$

14. $4t = \frac{24}{35}$ **15.** $\frac{5}{7}y = \frac{1}{3}$ **16.** $5\frac{1}{3} + v = -12$

17. $-\frac{8}{9}g = \frac{3}{5}$ **18.** $\frac{9}{10} = \frac{1}{4}w$ **19.** $1\frac{1}{2}d = \frac{5}{22}$

20. A jetliner is cruising at an altitude of 31,680 ft. What is the altitude in miles?

21. A car is travelling $\frac{11}{12}$ miles per minute. What is the speed of the car in miles per hour?

22. You spend $\frac{1}{3}$ of your money on lunch. Your friend then pays back a loan of $2.50. Later, you spend $4 on a movie ticket and $1.25 for a snack. You have $5.25 left. How much money did you have before lunch?

23. Open-Ended Describe an object you might measure using the customary system of measurement. Choose a unit of measure and estimate the measurement of the object using that unit.

In this book, there are many exercises that ask you to explain your work. One type of exercise that asks for an explanation is Error Analysis. For an Error Analysis exercise, you often need to do three things:

- Identify the error.
- Explain the error.
- Show a correct solution.

You do not have to do them in the above order, however. Often, showing a correct solution first will help you find and understand the error.

EXAMPLE

Error Analysis A student solved the equation $-\frac{7}{10}h = 5\frac{3}{5}$ and found the solution 8. Describe and correct the student's error.

- Show a correct solution.

$$-\frac{7}{10}h = 5\frac{3}{5}$$

$$-\frac{7}{10}h = \frac{28}{5}$$

$$\left(-\frac{\cancel{10}^1}{\cancel{7}_1}\right)\left(-\frac{\cancel{7}^1}{\cancel{10}_1}h\right) = \frac{\cancel{28}^4}{\cancel{5}^1}\left(-\frac{\cancel{10}^2}{\cancel{7}_1}\right)$$

$$h = -8$$

- Identify the error.
  The student lost the negative sign.
- Explain the error.
  You can only make a good guess as to the cause of the error.

> The student multiplied each side by $\frac{10}{7}$ and lost track of the negative sign.

EXERCISES

1. **Error Analysis** A student solved the equation $-\frac{7}{8}h = 3\frac{1}{2}$ and found the solution $-3\frac{1}{16}$. Describe and correct the student's error.

2. Explain why 0 is a solution and the only solution of $2x = 3x$.

5-9

Powers of Products and Quotients

What You'll Learn

OBJECTIVE 1

To find powers of products

OBJECTIVE 2

To find powers of quotients

. . . And Why

To solve real-world problems involving area

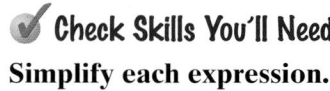
Check Skills You'll Need

Simplify each expression.

1. $(2^2)^3$ **2.** $(3^2)^2$ **3.** $(1^5)^4$

4. $(x^3)^6$ **5.** $(b^2)^5$ **6.** $(a^7)^4$

For help, go to Lesson 4-7.

OBJECTIVE

1 **Finding Powers of Products**

You can use the Commutative and Associative Properties of Multiplication to find a pattern in products raised to a power.

$$(4 \cdot 2)^3 = (4 \cdot 2) \cdot (4 \cdot 2) \cdot (4 \cdot 2) \quad \text{Write the factors.}$$

$$= 4 \cdot 4 \cdot 4 \cdot 2 \cdot 2 \cdot 2 \quad \text{Use the Commutative Property to arrange the factors.}$$

$$= (4 \cdot 4 \cdot 4) \cdot (2 \cdot 2 \cdot 2) \quad \text{Use the Associative Property to group the factors.}$$

$$= 4^3 \cdot 2^3 \quad \text{Write the powers.}$$

This result suggests a rule for simplifying products raised to a power.

Key Concepts **Rule for Raising a Product to a Power**

To raise a product to a power, raise each factor to the power.

Arithmetic	**Algebra**
$(5 \cdot 3)^4 = 5^4 \cdot 3^4$	$(ab)^m = a^m b^m$,
	for any positive integer m

To simplify an expression, you should eliminate as many parentheses as possible.

1 **EXAMPLE** **Simplifying a Power of a Product**

Simplify $(4x^2)^3$.

$$(4x^2)^3 = 4^3 \cdot (x^2)^3 \quad \text{Raise each factor to the third power.}$$

$$= 4^3 \cdot x^{2 \cdot 3} \quad \text{Use the Rule for Raising a Power to a Power.}$$

$$= 4^3 \cdot x^6 \quad \text{Multiply exponents.}$$

$$= 64x^6 \quad \text{Simplify.}$$

Need Help?

Rule for Raising a Power to a Power:
$(a^m)^n = a^{m \cdot n}$

Check Understanding **Example 1**

1. Simplify each expression.

a. $(2(3))^3$ **b.** $(2p)^4$ **c.** $(xy^2)^5$ **d.** $(5x^3)^2$

TEXT Interactive lesson includes instant self-check, tutorials, and activities.

The location of a negative sign affects the value of an expression.

2 EXAMPLE **Working With a Negative Sign**

a. **Simplify $(-5x)^2$.**
$$(-5x)^2 = (-5)^2(x)^2$$
$$= 25x^2$$

b. **Simplify $-(5x)^2$.**
$$-(5x)^2 = (-1)(5x)^2$$
$$= (-1)(5)^2(x)^2$$
$$= -25x^2$$

✓ **Check Understanding** Example 2

2. Simplify each expression.

    a. $(-2y)^4$ b. $-(2y)^4$ c. $(-5a^2b)^3$

OBJECTIVE

2 **Finding Powers of Quotients**

You can use repeated multiplication to write a power of a quotient.
$$\left(\frac{4}{5}\right)^3 = \left(\frac{4}{5}\right)\left(\frac{4}{5}\right)\left(\frac{4}{5}\right) = \frac{4 \cdot 4 \cdot 4}{5 \cdot 5 \cdot 5} = \frac{4^3}{5^3}$$

Key Concepts **Raising a Quotient to a Power**

To raise a quotient to a power, raise both the numerator and denominator to the power.

            Arithmetic   **Algebra**

        $\left(\frac{2}{3}\right)^4 = \frac{2^4}{3^4}$ $\left(\frac{a}{b}\right)^m = \frac{a^m}{b^m}$, for $b \neq 0$

                         and any positive integer m

> **Reading Math**
> You read $\left(\frac{2}{3}\right)^4$ as "two thirds to the fourth power." You read $\frac{2}{3^4}$ as "two divided by three to the fourth power."

3 EXAMPLE **Real-World** **Problem Solving**

Geometry Find the area of the square tile.

$$A = s^2 \qquad s = \text{length of a side}$$
$$= \left(\frac{3}{b}\right)^2$$
$$= \frac{3^2}{b^2} = \frac{9}{b^2}$$

The area of the tile is $\frac{9}{b^2}$ square units.

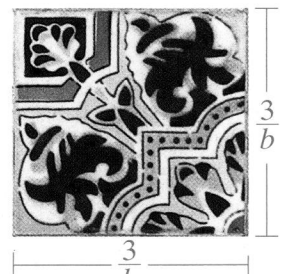

$\frac{3}{b}$

$\frac{3}{b}$

✓ **Check Understanding** Example 3

3. Simplify each expression.

    a. $\left(\frac{1}{2}\right)^3$ b. $\left(-\frac{2}{3}\right)^4$ c. $\left(\frac{2x^2}{3}\right)^3$

EXERCISES

For more exercises, see *Extra Practice*.

Practice and Problem Solving

A Practice by Example

Example 1
(page 274)

Simplify each expression.

1. $(3(2))^2$ **2.** $(3j)^3$ **3.** $(rs^3)^4$ **4.** $(7t^2)^3$

5. $(4a^5)^2$ **6.** $(2c^2)^5$ **7.** $(2x^2)^3$ **8.** $(a^2b^4)^3$

9. $(2a^5)^3$ **10.** $(c^3)^2$ **11.** $(2b)^3$ **12.** $(ac^2)^2$

Example 2
(page 275)

13. $(-10x^3)^4$ **14.** $-(xy)^2$ **15.** $(-5b)^3$ **16.** $-(3x)^2$

17. $(-5c^3)^2$ **18.** $-(x^2y^2)^2$ **19.** $(-3a^4b)^3$ **20.** $-(m^2 \cdot n)^4$

21. The side length of a square tablecloth is $5s^2$ cm.
  a. Find the area of the tablecloth.
  b. Will the tablecloth completely cover a square tabletop with area $20s^4$ cm^2? Explain.

Example 3
(page 275)

Simplify each expression.

22. $\left(\frac{2}{5}\right)^2$ **23.** $\left(-\frac{2}{5}\right)^3$ **24.** $\left(\frac{4}{7y}\right)^2$ **25.** $\left(\frac{3x^2}{10}\right)^4$ **26.** $\left(\frac{4}{9}\right)^2$

27. $\left(-\frac{3}{7}\right)^2$ **28.** $\left(-\frac{m}{b^3}\right)^6$ **29.** $\left(\frac{1}{3x^2}\right)^4$ **30.** $\left(-\frac{3}{4}\right)^3$ **31.** $\left(\frac{3t^2}{5}\right)^2$

B Apply Your Skills

Number Sense Complete each equation.

32. $(5 \cdot 2)^{\blacksquare} = 25 \cdot 4$ **33.** $(a^2)^{\blacksquare} = a^2$ **34.** $(4m)^{\blacksquare} = 256m^4$

35. $\left(-\frac{1}{2}\right)^{\blacksquare} = -\frac{1}{8}$ **36.** $\left(\frac{b^{\blacksquare}}{5}\right)^2 = \frac{b^{10}}{25}$ **37.** $\left(\frac{3}{7}\right)^{\blacksquare} = \frac{27}{343}$

Evaluate for $a = -1$, $b = 3$, and $c = \frac{1}{2}$.

38. $(-b^2)^2$ **39.** $\left(\frac{a}{b}\right)^3$ **40.** $(4c^2)^2$ **41.** $(a^2b)^2$

42. Geometry Find the area of a square with side length $4c$ units.

43. Furniture A table has sides that measure $3x^2$ ft. Write an expression for the area of the tabletop. Simplify your expression.

44. Writing in Math Explain why $(-xy)^2 = (xy)^2$.

Simplify each expression.

45. $(3 \cdot 4)^3$ **46.** $(-2 \cdot 5)^2$ **47.** $(3 \cdot 5)^2$ **48.** $(2ab^3)^2$

49. $\left(-\frac{5}{8}\right)^3$ **50.** $\left(-\frac{2}{x^3}\right)^5$ **51.** $\left(\frac{2c}{7d}\right)^2$ **52.** $\left(-\frac{3a}{b^2}\right)^3$

53. $\left(-\frac{2x}{7y}\right)^2$ **54.** $\left(\frac{2c}{d^2}\right)^4$ **55.** $\left(-\frac{xy}{2xy^4}\right)^5$ **56.** $\left(\frac{x^3}{2y^4}\right)^5$

C Challenge

Number Sense Complete each equation.

57. $(2b^{\blacksquare})^2 = 4b^8$ **58.** $(4 \cdot (-7))^{\blacksquare} = 64 \cdot (-343)$

59. $(gh^2)^{\blacksquare} = g^3h^{\blacksquare}$ **60.** $3(4c^3)^{\blacksquare} = \blacksquare c^{12}$

Geometry Use the formula $V = s^3$, where s is the length of a side, to find the volume of each cube.

61.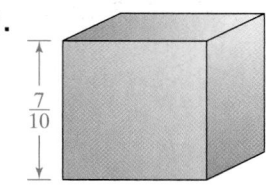
$\frac{7}{10}$

62.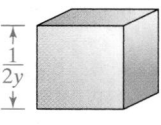
$\frac{1}{2}y$

63.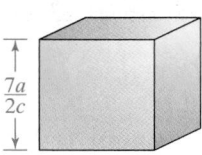
$\frac{7a}{2c}$

Multiple Choice

64. Which expression does NOT simplify to a^{36}?
 A. $(a^2)^{18}$ **B.** $(a^3)^6$ **C.** $(a^6)^6$ **D.** $(a^9)^4$

65. Which equation is FALSE?

 F. $\left|-\frac{1}{7}\right| = \left|\frac{1}{7}\right|$ **G.** $\left(\frac{3}{9}\right)^3 = \frac{3^3}{9^3}$

 H. $\left(-6 \cdot \frac{2}{3}\right)^2 = 6 \cdot \left(\frac{2}{3}\right)^2$ **I.** $\left(\frac{2}{5}\right)^3 = \frac{8}{125}$

66. What is the simplest form of $(2x^3)^4$?
 A. $8x^7$ **B.** $8x^{12}$ **C.** $16x^7$ **D.** $16x^{12}$

Take It to the NET
Online lesson quiz at
www.PHSchool.com
Web Code: ada-0509

Short Response

67. Does $(3y)^7$ equal $3y^7$? Explain.

68. The side length of a square rug is $7b$ ft.   **(a)** Will the rug cover a square floor with area $56b^2$ ft^2?   **(b)** Explain your reasoning.

Mixed Review

Lesson 5-8   **Solve each equation.**

69. $\frac{2}{7}h = \frac{7}{8}$ **70.** $7c = 1\frac{5}{9}$ **71.** $\frac{5}{8} = \frac{10}{12}x$ **72.** $10\frac{3}{4} = -5\frac{1}{2}y$

Lesson 3-5 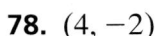 **73. Gardening** Delia bought three shrubs for $5.99, $12.99, and x. She paid a total of $34.97 for the shrubs. How much did the third shrub cost?

Lesson 1-10   Use the coordinate plane at the right. Write the coordinates of each point named below.

74. A 75. C

76. F 77. D

Write the name of each point with the given coordinates.

78. $(4, -2)$ 79. $(-4, 0)$

80. $(0, 4)$ 81. $(-2, -4)$

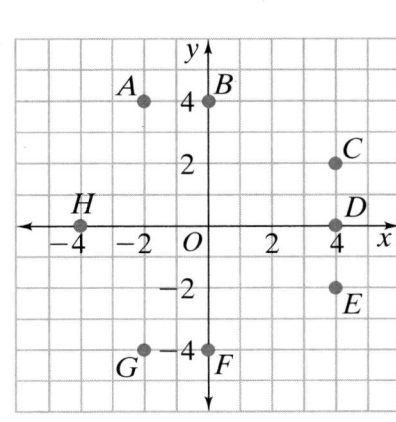

Answering the Question Asked

On a test item, be sure to answer the question that is asked. Some answer choices are there to "catch" those who read the question carelessly, or those who think carelessly about what they are to find.

1 EXAMPLE

What is the LCM of $4b^2$ and $6b^3$?

A. $2b^2$ **B.** $12b^2$ **C.** $12b^3$ **D.** $24b^3$

You are looking for the LCM, or *least common multiple*.
Choice A is the GCF, or greatest common factor, of $4b^2$ and $6b^3$.
Choice B shows the LCM of 4 and 6, but not of b^2 and b^3.
Choice D shows a common multiple of 4 and 6, but not one that's *least*.
● Choice C is the answer to the question asked.

2 EXAMPLE

Stan needed 6 lb of potatoes for the school picnic. He bought potatoes in 3-lb bags for $1.89 per bag. Zorn bought 10 lb of potatoes to make potato salad for the picnic. He paid $2.59 per 5-lb bag. How much more did Zorn pay for potatoes than Stan?

F. $.70 **G.** $1.40 **H.** $5.18 **I.** $8.96

Choice F is how much more Zorn paid *per bag* of potatoes.
Choice H is how much Zorn paid for 10 lb of potatoes.
Choice I is how much Zorn and Stan paid in all for potatoes.
● Choice G is the answer to the question asked.

EXERCISES

Answer the question asked. Then pick one other answer choice and tell why you might have (incorrectly) selected it as the answer.

1. What is the LCM of $4a$ and $10a^2$?
   A. $2a$ **B.** $4a$ **C.** $20a^2$ **D.** $30a^2$

2. Dante, a landscaper, purchased three trees. The first was $38.99. A second was $54.99. His total bill before tax was $152.98. How much more did he pay for the third tree than for the second one?
   F. $93.98 **G.** $59 **H.** $16 **I.** $4.01

Chapter Review

Vocabulary

dimensional analysis (p. 254)
least common denominator (LCD)
(p. 234)

least common multiple (LCM)
(p. 232)
multiple (p. 232)

reciprocals (p. 250)
repeating decimal (p. 238)
terminating decimal (p. 237)

Reading Math
Understanding
Vocabulary

Match each word or phrase with its definition.

1. For $\frac{5}{6}$ and $\frac{4}{9}$, this is equal to 18.

2. The pair of fractions $-\frac{13}{45}$ and $-\frac{45}{13}$ are these.

3. For 5, 6, and 12, this is equal to 60.

4. You can convert the fraction $\frac{1}{9}$ to one of these.

5. For 7, one of these is 35.

6. This tells you to multiply 8 ft by $\frac{12 \text{ in.}}{1 \text{ ft}}$ to find the number of inches in 8 ft.

7. You can convert the fraction $\frac{4}{5}$ to one of these.

a. least common multiple (LCM)

b. repeating decimal

c. reciprocals

d. dimensional analysis

e. terminating decimal

f. least common denominator (LCD)

g. multiple

Take It to the NET
Online vocabulary quiz
at www.PHSchool.com
Web Code: adj-0551

Skills and Concepts

5-1 Objectives

▼ To find the least common multiple (p. 232)

▼ To compare fractions (p. 233)

A **multiple** of a number is the product of that number and any nonzero whole number.

A *common multiple* of any group of numbers is a number that is a multiple of all the numbers. The common multiple with the least value is the **least common multiple (LCM)** of the numbers.

To compare fractions, use the LCM as the **least common denominator (LCD)** and write equivalent fractions.

Find the LCM of each group of numbers or expressions.

8. 12, 18   9. $8m^2, 14m$ 10. 3, 5, 7   11. $6x, 15y$

Compare. Use >, <, or = to complete each statement.

12. $\frac{5}{9}$ ■ $\frac{5}{11}$ 13. $\frac{2}{3}$ ■ $\frac{3}{4}$ 14. $-\frac{4}{5}$ ■ $-\frac{7}{8}$ 15. $\frac{1}{3}$ ■ $\frac{4}{12}$

5-2 Objectives

▼ To write fractions as decimals (p. 237)

▼ To write terminating and repeating decimals as fractions (p. 239)

To write a fraction as a decimal, divide the numerator by the denominator. If the division has a remainder of zero, the decimal is a **terminating decimal.** If the division produces a repeating block of digits, the decimal is a **repeating decimal.** The repeating part of the decimal is written with an overbar.

Reading a decimal correctly provides one way to write it as a fraction. To write a repeating decimal as a fraction, use algebra to eliminate the repeating part.

Write each fraction as a decimal.

16. $\frac{3}{5}$ **17.** $\frac{1}{6}$ **18.** $\frac{5}{8}$ **19.** $\frac{3}{10}$ **20.** $\frac{7}{100}$

Write each decimal as a fraction or mixed number.

21. 0.25 **22.** $0.8\overline{3}$ **23.** 5.6 **24.** $2.\overline{04}$

5-3 Objectives

▼ To add and subtract fractions (p. 243)

▼ To add and subtract mixed numbers (p. 244)

To add or subtract fractions and mixed numbers, write them with a common denominator. Then you can add or subtract the numerators. Change a mixed number to an improper fraction before adding or subtracting.

Add or subtract.

25. $2\frac{1}{3} + \frac{3}{4}$ **26.** $16\frac{4}{5} - 9\frac{2}{3}$ **27.** $\frac{6}{x} + \frac{3}{5}$ **28.** $1\frac{1}{2} - \frac{5}{8}$

29. An upholsterer cuts a piece of cording $1\frac{2}{3}$ ft long from a piece $2\frac{1}{4}$ ft long. How much cording is left?

5-4 Objectives

▼ To multiply fractions (p. 248)

▼ To divide fractions (p. 250)

To multiply fractions, multiply their numerators and their denominators. To divide fractions, multiply the first fraction by the **reciprocal** of the second fraction.

To multiply or divide mixed numbers, write them as improper fractions before multiplying or dividing.

Find each product or quotient.

30. $\frac{1}{4} \cdot \frac{7}{10}$ **31.** $-\frac{2}{3} \div \frac{5}{6}$ **32.** $1\frac{3}{5} \cdot \frac{3}{4}$ **33.** $9\frac{3}{4} \div 2\frac{3}{5}$ **34.** $\frac{3x}{5} \div \frac{6x}{5}$

5-5 Objectives

▼ To identify appropriate customary units (p. 253)

▼ To convert customary units (p. 254)

To convert units of measure in the customary system of measurement, use **dimensional analysis.**

Complete each statement.

35. 30 in. = ▨ ft   **36.** ▨ lb = 54 oz   **37.** 20 yd = ▨ ft

38. ▨ fl oz = $1\frac{1}{2}$ pt   **39.** 12 gal = ▨ pt   **40.** $2\frac{3}{4}$ t = ▨ lb

5-6 Objectives

▼ To solve problems by working backward (p. 259)

To solve some problems, you have to work backward.

41. Your family is planning a 4-h car trip. Along the way, you are planning to make three $\frac{1}{2}$-h stops. At what time should you leave home to arrive at the destination by 8:00 P.M.?

42. Buses bound for Los Angeles leave the station every hour from 6:00 A.M. to 8:00 P.M. How many buses is that in one day?

43. You sell used CDs at a local flea market. It costs $15 to rent a booth for the day. You spend $8 on lunch, and you make $140 selling CDs. If you have $162.50 at the end of the day, how much money did you have at the start of the day?

5-7 and 5-8 Objectives

▼ To solve equations by subtracting fractions (p. 264)

▼ To solve equations by adding fractions (p. 265)

▼ To solve equations by multiplying fractions (p. 268)

▼ To solve equations by multiplying mixed numbers (p. 269)

To solve equations with fractions, use inverse operations to undo addition or subtraction. You can undo multiplication by multiplying each side of the equation by the same fraction, usually a reciprocal of a fraction in the equation.

Solve each equation.

44. $\frac{1}{8} + x = 2\frac{1}{2}$ **45.** $x - \frac{5}{3} = \frac{4}{9}$ **46.** $x + 4\frac{2}{3} = 6$

47. $6x = \frac{1}{9}$ **48.** $-\frac{3}{4}x = \frac{2}{7}$ **49.** $2\frac{2}{5}x = \frac{8}{15}$

5-9 Objectives

▼ To find powers of products (p. 274)

▼ To find powers of quotients (p. 275)

To raise a product to a power, raise each factor to the power. To raise a quotient to a power, raise both the numerator and the denominator to the power.

Simplify each expression.

50. $(2d)^4$ **51.** $(-3(2))^2$ **52.** $(a^2b)^5$

53. $\left(-\frac{1}{2}\right)^3$ **54.** $\left(\frac{x}{3}\right)^2$ **55.** $\left(\frac{2a}{c^2}\right)^4$

Chapter Test

Take It to the NET
Online chapter test at
www.PHSchool.com
Web Code: ada-0552

Find the LCM of each pair.

1. $24, 36$

2. $50, 100$

3. $3x, 2y$

4. $16, 20$

Compare. Use > , < , or = to complete each statement.

5. $\frac{7}{8} \blacksquare \frac{7}{9}$

6. $\frac{2}{3} \blacksquare \frac{10}{15}$

7. $\frac{7}{10} \blacksquare 0.71$

8. $2\frac{3}{5} \blacksquare 2\frac{2}{3}$

9. $-0.87 \blacksquare -\frac{7}{8}$

10. $\frac{3}{4} \blacksquare \frac{14}{20}$

Order from least to greatest.

11. $0.5, \frac{1}{10}, 0, -\frac{1}{4}$

12. $-\frac{3}{5}, -0.\overline{6}, \frac{1}{6}, \frac{2}{3}$

Write each decimal as a fraction.

13. 0.4

14. $0.\overline{7}$

15. $12.\overline{36}$

16. 5.2

17. 0.002

18. $7.\overline{1}$

Write each fraction as a decimal.

19. $\frac{4}{15}$

20. $-\frac{2}{3}$

21. $\frac{3}{8}$

22. $\frac{1}{2}$

23. $\frac{6}{7}$

24. $\frac{5}{9}$

Add or subtract.

25. $\frac{1}{8} + \frac{3}{4}$

26. $\frac{2}{3} - \frac{1}{9}$

27. $-\frac{1}{6x} + \frac{1}{4}$

28. $11\frac{5}{6} - 5\frac{3}{8}$

29. $\frac{2}{3} - \left(-\frac{8y}{9}\right)$

30. $2\frac{1}{5} - \frac{3}{4}$

Multiply or divide.

31. $\frac{3}{5} \cdot \frac{1}{2}$

32. $-\frac{3}{4} \cdot \frac{5}{8}$

33. $\frac{5}{8x} \div \frac{7}{16}$

34. $\frac{4}{m} \div \frac{5m}{9}$

35. $3\frac{3}{4} \cdot 2\frac{4}{5}$

36. $-1\frac{1}{3} \div \left(-\frac{5}{9}\right)$

Complete each equation.

37. $10 \text{ yd} = \blacksquare \text{ ft}$

38. $20 \text{ oz} = \blacksquare \text{ lb}$

39. $\blacksquare \text{ lb} = 1\frac{3}{4} \text{ t}$

40. $6 \text{ pt} = \blacksquare \text{ qt}$

41. $3\frac{1}{2} \text{ qt} = \blacksquare \text{ c}$

42. $\blacksquare \text{ in.} = 1\frac{3}{4} \text{ yd}$

Solve each equation.

43. $m - \frac{2}{3} = \frac{1}{4}$

44. $h + \frac{3}{5} = \frac{9}{10}$

45. $x - \frac{5}{6} = -\frac{5}{6}$

46. $\frac{3}{5}a = 9$

47. $n + \frac{7}{8} = \frac{1}{3}$

48. $2\frac{1}{2}n = 3\frac{3}{4}$

49. $-5b = 3\frac{1}{3}$

50. $\frac{3}{8}y = -15$

Simplify each expression.

51. $(3(4))^2$

52. $(2a)^3$

53. $\left(\frac{3}{4}\right)^3$

54. $(3x^2)^3$

55. $-(2x^2y)^4$

56. $\left(\frac{2y}{5x}\right)^3$

Solve.

57. **Number Sense** Suppose you take a number, subtract 8, multiply by 7, add 10, and divide by 5. The result is 9. What is the original number?

58. You spend $\frac{3}{4}$ of your money on clothes and have $21 left. How much did you have before you bought the clothes?

59. **Writing in Math** Write a word problem for the equation $x - 1\frac{1}{4} = 5$.

60. Two packages each weigh $1\frac{7}{8}$ lb. How much do they weigh altogether?

61. You rode your bicycle a mile and a half to school. Then you rode to a friend's house. Altogether you rode $2\frac{1}{10}$ miles. Write and solve an equation to find how far it is from school to your friend's house.

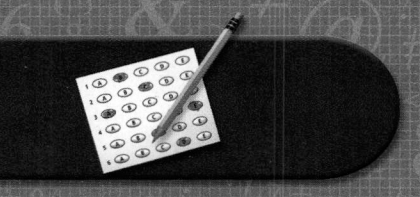

Reading Comprehension Read each passage below. Then answer the questions on the basis of what is *stated* or *implied* in the passage.

Patterns in the Sky The planet Mercury revolves around the sun about every 87.98 days and turns on its own axis about once every 58.65 (Earth) days. The planet Jupiter revolves around the sun about every 4,329.63 days. It rotates on its axis about once every 0.41 day.

Jupiter has 17 moons, among which four are Ganymede, Io, Castillo, and Europa. These satellites orbit Jupiter about once every 7.16, 1.77, 16.69, and 3.55 days, respectively.

1. How long does it take Castillo to orbit Jupiter?
   A. 7.16 days   **B.** 1.77 days
   C. 16.69 days   **D.** 3.55 days

2. Which of Jupiter's moons travels the fastest?
   F. Ganymede   **G.** Io
   H. Castillo   **I.** Europa

3. How many full rotations on its axis does Jupiter complete in 7 days?

4. Is the rotation of Mercury exactly 58.65 days? Explain.

5. What is a word that means "turns on its own axis"?

Bike Helmets Currently, 19 states and the District of Columbia require bike helmets for people who are under age 16. Even in the states that have no state law requiring helmets, there may be laws in specific counties and cities. Where such laws are in force, a typical fine for each offense is $50. According to the Consumer Product Safety Commission (CPSC), wearing a helmet can reduce the risk of head injury by 85%. The CPSC standard, which all bike helmets must meet, requires a helmet to protect the wearer against an impact on a flat surface at 14 miles per hour and on an irregular surface (such as rocks and curbs) at 11 mph. Recommended youth helmets range in price from $30 to $45.

6. How many states do NOT currently require bike helmets for people under age 16?
   A. 50   **B.** 31   **C.** 20   **D.** 19

7. Which inequality best represents the price range p of a recommended youth helmet?
   F. $p < \$45$ **G.** $\$30 < p < \$45$
   H. $p > \$30$ **I.** $\$30 \leq p \leq \$45$

8. About how much more than the price of a helmet is a fine for not wearing a helmet?
   A. $10   **B.** $30   **C.** $45   **D.** $50

9. What does *mph* stand for?

10. At what age do the bike helmet laws of these states no longer apply?

Real-World Snapshots

Quilt Tales

Applying Fractions Quilts are more than simple bed coverings. To historians, quilts are artifacts of the past. Fabrics and dyes provide information about the textile industry. Designs tell stories of life in America. The "Log Cabin" is a traditional quilt block. The red square in the center represents the chimney in the cabin. The strips around the red square symbolize the logs of the cabin. By rotating the blocks, a quilter can make various patterns appear in a quilt.

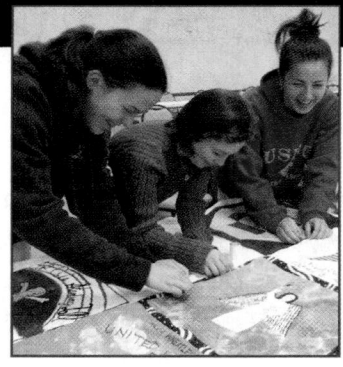

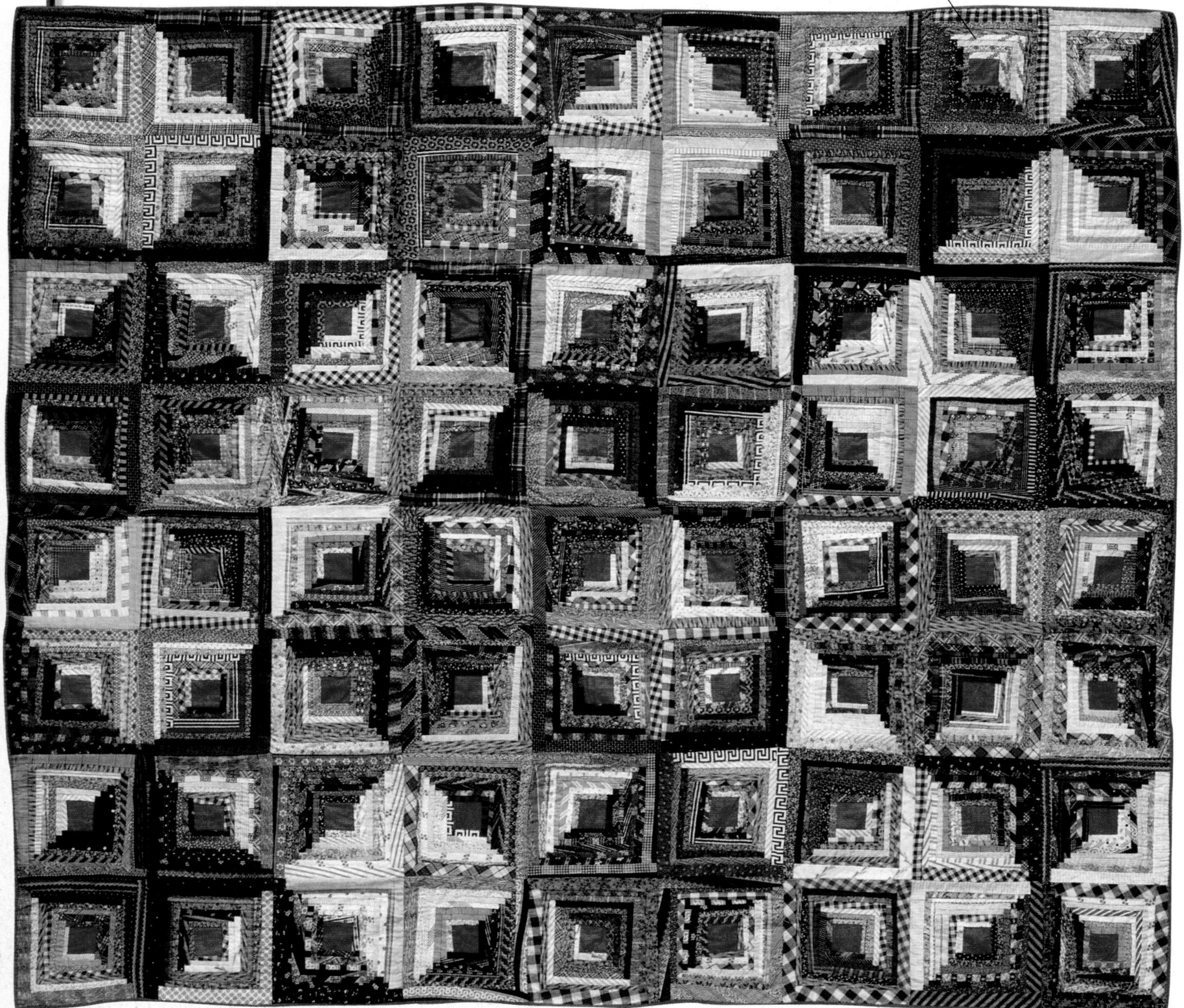

Log Cabin quilt, made around 1865

Activity

Use the pattern and the chart to answer the questions.

1. After you sew them together, the fabric pieces in a Log Cabin quilt are $1\frac{1}{2}$ in. wide. Copy and complete the table for one finished Log Cabin block.

One Log Cabin Block

Piece Number	Finished Dimensions (length × width)
1	$1\frac{1}{2}$ in. × $1\frac{1}{2}$ in.
2	3 in. × $1\frac{1}{2}$ in.
3	■
4	■
5	■
6	■
7	■

Pattern for One Log Cabin Block

2. A seam allowance is the fabric that overlaps when you sew two pieces of fabric together. In quilting, the seam allowance is $\frac{1}{4}$ in., which means that you make a seam $\frac{1}{4}$ in. from the edge of the fabric. Expand your table to include the original dimensions of each of the pieces.

3. a. What are the dimensions of one Log Cabin block?
 b. What are the dimensions of a Log Cabin quilt with four blocks? With nine blocks?

4. Fabric stores sell fabric in multiples of $\frac{1}{8}$ yd. The minimum amount of fabric you can buy is $\frac{1}{8}$ yd, which is a piece of fabric that measures $4\frac{1}{2}$ in. × 44 in. Suppose you decide to make all six blue pieces from the same fabric. How much fabric should you buy for nine blocks?

5. Suppose you have $5\frac{1}{2}$ yards of fabric left over from another quilt. You decide to make all six yellow pieces from this remnant. How much of the remnant will be left after you make a Log Cabin quilt with four blocks?

Take It to the NET For more information about quilting, go to **www.PHSchool.com**.
Web Code: ade-0553

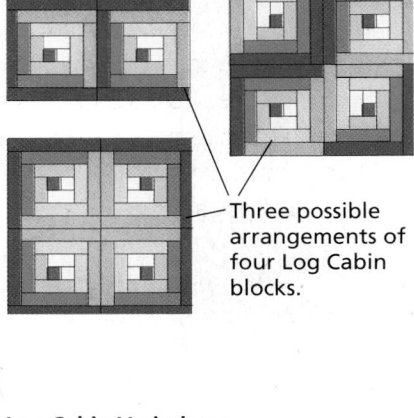

Three possible arrangements of four Log Cabin blocks.

Log Cabin Variations

Some Log Cabin quilts have center squares in colors other than red. When a Log Cabin quilt with black center squares hung on a clothesline, it meant the house was a stop on the Freedom Trail.

Log Cabin quilt, made around 1870

Where You've Been

● In Chapter 2, you solved equations by adding, subtracting, multiplying, and dividing.

● In Chapter 4, you investigated exponents.

● In Chapter 5, you learned how to work with fractions.

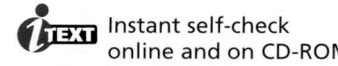 Instant self-check
online and on CD-ROM

 **Diagnosing Readiness**   (For help, go to the lesson in green.)

Solving Equations by Multiplying or Dividing (Lessons 2-6, 3-6, and 5-8)

Solve each equation.

1. $3x = 48$

2. $94.5 = 7r$

3. $\frac{3}{7}t = \frac{3}{8}$

4. $0.5y = 1.25$

5. $\frac{4}{5}x = 1$

6. $38.5 = 1.4m$

Simplifying Fractions (Lesson 4-4)

Find two fractions equivalent to each fraction.

7. $\frac{1}{4}$

8. $\frac{4}{10}$

9. $\frac{6}{14}$

10. $\frac{2}{9}$

11. $\frac{3}{8}$

12. $\frac{5}{6}$

Write each fraction in simplest form.

13. $\frac{2}{8}$

14. $\frac{6}{24}$

15. $\frac{12}{15}$

16. $\frac{6}{16}$

17. $\frac{18}{42}$

18. $\frac{25}{200}$

19. $\frac{80}{96}$

20. $\frac{40}{1,000}$

Writing Fractions and Decimals (Lesson 5-2)

Write each fraction as a decimal. Write each decimal as a fraction or a mixed number in simplest form.

21. $\frac{7}{20}$

22. 0.06

23. $\frac{30}{8}$

24. 0.35

25. 0.875

26. $3\frac{3}{5}$

27. 1.07

28. $\frac{12}{18}$

29. $11\frac{1}{9}$

30. $0.\overline{3}$

31. $\frac{100}{16}$

32. 3.98

Ratios, Proportions, and Percents

Chapter 6

Key Vocabulary

- certain event (p. 306)
- commission (p. 321)
- complement (p. 306)
- cross products (p. 294)
- discount (p. 329)
- event (p. 305)
- impossible event (p. 306)
- indirect measurement (p. 300)
- markup (p. 329)
- odds (p. 307)
- outcomes (p. 305)
- percent (p. 310)
- percent of change (p. 325)
- probability (p. 305)
- proportion (p. 294)
- rate (p. 289)
- ratio (p. 288)
- scale drawing (p. 300)
- similar figures (p. 299)
- unit rate (p. 289)

Where You're Going

In this chapter, you will learn how to

- Find and use ratios and unit rates.
- Write and solve proportions.
- Find and use percents.
- Solve a problem by making a table.

 **Real-World Snapshots** Applying what you learn, on pages 344–345 you will solve problems about stock trading.

Ratios and Unit Rates

What You'll Learn

OBJECTIVE 1 To write and simplify ratios

OBJECTIVE 2 To find rates and unit rates

. . . And Why

To solve real-world problems involving unit prices, gas mileage, and speed

 Check Skills You'll Need

Write in simplest form.

1. $\frac{30}{35}$ 2. $\frac{24}{40}$

3. $\frac{54}{60}$ 4. $\frac{12}{15}$

5. $\frac{14}{42}$ 6. $\frac{40}{24}$

 For help, go to Lesson 4-4.

New Vocabulary

• ratio
• rate
• unit rate

Reading Math

Regardless of how you write the ratio, you read 10 to 15, 10 : 15 and $\frac{10}{15}$ as "ten to fifteen."

TEXT Interactive lesson includes instant self-check, tutorials, and activities.

Statistics In the United States, about 10 out of every 15 people eligible to vote are registered to vote. The numbers 10 and 15 form a *ratio*.

Key Concepts **Ratio**

A **ratio** is a comparison of two quantities by division. You can write a ratio in different ways.

Arithmetic	Algebra
10 to 15 10 : 15 $\frac{10}{15}$	a to b $a : b$ $\frac{a}{b}$, for $b \neq 0$

1 EXAMPLE Real-World Problem Solving

Surveys A survey asked students whether they had after-school jobs. Write each ratio as a fraction in simplest form.

After-School Jobs

Response	Number
Have a Job	40
Don't Have a Job	60
Total	100

a. students with jobs to students without jobs

$$\frac{\text{students with jobs}}{\text{students without jobs}} = \frac{40}{60}$$

$$= \frac{2}{3}$$

b. students without jobs to all students surveyed

$$\frac{\text{students without jobs}}{\text{all students surveyed}} = \frac{60}{100}$$

$$= \frac{3}{5}$$

✓ **Check Understanding** Example 1

1. Write each ratio as a fraction in simplest form.

   a. students with jobs to all students surveyed

   b. students without jobs to students with jobs

2 Finding Rates and Unit Rates

A **rate** is a ratio that compares quantities in different units.
A **unit rate** is a rate that has a denominator of 1. Examples of
unit rates include unit prices, gas mileage, and speed.

2 EXAMPLE   Real-World 🌐 Problem Solving

Unit Prices The table shows prices for different sizes of the same
dish detergent. Which size has the lowest unit price?

Regular: $\dfrac{\text{price}}{\text{volume}}$ → $\dfrac{\$1.20}{12 \text{ fl oz}}$ = \$.10/fl oz

Family: $\dfrac{\text{price}}{\text{volume}}$ → $\dfrac{\$2.24}{28 \text{ fl oz}}$ = \$.08/fl oz   **Find the unit prices.**

Economy: $\dfrac{\text{price}}{\text{volume}}$ → $\dfrac{\$3.60}{40 \text{ fl oz}}$ = \$.09/fl oz

Dish Detergent Prices

Size	Volume (fl oz)	Price
Regular	12	$1.20
Family	28	$2.24
Economy	40	$3.60

● The family size has the lowest unit price.

✓ Check Understanding   Example 2

2. Find each unit rate.

   a. Two liters of spring water cost $1.98.
   b. A car goes 425 mi on 12.5 gal of gas.

You can use dimensional analysis to choose conversion factors for
converting rates.

3 EXAMPLE   Converting a Rate

Convert 10 mi/h to feet per minute.

$10 \text{ mi/h} = \dfrac{10 \text{ mi}}{1 \text{ h}} \cdot \dfrac{5{,}280 \text{ ft}}{1 \text{ mi}} \cdot \dfrac{1 \text{ h}}{60 \text{ min}}$ **Use conversion factors that convert miles to feet and hours to minutes.**

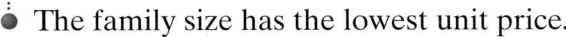

$= \dfrac{^1 10 \text{ mi}}{1 \text{ h}} \cdot \dfrac{\overset{880}{5{,}280} \text{ ft}}{1 \text{ mi}} \cdot \dfrac{1 \text{ h}}{\underset{6_1}{60} \text{ min}}$ **Divide the common factors and units.**

$= \dfrac{880 \text{ ft}}{\text{min}}$ **Simplify.**

● 10 mi/h equals 880 ft/min.

✓ Check Understanding   Example 3

3. Complete each statement.

   a. 3.5 qt/min = ■ gal/h   **b.** 12 cm/s = ■ m/h

EXERCISES

For more exercises, see *Extra Practice*.

Practice and Problem Solving

A Practice by Example

Example 1
(page 288)

Write each ratio as a fraction in simplest form.

1. $9:27$ **2.** 12 to 8 **3.** 2 to 18 **4.** $6:50$

5. $\dfrac{1,000}{10,000}$ **6.** $3:8$ **7.** 7 to 9 **8.** 8 out of 11

9. 3 out of 12 people live in a rural area.

10. 98 homes in 100 have a TV.

11. 70 homes out of 125 have a personal computer.

12. In one class, there are 6 girls for every 10 boys.

Example 2
(page 289)

Find each unit rate.

13. A skydiver falls 144 ft in 3 s. **14.** A pump moves 42 gal in 7 min.

15. A car travels 676 mi in 13 h. **16.** 20 c of water evaporate in 5 d.

Example 3
(page 289)

Complete each statement.

17. 720 m/day = ▊ m/min **18.** 1.5 gal/min = ▊ qt/h

19. 32 yd/min = ▊ in./s **20.** 0.85 km/s = ▊ m/min

21. 80 mi/h = ▊ ft/s **22.** 20 fl oz/min = ▊ qt/day

B Apply Your Skills

Write each ratio as a fraction in simplest form.

23. 36 to 48 **24.** 60 to 24 **25.** $16:12$ **26.** $15:27$

27. Cycling Anna and Julia each take a bicycle trip. Anna rides 20 miles in $1\frac{1}{3}$ hours. Julia rides 246 miles in 16 hours. Which rider has the slower unit rate? By how much?

28. Transportation What is the rate in meters per second of a jetliner that is traveling at a rate of 846 km/h?

29. Error Analysis A student converts 100 ft/min to 500 in./s. Use dimensional analysis to explain why the student's result is not reasonable.

Boys in Two Classes

Class	Number of Boys	Number of Students
A	6	30
B	4	24

Use the table at the left for Exercises 30 and 31.

30. For each class, write the ratio of the number of boys to the total number of students.

31. Which class has the greater ratio of boys to students?

C Challenge

32. Writing in Math A student claims that a ratio remains unchanged if 1 is added to both the numerator and the denominator of the fraction. Does $\frac{a}{b}$ equal $\frac{a+1}{b+1}$? Write an explanation, and give an example or a counterexample.

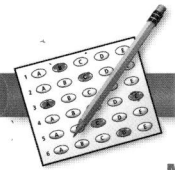

33. Science Density is the ratio of a substance's mass to its volume. A volume of 20 cubic centimeters of gold has a mass of 386 grams. Express the density of gold as a unit rate.

Test Prep

Multiple Choice

34. A 50-lb bag of Glossy Coat Horse Feed costs $23.50. A 25-lb bag costs $15.50. How much money per pound would you save by buying the bag with the lower unit price?
A. $.15   **B.** $.32   **C.** $.47   **D.** $.62

35. Karla and her dad were nailing up plywood. They started at 10:00. Karla drove 30 nails in 10 min, the time it took her dad to drive 50 nails. At that rate for each, when did they finish driving 392 nails in all?
F. 10:30   **G.** 10:39   **H.** 10:45   **I.** 10:49

Reading Comprehension   Read the passage below before doing Exercises 36–38.

A Sappy Story

Connecticut has more than 100 farms that produce maple syrup. Sugarers collect sap and boil it down to syrup. In a good year, one small sugarer in Connecticut averages 301 gallons of sap weekly from 200 trees. The sap boils down to just seven gallons of syrup. The syrup sells for $4.50 per half pint or $44 per gallon.

36. Write the ratio of sap to syrup in simplest form.

37. Find the unit prices for syrup sold by the half pint and syrup sold by the gallon. Which has the lower unit price?

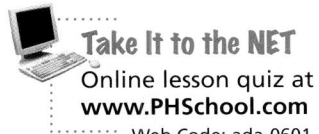

Take It to the NET
Online lesson quiz at
www.PHSchool.com
Web Code: ada-0601

38. If the sugarer sells the syrup by the half pint, how much income will there be for 10 weeks of sugaring in a good year?

Mixed Review

Lesson 5-9

Simplify each expression.

39. $(-3 \cdot 4)^3$ **40.** $(2x^2 y)^4$ **41.** $\left(-\dfrac{ab^3}{a^2 b}\right)^3$

Lesson 5-2

Compare. Use >, <, or = to complete each statement.

42. $\dfrac{7}{8} \ \blacksquare \ \dfrac{14}{24}$ **43.** $\dfrac{4}{12} \ \blacksquare \ \dfrac{10}{30}$ **44.** $\dfrac{13}{20} \ \blacksquare \ 0.6$

Lesson 2-1   **45. Vacation** Three friends shared the driving on a long trip. Marla drove 7 mi more than Guido. Guido drove five times as far as Juanita did. Juanita drove 112 mi. How long was the trip?

Converting Between Measurement Systems

For Use With Lesson 6-1

You can use conversion factors (dimensional analysis) to convert a unit of measure from one system to another. For example, since 1 mi ≈ 1.61 km, you can use $\frac{1 \text{ mi}}{1.61 \text{ km}}$ and $\frac{1.61 \text{ km}}{1 \text{ mi}}$ as conversion factors.

The table shows some useful conversion factors.

Customary Units and Metric Units	Conversion Factors
1 in. = 2.54 cm	$\frac{1 \text{ in.}}{2.54 \text{ cm}}$ or $\frac{2.54 \text{ cm}}{1 \text{ in.}}$
1 mi ≈ 1.61 km	$\frac{1 \text{ mi}}{1.61 \text{ km}}$ or $\frac{1.61 \text{ km}}{1 \text{ mi}}$
1.06 qt ≈ 1 L	$\frac{1.06 \text{ qt}}{1 \text{ L}}$ or $\frac{1 \text{ L}}{1.06 \text{ qt}}$
1 oz ≈ 28.4 g	$\frac{1 \text{ oz}}{28.4 \text{ g}}$ or $\frac{28.4 \text{ g}}{1 \text{ oz}}$
2.20 lb ≈ 1 kg	$\frac{2.20 \text{ lb}}{1 \text{ kg}}$ or $\frac{1 \text{ kg}}{2.20 \text{ lb}}$

In general, a conversion between systems results in an approximate measurement.

1 EXAMPLE

The longest track event at the Olympics is the 50-km walk. How long is the race in miles?

$50 \text{ km} \approx 50 \text{ km} \cdot \frac{1 \text{ mi}}{1.61 \text{ km}}$ **Use a conversion factor that changes kilometers to miles.**

$= 50 \text{ km} \cdot \frac{1 \text{ mi}}{1.61 \text{ km}}$ **Divide the common units.**

$= \frac{50 \text{ mi}}{1.61}$ **Multiply.**

$\approx 31 \text{ mi}$ **Divide.**

● The 50-km walk is about 31 mi long.

You can round within a conversion factor to get compatible numbers.

2 EXAMPLE

About how many ounces are in 60 grams?

$60 \text{ g} \approx 60 \text{ g} \cdot \frac{1 \text{ oz}}{28.4 \text{ g}}$ **Use the conversion factor that changes grams to ounces.**

$\approx 60 \text{ g} \cdot \frac{1 \text{ oz}}{30 \text{ g}}$ **Round within the conversion factor to a number compatible with 60.**

$= 60^{2} \text{ g} \cdot \frac{1 \text{ oz}}{130 \text{ g}}$ **Divide the common factors and units.**

$= 2 \text{ oz}$ **Simplify.**

● There are about 2 ounces in 60 grams.

Sometimes you may need to use two or more conversion factors.

3 **EXAMPLE**

A punch recipe calls for a gallon of sparkling water. How many 2-L bottles should you buy?

$1 \text{ gal} \approx 1 \text{ gal} \cdot \dfrac{4 \text{ qt}}{1 \text{ gal}} \cdot \dfrac{1 \text{ L}}{1.06 \text{ qt}}$ Use conversion factors that change gallons to quarts and quarts to liters.

$= 1 \text{ gal} \cdot \dfrac{4 \text{ qt}}{1 \text{ gal}} \cdot \dfrac{1 \text{ L}}{1.06 \text{ qt}}$ Divide the common units.

$= \dfrac{4 \text{ L}}{1.06}$ Multiply.

$\approx 3.8 \text{ L}$ Divide.

Now find the number of bottles you need for 3.8 L.

$\dfrac{3.8}{2} = 1.9$ Divide by 2, since there are 2 L per bottle.

You need about 1.9 bottles. You should buy two bottles.

EXERCISES

Convert. Where necessary, round to the nearest tenth.

1. 8 in. $\approx$ ▣ cm

2. 16 cm $\approx$ ▣ in.

3. ▣ mi $\approx$ 20 km

4. ▣ km $\approx$ 100 mi

5. ▣ L $\approx$ 50 qt

6. ▣ g $\approx$ 15 oz

7. 15 L $\approx$ ▣ qt

8. ▣ lb $\approx$ 14 kg

9. 44 lb $\approx$ ▣ kg

10. 100 oz $\approx$ ▣ kg

11. ▣ L $\approx$ 212 pt

12. 500 g $\approx$ ▣ lb

13. 1,000 mm $\approx$ ▣ in.

14. ▣ gal $\approx$ 20 L

15. ▣ km/h $\approx$ 10 mi/h

16. **Home Economics** A recipe calls for 8 oz of figs. The figs come in packages of 100 g. How many packages should you buy?

17. **Writing in Math** Explain how you would estimate the number of kilometers in 19 miles.

18. In Exercise 15, you may have found that 10 mi/h $\approx$ 16.1 km/h. Also, 10 mi/h = 880 ft/min (Example 3, p. 289). Convert both 16.1 km/h and 880 ft/min to meters per second and compare.

19. Restate Exercise 27 on page 290 in equivalent metric units and solve.

20. In Exercise 28 on page 290, you convert 846 km/h to meters per second. Convert 846 km/h to miles per hour and then to feet per second.

6-2 Proportions

What You'll Learn

OBJECTIVE 1
To solve proportions

OBJECTIVE 2
To use proportions to solve problems

...And Why

To solve real-world problems involving science

✓ Check Skills You'll Need

Solve each equation.

1. $4x = 52$ **2.** $3y = 18$

3. $5b = 75$ **4.** $7k = 21$

 For help, go to Lesson 2-6.

New Vocabulary

• proportion
• cross products

Reading Math

Read the proportion $\frac{6}{9} = \frac{8}{12}$ as "the ratio 6 to 9 equals the ratio 8 to 12," or as "6 is to 9 as 8 is to 12."

 TEXT Interactive lesson includes instant self-check, tutorials, and activities.

OBJECTIVE 1   Solving Proportions

A **proportion** is an equality of two ratios—for example, $\frac{6}{9} = \frac{8}{12}$. You can use the Multiplication Property of Equality to show an important property of all proportions.

$$\text{If } \frac{a}{b} = \frac{c}{d}$$

$$\text{then } \frac{a}{b} \cdot bd = \frac{c}{d} \cdot bd \qquad \textbf{Multiplication Property of Equality}$$

$$\frac{ab^1d}{{}_1b} = \frac{cbd^1}{{}_1d} \qquad \frac{b}{b} = 1 \text{ and } \frac{d}{d} = 1$$

and $ad = cb$, or $ad = bc$.

The products ad and bc are called the **cross products** of the proportion $\frac{a}{b} = \frac{c}{d}$.

Key Concepts   **Cross Products**

In a proportion, the cross products are equal.

Arithmetic	Algebra
$\dfrac{6}{9} \diagdown\!\!\!\!\diagup \dfrac{8}{12}$	$\dfrac{a}{b} \diagdown\!\!\!\!\diagup \dfrac{c}{d}$
$6 \cdot 12 = 9 \cdot 8 = 72$	$ad = bc$

To solve a proportion that contains a variable, you find the value that makes the equation true.

1 EXAMPLE   **Multiplying to Solve a Proportion**

Solve $\frac{x}{9} = \frac{4}{6}$.

Method 1 Multiplication Property of Equality

$$\frac{x}{9} = \frac{4}{6}$$

$$\frac{x}{9} \cdot 9 = \frac{4}{6} \cdot 9$$

$$x = \frac{36}{6}$$

$$x = 6$$

Method 2 Cross products

$$\frac{x}{9} = \frac{4}{6}$$

$$x \cdot 6 = 9 \cdot 4$$

$$6x = 36$$

$$\frac{6x}{6} = \frac{36}{6}$$

$$x = 6$$

✓ **Check Understanding**   Example 1

1. Solve each proportion.

    a. $\frac{h}{9} = \frac{2}{3}$ **b.** $\frac{4}{5} = \frac{t}{55}$ **c.** $\frac{22}{d} = \frac{6}{21}$

Two ratios form a proportion if their cross products are equal.

---

2   **EXAMPLE**   **Testing for a Proportion**

Do the ratios $\frac{4}{6}$ and $\frac{10}{14}$ form a proportion? Explain.

$$\frac{4}{6} \overset{?}{=} \frac{10}{14}$$ **Test by writing as a proportion.**

$$4 \cdot 14 \overset{?}{=} 6 \cdot 10$$ **Write cross products.**

$$56 \neq 60$$ **Simplify.**

● The ratios do not form a proportion. Cross products are not equal.

✓ **Check Understanding**   Example 2

2. Tell whether the two ratios form a proportion. Explain.

   a. $\frac{6}{9}, \frac{4}{6}$ **b.** $\frac{15}{20}, \frac{5}{7}$ **c.** $\frac{7}{12}, \frac{17.5}{30}$

OBJECTIVE

2   **Using Proportions to Solve Problems**

You can write and solve proportions for many real-world problems.

3   **EXAMPLE**   <u>Real-World</u> 🌐 <u>Problem Solving</u>

Navigation   **One hundred nautical miles equals about 115 standard, or statute, miles. To the nearest mile, how far in statute miles is 156 nautical miles?**

Let d = distance in statute miles.

distance in nautical miles → $\dfrac{100}{115} = \dfrac{156}{d}$ ← distance in nautical miles
distance in statute miles →   ← distance in statute miles

$$100d = 115(156)$$ **Write cross products.**

$$d = \frac{115(156)}{100}$$ **Divide each side by 100.**

$$d \approx 179$$ **A calculator may be useful.**

● 156 nautical miles is about 179 statute miles.

✓ **Check Understanding**   Example 3

3. To the nearest mile, how far in nautical miles is 100 statute miles?

Real-World 🌐 **Connection**

Sailors and astronauts measure distances in *nautical miles.* This photo of the Great Lakes was taken from the space shuttle at an altitude of 156 nautical miles.

EXERCISES

For more exercises, see *Extra Practice*.

Practice and Problem Solving

A Practice by Example

Example 1
(page 294)

Solve each proportion.

1. $\frac{2}{v} = \frac{1}{8}$ 　　 2. $\frac{z}{42} = \frac{25}{70}$ 　　 3. $\frac{4}{h} = \frac{8}{10}$ 　　 4. $\frac{4}{16} = \frac{s}{8}$

5. $\frac{4}{11} = \frac{x}{22}$ 　　 6. $\frac{2}{9} = \frac{r}{36}$ 　　 7. $\frac{12}{n} = \frac{2}{12}$ 　　 8. $\frac{1}{15} = \frac{3}{p}$

9. $\frac{4}{15} = \frac{a}{75}$ 　　 10. $\frac{3}{4} = \frac{21}{b}$ 　　 11. $\frac{13}{c} = \frac{39}{60}$ 　　 12. $\frac{3}{6} = \frac{7}{d}$

Example 2
(page 295)

Tell whether the two ratios form a proportion. Explain.

13. $\frac{2}{3}$ and $\frac{10}{20}$ 　　 14. $\frac{25}{80}$ and $\frac{5}{16}$ 　　 15. $\frac{4}{7}$ and $\frac{20}{25}$ 　　 16. $\frac{2}{3}$ and $\frac{10}{16}$

17. $\frac{3}{4}$ and $\frac{12}{15}$ 　　 18. $\frac{3}{8}$ and $\frac{21}{56}$ 　　 19. $\frac{9}{24}$ and $\frac{15}{40}$ 　　 20. $\frac{20}{32}$ and $\frac{12}{20}$

Example 3
(page 295)

21. **Photocopies** At the Copy Shoppe, 18 copies cost $1.08. At that rate, how much will 40 copies cost?

22. Three tea bags are needed to make a gallon of iced tea. How many tea bags are needed to make four gallons?

23. **Purchasing** Three posters cost $9.60. At that rate, how many posters can you buy for $48?

B Apply Your Skills

Tell whether the two ratios form a proportion. Explain.

24. $\frac{3.9}{5.4}$ and $\frac{13}{18}$ 　 25. $\frac{54}{60}$ and $\frac{118}{110}$ 　 26. $\frac{27}{72}$ and $\frac{48}{128}$ 　 27. $\frac{144}{120}$ and $\frac{75}{145}$

Mental Math Solve by mental math.

28. $\frac{1}{6} = \frac{a}{72}$ 　　 29. $\frac{120}{24} = \frac{y}{2}$ 　　 30. $\frac{10}{v} = \frac{3}{1.5}$ 　　 31. $\frac{n}{12} = \frac{12}{2}$

32. **Exchange Rates** On a recent day, the exchange rate for U.S. dollars to European euros was 0.89 dollar per euro. On that day, about how many euros would you get for 25 dollars?

33. **Error Analysis** Fancy ribbon costs $3 for 15 in. Your friend wants to find the cost of 3 ft of ribbon. He uses the proportion $\frac{3}{15} = \frac{x}{3}$ and gets an answer of $.60. Explain your friend's error.

Solve each proportion. Where necessary, round to the nearest tenth.

34. $\frac{4}{3} = \frac{b}{21}$ 　　 35. $\frac{6}{25} = \frac{e}{80}$ 　　 36. $\frac{4}{9} = \frac{f}{15}$ 　　 37. $\frac{3}{8} = \frac{50}{g}$

38. $\frac{24}{17} = \frac{109}{h}$ 　　 39. $\frac{7}{9} = \frac{j}{22.5}$ 　　 40. $\frac{6}{13} = \frac{7.8}{m}$ 　　 41. $\frac{20}{27} = \frac{1.1}{n}$

Estimation Estimate the solution of each proportion.

42. $\frac{11}{a} = \frac{9}{17}$ 　　 43. $\frac{w}{20} = \frac{6}{23}$ 　　 44. $\frac{3}{2} = \frac{29}{d}$ 　　 45. $\frac{20}{3.9} = \frac{s}{6}$

46. $\frac{1.5}{p} = \frac{2.1}{4.1}$ 　　 47. $\frac{f}{4} = \frac{12}{49}$ 　　 48. $\frac{60}{g} = \frac{24.1}{8.1}$ 　　 49. $\frac{9}{4.4} = \frac{x}{19}$

50. At the rate shown in the cartoon, how much would five potatoes cost?

51. Quality Control A microchip inspector found three defective chips in a batch containing 750 chips. At that rate, how many defective chips would there be in 10,000 chips?

52. Reasoning If $\frac{a}{b} = \frac{c}{d}$, will $\frac{a}{c} = \frac{b}{d}$? Assume that $b \neq 0$, $c \neq 0$, and $d \neq 0$. Explain your reasoning.

53. Geometry A rectangle that is 20 cm long and 28 cm wide is the same shape as one that is 9 cm long and z cm wide. Find z.

54. Baseball Your team scores 4 runs in the first three innings of a 9-inning baseball game. If it continues at that rate, how many runs will it score in the game?

REAL LIFE ADVENTURES by Gary Wise and Lance Aldrich

If the people who own the shops at the airport owned other things.

Write a proportion for each situation. Then solve.

55. 3 oz for $1.65; 5 oz for x dollars

56. 20 lb for $27.50; 12 lb for x dollars

57. 25 yd in $2\frac{1}{2}$ s; 100 yd in x seconds

58. 3 miles in 2.8 minutes; 33.3 miles in x minutes

59. $3\frac{1}{2}$ pounds in 4 cubic inches; x pound in 1 cubic inch

60. **Writing in Math** A truck driver estimates that it will take him 12 h to drive 1,160 km. After 5 h, he has driven 484 km. Is he on schedule? Explain.

C Challenge

For Exercises 61–64, use the table.

61. How many times does an adult's heart beat in 270 s?

62. In how many seconds will a newborn's heart beat 35 times?

63. In how many seconds will a 12-year-old's heart beat 17 times?

64. In 45 s, how many more times does a newborn's heart beat than a 6-year-old's heart?

Human Heart Rates

Age (years)	Beats per Minute
newborn	140
1	120
6	100
10	90
12	85
adult	80

Write a proportion for each situation. Then solve.

65. 5 km in 18 min 36 s; 8 km in v minutes

66. 96 oz for $2; y pounds for $10

67. 4 oz for $1.85; 1 lb for t dollars

68. $5.76 for 2 lb 4 oz; c dollars for 1 pound

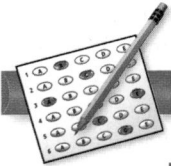

Test Prep

Multiple Choice

69. Four ounces of orange juice contain 50 calories. About how many calories are in 14 ounces of orange juice?
A. 1 cal   B. 14 cal   C. 175 cal   D. 700 cal

70. A lion's heart beats 12 times in 16 s. How many times does a lion's heart beat in 60 s?
F. 24   G. 32   H. 45   I. 192

71. An artist makes purple paint by mixing red and blue paint in the ratio of 2 parts red to 3 parts blue. What is the ratio of red paint to purple paint?
A. 3:2   B. 3:5   C. 2:3   D. 2:5

Extended Response

72. On Monday, the ratio of Tara's pocket money to her brother Seth's pocket money was $\frac{3}{1}$. On Tuesday, Tara gave $5 to Seth. Then Tara had twice as much money as Seth. Let $3x$ equal the amount Tara had on Monday and x equal the amount Seth had on Monday.
a. Write two ratios that each compare the amount of money Tara had on Tuesday to the amount Seth had on Tuesday. Use the ratios to write a proportion.
b. Solve for x.
c. Find the amount of money each person had on Monday.

Take It to the NET
Online lesson quiz at
www.PHSchool.com
Web Code: ada-0602

Mixed Review

Lesson 6-1   **Write each ratio as a fraction in simplest form.**

73. ten per thousand   **74.** 30 to 55   **75.** 125:70

Lesson 5-6 **76. Personal Finance** On Saturday afternoon, a student bought two music tapes for $8.95 each and a sweater for $24.95. She received $20 for mowing a lawn. On Saturday night, she had $45.12. How much money did the student have on Saturday morning?

Lessons 1-3 and 5-3   **Tell whether each equation is true or false.**

77. $\left| -2\frac{1}{4} \right| - \left| 2\frac{1}{4} \right| = 0$ **78.** $\left| -2\frac{1}{4} \right| + \left| 2\frac{1}{4} \right| = 0$

79. $-\left| -\frac{9}{4} \right| + \left| 2\frac{1}{4} \right| = 0$ **80.** $\left| -\frac{9}{4} \right| - \left| 2\frac{1}{4} \right| = 0$

Similar Figures and Scale Drawings

OBJECTIVE

1 Using Similar Figures

Similar figures have the same shape, but not necessarily the same size. Similar figures have *corresponding angles* and *corresponding sides*.

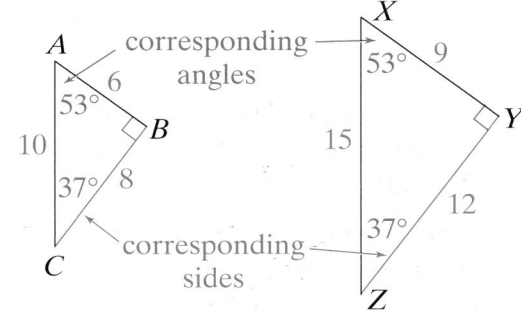

The symbol ~ means *is similar to*. At the right, $\triangle ABC \sim \triangle XYZ$.

Key Concepts   **Similar Figures**

Similar figures have two properties.

- The corresponding angles have equal measures.
- The lengths of corresponding sides are in proportion.

---

1 EXAMPLE   Using Similar Figures

Parallelogram $ABCD$ ~ parallelogram $EFGH$. Find the value of x.

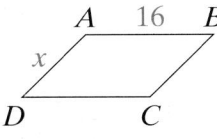 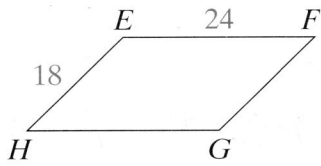

Write a proportion for corresponding sides.

Side *DA* corresponds to side *HE*. $\dfrac{x}{18} = \dfrac{16}{24}$ Side *AB* corresponds to side *EF*.

$x \cdot 24 = 18 \cdot 16$ Write cross products.

$\dfrac{24x}{24} = \dfrac{18 \cdot 16}{24}$ Divide each side by 24.

$x = 12$ Simplify.

✓ **Check Understanding** Example 1

1. Parallelogram $KLMN$ is similar to parallelogram $ABCD$ in Example 1. Find the value of y. Round to the nearest tenth.

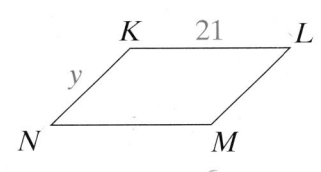

What You'll Learn

OBJECTIVE 1 To solve problems that involve similar figures

OBJECTIVE 2 To solve problems that involve scale drawings

... And Why

To solve real-world problems involving maps

✓ Check Skills You'll Need

Solve each proportion. Round to the nearest tenth where necessary.

1. $\dfrac{2}{3} = \dfrac{f}{21}$ **2.** $\dfrac{3}{8} = \dfrac{50}{p}$

3. $\dfrac{9}{4} = \dfrac{15}{p}$ **4.** $\dfrac{16}{3} = \dfrac{19}{g}$

❓ For help, go to Lesson 6-2.

New Vocabulary

- similar figures
- indirect measurement
- scale drawing

TEXT Interactive lesson includes instant self-check, tutorials, and activities.

You can use similar figures to compute distances that are difficult to measure directly. Such a process is called **indirect measurement.**

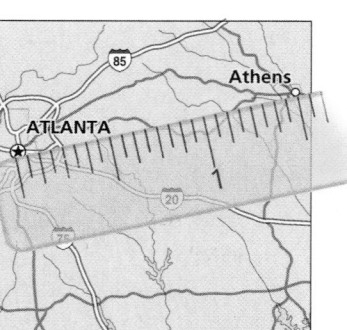

2 EXAMPLE   Real-World 🌐 Problem Solving

Indirect Measurement A tree casts a shadow 10 ft long. A 5-ft woman casts a shadow 4 ft long. The triangle shown for the woman and her shadow is similar to the triangle shown for the tree and its shadow. How tall is the tree?

$$\frac{4}{10} = \frac{5}{x}$$ Corresponding sides of similar triangles are in proportion.

$4x = 10 \cdot 5$ Write cross products.

$\frac{4x}{4} = \frac{10 \cdot 5}{4}$ Divide each side by 4.

$x = 12.5$ Simplify.

• The tree is 12.5 ft tall.

✓ Check Understanding   Example 2

2. **Indirect Measurement** A building 70 ft high casts a 150-ft shadow. A nearby flagpole casts a 60-ft shadow. Draw a diagram. Use similar triangles to find the height of the flagpole.

OBJECTIVE

2 Using Scale Drawings

A **scale drawing** is an enlarged or reduced drawing that is similar to an actual object or place. The ratio of a distance in the drawing to the corresponding actual distance is the *scale* of the drawing.

3 EXAMPLE   Real-World 🌐 Problem Solving

Maps The scale of the map is 1 in. : 40 mi. About how far from Atlanta is Athens?

Map distance = $1\frac{1}{2}$ in., or 1.5 in.   Measure the map distance.

$\frac{\text{map (in.)} \;\rightarrow}{\text{actual (mi)} \;\rightarrow}\quad \frac{1}{40} = \frac{1.5}{d} \;\;\begin{array}{l}\leftarrow \;\text{map (in.)}\\ \leftarrow \;\text{actual (mi)}\end{array}$ Write a proportion.

$1 \cdot d = 40 \cdot 1.5$ Write cross products.

$d = 60$ Simplify.

• Athens is about 60 mi from Atlanta.

✓ Check Understanding   Example 3

3. **Maps** The distance from Atlanta to Macon is about 75 mi. What is the approximate map distance between these two cities?

EXERCISES

For more exercises, see *Extra Practice*.

Practice and Problem Solving

A **Practice by Example**

Example 1
(page 299)

Trapezoid *EFGH* ~ trapezoid *MNOP*. Find the indicated value.

1. x

2. y

3. z

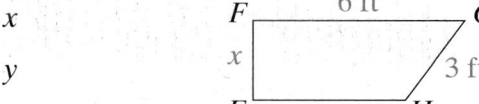
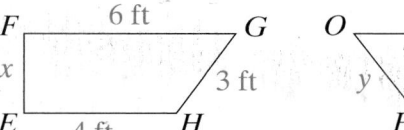

The triangles in each pair are similar. Find the missing length. Round to the nearest tenth where necessary.

4.

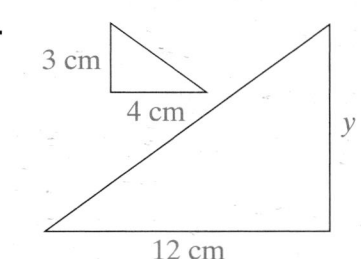

5.

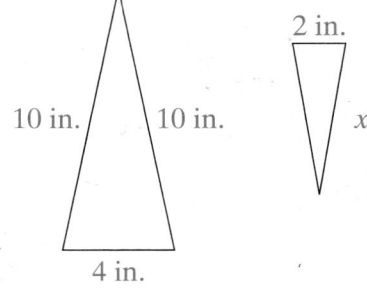

6.

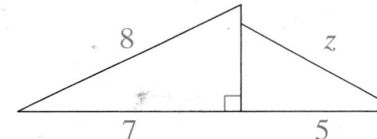

7.

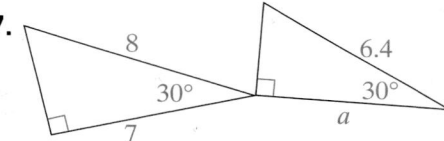

Example 2
(page 300)

8. Indirect Measurement A tree casts a shadow 8 ft long. A 6-ft man casts a shadow 4 ft long. The triangle formed by the tree and its shadow is similar to the triangle formed by the man and his shadow. How tall is the tree?

9. Projection An image on a slide is similar to its projected image. A slide is 35 mm wide and 21 mm high. Its projected image is 85 cm wide. To the nearest centimeter, how high is the image?

Example 3
(page 300)

The scale of a map is 1 cm : 12 km. Find the actual distance for each map distance.

10. 1.5 cm   **11.** 12 cm   **12.** 4.25 cm   **13.** 8.3 cm

14. Maps Duane is drawing a map with a scale of 1 in. : 3 mi. He knows that the distance from Center Point to Comfort is 9 miles. How far apart should Duane locate the two towns on his map?

The scale of a drawing is 1 in. : 25 yd. Find the length on the drawing for each actual length.

15. 100 yd   **16.** 375 yd   **17.** 512.5 yd   **18.** 20 yd

19. Indirect Measurement Jacques has a scale drawing of his bedroom with a scale of 1 cm : 0.4 m. On the drawing, the front window is 3 cm from the door. What is the actual distance in the room?

20. A scale drawing has a scale of 1 in. : 10 ft. What is the distance on the drawing for an actual distance of 20 ft? Of 45 ft?

B Apply Your Skills

The scale of a map is 2 cm : 15 km. Find the actual distance for each map distance.

21. 6 cm **22.** 2.1 cm **23.** 10 mm **24.** 17.4 cm

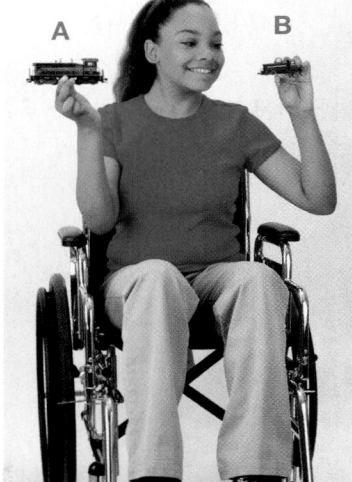

A   B

The length of each piece in a model railroad built on the HO scale is $\frac{1}{87}$ of the actual length. Another popular model is the N scale, for which the scale is $\frac{1}{160}$.

25. The student in the photograph is holding HO and N models of the same locomotive. Which type of model is labeled A? Which type of model is labeled B?

26. Each car on a full-size passenger train is 80 ft long. What is the length in inches of a model passenger car in the HO scale? In the N scale?

27. A diesel locomotive is 60 ft long. What is the length in inches of a model of the locomotive in the N scale?

28. In the O scale, a length is $\frac{1}{48}$ the actual length. An O-scale locomotive is 1.05 ft long. How long is the actual locomotive?

A scale drawing has a scale of $\frac{1}{2}$ in. : 10 ft. Find the length on the drawing for each actual length.

29. 40 ft **30.** 5 ft **31.** 35 ft **32.** $3\frac{1}{2}$ ft

33. Open-Ended Give some examples of similar figures you find in everyday life.

The cities of Jackson, Mississippi, and Carson City, Nevada, are 1,750 mi apart.

34. Geography A map of the United States has a scale of 1 in. : 250 mi. How far apart are the cities on the map?

35. On another map, the cities are 5 in. apart. What is the scale?

36. Reasoning A note at the bottom of a map says "not to scale." Explain why that is important information.

A 2-in. length in the scale drawing at the left represents an actual length of 20 ft.

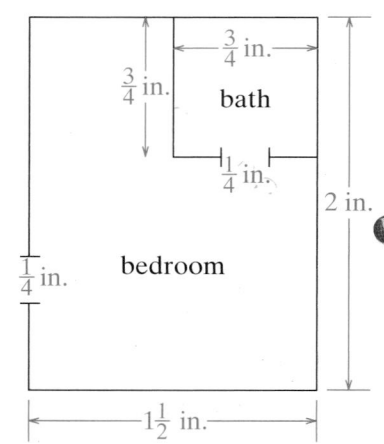

$\frac{3}{4}$ in.

$\frac{3}{4}$ in.   bath

$\frac{1}{4}$ in.

2 in.

$\frac{1}{4}$ in.   bedroom

$1\frac{1}{2}$ in.

37. Architecture What is the scale of the drawing?

38. What are the actual dimensions of the bath?

39. Find the actual width of the doorways that lead into the bedroom and the bathroom.

40. Find the actual area of the bedroom.

41. Can a bed 6 ft long and 3 ft wide fit into the narrow section of the bedroom? Justify your answer.

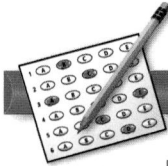 **Challenge** 🌐 **42. Architecture** The length of a room is 16 ft. The scale of a blueprint is $\frac{1}{2}$ in. : 1 ft. Find the room's length in the blueprint.

43. <u>Writing in Math</u> Explain why all squares are similar. For what other shape can you say that all figures are similar? Explain.

44. A boxcar on a freight train is 40 ft long. A model boxcar is 3 in. long. In which scale, HO, N, or O was the model built? (*Hint:* See Exercises 25–28.)

45. You are building a display shelf for your model train. You have 12 cars. Each car is 1.2 ft long. You want 1.2 in. of space between cars. How long must the shelf be?

Test Prep

Multiple Choice

46. The scale for a drawing of a garage is 1.5 in. : 12 ft. If one side of the garage is 40 ft, how long would that side be in the drawing?
A. 5 in.   **B.** 0.45 ft   **C.** 5 ft   **D.** 320 in.

47. The scale of a dollhouse is 1 in. : 2 ft. Which is *most likely* to be the measurement of the height of the dollhouse's front door?
F. $3\frac{1}{2}$ in.   **G.** $3\frac{1}{2}$ ft   **H.** 14 in.   **I.** 14 ft

Short Response

48. To plan a rectangular mural 90 ft long and 75 ft wide, you want to make a drawing with a scale of 1 in. : 9 ft. Can you fit the drawing on a piece of paper that is $8\frac{1}{2}$ in. by 11 in.? Explain.

49. Cheryl's goal is to ride 20 miles on a bike. The distance on a map from her house to the park is 4 in. The map scale is 1 in. : 2 mi. **(a)** Will Cheryl meet her goal if she rides from her house to the park and back? **(b)** Explain in words how you found your answer.

Take It to the NET
Online lesson quiz at
www.PHSchool.com
Web Code: ada-0603

Mixed Review

Lesson 6-2   **Solve each proportion.**

50. $\frac{x}{5} = \frac{32}{80}$ **51.** $\frac{3}{8} = \frac{r}{15}$ **52.** $\frac{40}{w} = \frac{50}{3}$ **53.** $\frac{24}{16} = \frac{204}{c}$

Lesson 6-1 🌐 **54. Gas Mileage** A car travels 264 mi on 12 gal of gas. Find the unit rate in miles per gallon.

Lesson 5-2   **Write each fraction as a decimal.**

55. $\frac{3}{8}$ **56.** $\frac{4}{9}$ **57.** $\frac{7}{16}$ **58.** $\frac{5}{12}$

Lesson 3-3   **Find the mean (to nearest tenth), median, and mode.**

59. 12, 10, 11, 7, 9, 8, 10, 5   **60.** 4.5, 3.2, 6.3, 5.2, 5, 4.8, 6, 3.9

You can use geometry software to make a scale drawing, or *dilation*, of a figure. First choose the Dilate command. Then choose a center of dilation and a scale, which is also known as a *scale factor*.

EXAMPLE

Draw a triangle. Then draw a dilation with scale factor 3.

Use geometry software. Draw $\triangle ABC$. Draw point D on one side of the triangle. Choose D as the center of a dilation with scale factor 3.

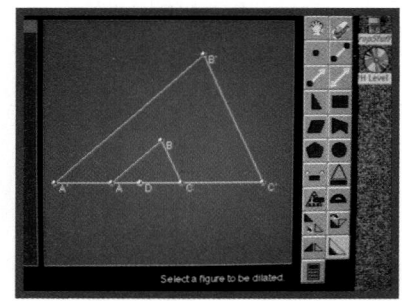

The result is an image like the one at the right. Each side of the dilation is 3 times as long as the corresponding side of $\triangle ABC$.

If you move point D, the dilation also will move. If instead you move A, B, or C, the dilation will change as $\triangle ABC$ changes.

EXERCISES

Use geometry software to draw $\triangle PQR$.

1. a. Draw a point S *outside* $\triangle PQR$. Draw a dilation of $\triangle PQR$ with center S and scale factor 2.5. Label the dilation $\triangle XYZ$. $\triangle XYZ$ is similar to $\triangle PQR$. Angle X corresponds to angle P, angle Y corresponds to angle Q, and angle Z corresponds to angle R.
  b. Compare the location of $\triangle XYZ$ to the location of $\triangle PQR$. Does the dilation lie inside the original triangle? Outside the triangle? Do the triangles overlap?
  c. Now move S to be *inside* $\triangle PQR$. Once again, compare the locations of the two triangles. How did moving the center of dilation change the relative locations of the triangles?

2. Change the location of point S so that $\triangle PQR$ and $\triangle XYZ$ have the given number of points in common. Print an example of each case.
  a. 0   **b.** 1   **c.** 2   **d.** more than 2

3. With S inside $\triangle PQR$, change the scale factor to 0.5. Describe the relative locations of the two triangles.

4. a. Keep the scale factor of the dilation at 0.5. Use the Area tool to find the area of $\triangle PQR$. Use the Area tool again to find the area of $\triangle XYZ$. Write a ratio to compare the areas.
  b. Move P, Q, or R to see how the area of $\triangle XYZ$ changes as the area of $\triangle PQR$ changes. Does the ratio of the areas change?
  c. **Reasoning** What do your results suggest about the areas of similar triangles that have a scale factor of 0.5?

Probability

OBJECTIVE
1   Finding Probability

Exploring Probability

Many board games involve rolling two number cubes and then adding the numbers on the cubes. Are certain sums more likely than others? The table shows the possible rolls and their sums.

Sums of 2 Number Cubes

	1	2	3	4	5	6
1	2	3	4		6	7
2	3	4	5	6		8
3	4	5		7	8	9
4	5		7	8	9	10
5	6	7	8	9	10	
6		8	9	10	11	12

1. Copy and complete the table.

2. What is the number of times each sum appears in the table?

3. Which sum appears most frequently?

4. There is a total of 36 sums in the table. Use your answer to Question 3 to write the ratio
$$\frac{\text{number of times the most frequent sum appears}}{\text{total number of sums}}.$$

Outcomes are the possible results of an action. There are six outcomes for rolling a single number cube: 1, 2, 3, 4, 5, and 6.

An **event** is any outcome or group of outcomes. The outcomes are called *favorable outcomes.* In rolling two number cubes, for example, rolling a sum of 4 is an event corresponding to the three favorable outcomes shown here.

Three outcomes result in the event *a sum of 4.*

The outcomes for rolling two number cubes are *random* and therefore *equally likely* to occur. When outcomes are equally likely, you can use a ratio to find the *probability of an event.*

probability of an event $= P(\text{event}) = \dfrac{\text{number of favorable outcomes}}{\text{number of possible outcomes}}$

What You'll Learn

OBJECTIVE 1   To find probability

OBJECTIVE 2   To find odds

. . . And Why

To solve real-world problems involving the likelihood of events

✓ Check Skills You'll Need

Simplify.

1. $1 - \dfrac{3}{8}$ **2.** $1 - \dfrac{17}{20}$

3. $1 - \dfrac{6}{11}$ **4.** $1 - \dfrac{1}{12}$

For help, go to Lesson 5-3.

New Vocabulary

- outcomes
- event
- probability
- impossible event
- certain event
- complement
- odds

 Interactive Interactive lesson includes instant self-check, tutorials, and activities.

1 EXAMPLE Finding Probability

Find P(rolling an even number) with one number cube.

$$\frac{\text{number of favorable outcomes}}{\text{number of possible outcomes}} = \frac{3}{6} \quad \leftarrow \text{ 3 even-number outcomes}$$
$$\leftarrow \text{ 6 possible outcomes}$$

● P(rolling an even number) $= \frac{3}{6}$, or $\frac{1}{2}$.

✓ Check Understanding Example 1

1. Find each probability for one roll of a number cube.

   a. P(odd number) **b.** P(2) **c.** P(5 or 6)

All probabilities range from 0 to 1.

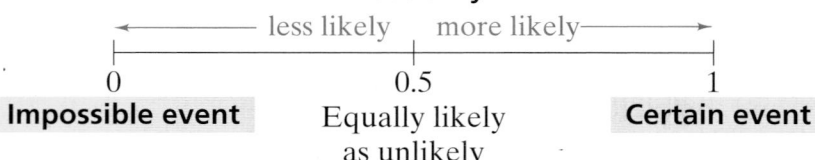

The **complement** of an event is the opposite of that event. The events *no rain* and *rain* are complements of each other. The probability of an event plus the probability of its complement always equals 1.

2 EXAMPLE Real-World 🌐 Problem Solving

Vital Statistics In the United States, the probability that a child is a twin is 2 in 90, or $\frac{2}{90}$. Find P(not a twin).

$$P(\text{twin}) + P(\text{not a twin}) = 1 \qquad \text{Write an equation.}$$

$$\frac{2}{90} + P(\text{not a twin}) = 1 \qquad \text{Substitute.}$$

$$\frac{2}{90} - \frac{2}{90} + P(\text{not a twin}) = 1 - \frac{2}{90} \qquad \text{Subtract } \frac{2}{90} \text{ from each side.}$$

$$P(\text{not a twin}) = \frac{88}{90} = \frac{44}{45} \qquad \text{Simplify.}$$

● The probability that a child is not a twin is $\frac{44}{45}$.

✓ Check Understanding Example 2

2. **a.** When you roll a number cube, what is P(not 2)?
   b. **Reasoning** What is the complement of an impossible event?

2 Finding Odds

You can think of probability as a ratio of $\frac{part}{whole}$. You can also use a $\frac{part}{part}$ ratio, called **odds,** to describe the likelihood of an event.

$$\text{odds in favor of an event} = \frac{\text{number of } \textit{favorable} \text{ outcomes}}{\text{number of } \textit{unfavorable} \text{ outcomes}}$$

$$\text{odds against an event} = \frac{\text{number of } \textit{unfavorable} \text{ outcomes}}{\text{number of } \textit{favorable} \text{ outcomes}}$$

3 EXAMPLE   Real-World Problem Solving

Coins The reverse sides of five quarters are shown below. If you select one of these quarters at random, what are the odds in favor of it showing at least one human figure on its reverse side?

odds in favor $= \frac{3}{2}$ ← **3 have a human figure.**
                     ← **2 do not.**

The odds are $\frac{3}{2}$, or 3 to 2, in favor.

> **Reading Math**
> Read odds of $\frac{3}{2}$ as "three to two."

✓ Check Understanding   Example 3

3. You choose a quarter at random from the five above.
  a. What are the odds in favor of it showing a horse?
  b. What are the odds against it showing a horse?
  c. Consider the event that the quarter shows the outline of a state.
    i. What are the odds in favor of the event?
    ii. What are the odds against the event?

EXERCISES

❓ For more exercises, see *Extra Practice*.

Practice and Problem Solving

A Practice by Example

Examples 1 and 2
(page 306)

Find each probability for one roll of a number cube.

1. $P(3)$ **2.** $P(3 \text{ or } 4)$ **3.** $P(1, 2, \text{ or } 3)$

4. $P(\text{not } 2, 3, \text{ or } 6)$ **5.** $P(\text{not } 1, 3, 4, \text{ or } 5)$ **6.** $P(\text{less than } 4)$

Find each probability for selecting a letter at random from the word ARKANSAS.

7. $P(A)$ **8.** $P(R)$ **9.** $P(S)$

10. $P(K \text{ or } N)$ **11.** $P(\text{vowel})$ **12.** $P(\text{consonant})$

13. A box of crayons contains one crayon of each of the following colors: red, orange, yellow, green, blue, purple, black, white, pink.
  a. What is the probability of NOT choosing a 6-letter color?
  b. What is the complement of choosing green?

Example 3
(page 307)

14. Suppose you choose a letter at random from the word ARITHMETIC. What are the odds in favor of selecting a vowel? What are the odds against selecting a vowel?

A teacher chooses a student at random from a class of 10 boys and 15 girls. Find the odds in favor of, and the odds against, each event.

15. choosing a girl   **16.** choosing a boy

B Apply Your Skills

Find each probability for one roll of a number cube.

17. $P(7)$ **18.** $P(\text{less than } 3)$ **19.** $P(\text{greater than } 2)$

Find each probability for choosing a letter at random from the word MATHEMATICS.

20. $P(K)$ **21.** $P(M, A, \text{ or } T)$ **22.** $P(\text{vowel})$ **23.** $P(\text{consonant})$

Lola's Socks

Color	Number of Socks
Pink	6
White	4
Green	3
Purple	2

24. Reasoning The table at the left describes the loose socks in Lola's drawer. One morning Lola pulls a sock from the drawer without looking. It is white. She pulls out another sock without looking. Find the probability that it also is white.

You have a set of 36 flash cards numbered from 1 to 36. A card is chosen at random. Find the odds in favor of, and the odds against, each selection.

25. even number   **26.** greater than 20   **27.** multiple of 3

28. prime number   **29.** multiple of 2 *or* 3   **30.** multiple of 2 *and* 3

31. It has only one digit.   **32.** It has more than one digit.

C Challenge

33. Open-Ended Give an example of an event for which the probability equals 1. Justify your answer.

34. Error Analysis Your friend is tossing a coin. He says that heads and tails are equally likely outcomes, so the probability of getting heads is $\frac{50}{50}$. Explain your friend's error.

35. Writing in Math Explain how you can use odds to find probability. Include an example.

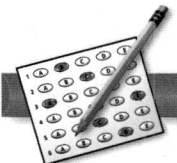
Multiple Choice

36. You draw a name at random from a hat holding the names of 6 girls and 8 boys. What are the odds in favor of choosing a boy?
   A. 3 to 4   **B.** 4 to 3   **C.** 3 to 7   **D.** 4 to 7

Take It to the NET
Online lesson quiz at
www.PHSchool.com
Web Code: ada-0604

37. Refer to the spinner. What is the probability of the complement of *stopping on either red or yellow*?
   F. $\frac{1}{8}$ **G.** $\frac{1}{4}$ **H.** $\frac{3}{8}$ **I.** $\frac{3}{4}$

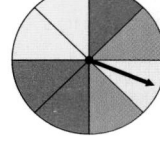

38. Suppose you roll a number cube. Which event has the same probability as $P(\text{not } 1, 2, \text{ or } 3)$?
   A. 3 or 4   **B.** less than 5   **C.** not odd   **D.** more than 4

Short Response

39. a. Can a probability be greater than 1?
   b. Explain your answer.

Mixed Review

Lesson 6-3

The scale of a map is 3 in. : 20 mi. Find the actual distance for each map distance.

40. 6 in.   **41.** 1 in.   **42.** 4.2 in.   **43.** $10\frac{1}{2}$ in.

Lesson 5-2

Write each decimal as a fraction or mixed number in simplest form.

44. 0.25   **45.** $0.\overline{6}$ **46.** 0.8125   **47.** 5.15

Lesson 2-6 🌐 **48. Ticket Sales** Students paid $855 for tickets to a dance. Each ticket cost $5. Write and solve an equation to find the number of tickets the students purchased.

✓ **Checkpoint Quiz 1**   **Lessons 6-1 through 6-4**

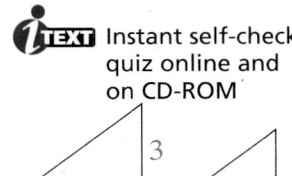
TEXT Instant self-check quiz online and on CD-ROM

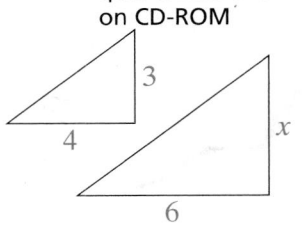

Write each phrase as a unit rate.

1. 20 mi in 5 h   **2.** 42 gal in 7 min   **3.** a fall of 144 ft in 3 s

4. Geometry The figures (left) are similar. Find the missing length.

5. A person blinks 112 times in 4 min. At that rate, how many times does the person blink in 1.5 min?

6. Suppose you roll a number cube. What is $P(2 \text{ or } 3)$?

6-5

Fractions, Decimals, and Percents

What You'll Learn

1 To write percents as fractions and decimals

OBJECTIVE

2 To write decimals and fractions as percents

. . . And Why

To solve real-world problems involving statistics

 Check Skills You'll Need

Write each fraction as a decimal.

1. $\frac{5}{8}$ 2. $\frac{9}{20}$ 3. $\frac{3}{4}$

4. $\frac{5}{6}$ 5. $\frac{2}{3}$ 6. $\frac{8}{11}$

 For help, go to Lesson 5-2.

New Vocabulary

• percent

Reading Math

Percent means "per hundred." The root *cent* shows up in many other words, such as centimeter, century, and centipede. In money, a cent is $\frac{1}{100}$ of a dollar, or $.01.

OBJECTIVE

1 ▸ **Writing Percents as Fractions and Decimals**

A **percent** is a ratio that compares a number to 100. Therefore, you can write a percent as a fraction with a denominator of 100.

1 EXAMPLE **Writing a Percent as a Fraction**

Write each percent as a fraction or a mixed number.

a. 5%

$\frac{5}{100}$ ◂—— Write as a fraction with a denominator of 100. ——▸ $\frac{125}{100}$

$\frac{1}{20}$ ◂—— Simplify. ——▸ $\frac{5}{4}$

Write as a mixed number. ——▸ $1\frac{1}{4}$

b. 125%

 Check Understanding Example 1

1. Write each percent as a fraction or mixed number in simplest form.

   a. 58%   **b.** 72%   **c.** 144%

To write a percent as a decimal, write the percent as a fraction with a denominator of 100. Then divide to convert the fraction to a decimal.

2 EXAMPLE **Writing a Percent as a Decimal**

Write 9.7% as a decimal.

$9.7\% = \frac{9.7}{100}$ Write as a fraction with a denominator of 100.

$= 009.7$ Divide by moving the decimal point left two places. You may need to write one or more zeros.

$= 0.097$

 Check Understanding Example 2

2. Write each percent as a decimal.

   a. 16%   **b.** 62.5%   **c.** 120%

   d. Biology About 45% of the people in the United States have type O blood. Write this percent as a decimal and as a fraction in simplest form.

---

 iTEXT Interactive lesson includes instant self-check, tutorials, and activities.

310   Chapter 6   Ratios, Proportions, and Percents

2 Writing Decimals and Fractions as Percents

Need Help?

For help on writing decimals as fractions, see Lesson 5-2.

To write a decimal as a percent, rewrite the decimal as a fraction with a denominator of 100. Then write the fraction as a percent.

Another way to change a decimal to a percent is to move the decimal point two places to the right and add a percent sign.

3 EXAMPLE   Writing a Decimal as a Percent

Write 0.333 as a percent.

Method 1
Rewrite as a fraction.

$$0.333 = \frac{333}{1,000}$$

$$= \frac{333 \div 10}{1,000 \div 10}$$

$$= \frac{33.3}{100}$$

$$= 33.3\%$$

Method 2
Move the decimal point.

$$0.333 = 33.3\%$$

✔ **Check Understanding**   Example 3

3. Write each decimal as a percent.

   a. 0.4   **b.** 0.023   **c.** 1.75

To write a fraction as a percent, divide the numerator by the denominator. Then convert the decimal quotient to a percent.

4 EXAMPLE   Real-World ⬤ Problem Solving

Pets Five out of sixteen families in the United States own dogs. What percent of families own dogs?

$\frac{5}{16}$ **Write a fraction.**

0.3125   **Divide the numerator by the denominator.**

31.25%   **Write as a percent.**

About 31% of families own dogs.

✔ **Check Understanding**   Example 4

4. Three out of eleven families in the United States own cats. To the nearest percent, what percent of families own cats?

Real-World ⬤ Connection

There are about 55 million dogs and 61 million cats in the United States.

EXERCISES

For more exercises, see *Extra Practice*.

Practice and Problem Solving

A Practice by Example

Example 1
(page 310)

Example 2
(page 310)

Example 3
(page 311)

Example 4
(page 311)

Write each percent as a fraction or mixed number in simplest form.

1. 40%   **2.** 28%   **3.** 39%   **4.** 55% $\frac{11}{20}$ **5.** 20%

6. 6%   **7.** 98%   **8.** 315%   **9.** 220%   **10.** 102%

Write each percent as a decimal.

11. 36%   **12.** 4.4%   **13.** 1%   **14.** 6.3%   **15.** 133%

16. 79.7%   **17.** 350%   **18.** 52%   **19.** 31.4%   **20.** 0.03%

21. Education In 2000, women made up 40% of freshmen studying computer science at a certain university. Write this percent as a decimal and as a fraction in simplest form.

Write each decimal as a percent.

22. 1.68   **23.** 0.36   **24.** 0.70   **25.** 0.002   **26.** 0.06

27. 1.88   **28.** 2.59   **29.** 1.11   **30.** 0.156   **31.** 0.043

Write each fraction as a percent. Round to the nearest tenth of a percent where necessary.

32. $\frac{23}{100}$ **33.** $\frac{1}{4}$ **34.** $\frac{11}{20}$ **35.** $\frac{3}{5}$ **36.** $\frac{5}{8}$

37. $\frac{4}{19}$ **38.** $\frac{1}{6}$ **39.** $\frac{7}{20}$ **40.** $\frac{2}{9}$ **41.** $\frac{7}{18}$

42. Populations In the United States, about one person in eight lives in California. To the nearest percent, what percent of people in the United States live in California?

43. Homework Ron has read 14 pages of his 22-page reading assignment. To the nearest percent, what percent of the assignment has Ron read?

B Apply Your Skills

Write each fraction as a percent. Round to the nearest tenth of a percent where necessary.

44. $\frac{8}{13}$ **45.** $\frac{5}{6}$ **46.** $\frac{111}{100}$ **47.** $\frac{9}{2}$ **48.** $\frac{12}{5}$

Estimation About what percent of each flag is red?

49.

Tennessee

50.

North Carolina

Probability Find each probability for one roll of a number cube. Write the probability as a percent. Round to the nearest tenth of a percent where necessary.

51. $P(6)$ **52.** $P(\text{even})$ **53.** $P(1 \text{ or } 2)$ **54.** $P(\text{not } 1)$

Copy and complete the table.

	Fraction	Decimal	Percent
55.	$\frac{4}{5}$	■	■
56.	■	0.10	■
57.	■	0.5	■
58.	$\frac{3}{4}$	■	■
59.	■	■	67%
60.	■	■	25%

Reasoning For Exercises 61–64, does each sentence make sense? Explain.

61. About 17% of Americans go camping. That means about 83% do not go camping.

62. A student correctly answered 200% of the items on a test.

63. Today a runner ran 150% of the distance she ran yesterday.

64. On a test, a student missed 12 items and correctly answered 96% of all items.

Compare. Use >, <, or = to complete each statement.

65. 0.05% ■ 50%   **66.** $\frac{7}{12}$ ■ 60%   **67.** 0.0325 ■ 32.5%

68. $\frac{7}{8}$ ■ 68%   **69.** 0.1756 ■ 176%   **70.** $\frac{140}{130}$ ■ 104%

🌐 **71. Maps** A map has a scale of 0.01%. Write the scale as a fraction.

72. Jeanette answered 32 questions correctly on a 45-question test. The passing grade was 70%. Did Jeanette pass? Justify your answer.

🌐 **73. Scale Drawings** A scale drawing has a scale of 1 : 12. Write the scale as a percent.

74. Writing in Math Explain how to write a decimal as a percent. Give examples.

🌐 **75. a. Test Grades** On his last math assignment, Kyle answered 5% of the questions incorrectly, or 1 question. How many questions did Kyle answer correctly?
   b. On the same test, Diana answered 16 questions correctly. What percent of the questions did she not answer correctly?

76. Open-Ended Use a percent to describe an everyday event. Then write the percent as a fraction and as a decimal.

77. Reasoning Explain why 0.25 is different from 0.25%.

A crowd filled the 8,000 seats in a stadium. There were 1,400 children and 4,800 men present. Write a ratio and a percent to describe how many seats were filled by each group.

78. men   **79.** children   **80.** women

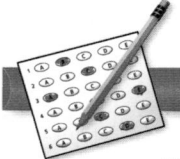

Test Prep

Multiple Choice

81. What is 0.2% written as a decimal?
A. 0.002   **B.** 0.2   **C.** 2   **D.** 20

82. If 12% of an iceberg is above water, what fraction is in the water?
F. $\frac{3}{25}$ **G.** $\frac{12}{88}$ **H.** $\frac{22}{25}$ **I.** $7\frac{1}{3}$

83. In a basketball free-throw contest, four players take the same number of free throws. Player A makes 33 of 40 free throws. Player B makes $\frac{3}{4}$ of his free throws, Player C makes 85% of her free throws, and Player D makes $\frac{4}{5}$ of his free throws. Which player makes the greatest number of free throws?
A. Player A   **B.** Player B   **C.** Player C   **D.** Player D

Short Response

84. A baseball player's batting average is the ratio of the number of hits to the number of times at bat.
  a. If Julienne's batting average is .392, what percent of her times at bat are hits?
  b. For part (a), explain your answer.

Take It to the NET
Online lesson quiz at
www.PHSchool.com
Web Code: ada-0605

85. A weather reporter predicts that at least 20% of the 11 counties in her area will get rain this weekend.
  a. If two counties get rain, is the reporter's prediction correct?
  b. Explain your answer.

Mixed Review

Lesson 6-4   **Find each probability for choosing a letter at random from the word PROBABLE.**

86. $P(\text{B})$ **87.** $P(\text{vowel})$ **88.** $P(\text{R})$ **89.** $P(\text{not L or R})$

Lesson 3-6   **Solve each equation.**

90. $0.85x = 39.95$ **91.** $4.8y = -0.84$

92. $100 = \frac{a}{13.2}$ **93.** $\frac{b}{-25} = 1.8$

Lesson 1-9 🌐 **94. Test Scores** The average of three test scores is 85. One test score is 90. Another is 72. What is the third?

Proportions and Percents

OBJECTIVE

1 Finding Part of a Whole

You can solve a percent problem by writing and solving a proportion.

A model can help you write a proportion. This model shows that 30 is 75% of 40.

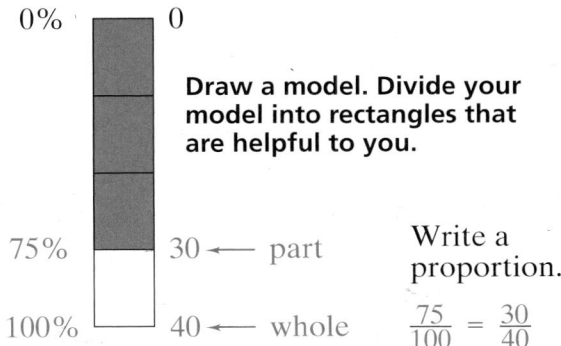

Draw a model. Divide your model into rectangles that are helpful to you.

Write a proportion.

$$\frac{75}{100} = \frac{30}{40}$$

1 EXAMPLE Finding Part of a Whole

Find 65% of 245.

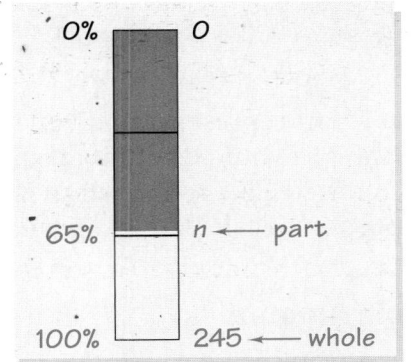

$$\frac{65}{100} = \frac{n}{245}$$ **Write a proportion.**

$$65(245) = 100n$$ **Write cross products.**

$$\frac{65(245)}{100} = \frac{100n}{100}$$ **Divide each side by 100.**

$$159.25 = n$$ **Simplify.**

• 65% of 245 is 159.25.

✓ Check Understanding Example 1

1. Draw a model and write a proportion. Then solve.

   a. 25% of 124 is ▪. **b.** 43% of 230 is ▪. **c.** 12.5% of 80 is ▪.

What You'll Learn

OBJECTIVE 1 To find a part of a whole and a percent

OBJECTIVE 2 To find a whole amount

. . . And Why

To solve real-world problems involving business data

✓ Check Skills You'll Need

Solve each proportion.

1. $\frac{25}{100} = \frac{x}{28}$

2. $\frac{98.9}{x} = \frac{43}{100}$

3. $\frac{52}{100} = \frac{13}{x}$

4. $\frac{x}{100} = \frac{27}{150}$

❓ For help, go to Lesson 6-2.

 Interactive lesson includes instant self-check, tutorials, and activities.

2 EXAMPLE Finding a Percent

What percent of 60 is 52? Round to the nearest tenth of a percent.

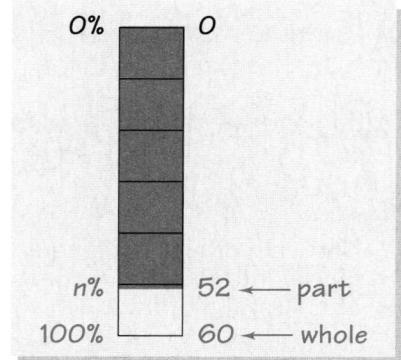

$$\frac{n}{100} = \frac{52}{60} \qquad \text{Write a proportion.}$$

$$60n = 100(52) \qquad \text{Write cross products.}$$

$$\frac{60n}{60} = \frac{100(52)}{60} \qquad \text{Divide each side by 60.}$$

$$n = 86.\overline{6} \qquad \text{Simplify.}$$

$$\approx 86.7 \qquad \text{Round.}$$

● 52 is approximately 86.7% of 60.

✓ Check Understanding Example 2

2. Round to the nearest tenth.

    a. What percent of 250 is 138?   **b.** 14 is what percent of 15?

OBJECTIVE

2 Finding a Whole Amount

Sometimes you know the percent that a part represents, and you want to find the whole amount. For example, your class fundraising committee might announce, "We've collected $207 so far, which is 46% of our goal!" You can use a proportion to calculate the goal.

3 EXAMPLE Finding the Whole Amount

207 is 46% of what number?

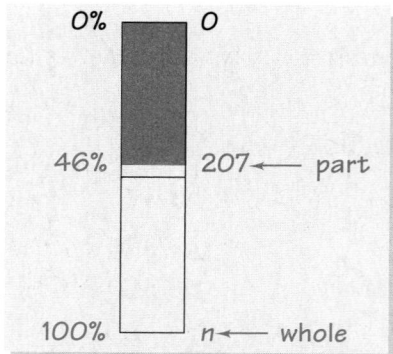

$$\frac{46}{100} = \frac{207}{n} \qquad \text{Write a proportion.}$$

$$46n = 100(207) \qquad \text{Write cross products.}$$

$$\frac{46n}{46} = \frac{100(207)}{46} \qquad \text{Divide each side by 46.}$$

$$n = 450 \qquad \text{Simplify.}$$

● 207 is 46% of 450.

✅ **Check Understanding**   Example 3

3. Round to the nearest tenth.

    a. 19 is 75% of what number?   **b.** 310 is 99% of what number?

4 EXAMPLE   <u>Real-World</u> 🌐 **Problem Solving**

Theaters In 2000, the number of drive-in movie screens in the United States was about 78% of the number in 1990. About how many drive-in screens were there in 1990?

Drive-In Movies

Year	Number of Screens
1990	■
1995	847
2000	717

SOURCE: Motion Picture Association of America

$$\frac{78}{100} = \frac{717}{n}$$ Write a proportion.

$78n = 100(717)$ Write cross products.

$$\frac{78n}{78} = \frac{100(717)}{78}$$ Divide each side by 78.

$n \approx 919$ Round to the nearest whole number.

There were about 919 drive-in screens in 1990.

Check Is the answer reasonable? The original problem says that the number of screens in 2000 was 78% of the number in 1990. Check by estimating:

78% of $919 \approx 0.8 \times 900 = 720$, which is close to 717, the number for 2000. So the answer is reasonable.

✅ **Check Understanding**   Example 4

4. Refer to the table in Example 4. In 2000, the number of drive-in movie screens was about 20.1% of the number in 1980. Find the number of drive-in screens in 1980.

Here is a summary of how to use proportions to solve percent problems.

Key Concepts Percents and Proportions		
Finding the Percent	**Finding the Part**	**Finding the Whole**
What percent of 40 is 6?	What number is 15% of 40?	6 is 15% of what number?
$\dfrac{n}{100} = \dfrac{6}{40} \begin{array}{l}\leftarrow \text{part} \\ \leftarrow \text{whole}\end{array}$	$\dfrac{15}{100} = \dfrac{n}{40} \begin{array}{l}\leftarrow \text{part} \\ \leftarrow \text{whole}\end{array}$	$\dfrac{15}{100} = \dfrac{6}{n} \begin{array}{l}\leftarrow \text{part} \\ \leftarrow \text{whole}\end{array}$

EXERCISES

For more exercises, see *Extra Practice*.

Practice and Problem Solving

A Practice by Example

Example 1
(page 315)

For Exercises 1–22, write and solve a proportion. Where necessary, round to the nearest tenth.

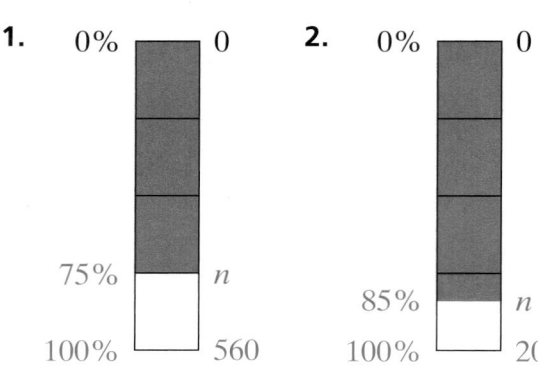

3. 80% of 20 is ■.

4. 40% of 60 is ■.

5. 53% of 70 is ■.

6. 18% of 150 is ■.

7. 16% of 75 is ■.

8. 92% of 625 is ■.

Example 2
(page 316)

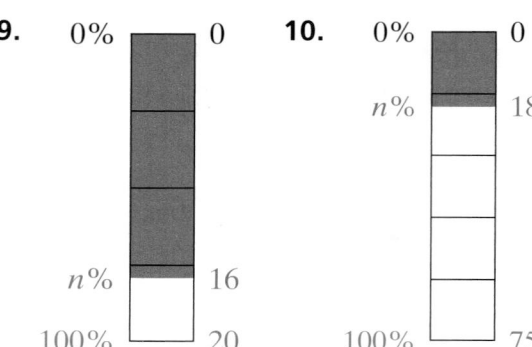

11. ■% of 40 is 30.

12. ■% of 20 is 4.

13. ■% of 25 is 13.

14. 75 is ■% of 250.

15. ■% of 92 is 17.

16. ■% of 80 is 14.

Example 3
(page 316)

17. 8 is 25% of ■.   **18.** 14 is 35% of ■.   **19.** 31 is 49% of ■.

20. 45 is 93% of ■.   **21.** 1 is 2% of ■.   **22.** 6 is 98% of ■.

Example 4
(page 317)

23. Population In 1950, the population of Alaska was about 128,535. That was about 20.5% of the population of Alaska in the year 2000. About how many people lived in Alaska in the year 2000?

24. Banking At the beginning of the summer Jeri had $480 in her savings account. That was only 15% of the amount in her savings account at the end of the summer. How much money did Jeri have in her account at the end of the summer?

B Apply Your Skills

Write and solve a proportion. Where necessary, round to the nearest whole amount.

25. Find 300% of 50.   **26.** 250% of ■ is 50.

27. Find 60% of 15.   **28.** 40,571 is ■% of 76,550.

29. 35% of ■ is 52.5.   **30.** 121.8 is ■% of 105.

31. Purchasing A bicycle cost $250 last year. The same bike costs $200 this year. What percent of last year's cost is this year's cost?

State	Sales Tax
Georgia	7%
Kansas	4.9%
Pennsylvania	6%
South Carolina	5%

32. Sales Tax The table shows sales tax rates for different states. For each state, find the following amount on a $15,000 car.
  a. the amount of sales tax **b.** the car's total cost

33. Profit You invested some money and made a profit of $55. Your profit was 11% of your investment. How much did you invest?

34. Nineteen members, or 38%, of the ski club are going on a ski trip. Find the total number of members in the club.

35. Error Analysis Your class has 26 students, which represents 5% of your school's enrollment. Your friend uses the proportion $\frac{5}{100} = \frac{n}{26}$ to find the number of students in your school. Explain your friend's error.

C Challenge

Write and solve a proportion. Where necessary, round to the nearest tenth.

36. Find $33\frac{1}{3}\%$ of 54.

37. $12\frac{1}{2}\%$ of ■ is 6.

38. ■% of 36,500 is 912.5.

39. What is $\frac{5}{4}\%$ of 145?

40. Open-Ended Write and solve a word problem involving percents.

41. Writing in Math At Pics, all posters are 30% off. At Pacs, all posters are marked $\frac{1}{3}$ off. Which is the greater discount rate? Explain.

42. Reasoning Do $a\%$ of b and $b\%$ of a represent the same amount? Justify your answer.

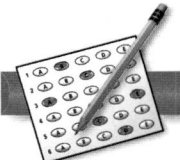

Test Prep

Gridded Response

43. 42 is 60% of what number?

44. 1.25 is what percent of 25?

45. What number is 30% of 75?

46. A student pole-vaulted 5 ft yesterday. Today she vaulted 20% higher. How many feet higher did she vault today?

Take It to the NET
Online lesson quiz at
www.PHSchool.com
Web Code: ada-0606

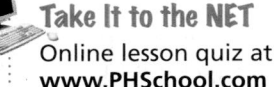

Mixed Review

Lesson 6-5

Write each number as a percent.

47. 0.08

48. 0.523

49. $\frac{7}{12}$

50. 4.56

Lesson 4-9

Order from least to greatest.

51. $10^3, 10^{-2}, 10^{-1}, 10^0$

52. $2.3 \times 10^4, 2.03 \times 10^5, 2.03 \times 10^4, 2.4 \times 10^3$

Lesson 1-1

53. Family Peter has four cousins. Paul has c cousins fewer than Peter. Write an expression for the number of Paul's cousins.

6-7

Percents and Equations

What You'll Learn

OBJECTIVE
1 To write and solve percent equations

OBJECTIVE
2 To use equations in solving percent problems

...And Why

To solve real-world problems involving earnings and surveys

✓ Check Skills You'll Need

Write each percent as a decimal.

1. 48%   **2.** 5%

3. 23.8%   **4.** 72.25%

5. 136%   **6.** 178.5%

 For help, go to Lesson 6-5.

New Vocabulary

• commission

Reading Math

For help with reading and solving percent equations, see page 324.

OBJECTIVE

1 Writing and Solving Percent Equations

You can solve a percent problem by writing and solving an equation. When you use a percent in an equation, write it as a decimal.

Key Concepts	Percent Equations	
Finding the Percent	**Finding the Part**	**Finding the Whole**
What percent of 40 is 6?	What is 15% of 40?	6 is 15% of what?
$n \cdot 40 = 6$	$n = 0.15 \cdot 40$	$6 = 0.15 \cdot n$

1 EXAMPLE   Solving a Percent Equation

What is 85% of 62?

$n = 0.85 \cdot 62$ **Write an equation. Write the percent as a decimal.**

$n = 52.7$ **Simplify.**

● 85% of 62 is 52.7.

✓ Check Understanding   Example 1

1. Write and solve an equation.

   a. 0.96 is what percent of 10?   **b.** 19.2 is 32% of what?

You can also write and solve equations having percents greater than 100%.

2 EXAMPLE   Percents Greater Than 100%

What percent of 48 is 54?

$n \cdot 48 = 54$ **Write an equation.**

$\frac{48n}{48} = \frac{54}{48}$ **Divide each side by 48.**

$n = 1.125$ **Simplify.**

$= 112.5\%$ **Change the decimal to a percent.**

● 54 is 112.5% of 48.

✓ Check Understanding   Example 2

2. Write and solve an equation.

   a. What is 145.5% of 20?   **b.** 380 is 125% of what number?

Interactive lesson includes instant self-check, tutorials, and activities.

2 Using Equations to Solve Percent Problems

Some sales jobs pay an amount based on how much you sell. This amount is called a **commission.**

3 EXAMPLE Real-World 🌐 Problem Solving

Commission A real-estate agent makes a 4.5% commission on property she sells. How much commission does she make on the sale of a house for $132,500?

Words	amount of commission	is	4.5%	of	$132,500

Let c = amount of commission.

Equation	c	=	0.045	·	132,500

$c = 0.045 \cdot 132,500$
$ = 5,962.50$

● The agent's commission is $5,962.50.

✔ **Check Understanding** Example 3

3. **Royalties** A singer receives a 5% royalty on each CD sale. To the nearest cent, find his royalty for a CD that sells for $16.99.

4 EXAMPLE Real-World 🌐 Problem Solving

Surveys The graph shows the results of a survey. There were 1,023 people who answered yes. How many people were surveyed?

Words	1,023	is	93%	of	number surveyed

Let n = number surveyed.

Equation	1,023	=	0.93	·	n

$0.93n = 1,023$
$\dfrac{0.93n}{0.93} = \dfrac{1,023}{0.93}$
$n = 1,100$

● 1,100 people were surveyed.

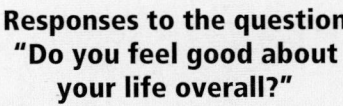

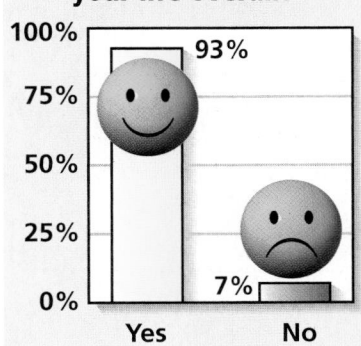

Responses to the question "Do you feel good about your life overall?"

✔ **Check Understanding** Example 4

4. In a survey, 922 people, or about 68.6%, preferred smooth peanut butter to chunky. How many people were surveyed?

EXERCISES

For more exercises, see *Extra Practice*.

Practice and Problem Solving

A Practice by Example

Example 1
(page 320)

Write an equation and solve.

1. Find 30% of 30.

2. What percent of 40 is 25?

3. 120 is 15% of what number?

4. What percent of 20 is 11?

5. Find 56% of 75.

6. 85% of *z* is 106,250. What is *z*?

7. What percent of 25 is 17?

8. Find 75% of 840.

Example 2
(page 320)

9. Find 150% of 90.

10. 300% of *a* is 297. What is *a*?

11. What percent of 4 is 9?

12. Find 500% of 12.

13. What percent of 150 is 96?

14. 3.5% of *d* is 0.105. What is *d*?

15. What percent of 1 is 4.7?

16. Find 15% of 150.

Example 3
(page 321)

17. Royalties Julius writes novels and receives 12% of the price for each book sold. To the nearest cent, find the royalty Julius receives for a book price of $7.99.

18. Sports An agent makes 16% commission on an athlete's signing bonus. If the bonus is $26,000, what is the agent's commission?

Example 4
(page 321)

For Exercises 19 and 20, the table gives information about videocassette recorders (VCRs) in the United States.

19. The number of households with VCRs in 1995 was about 93% of the number with VCRs in 1998. About how many households had VCRs in 1998?

20. The number of households with VCRs in 1990 was about 87.5% of the number with VCRs in 1993. About how many households had VCRs in 1993?

Households With VCRs

Year	Households (millions)
1980	1
1985	18
1990	63
1995	77
1998	■

SOURCE: Statistical Abstract of the United States. Go to **www.PHSchool.com** for a data update. Web Code: adg-2041

B Apply Your Skills

Write and solve an equation. Where necessary, round to the nearest tenth or tenth of a percent.

21. Find 225% of 3.6.

22. What percent of 45 is 24?

23. Find 5.5% of 44.

24. 24% of *w* is 3.6. What is *w*?

25. What percent of 8 is 20?

26. 9.2% of *b* is 27.6. What is *b*?

27. 135% of *t* is 63. What is *t*?

28. What is 264% of 12?

29. Commission A salesperson receives 5.4% commission. On one sale, she received $6.48. What was the amount of the sale?

30. Reasoning Describe a situation in which you would use a percent greater than 100%.

Mental Math Use mental math.

31. What percent of 60 is 30? **32.** 100% of t is 100. What is t?

33. Find 5% of 10. **34.** What percent of 55 is 11?

35. 50% of g is 24. What is g? **36.** Find 15% of 12.

 **Challenge**

For Exercises 37 and 38, use the table on page 322. Is each statement true or false? Explain.

37. Reasoning The number of households with VCRs in 1985 was less than 10% of the number of households with VCRs in 1990.

38. The number of households with VCRs in 1985 was more than 1,000% of the number in 1980.

39. Polly got a 20% discount on a computer that regularly cost x dollars. She paid sales tax of 5%. Later she sold the computer for 70% of what she paid for it. Write an expression for the amount Polly received for the computer.

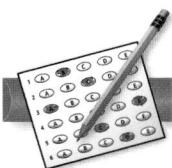

Writing in Math

Which approach do you prefer to use in solving percent problems—the approach you learned in this lesson, or the one you learned in Lesson 6-6? Explain.

 Test Prep

Multiple Choice

40. About what percent of 92 is 63?
A. 63% B. 68% C. 92% D. 146%

 **Take It to the NET**
Online lesson quiz at
www.PHSchool.com
Web Code: ada-0607

41. Seventy students voted for Tim, 25% voted for Li, and the other 40% voted for Mae. How many students voted in the election?
F. 200 G. 135 H. 100 I. 70

42. What is 158% of 35?
A. 12.64 B. 20.3 C. 42.6 D. 55.3

Short Response

43. Chan's team won 70% of the 20 games it played. Latisha's team played 15 games and won 80% of them.
a. Whose team won the greater number of games?
b. For part (a), explain your answer.

Mixed Review

Lesson 6-6 **Write a proportion. Then solve.**

44. ■% of 360 is 45. **45.** 35% of 60 is ■. **46.** 45 is 1.5% of ■.

Lesson 5-8 🌐 **47. Creative Writing** Ernest started writing a story on a Friday. He worked on the story for $\frac{1}{2}$ h each day. He took 7 h to finish it. On what day did Ernest finish his story?

Lesson 4-7 **Simplify each expression.**

48. $10^2 \cdot 10^4$ **49.** $9y^4 \cdot y^5$ **50.** $(x^3)^7$

To go from words to an equation, you first have to recognize a word equation. This requires that you recognize the variable, all operations, and the relationship. Percent problems can have various word equations, but each is equivalent to one of the three types in this table.

Key Concepts	**Percent Equations**	
Finding the Percent	**Finding the Part**	**Finding the Whole**
What percent of 40 is 6?	What is 15% of 40?	6 is 15% of what?
$n \cdot 40 = 6$	$n = 0.15 \cdot 40$	$6 = 0.15 \cdot n$

EXAMPLE

Six of 40 students wear at least one ring. What percent is this?

What percent of 40 is 6?   **Recognize the percent equation.**

n of 40 is 6   *What percent* **is what you must find.
Let a variable, *n*, represent this value.**

n $\cdot$ 40 is 6   **The word *of* suggests multiplication.**

n $\cdot$ 40 = 6   **The word *is* suggests equality.**

Now you have a math equation that you can solve.

$$\frac{n \cdot 40}{40} = \frac{6}{40}$$ **Divide each side by 40.**

$$n = 0.15$$ **Simplify.**

$$n = 15\%$$ **Write as a percent.**

EXERCISES

Restate, if necessary, the question to match a type of question in the table. Then solve.

1. Seven is what percent of 21?

2. Eighteen is thirty percent of what number?

3. How much is twenty percent of 50?

4. What percent of 6 is 40?

5. Sixty runners, or 80% of all entries, finished the course. How many entries were there?

6. Thirty students are in Ms. Payne's history class. Ninety percent of the students brought signed permission forms for a field trip. How many students brought permission forms?

Percent of Change

1   Finding Percent of Increase

Exploring Percent of Change

1. Find the change in population from 1980 to 1990 for each state.

2. Which state had the greater change in population?

Populations of Two States

State	1980	1990
California	23,668,000	29,786,000
Nevada	800,000	1,202,000

3. Write the ratio $\frac{\text{change in population}}{\text{1980 population}}$ for each state. Then write each ratio as a percent.

4. Compare the two percents. Which state had the greater population change in terms of percent?

The percent a quantity increases or decreases from its original amount is the **percent of change.**

$$\text{percent of change} = \frac{\text{amount of change}}{\text{original amount}}$$

1 EXAMPLE   Finding Percent of Increase

Find the percent of increase from 4 to 7.5.

amount of increase $= 7.5 - 4 = 3.5$

percent of increase $= \dfrac{\text{amount of increase}}{\text{original amount}}$

$\qquad\qquad\qquad = \dfrac{3.5}{4}$

$\qquad\qquad\qquad = 0.875 = 87.5\%$

The percent of increase from 4 to 7.5 is 87.5%.

✓ Check Understanding   Example 1

1. Find each percent of increase.

    a. from 100 to 114   **b.** from 2.0 to 3.2   **c.** from 4,000 to 8,500

What You'll Learn

OBJECTIVE 1   To find percent of increase

OBJECTIVE 2   To find percent of decrease

. . . And Why

To solve real-world problems involving environmental management

✓ Check Skills You'll Need

Write each decimal as a percent.

1. 0.46   **2.** 2.47

3. 0.03   **4.** 5.236

❓ For help, go to Lesson 6-5.

New Vocabulary

- **percent of change**

TEXT Interactive lesson includes instant self-check, tutorials, and activities.

2 EXAMPLE   Real-World Problem Solving

Waste Management
The annual production of municipal solid waste in the United States has more than doubled since 1960. Find the percent of increase from 1960 to 1990.

amount of increase
= 205 − 88 = 117

percent of increase

$= \dfrac{\text{amount of increase}}{\text{original amount}}$

$= \dfrac{117}{88}$

$= 1.329\overline{54} \approx 133\%$

Municipal Solid Waste

88 million tons — 1960
121 million tons — 1970
152 million tons — 1980
205 million tons — 1990
232 million tons — 2000

SOURCE: Environmental Protection Agency.
Go to **www.PHSchool.com** for a data update.
Web Code: adg-2041

• The percent of increase from 1960 to 1990 was about 133%.

✓ Check Understanding   Example 2

2. **Waste Management** Find the percent of increase in solid-waste production from 1970 to 1980. Round to the nearest percent.

OBJECTIVE

2 Finding Percent of Decrease

You also can find percent of decrease.

3 EXAMPLE   Finding Percent of Decrease

Find the percent of decrease from 1,500 to 1,416.

amount of decrease = 1,500 − 1,416 = 84

percent of decrease $= \dfrac{\text{amount of decrease}}{\text{original amount}}$

$= \dfrac{84}{1,500}$

$= 0.056 = 5.6\%$

• The percent of decrease is 5.6%.

✓ Check Understanding   Example 3

3. Find each percent of decrease. Where necessary, round to the nearest tenth of a percent.

   a. from 9.6 to 4.8   **b.** from 202 to 192   **c.** from 854.5 to 60.6

EXERCISES

For more exercises, see *Extra Practice*.

Practice and Problem Solving

A Practice by Example

Examples 1 and 2
(pages 325, 326)

Find each percent of increase.

1. from 30 to 39   **2.** from 50 to 66   **3.** from 4 to 4.5

4. from 48 to 60   **5.** from 32 to 76   **6.** from 5 to 5.5

7. from 55 to 176   **8.** from 38 to 95   **9.** from 2.5 to 3

 10. Life Spans In the United States in the 20th century, average life expectancy increased from about 47 years to about 77 years. Find the percent of increase to the nearest percent.

Example 3
(page 326)

Find each percent of decrease. Where necessary, round to the nearest tenth of a percent.

11. from 60 to 48   **12.** from 180 to 54   **13.** from 180 to 108

14. from 280 to 126   **15.** from 240 to 90   **16.** from 42 to 35

17. from 64 to 24   **18.** from 6.5 to 4.8   **19.** from 7.4 to 2.4

20. A computer that cost $1,099 last year costs $999 this year.

21. A racing bicycle that cost $1,500 new costs $845 used.

B Apply Your Skills

Find each percent of change. Tell whether the change is an increase or a decrease. Where necessary, round to the nearest tenth of a percent.

22. from 96 to 78   **23.** from 90 to 75   **24.** from 80 to 95

25. from 45 to 105   **26.** from 27 to 72   **27.** from 120 to 95

28. from 87 to 108   **29.** from 59 to 127   **30.** from 77 to 13

31. Error Analysis Eva's first step in finding the percent of change from 7 to 8 was to write $\frac{8-7}{8} = \frac{1}{8}$. Explain Eva's error.

 **32. Economics** The average cost of a gallon of gasoline was $1.29 in 1997 and $1.12 in 1998. Find the percent of decrease.

Mental Math Use mental math to find each percent of change. Tell whether the change is an increase or a decrease.

33. from 25 to 30   **34.** from 40 to 45   **35.** from 50 to 45

36. from 100 to 101.1   **37.** from 40 to 20   **38.** from 15 to 12

C Challenge

39. The population of Growtown increased from 10,000 to 13,000 in one year. In the same year, the population of Slowtown decreased from 30,000 to 24,000.
a. Find each town's percent of increase or decrease in population.
b. If each town maintains the same rate of change, within how many years will the population of Growtown exceed that of Slowtown?

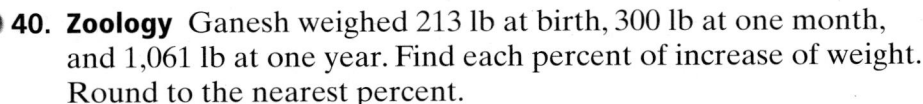

40. Zoology Ganesh weighed 213 lb at birth, 300 lb at one month, and 1,061 lb at one year. Find each percent of increase of weight. Round to the nearest percent.
 a. from birth to one month
 b. from one month to one year
 c. from birth to one year
 d. Writing in Math Explain why the sum of the percent increase from birth to one month and from one month to one year does not equal the percent increase from birth to one year.

Real-World Connection

Ganesh was the first elephant born at the Cincinnati Zoo.

41. a. Reasoning 100 is increased by 10%. The result is decreased by 10%. Is the final result 100? Explain.
 b. Compare the final result in part (a) to 100, the original number. Find the percent of change.

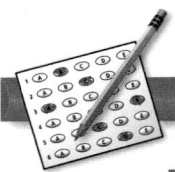

Test Prep

Multiple Choice

42. The price of an item is $5.99. With sales tax, you pay $6.35. About what percent of the price of the item is the sales tax?
 A. 3% **B.** 4% **C.** 5% **D.** 6%

43. Kayla was 36 in. tall at age 3. Today, at age 5, she is 42 in. tall. To the nearest percent, what is the percent of change in Kayla's height?
 F. 2% **G.** 8% **H.** 14% **I.** 17%

Take It to the NET
Online lesson quiz at
www.PHSchool.com
Web Code: ada-0608

44. A share of stock sold for $32.13 yesterday. Today, it is selling for $30.08. What is the approximate percent decline in the stock price?
 A. 5% **B.** 6% **C.** 7% **D.** 8%

45. What is the percent of change from 148 to 37?
 F. 3% **G.** 25% **H.** 75% **I.** 111%

Extended Response

46. 200 is decreased by 5%. The result is increased by 5%. What is the final result? Explain why the result is less than 200. Show your work.

Mixed Review

Lesson 6-7  **47. Astronomy** The Space Surveillance Center in Colorado tracks about 8,500 objects in orbit around Earth. All but about 500 objects are junk from past space missions. What percent are junk? Round to the nearest percent.

Lesson 5-3 **Find each sum or difference.**
 48. $5\frac{3}{4} - 2\frac{5}{8}$ **49.** $-4\frac{1}{3} + 2\frac{1}{2}$ **50.** $-6\frac{1}{3} - 6\frac{1}{3}$

Lesson 4-2 **Evaluate each expression.**
 51. $3x^2$ for $x = -5$ **52.** $[(3 + 12)4]^2$ **53.** $(7 + 4y)^2$ for $y = -2$

Markup and Discount

OBJECTIVE

1 Finding Markups

To make a profit, stores charge more for merchandise than they pay for it. The amount of increase is called the **markup.** The percent of increase is the *percent of markup*.

1 EXAMPLE Real-World Problem Solving

Music Sales A music store's percent of markup is 67%. A CD costs the store $10.15. Find the markup.

markup = percent of markup · store's cost

= 0.67 · 10.15

≈ 6.80   **Simplify. Round to the nearest cent.**

● The markup is $6.80.

✔ Check Understanding Example 1

1. A clothing store pays $56 for a jacket. The store's percent of markup is 75%. Find the markup for the jacket.

The store's cost plus the markup equals the *selling price*.

2 EXAMPLE Real-World Problem Solving

Retailing A computer store pays $6 for a computer mouse. The percent of markup is 75%. Find the mouse's selling price.

0.75 · 6 = 4.50   **Multiply to find the markup.**

6.00 + 4.50 = 10.50   **Cost + markup = selling price.**

● The selling price is $10.50.

✔ Check Understanding Example 2

2. A $5 cap has a 70% markup. Find the selling price.

OBJECTIVE

2 Finding Discounts

When an item goes on sale, the amount of the price decrease is the **discount.** The percent of decrease is the *percent of discount*.

Sale price = regular price − discount.

What You'll Learn

OBJECTIVE 1 To find markups

OBJECTIVE 2 To find discounts

. . . And Why

To solve real-world problems involving price markups and discounts

✔ Check Skills You'll Need

Write an equation and solve. Round to hundredths as needed.

1. What is 75% of $82?

2. What is 42% of $170?

3. What is 5.5% of $24?

4. What is 80% of $15.99?

❓ For help, go to Lesson 6-7.

New Vocabulary

- markup
- discount

📲 **iTEXT** Interactive lesson includes instant self-check, tutorials, and activities.

3 EXAMPLE **Finding Discount**

Reading Math

20% *off* means a discount of 20%.

Recreation Athletic shoes that regularly sell for $85.99 are on sale for 20% off. Find the discount.

$$\text{discount} = \text{percent of discount} \cdot \text{regular price}$$
$$= 0.20 \cdot 85.99$$
$$\approx 17.20 \qquad \textbf{Simplify. Round to the nearest cent.}$$

The discount is $17.20.

✓ **Check Understanding** Example 3

3. Pants priced at $21.99 are marked 15% off. Find the discount.

Here are two ways to use percent of discount to find a sale price.

More Than One Way

A video game that regularly sells for $39.95 is on sale for 20% off. What is the sale price?

Eric's Method

Find the discount. Then find the sale price.

$$\text{discount} = \text{percent of discount} \cdot \text{regular price}$$
$$= 0.20 \cdot 39.95$$
$$= 7.99$$
$$\text{sale price} = \text{regular price} - \text{discount}$$
$$= 39.95 - 7.99$$
$$= 31.96$$

The sale price is $31.96.

Michelle's Method

Find the sale price directly. The sale price equals 100% of the regular price minus 20% of the regular price.

$$\text{sale price} = (100\% - 20\%) \cdot \text{regular price}$$
$$= 80\% \cdot \text{regular price}$$
$$= 0.80(39.95)$$
$$= 31.96$$

The sale price is $31.96.

Choose a Method

1. Which method do you prefer? Explain.

2. Find the sale price if the percent of discount is 25%. Round to the nearest cent.

You can use the **TABLE** feature of a graphing calculator to show values that result from repeated operations.

EXAMPLE

The population of a town increases at the rate of 0.5% each year. Today the town's population is about 5,000. About what will the population be next year? in 5 years?

TABLE lets you show the first two columns of the following table for population $P = 5,000$. In the table, note that after each year, the population is 1.005 times the population at the start of the year.

Year	Population Start of Year	Population End of Year
0	P	$P(1.005)$
1	$P(1.005)$	$P(1.005)^2$
2	$P(1.005)^2$	$P(1.005)^3$
3	$P(1.005)^3$	$P(1.005)^4$
4	$P(1.005)^4$	$P(1.005)^5$
⋮	⋮	⋮

Press **Y=** . Enter $Y_1 = 5000(1.005)$^X.

In **TBLSET,** set TblStart $= 0$ and ΔTbl $= 1$.

Press **TABLE,** to view the first two columns of the table.

X	Y1	
0	5000	
1	5025	
2	5050.1	
3	5075.4	
4	5100.8	
5	5126.3	
6	5151.9	

X = 5

The table shows that after 1 year, the population will be 5,025. After 5 years, the population will be 5,126.

You can use a table like the one above as you work the Lesson 6-10 Example. Be sure to compare your table with the table on page 335.

EXERCISES

1. Find the population of the town above after 10 years.

2. In what year will the population exceed 5,500?

3. Suppose the growth rate of the town is 0.6%. What will its population be at the end of 1 year? 5 years? 10 years? In what year will its population exceed 5,500?

4. A nearby town has population 6,000 and a growth rate of 0.5%. What will its population be at the ends of 1, 5, and 10 years?

6-10 Problem Solving

Make a Table

What You'll Learn

OBJECTIVE 1 To solve problems by making a table

...And Why

To solve real-world problems involving population estimates

✔ Check Skills You'll Need

Solve.

1. For two weeks, you double the amount of money you save each day. You save $.01 the first day. How much money will you have at the end of the two weeks?

? For help, go to Lesson 1-8.

OBJECTIVE 1 Make a Table

Math Strategies in Action
Have you ever watched a baseball game at a field that doesn't have a scoreboard? It's hard to keep track of the score!

A scoreboard is a type of table. You can use tables to organize information. Tables are particularly helpful in solving problems that require several steps.

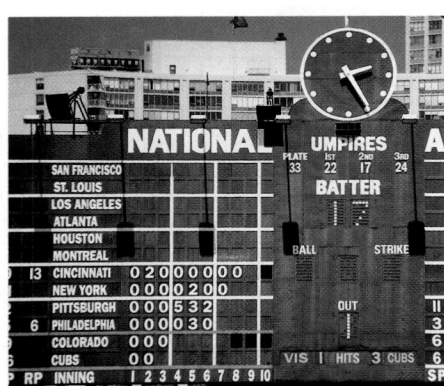

1 EXAMPLE   Real-World 🌐 Problem Solving

Population Growth At the beginning of the year 2000, the population of the United States was about 273.5 million. The rate of population growth was about 0.85% per year. If that rate continues, what will the population be at the beginning of 2010?

Read and Understand

Read the problem carefully.

1. What information are you asked to find?

2. What information will you need to use to solve the problem?

Plan and Solve

Decide on a strategy. You can use the percent of increase to predict the population increase for each year from 2000 to 2010. You can make a table to organize your predictions for each year.

3. How can you find the increase in population from the beginning of 2000 to the end of that year?

4. How can you find the population at the beginning of 2001?

5. The percent of increase is the same each year. Does that mean that the increase in population also will be the same each year? Explain your reasoning.

Copy and complete the table below.

6. Find the numbers for Column 4 by multiplying the numbers in Columns 2 and 3. Round to the nearest tenth of a million.

7. Find the numbers for Column 5 (and, hence, the next Column 2 entries) by adding the numbers in Columns 2 and 4.

1	2	3	4	5
Year	Population at Beginning of Year (millions)	Rate of Increase (0.85%)	Increase in Population (millions)	Population at End of Year (millions)
2000	273.5	0.0085	2.3	275.8
2001	275.8	0.0085	2.3	278.1
2002	278.1	0.0085	2.4	280.5
2003	280.5	0.0085	2.4	282.9
2004	282.9	0.0085	2.4	285.3
2005	285.3	0.0085	2.4	287.7
2006	287.7	0.0085	2.4	290.1
2007	290.1	0.0085	■	■
2008	■	0.0085	■	■
2009	■	0.0085	■	■
2010	■			

8. Sometimes the number in Column 4 changes from one year to the next, and sometimes it does not change. Explain.

9. What is your prediction for population at the beginning of 2010?

Look Back and Check

10. Your friend says that she knows a quicker way to find the answer. Simply multiply 273.5 · 0.0085 · 10 to find the increase for the ten-year period 2000 to 2010. Do you agree with your friend's approach? Explain your reasoning.

✔ Check Understanding

11. Suppose the annual percent of increase in population is 0.9%. At that rate, what will the population be at the beginning of 2010?

Practice and Problem Solving

 **Practice by Example**

Example 1
(page 334)

Make a table to solve each problem.

 1. Population The population of a town increases at the rate of 1% each year. Today the town's population is 8,500. What will the population be in five years?

2. Biology A microbe population increases 100% every 10 min. If you start with 1 microbe, how many will you have at the end of 1 h?

3. Cher has forgotten the combination to her locker. She knows it consists of four numbers—3, 5, 7, and 9—but she can't recall the order. She decides to try every possible order until she gets the right one. How many possible orders are there?

4. Banking At the beginning of the year 2000, Bob put $100 in a savings account. The bank pays Bob 5% interest on his total savings at the end of each year including all interest added to the account. Assume the interest rate continues and Bob does not deposit any additional money in the account. How much will he have in his savings account, to the nearest cent, after 5 interest payments?

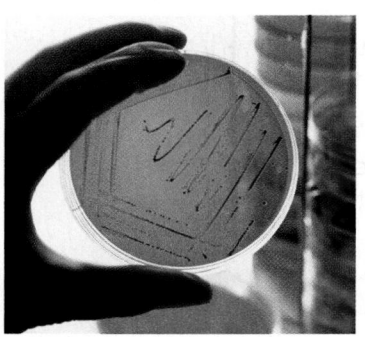

Real-World Connection

Microbe cultures grow on agar gel in petri dishes.

 **Apply Your Skills**

Use any strategy to solve each problem.

5. Paco has four pairs of jeans and four T-shirts. How many outfits of a T-shirt and a pair of jeans can Paco make?

6. Geometry The length of a rectangle is twice the width. The perimeter of the rectangle is 42 cm. Find the length and width.

7. Number Sense The difference of two numbers is 18. The sum of the two numbers is 34. What are the two numbers?

8. Capacity You fill a container $\frac{3}{4}$ full of water. The amount of water now in the container is 6 quarts. How much can the container hold?

9. Ticket Sales A family went to the movies. Tickets cost $4 for each child and $6 for each adult. The total admission charge for the family was $26. List all the possible numbers of adults and children in the family.

10. Number Sense A number n is multiplied by $\frac{5}{8}$. The product is subtracted from $\frac{2}{3}$. The result is $\frac{7}{12}$. What is n?

11. Geometry The height of a triangle is half the length of its base. The area of the triangle is 12.25 cm². Find the height.

12. Water Resources Water for irrigation is measured in *acre-feet*. One acre-foot is the volume of water that would cover one acre of land to a depth of one foot. How many acre-feet of water would it take to cover 600 acres to a depth of one inch?

Strategies

- Account for All Possibilities
- Draw a Diagram
- Look for a Pattern
- Make a Model
- Make a Table
- Simplify the Problem
- Simulate the Problem
- Solve by Graphing
- Try, Test, Revise
- Use Multiple Strategies
- Work Backward
- Write an Equation
- Write a Proportion

Challenge

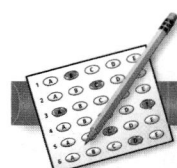

Multiple Choice

13. What is the percent of increase from 1.32 to 1.44, rounded to the nearest percent?

   A. 8%   **B.** 9%   **C.** 12%   **D.** 15%

Take It to the NET
Online lesson quiz at
www.PHSchool.com
Web Code: ada-0610

14. A store pays $50.00 for a coat. Its markup is 25%. Later, it puts the coat on sale at 20% off. What is the sale price of the coat?

   F. $40.00   **G.** $50.00   **H.** $52.50   **I.** $62.50

15. The width of a rectangle is half the length. The perimeter of the rectangle is 54 in. What is the length of the rectangle?

   A. 6 in.   **B.** 9 in.   **C.** 18 in.   **D.** 36 in.

Short Response

16. You must give a customer $.40 in change.

   a. In how many ways can you do this without using pennies?

   b. For part (a), make a table.

Mixed Review

Lesson 6-9   **Find each sale price.**

17. regular price: $39   **18.** regular price: $159.95
     percent of discount: 30%   percent of discount: 20%

Lesson 6-4   **19. Probability** What is the probability that a digit selected at random from the number 364,892 is a multiple of 3?

Lesson 4-4   **Write in simplest form.**

20. $\frac{16}{36}$ **21.** $\frac{10x}{65x}$ **22.** $\frac{8ab}{2bc}$ **23.** $\frac{12x^2y}{9xy^2}$

Math at Work

Caterer

Caterers provide food for parties, weddings, and other events. They plan the menu, buy the ingredients, cook the food, and provide the waitstaff. Some will even arrange for music and seating. For each event, a caterer determines the cost per guest.

The catering business requires a thorough knowledge of ratios, proportions, and percents.

Take It to the NET   For more information about caterers, go to **www.PHSchool.com**.
Web Code: adb-2031

Estimation may help you find an answer, check an answer, or eliminate answer choices. If, however, an incorrect choice is very close to the correct choice, you will still have to find the exact answer.

EXAMPLE

A coat regularly priced at $89.95 is on sale at 40% off. What is the sale price of the coat?

A. $35.98   **B.** $49.95   **C.** $53.97   **D.** $54.03

$89.95 \approx \$90$

40% is less than half. The discount will be less than $45, which is half of $90. So, the sale price will be more than $45.

This eliminates choice A.

$$40\% \text{ of } 90 = 0.4 \cdot 90$$
$$= 36$$

$90 - 36 = 54$, so the sale price is about $54. This eliminates choice B.

Choices C and D are both very close to $54, so you have to compute to find the answer is choice C.

EXERCISES

In Exercises 1–3, which answer choices can you eliminate by using estimation? Explain.

1. A store pays $8.50 for a case of scented candles. The store's percent of markup is 110%. What price will the store charge for the case of candles?
   A. $9.35   **B.** $16.15   **C.** $17.85   **D.** $18.15

2. A store is having a sale. Laverne looks at a $79.80 necklace that is on sale for $59.85. What is the percent of discount?
   F. 20%   **G.** 25%   **H.** $33\frac{1}{3}\%$ **I.** 40%

3. An entomologist noted that in the past five years in the local forest preserve, the population of bees decreased by 35%. In her study, she recorded that the number of active hives five years ago was 35. If the number of active hives decreased at the same rate as the bee population, how many hives are there today?
   A. 17 hives   **B.** 19 hives   **C.** 21 hives   **D.** 23 hives

4. For Exercise 3, explain how you can use estimation in two different ways to help you with the answer choices.

Chapter Review

Vocabulary

certain event (p. 306)
commission (p. 321)
complement (p. 306)
cross products (p. 294)
discount (p. 329)
event (p. 305)
impossible event (p. 306)

indirect measurement (p. 300)
markup (p. 329)
odds (p. 307)
outcomes (p. 305)
percent (p. 310)
percent of change (p. 325)
probability (p. 305)

proportion (p. 294)
rate (p. 289)
ratio (p. 288)
scale drawing (p. 300)
similar figures (p. 299)
unit rate (p. 289)

Reading Math
Understanding
Vocabulary

Match the vocabulary terms with their descriptions.

1. a comparison of two quantities by division

2. a ratio that compares a number to 100

3. the amount charged for an item above the cost

4. the amount of a price decrease

5. a ratio that compares quantities in different units

6. a rate that has a denominator of 1

7. two equal ratios

a. markup
b. percent
c. ratio
d. discount
e. unit rate
f. proportion
g. rate

Take It to the NET
Online vocabulary quiz
at **www.PHSchool.com**
Web Code: adj-0651

Skills and Concepts

6-1 Objectives

▼ To write and simplify ratios (p. 288)

▼ To find rates and unit rates (p. 289)

A **ratio** is a comparison of two quantities by division. A **rate** is a ratio that compares quantities in different units. A **unit rate** is a rate that has a denominator of 1.

Write each ratio as a fraction in simplest form.

8. $9 : 24$ **9.** $20 : 35$ **10.** $15 : 20$ **11.** $100 : 130$

Write each ratio as a unit rate.

12. 150 mi in 3 h   **13.** \$9.45 for 5 lb   **14.** 270 words in 3 min

6-2 Objectives

▼ To solve proportions (p. 294)

▼ To use proportions to solve problems (p. 295)

A **proportion** is an equality of ratios. To solve a proportion, write the cross products, and then solve.

Solve. Round to the nearest tenth where necessary.

15. $\dfrac{5}{6} = \dfrac{n}{42}$ **16.** $\dfrac{53}{2} = \dfrac{18}{x}$ **17.** $\dfrac{15}{a} = \dfrac{30}{98}$ **18.** $\dfrac{m}{150} = \dfrac{21}{25}$

6-3 Objectives

▼ To solve problems that involve similar figures (p. 299)

▼ To solve problems that involve scale drawings (p. 300)

Similar figures have the same shape, but not necessarily the same size. In similar figures, the corresponding angles have equal measures and the corresponding sides are proportional.

A **scale drawing** is an enlarged or reduced drawing of an object.

The figures in each pair are similar. Find _x_.

19.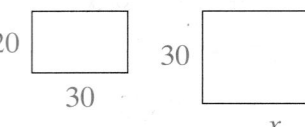

20.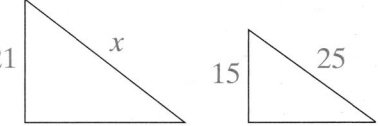

21. A map has a scale of 1 cm : 75 km. What is the distance on the map for an actual distance of 37.5 km?

6-4 Objectives

▼ To find probability (p. 305)

▼ To find odds (p. 307)

Outcomes are the possible results of an action. An **event** is any outcome or group of outcomes. When outcomes are equally likely, you can use formulas to find the **probability** of an event and the **odds** in favor of an event.

$$\text{probability} = \frac{\text{number of favorable outcomes}}{\text{number of possible outcomes}}$$

$$\text{odds} = \frac{\text{number of favorable outcomes}}{\text{number of unfavorable outcomes}}$$

Suppose you select a letter at random from the letters in the word EXPONENT. Find the probability of each event. Then find the odds in favor of the event.

22. selecting P   **23.** selecting N   **24.** selecting a vowel

6-5 Objectives

▼ To write percents as fractions and decimals (p. 310)

▼ To write decimals and fractions as percents (p. 311)

A **percent** is a ratio that compares a number to 100.

Write each percent as a fraction in simplest form and as a decimal.

25. 24%   **26.** 72%   **27.** 8%   **28.** 0.5%

Write each number as a percent. Round to the nearest tenth of a percent.

29. 0.3   **30.** 0.33   **31.** $\frac{1}{3}$ **32.** 0.35

33. $\frac{16}{18}$ **34.** 0.021   **35.** $\frac{120}{50}$ **36.** 0.0064

6-6 and 6-7 Objectives

▼ To find a part of a whole and a percent (p. 315)

▼ To find a whole amount (p. 316)

▼ To write and solve percent equations (p. 320)

▼ To use equations in solving percent problems (p. 321)

Solve percent problems by using a proportion or an equation.

Write and solve a proportion.

37. Find 15% of 48.

38. 20% of x is 30. What is x?

39. What percent of 300 is 90?

40. 125% of y is 100. What is y?

Write and solve an equation.

41. 35% of a is 70. What is a?

42. Find 68% of 300.

43. What percent of 180 is 9?

44. What percent of 56 is 3.5?

6-8 and 6-9 Objectives

▼ To find percent of increase (p. 325)

▼ To find percent of decrease (p. 326)

▼ To find find markups (p. 329)

▼ To find discounts (p. 329)

A **percent of change** is the percent by which a quantity increases or decreases from its original amount.

$$\text{percent of change} = \frac{\text{amount of change}}{\text{original amount}}$$

Markup is a real-world application of percent of increase. **Discount** is a real-world application of percent of decrease.

Find each percent of change. Tell whether the change is an increase or a decrease.

45. 120 to 90

46. 148 to 37

47. 285 to 342

48. 1,000 to 250

49. A cap that cost a retailer $5 was marked up by 75%. Find the selling price.

50. Peaches that are usually priced at $2/lb are on sale for 15% off. Find the sale price.

6-10 Objectives

▼ To solve problems by making a table (p. 334)

Make a table to organize information or to solve problems that have several steps.

51. Alicia bikes 25% of a 100-mi trip on the first day. She bikes $\frac{1}{3}$ of the remaining distance on the second day. On the third day, she bikes 40% of the remaining distance. Make a table to find the number of miles left in Alicia's trip.

52. Describe how you could use a table together with another problem-solving strategy that you have studied. Justify your answer with an example.

Chapter Test

Take It to the NET
Online chapter test at
www.PHSchool.com
Web Code: ada-0652

Find each unit rate.

1. A car travels 84 mi on 3 gal of gas.

2. A car travels 220 mi in 4 h.

Write = or ≠ to complete each statement.

3. $\frac{7}{8} \; \blacksquare \; \frac{40}{42}$

4. $\frac{3}{5} \; \blacksquare \; \frac{45}{75}$

5. $\frac{12}{18} \; \blacksquare \; \frac{18}{12}$

6. $\frac{5}{9} \; \blacksquare \; \frac{25}{81}$

Solve each proportion.

7. $\frac{x}{8} = \frac{90}{120}$

8. $\frac{0.8}{90} = \frac{5.6}{y}$

Write a proportion to describe each situation. Then solve.

9. Three cans of dog food sell for 99¢. Find the cost of 15 cans.

10. A photo that measures 5 in. by 7 in. is enlarged to 7.5 in. by b in.

11. A student reads 45 pages in 2 h and x pages in 3 h.

For Exercises 12–14, use the drawing below. The length of the kitchen in the drawing is $1\frac{1}{4}$ in. The actual length is 20 ft.

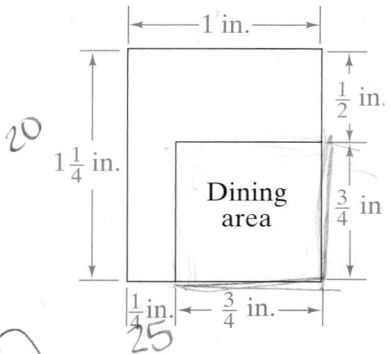

12. What is the scale of the drawing?

13. What is the actual width of the kitchen?

14. What are the actual length and width of the dining area?

Find each probability for one roll of a number cube.

15. $P(1)$

16. $P(1 \text{ or } 2)$

17. $P(\text{not } 2 \text{ or } 6)$

18. $P(\text{greater than } 1)$

Write each decimal as a percent.

19. 0.37

20. 0.005

21. 1.02

Write each fraction as a percent.

22. $\frac{5}{8}$

23. $\frac{7}{16}$

24. $\frac{5}{4}$

Solve.

25. What percent of 400 is 20?

26. Find 45% of 12.

27. 20% of c is 24. What is c?

28. What percent of 3 is 15?

29. Find 125% of 50.

30. 60% of y is 75. What is y?

Find each percent of change. Tell whether the change is an increase or a decrease. Round to the nearest tenth of a percent.

31. from 60 to 36

32. from 18 to 24

33. from 15 to 25

34. from 85 to 50

35. from 8.8 to 30

36. from 1.2 to 0.2

37. A salesperson made a $128 commission selling merchandise. His commission rate was 5%. Find the dollar amount of his sales.

38. A bicycle that usually sells for $230 is on sale for 15% off. Find the sale price.

39. **Writing in Math** Explain the difference between a markup and a discount.

40. In how many ways can you make $.35 in change without using pennies?

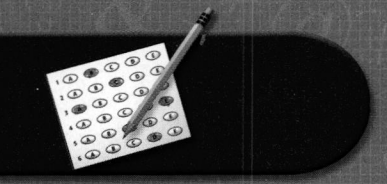

Multiple Choice

1. What is 56,500,000,000 written in scientific notation?
- **A.** $5.65 \cdot 10^8$
- **B.** $56.5 \cdot 10^{10}$
- **C.** $5.65 \cdot 10^{10}$
- **D.** $565 \cdot 10^9$

2. What is x when $\frac{2}{3}x = 2\frac{2}{9}$?
- **F.** $\frac{3}{10}$
- **G.** $2\frac{5}{8}$
- **H.** $3\frac{1}{3}$
- **I.** $7\frac{2}{3}$

3. What is the correct symbol?

$$\left|2\frac{4}{5}\right| \quad \blacksquare \quad \left|-\frac{9}{4}\right|$$

- **A.** $>$
- **B.** $<$
- **C.** $=$
- **D.** $\leq$

4. What is the unit rate for a ball moving 252 ft in 4 s?
- **F.** 252 : 4
- **G.** 63 ft/s
- **H.** 252 ft/s
- **I.** 1,008 ft/s

5. What percent of 63 is 41?
- **A.** about 82%
- **B.** about 65%
- **C.** about 41%
- **D.** about 0.65%

6. Which equation has -4 as a solution?
- **F.** $9z = 36$
- **G.** $-\frac{36}{z} = -9$
- **H.** $z + 9 = 5$
- **I.** $z - 9 = -5$

7. Which has the lowest unit price?
- **A.** 10 oz for $.30
- **B.** $.56 for 20 oz
- **C.** 30 oz for $.87
- **D.** $1.16 for 40 oz

Gridded Response

8. Evaluate $6x - 9$ for $x = 11$.

9. Simplify $(-1)^8 \cdot (-2)^0$.

10. Solve $y + 0.5 = 3$.

11. Find 40% of 40.

Write each fraction as a decimal.

12. $\frac{42}{50}$

13. $\frac{16}{20}$

14. $\frac{33}{55}$

15. $\frac{6}{80}$

16. $\frac{524}{200}$

17. $\frac{45}{1,000}$

Find each probability for one roll of a number cube.

18. $P(5 \text{ or } 6)$

19. $P(\text{less than } 4)$

The scale on a map is 1 in. = 5 mi. Find the actual distance in miles for each map distance.

20. 5.5 in.

21. 12 in.

22. 9.75 in.

Solve each proportion.

23. $\frac{5}{8} = \frac{15}{n}$

24. $\frac{28}{x} = \frac{14}{2.5}$

25. $\frac{n}{9} = \frac{40}{12}$

26. $\frac{6}{21} = \frac{s}{70}$

Write each ratio as a fraction in simplest form.

27. 20 : 45

28. 8 : 96

29. 30 : 36

30. 120 : 80

Short Response

31. For the similar figures, **(a)** write a proportion to solve for x. **(b)** Find x.

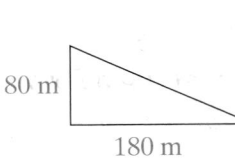 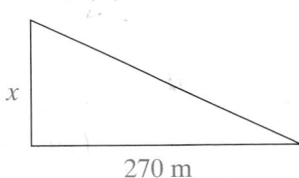

80 m   180 m x 270 m

In Exercises 32 and 33, **(a)** find the sale price. Round to the nearest cent where necessary. **(b)** Explain your answer.

32. regular price: $58
percent of discount: 45%

33. regular price: $15.98
percent of discount: 80%

Extended Response

34. Which is the better buy: **(a)** Brand A with a regular price of $15.98 and a 30% discount, or Brand B with a regular price of $18.50 and a 40% discount? **(b)** How much do you save with the better buy? **(c)** Show your work.

Calculating Change

Applying Percents When you buy a company's stock, you buy a small piece of the company. The amount you have to pay for a stock varies from day to day or even minute to minute. You can make money by selling the stock for more than you paid for it. You can lose money by selling it for less than you paid for it.

Wall Street

Since 1870, when continuous stock trading began at the New York Stock Exchange, the ringing of a bell signals the beginning (9:30 A.M. EST) and ending (4:00 P.M. EST) of trading each day.

Activity

1. Copy the table. Add another column for the percent of change in price from Monday to Friday. Indicate whether the percent of change is an increase or a decrease.

2. Suppose you and a friend buy stock on Monday and sell it on Friday. You buy 50 shares of Pat's Pastas and 25 shares of Leaping Lizards. Your friend buys 35 shares of Map Makers Plus and 25 shares of Wondermarts. Who made the better investment, you or your friend? Justify your answer.

3. Suppose you had $500 to invest on Monday.
   a. Which stock(s) would you buy on Monday, and how many shares of the stock(s) would you buy? Explain.
   b. You sell all your shares on Friday. How much money did you make?

4. a. **Research** Find the price of a stock in the newspaper or online. Find the price at least one day later.
   b. **Writing in Math** Would you invest in the company? Explain.

Seven Stocks

Company	Price per Share on Monday	Price per Share on Friday
All-Star Adventures	$6.25	$5.75
Fun Foods, Inc.	$28.00	$26.60
Leaping Lizards	$19.50	$23.40
Map Makers Plus	$13.00	$14.95
Nature's Nest	$3.80	$4.20
Pat's Pastas	$5.65	$4.45
Wondermarts	$34.00	$32.75

POS is the name of the stock.

3s means 300 shares sold.

$19.14 is the last traded price of the stock.

Stock Trader

A stock trader places orders or buys and sells securities or commodities. A successful trader is very interested in numbers and in investing and understands economic trends.

Stock Certificates

Most securities transactions today are done without stock certificates, although some people like to have the actual certificate in their possession.

Stock Market Floor

Runners at the Chicago Mercantile Exchange wear yellow jackets for visibility. They take orders to buy and sell stocks into and out of the trading areas.

Take It to the NET For more information about the stock market, go to **www.PHSchool.com**.
Web Code: ade-0653

Where You've Been

● In Chapter 2, you learned how to simplify variable expressions and to solve one-step equations and inequalities by adding, subtracting, multiplying, or dividing.

● In Chapter 3, you learned how to solve equations by adding, subtracting, multiplying, or dividing decimals.

● In Chapter 5, you learned how to solve equations by adding, subtracting, or multiplying fractions.

Diagnosing Readiness

i TEXT Instant self-check online and on CD-ROM

(For help, go to the lesson in green.)

Writing Variable Expressions (Lesson 1-1)

Write a variable expression for each situation.

1. three more than p points **2.** six fewer than q questions

3. the number of months in y years **4.** the value in cents of d dimes

5. twice as many as b baskets **6.** eight fewer than n nickels

Simplifying Expressions (Lesson 2-3)

Simplify each expression.

7. $3n + n$ **8.** $5b + 10 - 8b$ **9.** $12c + 9 + 7c + 4$

10. $3x + 2y - 7y - 10x$ **11.** $2(a + 3)$ **12.** $5(m - 7) + 4m$

Solving Equations (Lessons 2-5, 2-6)

Solve each equation.

13. $a - 3 = 8$ **14.** $-9 = 12 + x$ **15.** $\frac{m}{7} = -14$ **16.** $-10 = -2b$

17. $y \div 2 = 4$ **18.** $6.8 = c - 2.2$ **19.** $\frac{x}{-4} = 8$ **20.** $-40 = 5a$

Solving Inequalities (Lessons 2-9, 2-10)

Solve and graph each inequality.

21. $c + 6 \geq 7$ **22.** $y - 8 < -6$ **23.** $5b < 20$ **24.** $-3x < 0$

25. $12 \leq x + 18$ **26.** $-\frac{x}{3} \geq -5$ **27.** $b - 15 \leq 4$ **28.** $\frac{m}{4} \geq 20$

Solving Equations and Inequalities

Key Vocabulary

- balance (p. 383)
- compound inequality (p. 377)
- compound interest (p. 383)
- consecutive integers (p. 353)
- interest (p. 382)
- interest rate (p. 382)
- principal (p. 382)
- simple interest (p. 382)

Where You're Going

In this chapter, you will learn how to

- Write and solve multi-step equations.
- Write and solve two-step inequalities.
- Find simple interest and compound interest.
- Solve problems by writing equations.

Real-World Snapshots Applying what you learn, on pages 394–395 you will solve problems about cellular telephones.

Solving Two-Step Equations

What You'll Learn

OBJECTIVE
1 To solve two-step equations

OBJECTIVE
2 To use two-step equations to solve problems

. . . And Why

To solve problems involving savings

 Check Skills You'll Need

Solve each equation.

1. $9 + k = 17$

2. $d - 10 = 1$

3. $y - 5 = -4$

4. $x + 16 = 4$

5. $b + 6 = -4$

For help, go to Lesson 2-5.

Algebra tiles can help you understand the algebra behind solving the equation $2x + 1 = 5$.

$$2x + 1 = 5$$

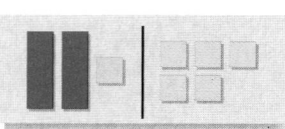

Model the equation.

$$2x + 1 - 1 = 5 - 1$$
$$2x = 4$$

Remove 1 tile from each side.

$$\frac{2x}{2} = \frac{4}{2}$$

Divide each side into two equal groups.

$$x = 2$$

Simplify.

To solve a two-step equation, first undo addition or subtraction. Then undo multiplication or division.

1 EXAMPLE Undoing an Operation

Solve $3n - 6 = 15$.

$$3n - 6 = 15$$
$$3n - 6 + 6 = 15 + 6 \qquad \text{Add 6 to each side.}$$
$$3n = 21 \qquad \text{Simplify.}$$
$$\frac{3n}{3} = \frac{21}{3} \qquad \text{Divide each side by 3.}$$
$$n = 7 \qquad \text{Simplify.}$$

Check

$$3n - 6 = 15$$
$$3(7) - 6 \stackrel{?}{=} 15 \qquad \text{Replace } n \text{ with 7.}$$
$$21 - 6 \stackrel{?}{=} 15 \qquad \text{Multiply.}$$
$$15 = 15 \checkmark \qquad \text{Simplify.}$$

TEXT Interactive lesson includes instant self-check, tutorials, and activities.

✓ Check Understanding   Example 1

1. Solve each equation.

    a. $15x + 3 = 48$　　　　　**b.** $\frac{t}{4} - 10 = -6$

    c. $\frac{b}{3} + 13 = 11$　　　　　**d.** $9g + 11 = 2$

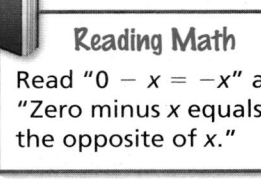

2 EXAMPLE   Negative Coefficients

Solve $5 - x = 17$.

$$5 - x = 17$$
$$-5 + 5 - x = -5 + 17 \qquad \text{Add } -5 \text{ to each side.}$$
$$0 - x = 12 \qquad \text{Simplify.}$$
$$-x = 12 \qquad 0 - x = -x$$
$$-1(-x) = -1(12) \qquad \text{Multiply each side by } -1.$$
$$x = -12 \qquad \text{Simplify.}$$

> **Reading Math**
> Read "$0 - x = -x$" as
> "Zero minus x equals
> the opposite of x."

✓ Check Understanding   Example 2

2. Solve each equation.

    a. $-a + 6 = 8$　　　**b.** $-9 - \frac{y}{7} = -12$　　**c.** $13 - 6f = 31$

OBJECTIVE

2   Solving Problems With Two-Step Equations

You can use two-step equations to model real-world situations.

3 EXAMPLE   Real-World 🌎 Problem Solving

Travel Planning Lynne wants to save \$900 to go to Puerto Rico.
She saves \$45 each week and now has \$180. To find how many
more weeks w it will take to have \$900, solve $180 + 45w = 900$.

$$180 + 45w = 900$$
$$180 + 45w - 180 = 900 - 180 \qquad \text{Subtract 180 from each side.}$$
$$45w = 720 \qquad \text{Simplify.}$$
$$\frac{45w}{45} = \frac{720}{45} \qquad \text{Divide each side by 45.}$$
$$w = 16 \qquad \text{Simplify.}$$

It will take Lynne 16 more weeks to have \$900.

Real-World 🌎 Connection

If you fly to San Juan, Puerto
Rico, it could cost you \$186
to leave from New York, New
York, \$590 to leave from
San Francisco, California,
\$914 to leave from Reno,
Nevada, or \$1,392 to leave
from Dallas, Texas.

✓ Check Understanding   Example 3

3. Jacob bought four begonias in 6-in. pots and a \$19 fern at a
fundraiser. He spent a total of \$63. Solve the equation
$4p + 19 = 63$ to find the price p of each begonia.

EXERCISES

❓ For more exercises, see *Extra Practice*.

Practice and Problem Solving

Ⓐ Practice by Example

Example 1
(page 348)

State the first step in solving each equation.

1. $2b + 9 = 3$ **2.** $\frac{a}{3} - 4 = 9$ **3.** $4b - 6 = -18$

Solve each equation.

4. $2d - 8 = -10$ **5.** $9x - 15 = 39$ **6.** $\frac{x}{3} + 2 = 0$

Example 2
(page 349)

7. $12 - 11a = 45$ **8.** $-8c + 1 = -3$ **9.** $5 = -\frac{x}{3} + 10$

10. $18 = -a + 2$ **11.** $4 - \frac{m}{5} = 18$ **12.** $-75 - k = -95$

Example 3 🌐 **13. Finance** Jose bought a new computer that cost $1,200. He paid
(page 349) $400 down and will pay $50 per week until the balance is paid
off. Solve the equation $400 + 50w = 1,200$ to find the number
of weeks it will take Jose to pay off the computer.

14. Thomas, Ardell, and Nichole baked muffins, which they shared
equally. Nichole ate a muffin on the way home. She then had
14 muffins left. Solve the equation $\frac{m}{3} - 1 = 14$ to find the number
of muffins m that Thomas, Ardell, and Nichole baked.

Ⓑ Apply Your Skills

Solve and check each equation.

15. $15 = -11b + 4$ **16.** $-35 = 4h + 1$ **17.** $10 = 3 + \frac{b}{2}$

18. $12y - 6 = 138$ **19.** $2x + 3 = 15$ **20.** $-6t + (-4) = 14$

21. You bought a CD for $16.95 and eight blank videotapes.
The total cost was $52.55 before the sales tax was added.
Solve the equation $8t + 16.95 = 52.55$ to find the cost of
each blank videotape.

🌐 **22. Savings** You had $235 in your savings account nine weeks ago.
You withdrew the same amount each week for eight weeks. Your
balance was then $75. Solve the equation $235 - 8m = 75$ to
find how much money m you withdrew each week.

Mental Math Solve each equation.

23. $\frac{n}{6} + 2 = -8$ **24.** $4a - 1 = 27$ **25.** $\frac{k}{5} + 3 = 6$

🌐 **26. Construction** A building contractor buys 525 metal bars. Because
he is buying more than 500 bars, the wholesaler gives him a
discount of $420. The total price is $3,780. Solve the equation
$525b - 420 = 3,780$ to find the cost of each metal bar.

27. Carmela wants to buy a digital camera for $249. She has $24 and
is saving $15 each week. Solve the equation $15w + 24 = 249$
to find how many weeks w it will take Carmela to save enough to
buy the digital camera.

28. Error Analysis A student solved the
equation $\frac{x}{4} + 5 = 1$ without showing all the
work. The student's solution is incorrect.
What error did the student make?

29. Writing in Math Explain how the processes
of solving $\frac{x}{4} - 2 = 8$ and $\frac{x}{4} = 8$ are different.

$$\frac{x}{4} + 5 = 1$$
$$\frac{x}{4} = -4$$
$$x = -1$$

Solve and check each equation.

30. $1.5x + 1.2 = 5.7$

31. $-1.7 = 2.2b - 6.1$

32. $3c - 3.2 = 4.6$

33. $\frac{y}{4} + 4.7 = 8.2$

 Challenge 🌐 **34. Nutrition** A soccer player wants to eat no more than 700 calories
at a meal that includes a Reuben sandwich and pickles. The
sandwich has 464 calories, and the pickles have 7 calories each.
  a. Solve the equation $464 + 7f = 700$ to find the number of
  pickles the soccer player can eat.
  b. Suppose the soccer player drinks a 200-calorie sports drink
  with the meal. Solve the equation $664 + 7f = 700$ to find the
  number of pickles the soccer player can eat now.

Test Prep

Multiple Choice

35. What is the solution of $\frac{x}{6} - 8 = 7$?
  A. -6 **B.** 6 **C.** 15 **D.** 90

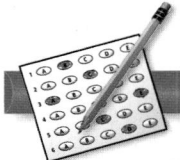

Take It to the NET
Online lesson quiz at
www.PHSchool.com
Web Code: ada-0701

36. What is the solution of $-11 = 4h - 3$?
  F. -5 **G.** -2 **H.** -1.25 **I.** 1

37. Which is the best estimate for the solution of $29x + 59.2 = 239$?
  A. 4 **B.** 5 **C.** 6 **D.** 7

Short Response

38. At a carnival, Bret buys game tokens for $.25 each. He spends
$7.50 for food and $14 in all. How many tokens did he buy?
  a. Write an equation to model this situation.
  b. Solve your equation and answer the question.

Mixed Review

Lesson 6-9   **Find each percent of markup.**

39. wholesale price: $34
selling price: $42.50

40. wholesale price: $45.95
selling price: $82.71

Lesson 6-4   **41. Probability** A student is chosen at random from a class of 20 boys
and 15 girls. Find the odds that a girl is chosen.

Lesson 2-3   **Simplify each expression.**

42. $a + 3b + 9a$

43. $2(c + 4) - 5c$

7-2 Solving Multi-Step Equations

What You'll Learn

OBJECTIVE 1 To combine like terms to simplify an equation

OBJECTIVE 2 To use the Distributive Property to simplify an equation

. . . And Why

To solve problems involving consecutive integers

 Check Skills You'll Need

Simplify each expression.

1. $2x + 4 + 3x$

2. $5y + y$

3. $8a - 5a$

4. $2 - 4c + 5c$

5. $4x + 3 - 2(5 + x)$

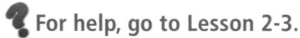 For help, go to Lesson 2-3.

New Vocabulary

• consecutive integers

OBJECTIVE

1 **Combining Like Terms**

 **Investigation**

Simplifying Equations

The tiles below model the equation $2x + 7 + x = 16$

1. How does this equation differ from others you have seen?

2. **a.** Group the tiles so that all the x tiles are together. This is the same as combining like terms. Write an equation to represent the tiles once the x tiles are grouped together.
   b. Solve your equation. Check your solution.

Combine like terms to simplify an equation before you solve it.

1 EXAMPLE **Real-World** **Problem Solving**

Model Airplanes Jake and Suki collect model airplanes. Suki has four fewer than twice as many model airplanes as Jake. Together they have 14 models. Solve the equation $m + 2m - 4 = 14$. Find the number of models each person has.

$$m + 2m - 4 = 14$$
$$3m - 4 = 14 \qquad \text{Combine like terms.}$$
$$3m - 4 + 4 = 14 + 4 \qquad \text{Add 4 to each side.}$$
$$3m = 18 \qquad \text{Simplify.}$$
$$\frac{3m}{3} = \frac{18}{3} \qquad \text{Divide each side by 3.}$$
$$m = 6 \qquad \text{Simplify.}$$

Jake has 6 models. Suki has $2(6) - 4 = 8$ models.

Check Is the solution reasonable? Jake and Suki have a total of 14 models. Since $6 + 8 = 14$, the solution is reasonable.

TEXT Interactive lesson includes instant self-check, tutorials, and activities.

✓ Check Understanding   Example 1

1. **Basketball Scores** One basketball team defeated another by 13 points. The total number of points scored by both teams was 171. Solve the equation $p + p - 13 = 171$ to find the number of points p scored by the winning team.

When you count by 1s from any integer, you are counting **consecutive integers.**

Reading Math
The definition of *consecutive* is "following one another in uninterrupted intervals."

two consecutive integers   three consecutive integers

120, 121 $-5, -4, -3$

2 EXAMPLE   Finding Consecutive Integers

Number Sense **The sum of three consecutive integers is 96. Find the integers.**

Words   sum of three consecutive integers   is   96

Let n = the least integer.
Then $n + 1$ = the second integer,
and $n + 2$ = the third integer.

Equation $n + n + 1 + n + 2$ =   96

$$n + (n + 1) + (n + 2) = 96$$

$$(n + n + n) + (1 + 2) = 96$$ Use the Commutative and Associative Properties of Addition to group like terms.

$$3n + 3 = 96$$ Combine like terms.

$$3n + 3 - 3 = 96 - 3$$ Subtract 3 from each side.

$$3n = 93$$ Simplify.

$$\frac{3n}{3} = \frac{93}{3}$$ Divide each side by 3.

$$n = 31$$ Simplify.

If $n = 31$, then $n + 1 = 32$, and $n + 2 = 33$.
The three integers are 31, 32, and 33.

• **Check** Is the solution reasonable? Yes, because $31 + 32 + 33 = 96$.

✓ Check Understanding   Example 2

2. **a. Number Sense** Find four consecutive integers with a sum of 358.
   b. For *consecutive even integers,* the first is n, and the second is $n + 2$. Find two consecutive even integers with a sum of 66.

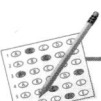
Test-Taking Tip
Always read problems carefully. It is easy to not see words such as *even* in *consecutive even integers* if you are reading too quickly.

2 | Using the Distributive Property

Need Help?

The Distributive Property:

$5(a + 4) = 5a + 20$

$3(6b - 2) = 18b - 6$

Sometimes you may need to use the Distributive Property when you solve a multi-step equation.

3 EXAMPLE | Using the Distributive Property

Solve each equation.

a. $2(5x - 3) = 14$

$2(5x - 3) = 14$	
$10x - 6 = 14$	Use the Distributive Property.
$10x - 6 + 6 = 14 + 6$	Add 6 to each side.
$10x = 20$	Simplify.
$\dfrac{10x}{10} = \dfrac{20}{10}$	Divide each side by 10.
$x = 2$	Simplify.

b. $38 = -3(4y + 2) + y$

$38 = -3(4y + 2) + y$	
$38 = -12y - 6 + y$	Use the Distributive Property.
$38 = -12y + y - 6$	Use the Commutative and Associative Properties of Addition to group like terms.
$38 = -11y - 6$	Combine like terms.
$38 + 6 = -11y - 6 + 6$	Add 6 to each side.
$44 = -11y$	Simplify.
$\dfrac{44}{-11} = \dfrac{-11y}{-11}$	Divide each side by –11.
$-4 = y$	Simplify.

✓ **Check Understanding**   Example 3

3. Solve each equation.

    a. $-3(m - 6) = 4$ **b.** $3(x + 12) - x = 8$

Key Concepts | **Steps for Solving a Multi-Step Equation**

Step 1   Use the Distributive Property, if necessary.

Step 2   Combine like terms.

Step 3   Undo addition or subtraction.

Step 4   Undo multiplication or division.

EXERCISES

 For more exercises, see *Extra Practice*.

Practice and Problem Solving

A Practice by Example

Example 1
(page 352)

Solve each equation.

1. $8a + 4a = 144$ **2.** $9x - 2x = -42$ **3.** $5b + 11 - 2b = 50$

4. $4a + 1 - a = 19$ **5.** $18 = b - 7b$ **6.** $4d + 2d - 3d = 27$

7. Collections Bill and Jasmine together have 94 glass marbles. Bill has 4 more than twice as many marbles as Jasmine. If Jasmine has m marbles, then Bill has $2m + 4$ marbles. Solve the equation $m + 2m + 4 = 94$. Find how many glass marbles each has.

Example 2
(page 353)

Number Sense Find the integers.

8. The sum of two consecutive integers is 131.

9. The sum of three consecutive even integers is 60.

Example 3
(page 354)

Solve each equation.

10. $3(n - 2) = 36$ **11.** $4(y - 1) = 36$

12. $2(8 + n) = 22$ **13.** $-2(a + 3) - a = 0$

14. $3(2x + 1) + x = -39$ **15.** $m + 4(2m - 3) = -3$

B Apply Your Skills

Solve and check each equation.

16. $5x - x = -12$ **17.** $-6 = a + a + 4$

18. $-9 - b + 8b = -23$ **19.** $36 = y - 5y - 12$

20. $-3(2y + 7) = -18$ **21.** $16 = 2(x - 1) - x$

22. $21 = 2(4a + 2)$ **23.** $8 - 3(x - 4) = 4$

Number Sense Find the integers.

24. The sum of four consecutive integers is -22.

25. The sum of five consecutive integers is -65.

26. Error Analysis A student solved the equation $7x - 5 - 5x = 15$ and found $x = 5$. What might be the student's error?

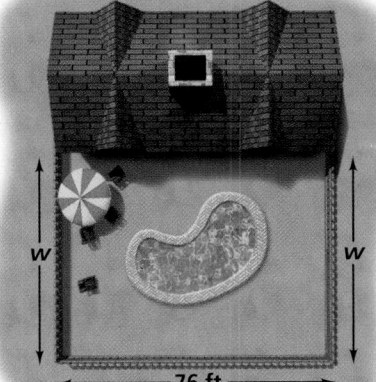

27. Construction A carpenter is building a fence around a swimming pool. One side of the pool is next to the house and does not need fencing. The carpenter has 120 feet of fencing and plans to use it all. Solve the equation $w + 76 + w = 120$ to find the unknown dimension of the enclosed rectangular area.

28. Number Sense Two numbers are w and $3w - 5$. Their sum is 23. Solve the equation $w + 3w - 5 = 23$ to find the numbers.

29. Writing in Math Explain how to solve $3(9 + 4a) - 19 = 32$.

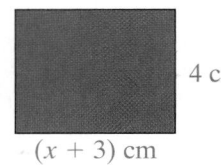

30. Birdhouses Together, Donal, Yolanda, and Iris made 27 birdhouses for a school fair. Yolanda made n birdhouses. Donal made one more birdhouse than Yolanda, and Iris made one more than Donal. Solve the equation $n + (n + 1) + (n + 1 + 1) = 27$. Find the number of birdhouses each one made.

Geometry For each rectangle, the area is 20 cm². Find the value of x.

31.

4 cm

$(x + 3)$ cm

32.

$(2x - 4)$ cm

10 cm

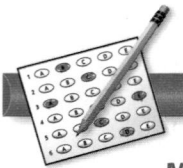 **Challenge** **Solve and check each equation.**

33. $\frac{1}{3}[2(x - 8) + 1] = 19$ **34.** $3 = \frac{1}{4}(m - 4) + \frac{1}{4}m$

Number Sense **Find the integers.**

35. The sum of four consecutive odd integers is -72.

36. The sum of five consecutive even integers is 0.

Test Prep

Multiple Choice

37. $3(2x + 5) = \underline{\ ?\ }$.
  A. $5x + 5$ **B.** $6x + 5$ **C.** $6x + 8$ **D.** $6x + 15$

38. A rectangle has base 5 cm and height $(x + 2)$ cm. Its area is 20 cm². What is the value of x?
  F. 2   **G.** 3.6   **H.** 4.4   **I.** 6

39. What is the solution of $-2(b - 4) = 12$?
  A. -4 **B.** -2 **C.** 2   **D.** 4

Take It to the NET
Online lesson quiz at
www.PHSchool.com
Web Code: ada-0702

Short Response

40. Three consecutive integers have a sum of 63.
  a. Write an equation to model this situation. Then solve.
  b. Show your work for part (a).

Mixed Review

Lesson 7-1 **Solve each equation.**

41. $10a - 32 = -28$ **42.** $5 - 2d = 15$ **43.** $\frac{c}{4} - 7 = 5$

Lesson 5-8 **44.** $\frac{7}{10}a = \frac{3}{5}$ **45.** $\frac{2}{7}x = \frac{5}{8}$ **46.** $-2\frac{3}{4} = 6\frac{3}{5}b$

Lesson 5-5 **47. Measurement** If you take $\frac{2}{3}$ c of flour from a bowl containing $2\frac{1}{2}$ c of flour, how much flour is left in the bowl?

Multi-Step Equations With Fractions and Decimals

OBJECTIVE

1 **Solving Multi-Step Equations With Fractions**

Remember, when the coefficient of a variable in an equation is a fraction, you can use the reciprocal to solve the equation.

$$\frac{4}{5}x = 12$$

$$\frac{5}{4} \cdot \frac{4}{5}x = \frac{5}{4} \cdot 12 \qquad \textbf{Multiply each side by } \frac{5}{4}, \textbf{ because } \frac{5}{4} \cdot \frac{4}{5} = 1.$$

$$x = 15$$

When you have a multi-step equation and the coefficient of the variable is a fraction, gather the variables on one side of the equation and the constants on the other before multiplying by the reciprocal.

1 **EXAMPLE** **Using the Reciprocal**

Solve $\frac{2}{3}n - 6 = 22$.

$$\frac{2}{3}n - 6 = 22$$

$$\frac{2}{3}n - 6 + 6 = 22 + 6 \qquad \textbf{Add 6 to each side.}$$

$$\frac{2}{3}n = 28 \qquad \textbf{Simplify.}$$

$$\frac{3}{2} \cdot \frac{2}{3}n = \frac{3}{2} \cdot 28 \qquad \textbf{Multiply each side by } \frac{3}{2}, \textbf{ the reciprocal of } \frac{2}{3}.$$

$$n = \frac{3 \cdot 28^{14}}{1^{}2} \qquad \textbf{Divide common factors.}$$

$$n = 42 \qquad \textbf{Simplify.}$$

Check $\frac{2}{3}n - 6 = 22$

$$\frac{2}{3}(42) - 6 \stackrel{?}{=} 22 \qquad \textbf{Replace } n \textbf{ with 42.}$$

$$\frac{2 \cdot 42^{14}}{1^{}3} - 6 \stackrel{?}{=} 22 \qquad \textbf{Divide common factors.}$$

$$28 - 6 \stackrel{?}{=} 22 \qquad \textbf{Multiply.}$$

$$22 = 22 \checkmark$$

Check Understanding **Example 1**

1. Solve each equation.

  a. $-\frac{7}{10}k + 14 = -21$ **b.** $\frac{2}{3}(m - 6) = 3$

What You'll Learn

 OBJECTIVE 1 To solve multi-step equations with fractions

 OBJECTIVE 2 To solve multi-step equations with decimals

. . . And Why

To solve problems involving cost of phone service

✓ Check Skills You'll Need

Solve each equation.

1. $2n + 53 = 47$

2. $4m - 37 = -28$

3. $-26x - 4 = 100$

4. $-3a + 15 = 13$

❓ For help, go to Lesson 7-1.

 Need Help?

For more help with fractions and reciprocals, see pages 250, 268, and Skills Handbook page 774.

---

iTEXT Interactive lesson includes instant self-check, tutorials, and activities.

You can use the Multiplication Property of Equality to simplify the solving of an equation involving fractions. Use the LCM of the denominators to clear the equation of fractions.

2 EXAMPLE   Using the LCM

Need Help?

For help with finding the least common multiple (LCM), see Lesson 5-1.

Solve $\frac{2}{5}x + 2 = \frac{3}{4}$.

$$\frac{2}{5}x + 2 = \frac{3}{4}$$

$$20\left(\frac{2}{5}x + 2\right) = 20\left(\frac{3}{4}\right)$$ **Multiply each side by 20, the LCM of 5 and 4.**

$$20 \cdot \frac{2}{5}x + 20 \cdot 2 = 20\left(\frac{3}{4}\right)$$ **Use the Distributive Property.**

$$8x + 40 = 15$$ **Simplify.**

$$8x + 40 - 40 = 15 - 40$$ **Subtract 40 from each side.**

$$8x = -25$$ **Simplify.**

$$\frac{8x}{8} = \frac{-25}{8}$$ **Divide each side by 8.**

$$x = -3\frac{1}{8}$$ **Simplify.**

✓ **Check Understanding**   Example 2

2. Solve each equation.

   a. $-\frac{7}{12} + y = \frac{1}{6}$ b. $\frac{1}{3}b - 1 = \frac{5}{6}$

OBJECTIVE

2 Solving Multi-Step Equations With Decimals

You can use the properties of equality to solve equations with decimals.

3 EXAMPLE   Real-World 🌐 Problem Solving

Cell Phones Suppose your cell phone plan is $20 per month plus $.15 per minute. Your bill is $37.25. Use the equation $20 + 0.15x = 37.25$ to find the number of minutes on your bill.

$$20 + 0.15x = 37.25$$

$$20 - 20 + 0.15x = 37.25 - 20$$ **Subtract 20 from each side.**

$$0.15x = 17.25$$ **Simplify.**

$$\frac{0.15x}{0.15} = \frac{17.25}{0.15}$$ **Divide each side by 0.15.**

$$x = 115$$ **Simplify.**

● There are 115 minutes on your bill.

✓ **Check Understanding**   Example 3

3. Solve each equation.

   a. $1.5x - 3.6 = 2.4$ b. $1.06p - 3 = 0.71$

You can solve multi-step equations containing decimals by calculating with the decimals or by multiplying by a power of 10 to clear the equation of decimals.

More Than One Way

Telephone Services For local telephone service, the McNeils pay $9.95/month plus $.035/min for local calls. Last month, they paid $12.75 for local service. To find the minutes m of local calls, solve the equation $0.035m + 9.95 = 12.75$.

Nicole's Method

I can work with decimals as I have before.

$$0.035m + 9.95 = 12.75$$
$$0.035m + 9.95 - 9.95 = 12.75 - 9.95$$
$$0.035m = 2.8$$
$$\frac{0.035m}{0.035} = \frac{2.8}{0.035}$$
$$m = 80$$

The McNeils made 80 min of local calls.

Daryl's Method

Use multiplication to clear the decimals. Use the decimals with the greatest number of decimal places to decide what power of 10 to use.

$$0.035m + 9.95 = 12.75$$
$$1{,}000(0.035m + 9.95) = 1{,}000(12.75)$$
$$35m + 9{,}950 = 12{,}750$$
$$35m + 9{,}950 - 9{,}950 = 12{,}750 - 9{,}950$$
$$35m = 2{,}800$$
$$\frac{35m}{35} = \frac{2{,}800}{35}$$
$$m = 80$$

The McNeils made 80 min of local calls.

Choose a Method

1. Which method would you use to find the number of minutes? Explain.

2. In Daryl's Method, why was each side of the equation multiplied by 1,000?

 For more exercises, see *Extra Practice*.

Practice and Problem Solving

A Practice by Example

Example 1
(page 357)

State the first step in solving each equation. Do not solve.

1. $\frac{1}{4}x + 3 = 2$ **2.** $-\frac{1}{5}y + 2 = -3$ **3.** $\frac{1}{2}(n - 8) = 6$

Solve each equation.

4. $\frac{5}{8}c - 8 = 12$ **5.** $-8 + \frac{3}{5}g = -2$ **6.** $\frac{3}{4}(b + 8) = 15$

Example 2
(page 358)

Mental Math By what number would you multiply each equation to get an equation without denominators? Do not solve.

7. $\frac{1}{2}h - 1 = \frac{3}{8}$ **8.** $\frac{1}{5}y + 3 = \frac{2}{3}$ **9.** $\frac{7}{10}c - 10 = \frac{2}{5}$

Solve each equation.

10. $\frac{1}{4}c + 2 = \frac{3}{4}$ **11.** $8 - \frac{w}{10} = \frac{3}{5}$ **12.** $\frac{2}{3}(a - 3) = \frac{1}{3}$

Example 3
(page 358)

13. $0.7c - 10 = 0.5$ **14.** $1.2n + 3.4 = 10$

15. $-0.8k - 3.1 = -8.3$ **16.** $0.4b + 9.2 = 10$

17. $0.9x + 2.3x = -6.4$ **18.** $-2d + 4.3 = 10.7$

19. Art Dwayne is taking a drawing class. The drawing pencils cost $.97 apiece and a sketchbook costs $5.95. Dwayne spent a total of $11.77. Solve the equation $0.97n + 5.95 = 11.77$ to find the number n of pencils he bought.

B Apply Your Skills

Solve and check each equation.

20. $\frac{5}{8}(p - 4) = 2$ **21.** $p + \frac{1}{3}p = \frac{2}{3}$ **22.** $0.07x + 9.95 = 12.47$

23. $-\frac{3}{4}y + \frac{1}{4} = \frac{1}{2}$ **24.** $\frac{x}{4} - \frac{3x}{2} = -\frac{1}{2}$ **25.** $2.4b + 5.6 = -11.2$

26. $4x + 2 = -28.4$ **27.** $-\frac{1}{3}(x - 9) = -1$ **28.** $\frac{2}{7}k - \frac{1}{14}k = -3$

29. $0.4(a + 2) = 2$ **30.** $\frac{1}{2}(x - 1) = \frac{1}{2}$ **31.** $1.2c + 2.6c = 4.56$

Real-World Connection

White-water rafting trips can be as short as two hours or as long as several days.

32. White-Water Rafting Six friends hire a raft and guide to go white-water rafting in Colorado. Each person also buys a souvenir photo of the trip for $25.75. The total each person pays is $90.30. To find the cost c of the raft and guide, solve the equation $\frac{c}{6} + 25.75 = 90.30$.

33. Writing in Math At a 15%-off sale, a customer pays $11.01 for a video. Explain how to solve the equation $p - 0.15p = 11.01$ to find the original price p of the video.

34. Sales A pair of athletic shoes is on sale for $\frac{1}{4}$ off the original cost. The sale price is $49.95. Solve the equation $c - \frac{1}{4}c = 49.95$ to find the original cost c of the shoes.

35. Geometry Use the rectangle at the right.
   a. Find the value of x if the area is 15 square units.
   b. Find the value of x if the perimeter is 24 units.

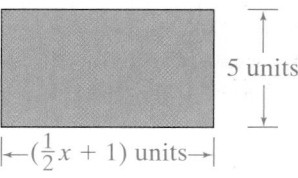

5 units

$\longleftarrow(\frac{1}{2}x + 1)$ units $\longrightarrow$

 **Challenge**   **Solve and check each equation.**

36. $12p + 7 = -15 + 6.5p$ **37.** $5(t - 0.4) = -6t$

38. a. A student has grades of 65, 80, 78, and 92 on four tests. Use s to represent the student's grade on the next test. Write an expression for the average of the five tests.
   b. The student wants to have an average of 80 after the fifth test. Use the expression you wrote in part (a) to write an equation.
   c. Solve the equation to find the grade the student must earn on the fifth test to have an average of 80 for the class.

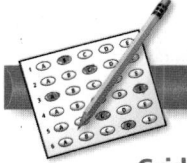

Test Prep

Gridded Response   **39.** What is the solution of $\frac{1}{2}(4a - 16) = 5$?

40. What is the solution of $7.1 = 3.8h + 5.2$?

41. Last season, you scored 48 points in basketball. This is 6 fewer than twice the number of points Gene scored. How many points did Gene score?

42. A cable television company charges $24.95 a month for basic service and $6.95 a month for each premium channel. If your monthly bill is $45.80, how many premium channels are you receiving?

43. A photograph is 4 in. wide and 5 in. long. You want to enlarge it to triple its dimensions. How many times the area of the original will the area of the enlargement be?

Take It to the NET
Online lesson quiz at
www.PHSchool.com
Web Code: ada-0703

Mixed Review

Lesson 7-2   **Solve each equation.**

44. $-9 = 3(y + 4)$ **45.** $x + 7 - 3x = 7$ **46.** $5(t - 8) = 10$

Lesson 6-2 🌐 **47. Commuting** Mrs. Milton travels 60 mi round-trip to work. She works five days a week. Her car gets about 25 mi/gal of gasoline. About how many gallons of gasoline does Mrs. Milton's car use during her weekly commute?

Lesson 4-2   **Write using exponents.**

48. $4 \cdot 4 \cdot 4$ **49.** $c \cdot c \cdot c \cdot c \cdot d$ **50.** $9 \cdot a \cdot a \cdot 2$

Write an Equation

OBJECTIVE
1 **Write an Equation**

What You'll Learn

OBJECTIVE
1 To write an equation to solve a problem

... And Why

To solve problems about renting moving vans

✔ **Check Skills You'll Need**

Write an equation to represent each situation.

1. Pierre bought a puppy for $48. This is $21 less than the original price. What was the original price of the puppy?

2. A tent weighs 6 lb. Together, your backpack and the tent weigh 33 lb. How much does your backpack weigh?

3. A veterinarian weighs 140 lb. She steps on a scale while holding a large dog. The scale shows 192 lb. What is the weight of the dog?

❓ For help, go to Lesson 2-4.

OBJECTIVE
1 **Write an Equation**

Math Strategies in Action You probably recognize Albert Einstein's famous formula, $E = mc^2$. Many scientists write and use equations and formulas every day. Banks use equations to calculate interest and loan information. Statisticians use equations to find sports and population statistics. Doctors use equations to calculate correct doses of medicines.

You have written one-step equations for word problems. Now you will extend your skills to more complex situations.

1 EXAMPLE **Real-World 🌐 Problem Solving**

Moving Vans A moving van rents for $29.95 a day plus $.12/mi. Ms. Smith's bill for a two-day rental was $70.46. How many miles did she drive?

[**Read and Understand**]

1. What is the goal of this problem?

2. For how long did Ms. Smith rent the van?

3. What does the van cost without mileage?

4. What is the mileage charge?

Write an equation.

Words	two days	·	$29.95/d	+	$.12/mi	·	number of miles	=	$70.46

Let m = the number of miles Ms. Smith drove the van.

Equation	2	·	29.95	+	0.12	·	m	=	70.46

Solve the equation.

$$2 \cdot 29.95 + 0.12 \cdot m = 70.46$$

$$59.9 + 0.12m = 70.46 \qquad \textbf{Multiply 2 and 29.95.}$$

$$59.9 - 59.9 + 0.12m = 70.46 - 59.9 \qquad \textbf{Subtract 59.9 from each side.}$$

$$0.12m = 10.56 \qquad \textbf{Simplify.}$$

$$\frac{0.12m}{0.12} = \frac{10.56}{0.12} \qquad \textbf{Divide each side by 0.12.}$$

$$m = 88 \qquad \textbf{Simplify.}$$

Ms. Smith drove the van 88 mi.

Look Back and Check

5. A student suggested that another way to solve the gas mileage problem was to use the strategy *Try, Test, Revise*. Suppose that Ms. Smith's bill for the two-day rental was $76.34. How many miles did she drive the van?
   a. Copy and complete the table below to keep track of your trials.

Miles	Cost	High/Low?
75	$2 \cdot 29.95 + 75 \cdot 0.12 = $ ■	low
100	$2 \cdot 29.95 + $ ■ $\cdot 0.12 = $ ■	■

   b. Extend the table to find the solution to the problem.
   c. Check your solution by writing and solving an equation.

✔ **Check Understanding**

6. **Reasoning** Which method do you prefer for solving this type of problem? Explain.

7. Mr. Jones rented the same van for three days. His bill was $104.49. How many miles did he drive?

EXERCISES

Fgit For more exercises, see *Extra Practice*.

Practice and Problem Solving

 Practice by Example

Example 1
(page 362)

Reading Math

For help with reading and solving Exercise 4, see page 366.

Use the *Write an Equation* strategy to solve each problem.

1. The sale price of a sweater is $48. The price is 20% less than the original price. What was the original price?

2. **Budgeting** Elena has $240 in the bank. She withdraws $15 each week to pay for piano lessons. How many lessons can she afford with her savings?

3. **Geometry** The perimeter of a rectangle is 64 cm. The length is 4 cm less than twice the width. Find the length and width.

4. Wendy bought a drill at a 10%-off sale. The sale price was $75.60. Find the original price *p*.

 **Apply Your Skills**

Solve using any strategy.

5. Lamar's summer job is mowing lawns for a landscaper. His pay is $7.50/h. Lamar also makes $11.25/h for any time over 40 h that he works in one week. He worked 40 h last week plus *n* overtime hours and made $339.38. How many overtime hours did he work?

6. **Number Sense** Find two whole numbers with a sum of 15 and a product of 54.

7. **Farming** A farmer is building a square pen 21 ft on each side. He puts one post at each corner and one post every 3 ft in between. How many posts will he use?

8. It takes 8 painters 6 hours to paint the walls of a gymnasium.
   a. How many person-hours does this job require?
   b. How many hours will 12 painters take to paint the gymnasium?

9. Cathy has a collection of dimes and quarters. The number of dimes equals the number of quarters. She has a total of $2.80. How many of each coin does Cathy have? (*Hint:* Let n = the number of dimes. Since each dime has a value of 10¢, the value of n dimes is $10n$. Since the number of quarters is also n, the value of n quarters is $25n$. Also change the value of $2.80 to its value in cents.)

Strategies

- Account for All Possibilities
- Draw a Diagram
- Look for a Pattern
- Make a Model
- Make a Table
- Simplify the Problem
- Simulate the Problem
- Solve by Graphing
- Try, Test, Revise
- Use Multiple Strategies
- Work Backward
- Write an Equation
- Write a Proportion

 **Challenge**

10. **Physics** The weight of an object on Venus is about $\frac{9}{10}$ of its weight on Earth. The weight of an object on Jupiter is about $\frac{13}{5}$ times its weight on Earth.
    a. If a rock weighs 23 lb on Venus, how much would it weigh on Earth?
    b. If the same rock were on Jupiter, how much would it weigh?

11. **Collections** Jackson, Petra, and Tyrone went to the beach and collected seashells over the weekend. Jackson collected *s* seashells. Petra and Tyrone each collected 13 fewer than twice the number of seashells Jackson collected. At the end of the weekend, they had 94 seashells. How many seashells did each person collect?

364 Chapter 7 Solving Equations and Inequalities

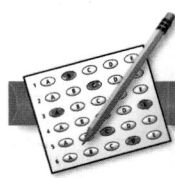

Multiple Choice

12. What is the solution of $49.95 + 0.6m + 9 = 93.23$ rounded to the nearest whole number?

A. 20   **B.** 57   **C.** 72   **D.** 155

13. What is the solution of $d + 3.95 + 0.25d = 7.70$?

F. 6   **G.** 5   **H.** 4   **I.** 3

Take It to the NET
Online lesson quiz at
www.PHSchool.com
Web Code: ada-0704

14. A car salesman makes a weekly salary of $260 plus 3% of the amount of sales he makes that week. Which equation could be used to find the amount of sales if one week's pay was $1,520?

A. $1,520 = 260 - 0.03x$ **B.** $260 = 1,520 + 0.3x$

C. $1,520 = 260 + 0.03x$ **D.** $260 = 1,520 - 0.3x$

Short Response

15. The perimeter of a rectangle is 15 ft. The height of the rectangle is 3 more than twice its base. **(a)** Write an equation to model this situation. **(b)** Solve the equation and find the height.

Mixed Review

Lesson 7-3   **Solve each equation.**

16. $\frac{3}{5}k + \frac{1}{5}k = 4$ **17.** $1.4x + 8.8 = 92.8$

Lesson 6-5   **Write each percent as a fraction in simplest form and as a decimal.**

18. 52% **19.** 20.5% **20.** 0.5% **21.** 205%

Lesson 6-1   **22.** You can buy 12 pencils for $.80. At this rate, how much will you pay for 27 pencils?

Checkpoint Quiz 1   Lessons 7-1 through 7-4

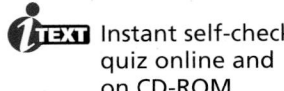

Instant self-check quiz online and on CD-ROM

Solve each equation.

1. $12n + 60 = 300$ **2.** $5y - 9 - 3y = 13$ **3.** $-44 = 3x + 10$

4. $\frac{a}{4} - \frac{3}{4} = \frac{1}{4}$ **5.** $\frac{4}{7}x - 3 = 13$ **6.** $-\frac{x}{6} - 8 = 0$

7. $0.6x + 1.9x = 5$ **8.** $10(5 + m) = 63$ **9.** $2c + 4 + 3c = -26$

10. $\frac{1}{5}(x + 10) = 2$ **11.** $7(2y - 1) = 7$ **12.** $3a + 9 = 27$

Write an equation for each situation. Then solve.

13. Gloria bought a suit at a 25%-off sale. The sale price was $82.50. Find the original price.

14. **Number Sense** Three consecutive integers have a sum of 132. Find the integers.

Read through the problem below. Then follow along with what Elena thinks as she solves the problem. Check your understanding with the exercise at the bottom of the page.

Wendy bought a drill at a 10%-off sale. The sale price was $75.60. Find the original price *p*.

What Elena Thinks	What Elena Writes
What information is given in the problem? I'll write it down.	A drill was on sale for 10% off. The sale price was $75.60.
What am I trying to find out? I'll write out the question.	What was the original price?
I know that 10% off means that you subtract 10% of the original price from the original price. I'll write this as an equation in words.	Original price minus 10% of the original price is the sale price, $75.60.
I'll use a variable for the original price. And I'll write 10% as the decimal 0.1.	$p - 0.1p = 75.60$
I can write *p* as 1*p* so that I can subtract like terms. Then I will simplify.	$1p - 0.1p = 75.60$ $0.9p = 75.60$
To finish solving the equation, I divide both sides by 0.9.	$\frac{0.9}{0.9}p = \frac{75.60}{0.9}$ $p = 84$
Is $84.00 a reasonable answer? 10% of 84 is about 8, and 84 − 8 is 76. This is close to $75.60. Yes, my answer is reasonable.	The original price of the drill was $84.00.

EXERCISE

1. Tanya got a 5% raise at her job at the video store. She now makes $6.51 per hour. How much did she make per hour before the raise?

Solving Equations With Variables on Both Sides

OBJECTIVE

1 Solving Equations With Variables on Both Sides

 **In**vestigation

Using Models to Solve Equations

Work in pairs.

1. Write an equation for the model at the right.

2. **a.** You must do the same thing to each side of the model. What can you do to get green tiles on only one side?
   b. Show what the model will look like when green tiles are on only one side. Write the new equation.
   c. Solve your new equation.

To solve an equation with a variable on both sides, use addition or subtraction to collect the variable on one side of the equation.

1 EXAMPLE Collecting the Variable on One Side

Solve $9a + 2 = 4a - 18$.

$$9a + 2 = 4a - 18$$
$$9a - 4a + 2 = 4a - 4a - 18 \quad \text{Subtract } 4a \text{ from each side.}$$
$$5a + 2 = -18 \quad \text{Combine like terms.}$$
$$5a + 2 - 2 = -18 - 2 \quad \text{Subtract 2 from each side.}$$
$$5a = -20 \quad \text{Simplify.}$$
$$\frac{5a}{5} = \frac{-20}{5} \quad \text{Divide each side by 5.}$$
$$a = -4 \quad \text{Simplify.}$$

Check $9a + 2 = 4a - 18$
$$9(-4) + 2 \stackrel{?}{=} 4(-4) - 18 \quad \text{Substitute } -4 \text{ for } a.$$
$$-36 + 2 \stackrel{?}{=} -16 - 18 \quad \text{Multiply.}$$
$$-34 = -34 \checkmark$$

✔ **Check Understanding** Example 1

1. Solve and check each equation.
   a. $4x + 4 = 2x + 36$ **b.** $-15 + 6b = -8b + 13$

What You'll Learn

 OBJECTIVE 1 To solve equations with variables on both sides

 OBJECTIVE 2 To use equations with variables on both sides

. . . And Why

To solve problems that involve time and distance

✔ **Check Skills You'll Need**

Solve each equation.

1. $k + 3k = 20$

2. $8x - 3x = 35$

3. $3b + 2 - b = -18$

4. $-8 - y + 7y = 40$

❓ For help, go to Lesson 7-2.

🖥 **TEXT** Interactive lesson includes instant self-check, tutorials, and activities.

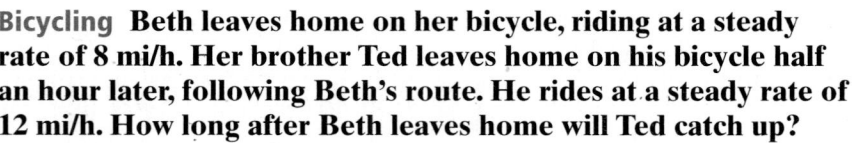

OBJECTIVE

2 Using Equations With Variables on Both Sides

You may need to use the Distributive Property to simplify one or both sides of an equation before you can get the variable alone on one side.

2 EXAMPLE Real-World 🌐 Problem Solving

Bicycling Beth leaves home on her bicycle, riding at a steady rate of 8 mi/h. Her brother Ted leaves home on his bicycle half an hour later, following Beth's route. He rides at a steady rate of 12 mi/h. How long after Beth leaves home will Ted catch up?

distance Beth travels = distance Ted travels

Words   8 mi/h · Beth's time = 12 mi/h · Ted's time

Let x = Beth's time.

Then $x - \frac{1}{2}$ = Ted's time.

Equation   8 · x = 12 · $\left(x - \frac{1}{2}\right)$

$$8x = 12\left(x - \frac{1}{2}\right)$$

$8x = 12x - 6$ **Use the Distributive Property.**

$8x - 12x = 12x - 12x - 6$ **Subtract 12x from each side.**

$-4x = -6$ **Combine like terms.**

$\frac{-4x}{-4} = \frac{-6}{-4}$ **Divide each side by −4.**

$x = \frac{6}{4}$, or $1\frac{1}{2}$ **Simplify.**

Ted will catch up with Beth $1\frac{1}{2}$ h after she leaves home.

Check Test the result.

At 8 mi/h, Beth will ride 12 mi in $1\frac{1}{2}$ h.

Ted's time is $\frac{1}{2}$ h less than Beth's. He rides for 1 h.

At 12 mi/h, he travels 12 mi in all.

● Since Beth and Ted each travel 12 mi, the answer checks.

✓ Check Understanding Example 2

2. Travel Time Car A leaves Eastown traveling at a steady rate of 50 mi/h. Car B leaves Eastown 1 h later following Car A. It travels at a steady rate of 60 mi/h. How long after Car A leaves Eastown will Car B catch up?

Real-World 🌐 Connection

An estimated 80.6 million people in the United States ride bicycles. About 14.5% of the nation's bicycle riders live in California.

EXERCISES

For more exercises, see *Extra Practice*.

Practice and Problem Solving

A Practice by Example

Example 1
(page 367)

Copy and complete the steps to each equation.

1.
$$-2a + 7 = a - 8$$
$$-2a + 7 - a = a - 8 - \blacksquare$$
$$\blacksquare + 7 = -8$$
$$\blacksquare + 7 - 7 = -8 - 7$$
$$\blacksquare = -15$$
$$\blacksquare = \frac{-15}{-3}$$
$$a = \blacksquare$$

2.
$$2x + 16 = -x - 5$$
$$2x + 16 + \blacksquare = -x - 5 + \blacksquare$$
$$\blacksquare + 16 = -5$$
$$3x + 16 - \blacksquare = -5 - \blacksquare$$
$$\blacksquare = -21$$
$$\frac{\blacksquare}{3} = \frac{-21}{3}$$
$$x = \blacksquare$$

Solve each equation.

3. $3y - 20 = 8y$

4. $x - 7 = 2x - 6$

5. $5x + 8 = 7x$

6. $3a = a + 22$

7. $2a + 6 = -a - 8$

8. $4w + 8 = 6w - 4$

9. $q + q + q = q + 6$

10. $b + b + 18 = 4b$

Example 2
(page 368)

11. $2(x - 4) = 3x$

12. $7a = 2(a - 10)$

13. $5(n - 3) = 2n - 6$

14. $4(8 - y) = 2y + 16$

15. $2n = 4(n - 8)$

16. $3(y + 7) = 10y$

17. Aviation A jet leaves an airport traveling at a steady rate of 600 km/h. Another jet leaves the same airport $\frac{3}{4}$ h later traveling at 800 km/h in the same direction. How long will it take the second jet to overtake the first?

B Apply Your Skills

Solve each equation.

18. $\frac{1}{2}(4d - 2) = d + 5$

19. $20.6 + 2.1x = -8.2x$

20. $-2(y + 6) = y + 3 + 2y$

21. $6(g + 3) = -2(g + 31)$

22. $7a - 4 + 2a = 3a - 2$

23. $3(2y - 0.3) = 19.4 - y$

24. Open-Ended Write a problem that you can represent with an equation with variables on both sides. Write and solve the equation.

Write an equation for each situation. Then solve.

25. Number Sense If a number n is subtracted from 18, the result is four less than n. What is the value of n?

26. Cell Phones A cellular phone company charges a $27.95 monthly fee and $.12/min for local calls. Another company charges $12.95 a month and $.32/min for local calls. For what number of minutes of local calls are the costs of the plans the same?

$$8x + 36 = 4(7 - x)$$
$$8x + 36 = 28 - 4x$$
$$4x + 36 = 28$$
$$4x = -8$$
$$x = -2$$

27. Error Analysis The student who solved the equation at the left made an error. Find the error. State the correct solution.

 **28. Boating** A group of campers and one group leader left a campsite in a canoe traveling at a steady 8 km/h. One hour later, the other group leader left the campsite in a motorboat with all of the supplies. The motorboat followed the canoe at a steady 20 km/h. How long after the canoe left the campsite did the motorboat overtake it?

29. Writing in Math Describe the steps you would use to solve the equation $5(2a - 3) = 20 + a$.

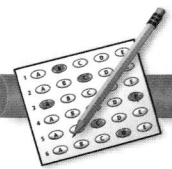 **Challenge**   **Solve each equation.**

30. $9 - (2k - 3) = k$ **31.** $2\left(2a + \frac{1}{2}\right) = 3\left(a - \frac{2}{3}\right)$

32. Mental Math Is the solution to $5b = 2b - 42 - 3b$ positive or negative? Explain.

 **33. Video Rental** A video store offers two types of rental cards. Each rental card is good for six months. The gold rental card costs $25 plus $1.75/rental. The silver rental card costs $10 plus $3.25/rental. Explain why someone would prefer one card over the other.

34. Reasoning To solve $\frac{2}{3}b = 10 - b$, you can first (a) multiply each side by $\frac{3}{2}$, (b) multiply each side by 3, or (c) add b to each side. Which first step do you prefer? Why? What is the solution?

Test Prep

Reading Comprehension   Read the passage below before doing Exercises 35 and 36.

An Algebraic Riddle

Diophantus was a Greek mathematician who lived in the third century. He was one of the first mathematicians to use algebraic symbols.

Most of what is known about Diophantus's life comes from an algebraic riddle from around the early sixth century. The riddle states, "Diophantus's youth lasted one sixth of his life. He grew a beard after one twelfth more. After one seventh more of his life he married. Five years later he and his wife had a son. The son lived exactly one half as long as his father, and Diophantus died four years after his son. All of this adds up to the years Diophantus lived." The riddle, the "facts" of which may or may not be true, results in the following equation:

$$\frac{1}{6}a + \frac{1}{12}a + \frac{1}{7}a + 5 + \frac{1}{2}a + 4 = a$$

where a is Diophantus's age at the time of his death.

35. How many years did Diophantus live?

36. How old was Diophantus when he married?

37. To which expression does $3(a + 2b) - 3a$ simplify?
A. $-6a + 6b$ **B.** $3a + 6b$ **C.** $2b$ **D.** $6b$

38. What is the solution of $6(k - 2) = 3k - 6$?
F. -6 **G.** 2 **H.** $-\frac{4}{3}$ **I.** $\frac{2}{3}$

39. What is the solution of $2(2x + 3) = -3(x + 5)$?
A. -7 **B.** $-\frac{21}{5}$ **C.** -3 **D.** $\frac{9}{7}$

40. The Garners rented a moving van for \$59.95 plus \$.50/mi. Before returning the van, they filled the gas tank, which cost \$21.50. The total cost for renting the van, including gas, was \$199.45. To the nearest mile, how many miles did the Garners drive the van?
F. 519 mi **G.** 279 mi **H.** 236 mi **I.** 70 mi

Take It to the NET
Online lesson quiz at
www.PHSchool.com
Web Code: ada-0705

Mixed Review

Lesson 6-9

Find the price after each discount or markup.

41. \$15; 25% discount **42.** \$88; 32% markup

43. \$24; 72% markup **44.** \$110; 75% discount

Lesson 2-10

Solve and graph each inequality.

45. $-4x < 32$ **46.** $\frac{a}{-9} \geq -3$ **47.** $-12 < 3y$ **48.** $12 \leq -2y$

Lesson 1-8 **49. Collections** In a collection of dimes and quarters, there are seven more quarters than there are dimes. How many dimes and quarters are there if the collection is worth \$3.50?

Math at Work

City Planner

City planners, also called urban planners or regional planners, determine the best use of a community's land and resources for homes, businesses, and recreation. They also work on community problems such as traffic congestion and air pollution. They study the effects of proposed changes in a community, such as the addition of a bus line or a new highway. Planners use mathematical analysis to evaluate different courses of action and to predict the impact of each course on a community.

Take It to the NET For more information about city planners, go to **www.PHSchool.com**
Web Code: adb-2031

Using Tables to Solve Equations

You can use tables on a graphing calculator to solve one-variable equations.

1 EXAMPLE

Solve $x + 9 = 3x - 7$.

Press **Y=** and enter

$Y_1 = x + 9$
$Y_2 = 3x - 7$

In **TBLSET**, set TBLStart = 0 and ΔTbl = 1.

In **TABLE**, compare the Y_1 and Y_2 values. $Y_1 = Y_2 = 17$ for X = 8.

● The solution of $x + 9 = 3x - 7$ is 8.

X	Y_1	Y_2
3	12	2
4	13	5
5	14	8
6	15	11
7	16	14
8	17	17
9	18	20

X=8

2 EXAMPLE

Solve $x + 3 = 3x - 4$.

Enter $Y_1 = x + 3$
$\quad\quad Y_2 = 3x - 4$

In **TABLE**, compare the Y_1 and Y_2 values. Y_1 values are greater than Y_2 values until X changes from 3 to 4. This suggests that $Y_1 = Y_2$ somewhere between 3 and 4.

In **TBLSET**, set TblStart = 3 and ΔTbl = 0.1.

In **TABLE**, compare the Y_1 and Y_2 values. $Y_1 = Y_2 = 6.5$ for X = 3.5.

● The solution of $x + 3 = 3x - 4$ is 3.5.

X	Y_1	Y_2
3	6	5
3.1	6.1	5.3
3.2	6.2	5.6
3.3	6.3	5.9
3.4	6.4	6.2
3.5	6.5	6.5
3.6	6.6	6.8

X=3.5

EXERCISES

Solve each equation. Round to the nearest tenth where necessary.

1. $p - 5 = 7$

2. $3x = 21$

3. $2y + 5 = 14$

4. $2x + x + 3 = 15$

5. $7m - 3m - 6 = 6$

6. $15 = -3(2q - 1)$

7. $6x - 2 = x + 13$

8. $3y + 12 = 5y - 3$

9. $2n - 5 = 8n + 7$

10. $6a - 9 = -a + 30$

11. $72 - 8c = 32 + 6c$

12. $-2b - 13 = 4b - 10$

13. Use graphing calculator tables to solve the equation $4(x - 2) = -3(x - 6)$. Find the solution to as many places as possible until "table breakdown" occurs. Then solve the equation using pencil and paper. Compare your two results.

Solving Two-Step Inequalities

OBJECTIVE

1 Solving Two-Step Inequalities

You solve two-step inequalities and equations using similar steps.

1 EXAMPLE Undoing Operations

Solve and graph $2y - 3 \leq -5$.

$$2y - 3 \leq -5$$
$$2y - 3 + 3 \leq -5 + 3 \qquad \text{Add 3 to each side.}$$
$$2y \leq -2 \qquad \text{Simplify.}$$
$$\frac{2y}{2} \leq \frac{-2}{2} \qquad \text{Divide each side by 2.}$$
$$y \leq -1 \qquad \text{Simplify.}$$

✓ Check Understanding Example 1

1. Solve and graph each inequality.

   a. $5a - 9 > 11$ **b.** $-10 \geq \frac{1}{2}x - 6$ **c.** $17 + \frac{1}{2}c < 14$

Remember to reverse the direction of the inequality symbol when you multiply or divide by a negative number.

2 EXAMPLE Reversing the Inequality Symbol

Solve $-9 > -\frac{1}{3}x + 6$.

$$-9 > -\frac{1}{3}x + 6$$
$$-9 - 6 > -\frac{1}{3}x + 6 - 6 \qquad \text{Subtract 6 from each side.}$$
$$-15 > -\frac{1}{3}x \qquad \text{Simplify.}$$
$$-3(-15) < -3\left(-\frac{1}{3}x\right) \qquad \begin{array}{l}\text{Multiply each side by } -3. \text{ Reverse the} \\ \text{direction of the inequality symbol.}\end{array}$$
$$45 < x, \text{ or } x > 45 \qquad \text{Simplify.}$$

✓ Check Understanding Example 2

2. Solve and graph each inequality.

   a. $-2m + 4 \leq 34$ **b.** $6 - x > 3$ **c.** $8.3 < -0.5b - 2.7$

What You'll Learn

 OBJECTIVE 1 To solve two-step inequalities

 OBJECTIVE 2 To use two-step inequalities to solve problems

. . . And Why

To solve problems involving camping and jobs

✓ Check Skills You'll Need

Solve each inequality. Graph the solutions.

1. $w + 4 \geq -5$

2. $7 < z - 3$

3. $4 > a + 6$

4. $x - 5 \leq -6$

❓ For help, go to Lesson 2-9.

Need Help?

If $a > b$ and $c > 0$, then $ac > bc$.

If $a > b$ and $c < 0$, then $ac < bc$.

 TEXT Interactive lesson includes instant self-check, tutorials, and activities.

Now that you know how to solve two-step inequalities, you can use them to solve real-world problems.

3 EXAMPLE <u>Real-World</u>  <u>Problem Solving</u>

Hiking **An expedition leader estimates that a group of hikers can carry less than 550 lb of food and equipment. The group must carry 336 lb of equipment as well as 25 lb of food for each climber. What is the greatest possible number of people in the expedition?**

Real-World  **Connection**

A pint of water weighs 1 lb. You need about a gallon of water per person per day.

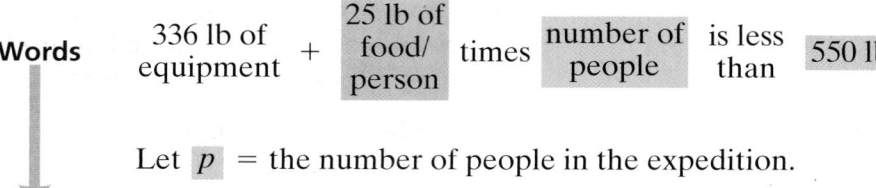

| **Words** | 336 lb of equipment | + | 25 lb of food/ person | times | number of people | is less than | 550 lb |

Let p = the number of people in the expedition.

Inequality $\quad$ 336 $\quad$ + $\quad$ 25 $\quad$ · $\quad$ p $\quad$ < $\quad$ 550

Solve the inequality.

$$336 + 25p < 550$$
$$336 + 25p - 336 < 550 - 336 \quad \textbf{Subtract 336 from each side.}$$
$$25p < 214 \quad \textbf{Simplify.}$$
$$\frac{25p}{25} < \frac{214}{25} \quad \textbf{Divide each side by 25.}$$
$$p < 8.56 \quad \textbf{Simplify.}$$

The greatest possible number of people in the expedition is 8.

Reading Math

Since $p < 8.56$, the "greatest number of people" must be the greatest whole number less than 8.56.

Check Is the answer reasonable? The original problem states that the total of the equipment plus 25 lb of food per person is less than 550 lb. Since $336 + 25(8) = 536$, the equipment plus the food is less than 550 lb. The answer is reasonable.

✓ **Check Understanding** Example 3

3. Commissions A stereo salesperson earns a salary of $1,200 per month, plus a commission of 4% of sales. The salesperson wants to maintain a monthly income of at least $1,500. How much must the salesperson sell each month?

EXERCISES

For more exercises, see *Extra Practice*.

Practice and Problem Solving

A Practice by Example

Example 1
(page 373)

Tell what you can do to the first inequality in order to get the second. Be sure to list *all* steps.

1. $4x - 2 \leq 6; x \leq 2$

2. $\frac{1}{2}a - 1 < 3; a < 8$

Solve and graph each inequality.

3. $10 + 4a < -6$

4. $2m + 8 > 0$

5. $6 + 3y > 5$

6. $4x - 9 > -7$

7. $\frac{1}{3}a - 4 \geq -1$

8. $4 + 7a \geq 32$

Example 2
(page 373)

9. $-2x - 1 < 11$

10. $-\frac{b}{7} + 7 \leq 6$

11. $2.1 - 0.6y \geq 0.9$

12. $10 \leq -8x - 6$

13. $-5y + 3 \geq 28$

14. $-21 - 3m < 0$

Example 3
(page 374)

15. Travel On a trip from Louisiana to Florida, your family wants to travel at least 420 miles in 8 hours of driving. Write and solve an inequality to find what your average speed must be.

16. Number Sense You divide a number x by -3. Then you subtract 1 from the quotient. The result is at most 5. Write and solve an inequality to find all possible solutions.

B Apply Your Skills

Solve each inequality.

17. $-\frac{1}{9}c + 13 \geq 5$

18. $\frac{x}{3} + 11 < 31$

19. $6y - 10 - y > 14$

20. $-\frac{x}{6} - 2 < 4$

21. $\frac{1}{2}c - \frac{1}{4} < -\frac{3}{4}$

22. $-4(2a + 7) \leq -12$

Write an inequality for each situation. Then solve.

23. Photography Maureen is ordering photographic reprints and enlargements. She can spend at most $11. She wants to order an 11-in. × 14-in. enlargement and some 3-in. × 5-in. reprints. How many reprints can she order using the price list at the left?

Photo Price List

Size	Price
3 in. x 5 in.	$.40
4 in. x 6 in.	$.45
5 in. x 7 in.	$1.95
8 in. x 10 in.	$4.95
8 in. x 12 in.	$6.45
11 in. x 14 in.	$7.00
16 in. x 20 in.	$13.95
20 in. x 30 in.	$16.95

24. You want to spend at most $10 for a taxi ride. Before you go anywhere, the taxi driver sets the meter at the initial charge of $2. The meter then adds $1.25 for every mile driven. If you plan on a $1 tip, what is the farthest you can go?

25. Test Scores Students in a math class need an average of at least 90 points to earn an A. One student's test scores are 88, 91, and 85. What must the student score on the next test to earn an A?

26. Error Analysis A student solved and graphed the inequality $-12x + 40 > 4$. What error did the student make?

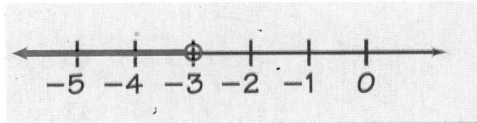

27. <u>Writing in Math</u> A friend was absent from class today. Write a letter to your friend telling how to solve two-step inequalities.

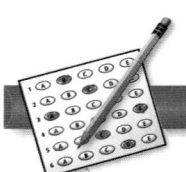 Challenge **28. Borrowing** Corey's parents agree to loan Corey $182 to help pay for the school's spring music trip to Florida. Corey agrees to monthly payback amounts of $2, $4, $6, $8, and so on. How long will it take Corey to pay back the $182?

29. Sightseeing You and a friend want to spend at most $20 each on a horse-carriage sightseeing ride. There is an initial charge of $5 and then $2.50 for each quarter-mile driven. You plan on giving a $6 tip. For how many miles can you ride in the carriage?

Test Prep

Multiple Choice

30. Which sign correctly completes
$$43(2) - (-3) \; \blacksquare \; -58 + (-4)12?$$
A. $\leq$ **B.** $<$ **C.** $=$ **D.** $>$

31. Which graph shows the solution of $-15 < -2x - 7$?

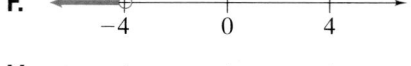

Take It to the NET
Online lesson quiz at
www.PHSchool.com
Web Code: ada-0706

32. Which graph shows the solution of $-15 \geq 7x + 20$?

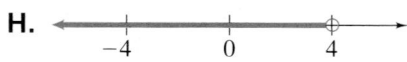

Extended Response

33. The perimeter of a triangle is at most 32 cm. One side is 11 cm long. The other two sides are the same length. **(a)** What are the possible lengths of the two congruent sides? **(b)** Draw a diagram and show your work. **(c)** Explain your process.

Mixed Review

Lesson 7-2 **Solve each equation.**

34. $a - 81 = 9a + 7$ **35.** $8x - 15 + 4x = 5x + 6$

Lesson 6-6  **36. Sales Tax** A stereo costs $262.99. The sales tax rate is 5%. What is the total cost of the stereo?

Lesson 3-4 **Use the distance formula, $d = rt$. Find each missing value.**

37. $r = 45$ mi/h, $t = 3.25$ h **38.** $d = 351$ mi, $r = 54$ mi/h

39. $d = 12$ cm, $t = 0.25$ h **40.** $d = 147.825$ mi, $t = 2.25$ h

Compound Inequalities

For Use With Lesson 7-6

A **compound inequality** is a statement in which two inequalities are joined by the word *and* or the word *or*.

$x > 4$ and $x \le 6$

$x \le -2$ or $x > 3$

A solution of a compound inequality joined by *and* is any number that makes both inqualities true.

A solution of a compound inequality joined by *or* is any number that makes either inequality true.

EXAMPLE

Graph each compound inequality on a number line.

a. $2 \le x$ and $x < 6$

A closed circle shows 2 is a solution.

An open circle shows 6 is not a solution.

$2 \le x$ and $x < 6$

b. $z > 4$ or $z \le 1$

closed circle   open circle

$z > 4$ or $z \le 1$

EXERCISES

Graph each compound inequality.

1. $x \ge 0$ and $x \le 7$

2. $z < -2$ and $z \ge -4$

3. $5 > a$ and $a \ge -6$

4. $b < -1$ or $b > 4$

5. $c < 2$ or $c > 3.5$

6. $y \ge 1$ or $y < -3$

7. $x \le 4$ and $x \ge 3$

8. $n \le -5$ or $n > 0$

9. $3 > m$ and $m > -3$

10. **Writing in Math** Explain why there are no solutions of the compound inequality $x > 2$ and $x \le 2$.

Transforming Formulas

What You'll Learn

OBJECTIVE 1
To solve a formula for a given variable

OBJECTIVE 2
To use formulas to solve problems

. . . And Why

To find travel times in real-world situations

✔ **Check Skills You'll Need**

Use each formula for the values given.

1. Use the formula $d = rt$ to find d when $r = 80$ km/h and $t = 4$ h.

2. Use the formula $P = 2\ell + 2w$ to find P when $\ell = 9$ m and $w = 7$ m.

3. Use the formula $A = \frac{1}{2}bh$ to find A when $b = 12$ ft and $h = 8$ ft.

❓ For help, go to Lesson 3-4.

OBJECTIVE

1 ▸ **Solving Formulas for a Given Variable**

Remember that a formula shows the relationship between two or more quantities. You can use the properties of equality to transform a formula to represent one quantity in terms of another.

1 EXAMPLE **Transforming in One Step**

Solve the area formula $A = \ell w$ for ℓ.

$A = \ell w$

$\dfrac{A}{w} = \dfrac{\ell w}{w}$ Divide each side by w.

$\dfrac{A}{w} = \ell$, or $\ell = \dfrac{A}{w}$ Simplify.

✔ **Check Understanding**   Example 1

1. Solve for the variable indicated in red.
   a. $p = s - c$
   b. $h = \dfrac{k}{j}$
   c. $I = prt$

Sometimes you need to use more than one step.

2 EXAMPLE **Using More Than One Step**

Solve the perimeter formula $P = 2\ell + 2w$ for ℓ.

$P = 2\ell + 2w$

$P - 2w = 2\ell + 2w - 2w$ Subtract $2w$ from each side.

$P - 2w = 2\ell$ Simplify.

$\frac{1}{2}(P - 2w) = \frac{1}{2}(2\ell)$ Multiply each side by $\frac{1}{2}$.

$\frac{1}{2}P - w = \ell$ Use the Distributive Property and simplify.

✔ **Check Understanding**   Example 2

2. Solve for the variable indicated in red.
   a. $5a + 7 = b$
   b. $P = 2\ell + 2w$
   c. $y = \dfrac{x}{3} + 8$

i⃝TEXT Interactive lesson includes instant self-check, tutorials, and activities.

OBJECTIVE

2 Using Formulas to Solve Problems

You can transform formulas to solve real-world problems.

3 EXAMPLE   Real-World Problem Solving

Travel You plan a 425-mi trip to Bryce Canyon National Park. You estimate you will average 50 mi/h. To find about how long the trip will take, solve the distance formula $d = rt$ for t. Then substitute to find the time.

$d = rt$

$\dfrac{d}{r} = \dfrac{rt}{r}$ **Divide each side by r.**

$\dfrac{d}{r} = t$, or $t = \dfrac{d}{r}$ **Simplify.**

$t = \dfrac{425}{50} = 8.5$ **Replace d with 425 and r with 50. Simplify.**

● It will take you about 8.5 h to complete the trip.

✓ Check Understanding   Example 3

3. Solve the distance formula in Example 3 for r.

4 EXAMPLE   Real-World Problem Solving

Temperature An exchange student in your class wants to know the Celsius equivalent of 77°F. First solve the formula $F = \frac{9}{5}C + 32$ for C. Then substitute to find the temperature.

$F = \frac{9}{5}C + 32$

$F - 32 = \frac{9}{5}C + 32 - 32$ **Subtract 32 from each side.**

$F - 32 = \frac{9}{5}C$ **Simplify.**

$\frac{5}{9}(F - 32) = \frac{5}{9} \cdot \frac{9}{5}C$ **Multiply each side by $\frac{5}{9}$.**

$\frac{5}{9}(F - 32) = C$, or $C = \frac{5}{9}(F - 32)$ **Simplify and rewrite.**

$C = \frac{5}{9}(77 - 32) = 25$ **Replace F with 77. Simplify.**

● 77°F is 25°C.

✓ Check Understanding   Example 4

4. Solve the batting average formula, $a = \frac{h}{n}$, for h. Find the number of hits h a batter needs in 40 times at bat n to have an average of 0.275.

Real-World Connection

Wind and water, rushing along stone plateaus, erode the stone and create shapes called "fins" and "hoodoos" in Bryce Canyon, Utah. Each year, more than 1.5 million people visit the national park.

EXERCISES

For more exercises, see *Extra Practice.*

Practice and Problem Solving

(A) Practice by Example

Examples 1 and 2
(page 378)

Complete the steps to solve each equation for the variable indicated in red.

1.
$$a = 6c + 3$$
$$a - \blacksquare = 6c + 3 - 3$$
$$a - \blacksquare = 6c$$
$$\frac{a - 3}{\blacksquare} = \frac{6c}{\blacksquare}$$
$$\frac{a - 3}{\blacksquare} = \blacksquare$$

2. $g = \frac{h}{j}$
$$\blacksquare g = j\left(\frac{h}{j}\right)$$
$$jg = \blacksquare$$
$$\frac{jg}{\blacksquare} = \frac{h}{g}$$
$$\blacksquare = \frac{h}{g}$$

Solve for the variable indicated in red.

3. $V = \ell w h$

4. $P = 4s$

5. $q = \frac{p}{d}$

6. $r = 2s - 8$

7. $\frac{2}{3}m - 5 = n$

8. $m = \frac{a + b}{2}$

Examples 3 and 4
(page 379)

9. Commissions LaTanya sells business suits and gets a 4% commission on her sales. Last week, she received a paycheck that included $196 in commissions. Solve the formula $C = 0.04s$ for s, where C is the amount of commission and s is the amount of sales. Substitute to find LaTanya's sales.

10. Renting You have $12.00 to rent a pair of in-line skates. They rent for $3.00 plus $1.50 per hour. To determine the maximum length of time you can rent the in-line skates, solve the formula $C = 3 + 1.5h$ for h. Then substitute 12 for C.

(B) Apply Your Skills

Solve for the variable indicated in red.

11. $V = \frac{1}{2}\pi r^2 h$

12. $d^2 = \frac{3}{2}h$

13. $A = \frac{1}{2}(a + b)h$

14. a. Construction Bricklayers use the formula $N = 7LH$ to estimate the number N of bricks needed in a wall. L is the length of the wall and H is the height. Solve the formula for H.
b. If 1,134 bricks are used to build a wall that is 18 ft long, how high is the wall?

15. Writing in Math A formula for the perimeter of a rectangle is $P = 2(b + h)$. Explain how you would find the height of the rectangle if you knew the perimeter and the base.

(C) Challenge

16. a. Economics Joe uses the formula $p = wh + 1.5wv$ to figure his weekly pay. In the formula, p is the weekly pay, w is the hourly wage, h is the number of regular hours, and v is the number of overtime hours. Solve the formula for v.
b. Joe's hourly wage is $6.24/h. If he earned $282.36 last week working 40 regular hours plus overtime, how many hours overtime did he work?

Multiple Choice

For Exercises 17–19, what is the correct result when you solve for the variable indicated in red?

17. $z = xy$

    A. $x = \frac{z}{y}$ **B.** $x = \frac{y}{z}$ **C.** $x = yz$ **D.** $y = xz$

18. $r = 2s - 8$

    F. $s = \frac{r + 2}{8}$ **G.** $s = r + 4$ **H.** $s = \frac{r + 8}{2}$ **I.** $s = 2r + 16$

19. $\frac{2}{3}m - 5 = n$

    A. $m = \frac{2}{3}(n + 5)$ **B.** $m = \frac{3}{2}(n + 5)$

    C. $m = \frac{3}{2}n + 5$ **D.** $m = \frac{2}{3}n + 5$

Take It to the NET
Online lesson quiz at
www.PHSchool.com
Web Code: ada-0707

20. Use the batting average formula, $a = \frac{h}{n}$. What is the number of hits h for $a = 0.245$ and $n = 25$?

    F. 98   **G.** 7   **H.** 6   **I.** 0

Extended Response

21. Solve $A = \frac{1}{2}(a + b)h$ twice, once for b and once for h. Explain your process for each solution. Then compare the two processes, stating similarities and differences.

Mixed Review

Lesson 7-5

Solve each inequality.

22. $3x - 12 > -6$ **23.** $17 \leq -4a + 5$ **24.** $-\frac{b}{2} + 9 < -3$

Lesson 7-1 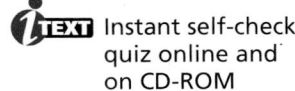 **25. Budgeting** Audrey wants to buy a dress for $54. She has $6 already and plans to save $8 each week. In how many weeks will she be able to buy the dress?

Lesson 6-7

Write and solve an equation. Where necessary, round to the nearest tenth or tenth of a percent.

26. What percent of 20 is 15?   **27.** 80% of what is 25?

✓ Checkpoint Quiz 2   Lessons 7-5 through 7-7

TEXT Instant self-check quiz online and on CD-ROM

Solve each equation or inequality.

1. $-8a - 6 = 10$ **2.** $9b + 42 = -12$ **3.** $2c + 6 + 7c = 8$

4. $18y = 12y + 24$ **5.** $2x + 5 = 9x - 16$ **6.** $12(m - 4) = 3m - 3$

7. $15 - 10y < 24$ **8.** $23 > -\frac{x}{2} - 5$ **9.** $1.8x - 3.4 > 5.6$

Solve for the variable indicated in red.

10. $s = g + h$ **11.** $3r + 4 = k$ **12.** $I = prt$

7-8 Simple and Compound Interest

What You'll Learn

OBJECTIVE 1 To solve simple-interest problems

OBJECTIVE 2 To solve compound-interest problems

. . . And Why

To find interest paid on investments using simple and compound interest

✓ Check Skills You'll Need

Find each amount.

1. 6% of $400

2. 55% of $2,000

3. 4.5% of $700

4. $5\frac{1}{2}$% of $325

🔎 For help, go to Lesson 6-6.

New Vocabulary

- principal
- interest
- interest rate
- simple interest
- compound interest
- balance

OBJECTIVE

1 Simple Interest

When you first deposit money in a savings account, your deposit is called **principal.** The bank takes the money and invests it. In return, the bank pays you **interest** based on the **interest rate.** **Simple interest** is interest paid only on the principal.

> **Key Concepts** Simple-Interest Formula
>
> $$I = prt,$$
> where I is the interest, p is the principal,
> r is the interest rate per year, and t is the time in years.

1 EXAMPLE Real-World 🌐 Problem Solving

Savings **Suppose you deposit $400 in a savings account. The interest rate is 5% per year.**

a. Find the simple interest earned in six years. Find the total of principal plus interest.

$I = prt$	Use the simple-interest formula.
$I = 400 \cdot 0.05 \cdot 6$	Replace p with 400, r with 0.05, and t with 6.
$I = 120$	Simplify.
total $= 400 + 120 = 520$	Find the total.

The account will earn $120 in six years. The total of principal plus interest will be $520.

b. Find the interest earned in three months. Find the total of principal plus interest.

$t = \frac{3}{12} = \frac{1}{4} = 0.25$	Write the months as part of a year.
$I = prt$	Use the simple-interest formula.
$I = 400 \cdot 0.05 \cdot 0.25$	Replace p with 400, r with 0.05, and t with 0.25.
$I = 5$	Simplify.
total $= 400 + 5 = 405$	Find the total.

The account will earn $5 in three months. The total of principal plus interest will be $405.

🖥️ **iTEXT** Interactive lesson includes instant self-check, tutorials, and activities.

✓ Check Understanding Example 1

1. Find the simple interest.

a. principal = $250
interest rate = 4%
time = 3 years

b. principal = $250
interest rate = 3.5%
time = 6 months

OBJECTIVE

2 Compound Interest

When a bank pays interest on the principal and on the interest an account has earned, the bank is paying **compound interest.** The principal plus the interest is the **balance,** which becomes the principal on which the bank figures the next interest payment.

2 EXAMPLE Real-World  Problem Solving

Banking **You deposit $400 in an account that earns 5% interest compounded annually (once per year). What is the balance in your account after 4 years? In your last calculation, round to the nearest cent.**

Principal at Beginning of Year	Interest	Balance
Year 1: $400.00	$400.00 \cdot 0.05 = 20.00$	$400 + 20 = 420.00$
Year 2: $420.00	$420.00 \cdot 0.05 = 21.00$	$420 + 21 = 441.00$
Year 3: $441.00	$441.00 \cdot 0.05 = 22.05$	$441 + 22.05 = 463.05$
Year 4: $463.05	$463.05 \cdot 0.05$ $= 23.1525$	$463.05 + 23.1525$ ≈ 486.20

● After four years, the balance is $486.20.

✓ Check Understanding Example 2

2. Make a table and find the balance. The interest is compounded annually.

a. principal = $500
interest rate = 3%
time = 2 years

b. principal = $625
interest rate = 2%
time = 4 years

You can find a balance using compound interest in one step with the compound interest formula and a calculator. An *interest period* is the length of time over which interest is calculated. The interest period can be a year or less than a year.

> **Reading Math**
> Interest periods:
> Annual—1 per year
> Semiannual—2 per year
> Quarterly—4 per year
> Monthly—12 per year
> Daily—360 per year
> (not 365)

Compound-Interest Formula

$$B = p(1 + r)^n,$$

where B is the final balance, p is the principal,
r is the interest rate for each interest period, and
n is the number of interest periods.

Calculator Hint

Remember to use the parentheses on your calculator when evaluating the compound-interest formula.

You can use this formula to solve Example 2.

$$B = p(1 + r)^n$$

$B = 400(1 + 0.05)^4$ **Replace p with 400, r with 0.05, and n with 4.**

$B \approx 486.20$ **Use a calculator. Round to the nearest cent.**

The balance is $486.20. Using the formula means there are fewer calculations and fewer chances for mistakes.

When interest is compounded semiannually (twice per year), you must *divide* the interest rate by the number of interest periods, which is 2.

$$\frac{6\% \text{ annual}}{\text{interest rate}} \div \frac{2 \text{ interest}}{\text{periods}} = \frac{3\% \text{ semiannual}}{\text{interest rate}}$$

To find the number of payment periods, *multiply* the number of years by the number of interest periods per year.

3 EXAMPLE **Real-World Problem Solving**

Investing Find the balance on a deposit of $1,000 that earns 6% interest compounded semiannually for 5 years.

The interest rate r for compounding semiannually is $0.06 \div 2$, or 0.03. The number of payment periods n is 5 years $\times$ 2 interest periods per year, or 10.

$B = p(1 + r)^n$ **Use the compound-interest formula.**

$B = 1,000(1 + 0.03)^{10}$ **Replace p with 1,000, r with 0.03, and n with 10.**

$B \approx 1,343.92$ **Use a calculator. Round to the nearest cent.**

The balance is $1,343.92.

✓ Check Understanding Example 3

3. Find the balance for each account.
   Amount deposited: $900, annual interest: 2%, time: 3 years

   a. compounding annually **b.** compounding semiannually

EXERCISES

For more exercises, see *Extra Practice.*

Practice and Problem Solving

A Practice by Example

Example 1 (page 382)

Find the simple interest. Then find the total of principal plus interest.

1. principal = \$200
interest rate = 7%
time = 2 years

2. principal = \$870
interest rate = 6%
time = 9 months

Example 2 (page 383)

Complete each table. Compound the interest annually. In your last calculation, round to the nearest cent.

3. \$3,000 at 4% for 3 years

Principal at Start of Year	Interest	Balance
Year 1: \$3,000	■	■
Year 2: ■	■	■
Year 3: ■	■	■

4. \$10,000 at 6% for 3 years

Principal at Start of Year	Interest	Balance
Year 1: \$10,000	■	■
Year 2: ■	■	■
Year 3: ■	■	■

Example 3 (page 384)

Find each balance.

5. \$495 at 8% compounded annually for 2 years

6. \$1,280 at 13% compounded annually for 3 years

7. \$2,000 at 5% compounded semiannually for 2 years

8. \$15,600 at 10% compounded semiannually for 3 years

B Apply Your Skills

9. Savings You deposit \$600 in a savings account for 3 years. The account pays 8% annual interest compounded quarterly.
- **a.** What is the quarterly interest rate?
- **b.** What is the number of payment periods?
- **c.** Find the final balance in the account.

Find each balance.

10. \$3,000 at 14% compounded annually for 4 years

11. \$500 at a simple-interest rate of 3% for 4 years

12. \$35 at a simple-interest rate of 2.5% for 1 year

13. \$8,900 at 9% compounded semiannually for 5 years

14. \$54,500 at 3% compounded semiannually for 9 years

15. \$900 at a simple-interest rate of 8% for 3 months

16. Mental Math Calculate the amount of simple-interest on \$9,000 deposited at an interest rate of 5% for 2 years.

17. Open-Ended Choose an amount of money to be invested and an interest rate. Find the value of the investment after 5 years if the interest is simple interest; if the interest is compounded annually.

18. Writing in Math Explain the difference between simple interest and compound interest.

Challenge **19. Borrowing** Leroy borrows $800 at 10% annual interest compounded semiannually. He makes no payments.
   a. How much will he owe after four years?
   b. How much interest will he owe in four years?

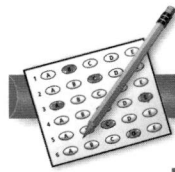

Writing in Math

Many banks compound interest on a daily basis. Explain what it means to compound interest daily.

🌐 **20. Investing** Ling invests $1,000 in an account paying 8% interest.
   a. Compare the account balances after 5 years of simple interest and after 5 years of interest compounded annually.
   b. After how many years of compounded interest will the account balance be about twice Ling's initial investment?
   c. Reasoning What would the simple interest rate have to be for the investment to double in the same amount of time?

Test Prep

Multiple Choice

21. Matthew invests $5,000 at 14% simple interest. About how much interest will he earn in eight months?
   A. $467   **B.** $700   **C.** $5,467   **D.** $5,700

22. Which formula could be used to find the balance on a deposit of $520, earning 7% interest compounded semiannually for 3 years?
   F. $B = 520(1 + 0.035)^3$ **G.** $B = 520(0.07)^3$
   H. $B = 520(1 + 0.035)^6$ **I.** $B = 520(0.07)^6$

23. What is the balance after 8 years on a deposit of $500, earning 7% interest compounded semiannually?
   A. $657.97   **B.** $658.40   **C.** $856.91   **D.** $859.09

Short Response

24. A savings account pays 4% simple interest.
   a. How much interest does an $800 deposit earn in 4 years?
   b. How much more would the $800 earn in 4 years at 5%?

25. Greg deposits $800 into a savings account that earns 10% interest compounded annually.
   a. What is Greg's balance after four years?
   b. Make a table to explain your answer.

📶 **Take It to the NET**
Online lesson quiz at
www.PHSchool.com
Web Code: ada-0708

Mixed Review

Lesson 7-6   **Solve for the variable indicated in red.**

26. $f = \frac{15m}{a}$ **27.** $y = 4x - 9$ **28.** $d = \frac{5}{8}k + 1$

Lesson 6-3 🌐 **29. Architecture** A floor plan has a scale of $\frac{1}{4}$ in. : 5 ft. Find the length on the drawing for an actual length of 60 ft.

Lesson 1-10   **Graph each point on a coordinate plane.**

30. $A(-2, 0)$ **31.** $C(-4, -5)$ **32.** $D(1, -3)$

 **Technology**

Credit-Card Interest

When you use a credit card, you are charged interest each month on the balance in your account. You can use a spreadsheet to investigate the interest charged on a credit-card account.

You use a credit card to buy a $450 airline ticket. You are charged 1.8% monthly interest on your account balance, and you make a $40 payment each month. Using a spreadsheet program, create a spreadsheet with the formulas shown in red.

	A	B	C	D	E	F
1	Month	Balance	Planned Monthly Payment	Interest	New Balance	Total Interest
2	1	450	40	=B2*0.018	=B2+D2−C2	=D2
3	=A2+1	=E2				=F2+D3
4						
	⋮	⋮	⋮	⋮	⋮	⋮

The arrows indicate you should use the Fill Down feature of your spreadsheet program. This will calculate successive months for you.

EXERCISES

Use your spreadsheet. Round any totals to the nearest cent.

1. a. In which month is the balance less than the monthly payment?
 b. Your last payment is the balance plus the interest in the month you found in part (a). What is the amount of the last payment?
 c. What is the total interest paid on this account?

2. a. Change the monthly payment to $60 a month. In which month is the balance less than the monthly payment?
 b. What is the total interest paid on this account?

3. a. Create a new spreadsheet using a beginning balance of $1,200, 2.1% monthly interest, and a monthly payment of $100. What is the total interest paid on this account in 5 months?
 b. Change the monthly payment to $200. What is the total interest paid on this account in 5 months?
 c. **Reasoning** What can you conclude about the relationship between the size of monthly payments and the amount of interest charges?

Eliminating Answers

Before you do all the work involved in solving a multiple-choice problem, you usually can eliminate some answer choices. This can save you time in finding the correct answer. Also, it improves your chances of making a correct guess.

1 EXAMPLE

What is the solution to $\frac{3}{4}(x - 2) = \frac{3}{2}$?

A. -2 **B.** 2 **C.** 3 **D.** 4

The product on the left must equal the positive number on the right. Thus, since $\frac{3}{4}$ is positive, the value of $(x - 2)$ must also be positive.

The choices -2 and 2 do not give positive values for $(x - 2)$. You can eliminate choices A and B. Then substitute 4 for x and use mental math to find that D is the correct choice.

2 EXAMPLE

What is the solution to $x + 0.05x = 420$?

F. 400 **G.** 410 **H.** 420 **I.** 450

On the left, a fraction of x is added to x and the result is 420. Thus the value of x must be less than 420. You can eliminate choices H and I. Then check 400 in the equation to find that F is the correct choice.

EXERCISES

Show how you can eliminate one or two of the answer choices for each multiple-choice question.

1. What is the solution to $\frac{x - 2}{-3} = -4$?
   A. -13 **B.** -10 **C.** 11 **D.** 14

2. What is the solution to $x - 0.15x = 680$?
   F. 620 **G.** 675 **H.** 760 **I.** 800

3. On a field trip to the zoo, 21 students voted to have sandwiches for lunch. This represents $\frac{7}{8}$ of the class. How many students are in the class?
   A. 24 **B.** 25 **C.** 38 **D.** 40

4. The area of a rectangle is 64 in.^{2}. If the area is increased by 25%, which of the following could be the dimensions of the new rectangle?
   F. 6 in. by 8 in. **G.** 10 in. by 8 in. **H.** 10 in. by 10 in. **I.** 8 in. by 8 in.

Chapter Review

Vocabulary

balance (p. 383)
compound inequality (p. 377)
compound interest (p. 383)

consecutive integers (p. 353)
interest (p. 382)
interest rate (p. 382)

principal (p. 382)
simple interest (p. 382)

Reading Math
Understanding
Vocabulary

Choose the vocabulary term that correctly completes the sentence.

1. A bank pays __?__ when it pays interest on the principal and on the interest an account has earned.

2. The amount of money first deposited into a savings account is called the __?__ .

3. The principal plus the interest is the __?__ of the account.

4. When you count by 1s from any integer, you are counting __?__ .

5. A bank pays interest based on its advertised __?__ .

6. __?__ is paid only on the principal of an account.

7. A bank pays you __?__ for the use of your money.

Take It to the NET
Online vocabulary quiz
at **www.PHSchool.com**
Web Code: adj-0751

Skills and Concepts

7-1 Objectives

▼ To solve two-step equations (p. 348)

▼ To use two-step equations to solve problems (p. 349)

To solve two-step equations, undo addition and subtraction, then undo multiplication and division.

Solve each equation.

8. $2a - 7 = -15$
9. $3 = -6x + 15$
10. $\frac{c}{4} + 10 = 22$
11. $1.5y + 3.4 = 7.9$
12. $\frac{2}{3}y - 9 = 5$
13. $8 = 9x - 7$

7-2 and 7-3 Objectives

▼ To combine like terms to simplify an equation (p. 352)

▼ To use the Distributive Property to simplify an equation (p. 354)

▼ To solve multi-step equations with fractions (p. 357)

▼ To solve multi-step equations with decimals (p. 358)

To solve multi-step equations, remove grouping symbols and combine like terms first. Then follow the steps for solving two-step equations.

Solve each equation.

14. $8m - 3m = 4$
15. $6 - 2y - y = 12$
16. $\frac{2}{3}q + 5 = \frac{3}{4}$
17. $\frac{1}{4}(b - 7) = 8$
18. $1.06x - 3 = 0.71$
19. $-2(5 + 6c) + 16 = -90$

20. **Number Sense** Find four consecutive integers with a sum of -66.

7-4 Objectives

▼ To write an equation to solve a problem (p. 362)

One strategy for solving problems is to write an equation and then solve the equation.

Write an equation. Then solve.

21. A pair of jeans is on sale for 15% off the original price. The sale price of the jeans is $29.74. What was the original price?

22. A bank teller is counting his money and notices that he has an equal number of tens and twenties. He also has $147 in other bills. If the total value of the bills he has is $1,167, how many tens and twenties does he have?

🌐 23. **Finance** Jalisha invested some money and made an 8% profit. The current value of her investment is $1,296. How much did she invest initially?

7-5 Objectives

▼ To solve equations with variables on both sides (p. 367)

▼ To use equations with variables on both sides (p. 368)

To solve equations with variables on both sides, first simplify both sides of the equation. Then use properties of equality to get the variable alone on one side of the equation.

Solve each equation.

24. $7x = 33 - 4x$ 25. $2a - 24 - 3a = 5a$

26. $5x + 7 = -5x + 19$ 27. $4x - 26 = 5(2 - x)$

28. $8(b + 3) = 4b - 4$ 29. $2x - (9 - 3x) = 8x - 11$

🌐 30. **Travel Time** A refrigerated truck leaves a rest stop traveling at a steady rate of 56 mi/h. A car leaves the same rest stop $\frac{1}{4}$ h later following the truck at a steady rate of 64 mi/h. How long after the truck leaves the rest stop will the car overtake the truck?

7-6 Objectives

▼ To solve two-step inequalities (p. 373)

▼ To use two-step inequalities to solve problems (p. 374)

Solving two-step inequalities involves the same steps as solving two-step equations. Reverse the direction of the inequality symbol when you multiply or divide by a negative number.

Solve and graph each inequality.

31. $2a - 3 > 11$ 32. $9y + 13 \leq -14$

33. $-6c + 12 \geq 8$ 34. $23 < 7 - 4x$

35. $\frac{8}{9}x + 5 < -3$ 36. $-\frac{b}{2} + 14 > 13$

37. $-17 > \frac{x}{3} - 19$ 38. $x + 4x + 9 \geq 6$

39. Computers Last year's computer model is on sale for $799. You can add more memory to the computer. Each chip of 8 megabytes of memory costs $25. How many megabytes of memory can you add if you have at most $1,000 to spend? Write and solve an inequality.

7-7 Objectives

▼ To solve a formula for a given variable (p. 378)

▼ To use formulas to solve problems (p. 379)

Use the properties of equality to transform a formula.

Solve for the variable indicated in red.

40. $r = 6km$

41. $8x = 6y$

42. $Q = gp$

43. $a = b - 2c$

44. $w = 3a + 5n$

45. $e = \frac{h}{6} + 11$

7-8 Objectives

▼ To solve simple-interest problems (p. 382)

▼ To solve compound-interest problems (p. 383)

You can calculate **simple interest** using the formula $I = prt$, where I is the interest, p is the **principal** (original amount deposited), r is the **interest rate** per year, and t is the time in years.

Compound interest is interest paid on both the principal and interest. It is found using the formula $B = p(1 + r)^n$, where B is the final **balance,** p is the principal, r is the interest rate for each interest period, and n is the number of interest periods.

Find the simple interest.

46. $150 deposited at an interest rate of 9% for 2 years

47. $2,525 deposited at an interest rate of 2.5% for 4 years

48. $6,000 deposited at an interest rate of 3% for 6 months

Find each balance.

49. $8,000 at 12% compounded annually for 3 years

50. $17,500 at 17% compounded annually for 6 years

51. $22,000 at 6% compounded semiannually for 8 years

52. $33,800 at 18% compounded semiannually for 5 years

53. The more interest periods there are, the more interest you make on an investment. Do you agree with this statement? Explain.

Take It to the NET

Online chapter test at
www.PHSchool.com
Web Code: ada-0752

Solve each equation.

1. $3x + 4 = 19$

2. $5 + \frac{c}{9} = -31$

3. $2y - 15 = 11$

4. $8a + 3 = -12.2$

5. $\frac{3}{5}b - 8 = 4$

6. $\frac{m}{2} - 5 = 7$

7. $-83 = 9x - 2$

8. $18 - \frac{a}{4} = -5$

9. $\frac{3}{5}y + \frac{2}{5} = \frac{4}{5}$

10. $-23 - c = -19$

11. $3x + 4x = 21$

12. $\frac{1}{2}(10y + 4) = 17$

13. $2(7b - 6) - 4 = 12$

14. $2m - 6 = m$

15. $\frac{2}{3}a - 5 + \frac{8}{9}a = -19$

16. $0.015x + 3.45 = 4.65$

17. $12y + 3 = 9y - 15$

18. $3(2b + 6) = 4b - 8$

Write an equation. Then solve.

19. Number Sense Find three consecutive integers with a sum of 267.

20. A rental car company charges $35 a day plus $.15/mi for a mid-size car. A customer owes $117.15 for a three-day rental. How many miles did the customer drive?

21. Travel Time A moving truck leaves a house and travels at a steady rate of 40 mi/h. The family leaves the house 1 h later following the same route in a car. They travel at a steady rate of 60 mi/h. How long after the moving truck leaves the house will the car catch up with the truck?

22. Coin Collections The Jaspers collect nickels, dimes, and quarters in a jar. When they count the change in the jar, there are twice as many nickels as there are quarters. If there is $15.30 in dimes and $74.80 in all, how many quarters are there?

Solve and graph each inequality.

23. $7m - 8 > 6$

24. $2x - 6 \geq -9$

25. $-9a - 1 \leq 26$

26. $22 < 6c + 4$

27. $\frac{b}{3} + 12 > -3$

28. $-\frac{2}{3}x + 8 \leq 2$

29. $11 > -3y + 2$

30. $16 - 4a > 8$

31. Commissions An insurance salesperson earns a salary of $1,200 per month plus a commission of 3% of sales. How much must the salesperson sell to have a monthly income of at least $1,500?

32. Writing in Math How is solving a two-step inequality different from solving a two-step equation?

Solve for the variable indicated in red.

33. $H = 3w + 2$

34. $g = cst$

35. $R = 6n + 4p$

36. $y = \frac{x}{5} - 4$

Find the simple interest.

37. $800 deposited at an interest rate of 1.5% for 3 years

38. $1,050 deposited at an interest rate of 2% for 9 months

39. $2,500 deposited at an interest rate of 8% for 5 years

Find each balance.

40. $12,000 at 8% compounded annually for 4 years

41. $1,950 at 5% compounded annually for 2 years

42. $18,500 at 9% compounded semiannually for 5 years

43. $75,000 at 15% compounded semiannually for 8 years

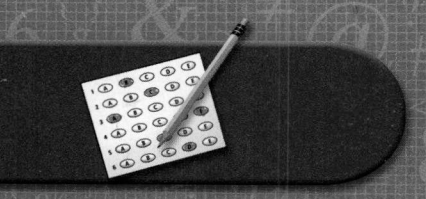

Test Prep

Reading Comprehension Read the passage below. Then answer the questions on the basis of what is *stated* or *implied* in the passage.

Income Tax The United States Tax Relief Act of 2001 lowered the percentage of tax that individuals must pay on their taxable income. The table below compares the tax rate for 2001 with the new, lower tax rate for 2002 for unmarried individuals.

Taxable Income	2001 Tax	2002 Tax
Up to $27,050	15% of taxable income	15% of taxable income
$27,051 to $65,550	$4,057.50 + 28% of excess over $27,050	$4,057.50 + 27.5% of excess over $27,050
$65,551 to $136,750	$14,837.50 + 31% of excess over $65,550	$14,465 + 30.5% of excess over $65,550
$136,751 to $297,350	$36,909.50 + 36% of excess over $136,750	$36,361 + 35.5% of excess over $136,750
Over $297,350	$94,725.50 + 39.6% of excess over $297,350	$93,374 + 39.1% of excess over $297,350

1. Why was the United States Tax Relief Act called a "Tax Relief" act?

2. Which expression shows the amount of tax owed by an unmarried person with taxable income of $40,000 for 2002?
   A. 0.275(40,000)
   B. 4,057.50 + 0.275(12,950)
   C. 4,057.50 + 0.275
   D. 4,057.50 + 0.275(40,000)

3. Which expression shows the amount of tax owed by an unmarried person with taxable income of $72,000 for 2002?
   F. 14,465 + 0.305(72,000)
   G. 0.305(65,500)
   H. 14,465 + 0.305(72,000 − 65,550)
   I. 0.305(72,000)

4. About how much tax will an unmarried person with taxable income of $27,500 owe for 2002?
   A. $0   B. $4,000 C. $7,500 D. $27,000

5. About how much tax will an unmarried person with taxable income of $300,000 owe for 2002?
   F. $90,000   G. $95,000
   H. $117,000   I. $210,000

6. About how much less tax would an unmarried person whose taxable income is $50,000 owe for 2002 than for 2001?
   A. $0   B. $10   C. $100   D. $1,000

7. In 2002, his first year out of high school, Joacquim expected to have a taxable income of $25,000. How much tax relief did Joacquim gain for 2002 compared to what he would have had to pay for 2001?

Wireless Style

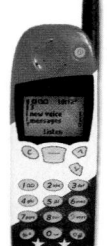

Applying Equations Cell-phone use has increased dramatically since the mid-1990s. Millions of people worldwide own cell phones. If you are one of them, you probably purchased a calling plan from a service provider. These providers charge different fees for a variety of services.

Throw It Away!

A credit-card-sized disposable cell phone offers approximately one hour of talk time.

The circuits are printed metallic ink instead of tiny wires.

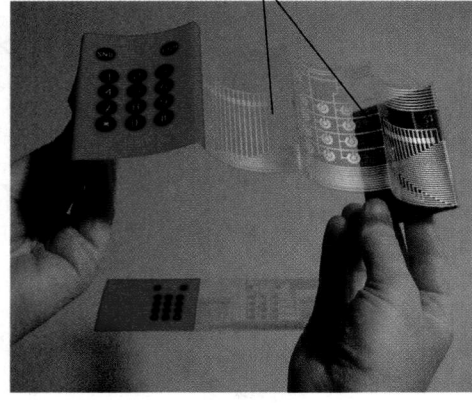

Activity

1. Suppose you are shopping for a calling plan. You expect to use 10 long-distance minutes per month.
   a. Use the table below and the total-cost equation to find out how much you will pay for the first month of each calling plan.
   b. **Writing in Math** Which plan would you choose? Explain.

2. Suppose a friend is also shopping for a calling plan. Your friend expects to use 60 long-distance minutes each month.
   a. Use the table below and the total-cost equation to find out how much your friend will pay for the first month of each calling plan.
   b. Which plan do you think your friend would choose? Explain.

3. **Number Sense** Without calculating, which plan would be the least expensive to use in the second month? Explain.

Calling Plan	A	B	C	D
Monthly Fee	$19.99	$34.99	$19.99	$29.99
Long-Distance Rate	$.15	$.15	$.00	$.20
Activation Fee	$36.00	$24.00	$30.00	$35.00

Total-Cost Equation

$$c = m + d\ell + a$$

c = total cost
m = monthly fee
ℓ = long-distance rate
d = long-distance minutes
a = activation fee

Monthly Fee The amount a customer pays each month for basic service

Long-Distance Rate The amount a customer pays for each minute of a call made outside the local calling area

Activation Fee A one-time fee paid to start phone service

Antenna

Antenna

Where's the Cell-Phone Tower?
Cell phone companies often camouflage their towers to make them blend in with the surrounding landscape.

Take It to the NET For more information about cell phones, go to **www.PHSchool.com**.
Web Code ade-0753

Where You've Been

- In Chapter 1, you used inductive reasoning to write rules for patterns. You also graphed points in a coordinate plane.

- In Chapter 4, you simplified fractions by finding the GCF of the numerator and denominator.

- In Chapter 7, you solved two-step and multi-step equations and inequalities using inverse operations.

Diagnosing Readiness

TEXT Instant self-check online and on CD-ROM

(For help, go to the lesson in green.)

Describing Number Patterns (Lesson 1-7)

Write the next two numbers in each pattern.

1. $8, 5, 2, -1, \ldots$ **2.** $43, 37, 31, 25, \ldots$ **3.** $4.5, 6, 7.5, 9, \ldots$ **4.** $-3, -5, -7, -9, \ldots$

Graphing Points (Lesson 1-10)

Write the coordinates of each point.

5. A **6.** B **7.** C

8. D **9.** E **10.** F

Draw a coordinate plane. Graph each point.

11. $M(0, -2)$ **12.** $H(-2, 4)$ **13.** $J(6, 1)$

14. $K(5, -3)$ **15.** $L(-4, -3)$ **16.** $G(3, 0)$

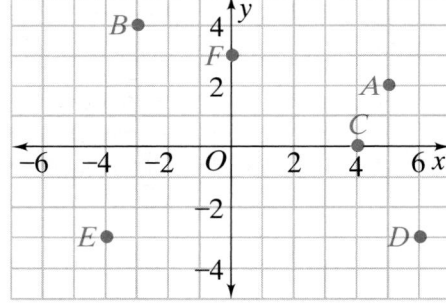

Simplifying Fractions (Lesson 4-4)

Write each fraction in simplest form.

17. $\dfrac{-5 - (-4)}{12 - (-6)}$ **18.** $\dfrac{15 - (-12)}{17 - 8}$ **19.** $\dfrac{-4 - 1}{-7 - (-2)}$ **20.** $\dfrac{4.3 - 3.5}{7.1 - 4.7}$

Transforming Equations (Lesson 7-7)

Solve each equation for y.

21. $4x + y = 3$ **22.** $y - 4 = -2x$ **23.** $2x - y = 6$ **24.** $8 + y + 6x = 0$

25. $12 - y = x$ **26.** $2y + x = 5$ **27.** $5y - 20 = x$ **28.** $3x + 4y = 12$

Linear Functions and Graphing

Key Vocabulary

Where You're Going

In this chapter, you will learn how to

- Determine whether a relation is a function.
- Solve linear equations.
- Solve systems of linear equations and inequalities.
- Solve a problem by graphing.

Real-World Snapshots Applying what you learn, on pages 454–455 you will solve problems about electronic devices.

You can use graphs to show real-world relationships visually. Labels can help explain the parts of a graph.

1 EXAMPLE

Transportation The graph at the right shows one trip from home to school and back. The trip combines walking and getting a ride from a neighbor. Tell what the graph shows by labeling each part.

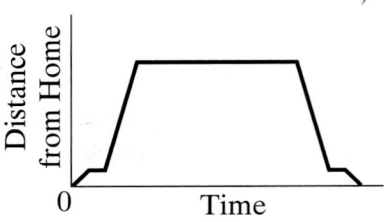

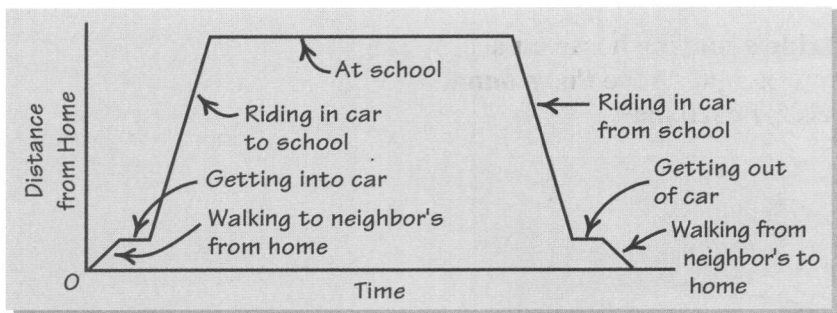

Label the parts of each graph.

1.

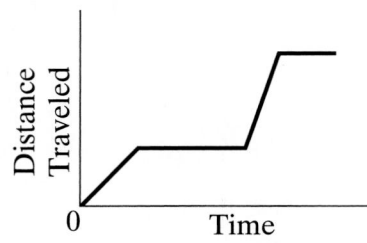

2.

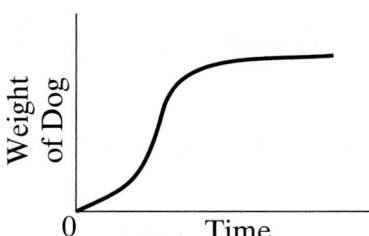

3. The graph at the right is a *step graph*. It shows the prices at a parking garage.
   a. How much does parking cost for an hour or less?
   b. How much does parking cost for 4 hours and 20 minutes?
   c. A receipt from the parking garage is for $7. What is the greatest length of time the car could have been in the garage?

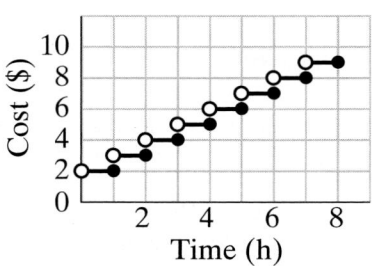

4. Reasoning Use the graph at the right. Jolene and Tamika were sprinting. Which girl ran faster? Explain.

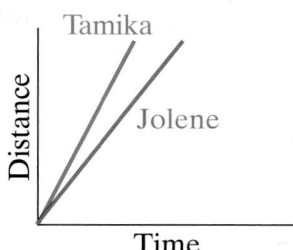

When you draw a graph without actual data, you are making a sketch. A sketch can help you visualize relationships.

2 EXAMPLE

You go to an amusement park and ride a moving horse on a carousel. Sketch a graph to show your height above the ground. Identify your axes and include labels for each part.

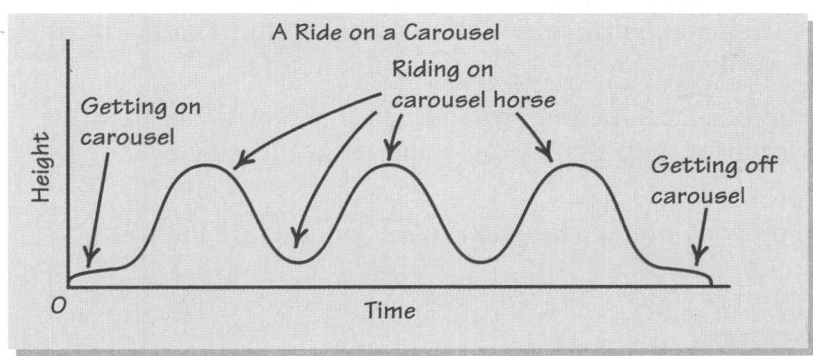

Sketch a graph for each situation. Identify your axes and include labels for each part.

5. the temperature outside during one 24-hour period

6. your speed as you take a trip on a train

7. the total distance you travel as you go to a concert and return home

8. the distance above ground of a pole vaulter's feet at a track meet

9. You pour water at a constant rate into the container shown at the right. Sketch a graph of the water level as you fill the container.

Relations and Functions

What You'll Learn

OBJECTIVE
1 To determine whether a relation is a function

OBJECTIVE
2 To graph relations and functions

. . . And Why

To solve real-world problems involving cooking

✓ **Check Skills You'll Need**

Graph each point.

1. $A(3, 4)$ **2.** $B(-3, 1)$

3. $F(2, 0)$ **4.** $D(2, -2)$

5. $C(-4, -3)$

6. $E(0, -4)$

For help, go to Lesson 1-10.

New Vocabulary

• relation
• domain
• range
• function
• vertical-line test

The table shows the results of a canned-food drive.

You can write the data in the table as a **relation,** a set of ordered pairs. The first coordinate of each ordered pair is the number of students in a homeroom. The second coordinate is the number of cans the students in that homeroom collected.

Food for Life Canned-Food Drive

Homeroom	Number of Students	Number of Cans
101	25	133
102	22	216
103	24	148
104	22	195
105	20	74
106	21	150

Here is the relation represented by the table:
   {(25, 133), (22, 216), (24, 148), (22, 195), (20, 74), (21, 150)}.
The braces, { }, indicate that these are all the ordered pairs in this relation. The first coordinates are the **domain** of the relation. The second coordinates are the **range** of the relation.

Some relations are functions. In a **function,** each member of the domain is paired with exactly one member of the range.

You can draw a *mapping diagram* to see whether a relation is a function.

1 EXAMPLE Identifying a Function

Is each relation a function? Explain.

a. {(0, 1), (1, 2), (1, 3), (2, 4)}

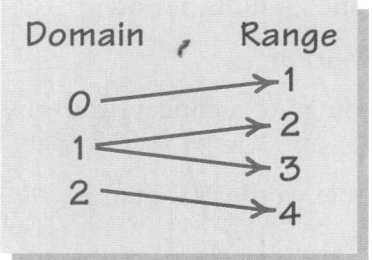

List the domain values and the range values in order.

Draw arrows from the domain values to their range values.

There are two range values for the domain value 1. This relation is *not* a function.

TEXT Interactive lesson includes instant self-check, tutorials, and activities.

b. {(0, 1), (1, 2), (2, 2), (3, 4)}

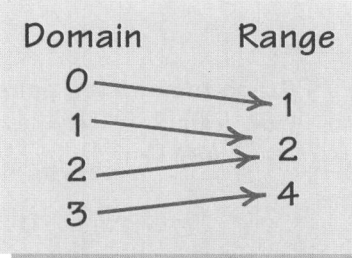

There is one range value
for each domain value.
This relation is a function.

c. {(0, 1), (1, 3), (2, 2), (3, 4)}

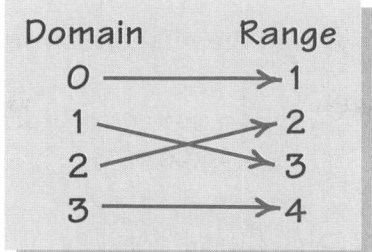

There is one range value
for each domain value.
This relation is a function.

✓ **Check Understanding** Example 1

1. Is each relation a function? Explain.

    a. {(−2, 3), (2, 2), (2, −2)}   **b.** {(−5, −4), (0, −4), (5, −4)}

Functions can model many everyday situations when one quantity
depends on another. One quantity *is a function of* the other.

2 EXAMPLE   **Real-World 🌐 Problem Solving**

Cooking **Is the time needed to cook a turkey a function of the
weight of the turkey? Explain.**

The time the turkey cooks (range value) is determined by the
weight of the turkey (domain value). This relation is a function.

✓ **Check Understanding** Example 2

2. **a.** For the United States Postal Service, is package weight
     a function of the postage paid to mail the package?
     Explain.
     b. Is the cost of postage a function of package weight?
     Explain.

Real-World 🌐 Connection

You can estimate the
cooking time of a turkey:
20 minutes per pound
unstuffed, or 30 minutes
per pound stuffed.

OBJECTIVE

2   **Graphing Relations and Functions**

Graphing a relation on a coordinate plane gives you a visual way to
tell whether the relation is a function. If the relation is a function, then
any vertical line passes through at most one point on the graph. If you
can find a vertical line that passes through two points on the graph,
then the relation is *not* a function. This is the **vertical-line test.**

3 EXAMPLE **Using the Vertical-Line Test**

Need Help?

The first value in an ordered pair, the *x*-coordinate, shows horizontal position.

The second value in an ordered pair, the *y*-coordinate, shows vertical position.

a. Graph the relation shown in the table.

x-coordinates   *y*-coordinates

Domain Value	Range Value
−4	−3
2	0
2	3
4	3
5	−4

Graph the ordered pairs (−4, −3), (2, 0), (2, 3), (4, 3), and (5, −4).

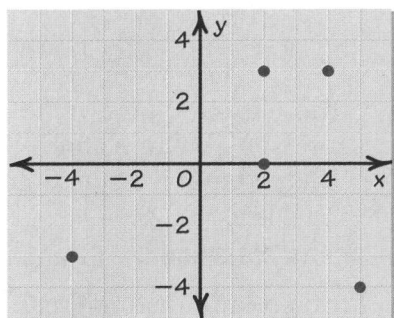

b. Use the vertical-line test. Is the relation a function? Explain.

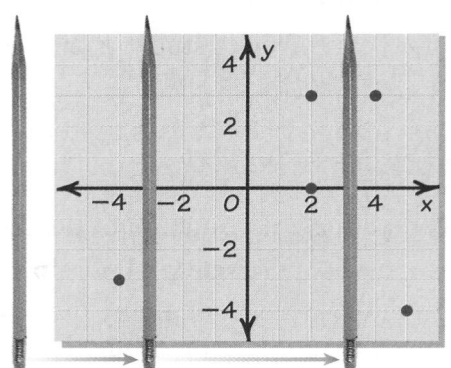

Pass a pencil across the graph as shown. Keep the pencil vertical (parallel to the *y*-axis) to represent a vertical line.

The pencil held vertically would pass through both $(2, 0)$ and $(2, 3)$, so the relation is *not* a function.

✓ Check Understanding   Example 3

3. **Algebra** Graph the relation shown in each table. Use the vertical-line test. Is the relation a function? Explain.

a.

x	y
−6	−5
−3	−2
0	−2
1	0
4	3
5	7

b.

x	y
−7	4
−2	6
−1	−1
−1	3
0	5
1	5

c.

x	y
−5	4
−4	4
−3	4
0	0
1	4
2	4

EXERCISES

 For more exercises, see *Extra Practice*.

Practice and Problem Solving

A Practice by Example

Is each relation a function? Explain.

Example 1
(page 400)

1. Domain Range   **2.** Domain Range   **3.** Domain Range

-5
-2 ——→ -2
2 ——→ 3
5

-5
-4 ——→ -1
-3 ——→ 2
6

3 ——→ -5
6 ——→ -2
      0
7 ——→ 1

4. $\{(3, -1), (3, 0), (-3, 4), (3, 8)\}$ **5.** $\{(-3, -2), (-1, 0), (1, 0), (5, -2)\}$

Example 2
(page 401)

6. Walking Is the time you take to go to the library a function of the distance to the library? Explain.

7. Is the price of a one-year subscription to your favorite magazine a function of the age of the subscriber? Explain.

8. Sewing Is the price of a piece of cloth a function of the length of the cloth? Explain.

9. Is the number of students on a field trip a function of the number of buses used? Explain.

10. Is the number of buses used for a field trip a function of the number of students on the field trip? Explain.

Example 3
(page 402)

Graph the relation shown in each table. Use the vertical-line test. Is the relation a function? Explain.

11.

x	y
-5	2
-1	4
2	-5
4	-1

12.

x	y
-5	-5
-3	-3
1	1
2	2

13.

x	y
-1	3
-1	2
0	-4
4	2

14.

x	y
3	-1
2	-1
-4	0
2	4

B Apply Your Skills

Graph each relation. Is the relation a function? Explain.

15. $\{(0, 1), (3, 5), (2, 2), \left(-\frac{1}{2}, \frac{4}{5}\right)\}$ **16.** $\{(-1, 9), (0, -1), (-1, 4), (4, 9)\}$

17. $\{(-1, 1), (-2, 1), (-2, 2), (0, 2)\}$

18. $\{(4, -8), (4, -6), (1, 2), (1, 5), (1, -6)\}$

19.

x	y
-5	6
-2	3
3	2
6	4

20.

x	y
3	-7
1	-5
-1	-5
-3	-7

21.

x	y
-7	3
-5	1
-5	-1
-7	-3

22.

x	y
6	-2
1	-1
0	-2
-1	-3

23. Writing in Math Is every relation a function? Is every function a relation? Explain.

24. Geometry Explain why the area of a square is a function of the length of a side of the square.

25. Error Analysis Your friend says that a relation is not a function when two ordered pairs have the same *y*-coordinate. Explain your friend's error.

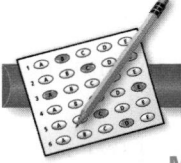 **Challenge**

Patterns In each function below, there is a pattern to how the range values relate to the domain values. Describe the pattern.

26. $\{(-2, 0), (0, 2), (3, 5), (8, 10)\}$ **27.** $\{(-5, 5), (-1, 1), (0, 0), (3, -3)\}$

28. $\{(-1, -0.5), (2, 1), (7, 3.5)\}$ **29.** $\{(1, 1), (2, 4), (3, 9), (4, 16)\}$

30. a. Open-Ended Write two different relations for which the domain is $\{-1, 0, 1\}$ and the range is $\{1, 2\}$.
   b. Graph your relations. Use the vertical-line test to tell whether each relation is a function.

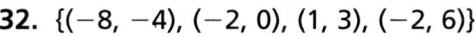

Test Prep

Multiple Choice

For Exercises 31 and 32, which choice best explains why the relation IS or IS NOT a function?

31. $\{(-5, 7), (-2, -1), (0, 3), (4, 7)\}$
   A. A function; only one range value exists for each domain value.
   B. A function; two domain values exist for range value 7.
   C. Not a function; the relation passes the vertical line test.
   D. Not a function; two domain values exist for range value 7.

Take It to the NET
Online lesson quiz at
www.PHSchool.com
Web Code: ada-0801

32. $\{(-8, -4), (-2, 0), (1, 3), (-2, 6)\}$
   F. A function; only one range value exists for each domain value.
   G. A function; two range values exist for domain value -2.
   H. Not a function; the relation passes the vertical line test.
   I. Not a function; two range values exist for domain value -2.

Short Response

33. Answer and explain.   **(a)** Is the number of people expected to attend a picnic a function of the number of sandwiches made for the picnic?   **(b)** Is the number of sandwiches made for a picnic a function of the number of people expected to attend?

Mixed Review

Lesson 7-8 **34. Banking** You invest $1,200 in an account that earns 3.5% interest compounded annually. Find the account balance after four years.

Lessons 7-1 and 7-3 **Solve each equation.**

35. $-42 + 3c = -6$ **36.** $\frac{3}{2}t - 4 = \frac{1}{2}$ **37.** $2m - 4.9 = -3.6$

Equations With Two Variables

OBJECTIVE

1 Finding Solutions of Two-Variable Equations

In previous chapters, you solved equations with one variable, such as $2x + 5 = 7x$. In this chapter, you will find solutions of equations with two variables, such as $y = 3x + 4$. An ordered pair that makes such an equation a true statement is a **solution** of the equation.

1 EXAMPLE   Finding a Solution

Find the solution of $y = 3x + 4$ for $x = -1$.

$$y = 3x + 4$$
$$y = 3(-1) + 4 \qquad \text{Replace } x \text{ with } -1.$$
$$y = -3 + 4 \qquad \text{Multiply.}$$
$$y = 1 \qquad \text{Add.}$$

● A solution of the equation is $(-1, 1)$.

✓ **Check Understanding**   Example 1

  1. Find the solution of each equation for $x = -3$.

   a. $y = 2x + 1$ **b.** $y = -4x + 3$ **c.** $y = 0x - 4$

You can use two-variable equations to model real-world situations.

2 EXAMPLE   Real-World Problem Solving

Meteorology The equation $t = 21 - 0.01n$ models the normal low July temperature in degrees Celsius at Mount Rushmore, South Dakota. In the equation, t is the temperature at n meters above the base of the mountain. Find the normal low July temperature at 300 m above the base.

$$t = 21 - 0.01n$$
$$t = 21 - 0.01(300) \qquad \text{Replace } n \text{ with 300.}$$
$$t = 21 - 3 \qquad \text{Multiply.}$$
$$t = 18 \qquad \text{Subtract.}$$

A solution of the equation is $(300, 18)$. The normal low July
● temperature at 300 m above the base of the mountain is $18°C$.

What You'll Learn

 OBJECTIVE 1 To find solutions of equations with two variables

 OBJECTIVE 2 To graph linear equations with two variables

. . . And Why

To solve real-world problems involving meteorology and oceanography

✓ **Check Skills You'll Need**

Evaluate each expression for $x = 2$.

1. $2 + x$ **2.** $x - 12$

3. $8x - 13$ **4.** $24 \div 2x$

❓ For help, go to Lesson 1-3.

New Vocabulary

• solution
• linear equation

 TEXT Interactive lesson includes instant self-check, tutorials, and activities.

✓ **Check Understanding** Example 2

2. Find the normal low July temperature at 700 m above the base of Mount Rushmore.

An equation with two variables can have many solutions. One way to show these solutions is to graph them, which also gives a graph of the equation. A **linear equation** is any equation whose graph is a line. All the equations in this lesson are linear equations.

3 EXAMPLE **Graphing a Linear Equation**

Graph $y = -\frac{1}{2}x + 3$.

Make a table of values to show ordered-pair solutions.

x	$-\frac{1}{2}x + 3$	(x, y)
-2	$-\frac{1}{2}(-2) + 3 = 1 + 3 = 4$	$(-2, 4)$
0	$-\frac{1}{2}(0) + 3 = 0 + 3 = 3$	$(0, 3)$
4	$-\frac{1}{2}(4) + 3 = -2 + 3 = 1$	$(4, 1)$

Graph the ordered pairs. Draw a line through the points.

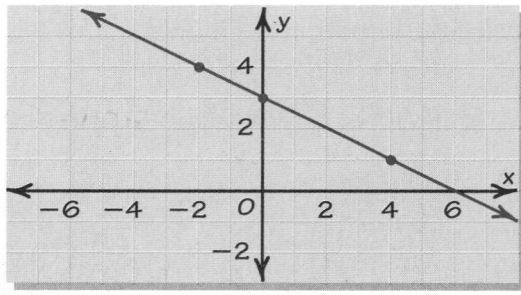

Need Help?

The expression $-\frac{1}{2}x$ means "the opposite of $\frac{1}{2}x$." So when the value of x is -2, the expression $-\frac{1}{2}x$ represents the opposite of one half of -2, which is 1.

✓ **Check Understanding** Example 3

3. Graph each linear equation.

  a. $y = 2x + 1$ **b.** $y = 3x - 2$ **c.** $y = -\frac{1}{2}x + 4$

If you use the vertical-line test on the graph in Example 3, you see that every x-value has exactly one y-value. This means that the relation $y = -\frac{1}{2}x + 3$ is a function. A linear equation is a function *unless* its graph is a vertical line.

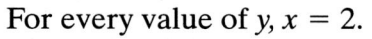

4 EXAMPLE Graphing $y = a$ and $x = b$

Graph each equation. Is the equation a function?

a. $y = 2$ **b.** $x = 2$

For every value of x, $y = 2$.   For every value of y, $x = 2$.

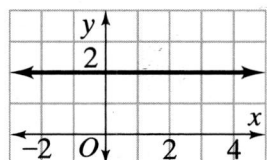   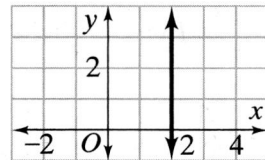

This is a horizontal line.   This is a vertical line.
The equation $y = 2$ is   The equation $x = 2$ is
a function.   *not* a function.

✓ **Check Understanding** Example 4

4. Graph each equation. Is the equation a function?

   a. $x = 1$ **b.** $y = -4$ **c.** $x = 0$

You may find it helpful to solve an equation for y before you find
solutions and graph the equation.

5 EXAMPLE Graphing by Solving for y

Solve $3x + y = -5$ for y. Then graph the equation.

Solve the equation for y.

$$3x + y = -5$$
$$3x + y - 3x = -5 - 3x \quad \textbf{Subtract 3x from each side.}$$
$$y = -3x - 5 \quad \textbf{Simplify.}$$

Make a table of values.   Graph.

x	$-3x - 5$	(x, y)
-2	$-3(-2) - 5 = 1$	$(-2, 1)$
-1	$-3(-1) - 5 = -2$	$(-1, -2)$
0	$-3(0) - 5 = -5$	$(0, -5)$

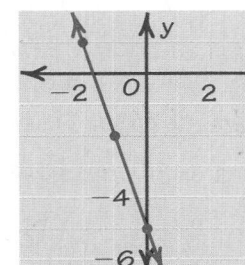

✓ **Check Understanding** Example 5

5. Solve each equation for y. Then graph the equation.

   a. $2x + y = 3$ **b.** $y - x = 5$ **c.** $-3x + 2y = 6$

EXERCISES

? For more exercises, see *Extra Practice*.

Practice and Problem Solving

 A Practice by Example

Example 1
(page 405)

Find the solution of each equation for $x = -5$.

1. $y = 4x + 2$ **2.** $y = -3x - 1$ **3.** $y = 8x$

Find the solution of $y = -x - 3$ for the given value of x.

4. -2 **5.** -1 **6.** 0 **7.** 1 **8.** 2 **9.** 3

Example 2
(page 405)

The equation $k = 1.6d$ gives an approximate relationship between d miles and k kilometers. Express each distance in kilometers.

10. the 430 miles between Boise, Idaho, and Reno, Nevada

11. the 665 miles between Columbus, Ohio, and Des Moines, Iowa

Examples 3 and 4
(pages 406 and 407)

Graph each linear equation. Is the equation a function?

12. $y = x - 3$ **13.** $y = -x - 2$ **14.** $y = \frac{2}{3}x - 2$

15. $y = x + 3$ **16.** $y = x - 10$ **17.** $y = 2x - 1$

18. $x = 7$ **19.** $y = 0$ **20.** $x = -2$

Example 5
(page 407)

Solve each equation for y. Then graph the equation.

21. $-4x + y = 16$ **22.** $-3y = 3x - 9$ **23.** $2x - 4y = 12$

24. $y - 6 = 0.5x$ **25.** $-3x = 2y$ **26.** $2y - 3x = 10$

B Apply Your Skills

27. Writing in Math Explain how you can determine from a linear equation whether the solutions of the equation form a function.

Is each ordered pair a solution of $4x - 3y = 6$? Explain.

28. $(3, 2)$ **29.** $(-3, -2)$ **30.** $(0, 2)$ **31.** $(2, 0)$

Find the solutions of each equation for $x = -2, 1,$ and 4.

32. $y = 7 - 3x$ **33.** $y = \frac{1}{4}x + 6$ **34.** $y = \frac{3}{5}x - 6$

$3x + 4y = 12$

$4y = 12 - 3x$

$y = 3 - 3x$

35. Error Analysis A student solved $3x + 4y = 12$ for y. Her work is at the left. What error did the student make?

36. José is driving on a highway. The equation $d = 55t$ relates the number of miles d and the amount of time in hours t. About how many hours does José spend driving 100 mi?

C Challenge

37. If you swim the backstroke, you burn 9 cal/min (calories per minute). If you swim the butterfly stroke, you burn 12 cal/min. The equation $9x + 12y = 360$ models how you can burn 360 cal by swimming the backstroke for x min and the butterfly for y min.
a. Find the solutions of the equation for $x = 0$ and $y = 0$. Explain what your solutions mean.

b. Graph the solutions you found in part (a). Draw a line through the two points.

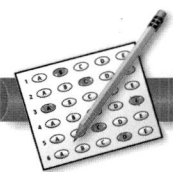**c. Language Arts** The solutions you found in part (a) are the *y-intercept* and the *x-intercept* of the line. Explain why these names are appropriate.

d. Use your graph from part (b). If you swim the butterfly stroke for 10 min, how long should you swim the backstroke to burn a total of 360 calories?

Test Prep

Multiple Choice

For Exercises 38 and 39, which ordered pair is a solution for the given equation?

38. $y = 2x + 7$
    A. (13, 3)   **B.** (3, 13)   **C.** (2, 8)   **D.** (8, 2)

39. $y = -3x - 4$
    F. (1, −1)   **G.** (1, 1)   **H.** (−7, 1)   **I.** (1, −7)

Reading Comprehension

Read the passage below before doing Exercises 40 and 41.

Mountains Under the Sea

There is a mountain range in the Pacific Ocean far beneath the surface. Jacques Piccard and Donald Walsh descended to 35,814 ft to make a record dive in these mountains in a submersible.

There is tremendous pressure at these depths. The pressure of the air at sea level is 14.7 lb/in.^{2}, and the pressure increases about 0.44 lb/in.^{2} for every foot an object descends below sea level.

40. What is the pressure at 10 ft below sea level?

41. The equation $y = 14.7 + 0.44x$ gives the pressure y in pounds per square inch at a depth of x feet below sea level.
    a. Find the pressure at the depth of the record dive.
    b. Find the pressure at half the depth of the record dive.

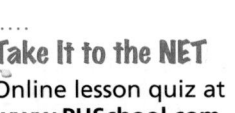

Take It to the NET
Online lesson quiz at
www.PHSchool.com
Web Code: ada-0802

Mixed Review

Lesson 8-1

Is each relation a function? Explain.

42. $\{(2, 4), (3, 6), (-3, 6), (1, 2)\}$ **43.** $\{(0, 3), (2, 1), (-7, 2), (1, 1)\}$

44. $\{(3, 4), (2.3, 6), (3, -7)\}$ **45.** $\{(0, -1), (0, 0), (-1, 0), (-2, -1)\}$

Lessons 4-9 and 5-5 **46. Astronomy** The sun orbits the Milky Way galaxy at about 135 mi/s. How far does the sun travel in an hour? In a week? Write your answers in scientific notation.

Direct Variation

A *direct variation* is a linear function modeled by the equation $y = kx$, where $k \neq 0$. The coefficient k is the *constant of variation*. In a direct variation, you can find k from one ordered pair (x, y). The graph of a direct variation always includes the origin.

1 EXAMPLE

Write an equation for the direct variation that includes $A(3, 5)$.

Step 1 First find the value of k.

$y = kx$	**direct-variation equation**
$5 = k(3)$	**Replace y with 5 and x with 3.**
$k = \frac{5}{3}$	**Solve for k.**

Step 2 Write the equation using the value of k.

$y = kx$	**direct-variation equation**
$y = \frac{5}{3}x$	**Replace k with $\frac{5}{3}$.**

You can write a direct variation to find the conversion factor between two measurement systems.

2 EXAMPLE

Measurement A segment measures 5 in., or 12.7 cm. Let x represent inches and let y represent centimeters. Write a direct variation to convert inches to centimeters. Then convert 24 in. to centimeters.

$y = kx$	**Use the equation for a direct variation.**
$12.7 = k(5)$	**Replace x with 5 and y with 12.7.**
$2.54 = k$	**Solve for k.**
$y = 2.54x$	**Replace k with 2.54 to write a direct variation.**
$y = 2.54(24)$	**Solve for $x = 24$.**
$y = 60.96$	**Multiply.**

24 in. is also 60.96 cm.

EXERCISES

Write an equation for a direct variation that includes each point.

1. $(4, 3)$ **2.** $(2, 3)$ **3.** $(8, 3)$ **4.** $(5.9, 22.42)$

5. Measurement A carton contains 2 qt, or 1.89 L, of juice. Write a direct variation for the relationship between quarts and liters. Find the number of liters in 8 quarts.

Slope and *y*-intercept

8-3

OBJECTIVE

1 **Finding the Slope of a Line**

**vestigation**

Understanding Slope

1. a. Graph $y = x$, $y = 2x$, and $y = 3x$ on one coordinate plane.
   b. How does the graph of $y = kx$ change as k, the coefficient of x, increases?

2. a. Graph $y = x$ and $y = -x$ on the same coordinate plane.
   b. How are the graphs of $y = x$ and $y = -x$ alike? Different?

The ratio that describes the tilt of a line is its slope. If a line slants upward from left to right, it has positive slope. If it slants downward, it has negative slope. To calculate slope, you use this ratio.

$$\text{slope} = \frac{\text{vertical change}}{\text{horizontal change}} = \frac{\text{rise}}{\text{run}}$$

1 **EXAMPLE** **Using Rise and Run to Find Slope**

Find the slope of each line.

a.

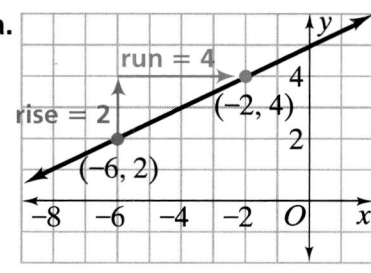

$$\text{slope} = \frac{\text{rise}}{\text{run}} = \frac{2}{4} = \frac{1}{2}$$

b.

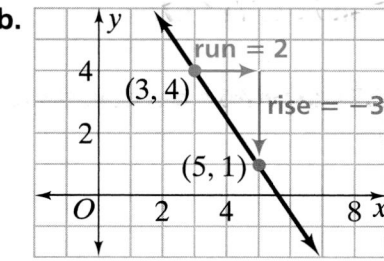

$$\text{slope} = \frac{\text{rise}}{\text{run}} = \frac{-3}{2} = -\frac{3}{2}$$

✓ **Check Understanding** **Example 1**

1. What is the slope of the ski trail at the right?

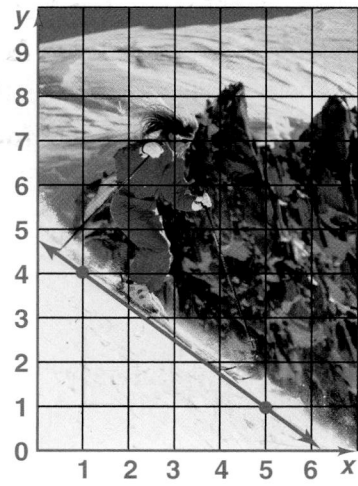

What You'll Learn

OBJECTIVE 1 To find the slope of a line

OBJECTIVE 2 To use slope-intercept form in graphing a linear equation

. . . And Why

To solve real-world problems involving the incline of a ramp or the slant of a roof

✓ **Check Skills You'll Need**

Find each difference.

1. $-4 - 5$ **2.** $3 - (-2)$

3. $6 - 9$ **4.** $-1 - (-1)$

❓ For help, go to Lesson 1-6.

New Vocabulary

• **slope**
• ***y*-intercept**
• **slope-intercept form**

ⓘ **TEXT** Interactive lesson includes instant self-check, tutorials, and activities.

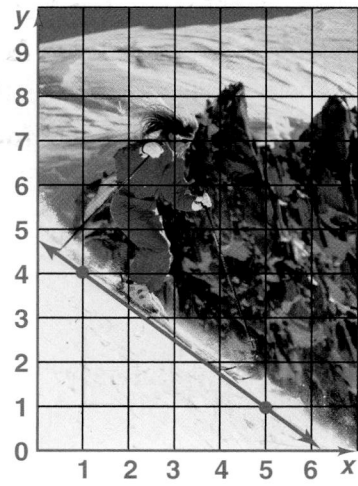

If you know two points of a line, you can find the slope of the line using the following formula.

$$\text{slope} = \frac{\text{difference in } y\text{-coordinates}}{\text{difference in } x\text{-coordinates}}$$

The y-coordinate you use first in the numerator must correspond to the x-coordinate you use first in the denominator.

2 EXAMPLE   Using Coordinates to Find Slope

Find the slope of the line through $C(-2, 6)$ and $D(4, 3)$.

$$\text{slope} = \frac{\text{difference in } y\text{-coordinates}}{\text{difference in } x\text{-coordinates}} = \frac{3 - 6}{4 - (-2)} = \frac{-3}{6} = \frac{-1}{2} = -\frac{1}{2}$$

✓ Check Understanding   Example 2

2. Find the slope of the line through each pair of points.

    a. $V(8, -1), Q(0, -7)$ **b.** $S(-4, 3), R(-10, 9)$

Horizontal and vertical lines are special cases for slope.

3 EXAMPLE   Finding Slope for Special Cases

Find the slope of each line.

a.
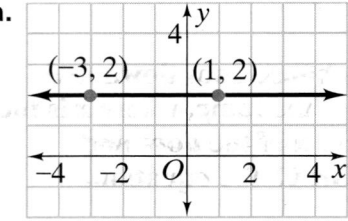

b.
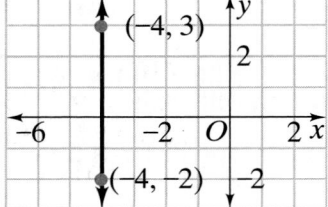

$$\text{slope} = \frac{2 - 2}{1 - (-3)} = \frac{0}{4} = 0$$

Slope is 0 for a horizontal line.

$$\text{slope} = \frac{-2 - 3}{-4 - (-4)} = \frac{-5}{0}$$

Division by zero is undefined. Slope is *undefined* for a vertical line.

Test-Taking Tip

You may say that a vertical line has *no slope*. But be sure that you do not confuse *no slope* with *slope 0*.

✓ Check Understanding   Example 3

3. Find the slope of each line.

a.
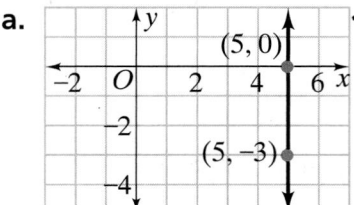

b.
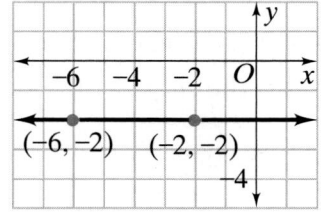

2 Using Slope to Graph Linear Equations

Here is the graph of $y = -\frac{1}{2}x + 3$.

The slope of the line is $\frac{-2}{4}$, or $-\frac{1}{2}$.

The **y-intercept** of the line is the point where the line crosses the *y*-axis. The constant in the equation is the *y*-intercept.

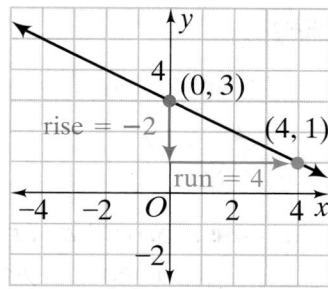

$$y = -\frac{1}{2}x + 3$$

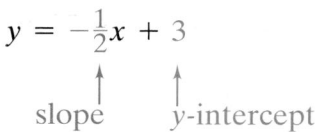

slope   *y*-intercept

Reading Math

The word *intercept* sounds like *intersect,* which means "to cross." Think of the *y*-intercept as where the line crosses the *y*-axis.

Key Concepts   Slope-Intercept Form

The equation $y = mx + b$ is the **slope-intercept form.** In this form, m is the slope of the line, and b is the *y*-intercept.

You can use slope-intercept form to help you graph an equation.

4 EXAMPLE   Real-World 🌐 Problem Solving

Engineering   A ramp slopes from a warehouse door down to a street. The function $y = -\frac{1}{3}x + 2$ models the ramp, where x is the horizontal distance in feet from the bottom of the door and y is the height in feet above the street. Graph the equation.

Step 1 Since the *y*-intercept is 2, graph $(0, 2)$.

Step 2 Since the slope is $-\frac{1}{3}$ or $\frac{-1}{3}$, move 1 unit down from $(0, 2)$. Then move 3 units right to graph a second point.

Step 3 Draw a line through the points.

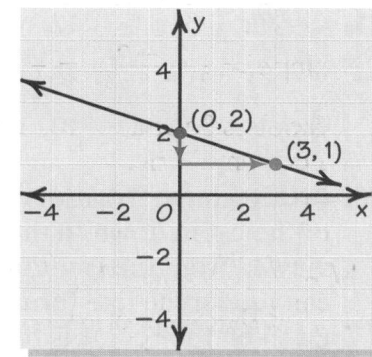

✓ Check Understanding   Example 4

4. Graph each equation.

a. $y = 2x - 3$ **b.** $y = -x + 4$

For more exercises, see *Extra Practice*.

Practice and Problem Solving

A Practice by Example

Example 1
(page 411)

Find the slope of each line.

1.

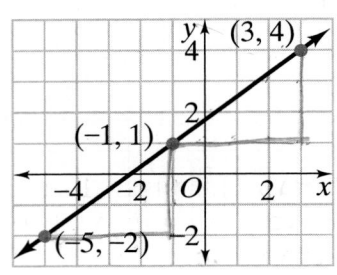

2.

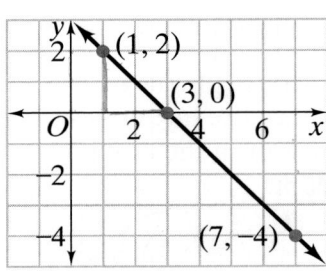

Example 2
(page 412)

Find the slope of the line through each pair of points.

3. $A(2, 6), B(8, 1)$

4. $E(1, -2), F(4, -8)$

5. $N(-5, 2), Q(1, -4)$

6. $G(3, 4), H(6, 10)$

7. $P(-3, 0), Q(4, -5)$

8. $A(2, 4), B(-1, -2)$

Example 3
(page 412)

Find the slope of each line.

9.

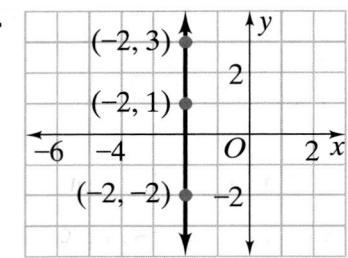

10.

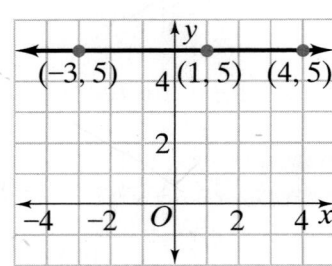

Example 4
(page 413)

Identify the slope and *y*-intercept of the graph of each equation. Then graph the equation.

11. $y = 7x + 3$

12. $y = -x$

13. $y = \frac{1}{2}x - 8$

14. $y = 2x + 1$

15. $y = -3x - 1$

16. $y = x - 4$

17. $y = 4$

18. $y = -3x + 3$

19. $y = -\frac{3}{2}x + 6$

20. Architecture The roof of an A-frame cabin slopes from the peak of the cabin down to the ground. It suggests the letter A when viewed from the front or the back. The equation $y = -3x + 15$ can model the line formed by one side of the roof. For a point (x, y) on the roof, x is the horizontal distance in feet from the center of the base of the house, and y is the height of the roof in feet. Graph the equation.

B Apply Your Skills

21. Error Analysis A student said that the slope of the line through $(8, 4)$ and $(2, 2)$ is 3. What error could this student have made?

22. Open-Ended Write equations for five different lines that intersect at $(0, 3)$.

Find the slope of each line.

23.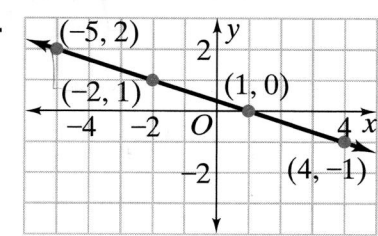

24.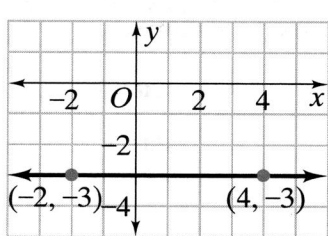

25. **Construction** The slope of a roof is its *pitch*. You indicate the pitch of a roof by a ratio $a : b$, where a is the number of feet of rise for every b feet of run. In the photos at the left, which house has a roof with steeper pitch? Explain.

Find the slope of the line through each pair of points.

26. $C\left(\frac{1}{2}, \frac{3}{4}\right), D\left(\frac{1}{4}, \frac{3}{4}\right)$

27. $L(7, -6.3), M(5, -1.3)$

28. $J(2.1, 3), K(2.1, 4.2)$

29. $A\left(\frac{2}{3}, 2\frac{2}{3}\right), B\left(2\frac{2}{3}, \frac{2}{3}\right)$

Solve each equation for y. Then graph the equation.

30. $y - 2x = 4$

31. $y + 3 = 5x$

32. $2y + 2x = 2$

33. $3y + 2x = 3$

34. $y - \frac{1}{2}x = 0$

35. $y + 3 = 0$

36. $2y = x - 8$

37. $-4y = x + 48$

38. $3y - 2x = 15$

39. Does the point $(-3, 4)$ lie on the graph of $y = -2x + 1$? Explain.

40. Does the point $(-2, -4)$ lie on the graph of $2y - 6x = 4$? Explain.

Ⓒ Challenge

Graph each line.

41. no slope, through $(4, -2)$

42. slope $\frac{2}{3}$, through $(0, -4)$

43. **a.** Graph the groups of equations on three coordinate planes.

Group 1	Group 2	Group 3
$y = 2x - 5$	$y = -3x - 1$	$y = -6$
$y = 2x$	$y = -3x$	$y = 1$
$y = 2x + 3$	$y = -3x + 4$	$y = 4.5$

b. **Writing in Math** How are the lines in each group related to each other? Explain.

c. **Reasoning** What is the coefficient of x in the equation of a graph that has slope 0?

44. **Construction** The slope of a road is its *grade*. What do you think it means for the grade of a road to be 4%?

45. Find the slope of the line at the left using two points. Then find the slope using two other points. Are the slopes the same? Explain.

Gridded Response

For Exercises 46–48, what is the slope of the line through the points of each pair?

46. $T(0, 5)$, $U(-3, -2)$ **47.** $Q(9, 5)$, $R(4, -5)$ **48.** $C(1, 7)$, $D(-8, 7)$

Take It to the NET
Online lesson quiz at
www.PHSchool.com
Web Code: ada-0803

For Exercises 49–51, what is the y-intercept of the graph of each equation?

49. $y = -4x + 7$ **50.** $y = -2x$ **51.** $y = 1.9$

Mixed Review

Lesson 7-6   **Solve and graph each inequality.**

52. $4x + 5 < 17$ **53.** $18 \leq 5 - 2x$ **54.** $-x + 6 > 31$

Lesson 6-8   **Find each percent of change. Tell whether the change is an increase or a decrease.**

55. from 10 to 9   **56.** from 20 to 30   **57.** from 52 to 39

Lesson 6-7  **58. Ticket Sales** During the 1998–1999 season, New York theater goers bought 11.7 million tickets for a total of $588.5 million. Theater goers spent a total of 5.5% more than the season before. What was the total amount spent during the 1997–1998 season?

Math at Work

Movie-Camera Operator

Lights . . . camera . . . action! These are familiar words for movie-camera operators. When the action begins, movie-camera operators are responsible for capturing the action on film. One scene in a movie can cost hundreds of thousands of dollars, so a scene has to be filmed correctly in as few tries as possible. Camera operators are trained in the effective use of lighting, lens filters, and camera angles. The operators determine the precise movements of the camera and its platform and the camera angles in advance of the actual shooting. It takes a good understanding of algebra and coordinate geometry to do that!

Take It to the NET For more information about movie-camera operators, go to **www.PHSchool.com**.
Web Code: adb-2031

Technology

Graphing Lines

You can use a graphing calculator to graph equations in slope-intercept form and find solutions.

EXAMPLE

Graph $y = 3x - 2$.

Step 1 Press the [Y=] key.
Enter $3x - 2$.

```
Plot1  Plot2  Plot3
\Y1=3X−2
\Y2=
\Y3=
\Y4=
```

Step 2 Press [ZOOM] **6** to graph your equation with the standard viewing window.

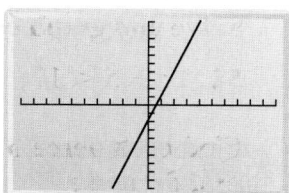

Step 3 Press **TABLE** to see solutions.

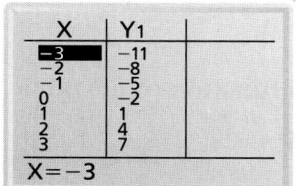

Step 4 Sketch the graph using values from the table of solutions.

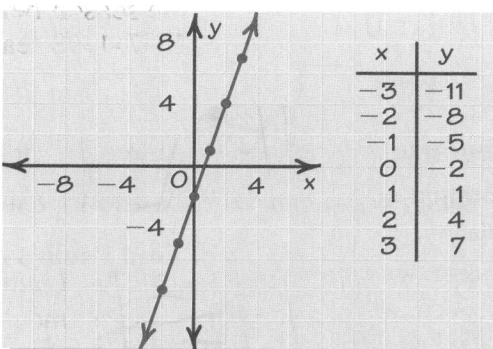

EXERCISES

Graph each equation.

1. $y = 2x + 1$

2. $y = x - 4$

3. $y = 3x + 2$

4. $y = -x$

5. $y = -x + 4$

6. $y = 4x - 3$

7. $y = -3x - 2$

8. $y = \frac{1}{2}x - 5$

9. $y = -\frac{1}{2}x + 2$

10. Graph $y = \frac{2}{3}x - 2$, $y = \frac{2}{3}x + 2$, and $y = \frac{2}{3}x + 6$, in the standard viewing window. Tell what you observe, and explain.

8-4

Writing Rules for Linear Functions

1 Writing Rules From Words

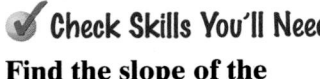
You can write a function using **function notation,** in which you use $f(x)$ instead of y. You read $f(x)$ as "f of x." You can think of a domain value as an *input* and the resulting range value as the *output*. A **function rule** is an equation that describes a function.

$$\overbrace{y = 3x + 7}^{\text{function rule}}$$

output input

$$\overbrace{f(x) = 3x + 7}^{\text{function rule}}$$

output input

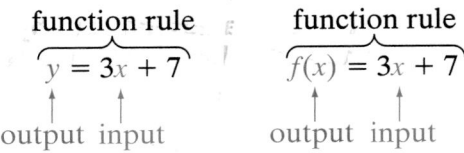

1 EXAMPLE   Real-World   Problem Solving

Sales Commissions Paulo works at a local store. Each week he earns a \$300 salary plus a 3% commission on his sales.

a. Write a function rule that relates total earnings to sales.

Words   total earnings   are   \$300   plus   3%   of   sales

Let s = the amount of his sales.

Let $t(s)$ = total earnings, a function of his sales.

Rule $t(s)$ =   300   +   0.03 · s

A rule for the function is $t(s) = 300 + 0.03s$.

b. Find Paulo's earnings for one week if his sales are \$2,500.

$t(s) = 300 + 0.03s$

$t(2,500) = 300 + 0.03(2,500)$ **Replace s with 2,500.**

$t(2,500) = 300 + 75$ **Multiply.**

$t(2,500) = 375$ **Add.**

Paulo earns \$375 if his sales are \$2,500.

✓**Check Understanding**   Example 1

1. Scrumptious Snack Mix is sold by mail order. It costs \$3/lb, plus \$4 for shipping and handling. Write a function rule for the total cost $c(p)$ based on the number of pounds p bought. Use your function to find the total cost of 5 lb of snack mix.

2 Writing Rules From Tables or Graphs

To write a function rule from a table, look for a pattern. The slope m is $\dfrac{\text{difference in } f(x) \text{ values}}{\text{difference in } x \text{ values}}$, and b is the value of $f(x)$ when $x = 0$.

2 EXAMPLE Writing a Function Rule From a Table

Write a rule for the linear function in the table below.

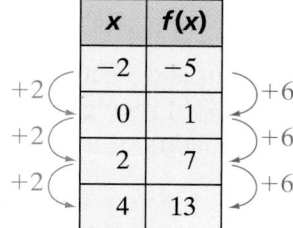

x	f(x)
−2	−5
0	1
2	7
4	13

+2 ... +6
+2 ... +6
+2 ... +6

As the x values increase by 2, the $f(x)$ values increase by 6.
So $m = \dfrac{6}{2} = 3$.

When $x = 0$, $f(x) = 1$. So $b = 1$.

$f(x) = m(x) + b$

● A rule for the function is $f(x) = 3x + 1$.

✓ Check Understanding Example 2

2. Write a rule for each linear function.

a.

x	f(x)
−1	−2
0	0
1	2
2	4

b.

x	f(x)
−3	6
0	0
3	−6
6	−12

c.

x	y
−6	−11
−4	−7
−2	−3
0	1

You can use slope-intercept form, $f(x) = mx + b$ or $y = mx + b$, when you write a rule for a linear function.

> **Reading Math**
> y and $f(x)$ may be used interchangeably in a function rule.

3 EXAMPLE Writing a Function Rule From a Graph

Write a rule for the linear function graphed below.

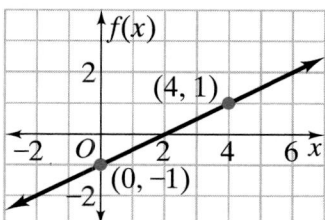

slope $= \dfrac{1 - (-1)}{4 - 0} = \dfrac{2}{4} = \dfrac{1}{2}$

y-intercept $= -1$

A rule for the function is $f(x) = \dfrac{1}{2}x - 1$.

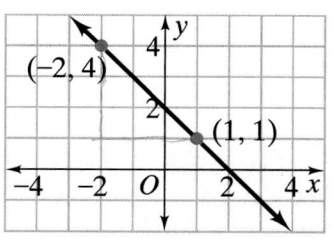

✓ Check Understanding Example 3

3. Write a rule for the function graphed at the right.

EXERCISES

For more exercises, see *Extra Practice*.

Practice and Problem Solving

A **Practice by Example**

Example 1
(page 418)

Write a function rule for each situation. Then use your function as indicated.

1. Money You give a salesperson $20 for a purchase and receive change. Use your function to find the amount of change from a $4.50 purchase.

2. Science The temperature *t* in *Kelvin* is 273.15 more than the temperature *c* in degrees *Celsius*. Use your function to find the equivalent temperature in Kelvin for 100°C.

3. Physics The force of gravity is less on Mars than it is on Earth. As a result, the weight of an object on Mars *m* is 40% of its weight on Earth *w*. Use your function to find the weight on Mars of a space probe that weighs 15 lb on Earth.

Example 2
(page 419)

In Exercises 4–8, write a rule for each linear function.

4.

x	f(x)
−9	−18
0	−9
9	0
18	9

5.

x	f(x)
−4	4
−2	2
0	0
2	−2

6.

x	y
0	−2.4
2	−4.8
4	−7.2
6	−9.6

Example 3
(page 419)

7.

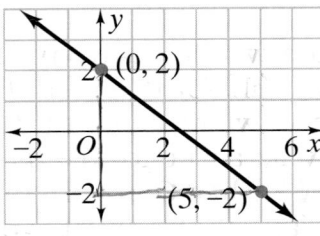

8.

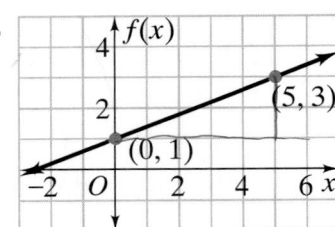

9. a. Writing in Math Describe the advantages you see in using a rule for a function rather than listing function values in a table.
   b. Describe the disadvantages.

B **Apply Your Skills**

10. Measurement Write a rule that expresses the number of quarts *q* of a liquid as a function of each of the following.
   a. the number of pints *p*   **b.** the number of fluid ounces *f*

11. a. Measurement Express the number of inches *n(d)* as a function of the number of yards *d*.
   b. Use your function to find the number of inches in 4 yards.

12. a. Geometry Write a rule that expresses the perimeter *p(s)* of a square as a function of the length *s* of one side.
   b. Use your function to find the perimeter of a square with side length 7 cm.

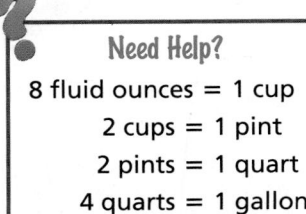

Need Help?

8 fluid ounces = 1 cup
2 cups = 1 pint
2 pints = 1 quart
4 quarts = 1 gallon

Examples 2 and 3 suggest that you can write a rule for a linear function if you know any of the following about its graph.
(a) the slope m and y-intercept b;
(b) the slope m and any point (p, q) of the graph;
(c) any two points (r, s) and (u, v) of the graph.

Sample A line through points $(-2, 6)$ and $(4, 3)$ has slope $\dfrac{3 - 6}{4 - (-2)} = -\dfrac{1}{2}$.

Using $-\dfrac{1}{2}$ for the slope, an equation of the line is $y = -\dfrac{1}{2}x + b$.

Using $(4, 3)$, substitute 4 for x and 3 for y: $3 = -\dfrac{1}{2}(4) + b$

So, $3 = -2 + b$, and the y-intercept b is 5. The rule is $y = -\dfrac{1}{2}x + 5$.

Write a rule for the linear function whose graph has slope m and y-intercept b.

13. $m = 2, b = -4$ **14.** $m = -\dfrac{1}{3}, b = -2$ **15.** $m = 0, b = 2$

Write a rule for the linear function whose graph has slope m and contains the given point.

16. $m = -\dfrac{1}{4}; (4, 0)$ **17.** $m = 3; (-2, -2)$ **18.** $m = \dfrac{3}{4}; (6, 4)$

Write a rule for the linear function whose graph contains the two given points.

19. $(1, 1), (2, 5)$ **20.** $(3, 0), (8, 2)$ **21.** $(11, 19), (-6, -15)$

22. $(-3, 2), (4, -1.5)$ **23.** $(1, -1), (4, -1)$ **24** $(1, 2.4), (-1, 3.8)$

C Challenge

25. a. Choose two points from the table and write a rule for the linear function.
b. Choose two other points from the table and write a rule for the linear function.
c. **Writing in Math** Compare the rules from parts (a) and (b). Justify your observations.

x	y
-6	-15
1	-1
7	11
11	19

Data Analysis For Exercises 26 and 27, use the data below.

26. Write a function rule for the total monthly cost for electric space heating.

27. a. Write a function rule for the total monthly bill of a home customer.
b. Suppose a home customer receives a bill for $22.52 one month. How many kilowatt-hours did the customer use that month?

Electricity Rates

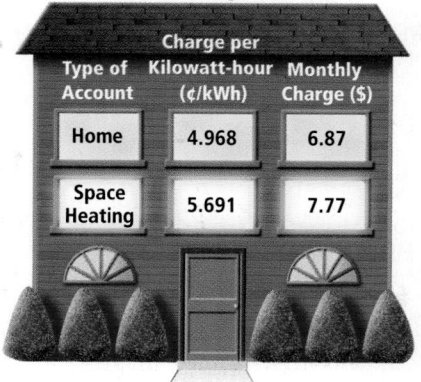

Type of Account	Charge per Kilowatt-hour (¢/kWh)	Monthly Charge ($)
Home	4.968	6.87
Space Heating	5.691	7.77

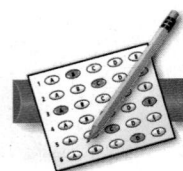

Test Prep

Multiple Choice

28. Which rule gives the same relationship between x and y as $x + y = 6$?
  A. $y = x + 6$ **B.** $y = x - 6$ **C.** $y = 6 - x$ **D.** $y = -6 - x$

29. Which function rule describes the number of centimeters y as a function of a number of millimeters x?
  F. $y = 100x$ **G.** $y = 10x$ **H.** $y = 0.1x$ **I.** $y = 0.01x$

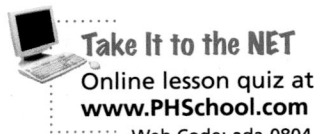

Take It to the NET
Online lesson quiz at
www.PHSchool.com
Web Code: ada-0804

30. Which rule shows the relationship of pounds, p, to ounces, z?
  A. $z = 16p$ **B.** $z = 32p$ **C.** $p = 16z$ **D.** $p = 32z$

Short Response

31. a. One gallon equals 4 quarts. Write a rule that expresses the number of quarts q as a function of the number of gallons g.
  b. Use your function from part (a) to find the number of quarts in 17 gallons.

Mixed Review

Lesson 8-3

Find the slope of the line through each pair of points.

32. $C(0, -2), D(2, 1)$ **33.** $J(3, -1), K(6, 1)$ **34.** $G(12, 8), H(6, 2)$

Lesson 6-4

Probability **Find each probability for choosing a letter at random from the letters in the word FUNCTION.**

35. $P(\text{N or C})$ **36.** $P(\text{consonant})$ **37.** $P(\text{not T})$

Lesson 3-5 **38. Sports** In 1999, Hicham El Guerrouj of Morocco ran the mile in world-record time. Had he taken 1.26 seconds longer, his time would have matched the previous record of 3 min, 44.39 s. Write and solve an equation to find the 1999 record time.

 ## Checkpoint Quiz 1   Lessons 8-1 through 8-4

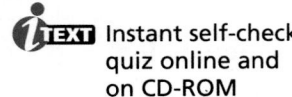 Instant self-check quiz online and on CD-ROM

1. Find three solutions of $9x - 2y = 18$.

2. Graph $3x - y = 5$ on a coordinate plane.

3. Is $\{(-2, 0), (-1, 3), (0, -2), (3, -1)\}$ a function? Explain.

4. **Writing in Math** Explain how to use the vertical-line test to determine whether a relation is a function.

Find the slope of the line through the given points.

5. $A(1, 5), B(3, 15)$ **6.** $D(-2, -4), F(0, -6)$ **7.** $G(-3, 4), H(-3, -6)$

8. What are the slope and the y-intercept of $y = -2x + 5$?

9. **Measurement** Write a rule to describe the number of pounds $p(n)$ as a function of a number of tons n.

Scatter Plots

8-5

OBJECTIVE

1 Interpreting and Drawing Scatter Plots

Making Scatter Plots

1. **Data Collection** For each person in your group, measure the height and *hand span,* the greatest distance possible between the tips of the thumb and little finger on one hand.

2. Graph the lengths as ordered pairs (height, hand span).

3. **a.** Share your data with the class. Make a graph of the class data.
   b. **Reasoning** Compare the two graphs you made. Does one graph show a relationship between heights and hand spans more clearly than the other? Explain.

A **scatter plot** is a graph that shows the relationship between two sets of data. To make a scatter plot, graph the data as ordered pairs.

1 EXAMPLE <u>Real-World</u> 🌐 <u>Problem Solving</u>

Income The scatter plot shows education and income data.

a. Describe the person represented by point A.

This person has 12 years of education and earns $20,000 in a year.

b. How many years of education does the person who earns $100,000 have?

The point (16, 100) has income coordinate 100. The person earning $100,000 in a year has 16 years of education.

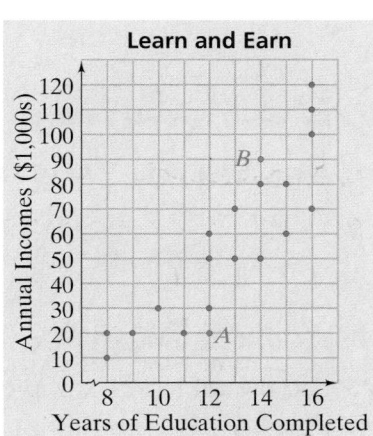

Learn and Earn

✓ **Check Understanding** Example 1

1. **a.** Describe the person represented by point B.
   b. How many people have exactly 12 years of education?

What You'll Learn

OBJECTIVE
1 To interpret and draw scatter plots

OBJECTIVE
2 To use scatter plots to find trends

. . . And Why

To solve real-world problems involving trends

✓ **Check Skills You'll Need**

Write the coordinates of each point.

1. A
2. B
3. C
4. D

❓ For help, go to Lesson 1-10.

New Vocabulary

- **scatter plot**
- **positive correlation**
- **negative correlation**
- **no correlation**

🅣🅔🅧🅣 Interactive lesson includes instant self-check, tutorials, and activities.

Climate Use the table to make a scatter plot of the latitude and temperature data.

Climate Data

City	Location (degrees north latitude)	Daily Mean Temperature (°F)	Mean Annual Precipitation (inches)
Atlanta, GA	34	61	51
Boston, MA	42	51	42
Chicago, IL	42	49	36
Duluth, MN	47	39	30
Honolulu, HI	21	77	22
Houston, TX	30	68	46
Juneau, AK	58	41	54
Miami, FL	26	76	56
Phoenix, AZ	33	73	8
Portland, ME	44	45	44
San Diego, CA	33	64	10
Wichita, KS	38	56	29

SOURCES: *The World Almanac* and *The Statistical Abstract of the United States*. Go to **www.PHSchool.com** for a data update. Web Code: adg-2041

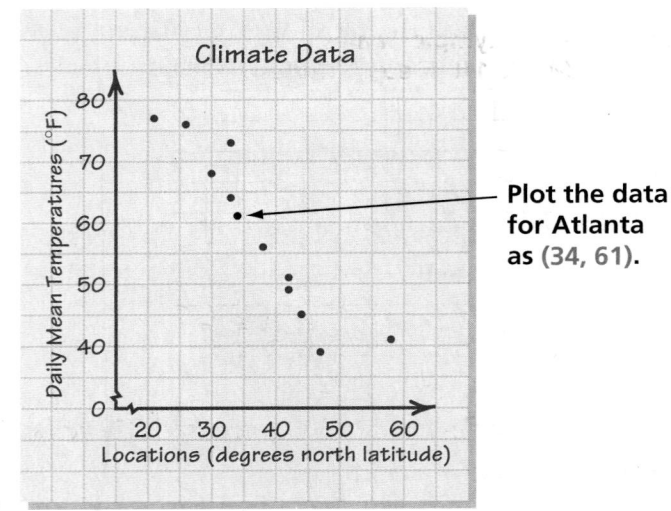

Plot the data for Atlanta as (34, 61).

✓ **Check Understanding** Example 2

2. Use the table in Example 2.

   a. Make a scatter plot of the latitude and precipitation data.

   b. Make a scatter plot of the temperature and precipitation data. Plot temperatures along the horizontal axis of the graph.

You can use scatter plots to look for trends. The next three scatter plots show the types of relationships two sets of data may have.

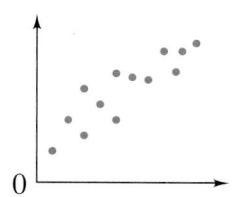

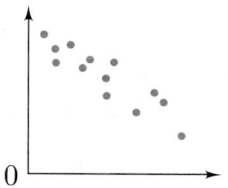

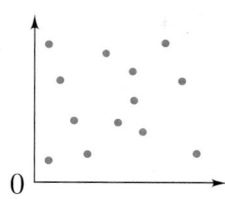

Positive correlation
As one set of values increases, the other set tends to increase.

Negative correlation
As one set of values increases, the other set tends to decrease.

No correlation
The values show no relationship.

> **Reading Math**
> "Positive slope" in a scatter plot suggests a positive correlation. "Negative slope" suggests a negative correlation.

3 **EXAMPLE** **Real-World** **Problem Solving**

Sports Use the scatter plot below. Is there a *positive correlation*, a *negative correlation*, or *no correlation* between the years and the winning times? Explain.

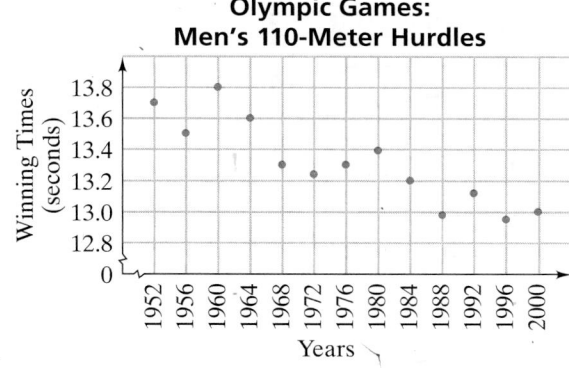

Since 1952, the winning times have generally decreased. There is a negative correlation.

✓ **Check Understanding** Example 3

3. Sports Use the scatter plot at the right. Is there a *positive correlation*, a *negative correlation*, or *no correlation* between the years and the winning distances? Explain.

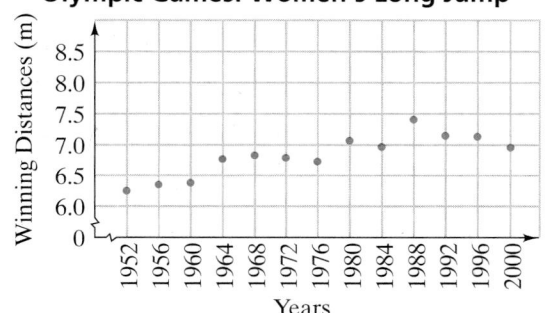

EXERCISES

For more exercises, see *Extra Practice*.

Practice and Problem Solving

A Practice by Example
Example 1
(page 423)

Reading Math
For help with reading and solving Exercises 1–3, see page 429.

Statistics The scatter plot shows the average times that 15 students spent watching television and on physical activities in a day.

1. Describe the student represented by point *A*.

2. How many students averaged 1 hour of physical activity?

3. How many students averaged 5 hours of watching television?

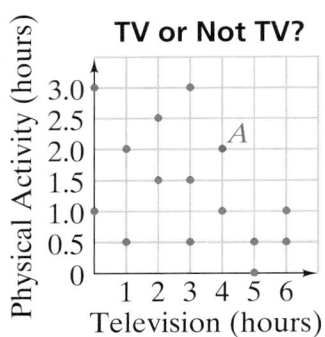

TV or Not TV?

Physical Activity (hours)
3.0
2.5
2.0
1.5
1.0
0.5
0
1 2 3 4 5 6
Television (hours)

Example 2
(page 424)

Nutrition For Exercises 4–6, use the table below. Make a scatter plot for the data indicated. Graph calories on the horizontal axis.

Nutritional Values for 100 Grams of Food

Food	Fat (grams)	Protein (grams)	Carbohydrate (grams)	Energy (calories)
Bread	4	8	50	267
Cheese	33	25	1	403
Chicken	4	31	0	165
Eggs	11	13	1	155
Ground beef	19	27	0	292
Milk	3	3	5	61
Peanuts	49	26	16	567
Pizza	5	12	33	223
Tuna	1	26	0	116

SOURCE: U. S. Department of Agriculture Nutrient Database for Standard Reference

4. calories and grams of protein

5. calories and grams of fat

6. calories and grams of carbohydrates

Example 3
(page 425)

Is there a *positive correlation,* a *negative correlation,* or *no correlation* between the sets of data in each scatter plot? Explain.

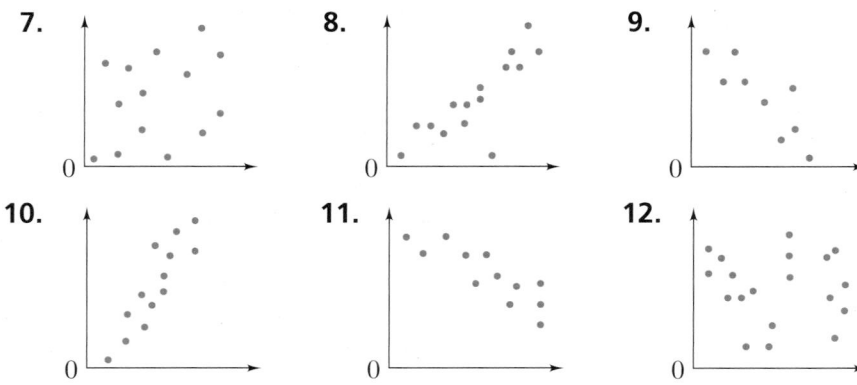

7.

8.

9.

10.

11.

12.

Data Analysis The scatter plot below shows the relationship between the distances from school and the times it takes to get to school for the students in one class.

13. How long does it take the student who lives 0.5 mi from school to get to school?

14. How many students live closer than 1 mi from school?

15. How many students take longer than 35 min to get to school?

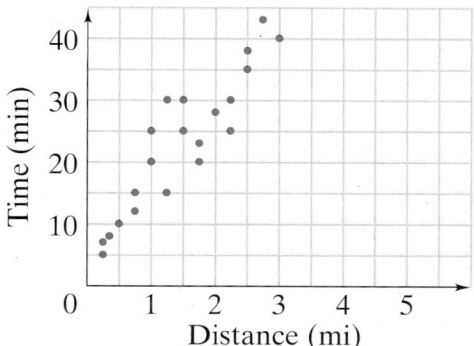

Would you expect a *positive correlation,* a *negative correlation,* or *no correlation* between each pair of data sets? Explain.

16. the age of pets in a home and the number of pets in that home

17. the temperature outside and the number of layers of clothing

18. your grade on a test and the amount of time you studied

19. the shoe sizes and the shirt sizes for men

20. the times candles take to burn and their original heights

21. the number of students in a school and the number of stores near a school

22. latitude and precipitation (see p. 424 Check Understanding 2a)

23. temperature and precipitation (see p. 424 Check Understanding 2b)

24. **Writing in Math** Describe a pair of data sets, different from any in this lesson, for which you would expect to see a scatter plot with a negative correlation. Explain.

25. **Ticket Prices** The table at the right shows the average prices of movie tickets and the numbers of movie admissions.

a. Make a scatter plot of the data in the table. Graph the prices of tickets on the horizontal axis.

b. **Data Analysis** Is there a *positive correlation,* a *negative correlation,* or *no correlation* between the numbers of admissions and the prices of tickets?

c. **Reasoning** Would your answer to part (b) be the same if you graphed ticket prices on the vertical axis instead? Explain.

Year	Number of Admissions (millions)	Average Ticket Price
1990	1,189	$4.23
1992	1,173	$4.15
1994	1,292	$4.18
1996	1,339	$4.42
1998	1,481	$4.69

SOURCE: Motion Picture Association of America

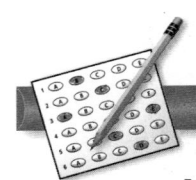

Multiple Choice

26. Which scatter plot shows that as the numbers of pages in magazines increase, the weights of the magazines increase?

A.

(scatter plot: Weights vs Pages, upward trend)

B.

(scatter plot: Weights vs Pages, downward trend)

Take It to the NET
Online lesson quiz at
www.PHSchool.com
Web Code: ada-0805

C.

(scatter plot: Pages vs Weights, downward trend)

D.

(scatter plot: Pages vs Weights, no correlation)

27. Which pair of data sets would most likely have no correlation?

 F. the distances cars can travel on full tanks of gasoline and the amounts of gasoline their tanks can hold

 G. the ages of children under 12 years old and their heights

 H. people's ring sizes and the numbers of rings they own

 I. the numbers of students and the numbers of teachers in each school in your state

Short Response

In Exercises 28–30, **(a)** describe a graph with each given type of correlation.   **(b)** Sketch a graph showing each type of correlation.

28. positive   **29.** negative   **30.** no correlation

Mixed Review

Lesson 8-5   **Write a rule for each function.**

31.

x	y
−4	−10
−2	−5
0	0
2	5

32.

x	y
−6	5
−3	3
0	1
3	−1

33.

x	f(x)
−2	9
1	6
4	3
7	0

Lesson 7-7   **Solve each formula for the variable indicated in red.**

34. $V = \frac{1}{3}Bh$ **35.** $A = \frac{1}{2}(b + c)h$ **36.** $S = \frac{a}{1 - r}$

Lesson 6-7 🌐 **37. Personal Finance** Ms. Jimenez earns $27,000 per year. She is paid weekly. She puts 8% of her salary in a retirement fund. How much money goes into this fund each week?

To read a graph, you must understand its parts. You must also be able to analyze what it shows. Graphs called *scatter plots* show correlations. They tell you how, if at all, pairs of data sets are related.

EXAMPLE

Statistics The scatter plot shows the average times that 15 students spent watching television and the average times they spent on physical activity in a day.

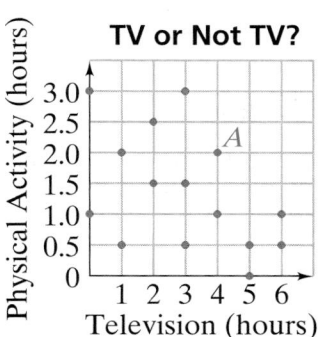

TV or Not TV?

1. Describe the student represented by point A.

2. How many students averaged 1 hour of physical activity?

3. How many students averaged 5 hours of watching television?

• **Understand the parts.**

The labeling of the axes provides the key to understanding the graph. You find hours of TV viewing on the horizontal axis. You find hours of physical activity on the vertical axis. A plotted point corresponds to an ordered pair (TV hours, activity hours).

1. **Describe the student represented by point A.**
   This student averaged 4 hours of TV viewing and 2 hours of physical activity daily.

2. **How many students averaged 1 hour of physical activity?**
   Find 1 hour of physical activity on the vertical axis. Look across and find three points. Three students averaged 1 hour of physical activity.

3. **How many students averaged 5 hours of watching TV?**
   Find 5 hours of television viewing on the horizontal axis. Look above and find two points. Two students averaged 5 hours watching TV.

• **Analyze what the graph shows.**

This graph is a scatter plot. You should decide what kind of correlation, if any, the graph shows.

EXERCISES

1. Would you expect there to be a positive correlation, a negative correlation, or no correlation between hours of physical activity and hours of watching television? Justify your choice.

2. Does the scatter plot suggest a positive correlation, a negative correlation, or no correlation? Explain.

Solve by Graphing

What You'll Learn

OBJECTIVE
1 To solve problems by graphing

. . . And Why

To solve real-world problems involving wildlife populations

✓ Check Skills You'll Need

Write a rule for each linear function.

1.

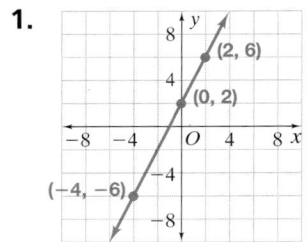

2.

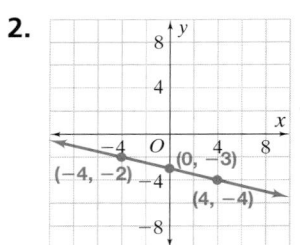

🔎 For help, go to Lesson 8–4.

New Vocabulary

• trend line

Math Strategies in Action
Businesses and government agencies use scatter plots to look for trends and make predictions.

For example, the park service at Isle Royale, Michigan, surveys the moose and wolf populations each spring. They use a scatter plot to show the relationship between them.

On the scatter plot they draw a **trend line** that closely fits the data points in the scatter plot. Using the trend line, they can predict the size of one population from the size of the other.

Real-World 🌐 Connection
Moose, like the one shown above, have wolves as a principal predator.

1 EXAMPLE Real-World 🌐 Problem Solving

Wildlife Use the data in the table below. Suppose there were 18 wolves one year. About how many moose would you expect to be on the island that year?

Isle Royale Populations

Year	Wolf	Moose	Year	Wolf	Moose	Year	Wolf	Moose
1982	14	700	1988	12	1,653	1994	15	1,800
1983	23	900	1989	11	1,397	1995	16	2,400
1984	24	811	1990	15	1,216	1996	22	1,200
1985	22	1,062	1991	12	1,313	1997	24	500
1986	20	1,025	1992	12	1,600	1998	14	700
1987	16	1,380	1993	13	1,880	1999	25	750

SOURCE: Isle Royale National Park Service

1. What are the two variables?

2. What are you trying to predict?

Plan and Solve

You can graph the data in a scatter plot. If the points show a correlation, you can draw a trend line. You can then use the line to predict other data values.

Step 1 Make a scatter plot by graphing the (wolf, moose) ordered pairs. Use the x-axis for wolves and the y-axis for moose.

Step 2 Sketch a trend line. The line should be as close as possible to each data point. There should be about as many points above the trend line as below it.

Step 3 To predict the number of moose when there are 18 wolves, find 18 along the horizontal axis. Look up to find the point on the trend line that corresponds to 18 wolves. Then look across to the value on the vertical axis, which is about 1,200.

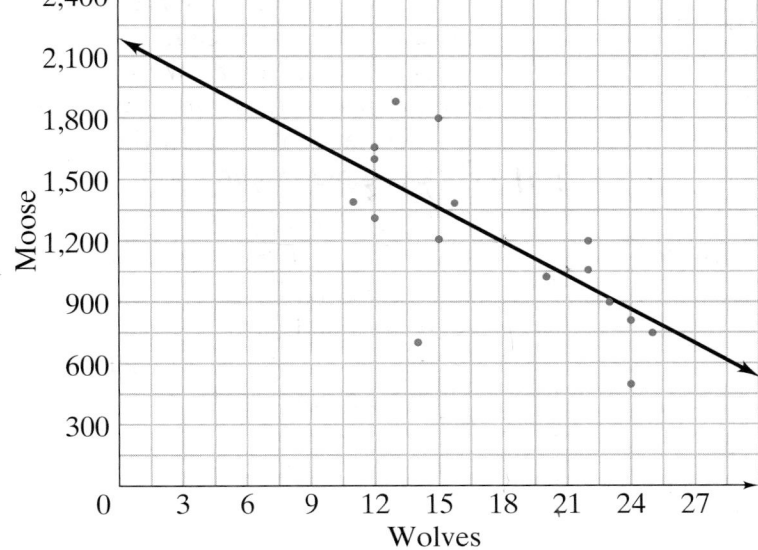

There will be about 1,200 moose when there are 18 wolves.

Look Back and Check

You can write an equation for a trend line. You can use the equation to make predictions.

Check Understanding

3. **a.** What is the y-intercept of the trend line above?
   b. Locate one other point on the trend line. Then find the slope of the trend line.
   c. Write an equation for the trend line in slope-intercept form.
   d. Use the equation you wrote in part (c). Find the solution of the equation when $x = 18$.

EXERCISES

For more exercises, see *Extra Practice.*

Practice and Problem Solving

 Practice by Example

Example 1
(page 430)

Solve each problem by graphing.

Statistics For Exercises 1 and 2, use the data below. The table shows the populations of some states and the numbers of cars registered in those states.

State Populations and Cars

State	Population (millions)	Registered Cars (millions)	State	Population (millions)	Registered Cars (millions)
FL	14.4	7.2	NY	18.1	7.9
GA	7.3	3.8	OH	11.2	6.6
IL	11.8	6.2	PA	12.0	5.9
KS	2.6	1.2	SC	3.7	1.8
ME	1.2	0.6	TN	5.3	3.0
MS	2.7	1.3	TX	19.1	7.4
NV	1.6	0.6	WA	5.5	2.6

SOURCE: *Statistical Abstract of the United States.* Go to **www.PHSchool.com** for a data update. Web Code: adg-2041

Strategies

- Account for All Possibilities
- Draw a Diagram
- Look for a Pattern
- Make a Model
- Make a Table
- Simplify the Problem
- Simulate the Problem
- Solve by Graphing
- Try, Test, Revise
- Use Multiple Strategies
- Work Backward
- Write an Equation
- Write a Proportion

1. a. Use the data to make a scatter plot of the data. Use the population data for the horizontal axis.
   b. Draw a trend line.
   c. Predict how many cars are registered by the 32.2 million people in California.
   d. Write an equation for your trend line. Predict the number of cars registered by the 7.3 million people in North Carolina.

2. Writing in Math Is there a correlation between the two data sets? Explain.

3. Data Analysis Use the data in the table below. Predict the number of gallons bought for $15.

Gasoline Purchases

Dollars Spent	12	14	11	12	10	6	10	8
Gallons Bought	7.3	8.0	5.9	6.5	5.7	3.5	5.1	4.4

B **Apply Your Skills** **Solve using any strategy.**

4. Elections Four candidates are running for president of the student council. Three other candidates are running for vice-president. How many different ways can the two offices be filled?

Writing in Math

For help with justifying your answer to Exercise 5, see page 434.

5. Business A supermarket charges $1.17 for a 12-oz jar of salsa and $1.89 for a 20-oz jar. Now the producer is introducing a 16-oz jar of the same salsa. What do you think would be a fair price for this new size? Justify your answer to the manager of the store.

432 Chapter 8 Linear Functions and Graphing

6. **Algebra** A plumber charges $45 for a service call, plus $70/h for her time.
   a. Find the cost of a two-hour service call.
   b. How long was a service call that cost $150?

7. **Engineering** To provide wheelchair access, a ramp with a slope of $\frac{1}{15}$ is being built to a door of a building. Suppose that the bottom of the door is 3 ft above street level. How far will the ramp extend from the building?

C Challenge 8. **Physics** As the weight held by a spring increases, the length of the spring increases proportionally. Suppose a 2-lb weight stretches a spring to 15 in., and a 12-lb weight stretches the same spring to 20 in. What is the length of the spring with no weight attached?

9. The data table on page 430 shows 18 data pairs. Its scatter plot (page 431) shows 17 plotted points. Make a conjecture as to why this is so. Study the table to verify or disprove your conjecture.

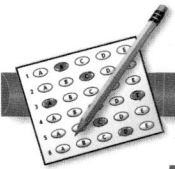

Test Prep

Multiple Choice

10. Which ordered pair is a solution for $4x - 3y = 6$?
    A. $(-3, 2)$ B. $(3, 2)$ C. $(3, -2)$ D. $(-3, -2)$

Take It to the NET
Online lesson quiz at
www.PHSchool.com
Web Code: ada-0806

11. What is the slope of the line through $A(2, 6)$ and $B(8, -1)$?
    F. $-\frac{6}{7}$ G. $-\frac{4}{9}$ H. $\frac{5}{6}$ I. $-\frac{7}{6}$

12. What is the slope of the graph of $3x - 2y = 6$?
    A. $-\frac{3}{2}$ B. $-\frac{2}{3}$ C. $\frac{2}{3}$ D. $\frac{3}{2}$

13. What is the y-intercept of the graph of $3x - 2y = 6$?
    F. -3 G. 2   H. 3   I. 6

Short Response

14. One gallon equals 4 quarts.   (a) Write a rule that expresses the number of gallons g of a liquid as a function of the number of quarts q.   (b) Use the rule to find the number of gallons in 30 quarts.

Mixed Review

Lesson 8-2   **Find the solutions of each equation for $x = -3, 0,$ and 2.**

15. $y = -3x$ 16. $y = \frac{1}{3}x + 4$ 17. $y = 0.5x - 2$

Lessons 7-2 and 7-5   **Solve each equation.**

18. $3x + 7 = 4x - 12$ 19. $7t + 3 - 4t = -6$

20. $8(2 - c) - 12 = -3c$ 21. $-2x + 3(5 - x) = 5$

Lesson 6-6 22. **Food** About 150 million of the 20 billion hot dogs consumed in the United States each year are eaten during the Fourth of July weekend. What percent of the hot dogs are eaten at this time?

When you present mathematical information to persuade someone to your point of view, you should do the following:

- Identify your audience and your goal.
- Summarize the mathematics behind your view.
- Create a graph or other visual display to support your view.

EXAMPLE

Business A supermarket charges $1.17 for a 12-oz jar of salsa and $1.89 for a 20-oz jar. Now the manufacturer is introducing a 16-oz jar of the same salsa. What do you think would be a fair price for this new size? Justify your answer.

- Identify your audience and your goal.

  Your audience is the manager. Your goal is to decide on a price for the 16-oz jar and then convince the manager that this price is fair.

- Summarize the mathematics behind your thinking.

  Writing solutions to word problems is excellent practice for this. Here, you find the unit price for each jar size.

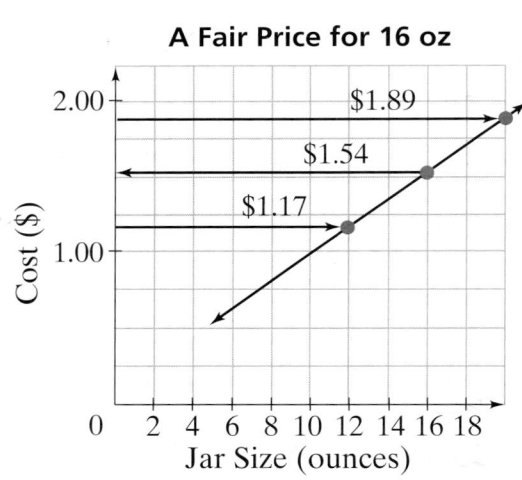

A Fair Price for 16 oz

  $\dfrac{\$1.17}{12 \text{ oz}} = \$.0975/\text{oz}$ **Find the 12-oz-jar unit price.**

  $\dfrac{\$1.89}{20 \text{ oz}} = \$.0945/\text{oz}$ **Find the 20-oz-jar unit price.**

  16 oz is halfway between 12 oz and 20 oz. A unit price halfway between $.0975 and $.0945 seems fair.

  $\dfrac{\$.0975 + \$.0945}{2} = \$.096$ **Find the average.**

  $16 \cdot \$.096 \approx \$1.54$ **Find the 16-oz-jar price.**

  A fair price for a 16-oz jar is $1.54.

- Make a visual display (at right) to support your view.

EXERCISES

1. What do you think would be a reasonable price for an 18-oz jar of the salsa in the example?

2. Your family eats two boxes of cereal each week. Your family buys 15-oz boxes costing $2.89 each. A 28-oz box of the same cereal is $4.79. You think that buying the larger size is better. Persuade your family to your point of view using mathematics, explanation, and a visual display. (*Hint:* Show what happens over an extended length of time, such as a year.)

Solving Systems of Linear Equations

OBJECTIVE

1 Graphing Systems of Linear Equations

Two or more linear equations form a **system of linear equations.**
A *solution of the system* is any ordered pair that is a solution of each
equation in the system.

You can solve some systems of equations by graphing the equations
on a coordinate plane and identifying the point(s) of intersection.

1 EXAMPLE Solving a System by Graphing

Solve the system $y = -x + 1$ and $y = 2x + 4$ by graphing.

Step 1 Graph each line.

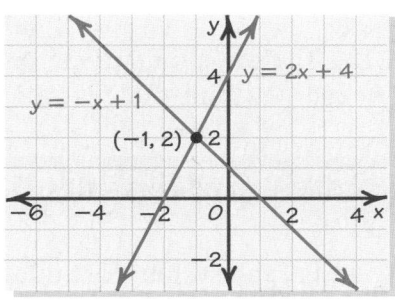

Step 2 Find the point of intersection.

The lines intersect at one point, $(-1, 2)$. The solution is $(-1, 2)$.

Check See whether $(-1, 2)$ makes both equations true.

$y = -x + 1$		$y = 2x + 4$
$2 \stackrel{?}{=} -(-1) + 1$	⟵ Replace x with -1 and y with 2. ⟶	$2 \stackrel{?}{=} 2(-1) + 4$
$2 = 2$ ✔	The solution checks.	$2 = 2$ ✔

✓ Check Understanding Example 1

1. Solve each system of equations by graphing. Check each solution.

   a. $y = x - 6$
   $\quad\;\; y = -2x$

   b. $y = 3x - 3$
   $\quad\;\; x + y = 1$

When the graphs of two equations are parallel, there is no point of
intersection. The system has *no solution*.

When the graphs of two equations are the same line, all the points
on the line are solutions. The system has *infinitely many solutions*.

What You'll Learn

OBJECTIVE
1 To solve systems of linear equations by graphing

OBJECTIVE
2 To use systems of linear equations to solve problems

. . . And Why

To solve real-world problems involving carpentry

✓ Check Skills You'll Need

Graph each equation.

1. $y = -x - 4$

2. $y = 2x - 1$

3. $-4x = 6y$

4. $3x - 2y = 5$

 For help, go to Lesson 8-2.

New Vocabulary

- **system of linear equations**

 Interactive lesson
includes instant self-check,
tutorials, and activities.

2 EXAMPLE Solving Special Systems

Solve each system of equations by graphing.

a. $x + y = 1; y = -x + 3$ **b.** $x - 2y = 4; 2x - 4y = 8$

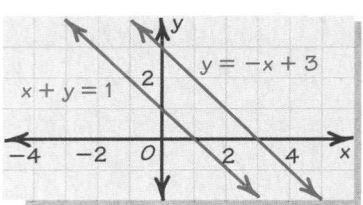

The lines are parallel.   The graphs are the same line.
They do not intersect.   There are infinitely many
There is no solution.   solutions.

✓ Check Understanding Example 2

2. Solve each system by graphing.

a. $y = x - 6;$ **b.** $y = x + 4;$
     $x - y = 6$ $y = x$

OBJECTIVE

2 Using Systems of Linear Equations

You can write and graph systems of equations to solve problems.

3 EXAMPLE Using a System of Equations

Find two numbers with a sum of 6 and a difference of 4.

Step 1 Write equations.

Let x = the greater number.
Let y = the lesser number.

Equation 1   Sum   is   6.
            $x + y$ =   6

Equation 2   Difference   is   4.
            $x - y$ =   4

Step 2 Graph the equations.

The lines intersect at $(5, 1)$.
The numbers are 5 and 1.

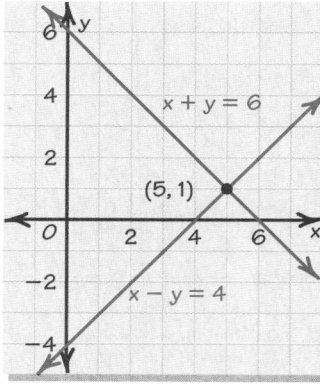

Check Since the sum of 5 and 1 is 6 and the difference of 5 and 1
is 4, the answer is correct.

✓ Check Understanding Example 3

3. Find two numbers with a difference of 2 and a sum of -8.

Graphing Calculator Hint

You can use a graphing
calculator to check
your solution of a
system. Write the
equations in slope-
intercept form,
press **Y=** , and enter
them as Y_1 and Y_2.
Then use the **CALC**
menu to find the
coordinates of the
intersection point.

You can solve some problems involving two variables by writing and graphing a system of equations, or you may be able to use one variable to write and solve an equation.

More Than One Way

Carpentry A carpenter cuts an 8-ft board into two pieces. One piece is three times as long as the other. What is the length of each piece?

Roberto's Method

Write and graph a system of equations.

Let x = length of longer piece; y = length of shorter piece.

Equation 1   Longer piece is three times shorter piece.

$$x \;=\; 3 \;\cdot\; y$$

Equation 2   Sum of lengths is eight.

$$x + y \;=\; 8$$

Graph the equations.

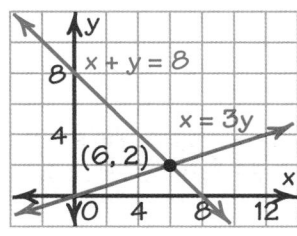

The lines intersect at (6, 2). The lengths are 6 ft and 2 ft.

Michelle's Method

Write a one-variable equation.

Let x = length of shorter piece; 3x = length of longer piece.

Equation   Shorter piece plus longer piece is 8 feet.

$$x \;+\; 3x = 8$$
$$4x = 8$$
$$x = 2$$

The shorter piece is 2 ft, and the longer piece is 3(2) = 6 ft.

Choose a Method

1. Which method would you use to find the lengths? Explain.

2. In Roberto's Method, suppose x = length of shorter piece. What difference would this make in the equations and the graph?

EXERCISES

For more exercises, see Extra Practice.

Practice and Problem Solving

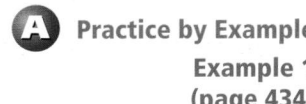 **Practice by Example**
Example 1
(page 434)

Check whether (−1, 5) is a solution of each system of equations. Show your work.

1. $x + y = 4$
$x − y = 6$

2. $y = −2x + 3$
$y = x − 4$

3. $2x = y − 7$
$2y = −x + 9$

Solve each system of equations by graphing. Check each solution.

4. $y = x + 1$
$y = 3x − 7$

5. $y = 2x + 5$
$x + y = 8$

6. $y = x + 1$
$y = −x − 3$

7. $y = x + 5$
$y = −2x + 8$

8. $y = x − 4$
$y = 3x$

9. $y = 2x − 2$
$y = 6$

Example 2
(page 435)

10. $−3x + y = 5$
$y = 3x − 7$

11. $y = −x − 3$
$y = −x + 2$

12. $y = −6 − 2x$
$2x + y = −6$

13. $y = −2x + 1$
$2x + y = −1$

14. $y = 3x$
$−y = −3x$

15. $y = x + 2$
$x − y = −2$

Example 3
(page 435)

16. Find two numbers with a sum of −8 and a difference of 4. Let x be the greater number and y be the lesser number.

B **Apply Your Skills**

Is each ordered pair a solution of the given system of equations? Show your work.

17. $2x + 5y = 3$
$y = 7.5x;\ (1.5, 0.2)$

18. $6x − 6y = 2$
$3x + 9y = −7;\ \left(−\frac{1}{3}, −\frac{2}{3}\right)$

19. Kites A four-foot-long wooden rod is cut into two pieces to make a kite. One piece is three times as long as the other.
a. Let x = the length of the longer piece.
Let y = the length of the shorter piece.
Write a system of equations to find the length of each piece.
b. Solve the system by graphing. State the length of each piece.

Solve each system of equations by graphing. Check each solution.

20. $x + y = 3$
$2x = 10 − 2y$

21. $y = 2x − 4$
$2x − y = 4$

22. $x − y = −4$
$x + y = 6$

23. $2x − 4y = 4$
$y = 0.5x − 1$

24. $y = x − 2$
$x + 3y = 6$

25. $3y − 2x = 3$
$6y = 4x + 6$

26. Geometry The perimeter of a rectangle is 24 ft. Its length is five times its width. Let x be the length and y be the width. What is the area of the rectangle?

27. The difference of two numbers is 5. The result when the greater number is decreased by twice the lesser is 9. Let x be the greater number and y be the lesser number. Find the numbers.

28. There are 11 animals in a barnyard. Some are chickens and some are cows. There are 38 legs in all. Let x be the number of chickens and y be the number of cows. How many of each animal are in the barnyard?

29. One sales position pays \$200/wk plus 10% commission. Another sales position pays \$150/wk plus 20% commission.
  a. For each job, write an equation that relates the amount of sales x for one week to the money earned y.
  b. Solve the system from part (a) to find the amount of sales in a week that will earn the same amount from each job. Show your work.
  c. If weekly sales at each job are about \$600, at which job can you earn more money? Explain.

30. a. Graph each system of equations on a separate coordinate plane.
  $$y = 3x + 1; y = 3x - 2 \qquad\qquad y = -2x - 1; y = -2x + 4$$
  b. Writing in Math Based on part (a), write a conjecture about solutions to systems of equations that have the same slope.

 **Challenge** **Open-Ended** **Write a system of equations with the given solutions.**

31. no solution   **32.** one solution   **33.** infinitely many

34. Geometry The graphs of $y = 3$, $y = 7$, $x = 2$, and $x = 5$ contain the sides of a rectangle. Find the area of the rectangle.

35. Solve the system $y = x + 2$, $y = 4x + 11$, and $y = -2x - 7$.

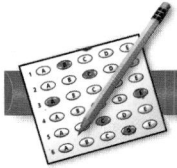

Test Prep

Multiple Choice

36. What is the solution of the system
  $y = x + 4$; $y = 4x + 1$?
  A. (0, 1)   **B.** (0, 4)   **C.** (1, 4)   **D.** (1, 5)

37. How many solutions does the system have
  $2x + 4y = 10$; $x + 2y = 10$?
  F. 0   **G.** 1   **H.** 2   **I.** infinitely many

38. Use the system $x + y = -6$; $x - y = 2$. How are the x-coordinate and the y-coordinate of the solution related?
  A. $y = -2x$ **B.** $y = 2x$ **C.** $x = -2y$ **D.** $x = 2y$

Extended Response

39. There are 16 questions on a test. Each question is worth either 5 points or 10 points. The total is 100 points.
  a. Let x = the number of 5-point questions.
    Let y = the number of 10-point questions.
    Write a system of equations to find the number of each type of question.
  b. Solve the system by graphing.
  c. How many questions of each type are on the test?

Take It to the NET
Online lesson quiz at
www.PHSchool.com
Web Code: ada-0807

Lesson 8-5

40. Use the scatter plot at the right.

   a. How much time did the person who saw four movies spend?

   b. How many people saw more than three movies?

   c. How many people spent less than three hours watching movies?

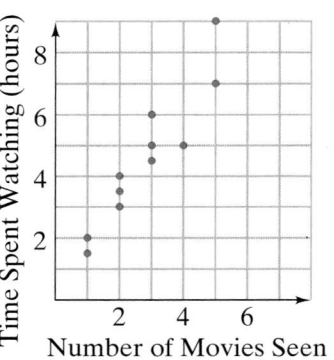

Lesson 7-6

Solve each inequality.

41. $1 - x < 5$

42. $3t - 1 \leq 17$

43. $-2c + 5 \geq 3$

44. $m + 4 > -10$

Lesson 6-4

Probability **Find each probability for one roll of a number cube.**

45. $P(2)$ **46.** $P(6 \text{ or } 5)$ **47.** $P(-1)$ **48.** $P(4, 2, \text{ or } 5)$

 Checkpoint Quiz 2   **Lessons 8-5 through 8-7**

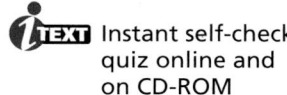 Instant self-check quiz online and on CD-ROM

1. a. Statistics Use the table at the right. Make a scatter plot relating daily newspaper circulation and television sets.

   b. Is there is a *positive correlation*, a *negative correlation*, or *no correlation* between daily newspaper circulation and the number of television sets in homes? Explain.

   c. Data Analysis Draw a trend line on your scatter plot. Use it to predict the number of television sets when newspaper circulation is 55 million.

Media in the United States

Year	Daily Newspaper Circulation (millions)	Television Sets in Homes (millions)
1980	62	128
1985	63	155
1990	62	193
1991	61	193
1992	60	192
1993	60	201
1994	59	211
1995	57	217
1996	57	223

Source: *Statistical Abstract of the United States.*
Go to **www.PHSchool.com** for a data update.
Web Code: adg-2041

Solve each system by graphing.

2. $y = -4x$
   $y = -x + 6$

3. $x - y = 1$
   $x + y = -7$

4. $6x + 2y = 12$
   $y = 3x$

5. Measurement One gallon of liquid occupies 231 cubic inches. Write a rule that expresses the number of gallons $g(c)$ as a function of the number of cubic inches c.

6. Find two numbers with a sum of -4 and a difference of 10.

Graphing Linear Inequalities

OBJECTIVE

1 Graphing Linear Inequalities

If you replace the equal sign in a linear equation with $>$, $<$, $\geq$, or $\leq$, the result is a **linear inequality.** The graph of a linear inequality is a region of the coordinate plane bounded by a line. Every point in the region is a solution of the inequality.

1 EXAMPLE   Graphing a Linear Inequality

Graph each inequality on a coordinate plane.

a. $y \leq x + 2$ **b.** $y < -2x$

Step 1 Graph the boundary line.

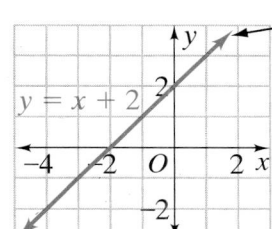

Points on the boundary line make $y \leq x + 2$ true. Use a solid line.

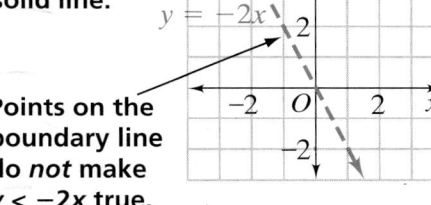

Points on the boundary line do *not* make $y < -2x$ true. Use a dashed line.

Step 2 Test a point not on the boundary line.

Test $(0, 0)$ in the inequality.

$$y \leq x + 2$$
$$0 \overset{?}{\leq} 0 + 2 \quad \textbf{Substitute.}$$
$$0 \leq 2 \quad \checkmark \text{ true}$$

Test $(1, 1)$ in the inequality.

$$y < -2x$$
$$1 \overset{?}{<} -2(1) \quad \textbf{Substitute.}$$
$$1 < -2 \quad \textbf{✗ false}$$

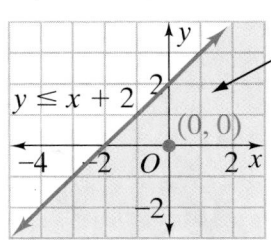

Since the inequality is true for (0, 0), shade the region containing (0, 0).

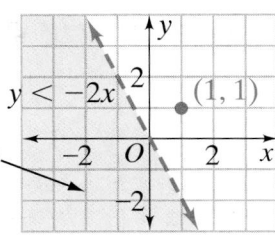

Since the inequality is false for (1, 1), shade the region that does *not* contain (1, 1).

1. Graph each inequality on its own coordinate plane.

a. $y \geq 3x - 1$ **b.** $y > -x + 3$ **c.** $y < 2x - 4$

Need Help?

< means "is less than."
> means "is greater than."
≤ means "is less than or equal to."
≥ means "is greater than or equal to."

---

2 **EXAMPLE** <u>Real-World</u> 🌐 <u>Problem Solving</u>

Grocery Shopping Apricots cost \$3/lb. Tomatoes cost \$1/lb. You plan to spend no more than \$10. How many pounds of each can you buy?

Step 1 Write an inequality.

Words		cost of apricots	plus	cost of tomatoes	is at most	ten dollars

Let x = number of pounds of apricots.

Let y = number of pounds of tomatoes.

Inequality	$3x$	$+$	y	$\leq$	10

Step 2 Write the equation of the boundary line in slope-intercept form.

$$3x + y \leq 10$$
$$y \leq -3x + 10$$
$$y = -3x + 10$$

Step 3 Graph $y = -3x + 10$ in Quadrant I since weight is not negative.

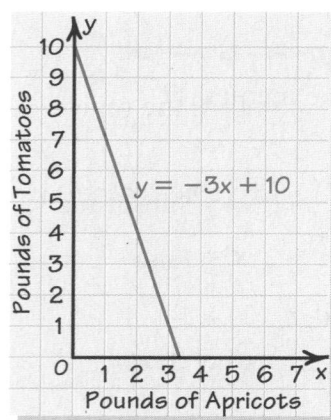

Step 4 Test $(1, 1)$.

$$y \leq -3x + 10$$
$$1 \stackrel{?}{\leq} -3(1) + 10$$
$$1 \leq 7 \ ✔$$

The inequality is true. $(1, 1)$ is a solution.

Step 5 Shade the region containing $(1, 1)$.

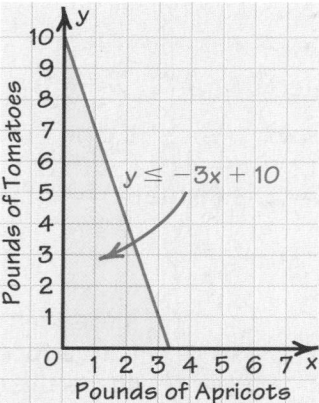

The graph shows the possible solutions. For example, you could buy 1 pound of apricots and 5 pounds of tomatoes.

Real-World 🌐 **Connection**

There are over 3,100 farmers markets in the United States.

✓ **Check Understanding** Example 2

2. Adult tickets to the school play cost $4. Children's tickets cost $2. Your goal is to sell tickets worth at least $30. Let x be the number of children's tickets and y be the number of adult tickets. Graph a linear inequality to show how many of each type of ticket you must sell to reach your goal.

OBJECTIVE

2 Graphing Systems of Linear Inequalities

Two or more linear inequalities form a **system of linear inequalities.** A *solution of a system of linear inequalities* is any ordered pair that makes each inequality in the system true. To solve a system, graph the inequalities on one coordinate plane.

3 EXAMPLE Solving a System of Linear Inequalities

Solve the system $y > x$ and $y \leq -x + 2$ by graphing.

Step 1 Graph $y > x$ on a coordinate plane.

Step 2 Graph $y \leq -x + 2$ on the same coordinate plane.

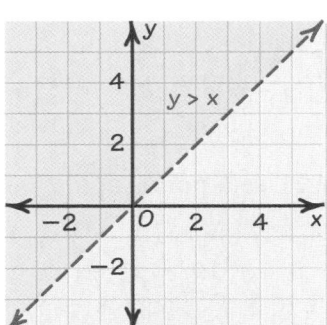 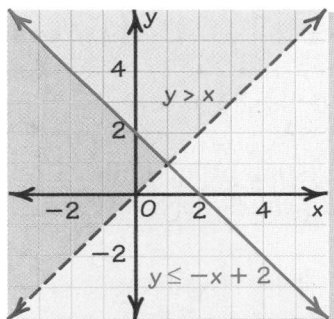

The solutions are the coordinates of all the points in the region that is shaded in both colors.

Check The point $(-1, 0)$ is in the solution region. Check whether $(-1, 0)$ makes both of the inequalities true.

$$y > x$$
$$0 \overset{?}{>} -1 \qquad \text{Replace } x \text{ with } -1 \text{ and } y \text{ with } 0.$$
$$0 > -1 ✔ \qquad \text{The solution checks.}$$

$$y \leq -x + 2$$
$$0 \overset{?}{\leq} -(-1) + 2$$
$$0 \leq 3 ✔$$

✓ **Check Understanding** Example 3

3. Solve each system by graphing.

   a. $y \leq -2x - 5$
   $\quad y < \frac{1}{2}x$

   b. $y > x - 1$
   $\quad y < 3x + 4$

EXERCISES

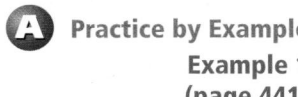 For more exercises, see *Extra Practice*.

Practice and Problem Solving

A Practice by Example
Example 1
(page 441)

The graph of each inequality is bounded by a line. State whether the boundary line is solid or dashed.

1. $y > x$ **2.** $y \leq -x + 1$ **3.** $y \geq x - 1$

Graph each inequality on its own coordinate plane.

4. $y > x - 6$ **5.** $y \leq -x + 8$ **6.** $y > x + 2$

7. $y \geq 2x - 1$ **8.** $y < -\frac{1}{3}x + 1$ **9.** $y \leq 2x + 1$

Example 2
(page 442)

Solve each inequality for y.

10. $4x + y < -3$ **11.** $-y \leq 2x$ **12.** $2x + 3y \leq 7$

For Exercises 13–15, show all the solutions by writing and graphing a linear inequality.

13. Find two nonnegative numbers with a sum greater than three.

14. A number is greater than or equal to three times another number. What are the numbers?

15. Collections Melissa has a collection of dimes and nickels with a total face value of less than one dollar. Let x be the number of dimes and y be the number of nickels. How many of each type of coin does she have?

Example 3
(page 443)

Solve each system of inequalities by graphing. Use a point on the x- or y-axis to check each solution.

16. $y > -x$ **17.** $y \leq x$ **18.** $y > -x$ **19.** $y \leq -x + 1$
      $y < x + 6$ $y \geq -x - 4$ $y > 2x + 3$ $y > x - 5$

B Apply Your Skills

Choose a linear inequality to match each graph.

20.

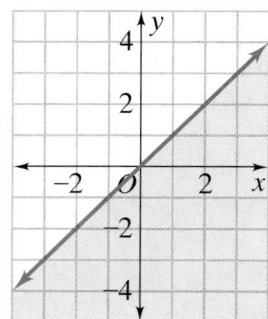

21.

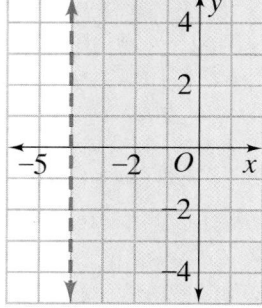

A. $-y \geq x$ **B.** $-y \leq x$ **F.** $x < -4$ **G.** $x > -4$
C. $-y \geq -x$ **D.** $-y \leq -x$ **H.** $-x < -4$ **I.** $-x > -4$

22. Writing in Math Describe the difference between the graph of $y < -x$ and the graph of $-y < x$.

Graph each inequality on its own coordinate plane.

23. $x - y > 10$ **24.** $y \leq 5$ **25.** $y \geq -\frac{2}{3}x$

26. $9x + 3y < 3$ **27.** $x - 2y \geq -12$ **28.** $-6x - 4y > 8$

29. a. Income You can earn $6/h mowing lawns and $3/h baby-sitting. You want to earn at least $45. Let x = number of hours mowing lawns and y = number of hours baby-sitting. Write a linear inequality to model this situation.
   b. Graph the linear inequality.
   c. If you baby-sit for 6 hours, what is the number of hours you will need to mow lawns to earn $45?

Write the equation of each boundary line in slope-intercept form. State whether the boundary line is solid or dashed.

30. $x + y < -3$ **31.** $x - y \geq 7$ **32.** $-y > 4x$

33. $-y \leq -\frac{1}{2}x$ **34.** $5x + 3y \leq 9$ **35.** $4x - 2y > 10$

36. Medium drinks cost $2 and large drinks cost $3. Let x be the number of medium drinks sold and y be the number of large drinks sold. How many drinks must the vendor sell to have at least $60 in sales? Show all possible solutions by graphing a linear inequality.

Solve each system of inequalities by graphing.

37. $2x + y \leq 4$ **38.** $x + y > -3$ **39.** $x < 6$
        $y + 1 \geq -2x$ $x - y < 5$ $y \leq 2x$

40. $y < 4$ **41.** $-2x + y > 1$ **42.** $3x + y > 5$
     $x > -5$ $x + 2y < 2$ $y \geq -2$

43. Writing in Math How is graphing an inequality on a coordinate plane similar to graphing an inequality on a number line? How is it different?

Ⓒ Challenge

Open-Ended Write a system of inequalities with the solutions indicated. If such a system is not possible, tell why.

44. no solutions   **45.** all real numbers   **46.** the points of a line

Reasoning Write a system of inequalities to describe each graph.

47.
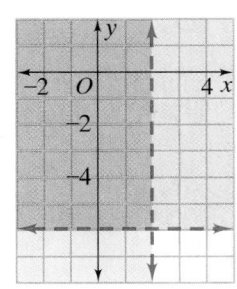

48.
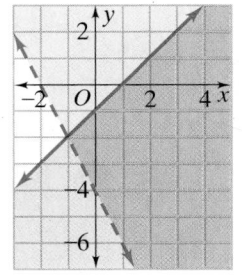

Multiple Choice

49. Which inequality has the same solutions as $y \geq -2x + 1$?
  A. $2x + y \leq 1$ **B.** $2x + y \geq 1$
  C. $2x - y \leq 1$ **D.** $2x - y \geq 1$

50. Which describes the graph of $y \leq -x + 2$?
  F. shading above a solid boundary line
  G. shading below a solid boundary line
  H. shading above a dashed boundary line
  I. shading below a dashed boundary line

Take It to the NET
Online lesson quiz at
www.PHSchool.com
Web Code: ada-0808

51. You want to spend less than $20 on asparagus and green beans. Asparagus costs $3.00 per pound and green beans cost $.50 per pound. Let a represent the asparagus and g represent the green beans. Which inequality models what you can spend?
  A. $3a + 0.5g > 20$ **B.** $3a + 0.5g \geq 20$
  C. $3a + 0.5g < 20$ **D.** $3a + 0.5g \leq 20$

52. Which inequality has a graph with shading below a dashed boundary line?
  F. $2x + y > -3$ **G.** $2x + y \geq -3$
  H. $2x + y \leq -3$ **I.** $2x + y < -3$

53. Which point is a solution of the system $y \geq 0$; $x \leq 0$?
  A. $(1, 1)$ **B.** $(-1, 1)$ **C.** $(1, -1)$ **D.** $(-1, -1)$

Short Response

54. Explain how to graph $y \geq 2x + 3$. Then graph the inequality.

Mixed Review

Lesson 8-7

Solve each system of equations by graphing. Check each solution.

55. $x + y = 8$
  $x - y = -2$

56. $y = 2x - 1$
  $2x - y = 3$

57. $3y = -2x - 3$
  $3y = x - 12$

Lesson 6-6 🌐 **58. Endangered Animals** In 1999, there were 162 California condors. Of these birds, 113 were in captivity, 29 were living free in California, and 20 were living free in Arizona.
  a. What percent of the condors were living free in Arizona? Round your answer to the nearest tenth of a percent.
  b. What percent of the condors were living free in all? Round your answer to the nearest tenth of a percent.

Lessons 5-7 and 5-8

Solve each equation.

59. $m - \frac{2}{3} = \frac{1}{6}$ **60.** $\frac{5}{4}c = \frac{3}{2}$ **61.** $\frac{3}{4} + w = \frac{9}{10}$

Lesson 4-6

Evaluate each expression for $c = 4$ and $m = -3$.

62. $\frac{c + m}{5}$ **63.** $\frac{m - c}{2}$ **64.** $\frac{2c - m}{-4}$ **65.** $\frac{4m}{2 - c}$

Technology

Graphing Inequalities

Graphing an inequality on a calculator is similar to graphing an equation. If your calculator does not graph dashed lines, you have to remember the type of boundary line you need for the inequality.

EXAMPLE

Graph $y > -x + 4$.

Step 1 Press the Y= key.
Enter $-x + 4$.

```
Plot1  Plot2  Plot3
\Y1☰ -X+4 ▪
\Y2=
\Y3=
\Y4=
```

Step 2 Press ◄ to move to the left of Y1.
Press ENTER twice when
y is greater than the right side of the equation.
Press ENTER three times when
y is less than the right side of the equation.

Step 3 Press ZOOM 6 to graph the inequality with the standard viewing window. Then sketch the inequality.

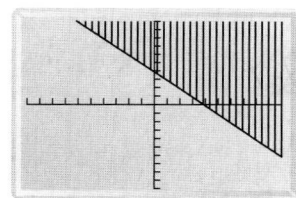
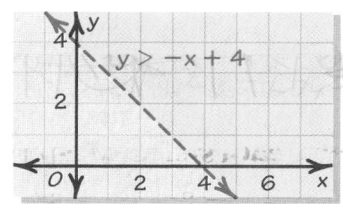

EXERCISES

Graph each inequality. Be sure your boundary line is correct.

1. $y > 3x + 1$ **2.** $y \leq 2x$ **3.** $y < -x - 5$ **4.** $y \geq 4x + 6$

5. $y \leq -2x - 4$ **6.** $y < x + 7$ **7.** $y > -3x + 4$ **8.** $y \geq -\frac{2}{5}x + 1$

Graph each system of inequalities. Sketch the solutions.

9. $y > -x$
    $y < x + 6$

10. $y \leq x$
    $y \geq -x - 4$

11. $y > -x$
    $y > 2x + 3$

12. $y \leq -x + 1$
    $y > x - 5$

13. Find and graph a system of inequalities that has no solution.

14. Find and graph a system of inequalities whose solutions are the points of a line.

A multiple-correct-answer test item presents you with a question and several possible answers labeled with Roman numerals. You have to decide which of the answers are correct. Then you pick your list of correct answers from the lettered choices given.

A good strategy to follow is to test each answer and mark it if correct.

EXAMPLE

For which equation(s) is $(4, 6)$ a solution?

I. $x - y = -2$ **II.** $-x - y = -10$ **III.** $x - y = 2$ **IV.** $y - x = 2$

A. I and II only   **B.** I, II, and III only   **C.** I, II, and IV only   **D.** III only

Test each answer.

Substitute 4 for x and 6 for y.

I. $x - y = -2$ **II.** $-x - y = -10$ **III.** $x - y = 2$ **IV.** $y - x = 2$

    $4 - 6 = -2$ $-4 - 6 = -10$ $4 - 6 = 2$ $6 - 4 = 2$

    true   true   not true   true

● Statements I, II, and IV (only) are correct; choice C.

EXERCISES

1. The slope of a line is -2. Through which pairs of points could the line pass?

    I. $(0, 3)$ and $(-2, 7)$ **II.** $(0, -1)$ and $(2, -5)$ **III.** $(0, 0)$ and $(3, 6)$ **IV.** $(2, -3)$ and $(-1, 3)$

    A. I and II only   **B.** I, II, and III only   **C.** I, II, and IV only   **D.** III only

2. For which system(s) of equations is $(2, 3)$ the solution?

    I. $y = x + 1$ and $y = -x + 5$ **II.** $y = 2x - 1$ and $y = \frac{1}{2}x + 2$

    III. $y = 3x - 3$ and $y = -2x + 7$ **IV.** $y = \frac{1}{4}x + \frac{5}{2}$ and $y = -3x + 3$

    F. I and III only   **G.** I, II, and III only   **H.** I, II, and IV only   **I.** III and IV only

3. Which system(s) of equations has no solution?

    I. $y = 3x - 1$ and $y = -3x + 1$ **II.** $y = 1.5x - 2$ and $y = \frac{3}{2}x + 2$

    III. $x + y = 1$ and $y = -x + 3$ **IV.** $2x + y = 4$ and $2y = 4x + 2$

    A. III only   **B.** II and III only   **C.** I, II, and III only   **D.** I, II, III, and IV

Chapter Review

Vocabulary

domain (p. 400)	**positive correlation** (p. 425)	**system of linear**
function (p. 400)	**range** (p. 400)	**equations** (p. 435)
function notation (p. 418)	**relation** (p. 400)	**system of linear**
function rule (p. 418)	**scatter plot** (p. 423)	**inequalities** (p. 443)
linear equation (p. 406)	**slope** (p. 411)	**trend line** (p. 430)
linear inequality (p. 441)	**slope-intercept form** (p. 413)	**vertical-line test** (p. 401)
negative correlation (p. 425)	**solution** (p. 405)	**y-intercept** (p. 413)
no correlation (p. 425)		

Reading Math
Understanding
Vocabulary

Choose the vocabulary term that correctly completes the sentence.

1. The tilt or slant of a line is its __?__.

2. To determine whether the graph shows a function, use the __?__.

3. On a scatter plot, when one set of values increases while the other decreases, the data is said to have a __?__.

4. When each member of a relation's domain is paired with exactly one member of the range, the relation is a __?__.

5. Any equation whose graph is a line is a __?__.

6. The first coordinates in a set of ordered pairs is the __?__ of the relation.

7. The second coordinates in a set of ordered pairs is the __?__ of the relation.

8. An ordered pair that makes an equation a true statement is a __?__ of the equation.

Take It to the NET
Online vocabulary quiz
at **www.PHSchool.com**
Web Code: adj-0851

Skills and Concepts

8-1 Objectives

▼ To determine whether a relation is a function (p. 400)

▼ To graph relations and functions (p. 401)

Any set of ordered pairs is a **relation.** The **domain** of a relation is the set of first coordinates of the ordered pairs. The **range** is the set of second coordinates. A **function** is a relation in which no two ordered pairs have the same first coordinate.

Is each relation a function? Explain.

9. $\{(2, 3), (4, 3), (0, 1), (-2, 3)\}$

10.

x	−3	4	−1	−4
y	0	2	0	1

11. Domain   Range
2 → −1
3 → 0
4 → 3

12. Is the amount of a long-distance telephone bill a function of time spent talking on the telephone? Explain.

8-2 Objectives

▼ To find solutions of equations with two variables (p. 405)

▼ To graph linear equations with two variables (p. 406)

A solution of an equation with two variables is any ordered pair that makes the equation true. The graph of a **linear equation** is a line.

Find the solutions of each equation for $x = -3, 0,$ and 2.

13. $y = x + 5$ **14.** $y = -4x$ **15.** $y = \frac{1}{2}x + 3$ **16.** $y = 6 - 2x$

8-3 Objectives

▼ To find the slope of a line (p. 411)

▼ To use slope-intercept form in graphing a linear equation (p. 413)

Slope is a measure describing the tilt of a line, which you can calculate using the ratio $\frac{\text{vertical change}}{\text{horizontal change}}$, or $\frac{\text{difference in } y\text{-coordinates}}{\text{difference in } x\text{-coordinates}}$.

One form of a linear equation is the slope-intercept form, $y = mx + b$, where m is the slope and b is the y-intercept.

Identify the slope and y-intercept of each equation. Then graph each equation.

17. $x + y = 7$ **18.** $x - y = -2$

19. $2x + 5y = 10$ **20.** $3x - 2y = 12$

Find the slope of each line.

21. 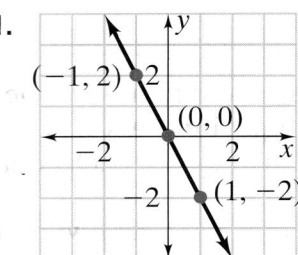   **22.** 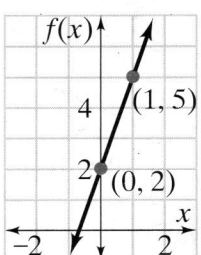   **23.**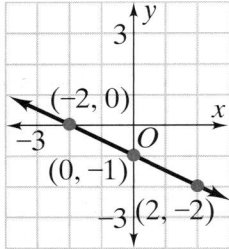

8-4 Objectives

▼ To write a function rule for a word relationship (p. 418)

▼ To write a function rule by analyzing a table or graph (p. 419)

You can write a **function rule** from a verbal description, from a table of values, or from a graph.

Write a rule for each function.

24.

x	f(x)
-2	2
-1	1
0	0
1	-1

25.

x	y
-3	-5
-2	-3
-1	-1
0	1

26.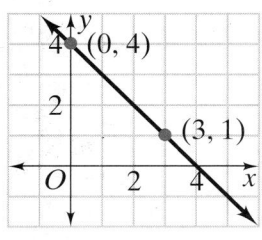

27. Tickets to a play cost $14 each by mail, plus a $2 processing fee for each order of one or more tickets. Write a rule to describe total cost $c(t)$ as a function of the number of tickets t.

A **scatter plot** is a graph that shows the relationship between two sets of data. A scatter plot can help you find trends between sets of data.

Use the scatter plot at the right.

28. How long did the person who used 240 calories ride a bicycle?

29. How many calories did the person who bicycled 50 minutes use?

Calories Used While Bicycling

30. **Data Analysis** Is there a positive correlation, a negative correlation, or no correlation between the time spent bicycling and the calories used? Explain.

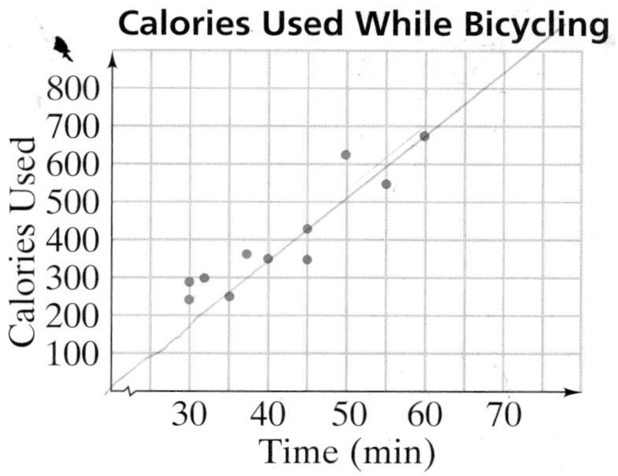

31. **Data Analysis** Carefully place a straightedge (preferably transparent) on the scatter plot to serve as a trend line. Use the trend line to predict the number of calories a person uses on a 70-min bicycle ride.

Two or more linear equations with the same variables form a **system of linear equations.** A solution of a system of equations is any ordered pair that makes each equation true.

Two or more linear inequalities with the same variables form a **system of linear inequalities.** A solution of a system of inequalities is any ordered pair that makes both inequalities true. You can solve a system by graphing.

Graph each inequality.

32. $y > 2x + 5$

33. $y \leq -x + 1$

34. $y \geq \frac{1}{2}x - 3$

35. $y < 3x - 2$

Solve each system by graphing.

36. $y = \frac{1}{2}x - 3$
$y = -\frac{1}{2}x + 1$

37. $3x + 2y = 6$
$x + 4y = -8$

38. $y = x - 5$
$y = -2x + 1$

39. $y < 3x + 2$
$y > 3x - 1$

40. Explain why it is possible for a system of linear equations to have no solutions.

Chapter Test

Take It to the NET
Online chapter test at
www.PHSchool.com
Web Code: ada-0852

Is each relation a function? Explain.

1. $\{(-2, -12), (-2, 0), (-2, 4), (-2, 11)\}$

2. $\{(8, 1), (4, 1), (0, 1), (-15, 1)\}$

3. $\{(-4, -6), (-3, -2), (1, -2), (1, 0), (1, 3)\}$

4. $\{(0, 1), (0, 2), (1, 2), (1, 3), (3, 1), (4, 2)\}$

Graph each equation.

5. $y = 2x$

6. $y = -x - 2$

7. $2x - y = 4$

8. $3y = x - 6$

Find the slope of the line through each pair of points.

9. $C(0, 1)$ and $D(-5, 1)$

10. $M(-4, 1)$ and $N(6, 3)$

11. $J(-1, -2)$ and $K(2, 7)$

12. $P(4, 9)$ and $Q(-6, 12)$

Write a rule for each function.

13.

x	f(x)
-2	-3
-1	-5
0	-7
1	-9

14.

x	f(x)
-3	4
0	1
3	-2
6	-5

Is there a *positive correlation*, a *negative correlation*, or *no correlation* between the sets of data in each scatter plot? Explain.

15.

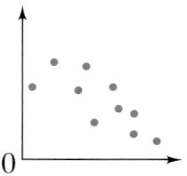

16.

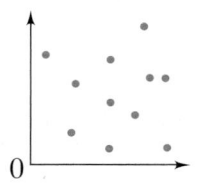

Graph each inequality.

17. $y \geq 3x - 1$

18. $y < -x + 5$

Solve each system by graphing.

19. $y = x - 1$
    $x = 2y$

20. $x + y = 4$
    $2x + 2y = 8$

21. $x + y = 3$
    $y = x - 5$

22. $y \leq 3x - 2$
    $y > x + 4$

23. **Writing in Math** Is the amount of sales tax paid a function of the labeled price of a taxable item? Explain.

24. **Writing in Math** Is a person's age a function of his or her height? Explain.

25. Use the data in the table below.

New York Thruway Tolls

Distance (miles)	Toll (dollars)	Distance (miles)	Toll (dollars)
112	3.50	125	3.90
137	3.75	100	3.10
112	3.40	22	0.70
69	1.65	58	1.80
69	2.15	137	4.25
169	5.70	43	1.80
90	2.80	84	3.05
188	5.85	164	5.10

a. Make a (distance, toll) scatter plot.

b. Draw a trend line. Predict the toll if a car travels 200 mi on the toll road.

c. Use your trend line to predict how far a car traveled on the toll road if there was a $4.50 toll.

d. Write an equation of your trend line.

26. **Open-Ended** The slope of a line through the origin is $-\frac{2}{3}$. Find the coordinates of two points on the line.

Multiple Choice

1. An empty pot weighs 1 lb 11 oz. With oatmeal in it, the pot weighs 3 lb 7 oz. How much does the oatmeal weigh?
   A. 5 lb 2 oz **B.** 2 lb 3 oz
   C. 1 lb 12 oz **D.** 1 lb 4 oz

2. Which equation has a solution of 8?
   F. $8x + 8 = 64$ **G.** $\frac{b}{2} + 7 = 10$
   H. $2z + 5 = 11$ **I.** $5n - 13 = 27$

3. Four friends split the cost of renting a car for a snorkeling trip. Each person also rents a snorkel for $2. Each person pays a total of $15. Which equation will help find the cost c of renting the car?
   A. $\frac{c}{4} + 2 = 15$ **B.** $15 - 2^4 = c$
   C. $15 - 4c = 2$ **D.** $\frac{c}{2} + 4 = 15$

4. Sara and Juan collect soccer cards. Sara has 6 fewer than three times the number of cards Juan has. Together they have 42 cards. Solve $c + (3c - 6) = 42$ to answer: How many cards does each have?
   F. Sara has 9 cards; Juan has 33 cards.
   G. Sara has 33 cards; Juan has 9 cards.
   H. Sara has 12 cards; Juan has 30 cards.
   I. Sara has 30 cards; Juan has 12 cards.

5. Which ordered pair is *not* a solution of $4x + 2y = 16$?
   A. $(-2, 12)$ **B.** $(5, -2)$
   C. $(2, 5)$ **D.** $(1, 6)$

6. Which function represents the number of kilograms $k(n)$ as a function of the number of grams n?
   F. $k(n) = 100n$ **G.** $k(n) = 0.01n$
   H. $k(n) = 1,000n$ **I.** $k(n) = 0.001n$

7. Which point is a solution of the system?
   $y = x + 2;\ y = 2x - 2$
   A. $(6, 4)$ **B.** $(1, 3)$
   C. $(4, 6)$ **D.** no solution

8. What is the solution of $-2(x - 1) \le -6$?
   F. $x \le 4$ **G.** $x \le -4$
   H. $x \ge 4$ **I.** $x \ge -4$

Gridded Response

9. The probability that a couple will give birth to a pair of twins is 1 in 90. About how many pairs of twins would you expect to find in 250,000 births?

10. Find the slope of the line through $(3, 2)$ and $(1, -2)$.

11. In the scatter plot below, each point represents an athlete who ran in the 100-m race. Greg won the race in the least amount of time. What is Greg's age in years?

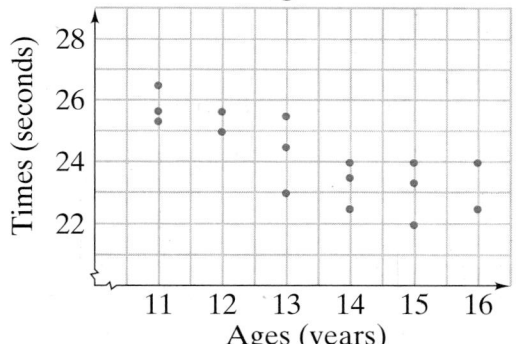

Athletes' Ages and Times

Short Response

Find the solutions of each equation for the given values of x. Show your work.

12. $y = x + 12;\ x = -3, 0,$ and 2

13. $4x - 4y = 8;\ x = 0, 2,$ and 4

Extended Response

14. **a.** Write the equation $x + \frac{1}{2}y = 4$ in slope-intercept form.
    b. Find the slope and the y-intercept of the line in part (a).
    c. Graph the equation in part (a).

Virtual Progress

Applying Graphs Technology changes every day. When your grandparents were kids, they watched black-and-white TVs, listened to records, and used typewriters. Today, people watch color TVs, listen to compact discs, and use computers. Tired of walking your dog? Robotic pets hit the market in 2000. Interested in becoming an astronaut? Pilots and astronauts train with virtual reality gear.

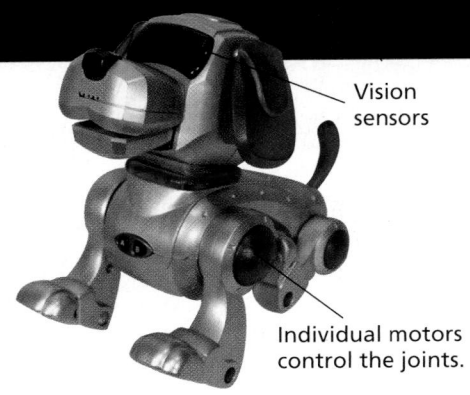

Vision sensors

Individual motors control the joints.

New and Different Pets
Robotic pets use computers and artificial intelligence to interact with their environments.

Activity

Use the information on these two pages to answer the questions.

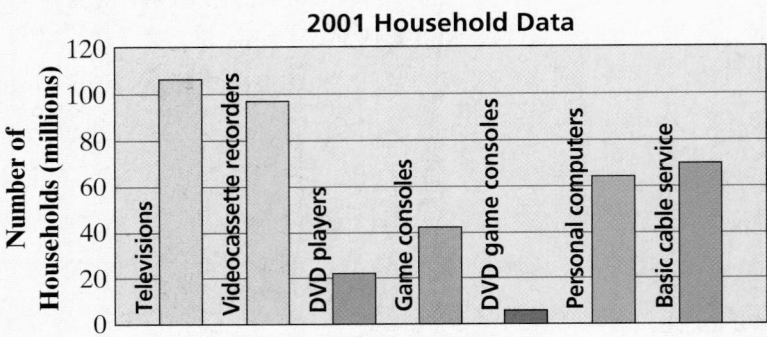

2001 Household Data

(Bar graph: y-axis "Number of Households (millions)" from 0 to 120; x-axis "Electronic Device" with bars for Televisions, Videocassette recorders, DVD players, Game consoles, DVD game consoles, Personal computers, Basic cable service)

1. How many households have a television and not a VCR?

2. How many households with televisions do not have basic cable?

3. The number of households with personal computers is how many times the number with DVD game consoles?

4. How many times as many households have a television as have a DVD player?

5. How many households will get their first DVD player between 2001 and 2006?

6. **a.** About 70% of DVD households rent at least one DVD movie per month. How many households is this?

   b. Suppose this percent stays constant. About how many households will rent at least one DVD movie in December 2006?

7. **Reasoning** What do you think is likely to happen to the number of households with VCRs by 2006? Explain.

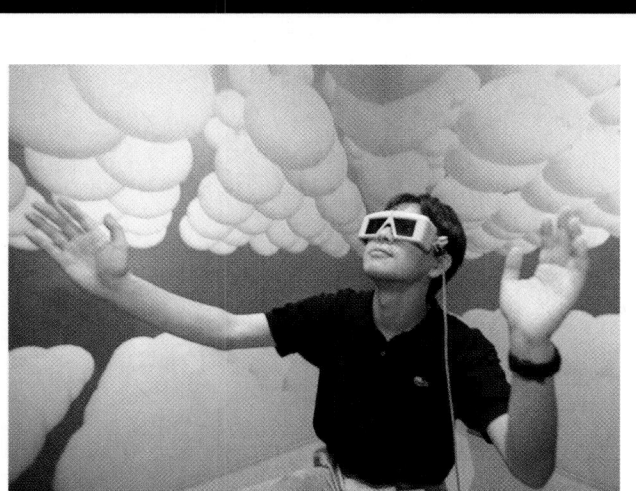

Intelligent Modeling
3-D glasses help this researcher "touch" carbon atoms from a microscopic world in a virtual reality room.

At Home Viewing
In 1997, most people watched movies at home on VCRs. Then DVDs hit the market. About 69 million households will have DVD players by the year 2006.

 **Take It to the NET** For more information about DVDs, go to **www.PHSchool.com**.
Web Code: ade-0853

Where You've Been

- In Chapter 3, you learned how to solve equations by multiplying or dividing decimals, and how to use formulas.

- In Chapter 5, you learned how to solve equations by multiplying fractions.

- In Chapter 7, you learned how to solve multi-step equations by using inverse operations.

 **Diagnosing Readiness** (For help, go to the lesson in green.)

Naming Polygons (Previous Course)

Match each polygon to its name.

1.

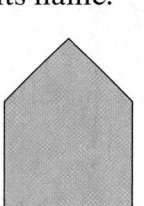
2.

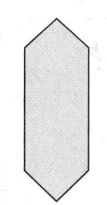
3.

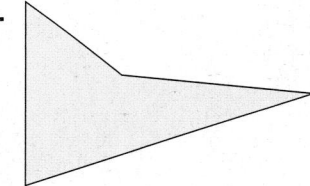
4.

A. quadrilateral   **B.** pentagon   **C.** octagon   **D.** hexagon

Identifying Radius (Previous Course)

Give the radius of each circle.

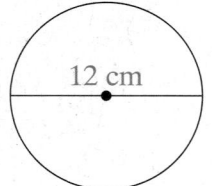
5. 12 cm

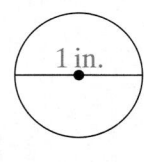
6. 1 in.

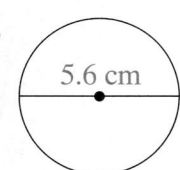
7. 5.6 cm

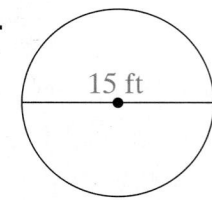
8. 15 ft

Graphing on the Coordinate Plane (Lesson 1-10)

Graph each point on the same coordinate plane.

9. $A(0, 7)$ **10.** $B(-2, 5)$ **11.** $E(4, 0)$ **12.** $D(2, -4)$ **13.** $C(-3, -1)$

14. $F\left(1\frac{1}{2}, -3\right)$ **15.** $G(0, 0)$ **16.** $J(0, -1)$ **17.** $I(-4, -5)$ **18.** $H(-5, -5)$

Spatial Thinking

Where You're Going

In this chapter, you will learn how to

● Use properties of figures to solve problems.

● Classify geometric figures.

● Construct figures.

● Solve a problem by drawing a diagram.

Real-World Snapshots Applying what you learn, on pages 518–519 you will solve problems about Ferris wheels.

Key Vocabulary

- adjacent angles (p. 465)
- alternate interior angles (p. 466)
- angle bisector (p. 493)
- complementary (p. 465)
- congruent angles (p. 465)
- congruent figures (p. 480)
- corresponding angles (p. 466)
- parallel (p. 459)
- perpendicular bisector (p. 492)
- perpendicular lines (p. 492)
- polygon (p. 470)
- reflection (p. 504)
- regular polygon (p. 472)
- rotation (p. 507)
- segment (p. 458)
- segment bisector (p. 492)
- supplementary (p. 465)
- symmetry (pp. 503, 508)
- translation (p. 497)
- vertical angles (p. 465)

9-1

Introduction to Geometry: Points, Lines, and Planes

OBJECTIVE
1 Points, Lines, and Planes

What You'll Learn

OBJECTIVE 1 To name basic geometric figures

OBJECTIVE 2 To recognize intersecting lines, parallel lines, and skew lines

. . . And Why

To build a basic vocabulary in geometry and to solve problems in architecture

✔ Check Skills You'll Need

Describe the number-line graph of each inequality.

1. $a \geq 3$ **2.** $a \leq 0$

3. $a \leq 5$ **4.** $a \geq -2$

🔑 For help, go to Lesson 2-8.

New Vocabulary

- **point**   - **line**
- **plane**   - **segment**
- **ray**   - **parallel**
- **skew**

Geometric shapes are evident in many human-made and natural structures. Notice the hexagonal shape of each cell of the honeycomb in the photo below. Two other examples of geometry in nature are the spiral structure of a snail's shell and the shape of a snowflake.

Basic Geometric Figures

Name	Sample	Symbolic Name	Description
Point	• A	Point A	A **point** is a location in space. It has no size.
Line	A, B, n	$\overleftrightarrow{AB}$, $\overleftrightarrow{BA}$, or n	A **line** is a series of points that extends in opposite directions without end. A lowercase letter can name a line.
Plane	A B M D C	$ABCD$ or M	A **plane** is a flat surface with no thickness. It contains many lines and extends without end in the directions of all its lines.
Line segment or segment	P Q	$\overline{PQ}$, or $\overline{QP}$	A **segment** is a part of a line. It has two endpoints. PQ represents the length of $\overline{PQ}$.
Ray	C R	$\overrightarrow{CR}$	A **ray** is a part of a line. It has exactly one endpoint. Name its endpoint first.

🅰️**TEXT** Interactive lesson includes instant self-check, tutorials, and activities.

You can combine the basic geometric figures to create many other geometric figures.

1 EXAMPLE **Naming Geometric Figures**

Name each figure in the diagram.

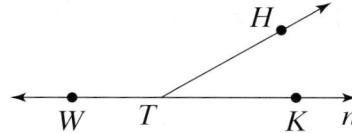

a. Name four points.
$H, K, T,$ and W
Name a point with a capital letter.

b. Name four different segments.
$\overline{HT}, \overline{WT}, \overline{TK},$ and $\overline{WK}$
Name a segment by its endpoints.

c. Write five other names for $\overleftrightarrow{WT}$.
$\overleftrightarrow{WK}, \overleftrightarrow{TK}, \overleftrightarrow{KT}, \overleftrightarrow{KW},$ or $\overleftrightarrow{TW}$
There is one line pictured. It has several names.

d. Name five different rays.
$\overrightarrow{TH}, \overrightarrow{TW}, \overrightarrow{TK}, \overrightarrow{WK},$ or $\overrightarrow{KW}$
The first letter names the endpoint of the ray.

✓ **Check Understanding** Example 1

1. Name each figure in the diagram.
   a. three points
   b. two segments
   c. two rays

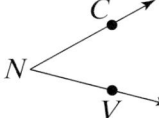

OBJECTIVE

2 Intersecting, Parallel, and Skew Lines

Two lines *intersect* if they have exactly one point in common. Two lines that lie in the same plane and do not intersect are **parallel.** You use the symbol $\parallel$ to indicate "is parallel to." Segments and rays are parallel if they lie in parallel lines.

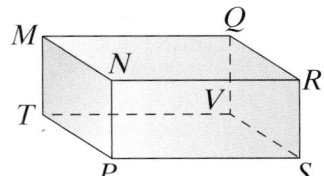

$\overline{MN}$ intersects $\overline{NP}$.
$\overline{MN} \parallel \overline{QR}$

Reading Math
The symbol $\parallel$ used for "parallel" looks like two parallel lines.

Skew lines are lines that do not lie in the same plane. They are not parallel and they do not intersect. Skew segments must be parts of skew lines. In the diagram above, $\overline{MN}$ and $\overline{RS}$ are skew.

Need Help?

One way to find skew segments in this figure is to look for a vertical segment and a horizontal segment that do not intersect.

2 EXAMPLE __Real-World__ 🌐 __Problem Solving__

Architecture **This structure is the frame of a room. Name the figures described below.**

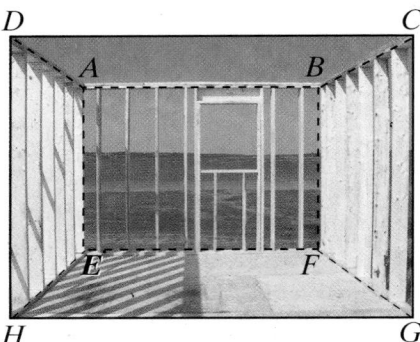

a. four segments that intersect $\overline{DH}$ $\overline{AD}, \overline{CD}, \overline{EH}, \overline{GH}$

b. three segments parallel to $\overline{DH}$ $\overline{AE}, \overline{BF}, \overline{CG}$

c. four segments skew to $\overline{DH}$ $\overline{AB}, \overline{BC}, \overline{EF}, \overline{FG}$

✓ **Check Understanding** Example 2

2. Use the diagram above. Name each of the following.

   a. four segments that intersect $\overline{EF}$
   b. three segments parallel to $\overline{EF}$
   c. four segments skew to $\overline{EF}$

3 EXAMPLE **Drawing Lines**

Draw two parallel lines. Then draw a segment that intersects the parallel lines.

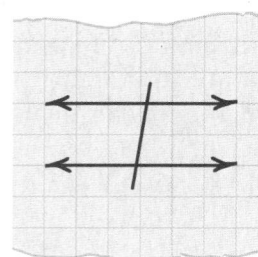

Use the lines on a piece of notebook paper or graph paper to help you draw parallel lines. Then draw a segment that intersects the two lines.

✓ **Check Understanding** Example 3

3. Use notebook paper or graph paper. Draw the figures indicated.

   a. three parallel segments
   b. a ray that intersects the parallel segments of part (a)
   c. a segment, $\overline{AB}$ **d.** a ray, $\overrightarrow{QR}$ **e.** a line, $\overleftrightarrow{LM}$

EXERCISES

For more exercises, see *Extra Practice*.

Practice and Problem Solving

A Practice by Example

Example 1
(page 459)

Name the indicated figures in each diagram.

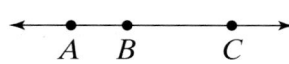

1. three points
2. three different segments
3. four different rays

4. all points
5. all segments
6. all lines

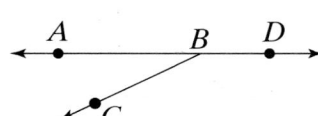

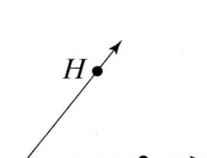

7. all segments
8. all lines
9. all rays

10. all rays
11. all points

Example 2
(page 460)

Name all indicated segments.

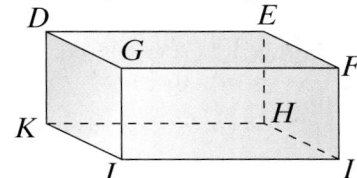

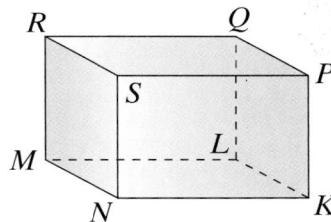

12. that intersect $\overline{DE}$
13. that are parallel to $\overline{DE}$
14. that are skew to $\overline{DE}$

15. that intersect $\overline{MN}$
16. that are parallel to $\overline{MN}$
17. that are skew to $\overline{MN}$

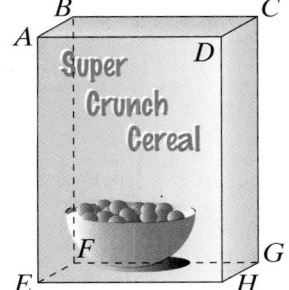

Packaging For the cereal box (left), name each of the following.

18. four segments that intersect $\overline{AE}$
19. three segments parallel to $\overline{AE}$
20. four segments skew to $\overline{AE}$

Example 3
(page 460)

21. Use notebook paper or graph paper. Draw three segments that are parallel to each other. Draw a line that intersects the parallel segments.

22. Draw two parallel rays.　　23. Draw $\overrightarrow{VB}$.

24. Draw $\overleftrightarrow{CD}$ so that it intersects two segments, $\overline{FG}$ and $\overline{HJ}$.

B Apply Your Skills

Modeling Draw each of the following. If not possible, explain.

25. $\overleftrightarrow{PQ} \parallel \overleftrightarrow{RS}$　　26. $\overrightarrow{AB} \parallel \overline{BC}$　　27. $\overline{JK}$ skew to $\overleftrightarrow{LM}$

9-1 Introduction to Geometry: Points, Lines, and Planes　**461**

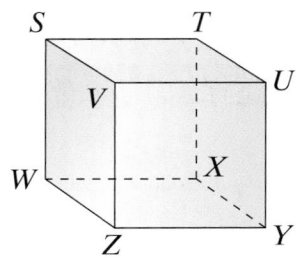

Use the figure at the left. Name a segment to make each statement true.

28. ▨ ∥ $\overline{XY}$ **29.** ▨ ∥ $\overline{YZ}$ **30.** ▨ ∥ $\overline{WX}$ **31.** ▨ ∥ $\overline{SV}$

Complete with *always, sometimes,* or *never* to make a true statement.

32. $\overrightarrow{AB}$ and $\overrightarrow{BC}$ are __?__ on the same line.

33. $\overrightarrow{AB}$ and $\overrightarrow{AC}$ are __?__ the same ray.

34. $\overline{AX}$ and $\overline{XA}$ are __?__ the same segment.

35. $\overleftrightarrow{TQ}$ and $\overleftrightarrow{QT}$ are __?__ the same line.

36. Skew lines are __?__ in the same plane.

37. Two lines in the same plane are __?__ parallel.

(**Algebra**) **Write an equation. Then find the length of each segment.**

38.
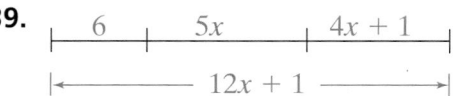

39.
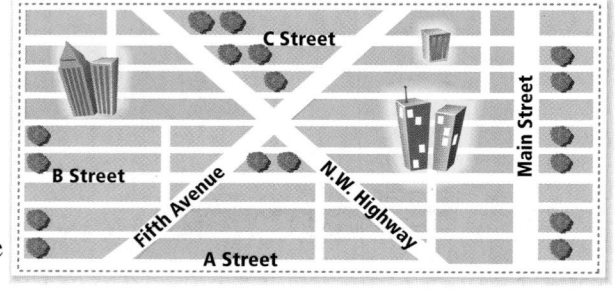

40. **Writing in Math** Explain what the symbols $\overline{AB}$ and AB represent. Use examples.

41. **Error Analysis** A student says that $\overrightarrow{AB}$ is the same ray as $\overrightarrow{BA}$. Explain the student's error.

🌐 **42. City Planning**
Use the map. Tell
whether the streets
in each pair appear
to be parallel or
intersecting.
   a. N.W. Highway
   and Fifth Avenue
   b. N.W. Highway
   and B Street
   c. A and C Streets   **d.** B and C Streets   **e.** C and Main Streets

Ⓒ Challenge

43. a. Suppose a town installs a mailbox at a point *P*. How many straight roads can the town build leading to *P*?
   b. Suppose a town installs mailboxes at points *P* and *R*. How many straight roads might the town build that pass by both mailboxes?

44. a. On a coordinate plane, draw a line through $\left(-\frac{1}{2}, -1\right)$ and $\left(1, 1\frac{1}{2}\right)$. Then draw a line through $(-1, 1)$ and $\left(\frac{1}{2}, 3\frac{1}{2}\right)$.
   b. What appears to be true of the two lines that you drew in part (a)?
   c. Find the slope of each line.
   d. **Inductive Reasoning** Make a conjecture based on your answer to parts (b) and (c).

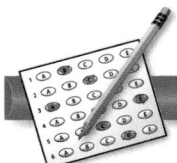
Multiple Choice

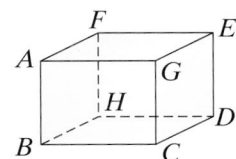

Use the figure at the left for Exercises 45–48.

45. Which segment is skew to $\overline{AB}$?

    A. $\overline{BC}$ **B.** $\overline{CD}$ **C.** $\overline{DE}$ **D.** $\overline{GC}$

46. Which segment is parallel to $\overline{ED}$?

    F. $\overline{BH}$ **G.** $\overline{AF}$ **H.** $\overline{AB}$ **I.** $\overline{GE}$

47. Which segment does NOT intersect $\overline{AG}$?

    A. $\overline{AB}$ **B.** $\overline{GC}$ **C.** $\overline{AF}$ **D.** $\overline{BC}$

Take It to the NET
Online lesson quiz at
www.PHSchool.com
Web Code: ada-0901

48. Which describes *BHDC*?

    F. point   **G.** line   **H.** plane   **I.** ray

Short Response

49. Draw a line and label three of its points as *A*, *B* and *C*.

    a. Explain why both $\overleftrightarrow{AB}$ and $\overleftrightarrow{BA}$ are names for your line.

    b. State another name for your line.

Mixed Review

Lesson 8-8

Graph each inequality in its own coordinate plane.

50. $y \geq -2x + 6$ **51.** $y > x + 1$ **52.** $x \leq -4$

Lessons 5-3 and 5-4

Simplify each expression.

53. $\frac{3}{8} + \frac{7}{12}$ **54.** $2\frac{3}{4} - 1\frac{5}{6}$ **55.** $1\frac{1}{3} + 2\frac{1}{6}$ **56.** $2\frac{1}{2} - 3\frac{2}{3}$

57. $\frac{5}{8} \cdot \frac{3}{4}$ **58.** $2\frac{2}{3} \div \frac{3}{8}$ **59.** $1\frac{1}{4} \cdot 3$ **60.** $4\frac{3}{8} \div 4$

Math at Work

········· **Choreographer**

Choreographers are usually experienced dancers whose hard work and dedication have earned them the opportunity to create original dances. Choreographers have an excellent sense of timing and spatial positioning.

Many choreographed dance numbers reflect geometric shapes such as triangles and quadrilaterals. Next time you see a dance group perform, be on the lookout for geometry—it will help you think like a choreographer!

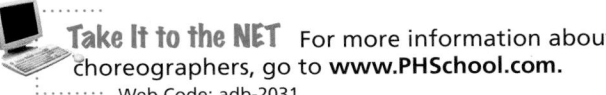

Take It to the NET For more information about choreographers, go to **www.PHSchool.com**.
Web Code: adb-2031

Drawing and Measuring Angles

An *angle* is formed by two rays with a common endpoint. The rays are the *sides* of the angle. The common endpoint is the *vertex*. You can name the angle at the right ∠ABC, ∠CBA, ∠B, or ∠1.

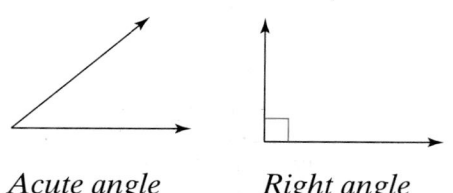

You can classify angles using their measures.

Acute angle
less than 90°

Right angle
90°

Obtuse angle
greater than 90°
and less than 180°

Straight angle
equal to 180°

You can use a protractor to draw and to measure angles.

Draw a 120° angle.

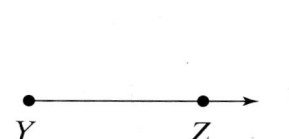

Step 1 Draw $\overrightarrow{YZ}$.

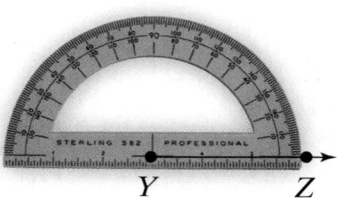

Step 2 Place the center of the protractor over Y. Make sure $\overrightarrow{YZ}$ passes through zero on the protractor scale.

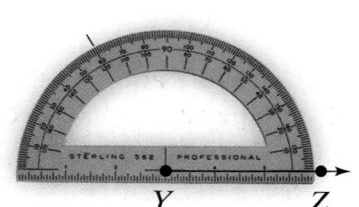

Step 3 Place a mark on your paper at 120° such that ∠XYZ will be obtuse.

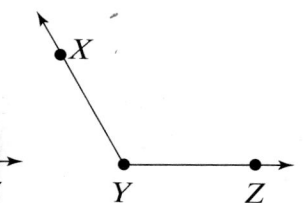

Step 4 Draw $\overrightarrow{YX}$. The measure of ∠XYZ is 120°.

EXERCISES

Draw an angle with the given measure.

1. 45°   **2.** 110°   **3.** 80°   **4.** 60°   **5.** 30°   **6.** 150°

Measure each angle. Then classify it as *acute*, *right*, or *obtuse*.

7.    **8.**    **9.** 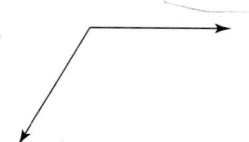   **10.**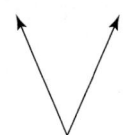

Angle Relationships and Parallel Lines

OBJECTIVE

1 Adjacent and Vertical Angles

In this lesson you will learn to identify special pairs of angles.

Adjacent angles share a vertex and a side but no points in their interiors.

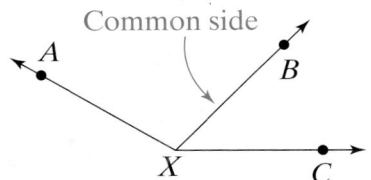

Common side

$\angle AXB$ and $\angle BXC$ are adjacent angles.

$\angle AXC$ and $\angle BXC$ are not adjacent angles.

Vertical angles are formed by two intersecting lines and are opposite each other. Vertical angles have the same measure.

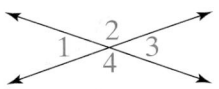

$\angle 1$ and $\angle 3$ are vertical angles.
$\angle 2$ and $\angle 4$ are vertical angles.

Angles that have the same measure are **congruent angles.** In the diagram above, $\angle 1$ is congruent to $\angle 3$. You can write this as $\angle 1 \cong \angle 3$. You can write *the measure of* $\angle 1$ as $m\angle 1$. Since $\angle 1 \cong \angle 3$, $m\angle 1 = m\angle 3$.

If the sum of the measures of two angles is $180°$, the angles are **supplementary.**

If the sum of the measures of two angles is $90°$, the angles are **complementary.**

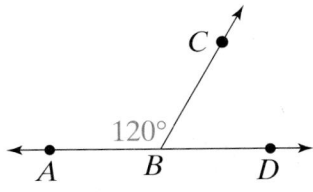

$\angle ABC$ and $\angle CBD$ are supplementary.

$\angle ABC$ and $\angle X$ are supplementary.
$\angle X$ and $\angle RQS$ are complementary.

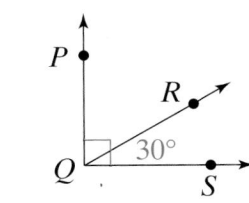

$\angle PQR$ and $\angle RQS$ are complementary.

What You'll Learn

OBJECTIVE 1 To identify adjacent and vertical angles

OBJECTIVE 2 To relate angles formed by parallel lines and a transversal

. . . And Why

To use the relationships of angles formed by parallel lines in real-world situations, such as setting leaded window panes

✔ Check Skills You'll Need

Solve.

1. $n + 45 = 180$

2. $75 + x = 90$

3. $3y = 2y + 90$

4. $2a + 15 = a + 45$

❓ For help, go to Lesson 7-5.

New Vocabulary

- adjacent angles
- vertical angles
- congruent angles
- supplementary
- complementary
- transversal
- corresponding angles
- alternate interior angles

ⓘ **TEXT** Interactive lesson includes instant self-check, tutorials, and activities.

1 EXAMPLE Finding the Measure of an Angle

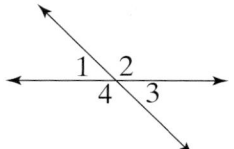

In the diagram at the left, find the measure of $\angle 1$ if $m\angle 4 = 135°$.

$m\angle 1 + m\angle 4 = 180°$	$\angle 1$ and $\angle 4$ are supplementary.
$m\angle 1 + 135° = 180°$	Replace $m\angle 4$ with 135°.
$m\angle 1 + 135° - 135° = 180° - 135°$	Solve for $m\angle 1$.
$m\angle 1 = 45°$	

✔ Check Understanding Example 1

1. If $m\angle 8 = 20°$, find the measures of $\angle 5$, $\angle 6$, and $\angle 7$.

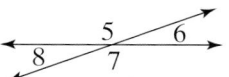

OBJECTIVE

2 Relating Angles and Parallel Lines

A line that intersects two other lines in different points is a **transversal.** Some pairs of angles formed by transversals and two lines have special names.

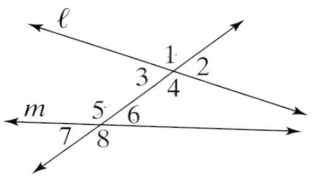

Corresponding angles lie on the same side of the transversal and in corresponding positions. $\angle 1$ and $\angle 5$, $\angle 3$ and $\angle 7$, $\angle 2$ and $\angle 6$, and $\angle 4$ and $\angle 8$ are corresponding angles.

Alternate interior angles are in the interior of a pair of lines and on opposite sides of the transversal. $\angle 3$ and $\angle 6$, and $\angle 4$ and $\angle 5$ are alternate interior angles.

When a transversal intersects two parallel lines, corresponding angles are congruent. Alternate interior angles are also congruent.

2 EXAMPLE Identifying Congruent Angles

In the diagram, $\ell \parallel m$. Identify each of the following.

a. congruent corresponding angles

$\angle 1 \cong \angle 3$, $\angle 2 \cong \angle 4$, $\angle 8 \cong \angle 6$, $\angle 7 \cong \angle 5$

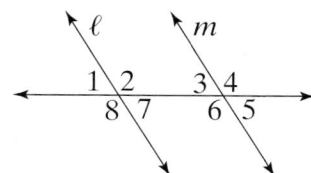

b. congruent alternate interior angles

$\angle 3 \cong \angle 7$, $\angle 2 \cong \angle 6$

2. In the diagram, $a \parallel b$. Name four pairs of congruent corresponding angles and two pairs of congruent alternate interior angles.

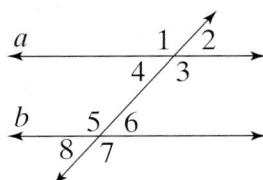

When solving a problem that involves parallel lines, you can often choose whether to use corresponding angles or alternate interior angles.

More Than One Way

The windowpanes at the right are held in place by parallel strips of lead. Lines r and s are parallel and line q is a tranversal. If $m\angle 1 = 65°$, what is $m\angle 4$?

Nicole's Method

Use corresponding angles.
$\angle 1 \cong \angle 3$ because they are corresponding angles, so $m\angle 3 = 65°$. $\angle 3$ and $\angle 4$ are supplementary, so $m\angle 3 + m\angle 4 = 180°$.

$$m\angle 3 + m\angle 4 = 180°$$
$$65° + m\angle 4 = 180°$$
$$65° + m\angle 4 - 65° = 180° - 65°$$
$$m\angle 4 = 115°$$

Eric's Method

Use alternate interior angles.
$\angle 1$ and $\angle 2$ are supplementary.

$$m\angle 1 + m\angle 2 = 180°$$
$$65° + m\angle 2 = 180°$$
$$65° + m\angle 2 - 65° = 180° - 65°.$$
$$m\angle 2 = 115°$$

$\angle 2$ and $\angle 4$ are alternate interior angles, so they are congruent. If $m\angle 2 = 115°$, then $m\angle 4 = 115°$.

Choose a Method

1. Which method do you prefer? Explain why.
2. What is another way to solve the problem?

EXERCISES

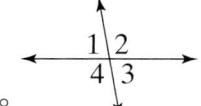 For more exercises, see *Extra Practice*.

Practice and Problem Solving

A Practice by Example

Example 1
(page 466)

For Exercises 1 and 2, copy and complete the sentence.

1. ∠1 and ∠2 are __?__ angles.

2. ∠1 and ∠3 are __?__ angles.

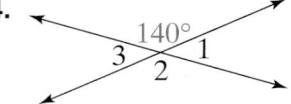

3. Find the measures of ∠1, ∠2, and ∠3 if $m\angle 4 = 100°$.

For Exercises 4 and 5, name the angle vertical to ∠1. Name an angle adjacent to ∠1. Then find $m\angle 1$.

4.

5.

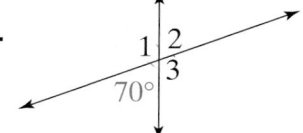

Example 2
(page 466)

For Exercises 6–8, use the figure at the right.

6. Name four pairs of corresponding angles.

7. Name the alternate interior angles.

8. Suppose $\overleftrightarrow{AB} \parallel \overleftrightarrow{MN}$. Name all angles congruent to ∠8.

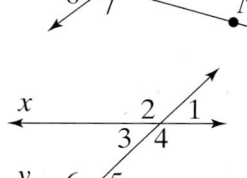

9. **a.** In the figure at the right, $x \parallel y$. List all angles that are congruent to ∠1.
   b. If $m\angle 5 = 45°$, what are the measures of the other angles?

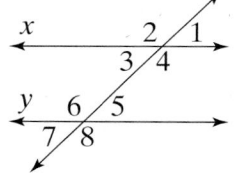

B Apply Your Skills

10. In the figure at the right, find the sum of the measures of ∠1, ∠2, and ∠3.

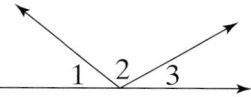

11. Fill in the blank. The sum of the measures of two angles is 90°. The angles are __?__ angles.

12. In the figure at the left, name the angle vertical to ∠1. Name an angle adjacent to ∠1. Then find $m\angle 1$.

13. **Writing in Math** Describe how you will keep from confusing the definitions of supplementary angles and complementary angles.

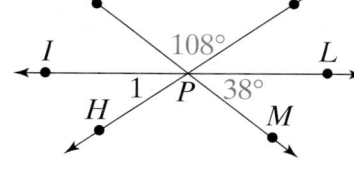

14. **Reasoning** Angles on the "outside" of two lines and on opposite sides of a transversal are called *alternate exterior angles*. The transversal *q* intersects two parallel lines *m* and *n*. If $m\angle 1 = 84°$, what is the measure of ∠5? Explain your reasoning.

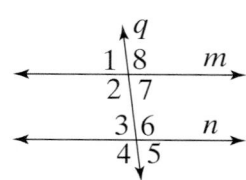

15. **Algebra** Use the figure for Exercise 14. If $m\angle 8 = 2x + 5$ and $m\angle 4 = x + 10$, what is the value of *x*?

16. (Algebra) Given $a \parallel b$ at the right, find the measures of $\angle 1$ and $\angle 2$.

C Challenge

17. a. (Algebra) Write an equation and find the value of x.
   b. Find $m\angle KQB$.
   c. Find $m\angle KQR$.

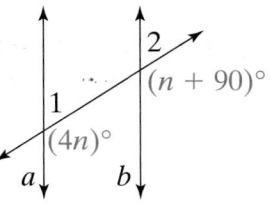

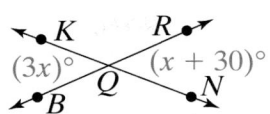

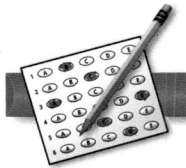

Test Prep

Multiple Choice

18. What is $m\angle 3$?
   A. 22°   **B.** 68°
   C. 158°   **D.** 202°

19. If $\ell \parallel m$, what is $m\angle 6$?
   F. 22°   **G.** 68°
   H. 158°   **I.** 202°

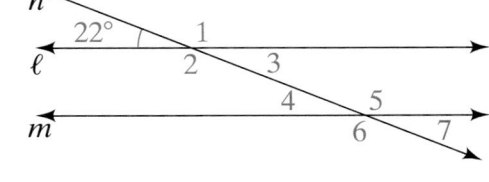

Reading Comprehension

Read the passage below before doing Exercises 20 and 21.

New Road Approved

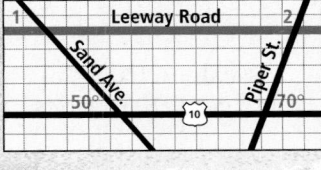

The Middleton City Board approved the proposal for a new road parallel to Highway 10. This new road, to be called Leeway Road, will help ease traffic flow in downtown Middleton during rush hour. Leeway Road will intersect both Sand Avenue and Piper Street.

20. When Leeway Road is built, what will $m\angle 1$ be? Justify your answer.

21. If $m\angle 2$ is 130° when Leeway Road is built, what criterion is Leeway Road NOT meeting?

Take It to the NET
Online lesson quiz at
www.PHSchool.com
Web Code: ada-0902

Mixed Review

Lesson 9-1

Draw each figure.

22. $\overline{AB}$ **23.** $\overrightarrow{CD}$ **24.** $\overrightarrow{DC}$ **25.** $\overleftrightarrow{EF}$ **26.** $\angle GHI$

Lesson 6-9

Find the sale price.

27. $25 at 10% discount

28. $324 at 20% discount

Lesson 4-5

29. In a single-elimination tournament, a team plays until it loses. Eight teams play in a tournament. How many games must be played to decide a tournament winner?

Classifying Polygons

OBJECTIVE
1 Classifying Triangles

What You'll Learn

OBJECTIVE
1 To classify triangles

OBJECTIVE
2 To classify quadrilaterals

. . . And Why

To use polygons in real-world situations involving design and construction

✔ **Check Skills You'll Need**

For the angle measures given, classify the angle as *acute, right,* or *obtuse.*

1. 85° **2.** 95° **3.** 160°

4. 90° **5.** 36° **6.** 127°

❓ For help, go to Lesson 9-2.

New Vocabulary

• polygon
• regular polygon

A **polygon** is a *closed* plane figure with at least three *sides*. The sides meet only at their endpoints.

A triangle is a polygon with three sides. You can classify triangles by angle measures. In the Review on page 464 you reviewed how to classify angles. You can also classify triangles by side lengths. Tick marks are used to indicate congruent sides of a figure.

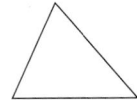

Acute triangle
three acute angles

Right triangle
one right angle

Obtuse triangle
one obtuse angle

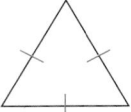

Equilateral triangle
three congruent sides

Isosceles triangle
at least two congruent sides

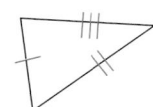

Scalene triangle
no congruent sides

1 EXAMPLE Classifying a Triangle

Classify the triangle by its sides and angles.

The triangle has two congruent sides and one right angle.

• The triangle is an isosceles right triangle.

8 in.

8 in.

✔ **Check Understanding** Example 1

1. Judging by appearance, classify each triangle by its sides and angles.

a.

b.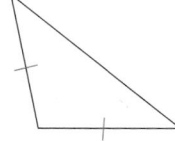

c.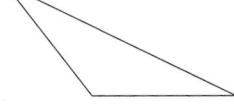

ℹ️ **TEXT** Interactive lesson includes instant self-check, tutorials, and activities.

2 Classifying Quadrilaterals

You can also classify quadrilaterals by their sides and angles.

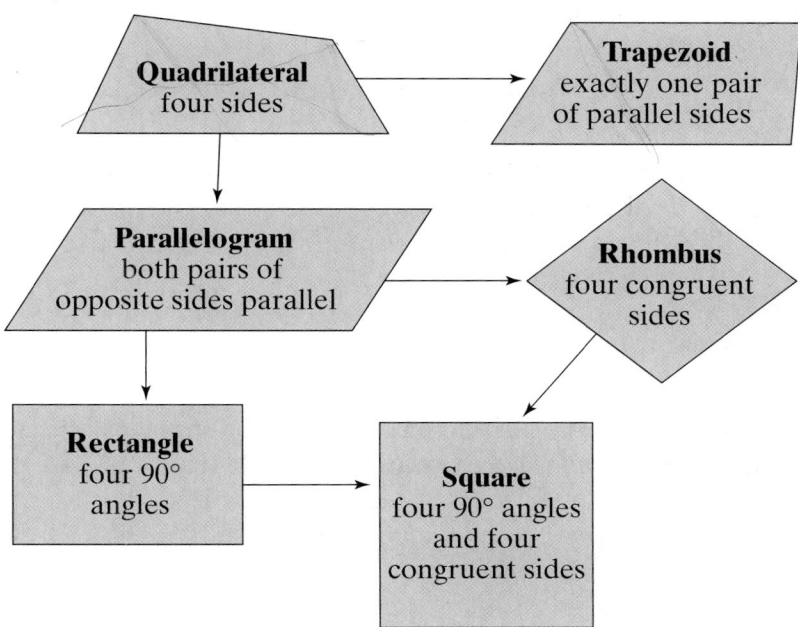

2 EXAMPLE Classifying Quadrilaterals

Name the types of quadrilaterals that have both pairs of opposite sides parallel.

All parallelograms have opposite sides parallel. Parallelograms include rectangles, rhombuses, and squares.

✓ **Check Understanding** Example 2

  2. Name the types of quadrilaterals that have four right angles.

In later math courses, you will prove that a parallelogram has opposite sides congruent and opposite angles congruent.

Polygons are named using their vertices. Start at one vertex and list them in consecutive order.

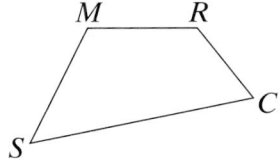

Starting from *M*, the name of this figure is quadrilateral *MRCS* or quadrilateral *MSCR*.

Reading Math
The plural of *vertex* is *vertices*.

A **regular polygon** has all sides congruent and all angles congruent. Some regular polygons are shown below.

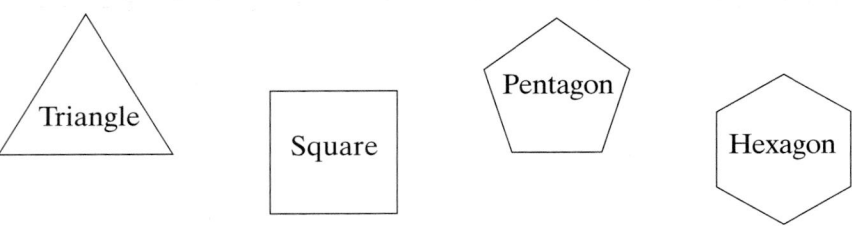

Triangle   Square   Pentagon   Hexagon

You can use algebra to write a formula for the perimeter of a regular polygon.

3 EXAMPLE   Real-World 🌐 Problem Solving

〔Algebra〕 **A contractor is framing a regular octagonal gazebo. Write a formula for the perimeter of the gazebo in terms of the length of a side. Evaluate the formula for a side length of 7 ft.**

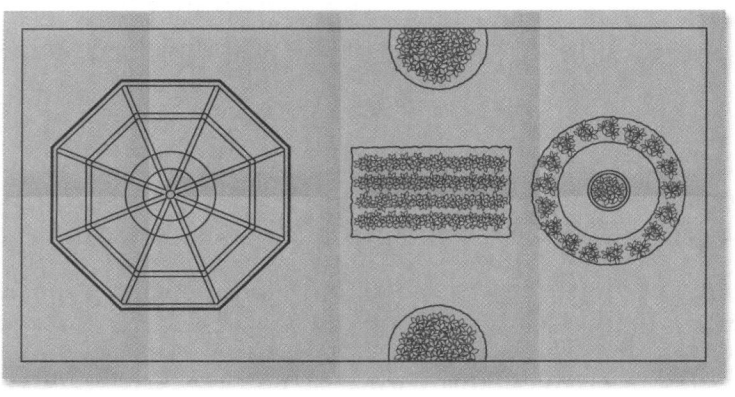

To write a formula, let x = the length of each side.
The perimeter of the regular octagon is
    $x + x + x + x + x + x + x + x$.
Therefore the formula for the perimeter is $P = 8x$.

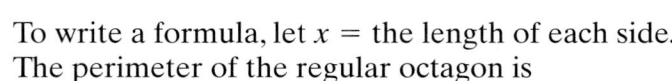

$P = 8x$ **Write the formula.**

$= 8(7)$ **Substitute 7 for x.**

$= 56$ **Simplify.**

● For a side length of 7 ft, the perimeter is 56 ft.

Real-World 🌐 Connection

Most gazebos are regular hexagons or regular octagons.

✔ **Check Understanding**   Example 3

3. a. 〔Algebra〕 Write a formula to find the perimeter of a regular hexagon.
   b. Use the formula to find the perimeter if one side is 16 cm.

EXERCISES

For more exercises, see *Extra Practice*.

Practice and Problem Solving

A Practice by Example

Example 1
(page 470)

Judging by appearance, classify each triangle by its sides and angles.

1.   2.   3.

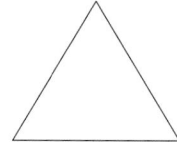

Example 2
(page 471)

Name the types of quadrilaterals that have the given property.

4. four congruent sides

5. exactly one pair of parallel sides

6. two pairs of parallel sides

7. opposite sides congruent

8. four congruent angles

9. opposite angles congruent

Example 3
(page 472)

[Algebra] **Write and use a formula for the perimeter of each figure. Use the formula to find the perimeter.**

10. an equilateral triangle with one side 3.5 cm

11. a square with one side 12.5 in.

12. a regular hexagon with one side $\frac{5}{8}$ in.

13. Architecture The Pentagon is a pentagonal-shaped building near Washington, D.C., that is home to the United States Department of Defense. Write a formula for the perimeter of a regular pentagon in terms of the length of a side. Evaluate the formula to find the perimeter of the Pentagon, which has a side length of 921 ft.

B Apply Your Skills

Open-Ended Sketch each figure.

14. an isosceles right triangle

15. a scalene obtuse triangle

16. an isosceles obtuse triangle

17. an isosceles acute triangle

18. a scalene right triangle

19. an equilateral triangle

20. Judging by appearance at the left, classify the triangle suggested by the edges of the piano, the piano lid, and the prop.

21. Draw a parallelogram without a right angle but with four congruent sides. What is another name for this figure?

Find the perimeter of each figure.

22. an isosceles triangle with congruent sides of 16.2 cm and a third side half that length

23. a scalene triangle with two side lengths of 8 in. and 5 in., and a third side length that is the average of the other two side lengths

Name the types of quadrilaterals that do *not* have the given property.

24. four congruent sides

25. four 90° angles

Name three different figures in each flag. For each triangle, state the type of triangle.

26.

Flag of Philippines

27.

Flag of Antigua

Are all equilateral triangles isosceles? Are all isosceles triangles equilateral? Explain.

The lengths of two sides of an isosceles triangle are given. What is the perimeter? Explain.

28. 10 cm, 12 cm
29. 5 cm, 12 cm
30. 12 cm, 12 cm

31. a. **Algebra** A decagon is a polygon with 10 sides. Write a formula for the perimeter of a regular decagon.
  b. Find the perimeter of a regular decagon with sides of 14.5 m.
  c. Find the length of a side of a regular decagon that has a perimeter of 22 ft.

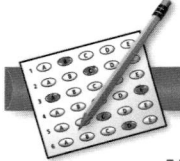

Test Prep

Multiple Choice

Take It to the NET
Online lesson quiz at
www.PHSchool.com
Web Code: ada-0903

Short Response

32. What is the perimeter of a regular pentagon with a side length of 4.9 cm?
  A. 4.9 cm   **B.** 14.7 cm   **C.** 24.5 cm   **D.** 29.4 cm

33. What is the perimeter of a square that has a side length of $\frac{3}{4}$ ft?
  F. $\frac{3}{16}$ ft   **G.** $\frac{3}{4}$ ft   **H.** 3 ft   **I.** 4 ft

34. Is a square a rhombus? Explain your answer.

35. Is a square a rectangle? Explain your answer.

Mixed Review

Lesson 9-2

36. A transversal intersects two parallel lines, forming eight angles. One angle measures 60°. Sketch a diagram showing the measures of all eight angles.

Lesson 8-7

37. **Parades** A town parade included modern and antique cycles. The modern cycles had two wheels and the antique cycles had three wheels. Altogether there were 64 wheels on the 28 cycles. How many of the cycles had three wheels?

Lessons 7-2 and 7-5

Solve each equation.

38. $x + 20 + 2x = 41$

39. $53 - 6x = 13 - 2x$

Angles of a Polygon

In previous courses, you learned that the sum of the measures of the angles of a triangle is 180°. Now you have the tools to prove that this is true with deductive reasoning.

In the figure, $\overleftrightarrow{AC} \parallel \overleftrightarrow{DE}$. If two parallel lines are cut by a transversal, then alternate interior angles are congruent. Therefore, $\angle 1 \cong \angle 4$, or $m\angle 1 = m\angle 4$.
Similarly, $m\angle 3 = m\angle 5$. $\angle ABC$ is a straight angle, so $m\angle 1 + m\angle 2 + m\angle 3 = 180°$.
Substitute $m\angle 4$ for $m\angle 1$ and $m\angle 5$ for $m\angle 3$ and you get $m\angle 4 + m\angle 2 + m\angle 5 = 180°$. These are the angles of $\triangle DBE$.

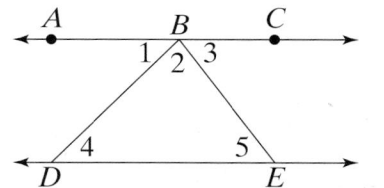

You can use triangles to find the sum of the measures of the angles of any polygon.

EXAMPLE

Find the sum of the measures of the angles of a hexagon.

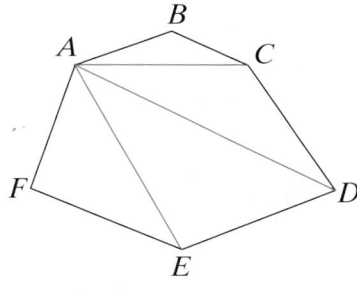

The hexagon has   **6** vertices.
From vertex A, there are **5** segments to the other vertices.
The segments determine **4** triangles.

number of triangles	·	number of degrees in angles of triangle	=	sum of measures of angles of hexagon
4	·	180°	=	720°

EXERCISES

Find the sum of the measures of the angles of each polygon.

1. a quadrilateral   **2.** a decagon (10 sides)

3. an octagon   **4.** a dodecagon (12 sides)

5. Reasoning Write a formula for the sum of the measures of the angles of an n-gon (n sides).

6. Find the value of x in the figure at the right.

7. Writing in Math The sum of the measures of the angles of a polygon is 1,260°. Explain how you can find the number of sides.

Find the number of sides in the polygon whose angle measures have the given sum.

8. 540°   **9.** 900°   **10.** 1,620°   **11.** 18,000°

Draw a Diagram

What You'll Learn

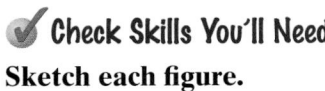

OBJECTIVE 1 To draw a diagram to solve a problem

. . . And Why

To find the number of diagonals in an octagon

✓ **Check Skills You'll Need**

Sketch each figure.

1. equilateral triangle

2. rectangle

3. pentagon

4. hexagon

5. octagon

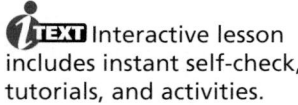

? For help, go to Lesson 9-3.

OBJECTIVE

1 Draw a Diagram

Math Strategies in Action
Car designers rely on computer-design programs to create, test, and modify their plans. The process of drawing a diagram helps them discover any problems they may have and see possible solutions.

Drawing a diagram is an important problem-solving tool.

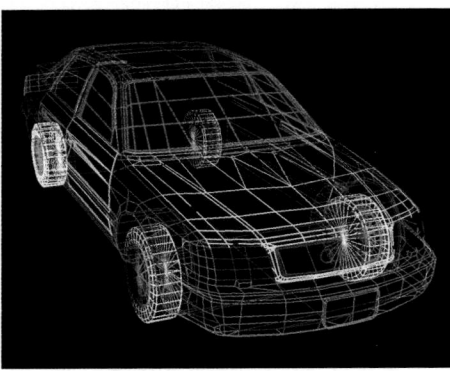

1 EXAMPLE Real-World Problem Solving

How many diagonals does an octagon have?

Read and Understand

In reading the problem, make sure you understand the meanings of all of the terms.

1. What is an octagon?

2. What is a diagonal?

Plan and Solve

One strategy for solving this problem is to draw a diagram and count the diagonals. An octagon has eight sides. You can draw five diagonals from one vertex of an octagon.

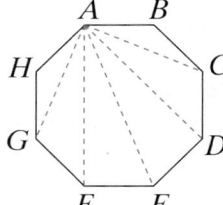

$\overline{AG}$, $\overline{AF}$, $\overline{AE}$, $\overline{AD}$, and $\overline{AC}$ are some of the diagonals.

3. There are 5 diagonals drawn from vertex *A*. Copy the diagram. Now find the number of diagonals you can draw from vertex *B*.

4. How many new diagonals can you draw from vertex *C*?

iText Interactive lesson includes instant self-check, tutorials, and activities.

It may be helpful to organize your results as you count the diagonals.

Make a table similar to the one below and fill in the number of diagonals from each vertex. Do not count a diagonal twice. (The segment from A to C is the same segment as the one from C to A.)

Then add to find the total number of diagonals.

Vertex	Number of Diagonals
A	5
B	5
C	4
D	■
E	■
F	■
G	■
H	■
Total	■

Look Back and Check

Counting the diagonals after they have all been drawn is not an easy task. To check your results, you may want to try a different approach.

Start with figures with fewer sides and see whether there is a pattern to the total numbers of diagonals as you increase the number of sides.

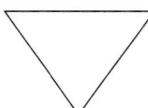 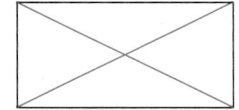 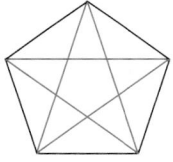 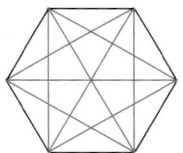

Figure	Number of Sides	Number of Diagonals
Triangle	3	0
Quadrilateral	4	2
Pentagon	5	5
Hexagon	6	9

Notice that the total number of diagonals increases as you increase the number of sides of the polygon. First the number increases by 2, then by 3, and then by 4. Continue this pattern to check your results.

✔ **Check Understanding**

5. How many diagonals does a decagon have?

EXERCISES

For more exercises, see *Extra Practice*.

Practice and Problem Solving

A Practice by Example

Example 1
(page 476)

Solve by drawing a diagram.

1. **Retail Delivery** A furniture delivery truck leaves the store at 8 A.M. It travels 6 miles east, then 4 miles south, then 2 miles west, and then 4 miles north. At the end of this route, how far is the truck from the store?

2. Bill is older than Jim and younger than Jose. Jose is older than Chris and younger than Tandala. Chris is older than Jim. Bill is younger than Tandala. Chris is older than Bill. Who is youngest?

3. **Geometry** How many triangles can you form in a hexagon if you draw all of the diagonals from only one vertex?

4. **Game Schedules** Eight soccer teams are to play each other two times in a season. How many games will be played?

5. There are 25 students in a math class. Ten students are in the math club. Twelve students are in the band. Five students are in both. How many students in the math class are members of neither club?

B Apply Your Skills

Solve using any strategy.

6. **Geometry** Snoozles are always born as twins, and each snoozle always moves in the opposite direction from its twin. Twin snoozles are at the origin of a coordinate plane. One follows the path $(0, 0)$ to $(1, 3)$ to $(2, 2)$ to $(4, 7)$. What path will its twin travel?

7. **Measurement** Maureen cut a 20-cm ribbon into exactly three pieces. The first piece is 3 cm shorter than the second piece. The third piece is 4 cm shorter than the second piece. Find the length of the shortest piece.

8. **Car Rental** A rental car costs $34.95 for the first 150 miles and $.35 for each additional mile. How much will the rental car cost for driving 275 miles?

9. A student was standing in the middle of a line. Twenty-three students were ahead of her. How many students were in the line?

10. **Writing in Math** Suppose you want to find the thickness of one sheet of paper. Describe the problem solving method you would use.

11. Shana has three pets, a dog, a cat, and a bird. One of them is named Sammy. Noodles is younger than both the bird and the dog. Fluffy is green. Which pet has the name Sammy?

12. **Geometry** You can draw one segment to connect two points and three distinct segments to connect three named points. How many segments can you draw to connect five points if no three of the points lie on the same line?

Strategies

- Account for All Possibilities
- Draw a Diagram
- Look for a Pattern
- Make a Model
- Make a Table
- Simplify the Problem
- Simulate the Problem
- Solve by Graphing
- Try, Test, Revise
- Use Multiple Strategies
- Work Backward
- Write an Equation
- Write a Proportion

13. Two friends rented a canoe for 10 days. One friend used the canoe for 6 days. The other friend used the canoe for 4 days. How much of the $150 rental fee should each friend pay?

C Challenge

14. Container A has twice the capacity of container B. Container A is full of sand and container B is empty. Suppose $\frac{1}{8}$ of the sand in container A is poured into container B. What fractional part of container B will contain sand?

15. Points P, Q, R, and S appear in that order on a line. The ratio $PQ : QR$ is $3 : 4$, and the ratio $QR : RS$ is $2 : 5$. The length PQ is 6 in. Find the length of PS.

Test Prep

Multiple Choice

16. How many diagonals does a hexagon have?
A. 6   **B.** 9   **C.** 12   **D.** 18

17. Some taxicabs begin each trip by setting the meter to $1.50. The meter then adds $.40 for each $\frac{1}{4}$ mi traveled. If a trip costs $7.90, how far did the cab travel?
F. 160 mi   **G.** 16 mi   **H.** 8 mi   **I.** 4 mi

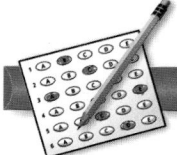

Take It to the NET
Online lesson quiz at
www.PHSchool.com
Web Code: ada-0904

18. What is the perimeter of a regular hexagon with side length of 6.3 cm?
A. 25.2 cm   **B.** 31.5 cm   **C.** 37.8 cm   **D.** 50.4 cm

Short Response

19. A coin collector has 53 rare coins. This is 12 fewer than 5 times the number there were a year ago. **(a)** Write an equation you could use to find out how many coins the collector had a year ago. **(b)** Solve the equation and show your work.

Mixed Review

Lesson 9-3

Classify each triangle by its sides and angles.

20. no congruent sides and one right angle

21. three congruent sides

22. one obtuse angle and no congruent sides

23. a 90° angle and two congruent sides

Lesson 8-8 **24. Ticket Sales** Adult tickets for the school musical sell for $8 and student tickets sell for $5 each. Let x be the number of adult tickets sold and y be the number of student tickets sold. The school hopes to make at least $1,000. Write an inequality to model the situation. Show all solutions by graphing the inequality.

Lesson 6-5

Write each decimal as a fraction in simplest form and as a percent.

25. 0.14   **26.** 4.5   **27.** 0.11   **28.** 0.02   **29.** 0.125   **30.** 1

9-5 Congruence

What You'll Learn

 OBJECTIVE **1** To identify corresponding parts of congruent triangles

 OBJECTIVE **2** To determine whether triangles are congruent

. . . And Why

To use congruent figures for finding distance

 **Check Skills You'll Need**

$\triangle ABC \sim \triangle XYZ$. For the given part of $\triangle ABC$, find the corresponding part of $\triangle XYZ$.

1. $\angle A$ **2.** $\angle C$

3. $\overline{AB}$ **4.** $\overline{CA}$

For help, go to Lesson 6-3.

New Vocabulary

• congruent figures

Exploring Congruence

1. Have each member of your group cut plastic straws 3 cm, 6 cm, and 7 cm long. String an 18-cm string through the three straws. Tie the string just tight enough to form a strong triangle without bending any straws.

2. Hold the triangles up to one another to compare. Are they the same size and shape? Describe how the angle measures compare.

Congruent figures have the same size and shape, and their corresponding parts have equal measures.

The triangles at the right are congruent. You use tick marks to indicate congruent segments, and arcs to mark congruent angles. You write a congruence statement by listing the corresponding angles in the same order.

You can use corresponding parts of congruent triangles to find distance.

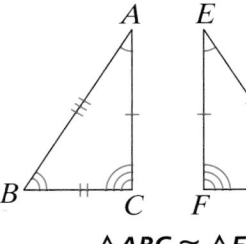

$\triangle ABC \cong \triangle EDF$

$\angle A \cong \angle E$	$\overline{AB} \cong \overline{ED}$
$\angle B \cong \angle D$	$\overline{BC} \cong \overline{DF}$
$\angle C \cong \angle F$	$\overline{AC} \cong \overline{EF}$

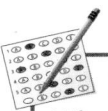 **Test-Taking Tip**

When two triangles are congruent, you can sketch the shapes side by side to help identify congruent parts.

TEXT Interactive lesson includes instant self-check, tutorials, and activities.

1 EXAMPLE **Real-World** 🌐 **Problem Solving**

Measurement $\triangle AMN \cong \triangle ABC$. **Name the corresponding parts.**

a. congruent angles
$\angle M \cong \angle B$, $\angle N \cong \angle C$,
$\angle MAN \cong \angle BAC$

b. congruent sides
$\overline{MN} \cong \overline{BC}$, $\overline{NA} \cong \overline{CA}$, $\overline{MA} \cong \overline{BA}$

c. Find the distance from M to N.
Since $\overline{MN} \cong \overline{BC}$ and $BC = 100$ yd, $MN = 100$ yd.

1. △*ABC* ≅ △*DEC*. List all pairs of congruent corresponding sides and angles. Then find *AC*.

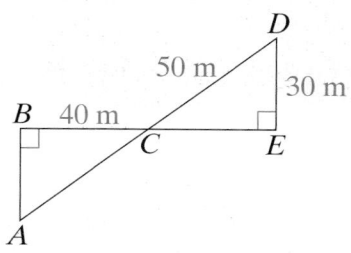

2 Identifying Congruent Triangles

You use corresponding parts of triangles to identify congruent triangles. Below are three of the ways to show that two triangles are congruent.

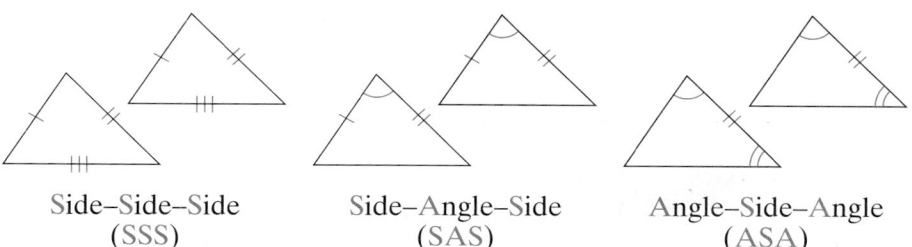

| Side–Side–Side (SSS) | Side–Angle–Side (SAS) | Angle–Side–Angle (ASA) |

2 EXAMPLE   Identifying Congruent Triangles

List the congruent corresponding parts of each pair of triangles. Write a congruence statement for the triangles.

a.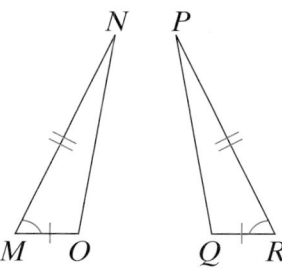

b.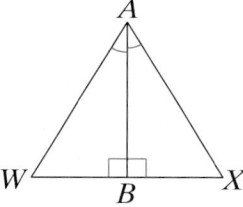

$\overline{MO} \cong \overline{RQ}$ **Side**

$\angle M \cong \angle R$ **Angle**

$\overline{MN} \cong \overline{RP}$ **Side**

△*MNO* ≅ △*RPQ* by SAS.

$\angle WAB \cong \angle XAB$ **Angle**

$\overline{AB} \cong \overline{AB}$ **Side**

$\angle ABW \cong \angle ABX$ **Angle**

△*WAB* ≅ △*XAB* by ASA.

✓ **Check Understanding** Example 2

2. For the two highlighted triangles, list the congruent corresponding parts. Write a congruence statement (and reason) for the triangles.

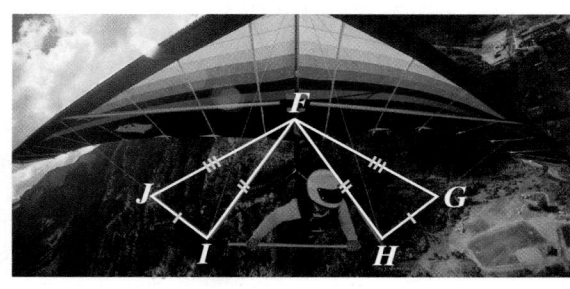

♀ For more exercises, see *Extra Practice*.

Practice and Problem Solving

Ⓐ Practice by Example

Example 1
(page 480)

$\triangle ABC \cong \triangle DEF$.
Complete each statement.

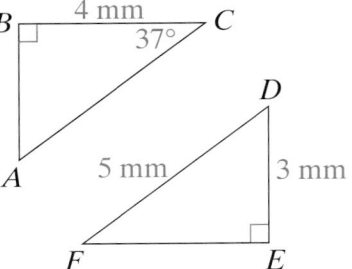

1. $\angle A \cong$ ■

2. $\angle B \cong$ ■

3. $m\angle C =$ ■

4. $m\angle B =$ ■

5. $m\angle A =$ ■

6. $\overline{AC} \cong$ ■

7. $\overline{EF} \cong$ ■

8. $\overline{BA} \cong$ ■

9. $AC =$ ■

10. $FE =$ ■

11. $\triangle CBA \cong$ ■

12. $\triangle BAC \cong$ ■

13. $\triangle ACB \cong$ ■

🌐 **Quilt Patterns** Use the quilt design for Exercises 14–16.

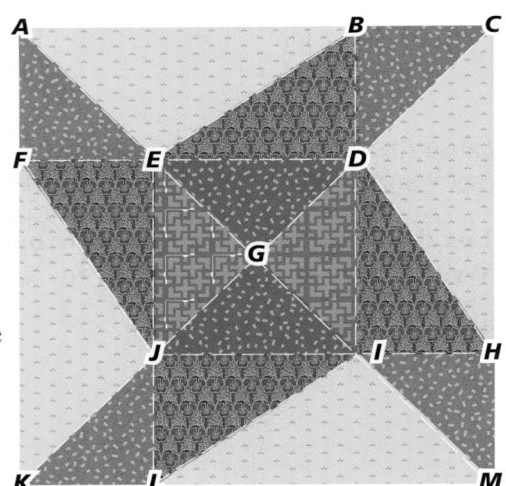

14. The yellow triangles are congruent. Name the corresponding congruent angles.

15. The red-and-blue triangles are congruent. Name the corresponding congruent sides.

16. The dark blue triangles are isosceles and congruent, and $GD = 10$ in. Find the distance from G to I.

Example 2
(page 481)

For each pair of triangles, list the congruent corresponding parts.
Write a congruence statement (and reason) for the triangles.

17.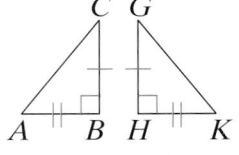

18.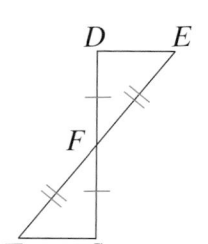

19.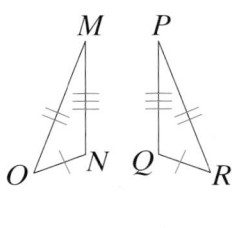

Ⓑ Apply Your Skills

Assume that $\triangle ABC \cong \triangle XYZ$. Answer the following.

20. Name the corresponding congruent angles.

21. Name the corresponding congruent sides.

22. If $AB = 12$ cm and $BC = 15$ cm, what is the length of $\overline{YZ}$?

Reading Math

For help with reading the diagram in Exercise 23, see page 485.

For each pair of triangles, list the congruent corresponding parts. Write a congruence statement (and reason) for the triangles.

23.

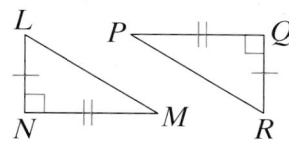

24.

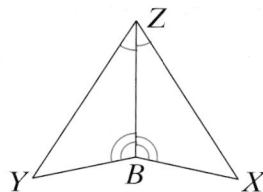

25.

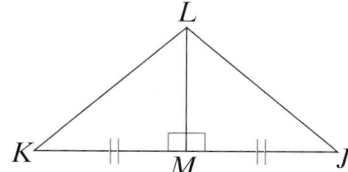

26.

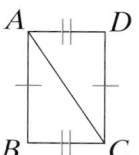

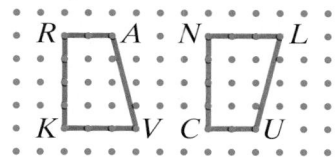

Error Analysis The two figures in the diagram (left) are congruent. State whether each congruence statement is correct and explain.

27. $RAVK \cong NLUC$

28. $RKVA \cong ULNC$

29. $ARKV \cong CULN$

30. $\overline{NL} \cong \overline{KV}$

31. $\angle V \cong \angle C$

32. $\angle VAR \cong \angle LUC$

 Challenge

Explain why the triangles in each pair are congruent. Then find the missing measures in each diagram.

33.

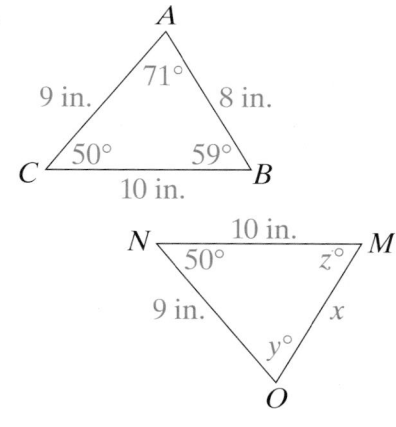

34.

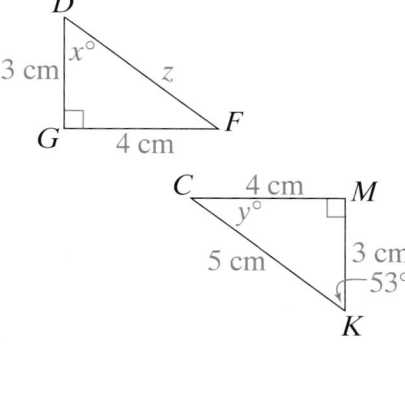

35. Containers The end of the shipping container at the left is a rectangle. The diagonals are congruent and intersect at point H. $\overline{HB} \cong \overline{HD}$ and $\overline{AH} \cong \overline{CH}$. Which triangle is congruent to the given triangle? Explain.
  a. $\triangle ABH$ **b.** $\triangle ADC$

36. Reasoning $\triangle KWR$ is *equiangular* (all angles are congruent). $\triangle ABJ$ is also equiangular. Can you use **A**ngle-**A**ngle-**A**ngle (**AAA**) to show that two triangles are congruent? Use diagrams to justify your conclusion.

37. Writing in Math $\triangle ABC \cong \triangle XYZ$. What can you conclude about the perimeters of the triangles? Explain.

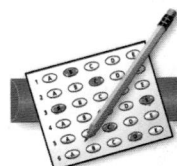
Multiple Choice

38. If $\triangle AND \cong \triangle PCK$, which statement must be true?
 A. $\overline{AN} \cong \overline{PK}$ **B.** $\angle N \cong \angle C$ **C.** $\overline{ND} \cong \overline{PC}$ **D.** $\angle AND \cong \angle PKC$

39. Which is the correct congruence statement?
 F. $\triangle BCD \cong \triangle FED$ by ASA
 G. $\triangle BCD \cong \triangle FED$ by SSS
 H. $\triangle CDB \cong \triangle DEF$ by ASA
 I. $\triangle BDC \cong \triangle FED$ by SAS

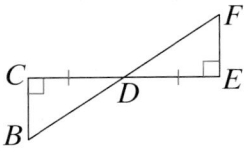

Take It to the NET
Online lesson quiz at
www.PHSchool.com
Web Code: ada-0905

40. Quadrilateral $JKLM \cong$ quadrilateral $PQRS$. Which is a correct congruence statement?
 A. $\overline{JK} \cong \overline{RS}$ **B.** $\overline{LM} \cong \overline{QR}$ **C.** $\angle K \cong \angle Q$ **D.** $\angle M \cong \angle P$

Mixed Review

Lesson 9-4

41. Students are evenly spaced as they sit around a round table. The fourth student is directly across from the eleventh student. How many students are seated at the table?

Lesson 6-7

Algebra   **Write and solve an equation.**

42. What percent of 50 is 20?

43. 15% of what number is 12?

44. Find 125% of 200.

Lesson 5-1

Order from least to greatest.

45. $\frac{1}{2}, \frac{5}{6}, \frac{3}{8}, \frac{2}{3}$

46. $\frac{3}{8}, \frac{2}{3}, \frac{3}{4}, \frac{4}{5}$

47. $\frac{1}{6}, \frac{1}{5}, \frac{1}{7}, \frac{1}{4}$

✓ Checkpoint Quiz 1   Lessons 9-1 through 9-5

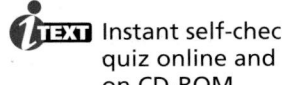 Instant self-check quiz online and on CD-ROM

Name the figure that has the properties described.

1. a part of a line with one endpoint

2. a series of points that extends in two directions without end

3. a segment congruent to $\overline{PR}$ when $\triangle LMN \cong \triangle PQR$

4. two rays with a common endpoint

5. **Algebra** In the diagram at the right, $a \parallel b$.
 a. Write an equation to find x.
 b. Find $m\angle TAV$.
 c. Find $m\angle TAN$.
 d. Find $m\angle DNK$.

6. Open-Ended Draw a triangle that is scalene and has a right angle.

Read the exercise below and then follow along with how Shelley reads the diagram. Check your understanding by solving the problem at the bottom of the page.

List the congruent corresponding parts of the triangles. Write a congruence statement (and reason) for the triangles.

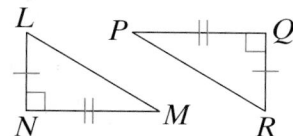

What Shelley Asks	What Shelley Thinks and Writes
What does the diagram show?	Two triangles The little squares show right angles. The tick marks show congruent sides.
What are the corresponding points?	Points L, N, M correspond to R, Q, and P.
What congruent parts do I know?	The single ticks show $\overline{LN} \cong \overline{RQ}$. The double ticks show $\overline{NM} \cong \overline{QP}$. I also know right angles are congruent. I'll write: $$\overline{LN} \cong \overline{RQ}$$ $$\overline{NM} \cong \overline{QP}$$ $$\angle N \cong \angle Q$$
Can I write a congruence statement?	I can write a congruence statement if I have SSS, SAS, or ASA.
Do I have SSS, SAS, or ASA?	I have congruence for two sides and an angle. SAS is the only possibility.
Do I have SAS?	The angles have to be between the sides. They are! I have SAS.
I must write the congruence statement (and reason).	I'll write: $$\triangle LNM \cong \triangle RQP \text{ by SAS}$$

EXERCISES

Write a congruence statement (and reason) for the triangles.

1.

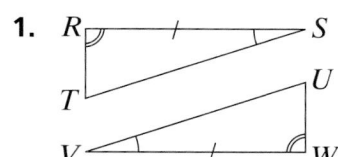

2.

3.

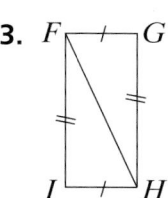

9-6

Circles

What You'll Learn

 OBJECTIVE 1 To find circumferences

 OBJECTIVE 2 To find central angles and to make circle graphs

. . . And Why

To display statistics using circle graphs

✓ Check Skills You'll Need

Solve each proportion. Round to the nearest whole number where necessary.

1. $\frac{10}{100} = \frac{x}{360}$

2. $\frac{75}{100} = \frac{x}{360}$

3. $\frac{0.8}{5.3} = \frac{x}{360}$

4. $\frac{1.6}{5.3} = \frac{x}{360}$

For help, go to Lesson 6-2.

New Vocabulary

- circle
- central angle

Investigation
Exploring Pi

1. Work in groups. Each member of your group should have a ruler, string, and several circular objects, such as jar lids. Make a chart similar to the chart below. Record your results.

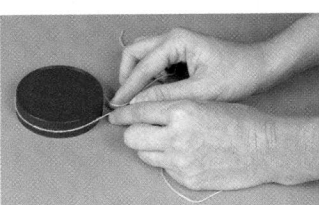

Object	Diameter	Circumference	Ratio $\frac{\text{Circumference}}{\text{Diameter}}$
▦	▦	▦	▦
▦	▦	▦	▦

2. Measure the diameter of each circle to the nearest millimeter.

3. Find the circumference of each circle by wrapping a string around the outside of the circle. Then straighten the string and measure its length to the nearest millimeter.

4. Calculate the ratio $\frac{\text{circumference}}{\text{diameter}}$ to the nearest tenth.

5. Make a conjecture about the relationship between the circumference of a circle and its diameter.

A **circle** is the set of all points in a plane that are the same distance from a given point, called the *center* of the circle.

Radius is a segment that has one endpoint at the center and the other point on the circle.

Diameter is a chord that passes through the center of a circle.

Circumference is the distance around the circle.

Chord is a segment whose endpoints are on the circle.

The ratio of every circle's circumference C to its diameter d is the same. It has a special symbol, π, which is pronounced "pie." Both 3.14 and $\frac{22}{7}$ are good approximations for this ratio. Use $\frac{22}{7}$ for π when calculations involve fractions, and use 3.14 when they do not.

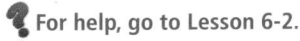 Interactive lesson includes instant self-check, tutorials, and activities.

If you multiply both sides of the equation $\frac{C}{d} = \pi$ by d, you get $C = \pi d$, which is a formula for the circumference of a circle.

Key Concepts	Circumference of a Circle

The circumference of a circle is π times the diameter.

$$C = \pi d \qquad C = 2\pi r$$

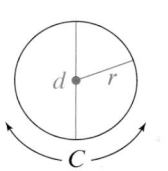

1 EXAMPLE   Finding Circumference

Find the circumference of the circle at the right.

$C = \pi d$ — **Write the formula.**

$C \approx (3.14)6$ — **Replace π with 3.14 and d with 6.**

$= 18.84$ — **Simplify.**

● The circumference of the circle is about 18.84 ft.

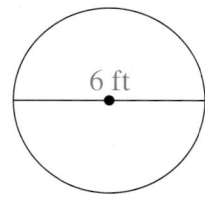

✓ Check Understanding   Example 1

1. Find the circumference of each circle.

   a. diameter $= 2\frac{4}{5}$ in.   **b.** radius $= 30$ mm   **c.** diameter $= 200$ mi

OBJECTIVE

2 Making Circle Graphs

To make a circle graph, you find the measure of each *central angle*. A **central angle** is an angle whose vertex is the center of a circle. There are $360°$ in a circle.

2 EXAMPLE   Real-World 🌐 Problem Solving

Budget **Make a circle graph for Juan's weekly budget shown at the right.**

Use proportions to find the measures of the central angles.

$$\frac{20}{100} = \frac{r}{360} \qquad \frac{25}{100} = \frac{\ell}{360} \qquad \frac{15}{100} = \frac{c}{360} \qquad \frac{40}{100} = \frac{s}{360}$$

$$r = 72° \qquad\quad \ell = 90° \qquad\quad c = 54° \qquad\quad s = 144°$$

- Use a compass to draw a circle.
- Draw the central angles with a protractor.
- Label each section.
● - Add a title and necessary information.

Juan's Weekly Budget

Recreation (r)	20%
Lunch (ℓ)	25%
Clothes (c)	15%
Savings (s)	40%

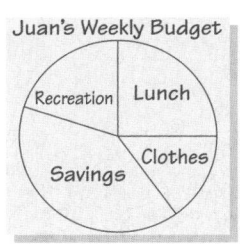

2. Make a circle graph for the data. Round the measure of each central angle to the nearest degree.

Blood Types of Population

Type A	Type B	Type AB	Type O
40%	12%	5%	43%

3 EXAMPLE Real-World 🌐 Problem Solving

National Parks Draw a circle graph of the data below.

First add to find the total number of visits (in millions).

$$0.3 + 0.4 + 1.3 + 1.8 = 3.8$$

Use proportions to find the measures of the central angles.

$$\frac{0.3}{3.8} = \frac{a}{360} \qquad \frac{0.4}{3.8} = \frac{b}{360}$$

$$a \approx 28° \qquad b \approx 38°$$

$$\frac{1.3}{3.8} = \frac{c}{360} \qquad \frac{1.8}{3.8} = \frac{d}{360}$$

$$c \approx 123° \qquad d \approx 171°$$

Visits to Kentucky's National Recreation Areas

Site	Visits (millions)
Abraham Lincoln's Birthplace	0.3
Big South Fork	0.4
Cumberland Gap	1.3
Mammoth Caves	1.8

Use a compass to draw a circle. Draw the central angles with a protractor. Label each section. Add a title and necessary information.

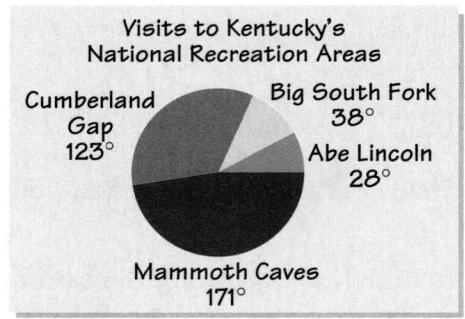

✔ **Check Understanding** Example 3

3. Students at Western High School work in the following places: restaurants, 140; library, 15; auto shop, 60; retail stores, 75; and other places, 30. Draw a circle graph to show where students at Western High School work. Round the measures of the central angles to the nearest degree.

EXERCISES

? For more exercises, see *Extra Practice*.

Practice and Problem Solving

A Practice by Example

Example 1
(page 487)

Find the circumference of each circle.

1.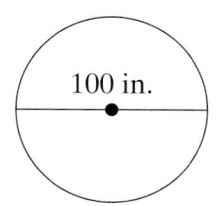
100 in.

2.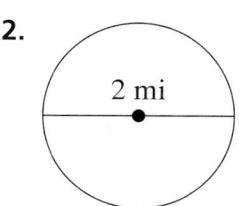
2 mi

3.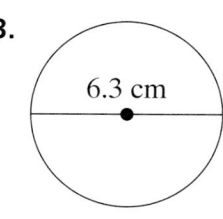
6.3 cm

Find the circumference of each circle with the given radius or diameter.

4. radius = 3.5 cm   **5.** radius = $4\frac{2}{3}$ ft   **6.** diameter = 0.1 m

7. radius = 18 in.   **8.** radius = 90 ft   **9.** diameter = $\frac{1}{2}$ yd

Examples 2 and 3
(pages 487 and 488)

Find the measures of the central angles that you would draw to represent each percent in a circle graph. Round to the nearest degree.

10. 35%   **11.** 50%   **12.** 30%   **13.** 1%   **14.** 25%   **15.** 75%

16. Income Make a circle graph for the data.

What College Students Earn

Monthly Income from Jobs	No job	Less than $200	$200 to $399	$400 or over
Percent of Total Number of Students	33%	14%	25%	28%

B Apply Your Skills

Find the circumference of each circle with the given radius or diameter.

17. radius = 0.6 in   **18.** radius = 10.25 mi   **19.** diameter = 4.6 yd

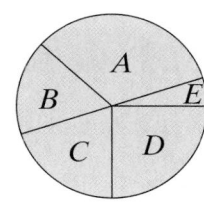

20. Personal Finance Nancy spends a third of her salary on rent, a fifth on utilities, a fourth on food, 5% on transportation, and she saves a sixth. Which section of the graph (at left) represents rent? Utilities? Food? Transportation? Savings?

21. The data below show how a group of students travel to school each day. Make a circle graph for the data.

How Students Travel to School

Transportation	Walk	Bicycle	Bus	Car	Other
Number of Students	55	80	110	40	15

22. Finance In a recent survey, families were asked how they spend extra income. Twenty-two families said they went to the movies, 34 said they eat out, 83 went on vacations, and the remaining 75 put it into savings. Make a circle graph for the data.

23. Writing in Math Write a paragraph to a student who was not in class describing how to make a circle graph.

24. A *tangent* to a circle is a line, segment, or ray in the same plane as the circle and which intersects the circle in exactly one point. A *secant* is a line, segment, or ray that intersects a circle in two points. Use the diagram to identify the following.

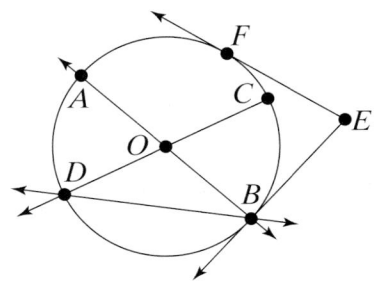

　a. one diameter　　　**b.** four radii
　c. two secants　　　**d.** three chords
　e. two tangents

Diameter	Circumference
1 in.	3.14 in.
5 in.	15.7 in.
8 in.	25.1 in.
10 in.	31.4 in.

25. The data at the left represent the circumference and the diameter of four circles of different sizes.
　a. Graph the points on a coordinate plane. Use the diameter as the *x*-coordinate and the circumference as the *y*-coordinate.
　b. Connect the points with a line.
　c. Find the slope of the line.
　d. **Reasoning** Explain the meaning of slope in this situation.

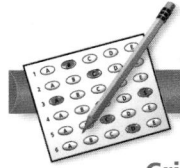 **Test Prep**

Gridded Response

26. To the nearest tenth of a degree, what is the measure of the central angle that represents 46% in a circle graph?

27. To the nearest tenth of a centimeter, what is the circumference of a circle with a radius of 2.5 cm? Use 3.14 for π.

Take It to the NET
Online lesson quiz at
www.PHSchool.com
Web Code: ada-0906

28. To the nearest hundredth of an inch, what is the circumference of a circle with a diameter of 8 in.? Use 3.14 for π.

Mixed Review

Lesson 9-5　**List the congruent corresponding parts of each pair of triangles. Write a congruence statement for the triangles.**

29. 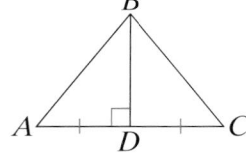　　　　**30.**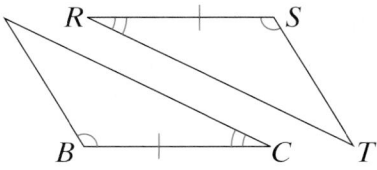

Lesson 8-1　**Is each relation a function? Explain.**

31. $\left\{\left(4, \frac{1}{2}\right), \left(6, \frac{1}{2}\right), \left(-2, \frac{1}{2}\right)\right\}$　　　**32.** $\left\{(1, 0), (1, 5), \left(1, 3\frac{1}{4}\right)\right\}$

Lesson 6-2 🌐 **33.** **Physical Fitness** While exercising, your heart beats 32 times in 15 s. At this rate, how many times will it beat in 2 min?

Constructions

OBJECTIVE

1 Congruent Segments and Angles

In constructions, you use only a *compass* and *straightedge* (an unmarked ruler) to accurately copy a segment or an angle, or draw an accurate bisector. A compass is a tool used to draw circles or parts of circles. An *arc* is part of a circle.

1 EXAMPLE — Constructing a Congruent Segment

Construct a segment congruent to $\overline{AB}$.

Step 1 Draw a ray with endpoint C.

Step 2 Open the compass to the length of $\overline{AB}$.

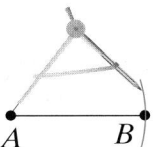

Step 3 With the *same* compass setting, put the compass tip on C. Draw an arc that intersects the ray. Label the intersection D.

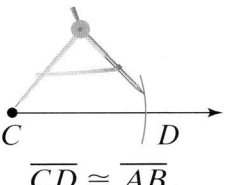

$$\overline{CD} \cong \overline{AB}$$

✓ Check Understanding   Example 1

1. Draw a segment. Construct a segment twice the length of the segment you drew.

What You'll Learn

OBJECTIVE 1 To construct a segment or an angle congruent to a given segment or angle

OBJECTIVE 2 To construct segment bisectors and angle bisectors

. . . And Why

To construct precise drawings such as those that architects use

✓ Check Skills You'll Need

State the meaning of each symbol.

1. B **2.** $\overline{AB}$

3. $\overrightarrow{AB}$ **4.** $\overleftrightarrow{AB}$

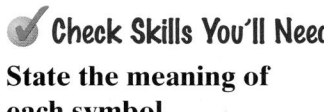

For help, go to Lesson 9-1.

New Vocabulary

- perpendicular lines
- segment bisector
- perpendicular bisector
- angle bisector

 **Interactive lesson** includes instant self-check, tutorials, and activities.

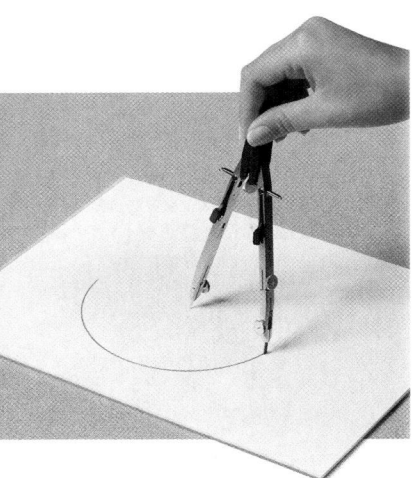

Real-World 🌐 Connection

To work with a compass easily, here is one way to hold it.

2 EXAMPLE **Constructing a Congruent Angle**

Construct an angle congruent to ∠E.

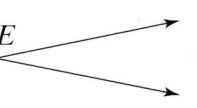

Step 1 Draw a ray with endpoint Q.

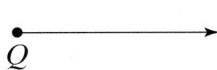

Step 2 With the compass point at E, draw an arc that intersects the sides of ∠E. Label the intersection points F and G.

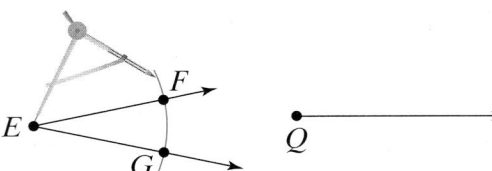

Step 3 With the *same* compass setting, put the compass tip on Q. Draw an arc intersecting the ray at point P.

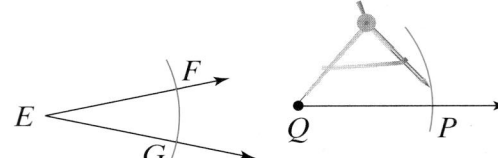

Step 4 Open the compass to the length of $\overline{FG}$. Using this setting, put the compass tip at P. Draw an arc to determine the point R. Draw $\overrightarrow{QR}$.

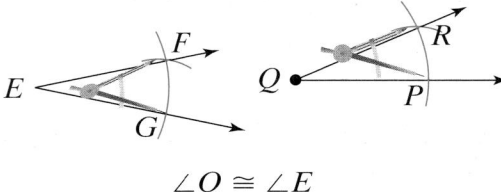

$\angle Q \cong \angle E$

✔ **Check Understanding** Example 2

2. Draw an obtuse angle. Construct an angle congruent to the angle you drew.

OBJECTIVE

2 **Constructing Bisectors**

The figures below show some special relationships intersecting lines may have.

Reading Math

To *bisect* means to divide into two equal parts. Therefore a bisector divides a segment or angle into two congruent parts.

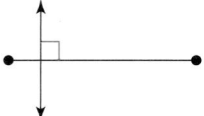

Perpendicular lines, segments, or rays intersect to form right angles.

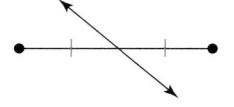

A **segment bisector** is a line, segment, or ray that divides a segment into two congruent segments.

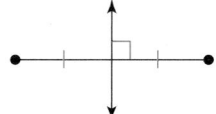

A **perpendicular bisector** is a line, segment, or ray that is perpendicular to the segment it bisects.

3 EXAMPLE Constructing a Perpendicular Bisector

Construct the perpendicular bisector of $\overline{PQ}$.

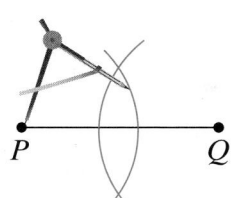

Step 1 Open the compass to more than half the length of $\overline{PQ}$. Put the compass tip at P. Draw an arc intersecting $\overline{PQ}$. With the same compass setting, repeat from point Q.

Step 2 Label the points of intersection of the two arcs as S and T. Draw $\overleftrightarrow{ST}$. Label the intersection of $\overleftrightarrow{ST}$ and $\overline{PQ}$ as point M.

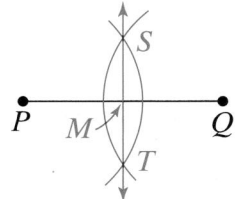

● $\overleftrightarrow{ST}$ is perpendicular to $\overline{PQ}$ and $\overleftrightarrow{ST}$ bisects $\overline{PQ}$.

✔ **Check Understanding Example 3**

3. Draw a segment. Construct its perpendicular bisector.

An **angle bisector** is a ray that divides an angle into two congruent angles.

4 EXAMPLE Constructing an Angle Bisector

Construct the bisector of $\angle A$.

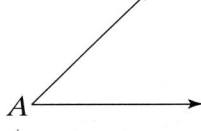

Step 1 Put the compass tip at A. Draw an arc that intersects the sides of $\angle A$. Label the points of intersection B and C.

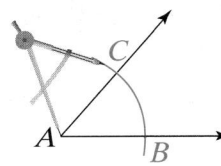

Step 2 Put the compass tip at B. Draw an arc. With the same compass setting, repeat with the compass tip at C. Make sure the arcs intersect. Label the intersection of the arcs D. Draw $\overrightarrow{AD}$.

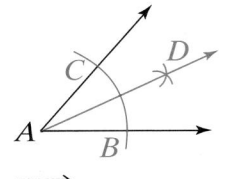

$\overrightarrow{AD}$ bisects $\angle BAC$.

✔ **Check Understanding Example 4**

4. Draw an obtuse angle. Construct its angle bisector.

EXERCISES

For more exercises, see *Extra Practice*.

Practice and Problem Solving

A Practice by Example

Example 1
(page 491)

For Exercises 1–4, draw a diagram similar to one that is given. Then construct each figure.

1. $\overline{EF}$ congruent to $\overline{XY}$

2. $\overline{GH}$ twice the length of $\overline{XY}$

Example 2
(page 492)

3. $\angle D$ congruent to $\angle A$

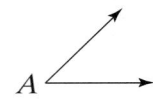

4. $\angle Y$ congruent to $\angle X$

5. Draw an acute angle. Construct an angle congruent to the angle you drew.

Example 3
(page 493)

For Exercises 6 and 7, first draw diagrams similar to ones shown.

6. Construct the perpendicular bisector of $\overline{MN}$.

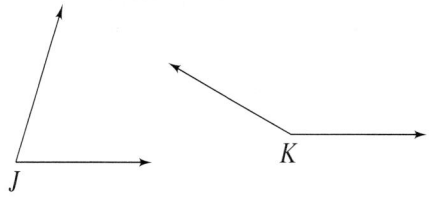

7. Construct the perpendicular bisector of $\overline{CD}$.

8. Draw $\overline{DE}$ at least 4 in. long. Then construct its perpendicular bisector.

Example 4
(page 493)

For Exercises 9 and 10, first draw diagrams similar to ones shown.

9. Construct the bisector of $\angle J$.

10. Construct the bisector of $\angle K$.

11. Use a protractor to draw a right angle. Construct its angle bisector.

B Apply Your Skills

For Exercises 12–14, draw a figure similar to the one that is given. Then construct each figure.

12. $\overline{MN}$ three times the length of $\overline{CD}$

13. $\overline{PQ}$ 1.5 times the length of $\overline{CD}$

14. $\triangle ABF$ with two angles congruent to $\angle X$

15. Draw an angle and label it $\angle A$. Then construct $\angle I$ so that $m\angle I = 2m\angle A$.

16. Construct a 90° angle.

17. **Writing in Math** How are constructing a segment bisector and constructing an angle bisector alike?

18. **Open-Ended** Use your compass to make a design. Decorate your design.

19. The bisector of $\angle XYZ$ is $\overrightarrow{YN}$. If the measure of $\angle XYN$ is 55°, what is the measure of $\angle XYZ$?

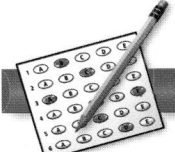 **Challenge**

20. **a.** Draw a point and a line. Construct the perpendicular segment from the point to the line. (*Hint:* Place your compass tip at the point. Open your compass far enough to draw an arc that intersects the line in two points. Construct the perpendicular bisector of the segment between the two points.)
 b. An *altitude* of a triangle is a perpendicular segment from a vertex to a line containing the side opposite the vertex. Draw a large acute triangle. Construct its three altitudes.

21. Draw $\triangle PQR$. To construct $\triangle ABC$ congruent to $\triangle PQR$, first construct $\overline{AB}$ congruent to $\overline{PQ}$. Use a compass setting the length of $\overline{PR}$. Draw an arc with the compass tip at A. Then use a compass setting the length of $\overline{QR}$. With the compass tip at B draw an arc that intersects the first arc. Label the intersection C. Draw $\overline{AC}$ and $\overline{BC}$.

 **Test Prep**

Multiple Choice

22. The bisector of $\angle ABC$ is $\overrightarrow{BD}$. If the measure of $\angle ABD$ is 50°, what is the measure of $\angle ABC$?
 A. 25°   **B.** 50°   **C.** 100°   **D.** 130°

Take It to the NET
Online lesson quiz at
www.PHSchool.com
Web Code: ada-0907

23. $\overrightarrow{DB}$ is the bisector of $\angle CDE$. Which statement must be true?
 F. $\angle CDE \cong \angle BDE$ **G.** $\angle CDB \cong \angle EDC$
 H. $\angle CDB \cong \angle BDE$ **I.** $\angle EDC \cong \angle EBC$

Extended Response

24. Explain how to construct each figure.
 a. a 45° angle   **b.** a $22\frac{1}{2}$° angle   **c.** a $67\frac{1}{2}$° angle
 d. Do one of the constructions (a)–(c).

Mixed Review

Lesson 9-6 **Find the measure of the central angle that would represent each percent in a circle graph. Round your answer to the nearest degree.**

25. 12%   26. 45%   27. 5%   28. 25%

Lesson 8-7 29. **Number Sense** Find two numbers with a sum of 25 and a difference of 15.

Lesson 7-8 **Find the simple interest.**

30. $1,000 deposited at an interest rate of 2% for 3 years

31. $150 deposited at an interest rate of 4% for 6 months

You can use geometry software to construct a geometric figure quickly and accurately. In such software, "construct" has a special meaning.

EXAMPLE

Construct $\overleftrightarrow{CD}$, the perpendicular bisector of $\overline{AB}$. Tell what happens when you do the following.

a. Drag A toward B.   **b.** Drag A in a path parallel to $\overleftrightarrow{CD}$.

Step 1   Use the Segment tool to draw a segment. Label its endpoints A and B.

Step 2   Highlight $\overline{AB}$. Use the Construct menu and construct the midpoint of $\overline{AB}$. Label the midpoint C.

Step 3   Highlight C and $\overline{AB}$. Use the Construct menu and construct a perpendicular through $\overline{AB}$ at C. Construct a second point on this perpendicular line and label it D.

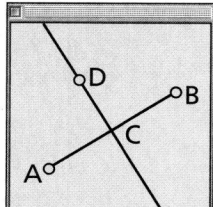

$\overleftrightarrow{CD}$ is the perpendicular bisector of $\overline{AB}$.

a.   As you drag A toward B, point C moves half as fast as A to remain the midpoint of $\overline{AB}$. $\overleftrightarrow{CD}$ moves to stay perpendicular to $\overline{AB}$.

b.   As you drag A in a path parallel to $\overleftrightarrow{CD}$, $\overline{AB}$ changes size and position, but $\overleftrightarrow{CD}$ moves also to remain the perpendicular bisector of $\overline{AB}$.

EXERCISES

1. Use the Segment tool to draw $\angle JKL$ as shown at the right. Then use the Construct menu and construct $\overrightarrow{KM}$, the bisector of $\angle JKL$.

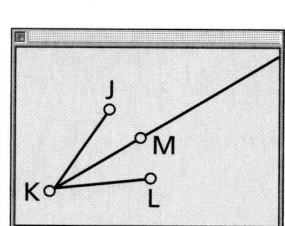

    a. Predict what will happen if you change the size of $\angle JKL$ by dragging point J. Use the software to test your prediction.

    b. Is there a way to move J so that $\overrightarrow{KM}$ does not change? Use the software to check your answer.

    c. Predict what will happen if you drag point K so that $\angle JKL$

        i. has measure 180°.

        ii. has measure 0°.

        Use the software to test each prediction.

2. **Writing in Math**   Describe what is special about a figure you *construct* with geometry software.

Translations

OBJECTIVE

1 Graphing Translations

You can move pattern blocks by sliding them, flipping them, or turning them. Each of these moves is a type of transformation. A **transformation** is a change of position or size of a figure.

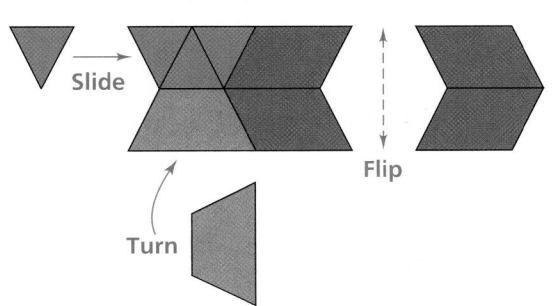

Slide

Flip

Turn

A **translation** is a transformation that moves points the same distance and in the same direction. A figure and its translated image are congruent. You can see examples of translations or slides in wallpaper, fabric, and wrapping paper.

The figure you get after a transformation is called the **image.** To name the image of a point, you use *prime* notation. The figure at the right shows the translation of A to its image A'.

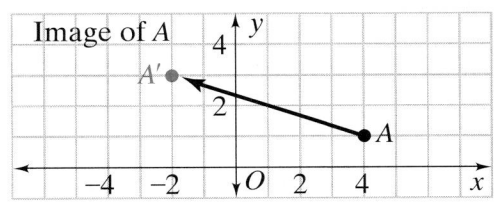

Image of A

1 EXAMPLE   Translating a Figure

Graph the image of △KRT after a translation 5 units to the right and 3 units down.

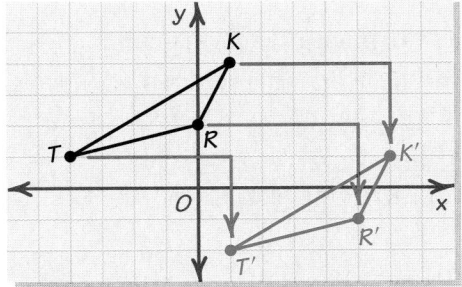

✓ Check Understanding   Example 1

1. On a coordinate plane, draw △KRT. Graph the image of △KRT after each translation.

   a. 4 units to the left   **b.** 5 units down

   c. 4 units to the left and 5 units down

2 Describing Translations

You can describe a transformation using arrow (→) notation, which describes the *mapping* of a figure onto its image.

2 EXAMPLE   Using Arrow Notation

The movement of point *P* is both horizontal and vertical. Use arrow notation to describe this translation.

The point moves from $P(-2, 2)$ to $P'(1, -1)$, so the translation is $P(-2, 2) \rightarrow P'(1, -1)$.

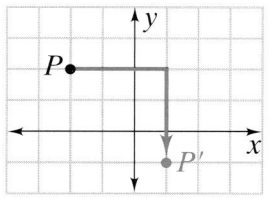

✔ Check Understanding   Example 2

2. Use arrow notation to describe a translation of $B(-1, 5)$ to $B'(3, 1)$.

Real-World ⊕ Connection

In chess, the move of a knight is a translation. The translation of piece *A* is $(x, y) \rightarrow (x + 1, y - 2)$.

You can also use arrow notation to write a general rule that describes a transformation. To write a rule for a translation, choose corresponding points on a figure and its image. Subtract the coordinates of the figure from the coordinates of its image.

3 EXAMPLE   Writing a Rule

Write a rule to describe the translation of △*PQR* to △*P'Q'R'*.

Use $P(3, 2)$ and its image $P'(-2, 5)$ to find the horizontal and vertical translations.

Horizontal translation: $-2 - 3 = -5$
Vertical translation: $5 - 2 = 3$

The rule is $(x, y) \rightarrow (x - 5, y + 3)$

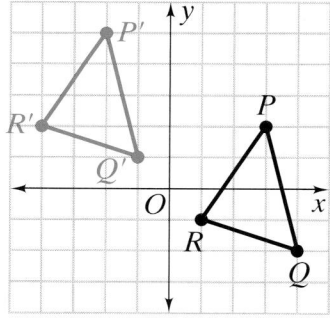

✔ Check Understanding   Example 3

3. Write a rule to describe the translation of quadrilateral *ABCD* to quadrilateral *A'B'C'D'*.

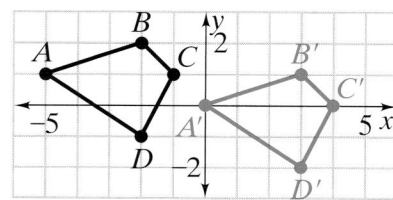

EXERCISES

 For more exercises, see *Extra Practice*.

Practice and Problem Solving

A Practice by Example

Example 1
(page 497)

Graph the image of △QRS for the given translation.

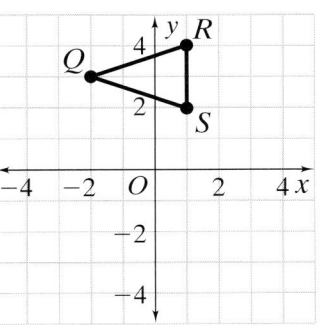

1. 2 units to the right

2. 5 units down

3. 3 units to the right and 5 units down

4. 1 unit to the left and 3 units down

5. 2 units to the right and 1 unit up

6. 3 units to the left and 2 units up

△HIJ has the coordinates given. Graph the triangle and its translation 3 units to the right and 2 units down.

7. $H(-1, 1), I(1, 4), J(1, 3)$ **8.** $H(0, 0), I(-3, -1), J(-1, -2)$

9. $H(-1, -2), I(0, 1), J(1, -2)$ **10.** $H(-4, 3), I(-2, 0), J(-4, 1)$

Use arrow notation to describe the translation.

Example 2
(page 498)

11. $A(1, 5)$ to $A'(2, 7)$ **12.** $W(-2, -6)$ to $W'(4, 9)$

13. $S(3, 3)$ to $S'(11, 1)$ **14.** $D(-9, -4)$ to $D'(0, 1)$

Example 3
(page 498)

Write a rule to describe each translation.

15.

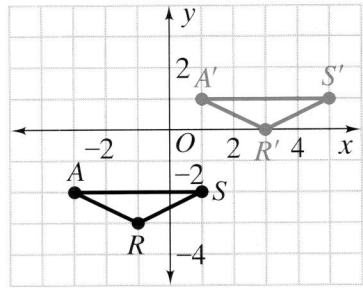

16.

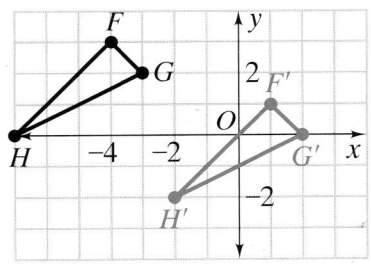

17.

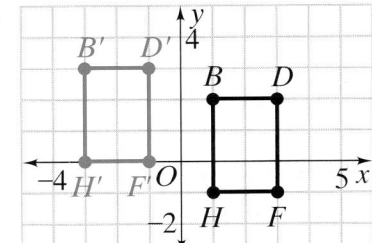

18.

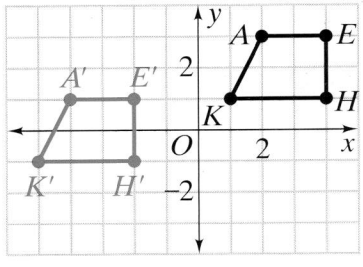

Write a description of each rule.

19. $(x, y) \longrightarrow (x - 11, y + 4)$ **20.** $(x, y) \longrightarrow (x + 5, y - 2)$

21. $(x, y) \longrightarrow (x - 6, y - 3)$ **22.** $(x, y) \longrightarrow (x + 3, y + 9)$

B Apply Your Skills

Complete with *horizontal* or *vertical* to make a true statement.

23. In a ? translation, the *y*-coordinate changes and the *x*-coordinate stays the same.

24. In a ? translation, the *x*-coordinate changes and the *y*-coordinate stays the same.

The endpoints of a segment are given. Graph each segment and its image for the given translation.

25. $A(0, 0), B(0, 5)$; 2 units left

26. $C(0, 0), D(0, 2)$; 2 units up

27. $E(0, 0), F(2, 0)$; 4 units down

28. $G(0, 0), H(-4, 0)$; 4 units up

29. $J(0, 0), K(5, 5)$; 1 unit right

30. $L(-1, 3), M(2, 1)$; 5 units left

Write a rule to describe each translation.

31.

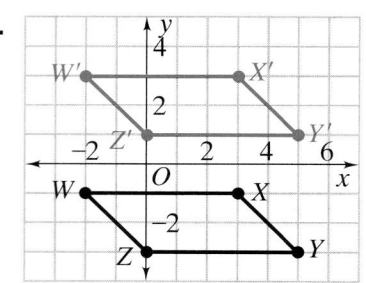

32.

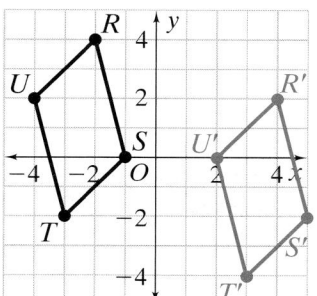

The endpoints of a segment are given. Graph each segment and its image for the given translation.

33. $N(3, 3), P(-3, 4)$;
3 units left, 2 units down

34. $Q(2, -1), R(-2, 1)$;
2 units right, 3 units up

35. $S(4, 3), T(1, -5)$;
4 units left, 1 unit up

36. $U(-4, -5), V(2, 1)$;
3 units right, 2 units down

37. Translate point $T(2, 5)$ 2 units to the right and 6 units up. Translate its image, point T', 4 units to the left and 1 unit down. What are the coordinates of the image of point T''?

C Challenge

38.  **Writing in Math** Describe and explain the result of moving a figure *a* units horizontally and then $-a$ units horizontally.

39. **Art** You can use translations to draw three-dimensional figures. First draw a figure on graph paper. Translate the figure. Connect each vertex with its image. Use dashes for sides that are not visible. Try this, first with a rectangle; then begin with a triangle.

40. A rule like $(x, y) \longrightarrow (2x, 2y)$ describes a dilation (see p. 304) of the coordinate plane. This dilation has center $(0, 0)$ and scale factor 2.
   a. $\overline{AB}$ has endpoints $A(4, 0)$ and $B(0, 3)$. Describe its image, $\overline{A'B'}$, for the dilation above. How do lengths AB and $A'B'$ compare?
   b. Describe a coordinate-plane dilation that has center $(0, 0)$ and scale factor $\frac{1}{2}$. Describe its effect on $\overline{AB}$ from part (a).

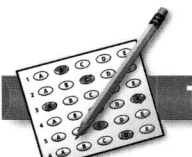

Multiple Choice

41. Which coordinates represent a translation of $B(-4, 1)$ 3 units to the right and 2 units down?

A. $B'(-7, 3)$ **B.** $B'(-6, 4)$ **C.** $B'(-1, -1)$ **D.** $B'(-2, -4)$

42. Which points show the translation $(x, y) \longrightarrow (x - 1, y + 4)$?

F. $A(4, 2), A'(5, -2)$ **G.** $A(4, 2), A'(3, 6)$

H. $A(4, 2), A'(8, 1)$ **I.** $A(4, 2), A'(0, 3)$

Take It to the NET

Online lesson quiz at **www.PHSchool.com**
Web Code: ada-0908

43. Quadrilateral $WXYZ$ has vertices $W(0, 0)$, $X(-4, 2)$, $Y(-4, 6)$, and $Z(0, 4)$. Quadrilateral $W'X'Y'Z'$ has vertices $W'(2, -3)$, $X'(-2, -1)$, $Y'(-2, 3)$, and $Z'(2, 1)$. Which rule describes the translation?

A. $(x, y) \longrightarrow (x - 3, y + 2)$ **B.** $(x, y) \longrightarrow (x + 2, y - 3)$

C. $(x, y) \longrightarrow (x - 2, y + 3)$ **D.** $(x, y) \longrightarrow (x + 3, y - 2)$

Short Response

44. You translate the graph of $y = 2x + 4$ by 3 units down and 4 units right.

a. Write a rule to describe the translation.

b. What is the slope of the graph of the image?

Mixed Review

Lesson 9-7

45. Draw an acute angle and construct its bisector.

Lesson 5-4

Simplify each product.

46. $\frac{3}{7} \cdot \frac{7}{9}$ **47.** $\frac{1}{2} \cdot \frac{8}{11}$ **48.** $\frac{1}{2} \cdot \frac{1}{8}$

Lesson 4-5

49. Amanda, Adam, and Ann ate salad, chicken, or tofu for lunch. Amanda did not eat chicken or tofu. Ann did not eat chicken. Each one had a different meal. What did each person eat?

 ## Checkpoint Quiz 2   **Lessons 9-6 through 9-8**

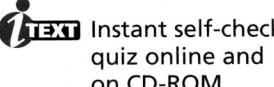 Instant self-check quiz online and on CD-ROM

Use the circle graph.

1. Eighty people attended a catered meal. Twenty-eight people ordered fish, half ordered chicken, and twelve ordered the vegetarian meal. Which section represents each of the meals?

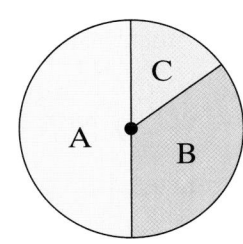

2. Determine the measure of the central angle of each section in the circle graph.

3. **Open-Ended** Draw a segment about $\frac{3}{4}$ in. long. Construct an equilateral triangle with sides of this length.

4. Graph $\overline{NR}$ with endpoints $N(2, 7)$ and $R(-4, 0)$. Then graph its image after a translation 4 units right and 3 units down.

Matrices and Translations

A matrix is a rectangular arrangement of numbers. Each number is a matrix entry. You can write the coordinates of the vertices of a figure as a matrix.

$$
\begin{array}{c} \\ x\text{-coordinate} \\ y\text{-coordinate} \end{array}
\begin{array}{ccc} A & B & C \end{array}
\begin{bmatrix} 0 & -1 & -4 \\ 0 & 4 & 0 \end{bmatrix}
$$

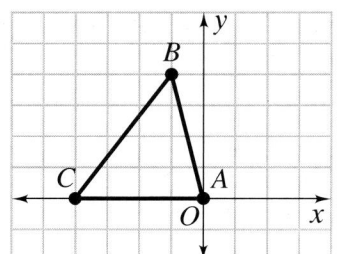

You can use matrices to translate figures.

EXAMPLE

Geometry Use a matrix to find the vertices of the image of quadrilateral $ABCD$ using the rule $(x, y) \longrightarrow (x + 3, y - 2)$.

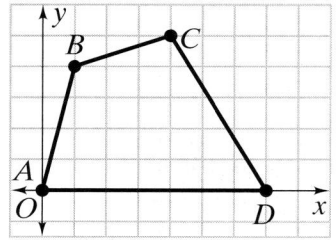

vertices of quadrilateral + translation matrix = vertices of image

Add 3 to each x-coordinate.

Add -2 to each y-coordinate.

$$
\begin{array}{cccc} A & B & C & D \end{array} \quad\quad\quad\quad\quad\quad \begin{array}{cccc} A' & B' & C' & D' \end{array}
$$
$$
\begin{bmatrix} 0 & 1 & 4 & 7 \\ 0 & 4 & 5 & 0 \end{bmatrix} + \begin{bmatrix} 3 & 3 & 3 & 3 \\ -2 & -2 & -2 & -2 \end{bmatrix} = \begin{bmatrix} 3 & 4 & 7 & 10 \\ -2 & 2 & 3 & -2 \end{bmatrix}
$$

The vertices of the image are $A'(3, -2)$, $B'(4, 2)$, $C'(7, 3)$, and $D'(10, -2)$.

EXERCISES

Use matrix addition to find the vertices of the image of the given figure under each translation.

1. $\triangle TRI$ with vertices
$T(-5, -5), R(-3, -1), I(-1, -3)$;
translation: $(x, y) \longrightarrow (x + 6, y + 6)$

2. square $SQRE$ with vertices
$S(1, 2), Q(4, 2), R(4, 5), E(1, 5)$;
translation: $(x, y) \longrightarrow (x + 1, y - 3)$

3. $\triangle NGL$ with vertices
$N(4, 4), G(7, 4), L(5, 0)$;
translation matrix: $\begin{bmatrix} -9 & -9 & -9 \\ -4 & -4 & -4 \end{bmatrix}$

4. square $RECT$ with vertices
$R(0, 0), E(0, -4), C(-4, -4), T(-4, 0)$;
translation matrix: $\begin{bmatrix} -1 & -1 & -1 & -1 \\ 2 & 2 & 2 & 2 \end{bmatrix}$

5. a. What matrix would you use to translate a triangle 1 unit to the left and 4 units down?

   b. Use your answer from part (a) to translate $\triangle ABC$ with vertices $A(2, 2), B(3, 5), C(3, 0)$

Symmetry and Reflections

OBJECTIVE

1 Identifying Lines of Symmetry

A figure has **reflectional symmetry** when one half is a mirror image of the other half. A **line of symmetry** divides a figure with reflectional symmetry into two congruent halves.

A pattern for the back of a shirt is shown below. To make a shirt, you place the pattern on a folded piece of material, with the dashed lines of the pattern on the fold. After cutting the material, the back of the shirt will look like this.

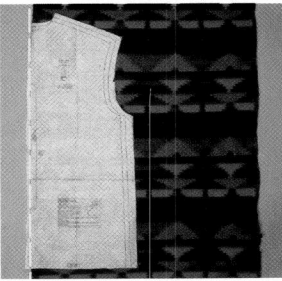

The fold is the line of symmetry.

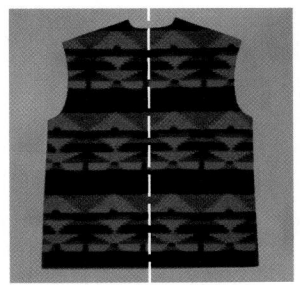

The shirt has one line of symmetry.

It is possible for a figure to have more than one line of symmetry.

1 EXAMPLE Finding Lines of Symmetry

Draw the lines of symmetry. Tell how many there are.

a.

one line of symmetry

b.

six lines of symmetry

✓ Check Understanding Example 1

1. Copy each figure. Draw all lines of symmetry.

   a. 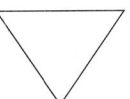   b.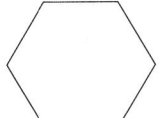

What You'll Learn

 OBJECTIVE 1 To identify a line of symmetry

 OBJECTIVE 2 To graph a reflection of a geometric figure

. . . And Why

To use symmetry and reflections in real-world situations, such as sewing

✓ Check Skills You'll Need

Graph each line.

1. $x = 0$ 2. $y = 0$

3. $x = 3$ 4. $y = 2$

5. $x = -1$ 6. $x = y$

🔍 For help, go to Lesson 8-3.

New Vocabulary

- reflectional symmetry
- line of symmetry
- reflection
- line of reflection

---

i TEXT Interactive lesson includes instant self-check, tutorials, and activities.

2 Graphing Reflections

A **reflection** is a transformation that flips a figure over a **line of reflection.** The reflected figure, or image, is congruent to the original figure. Together, an image and its reflection have line symmetry, the line of reflection being the line of symmetry.

2 EXAMPLE Reflecting Over an Axis

Graph the image of △ABC after a reflection over the y-axis.

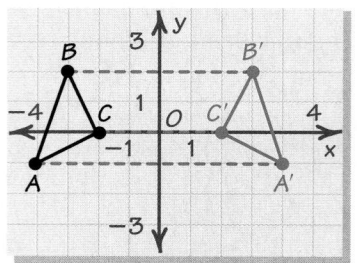

Since A is 4 units to the left of the y-axis, A′ is 4 units to the right of the y-axis. Reflect the other vertices. Draw △A′B′C′.

✔ **Check Understanding** Example 2

2. Graph the image of △ABC after a reflection over the x-axis.

You can reflect images over lines other than the axes.

3 EXAMPLE Reflecting Over a Line

Graph the image of △PQR after a reflection over y = 2.

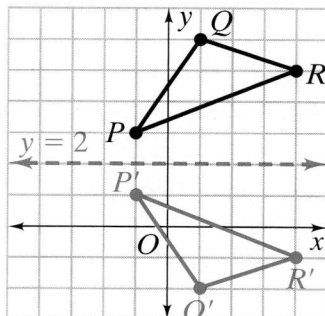

Graph y = 2. Since P is 1 unit above the red line, P′ is 1 unit below the red line.

Reflect the other vertices. Draw △P′Q′R′.

✔ **Check Understanding** Example 3

3. Graph the image △ABC with vertices A(3, 0), B(2, 3), and C(5, −1) after a reflection over each line.

    a. x = 2   **b.** y = −1

EXERCISES

For more exercises, see Extra Practice.

Practice and Problem Solving

A Practice by Example

Example 1
(page 503)

Copy each figure. Draw all lines of symmetry.

1. 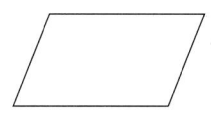 2. 3.

Example 2
(page 504)

In Exercises 4–8, graph each figure and its image after a reflection over the given line.

4. 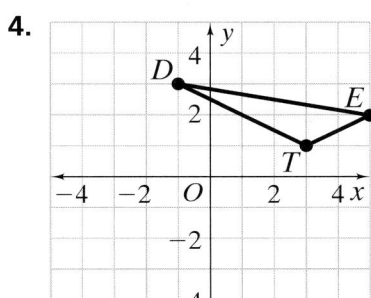 5.

the *x*-axis   the *y*-axis

Example 3
(page 504)

6. $\triangle ABC$ with $A(2, 0)$, $B(-6, 0)$, $C(2, -6)$; line $x = 1$

7. $\triangle KLM$ with $K(-1, 1)$, $L(3, 2)$, $M(0, 3)$; line $y = -1$

8. $\triangle WXY$ with $W(-1, -1)$, $X(0, 0)$, $Y(-5, 0)$; line $y = 2$

B Apply Your Skills

Draw each figure. Draw all the lines of symmetry.

9. rhombus   10. square   11. isosceles triangle

12. **Writing in Math** Can a reflection image of an angle have a measure that is different from the measure of the original angle? Explain.

Graph each point and its image after a reflection over the given line. Name the coordinates of the image.

13. $H(-8, 3)$; $y = 4$ 14. $J(-8, 3)$; $y = 2$ 15. $V(5, 0)$; $x = -2$

16. $A(2, 5)$; $y = x$ 17. $B(0, 3)$; $y = 0$ 18. $C(4, 0)$; $x = 0$

Reasoning Decide whether each statement is *always* true, *sometimes* true, or *never* true.

19. The image of a polygon reflected over a line is congruent to the original polygon.

20. When corresponding points of an original figure and its reflection are connected, the resulting segments are all perpendicular to the line of reflection.

21. When a point is reflected over a horizontal line, the *y*-coordinate of the point stays the same.

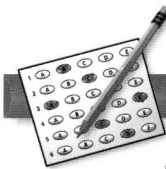 **Challenge**

The given point is reflected over line 1. Then the image is reflected over line 2. Name the coordinates of the second image.

22. $A(3, -2)$
line 1: y-axis
line 2: x-axis

23. $B(-1, 5)$
line 1: x-axis
line 2: $y = 3$

24. $C(-5, -1)$
line 1: $x = 2$
line 2: y-axis

25. a. On a coordinate plane, graph the line $y = x$ and $\triangle ABC$ with vertices $A(5, 3)$, $B(6, -1)$, and $C(2, -1)$.

b. To graph the image of $\triangle ABC$ over the line $y = x$, trace the axes and $\triangle ABC$ on tracing paper. Fold the paper along $y = x$. Trace over the triangle so that it makes an impression on your original graph. Label A', B', and C' appropriately and draw $\triangle A'B'C'$.

c. Connect A to A', B to B', and C to C'. What do you notice about the line $y = x$ and these segments?

d. Complete: The line of reflection is the __?__ of the segment that connects a point to its image.

Test Prep

Multiple Choice

26. Which type of figure has at least two lines of symmetry?
A. parallelogram   **B.** trapezoid
C. isosceles triangle   **D.** rhombus

27. How many lines of symmetry does a rectangle have?
F. 0   **G.** 1   **H.** 2   **I.** 4

Short Response

In Exercises 28 and 29, **(a)** state whether each statement is *always* true, *sometimes* true, or *never* true.   **(b)** Explain your reasoning.

28. When a point is reflected over a horizontal line, the x–coordinate stays the same.

29. When a point is reflected over a horizontal line and is NOT on the line, the y–coordinate stays the same.

Mixed Review

Lesson 9-8

The endpoints of a segment are given. Graph the segment and its image for the given translation.

30. $A(4, 3)$, $B(5, 7)$;
3 units left, 2 units down

31. $X(0, -1)$, $Y(2, 7)$;
2 units right, 3 units up

Lesson 8-2

Graph each equation.

32. $x + 3 = y$

33. $y - 8 = x$

34. $2y = x + 10$

Lesson 1-8

35. If six people meet, and each person shakes every other person's hand, how many handshakes are there in all?

Rotations

1 Graphing Rotations

A **rotation** is a transformation that turns a figure about a fixed point called the **center of rotation.** The angle measure of the rotation is the **angle of rotation.**

In the diagram, $\triangle QPR$ is rotated $90°$ about the center of rotation, point P. Notice that $m\angle QPQ' = 90°$ and $m\angle RPR' = 90°$. A figure and its rotation image are congruent.

In the diagram, the direction of the rotation is *counterclockwise.* All rotations in this book will be counterclockwise.

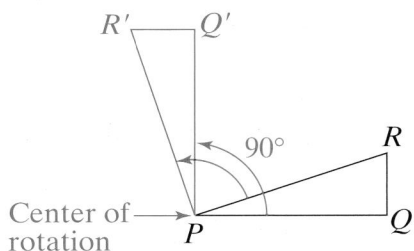

You can graph a rotation on a coordinate plane.

1 EXAMPLE   Finding a Rotation Image

Find the vertices of the image of $\triangle ABC$ after a rotation of $180°$ about the origin.

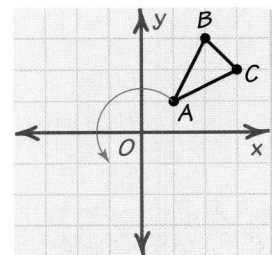   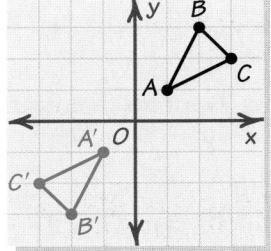

Step 1 Draw $\triangle ABC$. Place a piece of tracing paper over the graph. Trace the vertices of the triangle, the x-axis, and the y-axis. Then place your pencil at the origin to rotate the paper.

Step 2 Rotate the paper $180°$. Make sure the axes line up. Mark the position of each vertex by pressing through the paper. Connect the vertices of the rotated triangle.

The vertices of the image are $A'(-1, -1)$, $B'(-2, -3)$, and $C'(-3, -2)$.

What You'll Learn

OBJECTIVE
1 To graph rotations

OBJECTIVE
2 To identify rotational symmetry

. . . And Why

To use rotations in describing real objects

✔ Check Skills You'll Need

Graph each triangle.

1. $A(1, 3)$, $B(4, 1)$, $C(3, -2)$

2. $J(-2, 1)$, $K(1, -3)$, $L(1, 4)$

3. $X(4, 0)$, $Y(0, 2)$ $Z(-2, -3)$

For help, go to Lesson 1-10.

New Vocabulary

- rotation
- center of rotation
- angle of rotation
- rotational symmetry

 Interactive lesson includes instant self-check, tutorials, and activities.

✓ Check Understanding Example 1

1. Copy the graph of △*ABC* in Example 1. Draw its image after a rotation of 90° about the origin. Name the coordinates of the vertices of the image.

2 Identifying Rotational Symmetry

A figure has **rotational symmetry** if you can rotate it 180°, or less, so that its image matches the original figure. The angle (or its measure) through which the figure rotates is the angle of rotation.

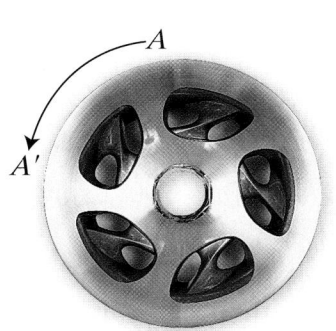

The wheel at the right has rotational symmetry. You can turn the wheel from its original position to four other positions (five positions in all) and its picture will be as you see here. The smallest such turn moves *A* to *A'*. The angle of rotation is 360° ÷ 5, or 72°.

2 EXAMPLE   Real-World 🌐 Problem Solving

Botany **Judging from appearance, state whether the flower has rotational symmetry. If so, what is the angle of rotation?**

> The flower can match itself in 3 positions.
>
> The pattern repeats in 3 equal intervals. 360° ÷ 3 = 120°

The figure has rotational symmetry.
● The angle of rotation is 120°.

✓ Check Understanding Example 2

2. Judging from appearance, tell whether each figure has rotational symmetry. If so, what is the angle of rotation?

a. 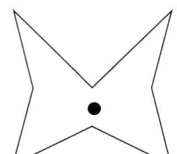   b. 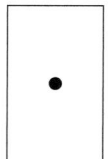   c.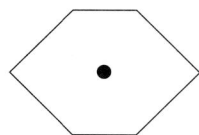

EXERCISES

For more exercises, see Extra Practice.

Practice and Problem Solving

A **Practice by Example**

Example 1
(page 507)

In Exercises 1–8, graph each figure and its image after a rotation of (a) 180° and (b) 90° about the origin.

1.
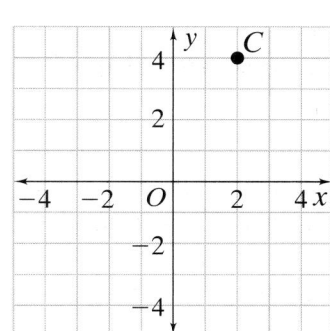

2.
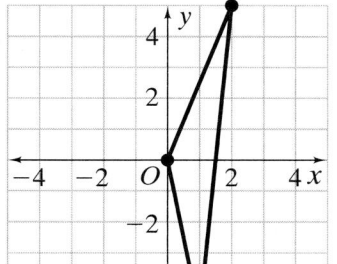

3. point $D(-1, -3)$

4. point $E(3, 2)$

5. $\triangle KLM$ with $K(3, 0)$, $L(2, 4)$, $M(2, 2)$

6. $\triangle STU$ with $S(0, -4)$, $T(-4, -4)$, $U(-4, -3)$

7. $\triangle CDE$ with $C(-2, 0)$, $D(-3, 5)$, $E(-1, 2)$

8. $\triangle GHI$ with $G(-4, -1)$, $H(-2, -5)$, $I(-2, -1)$

Example 2
(page 508)

🌐 **Natural Science** Judging from appearance, tell whether each figure has rotational symmetry. If so, what is the angle of rotation?

9.

10.

11.

12.

B **Apply Your Skills**

13. The vertices of a triangle are $V(0, 0)$, $W(2, 5)$, and $X(1, 5)$. On separate coordinate planes, graph the triangle and its images after rotations of (a) 90° and (b) 180° about $(1, 1)$.

14. **Writing in Math** Describe something in your classroom that has rotational symmetry. What is the angle of rotation?

Each figure below is an image formed by rotating the figure at the left. What is each angle of rotation?

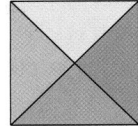

15.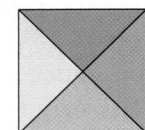

16.

17.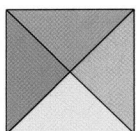

In Exercises 18–21, does the figure have rotational symmetry? If so, what is the angle of rotation?

18. equilateral triangle

19. rectangle

20. regular pentagon

21. trapezoid

22. For Exercises 18–21, tell (a) whether each figure has line symmetry and (b) the number of lines of symmetry.

C Challenge

23. $\triangle JKL$ has vertices $J(4, 4)$, $K(3, 2)$ and $L(5, 1)$.
   a. Graph its image, $\triangle J'K'L'$, after a rotation of 90° about the origin. Name the coordinates of the vertices of the image.
   b. Graph the image of $\triangle J'K'L'$ after a reflection over the y-axis.

24. Reasoning Is a rotation of 180° the same as a reflection over the y-axis? Justify your answer.

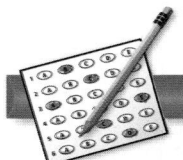

Test Prep

Take It to the NET
Online lesson quiz at
www.PHSchool.com
Web Code: ada-0903

Multiple Choice

25. Which letter has rotational symmetry?
   A. H **B.** J **C.** K **D.** L

26. Which number has rotational symmetry?
   F. 2 **G.** 4 **H.** 6 **I.** 8

27. Which object does NOT have rotational symmetry?
   A. daisy **B.** ceiling fan **C.** glove **D.** picture frame

Short Response

28. Which types of triangles have rotational symmetry? Explain.

Mixed Review

Lesson 9-9

The vertices of $\triangle ABC$ are $A(5, 6)$, $B(0, 3)$, and $C(3, 2)$. Graph $\triangle ABC$ and its image after a reflection over the given line.

29. $x = -2$ **30.** $y = -2$ **31.** x-axis

Lesson 8-3

Find the slope of the line through each pair of points.

32. $A(5, 9)$, $B(5, 14)$ **33.** $E(2, 1)$, $F(8, 4)$ **34.** $C(-2, 4)$, $D(-7, 14)$

Lesson 4-5

35. Number Sense How many three-digit numbers greater than 500 can you form using the digits 2, 6, and 8 exactly once each?

Tessellations

A tessellation is a repeating pattern of figures that completely covers a plane without gaps or overlaps. You can see tessellations in art, architecture, and nature.

You can use translations, rotations, and reflections to make a tessellation.

EXAMPLE

Show how the figure at the right forms a tessellation.

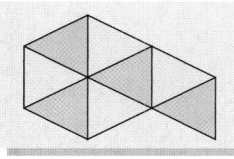

Rotate and translate the figure to cover the plane.

EXERCISES

Make multiple copies of each figure on graph paper. Determine whether each figure can form a tessellation. If it can, show the tessellation.

1. 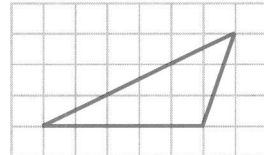 **2.** 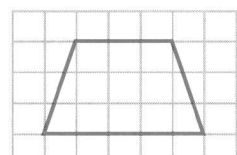 **3.** 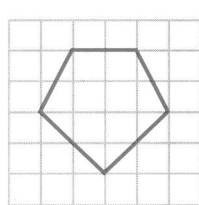 **4.**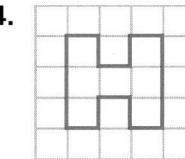

5. Open-Ended The diagram below shows how to make a shape to use as a repeating figure for a tessellation. Follow the diagram and make your own tessellation.

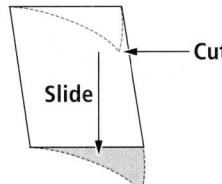 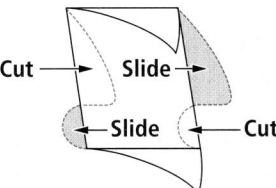  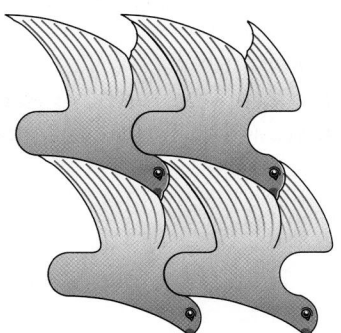

6. Reasoning Draw regular polygons with 3, 4, 5, 6, 7, and 8 sides. Which ones can you use to make a tessellation?

Test-Taking Strategies

Drawing a Diagram

Sometimes for a problem, you may find it helpful to draw a diagram to keep track of the facts and actually see how the given information is related. Then you can use the diagram to help you solve the problem.

1 EXAMPLE

Shayna has nearly completed the annual Walk for Hunger. She began at the Start/Finish line and walked south for $\frac{1}{2}$ mile. Then she walked $1\frac{1}{2}$ miles east. She walked 1 mile north and then walked $\frac{1}{4}$ mile west. She turned right and walked $\frac{1}{4}$ mile. Then she turned left and walked $1\frac{1}{4}$ miles. Then she walked $\frac{1}{2}$ mile south. How far is it directly back to the Start/Finish line?

A. $\frac{1}{4}$ mile **B.** $\frac{1}{2}$ mile **C.** $1\frac{1}{4}$ miles **D.** $1\frac{1}{2}$ miles

Draw a diagram on grid paper if possible. ⟶ Label each segment with its distance. If you draw the diagram carefully, it will show that Shayna is $\frac{1}{4}$ mile
• from the Start/Finish line. The correct choice is A.

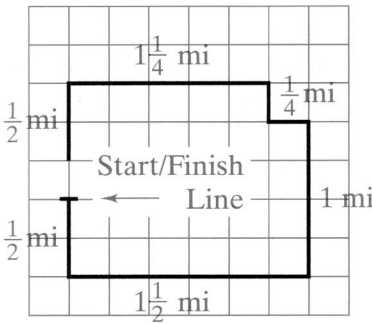

2 EXAMPLE

The endpoints of the diameter of a circle are at $(-4, 5)$ and $(4, 5)$ in a coordinate plane. At what points does the circle intersect the y-axis?

F. $(0, 0), (0, 8)$ **G.** $(0, 1), (0, 8)$ **H.** $(0, 0), (0, 9)$ **I.** $(0, 1), (0, 9)$

On grid paper locate the given points $(-4, 5)$ and $(4, 5)$. Sketch the diameter. Locate its midpoint, $(0, 5)$, the center of the circle. The radius is 4. Sketch the circle. The circle must intersect the y-axis 4 units above and below $(0, 5)$. The points of intersection
• are $(0, 1)$ and $(0, 9)$, choice I.

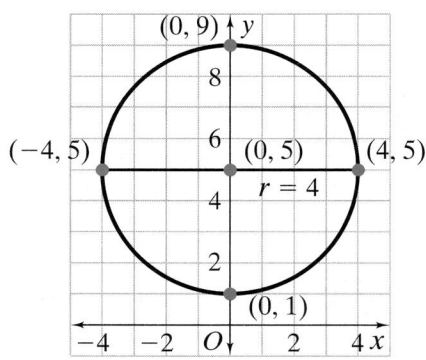

EXERCISES

1. In Example 1, how far has Shayna walked?
   A. $4\frac{1}{4}$ miles **B.** $4\frac{1}{2}$ miles **C.** $5\frac{1}{4}$ miles **D.** $5\frac{1}{2}$ miles

2. A triangle has vertices $(-2, 1), (5, 1),$ and $(0, 6)$. What is its area?
   F. $17\frac{1}{2}$ units^2 **G.** 21 units^2 **H.** 35 units^2 **I.** 42 units^2

Chapter Review

Vocabulary

adjacent angles (p. 465)	line (p. 458)	regular polygon (p. 472)
alternate interior angles (p. 466)	line of reflection (p. 504)	rotation (p. 507)
angle bisector (p. 493)	line of symmetry (p. 503)	rotational symmetry (p. 508)
angle of rotation (p. 507)	parallel (p. 459)	segment (p. 458)
center of rotation (p. 507)	perpendicular bisector (p. 492)	segment bisector (p. 492)
central angle (p. 487)	perpendicular lines (p. 492)	skew (p. 459)
circle (p. 486)	plane (p. 458)	supplementary (p. 465)
complementary (p. 465)	point (p. 458)	transformation (p. 497)
congruent angles (p. 465)	polygon (p. 470)	translation (p. 497)
congruent figures (p. 480)	ray (p. 458)	transversal (p. 466)
corresponding angles (p. 466)	reflection (p. 504)	vertical angles (p. 465)
image (p. 497)	reflectional symmetry (p. 503)	

Reading Math
Understanding Vocabulary

Match the vocabulary terms on the right with their descriptions on the left.

1. Angles that have the same measure, are opposite each other, and are formed by two intersecting lines

2. A flip of a figure over a line of reflection

3. A _?_ divides a figure with reflectional symmetry in half.

4. An angle whose vertex is the center of a circle

5. A change of position or size of a figure

6. A location in space

7. In a plane, all points the same distance from a given point

8. A line that intersects two other lines at different points

a. central angle
b. line of symmetry
c. reflection
d. transformation
e. vertical angles
f. transversal
g. point
h. circle

Take It to the NET
Online vocabulary quiz at www.PHSchool.com
Web Code: adj-0951

Skills and Concepts

9-1 Objectives

▼ To name basic geometric figures (p. 458)

▼ To recognize intersecting lines, parallel lines, and skew lines (p. 459)

A **point** is a position in space. All geometric figures are made up of points. A **line** is a series of points that extend in two directions without end. A **segment** is a part of a line and has two endpoints. A **ray** is a part of a line with exactly one endpoint. An angle is two rays that intersect at their endpoints.

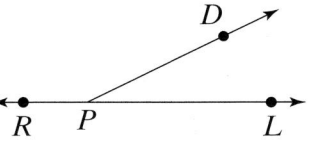

Name the following in the figure above.

9. 3 angles 10. 3 rays 11. a line 12. 4 points 13. 4 segments

9-2 Objectives

▼ To identify adjacent and vertical angles (p. 465)

▼ To relate angles formed by parallel lines and a transversal (p. 466)

Adjacent angles share a vertex and a side but no points in their interiors. **Vertical angles** are formed by intersecting lines and are **congruent.** If parallel lines are crossed by a **transversal** their **corresponding angles** are congruent. **Alternate interior angles** formed by a transversal and parallel lines are also congruent.

In the diagram at the right, $m \parallel n$.

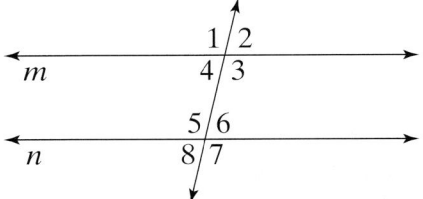

14. Name all angles congruent to $\angle 1$.

15. Name two pairs of supplementary angles.

16. Name all pairs of corresponding angles.

17. Name all pairs of alternate interior angles.

18. If $m \angle 2 = 75°$, find the measures of all the other angles.

9-3 and 9-5 Objectives

▼ To classify triangles (p. 470)

▼ To classify quadrilaterals (p. 471)

▼ To identify corresponding parts of congruent triangles (p. 480)

▼ To determine whether triangles are congruent (p. 481)

A **polygon** is a closed figure with at least three sides. Polygons with the same size and shape are **congruent.** A triangle can be classified by its angles and its sides. You can show two triangles are congruent using **Side-Side-Side, Side-Angle-Side,** and **Angle-Side-Angle.** You can classify some quadrilaterals as parallelograms, rectangles, squares, rhombuses, or trapezoids.

Use the most precise name for each figure described.

19. a triangle with all sides congruent

20. a parallelogram with all sides congruent and four 90° angles

21. a triangle with all acute angles and exactly two congruent sides

22. a quadrilateral with exactly one pair of parallel sides

List the congruent corresponding parts of each of the triangles below. Write a congruence statement (and reason) for the triangles.

23.

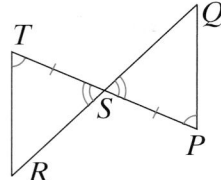

24.

9-4 Objectives

▼ To draw a diagram to solve a problem (p. 476)

Drawing a diagram can help you visualize a problem.

25. A house is to be built on a lot 70 ft wide by 100 ft deep. The shorter side of the lot faces the street. The house must be set back from the street at least 25 ft. It must be 20 ft from the back lot line and 10 ft from each side lot line. What are the maximum length and width of the house?

9-6 Objectives

▼ To find circumferences (p. 486)

▼ To find central angles and to make circle graphs (p. 487)

You can use these formulas to find the circumference of a circle:
$C = \pi d$ and $C = 2\pi r$.
There are 360° in a circle. An angle whose vertex is the center of a circle is a **central angle.**

26. Find the circumference of a circle with a diameter of 14 cm.

🌐 **27. Television Programming** Suppose a survey indicates that at 8 P.M. 40% of viewers watched channel X, 25% watched channel Y, and 35% watched channel Z. Make a circle graph of the data.

9-7 Objectives

▼ To construct a segment or angle congruent to a given segment or angle (p. 491)

▼ To construct segment bisectors and angle bisectors (p. 492)

You can use a compass and straightedge to construct congruent segments, congruent angles, **segment bisectors,** and **angle bisectors.**

Draw △*CDE* with an obtuse ∠*D*.

28. Construct the bisector of ∠*D*.

29. Construct the perpendicular bisector of $\overline{DE}$.

9-8, 9-9, and 9-10 Objectives

▼ To graph translations (p. 497)

▼ To describe translations (p. 498)

▼ To identify a line of symmetry (p. 503)

▼ To graph a reflection of a geometric figure (p. 504)

▼ To graph rotations (p. 507)

▼ To identify rotational symmetry (p. 508)

A **transformation** is a change of position or size of a figure. The figure after the transformation is called the **image.** You can transform figures in a plane by a **translation,** a **reflection,** or a **rotation.**

What is the image of point *A*(7, −2) after each transformation?

30. 4 units right, 3 units up

31. reflection over the *y*-axis

32. rotation of 90° about (0, 0)

33. reflection over the line $y = -1$

34. How do translations, reflections, and rotations affect the size and shape of an image? Explain.

Chapter Test

Take It to the NET
Online chapter test at
www.PHSchool.com
Web Code: ada-0952

Use the diagram to name the following.

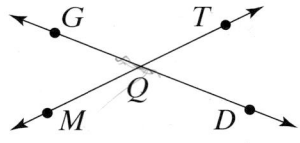

1. all segments containing point *G*

2. all pairs of vertical angles

3. all rays containing point *M*

4. a line containing point *T*

Use the diagram to name the following.

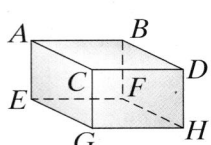

5. four segments that intersect $\overline{AB}$

6. three segments parallel to $\overline{AB}$

For Exercises 7 and 8, name all possible polygons for each description.

7. quadrilateral with at least one pair of parallel sides and at least two right angles

8. quadrilateral with one diagonal that divides it into two congruent equilateral triangles

9. Find the perimeter of an equilateral triangle that has a side measure of 60 cm.

10. Find the perimeter of a square that has a side measure of 60 cm.

11. The perimeter of a rectangle is 58 cm. One side is 18 cm. Find the lengths of the other three sides.

A segment has endpoints $A(-3, -6)$ and $M(-3, -4)$. Find the coordinates of the endpoints after each transformation.

12. a translation of 4 units right and 3 units up

13. a reflection over the *y*-axis

14. a rotation of 90° about the origin

15. Draw a segment. Construct its perpendicular bisector.

16. Draw an obtuse angle. Construct its angle bisector.

Use the diagram for Exercises 17 and 18.

17. If $m\angle 2 = 130°$, find $m\angle 4$.

18. **Writing in Math**
Describe how you can find $m\angle 1$ if you know $m\angle 2$.

19. **Statistics** Forty two-year-old children were asked to name their favorite color. Five chose yellow, seven chose blue, and fourteen chose red. The rest chose other colors.
a. To make a circle graph, what should be the measure of the central angle representing blue, red, and yellow? Round to the nearest degree.
b. Create a circle graph for the information.

20. If $\overline{AB} \cong \overline{CD}$, $\angle A \cong \angle D$, and $\angle B \cong \angle C$, what method can you use to show that $\triangle ABE \cong \triangle DCF$?

21. **Open-Ended** Draw and describe a figure that has rotational symmetry.

22. a. The measures of two angles of a triangle are 50° and 35°. What is the measure of the third angle?
b. Classify the triangle by its angles.

23. $\triangle CAB \cong \triangle DEB$. Find as many angle measures and side lengths as you can.

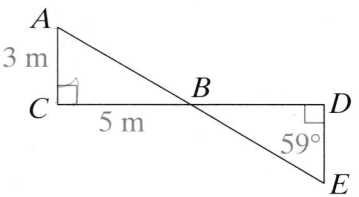

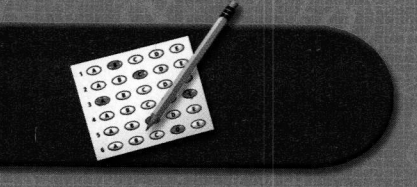
Reading Comprehension Read each passage below. Then answer the questions on the basis of what is *stated* or *implied* in the passage.

> **A Day in a Life** A market research firm studied the activities of a large group of people during a 24-hour day. The firm then found their average numbers of hours for certain activities. It found people spent 8 hours sleeping, 6 hours working, 3 hours on leisure activities, 1 hour eating, and the rest of the day on other activities.

1. On the average, how many hours did people spend daily doing other activities?
 A. 3 h   **B.** 4 h   **C.** 5 h   **D.** 8 h

2. On the average, how many hours did people spend sleeping each week?
 F. 7 h   **G.** 8 h   **H.** 48 h   **I.** 56 h

3. A circle graph for the daily activities would show how many regions?
 A. 4   **B.** 5   **C.** 6   **D.** 8

4. In a circle graph for the daily activities, what would be the measure of the central angle for time spent working?
 F. 6°   **G.** 45°   **H.** 90°   **I.** 120°

5. In a circle graph for the daily activities, what region would be half the size of another region?
 A. Working   **B.** Leisure activities
 C. Eating   **D.** Other activities

> **In Line With New Friends** Anna had doubts about her first day at the new school, but they faded quickly when she found herself next to Biff and Carly at lunch. They quickly discovered that Anna was the new girl who had moved into the house that sits between theirs on Poplar Road. Anna watched Biff scratch a line on a napkin. "Look Anna. My house is here, at B. Carly's is here at C. Carly's is five times as far from my house as your house is. She's 100 yards away from you. Guess that means you're going to have to be my next best friend!"

Let A, B, and C represent the homes of Anna, Biff, and Carly, respectively.

6. Which statements are true?
 I. A, B, and C are all on Poplar Road.
 II. B is between A and C.
 III. A is closer to B than to C.

 F. I only
 G. I and III only
 H. II and III only
 I. I, II, and III

7. How far apart are A and C?
 A. 25 yd   **B.** 50 yd
 C. 100 yd   **D.** 125 yd

8. How far apart are B and C? Show your work.

9. About how long did it take for Anna's doubts about her first day at the new school to fade?
 F. 1 h   **G.** 4 h   **H.** 8 h   **I.** 1 day

Circle Riding

Applying Circles Have you ever ridden on a Ferris wheel? Since its introduction in 1893, millions of people worldwide have enjoyed riding Ferris wheels. The basic structure of Ferris wheels remains quite similar to the one George W. Ferris created.

THE FERRIS WHEEL, CHICAGO.

The First Ferris Wheel

George W. Ferris built his ride for the 1893 World's Fair in Chicago. It was an instant success.

Each car held 60 people.

Ticket Sales

The ride sold more than $725,000 worth of tickets during the exposition.

Activity

Use the information on these two pages to answer these questions.

1. How far does a rider travel in one turn of each Ferris wheel?

2. For each wheel, estimate the number of turns needed for a rider to travel one mile.

3. Tickets for a ride on George W. Ferris's wheel cost $.50.
   a. At least how many tickets were sold?
   b. Suppose every ticket-holder rode for two turns of the wheel. At least how many turns did the wheel have to make?

4. Cosmo Clock 21 makes one rotation in 15 min. Find your car's location and the angle of rotation after the given time.
   a. 3 min   **b.** 5 min   **c.** 9 min   **d.** 12 min

5. **Writing in Math** Explain why 28 · 60 more people could ride at one time on the first Ferris wheel than on Cosmo Clock 21.

The Biggest Ride

With a maximum capacity of 480 riders, Cosmo Clock 21, in Yokohama, Japan, holds more riders than any other operating Ferris wheel. Even so, waiting time for this attraction is often more than one hour.

Ferris Wheel Statistics

Measure	First Ferris Wheel	Cosmo Clock 21
Diameter (ft)	250	328
Height, including base (ft)	264	369
Number of Passenger Cars	36	60
Number of People per Car	60	8

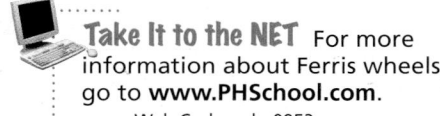

Take It to the NET For more information about Ferris wheels, go to **www.PHSchool.com**.
Web Code: ade-0953

Where You've Been

- In Chapter 7, you learned to solve multi-step equations and inequalities using inverse operations.

- In Chapter 8, you graphed and solved linear equations and inequalities.

- In Chapter 9, you learned how to classify polygons and identify corresponding parts of congruent triangles.

 **Diagnosing Readiness**

Instant self-check online and on CD-ROM

(For help, go to the lesson in green.)

Finding the Areas of Rectangles and Squares (Geometric Formulas, p. 780)

Find the area of each figure.

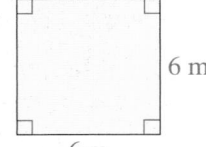
1. 6 m, 6 m

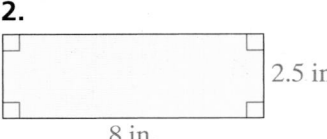
2. 8 in., 2.5 in.

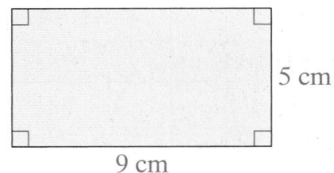
3. 9 cm, 5 cm

Simplifying Expressions With Exponents (Lesson 4-7)

Simplify each product.

4. $5 \cdot 3^2$ **5.** $3.14 \cdot 5^2$ **6.** $6 \cdot 12^2$ **7.** $4^2 \cdot 3$ **8.** $10^2 \cdot 3$ **9.** $3.14 \cdot 12^2$

Multiplying by a Fraction (Lesson 5-4)

Find each product.

10. $\frac{1}{2} \cdot 12$ **11.** $\frac{1}{2} \cdot 13 \cdot 3$ **12.** $\frac{1}{2}(10 + 8)$

13. $\frac{1}{2} \cdot 20x$ **14.** $\frac{1}{2} \cdot 5x \cdot 2x$ **15.** $\frac{1}{2}(10)(6 + 5)$

16. $\frac{1}{2}(62)(30 + 14)$ **17.** $\frac{1}{3}(20)(35 + 40)$ **18.** $\frac{1}{3}(3)(5 + 3)$

Finding the Circumferences of Circles (Lesson 9-6)

Find the circumference of each circle. Use 3.14 for π.

19. $d = 50$ yd   **20.** $r = 100$ m   **21.** $d = 5.5$ in.

EXERCISES

For more exercises, see *Extra Practice.*

Practice and Problem Solving

A Practice by Example
Examples 1 and 2
(page 533)

Find the area of each circle. Give the exact area, and an approximate area to the nearest square unit.

1.
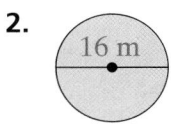
12 ft

2.
16 m

3.
60 cm

4. **Recreation** A standard dartboard has a diameter of 18 in. What is its area to the nearest square inch?

5. **Culinary Arts** A culinary student decorates an 8-in.-diameter round cake. What is the approximate area of the top of the cake?

Example 3
(page 534)

Find the area of each figure to the nearest square unit.

6.
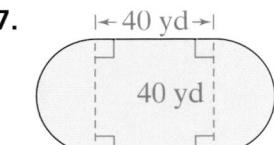
|← 10 in. →|
7 in.   3.5 in.

7.
|← 40 yd →|
40 yd

Find the area of each shaded region to the nearest square unit.

8.
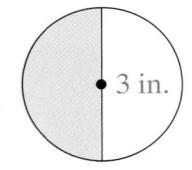
3 in.

9.
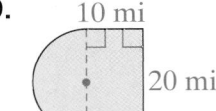
10 mi
20 mi

10.
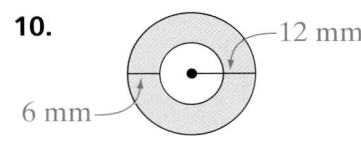
12 mm
6 mm

11. **Lawn Care** A groundskeeper wants to use sod to cover the lawn shown in green in the diagram. Each piece of sod covers 3 ft². About how many pieces of sod are needed?

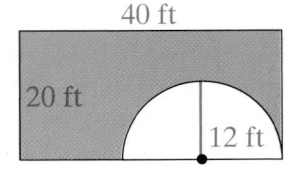
40 ft
20 ft
12 ft

B Apply Your Skills

Number Sense Match each object with its most likely area.

12. dinner plate

13. quarter

14. 12-in. circular pizza

15. jar lid

16. the center circle on a basketball court

A. 0.8 in.²

B. 110 in.²

C. 7 in.²

D. 16,000 in.²

E. 80 in.²

Pool
10 ft
15 ft
Border

17. **Pool Design** Covering for the pool border is sold by the square yard (whole-number amounts only). It costs $20/yd².
a. What is the area of the border in square feet?
b. About how much will the covering cost?

Find the area of each circle. Give the exact area, and an approximate area to the nearest tenth.

18. $r = 12$ mi   **19.** $r = 0.3$ m   **20.** $d = 1.5$ in.   **21.** $d = 8.4$ mm

22. Open-Ended Describe a real-life situation, not used in this lesson, where you might use the formula for the area of a circle.

23. Which has a greater area, four circles, each with radius 1 m, or one circle with radius 4 m? Explain.

24. How many circles with radius 2 cm will have the same total area as a circle with radius 4 cm?

Find the area of each shaded region to the nearest square unit.

25.
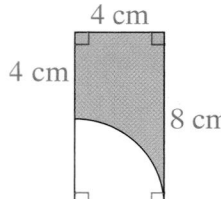
4 cm
4 cm
8 cm

26.
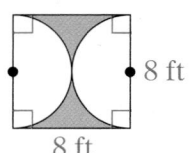
8 ft
8 ft

27.
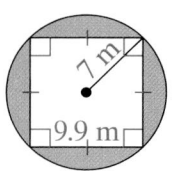
7 m
9.9 m

28. Writing in Math What is the area of the largest circle that will fit in a square with area 64 cm²? Explain.

C Challenge 🌐 **29. Can Lids** A manufacturer cuts lids for eight cans from one rectangular sheet of aluminum as shown at the left.
  a. What is the radius of each lid?
  b. How many square inches of aluminum do the lids require?
  c. How many square inches of aluminum are wasted?

24 in.
12 in.

🌐 **30. Consumer Issues** You can buy a 10-in. diameter pizza for $6.50, a 12-in. pizza for $8.50, or a 14-in. pizza for $10.50.
  a. What is the area of each pizza to the nearest square inch?
  b. What is the price per square inch of each pizza?
  c. Reasoning Is the largest pizza the best buy? Explain.

Test Prep

Multiple Choice

For Exercises 31–33, what is the exact area of each circle having radius r or diameter d?

31. $r = 11$ mi
  A. 5.5π mi²   **B.** 11π mi²   **C.** 22π mi²   **D.** 121π mi²

32. $r = \frac{1}{2}$ m
  F. $\frac{1}{4}\pi$ m²   **G.** $\frac{1}{2}\pi$ m²   **H.** π m²   **I.** 2π m²

33. $d = 1.2$ in.
  A. 2.4π in.²   **B.** 1.44π in.²   **C.** 0.36π in.²   **D.** 0.18π in.²

Short Response

34. Which has a greater area,   **(a)** a circle with radius 2 m or a square with side length 2 m?   **(b)** Explain your answer.

Lesson 10-2   **Find the area of each figure.**

35.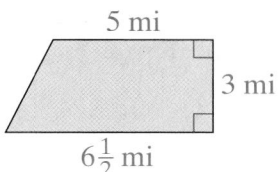

5 mi

3 mi

$6\frac{1}{2}$ mi

36.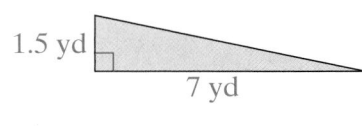

1.5 yd

7 yd

Lesson 9-4   **37.** Square *ABCD* has side length 8 in. △*BXY* is isosceles. Its congruent sides have length 2 in. How many triangles congruent to △*BXY* can you cut from square *ABCD*?

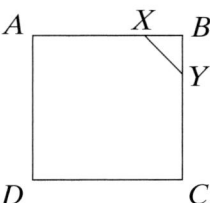

Lesson 5-3   **Find each sum or difference.**

38. $4\frac{3}{5} + 5\frac{2}{3}$ **39.** $5\frac{2}{3} - 4\frac{3}{5}$ **40.** $\frac{7}{8} + \frac{5}{6}$ **41.** $\frac{7}{8} - \frac{5}{6}$

✓ Checkpoint Quiz 1   Lessons 10-1 through 10-3

 Instant self-check quiz online and on CD-ROM

Find the area of each figure.

1.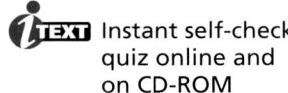

10 in.

10 in.

2.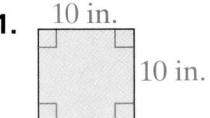

10 in.

10 in.

3.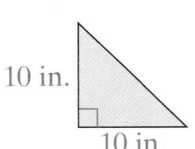

20 in.

15 in.

4.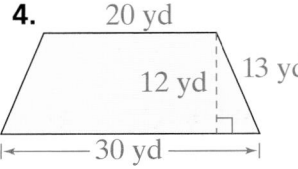

20 yd

12 yd   13 yd

30 yd

5.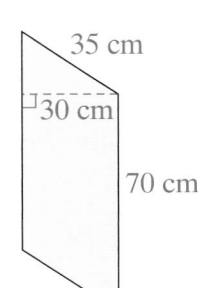

35 cm

30 cm

70 cm

6.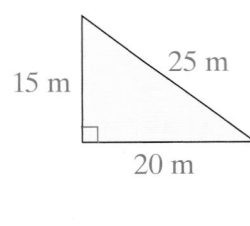

25 m

15 m

20 m

Find the area of each figure. Give the exact area, and an approximate area to the nearest square unit.

7.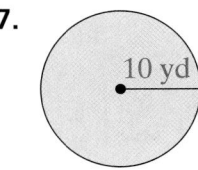

10 yd

8.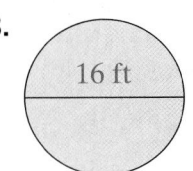

16 ft

9.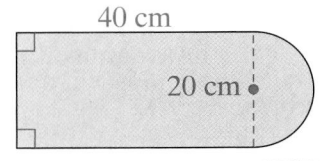

40 cm

20 cm

10. A trapezoid has an area of 45 cm². The two bases are 6 cm and 12 cm. What is the height of the trapezoid?

Three Views of an Object

A solid is a three-dimensional figure.

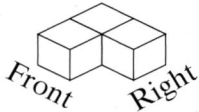

You can draw a solid *in perspective* (p. 542) to show that it is three-dimensional.

Isometric Dot Paper

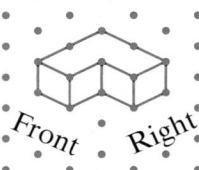

You can use isometric dot paper to draw a three-dimensional view.

Rectangular Graph Paper

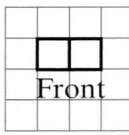

You can use rectangular graph paper to draw top, front, and side views.

EXAMPLE

Draw the top, front, and right-side views of the solid.

Isometric

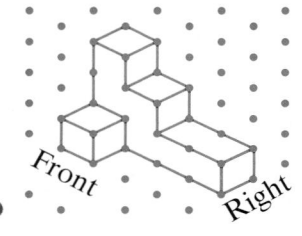

Top

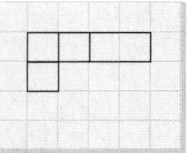

Front

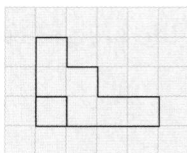

Right Side

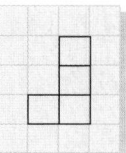

EXERCISES

Draw the top, front, and right-side views of each solid.

1.

2.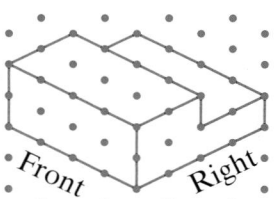

3.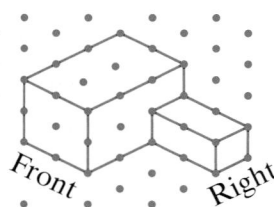

4.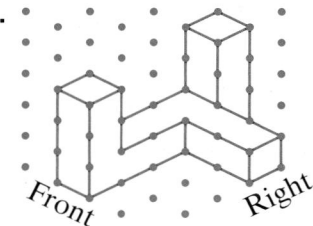

5. The top, front, and right-side views are given. Draw an isometric view on isometric dot paper.

Top

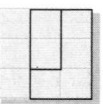

Front

Right Side

Space Figures

OBJECTIVE

1   Naming Space Figures

The figures below are common three-dimensional figures, also called **space figures** or solids. The space figures you will study in this book are prisms, pyramids, cylinders, cones, and spheres.

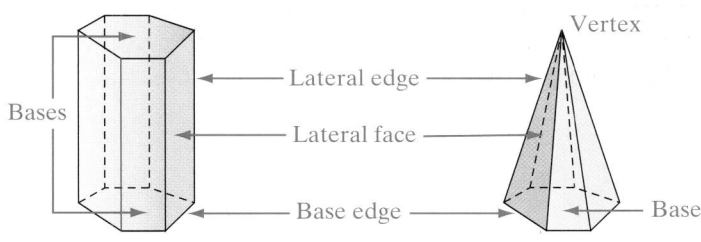

Prism

Pyramid

A **prism** has two parallel bases that are congruent polygons, and lateral faces that are parallelograms.

A **pyramid** has a base that is a polygon. The lateral faces are triangles.

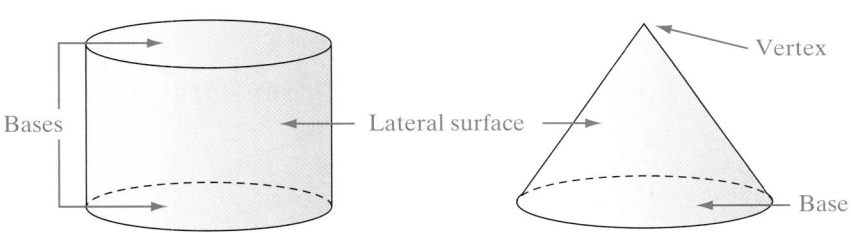

Cylinder

Cone

A **cylinder** has two parallel bases that are congruent circles.

A **cone** has one circular base and one vertex.

Sphere

A **sphere** is the set of all points in space that are a given distance from a given point called the center.

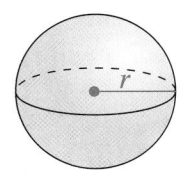

 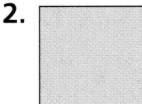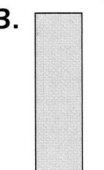 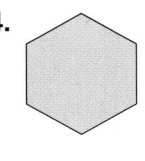
iTEXT Interactive lesson includes instant self-check, tutorials, and activities.

You can use the shape of a base to help you name a space figure.

Real-World Connection
This space figure displays the 73,000-ft² "Rainbow" by Corita Kent.

1 EXAMPLE **Naming Space Figures**

For each figure, describe the bases and name the figure.

a.

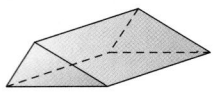

The bases are triangles. The figure is a triangular prism.

b.

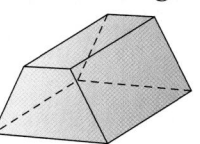

The bases of the prism are trapezoids. The figure is a trapezoidal prism.

✓ **Check Understanding** Example 1

1. Name each figure.

a.

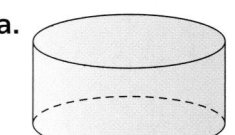

b.

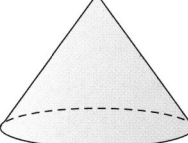

OBJECTIVE

2 **Identifying Space Figures From Nets**

A **net** is a pattern you can form into a space figure.

2 EXAMPLE **Naming Space Figures From Nets**

Name the space figure you can form from each net.

a.

With a hexagonal base and triangular sides, you can form a hexagonal pyramid.

b.

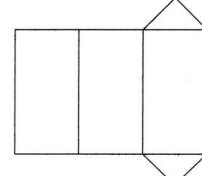

With two triangular bases and rectangular sides, you can form a triangular prism.

✓ **Check Understanding** Example 2

2. Name the space figure you can form from each net.

a.

b.

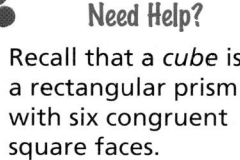

Need Help?

Recall that a *cube* is a rectangular prism with six congruent square faces.

EXERCISES

For more exercises, see *Extra Practice*.

Practice and Problem Solving

A Practice by Example

Example 1
(page 540)

For each figure, describe the base(s), if any, and name the figure.

1.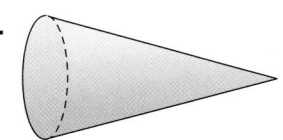

2.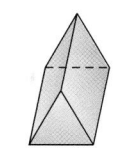

3.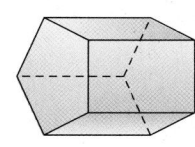

4.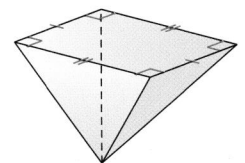

5.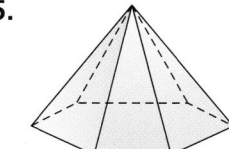

6.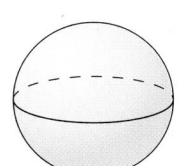

Example 2
(page 540)

Name the space figure you can form from each net.

7.

8.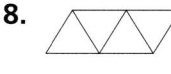

9.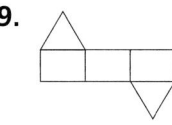

10.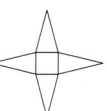

11.

12.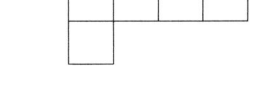

B Apply Your Skills

> **Reading Math**
> *Lateral* means "on the side." The lateral faces of a prism or pyramid are the surfaces that connect with a base. See page 539.

For Exercises 13–15, write the most precise name for each space figure that has the given properties.

13. four lateral faces that are triangles

14. three lateral faces that are rectangles

15. a lateral surface and one circular base

16. What type of space figure does each object suggest?
   a. a shoe box   **b.** a teepee   **c.** a basketball

Open Ended Draw a net for each space figure.

17. pentagonal pyramid   18. an object in your classroom

19. **Error Analysis** A student explains that since each figure below has six square faces, each can be folded to make a cube. Explain the error the student might have made.

Figure A   Figure B   Figure C   Figure D

20. A net is made of 4 congruent rectangles and 2 congruent squares whose sides are the same length as the shorter sides of the rectangles. Name a space figure you can form from this net.

Match each container with the correct net.

21. **22.** **23.**

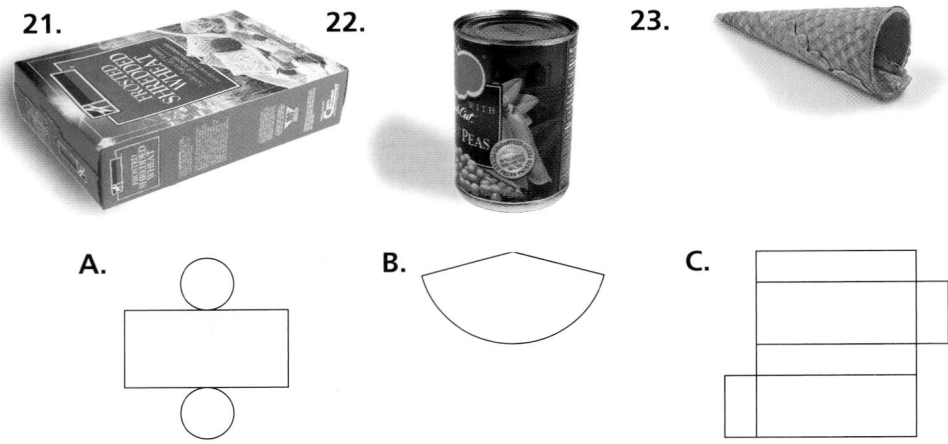

A. **B.** **C.**

24. <u>**Writing in Math**</u> Suppose you see a net for a rectangular prism and a net for a rectangular pyramid. Explain how you can match each net with its name.

25. Draw a net to represent a rectangular box that is 10 cm long, 8 cm wide, and 4 cm high. Label dimensions on the net.

 Challenge

26. A cube is easy to draw in *one-point perspective*. Draw a cube in one-point perspective by following the steps below.

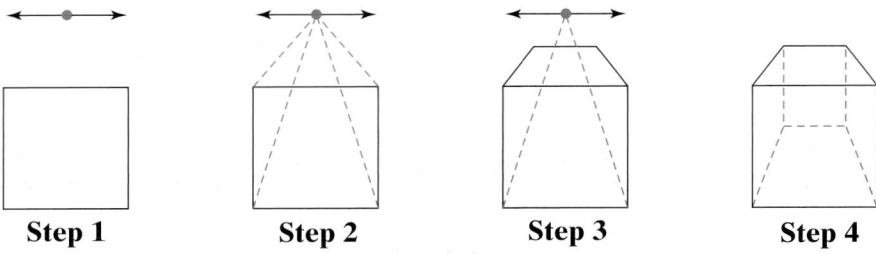

Step 1   Step 2   Step 3   Step 4

Step 1 Begin by drawing a square for the front. Draw a *horizon line* parallel to one horizontal edge of your square. Select a *vanishing point* on the horizon line.

Step 2 Draw lines, called *vanishing lines*, from the vertices of the square to the vanishing point.

Step 3 Draw a line segment parallel to the horizon line. Use this segment to determine the top and back edges.

Step 4 Draw dashed lines for the hidden back vertical and horizontal edges. Erase the horizon line and unnecessary parts of the vanishing lines.

27. Using steps like those suggested in Exercise 26, make a one-point perspective drawing of each figure.
a. triangular prism   **b.** cylinder

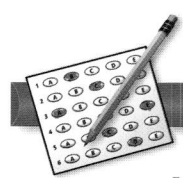
Multiple Choice

28. Which of the following is a net for a cylinder?

A. 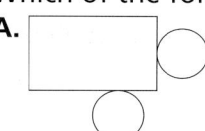   B.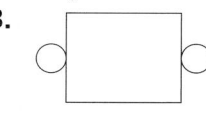

C.    D.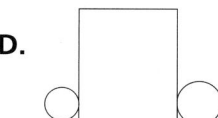

29. Which space figure can you form from the net?
  F. hexagonal pyramid
  G. triangular pyramid
  H. triangular prism
  I. hexagonal prism

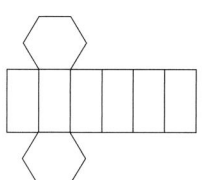

30. Which space figure has three lateral faces that are triangles?
  A. triangular pyramid   B. pentagonal prism
  C. square prism   D. triangular prism

31. Which space figure has 6 faces that are all regular quadrilaterals?
  F. triangular pyramid   G. pentagonal prism
  H. square prism   I. triangular prism

32. A rectangular prism has how many faces?
  A. 2   B. 4   C. 6   D. 8

Take It to the NET
Online lesson quiz at
www.PHSchool.com
Web Code: ada-1004

Short Response

33. **a.** Draw a net for a cylinder that has diameter 4 in. and height 6 in.
  b. Label your drawing.

Mixed Review

Lesson 10-3

For each circle, find the exact area and an approximate area.

34.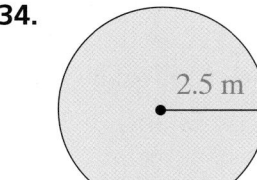
2.5 m

35.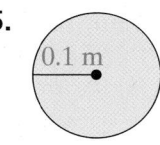
0.1 m

36.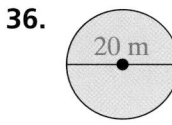
20 m

Lessons 9-4 🌐 **37. Mowing Lawns** A rectangular yard is 20 ft by 40 ft. Your lawn mower will mow a 2-ft-wide path. What is the least number of turns you must make to mow the lawn?

Lesson 8-3

Write each equation in slope-intercept form.

38. $3x - y = 6$ **39.** $2x - 2y = 10$ **40.** $-8y - 16 = 24x$

Cross Sections of Space Figures

The intersection of a plane and a space figure is a *cross section* of the space figure. This cross section of a block of cheese is a rectangle.

EXAMPLE

Sketch a plane intersecting a cube in three different ways to show a rectangular cross section.

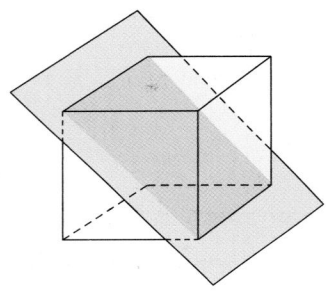 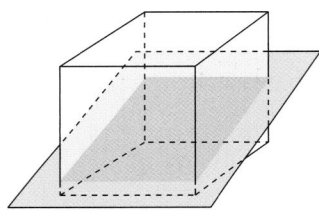 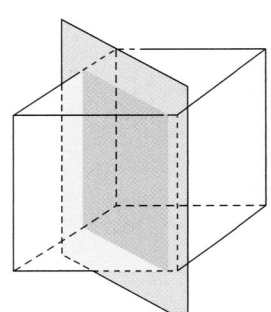

EXERCISES

Use the name of a polygon to describe each cross section of the cube. Points M, N, P, Q, and R are midpoints of edges.

1. through M, P, Q, and R

2. through E, A, C, and G

3. through B, E, and G

4. through M, N, D, and B

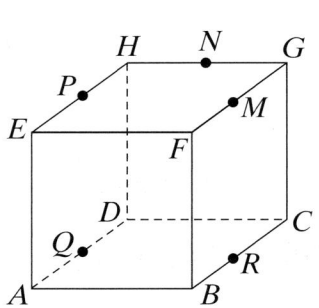

Sketch a cube to show each cross section.

5. a scalene triangle

6. a trapezoid

7. a square

8. an isosceles triangle

9. Describe the possible cross sections of a sphere.

10. Sketch and describe two possible cross sections of a cylinder.

Surface Area: Prisms and Cylinders

What You'll Learn

OBJECTIVE 1 To find surface areas of prisms

OBJECTIVE 2 To find surace areas of cylinders

. . . And Why

To find the amount of material needed in packaging

OBJECTIVE

1 Finding Surface Areas of Prisms

Prisms and cylinders can be *right* and *oblique*.

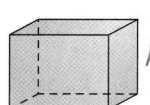 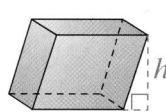 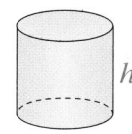 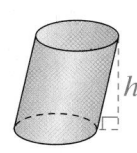

Right prism   Oblique prism   Right cylinder   Oblique cylinder

In this text, you may assume that prisms and cylinders are right unless otherwise stated.

Surface area (S.A.) is the sum of the areas of the base(s) and the lateral faces of a space figure. One way to find the surface area of a space figure is to find the area of its net. You measure surface area in square units.

✔ Check Skills You'll Need

Find the circumference of each circle with the given radius or diameter.

1. $r = 5$ in.

2. $r = 4.2$ cm

3. $d = 8$ ft

4. $d = 6.8$ in.

For help, go to Lesson 9-6.

New Vocabulary
- surface area
- lateral area

1 EXAMPLE Finding Surface Area Using a Net

Find the surface area of the rectangular prism using a net.

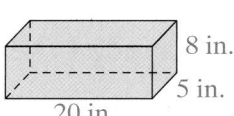

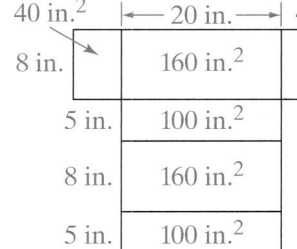

Draw and label a net.

Find the area of each rectangle in the net.

$40 + 40 + 160 + 100 + 160 + 100 = 600$ Add the areas.

• The surface area is 600 in.^{2}.

✔ Check Understanding Example 1

1. a. Find the surface area of the triangular prism.
   b. A similar triangular prism has dimensions twice those shown here. Find its surface area.
   c. How do surface areas of similar prisms compare when dimensions are doubled?

6 yd   5 yd   3 yd   4 yd

TEXT Interactive lesson includes instant self-check, tutorials, and activities.

Another way to find the surface area of a prism is to use the *lateral area* and the base areas. **Lateral area (L.A.)** of a prism is the sum of the areas of the lateral faces.

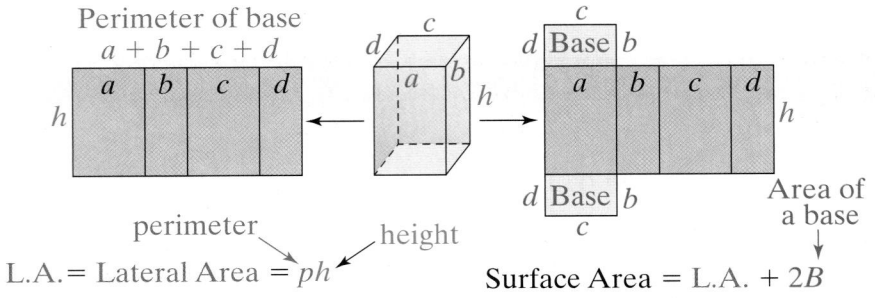

Perimeter of base
$a + b + c + d$

perimeter   height
L.A. = Lateral Area = ph

Area of a base

Surface Area = L.A. + $2B$

To find surface area, it is a good idea to find lateral area first.

Need Help?

B represents the area of a base. For a list of area formulas, see the table on page 780.

> **Key Concepts**   **Surface Area of a Prism**
>
> The lateral area of a prism is the product of the perimeter of the base and the height.
>
> $$\text{L.A.} = ph$$
>
> The surface area of a prism is the sum of the lateral area and the areas of the two bases.
>
> $$\text{S.A.} = \text{L.A.} + 2B$$
>
>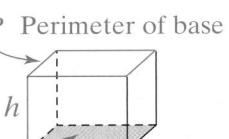
> P Perimeter of base
> h
> B Area of base

2 EXAMPLE   Finding Surface Area Using Formulas

Reading Math

For help with reading a formula, see page 551.

Find the surface area of the triangular prism at the right.

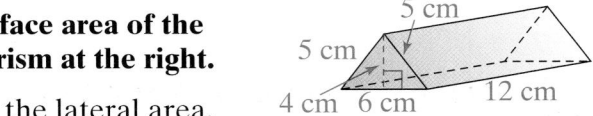
5 cm
5 cm
4 cm   6 cm   12 cm

Step 1 Find the lateral area.

$\text{L.A.} = ph$ **Use the formula for lateral area.**

$\quad = (5 + 5 + 6)12$ **$p = 5 + 5 + 6$ and $h = 12$.**

$\quad = 192$

Step 2 Find the surface area.

$\text{S.A.} = \text{L.A.} + 2B$ **Use the formula for surface area.**

$\quad = 192 + 2\left(\frac{1}{2} \cdot 6 \cdot 4\right)$ **L.A. = 192 and $B = \frac{1}{2} \cdot 6 \cdot 4$.**

$\quad = 192 + 24$

$\quad = 216$

● The surface area of the triangular prism is 216 cm².

✓ Check Understanding   Example 2

  2. Find the surface area of the prism at the right.

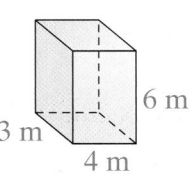
6 m
3 m
4 m

2 Finding Surface Areas of Cylinders

If you cut a label from a soup can, you will see that the label is a rectangle. The height of the rectangle is the height of the can. The base length of the rectangle is the circumference of the can.

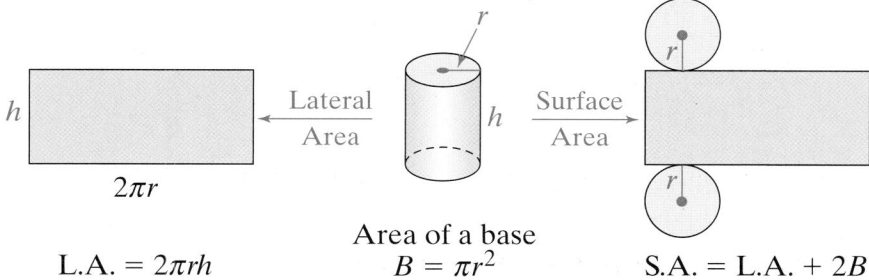

$$\text{L.A.} = 2\pi rh$$

Area of a base
$$B = \pi r^2$$

$$\text{S.A.} = \text{L.A.} + 2B$$

Key Concepts **Surface Area of a Cylinder**

The lateral area of a cylinder is the product of the circumference of the base and the height of the cylinder.

B is the area of a base.

$$\text{L.A.} = 2\pi rh$$

The surface area of a cylinder is the sum of the lateral area and the areas of the two bases.

$$\text{S.A.} = \text{L.A.} + 2B$$

---

3 EXAMPLE **Finding Surface Area of a Cylinder**

Packaging **Find the surface area of the can at the right.**

Step 1 Find the lateral area.

$$\text{L.A.} = 2\pi rh \qquad \text{Use the formula for lateral area.}$$
$$\approx 2(3.14)(3.5)(11.5) \quad \textbf{r = 3.5 and h = 11.5.}$$
$$\approx 253$$

3.5 cm

11.5 cm

Step 2 Find the surface area.

$$\text{S.A.} = \text{L.A.} + 2B \qquad \text{Use the formula for surface area.}$$
$$\approx 253 + 2(3.14)(3.5)^2 \quad \textbf{L.A.} \approx \textbf{253 and } B = \pi(3.5)^2.$$
$$\approx 253 + 77$$
$$= 330$$

• The surface area of the can is about 330 cm^2.

✓ **Check Understanding** **Example 3**

3. Find the surface area of a can with radius 5 cm and height 20 cm.

EXERCISES

For more exercises, see *Extra Practice*.

Practice and Problem Solving

A Practice by Example
Example 1
(page 545)

Find, to the nearest square unit, the surface area of the space figure represented by each net.

1.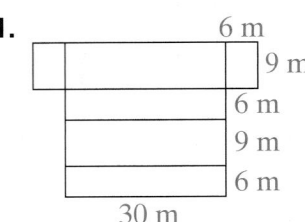

2.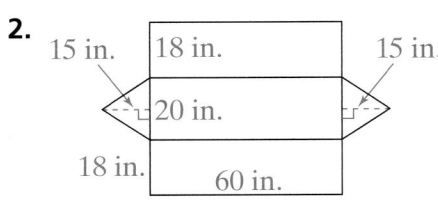

3. The base of a rectangular prism is 3 in. by 5 in. The height is 11 in.
   a. Draw and label a net for the prism.
   b. Find the surface area of the prism.
   c. A similar rectangular prism has dimensions three times the dimensions of the given prism. Find its surface area.
   d. How do surface areas of similar prisms compare when dimensions are tripled?

Example 2
(page 546)

Find the surface area of each prism.

4.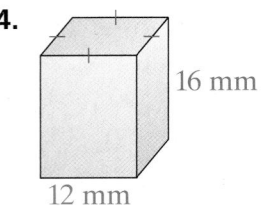

5.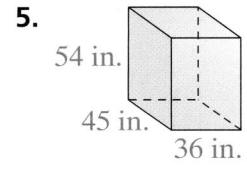

6.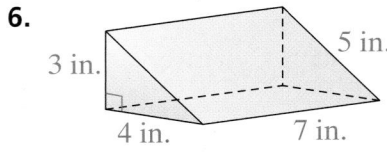

7.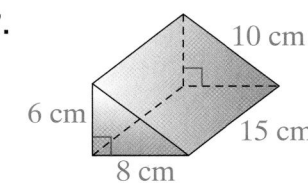

8.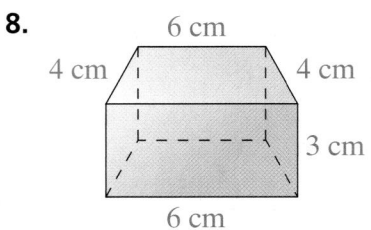

9.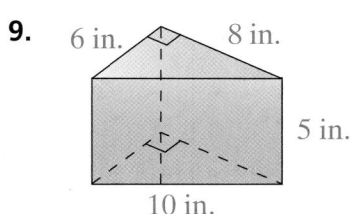

Example 3
(page 547)

Find the surface area of the cylinder shown or represented. Round to the nearest tenth.

10.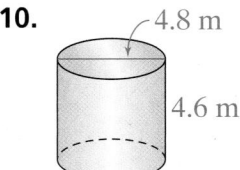

11.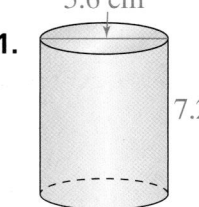

12.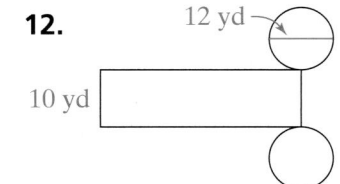

🌐 13. **Gift Wrapping** Juliet is trying to wrap a can of mixed nuts that is a birthday gift for her brother. The can has a radius of 8 cm and a height of 10 cm. Approximately how many square centimeters of wrapping paper will cover the gift?

Ⓑ Apply Your Skills

14. A cylinder has radius 8 ft and height 12 ft. Draw and label a net for the cylinder. Find its surface area.

15. Find the surface area of a square prism with base edge 7 m and height 15 m.

16. Find the area of the top and lateral surface of a cylindrical water tank with radius 20 ft and height 30 ft.

🌐 17. **Camping** A tent is approximately the shape of a triangular prism. Approximate the area of the tent, including the bottom, by finding the surface area of the prism.

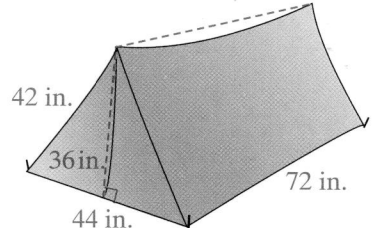

18. Find the surface area of a cylinder with radius 10 cm and height 8 cm.

🌐 19. **Painting** The neighborhood swimming pool needs to be painted. The pool is 40 ft by 60 ft. The depth of the pool is 6 ft throughout.
   a. How many sides need to be painted?
   b. What is the total number of square feet to be painted?
   c. The materials for painting the pool cost $1.50 per square yard. What is the cost of the materials for painting the pool?

20. **Error Analysis** A student explains that the two cylinders at the right have the same surface area. Explain the student's error.

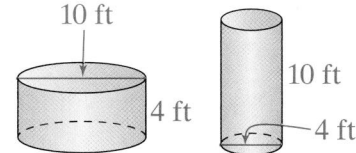

21. **Open-Ended** Describe a real-world situation in which you need to know the surface area of a space figure.

22. **Writing in Math** In a triangular prism, what is the difference between the height of a base and the height of the prism?

🌐 23. **Packaging** You have made two boxes with lids. Which box required more cardboard, a box 8 in. by 6.25 in. by 10.5 in., or a box 9 in. by 5.5 in. by 11.75 in.? Explain.

Ⓒ Challenge

24. **Reasoning** Use the cubes with side lengths of 1, 2, and 3 units.

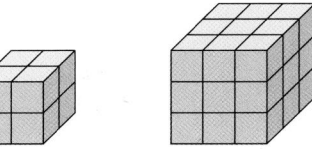

   a. Find the surface area of each cube.
   b. If the length of each side of a cube is doubled, how does that affect the surface area?
   c. If the length of each side of a cube is tripled, how does that affect the surface area?

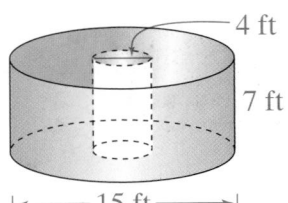
4 ft
7 ft
|← 15 ft →|

🌐 **25. Construction** The concrete figure at the left has a hole in it. The surface will be painted except for the inside of the hole. Find the total surface area to be painted to the nearest square foot.

26. Reasoning Which has the greater effect on the surface area of a cylinder: doubling the base radius or doubling the height? Justify your answer.

Test Prep

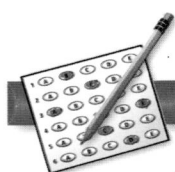

Multiple Choice

27. Which figure would cost more to paint?
  A. the square prism
  B. the cylinder
  C. They would cost the same.
  D. cannot be determined

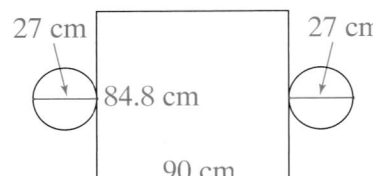
8 cm
5 cm
5 cm
10 cm
5 cm

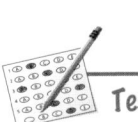
Test-Taking Tip
When a test question asks for the surface area of a prism, you can sketch the net of the prism to help visualize the entire surface.

28. What is the approximate surface area of the space figure represented by the net?
  F. 8,777 cm²
  G. 8,333 cm²
  H. 8,202 cm²
  I. 4,387 cm²

27 cm   27 cm
84.8 cm
90 cm

29. Each edge of cube is 40 cm long. What is the surface area of the cube? Use 2.5 cm ≈ 1 in.
  A. 256 in.²   **B.** 1,536 in.²   **C.** 3,840 in.²   **D.** 9,600 in.²

💻 **Take It to the NET**
Online lesson quiz at
www.PHSchool.com
Web Code: ada-1005

30. A cylinder has height 10 in. and base radius 2.5 in. What is its lateral area, to the nearest whole unit?
  F. 235 in.²   **G.** 215 in.²   **H.** 196 in.²   **I.** 157 in.²

● **Mixed Review**

Lesson 10-4   **Name each space figure.**

31. 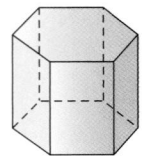   **32.** 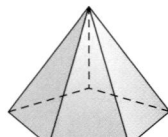   **33.**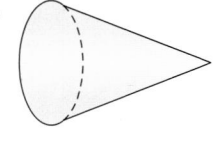

Lesson 9-9   **Graph each point and its image after a reflection over the given line.**

34. $A(0, 9)$; x-axis   **35.** $B(-3, 5)$; y-axis   **36.** $C(3, -1)$; $x = 2$

Lesson 6-2 🌐 **37. Recipes** A recipe that serves 6 people calls for $\frac{1}{2}$ teaspoon of salt. In preparing this recipe for 25 people, about how many teaspoons of salt should you use?

Reading Math

Reading a Formula

For Use With Page 546, Example 2

For the example below, follow along with how Diana reads and uses the formulas. Check your understanding by solving the exercises at the bottom of the page.

Find the surface area of the triangular prism at the right.

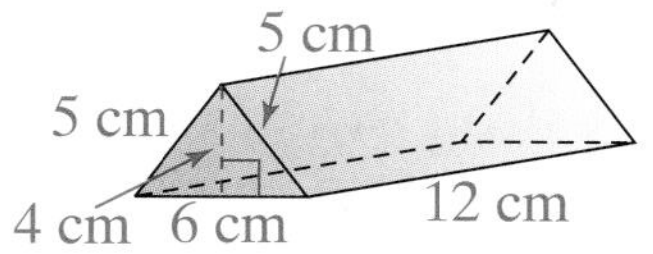

5 cm
5 cm
4 cm
6 cm
12 cm

What Diana Reads

Step 1 Find the lateral area.

$$\begin{aligned} \text{L.A.} &= ph \\ &= (5 + 5 + 6)12 \\ &= 192 \end{aligned}$$

Step 2 Find the surface area.

$$\begin{aligned} \text{S.A.} &= \text{L.A.} + 2B \\ &= 192 + 2\left(\tfrac{1}{2} \cdot 6 \cdot 4\right) \\ &= 192 + 24 \\ &= 216 \end{aligned}$$

The surface area of the triangular prism is 216 cm^2.

What Diana Thinks

Surface area means lateral area plus base areas.

In the Step 1 formula,

L.A. is the lateral area.

p is the perimeter of the base, so $p = 5 + 5 + 6$.

h is the height of the prism, so $h = 12$.

Using these values, the Step 1 formula gives L.A. = 192 cm^2.

In the Step 2 formula,

S. A. is the surface area.

L.A. is the lateral area, 192, from Step 1.

$2B$ is the area of the 2 bases.

Each base is a triangle with area B. Use the formula for area of a triangle and find $B = \frac{1}{2}(\text{base})(\text{height}) = \frac{1}{2}(6)(4)$.

Using these values, the Step 2 formula gives S.A. = 216 cm^2.

EXERCISES

Write the formulas you use to find the surface area of each figure. Give the meaning and value of each letter or letters in the formula.

1.

3 in.
5 in.
20 in.

2.

3 cm
5 cm
4 cm
10.5 cm

3.

1 m
2 m

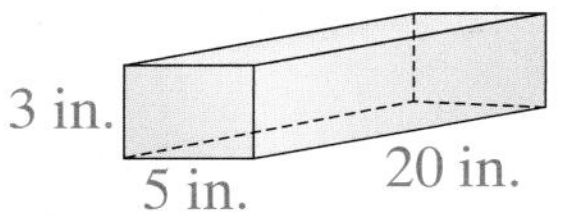

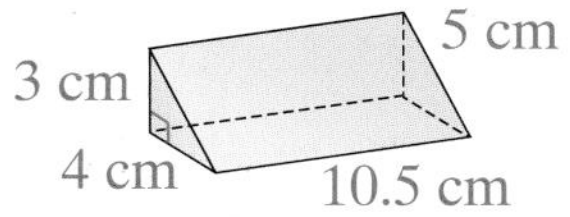

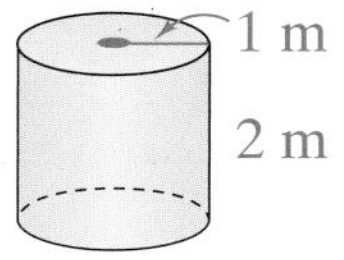

10-6 Surface Area: Pyramids, Cones, and Spheres

OBJECTIVE

1 Finding Surface Areas of Pyramids

What You'll Learn

OBJECTIVE
1 To find surface areas of pyramids

OBJECTIVE
2 To find surface areas of cones and spheres

. . . And Why

To find surface areas of real-world objects, such as a basketball

Check Skills You'll Need

Use the Order of Operations to simplify each expression.

1. $\frac{2}{3}(9\pi) + \frac{1}{2}(8\pi)$

2. $\frac{3}{4}(12\pi) + \frac{2}{5}(15\pi)$

3. $\frac{1}{6}(24\pi) + \frac{1}{3}(3\pi)$

4. $\frac{5}{8}(32\pi) + \frac{1}{7}(14\pi)$

For help, go to Lesson 5-4.

New Vocabulary

• slant height

In this text, all pyramids are *regular* pyramids. They have regular polygons for bases and congruent isosceles triangles for lateral faces.

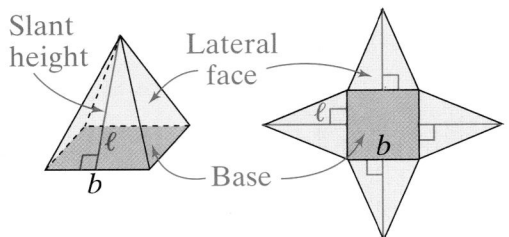

You can use the **slant height** ℓ, the height of a face, to find the area of the lateral faces. If n is the number of lateral triangular faces,

$$\text{L.A. is } n\left(\tfrac{1}{2}b\ell\right) \text{ or } \tfrac{1}{2}p\ell.$$

Key Concepts **Surface Area of a Pyramid**

The lateral area of a pyramid is one half the product of the perimeter of the base and the slant height.

The surface area of a pyramid is the sum of the lateral area and the area of the base.

$$\text{L.A.} = \tfrac{1}{2}p\ell \qquad \text{S.A.} = \text{L.A.} + B$$

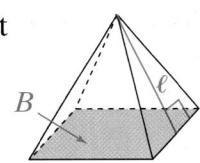

1 **EXAMPLE** **Finding Surface Area of a Pyramid**

Find the surface area of the square pyramid.

Step 1 Find the lateral area.

$\text{L.A.} = \tfrac{1}{2}p\ell$ **Use the formula for lateral area.**

$= \tfrac{1}{2} \cdot 48 \cdot 16$ **p = 4(12) and ℓ = 16.**

$= 384$

Step 1 Find the surface area.

$\text{S.A.} = \text{L.A.} + B$ **Use the formula for surface area.**

$= 384 + 12^2$ **L.A. = 384 and B = 12^2.**

$= 384 + 144$

$= 528$

• The surface area of the pyramid is 528 cm².

 Interactive lesson includes instant self-check, tutorials, and activities.

1. A pyramid has a square base with edge 20 ft. The slant height is 8 ft. Find the surface area.

OBJECTIVE

2 Finding Surface Areas of Cones and Spheres

In this text, every cone is a right circular cone with the vertex of the cone directly over the center of the circular base.

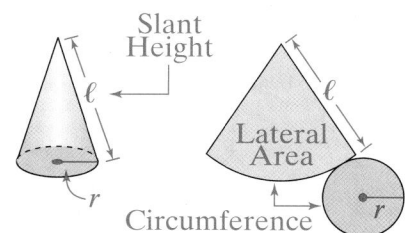

L.A. is $\frac{1}{2}(2\pi r)\ell$ or L.A. $= \pi r\ell$.

Key Concepts   **Surface Area of a Cone**

The surface area (S.A.) of a cone is the sum of the lateral area and base area.

$$\text{L.A.} = \pi r\ell \qquad \text{S.A.} = \text{L.A.} + B$$

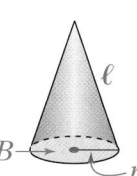

---

2 EXAMPLE   **Finding Surface Area of a Cone**

Find the surface area of the cone at the right.

L.A. $= \pi r\ell$ **Use the formula for lateral area.**
   $\approx 3.14(4)(10)$ $r = 4$ **and** $\ell = 10$.
   $= 125.6$

10 cm

4 cm

S.A. $=$ L.A. $+ B$ **Use the formula for surface area.**
   $\approx 125.6 + 3.14(4)^2$ **L.A.** $\approx$ **125.6 and** $B = \pi(4)^2$.
   $= 125.6 + 50.24$
   $= 175.84$

● The surface area of the cone is about 176 cm^2.

✔ **Check Understanding** Example 2

2. A cone has slant height 39 ft and radius 7 ft. Find it surface area.

A sphere has the same area as four circles with the same radius.

Key Concepts   **Surface Area of a Sphere**

The surface area of a sphere of radius r is
$$\text{S.A.} = 4\pi r^2.$$

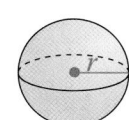

|— 10 in. —|

3 EXAMPLE — Real-World 🌐 Problem Solving

Basketball Calculate the surface area of a basketball.

$$\text{S.A.} = 4\pi r^2 \qquad \text{Use the formula for surface area.}$$

$$\approx 4(3.14)(5)^2 \qquad r = 5$$

$$= 314$$

● The surface area of the basketball is about 314 in.^{2}.

✓ Check Understanding Example 3

3. A sphere has a radius of 6 cm. Find its surface area.

You can find the surface area of a space figure that combines two or more figures you have studied.

More Than One Way

Find the surface area of the silo formed by a half sphere and a cylinder. The diameter of the silo is 20 ft.

10 ft

72 ft

Roberto's Method

Find the area of each space figure. Then find their sum.

One half sphere	Cylinder
$\text{S.A.} = \frac{1}{2}(4\pi r^2)$	$\text{L.A.} = 2\pi rh$
$\approx \frac{1}{2}(4)(3.14)(10^2)$	$\approx 2(3.14)(10)(72)$
$= 628$	$= 4{,}521.6$

Surface area of silo is about $628 + 4{,}521.6$, or $5{,}149.6$ ft^2.

Jasmine's Method

Combine formulas before substituting values.

$$\begin{aligned}
\text{Surface area} &= \tfrac{1}{2}\text{S.A.} \quad + \text{L.A.}\\
\text{of silo} &\quad\;\; \text{of sphere} \quad \text{of cylinder}\\
&= \tfrac{1}{2}(4\pi r^2) + 2\pi rh\\
&= 2\pi r^2 + 2\pi rh\\
&= 2\pi r(r + h)\\
&\approx 2(3.14)(10)(10 + 72)\\
&= 5{,}149.6
\end{aligned}$$

Surface area of silo is about $5{,}149.6$ ft^2.

Choose a Method

1. Which method do you prefer? Explain.

EXERCISES

❓ For more exercises, see *Extra Practice*.

Practice and Problem Solving

Ⓐ Practice by Example

Examples 1–3
(pages 552 and 553)

Find the surface area of each space figure, to the nearest square unit.

1.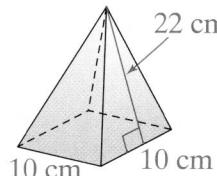
22 cm
10 cm   10 cm

2.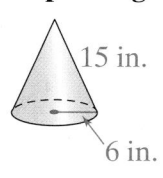
15 in.
6 in.

3.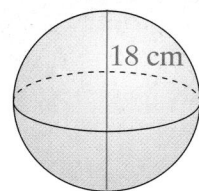
18 cm

4.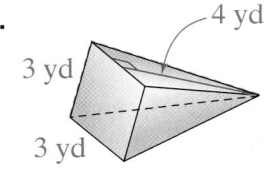
4 yd
3 yd
3 yd

5.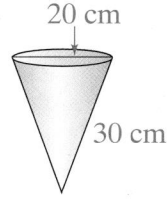
20 cm
30 cm

6.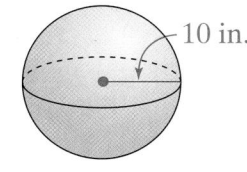
10 in.

7. The length of the base of a square pyramid is 5 cm. Its slant height is 8 cm. Find the surface area of the square pyramid.

8. The base of a cone has radius 3 ft. Its slant height is 8 ft. Find the surface area of the cone.

🌐 **9. Engineering** A spherical ball bearing has a radius of 8 mm. Find the surface area of the ball bearing.

Ⓑ Apply Your Skills

Find the surface area of each space figure, to the nearest square unit.

10.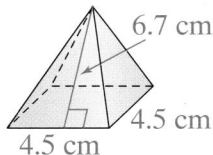
6.7 cm
4.5 cm
4.5 cm

11.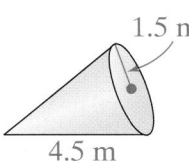
1.5 m
4.5 m

12.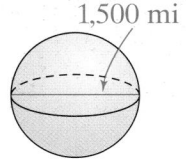
1,500 mi

🌐 **13. Geography** A globe has a diameter of 18 inches. What is the surface area of the globe to the nearest square inch?

14. Error Analysis A friend tells you that the surface area of a square prism with base length 4 m and height 5 m is the same as the surface area of a square pyramid with base length 4 m and height 5 m. Explain your friend's error.

15. Writing in Math Write a paragraph explaining how to find the surface area of a cone with slant height 10 in. and base radius 8 in.

Ⓒ Challenge

Find the surface area of each figure to the nearest square unit.

16.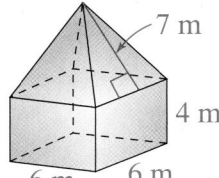
7 m
4 m
6 m   6 m

17.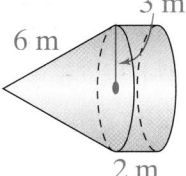
3 m
6 m
2 m

18.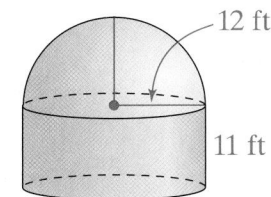
12 ft
11 ft

19. Architecture The spherical planetarium (left) at the American Museum of Natural History in New York City is 87 ft in diameter.
 a. What is the surface area of the sphere?
 b. The sphere is covered by 2,474 panels to absorb sound. What is the average area of each panel, to the nearest tenth of a square foot?

20. Reasoning Which has the greater surface area, a cylinder with height 2 in. and radius of base 2 in., or a sphere with radius 2 in.? Justify your answer.

21. Geography Approximately 70% of Earth's surface is covered by water. If the diameter of Earth is approximately 13,000 km, find the approximate surface area *not* covered by water.

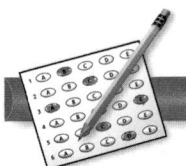

Test Prep

Multiple Choice

22. What is the surface area of the figure at the right?
 A. 2,150 in.^{2}
 B. 2,600 in.^{2}
 C. 3,000 in.^{2}
 D. 3,200 in.^{2}

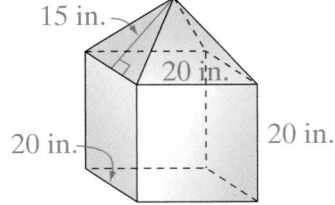

23. What is the ratio of the surface area of a sphere with radius 2 ft to the surface area of a sphere with radius 5 ft?
 F. 2 to 5   **G.** 4 to 25   **H.** 16 to 125   **I.** 18 to 20

Extended Response

24. A water storage tank with a roof that is in the shape of a cone has a diameter of 10 ft. The height of the cylindrical part of the tank is 15 ft. The slant height of the roof is 8 ft. **(a)** What is the radius of the tank?   **(b)** What is the lateral area of the cylindrical part of the tank?   **(c)** What is the surface area of the entire tank?

Mixed Review

Lesson 10-5

Find the surface area to the nearest square unit.

25.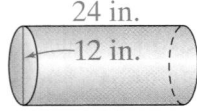

26.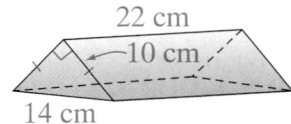

Lesson 8-7

27. Under rate plan A a new computer costs $200 down and $20 a month. Under rate plan B the computer costs $175 down and $25 a month. After how many months will the amount paid be the same for both plans?

Lesson 4-1

List all the factors of each number.

28. 21   **29.** 100   **30.** 25   **31.** 32

Volume: Prisms and Cylinders

1 Finding the Volumes of Prisms

The **volume** of a three-dimensional figure is the number of cubic units needed to fill it. A **cubic unit** is the space occupied by a cube with edges one unit long.

Consider filling the rectangular prism at the right with centimeter cubes.

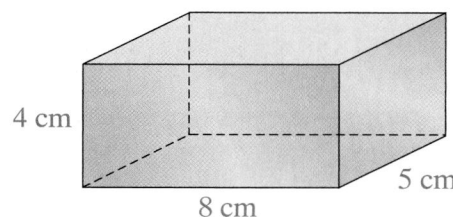

The bottom layer of the prism contains $8 \cdot 5 = 40$ centimeter cubes, or a volume of $40\ \text{cm}^3$ (cubic centimeters).

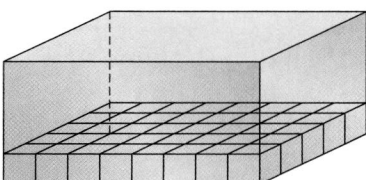

The prism has four layers of cubes, so it contains $4 \cdot 40$, or 160, centimeter cubes in all.

The volume of the prism is $160\ \text{cm}^3$.

The volume found for the rectangular prism above suggests the following formula.

Key Concepts **Volume of a Prism**

The volume V of a prism is the product of the base area B and the height h.

$$V = Bh$$

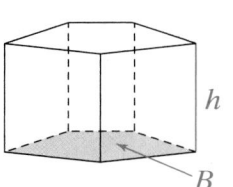

What You'll Learn

OBJECTIVE
1 To find volumes of prisms

OBJECTIVE
2 To find volumes of cylinders

... And Why

To solve real-world problems, such as finding volumes of containers

✔ Check Skills You'll Need

Find the area of each circle.

1. radius = 8 cm

2. radius = 12 cm

3. diameter = 20 cm

❓ For help, go to Lesson 10-3.

New Vocabulary

- volume
- cubic unit

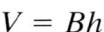TEXT Interactive lesson includes instant self-check, tutorials, and activities.

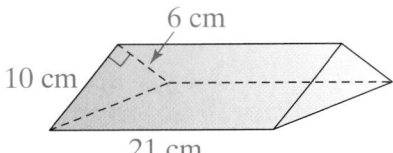
6 cm

10 cm

21 cm

1 EXAMPLE Finding Volume of a Prism

Find the volume of the triangular prism at the left.

$$V = Bh \qquad \text{Use the formula for volume.}$$

$$= 30 \cdot 21 \qquad B = \frac{1}{2} \cdot 10 \cdot 6 = 30 \text{ cm}^2$$

$$= 630 \qquad \text{Simplify.}$$

- The volume is 630 cm³.

✓ Check Understanding Example 1

1. Find the volume of the triangular prism.

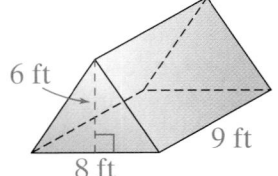
6 ft

9 ft

8 ft

OBJECTIVE

2 Finding the Volumes of Cylinders

You can calculate the volume of a cylinder in much the same way that you calculate the volume of a prism.

Key Concepts Volume of a Cylinder

The volume V of a cylinder is the base area B times the height h.

$$V = Bh$$

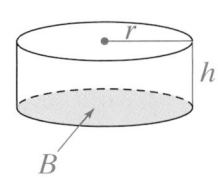
r

h

B

2 EXAMPLE Real-World 🌐 Problem Solving

Packaging Find the volume of the juice can to the nearest cubic centimeter.

$$V = Bh \qquad\qquad\quad \text{Use the formula for volume.}$$

$$V = \pi r^2 h \qquad\qquad B = \pi r^2$$

$$\approx 3.14 \cdot 3.4^2 \cdot 12 \qquad \begin{array}{l}\text{Replace } r \text{ with 3.4,}\\ \text{and } h \text{ with 12.}\end{array}$$

$$= 435.5808 \qquad\quad \text{Simplify.}$$

- The volume is about 436 cm³.

3.4 cm

12 cm

ORANGE JUICE

✓ Check Understanding Example 2

2. **a.** Find the volume of the cylinder to the nearest cubic foot.
   b. How does the volume of this cylinder compare with one having twice its dimensions?

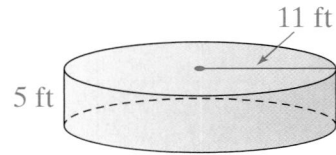
11 ft

5 ft

EXERCISES

For more exercises, see *Extra Practice*.

Practice and Problem Solving

A Practice by Example

Find the volume of each prism.

Example 1
(page 558)

1.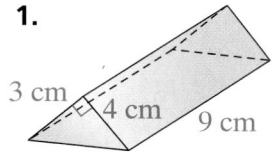
3 cm 4 cm 9 cm

2.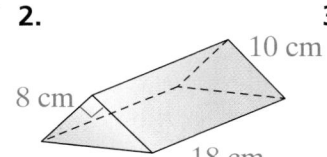
10 cm 8 cm 18 cm

3.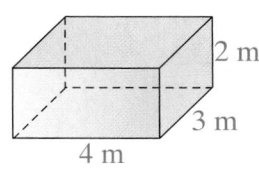
2 m 3 m 4 m

Example 2
(page 558)

For Exercises 4–7, find the volume of each cylinder to the nearest cubic unit.

4.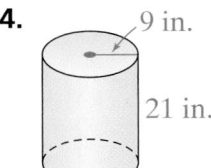
9 in. 21 in.

5.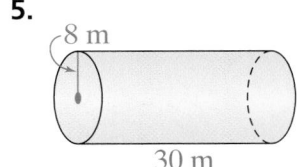
8 m 30 m

6.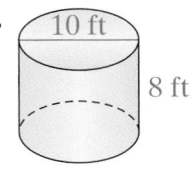
10 ft 8 ft

7. a. a mailing tube 25 in. long with a diameter of 4 in.
  b. a mailing tube with double the dimensions in part (a)
  c. How do the volumes of the two mailing tubes compare?

B Apply Your Skills

8. Firewood Wood for a fireplace is often sold by the cord. A cord is 8 ft by 4 ft by 4 ft. How many cubic feet are in a cord of wood?

9. Storage An under-the-bed storage box measures 24 in. by 12 in. by 3 in. Find its volume to the nearest cubic centimeter (1 in. = 2.54 cm).

Find each missing dimension. Use $\pi \approx 3.14$.

10.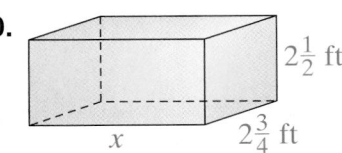
$2\frac{1}{2}$ ft x $2\frac{3}{4}$ ft

$V = 38.5$ ft^3
Length = ■

11.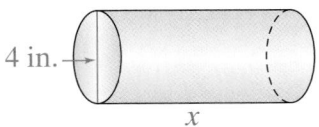
4 in. x

$V = 125.6$ in.^{3}
Height ≈ ■

12.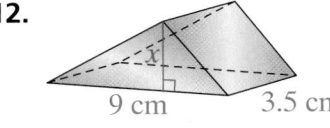
x 9 cm 3.5 cm

$V = 50.4$ cm^3
Height of triangle = ■

13.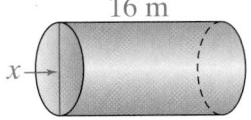
16 m x

$V = 1,256$ m^3
Diameter ≈ ■

Writing in Math Describe one real object with the given shape. Explain why you might want to find the volume of the object.

14. triangular prism   **15.** cylinder   **16.** rectangular prism

Challenge

17. Construction Concrete is sold by the yard, which means by the cubic yard. It costs $70 per yard. How many cubic feet are in a cubic yard? How much would it cost to pour a slab that is 14 ft by 16 ft by 6 in. for a patio?

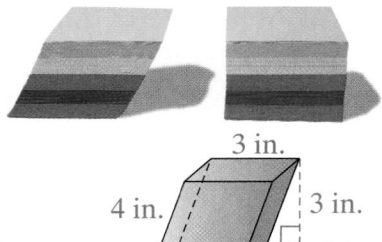

18. Reasoning The two stacks of paper in the photo at the left contain the same number of sheets. The first stack forms an oblique prism; the second forms a right prism. The stacks have the same height, base, and volume. Use this information to find the volume of the oblique prism shown below the stacks.

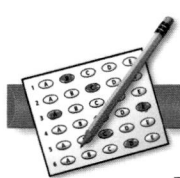

3 in.

4 in.   3 in.

3 in.

19. Error Analysis A student explains that a cylinder with radius 1 in. and height 3 in. has half the volume of one with radius 2 in. and height 3 in. Explain the student's error.

Test Prep

Multiple Choice

20. One side of a triangle is 5 cm and its corresponding height is 15 cm. The triangle is the base of a triangular prism with height 5 cm. What is the volume of the prism?
A. 12.5 cm³   B. 37.5 cm³   C. 187.5 cm³   D. 375.0 cm³

21. What is the height of a rectangular prism with length 5 ft, width 2 ft, and volume 120 ft³?
F. 12 ft   G. 10 ft   H. 6 ft   I. 2 ft

Extended Response

22. A manufacturer is deciding whether to package table salt in a cylinder or in a rectangular prism made of cardboard. The cylinder has radius 4 cm and height 13.5 cm. The prism is 7 cm by 7 cm by 13.5 cm.
a. What volume of salt will each package hold?
b. Each package will use how many square centimeters of cardboard?
c. Which seems to be the better type of package? Explain.

Take It to the NET
Online lesson quiz at
www.PHSchool.com
Web Code: ada-1007

Mixed Review

Lesson 10-6   **Find the surface area of each figure, to the nearest square unit.**

23.
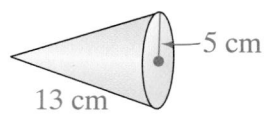
5 cm
13 cm

24.
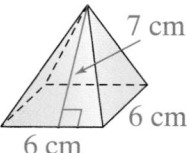
7 cm
6 cm
6 cm

25.
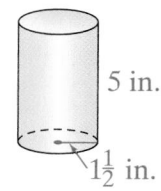
5 in.
1½ in.

Lesson 9-2   **26.** If $a \parallel b$ in the figure at the right, find the measures of angles 2–8 in terms of x.

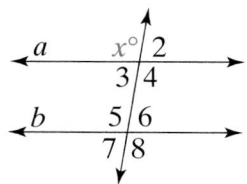
a $x°$ 2
3 4
b 5 6
7 8

Lesson 5-6   **27. Money** Juan has $3.80 in coins. He has 6 quarters and 12 dimes. The rest are nickels. How many nickels does he have?

Technology

Rounding Error

A calculator can help you avoid a *rounding error.* However, you have to know how to work with exact values in unsimplified form.

EXAMPLE

Find the volume of a cylinder with height 6 and circumference 15. Round to the nearest tenth.

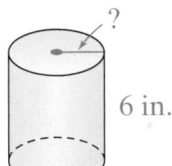

6 in.

Method 1

$C = 2\pi r$	**formula for circumference**
$15 = 2\pi r$	**C = 15**
$\frac{15}{2\pi} = r$	**Divide by 2π.**
$2.4 \approx r$	**Simplify (at left).**
$V = Bh$	**formula for volume**
$= \pi r^2 h$	**B = πr²**
$\approx \pi(2.4)^2(6)$	**Replace r and h.**
≈ 108.6	**Use a calculator.**

Method 2

$C = 2\pi r$

$15 = 2\pi r$

$\frac{15}{2\pi} = r$

$V = Bh$

$= \pi r^2 h$

$= \pi\left(\frac{15}{2\pi}\right)^2(6)$

≈ 107.4

In Method 1, the intermediate value $r \approx 2.4$ gives a final result that has a greater *rounding error.* In Method 2, note that the formula for volume uses the exact value of the radius, $\frac{15}{2\pi}$.

EXERCISES

What intermediate value must you find to solve the problem? Give its exact value and its approximate value to the nearest tenth.

1. Find the area of a circle with circumference 12.

2. Find the volume of a cylinder with radius 3 and lateral area 10.

Solve each problem to the nearest tenth by two methods. In one method, use an approximate intermediate value. In the other method, use the exact intermediate value.

3. Find the surface area of a cone with slant height 5 and lateral area 9.

4. Find the surface area of a sphere with circumference 13.

5. Find the surface area and volume of a cylinder with lateral area 10 and height 8.

6. **Writing in Math** In the Example, which method do you think makes better use of the calculator? Explain.

Make a Model

What You'll Learn
OBJECTIVE 1 To make a model

...And Why
To build the largest box possible from a given rectangle

✔ Check Skills You'll Need
Draw each figure described below.

1. a rectangle with small squares drawn in each corner

2. a rectangle divided into eight congruent rectangles

3. two parallelograms that have different shapes but the same perimeter

⚡ For help, go to Lesson 9-3.

Math Strategies in Action Architects build and use models when they plan. When they design buildings, they experiment with models. When they design packaging, they first create prototype models.

1 EXAMPLE Real-World 🌐 Problem Solving

Packaging A box company makes boxes to hold popcorn. Each box is made by cutting the square corners out of a rectangular sheet of cardboard. The rectangle is $8\frac{1}{2}$ in. by 11 in. What are the dimensions of the box that will hold the most popcorn if the square corners have side lengths 1 in., 2 in., 3 in., and 4 in.?

Read and Understand

1. What is the goal of the problem?

2. What information do you have to help you build a model?

Plan and Solve

To find the size that will hold the greatest amount of popcorn, you must find the dimensions that will give you the greatest volume.

Build four boxes using sheets of $8\frac{1}{2}$ in.-by-11 in. paper. Test four whole-number lengths of cuts.

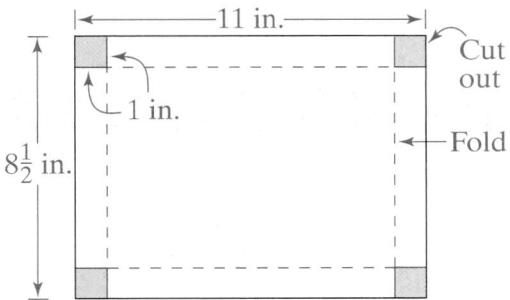

3. **a.** What are the dimensions of the box with corners 1 in. by 1 in.?
   b. What is the volume of this box?

4. When you cut a 2 in.-by-2 in. square from each corner, what effect does that have on the length, width, and height of the box?

Measure to find the dimensions of each of your boxes. Then find the volume of each box.

5. Which box has the greatest volume?

6. Is it possible to create a box that has 5 in.-by-5 in. corners? Explain.

Look Back and Check

A table is another way to organize your information and solve the problem.

7. List the size of the cut, and then find the length, width, and height of the box. Find each volume.

Size of Cut	Length	Width	Height	Volume
1 in.	9 in.	6.5 in.	1 in.	58.5 in.^{3}
2 in.	▦ in.	▦ in.	▦ in.	▦ in.^{3}
3 in.	▦ in.	▦ in.	▦ in.	▦ in.^{3}
4 in.	▦ in.	▦ in.	▦ in.	▦ in.^{3}

✔ Check Understanding

8. **a.** Use a table to find the volume of a box folded from an $8\frac{1}{2}$ in.-by-11 in. sheet of paper if the square corners are $1\frac{1}{2}$ in.; $2\frac{1}{2}$ in.; $3\frac{1}{2}$ in.
   b. Did you find dimensions of a box that holds a greater volume than you did in Question 7? Which dimensions are they?

EXERCISES

? For more exercises, see *Extra Practice*.

Practice and Problem Solving

A Practice by Example

Example 1
(page 562)

Solve by making a model.

1. You cut square corners off a piece of cardboard with dimensions 16 in. by 20 in. You then fold the cardboard to create a box with no lid. To the nearest inch, what dimensions will give you the greatest volume?

8-Page Signature

Side 1   Side 2

2. Publishing Newspapers, books, and magazines often are printed in groups of 8, 16, or 32 pages, called *signatures*. The diagram at the left shows how pages should be positioned for an 8-page signature. The pages are positioned to print on both sides of the paper that is fed through the printing press. When the paper is folded, the pages are in order. Make a model to show one way to position the pages in a 16-page book.

B Apply Your Skills

Solve using any strategy.

3. The length of a rectangle is twice its width. The perimeter of the rectangle is 90 cm. What are the length and width?

Strategies

- Account for All Possibilities
- Draw a Diagram
- Look for a Pattern
- Make a Model
- Make a Table
- Simplify the Problem
- Simulate the Problem
- Solve by Graphing
- Try, Test, Revise
- Use Multiple Strategies
- Work Backward
- Write an Equation
- Write a Proportion

4. Packaging A company packages snack mix in cylindrical tubes. Each tube is made from a rectangle of cardboard. The bases of the cylinder are plastic. The cardboard comes in $8\frac{1}{2}$ in.-by-11 in. sheets. To hold the greatest amount of mix, should the longer side or shorter side be the height? Justify your answer.

5. Pets A dog owner wants to use 200 ft of fencing to enclose the greatest possible area for his dog. He wants the fenced area to be rectangular. What dimensions should he use?

6. Writing in Math You want to find how the length of a pendulum affects the time the pendulum takes to swing back and forth. Explain how you would model the situation.

7. An alphabet book will have one letter on each page. Eight pages will be printed on a single piece of paper. You fold the paper in half. Then you fold it in half again and trim the edges. The eight pages appear in order. Draw the layout for two sides of the large sheet for the letters A–H. Explain why two layouts are possible.

C Challenge

8. Reasoning In the parts (a)–(c), how many of the indicated cubes are there in this 3-by-3-by-3 cube?
  a. 1-by-1-by-1 cubes
  b. 2-by-2-by-2-cubes
  c. 3-by-3-by-3 cubes
  d. How many 3-by-3-by-3 cubes would be in a 5-by-5-by-5 cube?

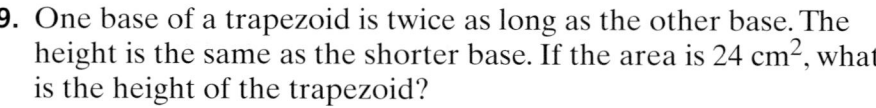

9. One base of a trapezoid is twice as long as the other base. The height is the same as the shorter base. If the area is 24 cm^2, what is the height of the trapezoid?

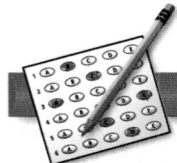
Multiple Choice

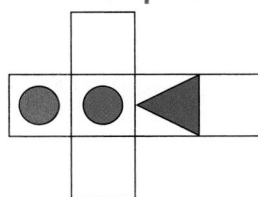

10. Which space figure below can you fold from the net at the left?

A.    **B.** 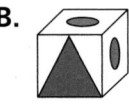   **C.** 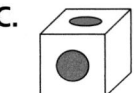   **D.**

11. A rectangle has a perimeter of 24. Both the length and width are whole numbers. If the rectangle has the least possible area, what are its dimensions?

  F. 1 by 11   **G.** 1 by 24   **H.** 2 by 4   **I.** 6 by 6

Take It to the NET
Online lesson quiz at
www.PHSchool.com
Web Code: ada-1008

12. A cone and a cylinder have the same base and height. The volume of the cylinder is how many times the volume of the cone?

  A. $\frac{1}{3}$ **B.** $\frac{1}{2}$ **C.** 2   **D.** 3

Mixed Review

Lesson 10-7   **Find the volume of each figure, to the nearest tenth.**

13. 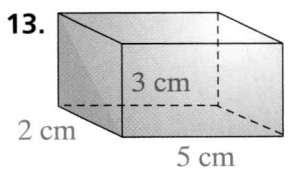   **14.** 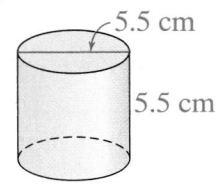   **15.**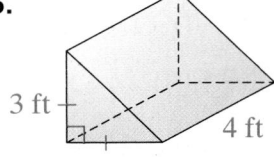

2 cm, 3 cm, 5 cm   5.5 cm, 5.5 cm   3 ft, 4 ft

Lesson 8-2   **Find the solutions of each equation when x is 0, 1, and -1.**

16. $2x - y = 10$ **17.** $5x + y = 15$ **18.** $2x + 3y = 6$

 Checkpoint Quiz 2   **Lessons 10-4 through 10-8**

Instant self-check
quiz online and
on CD-ROM

Name each space figure. Find its surface area, to the nearest square unit.

1. 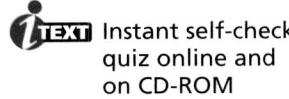   **2.** 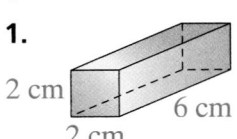   **3.**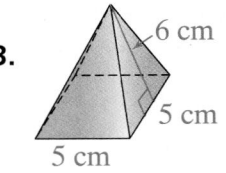

2 cm, 2 cm, 6 cm   3 in., 8 in.   6 cm, 5 cm, 5 cm

Find the volume of each figure to the nearest tenth.

4. 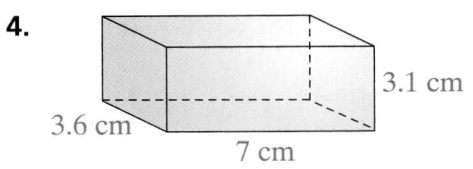   **5.**

3.6 cm, 7 cm, 3.1 cm   3 in., 6 in.

6. Open-Ended Choose a space figure. Draw its net.

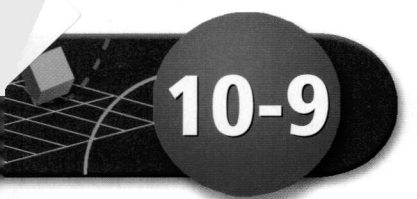

10-9

Volume: Pyramids, Cones, and Spheres

1 Finding Volumes of Cones and Pyramids

What You'll Learn

1 To find volumes of pyramids and cones

2 To find volumes of spheres

. . . And Why

To find out how much water is displaced by a space figure

✓ Check Skills You'll Need

Multiply.

1. $\frac{1}{3}(3.14)(2)^2(5)$

2. $\frac{1}{3}(4)^2(6)$

3. $\frac{4}{3}(3.14)(2)^3$

4. $\frac{4}{3}(3.14)(0.5)^3$

❓ For help, go to Lesson 5-4.

You can fill three cones with sand and pour the contents into a cylinder with the same height and radius. You will fill the cylinder evenly to the top.

The volume of the cone is one third the volume of the cylinder.

The same relationship is true of a pyramid and a prism with the same base and height.

Key Concepts   **Volume of a Cone and of a Pyramid**

The volume V of a cone or a pyramid is $\frac{1}{3}$ the product of the base area B and the height h.

$$V = \tfrac{1}{3}Bh$$

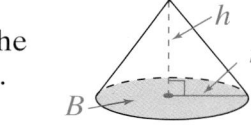

---

1 EXAMPLE   **Finding Volume of a Cone**

Find the volume of the cone.

$V = \frac{1}{3}Bh$ **Use the formula for volume.**

$V = \frac{1}{3}\pi r^2 h$ $B = \pi r^2$

$\approx \frac{1}{3}(3.14)(3)^2(10)$ **Replace r with 3 and h with 10. Simplify.**

$= 94.2$

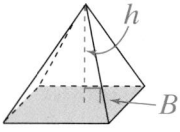

• The volume of the cone is about 94 ft^3.

✓ Check Understanding   Example 1

1. Find the volume, to the nearest cubic unit, of a cone with height 5 cm and radius of base 2 cm.

TEXT Interactive lesson includes instant self-check, tutorials, and activities.

2 EXAMPLE Finding Volume of a Pyramid

Find the volume of the square pyramid.

$V = \frac{1}{3}Bh$ **Use the formula for volume.**

$V = \frac{1}{3}s^2h$ $B = s^2$

$= \frac{1}{3}(6)^2(10)$ **Replace s with 6 and h with 10.**

$= 120$ **Simplify.**

● The volume of the pyramid is 120 ft^3.

 Check Understanding Example 2

2. Find the volume of a square pyramid that has a side of 5 ft and a height of 20 ft.

OBJECTIVE

2 Finding Volumes of Spheres

Below is the formula for the volume of a sphere.

Key Concepts **Volume of a Sphere**

The volume V of a sphere with radius r is $\frac{4}{3}\pi$ times the cube of the radius.

$$V = \frac{4}{3}\pi r^3$$

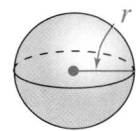

---

3 EXAMPLE Real-World 🌐 Problem Solving

Snow Spheres You build a snow statue with snow spheres. **What is the volume of the snow in the bottom sphere?**

$V = \frac{4}{3}\pi r^3$ **Use the volume formula.**

$\approx \frac{4}{3}(3.14)(1.5)^3$ **Replace r with 1.5.**

$= 14.13$ **Simplify.**

● The volume of the bottom snow sphere is about 14 ft^3.

 Check Understanding Example 3

3. Find the volume of each sphere to the nearest whole number.

    a. radius = 15 m   **b.** diameter = 7 mi

EXERCISES

For more exercises, see *Extra Practice.*

Practice and Problem Solving

A Practice by Example

Example 1
(page 566)

In Exercises 1–4, find the volume of each cone to the nearest cubic unit.

1.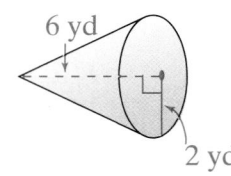
6 yd
2 yd

2.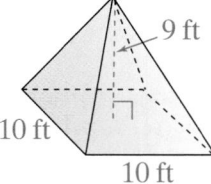
20 in.
25 in.

3. height 12 cm, radius 21 cm

4. height 7 in., radius 7 in.

Example 2
(page 567)

In Exercises 5–8, find the volume of each square pyramid.

5.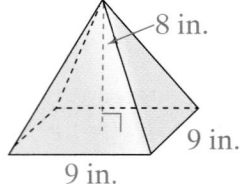
8 in.
9 in.
9 in.

6.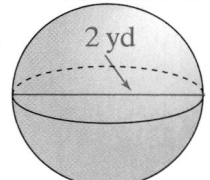
9 ft
10 ft
10 ft

7. edge 3.2 cm, height 6 cm

8. edge 90 mm, height 300 mm

Example 3
(page 567)

Find the volume of each sphere to the nearest whole number.

9.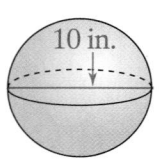
10 in.

10.
2 yd

11. $r = 12$ cm   **12.** $r = 3.5$ in.   **13.** $d = 60$ yd   **14.** $d = 30$ m

B Apply Your Skills

15. Plants A cone-shaped paper cup is 7 cm high with a diameter of 6 cm. If the ivy plant on Julia's desk needs 240 mL of water, about how many paper cups of water will she use to water it? (1 mL = 1 cm^3)

16. Snacks How much frozen yogurt can you pack inside a cone that is 5 in. high with a radius of 1.25 in.?

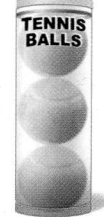

17. Packaging Tennis balls with a diameter of 2.5 in. are sold in cans of three (left). The can is a cylinder. What is the volume of the space in the can not occupied by tennis balls? Assume the balls touch the can on the sides, top, and bottom.

18. Writing in Math Explain how you remember formulas for finding volumes of prisms and pyramids, cylinders and cones, and spheres.

19. Physics You place a steel ball with diameter 4 cm in a water-filled cylinder that is 5 cm in diameter and 10 cm high. What volume of water will spill out of the cylinder?

Find the missing dimension. Round to the nearest unit.

20.
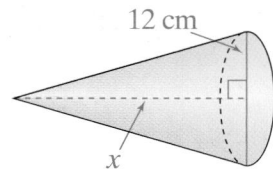

$V = 819 \text{ cm}^3$
Height ≈ ■

21.
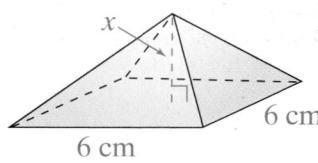

$V = 38 \text{ cm}^3$
Height = ■

22. Sphere: volume = $36\pi \text{ yd}^3$, diameter = ■

23. Cone: volume = 424 m^3, diameter = 18 m, height ≈ ■

C Challenge

24. You want to fill the top part of an hourglass $\frac{2}{3}$ full of salt. The height of the hourglass is 20 cm, and the radius of the base is 8 cm. Find the volume of salt needed.

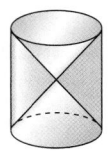

25. **Error Analysis** A student tells a class that if you double the radius of a sphere, the volume will be multiplied by 6. Explain the student's error.

Test Prep

Gridded Response

26. The eight segments from the center of a cube to the eight corners of the cube form the edges of six pyramids. If one edge of the cube is 4 in., what is the volume of each pyramid, to the nearest cubic inch?

27. What is the volume of a square pyramid with height 3.25 yd and base edge 5.5 yd, to the nearest tenth of a cubic yard?

28. What is the volume of a sphere with diameter 5.5 m, to the nearest cubic meter?

29. What is the volume of a cone with radius 4.8 cm and height 12 cm, to the nearest tenth of a cubic centimeter? Use 3.14 for π.

30. How many cones of radius 1 m and height 1 m have total volume equal to the volume of a sphere with radius 1 m?

Take It to the NET
Online lesson quiz at
www.PHSchool.com
Web Code: ada-1009

Mixed Review

Lesson 7-5

Solve each equation.

31. $\frac{5}{6}x = \frac{1}{6}x + 12$ 32. $5y + 2 = 3y - 10$ 33. $3a + 10 = 12 - 2a$

Lesson 5-9

Simplify each expression.

34. $(3ab^2)^3$ 35. $-(4x)^2$ 36. $(-2p^2)^4$ 37. $\left(-\frac{3}{8}\right)^2$ 38. $\left(\frac{2x}{y^3}\right)^2$

Some multiple-choice questions cannot be answered because there is insufficient information or there is more than one possible answer. If so, then one of the answer choices will be "cannot be determined."

1 EXAMPLE

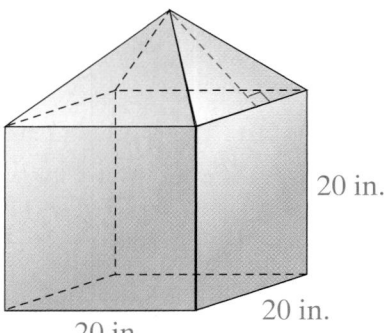

20 in.

20 in.

20 in.

What is the surface area of the figure at the right?

A. 2,600 in.^{2} **B.** 3,200 in.^{2} **C.** 8,600 in.^{2} **D.** cannot be determined

The bottom part is a cube. You know its length, width, and height, so you can find its base area and its lateral area. The top part is a pyramid. You know the perimeter of the base, but you need to know the slant height of its faces to find its lateral area.

● There is insufficient information. The correct choice is D.

2 EXAMPLE

A rectangular prism with height 5 cm has volume 60 cm^3. What is the perimeter of the base?

F. 14 cm   **G.** 16 cm   **H.** 26 cm   **I.** cannot be determined

You know $V = Bh$.

$$60 = B(5)$$ **Replace V with 60 and h with 5.**

$$12 = B$$ **Solve for B.**

For $B = 12$ cm^2, the rectangular base can be 1 cm by 12 cm, 2 cm by 6 cm, or 3 cm by 4 cm. The perimeter can be 26 cm (choice H), 16 cm (choice G), or 14 cm (choice A).

● There is more than one possible answer. The correct choice is I.

EXERCISES

If the answer to an exercise cannot be determined, choose "cannot be determined" and explain your reasoning.

1. The base of a square prism has sides of 14 in. What is the surface area of the prism?

A. 56 in.^{2} **B.** 196 in.^{2} **C.** 784 in.^{2} **D.** cannot be determined

2. A trapezoid has height 8 and area 28. What are the lengths of its bases?

F. 6 and 1   **G.** 5 and 2   **H.** 4 and 3   **I.** cannot be determined

Chapter Review

Vocabulary

Reading Math
Understanding Vocabulary

Choose the vocabulary term that correctly completes the sentence.

1. The sum of the areas of the lateral faces of a prism is the __?__ of a prism.

2. A __?__ is a space figure with one circular base and one vertex.

3. The __?__ of a parallelogram is a line segment drawn from the side opposite the base to the base, that is perpendicular to the base.

4. The __?__ of a three-dimensional figure is the number of cubic units needed to fill it.

5. The set of all points in space that are a given distance from a given point called the center is a __?__.

6. A __?__ has two parallel bases that are congruent circles.

7. The __?__ of a figure is the number of square units it encloses.

Take It to the NET
Online vocabulary quiz
at **www.PHSchool.com**
Web Code: adj-1051

Skills and Concepts

10-1 and 10-2 Objectives

▼ To find areas of rectangles (p. 522)

▼ To find areas of parallelograms (p. 523)

▼ To find areas of triangles (p. 527)

▼ To find areas of trapezoids (p. 528)

The **area** of a polygon is the number of square units enclosed by the polygon. To find the areas of parallelograms, triangles, or trapezoids, use the appropriate formulas.

parallelogram
$A = bh$

triangle
$A = \frac{1}{2}bh$

trapezoid
$A = \frac{1}{2}h(b_1 + b_2)$

Find the area of the shaded region in each figure.

8. Parallelogram
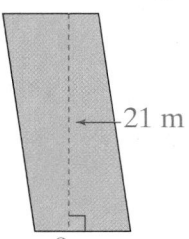
21 m
9 m

9. Trapezoid
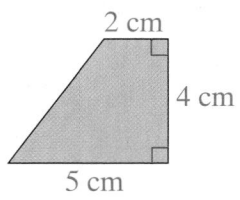
2 cm
4 cm
5 cm

10.
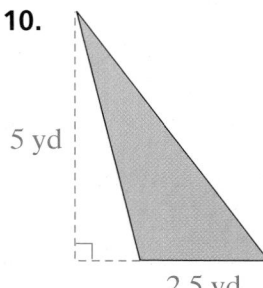
5 yd
2.5 yd

To find the area of a circle, use the formula $A = \pi r^2$. Use 3.14 for π.

Find the area of each figure to the nearest square unit.

11.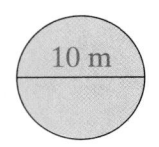
10 m

12.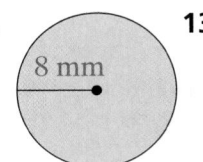
8 mm

13.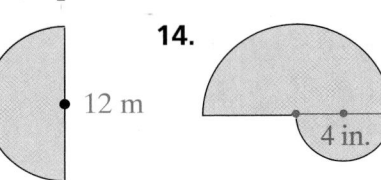
12 m

14.
4 in.

Name **pyramids** and **prisms** by the shapes of their bases. A **cylinder** is a space figure with two circular bases. **Cones** have one circular base and one vertex. **Nets** are flat patterns for space figures.

Name the space figure represented by each net.

15.

16.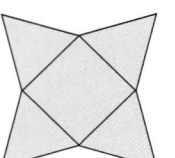

17.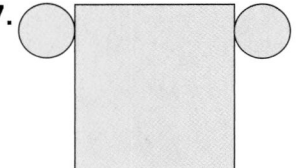

The **lateral area** of a prism is the sum of the areas of the lateral faces. The lateral area of a cylinder is the area of the curved surface. The **surface area** of a prism or a cylinder is the sum of the lateral area and the areas of the two bases.

To find surface area, use the appropriate formula.

prism	cylinder
L.A. = ph	L.A. = $2\pi rh$
S.A. = L.A. + $2B$	S.A. = L.A. + $2B$

Find the surface area to the nearest square unit. Use 3.14 for π.

18.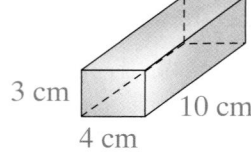
3 cm
10 cm
4 cm

19.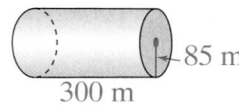
85 m
300 m

20.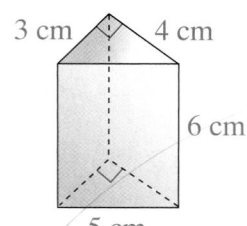
3 cm 4 cm
6 cm
5 cm

21.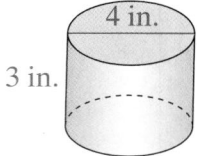
4 in.
3 in.

10-6 Objectives

▼ To find surface areas of pyramids (p. 552)

▼ To find surface areas of cones and spheres (p. 553)

For pyramids and cones, use **slant height** ℓ to find the lateral area. For a regular pyramid, if n is the number of lateral faces, you can find the area of one face and then multiply by n. The lateral area of a cone is the area of the curved surface. The surface area of a pyramid or a cone is the sum of the lateral area and the base area.

To find surface area, use the appropriate formula.

pyramid
$$\text{L.A.} = n\left(\tfrac{1}{2}b\ell\right)$$
$$\text{S.A.} = \text{L.A.} + B$$

cone
$$\text{L.A.} = \pi r\ell$$
$$\text{S.A.} = \text{L.A.} + B$$

sphere
$$\text{S.A.} = 4\pi r^2$$

Find the surface area of each figure, to the nearest square unit.

22.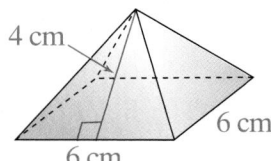
4 cm
6 cm
6 cm

23.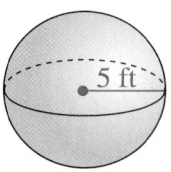
6 cm
6 cm
3 cm

24.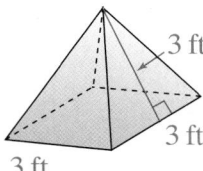
5 ft

25.
3 ft
3 ft
3 ft

10-8 Objective

▼ To make a model (p. 562)

To solve some problems, make a model.

26. A gift box measures 6 in. along each edge. You cut a rectangular sheet of wrapping paper to get a single piece with which you can cover the box without overlapping. What are the smallest possible dimensions of the original sheet of wrapping paper?

27. A 12 m-by-15 m rectangular garden has a walk 1 m wide around it. Describe how you would find the area of the walk.

10-7 and 10-9 Objectives

▼ To find volumes of prisms (p. 557)

▼ To find volumes of cylinders (p. 558)

▼ To find volumes of cones and pyramids (p. 566)

▼ To find volumes of spheres (p. 567)

Volume is the measure of how much a space figure can hold.

To find volume, use the appropriate formula.

prisms and cylinders
$$V = Bh$$

pyramids and cones
$$V = \tfrac{1}{3}Bh$$

spheres
$$V = \tfrac{4}{3}\pi r^3$$

Find each volume to the nearest cubic unit.

28.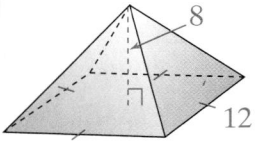
8
12

29.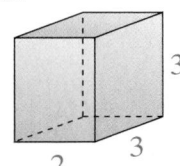
3
3
2

30.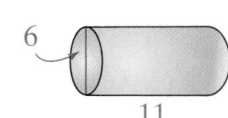
6
11

31.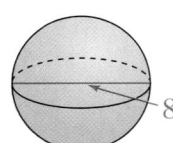
8

Use 3.14 for π as needed on this page.

Find the area of each figure.

1.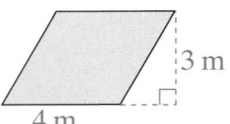

2.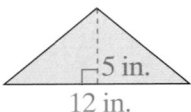

3.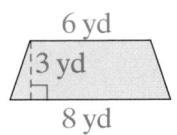

4.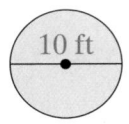

5.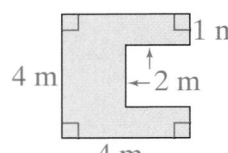

6.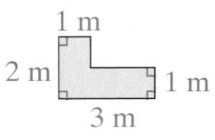

Find the missing measures.

7. circle
$d = 4$ cm
$A = \blacksquare$ cm^2

8. triangle
$b = 7$ m
$h = 4$ m
$A = \blacksquare$ m^2

Name the space figure for each net.

9.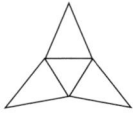

10.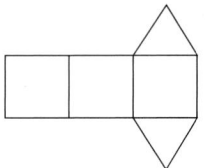

Find the surface area of each figure.

11.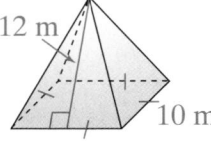

12.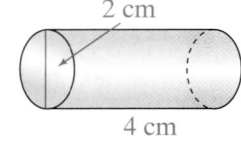

13.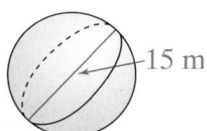

14.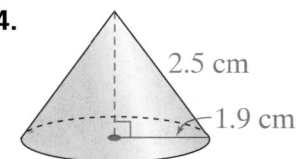

Find the volume of each figure to the nearest cubic unit.

15.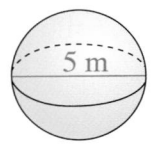

16.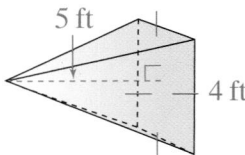

17.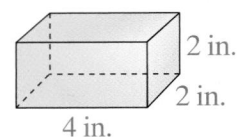

18.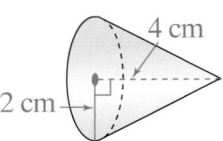

19. The height of a rectangle is doubled while the base is unchanged. How does this affect the area? Explain.

20. In cubic feet, how much greater is the volume of a cone with height 10 ft and radius 6 ft than the volume of a square pyramid with height 10 ft and base edge length 6 ft?

21. The diameter of Mars is about 4,000 mi.
a. Find the approximate surface area.
b. Find the approximate volume.

22. A box is 25.5 cm by 17 cm by 5 cm.
a. How much dry dishwashing detergent can it hold?
b. Without overlap, how much cardboard is needed to make the box?

23. **Writing in Math** How is the formula for volume of a prism like the formula for volume of a pyramid? How are the formulas different?

24. A rectangular piece of sheet metal measures 26 in. by 20 in. A square measuring 2 in. by 2 in. is cut out of each corner, and the sides are folded to form a box. What is the volume of the box?

25. **Open-Ended** Draw a net for a rectangular prism.

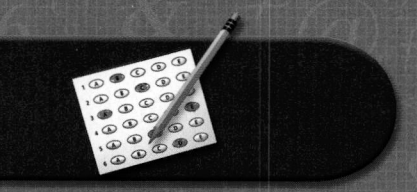

Test Prep

Multiple Choice

Choose the best answer.

1. The average nose has about 6,000,000 cells that detect odors. What is this number in scientific notation?
   A. $6 \cdot 10^5$ B. $6 \cdot 10^6$
   C. $6 \cdot 10^7$ D. $6 \cdot 10^8$

2. Which equation represents the statement *The sum of twice a number and five times another number is 40?*
   F. $40 = 2x + 5y$ G. $5y = \frac{40}{2x}$
   H. $2x \cdot 5y = 40$ I. $5y = \frac{1}{2}x + 40$

3. In which situation are two angles supplementary?
   A. The sum of their measures is 180°.
   B. They share a vertex.
   C. The sum of their measures is 90°.
   D. They have the same measure.

4. What space figure can you form from the net?
   F. square pyramid
   G. triangular pyramid
   H. triangular prism
   I. hexagonal prism

5. Figure A is a rectangle 10 in. long and 7.5 in. wide. Figure B is a parallelogram with height 12 in. and base length 7.5 in. Which statement is true?
   A. area of A > area of B
   B. area of A < area of B
   C. area of A = area of B
   D. cannot be determined

Gridded Response

Find each area.

6.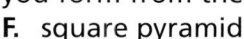
   6
   11.7
   10

7.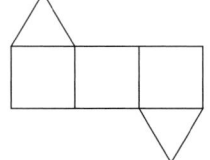
   4
   4
   10

Find each area to the nearest square unit.

8.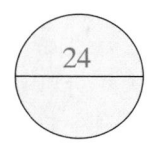
   24

9.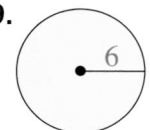
   6

Find the surface area of each figure to the nearest square unit.

10.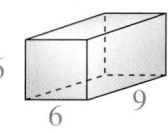
    6
    6   9

11.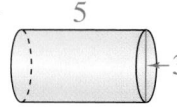
    5
    3

12.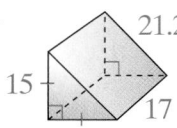
    21.2
    15
    17

13.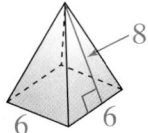
    8
    6   6

14.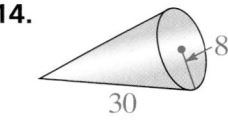
    8
    30

15.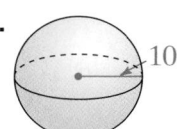
    10

Short Response

Find the volume of each figure, to the nearest cubic unit. Show your work.

16.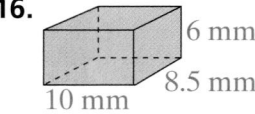
    6 mm
    8.5 mm
    10 mm

17.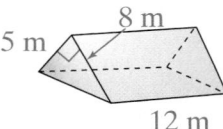
    8 m
    5 m
    12 m

18.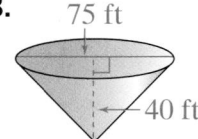
    75 ft
    40 ft

19.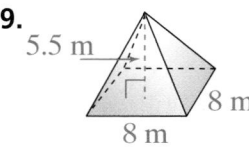
    5.5 m
    8 m
    8 m

20.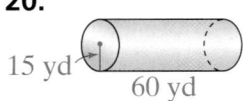
    15 yd
    60 yd

21.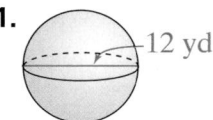
    12 yd

Extended Response

22. A cylinder has diameter 3 cm and height 6 cm.
    (a) Draw and label a net. **(b)** Find the surface area of the cylinder to the nearest square centimeter. **(c)** Find the volume.

Playing Fields

Applying Area Have you ever played a team sport such as soccer, basketball, or ice hockey? If so, you had to follow the rules of the game. You probably found that these include rules about your appearance and the equipment you use, as well as other game equipment such as goals, backboards, or hockey pucks. There are even rules for the space in which you play. One purpose of these rules is to provide all players with an equal chance of success.

Football Gridiron
Parallel lines run 5 yd apart from goal line to goal line along the playing area of a football field. The playing area, or gridiron, is 300 ft long.

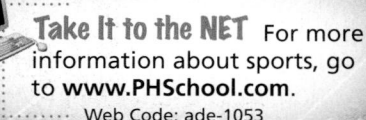

Take It to the NET For more information about sports, go to **www.PHSchool.com**.
Web Code: ade-1053

Hockey Rink

A hockey rink uses quarter circles with 28-ft radii to keep the puck from getting caught in the corners.

Basketball Court

A basketball court can be up to 2 yd shorter than regulation size and up to 4 yd narrower. Its dimensions must remain in proportion.

Soccer Field

Each soccer team plays both ends of the field during a game, switching goals after the first 45-min half.

Activity

1. Copy the table. Find the area of each field.

For Exercises 2 and 3, how many times the area of the smaller field is the area of the larger field?

2. a soccer field and a football field

3. a professional basketball court and a junior high basketball court

4. **Writing in Math** Why do you think the basketball courts are different sizes?

Playing Fields

Sport	Length	Width	Area
Basketball			
Professional and college	94 ft	50 ft	■
High school	82 ft	46 ft	■
Junior high school	74 ft	42 ft	■
Football (with end zones)	120 yd	$53\frac{1}{3}$ yd	■
Ice hockey	200 ft	85 ft	■
Soccer (maximum)	130 yd	100 yd	■

For Exercises 5–7, on each field, how much playing area is outside the indicated part? Round to the nearest whole number where necessary.

5. a professional basketball court, outside the two rectangular free-throw lanes, each 19 ft by 14 ft

6. a. a soccer field, outside two penalty areas, each 44 yd wide and 18 yd deep, in front of each goal
   b. the same field, outside the two penalty areas and the 10-yd-radius center circle

7. a hockey rink, outside its five face-off circles, each with a radius of 15 ft

8. In the New York Giants' football stadium, the grass surface is 433 ft long and 269 ft wide. What is the area of the grass surface outside the playing field?

Where You've Been

- In Chapter 7, you learned to solve two-step equations and inequalities, multi-step equations, equations with variables on both sides, and to transform formulas.

- In Chapter 9, you learned about points, lines, and planes; congruence, constructions, translations, symmetry, and reflections.

- In Chapter 10, you learned to calculate areas, surface areas, and volumes.

Understanding Coordinates (Lesson 1-10)

Name the point with the given coordinates.

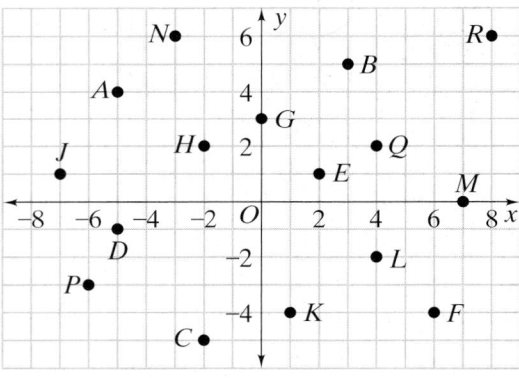

1. $(0, 3)$ **2.** $(1, -4)$ **3.** $(-2, 2)$

4. $(-5, -1)$ **5.** $(3, 5)$ **6.** $(6, -4)$

Write the coordinates of each point.

7. A **8.** E **9.** M

10. J **11.** L **12.** P

Simplifying Numbers With Exponents (Lesson 4-2)

Simplify each expression.

13. 10^2 **14.** 6^2 **15.** 2^2 **16.** 9^2 **17.** 11^2

18. 0.2^2 **19.** 7^2 **20.** 2.3^2 **21.** 4^2 **22.** 5^2

Solving Proportions (Lesson 6-2)

Solve each proportion.

23. $\frac{1}{3} = \frac{a}{12}$ **24.** $\frac{h}{5} = \frac{20}{25}$ **25.** $\frac{24}{6} = \frac{4}{x}$ **26.** $\frac{2}{7} = \frac{c}{35}$

27. $\frac{e}{5} = \frac{32}{80}$ **28.** $\frac{18}{g} = \frac{3}{10}$ **29.** $\frac{4}{11} = \frac{28}{m}$ **30.** $\frac{21}{13} = \frac{42}{a}$

31. $\frac{2}{15} = \frac{c}{75}$ **32.** $\frac{1}{4} = \frac{8}{x}$ **33.** $\frac{13}{p} = \frac{39}{51}$ **34.** $\frac{x}{20} = \frac{40}{100}$

Right Triangles in Algebra

Where You're Going

In this chapter, you will learn how to

- Find the square roots of numbers.
- Find the missing measures of right triangles.
- Use the Distance and Midpoint Formulas.
- Solve a problem by writing a proportion.

Real-World Snapshots Applying what you learn, on pages 626–627 you will apply ratios to solve problems about proportions in rectangles.

Square Roots and Irrational Numbers

What You'll Learn

 OBJECTIVE 1 To find square roots of numbers

 OBJECTIVE 2 To classify real numbers

...And Why

To use square roots in real-world situations, such as finding the distance to the horizon

 **Check Skills You'll Need**

Write the numbers in each list without using exponents.

1. $1^2, 2^2, 3^2, \ldots, 12^2$

2. $10^2, 20^2, 30^2, \ldots, 120^2$

🔖 For help, go to Lesson 4-2.

New Vocabulary

• perfect square
• square root
• irrational number

Reading Math

The symbol $\sqrt{100}$ is the positive square root of 100, so you may read $-\sqrt{100}$ as the negative square root of 100.

ⓘ **TEXT** Interactive lesson includes instant self-check, tutorials, and activities.

OBJECTIVE

1 Finding Square Roots

Consider the three squares shown below.

Each square has sides with integer length. The area of a square is the *square* of the length of a side. The square of an integer is a **perfect square.**

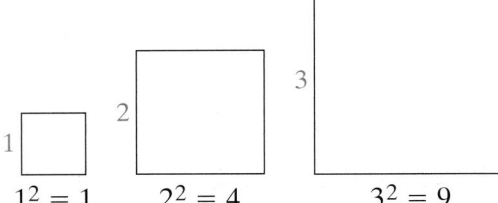

$1^2 = 1$ $2^2 = 4$ $3^2 = 9$

The inverse of squaring a number is finding a **square root.** The square-root radical, $\sqrt{}$, indicates the nonnegative square root of a number. In this book, you may assume that an expression under a square-root radical is greater than or equal to zero.

1 EXAMPLE Simplifying Square Roots

Simplify each square root.

a. $\sqrt{64}$ **b.** $-\sqrt{121}$

$\sqrt{64} = 8$ $-\sqrt{121} = -11$

✔ **Check Understanding** Example 1

1. Simplify each square root.

   a. $\sqrt{100}$ **b.** $-\sqrt{100}$ **c.** $\sqrt{16}$ **d.** $-\sqrt{16}$

The first thirteen perfect squares are
   $0, 1, 4, 9, 16, 25, 36, 49, 64, 81, 100, 121,$ and $144.$
Memorizing these will help you solve problems efficiently.

For an integer that is not a perfect square, you can estimate a square root. For example, 8 is between the perfect squares 4 and 9.

$$\sqrt{4} \qquad\qquad \sqrt{8}\ \sqrt{9}$$

$\sqrt{8}$ **is between** $\sqrt{4}$ **and** $\sqrt{9}$.

Since 8 is closer to 9 than to 4, $\sqrt{8}$ is closer to 3 than to 2. So, $\sqrt{8} \approx 3.$

2 **EXAMPLE** <u>Real-World</u> Problem Solving

Lifeguarding You can use the formula $d = \sqrt{1.5h}$ to estimate the distance d, in miles, to a horizon line when your eyes are h feet above the ground. Estimate the distance to the horizon seen by a lifeguard whose eyes are 10 feet above the ground.

$d = \sqrt{1.5h}$ Use the formula.

$d = \sqrt{15}$ Replace h with 10 and multiply.

$\sqrt{9} < \sqrt{15} < \sqrt{16}$ Find perfect squares close to 15.

$\sqrt{16} = 4$ Find the square root of the closest perfect square.

● The lifeguard can see about 4 miles to the horizon.

Real-World Connection

This lifeguard can see nearly 1 mile farther than he can standing on the beach.

✔ **Check Understanding**   Example 2

2. Estimate to the nearest integer.

    a. $\sqrt{27}$ **b.** $-\sqrt{72}$ **c.** $\sqrt{50}$ **d.** $-\sqrt{22}$

OBJECTIVE

2 **Classifying Real Numbers**

You can express a rational number as the ratio of two integers $\frac{a}{b}$, with $b \neq 0$. In decimal form, a rational number either terminates or repeats. An **irrational number** has decimal form that neither terminates nor repeats, and it cannot be written as the ratio of two integers. Together, rationals and irrationals form the real numbers.

If an integer is not a perfect square, its square root is irrational.

Need Help?

To review rational numbers, see Lesson 4-6.

3 **EXAMPLE** **Identifying Irrational Numbers**

Identify each number as rational or irrational. Explain.

a. $\sqrt{18}$ irrational, because 18 is not a perfect square

b. $\sqrt{121}$ rational, because 121 is a perfect square

c. 432.8   rational, because it is a terminating decimal

d. 0.1212 . . .   rational, because it is a repeating decimal

e. 0.120120012 . . .   irrational; it neither terminates nor repeats

f. π irrational; it cannot be represented as $\frac{a}{b}$, where a and b are integers

✔ **Check Understanding**   Example 3

3. Identify each number as rational or irrational. Explain.

    a. $\sqrt{2}$ **b.** $-\sqrt{81}$ **c.** 0.53   **d.** $\sqrt{42}$

EXERCISES

For more exercises, see *Extra Practice*.

Practice and Problem Solving

A **Practice by Example**

Example 1
(page 580)

Simplify each square root.

1. $\sqrt{4}$ 2. $-\sqrt{36}$ 3. $\sqrt{1}$ 4. $\sqrt{25}$

5. $-\sqrt{49}$ 6. $\sqrt{81}$ 7. $-\sqrt{9}$ 8. $-\sqrt{169}$

Example 2
(page 581)

Estimate to the nearest integer.

9. $\sqrt{10}$ 10. $\sqrt{17}$ 11. $-\sqrt{39}$ 12. $-\sqrt{55}$

13. **Viewing Distance** The observation
windows at the top of the Washington
Monument in Washington, D.C.,
are 500 ft high. Using the formula
$d = \sqrt{1.5h}$ of Example 2, estimate the
distance you can see to the horizon
from the observation windows.

Example 3
(page 581)

**Identify each number as rational or
irrational. Explain.**

14. 4.1010010001 . . .   15. $\sqrt{87}$

16. $-\sqrt{16}$ 17. $-0.\overline{3}$

18. $\sqrt{5}$ 19. 2,222,222

20. $\sqrt{144}$ 21. 0.31311 . . .

B **Apply Your Skills**

Simplify each square root.

22. $\sqrt{196}$ 23. $\sqrt{\frac{4}{9}}$ 24. $\sqrt{\frac{25}{49}}$ 25. $\sqrt{\frac{36}{64}}$

Estimate to the nearest integer.

26. $\sqrt{7}$ 27. $\sqrt{2}$ 28. $\sqrt{40}$ 29. $-\sqrt{80}$

30. $\sqrt{58}$ 31. $-\sqrt{98}$ 32. $\sqrt{14}$ 33. $\sqrt{105}$

Identify each number as rational or irrational. Explain.

34. $\sqrt{0}$ 35. 1.001001001 . . .   36. 2.3010010001 . . .

37. **Reasoning** What do you get when you square $\sqrt{x}$?

38. **Writing in Math** A classmate was absent for today's lesson.
Explain to him or her how to estimate $\sqrt{30}$.

39. a. **Patterns** You can create irrational numbers. For example, the
number 1.010010001 . . . shows a pattern, yet it is irrational.
What pattern do you see?
b. **Open-Ended** Name three irrational numbers between 9 and 10.

(Algebra) **Find two integers that make each equation true.**

40. $a^2 = 9$ **41.** $b^2 = 25$ **42.** $y^2 = 100$ **43.** $m^2 = \frac{100}{25}$

44. Geometry Find the length of a side of a square with area 81 cm^2.

45. Geometry The area of a circle is 12 in.^{2}. Estimate its radius to the nearest inch.

If a number is the product of three identical factors, each factor is the *cube root* of the number. Since $2^3 = 8$, 2 is the cube root of 8. In Exercises 46–49, find the number n that makes each equation true.

46. $n^3 = -8$ **47.** $n^3 = 27$ **48.** $n^3 = -27$ **49.** $n^3 = 343$

On your graphing calculator, press MATH 4 to show the cube-root radical $\sqrt[3]{}$. Use it to find each cube root.

50. $\sqrt[3]{-8}$ **51.** $\sqrt[3]{125}$ **52.** $\sqrt[3]{-1{,}331}$ **53.** $\sqrt[3]{15{,}625}$

Test Prep

Multiple Choice

Joe is hiking in national park wilderness. His radio transmits signals as far as the horizon. Use the formula $d = \sqrt{1.5h}$, where d is the line-of-sight distance to the horizon in miles and h is height in feet, to answer the following questions.

Take It to the NET
Online lesson quiz at
www.PHSchool.com
Web Code: ada-1101

54. Joe has the transmitter at a height of 6 ft. About how far is it from the transmitter to the horizon?
A. 3 mi   **B.** 5 mi   **C.** 7 mi   **D.** 9 mi

55. Joe sets his receiver on the ground. What is the farthest away that a transmitter 4 ft above the ground can be in order to reach Joe?
F. 0 mi   **G.** 1.2 mi   **H.** 2.4 mi   **I.** 6 mi

Short Response

56. Joe wants to talk with his base camp that he knows is 6 mi away. **(a)** Explain how Joe could find the height at which he should have the transmitter. **(b)** Find that height.

Mixed Review

Lesson 10-9   **Find the volume of each figure in cubic centimeters.**

57. sphere with $r = 0.03$ m   **58.** cone with $r = 4$ cm, $h = 10$ cm

Lesson 6-5   **59.** Shannon scored 17 correct on a 25-item test. The passing grade was 65%. Did Shannon pass? Explain.

Lesson 4-1   **List the positive factors of each number.**

60. 18   **61.** 22   **62.** 33   **63.** 45   **64.** 50   **65.** 90

11-2 The Pythagorean Theorem

What You'll Learn

 OBJECTIVE 1 To use the Pythagorean Theorem

 OBJECTIVE 2 To identify right triangles

... And Why

To use the Pythagorean Theorem in real-world situations, such as carpentry

✔ **Check Skills You'll Need**

Simplify.

1. $4^2 + 6^2$ 2. $5^2 + 8^2$

3. $7^2 + 9^2$ 4. $9^2 + 3^2$

❓ For help, go to Lesson 4-2.

New Vocabulary

• legs
• hypotenuse

OBJECTIVE

1 Using the Pythagorean Theorem

Investigation

Exploring Right Triangles

1. On graph paper, create right triangles with legs a and b. Measure the length of the third side c with another piece of graph paper.

   Copy and complete the table below.

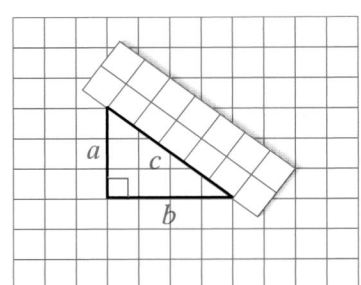

a	b	c	a^2	b^2	c^2
3	4	■	9	16	■
5	12	■	25	144	■
9	12	■	81	144	■

2. Based on your table, use $>$, $<$, or $=$ to complete the following statement.

$$a^2 + b^2 \ \blacksquare\ c^2$$

Need Help?

A right triangle is a triangle with a 90° angle.

In a right triangle, the two shortest sides are **legs.** The longest side, which is opposite the right angle, is the **hypotenuse.** The Pythagorean Theorem shows how the legs and hypotenuse of a right triangle are related.

Key Concepts   **Pythagorean Theorem**

In any right triangle, the sum of the squares of the lengths of the legs is equal to the square of the length of the hypotenuse.

$$a^2 + b^2 = c^2$$

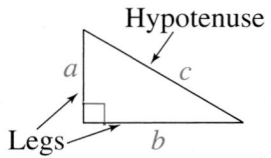

You will prove the Pythagorean Theorem in a future math class. For now, you will use the theorem to find the length of a leg or the length of a hypotenuse.

iTEXT Interactive lesson includes instant self-check, tutorials, and activities.

1 EXAMPLE Using the Pythagorean Theorem

Find c, the length of the hypotenuse, in the triangle at the right.

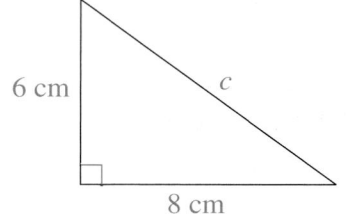

6 cm, 8 cm, c

$c^2 = a^2 + b^2$ Use the Pythagorean Theorem.

$c^2 = 6^2 + 8^2$ Replace a with 6 and b with 8.

$c^2 = 100$ Simplify.

$c = \sqrt{100} = 10$ Find the positive square root of each side.

● The length of the hypotenuse is 10 cm.

✓ Check Understanding Example 1

1. The lengths of two sides of a right triangle are given. Find the length of the third side.

a. legs: 3 ft and 4 ft   **b.** leg: 12 m; hypotenuse: 15 m

You can use a calculator or a table of square roots to find approximate values for square roots.

2 EXAMPLE Finding an Approximate Length

Find the value of x in the triangle at the right. Round to the nearest tenth.

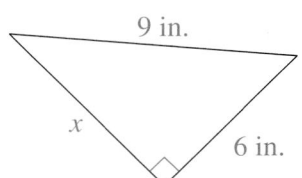

9 in., x, 6 in.

$a^2 + b^2 = c^2$ Use the Pythagorean Theorem.

$6^2 + x^2 = 9^2$ Replace a with 6, b with x, and c with 9.

$36 + x^2 = 81$ Simplify.

$x^2 = 45$ Subtract 36 from each side.

$x = \sqrt{45}$ Find the positive square root of each side.

Then use one of the two methods below to approximate $\sqrt{45}$.

Method 1 Use a calculator.
A calculator value for $\sqrt{45}$ is 𝟨.𝟩𝟢𝟪𝟤𝟢𝟥𝟫.

$x \approx 6.7$ Round to the nearest tenth.

Method 2 Use a table of square roots.
Use the table on page 778. Find 45 in the N column. Then find the corresponding value in the $\sqrt{N}$ column. It is 6.708.

$x \approx 6.7$ Round to the nearest tenth.

● The value of x is about 6.7 in.

✓ Check Understanding Example 2

2. In a right triangle, the length of the hypotenuse is 15 m and the length of a leg is 8 m. What is the length of the other leg, to the nearest tenth of a meter?

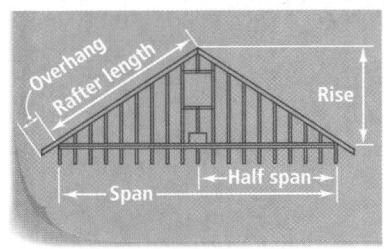

Overhang
Rafter length
Rise
Span
Half span

3 EXAMPLE Real-World Problem Solving

Carpentry The carpentry terms *span, rise,* and *rafter length* are illustrated in the diagram at the left. A carpenter wants to make a roof that has a span of 24 ft and a rise of 8.5 ft. What should the rafter length be?

$c^2 = a^2 + b^2$	Use the Pythagorean Theorem.
$c^2 = 12^2 + 8.5^2$	Use half the span, 12 ft. Replace a with 12 and b with 8.5.
$c^2 = 144 + 72.25$	Square 12 and 8.5.
$c^2 = 216.25$	Add.
$c = \sqrt{216.25}$	Find the positive square root.
$c \approx 14.7$	Round to the nearest tenth.

● The rafter length should be about 14.7 ft.

✓ Check Understanding Example 3

3. **Carpentry** What is the rise of a roof if the span is 22 feet and the rafter length is 14 feet? Round to the nearest tenth of a foot.

OBJECTIVE

2 Identifying Right Triangles

The *Converse of the Pythagorean Theorem* allows you to substitute the lengths of the sides of a triangle into the equation $a^2 + b^2 = c^2$ to check whether a triangle is a right triangle. If the equation is true, the triangle is a right triangle.

4 EXAMPLE Finding a Right Triangle

Is a triangle with sides 12 m, 15 m, and 20 m a right triangle?

$a^2 + b^2 = c^2$	Write the equation for the Pythagorean Theorem.
$12^2 + 15^2 \stackrel{?}{=} 20^2$	Replace a and b with the shorter lengths and c with the longest length.
$144 + 225 \stackrel{?}{=} 400$	Simplify.
$369 \neq 400$	

● The triangle is not a right triangle.

✓ Check Understanding Example 4

4. Can you form a right triangle with the three lengths given? Explain.

   a. 7 in., 8 in., $\sqrt{113}$ in.   **b.** 5 mm, 6 mm, 10 mm

EXERCISES

For more exercises, see *Extra Practice*.

Practice and Problem Solving

A Practice by Example

Examples 1 and 2
(page 585)

In each right triangle, find each missing length to the nearest tenth.

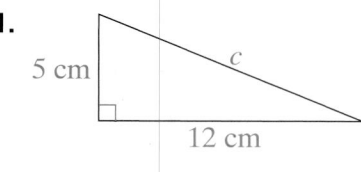

1. 5 cm, 12 cm, c

2. 8 m, 8 m, k

3. 6 in., 10 in., b

4. 6 mm, h, 3 mm

The lengths of two sides of a right triangle are given. Find the length of the third side. Round to the nearest tenth where necessary.

5. legs: 12 in. and 16 in.

6. legs: 21 ft and 28 ft

7. leg: 48 ft; hypotenuse: 50 ft

8. leg: 33 ft; hypotenuse: 55 ft

Example 3
(page 586)

Use the Pythagorean Theorem to solve each problem.

9. **Carpentry** Use the diagram in Example 3 on page 586. A carpenter wants to make a roof that has a rise of 5 ft and a rafter length of 16 ft. What is the half span? The span?

10. **House Painting** A painter places an 11-ft ladder against a house. The base of the ladder is 3 ft from the house. How high on the house does the ladder reach?

11. **Hiking** Darla hikes due north for 6 km. She then turns due east and hikes 3 km. What is the direct distance between her starting point and stopping point, rounded to the nearest tenth of a kilometer?

Example 4
(page 586)

Can you form a right triangle with the three lengths given? Explain.

12. 4 m, 6 m, 7 m

13. 4 mi, 5 mi, 6 mi

14. 7 in., 24 in., 25 in.

15. 6, 7, $\sqrt{85}$

16. 8 in., 10 in., 12 in.

17. 5 cm, 12 cm, 13 cm

B Apply Your Skills

Use the triangle at the right. Find the missing length to the nearest tenth of a unit.

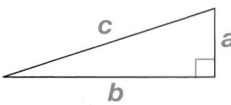

18. $a = 2$ in., $b = 4$ in., $c = $ ▓

19. $a = 1.4$ m, $b = 2.8$ m, $c = $ ▓

20. $a = 3$ ft, $c = 5$ ft, $b = $ ▓

21. $b = 2.7$ km, $c = 3.4$ km, $a = $ ▓

22. **Reasoning** Is a triangle with side lengths of $\sqrt{12}$ cm, $\sqrt{7}$ cm, and $\sqrt{5}$ cm a right triangle? Explain.

Any three positive integers that make $a^2 + b^2 = c^2$ true form a *Pythagorean triple*. Does each group of three integers below form a Pythagorean triple? Show your work.

23. $3, 4, 5$ **24.** $7, 24, 25$ **25.** $10, 24, 25$ **26.** $5, 12, 13$

27. For each group in Exercises 23–26 that forms a Pythagorean triple, multiply the integers by 2. Do the three new numbers form a Pythagorean triple? Show your work.

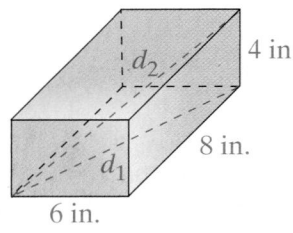

5 ft

2 ft

🌐 **28. Landscaping** Jim works for a landscaping company. He must plant and stake a tree. The stakes are 2 ft from the base of the tree. They are connected to wires that attach to the trunk at a height of 5 ft. If there is 6 in. of extra length at both ends of each wire, how long must each wire be, to the nearest tenth of a foot?

Can you form a right triangle having the three given lengths? Explain.

29. $\sqrt{5}$ yd, $\sqrt{3}$ yd, $\sqrt{2}$ yd   **30.** 1 m, 0.54 m, 0.56 m

🌐 **31. Quilting** The diagonals for a quilting frame must be the same length to ensure the frame is rectangular. What should the lengths of the diagonals be for a quilting frame 86 in. by 100 in.? Draw a sketch and then solve.

32. Writing in Math Can you form a right triangle having side lengths of $3p$ ft, $4p$ ft, and $5p$ ft? Explain.

C Challenge

33. Geometry In the rectangular prism at the left, d_1 is the diagonal of the base of the prism, and d_2 is the *diagonal of the prism*.
  a. Find d_1.
  b. The triangle formed by d_1, d_2, and the side that is 4 in. is a right triangle. Use your answer to part (a) to find d_2.
  c. Find the diagonal of a rectangular prism with dimensions 9 in., 12 in., and 5 in.

d_2

4 in.

8 in.

d_1

6 in.

Find the value of n in each diagram. Give your answer as a square root.

34.
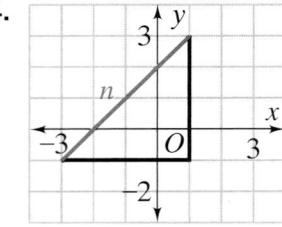

35.
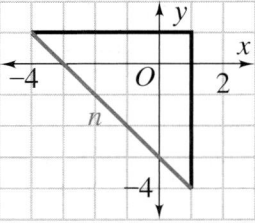

36.
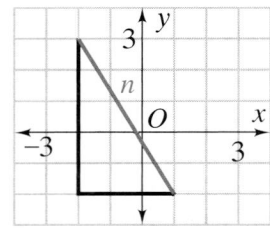

37.
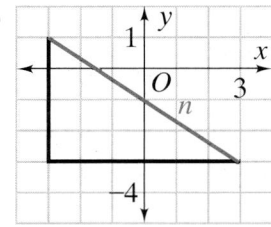

Multiple Choice   For Exercises 38 and 39, the lengths of two sides of a right triangle are given. What is the length of the third side?

38. legs: 36 m and 48 m

    A. 5 m   **B.** 12 m   **C.** 50 m   **D.** 60 m

39. leg: 6 m; hypotenuse: $\sqrt{85}$ m

    F. 7 m   **G.** 8 m   **H.** 9 m   **I.** 10 m

Extended Response   **40. a.** Can segments with lengths 3 ft, 4 ft, and 5 ft form a right triangle? Explain.

    b. Ancient builders are said to have used ropes with 12 equally-spaced knots to make sure that square corners were indeed right angles. How could you use such a rope to determine whether a corner in your room forms a right angle?

    c. Explain your answer in part (b).

Take It to the NET
Online lesson quiz at
www.PHSchool.com
Web Code: ada-1102

Mixed Review

Lesson 11-1   **Identify each number as rational or irrational.**

41. $\sqrt{36}$ **42.** $0.\overline{6}$ **43.** $-\sqrt{12}$ **44.** -33.3 **45.** $0.\overline{654}$

Lesson 5-9   **Simplify each expression.**

46. $(bc)^5$ **47.** $(2x^2)^4$ **48.** $(-3b)^3$ **49.** $(a^5b^2)^4$ **50.** $\left(\dfrac{3m}{5}\right)^2$

Lesson 4-9   **51. Geography** Greenland is the world's largest island and has an area of 2,175,600 km². Express this area in scientific notation.

Math at Work

      Air-Traffic Controller

When we think of airline safety, many of us think of pilots. But there is also a network of people, the air-traffic controllers, who work hard to ensure the safe operation of aircraft. Using radar and visual observation, they closely monitor the location of each plane. They coordinate the movement of air traffic to make certain that aircraft stay a safe distance apart. They also coordinate landings and takeoffs to keep delays at a minimum.

In their jobs, air-traffic controllers use angle measurements in some of the same ways you do when you solve problems in algebra and geometry.

Take It to the NET For more information about air-traffic controllers, go to **www.PHSchool.com**.
Web Code: adb-2031

The Pythagorean Theorem and Circles

For Use With Lesson 11-2

Follow the steps below to discover a characteristic of circle chords and their perpendicular bisectors.

Step 1 With a compass, construct a large circle. Label the center O.

Step 2 Draw a chord $\overline{AB}$ that is not a diameter.

Step 3 Construct the perpendicular bisector of the chord with a compass and straightedge or by folding the circle so that A lies on B.

Step 4 Label the point where the perpendicular bisector intersects the chord as point D.

1. Write a conjecture about the perpendicular bisector of a chord and the center of the circle.

2. Classify $\triangle AOD$ by its angles.

The distance from the center of a circle to a chord is the length of the perpendicular segment with endpoints at the center and on the chord. You can use the radius of a circle and the length of a chord to find the distance from the center of a circle to the chord.

1 EXAMPLE

Circle O has a radius of 10 cm. Chord FG is 12 cm long. $\overline{OM}$ is the perpendicular bisector of $\overline{FG}$. How far is $\overline{FG}$ from O?

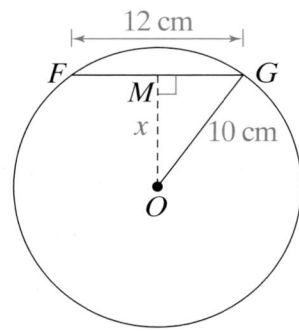

$\triangle OMG$ is a right triangle with legs $\overline{OM}$ and $\overline{MG}$, and hypotenuse $\overline{OG}$.

OM = distance to chord = x

OG = radius = 10 cm

$MG = \frac{1}{2}FG = \frac{1}{2}(12) = 6$

Use the Pythagorean Theorem to find x.

$$OG^2 = OM^2 + MG^2$$
$$10^2 = x^2 + 6^2$$
$$100 = x^2 + 36$$
$$100 - 36 = x^2 + 36 - 36$$
$$64 = x^2$$
$$8 = x$$

The distance from the center to the chord is 8 cm.

Find x, the distance from the center O of each circle to chord $\overline{JK}$. Round to the nearest tenth.

3.
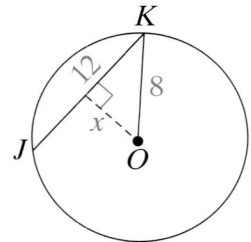

4.
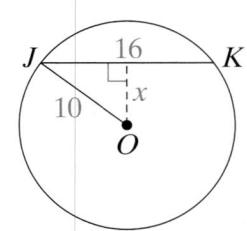

5.
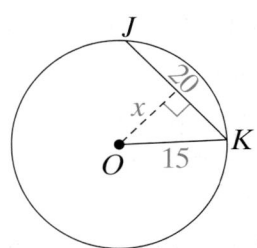

For a given circle, you can also find the length of a chord or the length of the radius if you know two other lengths.

2 EXAMPLE

Chord PT is 24 in. long and 5 in. from the center O of the circle. Find the length of the radius.

Use the Pythagorean Theorem to find the radius r.

$PM = \frac{1}{2}(PT) = 12$
$$r^2 = 12^2 + 5^2$$
$$r^2 = 144 + 25$$
$$r^2 = 169$$
$$r = 13$$

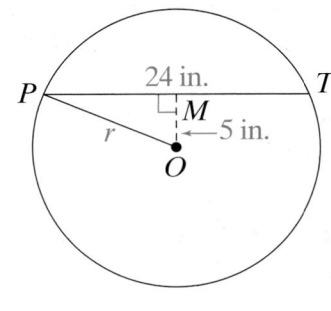

• The radius is 13 in.

Find x. If your answer is not an integer, round to the nearest tenth.

6.
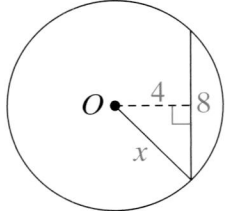

7.
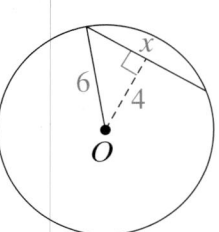

8.
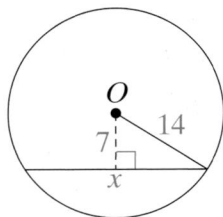

9.
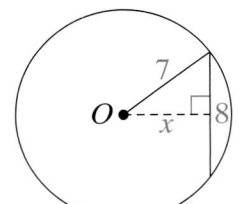

10.
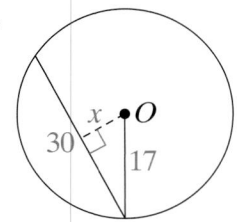

11.
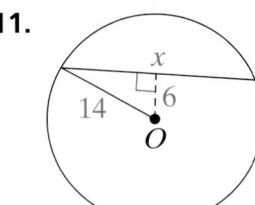

Distance and Midpoint Formulas

OBJECTIVE

1 Finding Distance

OBJECTIVE
1

What You'll Learn

To find the distance between two points using the Distance Formula

To find the midpoint of a segment using the Midpoint Formula

. . . And Why

To find the perimeters of figures on the coordinate plane

✔ **Check Skills You'll Need**

Write the coordinates of each point.

1. A **2.** D **3.** G **4.** J

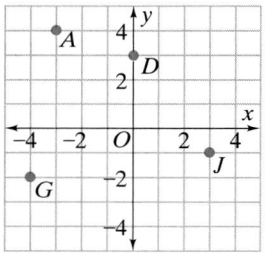

🐾 For help, go to Lesson 1-10.

New Vocabulary

• distance
• midpoint

In the graph at the right, you can locate point $C(7, 1)$ to form a right triangle with points $A(2, 1)$ and $B(7, 3)$. Using the Pythagorean Theorem, you can find AB.

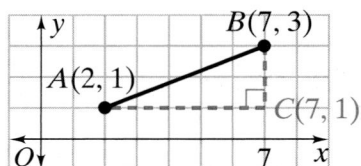

$$(AB)^2 = (AC)^2 + (BC)^2$$

$$(AB)^2 = (7 - 2)^2 + (3 - 1)^2$$ **AC equals the difference in x values.**
BC equals the difference in y values.

$$(AB)^2 = 5^2 + 2^2$$ **Simplify.**

$$AB = \sqrt{25 + 4} = \sqrt{29} \approx 5.4$$ **Find the square root.**

You can use the Pythagorean Theorem to find the length of a segment on a coordinate plane, or you can use the *Distance Formula*. The Distance Formula is based on the Pythagorean Theorem.

Key Concepts   **Distance Formula**

You can find the **distance** d between any two points (x_1, y_1) and (x_2, y_2):

$$d = \sqrt{(x_2 - x_1)^2 + (y_2 - y_1)^2}$$

1 EXAMPLE   Using the Distance Formula

Find the distance between $A(6, 3)$ and $B(1, 9)$.

$$d = \sqrt{(x_2 - x_1)^2 + (y_2 - y_1)^2}$$ **Use the Distance Formula.**

$$d = \sqrt{(1 - 6)^2 + (9 - 3)^2}$$ **Replace (x_2, y_2) with (1, 9) and (x_1, y_1) with (6, 3).**

$$d = \sqrt{(-5)^2 + 6^2}$$ **Simplify.**

$$d = \sqrt{61}$$ **Find the exact distance.**

$$d \approx 7.8$$ **Round to the nearest tenth.**

● The distance between A and B is about 7.8 units.

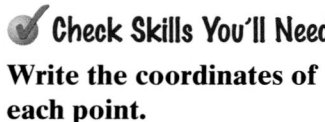Interactive lesson includes instant self-check, tutorials, and activities.

✓ **Check Understanding**   **Example 1**

1. Find the distance between the two points in each pair. Round to the nearest tenth.

a. $(3, 8), (2, 4)$ **b.** $(10, -3), (1, 0)$

You can also use the Distance Formula to solve geometry problems. Wait until the last step to round your answer.

Reading Math

The Distance Formula indicates that you subtract (twice), square (twice), and add before you find the square root.

2 EXAMPLE   **Finding Perimeter**

Find the perimeter of $ABCD$.

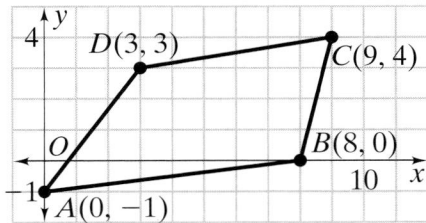

Use the Distance Formula to find the side lengths.

$AB = \sqrt{(8 - 0)^2 + (0 - (-1))^2}$ **Replace** (x_2, y_2) **with (8, 0) and** (x_1, y_1) **with (0, −1).**

$= \sqrt{64 + 1} = \sqrt{65}$ **Simplify.**

$BC = \sqrt{(9 - 8)^2 + (4 - 0)^2}$ **Replace** (x_2, y_2) **with (9, 4) and** (x_1, y_1) **with (8, 0).**

$= \sqrt{1 + 16} = \sqrt{17}$ **Simplify.**

$CD = \sqrt{(3 - 9)^2 + (3 - 4)^2}$ **Replace** (x_2, y_2) **with (3, 3) and** (x_1, y_1) **with (9, 4).**

$= \sqrt{36 + 1} = \sqrt{37}$ **Simplify.**

$DA = \sqrt{(0 - 3)^2 + ((-1) - 3)^2}$ **Replace** (x_2, y_2) **with (0, −1) and** (x_1, y_1) **with (3, 3).**

$= \sqrt{9 + 16} = \sqrt{25} = 5$ **Simplify.**

perimeter $= \sqrt{65} + \sqrt{17} + \sqrt{37} + 5 \approx 23.268126$

● The perimeter is about 23.3 units.

✓ **Check Understanding**   **Example 2**

2. Find the perimeter of $\triangle DEF$ at the right. Round to the nearest tenth.

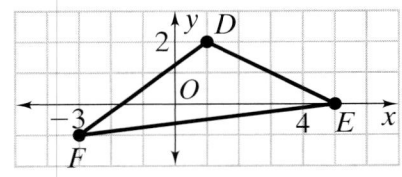

The **midpoint** of a segment $\overline{AB}$ is the point M on $\overline{AB}$ halfway between the endpoints A and B where $AM = MB$.

Key Concepts **Midpoint Formula**

You can find the midpoint of a line segment with endpoints $A(x_1, y_1)$ and $B(x_2, y_2)$:

$$M\left(\frac{x_1 + x_2}{2}, \frac{y_1 + y_2}{2}\right)$$

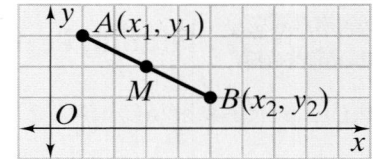

---

3 **EXAMPLE** **Finding the Midpoint of a Segment**

Find the midpoint of $\overline{GH}$.

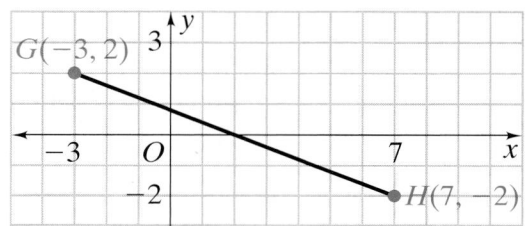

$$\left(\frac{x_1 + x_2}{2}, \frac{y_1 + y_2}{2}\right)$$ **Use the Midpoint Formula.**

$$= \left(\frac{-3 + 7}{2}, \frac{2 + (-2)}{2}\right)$$ **Replace (x_1, y_1) with $(-3, 2)$ and (x_2, y_2) with $(7, -2)$.**

$$= \left(\frac{4}{2}, \frac{0}{2}\right)$$ **Simplify the numerators.**

$$= (2, 0)$$ **Write the fractions in simplest form.**

● The coordinates of the midpoint of $\overline{GH}$ are $(2, 0)$.

✓ Check Understanding   **Example 3**

3. Find the midpoint of each segment.

a. 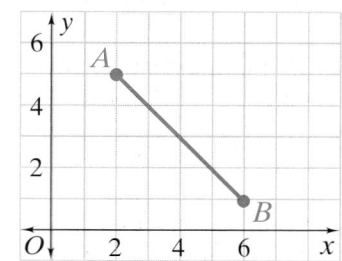   **b.**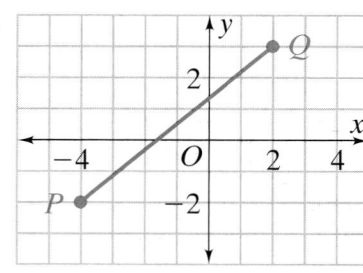

EXERCISES

For more exercises, see *Extra Practice*.

Practice and Problem Solving

A Practice by Example

Example 1
(page 592)

Find the distance between the two points of each pair. Round to the nearest tenth.

1. $(1, 5), (5, 2)$

2. $(6, 0), (-6, 5)$

3. $(-5, 10), (11, -7)$

4. $(-6, 12), (-3, -7)$

5. $(8, -1), (-5, 11)$

6. $(12, 3), (-12, 4)$

Example 2
(page 593)

Geometry Find the perimeter of each figure.

7.

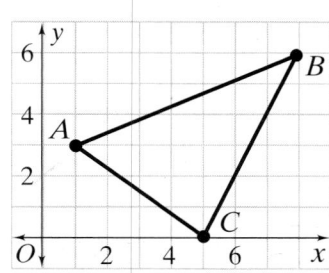

8.

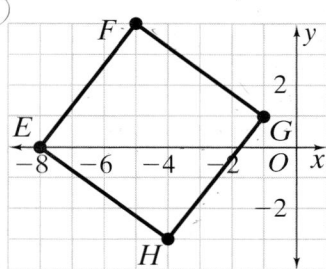

Example 3
(page 594)

Find the midpoint of each segment.

9.

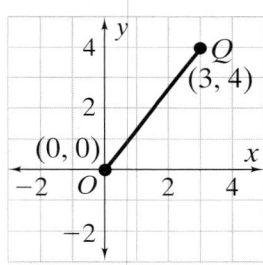

10.

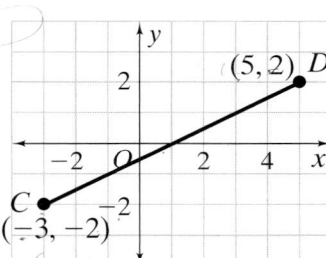

B Apply Your Skills

For Exercises 11 and 12, find both the length and the midpoint of the segment joining the two given points. Round to the nearest tenth.

11. $S(9, 12)$ and $U(-9, -12)$

12. $K(23, 4)$ and $W(-2, 16)$

13. **Error Analysis** A student's calculation of the midpoint of the segment with endpoints $A(-4, 2)$ and $B(6, 6)$ is shown at the right. What mistake did the student make?

$$\left(\frac{(6-(-4))}{2}, \frac{(6-2)}{2}\right)$$
$$= \left(\frac{10}{2}, \frac{4}{2}\right)$$
$$= (5, 2)$$

14. **Reasoning** The midpoint of $\overline{AB}$ is $(3, 5)$. The coordinates of A are $(-6, 1)$. What are the coordinates of B?

When you use the indicated formula, does it matter which point you choose as (x_1, y_1)? Explain.

15. the Midpoint Formula

16. the Distance Formula

Writing in Math

For help with writing a solution for Exercise 17, see page 597.

17. A segment has endpoints $A(-3, 5)$ and $B(2, 1)$.
   a. Find the midpoint M of the segment.
   b. Use the Distance Formula to verify that $AM = MB$.

11-3 Distance and Midpoint Formulas **595**

18. Geometry The three vertices of a triangle have coordinates $P(-3, 1)$, $Q(2, -5)$, and $R(4, 6)$. Determine whether the triangle is scalene, isosceles, or equilateral. Show your work.

19. Writing in Math Explain how using the Midpoint Formula involves finding averages.

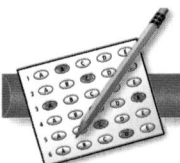

Test Prep

Gridded Response

Use the diagram for Exercises 20 and 21.

20. What is the number of square units in the square?

21. What is the perimeter of the square, to the nearest tenth?

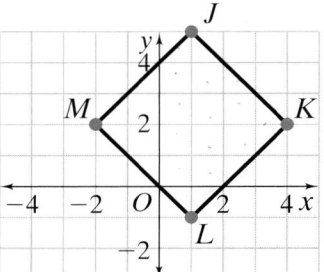

22. What is the length, to the nearest tenth, of the segment whose endpoints are $A(3, 7)$ and $B(8, 21)$?

Take It to the NET
Online lesson quiz at
www.PHSchool.com
Web Code: ada-1103

Mixed Review

Lesson 11-2   **Can you form a right triangle with the lengths given?**

23. 8 m, 15 m, 17 m   **24.** 5 in., 8 in., 5 in.   **25.** 20 yd, 12 yd, 16 yd

Lesson 10-4   **26. Geometry** Draw a net to represent a rectangular prism that is 4 in. long, 3 in. wide, and 2 in. high. Label dimensions on the net.

Lesson 6-2   **Solve each proportion.**

27. $\frac{3}{8} = \frac{a}{24}$ **28.** $\frac{11}{c} = \frac{66}{72}$ **29.** $\frac{5}{6} = \frac{n}{15}$ **30.** $\frac{b}{1.9} = \frac{7}{9.5}$

 Checkpoint Quiz 1   **Lessons 11-1 through 11-3**

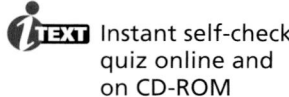 Instant self-check quiz online and on CD-ROM

Estimate to the nearest integer.

1. $-\sqrt{3}$ **2.** $\sqrt{14}$ **3.** $\sqrt{27}$ **4.** $\sqrt{90}$ **5.** $-\sqrt{45}$ **6.** $\sqrt{105}$

The lengths of two legs of a right triangle are given. Find the length of the hypotenuse. Round to the nearest tenth.

7. 6 ft, 8 ft   **8.** 8 m, 14 m   **9.** 7 yd, 24 yd   **10.** 5 cm, 5 cm

Find the length of $\overline{AB}$ and the midpoint of $\overline{AB}$. Round the length of $\overline{AB}$ to the nearest tenth.

11. $A(0, -2)$ and $B(-6, -9)$ **12.** $A(8, 11)$ and $B(-5, 2)$

13. Open-Ended Name three irrational numbers between 10 and 20.

One way to justify your solution of a problem is to give a reason for each step you take, keeping in mind the persons who will read your work. Acceptable reasons include properties and procedures that you and your audience have agreed upon.

EXAMPLE

A segment has endpoints $A(-3, 5)$ and $B(2, 1)$.
a. Find the midpoint M of the segment.
b. Use the Distance Formula to verify that $AM = MB$.

a. First find the midpoint of $\overline{AB}$.

Steps	Reasons
$\left(\dfrac{-3 + 2}{2}, \dfrac{5 + 1}{2}\right)$	**Use the Midpoint Formula. Replace (x_1, y_1) with $(-3, 5)$ and (x_2, y_2) with $(2, 1)$.**
$\left(-\dfrac{1}{2}, 3\right)$ or $(-0.5, 3)$	**Simplify.**

b. Next verify that this is the midpoint M by showing that $AM = MB$.

Steps	Reasons
$AM = \sqrt{(-0.5 - (-3))^2 + (3 - 5)^2}$	**Find AM. Use the Distance Formula.**
$AM = \sqrt{10.25}$	**Simplify.**
$MB = \sqrt{(2 - (-0.5))^2 + (1 - 3)^2}$	**Find MB. Use the Distance Formula.**
$MB = \sqrt{10.25}$	**Simplify.**

Since AM and MB are both $\sqrt{10.25}$, $AM = MB$ and $(-0.5, 3)$ is the midpoint of $\overline{AB}$.

EXERCISES

Solve each problem. Justify your steps to verify your answer.

1. Find the perimeter of the triangle with vertices located at $(5, 9)$, $(7, 4)$, and $(-3, 7)$.

2. The vertices of a triangle are located at $(-1, 5)$, $(2, 5)$, and $(2, 1)$. Show that this is a right triangle. (*Hint:* Use the Distance Formula and the Converse of the Pythagorean Theorem.)

Write a Proportion

What You'll Learn

OBJECTIVE
1 To write a
proportion from
similar triangles

. . . And Why

To solve problems of
unknown distance

✔ **Check Skills You'll Need**

Solve each proportion.

1. $\frac{1}{3} = \frac{a}{12}$ **2.** $\frac{h}{5} = \frac{20}{25}$

3. $\frac{1}{4} = \frac{8}{x}$ **4.** $\frac{2}{7} = \frac{c}{35}$

🔎 For help, go to Lesson 6-2.

Math Strategies in Action You can't measure distance across the
Grand Canyon with a tape measure. Yet, distances across it have been
measured. How were they measured?

Surveyors sometimes find such distances indirectly using similar
triangles and proportions. You learned about these in Lessons 6-2
and 6-3. Now let's see how you can use similar right triangles and
proportions to find measurements indirectly.

1 **EXAMPLE** **Real-World** 🌐 **Problem Solving**

Surveying To find the distance from Q to P across a canyon, a
surveyor picks points R and S such that $\overline{RS}$ is perpendicular to $\overline{RP}$.
He locates point T on $\overline{SP}$ such that $\overline{QT}$ is perpendicular to $\overline{RP}$. The
two triangles, $\triangle PRS$ and $\triangle PQT$, are similar. He then measures $\overline{RS}$,
$\overline{RQ}$, and $\overline{QT}$. What is the distance QP across the canyon?

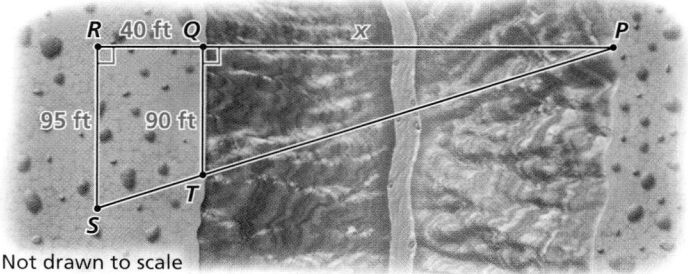

Not drawn to scale

Test-Taking Tip

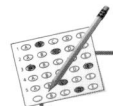

If problems involving
distance do not include
diagrams, draw your
own to help you solve
the problem.

Read and Understand

1. What information is given?

2. What are you asked to find?

🅘 **TEXT** Interactive lesson
includes instant self-check,
tutorials, and activities.

Plan and Solve

Since $\triangle PQT \sim \triangle PRS$ and you know three lengths, writing and solving a proportion is a good strategy to use. It is helpful to draw the triangles as separate figures.

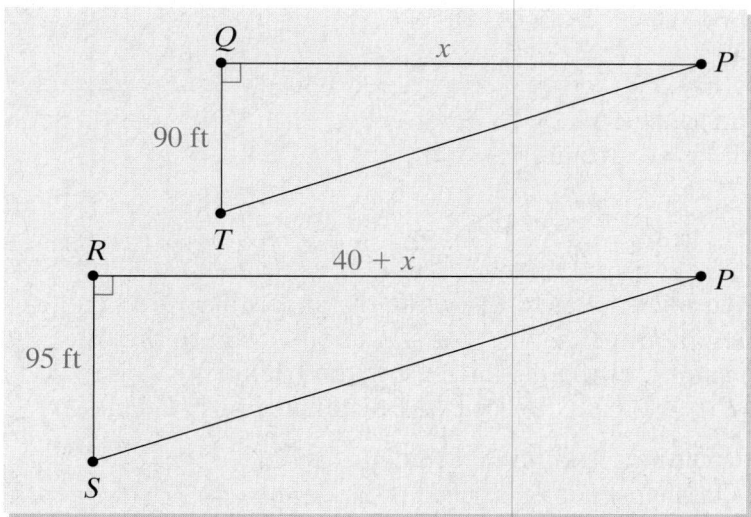

Write a proportion using the legs of the similar right triangles.

$$\frac{x}{40 + x} = \frac{90}{95} \qquad \text{Write a proportion.}$$

$$95x = 90(40 + x) \qquad \text{Write cross products.}$$

$$95x = 3,600 + 90x \qquad \text{Use the Distributive Property.}$$

$$5x = 3,600 \qquad \text{Subtract 90x from each side.}$$

$$x = 720 \qquad \text{Divide each side by 5.}$$

The distance QP across the canyon is 720 ft.

Look Back and Check

Solving problems that involve indirect measurement often makes use of figures that *overlap*. Use the diagram on page 598 to answer the following questions.

✓ Check Understanding

3. Which segments overlap?

4. A common error students make is to use part of a side in a proportion. For example, some students might think $\frac{40}{95}$ is equal to $\frac{x}{90}$. How does drawing the triangles as separate figures help you avoid this error?

EXERCISES

For more exercises, see *Extra Practice*.

Practice and Problem Solving

A Practice by Example

Example 1
(page 598)

In Exercises 1–5, write a proportion and find the value of each *x*.

1. $\triangle ABE \sim \triangle ACD$

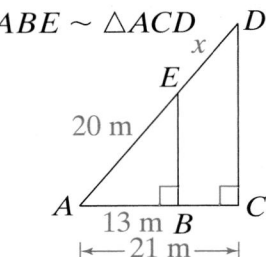

2. $\triangle GHI \sim \triangle KJI$

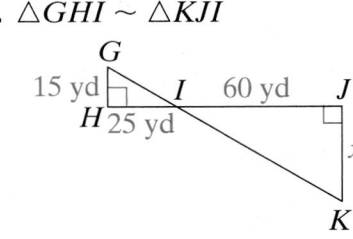

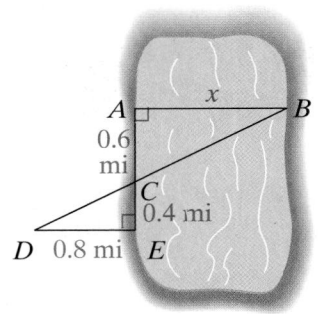

3. A swimmer needs to know the distance *x* across a lake (at left) to help her decide whether it is safe to swim to the other side. She estimates the distance using the triangles shown. $\triangle ABC \sim \triangle EDC$. What is the distance across the lake?

4. Landscaping A landscaper needs to find the distance *x* across a piece of land. She estimates the distance using the similar triangles at the right. What is the distance?

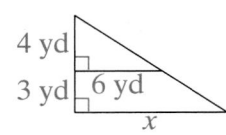

B Apply Your Skills

5. Indirect Measurement To estimate the height of a tree, Milton positions a mirror on the ground so he can see the top of the tree reflected in it. His height, his distance from the mirror, and his line of sight to the mirror determine a triangle. The tree's height, its distance from the mirror, and the distance from the top of the tree to the mirror form a similar triangle. Use the measurements shown to determine the height of the tree.

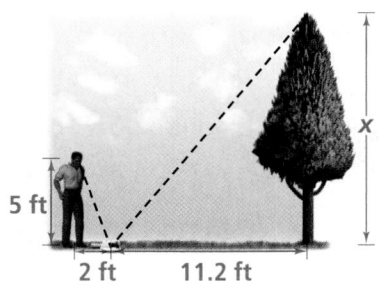

Strategies

- Account for All Possibilities
- Draw a Diagram
- Look for a Pattern
- Make a Model
- Make a Table
- Simplify the Problem
- Simulate the Problem
- Solve by Graphing
- Try, Test, Revise
- Use Multiple Strategies
- Work Backward
- Write an Equation
- Write a Proportion

Solve using any strategy.

6. There are 30 students in a math class. Twelve belong to the computer club, and eight belong to the photography club. Three belong to both clubs. How many belong to neither club?

7. Jake spent $\frac{3}{8}$ of his money on a book and $\frac{1}{2}$ of what was left on a magazine. He now has $6.25. How much money did he start with?

8. Hai takes 12 minutes to walk to school. He wants to get there 15 minutes early to meet with his lab partner. What time should he leave his house if school starts at 8:10 A.M.?

9. Number Sense Christa thought of a number. She added 4, multiplied the sum by −5, and subtracted 12. She then doubled the result and got −34. What number did Christa start with?

Real-World 🌐 **Connection**

The Eiffel Tower was named for its designer, Gustave Eiffel, who also designed the Statue of Liberty framework.

10. The height of the Eiffel Tower is 984 ft. A souvenir model of the tower is 6 in. tall. At 5 P.M. in Paris, the shadow of the souvenir model is 8 in. long. The Eiffel Tower and its shadow determine two legs of a right triangle that are similar to the two legs of a right triangle determined by the souvenir model and its shadow. About how long is the shadow of the Eiffel Tower?

🌐 11. **Architecture** Madison Square Garden in New York City is built in the shape of a circle. Its diameter is 404 ft and it accommodates 20,234 spectators. To the nearest tenth of a square foot, how much area is there for each spectator?

12. **Algebra** You serve a tennis ball from one end of a tennis court, 39 ft from the net. You hit the ball at 9 feet above the ground. It travels in a straight path down the middle of the court, and just clears the top of the 3-ft net. This is illustrated in the diagram. $\triangle PQR \sim \triangle MQS$. How far from the net does the ball land?

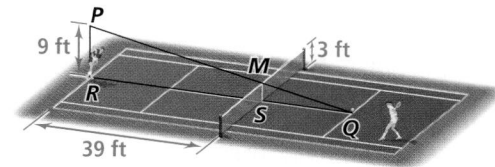

Test Prep

Multiple Choice

13. In the diagram at the right, what is x?
    A. 43.75   B. 28
    C. 26.25   D. 17

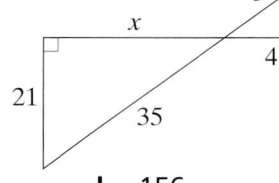

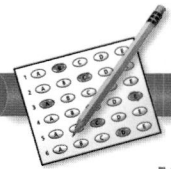

Take It to the NET
Online lesson quiz at
www.PHSchool.com
Web Code: ada-1104

14. What is the value of x in this proportion, $\frac{65}{50} = \frac{x + 36}{x}$?
    F. 15   G. 60   H. 120   I. 156

Short Response

15. Suppose a friend says to you "x is to $x + 1.5$ as 64 is to 72."
    a. Write a proportion to solve for x.
    b. Solve your proportion.

Mixed Review

Lesson 11-3

Find the midpoint of each segment with given endpoints.

16. $A(2, 3)$ and $B(4, 7)$ 17. $L(-1, 2)$ and $M(2, 6)$

Lessons 9-3

Sketch each figure.

18. isosceles right triangle   19. scalene obtuse triangle

Lesson 7-4 🌐 20. **Fundraising** Keith collected twice as much money as Lucy for a walkathon. Together they collected $120. How much money did each person collect?

11-5 Special Right Triangles

What You'll Learn

 OBJECTIVE 1 To use the relationships in 45°-45°-90° triangles

 OBJECTIVE 2 To use the relationships in 30°-60°-90° triangles

...And Why

To find distances in real-world situations, such as in sports

✔ Check Skills You'll Need

Find the missing side of each right triangle.

1. legs: 6 m and 8 m

2. leg: 9 m; hypotenuse: 15 m

3. legs: 27 m and 36 m

4. leg: 48 m; hypotenuse: 60 m

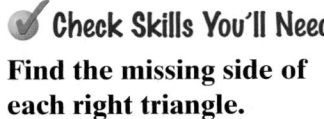 For help, go to Lesson 11-2.

OBJECTIVE

1 Using 45°-45°-90° Triangles

The Pythagorean Theorem requires that you understand square roots. The rule for Multiplying Square Roots will help you work with square roots more efficiently.

| Key Concepts | Multiplying Square Roots |

For nonnegative numbers, the square root of a product equals the product of the square roots.

Arithmetic

$$\sqrt{9 \cdot 2} = \sqrt{9} \cdot \sqrt{2}$$

Algebra

If $a \geq 0$ and $b \geq 0$, then $\sqrt{ab} = \sqrt{a} \cdot \sqrt{b}$.

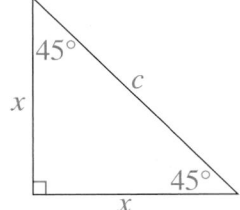

The rule for Multiplying Square Roots is especially useful with an isosceles right triangle, which is also known by its angle measures as a 45°-45°-90° triangle. You can use the rule to relate the lengths of the sides and the hypotenuse in such a triangle.

$c^2 = a^2 + b^2$	**Use the Pythagorean Theorem.**
$c^2 = x^2 + x^2$	**Replace a and b with x.**
$c^2 = 2x^2$	**Simplify.**
$c = \sqrt{2x^2}$	**Find the square root.**
$c = \sqrt{2} \cdot \sqrt{x^2}$	**Use the rule for Multiplying Square Roots.**
$c = \sqrt{2} \cdot x$, or $x\sqrt{2}$	**Simplify.**

This shows the following special relationship.

| Key Concepts | 45°-45°-90° Triangles |

In a 45°-45°-90° triangle, the legs are congruent and the length of the hypotenuse is the length of a leg times $\sqrt{2}$.

hypotenuse = leg $\cdot \sqrt{2}$

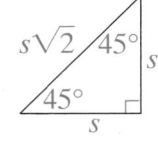

iTEXT Interactive lesson includes instant self-check, tutorials, and activities.

 **EXAMPLE** **Finding Length of the Hypotenuse**

Find the length of the hypotenuse in the triangle at the right.

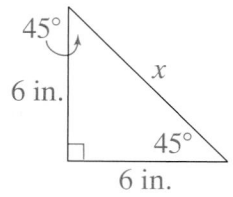

$$\text{hypotenuse} = \text{leg} \cdot \sqrt{2} \qquad \text{Use the 45°-45°-90° relationship.}$$
$$x = 6 \cdot \sqrt{2} \qquad \text{The length of the leg is 6.}$$
$$\approx 8.5 \qquad \text{Use a calculator.}$$

● The length of the hypotenuse is about 8.5 in.

✓ **Check Understanding** **Example 1**

1. The length of each leg of an isosceles right triangle is 4.2 cm. Find the length of the hypotenuse. Round to the nearest tenth.

You can use 45°-45°-90° triangles in real-world situations.

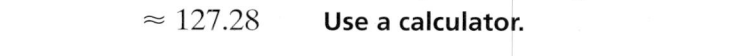 **EXAMPLE** **Real-World** 🌐 **Problem Solving**

Baseball **A baseball diamond is a square. The distance from any base to the next is 90 ft. How far is it from home plate to second base?**

$$\text{hypotenuse} = \text{leg} \cdot \sqrt{2} \qquad \text{Use the 45°-45°-90° relationship.}$$
$$= 90 \cdot \sqrt{2} \qquad \text{The length of the leg is 90.}$$
$$\approx 127.28 \qquad \text{Use a calculator.}$$

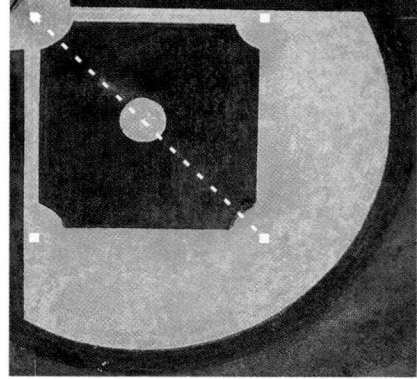

● The distance from home plate to second base is about 127 ft.

✓ **Check Understanding** **Example 2**

2. Gymnasts use mats that are 12 m by 12 m for floor exercises. A gymnast does cartwheels across the diagonal of a mat. What is the length of the diagonal to the nearest meter?

OBJECTIVE

 **Using 30°-60°-90° Triangles**

Another special right triangle is the 30°-60°-90° triangle. You can form two congruent 30°-60°-90° triangles by bisecting an angle of an equilateral triangle. This is shown in the diagram.

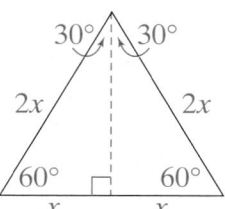

In the diagram, the length of the hypotenuse of each 30°-60°-90° triangle is twice the length of the shorter leg. You can use the Pythagorean Theorem to find the length of the longer leg.

For the figure at the right, find the length of the longer leg.

$(2x)^2 = x^2 + b^2$ **Use the Pythagorean Theorem.**

$4x^2 = x^2 + b^2$ **Simplify.**

$3x^2 = b^2$ **Subtract x^2 from each side.**

$\sqrt{3x^2} = b$ **Find the square root.**

$\sqrt{3} \cdot \sqrt{x^2} = b$ **Rule for Multiplying Square Roots**

$b = \sqrt{3} \cdot x$, or $x\sqrt{3}$ **Simplify.**

This shows the special relationship of the hypotenuse and the legs in a 30°-60°-90° triangle.

Key Concepts   **30°-60°-90° Triangle**

In a 30°-60°-90° triangle, the length of the hypotenuse is 2 times the length of the shorter leg. The length of the longer leg is the length of the shorter leg times $\sqrt{3}$.

hypotenuse = 2 · shorter leg

longer leg = shorter leg · $\sqrt{3}$

---

3 EXAMPLE   **Finding Lengths in a 30°-60°-90° Triangle**

Find the missing lengths in the triangle.

hypotenuse = 2 · shorter leg

$x = 2 \cdot 5$ **The length of the shorter leg is 5.**

$x = 10$ **Simplify.**

longer leg = shorter leg · $\sqrt{3}$

$y = 5 \cdot \sqrt{3}$ **The length of the shorter leg is 5.**

$y \approx 8.7$ **Use a calculator.**

The length of the hypotenuse is 10 ft, and the length of the longer leg is about 8.7 ft.

✓ **Check Understanding**   **Example 3**

3. Find the missing lengths in each 30°-60°-90° triangle.

a.
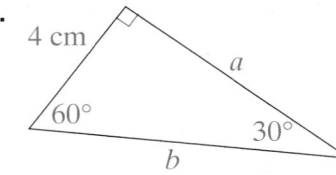

b.
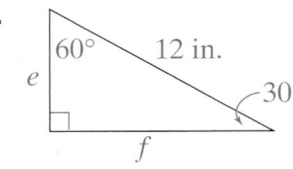

EXERCISES

For more exercises, see *Extra Practice*.

Practice and Problem Solving

A Practice by Example

Example 1
(page 603)

The lengths of the legs of an isosceles right triangle are given. Find the length of each hypotenuse to the nearest tenth.

1.
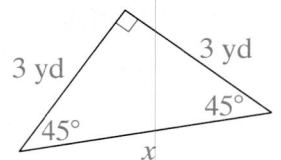

2.
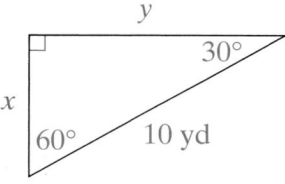

3. legs: 5.4 in.　　　**4.** legs: 17 ft　　　**5.** legs: 21 m

Example 2
(page 603)

6. Ballet A ballet teacher wants to divide his square classroom in half diagonally with masking tape. How much tape will he need if the side length of the classroom is 40 ft?

7. Flooring A square piece of tile with sides 12 in. is cut along a diagonal. What is the length of the diagonal rounded to the nearest inch?

Example 3
(page 604)

Find the missing lengths. Round to the nearest tenth.

8.
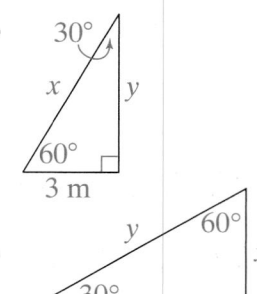

9.
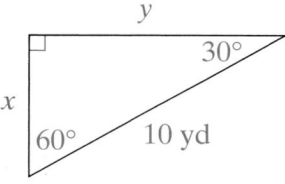

B Apply Your Skills

10.
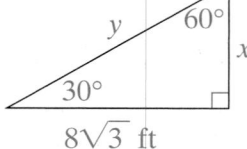

11.
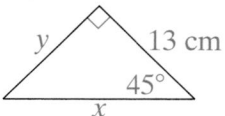

12. Error Analysis A student says that a right triangle with a hypotenuse of length $2\sqrt{2}$ in. has to be an isosceles right triangle. What mistake might the student have made?

13. Writing in Math Explain how to find the lengths of the longer leg and hypotenuse of a 30°-60°-90° triangle if the shorter leg is 10 ft.

14. Mrs. Fernandez wants to string a rope diagonally across her square classroom for her students to hang their completed art projects. If one side of the room measures 20 ft, what is the minimum length of rope she can use?

Simplify. Use the rule for Multiplying Square Roots.

15. $\sqrt{3} \cdot \sqrt{27}$　　　**16.** $\sqrt{50} \cdot \sqrt{2}$　　　**17.** $\sqrt{36} \cdot \sqrt{4}$

C Challenge

18. Reasoning The smaller angles of a 30°-60°-90° triangle are in the ratio 1:2. Are the shorter sides also in the ratio 1:2? Explain.

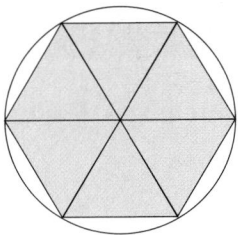

19. Geometry A polygon is inscribed in a circle if all of its vertices lie on the circle. To find the area of the hexagon inscribed in a circle with a diameter of 8 in., answer each of the following.
  a. The segments shown form 6 congruent equilateral triangles. What is the length of each side of each triangle?
  b. What is the height of one triangle?
  c. What is the area of one triangle?
  d. What is the area of the hexagon?

20. Geometry You can inscribe a regular hexagon in a circle using a compass and straightedge.
  a. Use your compass to construct a circle. Keep the compass at the same setting. Place the tip of the compass on the circle. Mark an arc on the circle. Place the tip of the compass where the arc intersects the circle and mark another arc. Continue around the circle until you have six arcs on the circle. Join consecutive arcs with segments.
  b. Measure the diameter of the circle. Use this measure and Exercise 19 to find the area of your hexagon.

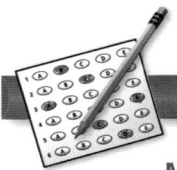

Writing in Math

Sketch a 45°-45°-90° triangle. Use x for the length of one leg. Explain how to find the lengths of the other sides of the triangle.

Test Prep

Multiple Choice

21. In the triangle at the right, what is x, to the nearest tenth?
  A. 8.7   **B.** 8   **C.** 5.7   **D.** 2

22. In a 30°-60°-90° triangle, the length of the longer leg is 10. What is the length of the hypotenuse, to the nearest tenth?
  F. 5.0   **G.** 5.8   **H.** 11.5   **I.** 17.3

Short Response

In Exercises 23–25, **(a)** tell whether a triangle with sides of the given lengths could be 45°-45°-90° or 30°-60°-90°. **(b)** Explain your answers.

23. 6, 8, 10   **24.** 5, 5, $5\sqrt{2}$ **25.** 15, $7.5\sqrt{3}$, 7.5

Mixed Review

Lesson 11-4

26. Surveying A surveyor needs to find the distance across a lake. He estimates the distance using the similar triangles at the right. What is the distance?

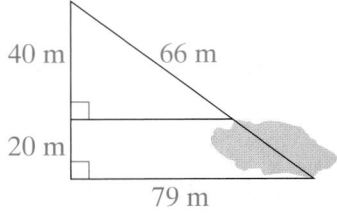

Lesson 9-6

Find the circumference of each circle with the given radius or diameter.

27. radius = 4 in.   **28.** diameter = 6 m   **29.** radius = 2.5 ft

Lesson 8-1

Is each relation a function? Explain.

30. $\{(-1, 3), (0, 4), (1, 5)\}$ **31.** $\{(2, 3), (3, 4), (4, 5), (5, 6)\}$

Square Roots of Expressions With Variables

For Use With Lesson 11-5

You can simplify square roots of expressions that contain variables. Assume that the value of each variable is not negative.

1 EXAMPLE

Write each square root without a radical sign.

a. $\sqrt{25x^2}$

$\sqrt{25x^2} = \sqrt{(5x)^2}$ **Write $25x^2$ as the square of $5x$.**

$= 5x$ **Simplify.**

b. $\sqrt{p^6}$

$\sqrt{p^6} = \sqrt{(p^3)^2}$ **Use the rule for the Power of a Power.**

$= p^3$ **Simplify.**

You can also simplify expressions that have nonsquare factors by using the rule for Multiplying Square Roots.

2 EXAMPLE

Simplify each square root.

a. $\sqrt{x^9}$

$\sqrt{x^9} = \sqrt{x^8 \cdot x}$ **Use the rule for Multiplying Powers with the Same Base.**

$= \sqrt{x^8} \cdot \sqrt{x}$ **Use the rule for Multiplying Square Roots.**

$= x^4 \sqrt{x}$ **Simplify.**

b. $\sqrt{48x}$

$\sqrt{48x} = \sqrt{16 \cdot 3x}$ **Find a perfect square factor.**

$= \sqrt{16} \cdot \sqrt{3x}$ **Use the rule for Multiplying Square Roots.**

$= 4\sqrt{3x}$ **Simplify.**

EXERCISES

Write each square root without the radical sign.

1. $\sqrt{49y^2}$ **2.** $\sqrt{100m^{12}}$ **3.** $-\sqrt{25x^6}$ **4.** $\sqrt{a^2b^{10}}$ **5.** $-\sqrt{169w^{26}}$

Simplify each square root.

6. $\sqrt{a^{12}}$ **7.** $\sqrt{36x^4}$ **8.** $\sqrt{81b^8}$ **9.** $-\sqrt{64a^{16}}$ **10.** $-\sqrt{x^4y^{12}}$

11. $\sqrt{c^7}$ **12.** $\sqrt{x^{23}}$ **13.** $-\sqrt{20m}$ **14.** $\sqrt{27b^{11}}$ **15.** $-\sqrt{72a^{19}}$

Sine, Cosine, and Tangent Ratios

✔ **Check Skills You'll Need**

Solve each problem.

1. A 6-ft man casts an 8-ft shadow while a nearby flagpole casts a 20-ft shadow. How tall is the flagpole?

2. When a 12-ft tall building casts a 22-ft shadow, how long is the shadow of a nearby 14-ft tree?

 For help, go to Lesson 6-3.

New Vocabulary

- trigonometry
- trigonometric ratio
- sine
- cosine
- tangent

OBJECTIVE

1 Finding Ratios in Right Triangles

Investigation

Exploring Ratios in Similar Right Triangles

1. In the diagram at the right, $\triangle PQR \sim \triangle XYZ$. Find the length of the hypotenuse of each triangle.

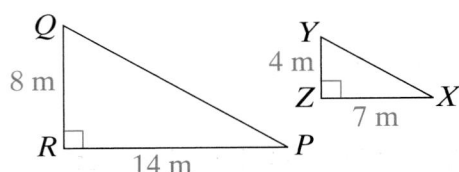

2. In the triangles above, $\angle P$ is the smallest angle of $\triangle PQR$ and $\angle X$ is the smallest angle of $\triangle XYZ$. For each figure, write the following ratios in simplest form.

a. $\dfrac{\text{length of leg opposite smallest angle}}{\text{length of hypotenuse}}$

b. $\dfrac{\text{length of leg adjacent to smallest angle}}{\text{length of hypotenuse}}$

c. $\dfrac{\text{length of leg opposite smallest angle}}{\text{length of leg adjacent to smallest angle}}$

3. What do you notice about the two ratios you wrote for each part of Question 2?

The word **trigonometry** means triangle measure. The ratio of the lengths of two sides of a right triangle is a **trigonometric ratio.** To write trigonometric ratios, you must identify sides that are opposite and adjacent to the acute angles of a triangle.

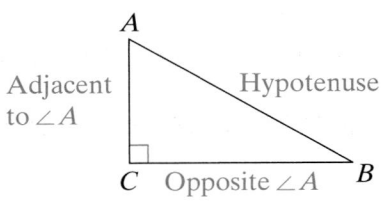

Trigonometric Ratios

sine $\angle A = \dfrac{\text{length of leg opposite } \angle A}{\text{length of hypotenuse}} = \dfrac{CB}{AB}$

cosine $\angle A = \dfrac{\text{length of leg adjacent to } \angle A}{\text{length of hypotenuse}} = \dfrac{AC}{AB}$

tangent $\angle A = \dfrac{\text{length of leg opposite } \angle A}{\text{length of leg adjacent to } \angle A} = \dfrac{CB}{AC}$

You can use these abbreviations when you find trigonometric ratios for a given acute $\angle N$.

$$\sin N = \frac{\text{opposite}}{\text{hypotenuse}} \qquad \cos N = \frac{\text{adjacent}}{\text{hypotenuse}} \qquad \tan N = \frac{\text{opposite}}{\text{adjacent}}$$

Reading Math

The abbreviations for sine, cosine, and tangent are sin, cos, and tan, respectively.

1 EXAMPLE Writing Trigonometric Ratios

For $\triangle XYZ$, find the sine, cosine, and tangent of $\angle X$.

$$\sin X = \frac{\text{opposite}}{\text{hypotenuse}} = \frac{5}{13}$$

$$\cos X = \frac{\text{adjacent}}{\text{hypotenuse}} = \frac{12}{13}$$

$$\tan X = \frac{\text{opposite}}{\text{adjacent}} = \frac{5}{12}$$

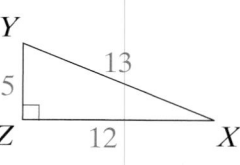

✓ Check Understanding Example 1

1. For $\triangle XYZ$ above, find the sine, cosine, and tangent of $\angle Y$.

Trigonometric ratios are usually expressed in decimal form as approximations. If you know the measure of an acute angle of a right triangle, you can use a calculator or a table of trigonometric ratios to find approximate values for the sine, cosine, and tangent of the angle.

2 EXAMPLE Using a Calculator

Find the trigonometric ratios of 42° using a calculator or the table on page 779. Round to four decimal places.

$\sin 42° \approx 0.6691$ **Scientific calculator: Enter 42 and press the key labeled SIN, COS, or TAN.**

$\cos 42° \approx 0.7431$ **Table: Find 42° in the first column.**

$\tan 42° \approx 0.9004$ **Look across to find the appropriate ratio.**

Graphing Calculator Hint

If you use a graphing calculator, enter the trigonometric ratio name before you enter the angle measure. Be sure the calculator is in degree mode.

✓ Check Understanding Example 2

2. Find each value. Round to four decimal places.

a. $\sin 10°$ **b.** $\cos 75°$ **c.** $\tan 53°$ **d.** $\cos 22°$

OBJECTIVE

2 Using Trigonometric Ratios to Solve Problems

You can use trigonometric ratios to find measures in right triangles indirectly. The advantage to using trigonometric ratios is that you need only an acute angle measure and the length of one side to find the lengths of the other two sides.

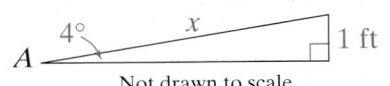

$4°$ x 1 ft

A

Not drawn to scale

3 EXAMPLE Real-World 🌐 Problem Solving

Ramps **What is the length of the wheelchair ramp at the left?**

You know the angle and the side opposite the angle. You want to find x, the length of the hypotenuse.

$$\sin A = \frac{\text{opposite}}{\text{hypotenuse}}$$ **Use the sine ratio.**

$$\sin 4° = \frac{1}{x}$$ **Substitute 4° for the angle and 1 for the side opposite.**

$$x(\sin 4°) = 1$$ **Multiply each side by x.**

$$x = \frac{1}{\sin 4°}$$ **Divide each side by sin 4°.**

$$x \approx 14.3$$ **Use a calculator.**

● The ramp is about 14.3 ft long.

✓ **Check Understanding**   Example 3

  3. How long is the longer leg under the ramp in Example 3?

More Than One Way

Ladders **Find the height, x, that the ladder reaches.**

8 ft   x

68°

3 ft

Kevin's Method

Use the Pythagorean theorem.
$$3^2 + x^2 = 8^2$$
$$9 + x^2 = 64$$
$$x^2 = 55$$
$$x = \sqrt{55} \approx 7.4$$
The ladder reaches about 7.4 ft.

Tina's Method

Use a trigonometric ratio.
$$\sin 68° = \frac{x}{8}$$
$$8(\sin 68°) = x$$
$$7.4 \approx x$$
The ladder reaches about 7.4 ft.

Choose a Method

  1. Which method do you prefer to use? Explain.

  2. What information is needed for each method?

EXERCISES

For more exercises, see *Extra Practice*.

Practice and Problem Solving

A **Practice by Example**

Example 1
(page 609)

For Exercises 1–3, find the length of the indicated side.

1. the leg opposite ∠A

2. the leg adjacent to ∠A

3. the hypotenuse of △ABC

4. Find the sine, cosine, and tangent of ∠A.

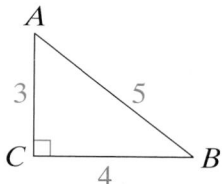

Use △QRS for Exercises 5 and 6.

5. Find the sine, cosine, and tangent of ∠R.

6. Find the sine, cosine, and tangent of ∠S.

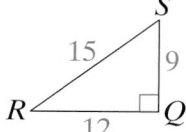

Example 2
(page 609)

Find each value. Round to four decimal places.

7. tan 89°   **8.** sin 30°   **9.** cos 14°   **10.** sin 67°

11. tan 28°   **12.** cos 89°   **13.** tan 11°   **14.** sin 83°

Example 3
(page 610)

15. Waterskiing The angle that a waterskiing ramp forms with the surface of the water is 15°, and the ramp rises 5 ft. Approximately how long is the ramp?

16. Loading Ramps The ramp on the back of a mover's truck is 12 ft long. If the angle of the ramp with the ground is 22°, about how high is the floor of the truck above the ground?

B **Apply Your Skills**

Use right triangles to find the ratios. Show your diagrams.

17. tan 45°   **18.** cos 60°   **19.** sin 30°   **20.** cos 30°

21. Writing in Math Tom says the missing length in the triangle at the right can be found using the tangent ratio. Jed says it can be found using the sine ratio. Who is correct? Explain.

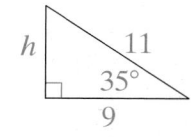

22. Hot-Air Balloons A hot-air balloon climbs continuously along a 30° angle to a height of 5,000 feet. To the nearest tenth of a foot, how far has the balloon traveled to reach 5,000 feet? Draw a sketch, and then solve.

C **Challenge**

23. Reasoning Find the sine of an angle and the cosine of its complement. Do this for several angles. Make a conjecture.

24. A wire from a radio tower is supported by a 23-ft brace.
 a. How tall is the radio tower?
 b. What is the measure of the angle formed by the wire and the ground?

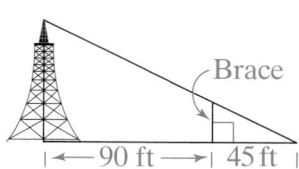

Multiple Choice   In Exercises 25 and 26, how high on a wall does a 12-ft ladder reach?

25. The base of the ladder is 3 ft from the wall.
   A. 4.0 ft   **B.** 10.0 ft   **C.** 11.6 ft   **D.** 12 ft

26. The ladder forms a 60° angle with the ground.
   F 10.4 ft   **G.** 8.0 ft   **H.** 6.9 ft   **I.** 6.0 ft

Reading Comprehension   Read the passage below before doing Exercises 27 and 28.

The Tilting Tower

Building began on the bell tower at Pisa, Italy, in 1173. Shortly after that, the 55.9-m tower began to lean and has continued to lean even more over the centuries. In 1993, the tower had a tilt that was 5.5° from the vertical. In the spring of 1999, engineering experts began work at the base to correct some of the lean. They completed the work in 2001 after decreasing the lean by 0.5°. The engineers hope their work will stabilize the tower for the next 300 years.

Take It to the NET
Online lesson quiz at
www.PHSchool.com
Web Code: ada-1106

27. In 2001, what was the tilt of the tower in degrees?

28. In 2001, about how many meters from the vertical was the top of the tower?

Mixed Review

Lesson 11-5   **Find the missing lengths.**

29.
45°
a
4 m   4 m

30.
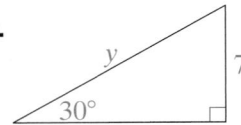
y
30°

31.
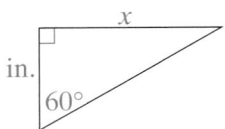
x
7 ft   13 in.
60°

Lesson 9-7   **32. Geometry** $\overleftrightarrow{GT}$ is the perpendicular bisector of $\overline{RA}$ at point *E*. Name two congruent segments.

Lesson 8-2   **Find the solutions of each equation for $x = -1, 0,$ and 3.**

33. $y = -3x + 2$ **34.** $x + y = 20$ **35.** $6x - 2y = 12$

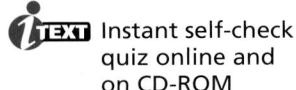
✓ Checkpoint Quiz 2   Lessons 11-4 through 11-6

TEXT Instant self-check quiz online and on CD-ROM

Tell whether a triangle with sides of the given lengths is 45°-45°-90°, 30°-60°-90°, or neither.

1. $8, 8, 8\sqrt{2}$ **2.** $1, 2, \sqrt{3}$ **3.** $12\sqrt{3}, 12, 24$

Find each value. Round to four decimal places.

4. cos 61°   **5.** tan 30°   **6.** sin 32°   **7.** sin 87°

Technology

Finding Angle Measures

You can use a calculator or a trigonometric-ratio table to find the degree measure of an acute angle of a right triangle if two sides of the triangle are known. If you are using a graphing calculator, be sure you are in degree mode.

EXAMPLE

You have a map charting a ship's course. The ship is traveling from the port along the course shown. What is the angle from due north of the ship's course?

The angle formed by due north, the port, and the ship is the angle at which the ship is traveling. This is angle X.

$$\cos X = \frac{191}{325}$$

To find $m\angle X$ with a calculator:

Press **TRIG cos⁻¹** 191 ÷ 325 [ENTER].

$$m\angle X \approx 54°$$

To find $m\angle X$ using the table of trigonometric ratios on page 779:

$\cos X = \frac{191}{325} \approx 0.5877$ **Divide.**

$m\angle X \approx 54°$ **In the cosine column, find the decimal closest to 0.5877, which is 0.5878. Read the angle measure across from 0.5878.**

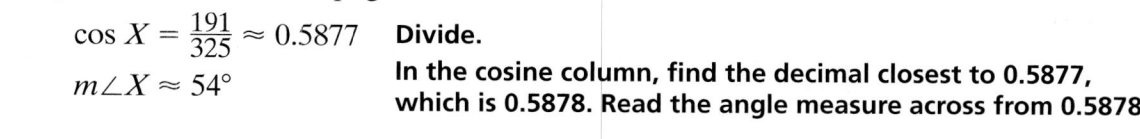

● The ship is traveling at a 54° angle from due north.

EXERCISES

Find the measure of each acute angle. Round to the nearest degree.

1.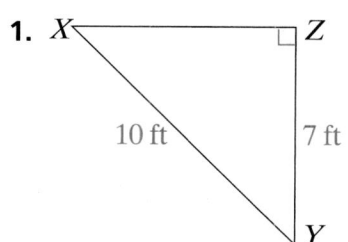

2.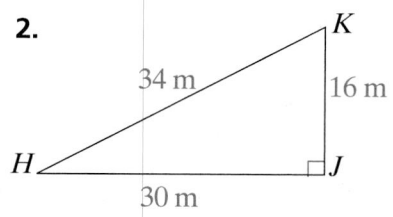

3.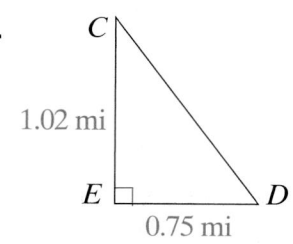

In $\triangle PQR$, $\angle Q$ is a right angle. Find the measures of $\angle P$ and $\angle R$ to the nearest tenth.

4. $PQ = 3$, $PR = 5$

5. $RQ = 12$, $PR = 13$

6. $PQ = 20$, $RQ = 21$

11-7

Angles of Elevation and Depression

What You'll Learn

OBJECTIVE
1 To use trigonometry to find angles of elevation

OBJECTIVE
2 To use trigonometry to find angles of depression

. . . And Why

To solve real-world problems in subjects such as surveying and navigation

 Check Skills You'll Need

Find each trigonometric ratio.

1. sin 45°   **2.** cos 32°

3. tan 18°   **4.** sin 68°

5. cos 88°   **6.** tan 84°

 For help, go to Lesson 11-6.

New Vocabulary

• angle of elevation
• angle of depression

 **Angles of Elevation**

Civil engineers and navigators use the terms *angle of elevation* and *angle of depression* to describe the angles at which they observe things. An **angle of elevation** is formed by a horizontal line and a line of sight above it. It is used when you must look up at an object.

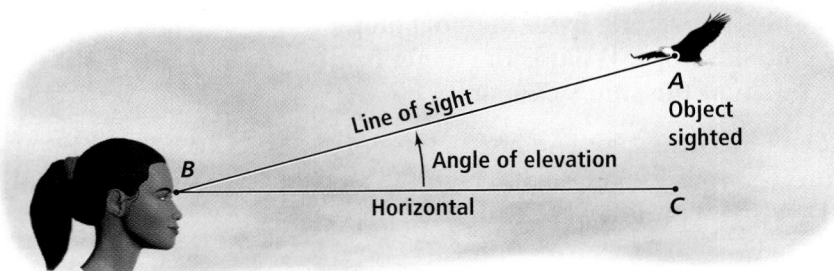

$\angle ABC$ is an angle of elevation.

1 **EXAMPLE**   **Real-World** 🌐 **Problem Solving**

Kite Flying Marcus is flying a kite. He lets out 40 yd of string and anchors it to the ground. He determines that the angle of elevation of the kite is 52°. What is the height x of the kite from the ground?

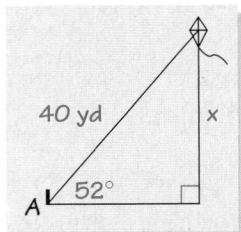   **Draw a picture.**

$\sin A = \dfrac{\text{opposite}}{\text{hypotenuse}}$ **Choose an appropriate trigonometric ratio.**

$\sin 52° = \dfrac{x}{40}$ **Substitute 52° for the angle measure and 40 for the hypotenuse.**

$40(\sin 52°) = x$ **Multiply each side by 40.**

$32 \approx x$ **Simplify.**

● The kite is about 32 yd from the ground.

 TEXT Interactive lesson includes instant self-check, tutorials, and activities.

✓ **Check Understanding** Example 1

1. The angle of elevation from a ship to the top of a lighthouse is 12°. The lighthouse is known to be 30 m tall. How far is the ship from the base of the lighthouse?

In real life, a person's line of sight is parallel to the ground at eye height. In some problems you must account for this.

2 EXAMPLE **Real-World** 🌐 **Problem Solving**

Indirect Measurement Felicia wants to determine the height of a tree. From her position 20 ft from the base of the tree, she sees the top of the tree at an angle of elevation of 73°. Felicia's eyes are 5 ft from the ground. How tall is the tree, to the nearest foot?

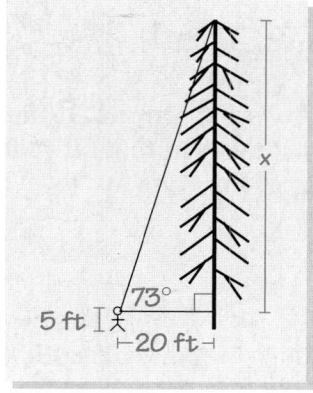

Draw a picture.

$$\tan = \frac{\text{opposite}}{\text{adjacent}}$$ **Choose an appropriate trigonometric ratio.**

$$\tan 73° = \frac{x}{20}$$ **Substitute 73 for the angle measure and 20 for the adjacent side.**

$$20(\tan 73°) = x$$ **Multiply each side by 20.**

$$65 \approx x$$ **Use a calculator or a table.**

$$65 + 5 = 70$$ **Add 5 to account for the height of Felicia's eyes from the ground.**

● The tree is about 70 ft tall.

✓ **Check Understanding** Example 2

2. A rock climber looks at the top of a vertical rock wall at an angle of elevation of 74°. He is standing 4.2 m from the base of the wall and his eyes are 1.5 m from the ground. How high is the wall, to the nearest tenth of a meter?

2 Angles of Depression

With an angle of elevation, the object sighted is elevated, or above the horizontal line. With an angle of depression, the object is depressed, or below the horizontal line.

An **angle of depression** is formed by a horizontal line and a line of sight below it. It is used when you must look down at an object.

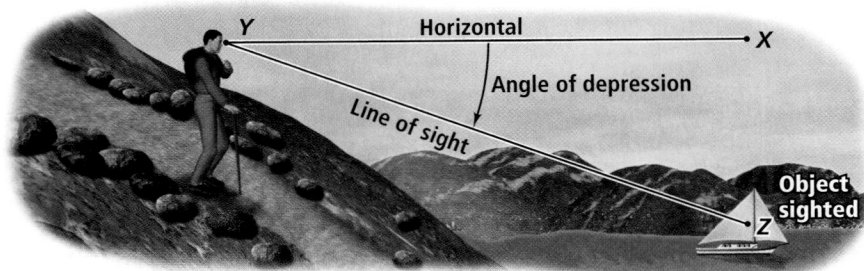

∠*XYZ* is an angle of depression.

3 EXAMPLE Real-World Problem Solving

Navigation **An airplane is flying 0.5 mi above the ground. If the pilot must begin a 3° descent to an airport runway at that altitude, how far is the airplane from the beginning of the runway (in ground distance)?**

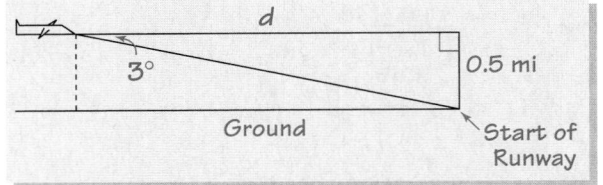

Not drawn to scale

$\tan 3° = \dfrac{0.5}{d}$ **Choose an appropriate trigonometric ratio.**

$d \tan 3° = 0.5$ **Multiply each side by *d*.**

$\dfrac{d \tan 3°}{\tan 3°} = \dfrac{0.5}{\tan 3°}$ **Divide each side by tan 3°.**

$d = \dfrac{0.5}{\tan 3°}$ **Simplify.**

$d \approx 9.5$ **Use a calculator.**

● The airplane is about 9.5 mi from the airport.

✓ Check Understanding Example 3

3. A group of people in a hang-gliding class are standing on top of a cliff 70 m high. They spot a hang glider landing on the beach below them. The angle of depression from the top of the cliff to the hang glider is 72°. How far is the hang glider from the base of the cliff?

EXERCISES

Practice and Problem Solving

For more exercises, see *Extra Practice*.

 A Practice by Example

Examples 1 and 2
(pages 614 and 615)

1. In Example 1, Marcus's kite drops so that the angle of elevation is 48°. Find the height of the kite above the ground.

2. In Example 2, Felicia spots a nest in the tree at an angle of elevation of 65°. How high above the ground is the nest?

Find *x* to the nearest tenth.

3.

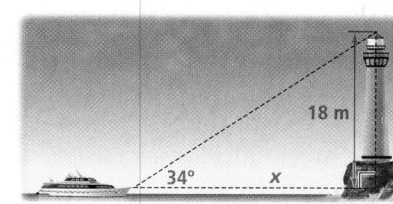

4.

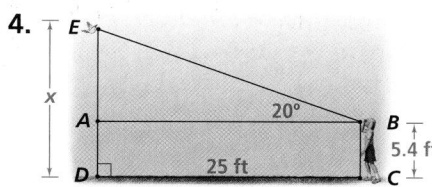

Example 3
(page 616)

For Exercises 5 and 6, draw a sketch and solve.

5. An airplane descends at an angle of 2°. Its altitude decreases by 2.5 miles. What is the ground distance covered by the airplane?

6. An airplane descends at an angle of 22.5° over a ground distance of 0.5 mi. By how many miles, to the nearest tenth, does its altitude decrease?

B Apply Your Skills

Name the angles of elevation and depression in each figure.

7.

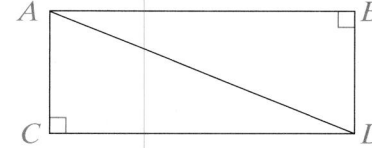

8.

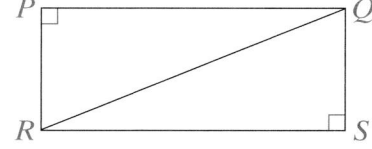

Reading Math
For help with reading and solving Exercise 9, see page 619.

9. Bird Watching A rare bird is spotted in a tree by a bird-watching group. The group is 9.5 yd from the base of the tree. The angle of elevation to the bird is 57°. How far is the bird from the group along the line of sight? Draw a sketch, and then solve.

10. Navigation The angle of elevation from a ship to the top of a lighthouse is 4°. If the top of the lighthouse is known to be 50 m above sea level, how far is the ship from the lighthouse?

11. Writing in Math How do you decide which trigonometric ratio to use to solve a problem?

12. Find the distance *x* of the car from the office building at the left.

13. Meteorology A meteorologist measures the angle of elevation of a weather balloon as 53°. A radio signal from the balloon indicates that it is 1,620 m (line-of-sight) from the meteorologist's location. How high above ground is the weather balloon?

11-7 Angles of Elevation and Depression **617**

14. Error Analysis A student made the drawing at the right to solve an angle-of-depression problem. What mistake has the student made?

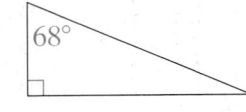

15. Aeronautics The pilot of a helicopter at an altitude of 6,000 ft sees a second helicopter at an angle of depression of 43°. The altitude of the second helicopter is 4,000 ft. What is the distance from the first helicopter to the second along the line of sight?

C Challenge **16. Astronomy** The diagram suggests a method for finding depths of moon craters from Earth. Astronomers calculate that the distance from R to H is 3 km when the angle of depression of the sun's rays is 12°.

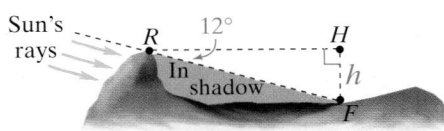

   a. How high is the rim of the crater from the floor of the crater?
   b. When the angle increases to 14°, how much shorter is the crater's shadow on the crater floor?

17. Surveying Surveyors find that a canyon is 4 km wide. From one canyon rim, the angle of depression to the base of the canyon wall below the other rim is 7°. The angle of depression to a river is 8°. How far is the river from the far canyon wall?

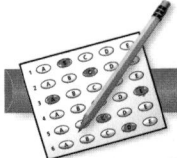

Test Prep

Multiple Choice

18. A ramp has an angle of elevation of 19° and a length of 35 ft. What is the height in inches of the ramp at its high end?
   A. 11 in.   **B.** 12 in.   **C.** 137 in.   **D.** 145 in.

19. A radio transmitting tower casts a shadow that extends 344 feet from the base of the tower. A line connecting the sun, the top of the tower, and the end of the shadow forms an angle of depression of 16°. Approximately how high is the tower?
   F. 344 ft   **G.** 99 ft   **H.** 1,200 ft   **I.** 1,248 ft

Take It to the NET
Online lesson quiz at
www.PHSchool.com
Web Code: ada-1107

Mixed Review

Lesson 11-6   **Find each value. Round to four decimal places.**

   20. $\tan 29°$ **21.** $\sin 80°$ **22.** $\cos 34°$ **23.** $\sin 76°$ **24.** $\cos 45°$

Lesson 10-3   **Find the area of each circle. Give an exact area using π and an approximate area to the nearest tenth.**

   25. $r = 8$ in.   **26.** $r = 1.9$ cm   **27.** $r = 10$ mm   **28.** $r = 4.5$ in.

Lesson 6-2   **29. Baking** A recipe that serves four people calls for $1\frac{1}{2}$ c of flour. How many cups of flour are needed to serve ten people?

Read the problem. Then follow along with what Cheryl thinks as she solves it. Check your understanding by solving the exercise at the bottom of the page.

Bird Watching A rare bird is spotted in a tree by a bird-watching group. The group is 9.5 yd from the base of the tree. The angle of elevation to the bird is 57°. How far is the bird from the group along the line of sight? Draw a sketch, and then solve.

What Cheryl Thinks	What Cheryl Writes

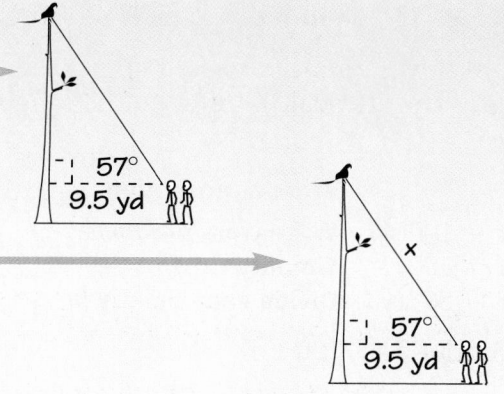

I'll draw a sketch. In it, I'll show:
angle of elevation = 57°,
distance from tree = 9.5 yd,
right angle near base of tree.

I must find the line-of-sight distance to the bird. That's along the hypotenuse of the right triangle. I'll name it x.

I know an angle and the adjacent leg. I want to find the hypotenuse. I'll use the cosine ratio.

$$\cos 57° = \frac{adjacent}{hypotenuse}$$

$$= \frac{9.5}{x}$$

I can solve this equation.

$$x(\cos 57°) = 9.5$$

$$\frac{x(\cos 57°)}{\cos 57°} = \frac{9.5}{\cos 57°}$$

$$x = \frac{9.5}{\cos 57°}$$

I'll use a calculator and round.

$$x \approx 17.4$$

Now I can write the answer.

The bird is about 17.4 yd from the group along the line of sight.

EXERCISE

1. A hot-air balloon is 150 feet high. The angle of depression from the pilot to her assistant on the ground is 25°. What is the line-of-sight distance from the pilot to her assistant, to the nearest foot?

You can solve many problems by letting a variable be an unknown quantity you want to find. Use the variable in an equation. Then solve the equation to help solve the problem.

1 EXAMPLE

When José visited France he saw a large model of the Statue of Liberty. He wondered how tall the model was, so he measured its shadow. The shadow was 100 feet. He measured the height and shadow of a vertical pole. The pole measured 4 feet and its shadow was 5 feet. How tall was the model of the Statue of Liberty?

The unknown quantity is the height of the model. Sketch similar triangles (not to scale). Let x be the height. Then write a proportion using x.

$\dfrac{5}{100} = \dfrac{4}{x}$ **Write a proportion.**

$5x = 100(4)$ **Write cross products.**

$5x = 400$ **Simplify.**

$x = 80$ **Divide each side by 5.**

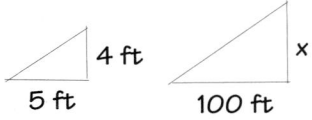

- The model was 80 ft tall.

2 EXAMPLE

City code requires that wheelchair ramps rise no more than 1 in. for every horizontal foot. To meet the code, you build a ramp the entire length of your house, 36 ft. What is the ramp's angle of elevation?

The unknown quantity is the measure of the angle that the ramp forms with the ground. Let x be that measure. You know the side opposite and the side adjacent the angle.

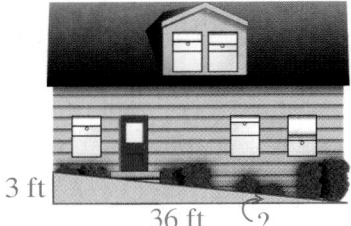

$\tan x = \dfrac{3}{36}$ **Use the tangent ratio.**

≈ 0.0833 **Write as a decimal.**

$x \approx 5$ **Use a calculator (see page 613).**

- The angle of elevation of the ramp is about 5°.

EXERCISE

1. You are flying a kite at the end of 200 ft of string. The angle of elevation is 30°. You are holding the end of the string at eye level, 5 ft above the ground. How high is the kite from the ground? Draw a diagram. Show how to use a variable. Then find how high the kite is.

Chapter Review

Vocabulary

angle of depression (p. 616)	**irrational number** (p. 581)	**square root** (p. 580)
angle of elevation (p. 614)	**legs** (p. 584)	**tangent** (p. 608)
cosine (p. 608)	**midpoint** (p. 594)	**trigonometric ratio** (p. 608)
distance (p. 592)	**perfect square** (p. 580)	**trigonometry** (p. 608)
hypotenuse (p. 584)	**sine** (p. 608)	

Reading Math
Understanding Vocabulary

Match the vocabulary terms on the right with their descriptions on the left.

1. the two shortest sides of a right triangle

2. an angle formed by a horizontal line and a line of sight above it

3. the ratio of the lengths of two sides of a right triangle

4. the longest side of a right triangle, opposite the right angle

5. a number that cannot be expressed as a ratio of two integers

6. The inverse of squaring a number is finding this.

a. irrational number
b. square root
c. legs
d. trigonometric ratio
e. hypotenuse
f. angle of elevation

Take It to the NET
Online vocabulary quiz at **www.PHSchool.com**
Web Code: adj-1151

Skills and Concepts

11-1 Objectives

▼ To find square roots of numbers (p. 580)

▼ To classify real numbers (p. 581)

The square of an integer is a **perfect square.** The inverse of squaring a number is finding a **square root.** The symbol $\sqrt{\ }$ indicates the positive square root of a number. A number that cannot be expressed as the ratio of two integers $\frac{a}{b}$, where b is not zero, is **irrational.** If a positive integer is not a perfect square, its square root is irrational.

Simplify each square root.

7. $\sqrt{1}$ 8. $-\sqrt{16}$ 9. $\sqrt{49}$ 10. $\sqrt{64}$ 11. $-\sqrt{36}$

Estimate to the nearest integer.

12. $\sqrt{5}$ 13. $\sqrt{11}$ 14. $\sqrt{33}$ 15. $\sqrt{62}$ 16. $\sqrt{91}$

Identify each number as rational or irrational. Explain.

17. 0.55 18. $\sqrt{64}$ 19. $0.\overline{45}$ 20. $\sqrt{15}$ 21. $0.123123\ldots$

22. Explain why $0.12122122212222\ldots$ is an irrational number.

11-2 Objectives

▼ To use the Pythagorean Theorem (p. 584)

▼ To identify right triangles (p. 586)

In a right triangle, the two shortest sides are the **legs.** The longest side, which is opposite the right angle, is the **hypotenuse.** The Pythagorean Theorem states that in any right triangle the sum of the squares of the lengths of the legs is equal to the square of the length of the hypotenuse ($a^2 + b^2 = c^2$).

Can you form a right triangle with the three lengths given? Show your work.

23. 1 mi, 3 mi, 3 mi

24. 8 yd, 15 yd, 17 yd

25. $\sqrt{6}$ ft, $\sqrt{10}$ ft, 4 ft

26. 30 m, 40 m, 50 m

11-3 Objectives

▼ To find the distance between two points using the Distance Formula (p. 592)

▼ To find the midpoint of a segment using the Midpoint Formula (p. 594)

The Distance Formula states that the **distance** d between any two points (x_1, y_1) and (x_2, y_2) is $d = \sqrt{(x_2 - x_1)^2 + (y_2 - y_1)^2}$.

The Midpoint Formula states that the **midpoint** of a line segment with endpoints $A(x_1, y_1)$ and $B(x_2, y_2)$ is $\left(\frac{x_1 + x_2}{2}, \frac{y_1 + y_2}{2} \right)$.

Find the distance between each pair of points. Round to the nearest tenth.

27. $(3, 0), (0, 2)$

28. $(-1, 7), (3, 10)$

29. $(4, -5), (-8, -1)$

30. $(-10, -12), (-8, -11)$

31. $(2, -14), (9, -20)$

32. $(10, 4), (-2, -2)$

Find the midpoint of each segment with the given endpoints.

33. $H(0, 1)$ and $J(4, 7)$

34. $K(2, 6)$ and $L(4, 2)$

35. $M(-7, 8)$ and $P(3, -4)$

36. $A(4, 9)$ and $B(5, 11)$

37. $X(-15, -12)$ and $Y(-9, -4)$

38. $D(20, 18)$ and $E(-15, -19)$

11-4 Objectives

▼ To write a proportion from similar triangles (p. 598)

You can write a proportion to solve indirect measurement problems using similar triangles.

🌐 **39. Engineering** An engineer needs to know what length to plan for a bridge across a river. She estimates the distance using the similar triangles $\triangle ABC$ and $\triangle DEC$ in the figure at the right. What is the distance a across the river?

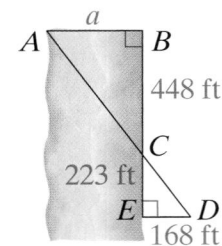

11-5 Objectives

▼ To use the relationships in 45°-45°-90° triangles (p. 602)

▼ To use the relationships in 30°-60°-90° triangles (p. 603)

In a 45°-45°-90° triangle, the length of the hypotenuse is the length of a leg times $\sqrt{2}$.

In a 30°-60°-90° triangle, the length of the hypotenuse is 2 times the length of the shorter leg, and the length of the longer leg is the length of the shorter leg times $\sqrt{3}$.

Find the values of the variables, rounded to the nearest tenth, if necessary.

40.

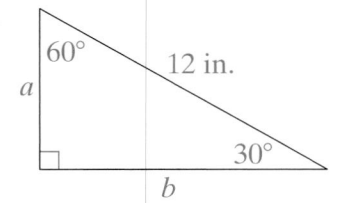

41.

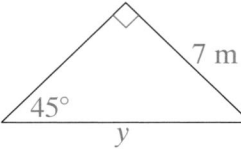

42.

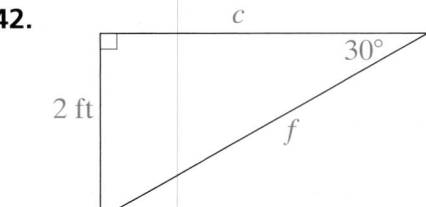

43.

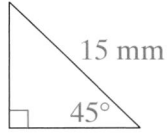

11-6 and 11-7 Objectives

▼ To find trigonometric ratios in right triangles (p. 608)

▼ To use trigonometric ratios to solve problems (p. 609)

▼ To use trigonometry to find angles of elevation (p. 614)

▼ To use trigonometry to find angles of depression (p. 616)

The ratios of the lengths of two sides of a right triangle are **trigonometric ratios.** Three trigonometric ratios are **sine, cosine,** and **tangent.** You can use these abbreviations when you find trigonometric ratios for a given acute $\angle N$.

$$\sin N = \frac{\text{opposite}}{\text{hypotenuse}} \qquad \cos N = \frac{\text{adjacent}}{\text{hypotenuse}} \qquad \tan N = \frac{\text{opposite}}{\text{adjacent}}$$

An **angle of elevation** is formed by a horizontal line and a line of sight above it. An **angle of depression** is formed by a horizontal line and a line of sight below it.

Find each value. Round to four decimal places.

44. $\sin 16°$ **45.** $\tan 82°$ **46.** $\cos 25°$ **47.** $\tan 3°$ **48.** $\sin 87°$

49. $\cos 73°$ **50.** $\cos 46°$ **51.** $\tan 45°$ **52.** $\sin 79°$ **53.** $\tan 13°$

Solve each problem. Round to the nearest unit.

54. A loading ramp forms a 28° angle with the ground. If the base of the ramp is 15 ft long, how high does the ramp reach?

55. Melanie is flying a kite and lets out 100 ft of string. Rosa determines that from Melanie's hands the angle of elevation of the kite is 71°. Melanie's hands are 4.3 ft from the ground. What is the height of the kite?

Chapter Test

 **Take It to the NET**
Online chapter test at
www.PHSchool.com
Web Code: ada-1152

Simplify each square root.

1. $\sqrt{25}$ **2.** $-\sqrt{81}$ **3.** $\sqrt{100}$

4. $-\sqrt{4}$ **5.** $\sqrt{16}$ **6.** $\sqrt{49}$

Estimate to the nearest integer.

7. $\sqrt{6}$ **8.** $\sqrt{12}$ **9.** $\sqrt{45}$

10. $\sqrt{78}$ **11.** $\sqrt{85}$ **12.** $\sqrt{118}$

Identify each number as rational or irrational.

13. $0.999\ldots$ **14.** $\sqrt{24}$

15. $\sqrt{100}$ **16.** $420{,}420$

Find each missing length to the nearest tenth of a unit.

17.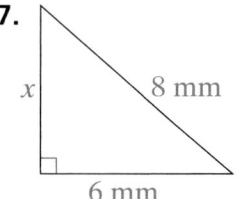

18.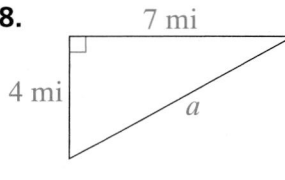

19.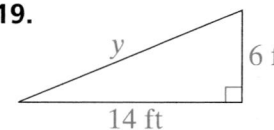

20.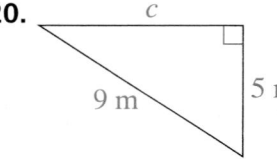

Find the distance between the points of each pair. Round to the nearest tenth.

21. $(0,0), (4,6)$ **22.** $(5,-3), (-6,2)$

23. $(-8,-9), (1,2)$ **24.** $(-1,-3), (-4,-7)$

Find the midpoint of each segment with the given endpoints.

25. $C(5,0)$ and $D(3,6)$

26. $M(9,-4)$ and $P(2,8)$

27. To estimate the height of a tree, Joan positions a mirror on the ground so she can see the top of the tree reflected in it. Joan's height, her distance from the mirror, and her line of sight to the mirror determine a triangle. The tree's height, its distance from the mirror, and the distance from the top of the tree to the mirror determine a similar triangle. Use the measurements below to find the height of the tree.

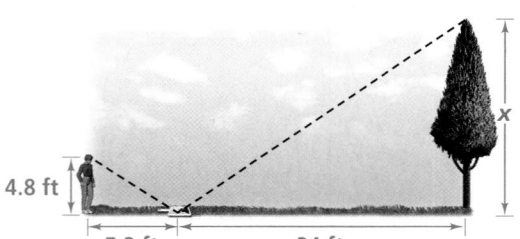

Find the missing lengths.

28.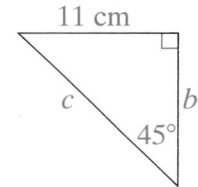

29.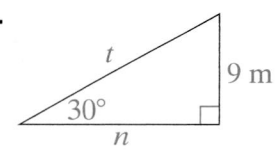

Find each value. Round to four decimal places.

30. $\sin 47°$ **31.** $\tan 75°$ **32.** $\cos 86°$

33. $\tan 29°$ **34.** $\cos 60°$ **35.** $\sin 67°$

36. **Writing in Math** Explain how a trigonometric ratio can be used to find a measurement indirectly.

37. **Navigation** The captain of a ship sights the top of a lighthouse at an angle of elevation of $12°$. The captain knows that the top of the lighthouse is 24 m above sea level. What is the distance from the ship to the lighthouse?

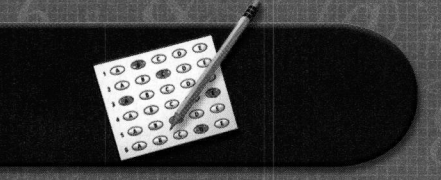

Test Prep

Reading Comprehension Read the passage below. Then answer the questions on the basis of what is *stated* or *implied* in the passage.

Early Geometry The early Babylonians and Egyptians used practical geometry in their buildings, but it was a Greek named Thales who first wrote down the formal abstract geometry that we know today.

Thales, an olive-oil merchant, lived from about 600 to 550 B.C. One of the unchanging properties of triangles that he discovered was that a triangle drawn in a semicircle (half a circle), with the diameter as a hypotenuse, will always be a right triangle.

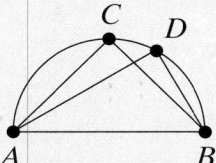

Around 540 B.C. a student of Thales, Pythagoras, founded a group that studied, among other things, mathematics. One of the rules of the *Pythagoreans* was never to eat beans! At first, they believed that the entire universe was made of only rational numbers, but working with right triangles convinced them that they could draw lines that have lengths equal to the square root of 2, the square root of 5, and so on.

1. What is the name of a teacher of Pythagoras?

2. What was the name of a group founded by Pythagoras?

3. What is the measure of $\angle C$?
   A. 360° **B.** 180° **C.** 90° **D.** 45°

4. Which term best describes $\overline{AC}$?
   F. leg   **G.** sine
   H. hypotenuse   **I.** tangent

5. If $AC = CB = 1$ in., what is AB?
   A. 2 in. **B.** $\sqrt{3}$ in. **C.** $\sqrt{2}$ in. **D.** 1 in.

6. If $AB = 6$ in. and $DB = 3$ in., what is AD?
   F. $3\sqrt{2}$ in.   **G.** $3\sqrt{3}$ in.
   H. $6\sqrt{2}$ in.   **I.** $6\sqrt{3}$ in.

7. If AB is $\sqrt{8}$ cm *and* $AC = CB$, what are AC and CB?

8. Which term does NOT apply to $\overline{AB}$?
   A. diameter   **B.** hypotenuse
   C. leg   **D.** line segment

9. How does the measure of $\angle D$ compare with the measure of $\angle C$?

10. What country was Thales from?

11. How long did Thales live?

12. What must be true of $\sqrt{2}$?
    I. It is not a rational number.
    II. A segment can have length $\sqrt{2}$.
    III. It is equal to $\sqrt{5}$.
    F. I only   **G.** I and II
    H. I and III   **I.** II and III only

Picture Perfect

Applying Ratios Ancient Greeks realized that rectangles with certain dimensions were especially pleasing to the eye. A golden rectangle has sides that form the proportion $\frac{a}{b} = \frac{a + b}{a}$. The ratio of two sides of a golden rectangle is called the *golden ratio*. Artists make paintings with dimensions close to the golden ratio. Photographers often *crop*, or cut, their photographs to be golden rectangles.

Golden Rectangle Proportion
a is to *b* as (*a* + *b*) is to *a*.

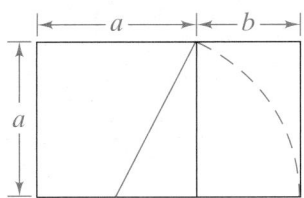

How to Make a Golden Rectangle

Start with a square with side length *a*. Open a compass the length from the midpoint of one side of the square to a corner on the opposite side. Make an arc. Extend the side containing the midpoint to intersect the arc. Make a rectangle using lengths *b* and *a*.

The Parthenon

The front of the Parthenon, in Athens, Greece, approximates a golden rectangle.

x

$1.62x$

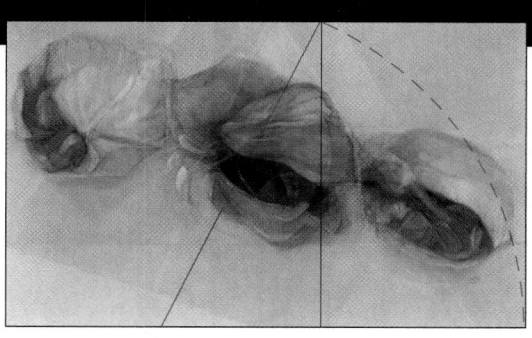

The Golden Rectangle in Art

Artist Sydney McGinley makes pastel paintings of flowers, such as *Pyramidal Fuschia*, using a golden rectangle to position the flowers within the painting.

The Villa Savoye

The Swiss architect Charles Le Corbusier designed the Villa Savoye, outside Paris, France, based on the golden rectangle, among other things. The house, built in 1930, looks different from each side.

Activity

1. a. Copy the table. For each rectangle, find the ratios $\frac{a}{b}$ and $\frac{a + b}{a}$. Write the ratios in decimal form, rounding to the nearest tenth. Write *yes* if the decimals are approximately equal.

    b. Which rectangles are close to a golden rectangle? Explain.

Rectangle Dimensions (inches)

Side a	Side $a + b$	$\frac{a}{b}$	$\frac{(a + b)}{a}$	Golden Ratio?
5	8	$\frac{5}{3} = 1.\overline{6} \approx 1.7$	$\frac{8}{5} = 1.6$	Yes
3	4	▦	▦	▦
6	10	▦	▦	▦
14	22	▦	▦	▦
12	16	▦	▦	▦
15	24	▦	▦	▦
18	26	▦	▦	▦
21	33	▦	▦	▦

2. Photo labs make prints in several sizes, including 3×5, 4×6, and 8×10. Which of these sizes is closest to a golden rectangle?

3. Open-Ended From the table, choose one pair of dimensions that do not form a golden rectangle. Change the value of a to a whole number that makes the rectangle closer to a golden rectangle. Justify your choice by showing your work.

4. Research Find at least three images from magazines or catalogs that you think approximate golden rectangles. Measure the images and calculate the ratio of length to width.

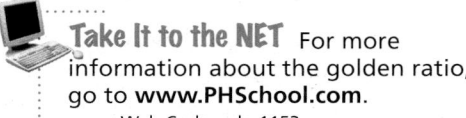

Take It to the NET For more information about the golden ratio, go to **www.PHSchool.com**.
Web Code: ade-1153

Where You've Been

- In Chapter 3, you investigated measures of central tendency for sets of data.

- In Chapter 4, you simplified fractions by dividing the numerator and denominator by the GCF.

- In Chapter 5, you performed operations with fractions.

- In Chapter 6, you found the probability of events. You also wrote fractions and decimals as percents.

iTEXT Instant self-check online and on CD-ROM

Diagnosing Readiness

(For help, go to the lesson in green.)

Finding the Median (Lesson 3-3)

Find the median.

1. 12, 14, 10, 9, 13, 12, 15, 12, 11   **2.** 55, 53, 67, 52, 50, 49, 51, 52, 52

3. 101, 100, 100, 105, 102, 101   **4.** 0.2, 0.5, 0.11, 0.25, 0.34, 0.19

Multiplying Fractions (Lesson 5-4)

Find each product.

5. $\frac{2}{3} \cdot \frac{1}{2}$ **6.** $\frac{7}{8} \cdot \frac{6}{7}$ **7.** $\frac{9}{10} \cdot \frac{8}{9}$ **8.** $\frac{5}{6} \cdot \frac{4}{5}$ **9.** $\frac{3}{4} \cdot \frac{2}{3}$ **10.** $\frac{7}{8} \cdot \frac{6}{7} \cdot \frac{5}{6}$

Finding Probability (Lesson 6-4)

Find the probability for one roll of a number cube.

11. $P(2)$ **12.** $P(5)$ **13.** $P(2 \text{ or } 5)$ **14.** $P(8)$

15. $P(1, 2, \text{ or } 3)$ **16.** $P(\text{less than } 1)$ **17.** $P(\text{not } 3)$ **18.** $P(\text{greater than } 4)$

A student is chosen at random from a class of 15 boys and 18 girls. Find each probability.

19. $P(\text{girl})$ **20.** $P(\text{boy})$ **21.** $P(\text{not a girl})$ **22.** $P(\text{not a boy})$

Fractions, Decimals, and Percents (Lesson 6-5)

Write each percent as a decimal, and each decimal or fraction as a percent.

23. 50%   **24.** 36%   **25.** 20%   **26.** 5%

27. $\frac{1}{5}$ **28.** $\frac{7}{8}$ **29.** 0.28   **30.** 0.3

Data Analysis and Probability

Where You're Going

In this chapter, you will learn how to

- Use graphs to represent data.
- Find theoretical probability and experimental probability.
- Find permutations and combinations.
- Solve problems by doing simulations.

Real-World Snapshots Applying what you learn, on pages 684–685 you will solve problems about goal scoring in World Cup soccer.

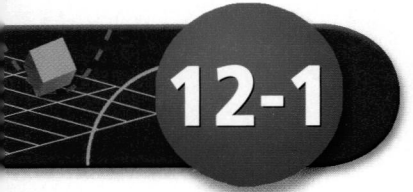

12-1

Frequency Tables and Line Plots

What You'll Learn

 OBJECTIVE 1 To display data in frequency tables

OBJECTIVE 2 To display data in line plots

. . . And Why

To solve real-world problems involving surveys

 Check Skills You'll Need

Find the median and mode of each data set.

1. 6, 9, 9, 5, 9

2. 73, 78, 77, 73, 79

3. 300, 100, 200, 150, 300

4. 3, 5, 7, 9, 3, 4, 6, 3, 7

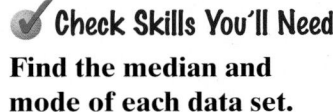 For help, go to Lesson 3-3.

New Vocabulary

• frequency table
• line plot
• range

 Investigation

Exploring Frequency Tables

Surveys Many people have favorite colors. Do people also have favorite numbers? Take a survey of your classmates.

1. Ask each person to choose an integer from 0 to 9. Use a table to record the responses.

2. Which number was chosen most frequently? How many times was each of the other numbers chosen?

3. Suppose you want to continue your survey by asking more people. Looking back, would you use the same type of table you used for Question 1? Can you make improvements? Explain.

You can display data in a **frequency table,** which lists each data item with the number of times it occurs.

 **1 EXAMPLE Building a Frequency Table**

A number cube was rolled 20 times. The results are shown at the right. Display the data in a frequency table.

| 5 | 2 | 5 | 4 | 1 | 6 | 5 | 2 | 5 | 1 |
| 3 | 6 | 1 | 3 | 4 | 5 | 3 | 5 | 3 | 4 |

List the numbers on the cube in order.	Use a tally mark for each result.	Count the tally marks and record the frequency.

Number	Tally	Frequency
1	III	3
2	II	2
3	IIII	4
4	III	3
5	HHT I	6
6	II	2

TEXT Interactive lesson includes instant self-check, tutorials, and activities.

✓ Check Understanding   Example 1

1. Display the data below in a frequency table.
   10 12 13 15 10 11 14 13 10 11 11 12 10 10 15

OBJECTIVE

2 Using Line Plots to Display Data

A **line plot** displays data with **X** marks above a number line.

The **range** of the data is the difference between the greatest and the least values in the data set.

Reading Math

This is the second use of the word *range*. The first appears in Lesson 8-1. You must read and use "range" *in context*, that is, according to the meanings of the words that appear with it.

2 EXAMPLE   Real-World 🌐 Problem Solving

Surveys Twenty-five students in a school hallway were asked how many books they were carrying. The frequency table at the right shows their responses. Display the data in a line plot. Then find the range.

"How many books are you carrying?"

Number	Frequency
0	3
1	7
2	6
3	2
4	4
5	3

For a line plot, follow steps ①,②, and ③.

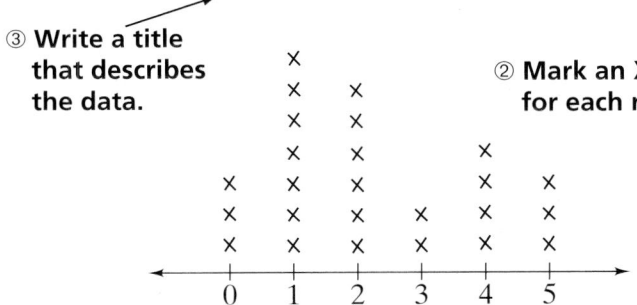

Students Carrying Books

③ Write a title that describes the data.

② Mark an X for each response.

① Draw a number line with the choices below it.

The greatest value in the data set is 5 and the least value is 0.
● So the range is 5 − 0, or 5.

✓ Check Understanding   Example 2

2. **a.** Display the data below in a line plot. Then find the range.
   miles from home to the mall: 2, 4, 3, 7, 3, 1, 4, 2, 2, 6, 3, 5, 1, 8, 3
   b. What is the range of the data below?
   prices of a gallon of regular gas at different gas stations:
   $1.48, $1.32, $1.30, $1.35, $1.41, $1.29, $1.32, $1.43, $1.36

EXERCISES

For more exercises, see *Extra Practice*.

Practice and Problem Solving

Ⓐ Practice by Example

Example 1
(page 630)

Display each set of data in a frequency table.

1. 1 4 0 3 0 1 3 2 2 4   **2.** 6 2 8 7 9 3 5 4 8 2 4 6 4 1

3. 10 30 20 30 50 10 40 30 50 40 30 50

4. 25 29 28 28 30 25 26 28 27 29 26 30

5. rolls of a number cube: 4 1 3 4 2 1 2 5 2 3 5 1 6 1 3 5 6

6. test scores: 100 90 70 60 95 65 85 70 70 75 80 85 75 70 100 90

Example 2
(page 631)

Draw a line plot for each frequency table.

7.

Number	1	2	3	4	5	6
Frequency	2	5	7	8	4	3

8.

Number	1	2	3	4	5	6
Frequency	1	3	5	8	8	5

In Exercises 9–14, display each set of data in a line plot. Find the range.

9. 0 2 1 1 4 0 4 3 2   **10.** 5 2 1 3 3 6 4 5 4 2

11. 5 0 2 1 4 3 4 0 2 5
    4 3 2 0 4   **12.** 4 2 4 12 8 12 10 6 4
    8 6 8 12

13. Literature the number of letters in each of the first twenty-five words of *Alice's Adventures in Wonderland* by Lewis Carroll:
4 3 10 5 3 9 2 3 4 5 2 7 2 3 6 2 3 4 3 2 6 7 2 2 4

Ⓑ Apply Your Skills

14. the weekly earnings in dollars of the employees at Industrial Enterprises: 320, 320, 320, 400, 400, 400, 400, 400, 400, 480, 480, 480, 720, 720, 720, 1000

Display each set of data in a frequency table and in a line plot. Find the range.

15. ages of club members:
14 16 14 16 14 13 12 15 16 12 12 15 14 15 15

16. heights of plants (inches):
25 25 20 25 16 20 25 30 25 31 26 28 30

17. 7 11 10 10 8 11 9 7 9 8 11 11

18. 17 20 16 17 19 18 17 20 17 18 18 19 18 17

19. Baseball In the World Series, the first team to win four games is the champion. Sometimes the Series lasts for seven games, but sometimes the Series ends in fewer games. Below are data for 1970–2002. Make a frequency table and use it to find the mode. Numbers of World Series Games, 1970–2002: 5, 7, 7, 7, 5, 7, 4, 6, 6, 7, 6, 6, 7, 5, 5, 7, 7, 7, 5, 4, 4, 7, 6, 6, 0, 6, 6, 7, 4, 4, 5, 7, 7

A frequency table or line plot may allow you to readily "see" the mode and find the median. Find the mode and the median for the data set in each exercise.

20. Exercise 11   **21.** Exercise 12   **22.** Exercise 13

23. Exercise 14   **24.** Exercise 15   **25.** Exercise 16

 **Challenge**

26. Reasoning A magazine line plot shows results of a survey. Explain how to use the line plot to find each of the following:
 a. the number of people who answered the survey.
 b. the mode, median, and mean

27. Writing in Math Describe a set of data that would be easier to display with a frequency table than with a line plot.

Multiple Choice

28. Below is a list of the ages of first-year teachers in one school system. What is the mode of the ages?
  23, 42, 21, 25, 23, 24, 23, 24, 37, 23, 39, 51, 63, 24, 55
 A. 23   **B.** 24   **C.** 37   **D.** 51

29. What is the range of the data below?
  99.2, 101.5, 97.9, 102.1, 98.6, 100.4, 102.2, 99.9
 F. 3.7   **G.** 3.9
 H. 4.0   **I.** 4.3

Short Response

The line plot (right) represents the results of a class survey in which students were asked to name their favorite lunch.

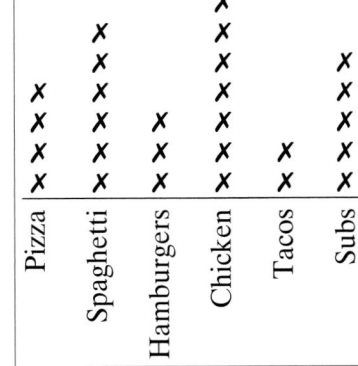

30. a. How many students were surveyed?
 b. How do you know?

Take It to the NET
Online lesson quiz at
www.PHSchool.com
Web Code: ada-1201

31. a. What is the mode of the survey?
 b. Explain your answer for part (a).

Lesson 11-7

32. Measurement The angle of elevation to a treetop from a point 10 ft out from the tree's base is 70°. Find the height of the tree.

Lesson 9-5

Given that $\triangle LMN \cong \triangle PQR$, complete each statement.

33. $\angle N \cong \blacksquare$ **34.** $\overline{MN} \cong \blacksquare$ **35.** $PQ = \blacksquare$

Lesson 3-3

Find the mean, median, and mode for each data set.

36. 12 13 14 16 16 17 18 18   **37.** 8 15 22 9 11 16 20 10

Making Histograms

For Use With Lesson 12-1

A histogram shows the frequencies of data items as a graph.
You can use a graphing calculator to make a histogram.

EXAMPLE

Make a histogram of the data below.
21, 23, 20, 22, 23, 21, 24, 26, 23, 21, 20, 23, 21, 23, 20, 24

Step 1 Press **LIST** to find list L_1.
Enter the data in L_1. (To first remove
any data already in L_1, select L_1, then
`CLEAR` `ENTER`.)

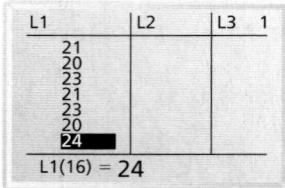

Step 2 In **PLOT**, enter 1 and select **On**.
Select the Type of graph that looks
like a histogram and `ENTER`.

Step 3 In the **ZOOM** menu, select item 7
"ZoomStat" and `ENTER`. In `WINDOW`, set
Xscl = 1. Then `GRAPH`.

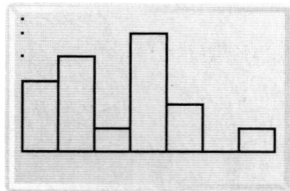

Step 4 To see the frequency of each number,
press `TRACE`, and move the cursor across the
histogram. Sketch the histogram.

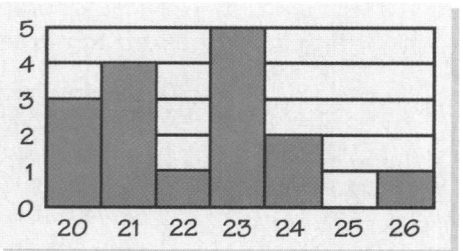

EXERCISES

Use a graphing calculator to make a histogram of each set of data.
Then sketch the histogram.

1. 11, 12, 12, 11, 10, 12, 13, 15, 9, 10, 12, 13

2. 9, 7, 6, 9, 8, 5, 9, 2, 2, 5, 8, 4, 6, 3, 8, 7, 8, 5

3. 23, 26, 25, 26, 23, 25, 25, 24, 21, 21, 22, 23

4. 95, 90, 92, 91, 95, 94, 93, 92, 94, 93, 95, 91

5. In Step 3 above, `ENTER` showed one histogram and then `GRAPH`
showed another. They are histograms of the same data. Explain
the difference in how they look.

Box-and-Whisker Plots

A **box-and-whisker plot** displays the distribution of data items along a number line. **Quartiles** divide the data into four equal parts. The median is the middle quartile.

Box-and-Whisker Plot

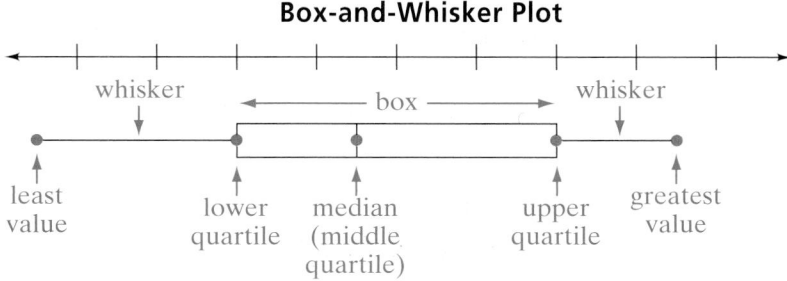

whisker   box   whisker

least value   lower quartile   median (middle quartile)   upper quartile   greatest value

1 EXAMPLE   Real-World 🌐 Problem Solving

Statistics The table, below right, shows United States crops harvested from 1988 to 2000. Make a box-and-whisker plot.

Step 1 Arrange the data in order from least to greatest. Find the median.

298 308 314 317 318 318 321 322 323 326 326 327 333

Step 2 Find the lower quartile and upper quartile, which are the medians of the lower and upper "halves."

298 308 314 317 318 318 321 322 323 326 326 327 333

$$\text{lower quartile} = \frac{314 + 317}{2} = \frac{631}{2} = 315.5$$

$$\text{upper quartile} = \frac{326 + 326}{2} = \frac{652}{2} = 326$$

Step 3 Draw a number line. Mark the least and greatest values, the median, and the quartiles. Draw a box from the first to the third quartiles. Mark the median with a vertical segment. Draw whiskers from the box to the least and greatest values.

Crops Harvested (millions of acres)

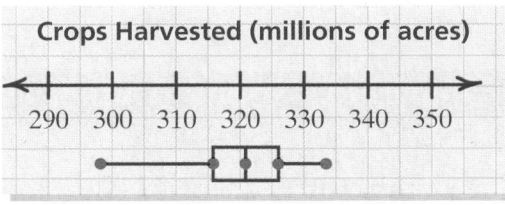

290 300 310 320 330 340 350

What You'll Learn

OBJECTIVE 1 To make box-and-whisker plots

OBJECTIVE 2 To analyze data in box-and-whisker plots

. . . And Why

To solve real-world problems involving large data sets

✔ Check Skills You'll Need

Find each median.

1. 12, 10, 11, 7, 9, 8, 10, 5

2. 4.5, 3.2, 6.3, 5.2, 5, 4.8, 6, 3.9

3. 55, 53, 67, 52, 50, 49, 51, 52, 52, 52

4. 101, 100, 100, 105, 102, 101

 For help, go to Lesson 3-3.

New Vocabulary

• box-and-whisker plot
• quartiles

Crops Harvested

Year	Acres (millions)	Year	Acres (millions)
1988	298	1995	314
1989	318	1996	326
1990	322	1997	333
1991	318	1998	326
1992	317	1999	327
1993	308	2000	323
1994	321		

SOURCE: *Statistical Abstract of the United States.* Go to to **www.PHSchool.com** for a data update. Web Code: adg-2041

iTEXT Interactive lesson includes instant self-check, tutorials, and activities.

✓ **Check Understanding** Example 1

1. Draw a box-and-whisker plot for the distances of migration of birds (thousands of miles): 5, 2.5, 6, 8, 9, 2, 1, 4, 6.2, 18, 7.

You can compare two sets of data by making two box-and-whisker plots below one number line.

Real-World Connection

DNA evidence suggests that whales and hippopotamuses are closely related genetically.

2 EXAMPLE Real-World 🌐 Problem Solving

Biology Use box-and-whisker plots to compare orca whale masses and hippopotamus masses.

Orca whale masses (kg)

3,900   2,750   2,600   3,100   4,200   2,600   3,700   3,000   2,200

Hippopotamus masses (kg)

1,800   2,000   3,000   2,500   3,600   2,700   1,900   3,100   2,300

Draw a number line for both sets of data. Use the range of data points to choose a scale.

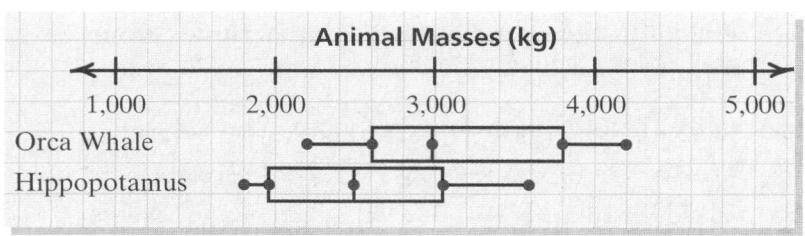

Draw the second box-and-whisker plot below the first one.

✓ **Check Understanding** Example 2

2. Compare annual video sales and CD sales by making two box-and-whisker plots below one number line.

videos (millions of units): 28, 24, 15, 21, 22, 16, 22, 30, 24, 17

CDs (millions of units): 16, 17, 22, 16, 18, 24, 15, 16, 25, 18

OBJECTIVE

2 Analyzing Box-and-Whisker Plots

Although you cannot see every data point in a box-and-whisker plot, you can use the quartiles and the greatest and least values to analyze and describe a data set.

3 EXAMPLE Describing Data

Describe the data in the box-and-whisker plot.

The highest score is 90 and the lowest is 50. At least half of the scores are within 10 points of the median, 75.

Exam Scores

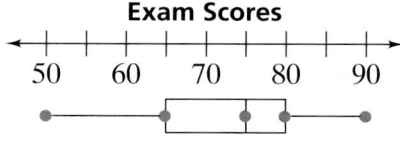

✓ Check Understanding Example 3

3. Describe the data in each box-and-whisker plot.

a.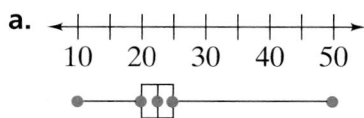

b.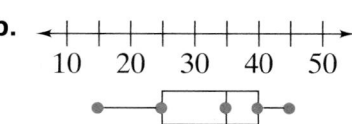

You can compare box-and-whisker plots to analyze two sets of data.

4 EXAMPLE Real-World 🌐 Problem Solving

Social Studies The plots below compare the percents of the voting-age population who said they registered to vote in U.S. elections to the percents who said they voted. What conclusions can you draw?

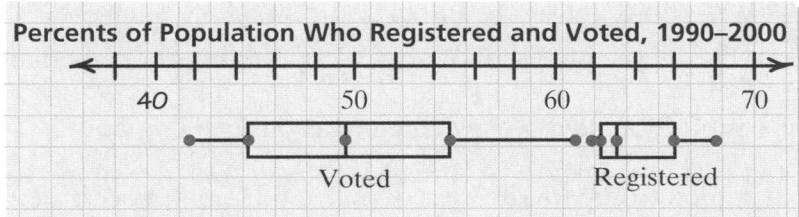

Percents of Population Who Registered and Voted, 1990–2000

Voted

Registered

The percent registered was fairly constant, since the box-and-whisker plot is narrow. The percent who voted varied more. You can conclude that in an election, on average, the percent of people who voted was about 15 less than the percent of people who were registered.

✓ Check Understanding Example 4

4. Use box-and-whisker plots below. What conclusions can you draw about heights of Olympic basketball players?

Olympic Basketball Players' Heights (in.)

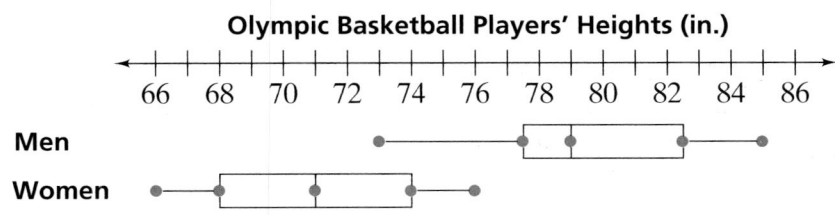

Men

Women

EXERCISES

For more exercises, see *Extra Practice*.

Practice and Problem Solving

A Practice by Example
Example 1
(page 635)

1. **Biology** Use the data at the right to make a box-and-whisker plot for the maximum speeds of animals.

2. Make a box-and-whisker plot for this set of data:
16, 18, 59, 75, 30, 34, 25, 49, 27, 16, 21, 58, 71, 19, 50

Example 2
(page 636)

3. Compare the data sets by making two box-and-whisker plots below one number line.
set A: 3, 7, 9, 12, 2, 1, 6, 5, 4, 3, 7, 10, 13, 8, 1, 9
set B: 9, 8, 1, 7, 6, 3, 7, 9, 8, 6, 4, 7, 8, 9, 10, 10

Maximum Speeds of Animals for a Quarter Mile

Animal	Maximum Speed (mi/h)
Cheetah	70
Lion	50
Quarter horse	47.5
Coyote	43
Hyena	40
Rabbit	35
Giraffe	32
Grizzly bear	30
Cat (domestic)	30
Elephant	25
Squirrel	12

SOURCE: *The World Almanac*

Example 3
(page 637)

Answer each question for the data in the box-and-whisker plot below.

4. What are the highest and lowest prices for the CD players?

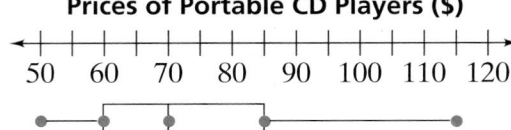

Prices of Portable CD Players ($)

5. What is the lower quartile price? The median price? The upper quartile price?

6. About half of the prices are within what amount of the median?

Example 4
(page 637)

7. In Example 2 on page 636, what conclusions can you draw?

B Apply Your Skills

8. a. **Olympics** Compare the ages of male and female soccer players by making two box-and-whisker plots below one number line.

Ages of U.S. Olympic Soccer Team Players

men: 22, 21, 22, 26, 20, 26, 23, 21, 22, 22, 22, 22, 21, 22, 23, 21, 20, 22

women: 30, 27, 28, 25, 31, 24, 31, 24, 21, 23, 27, 18, 19, 24, 23, 20

b. Compare the box-and-whisker plots. What can you conclude?

9. Use the box-and-whisker plot below. What can you conclude about acreages of state parks?

Areas of State Parks (acres)

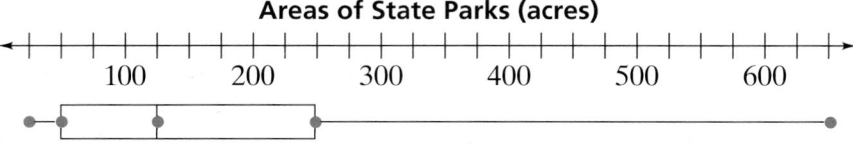

10. **Writing in Math** Explain how you can find the quartiles of a set of data.

11. **Error Analysis** A student made a box-and-whisker plot. The student marked the greatest and least data values and then divided the distance between those points into four equal parts. What error did the student make?

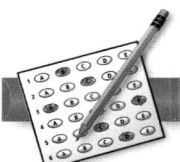 Challenge

12. **Open-Ended** Write a set of data whose box-and-whisker plot has a long box and short whiskers.

13. **Reasoning** Can you find the mean, median, and mode of a set of data by looking at a box-and-whisker plot? Explain.

 Test Prep

Multiple Choice

For Exercises 14–16, use the table.

14. What is the median of the maximum life spans of the animals in the table?
   A. 18 yr   B. 31 yr
   C. 34 yr   D. 50 yr

Take It to the NET
Online lesson quiz at
www.PHSchool.com
Web Code: ada-1202

15. What is the median of the maximum life spans of the animals if you exclude the mouse and chipmunk?
   F. 50 yr   G. 43 yr
   H. 26 yr   I. 18 yr

Short Response

16. a. Make a box-and-whisker plot to represent the maximum life spans.
   b. Identify and label the median, the lower and upper quartiles, and the least and greatest maximum life spans.

Animals' Maximum Life Spans

Animal	Years
Beaver	50
Black bear	36
Chimpanzee	53
Chipmunk	8
Elephant	77
Goat	18
Horse	50
Mouse	6
Squirrel	23
Tiger	26

Mixed Review

Lesson 12-1

Display each set of data in a frequency table.

17. 6 8 7 6 5 8 5 6 4 8 7 5
    4 7 6 8 6 7

18. 32 31 29 33 31 32 35 33
    32 31 32 30

Lesson 11-3

Find the distance between the points in each pair to the nearest tenth.

19. $D(3, -2), S(-3, 2)$

20. $A(0, 4), W(-7, -5)$

21. $Y(6, 4), K(-1, 3)$

22. $Z(9, 0), M(-8, 11)$

Lessons 4-9 and 5-5 🌐 23. Lawns can have 850 blades of grass per square foot.
   a. About how many blades of grass are in one square yard?
   b. The area of all lawns in the United States equals an area twice as large as that of Pennsylvania. Pennsylvania's area is 46,058 mi^2. Estimate the number of blades of grass in lawns in the United States. Write your answer in scientific notation. (*Hint:* A mile equals 5,280 feet.)

A *stem-and-leaf plot* organizes data
by showing the items in order.
The leaf is the last digit to the right.
The stem is the remaining digit or digits.

stem⟶ 15.7 ⟵leaf

stem⟶ 32 ⟵leaf

1 EXAMPLE

**Use the table at the right to construct a stem-and-leaf plot.
Then find the median, mode, and range.**

Choose the stems. For this data set,
use the values in the tens place.
Draw a line to the right of the stems.

stems ⟶
```
2|
3|
```

Leaves are single digits, so for this
data set the leaves will be the values
in the ones place.

```
2|9 8
3|7 8 7 3 9 7
```
⟵ leaves

Broadway Productions

```
2|9 8
3|7 8 7 3 9 7
2|8 means 28
```
⟵ key

Arrange the leaves on each stem
from least to greatest. Include a title
and a key that shows how to read
your stem-and-leaf plot.

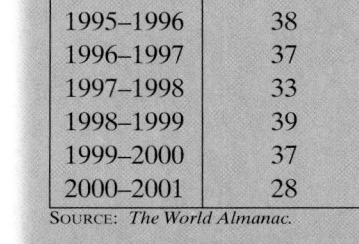

Broadway Productions

Season	New Shows
1993–1994	37
1994–1995	29
1995–1996	38
1996–1997	37
1997–1998	33
1998–1999	39
1999–2000	37
2000–2001	28

SOURCE: *The World Almanac.*

Since the data items are in order, the median is the midpoint.
The median is the mean of the fourth and fifth values, or 37.

The mode corresponds to the most repeated leaf. The mode is 37.

The range is the difference of the greatest and least values, or 11.

Average Longevity

Animal	Years	Animal	Years
Grizzly bear	25	Hippopotamus	41
Kangaroo	7	Pig	10
Cow	15	Lion	15
Dog	12	Opossum	1
Giraffe	10	Cat	12
Gorilla	20	Zebra	15

SOURCE: *The World Almanac*

1. **Biology** Use the table at the right.
   a. **Reasoning** What number should
      you use as the stem for the kangaroo
      and the opossum?
   b. Construct a stem-and-leaf plot.
   c. Find the median.
   d. Find the mode.
   e. Find the range.

**Make a stem-and leaf plot for each set of data.
Then find the median, the mode, and the range.**

2. 15, 22, 25, 10, 36, 15, 28, 35, 18

3. 47, 41, 60, 75, 85, 53, 57, 76, 79, 81, 84, 86

4. 785, 785, 776, 772, 792, 788, 761, 768, 768

5. 4.5, 4.3, 0.8, 3.5, 2.6, 1.4, 0.2, 0.8, 4.3, 6.0

A back-to-back stem-and-leaf plot uses two sets of data. The side-by-side display makes the data easier to compare.

2 EXAMPLE

Draw a back-to-back stem-and-leaf plot for the winning times in the Olympic 100-m dash. Find each median and mode.

Use seconds for the stem and tenths of seconds for the leaves. Put the leaves in ascending order starting at the stem.

Winning Times, 100-m Dash

Men's Times (tenths of second)	Stem (seconds)	Women's Times (tenths of second)
9 9 9 8	9	
3 2 1 1 0 0 0	10	5 8 8 9
	11	0 0 0 1 1 1 4

means 10.0 ← 0 | 10 | 5 → means 10.5

The median of the times for men is 10.0 s. The median of the times for women is 11.0 s. The modes of the times for men are 9.9 s and 10.0 s. The modes of the times for women are 11.0 s and 11.1 s.

Winning Times, 100-m Dash (seconds)

Year	Men	Women
1960	10.2	11.0
1964	10.0	11.4
1968	9.9	11.0
1972	10.1	11.1
1976	10.1	11.1
1980	10.3	11.1
1984	10.0	11.0
1988	9.9	10.5
1992	10.0	10.8
1996	9.8	10.9
2000	9.9	10.8

SOURCE: *Sports Illustrated Sports Almanac*

Make a back-to-back stem-and-leaf plot for each pair of data sets. Then find each median and mode.

6. set A: 9.1, 8.2, 7.3, 6.4, 7.3, 8.5   set B: 7.6, 9.2, 8.2, 8.3, 9.7, 7.6

7. set C: 236, 237, 241, 250, 242   set D: 262, 251, 248, 243, 257

8. Annual video sales (millions):   Annual CD sales (millions):
28, 24, 15, 21, 22, 16, 22, 30, 24, 17   16, 17, 22, 16, 18, 24, 15, 16, 25, 18

Use the stem-and-leaf plot at the right. The plot shows the time spent on homework by students in two classes.

9. Which numbers are the stems?

10. What is the least time spent for each set of data?

11. What is the median for each set of data?

12. What is the mode for each set of data?

13. What is the range for each set of data?

Time Spent on Homework (min)

Class A		Class B
7 4 3	6	1 1 3 5 5
9 9 8 5 4 4	7	0 2 2 4
5 2 1 0	8	4 5 8 9
7 6 6 4 2	9	3 6 7 9 9 9

means 63 ← 3 | 6 | 1 → means 61

12-3

Using Graphs to Persuade

What You'll Learn

OBJECTIVE

1 To recognize the use of breaks in the scales of graphs

OBJECTIVE

2 To recognize the use of different scales

...And Why

To solve real-world problems involving population and cost of living

✓ **Check Skills You'll Need**

Find the slope of $\overline{AB}$ in each graph.

1.

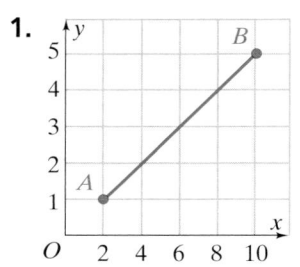

2.

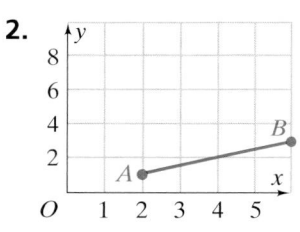

❓ For help, go to Lesson 8-3.

OBJECTIVE

1 | Using Breaks in Scales

You can draw graphs of a data set in different ways in order to give different impressions.

You can use a break in the scale on one or both axes of a line graph or a bar graph. This lets you show more detail and emphasize differences. However, it can also give a distorted picture of the data.

1 EXAMPLE Real-World 🌐 Problem Solving

Population Which title would be more appropriate for the graph below: "Los Angeles Overwhelms Chicago" or "Populations of Chicago and Los Angeles"? Explain.

Because of the break in the vertical axis, the bar for Los Angeles appears to be more than three times as tall as the bar for Chicago. Actually, the population of Los Angeles is a little less than 3.6 million, and the population of Chicago is about 2.7 million. So the population of Los Angeles is about 1.3 times that of Chicago.

The title "Los Angeles Overwhelms Chicago" could be misleading. "Populations of Chicago and Los Angeles" better describes the information in the graph.

✓ **Check Understanding** Example 1

1. Use the data in the graph in Example 1. Redraw the graph without a break.

ⓘ**TEXT** Interactive lesson includes instant self-check, tutorials, and activities.

2   Using Different Scales

You can use different scales or spacing along axes. This lets you emphasize (or de-emphasize) how changes in data are related.

2 EXAMPLE   <u>Real-World</u> 🌐 <u>Problem Solving</u>

Cost of Living **Study the graphs below. Which graph gives the impression of a sharper increase in price? Explain.**

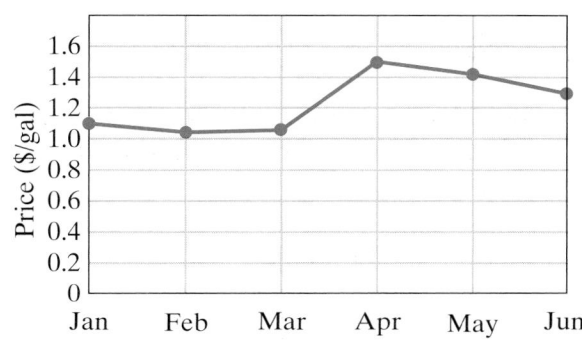

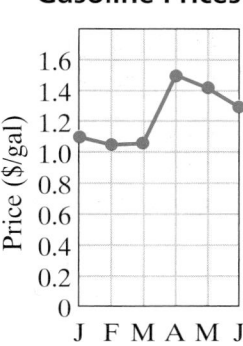

In the graph at the right, the months are much closer together, so the line appears to climb more rapidly. This graph suggests that prices are going up faster than suggested by the graph at the left.

✓ **Check Understanding**   Example 2

2. Use the data in the table at the right.

   a. Make a graph that suggests a rapid decrease in the total weight of fish caught.

   b. Make a graph that suggests a slow decrease in the total weight of fish caught.

   c. **Reasoning** A group is planning a campaign to protect the supply of fish. They are proposing a regulation that would limit the number of pounds of fish caught annually. Would they more likely use the graph from part (a) or part (b) in their proposal? Explain.

Fish Caught for Food in the U.S.

Year	Fish Caught (billions of pounds)
1993	8.2
1994	7.9
1995	7.7
1996	7.5

SOURCE: *Statistical Abstract of the United States.* Go to **www.PHSchool.com** for a data update. Web Code: adg-2041

There is a fine line between using graphs to persuade and using graphs to mislead.

Bar graphs can be misleading if their "bars" change in more than one dimension. This can happen when graphs use realistic images for the bars. These images make the graphs more interesting but also can give false impressions.

3 EXAMPLE   Real-World 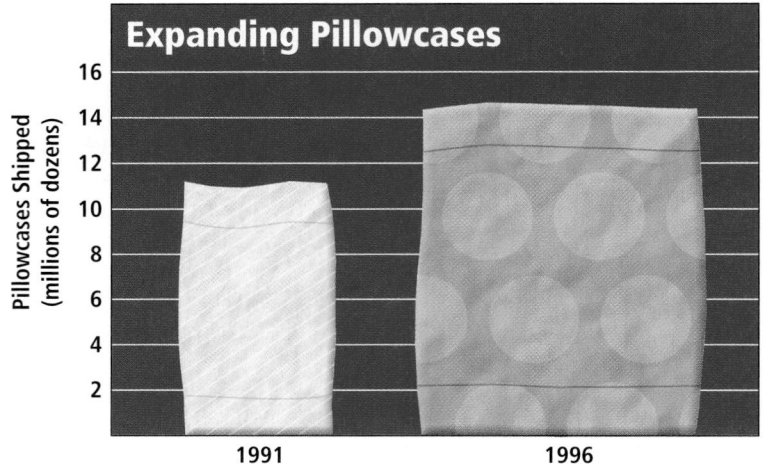 Problem Solving

Reasoning **What makes the graph misleading? Explain.**

By reading the vertical axis, you can see that the number of pillowcases shipped increased by about one fourth.

However, the bar on the right has not only increased in height, but has also nearly doubled in width. The area of the second bar is more than two times the area of the first bar.

Because of this, you might get the impression that the increase was much greater than it really was.

✔ Check Understanding   Example 3

3. Use the data in the table below.

Prices of Field-Grown Tomatoes in the United States

Year	Price of Tomatoes (cents per pound)
1990	86
1997	162

SOURCE: *Statistical Abstract of the United States*. Go to **www.PHSchool.com** for a data update. Web Code: adg-2041

a. Draw a graph that suggests that the price of tomatoes nearly doubled.
b. Draw a graph that suggests that the price of tomatoes more than doubled.

EXERCISES

For more exercises, see *Extra Practice*.

Practice and Problem Solving

A Practice by Example

Example 1
(page 642)

For Exercises 1–4, use the graph at the right.

Magazine Circulation

Circuitry Today
American Ampersand
Waffleball World
Fossil Week

7 9 11 13 15 17
Circulation (millions)

1. Which magazine *appears* to have about twice the circulation of *Circuitry Today?*

2. Which magazine *actually* has twice the circulation of *Circuitry Today?*

3. Explain why the graph might mislead you.

4. Redraw the graph without a break in the horizontal axis.

Example 2
(page 643)

Statistics For Exercises 5–7, use the graph at the right.

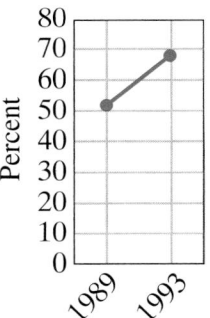

Percent of Students Using Computers at School

80
70
60
50
40
30
20
10
0

1989   1993
Year

Percent

5. **School Computers** Does the graph suggest a rapid increase or a slow increase in the percent of students using a computer at school?

6. Redraw the graph. Change the horizontal scale to suggest a slower increase from 1989 to 1993.

7. Redraw the graph. Suggest a slower increase from 1989 to 1993 by changing the vertical scale.

Example 3
(page 644)

Food Service For Exercises 8–10, use the graph below.

Milk Sales in the School Cafeteria

Cartons of Milk Sold

3,000
2,000
1,000
0

MILK   MILK

Jan   Feb
Month

8. What impression does the graph give you about milk sales in the school cafeteria? Is the graph misleading? Explain.

9. Redraw the graph to represent the data accurately.

10. Redraw the graph to suggest that milk sales changed very little.

Reading Math

For help with reading the table and drawing the graph in Exercise 11, see page 648.

11. a. Statistics Use the data at the right. Draw a graph with an axis break to suggest that enrollment in 2000 was many times the enrollment in 1990.
   b. Draw a second graph of the data, without using a break. Choose a scale that suggests that enrollment did not increase much from 1990 to 2000.

U.S. College Enrollment

Year	Enrollment
1990	13.8 million
1995	14.2 million
2000	14.9 million

SOURCE: U.S. Education Department

For Exercises 12–14, use the graph at the right.

12. Writing in Math The graph suggests that the number of students per computer in elementary schools is three times the number of students per computer in high schools. Is this true? Explain.

Average Number of Students per Computer

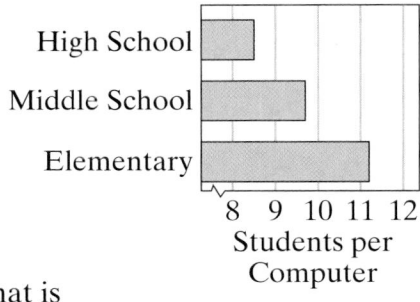

13. What does the graph suggest is the ratio of middle school students per computer to high school students per computer? What is the actual ratio?

14. Redraw the graph without a break. Describe the effect this has on what the graph suggests.

Average Annual Tuition and Fees for Four-Year Public Colleges

Year	Tuition and Fees
1980–1981	$1,647
1990–1991	$2,529
2000–2001	$3,535

SOURCE: The College Board

15. Use the data at the left. Draw a line graph that gives the impression of a gradual increase in college tuition and fees from 1980 to 2001.

16. Open-Ended Find a graph in a newspaper or magazine that could be misleading. Explain how it could be misleading.

 Challenge

Percent of Milk Sold That Was Low-Fat

Year	Percent
1980	38%
1990	59%

17. Use the data at the left to make two different graphs. Draw one of the graphs to suggest that the percent of low-fat milk sold in 1990 was double the percent in 1980.

18. Statistics Use the graph at the right. Explain why the intervals on the horizontal axis could make the graph misleading.

19. Tell how to scale the x- and y-axes so that $\overline{AB}$ joining points $A(4, 2)$ and $B(8, 6)$ appears to have the slope given.

   a. $\frac{1}{2}$ **b.** 1   **c.** 2

Test Prep

Multiple Choice   For Exercises 20 and 21, use the graph below.

20. The graph makes it appear that there are how many times as many students per teacher at North HS as there are at West HS?

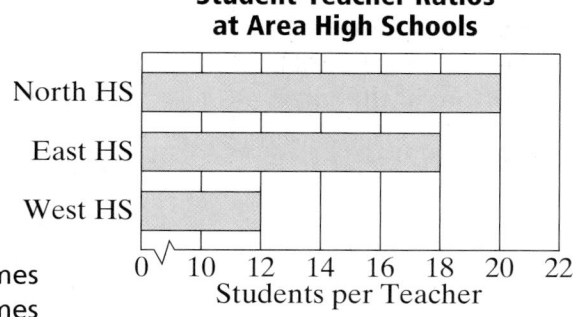

Student-Teacher Ratios at Area High Schools

A. 2 times   B. 3 times
C. 4 times   D. 5 times

21. Why might this graph give a distorted picture of the data?
    F. The longest horizontal bar is on top.
    G. The vertical lines are evenly spaced.
    H. There is a break in the horizontal axis.
    I. The horizontal bars are different lengths.

Short Response   22. Use the table at the right to make two different line graphs.
    a. Draw one graph to suggest that sales more than doubled from 1996 to 1999.
    b. Draw the other graph to suggest that sales increased only slightly during the same period.

Annual Sales

Year	Sales
1996	$87 million
1997	$87 million
1998	$88 million
1999	$90 million

Take It to the NET
Online lesson quiz at
www.PHSchool.com
Web Code: ada-1203

Mixed Review

Lesson 12-2   **Make a box-and-whisker plot for each set of data.**

23. 27, 25, 23, 29, 25, 28, 26, 27, 23, 21, 20, 24, 25, 28, 30, 19, 25

24. 2, 6, 3, 9, 15, 4, 9, 20, 6, 7, 2, 3, 8, 4, 1, 5, 6, 8, 5, 4, 9, 3, 2, 8, 7

25. 100, 95, 102, 101, 96, 100, 104, 115, 102, 108, 92, 97, 103, 106

Lessons 10-5   26. **Geometry** The Museum of Health and Medical Science in Houston, Texas, has one of the largest kaleidoscopes in the world. It is a cylinder 10 feet long and 22 inches in diameter. What is the surface area of the kaleidoscope?

Lesson 6-4   **Find each probability for choosing a letter at random from the word STATISTICS.**

27. $P(\text{vowel})$ 28. $P(S)$ 29. $P(\text{not } T)$ 30. $P(A \text{ or } C)$

Reading Math
Reading for Problem Solving

For Use With Page 646, Exercise 11

Read the problems below. Then follow along with what Kayla thinks as she solves them. Check your understanding by solving the exercise at the bottom of the page.

a. Statistics Use the data at the right. Draw a graph with a break to suggest that enrollment in 2000 was many times the enrollment in 1990.

b. Draw a second graph of the data without using a break. Choose a scale that suggests that enrollment did not increase much from 1990 to 2000.

U.S. College Enrollment

Year	Enrollment
1990	13.8 million
1995	14.2 million
2000	14.9 million

SOURCE: U.S. Education Department

What Kayla Thinks

Part (a) asks me to draw a graph with a break that makes enrollment in 2000 look *many times* the enrollment in 1990.

I'll use a bar graph. The table shows the 1990 enrollment was 13.8 million. I'll break the vertical scale right before 13.8 to make the 1990 bar look small.

The table shows a 2000 enrollment of 14.9 million. I'll use vertical intervals of 0.3. That makes the top mark 15.0.

The bar for 14.9 is as tall as possible. It looks nearly 4 times as tall as 1990!

Part (b) asks for no break. I'll scale by 2 on the vertical axis. This will make 1990 and 2000 almost the same height.

What Kayla Draws

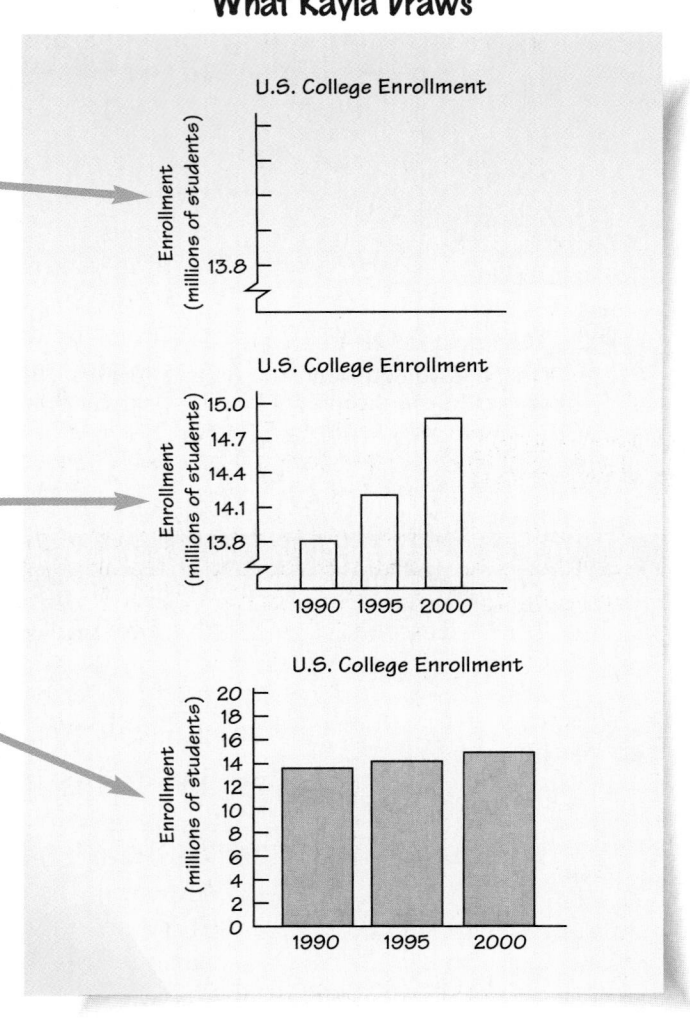

EXERCISE

1. Two months ago, the price for Technostar stock was $32. Last month it was $32.40. Now it is $32.80. Draw graphs suggesting each of the following about the stock price.

   a. a large increase   **b.** a small increase

Counting Outcomes and Theoretical Probability

OBJECTIVE

1 Counting Possible Choices

Exploring Possible Outcomes

Congratulations! Your application to run the pizza stand at school home games has been accepted. Now you have to decide which pizzas to sell. You plan to offer two or three choices in each of three categories—size, crust, and topping. The more types of pizza the better, but you're limited by kitchen space to a total of 18 types.

1. Decide which types of pizza you will offer. Make a menu that shows your customers their options.

2. **Reasoning** Suppose you decide to offer three choices of size and three choices of crust. How many choices of toppings can you offer?

You can use a tree diagram to display and count possible choices.

1 EXAMPLE   Drawing a Tree Diagram

A school team sells caps in two colors (blue or white), two sizes (child or adult), and two fabrics (cotton or polyester). Draw a tree diagram to find the number of cap choices.

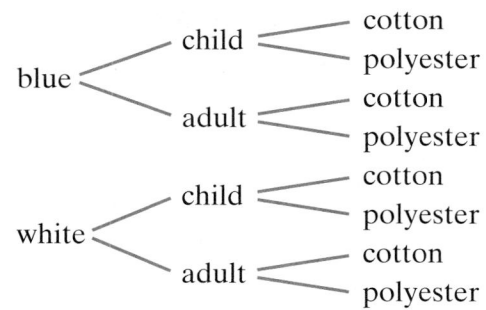

Each branch of the "tree" represents one choice—for example, blue-child-cotton.

• There are 8 possible cap choices.

✓ Check Understanding   Example 1

1. Suppose the caps in Example 1 also come in black. Draw a tree diagram. How many cap choices are there?

What You'll Learn

OBJECTIVE 1 To use a tree diagram and the Counting Principle to count possible choices

OBJECTIVE 2 To find theoretical probability by counting outcomes

... And Why

To solve real-world problems involving probabilities and outcomes

✓ Check Skills You'll Need

A bag has 5 blue (B) chips, 4 red (R) chips, and 3 tan (T) chips. Find each probability for choosing a chip at random from the bag.

1. $P(R)$ 2. $P(\text{not } R)$

3. $P(B)$ 4. $P(R \text{ or } B)$

5. $P(T)$ 6. $P(B \text{ or } T)$

 For help, go to Lesson 6-4

New Vocabulary

• counting principle
• theoretical probability
• sample space

TEXT Interactive lesson includes instant self-check, tutorials, and activities.

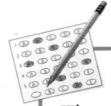

Another way to count choices is to use the **Counting Principle.**

| **Key Concepts** | **Counting Principle** |

If there are *m* ways of making one choice, and *n* ways of making a second choice, then there are $m \cdot n$ ways of making the first choice followed by the second.

The Counting Principle is particularly useful when a tree diagram would be too large to draw.

Real-World 🌐 Connection

A monogram is made up of two or more letters, such as your initials.

2 EXAMPLE **Using the Counting Principle**

How many two-letter monograms are possible?

first letter	second letter	**monograms**
possible choices	possible choices	possible choices
26	· 26 =	676

● There are 676 possible two-letter monograms.

✓ **Check Understanding** **Example 2**

2. **a.** How many three-letter monograms are possible?
   b. How many five-letter license plates can be made if the letters O and I cannot be used?

OBJECTIVE

2 **Finding Probability by Counting Outcomes**

You can count outcomes to help you find the **theoretical probability** of an event in which outcomes are equally likely.

| **Key Concepts** | **Theoretical Probability** |

$$P(\text{event}) = \frac{\text{number of favorable outcomes}}{\text{number of possible outcomes}}$$

A **sample space** is a list of all possible outcomes. You can use a tree diagram to find a sample space. Then you can calculate probability.

𝒊TEXT Interactive lesson includes instant self-check, tutorials, and activities.

3 EXAMPLE   Using a Tree Diagram

Use a tree diagram to find the sample space for tossing two coins. Then find the probability of tossing two tails.

heads — heads
heads — tails
tails — heads
tails — tails

The tree diagram shows there are four possible outcomes, one of which is tossing two tails.

$P(\text{event}) = \dfrac{\text{number of favorable outcomes}}{\text{number of possible outcomes}}$ Use the probability formula.

$P(\text{two tails}) = \dfrac{\text{number of two-tail outcomes}}{\text{number of possible outcomes}}$

$= \dfrac{1}{4}$

● The probability of tossing two tails is $\frac{1}{4}$.

✓ Check Understanding   Example 3

3. You toss two coins. Find $P(\text{one head and one tail})$.

You can also use the Counting Principle to find probability.

4 EXAMPLE   Real-World 🌐 Problem Solving

Many people play lottery games without knowing the probability of winning. In some state lotteries, the winning number is made up of four digits chosen at random. Suppose a player buys two tickets with different numbers. What is the probability that the player has a winning ticket?

First find the number of possible outcomes. For each digit, there are 10 possible outcomes, 0 through 9.

1st digit outcomes		2nd digit outcomes		3rd digit outcomes		4th digit outcomes		total outcomes
10	·	10	·	10	·	10	=	10,000

Then find the probability when there are two favorable outcomes.

$P(\text{winning ticket}) = \dfrac{\text{number of favorable outcomes}}{\text{number of possible outcomes}} = \dfrac{2}{10,000}$

● The probability is $\frac{2}{10,000}$, or $\frac{1}{5,000}$.

✓ Check Understanding   Example 4

4. A lottery uses five digits chosen at random. Find the probability of buying a winning ticket.

EXERCISES

For more exercises, see *Extra Practice*.

Practice and Problem Solving

 Practice by Example

Example 1
(page 649)

You can choose a burrito having one filling wrapped in one tortilla. Draw a tree diagram to count the number of burrito choices.

1. tortillas: flour or corn; fillings: beef, chicken, bean, cheese, or vegetable

2. tortillas: whole wheat flour, blue corn, or white corn; fillings: chicken, tofu, grilled fish, or vegetable

Example 2
(page 650)

There are four roads from Marsh to Taft and seven roads from Taft to Polk. Use the Counting Principle to find the number of routes below.

3. from Marsh to Polk through Taft

4. from Marsh to Polk after a new road opens from Marsh to Taft

Example 3
(page 651)

Use a tree diagram to find the sample space for tossing three coins. Then find each probability.

5. P(three heads)   6. P(two tails)   7. P(at least one head)

Example 4
(page 651)

Use the Counting Principle to help you find each probability.

8. Rolling a 3 on each of two number cubes

9. **Lottery** Choosing the three winning lottery numbers when the numbers are chosen at random from 1 to 50. Numbers can repeat.

 Apply Your Skills   10. **Snacks** You can choose chocolate, strawberry, or vanilla frozen yogurt, and red, blue, or green sprinkles. A sundae has one yogurt flavor and two different colors of sprinkles. How many different kinds of sundaes can you order? List them.

Sweaters

Colors	Styles
Blue	Cardigan
Pink	Crewneck
Red	V-neck
Brown	
Black	

You have one sweater of each possible color and style in the table (left).

11. How many sweaters do you have?

12. What is the probability of choosing a brown sweater at random?

13. What is the probability of choosing a cardigan at random?

Find the probability of each event.

14. You toss tails and roll an even number (when you toss a coin and roll a number cube).

15. You roll two odd numbers and pick a vowel (when you roll two number cubes and pick a letter of the alphabet at random).

Challenge

16. **Reasoning** You have a bag containing an equal number of nickels, dimes, and quarters. You reach into the bag and choose a coin. Are all outcomes equally likely? Explain.

17. **Writing in Math** Write a problem (unlike any in this lesson) that you can solve using the Counting Principle. Then solve.

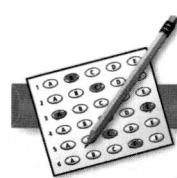

Test Prep

Multiple Choice

18. You are writing a three-digit number. The first digit must be 2 or 8. The second digit must be 1, 3, or 9. The third digit must be 4, 5, 6, 7, or 8. Which expression can you use to find how many different three-digit numbers you can write?
A. $2 \cdot 3 \cdot 5$ **B.** $5 \cdot 4 \cdot 3 \cdot 2 \cdot 1$
C. $(1 \cdot 2) + (2 \cdot 3) + (3 \cdot 5)$ **D.** $2 + 3 + 5$

19. An ice-cream vendor sells small or large cones and has chocolate, vanilla, rocky road, pecan, and strawberry flavors. To help a customer select a flavor and size, the vendor has a spinner. What is the probability that the spinner will choose a large strawberry for a customer?
F. $\frac{1}{14}$ **G.** $\frac{1}{10}$ **H.** $\frac{1}{7}$ **I.** $\frac{1}{3}$

Extended Response

Take It to the NET
Online lesson quiz at
www.PHSchool.com
Web Code: ada-1204

20. You roll two number cubes. List all possible outcomes. Find the probability of each event. Show your work.
a. rolling a 1 and a 2
b. rolling the same numbers
c. rolling different numbers

Mixed Review

Lesson 12-1

Display each data set in a line plot. Find the range.

21. 3 4 5 4 7 7 3 6 5   **22.** 19 18 19 17 17 16 19 18 17 19

Lesson 11-3

Find the midpoint of a segment with the given endpoints.

23. $X(3, -2)$ and $Y(-3, 6)$ **24.** $A(-1, 0)$ and $B(2, 1)$

Checkpoint Quiz 1   Lessons 12-1 through 12-4

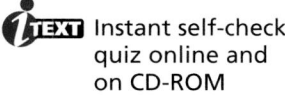 Instant self-check quiz online and on CD-ROM

1. Display the data below in a frequency table.
47 51 50 52 50 47 48 50 49 51 48 52

2. Make a box-and-whisker plot for the data below.
31, 33, 74, 90, 44, 49, 40, 64, 42, 31, 36, 73, 86, 34, 46, 65

3. Open-Ended Use the data in the table.
a. Draw a graph that could be misleading. Explain.
b. Draw a second graph that is not misleading.

Year	Hourly Minimum Wage
1996	$4.75
1997	$5.15

SOURCE: *Wall Street Journal Almanac*

4. Olivia and Oliver each choose a number from 1 to 10 at random. What is the probability that both numbers are odd numbers?

12-5

Independent and DObjective Events

What You'll Learn

OBJECTIVE 1
To calculate probabilities of independent events

OBJECTIVE 2
To calculate probabilities of dependent events

. . . And Why

To solve real-world problems involving games and science

✓ **Check Skills You'll Need**

Multiply.

1. $\frac{3}{5} \cdot \frac{1}{5}$ 2. $\frac{1}{4} \cdot \frac{2}{4}$

3. $\frac{4}{10} \cdot \frac{2}{10}$ 4. $\frac{5}{9} \cdot \frac{4}{8}$

5. $\frac{4}{7} \cdot \frac{3}{6}$ 6. $\frac{9}{10} \cdot \frac{8}{9}$

💬 For help, go to Lesson 5-4.

New Vocabulary

• **independent events**
• **dependent events**

OBJECTIVE 1   **Independent Events**

Exploring Probability in Games

You have four cards with an M written on them, two with an A, six with a T, and eight with an H.

1. You draw an M card at random and replace it. What is the probability that the next card you draw at random will also be an M card?

2. You draw an M card at random and do not replace the card. What is the probability that the next card you draw at random will also be an M card?

3. Make a table to find the probability of matching cards.

Probability **With** Replacement		Probability **Without** Replacement	
First Card	**Second Card Matches**	**First Card**	**Second Card Matches**
$P(M) = $ ▪	$P(M) = $ ▪	$P(M) = $ ▪	$P(M) = $ ▪
$P(A) = $ ▪	$P(A) = $ ▪	$P(A) = $ ▪	$P(A) = $ ▪
$P(T) = $ ▪	$P(T) = $ ▪	$P(T) = $ ▪	$P(T) = $ ▪
$P(H) = $ ▪	$P(H) = $ ▪	$P(H) = $ ▪	$P(H) = $ ▪

4. **Reasoning** For any letter, why is the probability for selecting the second card with replacement of the first card different from the probability of selecting the second card without replacement of the first card?

Suppose the numbers from 1 to 10 are written on 10 cards, one number to a card. You are interested in drawing one card at random and getting an even number, and then drawing a second card and getting an even number again.

If you *replace* your first card, the probability of getting an even number on the second card is unaffected.

Independent events are events for which the occurrence of one event *does not affect* the probability of the occurrence of the other.

📘 **TEXT** Interactive lesson includes instant self-check, tutorials, and activities.

Probability of Independent Events

For two independent events A and B, the probability of both events occurring is the product of the probabilities of each event occurring.

$$P(A, \text{then } B) = P(A) \cdot P(B)$$

1 EXAMPLE **Finding Probability for Independent Events**

You roll a number cube once. Then you roll it again. What is the probability that you get 2 on the first roll and a number greater than 4 on the second roll?

$P(2) = \frac{1}{6}$ **There is one 2 among 6 numbers on a number cube.**

$P(\text{greater than } 4) = \frac{2}{6}$ **There are two numbers greater than 4 on a number cube.**

$P(2, \text{then greater than } 4) = P(2) \cdot P(\text{greater than } 4)$

$$= \frac{1}{6} \cdot \frac{2}{6}$$

$$= \frac{2}{36}, \text{or } \frac{1}{18}$$

The probability is $\frac{1}{18}$.

✓ Check Understanding   **Example 1**

1. You toss a coin twice. Find the probability of getting two heads.

You can use fractions, decimals, or percents to represent probabilities and to find the probability of two events occurring.

2 EXAMPLE **Real-World**  **Problem Solving**

Botany Under the best conditions, a wild bluebonnet seed has a 20% probability of growing. If you select two seeds at random, what is the probability that both will grow, under the best conditions?

$P(\text{a seed grows}) = 20\%, \text{or } 0.20$ **Write the percent as a decimal.**

$P(\text{two seeds grow}) = P(\text{a seed grows}) \cdot P(\text{a seed grows})$

$$= 0.20 \cdot 0.20 \quad \textbf{Substitute.}$$

$$= 0.04 \quad \textbf{Multiply.}$$

$$= 4\% \quad \textbf{Write 0.04 as a percent.}$$

The probability that two seeds grow is 4%.

Real-World **Connection**

Bluebonnets grow wild in the southwestern United States.

2. **Botany** Chemically treated bluebonnet seeds have a 30% probability of growing. You select two such seeds at random. What is the probability that both will grow?

OBJECTIVE

2 **Dependent Events**

Suppose you want to draw two even-numbered cards from cards showing numbers from 1 to 10. You draw one card. Then, *without replacing* the first card, you draw a second card. The probability of drawing an even number on the second card is affected.

Dependent events are events for which the occurrence of one event *affects* the probability of the occurrence of the other.

Key Concepts **Probability of Dependent Events**

For two dependent events A and B, the probability of both events occurring is the product of the probability of the first event and the probability that, after the first event, the second event occurs.

$$P(A, \text{then } B) = P(A) \cdot P(B \text{ after } A)$$

3 **EXAMPLE** **Finding Probability for Dependent Events**

Three girls and two boys volunteer to represent their class at a school assembly. The teacher selects one name and then another from a bag containing the five students' names. What is the probability that both representatives will be girls?

$$P(\text{girl}) = \frac{3}{5} \quad \text{**Three of five students are girls.**}$$

$$P(\text{girl after girl}) = \frac{2}{4} \quad \text{**If a girl's name is drawn, two of the four remaining students are girls.**}$$

$P(\text{girl, then girl}) = P(\text{girl}) \cdot P(\text{girl after girl})$

$$= \frac{3}{5} \cdot \frac{2}{4} \quad \text{**Substitute.**}$$

$$= \frac{6}{20}, \text{or } \frac{3}{10} \quad \text{**Simplify.**}$$

● The probability that both representatives will be girls is $\frac{3}{10}$.

✓ **Check Understanding** Example 3

3. **a.** For Example 3, find $P(\text{boy, then girl})$.
   b. Find $P(\text{girl, then boy})$.

EXERCISES

For more exercises, see *Extra Practice*.

Practice and Problem Solving

 Practice by Example

Example 1
(page 655)

You roll a number cube twice. What is the probability that you roll each pair of numbers?

1. 6, then 5

2. 6, then a number less than 4

3. 6, then 2 or 5

4. an even number, then 2 or 5

5. 1, then 1

6. an even number, then an odd number

Example 2
(page 655)

7. Weather Forecasting Weather forecasters are accurate 91% of the time when predicting precipitation for the day. What is the probability that a forecaster will make correct precipitation predictions two days in a row?

Example 3
(page 656)

You select a card at random from those below. Without replacing the card, you select a second card. Find the probability of selecting each set of letters.

8. P, then G

9. E, then A

10. E, then a second vowel

11. G, then R or A

12. P or E, then A

13. a consonant, then a vowel

B **Apply Your Skills**

Are the events independent or dependent? Explain.

14. You select a card. Without putting the card back, you select a second card.

15. You roll a number cube. You roll it again.

You pick a marble from a bag containing 1 green marble, 4 red marbles, 2 yellow marbles, and 3 black marbles. You replace the first marble and then select a second one. Find each probability.

16. P(red, then yellow)

17. P(black, then black)

18. P(red, then black)

19. P(yellow, then black)

Gino has 5 blue socks and 4 black socks. He selects one sock at random. Without replacing the sock, he selects a second sock at random. Find each probability.

20. P(blue, then black)

21. P(black, then blue)

22. P(black, then black)

23. P(blue, then blue)

24.  **Writing in Math** Explain the difference between independent and dependent events.

25. A refrigerator contains 12 orange drinks, 4 grape drinks, and 25 apple drinks. Ann is first in the line for drinks. Mark is second. What is the probability that Ann gets an apple drink and Mark gets a grape drink, if they are given drinks at random?

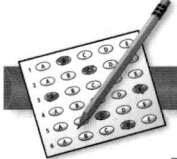 **Challenge**

26. On a multiple-choice test you randomly guess the answers to two questions. Each question has five choices.
  a. What is the probability that you get both answers correct?
  b. What is the probability that you get both answers incorrect?

27. Mrs. Kendall's wallet contains 3 one-dollar bills, 2 five-dollar bills, and 3 ten-dollar bills. She randomly selects one bill and then another. Find the probability that she selects the given bills.
  a. a one-dollar bill and then a ten-dollar bill
  b. a ten-dollar bill and then a five-dollar bill

Test Prep

Multiple Choice

28. There are 6 girls and 5 boys in a debate class. The teacher chooses two students at random to lead a class discussion. What is the probability of selecting a girl and then a boy?

  A. $\frac{30}{121}$ **B.** $\frac{3}{11}$ **C.** $\frac{36}{121}$ **D.** $\frac{6}{11}$

29. Mike asks Carolyn to pick a number at random from 1 to 100, and then asks Jamie to do the same. What is the probability that both girls will select 49?

  F. $\frac{1}{50}$ **G.** $\frac{1}{100}$ **H.** $\frac{1}{9,900}$ **I.** $\frac{1}{10,000}$

Short Response

30. **a.** Exercise 29 involves two events. What are they?
  b. Are they independent or dependent? Explain.

31. In a game, Teri and Hector take turns choosing cards at random from a basket. Each card shows a "T" or "H". A player chooses a card, records the letter, and puts the card in a discard pile.
  a. Are the letters drawn independent or dependent events?
  b. Explain your answer.

Take It to the NET
Online lesson quiz at
www.PHSchool.com
Web Code: ada-1205

Mixed Review

Lesson 12-4 **32. Travel** From Compt there are four ways to get to Murch. From Murch there are five ways to get to Toll. How many ways are there from Compt to Toll through Murch?

Lesson 11-6 **For each triangle, find the sine, cosine, and tangent of angle *A*.**

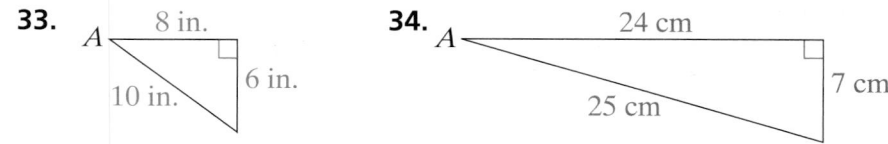

33.
8 in.
6 in.
10 in.

34.
24 cm
7 cm
25 cm

Permutations and Combinations

OBJECTIVE

1 Permutations

An arrangement in which order is important is a **permutation.**
For the letters O, P, S, and T, the permutations *STOP* and *POTS*
are different because the order of the letters is different.

You can use the Counting Principle to find the number of
possible permutations.

1 EXAMPLE Counting Permutations

**Find the number of permutations possible for the letters
O, P, S, and T.**

1st letter	2nd letter	3rd letter	4th letter
4 choices	3 choices	2 choices	1 choice

$$4 \cdot 3 \cdot 2 \cdot 1 = 24$$

● There are 24 permutations of the letters O, P, S, and T.

✓ Check Understanding Example 1

1. Use the Counting Principle to find the number of permutations
possible for the letters W, A, T, E, and R.

A track team has seven members. In how many ways could four
team members line up for a relay race?

You can use *permutation notation* to represent this problem.

7 members ─┐ ┌─ Choose 4.

$$_7P_4 = 7 \cdot 6 \cdot 5 \cdot 4 = 840$$

1st member 2nd member 3rd member 4th member

Four of seven team members could line up in 840 ways.

Key Concepts Permutation Notation

The expression $_nP_r$ stands for the number of permutations of
n objects chosen *r* at a time.

What You'll Learn

 OBJECTIVE 1 To use permutations

 OBJECTIVE 2 To use combinations

. . . And Why

To solve real-world
problems involving
sports and geography

✓ Check Skills You'll Need

**Use the Counting
Principle to find the
number of outcomes.**

1. Roll 2 number cubes.

2. Choose three
different letters.

3. Select a month and a
day of the week.

4. Toss a coin 4 times.

❓ For help, go to Lesson 12-4.

New Vocabulary

• permutation

• combination

💻 **TEXT** Interactive lesson
includes instant self-check,
tutorials, and activities.

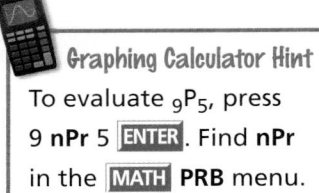

Graphing Calculator Hint

To evaluate $_9P_5$, press
9 nPr 5 ENTER . Find nPr
in the MATH PRB menu.

2 EXAMPLE **Simplifying Permutation Notation**

You have 9 books and want to display 5 on a shelf. How many different 5-book arrangements are possible?

9 books — ┌ Choose 5.

$$_9P_5 = 9 \cdot 8 \cdot 7 \cdot 6 \cdot 5 = 15{,}120 \qquad \textbf{Simplify.}$$

● There are 15,120 arrangements possible.

✓ Check Understanding Example 2

2. Simplify each expression.

    a. $_5P_2$ **b.** $_5P_3$ **c.** $_5P_4$ **d.** $_5P_5$

OBJECTIVE

2 **Combinations**

Sometimes the order of items is not important. For instance, a ham and cheese sandwich is the same as a cheese and ham sandwich. An arrangement in which order does not matter is a **combination.**

3 EXAMPLE **Real-World** **Problem Solving**

Inland Water

Country	Water Area (mi²)
Australia	26,610
Canada	291,573
Ethiopia	46,680
India	121,391
Tanzania	22,799
United States	79,541

SOURCE: *The Top 10 of Everything*

Geography In how many ways could you choose two countries from the table when you write reports about inland water?

Make an organized list of all the combinations.

AC	AE	AI	AT	AU
	CE	CI	CT	CU
		EI	ET	EU
			IT	IU
				TU

Abbreviate by using the first letter of each country's name. First, list all pairs containing Australia. Continue until every pair of countries is listed.

● There are fifteen ways to choose two countries from the list of six.

✓ Check Understanding Example 3

3. In how many ways could you choose three different items from a menu containing six items?

Key Concepts **Combination Notation**

The expression $_nC_r$ stands for the number of combinations of n objects chosen r at a time.

In general, there are fewer combinations than permutations. To find the number of combinations, $_nC_r$, of r items chosen from n items, find the total number of permutations $_nP_r$, and then divide by the number of possible permutations, $_rP_r$, for any group of r items.

$$_nC_r = \frac{_nP_r}{_rP_r}.$$

4 EXAMPLE   Simplifying Combination Notation

You have five choices of sandwich fillings. How many different sandwiches could you make by choosing three of the five fillings?

5 fillings ⌐ ⌐ Choose 3.

$$_5C_3 = \frac{_5P_3}{_3P_3}$$

$$= \frac{5 \cdot 4 \cdot 3}{3 \cdot 2 \cdot 1} = 10 \quad \textbf{Simplify.}$$

● You could make 10 different sandwiches.

Graphing Calculator Hint
To evaluate $_5C_3$, press 5 **nCr** 3 ENTER. Find **nCr** in the MATH **PRB** menu.

✓ Check Understanding   Example 4

4. Simplify each expression.

a. $_8C_2$ b. $_8C_3$ c. $_8C_4$ d. $_8C_5$

You can tell whether a problem requires permutations or combinations by asking yourself, *Does order matter?* If the answer is *yes*, use permutations. If it is *no*, use combinations.

5 EXAMPLE   Identifying Whether Order Is Important

Tell which type of arrangement each problem involves. Explain.

a. **How many different groups of three books could you choose from five books?**
   Combinations; the order of the books selected does not matter.

b. **In how many different orders could you play three CDs?**
   Permutations; the order in which you play the CDs matters.

✓ Check Understanding   Example 5

5. Tell which type of arrangment is involved. Explain.

a. A teacher selects a committee of 4 students from 25 students. How many different committees could the teacher select?
b. Class officers are president, vice-president, secretary, and treasurer. From a class of 25 students, how many different groups of officers could students elect?

EXERCISES

For more exercises, see *Extra Practice*.

Practice and Problem Solving

A Practice by Example

Example 1
(page 659)

Use the Counting Principle to find the number of permutations possible for all the letters in each group.

1. S, I, T   **2.** P, L, U, S   **3.** W, O, R, L, D

Example 2
(page 660)

Simplify each expression.

4. $_4P_2$ **5.** $_6P_4$ **6.** $_9P_4$ **7.** $_{10}P_8$

8. How many different arrangements of four books on a shelf could you make from eight books?

Example 3
(page 660)

In how many ways could you choose two different items from each group? Make an organized list of all the combinations.

9. C, A, T   **10.** M, A, T, H   **11.** V, A, L, U, E

Example 4
(page 661)

Simplify each expression.

12. $_4C_2$ **13.** $_6C_4$ **14.** $_9C_4$ **15.** $_{10}C_8$

16. Literature Louisa May Alcott published 13 novels during her lifetime. In how many ways could you select three of these books?

17. You have six choices of sandwich fillings. How many different sandwiches could you make by choosing three of the six fillings?

Example 5
(page 661)

Does each problem involve *permutations* or *combinations*? Explain.

18. In how many different ways could three students form a line?

19. In how many ways could you choose three shirts from seven shirts?

B Apply Your Skills

Find the number of possible 5-letter permutations of the given letters.

20. D, E, C, I, M, A, L   **21.** F, A, C, T, O, R   **22.** T, R, I, A, N, G, L, E

23. Use the different letters from your last name.
    a. Find the number of two-letter permutations.
    b. Find the number of two-letter combinations.

Simplify each expression.

24. $_6P_3$ **25.** $_6C_3$ **26.** $_2C_1$ **27.** $_2P_1$

28. $_{12}P_9$ **29.** $_{10}P_5$ **30.** $_{10}C_5$ **31.** $_{20}C_{19}$

C Challenge

32. Use the letters E, P, S, and T.
    a. How many possible arrangements of the letters are there?
    b. Add a second letter T to the list. How many distinct arrangements of the five letters are possible?

33. Writing in Math To open a combination lock, you turn a dial to match three whole numbers from 0 to 39. You alternate directions of the turns. Explain why 128,000 combinations are possible.

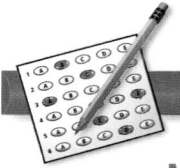

Test Prep

Multiple Choice

34. What is the value of $_{10}C_2$?

A. 45   **B.** 90   **C.** 180   **D.** 360

Take It to the NET
Online lesson quiz at
www.PHSchool.com
Web Code: ada-1205

35. A teacher is organizing a class of 24 students into eight groups of three. In how many different ways could she form groups of three?

F. 56   **G.** 2,024   **H.** 12,144   **I.** 735,471

Short Response

36. a. How many three-letter permutations are possible for the letters H, E, X, A, G, O, N?

b. How many four-letter permutations are possible?

Mixed Review

Lesson 12-5 **On each of five cards there is one of the letters A, B, C, D, and E. You select two cards. Find $P(A$, then $B)$ in each situation.**

37. with first card replaced   **38.** with first card not replaced

Lessons 10-2 and 11-2   **39.** Find the area of the triangle at the right.

Lesson 6-9  **40. Consumer Issues** A coat is on sale for $80. Its original price was $120. What is the percent of discount?

10 in.   26 in.

Math at Work

Wildlife Statistician

Wildlife statisticians study the growth or decline of plant and animal life in a geographical region. They make observations and collect data for a small portion, or sample, of an animal or plant population. Then they draw conclusions about the entire population. If you enjoy studying wildlife, this may be the job for you.

Take It to the NET For more information about statisticians, go to **www.PHSchool.com**.
Web Code: adb-2031

Extension — Pascal's Triangle

For Use With Lesson 12-6

The structure of Pascal's triangle is described below.

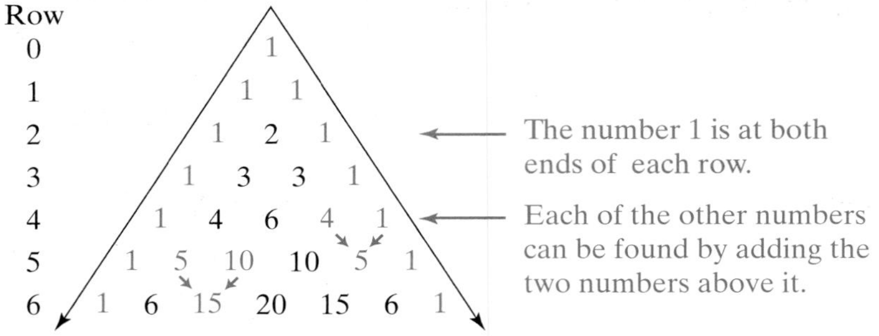
Row
0
1
2
3
4
5
6
1
1 1
1 2 1
1 3 3 1
1 4 6 4 1
1 5 10 10 5 1
1 6 15 20 15 6 1
The number 1 is at both ends of each row.
Each of the other numbers can be found by adding the two numbers above it.

You can use Pascal's triangle to find combinations.

EXAMPLE

Find $_5C_3$ using Pascal's triangle.

Row 5 of Pascal's triangle gives all the values of $_5C_r$, for $r = 0$ to 5.

1	**5**	**10**	**10**	**5**	**1**	← **row 5**
↕	↕	↕	↕	↕	↕	
$_5C_0$	$_5C_1$	$_5C_2$	$_5C_3$	$_5C_4$	$_5C_5$	← **combinations in the form $_5C_r$, for r = 0 to 5**

$$_5C_3 = 10$$

Note that $_nC_0$ equals 1.

EXERCISES

1. Copy and extend Pascal's triangle to Row 10.
2. a. Find the sum of the numbers in each row of the triangle.
   b. Write each sum as a power of 2.
   c. Complete: The sum of the numbers in row n is ■.

Use Pascal's triangle to find each value.

3. $_5C_2$ 4. $_3C_2$ 5. $_4C_3$ 6. $_6C_4$ 7. $_7C_2$

8. $_8C_6$ 9. $_9C_3$ 10. $_9C_5$ 11. $_{10}C_0$ 12. $_{10}C_{10}$

13. **Reasoning** Explain how to display the values in Row 27 of Pascal's triangle using a calculator.

Experimental Probability

OBJECTIVE

1 Finding Experimental Probability

Experimental probability is probability based on experimental data.

Key Concepts — Experimental Probability

$$P(\text{event}) = \frac{\text{number of times an event occurs}}{\text{number of times experiment is done}}$$

1 EXAMPLE — Real-World Problem Solving

Medical Science A medical study tests a new medicine on 3,500 people. It is effective for 3,010 people. Find the experimental probability that the medicine is effective.

$$P(\text{event}) = \frac{\text{number of times an event occurs}}{\text{number of times experiment is done}}$$

$$= \frac{3,010}{3,500} = 0.86, \text{ or } 86\%$$

✓ Check Understanding — Example 1

1. Another medicine is effective for 1,183 of 2,275 people. Find the experimental probability that the medicine is effective.

OBJECTIVE

2 Using Simulations

A **simulation** is a model used to find experimental probability.

2 EXAMPLE — Using a Simulation

Simulate the correct guessing of true-false answers.

Toss a coin to simulate each guess. Heads represents a correct guess. Here are the results of 50 trials:

HHTTT THHTT THTHH HTTTH TTHTT THTHT
HHTTT HTHHH THTHT THTHT

$$P(\text{heads}) = \frac{\text{number of heads}}{\text{number of tosses}} = \frac{22}{50} = \frac{11}{25}$$

The experimental probability of guessing correctly is $\frac{11}{25}$.

✓ Check Skills You'll Need

Write each decimal or fraction as a percent.

1. 0.8 2. 0.53 3. 0.625

4. $\frac{3}{5}$ 5. $\frac{7}{12}$ 6. $\frac{5}{8}$

❓ For help, go to Lesson 6-5.

New Vocabulary

- experimental probability
- simulation

TEXT Interactive lesson includes instant self-check, tutorials, and activities.

✓ **Check Understanding**   Example 2

   2. a. In Example 2, compare the experimental probability with the
        theoretical probability.
      b. If you try the experiment 100 times, what is likely to happen
        to the experimental probability?

More Than One Way ——————

**Use theoretical and experimental probabilities to find
a probability for correctly guessing all four answers on a
four-question true-false quiz.**

Nicole's Method

Each guess is independent. Find the probability of one correct
guess. Then find the probability of four independent correct guesses.

$$P(1 \text{ correct guess}) = \frac{1}{2}$$
$$P(4 \text{ correct guesses}) = \frac{1}{2} \cdot \frac{1}{2} \cdot \frac{1}{2} \cdot \frac{1}{2} = \frac{1}{16}$$

The theoretical probability is $\frac{1}{16}$.

Daryl's Method

Simulate the problem by tossing a coin. Let heads stand for a
correct guess and tails for an incorrect guess. Use the results
of 120 tosses given at the left. Separate the results into 30
groups of 4. Count the groups with 4 heads. There are two.

HTTT   HTTT   HHHT   TTTT   TTHT   THTT
THHH   THHH   HTTT   TTHH   HTTT   HTHH
HTHH   THTT   TTHT   THTH   HHTT   THTH
HHHH   TTHT   HHHH   THTT   TTTH   HHHT
HHTT   HTTT   THTT   HHTT   HHTH   HTHH

Find the experimental probability.

$$P(\text{event}) = \frac{\text{number of times an event occurs}}{\text{number of times experiment is done}}$$

$$= \frac{2}{30} = \frac{1}{15}$$

The experimental probability is $\frac{1}{15}$.

120 Coin Tosses

H T T T H T T T H H H T
T T T T T H T T T H T T
T H H H T H H H H T T T
T T H H H T T T H T H H
H T H H T H T T T T H T
T H T H H H T T T H T H
H H H H T T H T H H H H
T H T T T T H H H H T
H H T T H T T T T H T T
H H T T H H T H H H T H H

For Daryl's simulation, the experimental probability
is a little greater than the theoretical probability.

Choose a Method

   1. Which method would you use to solve the problem? Explain.

EXERCISES

For more exercises, see *Extra Practice*.

Practice and Problem Solving

A Practice by Example
Example 1
(page 665)

A student randomly selected 68 vehicles in a large parking lot and noted the color of each. Use the results to find the experimental probability that a vehicle chosen at random in the lot is the given color. Write the probability as a percent, to the nearest tenth of a percent.

Color	Number of Vehicles
Black	9
Blue	10
Brown	13
Green	7
Red	12
White	11
Gray	6

1. red
2. white
3. black
4. blue or green
5. not black or gray
6. purple

Example 2
(page 665)

7. In a multiple-choice test, each item has four choices.
 a. Tell how to simulate the correct guessing of the correct choice.
 b. Carry out your simulation. What do you find for the experimental probability?
 c. Compare your result to the theoretical probability.

8. A cereal company randomly puts one of six different stickers in each box of its cereal. Use a simulation to find the experimental probability of getting sticker 3 or sticker 4.

B Apply Your Skills

Students were surveyed about the numbers of pencils in their book bags. The table shows the results. Write each experimental probability as a fraction in simplest form.

Pencils in Students' Book Bags

Number of pencils	Number of students
0	4
1	16
2 or more	12

9. *P*(one pencil)

10. *P*(no pencils)

11. *P*(two or more pencils) **12.** *P*(at least one pencil)

13. a. How would you find the experimental probability of tossing three coins and getting three heads?
 b. Reasoning How would you compare the experimental probability of getting three heads to the theoretical probability? Would you expect the probabilities to be equal? Explain.

14. Error Analysis A student wants to do a simulation to find the probability of correctly guessing a number from 1 to 5 two times in a row. He decides to roll a number cube 100 times, separating the results into 50 groups of two and letting a roll of 1 stand for a correct guess. Explain why the student's simulation will not give good results.

15. Two players played a number-cube game. The table shows the results.
   a. Find P(A wins) and P(B wins).
   b. **Writing in Math** A *fair game* is one in which each player has the same chance of winning. Do you think the game that A and B played is fair? Explain.

Game Results

A Wins	B Wins
‖‖ ‖‖ ‖‖ ‖‖ ‖‖ ‖‖‖	‖‖ ‖‖ ‖‖ ‖‖ ‖‖ ‖‖ ‖‖ ‖‖ ‖‖ ‖‖

 **Challenge**

16. a. Open-Ended Write an experimental probability problem that you can solve with a simulation. Your problem should be different from any in this lesson.
   b. Solve the problem.

Gridded Response

17. A baseball manufacturer checked 250 of its baseballs and found that 8 were defective. What is the experimental probability, to the nearest tenth of a percent, that a baseball is NOT defective?

18. Suki tosses two number cubes 100 times. In 19 of the tosses, the sum of the two cubes equals 7. What is Suki's experimental probability of getting a sum of 7 when tossing two number cubes?

Take It to the NET
Online lesson quiz at
www.PHSchool.com
Web Code: ada-1207

19. A medical experiment finds that 232 out of 1,000 patients did NOT respond to the same medication. What is the experimental probability, to the nearest tenth of a percent, that a patient will respond to the medication?

Mixed Review

Lesson 12-6   **Evaluate each expression.**

20. $_4P_2$ **21.** $_{10}P_3$ **22.** $_4C_3$ **23.** $_6C_3$

Lesson 10-9   **24. Geometry** Find the volume of a spherical globe with a diameter of 0.9 m. Round to the nearest tenth.

Lesson 9-8   **Geometry Write a rule to describe each translation.**

25. 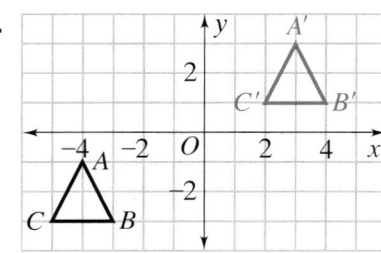   **26.**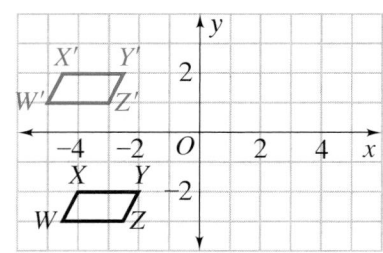

Random Samples and Surveys

OBJECTIVE

1 Choosing Samples for Surveys

How many books do you read each week? What are your hobbies? Statisticians use questions like these in surveys to get information about specific groups.

A **population** is a group about which you want information. A **sample** is a part of the population you use to make estimates about the population. The larger your sample, the more reliable your estimates will be.

For a **random sample** each member of the population has an equal chance to be selected. A random sample is likely to be representative of the whole population.

1 EXAMPLE   Real-World Problem Solving

Recycling You want to find out whether students will participate if you start a recycling program at your school. Tell whether each survey plan describes a good sample.

a. **Interview every tenth teenager you see at a mall.**
   This sample will probably include students who do not go to your school. It is not a good sample because it is not taken from the population you want to study.

b. **Interview the students in your ecology class.**
   The views of students in an ecology class may not represent the views about recycling of students in other classes. This is not a good sample because it is not random.

c. **Interview every tenth student leaving a school assembly.**
   This is a good sample. It is selected at random from the population you want to study.

Check Understanding   Example 1

1. Explain whether each plan describes a good sample.

   a. You want to know which bicycle is most popular. You plan to survey entrants in a bicycle race.
   b. You want to know how often teens rent videos. You plan to survey teens going into the local video rental store.
   c. You want to know the most popular breakfast cereal. You plan to survey people entering a grocery store.

What You'll Learn

OBJECTIVE
1 To choose a sample for a survey of a population

OBJECTIVE
2 To make estimates about populations

...And Why

To solve real-world problems involving recycling and quality control

✓ Check Skills You'll Need

Solve each proportion.

1. $\frac{8}{32} = \frac{n}{450}$

2. $\frac{7}{25} = \frac{n}{24,000}$

3. $\frac{2}{250} = \frac{n}{50,000}$

4. $\frac{4}{100} = \frac{n}{144,000}$

 For help, go to Lesson 6-2.

New Vocabulary

• population
• sample
• random sample

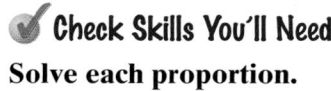 Interactive lesson includes instant self-check, tutorials, and activities.

2 Making Estimates About Populations

You can use a sample to make an estimate about a population by writing and solving a proportion.

2 EXAMPLE Real-World Problem Solving

Quality Control **From 20,000 calculators produced, a manufacturer takes a random sample of 500 calculators. The sample has 3 defective calculators. Estimate the total number of defective calculators.**

$$\frac{\text{defective sample calculators}}{\text{sample calculators}} = \frac{\text{defective calculators}}{\text{calculators}}$$ Write a proportion.

$$\frac{3}{500} = \frac{n}{20,000}$$ Substitute.

$$3(20,000) = 500n$$ Write cross products.

$$\frac{3(20,000)}{500} = \frac{500n}{500}$$ Divide each side by 500.

$$120 = n$$ Simplify.

● Estimate: About 120 calculators are defective.

✓ **Check Understanding** Example 2

2. Use the data in the table below.

Calculator Samples

Sample	Number Sampled	Number Defective
A	500	3
B	200	2
C	50	0

a. Using Sample B, how many of 20,000 calculators would you estimate to be defective?
b. **Reasoning** Would you expect an estimate based on Sample C to be more accurate or less accurate than one based on Sample B? Explain.
c. Explain why you would take a sample rather than counting or surveying an entire population.

In Example 2, you can think of the sample as giving an experimental probability ($\frac{3}{500} = 0.006$). Then you can multiply this probability by the total number of calculators ($0.006 \cdot 20,000$) to estimate the total number of defective calculators.

EXERCISES

For more exercises, see *Extra Practice*.

Practice and Problem Solving

A Practice by Example **Sports** You want to find how popular basketball is at your school. State whether each survey plan describes a good sample. Explain.

Example 1
(page 669)

1. Interview the 10 tallest students in the school.

2. Interview 20 students after picking their ID numbers at random.

3. Interview 30 students watching a basketball game.

Example 2
(page 670)

4. **Quality Control** A worker takes 100 eggs at random from a shipment of 120,000 eggs. The worker finds that four eggs are bad. Estimate the total number of bad eggs.

5. **Estimation** Of 75 pairs of jeans, 7 have flaws. Estimate how many of 24,000 pairs of jeans are flawed.

B Apply Your Skills

You want to find which restaurants in your city are most popular. State whether each survey plan describes a good sample. Explain.

6. Choose people to interview at random from the city phone book.

7. Interview every fifth person leaving a restaurant in the city.

8. Interview all the restaurant critics in the state.

9. **Error Analysis** Eight of the 32 students in your math class have a cold. The school population is 450. A student estimates that 112 students in the school have a cold.
   a. Why is your math class not representative of the population?
   b. Describe a survey plan you could use to better estimate the number of students who have a cold.

10. **Reasoning** You survey every fifth student leaving volleyball practice. Of those surveyed, 92% support a proposal to buy new bleachers for the gym. Should you report that there is overwhelming support for the proposal? Explain.

C Challenge

11. **Open-Ended** Describe a survey question, a population, and a sample you could use to make an estimate.

12. **Writing in Math** From 50,000 computer chips produced, you sample 250 chips and find that 0.8% are defective. Explain how you could estimate the total number of defective chips.

Test Prep

Multiple Choice

13. Out of 6,000 radios tested, 12 are defective. What is the estimated total number of defective radios in a group of 250,000?
    A. 60   **B.** 120   **C.** 200   **D.** 500

14. All students at a local elementary school eat lunch at school. You want to find how many students bring their lunches. Which group would be a good sample?
   F. students on one school bus   **G.** one first-grade classroom
   H. the cafeteria workers   **I.** all third-grade classrooms

Short Response For Exercises 15 and 16, **(a)** state whether each survey plan describes a good sample. **(b)** Explain your answer.

15. You want to find how often teens get haircuts. You plan to survey customers in a barbershop.

16. You want to find students' favorite foods. You plan to survey every fourth student leaving the library.

Take It to the NET
Online lesson quiz at
www.PHSchool.com
Web Code: ada-1208

Mixed Review

Lesson 12-7 **Use the survey data at the right. Write each experimental probability as a fraction.**

17. P(no pets)   **18.** P(two or more pets)

19. P(one pet)   **20.** P(at least one pet)

Students' Pets

Number of Pets	Number of Students
0	9
1	12
2 or more	5

Lesson 12-6 **21.** How many combinations of four flowers can you choose from a bouquet of one dozen different flowers?

Lesson 10-3 **Geometry** **Find the area of each circle. Give the exact area and area rounded to the nearest whole number of units. Use 3.14 for π.**

22. $r = 24$ cm   **23.** $d = 45$ in.   **24.** $r = 50$ mi

 Checkpoint Quiz 2   **Lessons 12-5 through 12-8**

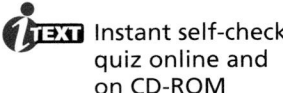 Instant self-check quiz online and on CD-ROM

1. A bag contains 10 cards labeled 1–10. You draw one card and then another, without replacing the first card before drawing the second. Find the probability of drawing two even numbers.

2. a. A club of 20 students chooses a president and a vice-president. How many different outcomes are possible?
   b. A club of 20 students chooses two committee members. How many different committees may be chosen?

3. A hockey player attempts 15 goals and makes 2. Find the experimental probability of making a goal. Predict the number of goals the player will make in the next game if the player attempts 23 goals.

4. Of 450 oranges from a crop of 50,000 oranges, 85 are "premium." Estimate the number of premium oranges in the whole crop.

Some calculators and computer programs can generate *random numbers*. You can use random numbers for simulations.

To make a list of random integers on a graphing calculator, highlight **randInt** in the MATH **PRB** menu. Press ENTER, and enter "0,9999." Press ENTER repeatedly for a list of four-digit random numbers. Note that the calculator suppresses any zeros at the front of a number. For example, 45 represents the four-digit number 0045.

EXAMPLE

There is a 30% probability of being stopped by a red light at each of four traffic lights. Use a simulation to find an experimental probability of being stopped by at least two red lights.

Use your calculator to generate 20 random 4-digit numbers.

There is a 30% chance of a red light, so let three of the ten digits represent a red light. For this simulation let 1, 2, and 3 represent a red light. Let 4, 5, 6, 7, 8, 9, and 0 represent a yellow or green light.

● P(at least two red lights) $= \frac{7}{20}$, or 35%

5186	8918	4275	4285
8124	9619	2517	9964
0912	2759	2329	1666
8938	0357	6755	2227
0201	6325	1905	6885

Any group with two or more of the digits 1, 2, or 3 represents being stopped by at least two red lights. There are seven such groups in this list.

EXERCISES

1. Use the information in the example. What is the experimental probability of being stopped by exactly three red lights? By four red lights?

2. What would be the result in the example if you had chosen 8, 9, and 0 instead of 1, 2, and 3 to represent red lights?

3. **a.** Make a new random number list by using randInt(0,999) in place of randInt(0,9999). How many digits are in each random number?
   b. How can you make a 6-digit random number?

4. **Writing in Math** Suppose the probability of being stopped by a red light at each of four lights is 50%. Describe how you would use random numbers to find the probability of getting a red light at two or more lights.

5. About 20% of high school students in the United States say they would like to be president. Use random numbers to find the probability that at least three of the next five high school students you see would like to be president.

Simulate the Problem

What You'll Learn

OBJECTIVE
1 To solve problems by simulation

. . . And Why

To solve real-world problems involving sports

✓ **Check Skills You'll Need**

Create a frequency table showing the number of times each letter of the alphabet appears in the sentence below.

A simulation is a model of a real experience.

? For help, go to Lesson 12-1.

OBJECTIVE

1 Simulate the Problem

Math Strategies in Action
Do you dream of flying your own airplane? Can you picture yourself in a space shuttle? Flight simulators help pilots train for real flying. Simulators are models of the real experience.

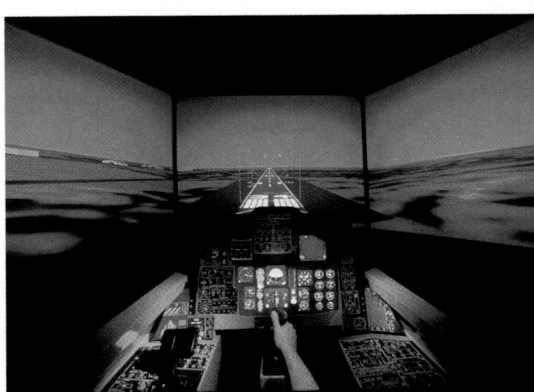

You can use simulations to investigate real-world problems. First develop a model, and then conduct an experiment.

1 EXAMPLE Real-World 🌐 Problem Solving

Basketball As time is running out in the basketball game, your team is behind by one point. You are fouled and go to the free-throw line. If you miss the shot, your team loses. If you make it, the score is tied and you get another shot. If you miss the second shot, the game ends in a tie. If you make both shots, your team wins. Your average at free throws is four out of five. Simulate the situation and find an experimental probability for each event.
• **a. You tie the game.   b. You win the game.   c. You tie or win the game.**

Read and Understand

Think about the problem.

1. Based on your average, what is the probability of making one free throw?

2. What methods could you use to simulate the problem?

Plan and Solve

You can use a spinner to simulate the problem. Construct a spinner with five congruent sections. Make four of the sections blue and one of them red. The blue section represents *makes the shot* and the red section represents *misses the shot*. Each spin represents one shot.

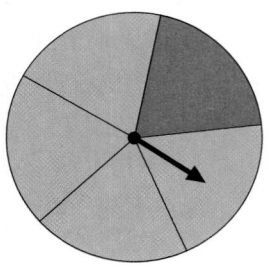

🖥**TEXT** Interactive lesson includes instant self-check, tutorials, and activities.

3. How many spins will you make for each experiment?

4. How many experiments will you do?

Use the results given in the table below. "B" stands for blue and "R" stands for red. Note that there is no second shot when the first shot is a miss (R).

Results of 100 Experiments

BR	BB	BB	BB	BB	BR	BB	BB	BB	BB
BR	BB	BR	BB	R	BB	R	BB	BR	BB
BB	BB	BB	R	BB	BB	BB	BB	BB	BB
BB	R	BB	BB	BB	BB	BB	BB	BB	BB
BB	R	BR	BR	BB	BB	BB	R	BB	BR
BB	BR	BB	BB	BB	R	BB	R	BB	BB
BB	R	BR	BB	BB	R	BB	BR	BB	R
BB	BB	BB	BB	BB	BB	BB	BR	BB	BB
BB	R	BR	BB	R	BB	BB	BB	R	BB
BR	BR	BB	R	BB	R	BB	BB	BB	BB

Make a frequency table.

Misses the first shot (R)	Makes the first shot and misses the second shot (BR)	Makes the first shot and makes the second shot (BB)
‖‖‖ ‖‖‖ ‖‖‖ ‖	‖‖‖ ‖‖‖ ‖‖‖	‖‖‖ ‖‖‖ ‖‖‖ ‖‖‖ ‖‖‖ ‖‖‖ ‖‖‖ ‖‖‖ ‖‖‖ ‖‖‖ ‖‖‖ ‖‖‖ ‖‖‖ ‖‖‖

5. Find each experimental probability.
  a. Your team ties the game.
  b. Your team wins the game.
  c. Your team ties or wins the game.

Look Back and Check

Simulations can give different results. You may find a different probability if you do another simulation. The more experiments you do, the closer the results of different simulations are likely to be.

✓ Check Understanding

6. Continue the simulation with another 100 experiments. Combine the results with the results of the first 100 experiments.

7. Based on the second simulation, what is the probability that your team wins?

For more exercises, see *Extra Practice.*

Practice and Problem Solving

 **Practice by Example**

Example 1
(page 674)

Solve by simulating the problem.

1. What is the experimental probability that exactly three children in a family of five children will be boys? Assume that $P(\text{boy}) = P(\text{girl})$.

2. You take a three-question multiple-choice test. Each question has four choices. You don't know any of the answers. What is the experimental probability that you will guess exactly two out of three correctly?

 Apply Your Skills

Solve using any strategy.

3. Thirteen of 25 students are going on a field trip. Six students are traveling in a van. What is the theoretical probability that a student chosen at random from those going on the trip is *not* traveling in the van?

4. A student draws a card at random from the cards below. What is the theoretical probability that the student will draw a card showing A or B?

5. Prices The original cost of a jacket is $72. During a sale, the store reduces the jacket price by 25%. After the sale, the store raises the reduced jacket price by 25%. What is the price of the jacket after it is increased?

6. Geometry A farmer uses 24 yd of fencing to make a rectangular pen. The pen is 6 yd longer than it is wide. What are the dimensions of the pen?

7. Reasoning The circumference of the peg is 3 in. Will the peg go through the hole? Explain.

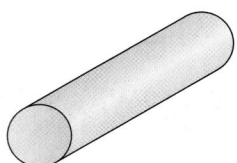 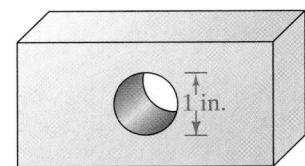

8. You toss five coins. What is the theoretical probability that you will get five heads?

9. Many sweepstakes contests have an elimination round. In the elimination round, half of the entrants are chosen at random to go on to the final round. Then one person is chosen as the winner. What is the theoretical probability that a person who enters a contest with 10,000 entrants will be the winner?

Strategies

- Account for All Possibilities
- Draw a Diagram
- Look for a Pattern
- Make a Model
- Make a Table
- Simplify the Problem
- Simulate the Problem
- Solve by Graphing
- Try, Test, Revise
- Use Multiple Strategies
- Work Backward
- Write an Equation
- Write a Proportion

 **Challenge**

10. On a TV game show, you try to win a prize that is hidden behind one of three doors. After you choose a door, but before it is opened, the host opens one of the other doors, behind which there is no prize. You can then switch to the remaining closed door or stay with your original choice.

    a. Find the experimental probability of winning if your strategy is to stay with your original choice. (*Hint:* Simulate by using one marked index card and two unmarked index cards.)

    b. Find the experimental probability of winning if your strategy is to switch to the other door.

    c. **Writing in Math** Should you stay or switch in this game? Explain.

11. Each box of Tastycrunch cereal contains a prize. There are four possible prizes. The prizes are equally likely. You purchase 10 boxes of Tastycrunch. Simulate the problem to find the experimental probability that you will get all four prizes.

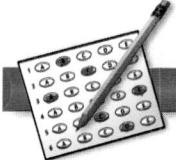

Test Prep

Multiple Choice

12. Raul has 4 pairs of shoes to choose from each day. He wants to find the experimental probability of choosing his favorite pair of shoes at random. Which simulation should Raul use?
    A. Tossing a coin
    B. Rolling a number cube
    C. Spinning a spinner with 4 congruent sections
    D. Drawing chips from a bag with 8 different-colored chips

13. Angela conducts a simulation in which she gets a favorable outcome 230 times out of 500 trials. What is the experimental probability of a favorable outcome?
    F. 2.3%   **G.** 23%   **H.** 46%   **I.** 230%

14. Jerome constructs a spinner that has 5 congruent sections. He writes "yes" in one section and "no" in the other four sections. Jerome uses this spinner to simulate making free-throw shots. What experimental probability is he most likely to find?
    A. 1%   **B.** 5%   **C.** 20%   **D.** 80%

Take It to the NET
Online lesson quiz at
www.PHSchool.com
Web Code: ada-1209

Mixed Review

Lesson 12-8   **15.** **Quality Control** Six out of every 80 wrenches are found to be defective. For a batch of 3,200 wrenches, estimate the number of wrenches that will *not* have any flaw.

Lesson 11-5   **16.** **Geometry** Each side of a square kite is to be 20 in. long. To the nearest inch, what length of wood do you need to make the diagonals?

Lesson 11-1   **Estimate to the nearest integer.**

    17. $\sqrt{15}$ **18.** $\sqrt{10}$ **19.** $\sqrt{50}$ **20.** $-\sqrt{82}$

Answering True/False Questions

In true/false questions, the entire statement must be true. Otherwise, the statement is false. A statement may be true for many cases and false for just one. This one case is called a *counterexample.* If you think a statement is false, try to find a counterexample.

1 EXAMPLE

True or False? The mean of a set of values is always different from the median of the same set of values.

Choose a simple example that has an odd number of values, and that is "evenly balanced" above and below the middle value.

8, 10, 12, 14, and 16

Find the median: 8, 10, **12**, 14, 16
Find the mean: $(8 + 10 + 12 + 14 + 16) \div 5 = 12$

● This is a counterexample to the statement, so the statement is false.

2 EXAMPLE

Suppose two events are independent and the probability of each is less than 1. Is the following statement true or false? The probability that the two events occur is less than the probability of either event.

Since the events are independent, $P(A \text{ and } B) = P(A) \cdot P(B)$. $P(A)$ and $P(B)$ are both less than 1. The product of two (proper) fractions is less than either fraction. Test some cases:

$\frac{1}{2} \times \frac{1}{4} = \frac{1}{8}$ $\frac{1}{8}$ is less than both $\frac{1}{2}$ and $\frac{1}{4}$.

$\frac{3}{4} \times \frac{1}{2} = \frac{3}{8}$ $\frac{3}{8}$ is less than both $\frac{3}{4}$ and $\frac{1}{2}$.

It seems likely that $P(A \text{ and } B) < P(A)$ and $P(A \text{ and } B) < P(B)$ are
● always true.

EXERCISES

Determine whether each statement is *true* or *false*. Explain.

1. The median of a data set is always one of the data values.

2. The number of permutations of two items from a data set is always two times the number of combinations when taking two objects at a time from the same data set.

3. In large data sets (1,000 or more values), the mean is always one of the data values.

Chapter Review

Vocabulary

box-and-whisker plot (p. 635)
combination (p. 660)
counting principle (p. 650)
dependent events (p. 656)
experimental probability (p. 665)
frequency table (p. 630)

independent events (p. 654)
line plot (p. 631)
permutation (p. 659)
population (p. 669)
quartiles (p. 635)
random sample (p. 669)

range (p. 631)
sample (p. 669)
sample space (p. 650)
simulation (p. 665)
theoretical probability (p. 650)

Reading Math
Understanding
Vocabulary

Choose the vocabulary term that correctly completes the sentence.

1. An arrangement in which order does not matter is a ? .

2. The part of a population used to make estimates about the entire population is a ? .

3. The ratio of the number of favorable outcomes to the number of possible outcomes is the ? of an event.

4. An arrangement in which order is important is a ? .

5. The difference between the greatest and the least values in a data set is the ? of the data set.

6. A listing of a data set that shows the number of times each data item occurs is a ? .

7. Events in which the first event *does* affect the second event are ? .

8. In a ? each member of the population has an equal chance of being selected.

Take It to the NET
Online vocabulary quiz
at **www.PHSchool.com**
Web Code: adj-1251

Skills and Concepts

12-1 Objectives

▼ To display data in frequency tables (p. 630)

▼ To display data in line plots (p. 631)

You can show data in a **frequency table,** which lists each data item with the number of times it occurs, or a **line plot,** which displays data with **X** marks on a number line. The **range** is the difference between the greatest and the least values in a set of data.

Display each set of data in a frequency table.

9. 11 10 12 10 12 11 13 12 11 9 12 10

10. 47 48 46 47 45 49 46 48 50 48 46 49

Draw a line plot for each frequency table. Find the range.

11.

Number	1	2	3	4	5	6
Frequency	6	4	5	2	3	1

12.

Number	1	2	3	4	5	6
Frequency	2	8	6	7	3	1

12-2 Objectives
▼ To make box-and-whisker plots (p. 635)

▼ To analyze data in box-and-whisker plots (p. 636)

A **box-and-whisker plot** displays data items below a number line. **Quartiles** divide the data into four parts. The median is the middle quartile. You can compare two sets of related data by making two box-and-whisker plots on one number line.

Make a box-and-whisker plot for each set of data.

13. 6 9 6 5 8 2 3 9 4 8 5 7 12 9 4

14. 21 35 26 32 24 30 29 38 27 32 51

12-3 Objectives
▼ To recognize the use of breaks in the scales of graphs (p. 642)

▼ To recognize the use of different scales (p. 643)

A graph can give a different impression if a break is used in the scale. A graph can be misleading when a scale is distorted.

For Exercises 15 and 16, use the graph showing wheat production.

15. What does the graph suggest about U.S. wheat production?

16. Explain how you could redraw the graph so that production seems to be increasing dramatically.

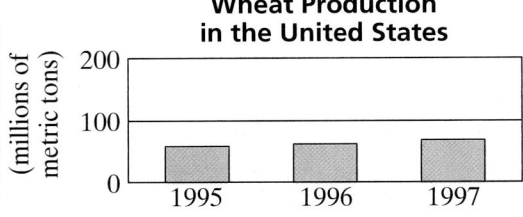

12-4 Objectives
▼ To use a tree diagram and the Counting Principle to count possible choices (p. 649)

▼ To find theoretical probability by counting outcomes (p. 650)

A **sample space** is all the possible outcomes of an event. Use a tree diagram or the **Counting Principle** to count the number of outcomes. You can count outcomes to help find **theoretical probability.**

17. Volunteers have made a large number of sandwiches for a school party. The sandwiches come on white bread, on whole wheat bread, or on a roll. Each contains one of five fillings: turkey, chicken, egg salad, cheese, or peanut butter.
   a. How many different types of sandwich are possible?
   b. There are 20 of each type of sandwich. You receive one sandwich at random. Find the theoretical probability of getting a sandwich on bread with a meat filling.

12-5 Objectives
▼ To calculate probabilities of independent events (p. 654)

▼ To calculate probabilities of dependent events (p. 656)

Independent events are events for which the occurrence of one event does not affect the probability of the occurrence of the other. If A and B are independent events, the probability that both A and B occur is $P(A \text{ and } B) = P(A) \cdot P(B)$.

Dependent events are events for which the occurrence of one event affects the probability of the occurrence of the other. If A and B are dependent events, the probability that A and then B occur is $P(A, \text{ then } B) = P(A) \cdot P(B \text{ after } A)$.

You select a card at random from those at the right. Find the probability of each event.

18. You select E, replace the card, and then select V.

19. You select T, do not replace the card, and then select N.

12-6 Objectives

▼ To use permutations (p. 659)

▼ To use combinations (p. 660)

An arrangement in which order is important is a **permutation.** An arrangement in which order does not matter is a **combination.**

Tell whether each question is a *permutation* or a *combination* problem. Explain. Then find each answer.

20. In how many different ways can five people line up for a photo?

21. How many groups of three pens can you select from a box of twelve pens?

12-7 and 12-9 Objectives

▼ To find experimental probability (p. 665)

▼ To use simulations (p. 665)

▼ To solve problems by simulation (p. 674)

Experimental probability is based on experimental data. You can use a simulation to model real-world problems.

Use the survey data at the right. Write each experimental probability as a fraction in simplest form.

22. P(one notebook)

23. P(at least two notebooks)

Notebooks in Students' Lockers

Number of Notebooks	Frequency
0	1
1	9
2	6
3 or more	4

24. You take a 3-question multiple-choice quiz. Each question has 3 choices. You don't know any of the answers. Use a simulation to find an experimental probability that you will guess exactly 2 out of 3 correctly.

12-8 Objectives

▼ To choose a sample for a survey of a population (p. 669)

▼ To make estimates about populations (p. 670)

A **population** is a group about which you want information. A **sample** is a part of the population you use to make estimates for the population. In a **random sample** each member of the population has an equal chance to be selected.

You want to find the favorite brand of in-line skates in your town. Does each survey plan describe a good sample? Explain.

25. You interview students in your homeroom.

26. You interview every tenth student entering the building.

For Exercises 1 and 2, use the box-and-whisker plot.

Test Grades

```
    65    70    75    80    85
```

1. What is the median grade on the test?

2. What is the range in grades?

3. Make a box-and-whisker plot for the data.
   75, 70, 80, 85, 85, 55, 60, 60, 65, 85, 75, 95, 50

4. Use the data below.
   8, 4, 5, 1, 8, 4, 7, 9, 10, 5, 0, 5, 3, 4, 2
   a. Display the data in a frequency table.
   b. Display the data in a line plot.
   c. Find the range of the data.

For Exercises 5 and 6, use the table. The table shows the money spent on movie tickets.

Year	Dollars (billions)
1994	5.6
1995	6.0
1996	6.3

5. Draw a graph that emphasizes the increase in money spent over time.

6. Draw a graph to suggest that the money spent has not changed much over time.

Use the word TRAIN. Find the probability of each event when a letter is drawn at random.

7. selecting an R, replacing it, and then selecting an N

8. selecting an R, not replacing it, and then selecting an N

9. **a.** Find the sample space for tossing 3 coins.
   b. Find the theoretical probability of tossing 2 heads and 1 tail.

Simplify each expression.

10. $_3P_2$

11. $_5C_2$

Find the number of three-letter permutations you can make using each group of letters.

12. F, O, U, R

13. L, U, N, C, H

A student has 4 blue shirts and 2 white shirts. He selects one shirt at random. Without replacing the shirt, he selects a second shirt at random. Find each probability.

14. P(blue, then white)   15. P(white, then blue)

16. P(blue, then blue)   17. P(white, then white)

For Exercises 18–21, use the table below. The table shows the colors of a random sample of the bicycles in a rack at school.

Color	Number of Bicycles
Black	9
Blue	10
Red	14

Find each experimental probability for a bicycle chosen at random from the rack. Write each probability as a percent, to the nearest tenth of a percent.

18. P(red)   19. P(blue)   20. P(black)

21. How many bicycles would you expect to be black if there are 50 bicycles in the rack?

22. You roll a pair of number cubes once. What is the probability of rolling doubles?
   a. Find the sample space. Then find the theoretical probability.
   b. Use a simulation to find the experimental probability.
   c. Writing in Math For parts (a) and (b), how close should you expect your answers to be? Explain.

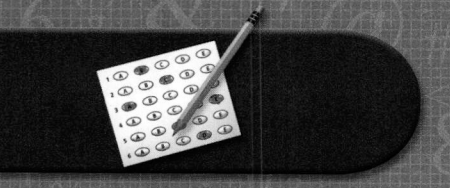

Test Prep

Multiple Choice

1. $\overleftrightarrow{MN} \parallel \overleftrightarrow{OP}$. Which angles are supplementary?

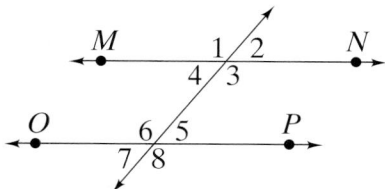

 A. ∠1 and ∠3   **B.** ∠4 and ∠6
 C. ∠2 and ∠5   **D.** ∠7 and ∠5

2. How many shaded triangles will exactly fill the trapezoid?

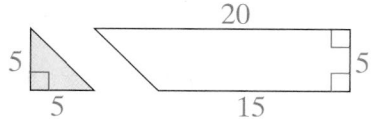

 F. four   **G.** five
 H. six   **I.** seven

3. Each of the six faces of a cube is painted either yellow or green. When the cube is tossed, the probability is $\frac{2}{3}$ that the cube will land with a green face up. How many faces are yellow?
 A. one   **B.** two
 C. three   **D.** four

Gridded Response

4. Simplify $_6P_3$.

5. A student has 3 blue T-shirts and 2 white T-shirts. He selects one T-shirt at random. Without replacing the T-shirt, he selects another T-shirt at random. What is the probability that the student will pick a white T-shirt and then a blue T-shirt?

6. A shoe manufacturer checks 150 pairs of walking shoes and finds three pairs to be defective. What is the estimated percent probability that a pair of walking shoes is defective?

Short Response

7. For the data listed below, **(a)** make a box-and-whisker plot. **(b)** Label the median and the lower and upper quartiles.
 55, 50, 60, 65, 65, 35, 40, 40, 45, 65, 55, 75, 30, 35, 55, 60, 45, 55

8. Use the data in the table. Make a graph that suggests each situation.
 a. sales decreasing sharply
 b. sales staying about the same

Year	Sales (dollars)
1997	18.2 million
1998	17.9 million
1999	17.7 million
2000	17.5 million

In Exercises 9 and 10, (a) state whether each survey plan describes a good sample. (b) Explain your reasoning.

9. To find how many people who buy stamps are buying them for a collection, you survey people in the post office.

10. To find how popular the U.S. women's soccer team is in your school, you survey all the girls in your English class.

11. ∠ABC is an acute angle.
 a. Write an inequality for x.
 b. Explain your answer for part (a).

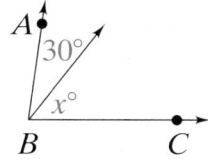

Extended Response

12. You roll two number cubes.
 a. What is P(6, then 6)?
 b. What is P(odd, then even)?
 c. Suppose you roll the two number cubes 50 times in a simulation. You roll double 3s six times. What is the experimental probability of NOT getting double 3s?

World Cup Soccer

Applying Data Analysis Anyone who has ever played soccer knows that controlling a rolling ball with your feet may be fun, but it isn't easy! Perhaps that's why the sport of soccer appeals to so many people of all ages all over the world. Soccer has been played in its current version since about 1863, and international competitions began before 1900. Today, Men's and Women's World Cup competitions are held every four years, one year apart.

Team Grin

Players from the United States women's soccer team pose with their gold medals after defeating China to win the 1999 Women's World Cup.

Final Gold

Mia Hamm (left) of the United States and Daniela Alves of Brazil get ready to kick the ball during the 2000 Women's Gold Cup Finals.

Take It to the NET For more information about soccer, go to **www.PHSchool.com**.
Web Code: ade-1253

FIFA World Cup™ Trophies

The Men's and Women's World Cup trophies are both made of gold. The United States won the FIFA Women's World Cup in 1999. Brazil won the Men's FIFA World Cup™ in 2002.

© 1998 FIFA

© 1974 FIFA

Following the Ball

Senegal midfielder Papa Bouba Diop (left) and Swedish forward Henrik Larsson go for the ball.

Activity

Use the table to answer the questions.

1. Make a line plot of the goals scored by the players.

2. What is the range of the data in the table?

3. Find the mean, median, and mode of the data. Which measure best represents the data? Explain.

4. **a.** Based on the data at the right, make a table showing the number of goals scored by each team.

   b. Find the mean and the mode of the data in your table.

   c. Why is the mean of this data different from the mean found in Exercise 3?

5. **Number Sense** Suppose you did not know which team won the 2002 FIFA World Cup™. From the data in the table, can you determine the top two teams? Explain.

2002 FIFA Men's World Cup™ Top Goal Scorers

Flag	Player	Team	Goals Scored
	Ronaldo	Brazil	8
	Rivaldo	Brazil	5
	Miroslav Klose	Germany	5
	Jon Dahl Tomasson	Denmark	4
	Christian Vieri	Italy	4
	Marc Wilmots	Belgium	3
	Pauleta	Portugal	3
	Papa Bouba Diop	Senegal	3
	Ilhan Mansiz	Turkey	3
	Robbie Keane	Ireland	3
	Michael Ballack	Germany	3
	Fernando Morientes	Spain	3
	Raul	Spain	3
	Henrik Larsson	Sweden	3

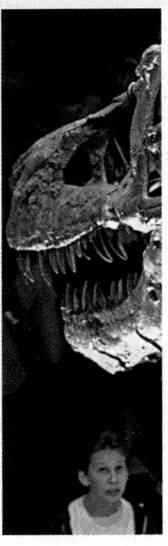

Where You've Been

- In Chapter 1, you wrote rules for patterns using inductive reasoning.

- In Chapter 2, you learned to simplify variable expressions by combining like terms.

- In Chapter 4, you learned how to multiply powers with the same base by adding the exponents.

- In Chapter 8, you graphed linear functions by making a table of values to show ordered-pair solutions.

Diagnosing Readiness

TEXT Instant self-check online and on CD-ROM

(For help, go to the lesson in green.)

Evaluating Expressions (Lesson 1-3)

Evaluate each expression.

1. $8b$, for $b = 5$ **2.** $(-h)^5$, for $h = 2$ **3.** $19 - (n - 6)$, for $n = 8$

4. $4a + 4$, for $a = 6$ **5.** n^2, for $n = 0.8$ **6.** $55 - 3mn$, for $m = 2, n = 5$

7. $\dfrac{120}{s + r}$, for $s = 25$ and $r = 35$ **8.** $\dfrac{j - k}{9}$, for $j = 75$ and $k = 12$

Using the Distributive Property (Lesson 2-2)

Simplify each expression.

9. $(d - 4)3$ **10.** $5(3x + 1)$ **11.** $3(u - 8)$ **12.** $-4(-2y - 7)$

13. $4(-3d + 1)$ **14.** $10(5 - 3s)$ **15.** $-3(7 - 2w)$ **16.** $(9 - 2b)3$

Simplifying Variable Expressions (Lesson 2-3)

Simplify each expression.

17. $5a - 4 + 6a$ **18.** $x - 4x + 3x + 5$ **19.** $g + 4 - 3g + g$

20. $5t + 5s + 5t$ **21.** $9b - 3d + 7d - 2b$ **22.** $-4(9c) + 2(-4c) - c$

Equations With Two Variables (Lesson 8-2)

Find the y values of each equation for $x = -2, 0$, and 2.

23. $y = 3x - 4$ **24.** $y = -3x$ **25.** $y = 4x - 2$ **26.** $y = \frac{3}{5}x - 5$

27. $y = 6 - 2x$ **28.** $y = -\frac{1}{4}x - 8$ **29.** $y = \frac{1}{2}x$ **30.** $y = -3x - 1$

Nonlinear Functions and Polynomials

Chapter 13

Where You're Going

In this chapter, you will learn how to

● Use arithmetic and geometric sequences.

● Graph nonlinear functions.

● Perform operations with polynomials.

● Solve a problem using multiple strategies.

Real-World Snapshots Applying what you learn, on pages 736–737 you will learn to solve problems about carbon-14 dating.

13-1 Patterns and Sequences

What You'll Learn

OBJECTIVE 1 To describe number patterns with arithmetic sequences

OBJECTIVE 2 To describe number patterns with geometric sequences

. . . And Why

To use sequences in making predictions

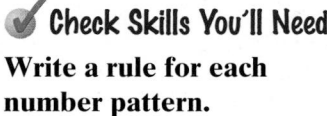 **Check Skills You'll Need**

Write a rule for each number pattern.

1. 60, 48, 36, 24, . . .

2. 7, 12, 17, 22, . . .

3. 6, 18, 54, 162, . . .

4. 60, 30, 15, $7\frac{1}{2}$, . . .

For help, go to Lesson 1-7.

New Vocabulary

- sequence
- term
- arithmetic sequence
- common difference
- geometric sequence
- common ratio

OBJECTIVE

1 Arithmetic Sequences

 **In**vestigation
Discovering a Pattern

You win a contest and can choose one of two options for 30 days.

Option A	Option B
You receive $500 the first day, $550 the second, $600 the third, $650 the fourth, and so on.	You receive $1 the first day, $2 the second, $4 the third, $8 the fourth, and so on.

1. Make a table of values for both options for the first 10 days.
  a. Which option gives you more money in 10 days?
  b. Which option would you choose for 30 days? Explain.

A **sequence** is a set of numbers that follow a pattern. Each number in the sequence is a **term** of the sequence. You find a term of an **arithmetic sequence** by *adding* a fixed number to the previous term. This fixed number is called the **common difference.**

Term Number	1st	2nd	3rd	4th
Arithmetic Sequence	2	6	10	14
Common Difference		+4	+4	+4

You can find the common difference for an arithmetic sequence by subtracting any term from the next term in the sequence.

1 EXAMPLE **Finding the Common Difference**

What is the common difference in the sequence 4, 2, 0, –2, . . . ?

4   2   0   –2   **Find the common difference.**
    –2   –2   –2

The common difference is −2.

 **Check Understanding** Example 1

1. What is the common difference in each sequence?

     a. 8, 13, 18, 23, . . .   **b.** 12, 9, 6, 3, . . .

TEXT Interactive lesson includes instant self-check, tutorials, and activities.

You can continue a sequence and write a rule to describe it.

2 EXAMPLE <u>Real-World</u> 🌐 **Problem Solving**

A runner training for a race runs 2 mi the first day, $2\frac{1}{4}$ mi the second day, $2\frac{1}{2}$ mi the third day, and so on. Find the next three terms of the sequence. Then write a rule to describe the sequence.

$$2 \quad 2\frac{1}{4} \quad 2\frac{1}{2} \quad 2\frac{3}{4} \quad 3 \quad 3\frac{1}{4}$$
$$+\frac{1}{4} \quad +\frac{1}{4} \quad +\frac{1}{4} \quad +\frac{1}{4} \quad +\frac{1}{4}$$

Find the common difference. Use it to find the next three terms.

The next three terms are $2\frac{3}{4}$, 3, and $3\frac{1}{4}$. The rule for the sequence is
● *Start with 2 and add $\frac{1}{4}$ repeatedly.*

✓ **Check Understanding** Example 2

2. Find the next three terms of each sequence. Then write a rule to describe the sequence.

   a. 23, 19, 15, 11, . . .   **b.** -6, $-4\frac{2}{3}$, $-3\frac{1}{3}$, -2, . . .

During a two-mile run, a runner's feet strike the ground about 3,000 times.

Real-World 🌐 **Connection**

You find a term of a **geometric sequence** by *multiplying* the previous term by a fixed number called the **common ratio**.

Term Number	1st	2nd	3rd	4th
Geometric Sequence	2	6	18	54
Common Ratio		×3	×3	×3

You can find the common ratio for a geometric sequence by dividing any term by the previous term in the sequence.

Reading Math
The word *common* means "shared." In a geometric sequence, all pairs of consecutive terms share the common ratio. In an arithmetic sequence, all pairs share the common difference.

3 EXAMPLE **Finding the Common Ratio**

Find the common ratio in the sequence 4, 8, 16, 32, . . . Find the next three terms of the sequence. Then write a rule to describe the sequence.

$$4 \quad 8 \quad 16 \quad 32 \quad 64 \quad 128 \quad 256$$
$$×2 \quad ×2 \quad ×2 \quad ×2 \quad ×2 \quad ×2$$

Find the common ratio. Use it to find the next three terms.

The next three terms are 64, 128, and 256. The rule for the
● sequence is *Start with 4 and multiply by 2 repeatedly.*

3. Find the common ratio and the next three terms of each sequence. Then write a rule to describe the sequence.

a. 4, 12, 36, 108, . . .   **b.** 4, 2, 1, 0.5, . . .

Not every sequence is arithmetic or geometric. You can determine whether any sequence of numbers is arithmetic or geometric by looking for a common difference or a common ratio. For other sequences, you can look for patterns.

Reading Math

Read both *geometric* and *arithmetic* (ayr ith MET ik) with the emphasis on the third syllable.

4   EXAMPLE   **Finding the Type of Sequence**

Tell whether each sequence is *arithmetic*, *geometric*, or *neither*. Find the next three terms of each sequence.

a. 4, 6, 8, 10, . . .

$$4 \quad 6 \quad 8 \quad 10 \quad 12 \quad 14 \quad 16$$
$$+2 \quad +2 \quad +2 \quad +2 \quad +2 \quad +2$$

There is a common difference of 2. The sequence is arithmetic. The next three terms are 12, 14, and 16.

b. 4, 6, 9, $13\frac{1}{2}$, . . .

$$4 \quad 6 \quad 9 \quad 13\frac{1}{2} \quad 20\frac{1}{4} \quad 30\frac{3}{8} \quad 45\frac{9}{16}$$
$$\times\frac{3}{2} \quad \times\frac{3}{2} \quad \times\frac{3}{2} \quad \times\frac{3}{2} \quad \times\frac{3}{2} \quad \times\frac{3}{2}$$

The ratios for the first four terms are $\frac{6}{4}, \frac{9}{6}$, and $\frac{27}{18}$. These equal $\frac{3}{2}$, which is the common ratio. The sequence is geometric. The next three terms are $20\frac{1}{4}, 30\frac{3}{8}$, and $45\frac{9}{16}$.

c. 4, 6, 9, 13, . . .

$$4 \quad 6 \quad 9 \quad 13 \quad 18 \quad 24 \quad 31$$
$$+2 \quad +3 \quad +4 \quad +5 \quad +6 \quad +7$$

The sequence is neither arithmetic nor geometric. Following the pattern above, the next three terms are 18, 24, and 31.

✓ **Check Understanding**   Example 4

4. Tell whether each sequence is *arithmetic*, *geometric*, or *neither*. Then find the next three terms of the sequence.

a. 3, 9, 27, 81, . . .   **b.** 10, 13, 18, 25, . . .
c. −12, 12, −12, 12, . . .   **d.** 50, 200, 350, 500, . . .

EXERCISES

For more exercises, see *Extra Practice*.

Practice and Problem Solving

 Practice by Example

Example 1
(page 688)

What is the common difference of each arithmetic sequence?

1. $5, 4, 3, 2, \ldots$ **2.** $4, 11, 18, 25, \ldots$ **3.** $7, 1, -5, -11, \ldots$

4. $80, 60, 40, 20, \ldots$ **5.** $3, 9, 15, 21, \ldots$ **6.** $-6, -5, -4, -3, \ldots$

Example 2
(page 689)

Find the next three terms of each sequence. Then write a rule to describe the sequence.

7. $0, 5, 10, 15, \ldots$ **8.** $21, 15, 9, 3, \ldots$ **9.** $-11, -8, -5, -2, \ldots$

10. Exercising You begin doing 20 sit-ups every day in November. You do 32 sit-ups every day in December, 44 sit-ups every day in January, and so on. Find the next three terms of the sequence. Then write a rule to describe the sequence.

Example 3
(page 689)

Find the common ratio and the next three terms of each sequence. Then write a rule to describe the sequence.

11. $3, 6, 12, 24, \ldots$ **12.** $5, 1, \frac{1}{5}, \frac{1}{25}, \ldots$ **13.** $45, 90, 180, 360, \ldots$

14. $2, 3, 4\frac{1}{2}, 6\frac{3}{4}, \ldots$ **15.** $12, 4, 1\frac{1}{3}, \frac{4}{9}, \ldots$ **16.** $8, 40, 200, 1{,}000, \ldots$

Example 4
(page 690)

Tell whether each sequence is *arithmetic*, *geometric*, or *neither*. Find the next three terms of the sequence.

17. $1, 3, 9, 27, \ldots$ **18.** $10, 5, 0, -5, \ldots$ **19.** $4.5, 4, 3.5, 3, \ldots$

20. $2, 2, 4, 6, \ldots$ **21.** $-1, 3, -9, 27, \ldots$ **22.** $0, 5, 12, 21, \ldots$

B **Apply Your Skills**

Tell whether each sequence is *arithmetic* or *geometric*. If arithmetic, give the common difference. If geometric, give the common ratio.

23. $1, 1\frac{1}{2}, 2, 2\frac{1}{2}, \ldots$ **24.** $-3, -15, -75, \ldots$ **25.** $-4, 12, -36, 108, \ldots$

26. $5, 6.4, 7.8, 9.2, \ldots$ **27.** $5, 15, 45, 135, \ldots$ **28.** $8.3, 5.7, 3.1, 0.5, \ldots$

Find the next three terms of each sequence. Then write a rule to describe the sequence.

29. $1, 4, 16, 64, \ldots$ **30.** $3, 1, -1, -3, \ldots$ **31.** $2, 20, 200, 2{,}000, \ldots$

32. $9, 18, 36, 72, \ldots$ **33.** $25, 50, 75, 100, \ldots$ **34.** $6.5, 6.7, 6.9, 7.1, \ldots$

Tell whether each sequence is *arithmetic*, *geometric*, or *neither*. Find the next three terms of each sequence.

35. $\frac{1}{2}, \frac{5}{6}, 1\frac{1}{6}, 1\frac{1}{2}, \ldots$ **36.** $1, 10, 2, 20, \ldots$ **37.** $13, 12, 10, 7, \ldots$

38. $7, 7.03, 7.06, 7.09, \ldots$ **39.** $-\frac{1}{5}, -\frac{1}{10}, -\frac{1}{20}, -\frac{1}{40}, \ldots$

40. Writing in Math The first two numbers of a sequence are 4 and 8. Can you tell what kind of sequence this is? Explain.

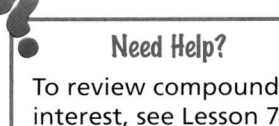

C Challenge

Evaluate each expression for $n = -2, -1, 0,$ and 1. Is the sequence formed *arithmetic*, *geometric*, or *neither*?

41. $3n$ **42.** $n(n + 1)$ **43.** 2^n **44.** n^2

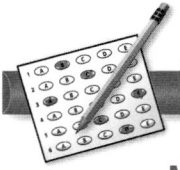

Need Help?

To review compound interest, see Lesson 7-8.

🌐 **45. Savings** You open a savings account with $2,000. The account earns 4% interest compounded semiannually.
  a. Write the balance in the savings account after each interest payment for two years.
  b. Does the pattern of balances form an arithmetic or geometric sequence? Explain.

46. Patterns In the Fibonacci sequence $1, 1, 2, 3, 5, 8, \ldots,$ you find each term (after the first two terms) by adding the two previous terms. Write the next three terms of the sequence.

Test Prep

Multiple Choice

47. If the first term of an arithmetic sequence is 35 and the fifth term is 67, what is the third term?
  A. 43   **B.** 51   **C.** 59   **D.** 75

48. If the rule for a sequence is "start with -7 and multiply by -2 repeatedly," what is the fourth term in the sequence?
  F. -112 **G.** -56 **H.** 56   **I.** 112

Reading Comprehension

Read the passage below before doing Exercises 49 and 50.

Population Watch

The population of the United States in 1980 was about 226 million, in 1985 it was about 238 million, in 1990 it was about 250 million, and in 1995 it was about 263 million.

49. What intervals of time are used with the given population data?

50. Which type of sequence, arithmetic or geometric, could you use to model the United States population data? Explain.

Take It to the NET
Online lesson quiz at
www.PHSchool.com
Web Code: ada-1301

Mixed Review

Lesson 12-8 🌐 **51. Surveys** You want to find out which presidential candidate is most popular in your city. You plan to interview people who visit the city's art museum. State whether the survey plan describes a good sample. Explain your reasoning.

Lesson 9-6 **Find the circumference of each circle rounded to the nearest tenth.**

52. radius = 8.5 m   **53.** radius = 5 in.   **54.** diameter = 14 cm

Displaying Sequences

For Use With Lesson 13-1

You can model rules for sequences mathematically and then display the sequences using graphing calculator tables.

1 EXAMPLE

Model the rule "Start with 23 and add −4 repeatedly" mathematically and then display the sequence in a calculator table.

Model: $23 + (-4)x$, or $23 - 4x$, with $x = 0, 1, 2, \ldots$

Display Method 1

Press ▣Y= and enter $Y_1 = 23 - 4x$.

● In **TBLSET,** set TblStart = 0 and ΔTbl = 1, then press **TABLE.**

X	Y_1	
0	23	
1	19	
2	15	
3	11	
4	7	
5	3	
6	−1	

X=6

Move down in either column to see more terms of the sequence.

2 EXAMPLE

Model the rule "Start with 4 and multiply by 2 repeatedly" mathematically and then display the sequence in a calculator table.

Model: $4(2)^x$, with $x = 0, 1, 2, \ldots$

Display Method 2

Clear your home screen. In **STAT**, use the **OPS** menu. Select the **seq** operator, and ENTER. Then

enter seq(X,X,0,10) STO▶ **STAT L₁** ENTER. In similar fashion,

enter seq(4(2)^X,X,0,10) STO▶ **STAT L₂** ENTER.

● Press LIST.

L1	L2	L3	1
0	4		
1	8		
2	16		
3	32		
4	64		
5	128		
6	256		

L1(7)=6

This list ends at 10.

EXERCISES

Use a graphing calculator table to display the first 11 terms of each sequence. Record the 11th term. Use Display Method 1 for some exercises and Display Method 2 for the others.

1. Start with 0 and add 5 repeatedly.

2. Start with 80 and subtract 30 repeatedly.

3. Start with 3 and add 6 repeatedly.

4. Start with −4 and multiply by −3 repeatedly.

5. $7, 7.3, 7.6, 7.9, \ldots$ **6.** $3, 1, -1, -3, \ldots$ **7.** $18 - 3x; x = 0, 1, 2, \ldots$ **8.** $6(3)^x$

9. In Example 1, the model gives the desired sequence for x having values $0, 1, 2, \ldots$ Find a model using x that gives the same sequence for x having values $1, 2, 3, \ldots$

13-2 Graphing Nonlinear Functions

What You'll Learn

OBJECTIVE 1 To graph quadratic functions

OBJECTIVE 2 To graph absolute value functions

. . . And Why

To use nonlinear functions in modeling real-world situations, such as finding the area of an enclosed space

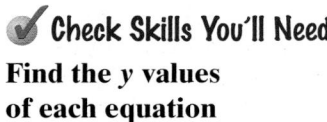
Check Skills You'll Need

Find the y values of each equation for x = −2, 0, and 2.

1. $y = 5x - 1$

2. $y = \frac{1}{2}x + 3$

3. $y = 3x + 2$

4. $y = \frac{1}{4}x - 5$

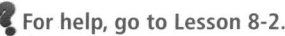
For help, go to Lesson 8-2.

New Vocabulary

• quadratic function
• absolute value function

OBJECTIVE

1 | **Graphing Quadratic Functions**

Investigation

Graphing Data

You can graph the area of a square as a function of the length of a side of the square.

1. Copy and complete the table at the right.

2. Draw a graph of the data. Does your graph appear to be a linear function? Explain.

Side x	Area f(x)
1	1
2	▪
3	▪
4	▪
5	▪
6	36

In a **quadratic function,** the input variable is squared. The graph of a quadratic function is a U-shaped curve called a *parabola*. The curve may open upward or downward.

1 EXAMPLE **Graphing a Quadratic Function**

For the function $y = 2x^2$, make a table with integer values of x from −2 to 2. Then graph the function.

Make a table.

x	$2x^2 = y$	(x, y)
−2	$2(-2)^2 = 8$	(−2, 8)
−1	$2(-1)^2 = 2$	(−1, 2)
0	$2(0)^2 = 0$	(0, 0)
1	$2(1)^2 = 2$	(1, 2)
2	$2(2)^2 = 8$	(2, 8)

Make a graph.

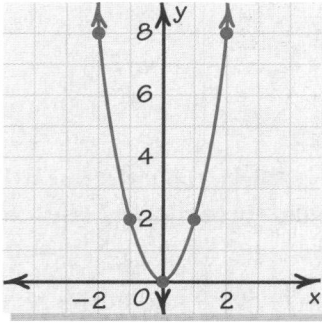

Check Understanding Example 1

1. For each function, make a table with integer values of x from −2 to 2. Then graph each function.

a. $y = -2x^2$ 　　　　　　　　**b.** $y = -x^2 + 3$

iTEXT Interactive lesson includes instant self-check, tutorials, and activities.

2 EXAMPLE Using a Graph to Solve a Problem

The function $A = 10x - x^2$, where x is the width in yards, gives the area A of a goat pen in square yards. Graph the function. Use the graph to find the width that gives the greatest area.

x	$10x - x^2 = y$	(x, y)
0	$10(0) - 0^2 = 0$	(0, 0)
1	$10(1) - 1^2 = 9$	(1, 9)
2	$10(2) - 2^2 = 16$	(2, 16)
3	$10(3) - 3^2 = 21$	(3, 21)
4	$10(4) - 4^2 = 24$	(4, 24)
5	$10(5) - 5^2 = 25$	(5, 25)
6	$10(6) - 6^2 = 24$	(6, 24)

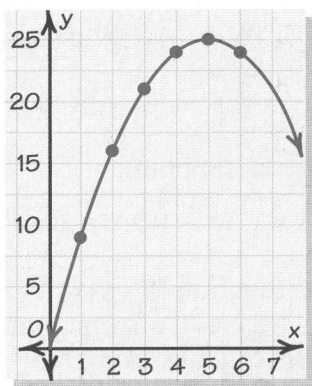

Real-World Connection

A goat pen with width 5 yd and area 25 yd^2 must have length 5 yd.

The ordered pair $(5, 25)$ shows what appears to be the highest point. So the width 5 yards gives the greatest area.

✓ Check Understanding Example 2

2. Graph each function.

a. $y = 3x + x^2$ **b.** $y = 6x - x^2$

OBJECTIVE

2 Graphing Absolute Value Functions

The equation $y = |x|$ is an **absolute value function.** The graph of $y = |x|$ is V-shaped.

Reading Math

Quadratic and absolute value functions are *nonlinear functions* because you cannot draw the graph of either in one line.

3 EXAMPLE Graphing an Absolute Value Function

Graph the function $y = |x|$.

x	$|x| = y$	(x, y)
−2	$|-2| = 2$	(−2, 2)
−1	$|-1| = 1$	(−1, 1)
0	$|0| = 0$	(0, 0)
1	$|1| = 1$	(1, 1)
2	$|2| = 2$	(2, 2)

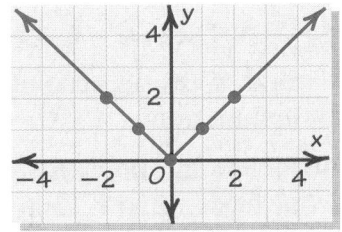

✓ Check Understanding Example 3

3. Graph each function.

a. $y = -|x| + 1$ **b.** $y = 2|x|$

EXERCISES

 For more exercises, see *Extra Practice*.

Practice and Problem Solving

A Practice by Example

Example 1
(page 694)

For each function, make a table with integer values of x from -2 to 2. Then graph the function.

1. $y = 4x^2$ **2.** $y = -x^2$ **3.** $y = -3x^2$ **4.** $y = x^2 + 1$

5. $y = -x^2 + 2$ **6.** $y = x^2 - 2$ **7.** $y = x^3 + 4$ **8.** $y = -x^2 + 3$

Example 2
(page 695)

Graph each function.

9. $y = x - x^2$ **10.** $y = 2x - x^2$ **11.** $y = 5x - x^2$ **12.** $y = 8x - x^2$

13. The function $A = 15x - x^2$, where x is the width in yards, gives the area A of a llama pen in square yards. Make a table with integer values from 0 to 10. Graph the function. Use the graph to find the width that gives the greatest area.

Example 3
(page 695)

For each function, make a table with integer values of x from -2 to 2. Then graph the function.

14. $y = 3|x|$ **15.** $y = |x| + 3$ **16.** $y = -3|x|$

17. $y = |x| - 4$ **18.** $y = -|x| - 1$ **19.** $y = -2|x|$

B Apply Your Skills

State whether the graph of the function has a U shape or a V shape. Make a table with integer values of x from -2 to 2. Then graph the function.

20. $y = |x| + 1$ **21.** $y = x^2 - 8$ **22.** $y = 3x - x^2$

23. $y = -4x^2$ **24.** $y = -|x| - 3$ **25.** $y = 2x^2 - 2$

26. $y = -\frac{1}{2}|x|$ **27.** $y = |x| - 2$ **28.** $y = -x^2 + 5$

Reading Math

For help with reading and solving Exercise 29, see page 698.

29. a. Graph $y = x^2$, $y = 2x^2$, and $y = \frac{1}{2}x^2$ on the same coordinate plane.
     b. Describe how the coefficients of x^2 affect the graphs.

30. Writing in Math Describe how the graphs of the functions $y = x^2$, $y = 2x + x^2$, and $y = 2x - x^2$ are alike and how they are different.

31. Open-Ended Write an absolute value function of your own. Graph the function.

C Challenge

32. Reasoning For the *cubing function*, $y = x^3$, make a table with integer values of x from -2 to 2. Then graph the function. Is the cubing function a quadratic function? Explain.

33. a. Geometry Make a table to show edge lengths and volumes of four cubes. Let the edge lengths be 1 m, 2 m, 3 m, and 4 m.
     b. Graph the ordered pairs from your table.
     c. Using your graph from part (b), estimate the volume of a cube with edge length 3.5 m.

Writing in Math

How are quadratic and absolute value functions alike? How are they different?

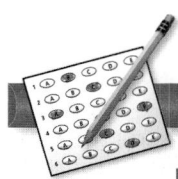

Multiple Choice

For Exercises 34–36, use the graph at the right.

34. The graph shows what type of function?
  A. quadratic   **B.** linear
  C. area   **D.** absolute value

35. Which point is NOT on the graph?
  F. $(1, -2)$ **G.** $(-2, 0)$
  H. $(0, -2)$ **I.** $(1, -1)$

Take It to the NET
Online lesson quiz at
www.PHSchool.com
Web Code: ada-1302

36. Which function matches the graph?
  A. $y = -2|x|$ **B.** $y = x^2 - 2$
  C. $y = |x - 2|$ **D.** $|x| - 2$

Short Response

37. For the function $y = 3x^2$, **(a)** make a table with integer values of x from -2 to 2.   **(b)** Graph the function.

Mixed Review

Lesson 13-1

Find the next three terms of each sequence. Then write a rule to describe the sequence.

38. $8, 4, 2, 1, \ldots$ **39.** $12, 27, 42, 57, \ldots$ **40.** $3, 4, 6, 9, \ldots$

Lesson 12-1

41. Statistics The table shows the prices of evening movies at 18 different theaters. Use the data to make a frequency table.

Costs of Movie Tickets

$7.00, $6.50, $7.50, $7.00, $7.50, $8.00, $7.00, $8.50, $8.00, $6.00, $7.00, $7.50, $8.00, $7.00, $7.50, $8.50, $7.50, $6.50

Math at Work

Systems Analyst

Systems analysts are responsible for upgrading hardware and designing and installing new software. They also respond to problems users have with hardware or software. Logic skills are necessary for writing programs and solving problems.

Systems analysts have backgrounds in computer programming. Since computer technology is constantly changing, they must continue their education throughout their careers.

Take It to the NET For more information about systems analysts, go to **www.PHSchool.com**.
Web Code: adb-2031

Sometimes you are asked to describe a graph or compare graphs. To do so, you must be able to read the graphs.

EXAMPLE

a. Graph $y = x^2$, $y = 2x^2$, and $y = \frac{1}{2}x^2$ on the same coordinate plane.
b. Describe how the coefficients of x^2 affect the graphs.

a. By the methods of Lesson 13-2, your graphs should look like these.
b. To describe how the coefficient of x^2 affects the graphs, ask these questions. Read the graphs for the answers.

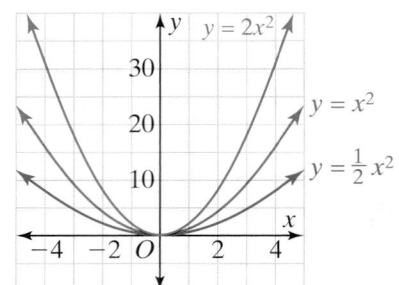

1. How are the graphs alike?

1. All three graphs are parabolas. All contain $(0, 0)$. All open upward.

2. How are the graphs different?

2. From the top down, they get wider.

3. How are the functions alike?

3. All contain x^2.

4. How are the functions different?

4. x^2 has different coefficients.

Now, make a connection and write your answer to part (b).

From the top down:
   Graphs get wider.

From the top down:
   $y = 2x^2$
   $y = x^2$
   $y = \frac{1}{2}x^2$

As the coefficients of x^2 get smaller, the graphs get wider.

EXERCISES

1. For $y = -x^2$, $y = -2x^2$, and $y = -\frac{1}{2}x^2$, describe how the coefficients of x^2 affect the graphs of the functions.

2. a. Graph $y = x^2$, $y = x^2 + 2$, and $y = x^2 - 3$ on the same coordinate plane.
   b. Describe how the constants affect the graphs of the functions.

3. For $y = k|x|$, describe how the values of k affect the graphs.

Exponential Growth and Decay

1 Exponential Growth

A function like $y = 2^x$ has input, or domain, values that are exponents. It models *exponential growth*. Its graph curves upward as input values increase.

1 EXAMPLE Real-World Problem Solving

Biology A warren of rabbits starts with one male and one female. The number of rabbits then doubles each month. The function $y = 2^x$ models the number of rabbits in the warren.

For the function $y = 2^x$, make a table with integer values of x from 2 to 5. Then graph the function.

x	2^x	y	(x, y)
2	2^2	4	$(2, 4)$
3	2^3	8	$(3, 8)$
4	2^4	16	$(4, 16)$
5	2^5	32	$(5, 32)$

✓ Check Understanding Example 1

1. For the function $y = 3^x$, make a table with integer values of x from 1 to 4. Then graph the function.

You can multiply the power in a function by a number. For example, in $y = 0.25(4^x)$, the power 4^x is multiplied by 0.25.

What You'll Learn

OBJECTIVE 1 To use tables, rules, and graphs with functions modeling growth

OBJECTIVE 2 To use tables, rules, and graphs with functions modeling decay

. . . And Why

To model real-world situations involving population growth

✓ Check Skills You'll Need

Evaluate each expression.

1. 5^2 **2.** 4^3 **3.** 3^5 **4.** 2^8

❓ For help, go to Lesson 4-2.

---

iTEXT Interactive lesson includes instant self-check, tutorials, and activities.

EXAMPLE   Graphing Exponential Growth

For the function $y = 0.25(4)^x$, make a table with integer values of x from 0 to 4. Then graph the function.

x	$0.25(4)^x$	y	(x, y)
0	$0.25(4)^0$	0.25	(0, 0.25)
1	$0.25(4)^1$	1	(1, 1)
2	$0.25(4)^2$	4	(2, 4)
3	$0.25(4)^3$	16	(3, 16)
4	$0.25(4)^4$	64	(4, 64)

✓ **Check Understanding**   Example 2

2. For the function $y = 0.5(2)^x$, make a table with integer values of x from 0 to 5. Then graph the function.

OBJECTIVE

2 Exponential Decay

A function like $y = \left(\frac{1}{2}\right)^x$ models *exponential decay*. Its graph slopes downward as input values increase.

3 **EXAMPLE**   Graphing Exponential Decay

For $y = 60\left(\frac{1}{2}\right)^x$, make a table with integer values of x from 0 to 5. Then graph the function.

x	$60\left(\frac{1}{2}\right)^x$	y	(x, y)
0	$60\left(\frac{1}{2}\right)^0$	60	(0, 60)
1	$60\left(\frac{1}{2}\right)^1$	30	(1, 30)
2	$60\left(\frac{1}{2}\right)^2$	15	(2, 15)
3	$60\left(\frac{1}{2}\right)^3$	7.5	(3, 7.5)
4	$60\left(\frac{1}{2}\right)^4$	3.75	(4, 3.75)
5	$60\left(\frac{1}{2}\right)^5$	1.875	(5, 1.875)

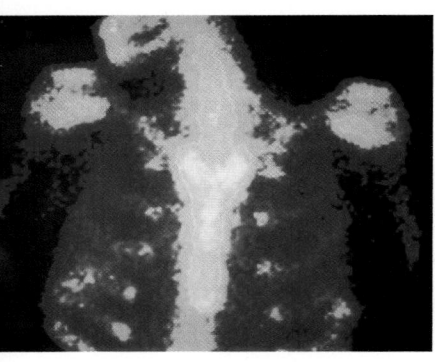

Real-World Connection

Doctors use the element technetium to make bone scans. Technetium decays exponentially. After 6 hours, only 15 mg of a 30-mg dose remain. After 12 hours, only 7.5 mg remain.

✓ **Check Understanding**   Example 3

3. For the function $y = 90\left(\frac{1}{3}\right)^x$, make a table with integer values of x from 0 to 5. Then graph the function.

EXERCISES

For more exercises, see *Extra Practice*.

Practice and Problem Solving

A Practice by Example

Examples 1 and 2
(pages 699 and 700)

Make a table with integer values of x from 0 to 4. Then graph the function.

1. $y = 4^x$ **2.** $y = 5^x$ **3.** $y = 6^x$

4. $y = 0.4(2)^x$ **5.** $y = 0.5(4)^x$ **6.** $y = 0.2(5)^x$

7. Biology A bacteria culture starts with ten cells and doubles every hour. The function $y = 10(2)^x$ models the number of cells y in the culture after x hours. Make a table with integer values of x from 0 to 3. Then graph the function.

Example 3
(page 700)

Make a table with integer values of x from 0 to 5. Then graph the function.

8. $y = \left(\frac{1}{2}\right)^x$ **9.** $y = 30\left(\frac{1}{3}\right)^x$ **10.** $y = 100\left(\frac{1}{5}\right)^x$

B Apply Your Skills

Match each graph with an equation.

11.

12.

     A. $y = 3^x$ **B.** $y = 2^x$ **A.** $y = 3\left(\frac{1}{3}\right)^x$ **B.** $y = 2\left(\frac{1}{2}\right)^x$

You put \$100 in a stock that increases in value by 20% each year. The function $v = 100(1.2)^x$ describes the value v of the stock after x years.

13. Evaluate the function for $x = 2$. What does the value represent?

14. For the function, make a table with integer values of x from 0 to 6. Graph the function.

15. Reasoning Use your graph from Exercise 14. Estimate how long it will take for the value to be twice the initial investment.

Make a table with integer values of x from 0 to 4. Then graph the function.

16. $y = 2 \cdot 3^x$ **17.** $y = \frac{1}{5} \cdot 5^x$ **18.** $y = 6(0.5)^x$

19. $f(x) = \frac{1}{2} \cdot 2^x$ **20.** $g(x) = 20\left(\frac{1}{2}\right)^x$ **21.** $g(x) = 3 \cdot 2^x$

Is the point (4, 16) on the graph of each function? Explain.

22. $y = 4x$ **23.** $y = 2^x$ **24.** $y = x^2$ **25.** $y = \left(\frac{1}{2}\right)^x$

 **Challenge**

26. a. For the functions $y = 2x$, $y = x^2$, and $y = 2^x$, make tables with integer values of x from 0 to 5. Then graph the functions.
b. Writing in Math Describe how the graphs are similar. Describe how they are different.

27. Reasoning Without graphing, predict whether each function shows exponential growth or exponential decay. Justify your prediction.
a. $y = 5^x$ **b.** $y = \left(\frac{1}{2}\right)^x$ **c.** $y = 3(0.2)^x$ **d.** $y = 3(2)^x$

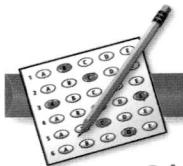 **Test Prep**

Gridded Response

For the given equation, what is the value of y for $x = 2$?

28. $y = 0.2(3)^x$ **29.** $y = 3\left(\frac{1}{3}\right)^x$ **30.** $y = 3x^2 - 6$ **31.** $y = 4|x| - 1$

For Exercises 32 and 33, use the formula $B = p(1.08)^n$ to find the balance B (in dollars and cents) for a principal p invested at a compound interest rate of 8% for n years.

32. $50 invested for 5 years **33.** $25 invested for 10 years

Take It to the NET
Online lesson quiz at
www.PHSchool.com
Web Code: ada-1303

Mixed Review

Lesson 13-2 **Graph each function.**

34. $y = |x| + 2$ **35.** $f(x) = 3|x|$ **36.** $g(x) = -x^2 + 1$

Lesson 12-4 **37. Shopping** Janelle is buying a sweatshirt. She has a choice of red, purple, or green; zipper or no zipper; and hooded or not hooded. How many different sweatshirt choices does she have?

Lesson 11-3 **Find the midpoint of each segment with the given endpoints.**

38. $A(4, -6)$ and $B(-2, 5)$ **39.** $X(-3, -8)$ and $Y(1, 6)$

 Checkpoint Quiz 1   **Lessons 13-1 through 13-3**

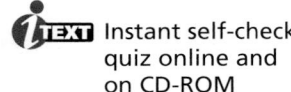 Instant self-check quiz online and on CD-ROM

Find the next three terms of each sequence. Then write a rule to describe the sequence.

1. $100, 85, 70, 55, \ldots$ **2.** $17, 24, 31, 38, \ldots$ **3.** $13, 26, 52, 104, \ldots$

4. A geometric sequence begins with 3 and has common ratio 2. Write its first five terms.

For each function, make a table with integer values of x. (Use –2 to 2 for Ex. 5 and 6; use 0 to 4 for Ex. 7.) Then graph the function.

5. $y = \frac{1}{4}x^2$ **6.** $f(x) = \frac{1}{4}|x|$ **7.** $f(x) = 0.5(3)^x$

Nonlinear Functions and Graphing Calculators

For Use With Lesson 13-3

You can use a graphing calculator to graph nonlinear functions. For the exponent 2, you can use the x^2 key or press $\wedge$ 2.

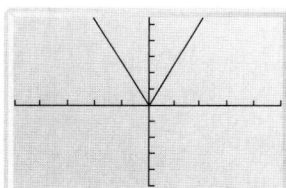

Graph $y = |3x|$.

Step 1 Press Y= CLEAR . Press MATH . In the **NUM** menu, select **abs** then ENTER . Enter Y_1 = abs (3x).

```
Plot1  Plot2  Plot3
\Y1■abs(3X)
\Y2=
\Y3=
\Y4=
```

Step 2 Set your viewing window.

```
WINDOW
 Xmin=−5
 Xmax=5
 ▵X=
 Xscl=1
 Ymin=−5
 Ymax=5
 Yscl=1
```

Step 3 Press GRAPH .

Step 4 Press **TABLE** to see solutions.

X	Y_1
−4	12
−3	9
−2	6
−1	3
0	0
1	3
2	6
X=2	

EXERCISES

Graph each equation using a graphing calculator. For each function, use TABLE and make a table on paper for integer values of x from −5 to 5. Then sketch the graph.

1. $y = |2x|$

2. $y = -|2x|$

3. $y = |2x| + 1$

4. $y = x^2 - 1$

5. $y = -x^2 - 1$

6. $y = 3(2)^x$

7. $y = -3(2)^x$

8. $y = 3\left(\frac{1}{2}\right)^x$

9. $y = -3\left(\frac{1}{2}\right)^x$

10. Compare your graphs for Exercises 1 and 2.
   a. Explain how they are related and why this is so.
   b. Compare the equations in Exercises 6 and 7. Should their graphs be related in the same way as in part (a)? Explain. Then check.

11. Open-Ended Write a nonlinear function that you can graph using a graphing calculator. Graph your function. Make a table of values and sketch your graph.

Polynomials

What You'll Learn

OBJECTIVE
1 To identify polynomials

OBJECTIVE
2 To evaluate polynomials

...And Why

To model real-world applications in science

 Check Skills You'll Need

Evaluate each expression.

1. $5n$ for $n = -8$

2. mn for $m = 6$ and $n = -4$

3. $x - 9$ for $x = 7$

4. $63 - 5x$ for $x = 7$

 For help, go to Lesson 1-3.

New Vocabulary

- monomial
- polynomial
- binomial
- trinomial

OBJECTIVE

1 **Identifying Polynomials**

You have seen how mathematics uses algebraic expressions to represent real-world situations. Some of these expressions are monomials. A **monomial** is a real number, a variable, or a product of a real number and variables with whole-number exponents.

Monomials: $\quad 3 \qquad m \qquad 5xy \qquad 0.35bc^3 \qquad \frac{w}{9} \qquad \frac{1}{4}p^2q$

Not monomials: $\qquad a - 8 \qquad \sqrt{m} \qquad y^{-1} \text{ (or } \frac{1}{y}) \qquad \frac{ab}{c}$

1 EXAMPLE **Recognizing a Monomial**

Is the expression a monomial? Explain.

a. $7x^2y$ — Yes, the expression is the product of the real number 7 and the variables x and y.

b. $8 + a$ — No, the expression is a sum.

c. $\frac{a}{7y}$ — No, the denominator contains a variable.

d. $\frac{5x}{4}$ — Yes, the expression is the product of the real number $\frac{5}{4}$ and the variable x.

✓ **Check Understanding** **Example 1**

1. Is the expression a monomial? Explain.

    a. $\frac{6}{m}$ **b.** $\frac{m}{6}$ **c.** 45   **d.** $mx + b$

A **polynomial** is a monomial or a sum or difference of monomials. We call the monomials that make up a polynomial its *terms*. You can name a polynomial by the number of its terms.

Polynomial	Number of terms	Examples
Monomial	1	$4,\ 32,\ x,\ 2x^2$
Binomial	2	$x - 3,\ 5x + 1,\ x^3 - x$
Trinomial	3	$x^2 + x + 1,\ x^4 - 2x - 5$

TEXT Interactive lesson includes instant self-check, tutorials, and activities.

2 EXAMPLE Naming a Polynomial

State whether the polynomial is a *monomial,* a *binomial,* or a *trinomial.*

a. $x - y$ b. $8xyz$ c. $y^2 + 8y + 18$
   binomial   monomial   trinomial

✓ **Check Understanding** Example 2

2. Is the polynomial a monomial, a binomial, or a trinomial?

   a. 10 **b.** $9x^2 + xy$ **c.** $8 - y$ **d.** $5 + x - 3y$

OBJECTIVE

2 Evaluating Polynomials

You evaluate polynomials by substituting values for the variables.

3 EXAMPLE Evaluating a Polynomial

Evaluate each polynomial for $m = 8$ and $p = -3$.

a. $2mp$ b. $3m - 2p$

   $2mp = 2(8)(-3)$ **Replace m with 8** $3m - 2p = 3(8) - 2(-3)$
                       and p with -3. $= 24 + 6$
        $= -48$ **Simplify.** $= 30$

✓ **Check Understanding** Example 3

3. Evaluate each polynomial for $x = -2$ and $y = 5$.

   a. $5xy$ **b.** $x + 3y$ **c.** $y^2 - 2y + x$

4 EXAMPLE Real-World 🌐 Problem Solving

Physics The polynomial $-16t^2 + 140t$ gives the height, in feet, reached by fireworks in t seconds. If the fireworks explode 4 seconds after launch, at what height do they explode?

   $-16t^2 + 140t$
   $-16(4)^2 + 140(4)$ **Replace t with 4.**
   304 **Simplify.**

The fireworks explode at 304 feet.

✓ **Check Understanding** Example 4

4. Fireworks are set to explode 6 seconds after launch. At what height will they explode?

Real-World 🌐 Connection

During a twenty-minute show, fireworks technicians can set off as many as 6,000 different fireworks.

EXERCISES

For more exercises, see *Extra Practice*.

Practice and Problem Solving

A Practice by Example

Example 1
(page 704)

Is the expression a monomial? Explain.

1. $2 + x$ **2.** $18ab^2$ **3.** $\frac{a}{3}$ **4.** $\frac{4}{b}$

5. 1 **6.** $0.82k$ **7.** $2x$ **8.** $-0.3y$

Example 2
(page 705)

State whether the polynomial is a *monomial*, a *binomial*, or a *trinomial*.

9. $3xy + 4y^2$ **10.** $5c - 2 + a$ **11.** $7y^2 + 2y - 9$

12. 658 **13.** $3x^2 + 2x$ **14.** 21

15. $7p^2$ **16.** $56 - x$ **17.** $a^2 + 7b - 3c$

Example 3
(page 705)

Evaluate each polynomial for $a = 2$ and $b = -4$.

18. $2ab$ **19.** $-4ab$ **20.** $7a + b$

21. $a - 3b$ **22.** $5a + 7b$ **23.** $ab^2 + 5$

24. $a^2 + 2b - 3$ **25.** $2a^2 - b + 4$ **26.** $10a + b^2 - 7$

Example 4
(page 705)

27. Sports The polynomial $-16t^2 + 32t + 4$ gives the height, in feet, that a tossed ball reaches in t seconds. If the ball reaches a maximum height after one second, what is that height?

B Apply Your Skills

Is the expression a monomial? Explain.

28. pq^{-3} **29.** 0 **30.** $\frac{3}{p}$ **31.** $10bc + b$

State whether the polynomial is a *monomial*, a *binomial*, a *trinomial* or *none* of these.

32. $4.5 + 3.7m$ **33.** $2x - 4^{-1}$ **34.** -42 **35.** $x^2 + 7x + 4$

36. $3a^2 - 6a^{-3}$ **37.** $15 + w$ **38.** abc **39.** $b^2 + \frac{2}{b} - 3$

40. Open-Ended Write a polynomial with four terms.

41. Geometry You can write the formula for the area of a trapezoid as $A = \frac{1}{2}b_1h + \frac{1}{2}b_2h$. What kind of polynomial is $\frac{1}{2}b_1h + \frac{1}{2}b_2h$?

42. a. Writing in Math Name other words with the prefixes *mono*, *bi*, *tri*, and *poly*. How do the prefixes help you understand the meanings of the words?
   b. What would you call a polynomial with four terms?

Evaluate each polynomial for $x = -5$ and $y = 3$.

43. $2x + 2y$ **44.** $7 + x^2y$ **45.** $7y^2 + 6x - 20$

46. $xy - y$ **47.** $x^2 + 2x - 3$ **48.** $\frac{x^2}{5} + x$

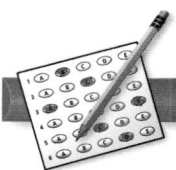

C Challenge

Reasoning Tell why each expression is not a polynomial.

49. $x^2 + 2x + \dfrac{1}{x}$ **50.** $2ab + b^2 + \sqrt{a}$ **51.** $(y^2 + 4) \div y$

52. a. Public Schools The polynomial $34x^2 - 945x + 46{,}971$ models U.S. public school enrollment, in thousands, from 1970 to 1998. The value of x for 1970 is 1 and the value of x for 1998 is 29. How many students were enrolled in public schools in 1970? In 1998?

    b. Use the polynomial to predict enrollment in 2010.

53. Geometry A polygon is convex if no diagonal has points outside the polygon. The polynomial $\dfrac{n^2}{2} - \dfrac{3n}{2}$ gives the number of diagonals that you can draw in a convex polygon with n sides. How many diagonals does a 20-sided convex polygon have?

Test Prep

Multiple Choice

54. Which of the following statements is NOT true?
- **A.** A monomial is a polynomial.
- **B.** A binomial is a sum or difference of two monomials.
- **C.** A polynomial must have more than one term.
- **D.** An integer is a monomial.

Take It to the NET
Online lesson quiz at
www.PHSchool.com
Web Code: ada-1304

55. The area of a trapezoid is $\frac{1}{2}b_1 h + \frac{1}{2}b_2 h$, where h is the height and b_1 and b_2 are the lengths of the bases. What is the area of a trapezoid with height 13 in., one base 4 in., and the other base twice as long?
- **F.** 39 in.^{2}
- **G.** 52 in.^{2}
- **H.** 78 in.^{2}
- **I.** 130 in.^{2}

Short Response

56. Is $\dfrac{4}{x}$ a monomial? Explain.

57. a. Write an example of a monomial, a binomial, and a trinomial.
    b. Explain why each is that type of polynomial.

Mixed Review

Lesson 13-3

For each function make a table with integer values of x from 1 to 4. Then graph each function.

58. $y = 2 \cdot 2^x$ **59.** $f(x) = \dfrac{1}{3} \cdot 3^x$ **60.** $y = 18(0.2)^x$

Lesson 11-7 **61. Navigation** A plane is flying 6.3 mi above the ground. The angle of depression to an airport is 14°. How far is the plane from the airport (in ground distance)?

Lesson 2-3 **Simplify each expression.**

62. $m + 5 + 3m$ **63.** $2y - 1 + 6x + 5$ **64.** $4a + 10b - 7a - 2$

Just as you can get information about a polynomial by counting the number of terms, you can get other information by looking at the exponents. The *degree of a term* is the sum of the exponents of the variables in the term. The *degree of a polynomial* is the greatest degree of its terms.

polynomial ⟶ $x^3 + 4x^2 + xy - 5x + 9$ ⟵ The degree of a nonzero constant is zero.

degree of each term ⟶   3   2   2   1   0

Degree of the polynomial is 3.

1 EXAMPLE

Identify each polynomial by name and by degree.

a. $2 - a$

   0   1 ⟵ degree of each term

Greatest degree of the two terms is 1.

The polynomial is a binomial of degree 1.

b. $3y^3x$

   4 ⟵ Add the exponents: $3 + 1 = 4$.

Degree of the one term is 4.

The polynomial is a monomial of degree 4.

c. $5x^2 + x + 4$

   2   1   0 ⟵ degree of each term

Greatest degree of the three terms is 2.

The polynomial is a trinomial of degree 2.

When you write a polynomial with the terms in order of decreasing degree, the polynomial is in *standard form*. If you need to move terms to do this, you can first write subtractions as additions and then use the Commutative Property of Addition. For example, first write $4 - x^2$ as $4 + (-x^2)$. Then rewrite the polynomial as $-x^2 + 4$.

2 EXAMPLE

Write each polynomial in standard form.

a. $x^4 + 2 - x^2$

    ↑   ↑   ↑

    4   0   2 ◄—— degree of each term

    standard form: $x^4 - x^2 + 2$

b. $-2y + y^3 + y^2 - 3$

    ↑   ↑   ↑   ↑

    1   3   2   0 ◄—— degree of each term

    standard form: $y^3 + y^2 - 2y - 3$

When you simplify a polynomial, write your result in standard form.

3 EXAMPLE

Simplify each polynomial.

a. $5a + a^2 + 3a^2 + 2$

    $5a + (1 + 3)a^2 + 2$ **Combine like terms.**

    $5a + 4a^2 + 2$ **Simplify.**

    $4a^2 + 5a + 2$ **Write in standard form.**

b. $3x - 8x + 2x^2 + 4x^2$

    $(3 - 8)x + (2 + 4)x^2$

    $-5x + 6x^2$

    $6x^2 - 5x$

EXERCISES

Identify each polynomial by name and by degree.

1. $9c + 5$
2. $12a^2b$
3. $6x^2 - 3x + 2$
4. p^2q^3
5. $d^4 + 6d$
6. $4a^3 + 8a^2 - 11$
7. $24x^3yz$
8. $15x - 2x^2$

Write each polynomial in standard form.

9. $8 + 5a$
10. $3y^2 + 16 + y$
11. $2c + 4c^2 - 7$
12. $5x - 4x^2 + 3$
13. $2b^2 - 2 + b^3 - b$
14. $11 + 6y^2 - y$
15. $4x^4 + 4x^5 + x^2 + 2x^3$
16. $p^6 - 4 + p + p^2 - 7p^3$
17. $9a - 5 + 6a^3 - 5a^2$

Simplify each polynomial.

18. $x + 3x^2 + x^2$
19. $3a + 5a^2 + 2a + 6$
20. $4m^2 + m^2 + 10 + 4m$
21. $6p - 5p^2 + 4p + 3p^2$
22. $c + 9c^2 - 7c - 8$
23. $-2x^2 + 5 + 3x^2 + 2x + 3$
24. $3b + 1 + 7b^2 - 3b - 2b^2$
25. $5m^3 + 8m^2 + 11m + 14$
26. $3a^4 - 5a^6 - 9a + 6$
27. $-11 - y^2 - 8y + 2y$
28. $6p + 8p^2 + 5p + 7p^2$
29. $22x + 18x^2 + 6 + 4x$

13-5

Adding and Subtracting Polynomials

What You'll Learn

OBJECTIVE
1 To add polynomials

OBJECTIVE
2 To subtract polynomials

. . . And Why

To solve problems involving area and volume

 Check Skills You'll Need

Simplify each expression.

1. $5x - 7 - 3x$

2. $a + 3b + 4a - 7b$

3. $8m - 4n - 7m - 8n$

4. $2x + 3y - 7 - 8x + 2$

 For help, go to Lesson 2-3.

Need Help?

Like terms are terms with the same variable(s), raised to the same power(s). You combine like terms by adding coefficients.

$3b + 12b = (3 + 12)b$
$= 15b$

iTEXT Interactive lesson includes instant self-check, tutorials, and activities.

OBJECTIVE

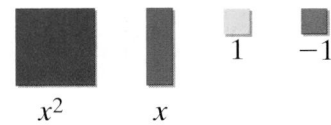

1 **Adding Polynomials**

In Chapter 2, you saw models for variables and numbers. You can also model the square, x^2, of a variable x.

x^2 x 1 -1

You can use models or properties to add polynomials.

1 EXAMPLE **Adding Polynomials**

Simplify $(2x^2 + 3x - 1) + (x^2 + x - 3)$.

Method 1 Add using tiles.

$2x^2 + 3x - 1$

$x^2 + x - 3$

The sum is $3x^2$ $+$ $4x$ $-$ 4

Method 2 Add by combining like terms.

$(2x^2 + 3x - 1) + (x^2 + x - 3)$

$= (2x^2 + x^2) + (3x + x) - 1 - 3$ **Use the Commutative and Associative Properties of Addition to group like terms.**

$= (2 + 1)x^2 + (3 + 1)x - 1 - 3$ **Use the Distributive Property to combine like terms.**

$= 3x^2 + 4x - 4$ **Simplify.**

✓ Check Understanding **Example 1**

1. Simplify.

  a. $(7d^2 + 7d) + (2d^2 + 3d)$
  b. $(x^2 + 2x + 5) + (3x^2 + x + 12)$

You can also add polynomials in a column by aligning like terms and then adding their coefficients.

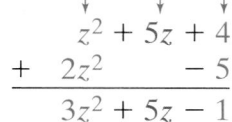

EXAMPLE **Aligning Like Terms**

Find the sum of $z^2 + 5z + 4$ and $2z^2 - 5$.

Align like terms.

$$\begin{array}{r}
z^2 + 5z + 4 \\
+\quad 2z^2\qquad - 5 \\
\hline
3z^2 + 5z - 1
\end{array}$$

Add the terms in each column.

✓ Check Understanding Example 2

2. Simplify each sum.

a. $\begin{array}{r} 4x + 9y \\ +\quad 3x - 5y \\ \hline \end{array}$

b. $\begin{array}{r} a^2 + 6a - 4 \\ +\quad 8a^2 - 8a \\ \hline \end{array}$

c. $(4g^2 - 2g + 2) + (2g^2 - 3)$
d. $(-2t^2 + t + 5) + (2t + 4)$

OBJECTIVE

2 **Subtracting Polynomials**

You subtract polynomials by adding the opposite of each term in the second polynomial.

3 EXAMPLE **Subtracting Polynominals**

Simplify $(5x^2 + 10x) - (3x - 12)$.

$(5x^2 + 10x) - (3x - 12)$

$= 5x^2 + 10x - 3x + 12$ Write the opposite of each term in the second polynomial.

$= 5x^2 + (10x - 3x) + 12$ Group like terms.

$= 5x^2 + (10 - 3)x + 12$ Use the Distributive Property.

$= 5x^2 + 7x + 12$ Simplify.

> **Test-Taking Tip**
>
> After you have *written* the sum or difference of two polynomials, make a mental check of your work, term by term.

✓ Check Understanding Example 3

3. Simplify each difference.

a. $(7a^2 - 2a) - (5a^2 + 3a)$
b. $(10z^2 + 6z + 5) - (z^2 - 8z + 7)$
c. $(3w^2 + 8 + v) - (5w^2 - 3 - 7v)$

EXERCISES

For more exercises, see *Extra Practice*.

Practice and Problem Solving

A Practice by Example

Example 1
(page 710)

Write the sum modeled in each exercise. Then simplify the sum.

1.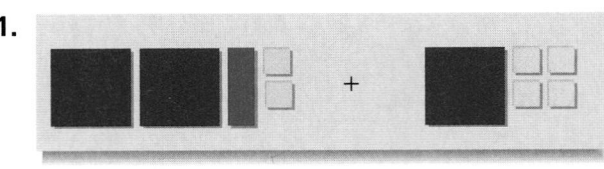

2.

Add by combining like terms.

3. $(x^2 + 3x + 1) + (x^2 + x + 6)$ **4.** $(x^2 + 5x + 2) + (3x^2 + x + 1)$

5. $(3x + 2) + (-4x + 3)$ **6.** $(5x^2 + 3x + 7) + (7x - 2)$

Example 2
(page 711)

Simplify each sum.

7.
$$\begin{array}{r} 5a + 7b \\ + \ -3a + 2b \\ \hline \end{array}$$

8.
$$\begin{array}{r} x^2 + 4x - 2 \\ + \ 8x^2 - 3x + 7 \\ \hline \end{array}$$

9.
$$\begin{array}{r} x^4 + 3x^3 - x^2 + \ x - 2 \\ + \qquad 7x^3 + x^2 - 5x - 9 \\ \hline \end{array}$$

10.
$$\begin{array}{r} xy + 5x - 2y + 4 \\ + \ 2xy - 3x - 3y - 8 \\ \hline \end{array}$$

11.
$$\begin{array}{r} x^3 + 5x^2 + 3x - 2 \\ + \ x^3 \qquad - 2x + 6 \\ \hline \end{array}$$

12.
$$\begin{array}{r} 4x^2 - 5xy \qquad + 7 \\ + \ 8x^2 + 3xy - 3y - 4 \\ \hline \end{array}$$
$-4x^2 + -2xy + {}^{-}3y + 3$

Example 3
(page 711)

Simplify each difference.

13. $(5x + 9) - (2x + 1)$ **14.** $(-11a^2 + 2a - 1) - (7a^2 + 4a)$

15. $(3x - \overset{-2+x}{2y}) - (5x + 4y)$ **16.** $(2x^2 + 3x - 7) - (x^2 - 6x - 9)$

17. $(ab - 4) - (3ab - 6)$ **18.** $(-4x^2 + x - 1) - (x^2 - x + 8)$

B Apply Your Skills

Simplify each sum or difference.

19. $(x^2 - 3x - 9) - (5x - 4)$ **20.** $(13a^2 - 3a) + (2a^2 + 5a)$

21. $(2x^2 + 3x) + (x^2 + 2x)$ **22.** $(8j - 3k + 6m) - (-2j + 3m)$

23. $(w^2 + 5w) + (2w - 6)$ **24.** $(3x^2 + x + 7) - (2x^2 + x + 2)$

25. $(6y - 8) - (2y + 7)$ **26.** $(x^2 + 3x + 5) + (x^2 + x + 2)$

27. a. Write an expression for the sum of three consecutive integers.
Let x be the first integer. Then simplify the expression.
b. What three consecutive integers have the sum 108?

Geometry Write the perimeter of each figure as a polynomial. Simplify.

28.
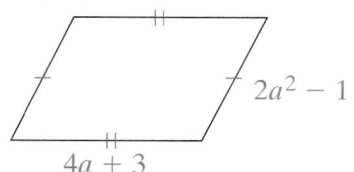

29.
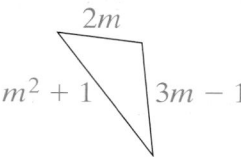

30.
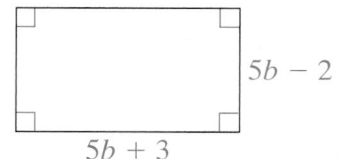

31.
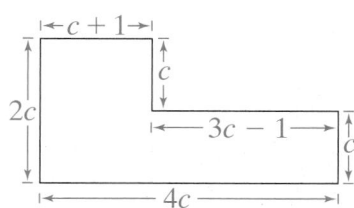

$5x^2 + 4x - 3$
$-\quad 2x^2 - x$
$\overline{\quad 3x^2 + 3x - 3\quad}$

32. Error Analysis Tian simplified $(5x^2 + 4x - 3) - (2x^2 - x)$ as shown at the left. What is his error?

33. The perimeter of a triangle is $11y - 2$. Two of the sides are represented by the expressions $3y - 1$ and $3y + 1$. Write an expression for the third side.

Geometry Find each missing length.

34. perimeter = $11x + 6$
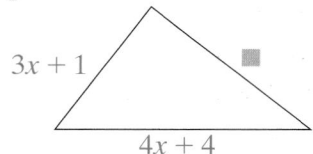

35. perimeter = $12b - 2$
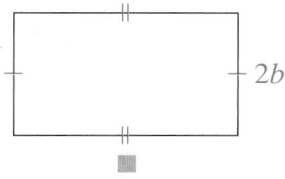

36. perimeter = $5m^2 + 3m$
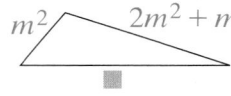

37. perimeter = $6a + 3$
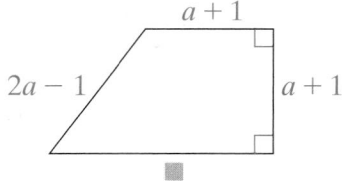

38. Writing in Math How is the process for adding two polynomials like the process for adding two integers? How is it different?

🅲 **Challenge**

39. Reasoning Justify each step.
$(x^2 + 2x + 1) - (2x^2 - 3x - 4)$
$(x^2 + 2x + 1) + (-2x^2) + 3x + 4$
$(x^2 + -2x^2) + (2x + 3x) + (1 + 4)$
$(1 + -2)x^2 + (2 + 3)x + (1 + 4)$
$-x^2 + 5x + 5$

40. Do Exercise 27 by letting x be the second integer.

41. a. Geometry The volume of a cube is $(3x^3 + 9)$ in.^{3}. A smaller cube with volume $(x^3 - 3)$ in.^{3} is cut out of the cube. Write a polynomial for the remaining volume.

b. Evaluate your polynomial for $x = 2$.

c. Reasoning When $x = 2$, will the large cube fit into a 5 in.-by-4 in.-by-6 in. box? Explain. (*Hint:* Recall cube roots, p. 583.)

42. a. What polynomial is the opposite of $2x^2 + 3x - 5$?

b. What is the sum of $2x^2 + 3x - 5$ and its opposite?

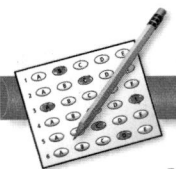

Test Prep

Multiple Choice

For Exercises 43 and 44 assume x is an integer.

43. What is the sum of x and the next two integers?
- **A.** $x + 2x + 3x$
- **B.** $x + x + 1 + x + 2$
- **C.** $x^3 + x^2 + x$
- **D.** $x + y + 1 + z + 2$

44. What is the sum of x and the previous two integers?
- **F.** $x + x - 1 + x - 2$
- **G.** $x - x - 1 - x - 2$
- **H.** $x + x + 1 + x + 2$
- **I.** $x + 2x + 3x$

45. What is the perimeter of the given figure?
- **A.** $4a + 4b$
- **B.** $4a + 3b$
- **C.** $7a + 4b$
- **D.** $6a + 4b$

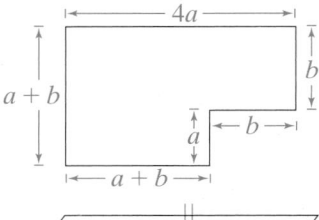

Short Response

46. The perimeter of the given figure is $8x^2 + 4$.

a. What is the missing length?

b. If $x = 3$ cm, what is the perimeter of the figure?

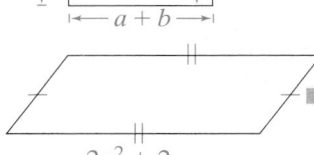

Take It to the NET
Online lesson quiz at
www.PHSchool.com
Web Code: ada-1305

Mixed Review

Lesson 13-4

Evaluate each polynomial for $a = 2$, $b = -1$, and $c = \frac{1}{2}$.

47. $8ab + 1$ **48.** $5 + 4ab - c$ **49.** $a^2 + ab + b^2$

Lesson 10-2

Find the area of each figure.

50.

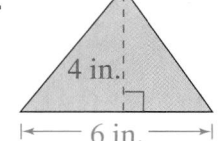

51.

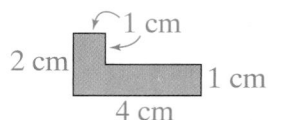

52.

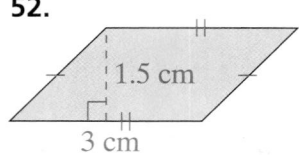

Lesson 3-6 **53. Charity** A student participated in a walk for charity. His friends pledged a total of $3.20 for each mile he walked. The student earned $22.40 for the charity. How many miles did he walk?

Multiplying a Polynomial by a Monomial

OBJECTIVE

1 Using an Area Model

You can model the product of a monomial and a polynomial using algebra tiles. You can find the area of a rectangle that is $2x$ units long and $(x + 4)$ units wide by counting the tiles.

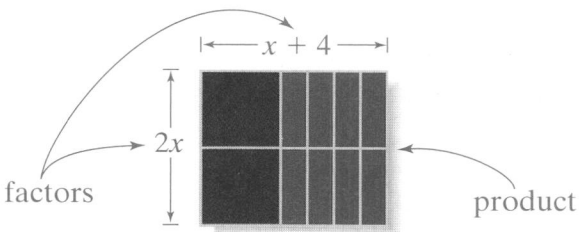

factors   product

The area is $2x^2 + 8x$. So $2x(x + 4) = 2x^2 + 8x$.

You can also use the Distributive Property to simplify a product of a monomial and a polynomial. Multiply each term of the polynomial by the monomial.

1 EXAMPLE   Real-World Problem Solving

Find the area of the garden. All measurements are in feet.

$$A = \ell w$$
$$= 2x(x - 5) \qquad \textbf{Substitute.}$$
$$= 2x(x) - 2x(5) \quad \textbf{Use the Distributive Property.}$$
$$= 2x^2 - 10x \qquad \textbf{Simplify.}$$

● The area of the garden is $(2x^2 - 10x)$ ft^2.

✓ Check Understanding   Example 1

1. Simplify each product.

    a. $3x(x + 4)$ **b.** $x(2x - 3)$

What You'll Learn

OBJECTIVE
1 To use an area model for multiplication

OBJECTIVE
2 To write a polynomial as the product of a monomial and a polynomial

. . . And Why

To use area formulas with polynomials

✓ Check Skills You'll Need

Simplify each expression.

1. $7(v + 3)$

2. $3(u - 8)$

3. $-5(6 - 3t)$

4. $(p + 8)9$

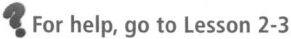 For help, go to Lesson 2-3.

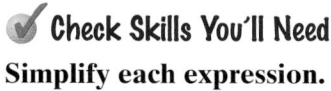 Interactive lesson includes instant self-check, tutorials, and activities.

You can often use other properties to simplify the product of a monomial and a polynomial.

2 EXAMPLE **Simplifying a Product**

Simplify $3x^2(8x^2 - 5x + 2)$.

$3x^2(8x^2 - 5x + 2)$

$= 3x^2(8x^2) + 3x^2(-5x) + 3x^2(2)$ **Use the Distributive Property.**

$= (3)(8)x^{2+2} + (3)(-5)x^{2+1} + (3)(2)x^2$ **Use the Commutative Property of Multiplication.**

$= (3)(8)x^4 + (3)(-5)x^3 + (3)(2)x^2$ **Add exponents.**

$= 24x^4 - 15x^3 + 6x^2$ **Simplify.**

Need Help?
To multiply powers with the same base, add exponents.

☑ **Check Understanding**   Example 2

  2. Simplify each product.

    a. $x(x^2 + 2x + 4)$ **b.** $2a^2(2a^3 - 3a^2 + 3)$

OBJECTIVE

2   **Writing a Polynomial as a Product**

You can sometimes use the Distributive Property to write a polynomial as the product of two factors. First, find the GCF of all the terms of the polynomial and then use it as one of the factors.

3 EXAMPLE **Finding Factors of a Polynomial**

Write $6x^3 + 3x^2 + 9x$ as a product of two factors.

$6x^3 = 2 \cdot 3 \cdot x \cdot x \cdot x$
$3x^2 = 3 \cdot x \cdot x$ **Write the prime factorization of each term.**
$9x = 3 \cdot 3 \cdot x$

$\text{GCF} = 3x$ **Find the GCF.**

Write each term as the product of $3x$ and another factor.

$6x^3 = 3x \cdot 2x^2$ $3x^2 = 3x \cdot x$ $9x = 3x \cdot 3$

$6x^3 + 3x^2 + 9x = 3x(2x^2 + x + 3)$ **Use the Distributive Property.**

Need Help?
To review prime factorization, see Lesson 4-3.

☑ **Check Understanding**   Example 3

  3. Use the GCF of the terms to write each polynomial as the product of two factors.

    a. $2x^2 + x$ **b.** $2b^3 + 6b^2 - 12b$

EXERCISES

🔔 For more exercises, see *Extra Practice.*

Practice and Problem Solving

Ⓐ Practice by Example

Example 1
(page 715)

Simplify each product. Use an area model as needed.

1. $3x(x + 1)$ **2.** $x(x + 5)$ **3.** $2x(x + 4)$

4. $2x(x + 3)$ **5.** $3y(y + 7)$ **6.** $2x(3x + 1)$

7. $2x(x + 6)$ **8.** $x(2x + 6)$ **9.** $3x(3x - 1)$

10. $3x(2x + 4)$ **11.** $5x(x + 3)$ **12.** $7c(4 + c)$

🌐 **13. City Property** Find the area of the city lot shown. All measurements are in feet.

🌐 **14. Sports** The length of an Olympic-size pool is 50 meters. If x represents the width of one lane, what is the area of a pool with five lanes?

Example 2
(page 716)

Simplify each product.

15. $5x(-3x^2 + 2x)$ **16.** $x(5x^2 + x - 4)$ **17.** $3a(a^2 + 2a + 1)$

18. $3b(2b^2 - b + 4)$ **19.** $a^3(a + a^2 + 5)$ **20.** $-3(2c^2 - 3c - 1)$

21. $5c(c + 5 - c^2)$ **22.** $4x^2(x^3 + x^2 - x)$ **23.** $7b^2(2b^2 + b - 3)$

Example 3
(page 716)

Use the GCF of the terms to write each polynomial as the product of two factors.

24. $3d^4 + d^2$ **25.** $4y^3 - 8y^2 - 12y$ **26.** $10x^5 - 5x^3 + 10x$

27. $7x^2 - 14x$ **28.** $14a^2 + 7a - 7$ **29.** $24y^3 + 6y^2 - 20y$

30. $7p^2 + p$ **31.** $5z^2 - 20z$ **32.** $15x^3 + 4x^2 - 7x$

Ⓑ Apply Your Skills

Simplify each product.

33. $3y(4y - 1)$ **34.** $a(a^2 + 3)$ **35.** $-14a(a^2 + 3a - 4)$

36. $\frac{1}{2}b(b - 8)$ **37.** $-8y(2y + 3)$ **38.** $6y^2\left(y^2 - 2y - \frac{1}{3}\right)$

39. $12x^2(5x + 2)$ **40.** $x(2x - 5)$ **41.** $17y(2y^2 - 8y + 9)$

42. Open-Ended Write a monomial and a polynomial with 4 terms. Multiply them and then simplify the product.

43. Open-Ended Write a polynomial whose terms have a GCF ≠ 1. Then write the polynomial as the product of two factors.

Write each polynomial as the product of two factors.

44. $-9b^2 - 3b$ **45.** $4x^5 - 4x^4 + 8x^2$ **46.** $18g^7 - 6g^4 + 3g^2$

47. $2a^3 - 6a^2 - 4a$ **48.** $6y^6 + 32y^4 - y^3$ **49.** $4m^9 + 6m^5 - 2m^2$

50. $2a^2 + ab$ **51.** $2m^3n - 6m^2n^2 + 8mn$

C Challenge

Simplify each product.

52. $4z(2z^6 - 3z^5 - 12z^2 + 8)$ **53.** $-3xy(2x^2y + xy + y^2 - 3)$

Geometry In Exercises 54–59, write an expression to represent the area of each figure. Then simplify the expression.

54.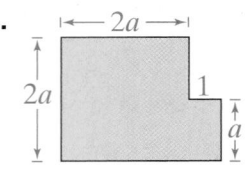

55.

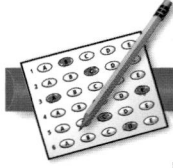

Writing in Math

Explain how to use the GCF to write the polynomial $15a^3 + 20a^2 + 45a$ as the product of two factors.

56. The width of a rectangle is 7 more than $\frac{1}{2}$ its length.

57. The length of a rectangle is 5 less than 4 times its width.

58. The base length of a triangle is $8x$. The triangle's height is twice the base length plus 5.

59. The height of an isosceles triangle is 3 less than $\frac{1}{3}$ its base.

Test Prep

Multiple Choice

Take It to the NET
Online lesson quiz at
www.PHSchool.com
Web Code: ada-1306

60. The length of a rectangular table is 35 inches greater than twice the width. If x is the width, what is the area of the table?
A. $2x^2 + 35x$ **B.** $x + 35$ **C.** $2x + 35$ **D.** $2x^2 + 35$

61. Which polynomial is the simplified form of $-3y(-6y^2 - 5y + 1)$?
F. $18y^3 - 15y^2 - 3y$ **G.** $18y^2 + 15y - 3$
H. $18y^3 + 15y^2 - 3y$ **I.** $18y^2 - 15y - 3$

Extended Response

62. The length of a rectangle is 2 inches more than the width w.
(a) What expressions in terms of w could you use for the length and the area of the rectangle?   **(b)** Explain.   **(c)** Draw a diagram of the rectangle and label it.   **(d)** Find the area of the rectangle.

Mixed Review

Lesson 13-5

Find each sum or difference.

63. $(2x + 8) + (3x^2 + 5x - 2)$

64. $(-7x^2 - 8x + 4) - (2x^2 - 3x - 9)$

Lesson 12-1

Display each set of data in a line plot.

65. 1.7, 2.1, 1.9, 2.1, 2.2, 2.4, 2.3, 2.1, 1.9

66. 13, 17, 15, 14, 12, 14, 11, 13, 15

Lesson 5-6 **67. Banking** A college student received a bank statement. The new balance was $200. It showed deposits of $400, interest of $1, and checks totaling $650. What was the beginning balance?

Multiplying Binomials

OBJECTIVE

1 Using Models

You can use tiles to model the product of two binomials.

1 EXAMPLE **Using a Model**

Simplify $(x + 2)(x + 4)$.

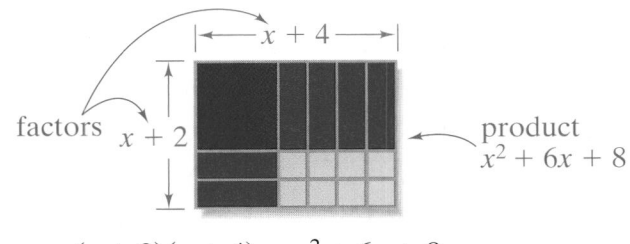

factors $x + 2$

$x + 4$

product $x^2 + 6x + 8$

$$(x + 2)(x + 4) = x^2 + 6x + 8$$

● The area is $x^2 + 6x + 8$.

✓ **Check Understanding** **Example 1**

1. Simplify each product using models.

a. $(x + 2)(x + 3)$ **b.** $(y + 1)(y + 4)$

OBJECTIVE

2 Multiplying Binomials

To simplify the product of two binomials, you can think of one binomial as a single expression and use the Distributive Property. Then you use the Distributive Property a second time.

2 EXAMPLE **Multiplying Two Binomials**

Simplify $(x + 4)(x - 3)$.

$(x + 4)(x - 3)$

$= x(x - 3) + 4(x - 3)$ **Use the Distributive Property.**

$= x^2 - 3x + 4x - 12$ **Use the Distributive Property again!**

$= x^2 + x - 12$ **Simplify.**

Check $(x + 4)(x - 3) = (x + 4)x - (x + 4)3$

$= x^2 + 4x - 3x - 12$

$= x^2 + x - 12$

What You'll Learn

 To use models in multiplying binomials

 To multiply two binomials

. . . And Why

To find the areas of geometric figures

✓ **Check Skills You'll Need**

Simplify each expression.

1. $-2(2x + 1)$

2. $3(7 + 4y)$

3. $(2a - b)5$

4. $(3m - 2n)4$

❓ For help, go to Lesson 2-2.

📱 **iTEXT** Interactive lesson includes instant self-check, tutorials, and activities.

2. Simplify each product.

    a. $(x + 2)(x - 5)$ **b.** $(m + 2)(2m + 3)$

More Than One Way

Write a polynomial to express the area of the square at the right.

$(2x + 1)$ in.

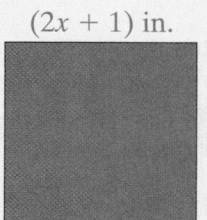

Eric's Method

Use a model.

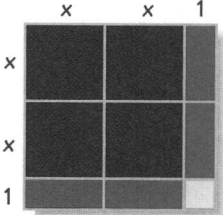

The area of the square is $(4x^2 + 4x + 1)$ in.^{2}.

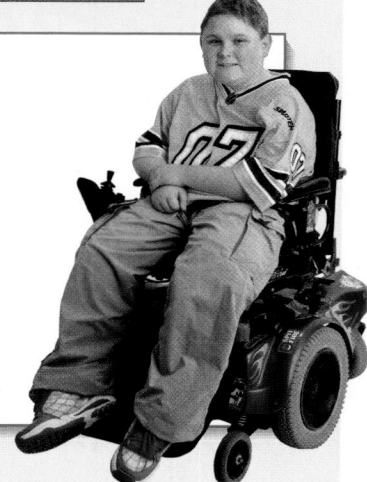

Jasmine's Method

Use the formula for the area of a square and the Distributive Property.

$$\text{Area} = \text{side}^2$$
$$A = (2x + 1)^2$$
$$= (2x + 1)(2x + 1)$$
$$= 2x(2x + 1) + 1(2x + 1)$$
$$= 2x(2x) + 2x(1) + 1(2x) + 1(1)$$
$$= 4x^2 + 2x + 2x + 1$$
$$= 4x^2 + 4x + 1$$

The area of the square is $(4x^2 + 4x + 1)$ in.^{2}.

Choose a Method

    1. Which method do you prefer to use? Explain.

    2. Which method would you use to simplify $(3x + 4)(3x + 4)$?

EXERCISES

For more exercises, see *Extra Practice*.

Practice and Problem Solving

 Practice by Example

Simplify each product using models. Sketch and label your models.

Example 1
(page 719)

1. $(x + 2)(x + 1)$ **2.** $(y + 2)(y + 2)$ **3.** $(w + 3)(w + 1)$

4. $(k + 3)(k + 4)$ **5.** $(x + 4)(x + 5)$ **6.** $(m + 9)(m + 3)$

7. $(s + 3)(s + 6)$ **8.** $(t + 2)(t + 5)$ **9.** $(m + 1)(m + 6)$

Example 2
(page 719)

Simplify each product using the Distributive Property.

10. $(x + 2)(x - 1)$ **11.** $(c + 7)(c + 9)$ **12.** $(x - 5)(x + 3)$

13. $(a - 4)(a - 2)$ **14.** $(x + 5)(x + 5)$ **15.** $(b + 6)(b - 6)$

16. $(c + 3)(c - 4)$ **17.** $(x + 3)(x - 2)$ **18.** $(y + 3)(y + 8)$

B **Apply Your Skills**

Find the area of each rectangle.

19.
$x + 3$
$2x + 1$

20.
$4n - 5$
$3n + 1$

21.
$2c + 4$
$5c + 3$

22.
$3x + 3$
$3x - 3$

Simplify each product.

23. $(x + 4)(2x + 1)$ **24.** $(n - 16)(n + 20)$ **25.** $(x + 2)(x + 8)$

26. $(b + 1)^2$ **27.** $(m - 8)(m - 3)$ **28.** $(2a + b)(4c - 2d)$

29. $(3c + 1)(2c - 4)$ **30.** $(3 + x)(5 - x)$ **31.** $\left(\frac{1}{2}x + 9\right)(4x + 8)$

32. Error Analysis A student simplifies $(x + 5)(x - 3)$ as shown at the right. Find the error in the student's work.

33. Writing in Math Explain the similarities between multiplying two binomials and multiplying a polynomial by a monomial.

$(x + 5)(x - 3)$
$x(x - 3) + 5(x - 3)$
$x^2 - 3x + 5x - 3$
$x^2 + 2x - 3$

C **Challenge**

Patterns Simplify the expressions. What pattern do you see?

34. $(y + 2)^2, (y + 3)^2, (y + 4)^2$

35. $(y + 1)(y - 1), (y + 2)(y - 2), (y + 5)(y - 5)$

36. Geometry The base of a parallelogram is $(w + 5)$ cm. The height is 2 cm less than the base. Find the area of the parallelogram.

37. Suppose x is an odd integer. What is the product of x and the next two odd integers?

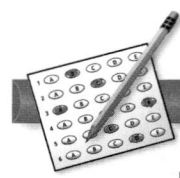

Multiple Choice

38. Suppose m is an even integer. What is the product of the next two consecutive even integers?

A. $m^2 + 3m + 2$ **B.** $m^2 + 6m + 8$

C. $m^2 + 2m$ **D.** $2m + 6$

39. If the length of a rectangular picture is $(2x + 3)$ inches and the width is $(x - 4)$ inches, which expression represents the area of the picture?

F. $(2x^2 + 5x - 12)$ in.^{2} **G.** $(2x^2 + 3x - 12)$ in.^{2}

H. $(2x^2 - 8x - 12)$ in.^{2} **I.** $(2x^2 - 5x - 12)$ in.^{2}

Short Response

40. a. Simplify $(3c - 1)(4c + 2)$ using the Distributive Property.
   b. Justify each step in part (a).

Mixed Review

Lesson 13-6

Find each product.

41. $7a(a + 5b + 2c)$ **42.** $-3xy(2x + 9y - 6)$

43. $8m^2(-4m^3 + mp + 2p^4)$ **44.** $2pq(5p + 8pq + 2)$

Lesson 12-6

45. Does the problem below require *permutations* or *combinations?* Explain.

> You select three colors from a choice of eight colors to paint a picture. How many 3-color choices are possible?

Lesson 12-2

Make a box-and-whisker plot for the data.

46. $8, 9, 27, 39, 14, 17, 13, 25, 15, 8, 11, 29, 36, 10, 15, 25$

Checkpoint Quiz 2   Lessons 13-4 through 13-7

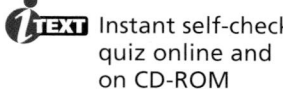
Instant self-check quiz online and on CD-ROM

Tell whether each polynomial is a *monomial*, a *binomial*, or a *trinomial*.

1. 178 **2.** $x + 15y$ **3.** $7pq$ **4.** $m^2 + 4m - 12$

Evaluate each polynomial for $x = -1$ and $y = 3$.

5. $5x - y$ **6.** $x + 3y$ **7.** $-7x + x^2y$ **8.** $4y^2 + 11x - 16$

Simplify each expression.

9. $(4a - b) + (3a - 5b)$ **10.** $(x^2 + 7x - 4) + (x^2 + 9)$

11. $(g + 6)(g + 4)$ **12.** $3m(-6m - 2m^2p - 10p)$

13. Open-Ended Write a binomial expression for the length of a side of a square. Use it to write a polynomial for the area of the square.

Binomial Factors of a Trinomial

You can sometimes write a trinomial as the product of two binomial factors. You can use algebra tiles to find the factors. Use tiles to form a rectangle. The lengths of the sides of the rectangle are the factors of the trinomial.

EXAMPLE

Write $x^2 + 4x + 3$ as the product of two binomial factors.

$x^2 + 4x + 3$

Model the trinomial.

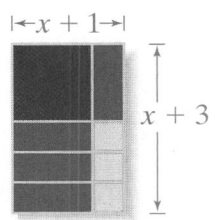

Use the tiles to form a rectangle. The length is $(x + 3)$ and the width is $(x + 1)$.

$x^2 + 4x + 3 = (x + 3)(x + 1)$

EXERCISES

Use tiles to find binomial factors of each trinomial.

1. $x^2 + 2x + 1$ **2.** $x^2 + 5x + 6$ **3.** $x^2 + 7x + 10$

4. $x^2 + 6x + 5$ **5.** $x^2 + 4x + 4$ **6.** $x^2 + 5x + 4$

7. $x^2 + 9x + 8$ **8.** $2x^2 + 5x + 3$ **9.** $2x^2 + 7x + 3$

10. $2x^2 + 9x + 4$ **11.** $2x^2 + 9x + 9$ **12.** $2x^2 + 9x + 10$

13. Reasoning Complete $x^2 + \blacksquare x + 12$ with three different integers so that each trinomial has two binomial factors. For each trinomial, write the binomial factors.

14. a. What two numbers have a sum of 11 and a product of 30?
    b. Reasoning Use your answer to part (a) to find the binomial factors of $x^2 + 11x + 30$.

15. $(x + 3)^2 = x^2 + 6x + 9$ is a *perfect-square trinomial.* What properties of a trinomial would reveal it as a perfect-square trinomial? Show how a perfect-square trinomial can be factored.

Use Multiple Strategies

OBJECTIVE

1 Combining Strategies

What You'll Learn

OBJECTIVE
1 To solve problems by combining strategies

. . . And Why

To solve problems about building a kite

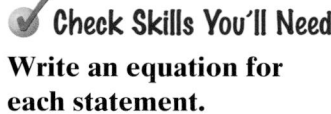 **Check Skills You'll Need**

Write an equation for each statement.

1. Seven times the opposite of twelve is negative 84.

2. Eleven times a number is 132.

3. A number divided by 45 is three.

4. A number squared is 64.

 For help, go to Lesson 2-4.

Math Strategies in Action

After a natural disaster such as an earthquake, a tornado, or a flood, relief workers help to rescue survivors. They also bring food, clothing, and blankets to people who need them. Relief organizers use multiple strategies as they plan and coordinate their efforts.

In many situations in your own life, you have already combined multiple strategies. Remember when you learned how to ride a bike or fly a kite. The more you practiced, the less you had to think about the steps required to be successful.

In mathematics, you can combine strategies to solve problems. The more strategies you learn and the more you use them, the better problem solver you will be. Solving problems can become as easy as riding a bike or flying a kite!

1 EXAMPLE **Real-World** **Problem Solving**

Hobbies Suppose you receive instructions for building a kite. The writer of the instructions presents them as a puzzle:

> I fly above the clouds with my tail flowing behind me. My tail is 12 ft plus twice my length. Together, our length is 21 ft. How long am I? How long is my tail?

Read and Understand

Read the problem carefully.

1. What do you want to find?

2. What is the relationship between the length of the kite's tail and the length of the kite's body?

 Interactive lesson includes instant self-check, tutorials, and activities.

Plan and Solve

To get a visual picture of the problem, draw a diagram. Then write an equation to solve the problem.

Draw a diagram.

Let b = length of the body of the kite.

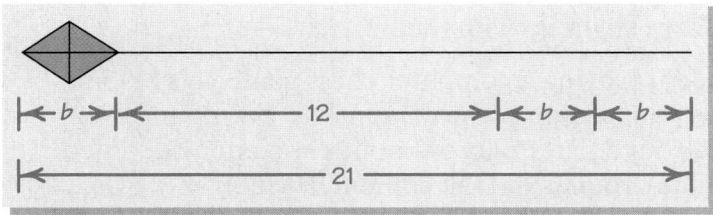

Write an equation.

$3b + 12 = 21$	Use the diagram to write an equation.
$3b + 12 - 12 = 21 - 12$	Subtract 12 from each side.
$3b = 9$	Simplify.
$\frac{3b}{3} = \frac{9}{3}$	Divide each side by 3.
$b = 3$	

The kite is 3 ft long. Now find the length of the tail.

length of tail $= 2b + 12$	Use the diagram to write an expression for the length of the tail.
$= 2(3) + 12$	Replace b with the length of the kite's body.
$= 18$	Simplify.

The tail is 18 ft long.

Look Back and Check

It is always good procedure to check your result in the context of the original problem.

✓ Check Understanding

3. The original problem says that the tail must be 12 ft plus twice the length of the kite's body. Show that the lengths found meet this condition.

4. The length of the kite's body plus the length of its tail must be 21 ft. Show that the lengths found meet this condition.

EXERCISES

For more exercises, see *Extra Practice*.

Practice and Problem Solving

Ⓐ Practice by Example

Example 1
(page 724)

Combine multiple strategies to solve each problem.

1. **Travel** A bus traveling 40 mi/h left Freetown at noon. A car following the bus at 60 mi/h left Freetown at 1:30 P.M.
   a. At what time did the car catch up with the bus?
   b. How many miles were the car and the bus from Freetown when the car caught up with the bus?

2. **Chess** A student playing a computer chess game gets 5 points every time he wins a round. The computer gets 3 points every time it wins a round. They play 64 rounds and end with a tied score. How many rounds did the computer win?

3. **Algebra** A kite and its tail total 36 ft in length. The tail is five times the length of the body. How long is the kite's tail?

Ⓑ Apply Your Skills

Solve using any strategy.

4. A student has $8 to spend on a phone call. The cost of a call is $.34 for the first minute and $.24 for each additional minute. How long can the student talk on the phone?

5. **Painting** A painter places an 8.5-ft-long ladder against a wall. The bottom of the ladder is 4 ft from the base of the wall. How high up the wall does the ladder reach?

6. **Geometry** A room has a floor area of 1,025 ft^2 and a 10-ft-high ceiling. The Housing Code requires at least 200 ft^3 per person. What is the maximum number of people allowed in the room?

7. **Pets** A student weighs her hamsters two at a time. Sandy and White Ears weigh 209 g together. White Ears and Sport weigh 223 g together. Sandy and Sport weigh 216 g together. How much does each hamster weigh?

8. **Geometry** There are 27 white cubes assembled to form a large cube. The outside surface of the large cube is painted red. The large cube is then separated into the 27 smaller cubes. How many of the small cubes will have red paint on exactly the following number of faces?
   a. three faces b. two faces c. one face d. no face

9. You decide to purchase a new telephone. You can choose from 8 different models, 2 different cord lengths, and 4 different colors. How many possible choices do you have?

10. **Geometry** A lot measures 50 ft by 100 ft. The house on the lot measures 25 ft by 50 ft. What is the area of the lawn?

11. **Algebra** A student spends $\frac{1}{3}$ of her money on a movie and $\frac{1}{4}$ of the remaining amount on a snack after the movie. She now has $12 left. How much money did she have originally?

Strategies

- Account for All Possibilities
- Draw a Diagram
- Look for a Pattern
- Make a Model
- Make a Table
- Simplify the Problem
- Simulate the Problem
- Solve by Graphing
- Try, Test, Revise
- Use Multiple Strategies
- Work Backward
- Write an Equation
- Write a Proportion

12. **Salaries** A clerk starts working at a beginning salary of $10,400 with an annual increase of $400. An assistant clerk who starts at the same time has a starting salary of $9,600 per year with an annual increase of $600.
    a. Who earns more after 3 years?
    b. After how many years will the assistant be earning more money than the clerk?

Challenge

13. **Geometry** You have three pieces of string, each 60 cm long. You form a circle with one piece, a square with another, and an equilateral triangle with the third piece. How do the areas of the three figures compare? Explain.

14. Each face of a cube can be painted either red or yellow. How many different ways can you paint the cube?

Test Prep

Multiple Choice

15. What is the product of $(x - 3)(x + 3)$?
    A. $x^2 + 6x - 9$ **B.** $x^2 - 6x + 9$
    C. $x^2 - 9$ **D.** $x^2 + 9$

16. A house lot measures 75 ft by 100 ft. It is all lawn except for the house on the lot. The house measures 30 ft by 50 ft. What is the area of the lawn?
    F. 1,500 ft^2 **G.** 6,000 ft^2 **H.** 7,500 ft^2 **I.** 8,000 ft^2

Short Response

17. A square has a perimeter of 24 inches and a rectangle has an area of 36 sq. inches. **(a)** Which figure has the greater area? **(b)** Explain.

Take It to the NET
Online lesson quiz at
www.PHSchool.com
Web Code: ada-1308

18. Aaron receives his allowance of $25. He spends $\frac{1}{5}$ of it on food, $\frac{1}{4}$ of it on magazines, and $\frac{11}{20}$ of it on movies. **(a)** How much of his allowance does Aaron have left? **(b)** Show your work.

Mixed Review

Lesson 13-7
Simplify each product.

19. $(x + 1)(x - 3)$ 20. $(d + 2)(2d + 5)$ 21. $(x + 3)^2$

Lesson 12-6
Make a list to find the number of two-letter combinations you can form from each group of letters.

22. G, O, A, T   23. A, P, E   24. H, Y, E, N, A

Lesson 5-1 25. **Jogging** A boy jogs in the park every other day. His sister jogs every third day. They both jogged together on April 2. On how many more of the 30 days in April will they jog together if they maintain this schedule?

You can solve many problems quickly using mental math and proven "shortcut" methods. One well-known shortcut is the FOIL method for multiplying binomials. With it, you multiply each term of the first binomial with each term of the second binomial, just as you did when you used the Distributive Property in Lesson 13-7.

EXAMPLE

Simplify the product $(2x + 3)(x + 6)$.

Think First terms, Outer terms,
      Inner terms, Last terms.
Notice that the first letters spell FOIL.

First Last

$$(2x+3)(x+6)$$

Inner

Outer

Identify the *First* terms in each binomial.	$2x$ and x	
Multiply them.	$2x \cdot x =$	$2x^2$
Identify the *Outer* terms.	$2x$ and 6	
Multiply them.	$2x \cdot 6 = 12x$	
Identify the *Inner* terms.	3 and x	
Multiply them.	$3 \cdot x = 3x$	
Add the outer and inner products.	$12x + 3x =$	$15x$
Identify the *Last* terms in each binomial.	3 and 6	
Multiply them.	$3 \cdot 6 =$	18

Your FOIL result will look like this: $(2x + 3)(x + 6) = 2x^2 + 15x + 18$

EXERCISES

Use FOIL and mental math to simplify the following.

1. $(x + 2)(x + 3)$ **2.** $(x + 6)(x + 6)$ **3.** $(x + 3)(x + 4)$

4. $(x + 2)^2$ **5.** $(x - 8)(x - 2)$ **6.** $(x - 6)(x - 3)$

7. $(x - 5)(x - 5)$ **8.** $(x - 4)^2$ **9.** $(x - 9)(x + 9)$

10. $(x + 4)(x - 7)$ **11.** $(x - 5)(x + 8)$ **12.** $(x + 6)(x - 6)$

13. $(2x + 2)(x + 6)$ **14.** $(7x + 7)(x + 3)$ **15.** $(6x - 5)(4x - 10)$

16. $(3x + 1)^2$ **17.** $(5x - 2)(4x + 3)$ **18.** $(8x + 5)(3x - 1)$

19. $(6x + 5)(4x - 10)$ **20.** $(3x - 2)(4x + 3)$ **21.** $(4x + 6)(4x - 6)$

22. $(3 - 3x)(5 + 4x)$ **23.** $(7 + 2x)(1 - x)$ **24.** $\left(\frac{1}{2}x + 5\right)(4x + 10)$

Chapter Review

Vocabulary

absolute value function (p. 695)	common ratio (p. 689)	quadratic function (p. 694)
arithmetic sequence (p. 688)	geometric sequence (p. 689)	sequence (p. 688)
binomial (p. 704)	monomial (p. 704)	term (p. 688)
common difference (p. 688)	polynomial (p. 704)	trinomial (p. 704)

 **Reading Math**
Understanding
Vocabulary

Match the vocabulary terms on the right with their descriptions on the left.

1. A monomial or a sum or difference of monomials

2. The graph of this is a parabola.

3. A sequence in which you find the terms by adding a fixed number to previous terms

4. An equation of the type $y = |x|$

5. A polynomial with two terms

6. A polynomial with three terms

7. Each number in a sequence

8. A set of numbers that follow a pattern

9. A real number, a variable, or a product of a real number and variables with whole-number exponents

a. arithmetic sequence
b. binomial
c. monomial
d. polynomial
e. quadratic function
f. absolute value function
g. term
h. trinomial
i. sequence

 **Take It to the NET**
Online vocabulary quiz
at www.PHSchool.com
Web Code: adj-1351

Skills and Concepts

13-1 Objectives

▼ To describe number patterns with arithmetic sequences (p. 688)

▼ To describe number patterns with geometric sequences (p. 689)

A **sequence** is a set of numbers that follow a pattern. Each number in the sequence is a **term** of the sequence. You find a term of an **arithmetic sequence** by adding a fixed number, called the **common difference,** to the previous term.

You find a term of a **geometric sequence** by multiplying the previous term by a fixed number. This fixed number is the **common ratio.**

Find the next three terms of each sequence. Then write a rule to describe the sequence.

10. $1, 5, 9, 13, \ldots$

11. $-60, -30, -15, -7.5, \ldots$

12. $100, 107, 114, 121, \ldots$

13. $0, -5, -10, -15, \ldots$

14. $26, 15, 4, -7, \ldots$

15. $\frac{1}{10}, \frac{1}{2}, 2\frac{1}{2}, 12\frac{1}{2}, \ldots$

**Tell whether each sequence is *arithmetic, geometric,* or *neither.*
Find the next three terms of the sequence.**

16. $9, 13, 17, 21, \ldots$

17. $-8, -4, -2, -1, \ldots$

18. $3, 4, 5, 6, \ldots$

19. $-22, -11, 0, 11, \ldots$

20. $10, 1, 20, 2, \ldots$

21. $\frac{1}{200}, \frac{1}{100}, \frac{1}{50}, \frac{1}{25}, \ldots$

22. Open-Ended Describe a situation that you can represent with an arithmetic sequence. Write a sequence of numbers for that situation and identify the common difference.

13-2 and 13-3 Objectives

▼ To graph quadratic functions (p. 694)

▼ To graph absolute value functions (p. 695)

▼ To use tables, rules, and graphs with functions modeling growth (p. 699)

▼ To use tables, rules, and graphs with functions modeling decay (p. 700)

Two types of nonlinear functions are **quadratic functions** and **absolute value functions.** The graph of a quadratic function is a U-shaped curve called a *parabola* that opens upward or downward. The graph of an absolute value function is V-shaped.

A function like $y = 2^x$ models *exponential growth.* Its graph curves upward as input values increase. A function like $y = \left(\frac{1}{2}\right)^x$ models *exponential decay.* Its graph slopes downward as input values increase.

For each function, make a table with integer values of x from -2 to 2. Then graph the function.

23. $y = \frac{1}{2}x^2$

24. $y = 2|x|$

25. $y = |x| + 1$

26. $y = x^2 + 5$

27. $y = -|x|$

28. $y = \frac{1}{2}|x|$

29. $y = -x^2 - 3$

30. $y = -x^2 + 4$

For each function, make a table with integer values of x from 0 to 4. Then graph the function.

31. $y = \left(\frac{1}{4}\right)^x$

32. $y = \frac{1}{2} \cdot 2^x$

33. $y = 3^x$

34. $y = \left(\frac{1}{2}\right)^x$

13-4 Objectives

▼ To identify polynomials (p. 704)

▼ To evaluate polynomials (p. 705)

A **monomial** is a real number, a variable, or a product of a real number and variables with whole-number exponents. A **polynomial** is a monomial or a sum or difference of monomials. You can name a polynomial by the number of its terms. A **binomial** has two terms and a **trinomial** has three terms.

**Tell whether each polynomial is a *monomial,* a *binomial,*
or a *trinomial.***

35. $3x$

36. $2x^2 - 1$

37. $\frac{2}{3}x$

38. $x^4 - x^3 + 2$

39. 15

40. mn

41. $z^2 + z$

42. $7d + f$

43. $-2x^2 - 12$

44. $3 + 2x - x^2$

Evaluate each polynomial for $x = -3$ and $y = 2$.

45. y^5

46. $x^2 - y$

47. $y^2 - x - 1$

48. $2xy$

49. $3 - xy$

13-5 Objectives

▼ To add polynomials (p. 710)

▼ To subtract polynomials (p. 711)

You can add polynomials by using models, combining like terms, or aligning like terms vertically and then adding their coefficients. You can subtract polynomials by adding the opposite of each term in the second polynomial.

Simplify each sum or difference.

50. $(a^2 + a + 1) + (2a^2 + a + 7)$

51. $(m^2 - 5m - 2) + (3m^2 + 3m - 10)$

52. $(3x^2 - 4) + (x^2 - 2x + 6)$

53. $(7p - 5q + 2) - (3p + 2q + 4)$

54. $(10w^2 + 6w) - (7w^2 - 3w + 5)$

55. $(9x - 3y) - (3x - 9y)$

13-6 and 13-7 Objectives

▼ To use an area model for multiplication (p. 715)

▼ To write a polynomial as the product of a monomial and a polynomial (p. 716)

▼ To use models in multiplying binomials (p. 719)

▼ To multiply two binomials (p. 719)

You can use properties to simplify the product of a monomial and a polynomial. You can sometimes use the Distributive Property to write a polynomial as the product of two factors.

You can use tiles to model the product of two binomials. When you use the Distributive Property to find the product of two binomials, you use the Distributive Property twice.

Simplify each product.

56. $a(2a + 5)$ **57.** $4c(3c - 7)$ **58.** $-6y(5y + 3)$

59. $3x(x^2 - x - 5)$ **60.** $x^2(x + 7)$ **61.** $2x^2(x^2 - 3x - 6)$

62. $(x + 3)(x + 4)$ **63.** $(x + 1)(x - 5)$ **64.** $(x - 2)(x - 4)$

Use the GCF of the terms to write each expression as the product of two factors.

65. $x^2 - x$ **66.** $9p^2 + 27$ **67.** $3x^3 - 9x^2 + 6x$

68. $5b^5 + 20b^3 - 30$ **69.** $8x^3 + 2x^2 + 4x$ **70.** $28a^2 - 4ab$

13-8 Objectives

▼ To solve problems by combining strategies (p. 724)

You can combine multiple strategies to solve problems.

71. A gardener plans to use 196 feet of fencing to enclose a garden. What is the largest possible area of the garden?

72. Explain your choice of strategies for Exercise 71.

Chapter 13

Chapter Test

Take It to the NET
Online chapter test at
www.PHSchool.com
Web Code: ada-1352

Find the next three terms of each sequence. Then write a rule to describe the sequence.

1. $5, 8, 11, 14, \ldots$ **2.** $-1.5, -3, -6, \ldots$

3. $50, 10, 2, 0.4, \ldots$ **4.** $100, 93, 86, 79, \ldots$

Tell whether each sequence is *arithmetic*, *geometric*, or *neither*. Find the next three terms of the sequence.

5. $5, 2, -1, -4, \ldots$ **6.** $1, 1, 2, 3, 5, \ldots$

7. $15, 13, 11, 9, \ldots$ **8.** $-48, -12, -3, \ldots$

9. $2, 4, 8, 16, \ldots$ **10.** $0, 7, 14, 21, \ldots$

For each function, make a table with integer values of x from -2 to 2. Then graph the function.

11. $y = x^2$ **12.** $y = x^2 - 1$

13. $y = -x^2 + 1$ **14.** $y = -x^2 - 2$

15. $y = |x| - 1$ **16.** $y = \frac{1}{2}|x|$

For each function, make a table with integer values of x from 0 to 4. Then graph the function.

17. $y = 2^x$ **18.** $y = 3^x$

19. $y = 2\left(\frac{1}{2}\right)^x$ **20.** $y = \left(\frac{1}{3}\right)^x$

Tell whether each polynomial is a *monomial*, a *binomial*, or a *trinomial*.

21. $4x - 1$ **22.** $c^2 + c + 1$

23. xyz **24.** $a^5 - 7$

25. $h^4 - h^3 - h$ **26.** ab

Evaluate each polynomial for $x = 4$ and $y = 10$.

27. $x + y$ **28.** $y - x^2$

29. $xy - 15$ **30.** $x^2 + xy - y^2$

31. Open-Ended Write a polynomial with two different variables. Assign a value to each variable. Evaluate your polynomial for those values.

Simplify each sum or difference.

32. $(x^2 + 4x + 3) + (x^2 - 3x + 7)$

33. $(2x^2 - 3) + (x + 4)$

34. $(3x^2 + 2x + 4) + (x^2 + 3)$

35. $(x^2 + 10x + 9) - (x^2 + x + 1)$

36. $(3x^2 - x + 3) - (2x^2 - 2x - 4)$

37. $(2x^2 - 4x) - (x^2 - 3x - 5)$

Simplify each product.

38. $x(x - 4)$

39. $2x(x^2 - x + 2)$

40. $x^2(3x^2 + 2x - 5)$

41. $(x + 2)(x + 4)$ **42.** $(x + 1)(x + 5)$

43. $(x + 3)(x - 1)$ **44.** $(x + 2)(x - 4)$

45. $(x - 1)(x - 6)$ **46.** $(x - 2)(x - 3)$

Write each expression as the product of a monomial and a polynomial.

47. $2x^3 + 4x^2 + 12x$

48. $x^2 - x$

49. $9x^3 - 18x^2 - 3x$

50. Writing in Math Explain how you can use the Distributive Property to write the expression $3x^2 + 6x$ as the product of a monomial and a polynomial.

51. A customer gives a clerk a $100 bill for a $76 purchase. In how many ways can the clerk give change using $20, $10, $5, and $1 bills?

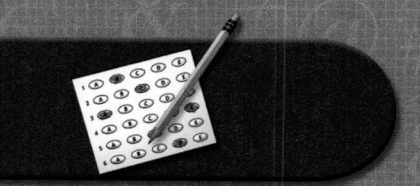

Test Prep

CUMULATIVE REVIEW
CHAPTERS 1–13

Take It to the NET
Online end-of-course test
at **www.PHSchool.com**
Web Code: ada-1154

Multiple Choice

1. What is the solution of $-3x + 1 < 25$?
- **A.** $x > 8$
- **B.** $x < -8$
- **C.** $x > -8$
- **D.** $x < 8$

2. 32% of b is 8,000. What is b?
- **F.** 250
- **G.** 2,560
- **H.** 25,000
- **I.** 25,600

3. What is the distance Joe traveled if he drove for $2\frac{1}{2}$ h at a rate of 62 mi/h?
- **A.** 24.8 mi
- **B.** 124 mi
- **C.** 154 mi
- **D.** 155 mi

4. Which decimal is between $(-0.1)^2$ and 0.05?
- **F.** 0.03
- **G.** 0.2
- **H.** 0.3
- **I.** -0.02

5. What is $\frac{a^5 b^3 c}{a^6 b^2}$ if $a = 2$, $b = -3$, and $c = -4$?
- **A.** -6
- **B.** -2
- **C.** 6
- **D.** 12

6. An artist created this scale drawing of a lighthouse. About how tall is the actual lighthouse? Use your centimeter ruler.

Scale:
1 cm = 12 m

- **F.** 36 m
- **G.** 48 m
- **H.** 72 m
- **I.** 120 m

7. Which ordered pair is a solution of $x - 2y = 3$ and $3x + y = 2$?
- **A.** $(1, -1)$
- **B.** $(-1, 1)$
- **C.** $(3, 2)$
- **D.** $\left(2, -\frac{1}{2}\right)$

8. What number is next in the pattern?
$-1, \sqrt{1}, -2, \sqrt{4}, -3, \ldots$
- **F.** $\sqrt{3}$
- **G.** $\sqrt{5}$
- **H.** $\sqrt{7}$
- **I.** $\sqrt{9}$

9. In $\triangle ABC$, $m\angle A = 55°$, and $m\angle C = 15°$. What type of triangle is $\triangle ABC$?
- **A.** acute
- **B.** equilateral
- **C.** right
- **D.** obtuse

10. If $\triangle ABC \sim \triangle DEF$. What is AC?

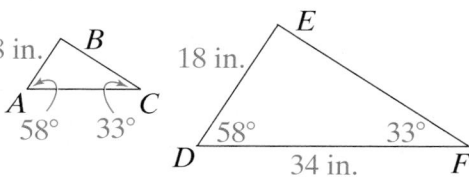

- **F.** 15.11 in.
- **G.** 17.25 in.
- **H.** 24 in.
- **I.** 76.5 in.

11. $ABCD$ is a rectangle. Which statement is NOT true?

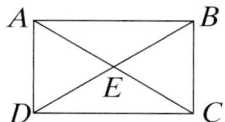

- **A.** $\overline{AC} \cong \overline{DB}$
- **B.** $\angle ADC \cong \angle CBA$
- **C.** $\triangle DAE \cong \triangle BCE$
- **D.** $\angle CBD \cong \angle DAB$

12. A cone has $r = 4$ and $h = 12$. What is its volume?
- **F.** 16π
- **G.** 64π
- **H.** 96π
- **I.** 192π

13. Which inequality represents *The number t is at least 35*?
- **A.** $t > 35$
- **B.** $t < 35$
- **C.** $t \geq 35$
- **D.** $t \leq 35$

14. What is the area of the shaded region?

2 ft

- **F.** 2.4 ft^2
- **G.** 3.4 ft^2
- **H.** 4.2 ft^2
- **I.** 4.3 ft^2

15. What is the area of $\triangle CDE$?

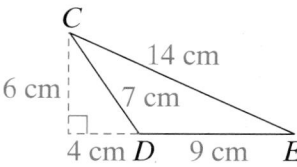

- **A.** 12 cm^2
- **B.** 27 cm^2
- **C.** 36 cm^2
- **D.** 39 cm^2

16. A bicycle company makes 3 different bicycle styles. Each style comes in 4 colors. Each style is made in 6 frame sizes with a choice of 2 types of seat. The bicycle shop would like to order one of each type of bicycle. How many bicycles is that?
  F. 60 bicycles **G.** 120 bicycles
  H. 144 bicycles **I.** 240 bicycles

17. In a box filled with 60 colored chips, $\frac{1}{6}$ are blue, $\frac{1}{12}$ are white, $\frac{1}{4}$ are yellow, and $\frac{1}{2}$ are purple. What is the probability of picking at random a purple chip or a white chip?
  A. $\frac{1}{24}$ **B.** $\frac{7}{12}$ **C.** $\frac{3}{5}$ **D.** $\frac{2}{3}$

18. If the first term in an arithmetic sequence is 15 and the fifth term is 39, what is the fourth term in the sequence?
  F. 32 **G.** 33 **H.** 34 **I.** 35

19. What is the simplest form $6z(4 - 2z^2)$?
  A. $24z - 12z^3$ **B.** $24z - 12z^2$
  C. $24z - 2z^2$ **D.** $24z + 12z^3$

20. Which expression is represented by the model shown below?

  F. $2(x^2 + 2x) + 3$ **G.** $2x^2 + 2 + 3^2$
  H. $x^2 + 2x + 3$ **I.** $2x^2 + 2x + 3$

21. What is $(x^4 + 2x^3 - x^2 + x - 3) + 6x^3 + x^2 - 4x - 8$?

  A. $x^4 + 4x^3 - 2x^2 - 5x - 5$
  B. $x^4 + 8x^3 - 4x - 5$
  C. $x^4 + 8x^3 + 2x^2 - 3x - 11$
  D. $x^4 + 8x^3 - 3x - 11$

22. What is $(5r - 4s) - (2r - s)$?
  F. $10r - 4s$ **G.** $3r - 3s$
  H. $10r^2 - 4s^2$ **I.** $3r - 5s$

23. Which phrase best describes the expression $9xyz$?
  A. monomial **B.** binomial
  C. trinomial **D.** polynomial

24. Which equation matches the graph?

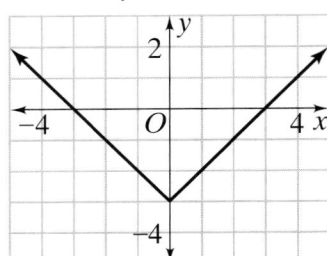

  F. $y = |x| - 3$ **G.** $y = x^2 - 3$
  H. $y = -3|x|$ **I.** $y = |x - 3|$

25. A submarine dove to a depth of 540 ft, then rose 84 ft. Which integer represents the final depth of the submarine?
  A. -624 **B.** -456
  C. 456 **D.** 624

26. Which property does $7(w + 8) = 7w + 56$ show?
  F. Commutative Property of Addition
  G. Associative Property of Multiplication
  H. Identity Property of Addition
  I. Distributive Property

27. Which of the following equations would you use to find out how far a satellite will travel in 2 minutes if it is traveling at a rate of 8 km per second?
  A. $d = 8(120)$ **B.** $d = \frac{8}{120}$
  C. $d = 8(2)$ **D.** $d = \frac{8}{2}$

28. What is the GCF of $18x^3y^4$ and $48xy^5$?
  F. $12xy^4$ **G.** $12x^2y$
  H. $6xy^4$ **I.** $6x^2y$

29. Which of the following is the simplified form of $\left(\frac{3a}{6b}\right)^3$?
  A. $\frac{a^3}{2b^3}$ **B.** $\frac{a^3}{6b^3}$
  C. $\frac{a^3}{8b^2}$ **D.** $\frac{a^3}{8b^3}$

30. Which of the following is a rule for the function described in the table?

x	f(x)
−2	−7
0	−3
2	1
4	5

F. $f(x) = 2x - 3$ **G.** $f(x) = 3x - 2$
H. $f(x) = 2x + 3$ **I.** $f(x) = 3x + 2$

31. Between which two integers is the value of $\sqrt{70}$?
A. 3 and 4   **B.** 8 and 9
C. 36 and 49   **D.** 64 and 81

32. Which polynomial is the product of the binomials $(x + 2)$ and $(x - 13)$?
F. $x^2 + 15x + 26$ **G.** $x^2 - 11x - 26$
H. $x^2 - 11x + 26$ **I.** $x^2 - 15x - 26$

Gridded Response

33. If $m\angle 2 = 110°$, what is $m\angle 3$ in degrees?

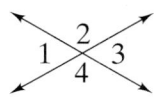

34. Small pieces of paper with the letters SKATES are placed in a bag. What is the probability of selecting a T from the bag at random, not replacing it, and then selecting an A?

35. A truck leaves a rest stop and travels at a steady rate of 65 mi/h. Later, a car leaves the rest stop, travels at a steady rate of 75 mi/h, and catches up with the truck in 3.25 hours. For how many hours had the truck been traveling?

36. What is the surface area of the figure to the nearest whole number of square feet?

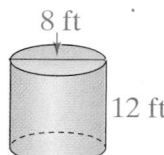

8 ft
12 ft

Short Response

37. An agent made a $7,500 commission for selling a house. The commission rate is 6%.
a. What was the price of the house?
b. If the commission rate is raised to 7%, what commission would the agent make for the house price in part (a)?

In Exercises 38 and 39, **(a) write the perimeter of each figure as a polynomial.   (b) Then simplify.**

38.

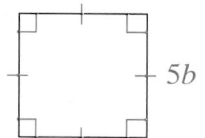

5b

39.

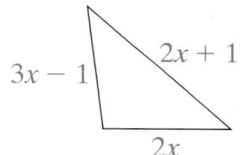

$3x - 1$ $2x + 1$
$2x$

40. A salesperson receives a 5% commission for each computer sold. **(a)** Is the value of the commission a function of the final sales price of each computer?   **(b)** Explain.

Extended Response

For each function, **(a) make a table with integer values of x from 0 to 4.   (b) Graph the function. (c) What exponential change does the graph show, growth or decay? Explain your answer.**

41. $y = 3^x$ **42.** $y = 20\left(\frac{1}{2}\right)^x$

43. Two electronics stores have the same television model on sale. The price of the television at Store A is $299 before a 25% discount. The price of the television at Store B is $279 before a 20% discount.
a. Which store has the greater discount?
b. Which store has the lower sale price?
c. What is the difference between the two sale prices?

Real-World Snapshots

Carbon Dating

Applying Algebra Have you ever wondered how a scientist can estimate the age of a fossil? When an organism is alive, it maintains carbon-14 in the same proportion as the atmosphere. When the organism dies, it stops replenishing its carbon-14. A scientist finds the amount of carbon-14 currently present in the fossil and calculates how long the amount that was present at death has been decaying.

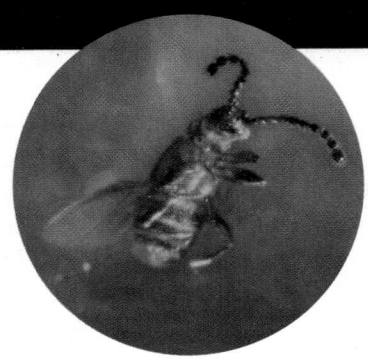

Amber Insects
Sometimes bees, flies, and other insects get stuck in the sap from a tree. Over time, the sap hardens and turns into amber.

How Old Is That?
Carbon-14 has a half-life of 5,730 years. Scientists use it to determine the age of bone, cloth, wood, and plant fibers.

Mammoth Model
The "woolly mammoth" was about 11 ft tall and weighed 4 to 6 tons, the same as an African elephant today, but had very small ears, a sloping back, and much longer tusks.

Shoulder hump

Mammoth hair was up to 3 ft long.

Activity

1. Copy and complete the table.

2. **Estimation** About how old is a fossil that has 40% carbon-14 present?

3. **Estimation** What percent of carbon-14 would you hope to find in a fossil that you think is 20,000 years old?

4. **Reasoning** Why do you think carbon-14 dating works only on fossils less than 60,000 years old?

Carbon-14 Dating

Percent of Carbon-14 Present	Age of Fossil (years)
100	0
50	5,730
▦	11,460
12.5	▦
▦	22,920
3.125	▦
▦	34,380
0.78125	▦

Remains of the Mammoth

Scientists have found several frozen mammoths, complete with hide and hair, in the frozen ground of Siberia and Alaska.

Take It to the NET For more information about fossils, go to **www.PHSchool.com**.
Web Code: ade-1353

Chapter Projects

Cure for the Common Code

A special sculpture stands outside the headquarters of the United States Central Intelligence Agency (CIA) in Langley, Virginia. Carved in the copper sculpture is a message in secret code. The code is so complex that for many years even CIA agents could not figure it out. The sculptor, James Sandborn, provided the secret agents with a challenge they could appreciate.

Chapter 1 *Algebraic Expressions and Integers*

Invent a Secret Code For the chapter project, you will decode computer writing and write in a code used by Julius Caesar. Then you'll invent a code of your own.

Take It to the NET To research more information about secret codes for your project, go to **www.PHSchool.com**.
········ Web Code: add-0161

DON'T LOSE YOUR BALANCE!

Have you ever used a balance in your science class? Balances make very precise measurements in science, industry, and government. The United States Mint, for example, ensures that the coins it produces meet exact specifications. You can make your own version of a balance and use it to compare the masses of different objects.

Chapter 2 *Solving One-Step Equations and Inequalities*

Make a Balance Scale For the chapter project, you will make a simple balance scale. You will use it to write and solve equations and inequalities for the masses of different coins.

Take It to the NET To research more information about balances for your project, go to **www.PHSchool.com**.
········ Web Code: add-0161

CURRENCY EVENTS

When you are shopping, of course you want to know how much an item costs before you decide to buy it! When you travel in another country, you need to "translate" the cost into its value in U.S. dollars.

Chapter 3 *Decimals and Equations*

Compare Currencies For the chapter project, you will research currency exchange rates and calculate prices in different currencies. You will make a poster that shows prices in U.S. dollars and in the currencies of three other countries.

Take It to the NET To research more information about currencies for your project, go to **www.PHSchool.com**.
Web Code: add-0161

TIME AFTER TIME

On the morning of the summer solstice, the sun rises directly over one of the stones at Stonehenge in southern England. Just as a sundial tells the time of day, Stonehenge tells the time of year.

A calendar may involve several astronomical events. For example, our day is based on Earth's rotation, whereas our year is based on Earth's movement around the sun. Over the centuries, people have come up with many different calendars.

Chapter 4 *Factors, Fractions, and Exponents*

Design a Calendar For the chapter project, you will investigate calendars and adjustments to calendars. Then you will design your own calendar. Your final project will be a sample and an explanation of your calendar.

Take It to the NET To research more information about calendars for your project, go to **www.PHSchool.com**.
Web Code: add-0161

If the Shoe Fits

What size shoe do you wear? As you grow, your shoe size can change rapidly. If your foot grows half an inch, does that mean you should get shoes that are a half-size larger?

The scale we use for sizing shoes is from the *duodecimal*, or base 12, number system. For that reason, a size chart could come in handy.

Make a Comparison Chart For the chapter project, you will make measurements and calculations that relate women's shoe sizes, men's shoe sizes, and shoe lengths. Your final project will be a convenient comparison chart that you can distribute to your friends and family and to shoe stores.

Take It to the NET To research more information about shoe sizes for your project, go to **www.PHSchool.com**.
Web Code: add-0161

STRING BAND

Guitars, fiddles, harps . . . people have been enjoying stringed instruments for thousands of years. The music from a stringed instrument follows rules of mathematics that you will learn in this chapter.

Make a Musical Instrument For the chapter project, you will construct and play a simple stringed instrument. You will make measurements that can be applied to a real instrument. Your final project will consist of drawings that show how to play notes on both instruments.

Take It to the NET To research more information about stringed instruments for your project, go to **www.PHSchool.com**.
Web Code: add-0161

The Intensity of DENSITY

Have you ever wondered why some objects sink while others float? People float in the salt water of the Dead Sea. Pebbles sink when tossed into a river. The densities of a liquid and an object influence whether the object sinks or floats in the liquid. Similarly, the densities of two liquids influence whether they combine or separate.

Chapter 7 *Solving Equations and Inequalities*

Find the Densities of Liquids For the chapter project, you will measure the masses and volumes of several liquids. You will use your measurements and an equation to calculate the density of each liquid.

Take It to the NET To research more information about densities for your project, go to **www.PHSchool.com**.
Web Code: add-0161

Rental Math

Your school is planning its graduation ceremony. Hundreds of people will be coming, and they need places to sit. Your school has some chairs, but not enough for this crowd! Better call a rental company.

Chapter 8 *Linear Functions and Graphing*

Compare Prices For the chapter project, you will research the cost of renting folding chairs. You do not yet know how many chairs you will need, so you will investigate the price per chair, as well as delivery charges. For your report to the graduation committee, you will write and graph equations to show the total costs of renting chairs from different companies.

Take It to the NET To research more information about chair rentals for your project, go to **www.PHSchool.com**.
Web Code: add-0161

TREASURE HUNT!

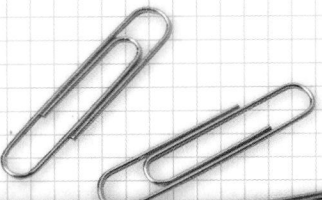

A mysterious map has come into your possession. The map shows the Sea Islands off the coast of Georgia. But that's not all! The map also contains three clues that tell where a treasure is supposedly buried.

Draw a Treasure Map Your project for this chapter will be to find the location of the treasure. Trace the map provided, and then add to the drawing by following the clues in the activities.

 Take It to the NET To research more information about treasure maps for your project, go to **www.PHSchool.com.**
Web Code: add-0161

MAKING A SPLASH

When you jump into a pool or step into a bathtub, you cause the water level to rise. That's an example of water displacement. The volume of water displaced is equal to the volume of the object submerged—you.

Use Water Displacement to Find Volume
For your chapter project, you will build a prism and a cylinder. You will calculate their volumes by using formulas. Then you will find their volumes by using water displacement.

Take It to the NET To research more information about water displacement for your project, go to **www.PHSchool.com.**
Web Code: add-0161

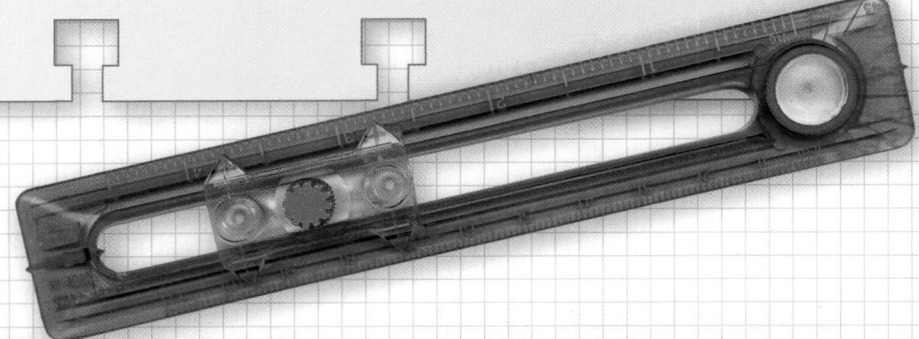

Tree Angles

Chapter 11 *Right Triangles in Algebra*

A giant sequoia in California is the largest living thing on Earth. It weighs about as much as 15 blue whales. What is the largest tree in your neighborhood? Maybe it is the largest of its species. You could nominate it to be in the National Register of Big Trees.

Measure a Big Tree The National Register of Big Trees has a formula to compare the sizes of trees of the same species: Big Tree Points $= C + H + \frac{S}{4}$, where C is the circumference in inches of the trunk at $4\frac{1}{2}$ feet above the ground, H is the tree's height in feet, and S is the average spread in feet of the tree's crown of branches.

For the chapter project, you will measure a tree and calculate its score in Big Tree Points.

 Take It to the NET To research more information about tree sizes for your project, go to **www.PHSchool.com**.
Web Code: add-0161

The Good Times POLL

Do you participate in an organized extracurricular activity, such as a sport or a club? How much time do you devote to such activities each week? How does the amount of time you spend compare to the averages for students in your class and your school?

Chapter 12 *Data Analysis and Probability*

Conduct a Survey For the chapter project, you will do a survey of your class and a survey of your school. You will use statistical measures and graphs to analyze and display the results.

 Take It to the NET To research more information about surveys for your project, go to **www.PHSchool.com**.
Web Code: add-0161

PRISM BUILDING

The prismatic shapes of tall buildings can be described using mathematical expressions such as $(a + b)^3$. Is $(a + b)^3$ equal to $a^3 + b^3$? No, but many students make that mistake. Sometimes it helps to have a concrete representation of a mathematical expression.

Chapter 13 *Nonlinear Functions and Polynomials*

Make a 3-D Polynomial Model For the chapter project, you will make a three-dimensional model of a polynomial. You will analyze the model and its parts. You will use the model to see how polynomials can represent real-world objects.

 Take It to the NET To research more information about polynomials for your project, go to **www.PHSchool.com**.
Web Code: add-0161

● **Lesson 1-1** **Write a variable expression for each word phrase.**

  1. 6 less than x

  2. y less than 12

  3. the sum of z and 2

  4. a number m increased by 34

  5. the product of 8 and p

  6. t divided by 5

● **Lesson 1-2** **Simplify each expression.**

  7. $15 + 20 \cdot 3$

  8. $46 - 4(2 + 8)$

  9. $16 \div 4 + 10 \div 2$

  10. $100 \div (30 + 20)$

  11. $5(8 + 4) \div 6 \div 2$

  12. $9 \cdot 6 - 12 \div 2$

● **Lesson 1-3** **Evaluate each expression.**

  13. $3x + 6$, for $x = 12$

  14. $15a - 2a$, for $a = 20$

  15. $38 - 3y$, for $y = 9$

  16. $25 - (t + 18)$, for $t = 7$

  17. $\frac{x + y}{10}$, for $x = 35$ and $y = 65$

● **Lesson 1-4** **Compare. Use >, <, or = to complete each statement.**

  18. $-12 \ \blacksquare \ -9$

  19. $|-4| \ \blacksquare \ |4|$

  20. $-|-7| \ \blacksquare \ |-7|$

  21. $0 \ \blacksquare \ -100$

● **Lessons 1-5 and 1-6** **Simplify each expression.**

  22. $-56 + 60$

  23. $18 + (-25)$

  24. $-34 + (-36)$

  25. $19 - (-5)$

  26. $80 - (-125)$

  27. $-82 - (-50)$

  28. $-7 + 35 + (-22)$

  29. $-44 - 20 - 80$

  30. $-8 + (-13) - (24)$

● **Lesson 1-7** **Write a rule for continuing each pattern. Find the next three numbers in the pattern.**

  31. $-12, -3, 6, 15, 24, \ldots$

  32. $0.15, 0.3, 0.45, 0.6, \ldots$

  33. $1, 1, 2, 3, 5, 8, 13, \ldots$

● **Lesson 1-9** **Simplify each expression.**

  34. $-4 \cdot 12$

  35. $-15(-8)$

  36. $30 \cdot (-5)$

  37. $-1(-2)(-3)(-4)$

  38. $-78 \div (-3)$

  39. $-150 \div 25$

  40. $\frac{120}{-15}$

  41. $-1{,}125 \div (-125)$

● **Lesson 1-10** **Draw a coordinate plane. Graph each point.**

  42. $A(0, 9)$

  43. $B(-3, -5)$

  44. $C(-9, 5)$

  45. $D(7, 2)$

  46. $E(0, 0)$

  47. $F(8, 0)$

  48. $G(7, -8)$

  49. $H(1, 1)$

  50. $K(-2, -2)$

Chapter 2

Extra Practice

● **Lesson 2-1** Simplify each expression. Justify each step.

1. $99 + (-46) + (-99) + 45$
2. $225 + 320 + 75$
3. $18 + 12 + (-25) + 13$
4. $5 \cdot 678 \cdot 2$
5. $58 \cdot 2 \cdot 50$
6. $20 \cdot 4 \cdot 5 \cdot 25$

● **Lessons 2-2 and 2-3** Use the Distributive Property to simplify.

7. $7(5) - 3(5)$
8. $3 \cdot 6 + 7 \cdot 6$
9. $15 \cdot 32 - 12 \cdot 32$
10. $7b + 25 - 4b$
11. $3(a - 2c)$
12. $3q + 2(q + 1)$
13. $-3(4y - 1) + 5(7 - y)$
14. $41 - 2(m + 1) - m$
15. $12 + 5x - 2(3x + 5)$

● **Lesson 2-4** Write an equation for each sentence. Is each equation *true*, *false*, or an *open sentence*?

16. Twice the sum of a number and one is twenty-two.

17. Negative three divided by negative one is three.

18. Forty-five plus five equals negative fifty.

● **Lessons 2-5 and 2-6** Solve each equation.

19. $40 + x = 25$
20. $-5 = y - 12$
21. $z + (-23) = -47$
22. $14 = a - 9$
23. $t - 453 = -520$
24. $78 = b + 100$
25. $4k = 96$
26. $300 = -15j$
27. $-12c = 180$
28. $\frac{d}{7} = -14$
29. $-4 = \frac{w}{6}$
30. $\frac{k}{-9} = -20$

● **Lesson 2-8** Graph the solutions of each inequality.

31. $x > -12$
32. $y \le 3$
33. $0 \ge z$
34. $p < -9$
35. $7 < n$
36. $f \le -3$

● **Lessons 2-9 and 2-10** Solve each inequality.

37. $a + 3 < -1$
38. $-2 > b - 4$
39. $5 + x > -8$
40. $-12 < -2 + y$
41. $w - 32 \le 15$
42. $-20 \ge z - 13$
43. $\frac{c}{5} \le -3$
44. $8p \ge -96$
45. $0 < 8r$
46. $\frac{t}{-6} < -3$
47. $\frac{a}{11} > -22$
48. $-12k \ge -144$

● **Lesson 3-1 Estimate. State the method you used.**

1. $5.35 + 7.953$

2. $25.68 - 3.7$

3. $6.877 + 3.521 + 8.5$

4. $103.890 - 25.6$

5. $42.875 + 36.982 + 45.7$

6. $42.651 - 12.8$

● **Lesson 3-2 Estimate each product or quotient.**

7. $9.5(12.31)$

8. $24.8 \div 5.03$

9. $2.8 \cdot 6.11$

10. $-5.78 \div 1.95$

11. $(-2.468)(-9.031)$

12. $-19.32 \div 4.025$

● **Lesson 3-3 Find the mean, median, and mode. When the answer is not an integer, round to the nearest tenth. Identify any outliers.**

13. 10 13 10 15 12 11 12 19 14

14. 85 86 80 85 90 90 50 88

15. \$25 \$30 \$32 \$28 \$30 \$15 \$28 \$30

16. 6.2 4.5 4.8 12.3 5.7 4.8 6.0

● **Lesson 3-4 Evaluate each formula for the values given.**

17. perimeter of a rectangle: $P = 2\ell + 2w$ when $\ell = 45$ yd and $w = 20$ yd

18. circumference of a circle: $C = 2\pi r$ when $r = 6.8$ in.; use 3.14 for π

19. distance traveled: $d = rt$ when $r = 50$ mi/h and $t = 3.5$ h

20. perimeter of a square: $P = 4s$ when $s = 12$ cm

● **Lessons 3-5 and 3-6 Solve each equation.**

21. $t + 4.5 = 17.2$

22. $15.5 + y = 10.5$

23. $x - 70.2 = 23.6$

24. $1.2b = 6$

25. $c \div 5.3 = 12$

26. $-21.2 = p - 12.7$

27. $f \div 5.25 = 7.8$

28. $6.4m = 38.4$

29. $-3.1 = -31a$

30. $h + 25.8 = 76$

31. $101.5 = j - 82.8$

32. $-50.8 = d + 36.2$

33. $4.5v = 13.5$

34. $s \div 10.5 = 42$

35. $26.2 = z - 6.55$

● **Lesson 3-7 Complete each statement.**

36. 0.95 m = ▇ cm

37. 250 mL = ▇ L

38. 2.5 kg = ▇ g

39. 60 g = ▇ kg

40. 0.54 L = ▇ mL

41. 5.62 m = ▇ cm

42. 58 cm = ▇ m

43. 564 mm = ▇ m

44. 345 g = ▇ mg

45. 36 mg = ▇ g

46. 234 cm = ▇ m

47. 567 mg = ▇ g

Chapter 4

Extra Practice

● **Lesson 4-1** **List all the factors of each number.**

1. 60   **2.** 45   **3.** 64   **4.** 46   **5.** 36   **6.** 100

● **Lesson 4-2** **Evaluate each expression.**

7. x^2, for $x = 8$ **8.** $-2v^3$, for $v = 2$ **9.** $5t^2 - 4$, for $t = 4$

10. $a^3 + 10$, for $a = -5$ **11.** mn^2, for $m = 3$ and $n = 4$ **12.** $6(2r - 4)^2$, for $r = 7$

● **Lesson 4-3** **Is each number *prime*, *composite*, or *neither*? For each composite number, write the prime factorization. Use exponents where possible.**

13. 25   **14.** 36   **15.** 47   **16.** 38   **17.** 1   **18.** 117

Find the GCF.

19. 20, 30   **20.** 8, 12, 18   **21.** $5x, 40x$ **22.** $6y, 108$

● **Lesson 4-4** **Write in simplest form.**

23. $\frac{12}{20}$ **24.** $\frac{4}{20}$ **25.** $\frac{35}{80}$ **26.** $\frac{18}{36}$

27. $\frac{13}{52}$ **28.** $\frac{75}{100}$ **29.** $\frac{16}{50}$ **30.** $\frac{5x}{65x^2}$

31. $\frac{3x^2}{45x}$ **32.** $\frac{50a^2}{5a}$ **33.** $\frac{36x}{16}$ **34.** $\frac{100pq}{625q}$

● **Lesson 4-6** **Graph each rational number on one number line.**

35. 0.2   **36.** $\frac{3}{10}$ **37.** -2 **38.** -1 **39.** $-\frac{1}{2}$

Evaluate each expression for $a = 10$ and $b = -4$. Write in simplest form.

40. $\frac{a + b}{a}$ **41.** $\frac{b}{a}$ **42.** $\frac{a - b}{3a}$ **43.** $\frac{b^2}{a^2}$

● **Lessons 4-7 and 4-8** **Simplify each expression.**

44. $8a^2 \cdot 3a^4$ **45.** $3y^2 \cdot 2y^3$ **46.** $(p^5)^6$ **47.** $(x^3)(y)(x^5)$

48. $\frac{6x^2}{2x^5}$ **49.** $\frac{18t^{20}}{6t^5}$ **50.** $\frac{b^2}{b^3}$ **51.** 12^0

● **Lesson 4-9** **Multiply. Express each result in scientific notation.**

52. $(5 \times 10^4)(8 \times 10^9)$ **53.** $(1.1 \times 10^6)(6 \times 10^{10})$ **54.** $(3 \times 10^{12})(4 \times 10^8)$

● **Lesson 5-1** **Find the LCM of each group of numbers or expressions.**

1. 15, 30   **2.** 4, 8, 10   **3.** $8x, 12y$ **4.** $3t^2, 5t$

Compare. Use >, <, or = to complete each statement.

5. $\frac{5}{8}$ ■ $\frac{3}{5}$ **6.** $\frac{3}{10}$ ■ $\frac{1}{3}$ **7.** $\frac{3}{4}$ ■ $\frac{6}{8}$ **8.** $-\frac{1}{5}$ ■ $-\frac{1}{4}$

● **Lesson 5-2** **Write each fraction or mixed number as a decimal.**

9. $\frac{7}{8}$ **10.** $2\frac{3}{5}$ **11.** $\frac{3}{11}$ **12.** $\frac{16}{5}$ **13.** $-\frac{7}{10}$ **14.** $-2\frac{1}{9}$

Write each decimal as a fraction or mixed number in simplest form.

15. 1.3 **16.** 0.605 **17.** $0.\overline{6}$ **18.** $-0.\overline{15}$ **19.** 0.35 **20.** 5.4

● **Lesson 5-3** **Add or subtract.**

21. $\frac{2}{5} + \frac{3}{5}$ **22.** $3\frac{3}{4} - 1\frac{5}{6}$ **23.** $-\frac{5}{8} + \frac{1}{4}$ **24.** $\frac{10}{x} - \frac{12}{x}$

25. $\frac{1}{2} - \frac{3}{4}$ **26.** $4\frac{5}{6} + 5\frac{2}{9}$ **27.** $\frac{5}{t} + \frac{3}{4}$ **28.** $5\frac{1}{3} - \frac{7}{8}$

● **Lesson 5-4** **Find each product or quotient.**

29. $\frac{3}{5} \cdot \frac{2}{3}$ **30.** $\frac{5}{6} \div 1\frac{2}{3}$ **31.** $-\frac{7}{10} \cdot 1\frac{3}{7}$ **32.** $\frac{5y}{6} \div \frac{2y}{3}$ **33.** $-\frac{2}{3} \cdot \left(-\frac{9}{22}\right)$

34. $10\frac{5}{8} \div \frac{5}{8}$ **35.** $\frac{5x}{7} \cdot \frac{1}{5}$ **36.** $\left(-\frac{1}{2}\right)\left(-\frac{3}{4}\right)$ **37.** $\frac{2}{5} \div \left(-\frac{1}{5}\right)$ **38.** $\frac{6}{7} \cdot \frac{3}{7}$

● **Lesson 5-5** **Complete each statement.**

39. 60 in. = ■ ft   **40.** 15 qt = ■ pt   **41.** 4 lb = ■ oz

● **Lessons 5-7 and 5-8** **Solve each equation.**

42. $\frac{3}{5} + a = 1\frac{2}{3}$ **43.** $b - 3\frac{1}{2} = 5$ **44.** $-\frac{4}{5}c = \frac{7}{10}$

45. $5d = \frac{3}{4}$ **46.** $1\frac{4}{7} = f + \frac{3}{14}$ **47.** $\frac{7}{8} = g - \frac{2}{3}$

● **Lesson 5-9** **Simplify each expression.**

48. $(8a^3)^2$ **49.** $(x^2y^3)^4$ **50.** $(-2v)^3$ **51.** $(abc^3)^5$ **52.** $(f^2g^3)^6$

53. $(2xy)^3$ **54.** $\left(\frac{2}{5}\right)^3$ **55.** $\left(\frac{2c}{d^3}\right)^2$ **56.** $\left(\frac{3t}{4v}\right)^2$ **57.** $\left(\frac{1}{4}\right)^3$

Extra Practice

● **Lesson 6-1** Write each ratio as a fraction in simplest form.

1. $15 : 30$
2. 25 to 10
3. 4 out of 16
4. $\frac{15}{35}$

Find each unit rate.

5. 40 mi/h = ■ ft/s
6. 8 cm/s = ■ m/h
7. 5.5 qt/min = ■ gal/h

● **Lesson 6-2** Solve each proportion. Round to the nearest tenth where necessary.

8. $\frac{3}{5} = \frac{a}{60}$
9. $\frac{8}{7} = \frac{96}{b}$
10. $\frac{8}{c} = \frac{40}{85}$
11. $\frac{d}{36} = \frac{2}{3}$

12. $\frac{105}{200} = \frac{x}{40}$
13. $\frac{8}{15} = \frac{y}{50}$
14. $\frac{z}{40} = \frac{11}{15}$
15. $\frac{t}{2} = \frac{1.5}{8}$

● **Lesson 6-3** The scale of a map is 4 in. : 25 mi. Find the actual distance for each map distance. Round to the nearest tenth where necessary.

16. 10 in.
17. 5.5 in.
18. $\frac{1}{2}$ in.
19. 3 in.

● **Lesson 6-4** Find each probability for one roll of a number cube. Then find the odds in favor of the event.

20. $P(4)$
21. $P(8)$
22. $P(\text{even number})$
23. $P(1 \text{ or } 2)$

● **Lesson 6-5** Write each percent as a fraction in simplest form and as a decimal.

24. 10%
25. 200%
26. 6%
27. 1.75%
28. 8.5%

Write each number as a percent. Where necessary, round to the nearest tenth of a percent.

29. 0.15
30. 1.2
31. $\frac{5}{12}$
32. $\frac{1}{8}$
33. 0.345

● **Lessons 6-6 and 6-7** Solve each percent problem by using a proportion or an equation.

34. Find 12% of 80.
35. 30% of x is 12. What is x?
36. What percent of 50 is 2.5?
37. Find 30% of 121.

● **Lesson 6-8** Find each percent of change. Tell whether the change is an increase or a decrease.

38. 120 to 80
39. 40 to 100
40. 175 to 231
41. $4 to $3.50

● **Lesson 6-9** Find each sale price.

42. regular price, $100; discount, 20%
43. regular price, $60; discount, 25%

● Lessons 7-1, 7-2, 7-3, and 7-5 Solve and check each equation.

1. $10 - 5x = 15$

2. $3y + 17 = -13$

3. $62 = -12z + 14$

4. $6x - 2x = 12$

5. $t + 5 - 2t = -10$

6. $24 = 2(b - 2) - 4b$

7. $5 - 2(y - 5) = 27$

8. $-56a + 90 + 58a = 92$

9. $8 = 3(c + 8)$

10. $8 - \frac{t}{2} = 53$

11. $75 = \frac{m}{3} + 10$

12. $\frac{3}{5}p + 18 = 24$

13. $0.05x - 0.08 + x = 0.97$

14. $2.5y + 3.5 = -1.5$

15. $6.3p + 1.2p = 22.5$

16. $2x + 6 = 5x$

17. $3a + 2 = a - 8$

18. $3(b - 2) = 9b$

19. $8(f + 3) = 10f - 32$

20. $\frac{1}{4}(x - 8) = \frac{3}{4}x$

21. $4(w - 2.1) = w + 0.6$

● Lesson 7-6 Solve and graph each inequality.

22. $3x + 18 > 12$

23. $4 + 9a \geq -23$

24. $10.5 < -4y + 2.5$

25. $19 - 3x \geq -2$

26. $-5(a - 3) \leq 45$

27. $\frac{1}{2}(t - 6) \leq 22$

28. $\frac{y}{4} - 6 < -9$

29. $-31.4 \leq 2x + 1$

30. $5.8 > 1 + 0.2m$

● Lesson 7-7 Solve for the variable indicated in red.

31. $s = p + c$

32. $x + y = 180$

33. $a - b = c$

34. $I = prt$

● Lesson 7-8 Find the simple interest.

35. $450 deposited at an interest rate of 2% for 4 years

36. $3,000 deposited at an interest rate of 3% for 10 years

37. $10,000 deposited at an interest rate of 9% for 5 years

Find each balance.

38. $9,000 at 6% compounded annually for 5 years

39. $25,000 at 7% compounded semiannually for 10 years

40. $12,000 at 3% compounded semiannually for 8 years

41. $1,000 at 4% compounded annually for 10 years

42. $500 at 1.5% compounded annually for 4 years

43. $2,000 at 5% compounded semiannually for 2 years

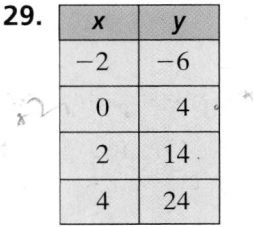 appears as a handwritten doodle in the margin.

- **Lesson 8-1 Is each relation a function? Explain.**

   1. $\{(3,5),(4,7),(4,8),(6,10)\}$ **2.** $\{(0,-1),(1,3),(-2,4),(3,6)\}$

   3. $\{(4,5),(5,2),(1,-3),(-2,-3),(0,2)\}$ **4.** $\{(1.5,0.6),(1.5,1.1),(2,1.9),(1,3.2)\}$

- **Lesson 8-2 Find the solution of each equation for $x = -3, 0,$ and 2.**

   5. $y = 3x - 2$ **6.** $y = 2x + 5$ **7.** $y = \frac{1}{2}x + 8$ **8.** $x = 3 - y$

   9. $y = -4$ **10.** $2y = 6x - 10$ **11.** $x - 2y = 3$ **12.** $y = -x - 1.5$

- **Lesson 8-3 Find the slope and y-intercept of the graph of each equation.**

   13. $y = 5x - 4$ **14.** $y = 10 - 3x$ **15.** $2y = 3x + 12$ **16.** $4x + y = 16$

   17. $y = \frac{3}{5}x - 1$ **18.** $12x + 6y = 30$ **19.** $y = x - \frac{1}{2}$ **20.** $x + y = -2$

   Graph each line.

   21. slope 3, through $(0, -5)$ **22.** slope -1, through $(3, 5)$ **23.** no slope, through $(2, -1)$

   24. $y = 2x + 1$ **25.** $x + y = 4$ **26.** $y = \frac{1}{2}x - 1$

- **Lesson 8-4 Write a rule for each linear function.**

   27.

x	y
0	-1
1	2
2	5
3	8

   28.

x	y
-1	4
0	6
1	8
2	10

   29.

x	y
-2	-6
0	4
2	14
4	24

   30. The graph has slope $-\frac{1}{2}$ and y-intercept 3.

   31. The graph has slope 2 and contains the point $(-1, 1)$.

   32. The graph contains the points $(-3, -2)$ and $(3, 0)$.

- **Lesson 8-5 Use the table to complete Exercises 33 and 34.**

   33. Make a scatter plot of (time studying, test grade).

   34. Is there a positive correlation, negative correlation, or no correlation between the sets of data? Explain.

   Study Time

Time Spent Studying (minutes)	40	30	20	50	75
Test Grade	85	80	60	80	90

- **Lessons 8-7 and 8-8 Solve each system by graphing.**

   35. $y = x + 3$
   $3x + y = 1$

   36. $x + y = -7$
   $x + y = 1$

   37. $y > 2x - 4$
   $y < -3x + 6$

   38. $x + y < 10$
   $x + y < -5$

● **Lesson 9-1 Use the figure at the right.**

1. Name the line in three ways.

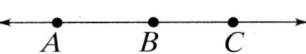

2. Name four different rays.

Use the figure at the right. Name each of the following.

3. four segments that intersect $\overline{MR}$

4. three segments parallel to $\overline{MR}$

5. three segments skew to $\overline{MR}$

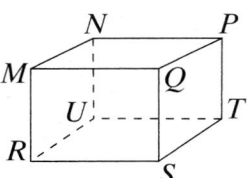

● **Lesson 9-2 In the figure at the right, $x \parallel y$.**

6. List all angles that are congruent to $\angle 1$.

7. If $m\angle 5 = 67°$, what are the measures of the other angles?

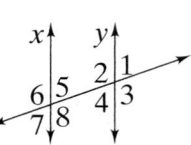

● **Lesson 9-3 Classify each figure.**

8.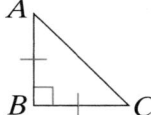

9.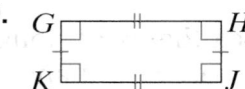

10.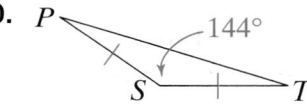

● **Lesson 9-5**

11. $\triangle XYZ \cong \triangle STU$. Which of the following must be true?
   a. $\overline{YZ} \cong \overline{TU}$
   b. $\angle X \cong \angle T$
   c. $\overline{ZX} \cong \overline{TS}$
   d. $\angle YZX \cong \angle STU$
   e. $\triangle YZX \cong \triangle UTS$

● **Lesson 9-6 Find the circumference of each circle with the given radius or diameter. Use 3.14 for π. Round to the nearest tenth.**

12. radius = 4 in.   13. diameter = 25 ft   14. radius = 7.8 cm   15. diameter = 100 m

● **Lesson 9-7 Draw $\triangle XYZ$ with acute $\angle Y$.**

16. Construct the angle bisector of $\angle Y$.   17. Construct a bisector of $\overline{XY}$.

● **Lessons 9-8, 9-9 and 9-10 Graph the image of $\triangle CDG$ with vertices $C(1, 3)$, $D(3, 5)$, and $G(5, 1)$ after each transformation.**

18. 3 units left, 2 units down   19. reflected over the x-axis   20. rotated 90° about the origin

Extra Practice

● **Lessons 10-1 and 10-2** Find the area of each figure.

1.
1 yd
6 ft

2.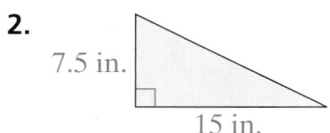
7.5 in.
15 in.

3.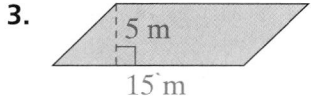
5 m
15 m

4.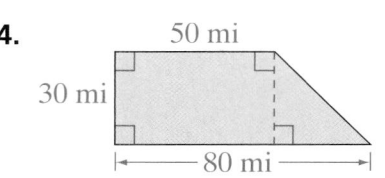
50 mi
30 mi
80 mi

5.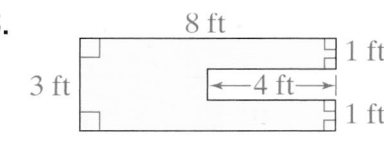
8 ft
1 ft
3 ft
4 ft
1 ft

6.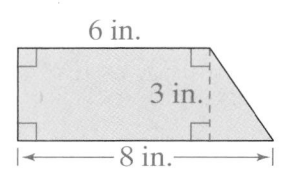
6 in.
3 in.
8 in.

● **Lesson 10-3** Find the area of each figure. Give an exact answer, and an approximate answer to the nearest tenth using 3.14 for π.

7.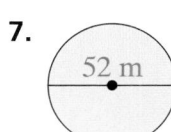
52 m

8.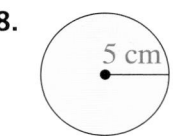
5 cm

9.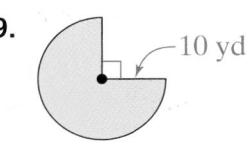
10 yd

● **Lesson 10-4**

10. Draw a net to represent a rectangular box that is 3 ft long, 5 ft wide, and 2 ft high. Label dimensions on the net and find the surface area.

● **Lessons 10-5, 10-6, 10-7, and 10-9** Find the surface area and volume of each space figure, to the nearest tenth. Use 3.14 for π.

11.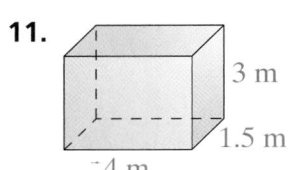
3 m
1.5 m
4 m

12.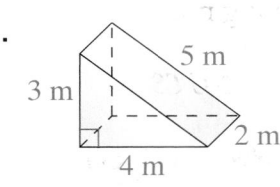
5 m
3 m
2 m
4 m

13.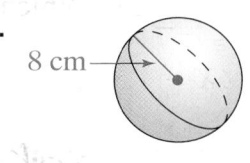
8 cm

14.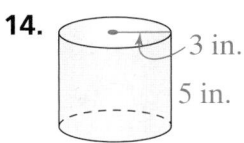
3 in.
5 in.

15.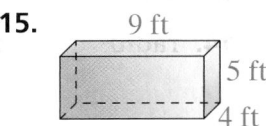
9 ft
5 ft
4 ft

16.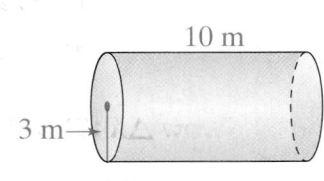
10 m
3 m

17.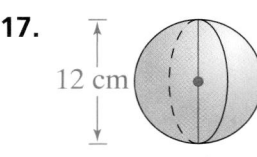
12 cm

18.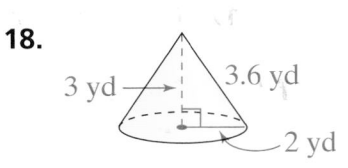
3 yd
3.6 yd
2 yd

19.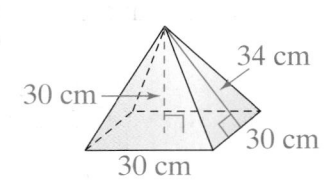
34 cm
30 cm
30 cm
30 cm

Chapter 11

Extra Practice

● **Lesson 11-1** Simplify each square root.

1. $\sqrt{4}$ **2.** $\sqrt{100}$ **3.** $-\sqrt{36}$ **4.** $\sqrt{121}$ **5.** $\sqrt{25}$

Estimate to the nearest integer.

6. $\sqrt{50}$ **7.** $\sqrt{12}$ **8.** $\sqrt{40}$ **9.** $\sqrt{105}$ **10.** $\sqrt{55}$

Identify each number as rational or irrational.

11. $\sqrt{9}$ **12.** 0.6 **13.** $\sqrt{5}$ **14.** $0.\overline{6}$ **15.** $0.010010001\ldots$

● **Lesson 11-2** Find each missing length, to the nearest tenth of a unit.

16. 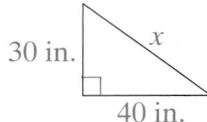   **17.** 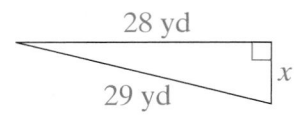   **18.**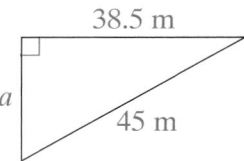

● **Lesson 11-3** Find the distance between each pair of points. Round to the nearest tenth.

19. $(4, 6), (8, 2)$ **20.** $(0, -4), (-5, 1)$ **21.** $(20, -5), (10, -8)$

Find the midpoint of each segment with the given endpoints.

22. $A(5, 4)$ and $B(3, 0)$ **23.** $C(-2, -4)$ and $D(3, 1)$ **24.** $E(-1, 5)$ and $F(2, -1)$

● **Lesson 11-5** Find the missing lengths.

25. 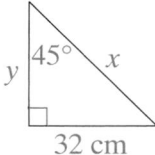   **26.** 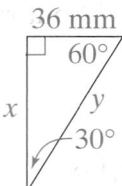   **27.**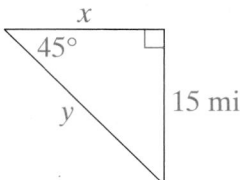

● **Lessons 11-6 and 11-7** Find each value. Round to four decimal places.

28. $\sin 10°$ **29.** $\tan 85°$ **30.** $\cos 33°$

31. $\tan 5°$ **32.** $\sin 78°$ **33.** $\cos 65°$

34. $\cos 52°$ **35.** $\tan 50°$ **36.** $\sin 30°$

37. A right triangle has one leg of 10 cm and an angle whose measure is 25°. What lengths are possible for the other leg and the hypotenuse, to the nearest tenth?

Chapter 12 Extra Practice

● **Lesson 12-1** Display each set of data in a frequency table. Then draw a line plot for each frequency table. Find the range.

1. 21 22 20 21 21 20 23 22 21 21

2. 95 100 95 95 90 80 85 80 95 100

● **Lesson 12-2** Use box-and-whisker plots to compare data sets. Use a single number line.

3. 1st set: 26 60 36 44 62 24 29 50 37 52 40 41 18 39 64 42
2nd set: 78 22 29 67 10 62 50 72 8 63 35 80 52 60 18 65 61

● **Lesson 12-3** Use the graph at the right for Exercises 4 and 5.

4. The graph suggests that the number of farms in 1982 was three times the number in 1992. Is this true? Explain.

5. Redraw the graph without a break.

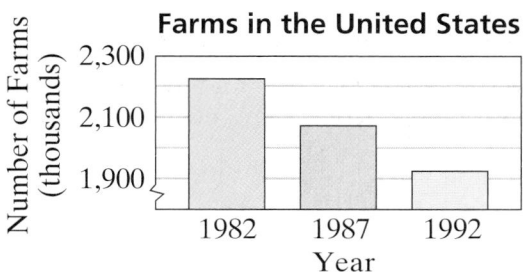

● **Lesson 12-4**

6. A menu shows that you can pick one vegetable from four choices, one potato dish from five choices, and one main dish from two choices. How many different choices of meals do you have?

● **Lesson 12-5** You select letters at random from the word MATHEMATICS.

7. Find the probability that you select A and then, after replacing A, select T.

8. Find the probability that you select A and then, without replacing A, select T.

● **Lesson 12-6** Simplify each expression.

9. $_3C_2$ **10.** $_3P_2$ **11.** $_5P_2$ **12.** $_7C_3$ **13.** $_{10}C_3$ **14.** $_8P_3$

● **Lessons 12-7 and 12-8** Some students were surveyed about the number of books in their lockers. The table shows the results.

15. Find the experimental probability that a locker will have 3 books.

16. In a school of 600 students, how many lockers would you expect to have one book?

Number of Books in Students' Lockers

Number of Books	1	2	3	4	5
Number of Students	12	21	10	7	10

● **Lesson 13-1 Find the next three terms of each sequence. Then write a rule to describe each sequence.**

1. $100, 80, 60, 40, \ldots$
2. $6, 12, 18, 24, \ldots$
3. $8, 16, 24, 32, \ldots$
4. $50, 500, 5,000, 50,000, \ldots$
5. $-5, 25, -125, 625, \ldots$
6. $50, 10, -30, -70, \ldots$

● **Lesson 13-2 Graph each function, for x values from -2 to 2.**

7. $y = x^2 - 1$
8. $y = -x^2 + 6$
9. $y = |x| - 3$
10. $y = -|x| + 2$
11. $y = -3x^2$
12. $y = -3|x| - 1$
13. $y = 2x^2 - 2$
14. $y = \frac{1}{2}|x|$

● **Lesson 13-3 For each function, make a table with integer values of x from 0 to 4. Then graph each function.**

15. $y = 4^x$
16. $y = \frac{1}{2} \cdot 10^x$
17. $y = 10(0.5)^x$
18. $y = 2^x$

● **Lesson 13-4 Tell whether each polynomial is a *monomial,* a *binomial,* or a *trinomial*.**

19. $2x^2 - 3x - 1$
20. $3xy$
21. $5x^3 - 15$
22. $10 - 2x + 5y$
23. xyz^2
24. $56 - y$
25. $3ab - a^2 - b$
26. 80

● **Lesson 13-5 Simplify each sum or difference.**

27. $(5y - 12) + (2y + 10)$
28. $(x^2 + 3x + 4) + (2x^2 + x + 6)$
29. $(x^2 - 7x + 2) + (-x^2 + 6x - 2)$
30. $(4a^2 - 3a - 2) - (2a^2 + 5a + 10)$
31. $(5x - 3) + (6x^2 - 9)$
32. $(15y^2 + 12y) - (12y^2 - 20)$
33. $(3ab + a^2 + b^2) - (a^2 - 3b^2 - 5ab)$
34. $(10t - t^2 - 15) + (3t^2 + 12)$

● **Lessons 13-6 and 13-7 Simplify each product.**

35. $2x(5x^2 + 6)$
36. $y^2(x + y)$
37. $6t^2(2t^2 - 3 + 8t)$
38. $(x - 8)(x + 1)$
39. $(y + 6)(2y + 4)$
40. $3b(5ab + 2ab^2 + 6b)$

Use the GCF of the terms to write each expression as the product of two factors.

41. $4x^2 - 12$
42. $5z^2 - 20z + 30$
43. $2a^2b - 4a + 6b$
44. $t^2 - 3t$
45. $6xy + 2x + 3x^2y$
46. $5w^3 + 6w^2 - 3w$

Skills Handbook

Comparing and Ordering Whole Numbers

The numbers on a number line are in order from least to greatest.

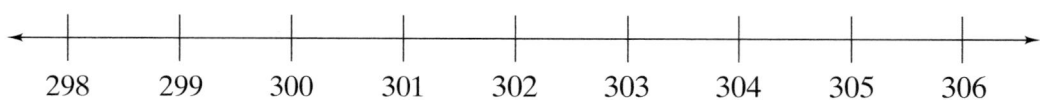

298   299   300   301   302   303   304   305   306

You can use a number line to compare whole numbers. Use the symbols > (is greater than) and < (is less than).

1 EXAMPLE

Use > or < to compare the numbers.

a. 303 ■ 299
303 is to the right of 299.
303 > 299

b. 301 ■ 305
301 is to the left of 305.
301 < 305

The value of a digit depends on its place in a number. Compare digits starting from the left.

2 EXAMPLE

Use > or < to compare the numbers.

a. 12,060,012,875 ■ 12,060,012,675
8 hundreds > 6 hundreds, so
12,060,012,875 > 12,060,012,675.

b. 465,320 ■ 4,653,208
0 millions < 4 millions, so
465,320 < 4,653,208.

EXERCISES

Use > or < to compare the numbers.

1. 3,660 ■ 360
2. 74,328 ■ 74,238
3. 88,010 ■ 8,101
4. 87,524 ■ 9,879

5. 295,286 ■ 295,826
6. 829,631 ■ 842,832
7. 932,401 ■ 932,701
8. 60,000 ■ 500,009

9. 1,609,372,002 ■ 609,172,002
10. 45,248,315,150 ■ 45,283,718,150

Write the numbers from least to greatest.

11. 3,747; 3,474; 3,774; 3,347; 3,734
12. 70,903; 70,309; 73,909; 73,090

13. 32,056,403; 302,056,403; 30,265,403; 30,256,403
14. 884,172; 881,472; 887,142; 881,872

Rounding Whole Numbers

You can use number lines to help you round numbers.

1 EXAMPLE

a. **Round 7,510 to the nearest thousand.**

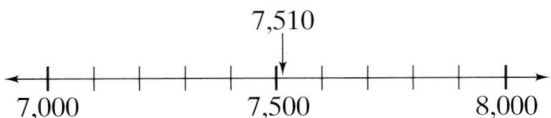

7,510 is between 7,000 and 8,000 and closer to 8,000.
7,510 rounds to 8,000.

b. **Round 237 to the nearest ten.**

237 is between 230 and 240 and closer to 240.
237 rounds to 240.

To round a number to a particular place, look at the digit to the right of that place. If the digit is less than 5, round down. If the digit is 5 or greater, round up.

2 EXAMPLE

Round to the place of the underlined digit.

a. **3,4_6_3,280**
The digit to the right of the 6 is 3, so 3,463,280 rounds down to 3,460,000.

b. **28_9_,543**
The digit to the right of the 9 is 5, so 289,543 rounds up to 290,000.

EXERCISES

Round to the nearest ten.

1. 42   **2.** 89   **3.** 671   **4.** 3,482   **5.** 7,029   **6.** 661,423

Round to the nearest thousand.

7. 5,800   **8.** 3,100   **9.** 44,280   **10.** 9,936   **11.** 987   **12.** 313,591

13. 5,641   **14.** 37,896   **15.** 82,019   **16.** 808,155   **17.** 34,501   **18.** 650,828

Round to the place of the underlined digit.

19. 68,_8_52   **20.** _4_51,006   **21.** 3,40_7_,481   **22.** 2_8_,512,030   **23.** 71,2_2_5,003

24. 96,_4_49   **25.** 4_0_1,223   **26.** _8_,902   **27.** 3,6_7_7   **28.** 2,551,_7_50

29. 6_8_,663   **30.** 70_1_,803,229   **31.** 56_5_,598   **32.** 32,_8_10   **33.** 1,_4_46,300

Multiplying Whole Numbers

When you multiply by a two-digit number, first multiply by the ones and then multiply by the tens. Add the products.

1 EXAMPLE

Multiply 62 × 704.

Step 1	Step 2	Step 3
704	704	704
× 62	× 62	× 62
‾‾‾‾	‾‾‾‾	‾‾‾‾
1408	1408	1 408
	42240	+ 42 240
		‾‾‾‾‾‾
		43,648

2 EXAMPLE

Find each product.

a. **93 × 6**

$$\begin{array}{r} 93 \\ \times\ 6 \\ \hline 558 \end{array}$$

b. **25 × 48**

$$\begin{array}{r} 48 \\ \times\ 25 \\ \hline 240 \\ +\ 960 \\ \hline 1,200 \end{array}$$

c. **80 × 921**

$$\begin{array}{r} 921 \\ \times\ 80 \\ \hline 73,680 \end{array}$$

EXERCISES

Find each product.

1. $\begin{array}{r} 74 \\ \times\ 6 \end{array}$
2. $\begin{array}{r} 35 \\ \times\ 9 \end{array}$
3. $\begin{array}{r} 53 \\ \times\ 7 \end{array}$
4. $\begin{array}{r} 80 \\ \times\ 8 \end{array}$
5. $\begin{array}{r} 98 \\ \times\ 4 \end{array}$
6. $\begin{array}{r} 65 \\ \times\ 8 \end{array}$

7. $\begin{array}{r} 512 \\ \times\ 3 \end{array}$
8. $\begin{array}{r} 407 \\ \times\ 9 \end{array}$
9. $\begin{array}{r} 225 \\ \times\ 6 \end{array}$
10. $\begin{array}{r} 340 \\ \times\ 5 \end{array}$
11. $\begin{array}{r} 816 \\ \times\ 7 \end{array}$
12. $\begin{array}{r} 603 \\ \times\ 3 \end{array}$

13. $\begin{array}{r} 70 \\ \times\ 36 \end{array}$
14. $\begin{array}{r} 41 \\ \times\ 55 \end{array}$
15. $\begin{array}{r} 38 \\ \times\ 49 \end{array}$
16. $\begin{array}{r} 601 \\ \times\ 87 \end{array}$
17. $\begin{array}{r} 271 \\ \times\ 34 \end{array}$
18. $\begin{array}{r} 450 \\ \times\ 67 \end{array}$

19. 6×82
20. 405×5
21. 81×9
22. 3×274
23. 552×4

24. 60×84
25. 52×17
26. 31×90
27. 78×52
28. 43×66

29. 826×3
30. 702×4
31. 8×180
32. 6×339
33. 781×7

Dividing Whole Numbers

First estimate the quotient by rounding the divisor, the dividend, or both. When you divide, after you bring down a digit, you must write a digit in the quotient.

EXAMPLE

Find each quotient.

a. $741 \div 8$

Estimate:

$720 \div 8 \approx 90$

$$\begin{array}{r} 92 \text{ R5} \\ 8\overline{)741} \\ -72 \\ \hline 21 \\ -16 \\ \hline 5 \end{array}$$

b. $838 \div 43$

Estimate:

$800 \div 40 \approx 20$

$$\begin{array}{r} 19 \text{ R21} \\ 43\overline{)838} \\ -43 \\ \hline 408 \\ -387 \\ \hline 21 \end{array}$$

c. $367 \div 9$

Estimate:

$360 \div 9 \approx 40$

$$\begin{array}{r} 40 \text{ R7} \\ 9\overline{)367} \\ -360 \\ \hline 7 \end{array}$$

EXERCISES

Divide.

1. $4\overline{)61}$
2. $8\overline{)53}$
3. $7\overline{)90}$
4. $3\overline{)84}$
5. $6\overline{)81}$

6. $6\overline{)469}$
7. $3\overline{)653}$
8. $8\overline{)645}$
9. $9\overline{)231}$
10. $4\overline{)415}$

11. $60\overline{)461}$
12. $40\overline{)213}$
13. $70\overline{)517}$
14. $30\overline{)432}$
15. $80\overline{)276}$

16. $43\overline{)273}$
17. $52\overline{)281}$
18. $69\overline{)207}$
19. $38\overline{)121}$
20. $81\overline{)433}$

21. $94\overline{)1,368}$
22. $62\overline{)1,147}$
23. $55\overline{)2,047}$
24. $85\overline{)1,450}$
25. $46\overline{)996}$

26. $94 \div 4$
27. $66 \div 9$
28. $90 \div 5$
29. $69 \div 6$
30. $58 \div 8$

31. $323 \div 5$
32. $849 \div 7$
33. $404 \div 8$
34. $934 \div 3$
35. $619 \div 6$

36. $777 \div 50$
37. $528 \div 20$
38. $443 \div 70$
39. $312 \div 40$
40. $335 \div 60$

41. $382 \div 72$
42. $580 \div 68$
43. $279 \div 43$
44. $232 \div 27$
45. $331 \div 93$

46. $614 \div 35$
47. $423 \div 28$
48. $489 \div 15$
49. $1,134 \div 51$
50. $1,103 \div 26$

Decimals and Place Value

Each digit in a whole number or a decimal has both a place and a value. The value of any place is one tenth the value of the place to its left. The chart below can help you read and write decimals.

Billions	Hundred millions	Ten millions	Millions	Hundred thousands	Ten thousands	Thousands	Hundreds	Tens	Ones	.	Tenths	Hundredths	Thousandths	Ten-thousandths	Hundred-thousandths	Millionths
2	4	0	1	2	6	2	8	3	0	.	7	5	0	1	9	1

EXAMPLE

a. **What is the value of the digit 8 in the number above?**
   The digit 8 is in the hundreds place.
   So, its value is 8 hundreds.

b. **Write 2.006 in words.**
   The digit 6 is in the thousandths place.
   So, 2.006 is read two and six thousandths.

c. **Write five and thirty-four ten-thousandths as a decimal.**
   Ten-thousandths is 4 places to the right of the decimal point.
   So, the decimal will have 4 places after the decimal point.
   The answer is 5.0034.

EXERCISES

Use the chart above. Write the value of each digit.

1. the digit 9
2. the digit 7
3. the digit 5
4. the digit 6
5. the digit 4
6. the digit 3

Write a decimal for the given words.

7. forty-one ten-thousandths
8. eighteen and five hundred four thousandths
9. eight millionths
10. seven and sixty-three hundred-thousandths
11. thirteen thousandths
12. sixty-five and two hundred one thousandths

Write each decimal in words.

13. 0.06
14. 4.7
15. 0.00011
16. 0.9
17. 0.012
18. 0.000059
19. 0.0042
20. 6.020

Comparing and Ordering Decimals

To compare two decimals, use the symbols > (is greater than),
< (is less than), or = (is equal to). When you compare, start at the left
and compare the digits.

1 EXAMPLE

Use >, <, or = to compare the decimals.

a. 0.1 ■ 0.06
   1 tenth > 0 tenths, so
   0.1 > 0.06.

b. 2.4583 ■ 2.48
   5 hundredths < 8 hundredths,
   so 2.4583 < 2.48.

c. 0.30026 ■ 0.03026
   3 tenths > 0 tenths, so
   0.30026 > 0.03026.

2 EXAMPLE

Draw number lines to compare the decimals.

a. 0.1 ■ 0.06

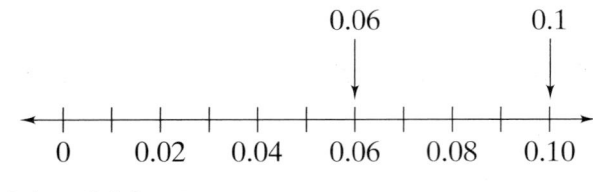

0.1 > 0.06

b. 2.4583 ■ 2.48

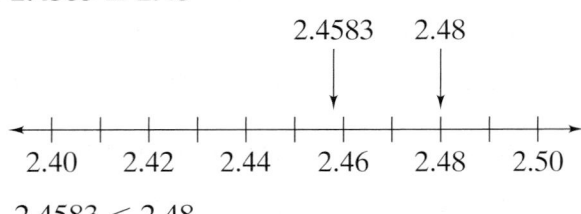

2.4583 < 2.48

EXERCISES

Use >, <, or = to compare the decimals. Draw number
lines if you wish.

1. 0.003 ■ 0.02
2. 84.2 ■ 842
3. 0.162 ■ 0.106
4. 0.0659 ■ 0.6059

5. 2.13 ■ 2.99
6. 3.53 ■ 3.529
7. 2.01 ■ 2.010
8. 0.00072 ■ 0.07002

9. 0.458 ■ 0.4589
10. 8.627 ■ 8.649
11. 0.0019 ■ 0.0002
12. 0.19321 ■ 0.19231

Write the decimals in order from least to greatest.

13. 2.31, 0.231, 23.1, 0.23, 3.21
14. 1.02, 1.002, 1.2, 1.11, 1.021

15. 0.02, 0.002, 0.22, 0.222, 2.22
16. 55.5, 555.5, 55.555, 5.5555

17. 0.07, 0.007, 0.7, 0.71, 0.72
18. 2.78, 2.7001, 2.701, 2.71, 2.7

19. 7, 7.3264, 7.3, 7.3246, 7.0324
20. 0.0101, 0.0099, 0.011, 0.00019

Rounding

When you round to a particular place, look at the digit to the right of that place. If it is 5 or greater, you increase the digit in the place you are rounding to by 1. If it is less than 5, you leave the digit in the place you are rounding to unchanged.

Skills Handbook

EXAMPLE

a. **Round 1.627 to the nearest whole number.**
The digit to the right of the units place is 6, so 1.627 rounds up to 2.

b. **Round 12,034 to the nearest thousand.**
The digit to the right of the thousands place is 0, so 12,034 rounds down to 12,000.

c. **Round 2.7195 to the nearest hundredth.**
The digit to the right of the hundredths place is 9, so 2.7195 rounds up to 2.72.

d. **Round 0.060521 to the nearest thousandth.**
The digit to the right of the thousandths place is 5, so 0.060521 rounds up to 0.061.

EXERCISES

Round to the nearest thousand.

1. 105,099   **2.** 10,400   **3.** 79,527,826   **4.** 79,932   **5.** 4,312,349

Round to the nearest whole number.

6. 135.91   **7.** 3.001095   **8.** 96.912   **9.** 101.167   **10.** 299.9

Round to the nearest tenth.

11. 82.01   **12.** 4.67522   **13.** 20.397   **14.** 399.95   **15.** 129.98

Round to the nearest hundredth.

16. 13.458   **17.** 96.4045   **18.** 0.699   **19.** 4.234   **20.** 12.09531

Round to the place of the underlined digit.

21. 7.0$\underline{6}$15   **22.** $\underline{5}$.77125   **23.** 1,5$\underline{2}$2   **24.** 0.919$\underline{5}$2   **25.** 4.$\underline{2}$43

26. 2$\underline{3}$6.001   **27.** $\underline{3}$52   **28.** 3.4953$\underline{6}$6   **29.** 8.0$\underline{7}$092   **30.** $\underline{0}$.6008

31. 4$\underline{0}$9   **32.** 23,$\underline{9}$51,888   **33.** 2.5$\underline{7}$84   **34.** 8$\underline{6}$2   **35.** 19.3$\underline{2}$

36. $\underline{9}$18   **37.** 7,$\underline{7}$35   **38.** 25.66$\underline{0}$47   **39.** 9$\underline{8}$3,240,631   **40.** $\underline{2}$7

41. 0.0037$\underline{7}$1   **42.** 0.$\underline{0}$649   **43.** 12.$\underline{7}$77   **44.** 1,75$\underline{9}$,230   **45.** 2$\underline{0}$,908

Adding and Subtracting Decimals

You add or subtract decimals just as you do whole numbers. You line up the decimal points and then add or subtract. If you wish, you can use zeros to make the columns even.

EXAMPLE

Find each sum or difference.

a. 37.6 + 8.431

$$
\begin{array}{r} 37.6 \\ + 8.431 \end{array} \rightarrow
\begin{array}{r} 37.600 \\ + 8.431 \\ \hline 46.031 \end{array}
$$

b. 8 − 4.593

$$
\begin{array}{r} 8 \\ - 4.593 \end{array} \rightarrow
\begin{array}{r} 8.000 \\ - 4.593 \\ \hline 3.407 \end{array}
$$

c. 8.3 + 2.99 + 17.5

$$
\begin{array}{r} 8.3 \\ 2.99 \\ + 17.5 \end{array} \rightarrow
\begin{array}{r} 8.30 \\ 2.99 \\ + 17.50 \\ \hline 28.79 \end{array}
$$

EXERCISES

Find each sum or difference.

1. $\begin{array}{r} 39.7 \\ - 36.03 \end{array}$
2. $\begin{array}{r} 1.08 \\ - 0.9 \end{array}$
3. $\begin{array}{r} 6.784 \\ + 0.528 \end{array}$
4. $\begin{array}{r} 5.01 \\ - 0.87 \end{array}$
5. $\begin{array}{r} 13.02 \\ + 23.107 \end{array}$

6. $\begin{array}{r} 8.634 \\ + 1.409 \end{array}$
7. $\begin{array}{r} 2.1 \\ - 0.5 \end{array}$
8. $\begin{array}{r} 8.23 \\ - 3.1 \end{array}$
9. $\begin{array}{r} 1.05 \\ + 12.9 \end{array}$
10. $\begin{array}{r} 2.6 \\ + 0.003 \end{array}$

11. $\begin{array}{r} 0.1 \\ 58.21 \\ + 1.9 \end{array}$
12. $\begin{array}{r} 12.2 \\ 3.06 \\ + 0.5 \end{array}$
13. $\begin{array}{r} 9.42 \\ 3.6 \\ + 21.003 \end{array}$
14. $\begin{array}{r} 15.22 \\ 7.4 \\ + 8.125 \end{array}$
15. $\begin{array}{r} 3.7 \\ 20.06 \\ + 16.19 \end{array}$

16. $76.39 - 8.47$
17. $8.7 + 17.03$
18. $32.403 + 12.06$
19. $20.5 + 11.45$

20. $8.9 - 4.45$
21. $1.245 + 5.8$
22. $3.9 + 6.57$
23. $14.81 - 8.6$

24. $11.9 - 2.06$
25. $3.45 + 4.061$
26. $8.29 + 4.3$
27. $7.06 - 4.235$

28. $6.02 + 4.005$
29. $7.05 - 3.5$
30. $1.18 + 3.015$
31. $2.304 - 0.87$

32. $5.002 - 3.45$
33. $6.8 + 3.57$
34. $0.23 + 0.091$
35. $0.5 - 0.18$

36. $8.3 + 2.99 + 17.52$
37. $9.5 + 12.32 + 6.4$
38. $4.521 + 1.8 + 3.07$

39. $3.602 + 9.4 + 24$
40. $11.6 + 8.05 + 5.13$
41. $7.023 + 1.48 + 3.9$

42. $57 + 0.6327 + 189.007$
43. $741 + 6.08 + 0.0309$
44. $0.045 + 16.32 + 8.6$

45. $4.27 + 6.18 + 0.91$
46. $3.856 + 14.01 + 1.72$
47. $11.45 + 3.79 + 23.861$

Multiplying Decimals

Multiply decimals as you would whole numbers. Then place the decimal point in the product. To do this, add the number of decimal places in the factors.

1 EXAMPLE

Multiply 0.068 × 2.3.

Step 1 Multiply.

$$
\begin{array}{r}
0.068 \\
\times\ 2.3 \\
\hline
204 \\
+\ 1360 \\
\hline
1564
\end{array}
$$

Step 2 Place the decimal point.

$$
\begin{array}{r}
0.068 \\
\times\ 2.3 \\
\hline
204 \\
+\ 1360 \\
\hline
0.1564
\end{array}
$$

0.068 ← three decimal places
× 2.3 ← one decimal place
0.1564 ← four decimal places

2 EXAMPLE

Find each product.

a. 3.12 × 0.9

$$
\begin{array}{r}
3.12 \\
\times\ 0.9 \\
\hline
2.808
\end{array}
$$

b. 5.75 × 42

$$
\begin{array}{r}
5.75 \\
\times\ 42 \\
\hline
11\ 50 \\
+\ 230\ 00 \\
\hline
241.50
\end{array}
$$

c. 0.964 × 0.28

$$
\begin{array}{r}
0.964 \\
\times\ 0.28 \\
\hline
7712 \\
+\ 19280 \\
\hline
0.26992
\end{array}
$$

EXERCISES

Multiply.

1. $\begin{array}{r} 1.48 \\ \times\ 3.6 \end{array}$

2. $\begin{array}{r} 191.2 \\ \times\ 3.4 \end{array}$

3. $\begin{array}{r} 0.05 \\ \times\ 43 \end{array}$

4. $\begin{array}{r} 0.27 \\ \times\ 5 \end{array}$

5. $\begin{array}{r} 1.36 \\ \times\ 3.8 \end{array}$

6. $\begin{array}{r} 6.23 \\ \times\ 0.21 \end{array}$

7. $\begin{array}{r} 0.512 \\ \times\ 0.76 \end{array}$

8. $\begin{array}{r} 0.04 \\ \times\ 7 \end{array}$

9. $\begin{array}{r} 0.136 \\ \times\ 8.4 \end{array}$

10. $\begin{array}{r} 3 \\ \times\ 0.05 \end{array}$

11. 2.07×1.004

12. 0.12×6.1

13. 3.2×0.15

14. 0.74×0.23

15. 2.6×0.14

16. 0.77×51

17. 9.3×0.706

18. 71.13×0.4

19. 0.42×98

20. 6.3×85

21. 45×0.028

22. 76×3.3

23. 9×1.35

24. 4.56×7

25. 5×2.41

26. 704×0.3

27. 8.003×0.6

28. 42.2×0.9

29. 0.6×30.02

30. 0.05×11.8

Zeros in a Product

When you multiply with decimals, you may have to write one or more zeros to the left of a product before you can place the decimal point.

1 EXAMPLE

Multiply 0.06 × 0.015.

Step 1 Multiply.

$$\begin{array}{r} 0.015 \\ \times\ 0.06 \\ \hline 90 \end{array}$$

Step 2 Place the decimal point.

$$\begin{array}{r} 0.015 \\ \times\ 0.06 \\ \hline 0.00090 \end{array}$$ ← **The product should have 5 decimal places, so you must write three zeros before placing the decimal point**

2 EXAMPLE

a. 0.02 × 1.3

$$\begin{array}{r} 1.3 \\ \times\ 0.02 \\ \hline 0.026 \end{array}$$

b. 0.012 × 2.4

$$\begin{array}{r} 2.4 \\ \times\ 0.012 \\ \hline 48 \\ +\ 240 \\ \hline 0.0288 \end{array}$$

c. 0.022 × 0.051

$$\begin{array}{r} 0.051 \\ \times\ 0.022 \\ \hline 102 \\ +\ 1020 \\ \hline 0.001122 \end{array}$$

EXERCISES

Multiply.

1. $\begin{array}{r} 0.03 \\ \times\ 0.9 \\ \hline \end{array}$
2. $\begin{array}{r} 0.06 \\ \times\ 0.5 \\ \hline \end{array}$
3. $\begin{array}{r} 2.4 \\ \times\ 0.03 \\ \hline \end{array}$
4. $\begin{array}{r} 7 \\ \times\ 0.01 \\ \hline \end{array}$
5. $\begin{array}{r} 0.05 \\ \times\ 0.05 \\ \hline \end{array}$

6. $\begin{array}{r} 0.016 \\ \times\ 0.12 \\ \hline \end{array}$
7. $\begin{array}{r} 0.031 \\ \times\ 0.08 \\ \hline \end{array}$
8. $\begin{array}{r} 0.03 \\ \times\ 0.2 \\ \hline \end{array}$
9. $\begin{array}{r} 0.27 \\ \times\ 0.033 \\ \hline \end{array}$
10. $\begin{array}{r} 0.014 \\ \times\ 0.25 \\ \hline \end{array}$

11. 0.003 × 0.55
12. 0.01 × 0.74
13. 0.47 × 0.08
14. 0.76 × 0.1

15. 0.3 × 0.27
16. 0.19 × 0.05
17. 0.018 × 0.04
18. 0.43 × 0.2

19. 0.03 × 0.03
20. 4.003 × 0.02
21. 0.5 × 0.08
22. 0.06 × 0.7

23. 0.047 × 0.008
24. 0.05 × 0.06
25. 0.03 × 0.4
26. 0.05 × 0.036

27. 0.4 × 0.23
28. 0.3 × 0.017
29. 0.3 × 0.24
30. 0.67 × 0.09

31. 3.02 × 0.006
32. 0.31 × 0.08
33. 0.14 × 0.05
34. 0.07 × 0.85

Dividing Decimals by Whole Numbers

When you divide a decimal by a whole number, the decimal point in the quotient goes directly above the decimal point in the dividend. You may need extra zeros to place the decimal point.

1 EXAMPLE

Divide 2.432 ÷ 32.

Step 1 Divide.

$$
\begin{array}{r}
76 \\
32\overline{)2.432} \\
-2\,24 \\
\hline
192 \\
-192 \\
\hline
0
\end{array}
$$

Step 2 Place the decimal point.

$$
\begin{array}{r}
0.076 \\
32\overline{)2.432} \\
-2\,24 \\
\hline
192 \\
-192 \\
\hline
0
\end{array}
$$
← **Put extra zeros to the left. Then place the decimal point.**

2 EXAMPLE

a. 37.6 ÷ 8

$$
\begin{array}{r}
4.7 \\
8\overline{)37.6} \\
-32 \\
\hline
5\,6 \\
-5\,6 \\
\hline
0
\end{array}
$$

b. 39.33 ÷ 69

$$
\begin{array}{r}
0.57 \\
69\overline{)39.33} \\
-34\,5 \\
\hline
4\,83 \\
-4\,83 \\
\hline
0
\end{array}
$$

c. 4.482 ÷ 54

$$
\begin{array}{r}
0.083 \\
54\overline{)4.482} \\
-4\,32 \\
\hline
162 \\
-162 \\
\hline
0
\end{array}
$$

EXERCISES

Divide.

1. $7\overline{)17.92}$ **2.** $5\overline{)16.5}$ **3.** $9\overline{)6.984}$ **4.** $6\overline{)91.44}$ **5.** $4\overline{)35.16}$

6. $56\overline{)8.848}$ **7.** $22\overline{)2.42}$ **8.** $26\overline{)1,723.8}$ **9.** $83\overline{)15.272}$ **10.** $39\overline{)26.91}$

11. 14.49 ÷ 7   **12.** 10.53 ÷ 9   **13.** 17.52 ÷ 2   **14.** 37.14 ÷ 6

15. 0.1352 ÷ 8   **16.** 0.0324 ÷ 9   **17.** 0.0882 ÷ 6   **18.** 0.8682 ÷ 6

19. 12.342 ÷ 22   **20.** 29.792 ÷ 32   **21.** 22.568 ÷ 26   **22.** 11.340 ÷ 36

23. 45.918 ÷ 18   **24.** 79.599 ÷ 13   **25.** 58.5 ÷ 15   **26.** 74.664 ÷ 12

27. 21.0 ÷ 84   **28.** 89.378 ÷ 67   **29.** 0.0672 ÷ 48   **30.** 171.031 ÷ 53

Multiplying and Dividing by Powers of Ten

You can use shortcuts to multiply or divide by powers of ten.

When you multiply by	Move the decimal point	When you divide by	Move the decimal point
10,000	4 places to the right	10,000	4 places to the left
1,000	3 places to the right	1,000	3 places to the left
100	2 places to the right	100	2 places to the left
10	1 place to the right	10	1 place to the left
0.1	1 place to the left	0.1	1 place to the right
0.01	2 places to the left	0.01	2 places to the right
0.001	3 places to the left	0.001	3 places to the right

EXAMPLE

Multiply or divide.

a. 0.7×0.001

Move the decimal point 3 places to the left.
0.000.7

$0.7 \times 0.001 = 0.0007$

b. $0.605 \div 100$

Move the decimal point 2 places to the left.
0.00.605

$0.605 \div 100 = 0.00605$

EXERCISES

Multiply or divide.

1. $10,000 \times 0.056$ **2.** 0.001×0.09 **3.** 5.2×10 **4.** $0.03 \times 1,000$

5. $236.7 \div 0.1$ **6.** $45.28 \div 10$ **7.** $0.9 \div 1,000$ **8.** $1.07 \div 0.01$

9. 100×0.08 **10.** $1.03 \times 10,000$ **11.** 1.803×0.001 **12.** 4.1×100

13. $13.7 \div 0.001$ **14.** $203.05 \div 0.01$ **15.** $4.7 \div 10$ **16.** $0.05 \div 100$

17. 23.6×0.01 **18.** $1,000 \times 0.12$ **19.** 0.41×0.001 **20.** 0.01×6.2

21. $42.3 \div 0.1$ **22.** $0.4 \div 10,000$ **23.** $5.02 \div 0.01$ **24.** $16.5 \div 100$

25. $0.27 \div 0.01$ **26.** 1.05×0.001 **27.** 10×0.04 **28.** $2.09 \div 100$

29. 0.65×0.1 **30.** $0.03 \div 100$ **31.** $2.6 \div 0.1$ **32.** $12.6 \times 10,000$

33. $0.3 \div 1,000$ **34.** 0.01×6.7 **35.** 100×0.158 **36.** $23.1 \div 10$

Dividing Decimals by Decimals

To divide with a decimal divisor, multiply it by the smallest power of ten that will make the divisor a whole number. Then multiply the dividend by that same power of ten.

Find each quotient.

a. $3.348 \div 6.2$
  Multiply by 10.

$$
\begin{array}{r}
0.54 \\
6.2\overline{)3\,3.48} \\
-3\ 1\ 0 \\
\hline
2\ 48 \\
-2\ 48 \\
\hline
0
\end{array}
$$

b. $2.4885 \div 0.35$
  Multiply by 100.

$$
\begin{array}{r}
7.11 \\
0.35\overline{)2\,48.85} \\
-2\ 45 \\
\hline
3\ 8 \\
-3\ 5 \\
\hline
35 \\
-35 \\
\hline
0
\end{array}
$$

c. $0.0576 \div 0.012$
  Multiply by 1,000.

$$
\begin{array}{r}
4.8 \\
0.012\overline{)0\,057.6} \\
-48 \\
\hline
96 \\
-96 \\
\hline
0
\end{array}
$$

EXERCISES

Divide.

1. $3.2\overline{)268.8}$ **2.** $1.9\overline{)123.5}$ **3.** $0.3\overline{)135.6}$ **4.** $2.3\overline{)170.2}$ **5.** $7.9\overline{)252.8}$

6. $5.7\overline{)10.26}$ **7.** $2.3\overline{)71.53}$ **8.** $3.1\overline{)16.12}$ **9.** $7.8\overline{)24.18}$ **10.** $6.3\overline{)14.49}$

11. $134.42 \div 5.17$ **12.** $89.96 \div 3.46$ **13.** $160.58 \div 5.18$ **14.** $106.59 \div 6.27$

15. $62.4 \div 3.9$ **16.** $260.4 \div 8.4$ **17.** $316.8 \div 7.2$ **18.** $162.4 \div 2.9$

19. $1.512 \div 0.54$ **20.** $3.225 \div 0.43$ **21.** $2.484 \div 0.69$ **22.** $511.5 \div 5.5$

23. $0.992 \div 0.8$ **24.** $4.53 \div 0.05$ **25.** $3.498 \div 0.06$ **26.** $59.2 \div 0.8$

27. $2.198 \div 0.07$ **28.** $14.28 \div 0.7$ **29.** $1.98 \div 0.5$ **30.** $26.36 \div 0.04$

31. $3.922 \div 7.4$ **32.** $23.52 \div 0.98$ **33.** $71.25 \div 7.5$ **34.** $114.7 \div 3.7$

35. $0.832 \div 0.52$ **36.** $1.125 \div 0.09$ **37.** $9.666 \div 2.7$ **38.** $1.456 \div 9.1$

39. $0.4374 \div 1.8$ **40.** $2.3414 \div 0.46$ **41.** $0.07224 \div 0.021$ **42.** $0.1386 \div 0.18$

43. $0.16926 \div 0.091$ **44.** $0.6042 \div 5.3$ **45.** $2.3374 \div 0.62$ **46.** $1.0062 \div 0.078$

Zeros in Decimal Division

When you are dividing by a decimal, sometimes you need to use extra zeros in the dividend or the quotient, or both.

1 EXAMPLE

Divide 0.045 ÷ 3.6.

Step 1 Multiply by 10.

$$3.6.\overline{)0.0.45}$$

Step 2 Divide.

$$\begin{array}{r} 125 \\ 3.6.\overline{)0.0.4500} \\ -36 \\ \hline 90 \\ -72 \\ \hline 180 \\ -180 \\ \hline 0 \end{array}$$

Step 3 Place the decimal point.

$$\begin{array}{r} 0.0125 \\ 3.6.\overline{)0.0.4500} \\ -36 \\ \hline 90 \\ -72 \\ \hline 180 \\ -180 \\ \hline 0 \end{array}$$

2 EXAMPLE

Find each quotient.

a. **0.4428 ÷ 8.2**

Multiply by 10.

$$\begin{array}{r} 0.054 \\ 8.2.\overline{)0.4.428} \end{array}$$

b. **0.00434 ÷ 0.07**

Multiply by 100.

$$\begin{array}{r} 0.062 \\ 0.07.\overline{)0.00.434} \end{array}$$

c. **0.00306 ÷ 0.072**

Multiply by 1,000.

$$\begin{array}{r} 0.0425 \\ 0.072.\overline{)0.003.0600} \end{array}$$

EXERCISES

Divide.

1. $0.05\overline{)0.0023}$

2. $0.02\overline{)0.000162}$

3. $0.12\overline{)0.009}$

4. $2.5\overline{)0.021}$

5. $0.0019 \div 0.2$

6. $0.9 \div 0.8$

7. $0.000175 \div 0.07$

8. $0.142 \div 0.04$

9. $0.0017 \div 0.02$

10. $0.003 \div 0.6$

11. $0.0105 \div 0.7$

12. $0.034 \div 0.05$

13. $0.00056 \div 0.16$

14. $0.0612 \div 7.2$

15. $0.217 \div 3.1$

16. $0.052 \div 0.8$

17. $0.000924 \div 0.44$

18. $0.05796 \div 0.63$

19. $0.00123 \div 8.2$

20. $0.0954 \div 0.09$

21. $0.0084 \div 1.4$

22. $0.259 \div 3.5$

23. $0.00468 \div 0.52$

24. $0.104 \div 0.05$

25. $0.00063 \div 0.18$

26. $0.011 \div 0.25$

27. $0.3069 \div 9.3$

28. $0.00045 \div 0.3$

Writing Equivalent Fractions

If you multiply or divide both the numerator and the denominator of a fraction by the same number, you get an equivalent fraction.

1 EXAMPLE

a. Find the missing number in $\frac{5}{6} = \frac{20}{\blacksquare}$.

$$\frac{5}{6} = \frac{20}{\blacksquare}$$

$$\frac{5}{6} = \frac{20}{24}$$

$\times 4$

b. Find the missing number in $\frac{12}{30} = \frac{\blacksquare}{15}$.

$$\frac{12}{30} = \frac{\blacksquare}{15}$$

$$\frac{12}{30} = \frac{6}{15}$$

$\div 2$

To write a fraction in simplest form, divide both the numerator and the denominator by the greatest common factor.

2 EXAMPLE

a. Write $\frac{6}{15}$ in simplest form.

3 is the greatest common factor.

$$\frac{6}{15} = \frac{6 \div 3}{15 \div 3} = \frac{2}{5}$$

The simplest form of $\frac{6}{15}$ is $\frac{2}{5}$.

b. Write $\frac{36}{42}$ in simplest form.

6 is the greatest common factor.

$$\frac{36}{42} = \frac{36 \div 6}{42 \div 6} = \frac{6}{7}$$

The simplest form of $\frac{36}{42}$ is $\frac{6}{7}$.

EXERCISES

Find each missing number.

1. $\frac{1}{3} = \frac{\blacksquare}{6}$

2. $\frac{3}{4} = \frac{\blacksquare}{16}$

3. $\frac{18}{30} = \frac{6}{\blacksquare}$

4. $\frac{2}{3} = \frac{\blacksquare}{21}$

5. $\frac{3}{4} = \frac{9}{\blacksquare}$

6. $\frac{3}{10} = \frac{9}{\blacksquare}$

7. $\frac{4}{5} = \frac{\blacksquare}{30}$

8. $\frac{2}{3} = \frac{8}{\blacksquare}$

9. $\frac{33}{55} = \frac{\blacksquare}{5}$

10. $\frac{27}{72} = \frac{9}{\blacksquare}$

11. $\frac{2}{3} = \frac{\blacksquare}{24}$

12. $\frac{11}{12} = \frac{55}{\blacksquare}$

13. $\frac{3}{5} = \frac{18}{\blacksquare}$

14. $\frac{60}{72} = \frac{10}{\blacksquare}$

15. $\frac{7}{8} = \frac{\blacksquare}{24}$

Write each fraction in simplest form.

16. $\frac{12}{36}$

17. $\frac{25}{30}$

18. $\frac{14}{16}$

19. $\frac{27}{36}$

20. $\frac{21}{35}$

21. $\frac{40}{50}$

22. $\frac{24}{40}$

23. $\frac{32}{64}$

24. $\frac{15}{45}$

25. $\frac{27}{63}$

26. $\frac{44}{77}$

27. $\frac{45}{75}$

28. $\frac{60}{72}$

29. $\frac{77}{84}$

30. $\frac{12}{24}$

31. $\frac{24}{32}$

32. $\frac{7}{21}$

33. $\frac{18}{42}$

Mixed Numbers and Improper Fractions

A fraction, such as $\frac{10}{7}$, in which the numerator is greater than or equal to the denominator is an improper fraction. You can write an improper fraction as a mixed number that shows the sum of a whole number and a fraction.

Sometimes it is necessary to do the opposite and write a mixed number as an improper fraction.

EXAMPLE

a. **Write $\frac{11}{5}$ as a mixed number.**

$$\frac{11}{5} \rightarrow \begin{array}{r} 2 \\ 5\overline{)11} \\ -10 \\ \hline 1 \end{array} \begin{array}{l} \leftarrow \text{whole number} \\ \\ \leftarrow \text{remainder} \end{array}$$

$\frac{11}{5} = 2\frac{1}{5}$ $\leftarrow$ whole number $+\frac{\text{remainder}}{\text{denominator}}$

b. **Write $2\frac{5}{6}$ as an improper fraction.**

$$2\frac{5}{6} = 2 + \frac{5}{6}$$
$$= \frac{12}{6} + \frac{5}{6} \quad \leftarrow \text{Write 2 as } \frac{12}{6}.$$
$$= \frac{12 + 5}{6} \quad \leftarrow \text{Add the numerators.}$$
$$2\frac{5}{6} = \frac{17}{6}$$

EXERCISES

Write each improper fraction as a mixed number.

1. $\frac{7}{5}$ **2.** $\frac{9}{2}$ **3.** $\frac{13}{4}$ **4.** $\frac{21}{5}$ **5.** $\frac{13}{10}$ **6.** $\frac{49}{5}$

7. $\frac{21}{8}$ **8.** $\frac{13}{7}$ **9.** $\frac{17}{5}$ **10.** $\frac{49}{6}$ **11.** $\frac{17}{4}$ **12.** $\frac{5}{2}$

13. $\frac{27}{5}$ **14.** $\frac{12}{9}$ **15.** $\frac{30}{8}$ **16.** $\frac{37}{12}$ **17.** $\frac{8}{6}$ **18.** $\frac{19}{12}$

19. $\frac{45}{10}$ **20.** $\frac{15}{12}$ **21.** $\frac{11}{2}$ **22.** $\frac{20}{6}$ **23.** $\frac{34}{8}$ **24.** $\frac{21}{9}$

Write each mixed number as an improper fraction.

25. $1\frac{1}{2}$ **26.** $2\frac{2}{3}$ **27.** $1\frac{1}{12}$ **28.** $3\frac{1}{5}$ **29.** $2\frac{2}{7}$ **30.** $4\frac{1}{2}$

31. $2\frac{7}{8}$ **32.** $1\frac{2}{9}$ **33.** $5\frac{1}{5}$ **34.** $4\frac{7}{9}$ **35.** $9\frac{1}{4}$ **36.** $2\frac{3}{8}$

37. $7\frac{7}{8}$ **38.** $1\frac{5}{12}$ **39.** $3\frac{3}{7}$ **40.** $6\frac{1}{2}$ **41.** $3\frac{1}{10}$ **42.** $4\frac{6}{7}$

Adding and Subtracting Fractions With Like Denominators

When you add or subtract fractions with the same denominator, add or subtract the numerators and then write the answer over the denominator.

1 EXAMPLE

Add or subtract. Write each answer in simplest form.

a. $\frac{5}{8} + \frac{7}{8}$

$$\frac{5}{8} + \frac{7}{8} = \frac{5+7}{8}$$
$$= \frac{12}{8} = 1\frac{4}{8} = 1\frac{1}{2}$$

b. $\frac{11}{12} - \frac{2}{12}$

$$\frac{11}{12} - \frac{2}{12} = \frac{11-2}{12}$$
$$= \frac{9}{12} = \frac{3}{4}$$

To add or subtract mixed numbers, add or subtract the fractions first. Then add or subtract the whole numbers.

2 EXAMPLE

Add or subtract. Write each answer in simplest form.

a. $3\frac{4}{6} + 2\frac{5}{6}$

$$\begin{array}{r} 3\frac{4}{6} \\ + 2\frac{5}{6} \\ \hline 5\frac{9}{6} = 5 + 1 + \frac{3}{6} = 6\frac{1}{2} \end{array}$$

b. $6\frac{1}{4} - 1\frac{3}{4}$

$$6\frac{1}{4} \rightarrow 5\frac{5}{4} \quad \leftarrow \text{Rewrite 1 unit as } \frac{4}{4} \text{ and add it to } \frac{1}{4}.$$

$$\begin{array}{r} -1\frac{3}{4} \quad -1\frac{3}{4} \\ \hline 4\frac{2}{4} = 4\frac{1}{2} \end{array}$$

EXERCISES

Add or subtract. Write each answer in simplest form.

1. $\frac{4}{5} + \frac{3}{5}$
2. $\frac{2}{6} - \frac{1}{6}$
3. $\frac{2}{7} + \frac{2}{7}$
4. $\frac{7}{8} + \frac{2}{8}$
5. $1\frac{2}{5} - \frac{1}{5}$

6. $\frac{3}{6} - \frac{1}{6}$
7. $\frac{6}{8} - \frac{3}{8}$
8. $\frac{2}{9} + \frac{1}{9}$
9. $\frac{4}{5} - \frac{1}{5}$
10. $\frac{5}{9} + \frac{7}{9}$

11. $9\frac{1}{3} - 8\frac{1}{3}$
12. $8\frac{6}{7} - 4\frac{2}{7}$
13. $3\frac{1}{10} + 1\frac{3}{10}$
14. $2\frac{2}{9} + 3\frac{4}{9}$

15. $4\frac{5}{12} - 3\frac{1}{12}$
16. $9\frac{5}{9} + 6\frac{7}{9}$
17. $5\frac{7}{8} + 2\frac{3}{8}$
18. $4\frac{4}{7} - 2\frac{1}{7}$

19. $9\frac{3}{4} + 1\frac{3}{4}$
20. $8\frac{2}{3} - 4\frac{1}{3}$
21. $8\frac{7}{10} + 2\frac{3}{10}$
22. $1\frac{4}{5} + 3\frac{3}{5}$

23. $7\frac{1}{5} - 2\frac{3}{5}$
24. $4\frac{1}{3} - 1\frac{2}{3}$
25. $4\frac{3}{8} - 3\frac{5}{8}$
26. $5\frac{1}{12} - 2\frac{7}{12}$

Multiplying and Dividing Fractions

To multiply fractions, multiply the numerators and the denominators.
To divide fractions, multiply by the reciprocal of the divisor.

EXAMPLE

Multiply. Write each answer in simplest form.

a. $\dfrac{8}{9} \times \dfrac{3}{10} = \dfrac{\cancel{8}^{4}}{\cancel{9}^{3}} \times \dfrac{\cancel{3}^{1}}{\cancel{10}_{5}} = \dfrac{4}{15}$

b. $3\dfrac{1}{8} \times 1\dfrac{3}{4} = \dfrac{25}{8} \times \dfrac{7}{4}$

$= \dfrac{175}{32} = 5\dfrac{15}{32}$ ← Rewrite as a mixed number.

Divide. Write each answer in simplest form.

c. $\dfrac{2}{3} \div \dfrac{4}{5} = \dfrac{2}{3} \times \dfrac{5}{4}$

$= \dfrac{\cancel{2}^{1}}{3} \times \dfrac{5}{\cancel{4}_{2}} = \dfrac{5}{6}$

d. $3\dfrac{1}{8} \div 1\dfrac{3}{4} = \dfrac{25}{8} \div \dfrac{7}{4}$

$= \dfrac{25}{\cancel{8}_{2}} \times \dfrac{\cancel{4}^{1}}{7} = \dfrac{25}{14} = 1\dfrac{11}{14}$ ← Rewrite as a mixed number.

EXERCISES

Multiply. Write each answer in simplest form.

1. $\dfrac{3}{4} \times \dfrac{3}{5}$ 2. $\dfrac{2}{3} \times \dfrac{3}{4}$ 3. $6 \times \dfrac{2}{3}$

4. $\dfrac{3}{4} \times \dfrac{5}{6}$ 5. $\dfrac{5}{8} \times \dfrac{2}{3}$ 6. $\dfrac{9}{16} \times \dfrac{2}{3}$

7. $\dfrac{3}{10} \times \dfrac{2}{15}$ 8. $\dfrac{3}{4} \times \dfrac{1}{6}$ 9. $\dfrac{1}{4} \times \dfrac{5}{20}$

10. $\dfrac{9}{10} \times \dfrac{1}{3}$ 11. $1\dfrac{1}{3} \times 2\dfrac{2}{3}$ 12. $\dfrac{3}{5} \times 2\dfrac{3}{4}$

13. $2\dfrac{1}{4} \times 3\dfrac{1}{3}$ 14. $\dfrac{1}{4} \times 3\dfrac{1}{3}$ 15. $6\dfrac{1}{4} \times 7$

16. $1\dfrac{3}{4} \times 2\dfrac{1}{5}$ 17. $2\dfrac{3}{4} \times \dfrac{1}{2}$ 18. $3\dfrac{4}{5} \times 2\dfrac{1}{3}$

Divide. Write each answer in simplest form.

19. $\dfrac{5}{8} \div \dfrac{5}{7}$ 20. $\dfrac{5}{7} \div \dfrac{5}{8}$ 21. $\dfrac{3}{4} \div \dfrac{6}{11}$

22. $\dfrac{1}{9} \div \dfrac{1}{9}$ 23. $\dfrac{1}{9} \div 9$ 24. $\dfrac{9}{10} \div \dfrac{3}{5}$

25. $\dfrac{2}{3} \div \dfrac{1}{9}$ 26. $\dfrac{4}{5} \div \dfrac{5}{6}$ 27. $\dfrac{1}{5} \div \dfrac{8}{9}$

28. $\dfrac{7}{8} \div \dfrac{1}{3}$ 29. $4\dfrac{1}{5} \div 2\dfrac{2}{5}$ 30. $6\dfrac{1}{4} \div 4\dfrac{3}{8}$

31. $2\dfrac{1}{3} \div 5\dfrac{5}{6}$ 32. $1\dfrac{1}{2} \div 4\dfrac{1}{2}$ 33. $15\dfrac{2}{3} \div 1\dfrac{1}{3}$

34. $10\dfrac{1}{3} \div 2\dfrac{1}{5}$ 35. $6\dfrac{1}{4} \div 1\dfrac{3}{4}$ 36. $6\dfrac{2}{3} \div 3\dfrac{1}{8}$

Working With Integers

Quantities less than zero can be written using negative integers. For example, a temperature of 5 degrees below zero can be written as -5. Positive integers are used for quantities greater than zero.

1 EXAMPLE

Write an integer for each situation.

a. **10 degrees above zero**
$+10$, or 10

b. **a loss of $20**
-20

c. **15 yards lost**
-15

A number line can be used to compare integers. The integer to the right is greater.

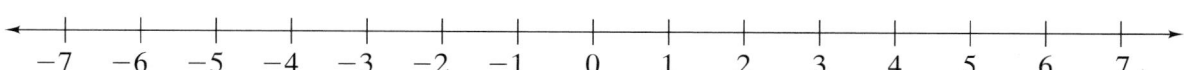

2 EXAMPLE

Compare. Use >, <, or = to complete each statement.

a. **0 ▦ −3**
0 is to the right, so it is greater.
$0 > -3$

b. **−2 ▦ −6**
-2 is to the right, so it is greater.
$-2 > -6$

c. **−7 ▦ 3**
-7 is to the left, so it is less.
$-7 < 3$

EXERCISES

Write an integer for each situation.

1. 6 yards gained
2. 10 yards lost
3. 5 steps forward
4. 4 steps backward

5. find $3
6. lose $8
7. 12 floors up
8. 4 floors down

Compare. Use >, <, or = to complete each statement.

9. 0 ▦ −1
10. −9 ▦ 0
11. −3 ▦ 3
12. 7 ▦ −3
13. 0 ▦ 1

14. 3 ▦ 0
15. 1 ▦ −4
16. −2 ▦ −9
17. 6 ▦ −1
18. 3 ▦ −10

19. −7 ▦ 3
20. 4 ▦ 6
21. −16 ▦ −25
22. −15 ▦ −12
23. 7 ▦ −8

24. 2 ▦ 3
25. −7 ▦ −8
26. 35 ▦ −40
27. −30 ▦ −20
28. 25 ▦ −25

29. 9 ▦ −9
30. −6 ▦ −5
31. −23 ▦ −15
32. −17 ▦ −19
33. −15 ▦ −25

Tables

Table 1 Measures

Metric

Length

10 millimeters (mm) = 1 centimeter (cm)

100 cm = 1 meter (m)

1,000 m = 1 kilometer (km)

Area

100 square millimeters (mm^2) =
    1 square centimeter (cm^2)

10,000 cm^2 = 1 square meter (m^2)

1,000,000 m^2 = 1 square kilometer (km^2)

Volume

1,000 cubic millimeters (mm^3) =
    1 cubic centimeter (cm^3)

1,000,000 cm^3 = 1 cubic meter (m^3)

Mass

1,000 milligrams (mg) = 1 gram (g)

1,000 g = 1 kilogram (kg)

Volume (Capacity)

1,000 milliliters (mL) = 1 liter (L)

1 mL = 1 cm^3

Customary

Length

12 inches (in.) = 1 foot (ft)

3 ft = 1 yard (yd)

36 in. = 1 yd

5,280 ft = 1 mile (mi)

1,760 yd = 1 mi

Area

144 square inches ($in.^2$) = 1 square foot (ft^2)

9 ft^2 = 1 square yard (yd^2)

4,840 yd^2 = 1 acre

Volume

1,728 cubic inches ($in.^3$) = 1 cubic foot (ft^3)

27 ft^3 = 1 cubic yard (yd^3)

Weight

16 ounces (oz) = 1 pound (lb)

2,000 lb = 1 ton (t)

Volume (Capacity)

8 fluid ounces (fl oz) = 1 cup (c)

2 c = 1 pint (pt)

2 pt = 1 quart (qt)

4 qt = 1 gallon (gal)

Time

1 minute (min) = 60 seconds (s)

1 hour (h) = 60 min

1 day (d) = 24 h

1 year (yr) = 365 d

Table 2 📖 Reading Math Symbols

$>$	is greater than	p. 103
$<$	is less than	p. 103
$\geq$	is greater than or equal to	p. 103
$\leq$	is less than or equal to	p. 103
$=$	is equal to	p. 80
$\neq$	is not equal to	p. 80
$\approx$	is approximately equal to	p. 128
$\stackrel{?}{=}$	is this statement true?	p. 81
$+$	plus (addition)	p. 5
$-$	minus (subtraction)	p. 5
$\times, \cdot$	times (multiplication)	p. 5
$\div, \overline{)}$	divide (division)	p. 5
$\sqrt{x}$	nonnegative square root of x	p. 580
$\circ$	degrees	p. 464
$\%$	percent	p. 310
$(\ )$	parentheses for grouping	p. 9
$\lvert a \rvert$	absolute value of a	p. 19
$a:b, \frac{a}{b}$	ratio of a to b	p. 288
(a, b)	ordered pair with x-coordinate a and y-coordinate b	p. 50
$\cong$	is congruent to	p. 465
$\sim$	is similar to	p. 299
$\parallel$	is parallel to	p. 459
π	pi, an irrational number approximately equal to 3.14	p. 486
$f(n)$	function value at n, f of n	p. 418
b	y-intercept	p. 413
m	slope of a line	p. 413
$\begin{bmatrix} 1 & 3 \\ 2 & 4 \end{bmatrix}$	matrix	p. 502
$-a$	opposite of a	p. 19
$\frac{1}{a}$	reciprocal of a	p. 250
a^n	nth power of a	p. 182
d	diameter	p. 486
	distance	pp. 143, 592
A'	image of A, A prime	p. 497
A	Area	p. 522

b_1, b_2	base lengths of a trapezoid	p. 529
b	base length	p. 523
h	height	p. 523
p or P	perimeter	p. 144
ℓ	length	p. 144
	slant height	p. 552
w	width	p. 144
C	circumference	p. 486
S.A.	surface area	p. 545
L.A.	lateral area	p. 546
B	area of a base	p. 546
V	volume	p. 557
r	rate	p. 143
	radius	p. 487
$\overline{AB}$	segment AB	p. 458
$\overrightarrow{AB}$	ray AB	p. 458
$\overleftrightarrow{AB}$	line AB	p. 458
$\triangle ABC$	triangle with vertices A, B, and C	p. 299
$\angle A$	angle with vertex A	p. 464
$\angle ABC$	angle with sides $\overrightarrow{BA}$ and $\overrightarrow{BC}$	p. 464
$m\angle ABC$	measure of angle ABC	p. 465
AB	length of segment $\overline{AB}$	p. 458
$\sin A$	sine of $\angle A$	p. 609
$\cos A$	cosine of $\angle A$	p. 609
$\tan A$	tangent of $\angle A$	p. 609
$P(\text{event})$	probability of an event	p. 305
${}_nP_r$	number of permutations of n things taken r at a time	p. 659
${}_nC_r$	number of combinations of n things taken r at a time	p. 660
$\wedge$	raised to a power (in software or a calculator)	p. 209
$*$	multiply (in software or a calculator)	p. 147
$/$	divide (in software or a calculator)	p. 147

Table 3 Squares and Square Roots

N	N²	√N	N	N²	√N
1	1	1	51	2,601	7.141
2	4	1.414	52	2,704	7.211
3	9	1.732	53	2,809	7.280
4	16	2	54	2,916	7.348
5	25	2.236	55	3,025	7.416
6	36	2.449	56	3,136	7.483
7	49	2.646	57	3,249	7.550
8	64	2.828	58	3,364	7.616
9	81	3	59	3,481	7.681
10	100	3.162	60	3,600	7.746
11	121	3.317	61	3,721	7.810
12	144	3.464	62	3,844	7.874
13	169	3.606	63	3,969	7.937
14	196	3.742	64	4,096	8
15	225	3.873	65	4,225	8.062
16	256	4	66	4,356	8.124
17	289	4.123	67	4,489	8.185
18	324	4.243	68	4,624	8.246
19	361	4.359	69	4,761	8.307
20	400	4.472	70	4,900	8.367
21	441	4.583	71	5,041	8.426
22	484	4.690	72	5,184	8.485
23	529	4.796	73	5,329	8.544
24	576	4.899	74	5,476	8.602
25	625	5	75	5,625	8.660
26	676	5.099	76	5,776	8.718
27	729	5.196	77	5,929	8.775
28	784	5.292	78	6,084	8.832
29	841	5.385	79	6,241	8.888
30	900	5.477	80	6,400	8.944
31	961	5.568	81	6,561	9
32	1,024	5.657	82	6,724	9.055
33	1,089	5.745	83	6,889	9.110
34	1,156	5.831	84	7,056	9.165
35	1,225	5.916	85	7,225	9.220
36	1,296	6	86	7,396	9.274
37	1,369	6.083	87	7,569	9.327
38	1,444	6.164	88	7,744	9.381
39	1,521	6.245	89	7,921	9.434
40	1,600	6.325	90	8,100	9.487
41	1,681	6.403	91	8,281	9.539
42	1,764	6.481	92	8,464	9.592
43	1,849	6.557	93	8,649	9.644
44	1,936	6.633	94	8,836	9.695
45	2,025	6.708	95	9,025	9.747
46	2,116	6.782	96	9,216	9.798
47	2,209	6.856	97	9,409	9.849
48	2,304	6.928	98	9,604	9.899
49	2,401	7	99	9,801	9.950
50	2,500	7.071	100	10,000	10

Table 4 Trigonometric Ratios

Angle	Sine	Cosine	Tangent	Angle	Sine	Cosine	Tangent
1°	0.0175	0.9998	0.0175	46°	0.7193	0.6947	1.0355
2°	0.0349	0.9994	0.0349	47°	0.7314	0.6820	1.0724
3°	0.0523	0.9986	0.0524	48°	0.7431	0.6691	1.1106
4°	0.0698	0.9976	0.0699	49°	0.7547	0.6561	1.1504
5°	0.0872	0.9962	0.0875	50°	0.7660	0.6428	1.1918
6°	0.1045	0.9945	0.1051	51°	0.7771	0.6293	1.2349
7°	0.1219	0.9925	0.1228	52°	0.7880	0.6157	1.2799
8°	0.1392	0.9903	0.1405	53°	0.7986	0.6018	1.3270
9°	0.1564	0.9877	0.1584	54°	0.8090	0.5878	1.3764
10°	0.1736	0.9848	0.1763	55°	0.8192	0.5736	1.4281
11°	0.1908	0.9816	0.1944	56°	0.8290	0.5592	1.4826
12°	0.2079	0.9781	0.2126	57°	0.8387	0.5446	1.5399
13°	0.2250	0.9744	0.2309	58°	0.8480	0.5299	1.6003
14°	0.2419	0.9703	0.2493	59°	0.8572	0.5150	1.6643
15°	0.2588	0.9659	0.2679	60°	0.8660	0.5000	1.7321
16°	0.2756	0.9613	0.2867	61°	0.8746	0.4848	1.8040
17°	0.2924	0.9563	0.3057	62°	0.8829	0.4695	1.8807
18°	0.3090	0.9511	0.3249	63°	0.8910	0.4540	1.9626
19°	0.3256	0.9455	0.3443	64°	0.8988	0.4384	2.0503
20°	0.3420	0.9397	0.3640	65°	0.9063	0.4226	2.1445
21°	0.3584	0.9336	0.3839	66°	0.9135	0.4067	2.2460
22°	0.3746	0.9272	0.4040	67°	0.9205	0.3907	2.3559
23°	0.3907	0.9205	0.4245	68°	0.9272	0.3746	2.4751
24°	0.4067	0.9135	0.4452	69°	0.9336	0.3584	2.6051
25°	0.4226	0.9063	0.4663	70°	0.9397	0.3420	2.7475
26°	0.4384	0.8988	0.4877	71°	0.9455	0.3256	2.9042
27°	0.4540	0.8910	0.5095	72°	0.9511	0.3090	3.0777
28°	0.4695	0.8829	0.5317	73°	0.9563	0.2924	3.2709
29°	0.4848	0.8746	0.5543	74°	0.9613	0.2756	3.4874
30°	0.5000	0.8660	0.5774	75°	0.9659	0.2588	3.7321
31°	0.5150	0.8572	0.6009	76°	0.9703	0.2419	4.0108
32°	0.5299	0.8480	0.6249	77°	0.9744	0.2250	4.3315
33°	0.5446	0.8387	0.6494	78°	0.9781	0.2079	4.7046
34°	0.5592	0.8290	0.6745	79°	0.9816	0.1908	5.1446
35°	0.5736	0.8192	0.7002	80°	0.9848	0.1736	5.6713
36°	0.5878	0.8090	0.7265	81°	0.9877	0.1564	6.3138
37°	0.6018	0.7986	0.7536	82°	0.9903	0.1392	7.1154
38°	0.6157	0.7880	0.7813	83°	0.9925	0.1219	8.1443
39°	0.6293	0.7771	0.8098	84°	0.9945	0.1045	9.5144
40°	0.6428	0.7660	0.8391	85°	0.9962	0.0872	11.4301
41°	0.6561	0.7547	0.8693	86°	0.9976	0.0698	14.3007
42°	0.6691	0.7431	0.9004	87°	0.9986	0.0523	19.0811
43°	0.6820	0.7314	0.9325	88°	0.9994	0.0349	28.6363
44°	0.6947	0.7193	0.9657	89°	0.9998	0.0175	57.2900
45°	0.7071	0.7071	1.0000				

Formulas and Properties

Geometric Formulas

Perimeter and Circumference

Rectangle

$P = 2\ell + 2w$

Circle

$C = \pi d$ or $C = 2\pi r$

Area

Square

$A = s^2$

Parallelogram and Rectangle

$A = bh$

Triangle

$A = \frac{1}{2}bh$

Trapezoid

$A = \frac{1}{2}h(b_1 + b_2)$

Circle

$C = \pi r^2$

Triangle Formulas

Pythagorean Theorem

In a right triangle with legs of lengths a and b and hypotenuse of length c, $a^2 + b^2 = c^2$.

Trigonometric Ratios

$\text{sine of } \angle A = \dfrac{\text{length of leg opposite } \angle A}{\text{length of hypotenuse}}$

$\text{cosine of } \angle A = \dfrac{\text{length of leg adjacent to } \angle A}{\text{length of hypotenuse}}$

$\text{tangent of } \angle A = \dfrac{\text{length of leg opposite } \angle A}{\text{length of leg adjacent to } \angle A}$

Triangle Angle Sum

For any $\triangle ABC$,

$m\angle A + m\angle B + m\angle C = 180°$.

Surface Area

Rectangular Prism

$\text{L.A.} = ph$

$\text{S.A.} = \text{L.A.} + 2B$

Cylinder

$\text{L.A.} = 2\pi rh$

$\text{S.A.} = \text{L.A.} + 2B$

Pyramid

$\text{L.A.} = \frac{1}{2}p\ell = n\left(\frac{1}{2}b\ell\right)$, where n is the number of faces

$\text{S.A.} = \text{L.A.} + B$

Cone

$\text{L.A.} = \pi r\ell$

$\text{S.A.} = \text{L.A.} + B$

Sphere

$\text{S.A.} = 4\pi r^2$

Volume

Prism

$V = Bh$

Cylinder

$V = Bh$, or $\pi r^2 h$

Pyramid

$V = \frac{1}{3}Bh$

Cone

$V = \frac{1}{3}Bh$, or $\frac{1}{3}\pi r^2 h$

Sphere

$V = \frac{4}{3}\pi r^3$

Properties of Real Numbers

Unless otherwise stated, $a, b, c,$ and d are real numbers.

Identity Properties

Addition $a + 0 = a$ and $0 + a = a$

Multiplication $a \cdot 1 = a$ and $1 \cdot a = a$

Commutative Properties

Addition $a + b = b + a$

Multiplication $a \cdot b = b \cdot a$

Associative Properties

Addition $(a + b) + c = a + (b + c)$

Multiplication $(a \cdot b) \cdot c = a \cdot (b \cdot c)$

Inverse Properties

Addition

$a + (-a) = 0$ and $-a + a = 0$

Multiplication

$a \cdot \frac{1}{a} = 1$ and $\frac{1}{a} \cdot a = 1 (a \neq 0)$

Distributive Properties

$a(b + c) = ab + ac$ $(b + c)a = ba + ca$

$a(b - c) = ab - ac$ $(b - c)a = ba - ca$

Properties of Equality

Addition   If $a = b$, then $a + c = b + c$.

Subtraction   If $a = b$, then $a - c = b - c$.

Multiplication If $a = b$, then $a \cdot c = b \cdot c$.

Division   If $a = b$, and $c \neq 0$, then $\frac{a}{c} = \frac{b}{c}$.

Substitution   If $a = b$, then b can replace a in any expression.

Reflexive $a = a$

Symmetric   If $a = b$, then $b = a$.

Transitive   If $a = b$ and $b = c$, then $a = c$.

Zero-Product Property

If $ab = 0$ then $a = 0$ or $b = 0$.

Zero Property of Multiplication

$a \cdot 0 = 0 \cdot a = 0$

Cross Product Property

$\frac{a}{b} = \frac{c}{d}$ is equivalent to $ad = bc$.

Closure Properties

$a + b$ is a unique real number.

ab is a unique real number.

Density Property

Between any two rational numbers, there is at least one other rational number.

Properties of Inequality

Addition   If $a > b$, then $a + c > b + c$.
                    If $a < b$, then $a + c < b + c$.

Subtraction   If $a > b$, then $a - c > b - c$.
                    If $a < b$, then $a - c < b - c$.

Multiplication

If $a > b$ and $c > 0$, then $ac > bc$.

If $a < b$ and $c > 0$, then $ac < bc$.

If $a > b$ and $c < 0$, then $ac < bc$.

If $a < b$ and $c < 0$, then $ac > bc$.

Division

If $a > b$ and $c > 0$, then $\frac{a}{c} > \frac{b}{c}$.

If $a < b$ and $c > 0$, then $\frac{a}{c} < \frac{b}{c}$.

If $a > b$ and $c < 0$, then $\frac{a}{c} < \frac{b}{c}$.

If $a < b$ and $c < 0$, then $\frac{a}{c} > \frac{b}{c}$.

Transitive   If $a > b$ and $b > c$, then $a > c$.

Comparison   If $a = b + c$ and $c > 0$, then $a > b$.

Properties of Exponents

For $a \neq 0$ and any integers m and n:

Zero Exponent $a^0 = 1$

Negative Exponent $a^{-n} = \frac{1}{a^n}$

Product of Powers $a^m \cdot a^n = a^{m+n}$

Quotient of Powers $\frac{a^m}{a^n} = a^{m-n}$

Power of a Power $(a^m)^n = a^{m \cdot n}$

English/Spanish Illustrated Glossary

EXAMPLES

Absolute value (p. 19) Absolute value is the distance of a number from zero on a number line. You write *the absolute value* of −3 as $|-3|$.

The absolute value of −3 is 3 because −3 is 3 units from zero on a number line.

Valor absoluto (p. 19) El valor absoluto de un número es la distancia desde cero hasta ese número en una recta numérica. Escribe "el valor absoluto de 23" como $|-3|$.

Absolute value function (p. 695) An absolute value function is a function with a graph that is V-shaped and opens up or down.

EXAMPLE The absolute value function $y = |x| - 3$ has the graph shown here.

Función de valor absoluto (p. 695) Una función de valor absoluto es una función con una gráfica en forma de V abierta hacia arriba o hacia abajo.

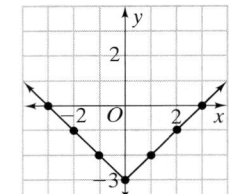

Acute angle (p. 464) An acute angle is an angle with a measure less than 90°.

EXAMPLE $0° < m\angle 1 < 90°$

Ángulo agudo (p. 464) Un ángulo agudo es cualquier ángulo que mide menos de 90°.

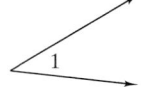

Acute triangle (p. 470) An acute triangle is a triangle with three acute angles.

EXAMPLE $\angle 1$, $\angle 2$, and $\angle 3$ are acute.

Acutángulo (p. 470) Acutángulo es un triángulo que tiene sus tres ángulos agudos.

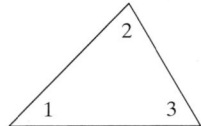

Addition Property of Equality (p. 88) If $a = b$ then $a + c = b + c$.

$8 = 2(4)$, so $8 + 3 = 2(4) + 3$

Propiedad aditiva de la igualdad (p. 88) Si $a = b$, entonces $a + c = b + c$.

Addition Property of Inequality (p. 107) If $a > b$, then $a + c > b + c$. If $a < b$, then $a + c < b + c$.

$7 > 3$, so $7 + 4 > 3 + 4$
$2 < 5$, so $2 + 6 < 5 + 6$

Propiedad aditiva de la desigualdad (p. 107) Si $a > b$, entonces $a + c > b + c$. Si $a < b$, entonces $a + c < b + c$.

Additive identity (p. 67)   The additive identity is zero. When you add a number and 0, the sum equals the original number.

$a + 0 = a$

Identidad aditiva (p. 67)   La identidad aditiva es cero. Cuando se suman un número y 0, la suma es idéntica al número original.

Additive inverses (p. 24)   Additive inverses are two numbers with a sum of zero.

23 and -23 are additive inverses because $-23 + 23 = 0$.

Inversos aditivos (p. 24)   Se llaman inversos aditivos a los números cuya suma es igual a cero.

Adjacent angles (p. 465)   Adjacent angles are two angles that share a vertex and a side but no points in their interiors.

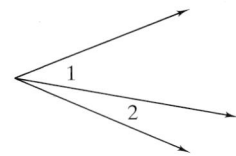

$\angle 1$ and $\angle 2$ are adjacent angles.

Ángulos adyacentes (p. 465)   Ángulos adyacentes son dos ángulos que tienen un mismo vértice y un lado común, pero no tienen puntos interiores comunes.

Alternate interior angles (p. 466)   Alternate interior angles are angles between two lines and on opposite sides of a transversal.

EXAMPLE $\angle 2$ and $\angle 3$ are alternate interior angles. $\angle 1$ and $\angle 4$ are also alternate interior angles.

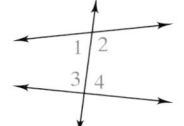

Ángulos alternos internos (p. 466)   Ángulos alternos internos son los pares de ángulos no adyacentes, ambos interiores, en lados opuestos de una transversal.

Altitude (p. 523)   An altitude is any segment perpendicular to the line containing the base of a figure, and drawn from the side opposite the base.

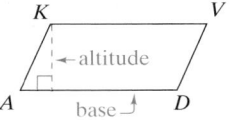

Altura (p. 523)   La altura es cualquier segmento perpendicular a la recta de la base de la figura y se dibuja desde el lado opuesto a la base.

Angle (p. 464)   An angle is a figure formed by two rays with a common endpoint.

EXAMPLE $\angle 1$ is made up of $\overrightarrow{GP}$ and $\overrightarrow{GS}$ with common endpoint G.

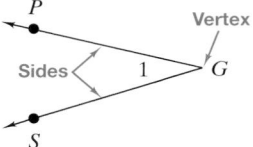

Ángulo (p. 464)   Un ángulo es una figura formada por dos rayos que parten de un origen común.

Angle bisector (p. 493)   An angle bisector is a ray that divides a given angle into two congruent angles, each half the size of the given angle.

EXAMPLE $\overrightarrow{BD}$ is the angle bisector of $\angle ABC$.

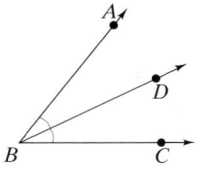

Bisectriz de un ángulo (p. 493)   La bisectriz de un ángulo es el rayo que divide un ángulo dado en dos ángulos congruentes, cada uno de los cuales tiene la mitad de tamaño que el ángulo dado.

English/Spanish Glossary

Angle of depression (p. 616)   An angle of depression is an angle formed by a horizontal line and a line of sight below it.

EXAMPLE $\angle XYZ$ is an angle of depression.

Ángulo de depresión (p. 616)   Un ángulo de depresión es un ángulo que está formado por una recta horizontal y una línea de visión por debajo de ella.

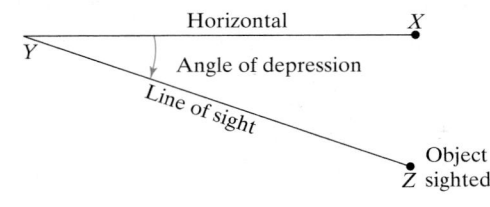

Angle of elevation (p. 614)   An angle of elevation is an angle formed by a horizontal line and a line of sight above it.

EXAMPLE $\angle ABC$ is an angle of elevation.

Ángulo de elevación (p. 614)   Una ángulo de elevación es un ángulo que está formado por una recta horizontal y una línea de visión por arriba de ella.

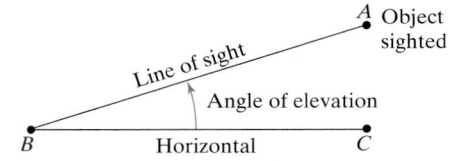

Angle of rotation (p. 507)   See *Rotation*.

Ángulo de rotación (p. 507)   Ver *Rotation*.

Area (p. 522)   The area of a figure is the number of square units it encloses.

EXAMPLE $b = 4$ ft and $h = 6$ ft, so the area is 24 ft^2.

Área (p. 522)   El área de una figura es el número de unidades cuadradas en su interior.

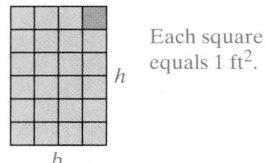

Each square equals 1 ft^2.

Arithmetic sequence (p. 688)   An arithmetic sequence is a sequence of numbers in which each term after the first is the result of adding a fixed number (called the common difference) to the previous term.

The sequence 4, 10, 16, 22, 28, 34, . . . is an arithmetic sequence. The common difference is 6.

Progresión aritmética (p. 688)   Una progresión aritmética es una sucesión de números en la que cada término después del primero resulta de la suma de un mismo número (llamado diferencia común) al término anterior.

Associative Properties of Addition and Multiplication (p. 66)
For any numbers $a, b,$ and $c, (a + b) + c = a + (b + c)$ and $(ab)c = a(bc)$.

$(2 + 7) + 3 = 2 + (7 + 3)$
$(9 \cdot 4)5 = 9(4 \cdot 5)$

Propiedad asociativa de la suma y de la multiplicación (p. 66)   Para cualesquiera números a, b y $c, (a + b) + c = a + (b + c)$ y $(ab)c = a(bc)$.

Balance (p. 383)   The balance in an account is the principal plus the earned interest.

See *Compound interest*.

Balance (p. 383)   El balance de una cuenta es el capital más el interés ganado.

Bar graph (p. 101)   A bar graph is a graph that compares amounts.

EXAMPLE This bar graph compares the numbers of students in grades 6, 7, and 8.

Gráfica de barras (p. 101)   Una gráfica de barras es una gráfica que compara cantidades.

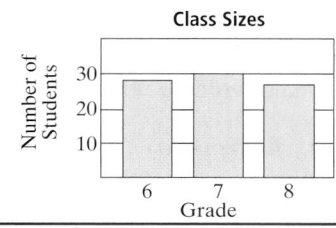

Base (p. 182)   The base is the repeated factor of a number written in exponential form.

Base (p. 182)   La base es el factor repetido de un número que se escribe en forma exponencial.

$$5^4 = 5 \cdot 5 \cdot 5 \cdot 5$$
5 is the base.

Bases of three-dimensional figures (p. 539)   See *Cone, Cylinder, Prism,* and *Pyramid.*

Bases de figuras tridimensionales (p. 539)   Ver *Cone, Cylinder, Prism* y *Pyramid.*

Bases of two-dimensional figures (pp. 522, 527)   See *Parallelogram, Triangle,* and *Trapezoid.*

Bases de figuras bidimensionales (p. 522, 527)   Ver *Parallelogram, Triangle,* y *Trapezoid.*

Binomial (p. 704)   A binomial is a polynomial with two terms.

Binomio (p. 704)   Un binomio es un polinomio con dos términos.

$3x^2 - 1$ is a binomial.

Box-and-whisker plot (p. 635)   A box-and-whisker plot is a graph that shows the distribution of data along a number line. Quartiles divide the data into four equal parts.

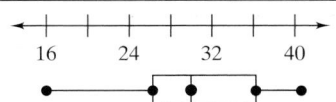

EXAMPLE The box-and-whisker plot at the right is for the data
16 19 26 27 27 29 30 31 34 35 37 39 40.

The lower quartile is 26.5. The median is 30. The upper quartile is 36.

Gráfica de caja y brazos (p. 635)   Una gráfica de caja y brazos presenta la distribución de datos en una recta numérica. Los cuartiles dividen los datos en cuatro partes iguales.

Center of rotation (p. 507)   See *Rotation.*

Centro de rotación (p. 507)   Ver *Rotation.*

Central angle (p. 487)   A central angle is an angle whose vertex is the center of a circle.

Ángulo central (p. 487)   Un ángulo central es un ángulo cuyo vértice está en el centro del círculo.

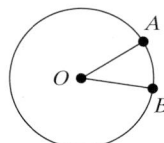

$\angle AOB$ is a central angle.

Chord (p. 486)   A chord of a circle is a segment whose endpoints are on the circle.
EXAMPLE $\overline{AB}$ is a chord of circle O.

Cuerda (p. 486)   Una cuerda es un segmento cuyos extremos se hallan en un círculo.

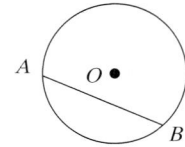

Circle (p. 486)   A circle is the set of all points in a plane that are equidistant from a given point, called the center.
EXAMPLE Circle O

Círculo (p. 486)   Un círculo es un conjunto de puntos en un plano que se hallan a la misma distancia de un punto dado llamado el centro.

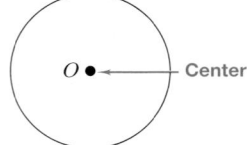

Circle graph (p. 487)   A circle graph is a graph that represents parts of a whole. The total must be 100% or 1.
EXAMPLE This circle graph represents the different types of the plays that William Shakespeare wrote.

Gráfica circular (p. 487)   Una gráfica circular es la gráfica que representa partes de un todo. El total debe ser cien por ciénto o uno.

Circumference (p. 486)   Circumference is the distance around a circle. You calculate the circumference of a circle by multiplying the diameter by π.

Circunferencia (p. 486)   La circunferencia es la distancia alrededor de un círculo. La circunferencia de un círculo se calcula multiplicando el diámetro por π.

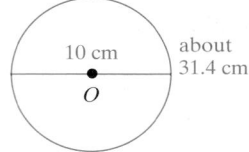

The circumference of the circle is 10π cm, or approximately 31.4 cm.

Coefficient (p. 76)   A coefficient is a number that multiplies a variable.

Coeficiente (p. 76)   Coeficiente es el número que multiplica una variable.

In the expression $2x + 3y - 16$, 2 is the coefficient of x and 3 is the coefficient of y.

Combination (p. 660)   A combination is a group of items in which the order of the items is *not* important. You can use the notation $_nC_r$ to express the number of combinations of n objects chosen r at a time.

Combinación (p. 660)   Una combinación es un conjunto de datos en el cual el orden de sus componentes no es importante. Se puede usar la notación $_nC_r$ para expresar el número de combinaciones de n objetos elegidos r veces a la vez.

The combination (pots and pans) is the same as the combination (pans and pots).

Commission (p. 321)   Commission is pay that is equal to a percent of sales.

Comisión (p. 321)   Una comisión es un pago que equivale a un porcentaje de las ventas.

A saleswoman received a 5% commission on sales of $120. Her commission was $6.

Common difference (p. 688)   See *Arithmetic sequence.*

Diferencia común (p. 688)   Ver *Arithmetic sequence.*

Common ratio (p. 689)   See *Geometric sequence.*

Razón común (p. 689)   Ver *Geometric sequence.*

Commutative Properties of Addition and Multiplication (p. 66)
For any numbers a and b, $a + b = b + a$ and $ab = ba$.

Propiedad conmutativa de la suma (p. 66)   Para cualquier número a y b, $a + b = b + a$, y $ab = ba$.

$6 + 4 = 4 + 6$
$9 \cdot 5 = 5 \cdot 9$

Compass (p. 491)   A compass is a geometric tool used to draw circles and arcs.

Compás (p. 491)   Un compás es un instrumento de geometría que se emplea para trazar círculos y arcos.

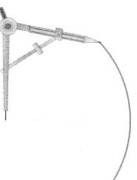

Compatible numbers (p. 133)   Compatible numbers are numbers that are close in value to the numbers you want to add, subtract, multiply, or divide, and for which the operation is easy to perform mentally. Estimating sums, differences, products, and quotients is easy to do mentally when you use compatible numbers.

Números compatibles (p. 133)   Los números compatibles son aquéllos con un valor cercano a los números que deseas sumar, restar, multiplicar o dividir, y con los cuales es fácil hacer los cáculos mentalmente. Cuando calculas sumas, diferencias, productos y cocientes, te resulta más fácil utilizar números compatibles.

Estimate $151 \div 14.6$.
$151 \approx 150$
$14.6 \approx 15$
$150 \div 15 = 10$
$151 \div 14.6 \approx 10$
For $155 \div 14.6$, 150 and 15 are compatible numbers.

Complement of an event (p. 306)   The complement of an event is the opposite of that event. The probability of an event plus the probability of its complement equals 1.

Complemento de un suceso (p. 306)   El complemento de un suceso es el opuesto de ese suceso. La probabilidad de un suceso más la probabilidad de su complemento es igual a 1.

The event *no rain* is the complement of the event *rain*.

English/Spanish Glossary

Complementary angles (p. 465)   Complementary angles are two angles whose measures add to 90°.

EXAMPLE $\angle BCA$ and $\angle CAB$ are complementary angles.

Ángulos complementarios (p. 465)   Dos ángulos son complementarios cuando la suma de sus medidas es 90°.

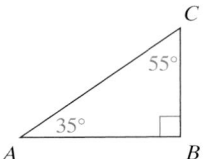

Composite number (p. 186)   A composite number is an integer greater than 1 with more than two positive factors.

Número compuesto (p. 186)   Un número compuesto es el número entero mayor que uno, que tiene más de dos factores positivos.

24 is a composite number that has 1, 2, 3, 4, 6, 8, 12, and 24 as factors.

Compound inequalities (p. 377)   Compound inequalities are two inequalities joined by the word *and* or the word *or*.

Desigualdades compuestas (p. 377)   Desigualdades compuestas son dos desigualdades que están enlazadas por medio de una *y* o una *o*.

$x > 4$ and $x \le 6$

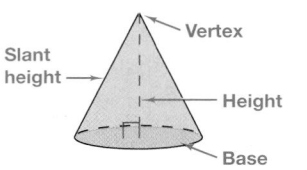

$x \le -2$ or $x > 3$

Compound interest (p. 383)   Compound interest is interest paid on both the principal and the interest earned in previous interest periods. You can use the formula $B = p(1 + r)^n$ where B is the final balance, p is the principal, r is the interest rate for each interest period, and n is the number of interest periods.

Interés compuesto (p. 383)   Interés compuesto es el interés pagado sobre el principal y sobre el interés ganado en previos períodos de interés. Para calcular el interés compuesto, se puede usar la formula $B = p(1 + r)^n$, en donde B es el balance en la cuenta, p es el principal, r es la tasa de interés para cada período y n es el número de períodos de interés.

You deposit $500 in an account earning 5% annual compound interest. The balance after six years is $500(1 + 0.05)^6$, or $670.05. The compound interest is $670.05 - 500$, or $170.05.

Cone (p. 539)   A cone is a space figure with one circular base and one vertex.

Cono (p. 539)   Un cono es una figura tridimensional con una base circular y un vértice.

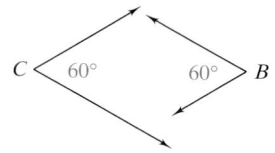

Congruent angles (p. 465)   Congruent angles are angles that have the same measure.

EXAMPLE $\angle B \cong \angle C$

Ángulos congruentes (p. 465)   Ángulos congruentes son los ángulos que tienen la misma medida.

Congruent figures (p. 480) Congruent figures are figures that have the same size and shape. Congruent polygons have congruent corresponding sides and congruent corresponding angles. The symbol $\cong$ means "is congruent to."

EXAMPLE $\overline{AB} \cong \overline{QS}$, $\overline{BC} \cong \overline{SR}$, and $\overline{AC} \cong \overline{QR}$.
$\angle A \cong \angle Q$, $\angle B \cong \angle S$, and $\angle C \cong \angle R$.
Triangles ABC and QSR are congruent.
$\triangle ABC \cong \triangle QSR$

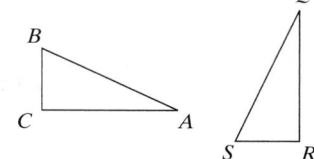

Figuras congruentes (p. 480) Figuras congruentes son las figuras que tienen el mismo tamaño y la misma forma. Los polígonos congruentes tienen lados correspondientes congruentes y ángulos correspondientes congruentes. El símbolo $\cong$ significa "es congruente con."

Congruent segments (p. 491) Congruent segments are segments that have the same length.

Segmentos congruentes (p. 491) Segmentos congruentes son aquéllos que tienen la misma longitud.

$A \bullet\!\!\!-\!\!\!-\!\!\!-\!\!\!-\!\!\!-\!\!\!-\!\!\!-\!\!\!-\!\!\!-\!\!\!\bullet B$

$W \bullet\!\!\!-\!\!\!-\!\!\!-\!\!\!-\!\!\!-\!\!\!-\!\!\!-\!\!\!\bullet X$

$\overline{AB} \cong \overline{WX}$

Conjecture (p. 35) A conjecture is a conclusion reached through inductive reasoning.

Conjectura (p. 35) Una conjectura es una conclusión obtenida usando el razonamiento inductivo.

A dropped piece of toast always lands with its buttered side down.

Consecutive integers (p. 353) Consecutive integers are a sequence of integers obtained by counting by ones from any integer.

Numeros enteros consecutivos (p. 353) Los números enteros consecutivos son una sucesión de enteros que se obtiene al contar en unidades comenzando en cualquier entero.

Three consecutive integers are -5, -4, and -3.

Constant (p. 76) A constant is a term that has no variable.

Constante (p. 76) Constante es un término que no tiene variable.

In the expression $4x - 13y + 17$, 17 is the constant.

Constant of variation (p. 410) A constant of variation is the coefficient k in a direct variation $y = kx$.

Constante de variación (p. 410) Una constante de variación es el coeficiente k en una variación directa $y = kx$.

In the direct variation $y = 3x$, the constant of variation is 3.

Coordinate plane (p. 50)   The coordinate plane is the plane formed by two number lines that intersect at their zero points. The horizontal number line is called the *x*-axis. The vertical number line is called the *y*-axis. The two axes meet at the origin, $O(0, 0)$, and divide the coordinate plane into four quadrants.

Plano de coordenadas (p. 50)   El plano de coordenadas está formado por la intersección de una recta numérica horizontal, llamada el eje de *x*, y una recta numérica vertical, llamada el eje de *y*. Los dos ejes se intersecan en el origen, O $(0, 0)$, y divide el plano de coordenadas en cuatro cuadrantes.

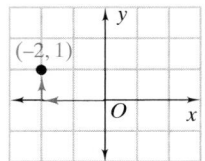

Coordinates (p. 50)   Coordinates are ordered pairs (x, y) that identify points in a coordinate plane. The *x*-coordinate (the first coordinate) shows the horizontal position. The *y*-coordinate (the second coordinate) shows the vertical position.

Coordenadas (p. 50)   Las coordenadas son pares ordenados (x, y), que identifican puntos en el plano de coordenadas. La coordenada *x*, (la primera coordenada) muestra la posición horizontal. La coordenada *y* (la segunda coordenada) muestra la posición vertical.

The ordered pair $(-2, 1)$ describes the point that is found by moving 2 units to the left from the origin and one unit up from the *x*-axis.

Correlation (p. 425)   A correlation is a relation between two sets of data. The data have a *positive correlation* if, as one set of values increases, the other set tends to increase. The data have a *negative correlation* if, as one set of values increases, the other set tends to decrease. The data have little or *no correlation* if the values show no relationship.

Correlación (p. 425)   Una correlación es la relación que hay entre dos conjuntos de datos. Los datos tienen una *correlación positiva* si, a medida que aumenta un conjunto de valores, el otro conjunto tiende a aumentar. Los datos tienen una *correlación negativa* si, a medida que aumenta un conjunto de valores, el otro conjunto tiende a disminuir. Los datos tienen correlación débil o *no tienen correlación* si los valores no muestran relación entre ellos.

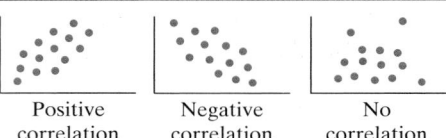

Positive correlation   Negative correlation   No correlation

Corresponding angles (p. 466)   Corresponding angles are pairs of nonadjacent angles that lie on the same side of a transversal of two lines and in corresponding positions.

EXAMPLE $\angle 1$ and $\angle 3$ are corresponding angles.
$\angle 2$ and $\angle 4$ are corresponding angles.

Ángulos correspondientes (p. 466)   Ángulos correspondientes son los pares de ángulos no adyacentes, uno interior y el otro exterior, en el mismo lado de la transversal.

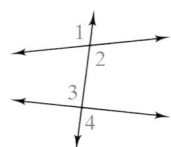

Corresponding angles of polygons (p. 480) Corresponding angles are matching angles of similar or congruent figures.

Ángulos correspondientes de polígonos (p. 480) Ángulos correspondientes son los ángulos equivalentes de figuras semenjantes o congruentes.

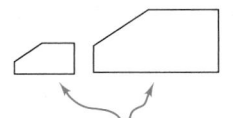

Corresponding angles of similar trapezoids

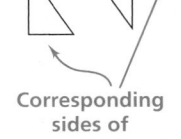

Corresponding angles of congruent triangles

Corresponding sides of polygons (p. 480) Corresponding sides are matching sides of similar or congruent figures.

Lados correspondientes de polígonos (p. 480) Lados correspondientes son los lados equivalentes de figuras semejantes o congruentes.

Corresponding sides of similar polygons

Corresponding sides of congruent triangles

Cosine (p. 608) See *Trigonometric ratios*.

Razón coseno (p. 608) Ver *Trigonometric ratios*.

Counterexample (p. 37) A counterexample is an example that proves a statement false.

Contraejemplo (p. 37) Contraejemplo es todo ejemplo que pruebe la falsedad de un enunciado.

Statement: Motor vehicles have four wheels.

Counterexample: A motorcycle is a motor vehicle with two wheels.

Counting Principle (p. 650) If there are m ways of making one choice and n ways of making a second choice, then there are $m \times n$ ways of making the first choice followed by the second.

Principio de conteo (p. 650) Si hay m maneras de realizar una elección y n maneras de realizar una segunda elección, por lo tanto hay $m \times n$ maneras de realizar la primera elección seguida de la segunda elección.

There are 26 possible choices for each letter of a monogram. Thus, there are $26 \cdot 26$, or 676, possible two-letter monograms.

Cross products (p. 294) Cross products are products formed from a proportion. They are the product of the numerator of the first ratio and the denominator of the second ratio, and the product of the denominator of the first ratio and the numerator of the second ratio. For a proportion, these products are equal.

Productos cruzados (p. 294) Los productos cruzados son los productos formados a partir de una proporción. Son el producto del numerador de la primera razón y del denominador de la segunda razón, y el producto del denominador de la primera razón y del numerador de la segunda razón. Para una proporción, estos productos son iguales.

The cross products for the proportion $\frac{3}{4} = \frac{6}{8}$ are $3 \cdot 8$ and $4 \cdot 6$.
$3 \cdot 8 = 24$ and $4 \cdot 6 = 24$.

Cross section (p. 544)   A cross section is the intersection of a plane and a space figure.

Sección de corte (p. 544)   Una sección de corte es la intersección de un plano y una figura tridimensional.

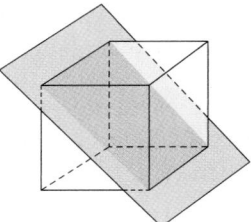

Cube (p. 540)   A cube is rectangular prism with six congruent faces.

Cubo (p. 540)   Un cubo es un prisma rectangular con seis caras congruentes.

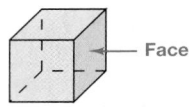

Cubic root (p. 583)   The cube root of a given number is a number whose third power is the given number. The symbol for the cube root of a number is $\sqrt[3]{}$.

Raíz cúbica (p. 583)   La raíz cúbica de un número dado es un número cuya tercera potencia es el número dado. El símbolo de la raíz cúbica de un número es $\sqrt[3]{}$.

$\sqrt[3]{8} = 2$ because $2^3 = 8$.
$\sqrt[3]{-8} = -2$ because $(-2)^3 = -8$.

Cubic unit (p. 557)   A cubic unit is the amount of space occupied by a cube with edges one unit long.

Unidad cúbica (p. 557)   Una unidad cúbica es el espacio que ocupa un cubo cuyos lados tienen una unidad de longitud.

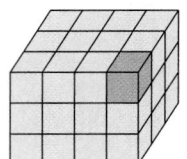

Cylinder (p. 539)   A cylinder is a space figure with two circular, parallel, and congruent bases.

Cilindro (p. 539)   Un cilindro es una figura tridimensional con dos bases circulares, paralelas y congruentes.

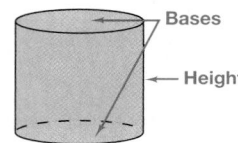

Decagon (p. 474)   A decagon is a polygon with ten sides.

Decágono (p. 474)   Un decágono es un polígono que tiene diez lados.

See *Polygon*.

Deductive reasoning (p. 77)   Deductive reasoning is the process of reasoning logically from given facts to a conclusion.
EXAMPLE   Deductive reasoning is used to simplify the expression $4c + 3(3 + c)$.

Razonamiento deductivo (p. 77)   El razonamiento deductivo es el proceso de razonar lógicamente para llegar a una conclusión a partir de datos dados.

$$4c + 3(3 + c) = 4c + 9 + 3c$$
$$= 4c + 3c + 9$$
$$= (4 + 3)c + 9$$
$$= 7c + 9$$

Dependent events (p. 656)   Dependent events are events for which the occurrence of one event affects the probability of the occurrence of the other.

Sucesos dependientes (p. 656)   Cuando el resultado de un seceso afecta el resultado de un segundo suceso, los sucesos son dependientes.

A bag contains 10 pieces of paper and on each piece is a different number from 1 to 10. A paper is picked and not returned to the bag. The probability of the outcome of the second pick is dependent on the outcome of the first pick.

Diagonal (p. 476)   A diagonal of a polygon is a segment that connects two nonconsecutive vertices.

Diagonal (p. 476)   Una diagonal de un polígono es un segmento que conecta dos vértices no consecutivos.

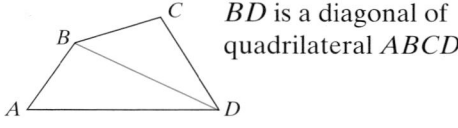

$\overline{BD}$ is a diagonal of quadrilateral $ABCD$.

Diameter (p. 486)   A diameter of a circle is a chord that passes through the center of the circle.

EXAMPLE $\overline{RS}$ is a diameter of circle O.

Diámetro (p. 486)   Un diámetro de un círculo es una cuerda que pasa a través del centro de un círculo.

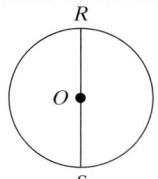

Dilation (p. 304)   A dilation is a transformation that results in a size change. The scale factor, r, describes the size of the change from the original figure to its image. If $r > 1$, the dilation is an enlargement. If r is positive and $r < 1$, the dilation is a reduction.

Dilatación (p. 304)   Una dilatación es una transformación que da como resultado un cambio de tamaño. El factor de escala r describe el tamaño del cambio de la figura original a su reproducción. Si $r > 1$, la dilatación es un agrandamiento. Si $r < 1$, la dilatación es una reducción.

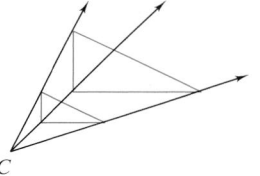

The blue triangle is an enlargement of the red triangle. The red triangle is a reduction of the blue triangle.

Dimensional analysis (p. 254)   Dimensional analysis is a process of analyzing units to decide which conversion factors to use.

Análisis dimensional (p. 254)   El análisis dimensional es el proceso de analizar unidades para decidir qué factores de conversión usar.

$$0.5 \text{ mi} = \frac{0.5 \text{ mi}}{1} \cdot \frac{5,280 \text{ ft}}{1 \text{ mi}} = 2,640 \text{ ft}$$

Direct variation (p. 410)   A direct variation is a linear function modeled by the equation $y = kx$, where $k \neq 0$.

Variación directa (p. 410)   Una variación directa es una función lineal representada por una ecuación $y = kx$, donde $k \neq 0$.

$y = 3x$

Discount (p. 329)   A discount is the amount by which a price is decreased.

Descuento (p. 329)   Descuento es la cantidad en la cual un precio es reducido.

The price of a $10 book is reduced by a discount of $1.50 to sell for $8.50.

English/Spanish Glossary

EXAMPLES

Distance Formula (p. 592)   The distance d between any two points (x_1, y_1) and (x_2, y_2) is $d = \sqrt{(x_2 - x_1)^2 + (y_2 - y_1)^2}$.

Fórmula de distancia (p. 592)   La distancia d entre cualesquiera dos puntos (x_1, y_1) y (x_2, y_2) es $d = \sqrt{(x_2 - x_1)^2 + (y_2 - y_1)^2}$.

The distance between $(6, 3)$ and $(1, 9)$ is d:

$$d = \sqrt{(1 - 6)^2 + (9 - 3)^2}$$
$$= \sqrt{(-5)^2 + 6^2}$$
$$= \sqrt{61}$$
$$\approx 7.8$$

Distributive Property (p. 71)   For any numbers a, b, and c, $a(b + c) = ab + ac$ and $a(b - c) = ab - ac$.

Propiedad distributiva (p. 71)   Para cualquier número a, b y c, $a(b + c) = ab + ac$ y $a(b - c) = ab - ac$

$$2\left(3 + \tfrac{1}{2}\right) = 2 \cdot 3 + 2 \cdot \tfrac{1}{2}$$
$$8(5 - 3) = 8(5) - 8(3)$$

Divisible (p. 178)   Divisible means that the remainder is 0 when you divide one integer by another.

Divisible (p. 178)   Un número entero es divisible por otro número si el residuo es cero.

15 is divisible by 5 because $15 \div 5 = 3$ with remainder 0.

Division Property of Equality (p. 92)   If $a = b$ and $c \neq 0$, then $\frac{a}{c} = \frac{b}{c}$.

Propiedad de igualdad en la división (p. 92)   Si $a = b$ y $c \neq 0$, entonces $\frac{a}{c} = \frac{b}{c}$.

$6 = 3(2)$, so $\frac{6}{3} = \frac{3(2)}{3}$

Division Properties of Inequality (p. 110)   If $a < b$ and c is positive, then $\frac{a}{c} < \frac{b}{c}$. If $a > b$ and c is positive, then $\frac{a}{c} > \frac{b}{c}$. If you divide each side of an inequality by a negative number, you reverse the inequality symbol.
If $a < b$ and c is negative, then $\frac{a}{c} > \frac{b}{c}$.
If $a > b$ and c is negative, then $\frac{a}{c} < \frac{b}{c}$.

Propiedad de división de la desigualdad (p. 110)   Si $a < b$ y c es positivo, entonces $\frac{a}{c} < \frac{b}{c}$. Si $a > b$ y c es positivo, entonces $\frac{a}{c} > \frac{b}{c}$. Si se divide cada lado de una desigualdad por un número negativo, se invierte la dirección del símbolo de desigualdad.

Si $a < b$, y c es negativo, entonces $\frac{a}{c} > \frac{b}{c}$.

Si $a > b$, y c es negativo, entonces $\frac{a}{c} < \frac{b}{c}$.

$3 < 6$, so $\frac{3}{3} < \frac{6}{3}$

$8 > 2$, so $\frac{8}{2} > \frac{2}{2}$

$6 < 12$, so $\frac{6}{-3} > \frac{12}{-3}$

$16 > 8$, so $\frac{16}{-4} < \frac{8}{-4}$

Domain (p. 400)   A domain is the set of first coordinates of the ordered pairs of a relation.

Dominio (p. 400)   Un dominio es el conjunto que comprende todas las primeras coordenadas de los pares ordenados de una relación.

In the relation $\{(0, 1), (-3, 2), (0, 2)\}$, the domain is $\{0, -3\}$.

Edge (p. 539)   An edge is the intersection of two faces of a space figure.

Arista (p. 539)   Un arista es el segmento en donde se intersecan dos caras de una figura tridimensional.

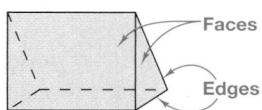

Equation (p. 80)   An equation is a mathematical sentence with an equal sign, =. An equation says that the side to the left of the equal sign has the same value as the side to the right of the equal sign.

$2(6 + 17) = 46$

Ecuación (p. 80)   Una ecuación es un enunciado matemático que contiene un signo igual, =. Una ecuacíon dice que el lado izquierdo del signo igual tiene el mismo valor que el lado derecho del signo igual.

Equilateral triangle (p. 470)   An equilateral triangle is a triangle with three congruent sides.

Triángulo equilátero (p. 470)   Un triángulo es equilátero cuando sus tres lados son congruentes.

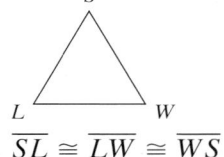

$\overline{SL} \cong \overline{LW} \cong \overline{WS}$

Equivalent fractions (p. 192)   Equivalent fractions are fractions that describe the same part of a whole.

$\frac{3}{4}$ and $\frac{6}{8}$

Fracciones equivalentes (p. 192)   Fracciones equivalentes son fracciones que describen la misma parte de un todo.

Evaluate an expression (p. 14)   To evaluate an expression is to replace each variable with a number, and then follow the order of operations.

To evaluate the expression $3x + 2$ for $x = 4$, substitute 4 for x.
$3x + 2 = 3(4) + 2 = 12 + 2 = 14$

Evaluación de una expresión (p. 14)   Una expresión se evalúa, sustituyendo cada variable con un número. Luego se sigue el órden de las operaciones.

Event (p. 305)   An event is any outcome or group of outcomes.

In a game that includes tossing a coin and rolling a number cube, *tossing heads and rolling a 2* is an event.

Suceso (p. 305)   Un suceso es cualquier resultado o grupo de resultados.

Experimental probability (p. 665)   See *Probability*.

Probabilidad experimental (p. 665)   Ver *Probability*.

Exponent (p. 182)   An exponent is a number that shows how many times a base is used as a factor.

$3^4 = 3 \cdot 3 \cdot 3 \cdot 3$

4 is the exponent.

Exponente (p. 182)   Un exponente es un número que indica las veces que una base se usa como factor.

English/Spanish Glossary

Exponential decay (p. 700) Exponential decay is any function of the form $y = b^x$, where $0 < b < 1$. The graph of the function slopes downward as input values increase.

EXAMPLE The function $y = 10\left(\frac{1}{2}\right)^x$ is graphed for integer values of x from 1 to 5.

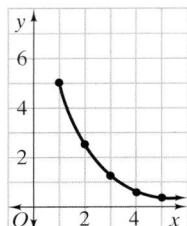

Decremento exponencial (p. 700) Decremento exponencial es cualquier función de la forma $y = b^x$, donde $0 < b < 1$. La gráfica de la función tiene pendiente hacia abajo a medida que aumentan los valores de entrada.

Exponential growth (p. 699) Exponential growth is any function of the form $y = b^x$, where $b > 1$. The graph of the function curves upward as input values increase.

EXAMPLE The function $y = 2^x$ is graphed for integer values of x from 0 to 4.

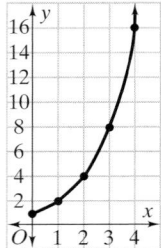

Incremento exponencial (p. 699) Incremento exponencial es cualquier función de la forma $y = b^x$, donde $b > 1$. La gráfica de la función se curva hacia arriba a medida que aumentan los valores de entrada.

Face (p. 539) A face is a surface of a space figure.

Cara (p. 539) Cara es la superficie plana de una figura tridimensional.

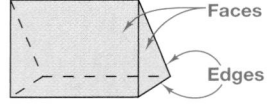

Factor (p. 179) A factor of a nonzero integer is an integer that divides the nonzero integer with remainder zero.

1, 2, 3, 4, 6, 9, 12, 18, and 36 are factors of 36.

Factor (p. 179) Un número entero es factor de otro número entero distinto de cero, cuando lo divide y el residuo es cero.

Formula (p. 143) A formula is an equation that shows a relationship between quantities that are represented by variables.

The formula $P = 4s$ gives the perimeter of a square in terms of the length s of a side.

Fórmula (p. 143) Una fórmula es una ecuación que muestra una relación entre las cantidades que representan las variables.

Frequency table (p. 630) A frequency table is a list of items that shows the number of times, or frequency, with which they occur.

EXAMPLE This frequency table shows the number of household telephones for the students in one school class.

Household Telephones

Phones	Tally	Frequency
1	ⅢⅠ ⅠⅠⅠ	8
2	ⅢⅠ Ⅰ	6
3	ⅠⅠⅠⅠ	4

Tabla de frecuencia (p. 630) Una tabla de frecuencia registra el número de veces, o frecuencia, con que se ha producido un determinado tipo de resultado.

Front-end estimation (p. 128) Front-end estimation is a way to estimate a sum. First add the front-end digits. Round to estimate the sum of the remaining digits. Then combine estimates.

Estimate $3.49 + $2.29.
$3 + 2 = 5$
$0.49 + 0.29 \approx 0.50 + 0.30 = 0.80$
$\$3.49 + \$2.29 \approx \$5 + \$0.80 = \$5.80$

Estimación por la izquierda (p. 128) La estimación por la izquierda se emplea para estimar sumas. Primero, se suman los dígitos delanteros. Luego, se redondea para estimar la suma de los dígitos restantes. Por último se combinan las estimaciones.

Function (p. 400) A function is a relationship in which each member of the domain is paired with exactly one member of the range. A number of the domain is an input and the related number of the range is an output.

Earned income is a function of the number of hours worked (n). If you earn $5/h, then your income is expressed by the function $f(n) = 5n$.

Función (p. 400) Una función es una relación en la que a cada miembro de un dominio le corresponde exactamente un miembro dominio. Un número del dominio es el valor de entrada y el número relacionado del dominio es el valor de salida.

Function notation (p. 418) Function notation is notation that represents a function as $f(x)$ instead of y.

$f(x) = -2x + 1$

Notación de una función (p. 418) La notación de una función es aquélla que representa una función $f(x)$ en vez de y.

Function rule (p. 418) A function rule is an equation that describes a function.

$y = 2x + 5, f(x) = -4x + 3$

Regla de una función (p. 418) La regla de una función es la ecuación que describe una función.

G

Geometric sequence (p. 689) A geometric sequence is a sequence of numbers in which each term after the first is the result of multiplying the previous term by a fixed number (called the common ratio).

The sequence $1, 3, 9, 27, 81, \ldots$ is a geometric sequence. The common ratio is 3.

Progresión geométrica (p. 689) Una progresión geométrica es una sucesión de números en la que cada término, después del primero, es el resultado de la multiplicación del término anterior por un número fijo (llamando razón común).

Greatest common factor (GCF) (p. 187) The greatest common factor of two or more numbers is the greatest factor that the numbers have in common.

The greatest common factor (GCF) of 12 and 30 is 6.

Máximo común divisor (MCD) (p. 187) El máximo común divisor de dos o más números es el mayor divisor que los números tienen en común.

Greatest possible error (p. 258)   The greatest possible error of a measurement is half the unit used for measuring.

Máximo error posible (p. 258)   El máximo error posible de una medida es la mitad de la unidad usada para medir.

The measurement 400 kg is rounded to the nearest hundred kilograms. So, the greatest possible error is 50 kg.

Height of a three-dimensional figure (pp. 546, 547, 566)
See *Cone*, *Cylinder*, *Prism*, and *Pyramid*.

Altura de figuras tridimensionales (pp. 546, 547, 566)
Ver *Cone*, *Cylinder*, *Prism* y *Pyramid*.

Height of a two-dimensional figure (pp. 523, 527, 529)
See *Parallelogram*, *Triangle*, and *Trapezoid*.

Altura de figuras bidimensionales (pp. 523, 527, 529)
Ver *Parallelogram*, *Triangle* y *Trapezoid*.

Hexagon (p. 472)   A hexagon is a polygon with six sides.

Hexágono (p. 472)   Un hexágono es un polígono que tiene seis lados.

See *Polygon*.

Histogram (p. 634)   A histogram is a bar graph in which the heights of the bars give the frequencies of the data. There are no spaces between bars.

EXAMPLE This histogram gives the frequencies of board-game purchases at a local toy store.

Histograma (p. 634)   Un histograma es una gráfica de barras en la cual la altura de las barras representa la frecuencia de los datos. No hay espacio entre las barras.

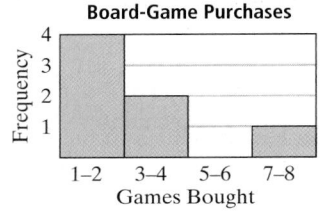

Hypotenuse (p. 584)   In a right triangle, the hypotenuse is the longest side, which is opposite the right angle.

Hipotenusa (p. 584)   La hipotenusa es el lado más largo de un triángulo rectángulo. Es el lado opuesto al ángulo recto.

See *Right triangle*.

Identity Properties of Addition and Multiplication (p. 67)   For any number *a*, the sum of *a* and 0 is *a*. The product of *a* and 1 is 1.

$a + 0 = a$
$a \cdot 1 = a$

Propiedad de identidad de la suma y de la multiplicación (p. 67)
La suma de cero y cualquier número *a* es *a*. El producto de cualquier número *a* y uno es *a*.

Image (p. 497)   An image is the result of the transformation of a point, line, or figure to a new set of coordinates.

See *Transformation*.

Imagen (p. 497)   Una imagen es el resultado de la transformación de un punto, una recta o una figura a un nuevo conjunto de coordenadas.

Improper fraction (p. 244)   An improper fraction is a fraction with a numerator that is greater than or equal to the denominator.

$\frac{24}{15}$ and $\frac{16}{16}$ are improper fractions.

Fracción impropia (p. 244)   Una fracción impropia es una fracción cuyo numerador es mayor o igual que su denominador.

Independent events (p. 654)   Two events are independent events if the occurrence of one event does not affect the probability of the occurrence of the other.

When a number cube is rolled twice, the events rolling 6 and then rolling 3 are independent.

Sucesos independientes (p. 654)   Dos sucesos son independientes si el acontecimiento de uno no afecta la probabilidad de que el otro suceso ocurra.

Indirect measurement (p. 300)   Indirect measurement is a method of determining length or distance without measuring directly.

EXAMPLE   By using the distances shown in the diagram and using properties of similar figures, you can find the height of the taller tower.

$\frac{240}{540} = \frac{x}{1,192} \rightarrow x \approx 529.8$ ft

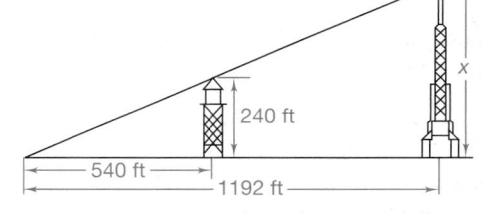

Medición indirecta (p. 300)   La medición indirecta es un método para determinar la longitud o distancia sin medir directamente.

Inductive reasoning (p. 35)   Inductive reasoning is making conclusions based on patterns you observe.

By inductive reasoning, the next number in the pattern $2, 4, 6, 8, \ldots$ is 10.

Razonamiento inductivo (p. 35)   El razonamiento inductivo es sacar conclusiones a partir de patrones observados.

Inequality (p. 102)   An inequality is a sentence that uses one of the symbols $>, <, \geq, \leq,$ or $\neq$.

$0 \leq 2, k > -3, 10 < t$

Desigualdad (p. 102)   Una desigualdad es un enunciado que usa uno de los siguientes símbolos $>, <, \geq, \leq,$ o $\neq$.

Integer (p. 19)   The integers are the whole numbers and their opposites.

$-45, 0,$ and 289 are integers.

Números enteros (p. 19)   Los números enteros son el conjunto de los números enteros positivos (naturales) y sus opuestos.

English/Spanish Glossary

Interest (p. 382)   See *Compound interest* and *Simple interest*.

Interés (p. 382)   Ver *Compound interest* y *Simple interest*.

Interest rate (p. 382)   An interest rate is the percentage of the balance that an account or investment earns in a fixed period of time.

A savings account pays $2\frac{1}{4}\%$ per year.

Tasa de interés (p. 382)   Una tasa de interés es el porcentaje del saldo que gana una cuenta o inversión durante un período fijo.

Inverse operations (p. 86)   Inverse operations are operations that undo each other.

Multiplication and division are inverse operations.

Operaciones inversas (p. 86)   Operaciones inversas son las operaciones que se cancelan una a la otra.

Irrational number (p. 581)   An irrational number is a number whose decimal form neither terminates nor repeats.

The number π, which is approximately equal to 3.141592654, is an irrational number.

Número irracional (p. 581)   Un número irracional es aquél cuyas cifras decimales son infinitas y no se repiten.

Isosceles triangle (p. 470)   An isosceles triangle is a triangle with at least two congruent sides.

EXAMPLE $\overline{LM} \cong \overline{LB}$

$\triangle MLB$ is an isosceles triangle.

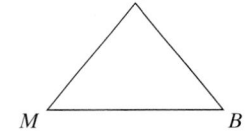

Triángulo isósceles (p. 470)   Un triángulo isósceles es aquel que tiene al menos dos lados congruentes.

Lateral area (p. 546)   The lateral area of a prism is the sum of the areas of the lateral faces.

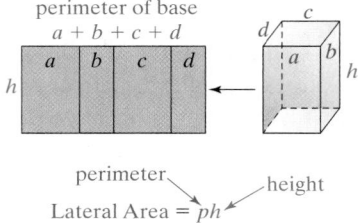

Área lateral (p. 546)   El área lateral de un prisma es la suma de las áreas de las caras laterales.

Lateral face (p. 539)   See *Prism* and *Pyramid*.

Cara lateral (p. 539)   Ver *Prism* y *Pyramid*.

Least common denominator (LCD) (p. 234)   The least common denominator of two or more fractions is the least common multiple (LCM) of their denominators.

The least common denominator (LCD) of the fractions $\frac{3}{8}$ and $\frac{7}{10}$ is $2 \cdot 2 \cdot 2 \cdot 5$, or 40.

Mínimo común denominador (mcd) (p. 234)   El mínimo común denominador de dos o más fracciones es el mínimo común múltiplo (mcm) de sus denominadores.

Least common multiple (LCM) (p. 232)   The least common multiple of two or more numbers is the least number that is a common multiple.

The least common multiple (LCM) of 6 and 15 is $2 \cdot 3 \cdot 5$, or 30.

Mínimo común múltiplo (mcm) (p. 232)   El número menor que es múltiplo común de dos o más números es el mínimo común múltiplo.

Legs of a right triangle (p. 584)   The legs of a right triangle are the two shorter sides of the triangle.

See *Right triangle.*

Catetos de un triángulo rectángulo (p. 584)   Los catetos de un triángulo rectángulo son los lados más cartos del triángulo.

Like terms (p. 76)   Like terms are terms with the same variable(s), raised to the same power(s).

EXAMPLE $3b$ and $12b$ are like terms. Like terms can be combined by using the Distributive Property.

$$3b + 12b = (3 + 12)b$$
$$= 15b$$

Términos semejantes (p. 76)   Términos semejantes son aquellos que tienen la o las mismas variables elevadas a las mismas potencias.

Line (p. 458)   A line is a series of points that extends in opposite directions without end.

EXAMPLE $\overleftrightarrow{AB}, \overleftrightarrow{BA}$, or n represent a line.

Recta (p. 458)   Una recta es una serie de puntos que se extiende infinitamente en direcciones opuestas.

Line graph (p. 100)   A line graph is a graph that shows a relationship between two quantities.

EXAMPLE This line graph shows the change in the number of listeners to station KLZR during the day.

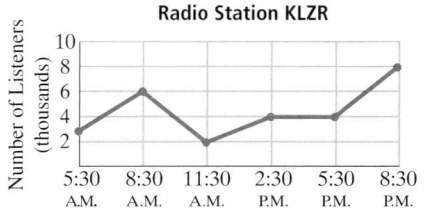

EXAMPLE This multiple line graph represents seasonal air conditioner and snowblower sales (in thousands) for a large chain of stores.

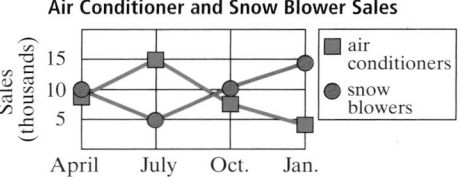

Gráfica lineal (p. 100)   Una gráfica lineal representa la relación que existe entre dos cantidades.

English/Spanish Glossary

Line of reflection (p. 504)   A line of reflection is a line across which a figure is reflected.

See *Reflection*.

Eje de reflexión (p. 504)   Un eje de reflexión es una recta sobre la cual una figura es reflejada.

Line of symmetry (p. 503)   A line of symmetry is a line that divides a figure with reflectional symmetry into two congruent halves.

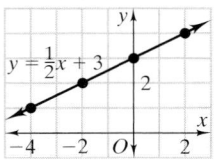
Line of symmetry

Eje de simetría (p. 503)   Un eje de simetría es una recta que divide una figura que tiene simetría de reflexión en dos mitades congruentes.

Line plot (p. 631)   A line plot is a graph that displays data by using X's above a number line.

Heights of Girls

EXAMPLE This line plot shows the numbers of girls on a field hockey team who are at the indicated heights.

```
                    ×
              ×     ×
        ×     ×  ×  ×
  ×  ×  ×  ×  ×  ×
  ─────────────────────→
  45  46  47  48  49  50
      Height in Inches
```

Diagrama de puntos (p. 631)   Un diagrama de puntos es una gráfica que muestra datos marcando una X sobre una recta numérica.

Linear equation (p. 406)   A linear equation is any equation whose graph is a line.

EXAMPLE $y = \frac{1}{2}x + 3$ is linear because its graph is a line.

Ecuación lineal (p. 406)   Una ecuación lineal es cualquier ecuación cuya gráfica de todas sus soluciones es una recta.

Linear inequality (p. 441)   A linear inequality is a number sentence in which the equal sign of a linear equation is replaced with $>$, $<$, $\geq$, or $\leq$.

$y \geq 2x + 3$
$y < -4x - 1$

Desigualdad lineal (p. 441)   Una desigualdad lineal es una proposición numérica en la cual el signo igual de una ecuación lineal se reemplaza con un signo $>$, $<$, $\geq$ o $\leq$.

Lower quartile (p. 635)   The lower quartile is the median of the lower half of a data set.

See *Box-and-whisker plot*.

Cuartil inferior (p. 635)   El cuartil inferior es la mediana de la mitad inferior del conjunto de datos.

M

Markup (p. 329)   Markup is the amount of increase in price. Markup is added to the cost of merchandise to arrive at the selling price.

A store buys a coat for $60 and sells it for $100. The markup is $40.

Sobrecosto (p. 329)   El sobrecosto es la cantidad que se aumenta en precio. El sobrecosto se agrega al costo de la mercadería y eso da el precio de venta.

Matrix (p. 502) A matrix is a rectangular arrangement of numbers.

Matriz (p. 502) Una matriz es una organización de números dispuestos en forma rectangular.

$$\begin{bmatrix} 0 & -1 & -4 \\ 0 & 4 & 0 \end{bmatrix}$$

Mean (p. 137) The mean of a collection of data is the sum of the data items divided by the number of data items.

Media (p. 137) La media de un conjunto de datos resulta de la suma de los datos dividida entre el número de componentes de los datos.

The mean temperature (°F) for the temperatures 44, 52, 48, 55, 61, 67, and 58 is 55.

Measures of central tendency (p. 137) Measures of central tendency in statistics are *mean*, *median*, and *mode*.

Medidas de tendencia central (p. 137) En estadistia, la *media*, la *mediana* y la *moda* son medidas de tendencia central en la estadística.

See *Mean*, *Median*, and *Mode*.

Median (p. 137) The median of a collection of data is the middle number when there is an odd number of data items and they are written in order. For an even number of data items, the median is the mean of the two middle numbers.

Mediana (p. 137) La mediana es el número central de un conjunto de datos, cuando hay un número impar de datos y éstos están dispuestos en orden. Si hay un número par de datos, la mediana es la media de los dos números centrales.

The median temperature (°F) for the temperatures 44, 48, 52, 55, 58, 61, and 67 is 55.

Midpoint Formula (p. 594) The midpoint of a line segment with endpoints $A(x_1, y_1)$ and $B(x_2, y_2)$ is $\left(\frac{x_1 + x_2}{2}, \frac{y_1 + y_2}{2}\right)$.

Fórmula del punto medio (p. 594) El punto medio de un segmento con puntos extremos $A(x_1, y_1)$ y $B(x_2, y_2)$ es $\left(\frac{x_1 + x_2}{2}, \frac{y_1 + y_2}{2}\right)$.

The midpoint of $A(-3, 2)$ and $B(7, -2)$ is $\left(\frac{-3 + 7}{2}, \frac{2 + -2}{2}\right)$, or $(2, 0)$.

Mixed number (p. 237) A mixed number is the sum of a whole number and a fraction.

Número mixto (p. 237) Un número mixto es la suma de un número entero y una fracción.

$3\frac{11}{16}$ is a mixed number.
$3\frac{11}{16} = 3 + \frac{11}{16}$

Mode (p. 137) The mode of a collection of data is the data item that occurs most often. There can be no mode, one mode, or more than one mode.

Moda (p. 137) La moda de un conjunto de datos es el dato que se presenta con mayor frecuencia. Puede no haber moda, una moda o más de una moda.

The mode of the collection of numbers 3, 4, 1, 3, 2, 2, 5, 3 is 3.

English/Spanish Glossary

Monomial (p. 704)   A monomial is a real number, a variable, or a product of a real number and variables with whole number exponents.

$5x$, -4, and y^3 are all monomials.

Monomio (p. 704)   Un monomio es un número real, una variable o el producto de un número real y variables con exponentes que sean números enteros.

Multiple (p. 232)   A multiple of a number is the product of that number and any nonzero whole number.

The multiples of 13 are 13, 26, 39, 52, and so on.

Múltiplo (p. 232)   El múltiplo de un número es el producto de dicho número y cualquier otro número entero distinto de cero.

Multiple line graph (p. 100)   A multiple line graph is a graph that shows more than one data set changing over time.

See *Line graph.*

Gráfica multilineal (p. 100)   Una gráfica multilineal representa las variaciones de más de un conjunto de datos en el tiempo.

Multiplication Property of Equality (p. 93)   If $a = b$, then $ac = bc$.

$12 = 3(4)$, so $12 \cdot 2 = 3(4) \cdot 2$

Propiedad multiplicativa de la igualdad (p. 93)   Si $a = b$, entonces $ac = bc$.

Multiplication Properties of Inequality (p. 111)   If $a < b$, and c is positive, then $ac < bc$. If $a > b$, and c is positive, then $ac > bc$.

$3 < 4$, so $3(5) < 4(5)$
$7 > 2$, so $7(6) > 2(6)$

If you multiply each side of an inequality by a negative number, you reverse the inequality symbol.

If $a < b$, and c is negative, then $ac > bc$. If $a > b$, and c is negative, then $ac < bc$.

$6 < 9$, so $6(-2) > 9(-2)$
$7 > 5$, so $7(-3) < 5(-3)$

Propiedad multiplicativa de la desigualdad (p. 111)   Si $a < b$, y c es positivo, entonces $ac < bc$. Si $a > b$, y c es positivo, entonces $ac > bc$. Si se multiplica cada lado de una desigualdad por un número negativo, se invierte la dirección del signo de la desigualdad. Si $a < b$, y c es negativo, entonces $ac > bc$. Si $a > b$, y c es negativo, entonces $ac < bc$.

Multiplicative identity (p. 67)   The multiplicative identity is 1. For any number a, the product of a and 1 is a.

$a \cdot 1 = a$

Identidad multiplicativa (p. 67)   La identidad multiplicativa es 1. Cuando se multiplica un número por uno, el producto es igual al número original.

Multiplicative inverse (p. 250)   The multiplicative inverse of a number is its reciprocal.

The multiplicative inverse of $\frac{4}{9}$ is $\frac{9}{4}$.

Inverso multiplicativo (p. 250)   El inverso multiplicativo de un número es su recíproco.

Negative correlation (p. 425)   See *Correlation*.

Correlación negativa (p. 425)   Ver *Correlation*.

Net (p. 540)   A net is a pattern that can be folded to form a space figure.
EXAMPLE This net can be folded to form a cube.

Plantilla (p. 540)   Una plantilla es un patrón que se puede doblar para formar una figura tridimensional.

No correlation (p. 425)   See *Correlation*.

Sin correlación (p. 425)   Ver *Correlation*.

O

Obtuse angle (p. 464)   An obtuse angle is an angle with a measure greater than 90° and less than 180°.

Ángulo obtuso (p. 464)   Un ángulo obtuso es un ángulo que mide más de 90° y menos de 180°.

Obtuse triangle (p. 470)   An obtuse triangle is a triangle with one obtuse angle.
EXAMPLE $\triangle NJX$ is an obtuse triangle, since $\angle J$ is an obtuse angle.

Triángulo obtusángulo (p. 470)   Un triángulo es obtusángulo cuando contiene un ángulo obtuso.

Octagon (p. 476)   An octagon is a polygon with eight sides.

Octágono (p. 476)   Un octágono es un polígono que tiene ocho lados.

See *Polygon*.

Odds (p. 307)   Odds are a ratio that describe the likelihood of an event. Odds in favor of an event $= \frac{\text{number of favorable outcomes}}{\text{number of unfavorable outcomes}}$.

For the toss of a coin, the odds in favor of tossing heads are 1 to 1.

Posibilidades (p. 307)   Las posibilidades son la razón que describe la probabilidad de que ocurra un suceso. Posibilidades favorables de que ocurra un evento $= \frac{\text{número de sucesos favorables}}{\text{número de resultados no favorables}}$.

Open sentence (p. 80)   An open sentence is an equation with one or more variables.

$3a = 5a + 8$

Proposición abierta (p. 80)   Una proposición abierta es una ecuación con una o más variables.

Opposites (p. 19)   Opposites are numbers that are the same distance from zero on the number line but in opposite directions.

Números opuestos (p. 19)   Números opuestos son los números que se hallan a la misma distancia de cero en una recta, numérica pero en direcciones opuestas.

-17 and 17 are opposites because they are both 17 units from zero on the number line.

Order of operations (pp. 9, 183)
  1. Work inside grouping symbols.
  2. Simplify any terms with exponents.
  3. Multiply and divide in order from left to right.
  4. Add and subtract in order from left to right.

Orden de las operaciones (pp. 9, 183)
  1. Efectúa las operaciones que están dentro de los signos de agrupación.
  2. Trabaja con los exponentes.
  3. Multiplica y divide en orden de izquierda a derecha.
  4. Suma y resta en orden de izquierda a derecha.

$2^3(7 - 4) = 2^3(3) = 8 \cdot 3 = 24$

Ordered pair (p. 50)   An ordered pair is a pair of numbers that gives the location of a point in a coordinate plane. The first number is the x-coordinate and the second number is the y-coordinate.

Par ordenado (p. 50)   Un par ordenado es un par de números que describe la localización de un punto en un plano de coordenadas. El primer número es la coordenada x y el segundo número es la coordenada y.

See *Coordinates*.

Origin (p. 50)   The origin is the intersection of the x-axis and the y-axis in a coordinate plane. The ordered pair $(0, 0)$ describes the origin.

Origen (p. 50)   El origen el punto de intersección de los ejes de x y de y en un plano de coordenadas. El par ordenado $(0, 0)$ describe el origen.

See *Coordinate plane*.

Outcomes (p. 305)   Outcomes are the possible results of an action.

Resultados (p. 305)   Se llama resultados a los posibles efectos o consecuencias de una acción.

Heads is an outcome of tossing a coin.

Outlier (p. 138)   An outlier is a data value that is much higher or lower than the other data values in a collection of data.

Extremo (p. 138)   Un extremo es el valor de un conjunto de datos que es mucho mayor o menor que el resto de los datos.

An outlier in the data $1, 1, 2, 3, 4, 4, 6, 7, 7, 52$ is 52.

Parabola (p. 694) A parabola is the graph of a quadratic function. It is U-shaped.

EXAMPLE This parabola is the graph of the equation $y = x^2 - 2$.

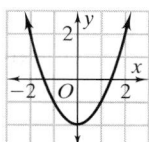

Parábola (p. 694) Una parábola es la gráfica de una ecuación cuadrática. Tiene la forma de U.

Parallel lines (p. 459) Parallel lines are lines that lie in the same plane and do not intersect. The symbol $\parallel$ means "is parallel to."

EXAMPLE $\overleftrightarrow{EF} \parallel \overleftrightarrow{HI}$

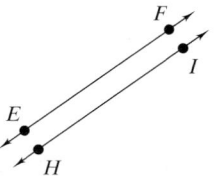

Rectas paralelas (p. 459) Rectas paralelas son las rectas que se encuentran en un mismo plano y no se cortan. El símbolo de dos rectas verticales paralelas significa "es paralelo a".

Parallelogram (p. 471) A parallelogram is a quadrilateral with both pairs of opposite sides parallel.

EXAMPLE $KVDA$ is a parallelogram.

$\overline{KV} \parallel \overline{AD}$ and $\overline{AK} \parallel \overline{DV}$.

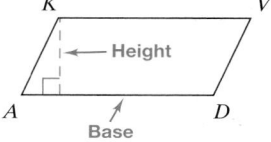

Paralelogramo (p. 471) Un paralelogramo es un cuadrilátero en el cual los lados opuestos son paralelos.

Pentagon (p. 472) A pentagon is a polygon with five sides.

See *Polygon*.

Pentágono (p. 472) Un pentágono es un polígono que tiene cinco lados.

Percent (p. 310) A percent is a ratio that compares a number to 100. The symbol for percent is %.

$\dfrac{50}{100} = 50\%$

Porcentaje (p. 310) Un porcentaje es una razón que compara un número con cien. El símbolo de porcentaje es %.

Percent of change (p. 325) Percent of change is the percent something increases or decreases from its original amount.

A school's population increases from 500 to 520 students. The percent of change is $\dfrac{520 - 500}{500} = 4\%$.

Porcentaje de cambio (p. 325) El porcentaje de cambio es el porcentaje en que algo aumenta o disminuye en relación con su valor original.

Perfect square (p. 580) A perfect square is the square of an integer.

$3^2 = 9$, so 9 is a perfect square.

Cuadrado perfecto (p. 580) Un cuadrado perfecto es un número natural que es igual a la segunda potencia de un número entero.

English/Spanish Glossary

Perimeter (p. 144)   The perimeter of a figure is the distance around the figure. To find the perimeter of a rectangle, find the sum of the lengths of all its sides, or use the formula $P = 2\ell + 2w$.
EXAMPLE The perimeter of $ABCD$ is 12 ft.

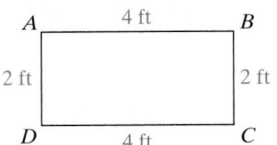

Perímetro (p. 144)   El perímetro de una figura es la suma de las longitudes de sus lados. Para hallar el perímetro de un rectángulo, halla la suma de los largos de todos los lados o usa la fórmula $P = 2\ell + 2w$.

Permutation (p. 659)   A permutation is an arrangement of items in a particular order. You can use the notation $_nP_r$ to express the number of permutations of n objects chosen r at a time.

The seating plans (Judith, Ann, Adrian) and (Ann, Judith, Adrian) are two different permutations.

Permutación (p. 659)   Una permutación es una colocación de objetos en un determinado orden. Se puede usar la notación $_nP_r$ para expresar el número de permutaciónes de n objetos elegidos r a la vez.

Perpendicular bisector (p. 492)   A perpendicular bisector is a line, segment, or ray that is perpendicular to a segment at its midpoint.
EXAMPLE $\overleftrightarrow{FG}$ is the perpendicular bisector of $\overline{DE}$.

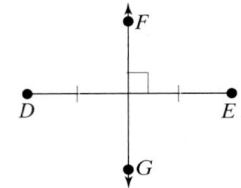

Mediatriz (p. 492)   Una mediatriz es una recta, segmento o rayo que es perpendicular a un segmento en su punto medio.

Perpendicular lines (p. 492)   Perpendicular lines are lines that intersect to form right angles.

Rectas perpendiculares (p. 492)   Rectas perpendiculares son aquellas que se cortan para formar ángulos rectos.

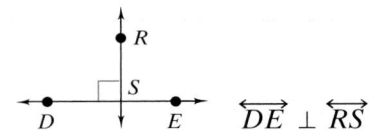

$$\overleftrightarrow{DE} \perp \overleftrightarrow{RS}$$

Pi (p. 486)   Pi (π) is the name for the ratio of the circumference C to the diameter d of a circle.

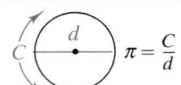

$$\pi = \frac{C}{d}$$

Pi (p. 486)   Pi (π) es el nombre de la razón de la circumferencia C al diámetro d de un círculo.

Plane (p. 458)   A plane is a flat surface that has no thickness and extends without end in the directions of all the lines it contains.

Plano (p. 458)   Un plano es una superficie plana que no tiene grosor y que se extiende indefinidamente en las direcciónes de todas las líneas que contiene.

$ABCD$ or M is a plane.

Point (p. 458)   A point is a location in space that has no size.

$\cdot\,A$

Punto (p. 458)   Un punto es una posición en el espacio. No tiene dimensiones, solamente tiene localización.

A is a point.

Polygon (p. 470)   A polygon is a closed plane figure with at least three sides.

Polígono (p. 470)   Un polígono es una figura plana cerrada formada por tres o más lados.

Polynomial (p. 704)   A polynomial is a monomial or a sum or difference of monomials.

Polinomio (p. 704)   Un polinomio es un monomio o la suma o la diferencia de dos o más monomios.

$4x^2 - 3x + 7$ is a polynomial.

Population (p. 669)   A population is a group about which you want information.

Población (p. 669)   Una población es un grupo sobre el cual se reúne información.

See *Sample*.

Positive correlation (p. 425)   See *Correlation*.

Correlación positiva (p. 425)   Ver *Correlation*.

Power (p. 182)   A power is any expression in the form a^n. *Power* is also used to refer to the exponent.

Potencia (p. 182)   Una potencia es cualquier expresión de la forma a^n. La potencia también se usa para referirse al exponente.

5^4 is a power and can be read as "five to the fourth power."

Precision in measurement (p. 162)   The precision of a measurement is its exactness. A measurement cannot be more precise than the precision of the measuring tool used.

Precisión de una medición (p. 162)   La precisión de una medición se refiere a su grado de exactitud. Una medida no puede ser más precisa que la precisión del instrumento de medida utilizado.

A hundredth of a meter is a smaller unit than a tenth of a meter. So, 2.72 m is more precise than 2.7 m.

Prime factorization (p. 187)   The prime factorization of a number is the expression of the number as the product of its prime factors.

Descomposición en factores primos (p. 187)   La descomposición en factores primos de un número es la expresión de dicho número como el producto de sus factores primos.

The prime factorization of 30 is $2 \cdot 3 \cdot 5$.

Prime number (p. 186)   A prime number is an integer greater than 1 with only two positive factors, 1 and itself.

Número primo (p. 186)   Un número primo es un número natural que tiene exactamente dos factores positivos, 1 y él mismo.

13 is a prime number because its only factors are 1 and 13.

Principal (p. 382)   The principal is the initial amount of an investment or loan.

See *Simple interest*.

Capital (p. 382)   El capital es el monto inicial de una inversión o préstamo.

Prism (p. 539)   A prism is a space figure with two parallel and congruent polygonal faces, called bases, and lateral faces that are parallelograms. A prism is named for the shape of its base.

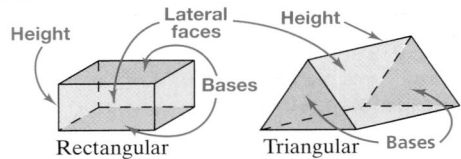

Prisma (p. 539)   Un prisma es una figura tridimensional con dos caras poligonales congruentes y paralelas llamadas bases, y caras laterales paralelas. Un prisma recibe su nombre de acuerdo a la forma de las bases.

Probability (p. 305)   The *theoretical probability* of an event E is $P(E) = \frac{\text{number of favorable outcomes}}{\text{number of possible outcomes}}$ when outcomes are equally likely. The *experimental probability* of an event E is $P(E) = \frac{\text{number of times an event occurs}}{\text{number of times experiment is done}}$. Experimental probability is based on experimental data.

The theoretical probability of spinning the number 4 is $\frac{1}{8}$.

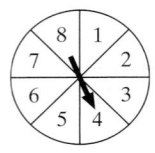

Probabilidad (p. 305)   La *probabilidad teorica* de un suceso E es $P(E) = \frac{\text{número de resultados favorables}}{\text{número de resultados posibles}}$ cuando los resultados tienen la misma posibilidad de producirse.

La *probabilidad experimental* de un suceso E es $P(E) = \frac{\text{número de veces que ocurre un suceso}}{\text{número de veces que se realiza un experimento}}$. La probabilidad experimental se basa en datos experimentales.

In 100 trials, you spin the number 4 ten times. The experimental probability of spinning 4 is $\frac{10}{100}$, or $\frac{1}{10}$.

Proportion (p. 294)   A proportion is an equality of two ratios.

$\frac{3}{12} = \frac{12}{48}$ is a proportion.

Proporción (p. 294)   Una proporción es una igualdad de dos razones.

Pyramid (p. 539)   A pyramid is a space figure with triangular faces that meet at a vertex, and a base that is a polygon. A pyramid is named for the shape of its base.

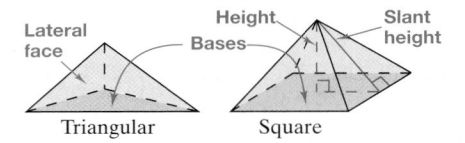

Pirámide (p. 539)   Una pirámide es una figura tridimensional con caras triangulares que convergen en un vértice, y una base que es un polígono. Una pirámide recibe su nombre de acuerdo a la forma de la base.

Pythagorean Theorem (p. 584)   In any right triangle, the sum of the squares of the lengths of the legs (a and b) is equal to the square of the length of the hypotenuse (c): $a^2 + b^2 = c^2$.

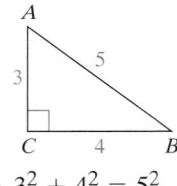

Teorema de Pitágoras (p. 584)   Para cualquier triángulo rectángulo, la suma del cuadrado de las longitudes de los catetos (a y b) es igual al cuadrado de la longitud de la hipotenusa (c): $a^2 + b^2 = c^2$.

$3^2 + 4^2 = 5^2$

Quadrants (p. 50)   Quadrants are the four regions determined by the x- and y-axes of the coordinate plane.

See *Coordinate plane.*

Cuadrante (p. 50)   El eje de x y el eje de y dividen el plano de coordenadas en cuatro regiones llamadas cuadrantes.

Quadratic function (p. 694)   A quadratic function is a function based on squaring the input variable. The graph of a quadratic function is a parabola.

See *Parabola.*

Función cuadrática (p. 694)   Una función cuadrática es la función que tiene una variable elevada a la segunda potencia. La gráfica de una función cuadrática es una párabola.

Quadrilateral (p. 471)   A quadrilateral is a polygon with four sides.

See *Polygon.*

Cuadrilátero (p. 471)   Un cuadrilátero es un polígono con cuatro lados.

Quartiles (p. 635)   Quartiles are numbers that divide a data set into four equal parts.

See *Box-and-whisker plot.*

Cuartiles (p. 635)   Los cuartiles son números que dividen un conjunto de datos en cuatro partes iguales.

Radius (plural is radii) (p. 486)   A radius of a circle is a segment that has one endpoint at the center of the circle and the other endpoint on the circle.
EXAMPLE $\overline{OA}$ is a radius of circle O.

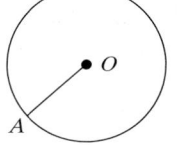

Radio (p. 486)   El radio de un círculo es un segmento que tiene un extremo en el centro y el otro en el círculo.

Random sample (p. 669)   A random sample is a sample of a population for which each member of the population has an equal chance of being selected.

For the population *customers at a mall,* a random sample could be every 20th customer entering for a 2-hour period.

Muestra aleatoria (p. 669)   Una muestra aleatoria es una muestra de una población, de la cual cada miembro tiene la misma probabilidad de ser escogido.

Range of a relation (p. 400)   A range is the set of second coordinates of the ordered pairs of a relation.

In the relation $\{(0, 1), (-3, 2), (0, 2)\}$, the range is $\{1, 2\}$.

Recorrido de una relación (p. 400)   Un recorrido es el conjunto que comprende todas las segundas coordenadas de los pares ordenados de una relación.

English/Spanish Glossary

Range of a set of data (p. 631)   The range is the difference between the greatest and least values in a set of data.

The range of the data 7 9 15 3 18 2 16 14 14 20 is $20 - 2 = 18$.

Amplitud de un conjunto de datos (p. 631)   La amplitud es la diferencia entre los valores mayor y menor de un conjunto de datos.

Rate (p. 289)   A rate is a ratio that compares quantities measured in different units.

A student typed 1,100 words in 50 minutes for a typing rate of 1,100 words per 50 minutes, or 22 words/minute.

Tasa (p. 289)   Una tasa es una razón que compara dos cantidades medidas en unidades diferentes.

Ratio (p. 288)   A ratio is a comparison of two quantities by division.

There are three ways to write a ratio: 72 to 100, 72 : 100, and $\frac{72}{100}$.

Razón (p. 288)   Una razón es la comparación de dos números mediante una división.

Rational number (p. 201)   A rational number is any number you can write as a quotient of two integers $\frac{a}{b}$, where b is not zero.

$\frac{3}{5}$, -8, 8.7, $0.333\ldots$, $-5\frac{3}{11}$, 0, and $\frac{17}{4}$ are rational numbers.

Número racional (p. 201)   Un número racional es cualquier número que puede escribirse como el cociente de dos enteros $\frac{a}{b}$, donde b es distinto de cero.

Ray (p. 458)   A ray is a part of a line. It has exactly one endpoint. Its endpoint is named first.

Rayo (p. 458)   Un rayo es una parte de una recta. Tiene exactamente un extremo. El extremo se nombre primero.

$\overrightarrow{SW}$ represents a ray.

Real number (p. 581)   A real number is a rational number or an irrational number.

3, -5.25, $3.141592653\ldots$, and $\frac{7}{8}$ are real numbers.

Números reales (p. 581)   Un número real es un número racional o un número irracional.

Reciprocal (p. 250)   Reciprocals are two numbers with a product of 1.

$\frac{4}{9}$ and $\frac{9}{4}$ are reciprocals.

$\frac{4}{9} \cdot \frac{9}{4} = 1$.

Recíprocos (p. 250)   Dos números son recíprocos cuando su producto es 1.

Rectangle (p. 471)   A rectangle is a parallelogram with four right angles.

EXAMPLE *RSWH* is a rectangle.

Rectángulo (p. 471)   Un rectángulo es un paralelogramo con cuatro ángulos rectos.

Reflection (p. 504)   A reflection is a transformation that flips a figure over a line of reflection.

EXAMPLE   *K'L'M'N'* is the reflection of *KLMN* across the *y*-axis. The *y*-axis is the line of reflection.

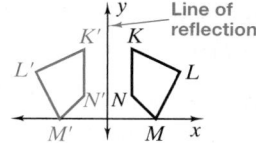

Reflexión (p. 504)   Una reflexión es una transformación que invierte una figura a través de un eje de reflexión.

Reflectional symmetry (p. 503)   A figure has reflectional symmetry when one half of the figure is a mirror image of the other half. The line of reflection is also called the line of symmetry.

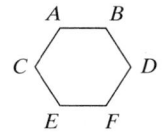

Simetría de reflexión (p. 503)   Una figura tiene simetría de reflexión cuando la mitad de la figura es una imagen refleja de la otra mitad. El eje de reflexión también se llama eje de simetría.

Regular polygon (p. 472)   A regular polygon is a polygon with all its sides congruent and all its angles congruent.

EXAMPLE   *ABDFEC* is a regular hexagon.

Polígono regular (p. 472)   Un polígono regular tiene todos sus lados congruentes y todos sus ángulos son congruentes.

Relation (p. 400)   A relation is a set of ordered pairs.

$\{(0, 2), (-3, 2), (0, 1)\}$ is a relation.

Relación (p. 400)   Una relación es un conjunto de pares ordenados.

Relatively prime (p. 190)   Two numbers are relatively prime if their GCF is 1.

9 and 20 are relatively prime.

Números primos entre sí (p. 190)   Dos números son primos entre sí, si su máximo conúm divisor es 1.

Repeating decimal (p. 238)   A repeating decimal is a decimal in which the same block of digits repeats without end. The symbol for a repeating decimal is a bar drawn over the digit or digits that repeat.

$0.8888 \ldots = 0.\overline{8}$

Decimal periódico (p. 238)   Un decimal periódico es un decimal cuyos dígitos se repiten indefinidamente. El símbolo de un decimal periódico es una raya trazada encima del dígito o dígitos que se repiten.

Rhombus (p. 471)   A rhombus is a parallelogram with four congruent sides.

EXAMPLE   *GHJI* is a rhombus.
$$GH = HJ = IJ = GI$$

Rombo (p. 471)   Un rombo es un paralelogramo con cuatro lados congruentes.

Right angle (p. 464) A right angle is an angle with a measure of 90°.
EXAMPLE ∠*CDE* is a right angle.

Ángulo recto (p. 464) Un ángulo recto es un ángulo que mide 90°.

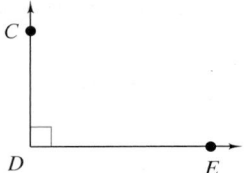

Right triangle (p. 470) A right triangle is a triangle with one right angle.
EXAMPLE △*ABC* is a right triangle, since ∠*B* is a right angle.

Triángulo rectángulo (p. 470) Un triángulo rectángulo es aquél que posee un ángulo recto.

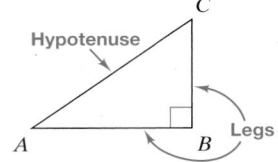

Rotation (p. 507) A rotation is a transformation that turns a figure about a fixed point, called the center of rotation. The angle measure of the rotation is the angle of rotation.
EXAMPLE The image of △*PQR* after a 90° rotation is △*PQ'R'*. Point *P* is the center of rotation.

Rotación (p. 507) Una rotación es una transformación en la cual una figura se mueve sin deformación alrededor de un punto fijo, llamado centro de rotación. La medida del ángulo de la rotación es el ángulo de rotación.

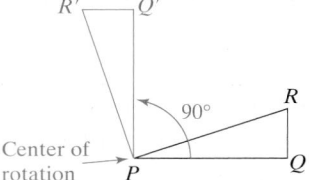

Rotational symmetry (p. 508) A figure has rotational symmetry if the figure can be rotated 180° or less and match the original figure.

Simetría rotacional (p. 508) Una figura tiene simetría rotacional si la figura se puede rotar 180° o menos y coincide exactamente con la figura original.

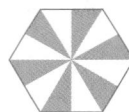

This figure has 60° rotational symmetry.

Sample (p. 669) A sample is a part of a population.

Muestra (p. 669) Una muestra es una parte de una población.

A class of 25 students is a sample of the population of a large school.

Sample space (p. 650) A sample space is all possible outcomes of an experiment.

Espacio muestral (p. 650) Un espacio muestral es el conjunto de todos los resultados posibles de un experimento.

The sample space for tossing two coins is HH, HT, TH, TT.

Scale drawing (p. 300) A scale drawing is an enlarged or reduced drawing that is similar to an actual object or place.

Dibujo a escala (p. 300) Un dibujo a escala es un dibujo aumentado o reducido que es similar al objeto o lugar real.

A map is a scale drawing.

Scalene triangle (p. 470)   A scalene triangle is a triangle with no congruent sides.

EXAMPLE $\triangle NPO$ is a scalene triangle.

Triángulo escaleno (p. 470)   Un triángulo escaleno es un triángulo que no tiene lados congruentes.

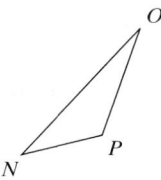

Scatter plot (p. 423)   A scatter plot is a graph that displays data from two related sets as ordered pairs.

EXAMPLE This scatter plot displays the amount various companies spent on advertising (in dollars) versus product sales (in thousands of dollars).

Diagrama de dispersión (p. 423)   Un diagrama de dispersión es una gráfica que muestra datos de dos conjuntos relacionados, como pares ordenados.

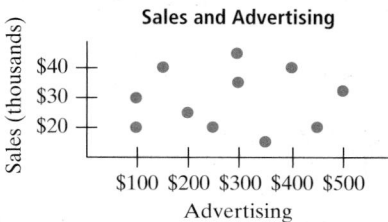

Scientific notation (p. 215)   Scientific notation is a way of expressing a number. A number is expressed in scientific notation when it is written as the product of a number greater than or equal to 1 and less than 10, and a power of 10.

Notación científica (p. 215)   La notación científica es una forma de expresar un número. Un número se expresa en notación científica cuando se escribe como el producto de un número mayor o igual a 1 y menor que 10 y el segundo es una potencia de 10.

In scientific notation, 37,000,000 is written as 3.7×10^7.

Segment (p. 458)   A segment is part of a line. It has two endpoints.

Segmento (p. 458)   Un segmento es parte de una recta. Tiene dos puntos extremos.

$\overline{CB}$ represents the segment shown.

Segment bisector (p. 492)   A segment bisector is a line, segment, or ray that separates a segment into two congruent segments.

Mediatriz de un segmento (p. 492)   La mediatriz de un segmento es una recta, segmento o rayo que divide el segmento en dos segmentos congruentes.

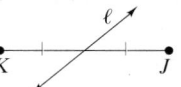

Line ℓ bisects $\overline{KJ}$.

Sequence (p. 688)   A sequence is a set of numbers that follow a pattern.

Progresión (p. 688)   Una progresión es un conjunto de números que sigue un patrón.

2, 2.3, 2.34, 2.345, . . .

Side (pp. 464, 470)   See *Angle* and *Polygon*.

Cara (p. 464, 470)   Ver *Angle* y *Polygon*.

Significant digits (p. 162) Significant digits are the digits that represent an actual measurement.

Dígitos significativos (p. 162) Dígitos significativos son los dígitos que representan una medida real.

Similar figures (p. 299) Similar figures are figures with corresponding angles that have equal measures and corresponding sides that have proportional lengths. The symbol ~ means "is similar to."
EXAMPLE $\triangle ABC \sim \triangle RTS$

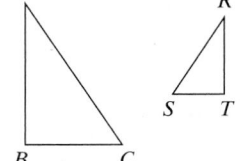

Figuras semejantes (p. 299) Figuras semejantes son figuras con ángulos correspondients que tienen la misma medida y lados correspondientes que tienen longitudes proporcionales. El símbolo ~ significa "es semejante a."

Simple interest (p. 382) Simple interest is interest paid only on the principal, the initial amount of money invested or borrowed. The formula for simple interest is $I = prt$, where I is the interest, p is the principal, r is the interest rate per year, and t is the time in years.

The simple interest on $1,000 at 5% for 2 years is $1,000 $\cdot$ 0.05 $\cdot$ 2, or $100.

Interés simple (p. 382) Interés simple es aquel que se paga sólo por el capital, el monto inicial de dinero que se invierte o se pide prestado. La fórmula de interés simple es $I = prt$, donde I es el interés, p es el capital, r es la tasa de interés anual y t es el tiempo en años.

Simplest form of a fraction (p. 192) The simplest form of a fraction is the form in which the only common factor of the numerator and denominator is 1.

The simplest form of the fraction $\frac{15}{20}$ is $\frac{3}{4}$.

Mínima expresión de una fracción (p. 192) La mínima expresión de una fracción es la expresión en que el único factor común del numerador y del denominador es 1.

Simplify a variable expression (p. 76) To simplify a variable expression is to replace it with an equivalent expression having as few terms as possible.

$2x + 5 + 4x$ simplifies to $6x + 5$.

Simplificar una expresión variable (p. 76) Se simplifica una expresión variable al reemplazarla con una expresión equivalente que tiene el menor número posible de términos.

Simulation (p. 665) A simulation is a model used to find experimental probability.

Your baseball team has an equal chance of winning or losing each of its next five games. You can toss a coin to simulate the outcomes of the next five games.

Simulación (p. 665) Una simulación es un modelo que se usa para hallar la probabilidad experimental.

Sine (p. 608)   See *Trigonometric ratios*.

Razón del seno (p. 608)   Ver *Trigonometric ratios*.

Skew lines (p. 459)   Skew lines are lines in space that do not intersect and are not parallel. They do not lie in the same plane. Skew segments must be parts of skew lines.

Rectas cruzadas (p. 459)   Las rectas cruzadas son rectas en el espacio, que no se intersecan y que no son paralelas. No están en el mismo plano. Los segmentos cruzados son partes de rectas cruzadas.

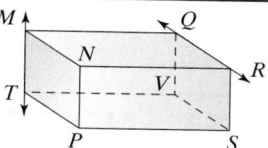

$\overleftrightarrow{MT}$ and $\overleftrightarrow{QR}$ are skew lines.

Slant height (p. 552)   See *Cone* and *Pyramid*.

Altura inclinada (p. 552)   Ver *Cone* y *Pyramid*.

Slope (p. 411)   Slope is a ratio that describes the tilt of a line.

$$\text{slope} = \frac{\text{vertical change}}{\text{horizontal change}} = \frac{\text{difference in } y\text{-coordinates}}{\text{difference in } x\text{-coordinates}}$$

Pendiente (p. 411)   La pendiente de una recta es la razón que describe su inclinación.

$$\text{Pendiente} = \frac{\text{variación vertical}}{\text{variación horizontal}} = \frac{\text{diferencia en las coordenadas } y}{\text{diferencia en las coordenadas } x}$$

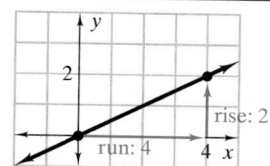

The slope of the given line is $\frac{2}{4}$, or $\frac{1}{2}$.

Slope-intercept form of an equation (p. 413)   The slope-intercept form of an equation is $y = mx + b$, where m is the slope and b is the y-intercept of the line.

Forma pendiente-intercepto de una ecuación (p. 413)   La forma pendiente-intercepto de una ecuación es $y = mx + b$ donde m es la pendiente y b es el intercepto en y de la recta.

The equation $y = 2x + 1$ is in slope-intercept form with $m = 2$ and $b = 1$.

Solid (p. 538)   A solid is a three-dimensional figure.

Sólido (p. 538)   Un sólido es una figura tridimensional.

See *Space figure*.

Solution (p. 81)   A solution is any value or values that make an equation or an inequality true.

Solución (p. 81)   Una solución es cualquier valor o valores que hacen verdadera una ecuación o una desigualdad.

4 is the solution of $x + 5 = 9$.

$(8, 4)$ is a solution of $y = -1x + 12$ because $4 = -1(8) + 12$.

-4 is a solution of $2x < -3$, because $2 \cdot -4 < -3$.

$(-1, 3)$ is a solution of $y > x - 4$, because $3 > -1 - 4$.

Space figure (p. 539)   A space figure is a three-dimensional figure, or solid.

EXAMPLE A cylinder, a cone, and a prism are space figures.

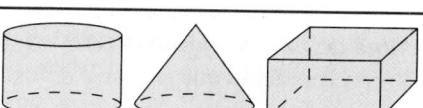

Cuerpos geométricos (p. 539)   Un cuerpo geométrico es una figura tridimensional o sólido.

English/Spanish Glossary

Sphere (p. 539)   A sphere is the set of points in space that are a given distance from a point, called the center.

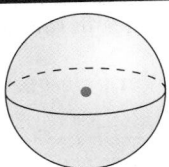

Esfera (p. 539)   Una esfera es el conjunto de todos los puntos del espacio que se hallan a una misma distancia de un punto dado llamado el centro.

Square (p. 471)   A square is a parallelogram with four right angles and four congruent sides.

EXAMPLE $QRTS$ is a square.
$\angle Q$, $\angle R$, $\angle T$, and $\angle S$ are right angles.
$QR = RT = ST = SQ$

Cuadrado (p. 471)   Un cuadrado es un paralelogramo con cuatro ángulos rectos y cuatro lados congruentes.

Square root (p. 580)   The square root of a given number is a number that when multiplied by itself equals the given number.

The symbol for the nonnegative square root of a number is $\sqrt{}$.

$\sqrt{25} = 5$ because $5^2 = 25$.

Raíz cuadrada (p. 580)   La raíz cuadrada de un número dado es un número que cuando es multiplicado por sí mismo, es igual al número dado.

Standard form (p. 708)   Standard form of a polynomial is the form in which the terms are in order of decreasing degree.

$3y^2 + 8y - 2$ is in standard form.

Forma general de un polinomio (p. 708)   Un polinomio está en forma general cuando sus términos están en orden descendente.

Standard notation (p. 216)   Standard notation is the usual form for representing a number.

The standard notation of 8.9×10^5 is 890,000.

Notación normal (p. 216)   La notación normal es la forma común de representar un número.

Stem-and-leaf plot (p. 640)   A stem-and-leaf plot is a display that shows numeric data arranged in order. The leaf of each data item is its last digit. The stem is its other digits. The stems are stacked in order and the leaves are arranged in order to the side of each stem.

EXAMPLE This stem-and-leaf plot displays recorded times in a race. The stem records the whole number of seconds. The leaf represents tenths of a second. So, 27 | 7 represents 27.7 seconds.

Stem	Leaf
27	7
28	5 6 8
29	6 9
30	8

27 | 7 means 27.7.

Diagrama de tallo y hojas (p. 640)   Un diagrama de tallo y hojas es una representación que muestra datos numéricos en orden de valor relativo. La hoja de cada dato es su último dígito. El tallo son sus otros dígitos. Los tallos están organizados en columnas ordenadas y las hojas están organizadas en orden al lado de cada tallo.

Straight angle (p. 464)   A straight angle is an angle with a measure of 180°.

Ángulo llano (p. 464)   Un ángulo llano es un ángulo cuya medida es 180°.

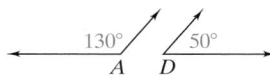

Subtraction Property of Equality (p. 86)   If $a = b$, then $a - c = b - c$.

$10 = 2(5)$, so $10 - 5 = 2(5) - 5$

Propiedad sustrativa de la igualdad (p. 86)   Si $a = b$, entonces $a - c = b - c$.

Subtraction Property of Inequality (p. 106)   If $a > b$, then $a - c > b - c$. If $a < b$, then $a - c < b - c$.

$7 > 4$, so $7 - 3 > 4 - 3$
$6 < 9$, so $6 - 2 < 9 - 2$

Propiedad sustractiva de la desigualdad (p. 106)   Si $a > b$, entonces $a - c > b - c$. Si $a < b$, entonces $a - c < b - c$.

Supplementary angles (p. 465)   Supplementary angles are two angles whose measures add to 180°.

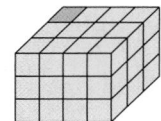

Ángulos suplementarios (p. 465)   Dos ángulos son suplementarios si la suma de sus medidas es 180°.

$\angle A$ and $\angle D$ are supplementary.

Surface area (p. 545)   Surface area is the sum of the areas of the base(s) and lateral faces of a space figure.

Each square $= 1$ in.^{2}

EXAMPLE   The surface area of the prism is the sum of the areas of its faces.
$(12 + 12 + 12 + 12 + 9 + 9)$ in.$^2 = 66$ in.^{2}

Área total (p. 545)   El área total es la suma de las áreas de la o las bases y de las caras laterales de una figura tridimesional.

System of linear equations (p. 435)   A system of linear equations is two or more linear equations.

$y = 3x + 1$ and $y = -2x - 3$ form a system of linear equations.

Sistema de ecuaciones lineales (p. 435)   Dos o más ecuaciones lineales forman un sistema de ecuaciones lineales.

System of linear inequalities (p. 443)   A system of linear inequalities is two or more linear inequalities.

$y \geq 3x + 1$ and $y < -2x - 3$ form a system of linear inequalities.

Sistema de desigualdades lineales (p. 443)   Dos o más desigualdades lineales forman un sistema de desigualdades lineales.

Tangent (p. 608)   See *Trigonometric ratios*.

Tangente (p. 608)   Ver *Trigonometric ratios*.

English/Spanish Glossary

Term of an expression (p. 76)   A term is a number, a variable, or the product of a number and variable(s).

The expression $7x + 12 + (-9y)$ has three terms: $7x$, 12, and $-9y$.

Término de una expresión (p. 76)   Un término es un número, una variable o el producto de un número y una o mas variables.

Term of a sequence (p. 688)   A term of a sequence is any number in the sequence.

$1, 2, 3, 4, \ldots$

EXAMPLE In this sequence, 1 is the first term, 2 is the second term, 3 is the third term, and 4 is the fourth term.

Término de una progresión (p. 688)   Un término de una progresión es cualquier número de la progresión.

Terminating decimal (p. 237)   A terminating decimal is a decimal with a finite number of digits.

Both 0.6 and 0.7265 are terminating decimals.

Decimal finito (p. 237)   Un decimal finito es un decimal que tiene un número finito de digitos.

Tessellation (p. 511)   A tessellation is a repeated pattern of figures that completely covers a plane without gaps or overlaps.

Teselación (p. 511)   Una teselación es un patrón repetido de figuras que cubre completamente un plano sin dejar espacios ni sobreponerse.

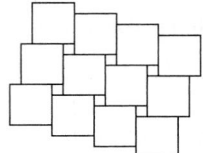

This tessellation consists of small squares and large squares.

Theoretical Probability (p. 650)   See *Probability*.

Probabilidad teórica (p. 650)   Ver *Probability*.

Three-dimensional figure (p. 539)   A three-dimensional figure is a figure that does not lie in a plane.

See *Space figure*.

Figura tridimensional (p. 539)   Una figura tridimensional es una figura que no está situada en un plano.

Transformation (p. 497)   A transformation is a change of position or size of a figure. Four types of transformations are translations, reflections, rotations, and dilations.

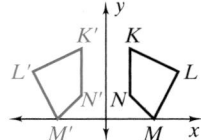

EXAMPLE $K'L'M'N'$ is a reflection of $KLMN$ across the y-axis.

Transformación (p. 497)   Una transformación es un cambio de posición o tamaño de una figura. Una transformación puede ser una traslacion, una reflexión, una rotación o una dilatación.

Translation (p. 497)   A translation is a transformation that moves points the same distance and in the same direction.

EXAMPLE $A'B'C'D'$ is the translation image of $ABCD$.

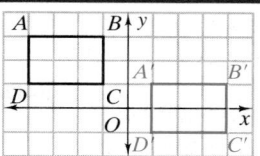

Traslación (p. 497)   Una traslación es una transformación que mueve puntos la misma distancia y en la misma dirección.

Transversal (p. 466)   A transversal is a line that intersects two other lines in different points.

EXAMPLE $\overleftrightarrow{RI}$ is a transversal of $\overleftrightarrow{QS}$ and $\overleftrightarrow{HJ}$.

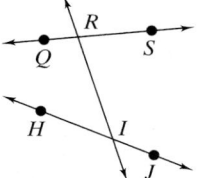

Transversal (p. 466)   Transversal es una recta que interseca a otras dos rectas en puntos distintos.

Trapezoid (p. 471)   A trapezoid is a quadrilateral with exactly one pair of parallel sides.

EXAMPLE $UVYW$ is a trapezoid.
$\overleftrightarrow{UV} \parallel \overleftrightarrow{WY}$

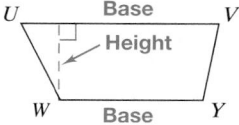

Trapecio (p. 471)   Un trapecio es un cuadrilátero que tiene exactamente un par de lados paralelos.

Tree diagram (p. 649)   A tree diagram is a diagram that displays all the possible outcomes of an event.

EXAMPLE   There are for 4 possible outcomes for tossing 2 coins: HH, HT, TH, and TT.

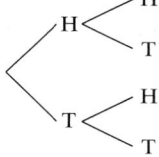

Diagrama de árbol (p. 649)   Un diagrama de árbol presenta todos los resultados posibles de un suceso.

Trend line (p. 430)   A trend line is a line that closely fits the data points in a scatter plot.

Línea de tendencia (p. 430)   Una línea de tendencia es la recta que más corresponde con los puntos de los datos en una diagrama de dispersión.

Triangle (p. 472)   A triangle is a polygon with three sides.

Triángulo (p. 472)   Un triángulo es un polígono con tres lados.

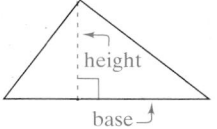

English/Spanish Glossary

Trigonometric ratios (p. 608) Trigonometric ratios are the sine, cosine, and tangent. In $\triangle ABC$ with right $\angle C$,

$$\text{sine } \angle A = \frac{\text{length of leg opposite } \angle A}{\text{length of hypotenuse}} = \frac{a}{c},$$

$$\text{cosine } \angle A = \frac{\text{length of leg adjacent to } \angle A}{\text{length of hypotenuse}} = \frac{b}{c},$$

$$\text{tangent } \angle A = \frac{\text{length of leg opposite } \angle A}{\text{length of leg adjacent to } \angle A} = \frac{a}{b}.$$

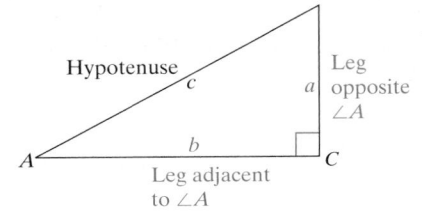

Razones trigonométricas (p. 608) Las razónes trigonoméricas son seno, coseno y tangente. En $\triangle ABC$, con ángulo recto C,

$$\text{seno } \angle A = \frac{\text{longitud del cateto opuesto a } \angle A}{\text{longitud de la hipotenusa}} = \frac{a}{c},$$

$$\text{coseno } \angle A = \frac{\text{longitud del cateto adyacente a } \angle A}{\text{longitud de la hipotenusa}} = \frac{b}{c},$$

$$\text{tangente } \angle A = \frac{\text{longitud del cateto opuesto a } \angle A}{\text{longitud del cateto adyacente a } \angle A} = \frac{a}{b}.$$

Trigonometry (p. 608) Trigonometry is a branch of mathematics involving triangle measures.

Trigonometría (p. 608) La trigonometría es la rama de las matemáticas que se relaciona con la medida de triángulos.

Trinomial (p. 704) A trinomial is a polynomial with three terms.

$x^2 - 5x + 6$ is a trinomial.

Trinomio (p. 704) Un trinomio es un polinomio compuesto de tres términos.

Unit rate (p. 289) A unit rate is a rate that has denominator 1.

If you drive 165 mi in 3 h, your unit rate of travel is 55 mi in 1 h or 55 mi/h.

Tasa unitaria (p. 289) Una tasa unitaria es la tasa cuyo denominador es 1.

Upper quartile (p. 635) The upper quartile is the median of the upper half of a data set.

See *Quartile*.

Cuartil superior (p. 635) El cuartil superior es la mediana de la mitad superior de un conjunto de datos.

Variable (p. 4) A variable is a letter that stands for a number.

x is a variable in the equation $9 - x = 3$.

Variable (p. 4) Una variable es una letra que representa a un número.

Variable expression (p. 4) A variable expression is a mathematical phrase that uses variables, numbers, and operation symbols.

$7 + x, 2y - 4, \frac{3}{5}g$, and $\frac{7}{k}$ are variable expressions.

Expresión algebraica (p. 4) Una expresión algebraica es una expresión en la que se usan variables, números y símbolos de operaciones.

Venn diagram (p. 191) A Venn diagram is a diagram that illustrates the relationships among collections of objects or numbers. The intersection, or overlap, of two circles indicates what is common to both collections.

EXAMPLE The Venn diagram shows the activities of 67 music students.

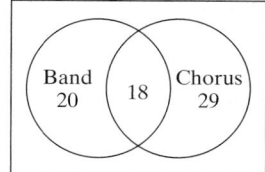

Diagrama Venn (p. 191) Un diagrama Venn es un diagrama que muestra la relación entre dos conjuntos de objetos o números. La intersección o sobreposición de dos círculos indica lo que tienen en común ambos conjuntos.

Vertex (pp. 464, 471) See *Angle* and *Polygon*.

Vértice (pp. 464, 471) Ver *Angle* y *Polygon*.

Vertical angles (p. 465) Vertical angles are angles formed by two intersecting lines, and are opposite each other. Vertical angles are congruent.

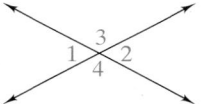

$\angle 1$ and $\angle 2$ are vertical angles, as are $\angle 3$ and $\angle 4$.

Ángulos verticales (p. 465) Ángulos verticales son aquellos formados por dos rectas que se intersecan y que son opuestos entre sí. Los ángulos verticales son congruentes.

Vertical-line test (p. 401) The vertical-line test is a test that allows you to describe graphically whether a relation is a function.

EXAMPLE Since the vertical line $x = 2$ passes through two points of the graph, the relation is not a function.

Prueba de la línea vertical (p. 401) Método que permite determinar gráficamente si una relación es o no es una función.

Volume (p. 557) The volume of a space figure is the number of cubic units needed to fill it.

EXAMPLE The volume of the rectangular prism is 36 in.³.

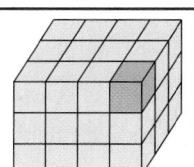

Each cube is 1 in.³.

Volumen (p. 557) El volumen de una figura tridimensional es el número de unidades cúbicas necesarias para llenar el espacio interior de dicha figura.

English/Spanish Glossary

x-axis (p. 50)   The *x*-axis is the horizontal number line that, together with the *y*-axis, establishes the coordinate plane.

See *Coordinate plane.*

Eje de *x* (p. 50)   El eje de *x* es la recta numérica horizontal que, junto al eje de *y*, forma el plano de coordenadas.

---

x-coordinate (p. 50)   The *x*-coordinate is the horizontal position of a point in the coordinate plane.

See *Coordinates.*

Coordenada *x* (p. 50)   La coordenada *x* muestra la ubicación horizontal de un punto en el plano de coordenadas.

---

x-intercept (p. 409)   The *x*-intercept of a line is the *x*-coordinate of the point where the line crosses the *x*-axis.

EXAMPLE   The *x*-intercept is 2. The *y*-intercept is −3.

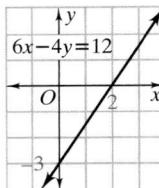

Intercepto *x* (p. 409)   El intercepto *x* de una recta es la coordenada *x* del punto de intercepción de la recta con el eje de *x*.

---

y-axis (p. 50)   The *y*-axis is the vertical number line that, together with the *x*-axis, forms the coordinate plane.

See *Coordinate plane.*

Eje de *y* (p. 50)   El eje de *y* es la recta numérica vertical que, junto al eje de *x*, forma el plano de coordenadas.

---

y-coordinate (p. 50)   The *y*-coordinate is the vertical position of a point in the coordinate plane.

See *Coordinates.*

Coordenada *y* (p. 50)   La coordenada *y* muestra la ubicación vertical de un punto en el plano de coordenadas.

---

y-intercept (pp. 409, 413)   The *y*-intercept of a line is the *y*-coordinate of the point where the line crosses the *y*-axis.

See *x-intercept.*

Intercepto *y* (pp. 409, 413)   El intercepto *y* de una recta es la coordenada *y* del punto de intercepción de la recta con el eje de *y*.

Zero pair (p. 23)   A zero pair is a positive algebra tile paired with a negative algebra tile.

Par cero (p. 23)   Un par cero es un ficha de álgebra positiva que se empareja con una ficha de álgebra negativa.

Answers to Instant Check System™

Chapter 1

1. 1 **2.** 11 **3.** 11 **4.** 19 **5.** 13 **6.** 40 **7.** 17 **8.** 43 **9.** 176 **10.** 28 **11.** 166 **12.** 75 **13.** > **14.** > **15.** < **16.** < **17.** < **18.** = **19.** 12 **20.** 30 **21.** 28 **22.** 5 **23.** 96 **24.** 5 **25.** 200 **26.** 80 **27.** 31 **28.** 13 **29.** 480 **30.** 12 **31.** 1 **32.** 4 **33.** 7 **34.** 10

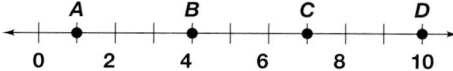

Lesson 1-1 pp. 4–7

Check Skills You'll Need 1. 7 **2.** 12 **3.** 5 **4.** 4 **5.** 3

Check Understanding 1a. Variable expression; *x* is the variable. **b.** numerical expression **c.** Variable expression.; *d* is the variable **2a.** 0.50*b* **b.** $\frac{m}{60}$

Lesson 1-2 pp. 8–12

Check Skills You'll Need 1. 82 **2.** 43 **3.** 71 **4.** 19 **5.** 14 **6.** 26

Check Understanding 1a. 17 **b.** 3 **c.** 3 **2a.** 4 **b.** 12 **3a.** 6 **b.** 3

Lesson 1-3 pp. 14–17

Check Skills You'll Need 1. 60 **2.** 18 **3.** 29 **4.** 32

Check Understanding 1a. 28 **b.** 45 **2a.** 90 **b.** 23 **c.** 12 **3.** 29*c*; $145 **4.** $104

Lesson 1-4 pp. 18–22

Check Skills You'll Need 1. −7 **2.** 9 **3.** 8 **4.** 3 **5.** −5

Check Understanding 1. −2

2.
−6, 0, 2 **3.** the absolute value of negative ten; 10

Checkpoint Quiz 1 1. *f* + 23 **2.** $\frac{g}{34}$ **3.** 9*p* **4.** 20 **5.** 2 **6.** 19 **7.** 0 **8.** 54 **9.** 15

10a.

 b. Tuesday, Wednesday, Monday, Thursday

Lesson 1-5 pp. 24–29

Check Skills You'll Need 1. < **2.** > **3.** < **4.** = **5.** > **6.** >

Check Understanding 1a. 3 **b.** 4 **c.** −4 **2a.** −4 **b.** 5 **c.** −6 **3a.** −38 **b.** 47 **c.** −90 **4.** 1,280 m **5a.** −10 **b.** 70

Lesson 1-6 pp. 30–34

Check Skills You'll Need 1. −1 **2.** −29 **3.** −10 **4.** 11 **5.** 0 **6.** −23

Check Understanding 1a. −5 **b.** −1 **c.** −3 **2a.** −4 **b.** −6 **c.** 5 **3a.** 35 **b.** −106 **c.** −46 **3d.** −81°C

Lesson 1-7 pp. 35–39

Check Skills You'll Need 1. −7 **2.** −11 **3.** −15 **4.** −19

Check Understanding 1. A six-sided figure with all vertices on a circle. **2a.** Start with 4 and add 5 repeatedly. **b.** Start with 3 and multiply by 3 readily **c.** Start with 1, 1. Then each number is the sum of the previous two numbers. **3.** Start with 1 and add 2 repeatedly; 9, 11. **4.** No; if the coin is fair, the coin can come up tails on any toss. **5a.** correct **b.** Incorrect; 8 and |8| are not opposites. **c.** correct

Lesson 1-8 pp. 40–43

Check Skills You'll Need 1. Start with 8 and add 3 repeatedly; 20, 23, 26 **2.** Start with 1, then alternately add 4 and subtract 1; 11, 10, 14 **3.** Start with 3, then alternately add 2 and multiply by 2; 26, 52, 54 **4.** Start with 1, then add 3 repeatedly; 13, 16, 19

Check Understanding 8. 127

Lesson 1-9 pp. 44–49

Check Skills You'll Need 1. 20 **2.** 24 **3.** 25 **4.** 28 **5.** 30 **6.** 140

Check Understanding 1a. −12 **b.** −12 **c.** −14 **2.** 12 **3a.** 64 **b.** −90 **c.** 0 **4a.** −4 **b.** 8 **c.** 14 **d.** −2

Checkpoint Quiz 2 1. −8 **2.** 20 **3.** −45 **4.** 8 **5.** −12 **6.** 72 **7–9.** Answers may vary. Samples are given. **7.** −7 **8.** 22 **9.** −40 **10.** 13, 18, 23 **11.** 81, 243, 729

Lesson 1-10 pp. 50–54

Check Skills You'll Need

1.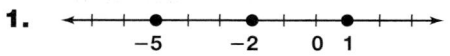

2.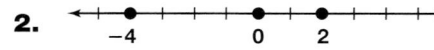

3.

4.

Check Understanding 1a. (2, −3); (3, 3) **b.** Quadrant IV; Quadrant I

2a–b.

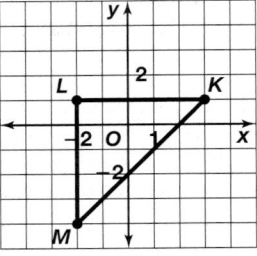

b. a triangle

Chapter 2

Diagnosing Readiness   p. 64

1. 11, 11 **2.** 5, 5 **3.** −3, −3 **4.** −19, −19 **5.** 25, 25
6. 6, 6 **7.** 6, 6 **8.** 7, 7 **9.** < **10.** > **11.** < **12.** >
13. < **14.** = **15.** = **16.** < **17.** > **18.** < **19.** <
20. > **21.** 25 **22.** 28 **23.** 15 **24.** −110 **25.** 36
26. 16 **27.** −24 **28.** 45 **29.** −20 **30.** −27 **31.** −5
32. −45

Lesson 2-1   pp. 66–70

Check Skills You'll Need 1. −25 **2.** 35 **3.** −7 **4.** −46

Check Understanding
1. $18; 6 + 8 + 4
   = 6 + (8 + 4)   Assoc. Prop. of Add.
   = 6 + (4 + 8)   Comm. Prop. of Add.
   = (6 + 4) + 8   Assoc. Prop. of Add.
   = 10 + 8   Add within parentheses.
   = 18   Add.
2a. Comm. Prop. of Add **b.** Ident. Prop of Mult.
c. Assoc. Prop. of Mult. **3a.** 27 **b.** 3 **c.** 40 **d.** 10
4. $6.30 **5a.** 300 **b.** −120 **c.** 240 **d.** 540

Lesson 2-2   pp. 71–75

Check Skills You'll Need 1. 12 **2.** 24 **3.** 20 **4.** 6 **5.** 8
6. 4

Check Understanding 1a. 2,650 **b.** 3,120 **c.** 1,791
2. $1,428 **3a.** 210 **b.** −120 **c.** 35 **4a.** $8x − 12$
b. $3x + 12$ **c.** $6x + 2$ **5a.** $14 − 6d$ **b.** $18m + 3$
c. $−15t + 6$

Lesson 2-3   pp. 76–79

Check Skills You'll Need 1. $5b + 20$ **2.** $−6x − 15$
3. $−32 − 12q$ **4.** $−12b + 42$

Check Understanding 1a. 2, 4; $2s$, $4s$; 6 **b.** −4; none;
none **c.** 9, 2, −2, 1; $9m$ and $−2m$, $2r$ and r; none
2. $7a + 1$ **3a.** $2b$ **b.** $−13m$ **c.** $3p$ **4a.** $−y + 5m$
b. $2x − 7$

Checkpoint Quiz 1 1. Comm. Prop of Mult.
2. Assoc. Prop. of Mult. **3.** Ident. Prop. of Mult.
4. Comm. Prop. of Add. **5.** Comm. Prop. of Mult.
6. Dist. Prop. **7.** $9a$ **8.** $18y$ **9.** $16w − 6$

Lesson 2-4   pp. 80–83

Check Skills You'll Need 1. $x + 46$ **2.** $g − 4$ **3.** $t − 5$
4. $\frac{z}{26}$

Check Understanding 1a. false; 2 ≠ 3 **b.** open; has a
variable **c.** true; 20 = 20 **2.** $20 − x = 3$; open
because there is a variable **3a.** no **b.** yes
4. $b + 6 = 33$; $27 + 6 = 33$; Yes, the backpack
weighs 27 lb.

Lesson 2-5   pp. 86–90

Check Skills You'll Need 1. 3 **2.** 9 **3.** 8 **4.** 6

Check Understanding 1a. −5 **b.** 4 **c.** −1
2. $123 = r + 55$; 68 beats/min **3a.** 13 **b.** 72
c. 112 **4.** $5 = h − 17$; $22

Lesson 2-6   pp. 92–95

Check Skills You'll Need 1. 1 **2.** −1 **3.** −1 **4.** 1

Check Understanding 1a. 21 **b.** 13 **c.** 9 **2a.** −8
b. −12 **c.** 14 **3a.** −50 **b.** 324 **c.** −600

Lesson 2-7   pp. 96–99

Check Skills You'll Need 1. 178 **2.** 188 **3.** 183 **4.** 180

Check Understanding 6. 53 adult tickets, 80 student
tickets

Lesson 2-8   pp. 102–105

Check Skills You'll Need

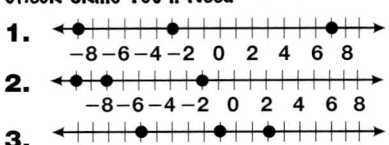

Check Understanding

1a.
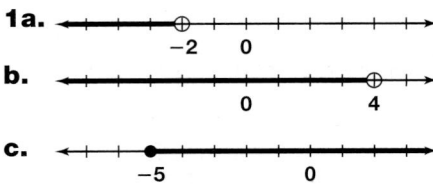
b.

c.

d.

2. $x \geq 3$ **3.** $n < 5$

Lesson 2-9
pp. 106–109

Check Skills You'll Need 1. -2 **2.** 19 **3.** 9 **4.** 29

Check Understanding 1a. $m > 3$

b. $t < 7$

c. $x \geq -10$

2. ≤ 28 lb **3a.** $m > 42$ **b.** $v \leq 11$ **c.** $t \geq 16$

Checkpoint Quiz 2 1. true; $19 = 19$ **2.** open; variable
3. false; $1 \neq -1$ **4.** -4 **5.** 4 **6.** 6 **7.** -32 **8.** -9
9. $a \geq 6$ **10.** $r < 19$ **11.** $m > -19$
12. 1 quarter, 5 dimes, 2 pennies

Lesson 2-10
pp. 110–114

Check Skills You'll Need 1. 4 **2.** -9 **3.** -20 **4.** 288

Check Understanding 1a. $x > 10$ **b.** $m < -7$
c. $t > -4$ **2a.** $m \geq 8$ **b.** $t > -21$ **c.** $r > 35$

Chapter 3

Diagnosing Readiness
p.124

1. 40 **2.** 10 **3.** 0 **4.** 600 **5.** 830 **6.** 6,010 **7.** $<$
8. $>$ **9.** $<$ **10.** $<$ **11.** $>$ **12.** $>$ **13.** 8,349, 8.35,
8.351, 9.25 **14.** 0.017, 0.02, 0.0201, 0.201
15. $-14.1, -1.401, -1.4, -1.04$ **16.** $-3.2, -3.19,$
$-2.8, -2.3$ **17.** 11.49 **18.** 3.07 **19.** 3.65 **20.** 1.206
21. 6.7067 **22.** 6.9 **23.** 55.12 **24.** 10.6 **25.** 98.7
26. 532 **27.** 300 **28.** 154,070 **29.** 0.08 **30.** 0.0842
31. 0.0161 **32.** 0.001209

Lesson 3-1
pp. 127–131

Check Skills You'll Need 1. 2 tens **2.** 3 tenths
3. 8 hundredths **4.** 6 thousandths

Check Understanding 1a. tenths; 38.4 **b.** ones; 1
c. tenths; 7,098.6 **d.** thousandths; 274.943
e. tenths; 5.0 **f.** hundredths; 9.85 **2a.** about 560
b. about 220 **3a.** about 18.6 **b.** about $11
4a. about $15 **b.** about 125

Lesson 3-2
pp. 132–135

Check Skills You'll Need 1. 146 **2.** 199 **3.** 101 **4.** 28

Check Understanding 1a. about 10 **b.** about 68
c. about 160 **2.** about $40 **3a.** about 20
b. about 6 **c.** about 20 **4a.** Yes; 0.68 is close to
an estimate of 0.8. **b.** No; 52.3 is not close to an
estimate of 5.

Lesson 3-3
pp. 137–141

Check Skills You'll Need 1. 3, 4, 5, 6, 6, 8, 9
2. 68, 69, 71, 72, 72 **3.** 98, 101, 101, 112, 120
4. 3, 3.3, 3.7, 3.74, 37

Check Understanding 1. 2.95, 2.8, 2.3 **2a.** 3 modes
b. 1 mode **3a.** 31; raises the mean by 2.6
b. 1; lowers the mean by 2.8 **4a.** $25.25, $23.50,
$20 **b.** Answers may vary. Sample: Median; the
mode is equal to two of the smaller data values,
and the outlier ($42) affects the mean too much.

Lesson 3-4
pp. 143–146

Check Skills You'll Need 1. 14 **2.** 10 **3.** 14 **4.** 3.5

Check Understanding 1a. $r = 28$ mi/h **b.** $t = 51.5$ yr
2a. 61°F **b.** 59°F **c.** 53.5°F **3a.** 88.2 cm **b.** 52 in.

Checkpoint Quiz 1 1. 15.66 **2.** 0.891 **3.** 7,023 **4.** 345.7
5. about 32 **6.** about 24 **7.** about -1 **8.** about 6
9. 56, 57, no mode **10.** 2, 2, 1 **11.** 8.5 h

Lesson 3-5
pp. 148–151

Check Skills You'll Need 1. 9.86 **2.** 2.45 **3.** 2.04 **4.** 3.08

Check Understanding 1a. 13.9 **b.** 38.96
2. $35.48 + m = 70$; $34.52 **3a.** 21.1 **b.** -7.4
4. $x - 14.95 = 12.48$; $27.43

Lesson 3-6
pp. 152–155

Check Skills You'll Need 1. 11.7 **2.** 0.48 **3.** 6.618
4. 4.8018

Check Understanding 1a. -2 **b.** 0.5 **c.** 90.9
2. $5.5p = 7.70$; $1.40 **3a.** -3 **b.** 12.5 **c.** -360
4. 12 hits

Lesson 3-7
pp. 156–161

Check Skills You'll Need 1. 500 **2.** 0.01406 **3.** 2.94
4. 0.009

Check Understanding 1a. Centimeter; a meter is too
large unless you use fractional parts of a meter;
millimeters are too small. **b.** Gram; an energy bar
has a mass of several grams, but it is much less
than 1 kilogram. **c.** Kilogram; a horse is very
heavy, so grams are too small. **d.** Liter; a gas tank
holds several liters, so milliliters are too small.
2a. 50 km; millimeters are used to measure very
small lengths. **b.** 10 mL; the eyedropper holds
several drops of water but much less than a quart.
3a. 0.035 **b.** 250,000 **c.** 6,000 **4a.** 3,800 m
b. 250 mL

Checkpoint Quiz 2 **1.** 0.25 **2.** 8.55 **3.** 130 **4.** 3.05 **5.** 6.5 **6.** 129.6 **7.** 1.5 m; 1.5 cm is a little wider than the width of a thumbnail. **8.** 500 mL; 500 L would be about 500 qt. **9.** 0.095 **10.** 7,650,000 **11.** 0.675 **12.** 7,100 **13.** 9,100 g

Lesson 3-8	pp. 164–167

Check Skills You'll Need **1.** Start with 0 and add 6 repeatedly; 24, 30, 36 **2.** Start with −18 and add 9 repeatedly; 18, 27, 36 **3.** Start with 0. Alternately add 2 and subtract 1; 5, 4, 6 **4.** Start with 7. Alternately subtract 1 and add 2; 9, 11, 10

Check Understanding

6.

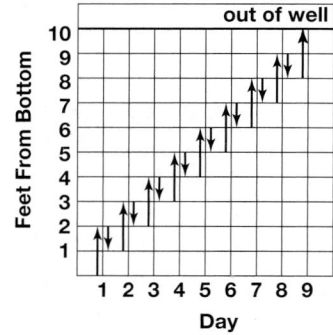

Chapter 4

Diagnosing Readiness	p. 176

1. 1,728 **2.** −64 **3.** 6,561 **4.** 15,625 **5.** 512 **6.** 64 **7.** 2, 6 **8.** 9, 5 **9.** 3, 6 **10.** 9, 7 **11.** 6, 4 **12.** 2, 25 **13.** 16, 2 **14.** 9, 9 **15.** 6, 9 **16.** 6, 10 **17.** 4, 7 **18.** 7, 8 **19.** 4, 11 **20.** 9, 4 **21.** 8, 9 **22.** 90 **23.** 900 **24.** 22 **25.** 49 **26.** 21 **27.** 45 **28.** 212 **29.** 140 **30.** 23 **31.** 27 **32.** 91 **33.** 130

Lesson 4-1	pp. 178–181

Check Skills You'll Need **1.** 160 **2.** 73 **3.** 51 **4.** 48 **5.** 177 **6.** 118

Check Understanding **1a.** Yes; 160 ends in 0. **b.** No; 56 does not end in 0. **c.** No; 53 does no end in 0, 2, 4, 6, or 8. **d.** Yes; 1,118 ends in 8. **2a.** No; the sum of the digits, 10, is not divisible by 9. **b.** No; the sum of the digits, 13, is not divisible by 3. **c.** Yes; the sum of the digits, 12, is divisible by 3. **d.** Yes; the sum of the digits, 18, is divisible by 9. **3a.** 1, 2, 5, 10 **b.** 1, 3, 7, 21 **c.** 1, 2, 3, 4, 6, 8, 12, 24 **d.** 1, 31 **e.** 1 row of 36 students, 2 rows of 18 students, 3 rows of 12 students, 4 rows of 9 students, or 6 rows of 6 students

Lesson 4-2	pp. 182–185

Check Skills You'll Need **1.** 81 **2.** 144 **3.** −64 **4.** 10,000

Check Understanding **1a.** 6^3 **b.** $4xy^2$ **c.** $(-3)^4$ **2a.** 49 **b.** −16, 16 **3a.** −58 **b.** 81

Lesson 4-3	pp. 186–190

Check Skills You'll Need **1.** 1, 3, 5, 15 **2.** 1, 5, 7, 35 **3.** 1, 7 **4.** 1, 2, 4, 5, 10, 20 **5.** 1, 2, 4, 5, 10, 20, 25, 50, 100 **6.** 1, 11, 121

Check Understanding **1a.** 11, 13, 17, 19 **b.** 10, 12, 14, 15, 16, 18, 20 **2a.** $2^3 \cdot 3^2$ **b.** 11^2 **c.** $3^2 \cdot 5^2$ **b.** $2^2 \cdot 59$ **3a.** 4 **b.** 3 **c.** $4r$ **d.** $15m$

Lesson 4-4	pp. 192–195

Check Skills You'll Need **1.** 7 **2.** 12 **3.** $5mn$ **4.** 3

Check Understanding **1a–c.** Answers may vary. Samples are given. **1a.** $\frac{1}{3}, \frac{10}{30}$ **b.** $\frac{5}{6}, \frac{20}{24}$ **c.** $\frac{7}{10}, \frac{28}{40}$ **2a.** $\frac{3}{4}$ **b.** $\frac{3}{4}$ **c.** $\frac{4}{5}$ **3a.** $\frac{1}{ac}$ **b.** $\frac{n}{3}$ **c.** $3x$

Checkpoint Quiz 1 **1.** 2, 3, 5, 10 **2.** 2, 3, 9 **3.** 2, 3 **4.** none **5.** 3, 9 **6.** 64 **7.** 125 **8.** −18 **9.** $\frac{1}{2}$ **10.** $\frac{2}{3}$ **11.** $\frac{4}{7}$ **12.** $\frac{1}{4}$ **13.** $2y$ **14.** Answers may vary. Samples: $5a^2$, $10a^2$; $25a^3b$, $30a^2$

Lesson 4-5	pp. 197–200

Check Skills You'll Need **1.** > **2.** > **3.** < **4.** <

Check Understanding **7.** 45 pictures

Lesson 4-6	pp. 201–204

Check Skills You'll Need **1.** $\frac{1}{5}$ **2.** $\frac{2}{3}$ **3.** $\frac{4}{5}$ **4.** $\frac{3}{4}$

Check Understanding **1a–d.** Answers may vary. Samples are given. **1a.** $\frac{2}{6}, \frac{-2}{-6}, \frac{-1}{-3}$ **b.** $-\frac{8}{10}, \frac{-4}{5}, \frac{4}{-5}$ **c.** $\frac{10}{16}, \frac{-10}{-16}, \frac{-5}{-8}$ **d.** $-\frac{2}{4}, \frac{-1}{2}, \frac{1}{-2}$

2a–d.

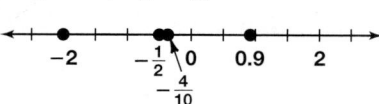

3a. $-\frac{1}{3}$ **b.** $\frac{2}{3}$ **c.** −3

Lesson 4-7	pp. 205–208

Check Skills You'll Need **1.** k^4 **2.** m^2n^2 **3.** 2^4 **4.** 5^3

Check Understanding **1a.** 32 **b.** m^{12} **c.** x^5y^5 **2a.** $18a^4$ **b.** $15c^9$ **c.** $12x^6$ **3a.** 256 **b.** c^{20} **c.** m^6

Lesson 4-8	pp. 210–214

Check Skills You'll Need **1.** x **2.** $\frac{1}{y}$ **3.** $\frac{2x}{3}$ **4.** $\frac{ab}{4}$

Check Understanding **1a.** 1,000 **b.** x^7 **c.** $4m^4$ **2a.** 1 **b.** 5 **c.** y^3 **d.** 5 **3a.** $\frac{1}{16}$ **b.** $\frac{1}{a^2}$ **c.** $\frac{1}{3y^4}$ **4a.** b^{-6} **b.** $m^{-3}n^{-6}$ **c.** $x^{-4}y^2$

Checkpoint Quiz 2 **1–5. Answers may vary. Samples are given. 1.** $\frac{1}{4}, \frac{-1}{-4}, \frac{2}{8}$ **2.** $\frac{1}{3}, \frac{-1}{-3}, \frac{2}{6}$ **3.** $\frac{7}{10}, \frac{-7}{-10}, \frac{14}{20}$

4. $\frac{9}{14}, \frac{-9}{-14}, \frac{-18}{-28}$ **5.** $\frac{8}{10}, \frac{-8}{-10}, \frac{-4}{-5}$ **6.** $-\frac{1}{3}$ **7.** $-\frac{1}{2}$ **8.** $\frac{2}{3}$

9. $-\frac{5}{8}$ **10.** $\frac{1}{4}$

11–15.

16. 128 **17.** x^{50} **18.** $6a^2$ **19.** $\frac{1}{x^5}$ **20.** $\frac{1}{a^6}$ **21.** $\frac{3}{4}$

Lesson 4-9   pp. 215–220

Check Skills You'll Need **1.** 10^8 **2.** 10^{16} **3.** 10^2 **4.** 10^{-3}

Check Understanding **1a.** 5.45×10^7 **b.** 7.23×10^5 **c.** 6.02×10^{11} **2a.** 2.1×10^{-4} **b.** 5×10^{-8} **c.** 8.03×10^{-11} **3a.** 32,100,000 **b.** 0.000000059 **c.** 10,060,000,000 **4a.** 1.6×10^6 **b.** 2.03×10^5 **c.** 7.243×10^{15} **5a.** $18.3 \times 10^6, 0.098 \times 10^9, 526 \times 10^7$ **b.** $0.22 \times 10^{-10}, 8 \times 10^{-9}, 14.7 \times 10^{-7}$ **6a.** 2.4×10^{11} **b.** 5.68×10^{-3}

Chapter 5

Diagnosing Readiness   p. 230

1. 1.2 **2.** 60 **3.** −45 **4.** −40 **5.** 1.5 **6.** 74 **7.** 8 **8.** −1.78 **9.** 3 **10.** 4 **11.** 12 **12.** 1 **13.** 10 **14.** 5 **15.** 9 **16.** 1 **17.** 10 **18.** 14 **19–21. Answers may vary. Samples are given. 19.** $\frac{1}{2}, \frac{3}{6}$ **20.** $\frac{8}{12}, \frac{2}{3}$ **21.** $\frac{3}{4}, \frac{6}{8}$ **22.** $\frac{5}{6}$ **23.** $\frac{2}{5}$ **24.** −2 **25.** $\frac{1}{4}$ **26.** $-\frac{24}{25}$ **27.** $\frac{1}{3}$ **28.** $\frac{4}{15}$ **29.** $\frac{4}{31}$ **30.** $-\frac{2}{9}$ **31.** $-\frac{2}{13}$ **32.** $\frac{1}{6}$ **33.** $\frac{5}{7}$ **34.** 5.4 **35.** 0.6 **36.** 0.625 **37.** 0.75 **38.** 0.375

Lesson 5-1   pp. 232–236

Check Skills You'll Need **1.** $2^2 \cdot 5$ **2.** 5^3 **3.** $3^2 \cdot 5$ **4.** $2 \cdot 3 \cdot 31$ **5.** $3^3 \cdot 23$ **6.** $3^2 \cdot 5^2 \cdot 7$

Check Understanding **1a.** 12 **b.** 20 **c.** 60 **2a.** 48 **b.** 45 **c.** 180 **3a.** $60xy$ **b.** $56m^4$ **c.** $75xy^2$ **4a.** $\frac{4}{9} > \frac{2}{9}$ **b.** $-\frac{4}{9} < -\frac{2}{9}$ **c.** $-\frac{4}{9} < \frac{2}{9}$ **5a.** $\frac{6}{7} > \frac{4}{5}$ **b.** $\frac{2}{3} < \frac{3}{4}$ **c.** $-\frac{3}{4} < -\frac{7}{10}$ **6a.** $\frac{1}{6} < \frac{5}{12} < \frac{2}{3}$ **b.** $\frac{1}{5} < \frac{3}{10} < \frac{1}{2} < \frac{7}{12}$

Lesson 5-2   pp. 237–241

Check Skills You'll Need **1.** 0.241, 2.41, 12.4, 24.1 **2.** 1.003, 1.030, 1.300, 13.03 **3.** −0.1, −0.01, 0.01, 0.1

Check Understanding **1a.** 0.25 **b.** 1.875 **c.** 3.3 **d.** 0.6 **2a.** $0.\overline{7}$; repeating 7 **b.** $0.9\overline{54}$; repeating; 54 **c.** 1.375; terminating **d.** $0.\overline{72}$; repeating; 72 **3a.** $0.2, 0.5, \frac{7}{10}, \frac{4}{5}$ **b.** $-0.75, -0.375, -\frac{1}{4}, -\frac{1}{8}$ **4a.** $1\frac{3}{4}$ **b.** $2\frac{8}{25}$ **c.** $\frac{13}{20}$ **5a.** $\frac{7}{9}$ **b.** $\frac{6}{11}$ **c.** $\frac{71}{333}$

Lesson 5-3   pp. 243–247

Check Skills You'll Need **1.** 8 **2.** 18 **3.** $10n$ **4.** 18 **5.** 40 **6.** $10n$

Check Understanding **1a.** $\frac{4}{7}$ **b.** $\frac{5}{k}$ **c.** $\frac{2}{5}$ **d.** $\frac{6}{y}$ **2a.** $\frac{7}{15}$ **b.** $-\frac{1}{8}$ **c.** $\frac{3m-14}{7m}$ **3a.** $6\frac{5}{8}$ **b.** $2\frac{1}{4}$ **c.** $3\frac{1}{4}$ **d.** $3\frac{1}{2}$ qt

Checkpoint Quiz 1 **1.** > **2.** = **3.** < **4.** < **5.** 0.51 **6.** $\frac{3}{250}$ **7.** 1.25 **8.** $\frac{1}{3}$ **9.** $0.8\overline{3}$ **10.** $\frac{17}{33}$ **11.** $\frac{11}{13}$ **12.** $\frac{5}{36}$ **13.** $4\frac{19}{40}$ **14.** $\frac{2}{3}$

Lesson 5-4   pp. 248–252

Check Skills You'll Need **1.** $\frac{7}{3}$ **2.** $\frac{33}{10}$ **3.** $\frac{13}{9}$ **4.** $\frac{24}{5}$ **5.** $\frac{63}{8}$ **6.** $\frac{36}{7}$

Check Understanding **1a.** $\frac{2}{15}$ **b.** $-\frac{5}{9}$ **c.** $\frac{35}{72}$ **d.** $\frac{3}{32}$ **2a.** $\frac{4}{7}$ **b.** $-\frac{7}{25}$ **c.** $\frac{x}{6}$ **3a.** $1\frac{1}{2}$ **b.** $\frac{6}{7}$ **c.** $-4\frac{8}{15}$ **4a.** $-\frac{1}{2}$ **b.** $\frac{15a}{16}$ **c.** $\frac{b}{2}$ **5a.** $1\frac{3}{5}$ **b.** $-1\frac{1}{3}$ **c.** $7\frac{1}{2}$

Lesson 5-5   pp. 253–257

Check Skills You'll Need **1.** $\frac{1}{3}$ **2.** 52 **3.** 10 **4.** $1\frac{1}{2}$

Check Understanding **1a.** Feet; inches are too small and miles are too large. **b.** Pounds; the weight is too great to measure in ounces. **c.** Inches; the pencil is too small to measure in feet. **d.** Fluid ounces; the capacity of a cup is too large. **2a.** $\frac{7}{8}$ **b.** $1\frac{1}{6}$ **c.** 7 **3a.** 56 **b.** $10\frac{1}{2}$ **c.** 7

Lesson 5-6   pp. 259–262

Check Skills You'll Need **1.** $\frac{1}{10}, \frac{1}{5}, \frac{1}{4}, \frac{1}{3}, \frac{1}{2}$ **2.** $\frac{3}{3}, \frac{5}{3}, \frac{7}{3}, \frac{13}{3}$ **3.** $\frac{3}{13}, \frac{3}{7}, \frac{3}{5}, \frac{3}{3}$ **4.** $-\frac{3}{3}, -\frac{3}{5}, -\frac{3}{7}, -\frac{3}{13}$

Check Understanding **7.** 3 h 55 min

Lesson 5-7   pp. 264–267

Check Skills You'll Need **1.** $-1\frac{1}{8}$ **2.** $8\frac{5}{24}$ **3.** $2\frac{5}{8}$ **4.** $-7\frac{7}{18}$

Check Understanding **1a.** $-\frac{1}{3}$ **b.** $\frac{1}{15}$ **c.** $\frac{13}{30}$ **2a.** $\frac{4}{5}$ **b.** $1\frac{1}{7}$ **3a.** $7\frac{5}{12}$ **b.** $2\frac{1}{18}$

Lesson 5-8   pp. 268–272

Check Skills You'll Need **1.** $\frac{5}{14}$ **2.** $-1\frac{1}{2}$ **3.** $6\frac{1}{4}$ **4.** 3

Check Understanding **1a.** $\frac{5}{56}$ **b.** $\frac{7}{18}$ **c.** $\frac{4}{15}$ **2a.** $3\frac{3}{4}$ **b.** $1\frac{5}{27}$ **c.** 1 **3a.** $-\frac{7}{8}$ **b.** $\frac{13}{15}$ **c.** $-\frac{1}{14}$ **4a.** 8 **b.** $-\frac{3}{10}$ **c.** $4\frac{6}{11}$

Checkpoint Quiz 2 **1.** 14 **2.** $\frac{1}{2}$ **3.** $-\frac{4}{27}$ **4.** $1\frac{1}{3}$ **5.** -2 **6.** 34 **7.** $2\frac{1}{4}$ **8.** 90 **9.** $1\frac{1}{2}$ **10.** $\frac{1}{3}$ **11.** $\frac{1}{5}$ **12.** $1\frac{5}{8}$ **13.** $11\frac{1}{4}$ **14.** $\frac{6}{35}$ **15.** $\frac{7}{15}$ **16.** $-17\frac{1}{3}$ **17.** $-\frac{27}{40}$ **18.** $3\frac{3}{5}$ **19.** $\frac{5}{33}$ **20.** 6 miles **21.** 55 mi/h **22.** $12 **23.** Answers may vary. Sample: A desktop can be measured in inches; 48 inches.

Lesson 5-9   pp. 274–277

Check Skills You'll Need **1.** 64 **2.** 81 **3.** 1 **4.** x^{18} **5.** b^{10} **6.** a^{28}

Check Understanding **1a.** 216 **b.** $16p^4$ **c.** x^5y^{10} **d.** $25x^6$ **2a.** $16y^4$ **b.** $-16y^4$ **c.** $-125a^6b^3$ **3a.** $\frac{1}{8}$ **b.** $\frac{16}{81}$ **c.** $\frac{8x^6}{27}$

Chapter 6

Diagnosing Readiness   p. 286

1. 16 **2.** 13.5 **3.** $\frac{7}{8}$ **4.** 2.5 **5.** $1\frac{1}{4}$ **6.** 27.5 **7–12.** Answers may vary. Samples are given. **7.** $\frac{2}{8}, \frac{4}{16}$ **8.** $\frac{2}{5}, \frac{8}{20}$ **9.** $\frac{3}{7}, \frac{12}{28}$ **10.** $\frac{4}{18}, \frac{6}{27}$ **11.** $\frac{6}{16}, \frac{9}{24}$ **12.** $\frac{10}{12}, \frac{15}{18}$ **13.** $\frac{1}{4}$ **14.** $\frac{1}{4}$ **15.** $\frac{4}{5}$ **16.** $\frac{3}{8}$ **17.** $\frac{3}{7}$ **18.** $\frac{1}{8}$ **19.** $\frac{5}{6}$ **20.** $\frac{1}{25}$ **21.** 0.35 **22.** $\frac{3}{50}$ **23.** 3.75 **24.** $\frac{7}{20}$ **25.** $\frac{7}{8}$ **26.** 3.6 **27.** $1\frac{7}{100}$ **28.** $0.\overline{6}$ **29.** $11.\overline{1}$ **30.** $\frac{1}{3}$ **31.** 6.25 **32.** $3\frac{49}{50}$

Lesson 6-1   pp. 288–291

Check Skills You'll Need **1.** $\frac{6}{7}$ **2.** $\frac{3}{5}$ **3.** $\frac{9}{10}$ **4.** $\frac{4}{5}$ **5.** $\frac{1}{3}$ **6.** $\frac{5}{3}$, or $1\frac{2}{3}$

Check Understanding **1a.** $\frac{2}{5}$ **b.** $\frac{3}{2}$ **2a.** $.99/L **b.** 34 mi/gal **3a.** 52.5 **b.** 432

Lesson 6-2   pp. 294–298

Check Skills You'll Need **1.** 13 **2.** 6 **3.** 15 **4.** 3

Check Understanding **1a.** 6 **b.** 44 **c.** 77 **2a.** yes, cross products equal **b.** no, cross products not equal **c.** yes, cross products equal **3.** 87 nautical miles

Lesson 6-3   pp. 299–303

Check Skills You'll Need **1.** 14 **2.** 133.3 **3.** 6.7 **4.** 3.6

Check Understanding **1.** 15.8 **2.** 28 ft

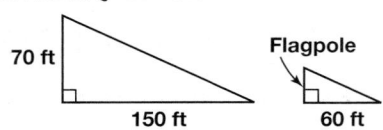

3. $1\frac{7}{8}$ in.

Lesson 6-4   pp. 305–309

Check Skills You'll Need **1.** $\frac{5}{8}$ **2.** $\frac{3}{20}$ **3.** $\frac{5}{11}$ **4.** $\frac{11}{12}$

Check Understanding **1a.** $\frac{3}{6}$, or $\frac{1}{2}$ **b.** $\frac{1}{6}$ **c.** $\frac{2}{6}$, or $\frac{1}{3}$ **2a.** $\frac{5}{6}$ **b.** a certain event **3a.** 1 to 4 **b.** 4 to 1 **ci.** 2 to 3 **cii.** 3 to 2

Checkpoint Quiz 1 **1.** 4 mi/h **2.** 6 gal/min **3.** 48 ft/s **4.** 4.5 **5.** 42 times **6.** $\frac{2}{6}$, or $\frac{1}{3}$

Lesson 6-5   pp. 310–314

Check Skills You'll Need **1.** 0.625 **2.** 0.45 **3.** 0.75 **4.** $0.8\overline{3}$ **5.** $0.\overline{6}$ **6.** $0.\overline{72}$

Check Understanding **1a.** $\frac{29}{50}$ **b.** $\frac{18}{25}$ **c.** $1\frac{11}{25}$ **2a.** 0.16 **b.** 0.625 **c.** 1.2 **d.** 0.45, $\frac{9}{20}$ **3a.** 40% **b.** 2.3% **c.** 175% **4.** 27%

Lesson 6-6   pp. 315–319

Check Skills You'll Need **1.** 7 **2.** 230 **3.** 25 **4.** 18

Check Understanding

1a. 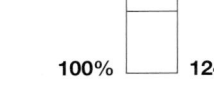 $\frac{25}{100} = \frac{n}{124}$; 31

b. 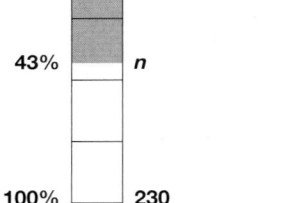 $\frac{43}{100} = \frac{n}{230}$; 98.9

c. 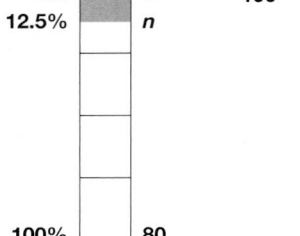 $\frac{12.5}{100} = \frac{n}{80}$; 10

2a. 55.2% **b.** 93.3% **3a.** 25.3 **b.** 313.1 **4.** about 3,567 screens

Lesson 6-7   pp. 320–323

Check Skills You'll Need **1.** 0.48 **2.** 0.05 **3.** 0.238 **4.** 0.7225 **5.** 1.36 **6.** 1.785

Check Understanding **1a.** $0.96 = n \cdot 10$; 9.6%
b. $19.2 = 0.32 \cdot n$; 60 **2a.** $n = 1.455 \cdot 20$; 29.1
b. $380 = 1.25n$; 304 **3.** $.85 **4.** 1,344 people

Lesson 6-8   pp. 325–328

Check Skills You'll Need **1.** 46% **2.** 247% **3.** 3%
4. 523.6%

Check Understanding **1a.** 14% **b.** 60% **c.** 112.5%
2. 26% **3a.** 50% **b.** 5.0% **c.** 92.9%

Lesson 6-9   pp. 329–332

Check Skills You'll Need **1.** $61.50 **2.** $71.40 **3.** $1.32
4. $12.79

Check Understanding **1.** $42 **2.** $8.50 **3.** $3.30

Checkpoint Quiz 2 **1.** = **2.** < **3.** > **4.** $0.33 \cdot 120 = n$;
39.6 **5.** $1.25 \cdot 42 = n$; 52.5 **6.** $n \cdot 5.6 = 1.4$; 25%
7. $0.15 \cdot q = 9.75$; 65 **8.** $9,600

Lesson 6-10   pp. 334–337

Check Skills You'll Need **1.** $163.83

Check Understanding **11.** about 299 million people

Chapter 7

Diagnosing Readiness   p. 346

1. $p + 3$ **2.** $q - 6$ **3.** $12y$ **4.** $10d$ **5.** $2b$ **6.** $n - 8$
7. $4n$ **8.** $-3b + 10$ **9.** $19c + 13$ **10.** $-7x - 5y$
11. $2a + 6$ **12.** $9m - 35$ **13.** 11 **14.** -21 **15.** -98
16. 5 **17.** 8 **18.** 9 **19.** -32 **20.** -8 **21.** $c \geq 1$
22. $y < 2$ **23.** $b < 4$ **24.** $x > 0$ **25.** $x \geq -6$
26. $x \leq 15$ **27.** $b \leq 19$ **28.** $m \geq 80$

Lesson 7-1   pp. 348–351

Check Skills You'll Need **1.** 8 **2.** 11 **3.** 1 **4.** -12 **5.** -10

Check Understanding **1a.** 3 **b.** 16 **c.** -6 **d.** -1 **2a.** -2
b. 21 **c.** -3 **3.** $11

Lesson 7-2   pp. 352–356

Check Skills You'll Need **1.** $5x + 4$ **2.** $6y$ **3.** $3a$ **4.** $2 + c$
5. $2x - 7$

Check Understanding **1.** 92 points **2a.** 88, 89, 90, 91
b. 32, 34 **3a.** $4\frac{2}{3}$ **b.** -14

Lesson 7-3   pp. 357–361

Check Skills You'll Need **1.** -3 **2.** $2\frac{1}{4}$ **3.** -4 **4.** $\frac{2}{3}$

Check Understanding **1a.** 50 **b.** $10\frac{1}{2}$ **2a.** $\frac{3}{4}$ **b.** $5\frac{1}{2}$
3a. 4 **b.** 3.5

Lesson 7-4   pp. 362–365

Check Skills You'll Need **1.** $p - 21 = 48$ **2.** $b + 6 = 33$
3. $140 + d = 192$

Check Understanding **6.** Answers may vary. Sample:
Write and solve an equation because it is faster.
7. 122 mi

Checkpoint Quiz 1 **1.** 20 **2.** 11 **3.** -18 **4.** 4 **5.** 28
6. -48 **7.** 2 **8.** 1.3 **9.** -6 **10.** 0 **11.** 1 **12.** 6
13. $p - 0.25p = 82.50$; $110
14. $n + (n + 1) + (n + 2) = 132$; 43, 44, 45

Lesson 7-5   pp. 367–371

Check Skills You'll Need **1.** 5 **2.** 7 **3.** -10 **4.** 8

Check Understanding **1a.** 16 **b.** 2 **2.** 6 h

Lesson 7-6   pp. 373–376

Check Skills You'll Need

1. $w \geq -9$
2. $z > 10$
3. $a < 2$
4. $x \leq -1$

Check Understanding

1a. $a > 4$
1b. $x \leq -8$
1c. $c < -6$
2a. $m \geq -15$
2b. $x < 3$
2c. $b < -22$

3. $\geq$ $7,500

Lesson 7-7   pp. 378–381

Check Skills You'll Need **1.** 320 km **2.** 32 m **3.** 48 ft^2

Check Understanding **1a.** $s = p + c$ **b.** $k = hj$
c. $p = \frac{I}{rt}$ **2a.** $a = \frac{1}{5}b - \frac{7}{5}$ **b.** $w = \frac{1}{2}P - \ell$
c. $x = 3(y - 8)$ **3.** $r = \frac{d}{t}$ **4.** $h = an$; 11 hits

Checkpoint Quiz 2 1. -2 **2.** -6 **3.** $\frac{2}{9}$ **4.** 4 **5.** 3 **6.** 5
7. $y > -\frac{9}{10}$ **8.** $x > -56$ **9.** $x > 5$ **10.** $h = s - g$
11. $r = \frac{1}{3}k - \frac{4}{3}$ **12.** $t = \frac{I}{pr}$

Lesson 7-8   pp. 382–386

Check Skills You'll Need 1. $24 **2.** $1,100 **3.** $31.50
4. $17.88

Check Understanding 1a. $30 **b.** $4.38

2a.

Bal. at Yr Start	Interest	Bal. at Yr End
$500.00	$15.00	$515.00
$515.00	$15.45	$530.45

2b.

Bal. at Yr Start	Interest	Bal. at Yr End
$625.00	$12.50	$637.50
$637.50	$12.75	$650.25
$650.25	$13.01	$663.26
$663.26	$13.27	$676.53

3a. $955.09 **b.** $955.37

Chapter 8

Diagnosing Readiness   p. 396

1. $-4, -7$ **2.** 19, 13 **3.** 10.5, 12 **4.** $-11, -13$
5. (5, 2) **6.** $(-3, 4)$ **7.** (4, 0) **8.** $(6, -3)$ **9.** $(-4, -3)$
10. (0, 3)   **11–16.**
17. $-\frac{1}{18}$ **18.** 3 **19.** 1 **20.** $\frac{1}{3}$
21. $y = -4x + 3$
22. $y = -2x + 4$
23. $y = 2x - 6$
24. $y = -6x - 8$
25. $y = -x + 12$
26. $y = \frac{-x + 5}{2}$
27. $y = \frac{x + 20}{5}$
28. $y = \frac{-3x + 12}{4}$

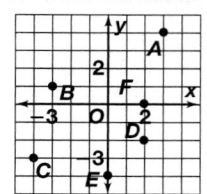

Lesson 8-1   pp. 400–404

Check Skills You'll Need 1–6.

Check Understanding 1a. No; there are two range values for the domain value 2. **b.** Yes; there is one range value for each domain value.
2a. No; a specific postage cost (domain value) can mail packages of different weights (range values). **b.** Yes; for each package weight (domain value) there is one postage cost to the same zip code (range value).

3a. A function; no vertical line passes through two graphed points.

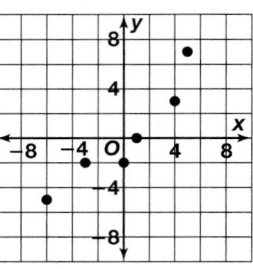

b. Not a function; a vertical line passes through both $(-1, 1)$ and $(-1, 3)$.

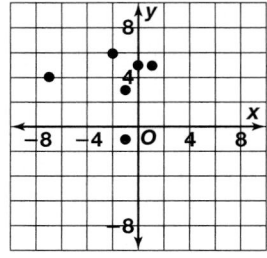

c. A function; no vertical line passes through two graphed points.

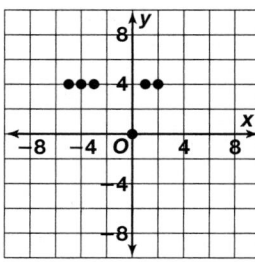

Lesson 8-2   pp. 405–409

Check Skills You'll Need 1. 4 **2.** -10 **3.** 3 **4.** 6

Check Understanding 1a. $(-3, -5)$ **b.** $(-3, 15)$
c. $(-3, -4)$ **2.** 14°C
3a.

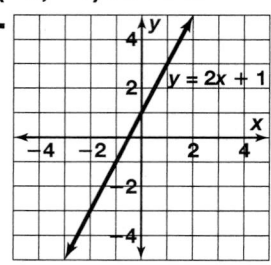

b.

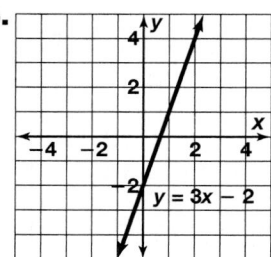

c.

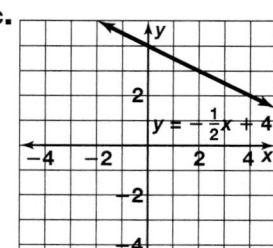

4a. no

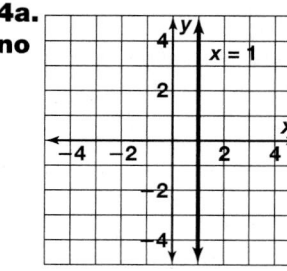

b. yes

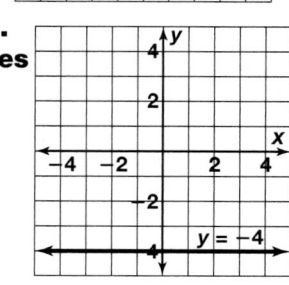

c. no

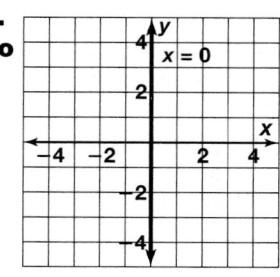

5a.

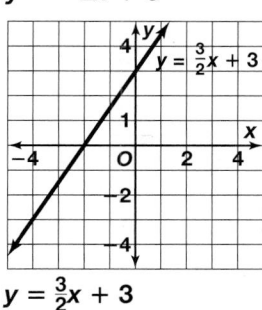

$y = -2x + 3$

b.

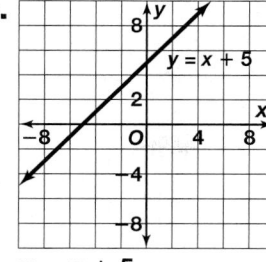

$y = x + 5$

c.

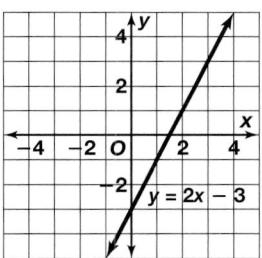

$y = \frac{3}{2}x + 3$

Lesson 8-3   pp. 411–416

Check Skills You'll Need 1. -9 **2.** 5 **3.** -3 **4.** 0

Check Understanding 1. $-\frac{3}{4}$ **2a.** $\frac{3}{4}$ **b.** -1
3a. undefined **b.** 0

4a.

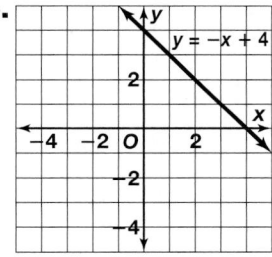

b.

$y = 2x - 3$ $y = -x + 4$

Lesson 8-4   pp. 418–422

Check Skills You'll Need 1. 0 **2.** 1 **3.** undefined **4.** $-\frac{1}{3}$

Check Understanding 1. $c(p) = 3p + 4$; $19
2a. $f(x) = 2x$ **b.** $f(x) = -2x$ **c.** $y = 2x + 1$
3. $y = -x + 2$

Checkpoint Quiz 1 1. Answers may vary. Sample:
$(0, -9)$, $(2, 0)$, $(1, -4\frac{1}{2})$ **2.**
3. Yes; there is one range
value for each domain
value.
4. Answers may vary.
Sample: If every vertical
line passes through just
one graphed point, then
the relation is a function.
5. 5 **6.** -1 **7.** undefined
8. $-2, 5$ **9.** $p(n) = 2,000n$

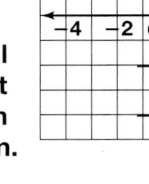

$3x - y = 5$

Lesson 8-5   pp. 423–428

Check Skills You'll Need 1. $(-2, 2)$ **2.** $(0, 3)$ **3.** $(-3, 0)$
4. $(2, 3)$

Check Understanding 1a. The person has 14 years of
education and earns \$90,000 in a year. **b.** 4 people
2a.

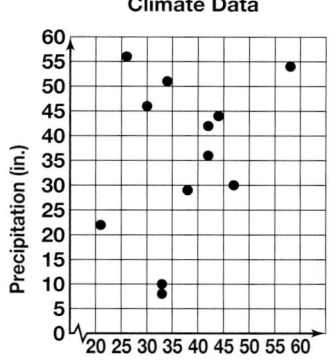

Climate Data

2b.

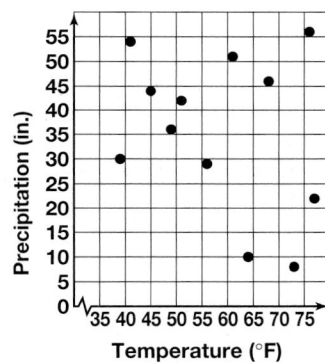

Climate Data

3a. Positive correlation; as time goes by, the
winning distances have tended to increase.

Lesson 8-6   pp. 430–433

Check Skills You'll Need 1. $y = 2x + 2$ **2.** $y = -\frac{1}{4}x - 3$

Check Understanding 3a–d. Answers may vary.
Samples are given. **a.** about 2,175 **b.** about -55
c. $y = -55x + 2,175$ **d.** 1,185

Lesson 8-7   pp. 435–440

Check Skills You'll Need
1.

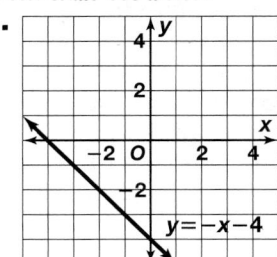

$y = -x - 4$

2.

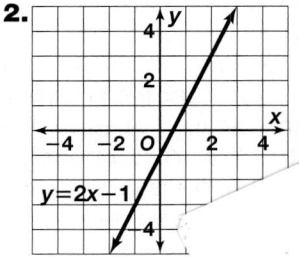

$y = 2x - 1$

3.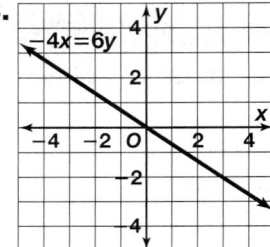

$-4x = 6y$

4.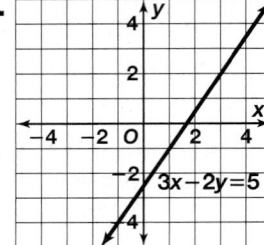

$3x - 2y = 5$

Check Understanding

1a. (2, −4)

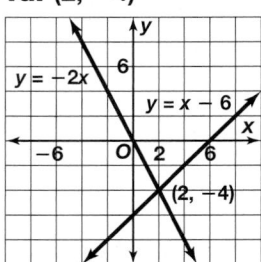

$y = -2x$

$y = x - 6$

$(2, -4)$

b. (1, 0)

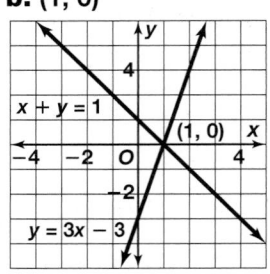

$x + y = 1$

$(1, 0)$

$y = 3x - 3$

2a. infinitely many solutions

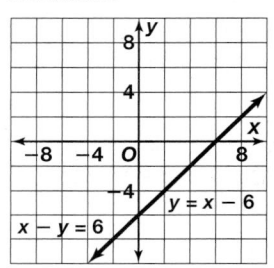

$x - y = 6$

$y = x - 6$

b. no solutions

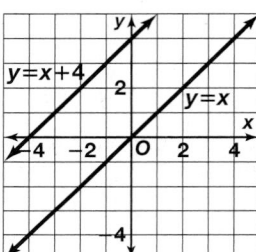

$y = x + 4$

$y = x$

3. −3, −5

Checkpoint Quiz 2

1a.

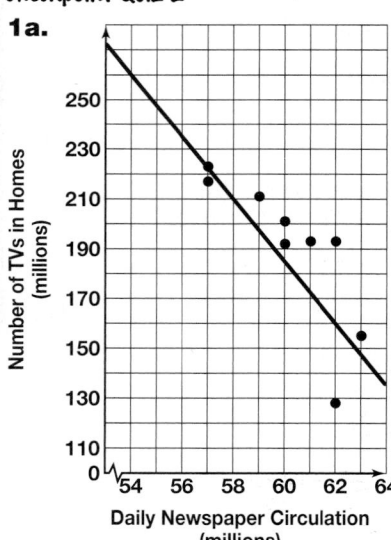

Number of TVs in Homes (millions)

Daily Newspaper Circulation (millions)

1b. Negative correlation; as the number of television sets increases, the newspaper circulation decreases.
1c. Trend lines may vary. Sample: See scatterplot; 250 million television sets.

2. (−2, 8)

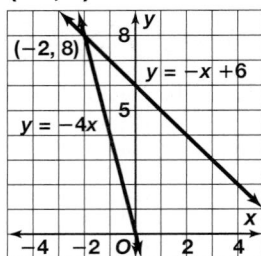

$(-2, 8)$

$y = -x + 6$

$y = -4x$

3. (−3, −4)

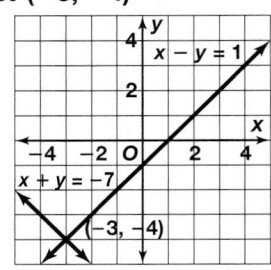

$x - y = 1$

$x + y = -7$

$(-3, -4)$

4. (1, 3)

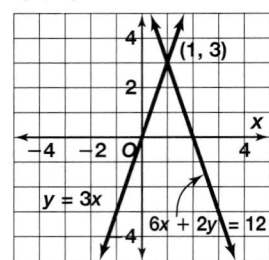

$(1, 3)$

$y = 3x$

$6x + 2y = 12$

5. $g(c) = \frac{c}{231}$ **6.** 3, −7

Lesson 8-8   **pp. 441–446**

Check Skills You'll Need 1. yes; $-5 + 3 \geq -2$
2. no; $5 - 1 \not< 4$ **3.** yes; $-2 - 2(-4) \leq 6$
4. no; $4(-2) + 1 \not> -7$

Check Understanding

1a.

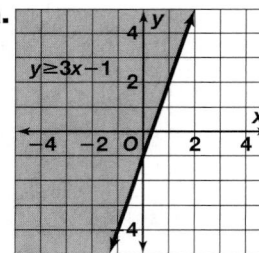

$y \geq 3x - 1$

b.

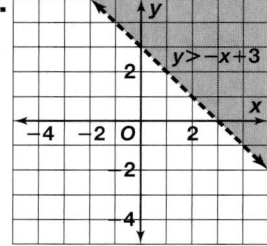

$y > -x + 3$

c.

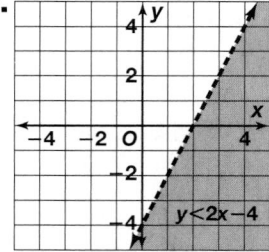

$y < 2x - 4$

2a.

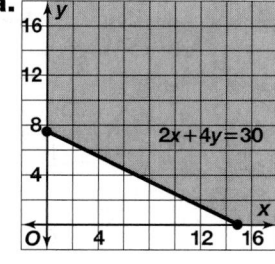

$2x + 4y = 30$

$2x + 4y \geq 30$

3a.

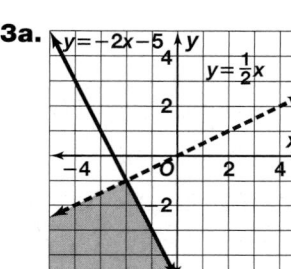

$y = -2x - 5$

$y = \frac{1}{2}x$

b.

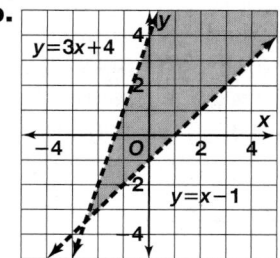

$y = 3x + 4$

$y = x - 1$

Answers to Instant Check System™

Chapter 9

1. C 2. B 3. D 4. A 5. 6 cm 6. $\frac{1}{2}$ in. 7. 2.8 cm
8. 7.5 ft

9–18.

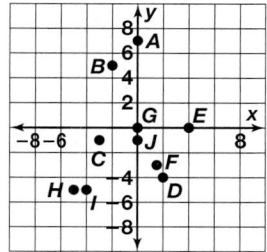

Check Skills You'll Need 1. The graph is a line that starts at 3 and extends to the right without end. **2.** The graph is a line that starts at 0 and extends to the left without end. **3.** The graph is a line that starts at 5 and extends to the left without end. **4.** The graph is a line that starts at −2 and extends to the right without end.

Check Understanding 1a. C, N, V **b.** $\overline{NC}$, $\overline{NV}$
c. $\overrightarrow{NC}$, $\overrightarrow{NV}$ **2a.** $\overline{EH}$, $\overline{FG}$, $\overline{AE}$, $\overline{BF}$
b. $\overline{HG}$, $\overline{DC}$, $\overline{AB}$ **c.** $\overline{DH}$, $\overline{CG}$, $\overline{AD}$, $\overline{BC}$

3a.

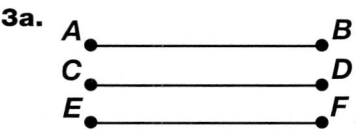

b.

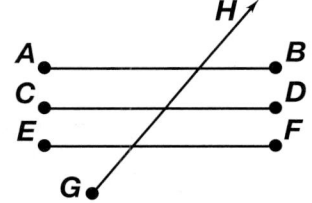

c.

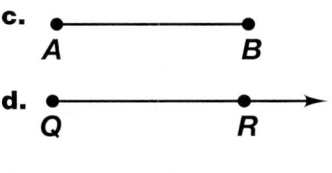

Check Skills You'll Need 1. 135 **2.** 15 **3.** 90 **4.** 30

Check Understanding 1. 160°, 20°, 160° **2.** ∠1 ≅ ∠5,
∠2 ≅ ∠6, ∠3 ≅ ∠7, ∠4 ≅ ∠8; ∠3 ≅ ∠5, ∠4 ≅ ∠6

Check Skills You'll Need 1. acute **2.** obtuse **3.** obtuse
4. right **5.** acute **6.** obtuse

Check Understanding 1a. scalene right triangle
b. isosceles obtuse triangle **c.** scalene obtuse
triangle **2.** rectangles and squares **3a.** $P = 6x$
b. 96 cm

Check Skills You'll Need 1.   **2.**

3.   **4.**   **5.**

Check Understanding 5. 35

Check Skills You'll Need 1. ∠X **2.** ∠Z **3.** $\overline{XY}$ **4.** $\overline{ZX}$

Check Understanding 1. $\overline{AB} \cong \overline{DE}$, $\overline{BC} \cong \overline{EC}$,
$\overline{AC} \cong \overline{DC}$, ∠A ≅ ∠D, ∠B ≅ ∠E, ∠BCA ≅ ∠ECD,
$AC = 50$ m **2.** $\overline{FJ} \cong \overline{FG}$, $\overline{JI} \cong \overline{GH}$, $\overline{FI} \cong \overline{FH}$,
△JFI ≅ △GFH by SSS

Checkpoint Quiz 1 1. ray **2.** line **3.** $\overline{LN}$ **4.** angle
5a. $6x + 16 + 2x + 12 = 180$, $x = 19$ **b.** 50°
c. 130° **d.** 130° **6.**

Check Skills You'll Need 1. 36 **2.** 270 **3.** 54 **4.** 109

Check Understanding 1a. about $8\frac{4}{5}$ in.
b. about 188.4 mm **c.** about 628 mi

2. Blood Types of Population

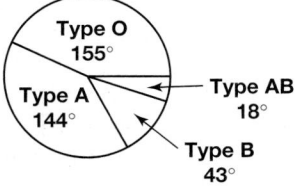

3. Student Jobs at Western High School

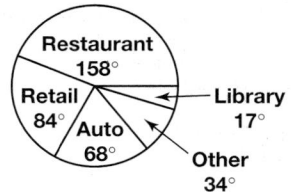

Instant Check System™ Answers

Lesson 9-7   pp. 491–495

Check Skills You'll Need 1. point *B* **2.** a line segment with end points *A* and *B* **3.** a ray with endpoint *A* and containing *B* **4.** a line containing point *A* and point *B*

Check Understanding

1.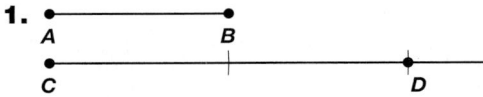

2.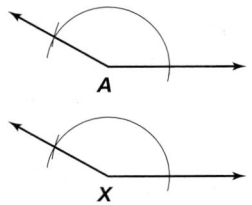

3.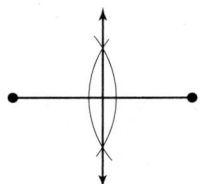

4.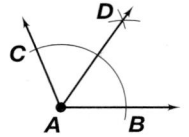

b.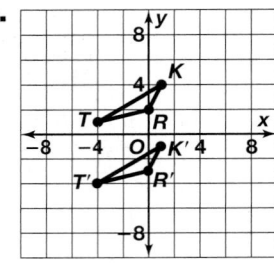

c.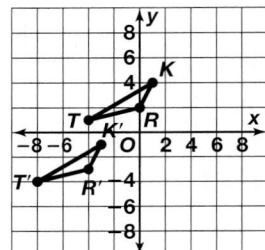

2. $B(-1, 5) \rightarrow B'(3, 1)$ **3.** $(x, y) \rightarrow (x + 5, y - 1)$

Checkpoint Quiz 2 1. A is chicken, B is fish, and C is vegetarian. **2.** The central angle for A is 180°, B is 126°, and C is 54°.

3.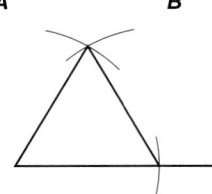

4.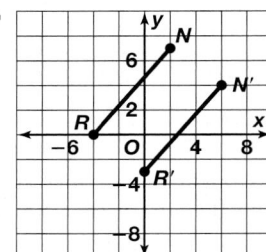

Lesson 9-9   pp. 503–506

Check Skills You'll Need

1. 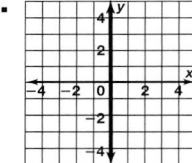   **2.**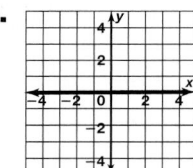

3. 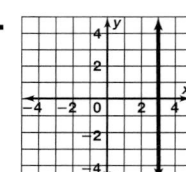   **4.**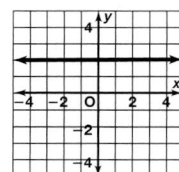

5. 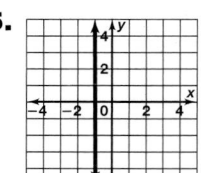   **6.**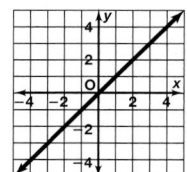

Check Understanding

1a. 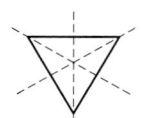   **b.**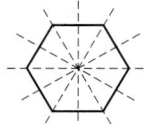

Lesson 9-8   pp. 497–501

Check Skills You'll Need 1–5.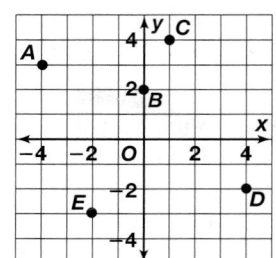

Check Understanding 1a.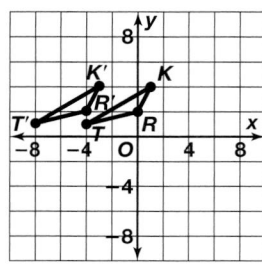

2.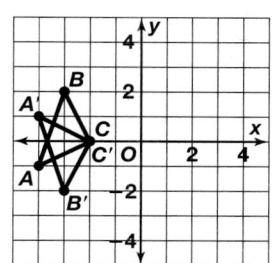

3a.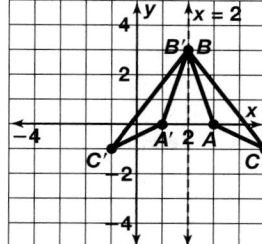

b.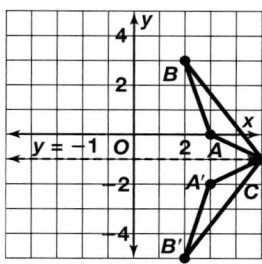

Chapter 10

Diagnosing Readiness

1. 36 m² **2.** 20 in.² **3.** 45 cm² **4.** 45
6. 864 **7.** 48 **8.** 300 **9.** 452.16 **10.** 6 **11.** $19\frac{1}{2}$
12. 9 **13.** 10x **14.** 5x² **15.** 55 **16.** 1,364 **17.** 500
18. 8 **19.** 157 yd **20.** 628 m **21.** 17.27 in.

Lesson 10-1	**pp. 522–526**

Check Skills You'll Need 1. $\ell = 9$ in. **2.** $A = 245$ m²
3. $w = 10$ cm **4.** $A = 51.84$ ft²

Check Understanding 1a. 1,000 cm², or 0.1 m²
b. 12 ft², or $1\frac{1}{3}$ yd² **2a.** 6 m² **b.** 24 in.² **c.** The larger
parallelogram is 4 times the area of the smaller
parallelogram.

Lesson 10-2	**pp. 527–531**

Check Skills You'll Need 1. 8 **2.** 42 **3.** $37\frac{1}{2}$ **4.** 10

Check Understanding 1a. 7.38 ft² **b.** 5 m² **2.** 24 yd²
3. 13 ft² **b.** 342 mm²

Lesson 10-3	**pp. 532–537**

Check Skills You'll Need 1. 50.24 **2.** 78.5 **3.** 254.34
4. 0.785

Check Understanding 1. 2,500π in.² **2.** about
113 mi² **3.** 40.2 cm²

Checkpoint Quiz 1 1. 100 in.² **2.** 50 in.² **3.** 300 in.²
4. 300 yd² **5.** 2,100 cm² **6.** 150 m² **7.** 100π yd²;
314 yd² **8.** 64π ft²; 201 ft² **9.** (800 + 50π) cm²;
957 cm² **10.** 5 cm

Lesson 10-4	**pp. 539–543**

Check Skills You'll Need 1. triangle **2.** square
3. rectangle **4.** hexagon

Check Understanding 1a. cylinder **b.** cone **2a.** With a
triangular base and three faces that are triangles,
you can form a triangular pyramid. **b.** With two
square bases and 4 faces that are squares, you
can form a cube.

Lesson 9-10	**pp. 507–510**

Check Skills You'll Need

1. 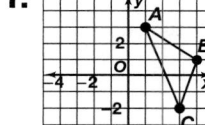 **2.**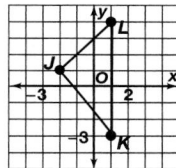

3.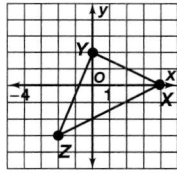

Check Understanding

1.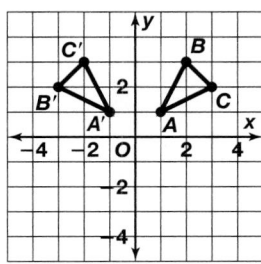
2a. no **b.** yes, 180°
c. yes, 180°

The vertices of the image are $A'(-1, 1)$,
$B'(-3, 2)$, and $C'(-2, 3)$.

Instant Check System™ Answers

Check Skills You'll Need

1. 31.4 in.
2. 26.4 cm
3. 25.1 ft
4. 21.3 in.

Check Understanding 1a. 84 yd^2 **b.** 336 yd^2 **c.** The surface area of the larger prism is 4 times the surface area of the smaller prism. **2.** 108 m^2 **3.** about 785 cm^2

Lesson 10-6   pp. 552–556

Check Skills You'll Need 1. 10π **2.** 15π **3.** 5π **4.** 22π

Check Understanding 1. 720 ft^2 **2.** about 1,011 ft^2 **3.** about 452 cm^2

Lesson 10-7   pp. 557–560

Check Skills You'll Need 1. about 201 cm^2 **2.** about 452 cm^2 **3.** about 314 cm^2

Check Understanding 1. 216 ft^3 **2a.** 1,900 ft^3 **b.** The volume of the larger cylinder is 8 times the volume of the smaller cylinder.

Lesson 10-8   pp. 562–565

Check Skills You'll Need

1.    2.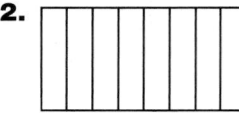

3.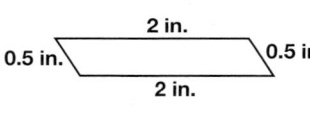

Check Understanding 8a. 66 in.^{3}; 52.5 in.^{3}; 21 in.^{3} **b.** Yes; $5\frac{1}{2}$ in. by 8 in. by $1\frac{1}{2}$ in.

Checkpoint Quiz 2 1. square prism, 56 cm^2 **2.** cylinder, 207 in.^{2} **3.** square pyramid, 85 cm^2 **4.** 78.1 cm^3 **5.** 169.6 in.^{3} **6.** Check students' work.

Lesson 10-9   pp. 566–569

Check Skills You'll Need

1. 20.9$\overline{3}$ **2.** 32 **3.** 33.49$\overline{3}$ **4.** 0.52$\overline{3}$

Check Understanding 1. 21 cm^3 **2.** 167 ft^3 **3a.** 14,130 m^3 **b.** 180 mi^3

Chapter 11

Diagnosing Readiness   p. 578

1. *G* **2.** *K* **3.** *H* **4.** *D* **5.** *B* **6.** *F* **7.** (−5, 4) **8.** (2, 1) **9.** (7, 0) **10.** (−7, 1) **11.** (4, −2) **12.** (−6, −3) **13.** 100 **14.** 36 **15.** 4 **16.** 81 **17.** 121 **18.** 0.04 **19.** 49 **20.** 5.29 **21.** 16 **22.** 25 **23.** 4 **24.** 4 **25.** 1 **26.** 10 **27.** 2 **28.** 60 **29.** 77 **30.** 26 **31.** 10 **32.** 32 **33.** 17 **34.** 8

Lesson 11-1   pp. 580–583

Check Skills You'll Need 1. 1, 4, 9, 16, 25, 36, 49, 64, 81, 100, 121, 144 **2.** 100; 400; 900; 1,600; 2,500; 3,600; 4,900; 6,400; 8,100; 10,000; 12,100; 14,400

Check Understanding 1a. 10 **b.** −10 **c.** 4 **d.** −4 **2a.** 5 **b.** −8 **c.** 7 **d.** −5 **3a.** irrational; because 2 is not a perfect square **b.** rational; because 81 is a perfect square **c.** rational; because it is a terminating decimal **d.** irrational; because 42 is not a perfect square

Lesson 11-2   pp. 584–589

Check Skills You'll Need 1. 52 **2.** 89 **3.** 130 **4.** 90

Check Understanding 1a. 5 ft **b.** 9 m **2.** 12.7 m **3.** 8.7 ft **4a.** Yes, $7^2 + 8^2 = 113$. **b.** No, $5^2 + 6^2 \neq 10^2$.

Lesson 11-3   pp. 592–596

Check Skills You'll Need 1. (−3, 4) **2.** (0, 3) **3.** (−4, −2) **4.** (3, −1)

Check Understanding 1a. 4.1 **b.** 9.5 **2.** 17.5 **3a.** (4, 3) **b.** (−1, 0.5)

Checkpoint Quiz 1 1. −2 **2.** 4 **3.** 5 **4.** 9 **5.** −7 **6.** 10 **7.** 10 ft **8.** 16.1 m **9.** 25 yd **10.** 7.1 cm **11.** 9.2; (−3, −5.5) **12.** 15.8; (1.5, 6.5) **13.** Answers may vary.

Sample: $\sqrt{120}$, $\sqrt{299}$, 15.010010001 . . .

Lesson 11-4   pp. 598–601

Check Skills You'll Need 1. 4 **2.** 4 **3.** 32 **4.** 10

Check Understanding 3. $\overline{RQ}$ and $\overline{RP}$, $\overline{ST}$ and $\overline{SP}$ **4.** It allows you to draw the entire 40 + *x* side to complete the larger triangle.

Lesson 11-5   pp. 602–606

Check Skills You'll Need 1. 10 m **2.** 12 m **3.** 45 m **4.** 36 m

Check Understanding 1. 5.9 cm **2.** 17 m **3a.** $a \approx 6.9$ cm, $b = 8$ cm **b.** $e = 6$ in., $f \approx 10.4$ in.

Lesson 11-6
pp. 608–612

Check Skills You'll Need **1.** 15 ft **2.** $25\frac{2}{3}$ ft

Check Understanding **1.** $\sin Y = \frac{12}{13}$, $\cos Y = \frac{5}{13}$, $\tan Y = \frac{12}{5}$ **2a.** 0.1736 **b.** 0.2588 **c.** 1.3270 **d.** 0.9272 **3.** about 14.3 ft

Checkpoint Quiz 2 **1.** 45°-45°-90° **2.** 30°-60°-90° **3.** 30°-60°-90° **4.** 0.4848 **5.** 0.5774 **6.** 0.5299 **7.** 0.9986

Lesson 11-7
pp. 614–618

Check Skills You'll Need **1.** 0.7071 **2.** 0.8480 **3.** 0.3249 **4.** 0.9272 **5.** 0.0349 **6.** 9.5144

Check Understanding **1.** about 141 m **2.** 16.1 m **3.** about 22.7 m

Chapter 12

Diagnosing Readiness
p. 628

1. 12 **2.** 52 **3.** 101 **4.** 0.225 **5.** $\frac{1}{3}$ **6.** $\frac{3}{4}$ **7.** $\frac{4}{5}$ **8.** $\frac{2}{3}$ **9.** $\frac{1}{2}$ **10.** $\frac{5}{8}$ **11.** $\frac{1}{6}$ **12.** $\frac{1}{6}$ **13.** $\frac{2}{6}$ or $\frac{1}{3}$ **14.** 0 **15.** $\frac{3}{6}$, or $\frac{1}{2}$ **16.** 0 **17.** $\frac{5}{6}$ **18.** $\frac{2}{6}$, or $\frac{1}{3}$ **19.** $\frac{18}{33}$, or $\frac{6}{11}$ **20.** $\frac{15}{33}$, or $\frac{5}{11}$ **21.** $\frac{15}{33}$, or $\frac{5}{11}$ **22.** $\frac{18}{33}$, or $\frac{6}{11}$ **23.** 0.50 **24.** 0.36 **25.** 0.20 **26.** 0.05 **27.** 20% **28.** 87.5% **29.** 28% **30.** 30%

Lesson 12-1
pp. 630–633

Check Skills You'll Need **1.** 9; 9 **2.** 77; 73 **3.** 200; 300 **4.** 5; 3

Check Understanding

1.

Number	Frequency
10	5
11	3
12	2
13	2
14	1
15	2

2a.

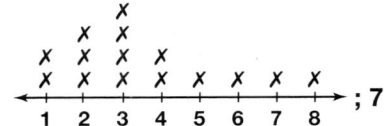

Miles to the Mall

b. \$.19

Lesson 12-2
pp. 635–639

Check Skills You'll Need **1.** 9.5 **2.** 4.9 **3.** 52 **4.** 101

Check Understanding

1.

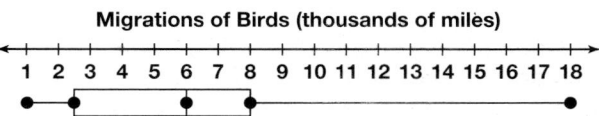

Migrations of Birds (thousands of miles)

2.

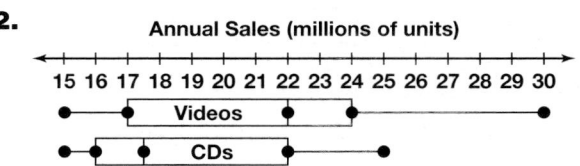

Annual Sales (millions of units)

3a. The highest value is 50 and the lowest is 10. The median is 22.5. At least half of the values are within 2.5 units of the median. **b.** The highest value is 45 and the lowest is 15. The median is 35. At least half of the values are within 10 units of the median. **4.** The women's heights have a median of 71 in. and a range of 10 in. The men's heights have a median of 79 in. and a range of 12 in. Most of the men are taller than the tallest woman.

Lesson 12-3
pp. 642–647

Check Skills You'll Need **1.** $\frac{1}{2}$ **2.** $\frac{1}{2}$

Check Understanding

1.

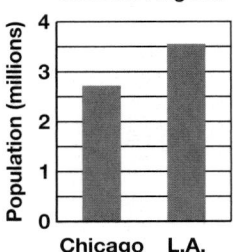

Populations of Chicago and Los Angeles

2a. Answers may vary. Sample:

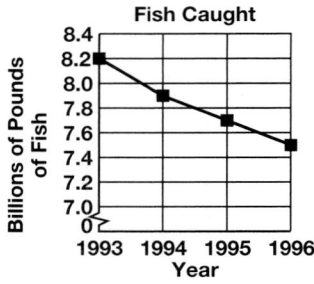

b. Answers may vary. Sample:

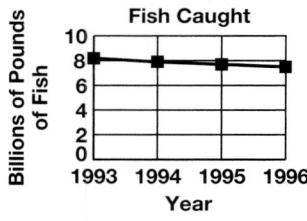

c. Answers may vary. Sample: They would use the graph from part (a) to show that the supply of fish is decreasing rapidly. Using this graph emphasizes the need for the limit.

3a. Answers may vary. Sample:

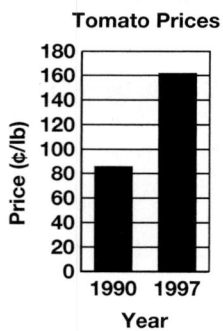

b. Answers may vary. Sample:

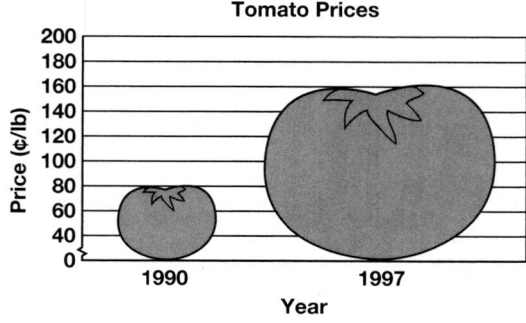

Check Skills You'll Need   **1.** $\frac{4}{12}$, or $\frac{1}{3}$ **2.** $\frac{8}{12}$, or $\frac{2}{3}$ **3.** $\frac{5}{12}$
4. $\frac{9}{12}$, or $\frac{3}{4}$ **5.** $\frac{3}{12}$, or $\frac{1}{4}$ **6.** $\frac{8}{12}$, or $\frac{2}{3}$

Check Understanding

1. 12 choices;

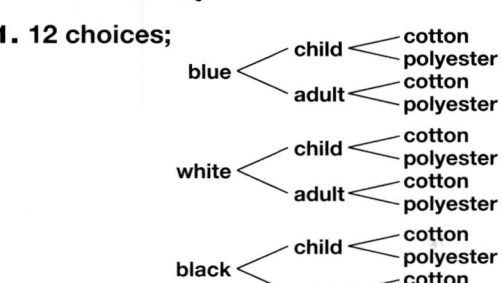

2a. 17,576 three-letter monograms **b.** 7,962,624 license plates **3.** $\frac{1}{2}$ **4.** $\frac{1}{100,000}$

Checkpoint Quiz 1

1.

Number	Frequency
47	2
48	2
49	1
50	3
51	2
52	2

2.

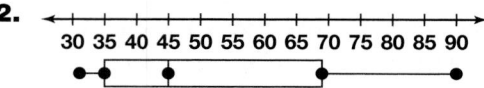

3a.

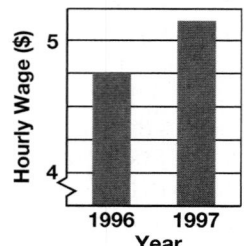

A break in the graph makes it look like there is a significant increase in minimum wage.

3b.

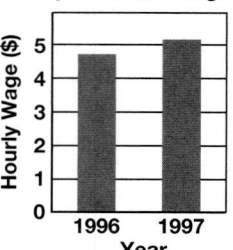

4. $\frac{1}{4}$

Lesson 12-5   pp. 654–658

Check Skills You'll Need 1. $\frac{3}{25}$ 2. $\frac{1}{8}$ 3. $\frac{2}{25}$ 4. $\frac{5}{18}$ 5. $\frac{2}{7}$ 6. $\frac{4}{5}$

Check Understanding 1. $\frac{1}{4}$ 2. 9% 3a. $\frac{3}{10}$ b. $\frac{3}{10}$

Lesson 12-6   pp. 659–663

Check Skills You'll Need 1. 36 outcomes 2. 15,600 outcomes 3. 84 outcomes 4. 16 outcomes

Check Understanding 1. 120 2a. 20 b. 60 c. 120 d. 120 3. 20 ways 4a. 28 b. 56 c. 70 d. 56 5a. Combinations; the order in which the teacher selects the students does not matter. b. Permutations; the order in which students are chosen matters.

Lesson 12-7   pp. 665–668

Check Skills You'll Need 1. 80% 2. 53% 3. 62.5% 4. 60% 5. 58.$\overline{3}$% 6. 62.5%

Check Understanding 1. 52% 2a. The experimental probability is less than the theoretical probability. b. The experimental probability is likely to get closer to the theoretical probability of $\frac{1}{2}$.

Lesson 12-8   pp. 669–672

Check Skills You'll Need 1. 112.5 2. 6,720 3. 400 4. 5,760

Check Understanding 1a. Not a good sample; these students would be most interested in racing bikes. b. Not a good sample; this sample would not include teens who do not rent videos. c. This is a good sample, because there is little built-in bias for or against any cereal. 2a. 200 calculators b. Less accurate; a larger sample is likely to be more representative of the population. c. The entire population might be too large to be surveyed. Also, the testing might be destructive, as would occur in testing light-bulb life.

Checkpoint Quiz 2 1. $\frac{2}{9}$ 2a. 380 outcomes b. 190 committees 3. $\frac{2}{15}$; 3 goals 4. 9,444 premium oranges

Lesson 12-9   pp. 674–677

Check Skills You'll Need

1.

letter	tally	frequency
a	ⅢⅢ	5
c	I	1
d	I	1
e	ⅢⅢ I	6
f	I	1
i	IIII	4
l	III	3
m	II	2
n	II	2
o	III	3
p	I	1
r	II	2
s	II	2
t	I	1
u	I	1
x	I	1

Check Understanding 6. Check students' work. 7. Check students' work.

Chapter 13

Diagnosing Readiness   p. 686

1. 40 2. −32 3. 17 4. 28 5. 0.64 6. 25 7. 2 8. 7 9. $3d - 12$ 10. $15x + 5$ 11. $3u - 24$ 12. $8y + 28$ 13. $-12d + 4$ 14. $50 - 30s$ 15. $-21 + 6w$ 16. $27 - 6b$ 17. $11a - 4$ 18. 5 19. $-g + 4$ 20. $10t + 5s$ 21. $7b + 4d$ 22. $-45c$ 23. −10, −4, 2 24. 6, 0, −6 25. −10, −2, 6 26. $-6\frac{1}{5}$, −5, $-3\frac{4}{5}$, 27. 10, 6, 2 28. $-7\frac{1}{2}$, −8, $-8\frac{1}{2}$ 29. −1, 0, 1 30. 5, −1, −7

Lesson 13-1   pp. 688–692

Check Skills You'll Need 1. Start with 60 and subtract 12 repeatedly. 2. Start with 7 and add 5 repeatedly. 3. Start with 6 and multiply by 3 repeatedly. 4. Start with 60 and divide by 2 repeatedly.

Check Understanding 1a. 5 b. −3 2a. 7, 3, −1; start with 23 and add −4 repeatedly. b. $-\frac{2}{3}$, $\frac{2}{3}$, 2; start with −6 and add $1\frac{1}{3}$ repeatedly. 3a. 3; 324, 972, 2,916; start with 4 and multiply by 3 repeatedly. b. 0.5; 0.25, 0.125, 0.0625; start with 4 and multiply by 0.5 repeatedly. 4a. geometric; 243, 729, 2,187 b. neither; 34, 45, 58 c. geometric; −12, 12, −12 d. arithmetic; 650, 800, 950

Check Skills You'll Need   **1.** −11, −1, 9 **2.** 2, 3, 4
3. −4, 2, 8 **4.** $-5\frac{1}{2}$, −5, $-4\frac{1}{2}$

Check Understanding

1a.

x	$-2x^2 = y$	(x, y)
−2	$-2(-2)^2 = -8$	(−2, −8)
−1	$-2(-1)^2 = -2$	(−1, −2)
0	$-2(0)^2 = 0$	(0, 0)
1	$-2(1)^2 = -2$	(1, −2)
2	$-2(2)^2 = -8$	(2, −8)

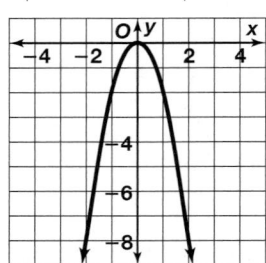

b.

x	$-x^2 + 3 = y$	(x, y)
−2	$-(-2)^2 + 3 = -1$	(−2, −1)
−1	$-(-1)^2 + 3 = 2$	(−1, 2)
0	$-0^2 + 3 = 3$	(0, 3)
1	$-1^2 + 3 = 2$	(1, 2)
2	$-2^2 + 3 = -1$	(2, −1)

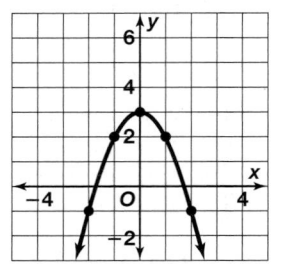

2a.

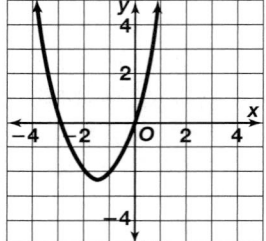

b.

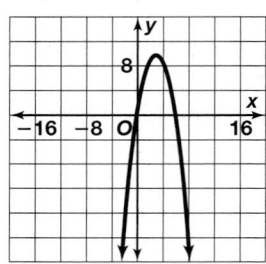

3a.

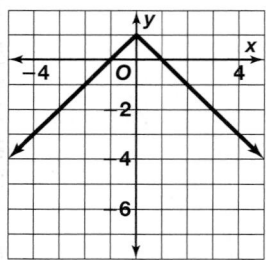

b.

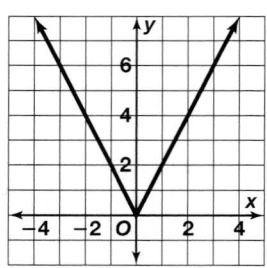

Check Skills You'll Need   **1.** 25 **2.** 64 **3.** 243 **4.** 256

Check Understanding

1.

x	3^x	y	(x, y)
1	3^1	3	(1, 3)
2	3^2	9	(2, 9)
3	3^3	27	(3, 27)
4	3^4	81	(4, 81)

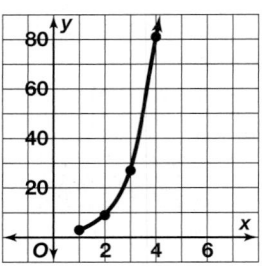

2.

x	$0.5(2)^x$	y	(x, y)
0	$0.5(2)^0$	0.5	(0, 0.5)
1	$0.5(2)^1$	1	(1, 1)
2	$0.5(2)^2$	2	(2, 2)
3	$0.5(2)^3$	4	(3, 4)
4	$0.5(2)^4$	8	(4, 8)
5	$0.5(2)^5$	16	(5, 16)

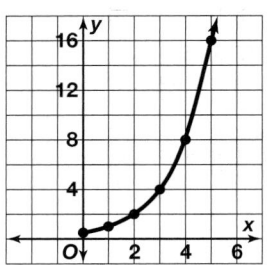

3.

x	$90(\frac{1}{3})^x$	y	(x, y)
0	$90(\frac{1}{3})^0$	90	(0, 90)
1	$90(\frac{1}{3})^1$	30	(1, 30)
2	$90(\frac{1}{3})^2$	10	(2, 10)
3	$90(\frac{1}{3})^3$	$3\frac{1}{3}$	$(3, 3\frac{1}{3})$
4	$90(\frac{1}{3})^4$	$1\frac{1}{9}$	$(4, 1\frac{1}{9})$
5	$90(\frac{1}{3})^5$	$\frac{10}{27}$	$(5, \frac{10}{27})$

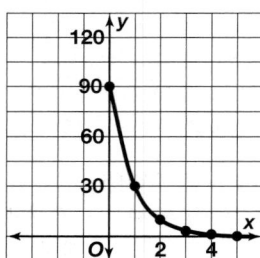

Checkpoint Quiz 1   **1.** 40, 25, 10; start with 100 and add −15 repeatedly. **2.** 45, 52, 59; start with 17 and add 7 repeatedly. **3.** 208, 416, 832; start with 13 and multiply by 2 repeatedly. **4.** 3, 6, 12, 24, 48

5.

x	$\frac{1}{4}x^2$	y	(x, y)
-2	$\frac{1}{4} \cdot (-2)^2$	1	$(-2, 1)$
-1	$\frac{1}{4} \cdot (-1)^2$	$\frac{1}{4}$	$(-1, \frac{1}{4})$
0	$\frac{1}{4} \cdot 0^2$	0	$(0, 0)$
1	$\frac{1}{4} \cdot 1^2$	$\frac{1}{4}$	$(1, \frac{1}{4})$
2	$\frac{1}{4} \cdot 2^2$	1	$(2, 1)$

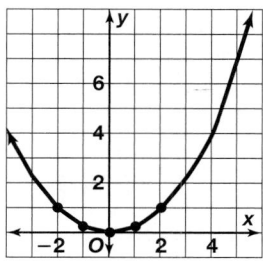

6.

x	$\frac{1}{4}|x|$	y	(x, y)
-2	$\frac{1}{4} \cdot |-2|$	$\frac{1}{2}$	$(-2, \frac{1}{2})$
-1	$\frac{1}{4} \cdot |-1|$	$\frac{1}{4}$	$(-1, \frac{1}{4})$
0	$\frac{1}{4} \cdot |2|$	0	$(0, 0)$
1	$\frac{1}{4} \cdot |1|$	$\frac{1}{4}$	$(1, \frac{1}{4})$
2	$\frac{1}{4} \cdot |2|$	$\frac{1}{2}$	$(2, \frac{1}{2})$

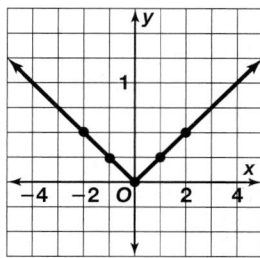

7.

x	$0.5(3)^x$	y	(x, y)
0	$0.5(3)^0$	0.5	$(0, 0.5)$
1	$0.5(3)^1$	1.5	$(1, 1.5)$
2	$0.5(3)^2$	4.5	$(2, 4.5)$
3	$0.5(3)^3$	13.5	$(3, 13.5)$
4	$0.5(3)^4$	40.5	$(4, 40.5)$

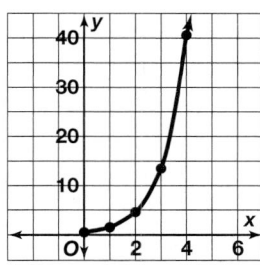

Lesson 13-4   pp. 704–707

Check Skills You'll Need 1. -40 **2.** -24 **3.** -2 **4.** 28

Check Understanding 1a. No; the denominator contains a variable. **b.** Yes; it is the product of the variable m and the real number $\frac{1}{6}$. **c.** Yes, it is a real number. **d.** No, it is a sum. **2a.** monomial **b.** binomial **c.** binomial **d.** trinomial **3a.** -50 **b.** 13 **c.** 13 **4.** 264 ft

Lesson 13-5   pp. 710–714

Check Skills You'll Need 1. $2x - 7$ **2.** $5a - 4b$
3. $m - 12n$ **4.** $-6x + 3y - 5$

Check Understanding 1a. $9d^2 + 10d$ **b.** $4x^2 + 3x + 17$
2a. $7x + 4y$ **b.** $9a^2 - 2a - 4$ **c.** $6g^2 - 2g - 1$
d. $-2t^2 + 3t + 9$ **3a.** $2a^2 - 5a$ **b.** $9z^2 + 14z - 2$
c. $-2w^2 + 11 + 8v$

Lesson 13-6   pp. 715–718

Check Skills You'll Need 1. $7v + 21$ **2.** $3u - 24$
3. $-30 + 15t$ **4.** $9p + 72$

Check Understanding 1a. $3x^2 + 12x$ **b.** $2x^2 - 3x$
2a. $x^3 + 2x^2 + 4x$ **b.** $4a^5 - 6a^4 + 6a^2$
3a. $x(2x + 1)$ **b.** $2b(b^2 + 3b - 6)$

Lesson 13-7   pp. 719–722

Check Skills You'll Need 1. $-4x - 2$ **2.** $21 + 12y$
3. $10a - 5b$ **4.** $12m - 8n$

Check Understanding 1a. $x^2 + 5x + 6$ **b.** $y^2 + 5y + 4$
2a. $x^2 - 3x - 10 + 4x$ **b.** $2m^2 + 7m + 6$

Checkpoint Quiz 2 1. monomial **2.** binomial
3. monomial **4.** trinomial **5.** -8 **6.** 8 **7.** 10 **8.** 9
9. $7a - 6b$ **10.** $2x^2 + 7x + 5$ **11.** $g^2 + 10g + 24$
12. $-18m^2 - 6m^3p - 30mp$ **13.** Answers may vary. Sample: $x + 3$; $x^2 + 6x + 9$

Lesson 13-8   pp. 724–727

Check Skills You'll Need 1. $7(-12) = -84$ **2.** $11x = 132$
3. $\frac{x}{45} = 3$ **4.** $x^2 = 64$

Check Understanding 1. the length of the kite and the length of the tail **2.** The tail is 12 ft plus twice the length of the kite. Together, the two lengths total 21 ft. **3.** $18 = 12 + 2 \cdot 3$ **4.** $3 + 18 = 21$

Selected Answers

Chapter 1

Lesson 1-1   pp. 6–7

EXERCISES 3. Variable expression; *n* is the variable. **5.** Variable expression; *x* is the variable. **11.** 3*b* **15.** 2 − *x* **17.** 2 · 12 **21.** 4 · 3 **23.** Variable expression; *d* is the variable. **25.** Variable expression; *g* is the variable. **29.** $\frac{160}{16}$ **31.** $\frac{100}{12}$ **35.** 70*a* + 100*b* **37.** C **39.** A **47.** 72 **51.** 9,563

Lesson 1-2   pp. 11–12

EXERCISES 15. 49 **23.** We must agree on an order of operations to ensure that everyone gets the same value for an expression. **25.** 24 **31.** 22 **33.** > **37.** > **39.** (7 + 4) · 6 = 66 **41.** (3 + 8 − 2) · 5 = 45 **43.** 4 · 9 + 5; 41 **45.** 17 − (25 ÷ 5); 12 **57.** $\frac{k}{20}$ **59.** 10*d*

Lesson 1-3   pp. 16–17

EXERCISES 1. 35 **5.** 1 **9.** 4 **13.** 14 **15a.** 55*m* **b.** 1,100 words **23.** 99 **29.** Answers may vary. Sample: You did not work within the grouping symbols first. **39.** 53 **41.** 19 − *t* **43.** 8 + *n*

Lesson 1-4   pp. 20–22

EXERCISES 3. −45 **5.** −50 **11.** 5 **13.** −9, −2, 8 **15.** −6, 0, 6 **17.** 2, 2 **21.** 4, 4 **23.** 9 **27.** 2 **29.** Answers may vary. Sample: 28 golf strokes over par **31.** 6 **33.** 2 **37.** −13 **39.** −23 **43.** < **45.** < **47.** 10*h* **49.** *r* + *n* **51.** Answers may vary. Sample: My friend did not take into account the signs of the numbers. **53.** negative **55.** negative **67.** 24 **69.** > **71.** *c* + 6

Lesson 1-5   pp. 27–29

EXERCISES 1. −4 + 7; 3 **3.** −4 + (−2); −6 **7.** 3 **11.** −1 **15.** −13 **19.** 100 **23.** 23 **25.** −61 **27.** Negative; both numbers are negative. **29.** Zero; the numbers are opposites. **31.** 0 **35.** −40 **39.** > **41.** > **43.** −8 **45.** −20 + 18; −2 **47.** 120 + (−25); 95 **49.** 1 **53.** $158 **65.** > **69.** < **71.** 25 + 10*n*; $55

Lesson 1-6   pp. 32–34

EXERCISES 1. −9 − (−2) = −7 **5.** 1 **13.** −6 **21.** 2 + (−6); −4 **31.** −15 **35.** 170 **39.** −68 **41.** −30 **43.** 10 **45–47.** Answers may vary. Samples are given. **45.** 3 − 3 = 0; (−4) − (−4) = 0 **47.** 1 − 7 = −6; −10 − (−4) = −6 **51.** It decreases. **53.** −8°C **55.** −60 **59.** 66 **61.** −40 **87.** 7 **89–92.** Answers may vary. Samples are given. **89.** −7 **91.** 0 **93.** 100 + 6 · 9; 154

Lesson 1-7   pp. 38–39

EXERCISES 1. 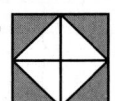 a square with four shaded corners

5. Start with 2 and add 5 repeatedly; 22, 27 **7.** Start with 1 and add 3 repeatedly; 13, 16 **11.** correct **13.** an eight-sided figure with bottom right eighth shaded

15. Start with 1 and add 0.5 repeatedly; 3.5, 4, 4.5 **17.** Start with 6 and add −2 repeatedly; −2, −4, −6 **19.** Incorrect; 8 + (−6) is 2, 2 < 8. **27.** −7 **29.** 103 **31.** −2 **33.** 1,500*n*; 36,000

Lesson 1-8   pp. 42–43

EXERCISES 1. 36 laps/day **3.** $10.23 **5.** 11 pieces; 16 pieces **7a.** $59; $21 **b.** 10 people **13.** a circle divided into 5 pieces **15.** 0 **17.** 25

Lesson 1-9   pp. 47–49

EXERCISES 1. 5 · (−2) = −10 **3.** 5(−5); −25 **9.** −18 **17.** −360 **23.** −7 **27.** −12 **29.** −2°C **31.** 0 **33.** Positive; the integers have the same sign. **35.** Negative; the integers have opposite signs. **37.** *A* **39.** *C* **43.** 4,661 **47.** −76 **53.** > **55.** = **57.** 12 **59.** −27 **73.** < **75.** < **77.** 60*y* **78.** *x* + *y*

Lesson 1-10 pp. 52–54

EXERCISES 1. III **5.** II **9.** (−2, 4) **11.** (−8, 3)
15, 18.

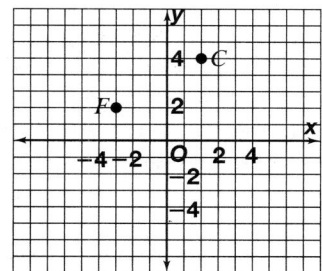

33. *P* **37.** (6, 6) **39.** (0, −4) **41.** IV **43.** II
47. III **49.** *y*-axis
51. triangle **53.** parallelogram

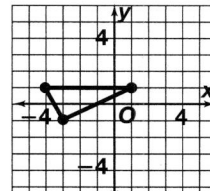 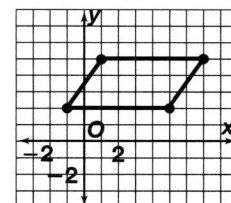

55. (0, −5) **57.** about 90° W, 32° N
59. Frankfort, Kentucky **61.**

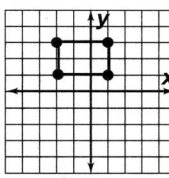

63. Answers may vary.
Sample: 62a flips the figure
across the *y*-axis. 62b flips the figure across the
x-axis. 62c flips the figure across one axis and then
the other. 62d doubles the lengths of the sides.
73. −9 **75.** −925 ft **77.** −95 **81.** 3

Chapter 1 Review pp. 57–59

1. origin **2.** variable **3.** *y*-axis **4.** quadrants
5. integers **6.** *x*-coordinate **7.** absolute value
8. $x - 25$ **9.** $3n$ **10.** $10 - t$ **11.** $\frac{x}{4}$ **12.** $n + 5$
13. $y + 2$ **14.** 24 **15.** 12 **16.** 37 **17.** 19 **18.** 17
19. 20 **20.** 40 **21.** 450 **22.** 16 **23.** −17
24. 1,000 **25.** 9 **26.** −12 **27.** > **28.** > **29.** <
30. = **31.** −30 **32.** −7 **33.** 12 **34.** 14 **35.** −15
36. −27 **37.** −11 **38.** −1 **39.** −20 ft **40.** Start
with 0 and add 6 repeatedly; 24, 30, 36 **41.** Start
with −18 and add 9 repeatedly; 18, 27, 36
42. Start with $\frac{1}{2}$ and add $\frac{1}{2}$ repeatedly; $2\frac{1}{2}$, 3, $3\frac{1}{2}$
43. 8 weeks **44.** $112 **45.** −42 **46.** −5 **47.** 72
48. 7 **49.** −3 **50.** −165 **51.** −8 **52.** 35 **53.** 102
54. (1, −3) **55.** (−2, 1) **56.** (−3, −3) **57.** (2, 2)

Chapter 2

Lesson 2-1 pp. 69–70

EXERCISES 1. (1 + 3) + 25; 1 + (3 + 25)
3. $215; Answers may vary.
Sample: 120 + 15 + 80
= 120 + (15 + 80) Assoc. Prop. of Add.
= 120 + (80 + 15) Comm. Prop. of Add.
= (120 + 80) + 15 Assoc. Prop. of Add.
= 200 + 15 Add within parentheses.
= 215 Add.
5. Ident. Prop. of Add. **9.** Comm. Prop. of Mult.
15. 3 **19.** 7.88 **23.** 90 **25.** 800 **27.** Assoc. Prop.
of Mult. **31.** Ident. Prop. of Add. **35.** −10,000
37. $352 **47.** III **49.** II **51.** 12 h **53.** 72

Lesson 2-2 pp. 74–75

EXERCISES 7. 784 **9.** 1,176 people **11.** −9
13. 21 **17.** 3(3*x* − 1); 9*x* − 3 **19.** 4*v* − 12
21. −14*z* − 6 **23.** 12*a* + 36 **27.** −7*t* + 28
31. −55 **35.** −104 **37.** 1,792 miles
43. −15*y* − 24 **45.** My friend didn't distribute
the 7 to the *t*. **55.** Comm. Prop. of Mult.
57. Assoc. Prop. of Mult. **59.** 1 **61.** −3

Lesson 2-3 pp. 78–79

EXERCISES 1. 3, 5; none; −3 **5.** −3; none;
none **7.** 7*x* + 10 **9.** 4*x* + 2 **13.** *b* **15.** 8*r* − 5
17. 5*g* + 15 **19.** −*m* + 4*d* **25.** −5*a* − 12
33. Answers may vary. Sample: My friend added
x + *y* to get *xy*.

Lesson 2-4 pp. 82–83

EXERCISES 5. false; 7 ≠ 8 **7.** true; 20 = 20
11. 25 = *v* + 15; open; variable **15.** yes **19.** no
21. 140 + *d* = 192; yes **23.** True; for example
3 + 2 = 7. **25.** True; by definition, an open
sentence is one that contains a variable.
29. open; variable **31.** true; 12 = 12
33. (−20)(9) = −11; false; −180 ≠ −11
35. 48 ÷ 12 = 3; false; 4 ≠ 3 **37.** yes; −9 = −9
39. no; −6 ≠ 6 **47.** 4*m* + 7 **49.** 6*k* − *w* **51.** 16
53. 8

Lesson 2-5 pp. 89–90

EXERCISES 5. 28 **11.** 5,200 = *s* + 2,520;
2,680 m/s **13.** 54 **21.** 108 = *d* − 42;
150 million km **23.** 35; 35; −125 **31.** −49
35. Answers may vary. Sample: This year the
Tigers won 22 games in all. **37.** 100 **39.** The
student subtracted (rather than added) 6 on the
right side. **53.** open; variable **55.** false; 2 ≠ 3
57. 48 **59.** 400

Lesson 2-6   pp. 94–95

EXERCISES **17.** 23 **19.** 36 h **23.** 105 **27.** 40
33. 300 **37.** Dividing by 0 would result in 4 = 5, which is not a true statement. **39.** no; $\frac{-18}{-3} \neq -6$
41. $-20y = 100$; -5 **43.** $7k = -168$; -24
49. $-15,000$ **61.** -11 **63.** -19 **65.** increase of 1,765 ft **67.** $7n$

Lesson 2-7   pp. 98–99

EXERCISES **1.** Answers may vary. Samples:
14 dimes, 2 nickels; 2 quarters, 6 dimes, 8 nickels
3. 11 years and 12 years **5.** 16 ft^2 **11.** 2 CDs, 3 books **19.** -6 **21.** 2 **23.** Ident. Prop. of Mult.
25. Comm. Prop. of Add.

Lesson 2-8   pp. 104–105

EXERCISES **1.**

3.   **13.** $x \leq -2$

15. $x < 0$ **17.** $t \leq 3$ **23.** $t > 7$ **27.** Use a solid dot for $\geq$ and $\leq$; use an open dot for $>$ and $<$.
29. $x \leq -10$ **31.** $x < -\frac{1}{2}$ **43.** 5 **45.** $9 - s$ **47.** $52y$

Lesson 2-9   pp. 108–109

EXERCISES **3.** $x \geq 1$

9. 64,000 lb **15.** $c > 14$ **19.** $y \leq 8$ **21.** Add 3 to each side.
23. $y > -13$

29. $b > 5$

31. $13 + n > 15$; $n > 2$ **33.** $\leq$ \$49
41.

43.

45. $2x + 12$ **47.** -35

Lesson 2-10   pp. 113–114

EXERCISES **7.** $k \leq -8$ **11.** $f \geq -3$ **19.** $q > -18$
25. $h < 80$ **27.** unchanged **29.** reverses

31. $r \leq -21$ **37.** $x \geq 4$ **41.** $7t \leq 21$; $t \leq 3$
45. You have to divide by -4 instead of 4. The direction of each inequality sign is different when you solve each inequality. **55.** $t > 11$ **57.** $r \leq -14$
59. Dist. Prop. **61.** Assoc. Prop. of Add.

Chapter 2 Review   pp. 117–119

1. d **2.** b **3.** e **4.** a **5.** c **6.** h **7.** j **8.** f **9.** g **10.** i
11. 80 **12.** 700 **13.** 547 **14.** 6,500 **15.** 300
16. 105 **17.** 864 **18.** 496 **19.** 387 **20.** $4w + 36$
21. $24 + 48a$ **22.** $-42 + 14m$ **23.** You can write 15 as $5 \cdot 3$. $5x + 5 \cdot 3 = 5(x + 3)$ by the Distributive Property. **24.** $-3a + 7$ **25.** $7w + 9$
26. $9 - 3x$ **27.** $15 - 24n$ **28.** k **29.** $-17r + 31$
30. They have the same variable or no variable and are separated by addition or subtraction signs. **31.** $32 + 5 = 6 \cdot 6$; false **32.** $\frac{t}{17} = -3$; open **33.** $4 \cdot 20 = 80$; true **34.** $p + 1.75 = 6.50$
35. 11 **36.** 8 **37.** -5 **38.** 27 **39.** 128 **40.** -8
41. \$6.50 **42.**

43.

44.

45.

46. $t < 0$ **47.** $h > 12$ **48.** $n > 14$ **49.** $k \geq 2$
50. $s \leq 3$ **51.** $m < -6$ **52.** $d < -14$ **53.** $c \leq 36$

Chapter 3

Lesson 3-1   pp. 130–131

EXERCISES **1.** hundredths; 27.39 **3.** ones; 1,046
5. 345.7 **7.** 215 **11.** about 40 **13.** about \$28
15. about \$13.90 **19.** about 7.10 miles **21.** about \$27 **23.** about 80 **27.** about 400 **33.** about 22,000 mi^2 **37, 39.** Answers may vary. Samples are given. **37.** about 30; rounding **39.** about 90; front-end **47.** $x \leq 3$ **49.** $y \geq 0$ **51.** 7 bikes; 3 trucks **53.** -12 **55.** -30

Lesson 3-2   pp. 134–135

EXERCISES **1.** about 35 **5.** about 180
7. about \$18 **9.** about 2 **15.** about \$2.00 per pound **19.** about 380 **23.** about \$6 **25.** Answers may vary: Samples are given. physical therapist: about \$18/h in Dallas, about \$16/h in Washington, D.C.; pharmacist: about \$20/h in Dallas, about \$21/h in Washington, D.C.; nurse: about \$15/h in Dallas, about \$18/h in Washington, D.C.
27. about \$2 **29.** reasonable; $72 \div 12 = 6$
41. about 39 **43.** about 12 **45.** Quadrant I
47. Quadrant IV

Lesson 3-3   pp. 140–141

EXERCISES **1.** 58.9, 56, 56 **5.** 1.8 h, 1.8 h, 1.5 h
7. 1 mode **9.** 1 mode **11.** 115; lowers mean by about 1.9 **13.** Mean; there likely are no outliers.

15. Mean; there likely are no outliers. **17.** Mean, median, or mode **19.** 5.8, 6.5, 6.5; median (or mode); the outlier (1.2) affects the mean too much. **21.** 7.8, 8, none; there is no mode and the mean and median are nearly the same. **23.** Mode; the data are not numerical. **25.** Median; there could easily be outliers. **33.** about 6 **35.** about $39.00 **37.** $6x + 10$ **39.** $x - 2t + 5$

Lesson 3-4 pp. 145–146

EXERCISES **1.** $d = 481.25$ m **3.** $t = 259.3$ s **5.** 67°F **7.** 60°F **9.** 55.4 mm **11.** 136.4°F **13.** 161.6°F **17.** 21 m; 24.5 m² **29.** 306 mL, 303 mL, 250 mL; mean **31.** −13 **33.** $n = 2t$; each n value is twice the t value below it.

Lesson 3-5 pp. 150–151

EXERCISES **3.** 26.1 **7.** $s + 599.01 = 686.98$; 87.97 days **9.** 23.7 **15.** $x - 13.50 = 26.50$; $40 **17.** 13.8 **19.** $r - 23.86 = 19.32$; 43.18 s **21.** 7.285 **25.** −10.5 **27.** 1.2 **31.** Add −1.8 to each side. **39.** 38.5 cm² **41.** −30 **43.** $1.30

Lesson 3-6 pp. 154–155

EXERCISES **5.** −25.1 **11.** $2.5m = 5.30$; $2.12 **13.** −1.94 **21.** 179 hits **23.** 2.3 **27.** −5.4 **29.** $-7.3n = 30.66$; −4.2 **31.** $\frac{n}{-2.35} = 400.9$; −942.115 **41.** − 5.3 **43.** 7.285 **45.** no; $8 \neq 3$

Lesson 3-7 pp. 159–161

EXERCISES **1.** C **5.** A **7.** 5 kg; the mass of a dog is much greater than the mass of 5 paper clips. **9.** 350 g; 350 mg is less than the mass of a paper clip. **13.** 3,010 **19.** 5.18 m **23.** Centimeter; the length is much less than a meter and much more than a millimeter, so meters are too large and millimeters are too small. **27.** Camille multiplied 6,392 g by 1,000, so she changed grams to milligrams. To change grams to kilograms she should have *divided* 6,392 by 1,000 to get 6.392 kg. **29.** mm **31.** cm **33.** 150 cm; 150 m is greater than the length of a football field. **35.** 1 g; 1 mg is closer to the mass of a speck of sawdust. **43.** 301,000,000 **45.** 3.068 kg **51.** A **53a.** 33,580 mm **b.** 0.03358 km **61.** $6t = 8.1$ or $t = \frac{8.1}{6}$; 1.35 s/knot **63.** about 90 **65.** $a \geq 21$ **67.** $r \geq -7$

Lesson 3-8 pp. 166–167

EXERCISES **1.** 107 digits **3.** 13 triangles **5.** 3.25 ft **7.** 80 sketches **17.** 0.27 **21.** 300 **23.** 91 **25.** about $12

Chapter 3 Review pp. 169–171

1. mean **2.** compatible numbers **3.** mode **4.** outlier **5.** median **6.** formula **7.** measures of central tendency **8.** perimeter **9–18.** Answers may vary. Samples are given. **9.** about 10; front-end **10.** about 4; rounding **11.** about 24; rounding **12.** about 10; rounding **13.** about 60; clustering **14.** about 7; rounding **15.** about 11.7; front-end **16.** about 6; rounding **17.** about 18; clustering **18.** about 6; rounding **19.** Answers may vary. Sample: You use rounding when only a rough answer is needed and the numbers are not clustered. You use front-end estimation when you need a better estimate of a sum. You use clustering when there are 3 or more numbers and there is one number that they are all close to. **20.** about 40 feet **21.** about 48 **22.** about 4 **23.** about 10 **24.** about 5 **25.** about 12 **26.** about 5 **27.** about −8 **28.** about −6 **29.** about 12 **30.** 5.4, 5, 2 and 5; no outliers **31.** 16.1, 16.2, 16.3; no outliers **32.** 36, 33, none; outlier: 57 **33.** 1.0, 0.2, 0.1; outlier: 7.9 **34–36.** Answers may vary. Samples are given. **34.** Mode; the data are not numerical. **35.** Median; there could easily be outliers. **36.** Mean; there likely are no outliers. **37.** 70 mi **38.** 384 mm² **39.** 37.68 in. **40.** 52 cm **41.** 7.1 **42.** 9.25 **43.** −2.01 **44.** 26.2 **45.** −9.1 **46.** 10.6 **47.** 2.5 **48.** 40.817 **49.** 11.3 **50.** 968.75 **51.** −19.4 **52.** −185.0125 **53a.** $3.2 + x = 2.64$ **b.** −$.56 **54.** Meter; a kilometer is too large unless you use fractional parts of a kilometer; centimeters are too small. **55.** Kilogram; a bicycle is heavy, so grams are too small. **56.** Milliliter; a liter is about the same as a quart, so liters are too large. **57.** 85 **58.** 0.16 **59.** 230 **60.** 1,600 **61.** 620 **62.** 0.08 **63.** A mature oak tree would be a number of meters tall. Centimeters is too small a unit. **64.** 1, 4, 9, 16, 25, 36, 49, 64, 81, 100

Chapter 4

Lesson 4-1 pp. 180–181

EXERCISES **5.** yes; ends in 0 **15.** yes; sum of digits is divisible by 3 **17.** 1, 2, 4 **21.** 1 row of 32; 2 rows of 16; 4 rows of 8 **23.** none **27.** 3, 9; $8 + 9 + 1 = 18$; 18 is divisible by 3 and 9 **33.** $1 \cdot 32, 2 \cdot 16, 4 \cdot 8$ **37.** $1 \cdot 53$ **39.** 7 **43.** Explanations may vary. Sample: Yes; a number divisible by 9 has 3 as a factor. **55.** cm **57.** 27

Lesson 4-2 pp. 184–185

EXERCISES 1. 8^3 **5.** 9^5 **9.** 64 **13.** 1,000,000
15. −15 **19.** 42 **21.** −212 **23.** 22 **25.** d^3
27. The student didn't multiply $a \cdot a \cdot a$. **29.** −16
and 16 **31.** −288 **37.** 243 **41.** Yes; $-a^2 = (-a)^2$
only when $a = 0$. **59.** none **63a.** 83 **b.** 82
65. $-3w - 7$

Lesson 4-3 pp. 189–190

EXERCISES 3. Prime; it has only two factors,
1 and 31. **7.** Composite; it has more than two
factors, 1, 3, 29, and 87. **11.** $2 \cdot 17$ **15.** $2 \cdot 3 \cdot 31$
19. 25 **23.** $6c^3$ **25.** prime **29.** 8 groups **33.** 4
43. Answers may vary. Sample: 6, 30 **63.** 20
65. 29 **67.** 1.8 **71.** 81 books

Lesson 4-4 pp. 194–195

EXERCISES 1. $\frac{1}{4}, \frac{4}{16}$ **5.** $\frac{1}{3}, \frac{12}{36}$ **9.** $\frac{1}{4}$ **13.** $\frac{1}{3}$ **17.** $\frac{3x}{2}$
21. $8b$ **25.** $\frac{5}{8}, \frac{20}{32}$ **27.** $\frac{1}{4}, \frac{2}{8}$ **31.** $\frac{3}{4}$
41. Answers may vary. Sample: $\frac{6x}{10}, \frac{3xy}{5y}$ **51.** 2
53. $7a$ **55.** 2.62 **57.** −6.33

Lesson 4-5 pp. 199–200

EXERCISES
1. 15 days;

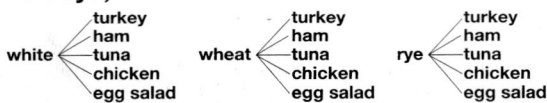

3. 15 pizzas **5.** 28 handshakes **7.** 36 blocks **17.** $\frac{1}{2}$
19. $\frac{2a^2}{5}$ **21.** Start with 10; add 10 repeatedly.
23. Start with 2; multiply by 3 repeatedly.

Lesson 4-6 pp. 203–204

EXERCISES 1. $\frac{4}{8}, \frac{5}{10}, \frac{6}{12}$ **5, 7.** Answers may vary.
Samples are given. **5.** $-\frac{10}{18}, \frac{-5}{9}, \frac{5}{-9}$ **7.** $\frac{-4}{6}, \frac{-2}{3}, \frac{2}{-3}$
9, 13.

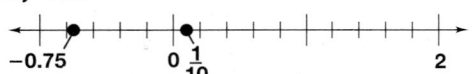

15. $\frac{2}{3}$ **21.** 44 ft/s² **25, 27, 29.** Answers may
vary. Samples are given. **25.** $-\frac{4}{9}, \frac{-12}{27}, \frac{12}{-27}$
27. $\frac{-10}{26}, \frac{-5}{13}, \frac{10}{-26}$ **29.** $\frac{8}{8}$ **33.** $-\frac{1}{4}$ **37.** $\frac{4}{-5}, \frac{-12}{15}, -\frac{16}{20}$
57. −28 **59.** 31 **61.** −1 **63.** −4

Lesson 4-7 pp. 207–208

EXERCISES 9. x^6y^5 **21.** m^{24} **29.** 7 **33.** 3
35. < **39.** $2x^4$; the two terms are being added,
not multiplied. **49.** −4 **53.**

![number line marked at −4, 0, 4 with point at −4]
−4   0   4

55. 8(1.50) + 10(1.25); $24.50

Lesson 4-8 pp. 213–214

EXERCISES 3. $\frac{5y^5}{3}$ **23.** $\frac{1}{1,296}$ **25.** y^{-3}
27. $m^{-2}n^{-2}$ **31.** 5 **35.** 900 times as much
39. x^{-2} **41.** m^7n^{-7} **51.** 125 **53.** $16a^{16}$
55. about 20.2 **57.** 87, 88, 89

Lesson 4-9 pp. 219–220

EXERCISES 5. 2.09×10^{-1} **7.** 5×10^9 km
9. 0.00000002104 **13.** 0.0060502 **15.** 7.2×10^{-5}
17. 3.508×10^{-4} **19.** $3.7 \times 10^{-8}, 253 \times 10^{-9}$,
12.9×10^{-7} **21.** 3×10^9 **25.** 2×10^{10} lb
27. 8,430,000 **29.** 5,880,000,000,000 mi
31. $10^{-8}, 10^{-6}, 10^0, 10^5, 10^9$ **33a–b.** Answers
may vary. Samples are given. Move the decimal
point 4 places to the right and write 4.3×10^{-4}.
Write $523.4 \times 10^5 = 5.234 \times 10^2 \times 10^5 =$
5.234×10^7. **41.** x^2 **43.** $\frac{3m^2}{n}$ **45.** 0.9 ft/h
47. 78 chimes

Chapter 4 Review pp. 223–225

1. factor **2.** simplest form **3.** rational number
4. scientific notation **5.** exponents **6.** prime
number **7.** 1, 2, 3, 4, 6, 12 **8.** 1, 2, 3, 5, 6, 10, 15,
30 **9.** 1, 2, 3, 6, 7, 14, 21, 42 **10.** 1, 2, 3, 4, 6, 8, 9,
12, 18, 24, 36, 72 **11.** 1, 3, 37, 111 **12.** 1, 2, 3, 4, 6,
7, 9, 12, 14, 18, 21, 28, 36, 42, 63, 84, 126, 252
13. 8 **14.** 27 **15.** 172 **16.** −25 **17.** 121 **18.** 58
19. 49 **20.** 16 **21.** prime **22.** composite; $2^2 \cdot 5$
23. prime **24.** composite; $2 \cdot 5 \cdot 11$
25. composite; $3 \cdot 29$ **26.** 4 **27.** 9 **28.** 1 **29.** $3x^2$
30. $2ab$ **31.** $3cd$ **32.** No factor of a positive
integer is greater than the integer. **33.** $\frac{1}{5}$ **34.** $\frac{1}{2}$
35. $\frac{4}{13}$ **36.** $\frac{7}{10}$ **37.** $\frac{7}{11}$ **38.** $\frac{1}{6}$ **39.** x **40.** 5 **41.** $\frac{1}{4}$
42. $\frac{2}{5}$ **43.** $\frac{x}{3}$ **44.** $4b$ **45.** 24 days
46–49.

![number line from −2 to 2 with points marked at −0.6 and 2/10]
−2   −0.6   0 $\frac{2}{10}$ 1   2

50. $\frac{2}{5}$
51. $\frac{7}{8}$ **52.** −1 **53.** $-\frac{4}{5}$ **54.** 128 **55.** $21a^6$ **56.** b^7c^4
57. x^{15} **58.** y^{20} **59.** 4,096 **60.** $\frac{1}{b^2}$ **61.** $\frac{7}{8y^5}$
62. 2×10^6 **63.** 4.58×10^8 **64.** 7×10^{-7}
65. 5.9×10^{-9} **66.** 800,000,000,000
67. 0.0000032 **68.** 11,190,000
69. 0.000000000005 **70.** $4.3 \times 10^{10}, 12 \times 10^{11}$,

$3{,}644 \times 10^9$ **71.** 8×10^{-10}, 58×10^{-10}, 716×10^{-10} **72.** 2.4×10^{16} **73.** 1.8×10^{11}

Chapter 5

Lesson 5-1 pp. 235–236

EXERCISES 1. 90 **9.** in 21 days **13.** 60 **17.** $24a^3$
19. $\frac{-2}{3} < -\frac{1}{3}$

21. $\frac{11}{12} > \frac{7}{12}$

23. < **25.** > **27.** $\frac{3}{9} < \frac{5}{9} < \frac{7}{9}$ **29.** $\frac{2}{7} < \frac{2}{5} < \frac{2}{3}$ **35.** =
39. Yes; $\frac{2}{3} > \frac{5}{8}$ **41.** 1,800 **45.** $72xy$ **49.** =
57. Answers may vary. Sample: I would prefer Fran's method. The LCD of $\frac{5}{8}$ and $\frac{9}{12}$ is 24. It would be easier to work with smaller numbers.
65. 1.394×10^{-3} **67.** 5×10^{-6} **69.** 4 **71.** $45x$

Lesson 5-2 pp. 240–241

EXERCISES 1. 0.28 **5.** Yes,
$\frac{5}{16} = 5 \div 16 = 0.3125$, so $10\frac{5}{16} = 10.3125$.
7. $-0.1\overline{6}$; repeating; 6 **9.** $0.\overline{81}$ repeating; 81
13. $0.06, \frac{2}{5}, \frac{6}{5}, \frac{3}{2}$ **15.** $\frac{22}{11}, 2.01, 2.1, \frac{22}{10}$ **21.** $6\frac{37}{100}$
27. $-\frac{1}{3}$ **29.** = **31.** < **33.** 5.375 **37.** -0.31
39. $\frac{7}{20}$ **43a.** Sarah: 0.286; Lizzie: 0.302 **b.** Lizzie;
$0.302 > 0.286$ **55.** $-\frac{5}{6}, -\frac{1}{3}, \frac{1}{6}, \frac{2}{3}$ **57.** $-\frac{6}{7}, -\frac{4}{7}, -\frac{3}{14}, -\frac{1}{14}$
61. $\frac{73}{7}$ **63.** $\frac{47}{10}$

Lesson 5-3 pp. 246–247

EXERCISES 3. $\frac{7}{q}$ **7.** $-\frac{2}{5}$ **9.** $\frac{1}{12}$ **11.** $-\frac{7}{20}$ **15.** $13\frac{7}{8}$
21. $3\frac{13}{20}$ h **23.** Sample answer: 15 **27.** $1\frac{7}{8}$ in.
29. $\frac{30 - 3n}{10n}$ **31.** $1\frac{11}{18}$ **33.** $7\frac{2}{5}$ **35.** $20\frac{3}{4}$ **45.** $\frac{3}{6}, \frac{4}{7}, \frac{5}{8}$
47. $-\frac{10}{9}, -\frac{9}{10}, \frac{9}{10}, \frac{10}{9}$ **49.** x^{12}

Lesson 5-4 pp. 251–252

EXERCISES 5. $\frac{7}{10}$ **13.** $1\frac{1}{4}$ hours **17.** $-1\frac{1}{21}$ **25.** $1\frac{1}{2}$
31. $-\frac{3}{5}$ **37.** $\frac{35}{72}$ **41.** $-1\frac{7}{8}$ **45.** $\frac{2}{3w}$ **49.** $2\frac{1}{2}$
57. 4 mi; $2\frac{2}{15}$ mi **67.** $1\frac{23}{35}$ **69.** $\frac{3}{10}$ **73.** $4\frac{1}{2}$
77. 24 years old

Lesson 5-5 pp. 255–257

EXERCISES 1. Ounces; it is closest to the weight of a paper clip. **3.** Miles; distances to continents would be measured in miles. **7.** $\frac{1}{2}$ **9.** $1\frac{1}{2}$ **13.** C
17. E **21.** 78 **25.** 7 **31.** C **37.** 9,560 ft **39.** weight
43. volume **45.** Pounds or ounces; tons are too large. **49a.** mile; about 3,740 mi **51.** yes
55. no; 1 lb **59.** 10,000 **67.** $3\frac{1}{8}$ **85.** $\frac{9}{29}$ **87.** $1\frac{1}{5}$
89. $x + 3y$ **91.** $-3y$

Lesson 5-6 pp. 261–262

EXERCISES 1. 8:30 A.M. **3.** the 12:15 P.M. bus
5. 6 different amounts; \$.40, \$.45, \$.50, \$.55, \$.60, and \$.65 **7.** \$30 **19.** $\frac{3}{32}$ **27.** about \$48

Lesson 5-7 pp. 266–267

EXERCISES 5. $\frac{1}{8}$ **7.** $\frac{1}{6}$ of the book **11.** $1\frac{1}{8}$ **15.** $2\frac{3}{4}$
21. Negative; $\frac{9}{10} > \frac{1}{2}$, so $\frac{1}{2} - \frac{9}{10} < 0$. **23b.** $60\frac{7}{8}$ in.
27. $-\frac{7}{9}$ **33.** $13\frac{3}{8}$ lb. **45.** c **49.** yd **51.** 2.5
53. -28.125

Lesson 5-8 pp. 270–272

EXERCISES 13. $\frac{1}{2}$ **21.** $\frac{3}{4}s = 9$; 12 sheets **25.** $\frac{7}{15}$
29. $7\frac{7}{15}$ **31.** Positive; a positive product means the two factors have the same sign. **35.** 20 weeks
39. $3\frac{9}{13}$ **47.** 4 **63.** $\frac{1}{8}$ **65.** $3\frac{5}{8}$ **67.** $3r^5$ **71.** x^{13}

Lesson 5-9 pp. 276–277

EXERCISES 7. $8x^6$ **21a.** $25s^4$ cm² **b.** Yes; The area of the tablecloth is $25s^4$ cm² which is greater than $20s^4$ cm². **25.** $\frac{81x^8}{10{,}000}$ **31.** $\frac{9t^4}{25}$ **33.** 1
37. 3 **39.** $-\frac{1}{27}$ **43.** $(3x^2)_2 = 9x^4$ ft² **49.** $-\frac{125}{512}$
55. $-\frac{1}{32y^{15}}$ **69.** $3\frac{1}{16}$ **73.** \$15.99 **75.** (4, 2)
77. (4, 0) **79.** H **81.** G

Chapter 5 Review pp. 279–281

1. f **2.** c **3.** a **4.** b **5.** g **6.** d **7.** e **8.** 36 **9.** $56m^2$
10. 105 **11.** $30xy$ **12.** > **13.** < **14.** > **15.** =
16. 0.6 **17.** $0.1\overline{6}$ **18.** 0.625 **19.** 0.3 **20.** 0.07
21. $\frac{1}{4}$ **22.** $\frac{5}{6}$ **23.** $5\frac{3}{5}$ **24.** $2\frac{4}{99}$ **25.** $3\frac{1}{12}$ **26.** $7\frac{2}{15}$
27. $\frac{30 + 3x}{5x}$ **28.** $\frac{7}{8}$ **29.** $\frac{7}{12}$ ft, or 7 in. **30.** $\frac{7}{40}$ **31.** $-\frac{4}{5}$
32. $1\frac{1}{5}$ **33.** $3\frac{3}{4}$ **34.** $\frac{1}{2}$ **35.** $2\frac{1}{2}$ **36.** $3\frac{3}{8}$ **37.** 60
38. 24 **39.** 96 **40.** 5,500 **41.** 2:30 P.M.
42. 15 buses **43.** \$45.50 **44.** $2\frac{3}{8}$ **45.** $1\frac{2}{15}$ **46.** $1\frac{1}{3}$
47. $\frac{1}{54}$ **48.** $-\frac{8}{21}$ **49.** $\frac{2}{9}$ **50.** $16d^4$ **51.** 36 **52.** $a^{10}b^5$
53. $-\frac{1}{8}$ **54.** $\frac{x^2}{9}$ **55.** $\frac{16a^4}{c^8}$

Chapter 6

Lesson 6-1 — pp. 290–291

EXERCISES 5. $\frac{1}{10}$ **11.** $\frac{14}{25}$ **13.** 48 ft/s **15.** 52 mi/h
17. $\frac{1}{2}$ **21.** $117\frac{1}{3}$ **25.** $\frac{4}{3}$ **27.** Anna; $\frac{3}{8}$ mi/h
31. class A **39.** −1,728 **41.** $\frac{b^6}{a^3}$ **43.** =

Lesson 6-2 — pp. 296–298

EXERCISES 5. 8 **11.** 20 **17.** no, cross products not equal **23.** 15 posters **25.** no, cross products not equal **27.** no, cross products not equal **29.** 10 **31.** 72 **35.** 19.2 **39.** 17.5 **47.** 1 **51.** 40 defective chips **55.** $\frac{3}{1.65} = \frac{5}{x}$; $2.75 **57.** $\frac{25}{2.5} = \frac{100}{x}$; 10 s **73.** $\frac{1}{100}$ **75.** $\frac{25}{14}$ **77.** true

Lesson 6-3 — pp. 301–303

EXERCISES 1. $2\frac{2}{5}$ ft **3.** $3\frac{1}{3}$ ft **7.** 5.6 ft **9.** 51 cm **11.** 144 km **13.** 99.6 cm **15.** 4 in. **19.** 1.2 m **21.** 45 km **23.** 7.5 km **25.** HO model; N model **27.** 4.5 in. **29.** 2 in. **31.** $1\frac{3}{4}$ in. **35.** 1 in. : 350 mi **37.** 1 in. : 10 ft **39.** 2.5 ft **51.** $5\frac{5}{8}$ **53.** 136 **55.** 0.375 **57.** 0.4375 **59.** 9, 9.5, 10

Lesson 6-4 — pp. 308–309

EXERCISES 3. $\frac{3}{6}$, or $\frac{1}{2}$ **5.** $\frac{2}{6}$, or $\frac{1}{3}$ **9.** $\frac{2}{8}$, or $\frac{1}{4}$ **13a.** $\frac{2}{3}$ **b.** not choosing green **15.** 3 to 2; 2 to 3 **17.** 0 **21.** $\frac{6}{11}$ **23.** $\frac{7}{11}$ **27.** 1 to 2; 2 to 1 **31.** 1 to 3; 3 to 1 **41.** $6\frac{2}{3}$ mi **43.** 70 mi **45.** $\frac{2}{3}$ **47.** $5\frac{3}{20}$

Lesson 6-5 — pp. 312–314

EXERCISES 5. $\frac{1}{5}$ **9.** $2\frac{1}{5}$ **17.** 3.5 **21.** 0.4; $\frac{2}{5}$ **23.** 36% **29.** 111% **41.** 38.9% **43.** 64% **45.** 83.3% **47.** 450% **49.** about 80% **51.** 16.7% **53.** 33.3% **55.** 0.8, 80% **59.** $\frac{67}{100}$, 0.67 **61.** Yes; 100% − 17% = 83% **63.** Yes; the runner ran $1\frac{1}{2}$ times as far as she ran yesterday. **69.** < **75a.** 19 questions **b.** 20% **87.** $\frac{3}{8}$ **89.** $\frac{6}{8}$ or $\frac{3}{4}$ **91.** −0.175 **93.** −45

Lesson 6-6 — pp. 318–319

EXERCISES 5. 37.1 **23.** 627,000 people **25.** 150 **31.** 80% **47.** 8% **49.** 58.$\overline{3}$% **51.** 10^{-2}, 10^{-1}, 10^0, 10^3 **53.** 4 − c

Lesson 6-7 — pp. 322–323

EXERCISES 9. $n = 1.5 \cdot 90$; 135 **17.** $.96 **19.** about 83 million households **25.** $n \cdot 8 = 20$; 250% **29.** $120 **31.** 50% **35.** 48 **45.** $\frac{35}{100} = \frac{n}{60}$; 21 **47.** Thursday

Lesson 6-8 — pp. 327–328

EXERCISES 5. 137.5% **9.** 20% **13.** 40% **21.** 43.7% **27.** 20.8% decrease **31.** Eva should compare 8 − 7 to 7, not 8. **33.** 20% increase **37.** 50% decrease **47.** 94% **49.** $-1\frac{5}{6}$ **51.** 75 **53.** 1

Lesson 6-9 — pp. 331–332

EXERCISES 3. $55.50 **5.** $8.55 **7.** $3.99 **9.** $73.92 **11.** $27; $73 **15.** $37.50; $87.50 **19.** $17.25 **21.** store B; $.11 **29.** 22.2% **34.** 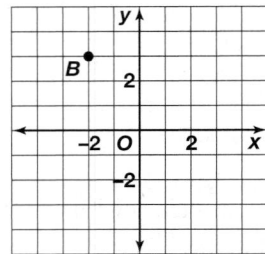 **35.** 7%

Lesson 6-10 — pp. 336–337

EXERCISES 1. about 8,934 people **3.** 6 orders **5.** 16 outfits **7.** 8 and 26 **11.** 3.5 cm **17.** $27.30 **19.** $\frac{1}{2}$ **21.** $\frac{2}{13}$ **23.** $\frac{4x}{3y}$

Chapter 6 Review — pp. 339–341

1. c **2.** b **3.** a **4.** d **5.** g **6.** e **7.** f **8.** $\frac{3}{8}$ **9.** $\frac{4}{7}$ **10.** $\frac{3}{4}$ **11.** $\frac{10}{13}$ **12.** 50 mi/h **13.** $1.89/lb **14.** 90 words/min **15.** 35 **16.** 0.7 **17.** 49 **18.** 126 **19.** 45 **20.** 35 **21.** 0.5 cm **22.** $\frac{1}{8}$; 1 to 7 **23.** $\frac{2}{8}$, or $\frac{1}{4}$; 1 to 3 **24.** $\frac{3}{8}$; 3 to 5 **25.** $\frac{6}{25}$; 0.24 **26.** $\frac{18}{25}$; 0.72 **27.** $\frac{2}{25}$; 0.08 **28.** $\frac{1}{200}$; 0.005 **29.** 30% **30.** 33% **31.** 33.3% **32.** 35% **33.** 88.9% **34.** 2.1% **35.** 240% **36.** 0.6% **37.** $\frac{15}{100} = \frac{n}{48}$; 7.2 **38.** $\frac{20}{100} = \frac{30}{x}$; 150 **39.** $\frac{n}{100} = \frac{90}{300}$; 30% **40.** $\frac{125}{100} = \frac{100}{y}$; 80 **41.** $0.35 \cdot a = 70$; 200 **42.** $n = 0.68 \cdot 300$; 204 **43.** $n \cdot 180 = 9$; 5% **44.** $n \cdot 56 = 3.5$; 6.25% **45.** 25% decrease **46.** 75% decrease **47.** 20% increase **48.** 75% decrease **49.** $8.75 **50.** $1.70/lb **51.** 30 mi **52.** Check students' work.

Chapter 7

Lesson 7-1 — pp. 350–351

EXERCISES 1. Subtract 9 from each side. **3.** Add 6 to each side. **7.** −3 **13.** 16 weeks **19.** 6 **21.** $4.45 **23.** −60 **25.** 15 **31.** 2 **33.** 14 **39.** 25% **41.** 3 to 4 **43.** $-3c + 8$

Lesson 7-2   pp. 355–356

EXERCISES 1. 12 **7.** Jasmine: 30 marbles, Bill: 64 marbles **9.** 18, 20, 22 **11.** 10 **15.** 1 **19.** −12 **21.** 18 **25.** −15, −14, −13, −12, −11 **29.** First, use the Distributive Property and combine like terms. Next, subtract 8 from each side. Finally, divide each side by 12. **31.** 2 **41.** $\frac{2}{5}$ **43.** 48

Lesson 7-3   pp. 360–361

EXERCISES 1. Subtract 3 from each side or multiply each side by 4. **3.** Multiply each side by 2. **5.** 10 **7.** 8 **9.** 10 **11.** 74 **15.** 6.5 **19.** 6 pencils **21.** $\frac{1}{2}$ **25.** −7 **33.** Answers may vary. Sample: First, combine like terms. Then divide each side by 0.85. **45.** 0 **47.** 12 gal **49.** $c^4 d$

Lesson 7-4   pp. 364–365

EXERCISES 1. $60 **3.** 20 cm by 12 cm **7.** 28 posts **9.** 8 quarters and 8 dimes **17.** 60 **19.** $\frac{41}{200}$, 0.205 **21.** $\frac{41}{20}$, or $2\frac{1}{20}$; 2.05

Lesson 7-5   pp. 369–371

EXERCISES 1. a, −3a, −3a, −3a, $\frac{-3a}{-3}$, 5 **9.** 3 **17.** 3 h **19.** −2 **23.** 2.9 **27.** The student subtracted 4x from the left side of the equation instead of adding 4x; $x = -\frac{2}{3}$ **41.** $11.25 **43.** $41.28
45. $x > -8$

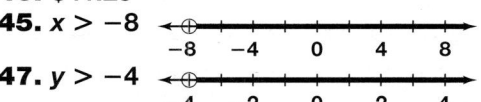

47. $y > -4$

Lesson 7-6   pp. 375–376

EXERCISES 1. Add 2 to each side, simplify, divide each side by 4, and simplify.
3. $a < -4$

7. $a \geq 9$

13. $y \leq -5$ **15.** $8t \geq 420$; $t \geq 52.5$; at least 52.5 mi/h **17.** $c \leq 72$ **19.** $y > 4\frac{4}{5}$ **35.** 3 **37.** 146.25 mi **39.** 48 cm/h

Lesson 7-7   pp. 380–381

EXERCISES 1. 3; 3; 6, 6; 6, c **3.** $w = \frac{V}{\ell h}$ **9.** $4,900 **11.** $h = \frac{2V}{\pi r^2}$ **15.** Answers may vary. Sample: Solve the equation for h and substitute the known values. **23.** $a \leq -3$ **25.** 6 weeks **27.** 31.3

Lesson 7-8   pp. 385–386

EXERCISES 1. $28; $228 **3.** $120.00 $3,120.00 $3,120.00 $124.80 $3,244.80 $3,244.80 $129.79 $3,374.59 **7.** $2,207.63 **9a.** 2%, **b.** 12 periods, **c.** $760.95 **13.** $13,821.43 **17.** Answers may vary. Sample: $10,000 at 6%; $13,000; $13,382.26 **27.** $x = \frac{1}{4}y + \frac{9}{4}$ **29.** 3 in.

31.
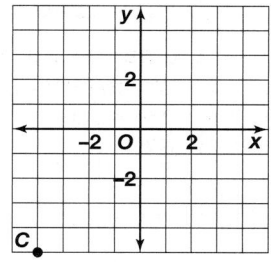

Chapter 7 Review   pp. 389–391

EXERCISES 1. compound interest **2.** principal **3.** balance **4.** consecutive integers **5.** interest rate **6.** simple interest **7.** interest **8.** −4 **9.** 2 **10.** 48 **11.** 3 **12.** 21 **13.** $1\frac{2}{3}$ **14.** $\frac{4}{5}$ **15.** −2 **16.** $-6\frac{3}{8}$ **17.** 39 **18.** 3.5 **19.** 8 **20.** −18, −17, −16, −15 **21.** $p - 0.15p = 29.74$; $34.99 **22.** $10n + 20n + 147 = 1,167$; 34 tens, 34 twenties **23.** $a + 0.08a = 1,296$; $1,200 **24.** 3 **25.** −4 **26.** $1\frac{1}{5}$ **27.** 4 **28.** −7 **29.** $\frac{2}{3}$ **30.** 2 h
31. $a > 7$

32. $y \leq -3$

33. $c \leq \frac{2}{3}$

34. $x < -4$

35. $x < -9$

36. $b < 2$

37. $x < 6$

38. $x \geq -\frac{3}{5}$

39. $799 + 25\left(\frac{c}{8}\right) \leq 1,000$; about 64 megabytes
40. $m = \frac{r}{6k}$ **41.** $y = \frac{4}{3}x$ **42.** $g = \frac{Q}{p}$ **43.** $b = a + 2c$
44. $a = \frac{1}{3}w - \frac{5}{3}n$ **45.** $h = 6e - 66$ **46.** $27
47. $252.50 **48.** $90.00 **49.** $11,239.42
50. $44,890.37 **51.** $35,303.54 **52.** $80,016.89
53. Answers may vary. Sample: Yes; with more interest periods, the interest would start earning interest earlier.

Chapter 8

EXERCISES **1a.** Yes; there is one range value for each domain value. **7.** No; subscribers of a specific age (domain value) may pay different subscription prices (range values).

11.

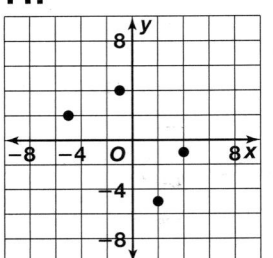

A function; no vertical line passes through two graphed points.

13.

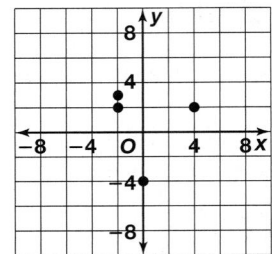

Not a function; a vertical line passes through both (−1, 3) and (−1, 2).

15.

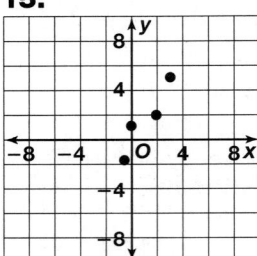

A function; there is only one range value for each domain value.

21.

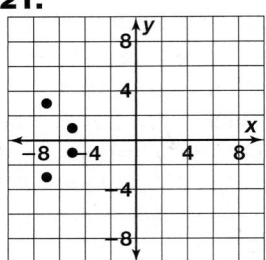

Not a function; a vertical line passes through both (−7, 3) and (−7, −3).

35. 12 **37.** 0.65

EXERCISES **1.** (−5, −18) **3.** (−5, −40) **5.** −2 **9.** −6 **11.** about 1,064 km

13.

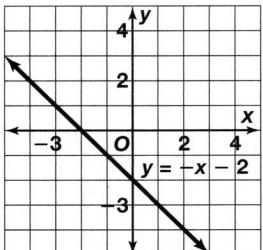

23. $y = \frac{1}{2}x - 3$

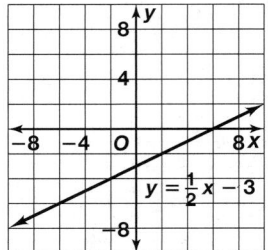

27. Answers may vary. Sample: If you can solve the equation for y, you have a function.

29. no; $-12 + 6 \neq 6$ **31.** no; $8 - 0 \neq 6$
33. $(-2, 5\frac{1}{2})$, $(1, 6\frac{1}{4})$, $(4, 7)$ **35.** The student forgot to divide $-3x$ by 4. **43.** Yes; there is one range value for each domain value. **45.** No; there are two range values for the domain value 0.

EXERCISES **1.** $\frac{3}{4}$ **3.** $-\frac{5}{6}$ **5.** −1 **9.** undefined
11. 7; 3

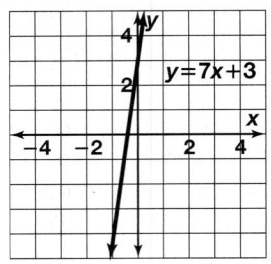

21. The student could have calculated $\frac{\text{difference in } x\text{-coordinates}}{\text{difference in } y\text{-coordinates}}$.

23. $-\frac{1}{3}$ **25.** The upper roof has the steeper pitch because it has the greater slope. **27.** $-\frac{5}{2}$ **29.** −1

31. $y = 5x - 3$

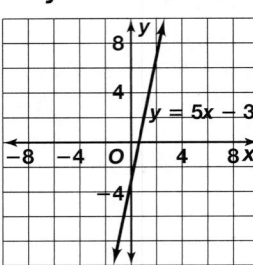

39. no; $4 \neq -2(-3) + 1$

53. $x \leq -6\frac{1}{2}$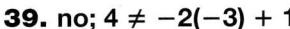

55. 10% decrease **57.** 25% decrease

EXERCISES **1.** $a(c) = 20 - c$; $15.50
3. $m(w) = 0.4w$; 6 lb **5.** $f(x) = -x$ **11a.** $n(d) = 36d$
13. $y = 2x - 4$ **19.** $y = 4x - 3$ **33.** $\frac{2}{3}$ **35.** $\frac{3}{8}$ **37.** $\frac{7}{8}$

EXERCISES **1.** averaged 4 h watching television and 2 h of physical activity daily **3.** 2 students
5.

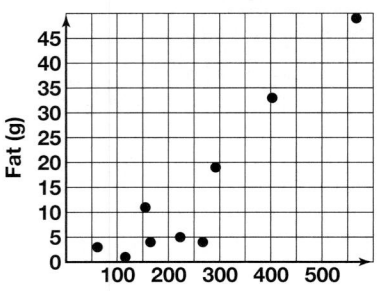

Nutritional Values

7. No correlation; there is no apparent relationship. **11.** Negative; as one set of values increases, the other set tends to decrease. **13.** 10 min **15.** 3 students **17.** Negative; the lower the temperature, the more layers of clothing you wear. **21.** No correlation; the sets of data are not related. **31.** $y = \frac{5}{2}x$

33. $f(x) = -x + 7$ **35.** $h = \frac{2A}{b + c}$ **37.** $41.54

Lesson 8-6 pp. 432–433

EXERCISES 1a–b. Trend lines may vary. Sample is given.

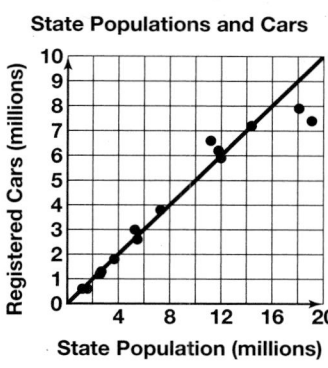

State Populations and Cars

c. about 14.5 million cars **d.** $y = 0.4x + 0.4$; about 3.6 million cars **3.** Answers may vary. Sample: 8.4 gal **5.** Answers may vary. Sample: $1.55; (16, 1.55) is on the line through the two points (12, 1.17) and (20, 1.89). **7.** 45 ft **15.** (−3, 9), (0, 0), (2, −6)

19. −3 **21.** 2

Lesson 8-7 pp. 438–440

EXERCISES 1. no **3.** yes **5.** (1, 7) **9.** (4, 6) **17.** no **19a.** $x + y = 4$, $x = 3y$ **b.** (3, 1); 3 ft, 1 ft **21.** infinitely many solutions **41.** $x > -4$ **43.** $c \le 1$ **45.** $\frac{1}{6}$ **47.** 0

Lesson 8-8 pp. 444–446

EXERCISES 1. dashed **3.** solid **5.**

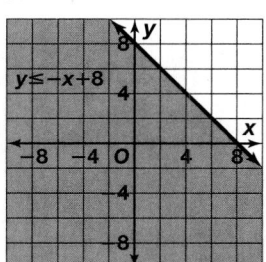

11. $y \ge -2x$
15. $10x + 5y < 100$

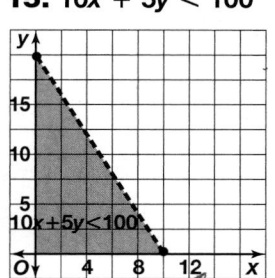

19.

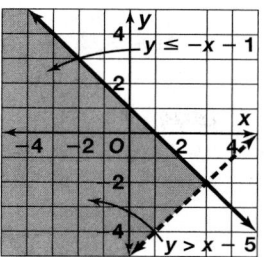

25.

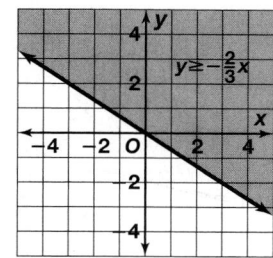

31. $y = x - 7$; solid **35.** $y = 2x - 5$; dashed
41.

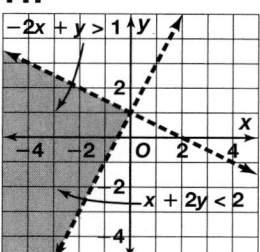

55. (3, 5)
59. $\frac{5}{6}$ **61.** $\frac{3}{20}$ **63.** $-3\frac{1}{2}$
65. 6

Chapter 8 Review pp. 449–457

1. slope **2.** vertical-line test **3.** negative correlation **4.** function **5.** linear equation **6.** domain **7.** range **8.** solution **9.** Yes; there is one range value for each domain value. **10.** Yes; there is one range value for each domain value. **11.** No; there are domain values for which there is more than one range value. **12.** No; one length of time (for different distances) could result in different costs. **13.** (−3, 2), (0, 5), (2, 7) **14.** (−3, 12), (0, 0), (2, −8) **15.** (−3, 1$\frac{1}{2}$), (0, 3), (2, 4) **16.** (−3, 12), (0, 6), (2, 2)

17. −1, 7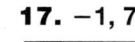

18. 1, 2

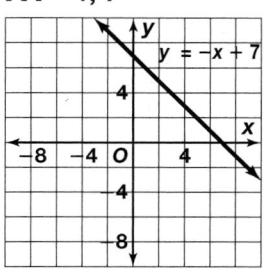

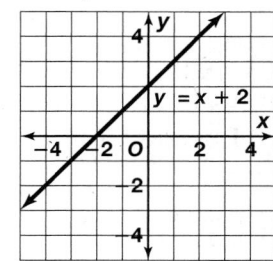

19. $-\frac{2}{5}$, 2

20. $\frac{3}{2}$, −6

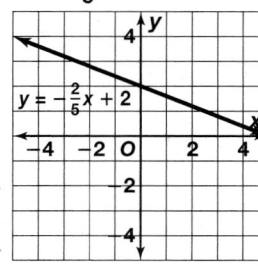

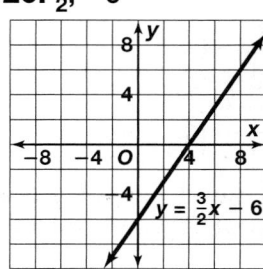

21. −2 **22.** 3 **23.** $-\frac{1}{2}$ **24.** $f(x) = -x$

25. $y = 2x + 1$ **26.** $y = -x + 4$ **27.** $c(t) = 14t + 2$
28. 30 min **29.** about 620 calories **30.** Positive correlation; as the time bicycling increases, the calories used increases.
31. about 800 calories
32.

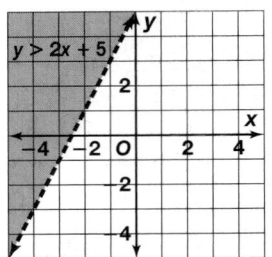

33.

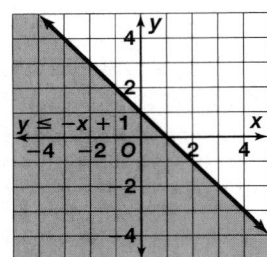

34.

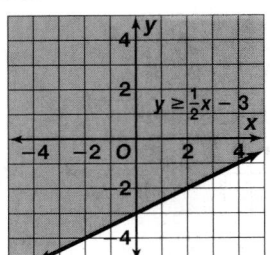

35.

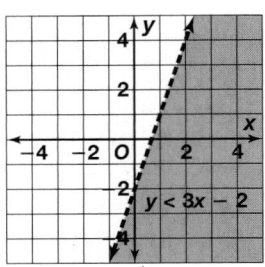

36. (4, −1)

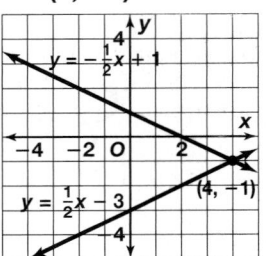

37. (4, −3)

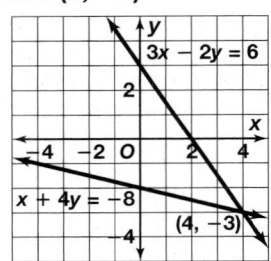

38. (2, −3)

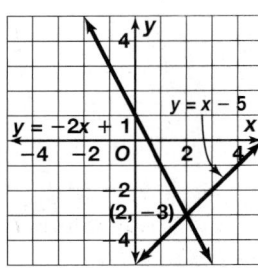

39. infinitely many solutions

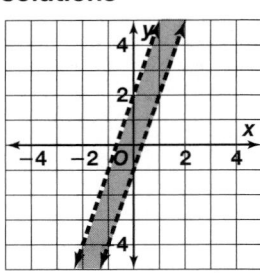

40. The graphs could be parallel lines, so there is no common solution.

Chapter 9

Lesson 9-1   pp. 461–463

EXERCISES 1. A, B, C **3.** $\overrightarrow{AC}, \overrightarrow{BC}, \overrightarrow{BA}, \overrightarrow{CA}$
13. $\overline{GF}, \overline{JI}, \overline{KH}$ **17.** $\overline{PS}, \overline{RQ}, \overline{PK}, \overline{QL}$
19. $\overline{BF}, \overline{CG}, \overline{DH}$
23.

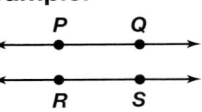

25. Answers may vary. Sample:

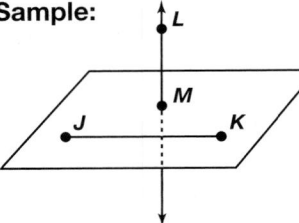

27. Answers may vary. Sample:

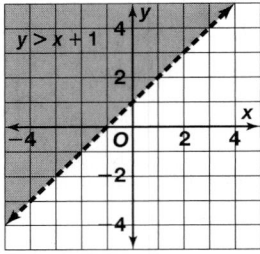

29. $\overleftrightarrow{WX}$ **31.** $\overline{TU}$
33. sometimes
35. always
39. $6 + 5x + 4x + 1 = 12x + 1$; 6, 10, 9, 25
41. Answers may vary. Sample: $\overrightarrow{AB}$ and $\overrightarrow{BA}$ have different endpoints.

51.

53. $\frac{23}{24}$ **55.** $3\frac{1}{2}$

Lesson 9-2   pp. 468–469

EXERCISES 1. supplementary **3.** $m\angle 1 = 80°$, $m\angle 2 = 100°$, $m\angle 3 = 80°$ **5.** $\angle 3$ is vertical to $\angle 1$. $\angle 2$ is adjacent to $\angle 1$. $m\angle 1 = 110°$ **7.** $\angle 2$ and $\angle 8$, $\angle 3$ and $\angle 5$ **9a.** $\angle 5, \angle 3, \angle 7$ **b.** $m\angle 6 = 135°$, $m\angle 7 = 45°$, $m\angle 8 = 135°$, $m\angle 3 = 45°$, $m\angle 2 = 135°$, $m\angle 1 = 45°$, $m\angle 4 = 135°$

11. complementary **15.** 5

23.   C   D   **25.**   E   F

27. $22.50 **29.** seven games

Lesson 9-3   pp. 473–474

EXERCISES 1. equilateral acute triangle
3. scalene acute triangle **5.** trapezoid
9. rectangle, parallelogram, square, rhombus
11. $P = 4x$; 50 in. **13.** $P = 5x$; 4,605 ft

15.

19.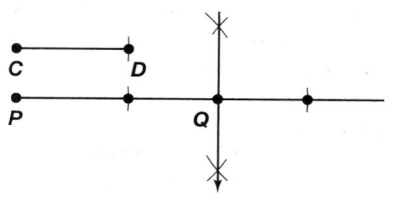

23. 19.5 in. **25.** trapezoid, parallelogram, rhombus **37.** 8 antique cycles **39.** 10

Lesson 9-4   pp. 478–479

EXERCISES 1. 4 mi **5.** 8 students **7.** 5 cm
11. the dog **21.** equilateral triangle
23. isosceles right triangle **25.** $\frac{7}{50}$, 14%
29. $\frac{1}{8}$, 12.5%

Lesson 9-5   pp. 482–484

EXERCISES 1. $\angle D$ **5.** $m\angle D$, or 53°
15. $\overline{EB} \cong \overline{JF} \cong \overline{IL} \cong \overline{DH}$, $\overline{BD} \cong \overline{FE} \cong \overline{LJ} \cong \overline{HI}$,
$\overline{DE} \cong \overline{EJ} \cong \overline{JI} \cong \overline{ID}$ **17.** $\overline{BC} \cong \overline{HG}$, $\overline{AB} \cong \overline{KH}$,
$\angle B \cong \angle H$, $\triangle ABC \cong \triangle KHG$ by SAS **19.** $\overline{ON} \cong \overline{RQ}$,
$\overline{OM} \cong \overline{RP}$, $\overline{NM} \cong \overline{QP}$, $\triangle ONM \cong \triangle RQP$ by SSS
21. $\overline{AB} \cong \overline{XY}$, $\overline{BC} \cong \overline{YZ}$, $\overline{AC} \cong \overline{XZ}$ **23.** $\overline{NL} \cong \overline{QR}$,
$\overline{NM} \cong \overline{QP}$, $\angle N \cong \angle Q$, $\triangle LNM \cong \triangle RQP$ by SAS
25. $\overline{KM} \cong \overline{JM}$, $\overline{ML} \cong \overline{ML}$, $\angle KML \cong \angle JML$,
$\triangle KML \cong \triangle JML$ by SAS **27.** Incorrect; $\angle R$ does
not correspond with $\angle N$. **31.** Incorrect; $\angle V$ and
$\angle C$ are not corresponding angles. **41.** 14 students
43. $0.15 \cdot x = 12$, 80 **45.** $\frac{3}{8}, \frac{1}{2}, \frac{2}{3}, \frac{5}{6}$ **47.** $\frac{1}{7}, \frac{1}{6}, \frac{1}{5}, \frac{1}{4}$

Lesson 9-6   pp. 489–490

EXERCISES 1. about 314 in. **3.** about 19.8 cm
5. about $29\frac{1}{3}$ m **7.** about 113 in. **11.** 180°
15. 270° **19.** about 14.4 yd
29. $\overline{AD} \cong \overline{CD}$, $\overline{BD} \cong \overline{BD}$, $\angle ADB \cong \angle CDB$,
$\triangle ADB \cong \triangle CDB$ by SAS **31.** Yes; there is one
range value for each domain value. **33.** 256 times

Lesson 9-7   pp. 494–495

EXERCISES

1.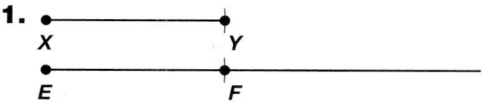

5.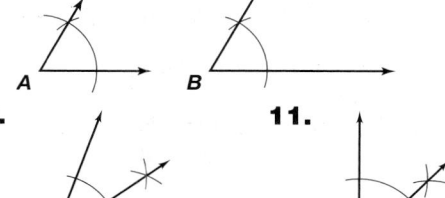

9. **11.**

13.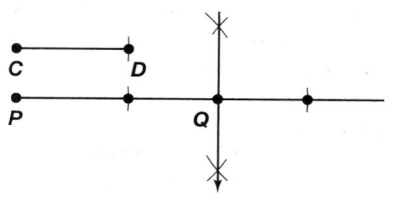

17. Answers may vary. Sample: In both
constructions, you use the compass to draw
intersecting arcs, and then use the points of
intersection to draw the bisectors. **25.** 43°
27. 18° **29.** 5 and 20 **31.** $36

Lesson 9-8   pp. 499–501

EXERCISES

3.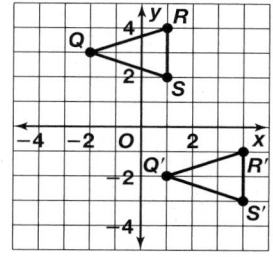

7.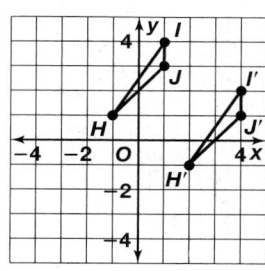

11. $A(1, 5) \rightarrow A'(2, 7)$ **13.** $S(3, 3) \rightarrow S'(11, 1)$
15. $(x, y) \rightarrow (x + 4, y + 3)$ **17.** $(x, y) \rightarrow (x - 4, y + 1)$
19. translation 11 units to the left and 4 units up
21. translation 6 units to the left and 3 units down
23. vertical
25.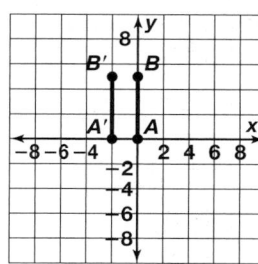

31. $(x, y) \rightarrow (x, y + 4)$
35.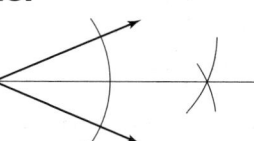

45.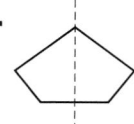

47. $\frac{4}{11}$ **49.** Amanda had
salad, Adam had chicken,
and Ann had tofu.

Lesson 9-9   pp. 503–506

EXERCISES

1. no line of symmetry
because no half is a
mirror reflection of
the other half

3.

7.

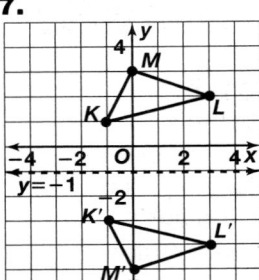

9.

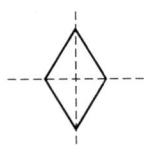

11.

15. $V'(-9, 0)$

19. always

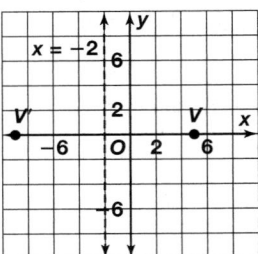

31. $X'(2, 2), Y'(4, 10)$

33.

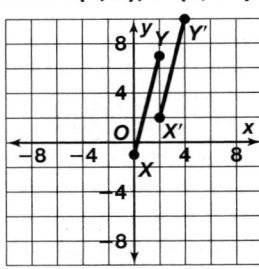

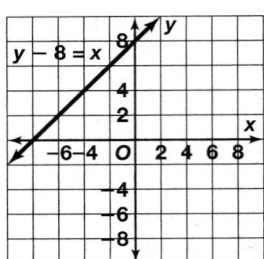

35. 15 handshakes

Lesson 9-10   **pp. 509–510**

EXERCISES

3a.

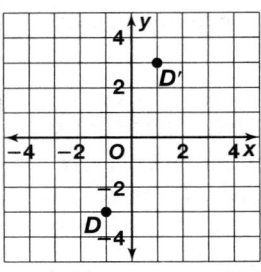

3b.

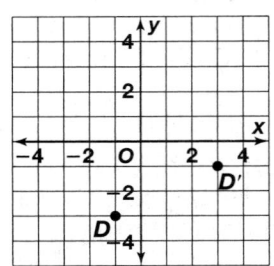

9. yes, 90° **11.** yes, 60° **15.** 90° **17.** 180°
19. yes, 180° **21.** no
29.

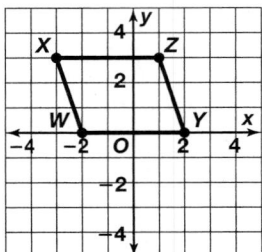

33. $\frac{1}{2}$ **35.** four

Chapter 9 Review   **pp. 513–515**

1. e **2.** c **3.** b **4.** a **5.** d **6.** g **7.** h **8.** f
9. $\angle RPD, \angle DPL, \angle RPL$ **10.** $\overrightarrow{PR}, \overrightarrow{PD}, \overrightarrow{PL}$
11. Answers may vary. Sample: $\overleftrightarrow{RL}$ **12.** R, P, D, L
13. $\overline{RP}, \overline{PD}, \overline{PL}, \overline{RL}$ **14.** $\angle 3, \angle 5, \angle 7$ **15.** Answers
may vary. Samples: $\angle 2$ and $\angle 3, \angle 5$ and $\angle 6$
16. $\angle 1$ and $\angle 5, \angle 2$ and $\angle 6, \angle 3$ and $\angle 7, \angle 4$ and
$\angle 8$ **17.** $\angle 4$ and $\angle 6, \angle 3$ and $\angle 5$ **18.** $m\angle 1 = 105°$,
$m\angle 3 = 105°, m\angle 4 = 75°, m\angle 5 = 105°, m\angle 6 = 75°$,
$m\angle 7 = 105°, m\angle 8 = 75°$ **19.** equilateral triangle
20. square **21.** isosceles acute triangle
22. trapezoid **23.** $\angle T \cong \angle P, \overline{ST} \cong \overline{SP}$,
$\angle RST \cong \angle QSP, \triangle RST \cong \triangle QSP$ by ASA
24. $\overline{DE} \cong \overline{FE}, \overline{CE} \cong \overline{GE}, \angle DEC \cong \angle FEG$,
$\triangle CDE \cong \triangle GFE$ by SAS **25.** 50 ft wide by
55 ft long **26.** about 43.96 cm
27. Television Programming

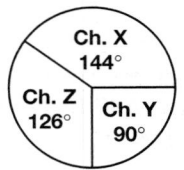

28–29. Drawings may vary. Samples:

28.

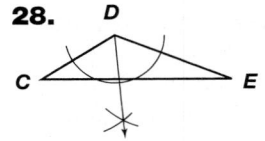

29.

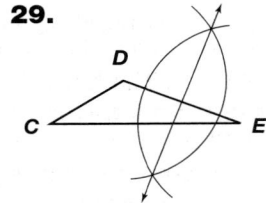

30. $A'(11, 1)$ **31.** $A'(-7, -2)$ **32.** $A'(2, 7)$
33. $A'(7, 0)$ **34.** They have no effect on size or
shape. In each case the image is congruent to the
original figure. None of these transformations
affect size or shape.

Chapter 10

Lesson 10-1   **pp. 524–525**

EXERCISES 3. 12 ft², or $1\frac{1}{3}$ yd² **11.** 48,000 ft²

13. 1,400 mm², or 14 cm² **15.** 1,694 in.²
17.

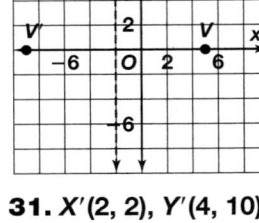

12 square units

19. No; the left
parallelogram has
an area of 6 m² while
the right parallelogram
has 4.5 m².

32.

37. $\frac{4}{25}$ **39.** $4\frac{8}{9}$

Lesson 10-2   pp. 530–531

EXERCISES 1. 8 in.^{2} **3.** 60 m^2 **5.** 130 m^2
7. 77 ft^2 **9.** 63 ft^2 **13.** 5 in. **15.** $\overline{34}$ cm^2
25. 0.5 m^2, or 5,000 cm^2 **27.** $1.\overline{54}$ **29.** $10

Lesson 10-3   pp. 535–537

EXERCISES 3. 900π cm^2; 2,826 cm^2 **5.** 50 in.^{2}
7. 2,856 yd^2 **9.** 357 mi^2 **11.** about 248 pieces
13. A **17a.** about 392.5 ft^2 **b.** about $880
21. 17.64π mm^2; 55.4 mm^2 **23.** The circle with
radius 4 m has greater area because the four
circles have a total area of 4π m^2, but the circle
with radius 4 m has an area of 16π m^2.
25. 19 cm^2 **27.** 56 m^2 **35.** 17.25 mi^2
37. 32 triangles **39.** $1\frac{1}{15}$ **41.** $\frac{1}{24}$

Lesson 10-4   pp. 541–543

EXERCISES 3. The bases are pentagons. The
figure is a pentagonal prism. **5.** The base is a
hexagon. The figure is a hexagonal pyramid.
7. square prism **11.** rectangular prism
13. pyramid **15.** cone
17.

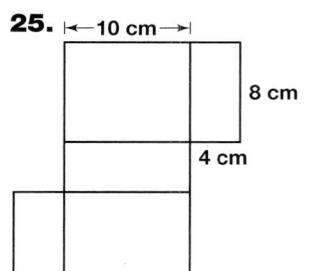

19. Figures A and C will not form
a cube because bases need to be
on both ends of the vertical faces.
21. C

25. |←—10 cm—→|

8 cm

4 cm

35. 0.01π m^2; 0.0314 m^2
37. 9 turns **39.** $y = x - 5$

Lesson 10-5   pp. 548–550

EXERCISES 1. 1,008 m^2
3a. |←11 in.→|

5 in.

3 in.

3b. 206 in.^{2}
3c. 1,854 in.^{2}
3d. The surface area
of the larger prism is
9 times the surface
area of the smaller
prism.

5. 11,988 in.^{2} **9.** 168 in.^{2} **11.** 175.8 cm^2
13. 904 cm^2 **19a.** 5 sides **b.** 3,600 ft^2 **c.** $600
31. hexagonal prism **33.** cone

35.

37. 2 teaspoons

Lesson 10-6   pp. 555–556

EXERCISES 3. 1,017 cm^2 **7.** 105 cm^2 **11.** 28 m^2
15. Use the slant height to find the lateral area
using the formula L.A. $= \pi r \ell$: $3.14 \cdot 8 \cdot 10$. Then
add the area of the base, $3.14 \cdot 8^2$ to the lateral
area to find the total surface area. **25.** 1,130 in.^{2}
27. 5 months **29.** 1, 2, 4, 5, 10, 20, 25, 50, 100
31. 1, 2, 4, 8, 16, 32

Lesson 10-7   pp. 559–560

EXERCISES 1. 54 cm^3 **3.** 24 m^3 **5.** 6,029 m^3
9. 14,158 cm^3 **11.** 10 in. **13.** 10 m **23.** 283 cm^2
25. 61 in.^{2} **27.** 22 nickels

Lesson 10-8   pp. 564–565

EXERCISES 1. 10 in. by 14 in. by 3 in. **3.** 30 cm,
15 cm **5.** 50 ft by 50 ft **13.** 30 cm^3 **15.** 18 ft^3
17. 15, 10, 20

Lesson 10-9   pp. 568–569

EXERCISES 1. 25 yd^3 **3.** 5,539 cm^3 **5.** 216 in.^{3}
7. 20.48 cm^3 **11.** 7,235 cm^3 **13.** 113,040 yd^3
15. 4 cups **19.** about 33.5 cm^3 **21.** 3 cm
23. 5 m **31.** 18 **33.** $\frac{2}{5}$ **35.** $-16x^2$ **37.** $\frac{9}{64}$

Chapter 10 Review   pp. 571–573

EXERCISES 1. lateral area **2.** cone **3.** altitude
4. volume **5.** sphere **6.** cylinder **7.** area

8. 189 m² **9.** 14 cm² **10.** 6.25 yd² **11.** 79 m²
12. 201 mm² **13.** 57 m² **14.** 31 in.²
15. triangular prism **16.** square pyramid
17. cylinder **18.** 164 cm² **19.** 205,513 m²
20. 84 cm² **21.** 63 in.² **22.** 84 cm² **23.** 85 cm²
24. 314 ft² **25.** 27 ft² **26.** 24 in. by 18 in.
27. Find the area of the walk and garden, and
then subtract the area of the garden.
28. 384 units³ **29.** 18 units³ **30.** 311 units³
31. 268 units³

Chapter 11

Lesson 11-1 pp. 582–583

EXERCISES **3.** 1 **7.** −3 **9.** 3 **13.** 27 mi
17. rational; because it is a repeating decimal
21. irrational; it neither terminates nor repeats
23. $\frac{2}{3}$ **25.** $\frac{3}{4}$ **31.** −10 **33.** 10 **35.** rational;
repeating decimal **37.** x **41.** 5, −5 **43.** 2, −2
57. about 113 cm³ **59.** Yes; $\frac{17}{25}$ is 0.68, or 68%.
Since 68% ≥ 65%, Shannon passed the test.
61. 1, 2, 11, 22 **63.** 1, 3, 5, 9, 15, 45

Lesson 11-2 pp. 587–589

EXERCISES **1.** 13 cm **3.** 8 in. **5.** 20 in. **7.** 14 ft
9. about 15.2 ft; about 30.4 ft **11.** 6.7 km **15.** yes;
$6^2 + 7^2 = 85$ **17.** yes; $5^2 + 12^2 = 13^2$ **19.** 3.1 m
21. 2.1 km **23.** yes; $3^2 + 4^2 = 5^2$ **25.** no;
$10^2 + 24^2 \neq 25^2$ **29.** yes; $\left(\sqrt{2}\right)^2 + \left(\sqrt{3}\right)^2 =$
$\left(\sqrt{5}\right)^2$ **31.** about 131.9 in. **43.** irrational; because
12 is not a perfect square **45.** rational; because
it is a terminating decimal **47.** $16x^8$
51. 2.1756×10^6 km²

Lesson 11-3 pp. 595–596

EXERCISES **1.** 5 **5.** 17.7 **7.** 19.3 **9.** (1.5, 2)
11. 30; (0, 0) **13.** The student used subtraction in
the numerators instead of addition. **15.** No;
addition is commutative. **17a.** (−0.5, 3)
b. $AM = \sqrt{(-3 - (-0.5))^2 + (5 - 3)^2}$
$MB = \sqrt{(2 - (-0.5))^2 + (1 - 3)^2}$
$\sqrt{10.5} = \sqrt{10.5}$
23. yes; $8^2 + 15^2 = 17^2$ **25.** yes; $12^2 + 16^2 = 20^2$
27. 9 **29.** 12.5

Lesson 11-4 pp. 600–601

EXERCISES **1.** $\frac{20}{x + 20} = \frac{13}{21}$; 12.3 m **3.** 1.2 mi
7. $20 **11.** 6.3 ft² **17.** (0.5, 4)

19.

Lesson 11-5 pp.605–606

EXERCISES **3.** 7.6 in. **7.** 17 in. **11.** $x \approx 18.4$ cm,
$y = 13$ cm **13.** Answers may vary. Sample: The
hypotenuse is twice the shorter leg. Since the
shorter leg is 10 ft, the hypotenuse is 20 ft. The
longer leg is $\sqrt{3}$ times the shorter leg, which is
$10\sqrt{3}$, or about 17.3 ft. **26.** 33 m **27.** about
25.1 in. **31.** Yes; for each domain value there
is only one range value.

Lesson 11-6 pp. 611–612

EXERCISES **1.** 4 **3.** 5 **5.** $\frac{9}{15}$ or $\frac{3}{5}$, $\frac{12}{15}$ or $\frac{4}{5}$, $\frac{9}{12}$ or $\frac{3}{4}$
9. 0.9703 **15.** 19.3 ft
17. 1 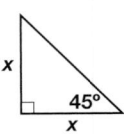 **21.** Both are correct. The ratios
include h, a known side
length, and a known angle
measure.

29. $4\sqrt{2}$ m, or about 5.7 m **31.** $13\sqrt{3}$ in., or
about 22.5 in. **33.** 5, 2, −7

Lesson 11-7 pp. 617–618

EXERCISES **1.** about 30 yd **3.** 26.7 m
5. about 71.6 mi **7.** angle of elevation = $\angle ADC$,
angle of depression = $\angle BAD$ **13.** about 1,293.8 m
21. 0.9848 **23.** 0.9703 **27.** 100π mm²; 314.0 mm²
29. $3\frac{3}{4}$ c

Chapter 11 Review pp. 621–623

EXERCISES **1.** c **2.** f **3.** d **4.** e **5.** a **6.** b **7.** 1
8. −4 **9.** 7 **10.** 8 **11.** −6 **12.** 2 **13.** 3 **14.** 6
15. 8 **16.** 10 **17.** rational; because it is a
terminating decimal **18.** rational; because 64
is a perfect square **19.** rational; because it is a
repeating decimal **20.** irrational; because 15 is
not a perfect square **21.** rational; because it is a
repeating decimal **22.** It is irrational because the
decimal neither terminates nor repeats. **23.** no;
$1^2 + 3^2 \neq 3^2$ **24.** yes; $8^2 + 15^2 = 17^2$ **25.** yes;
$(\sqrt{6})^2 + (\sqrt{10})^2 = 4^2$ **26.** yes; $30^2 + 40^2 = 50^2$
27. 3.6 **28.** 5 **29.** 12.6 **30.** 2.2 **31.** 9.2 **32.** 13.4
33. (2, 4) **34.** (3, 4) **35.** (−2, 2) **36.** (4.5, 10)
37. (−12, −8) **38.** (2.5, −0.5) **39.** about 337.5 ft
40. $a = 6$ in., $b \approx 10.4$ in. **41.** $y \approx 9.9$ m
42. $f = 4$ ft, $c \approx 3.5$ ft **43.** $g \approx 10.6$ mm
44. 0.2756 **45.** 7.1154 **46.** 0.9063 **47.** 0.0524
48. 0.9986 **49.** 0.2924 **50.** 0.6947 **51.** 1.0000
52. 0.9816 **53.** 0.2309 **54.** 8 ft **55.** 99 ft

Chapter 12

EXERCISES

1.

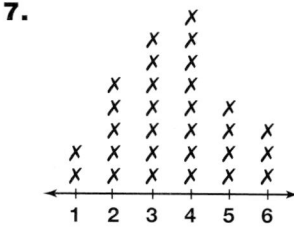

Number	Frequency
0	2
1	2
2	2
3	2
4	2

5. Rolls of a Number Cube

Number	Frequency
1	4
2	3
3	3
4	2
5	3
6	2

7.

(dot plot with X's over 1–6, peak at 3)

9.

(dot plot over 0–4) ; 4

13.

Numbers of Letters

(dot plot over 2–10) ; 8

15. Ages of Club Members

Age	Frequency
12	3
13	1
14	4
15	4
16	3

Ages of Club Members

(dot plot over 12–16) ; 4

21. 4, 8, 12; 8   **23.** 400; 400   **25.** 25; 25   **33.** $\angle R$
35. *LM*   **37.** 13.875, 13, no mode

EXERCISES 1. Maximum Speeds of Animals (mi/h)

(box plot over 0–100 scale)

3.

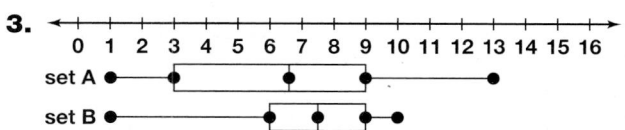

(box plots for set A and set B over 0–16 scale)

5. $60; $70; $85   **7.** Answers may vary. Sample:
The orca weights have a median of 3,000 lb and
a range of 2,000 lb. The hippopotamus weights
have a median of 2,500 lb and a range of 1,800 lb.
A significant number of the orcas and hippos in this
comparison fall within the same weight range.

9. The acreages vary considerably, from about 25
acres to about 650 acres. However, about half of the
parks are between 50 and 250 acres, with a median
of 125 acres. **11.** Answers may vary. Sample: The
student assumed that the lower value, the upper
value, and the quartiles are equally spaced.

17.

Number	Frequency
4	2
5	3
6	5
7	4
8	4

19. 7.2   **23a.** 7,650
blades of grass
23b. about 2.18×10^{15}
blades of grass

EXERCISES 1. *American Ampersand* **3.** You might
compare the lengths of the bars without noticing
the break in the scale. **5.** It suggests that the
percent is rising rapidly, by putting 1989 and 1993
very close together.

7.

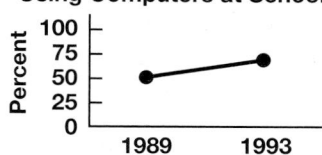

Percent of Students
Using Computers at School

11a.

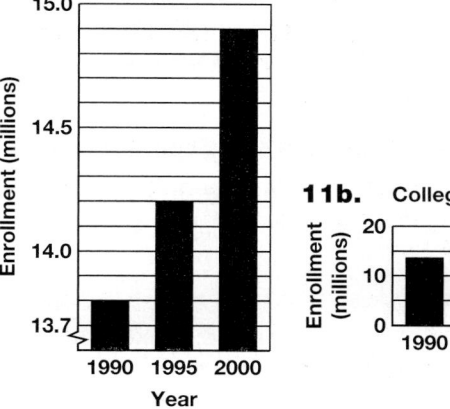

College Enrollment

11b. College Enrollment

13. nearly 2 to 1; about 1.14 to 1

23.

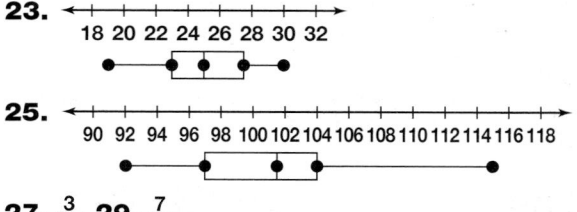

(box plot over 18–32 scale)

25.

(box plot over 90–118 scale)

27. $\frac{3}{10}$ **29.** $\frac{7}{10}$

Lesson 12-4　　　　　　　　　pp. 652–653

EXERCISES
1. 10 choices

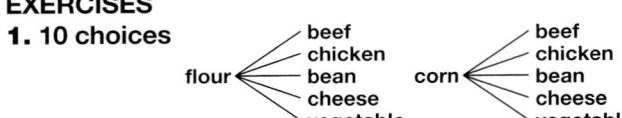

3. 28 routes **5.** $\frac{1}{8}$ **7.** $\frac{7}{8}$ **9.** $\frac{1}{125,000}$
11. 15 sweaters **13.** $\frac{3}{15}$, or $\frac{1}{3}$ **15.** $\frac{5}{104}$
21.
X X X　　　X
X　X X X　X
3 4 5 6 7 ; 4
23. (0, 2)

Lesson 12-5　　　　　　　　　pp. 657–658

EXERCISES 3. $\frac{2}{30}$, or $\frac{1}{18}$ **7.** about 83% **11.** $\frac{4}{90}$, or $\frac{2}{45}$
13. $\frac{24}{90}$, or $\frac{4}{15}$ **15.** Independent; the possibilities on
the second roll are the same as on the first.
17. $\frac{9}{100}$ **19.** $\frac{6}{100}$, or $\frac{3}{50}$ **21.** $\frac{20}{72}$, or $\frac{5}{18}$ **23.** $\frac{20}{72}$, or $\frac{5}{18}$
33. $\frac{6}{10}$ or $\frac{3}{5}$, $\frac{8}{10}$, or $\frac{4}{5}$, $\frac{6}{8}$, or $\frac{3}{4}$

Lesson 12-6　　　　　　　　　pp. 662–663

EXERCISES 1. 6 **3.** 120 **5.** 360 **7.** 1,814,400
9. 3; CA, CT, AT **11.** 10; VA, VL, VU, VE, AL, AU,
AE, LU, LE, UE **15.** 45 **17.** 20 sandwiches
19. Combinations; the order of the shirts selected
does not matter. **21.** 720 **27.** 2 **31.** 20 **37.** $\frac{1}{25}$
39. 120 in.^{2}

Lesson 12-7　　　　　　　　　pp. 667–668

EXERCISES 3. 13.2% **5.** 77.9% **9.** $\frac{1}{2}$ **11.** $\frac{3}{8}$
21. 720 **23.** 20 **25.** $(x, y) \rightarrow (x + 7, y + 4)$

Lesson 12-8　　　　　　　　　pp. 671–672

EXERCISES 3. Not a good sample; it excludes
students not interested in basketball.
5. 2,240 pairs **7.** Not a good sample; it excludes
people who dislike that particular restaurant.
9a. The cold virus may be passed from student to
student in that class so that more of them have
colds than in the total school population.
9b. Answers may vary. Sample: Survey
students as they enter the school cafeteria.
17. $\frac{9}{26}$ **21.** 495 combinations
23. 506.25π in.^{2}; 1,590 in.^{2}

Lesson 12-9　　　　　　　　　pp. 676–677

EXERCISES 1. Answers may vary. Sample:
Simulate the problem by tossing a coin. Let
heads be a girl and tails be a boy. Toss the coin
100 times and organize the results into 20 groups
of five. Count the number of groups with exactly

---

three tails. Divide this number by 20 to get the
experimental probability. **5.** $67.50 **9.** $\frac{1}{10,000}$
15. 2,960 wrenches **17.** 4 **19.** 7

Chapter 12 Review　　　　　　pp. 679–681

EXERCISES 1. combination **2.** sample
3. theoretical probability **4.** permutation
5. range **6.** frequency table **7.** dependent events
8. random sample

9.
Number	Frequency
9	1
10	3
11	3
12	4
13	1

10.
Number	Frequency
45	1
46	3
47	2
48	3
49	2
50	1

11.
X
X　　X
X X X
X X X　　X
X X X X X
X X X X X X ; 5
1 2 3 4 5 6

12.
X
X　X
X X X
X X X
X X X
X X X X
X X X X X
X X X X X X ; 5
1 2 3 4 5 6

13.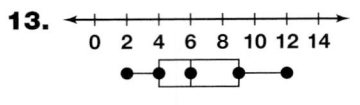
0 2 4 6 8 10 12 14

14.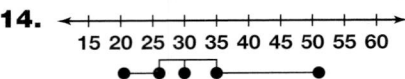
15 20 25 30 35 40 45 50 55 60

15. It increased gradually. **16.** Answers may
vary. Sample: Break the vertical axis and mark
a scale from 50 to 60 above the break.
17a. 15 types **b.** $\frac{4}{15}$ **18.** $\frac{2}{25}$ **19.** $\frac{1}{20}$
20. permutation, since order is important;
120 ways **21.** combination, since order does not
matter; 220 groups **22.** $\frac{9}{20}$ **23.** $\frac{1}{2}$ **24.** Answers
may vary. Sample: Simulate the problem by making
a spinner with 3 congruent sections. Make one
section red, to represent a correct answer. Spin 60
times and organize the results into 20 groups of 3.
Count the number of groups with exactly 2 red
spins. Divide this number by 20 to get the
experimental probability. **25.** Not a good sample;
it includes people not in the town's skating
population. **26.** Not a good sample; it includes
people not in the town's skating population.

Chapter 13

Lesson 13-1　　　　　　　　　pp. 691–692

EXERCISES 1. −1 **3.** −6 **7.** 20, 25, 30; start with
0 and add 5 repeatedly. **9.** 1, 4, 7; Start with −11

and add 3 repeatedly. **11.** 2; 48, 96, 192; start with 3 and multiply by 2 repeatedly. **13.** 2; 720, 1440, 2880; start with 45 and multiply by 2 repeatedly. **17.** geometric; 81, 243, 729 **21.** geometric; −81, 243, −729 **23.** arithmetic; $\frac{1}{2}$ **27.** geometric; 3 **29.** 256, 1,024, 4,096; start with 1 and multiply by 4 repeatedly. **33.** 125, 150, 175; start with 25 and add 25 repeatedly. **35.** arithmetic; $1\frac{5}{6}$, $2\frac{1}{6}$, $2\frac{1}{2}$ **39.** geometric; $-\frac{1}{80}$, $-\frac{1}{160}$, $-\frac{1}{320}$ **51.** Not a good sample; it excludes many groups, such as people with no interest in art. **53.** 31.4 in.

Lesson 13-2 pp. 696–697

EXERCISES

1.

x	$4(x)^2$	y	(x, y)
−2	$4(−2)^2$	16	(−2, 16)
−1	$4(−1)^2$	4	(−1, 4)
0	$4(0)^2$	0	(0, 0)
1	$4(1)^2$	4	(1, 4)
2	$4(2)^2$	16	(2, 16)

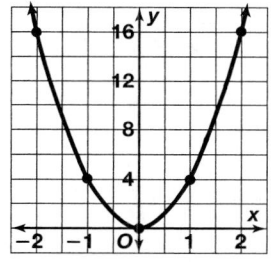

7.

x	$x^2 + 4$	y	(x, y)
−2	$(−2)^2 + 4$	8	(−2, 8)
−1	$(−1)^2 + 4$	5	(−1, 5)
0	$0^2 + 4$	4	(0, 4)
1	$1^2 + 4$	5	(1, 5)
2	$2^2 + 4$	8	(2, 8)

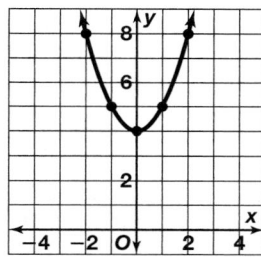

15. V shape

x	$|x| + 3$	y	(x, y)
−2	$|−2| + 3$	5	(−2, 5)
−1	$|−1| + 3$	4	(−1, 4)
0	$|0| + 3$	3	(0, 3)
1	$|1| + 3$	4	(1, 4)
2	$|2| + 3$	5	(2, 5)

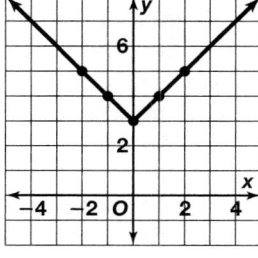

21. U shape

x	$x^2 − 8$	y	(x, y)
−2	$(−2)^2 − 8$	−4	(−2, −4)
−1	$(−1)^2 − 8$	−7	(−1, −7)
0	$(0)^2 − 8$	−8	(0, −8)
1	$(1)^2 − 8$	−7	(1, −7)
2	$(2)^2 − 8$	−4	(2, −4)

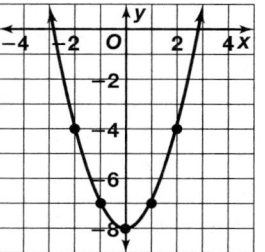

30. The graphs of the functions have the same shape, but $y = x^2 + 2$ is shifted up 2 from the origin and $y = x^2 − 3$ is shifted down 3 from the origin. **38.** $\frac{1}{2}$, $\frac{1}{4}$, $\frac{1}{8}$; start with 8 and multiply by $\frac{1}{2}$ repeatedly. **40.** 15, 18, 21; start with 3 and add 3 repeatedly.

Lesson 13-3 pp. 701–702

EXERCISES

1.

x	4^x	y	(x, y)
0	4^0	1	(0, 1)
1	4^1	4	(1, 4)
2	4^2	16	(2, 16)
3	4^3	64	(3, 64)
4	4^4	256	(4, 256)

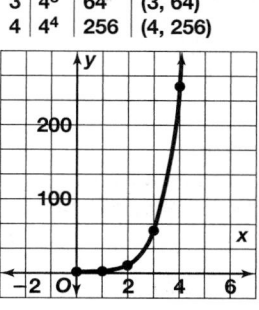

9.

x	$30(\frac{1}{3})^x$	y	(x, y)
0	$30(\frac{1}{3})^0$	30	(0, 30)
1	$30(\frac{1}{3})^1$	10	(1, 10)
2	$30(\frac{1}{3})^2$	$3\frac{1}{3}$	(2, $3\frac{1}{3}$)
3	$30(\frac{1}{3})^3$	$1\frac{1}{9}$	(3, $1\frac{1}{9}$)
4	$30(\frac{1}{3})^4$	$\frac{10}{27}$	(4, $\frac{10}{27}$)
5	$30(\frac{1}{3})^5$	$\frac{10}{81}$	(5, $\frac{10}{81}$)

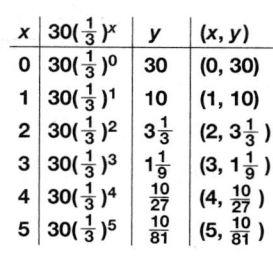

11. B **13.** 144; this is the value of the stock after 2 years.
15. Answers may vary. Sample: 3 yr 10 months
17.

x	$\frac{1}{5} \cdot 5^x$	y	(x, y)
0	$\frac{1}{5} \cdot 5^0$	$\frac{1}{5}$	(0, $\frac{1}{5}$)
1	$\frac{1}{5} \cdot 5^1$	1	(1, 1)
2	$\frac{1}{5} \cdot 5^2$	5	(2, 5)
3	$\frac{1}{5} \cdot 5^3$	25	(3, 25)
4	$\frac{1}{5} \cdot 5^4$	125	(4, 125)

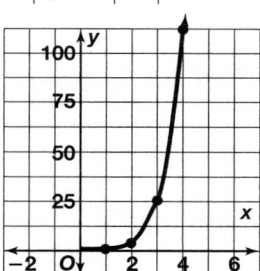

23. yes; $2^4 = 16$
25. no; $\left(\frac{1}{2}\right)^4 \neq 16$
35.

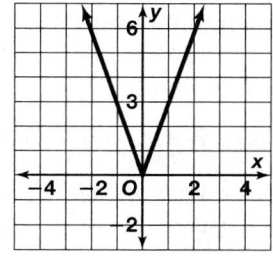

37. 12 choices
39. (−1, −1)

Lesson 13-4 pp. 706–707

EXERCISES 1. No; it is a sum. **3.** Yes; it is a product of the real number $\frac{1}{3}$ and the variable a. **9.** binomial **15.** monomial **19.** 32 **23.** 37 **29.** Yes; it is a real number. **31.** No; it is a sum. **33.** binomial **37.** binomial **43.** −4 **47.** 12
59.

x	$\frac{1}{3} \cdot 3^x$	y	(x, y)
1	$\frac{1}{3} \cdot 3^1$	1	(1, 1)
2	$\frac{1}{3} \cdot 3^2$	3	(2, 3)
3	$\frac{1}{3} \cdot 3^3$	9	(3, 9)
4	$\frac{1}{3} \cdot 3^4$	27	(4, 27)

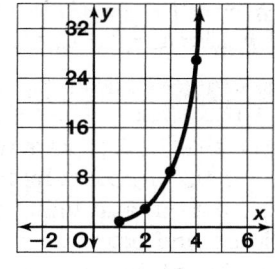

61. about 25.3 mi **63.** $2y + 6x + 4$

Lesson 13-5   pp. 712–714

EXERCISES 1. $(2x^2 + x + 2) + (x^2 + 4) =$
$3x^2 + x + 6$ **3.** $2x^2 + 4x + 7$ **5.** $-x + 5$
7. $2a + 9b$ **11.** $2x^3 + 5x^2 + x + 4$ **13.** $3x + 8$
17. $-2ab + 2$ **19.** $x^2 - 8x - 5$ **23.** $w^2 + 7w - 6$
29. $m^2 + 5m$ **33.** $5y - 2$ **35.** $4b - 1$ **37.** $2a + 2$
47. -15 **49.** 3 **51.** 5 cm^2 **53.** 7 mi

Lesson 13-6   pp. 717–718

EXERCISES 5. $3y^2 + 21y$ **13.** $(3x^2 - 135x) \text{ ft}^2$
15. $-15x^3 + 10x^2$ **19.** $a^4 + a^5 + 5a^3$
25. $4y(y^2 - 2y - 3)$ **31.** $5z(z - 4)$
35. $-14a^3 - 42a^2 + 56a$ **39.** $60x^3 + 24x^2$
45. $4x^2(x^3 - x^2 + 2)$ **51.** $2mn(m^2 - 3mn + 4)$
63. $3x^2 + 7x + 6$
65.

```
                x
        x       x
  x     x       x   x   x   x
  +---+---+---+---+---+---+---+--->
 1.7 1.8 1.9 2.0 2.1 2.2 2.3 2.4
```

67. $449

Lesson 13-7   pp. 721–722

EXERCISES 1. $x^2 + 3x + 2$ **5.** $x^2 + 9x + 20$
11. $c^2 + 16c + 63$ **17.** $x^2 + x - 6$
19. $2x^2 + 7x + 3$ **21.** $10c^2 + 26c + 12$
25. $x^2 + 10x + 16$ **29.** $6c^2 - 10c - 4$
41. $7a^2 + 35ab + 14ac$
43. $-32m^5 + 8m^3p + 16m^2p^4$
45. Combinations, since the order of the colors is
not important.

Lesson 13-8   pp. 726–727

EXERCISES 1a. 4:30 P.M. **b.** 180 mi **3.** 30 ft
7. Sandy 101 g, White Ears 108 g, Sport 115 g
9. 64 choices **19.** $x^2 - 2x - 3$ **21.** $x^2 + 6x + 9$
23. AP, AE, PE; 3 **25.** four more days

Chapter 13 Review   pp. 729–731

EXERCISES 1. d **2.** e **3.** a **4.** f **5.** b **6.** h **7.** g
8. i **9.** c **10.** 17, 21, 25; start with 1 and add 4
repeatedly. **11.** -3.75, -1.875, -0.9375; start
with -60 and multiply by 0.5 repeatedly. **12.** 128,
135, 142; start with 100 and add 7 repeatedly.
13. -20, -25, -30; start with 0 and add -5
repeatedly. **14.** -18, -29, -40; start with 26
and add -11 repeatedly. **15.** $62\frac{1}{2}$, $312\frac{1}{2}$, $1{,}562\frac{1}{2}$;
start with $\frac{1}{10}$ and multiply by 5 repeatedly.
16. arithmetic; 25, 29, 33 **17.** geometric; $-\frac{1}{2}$, $-\frac{1}{4}$,
$-\frac{1}{8}$ **18.** arithmetic; 7, 8, 9 **19.** arithmetic; 22, 33,
44 **20.** neither; 30, 3, 40 **21.** geometric; $\frac{2}{25}$, $\frac{4}{25}$, $\frac{8}{25}$
22. Sample: A club starts with 10 members and
adds 1 new member every week; 10, 11, 12, . . .; 1

23.

x	$\frac{1}{2}x^2$	y	(x, y)
-2	$\frac{1}{2} \cdot (-2)^2$	2	$(-2, 2)$
-1	$\frac{1}{2} \cdot (-1)^2$	$\frac{1}{2}$	$(-1, \frac{1}{2})$
0	$\frac{1}{2} \cdot (0)^2$	0	$(0, 0)$
1	$\frac{1}{2} \cdot (1)^2$	$\frac{1}{2}$	$(1, \frac{1}{2})$
2	$\frac{1}{2} \cdot (2)^2$	2	$(2, 2)$

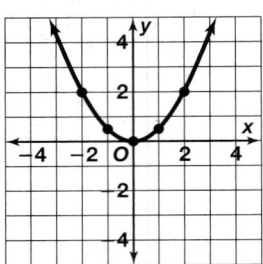

24.

x	$2|x|$	y	(x, y)
-2	$2|-2|$	4	$(-2, 4)$
-1	$2|-1|$	2	$(-1, 2)$
0	$2|0|$	0	$(0, 0)$
1	$2|1|$	2	$(1, 2)$
2	$2|2|$	4	$(2, 4)$

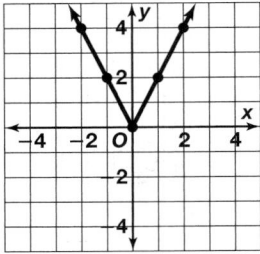

25.

x	$|x| + 1$	y	(x, y)
-2	$|-2| + 1$	3	$(-2, 3)$
-1	$|-1| + 1$	2	$(-1, 2)$
0	$|0| + 1$	1	$(0, 1)$
1	$|1| + 1$	2	$(1, 2)$
2	$|2| + 1$	3	$(2, 3)$

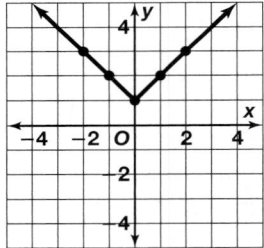

26.

x	$x^2 + 5$	y	(x, y)
-2	$(-2)^2 + 5$	9	$(-2, 9)$
-1	$(-1)^2 + 5$	6	$(-1, 6)$
0	$0^2 + 5$	5	$(0, 5)$
1	$1^2 + 5$	6	$(1, 6)$
2	$2^2 + 5$	9	$(2, 9)$

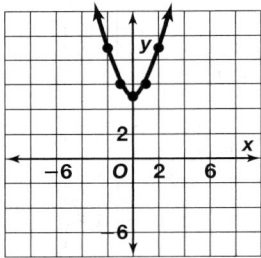

27.

x	$-|x|$	y	(x, y)
-2	$-|-2|$	-2	$(-2, -2)$
-1	$-|-1|$	-1	$(-1, -1)$
0	$-|0|$	0	$(0, 0)$
1	$-|1|$	-1	$(1, -1)$
2	$-|2|$	-2	$(2, -2)$

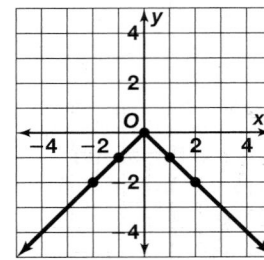

28.

x	$\frac{1}{2}|x|$	y	(x, y)
-2	$\frac{1}{2}|-2|$	1	$(-2, 1)$
-1	$\frac{1}{2}|-1|$	$\frac{1}{2}$	$(-1, \frac{1}{2})$
0	$\frac{1}{2}|0|$	0	$(0, 0)$
1	$\frac{1}{2}|1|$	$\frac{1}{2}$	$(1, \frac{1}{2})$
2	$\frac{1}{2}|2|$	1	$(2, 1)$

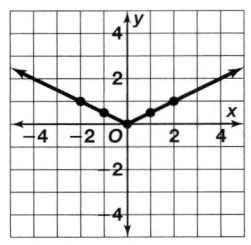

29.

x	$-x^2 - 3$	y	(x, y)
-2	$-(-2)^2 - 3$	-7	$(-2, -7)$
-1	$-(-1)^2 - 3$	-4	$(-1, -4)$
0	$-(0)^2 - 3$	-3	$(0, -3)$
1	$-(1)^2 - 3$	-4	$(1, -4)$
2	$-(2)^2 - 3$	-7	$(2, -7)$

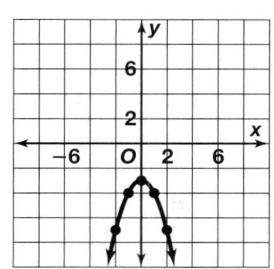

30.

x	$-x^2 + 4$	y	(x, y)
-2	$-(-2)^2 + 4$	0	$(-2, 0)$
-1	$-(-1)^2 + 4$	3	$(-1, 3)$
0	$-(0)^2 + 4$	4	$(0, 4)$
1	$-(1)^2 + 4$	3	$(1, 3)$
2	$-(2)^2 + 4$	0	$(2, 0)$

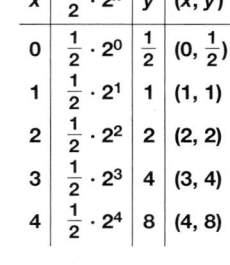

31.

x	$\left(\frac{1}{4}\right)^x$	y	(x, y)
0	$\left(\frac{1}{4}\right)^0$	1	$(0, 1)$
1	$\left(\frac{1}{4}\right)^1$	$\frac{1}{4}$	$\left(1, \frac{1}{4}\right)$
2	$\left(\frac{1}{4}\right)^2$	$\frac{1}{16}$	$\left(2, \frac{1}{16}\right)$
3	$\left(\frac{1}{4}\right)^3$	$\frac{1}{64}$	$\left(3, \frac{1}{64}\right)$
4	$\left(\frac{1}{4}\right)^4$	$\frac{1}{256}$	$\left(4, \frac{1}{256}\right)$

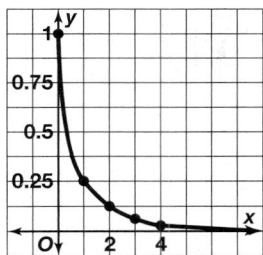

32.

x	$\frac{1}{2} \cdot 2^x$	y	(x, y)
0	$\frac{1}{2} \cdot 2^0$	$\frac{1}{2}$	$\left(0, \frac{1}{2}\right)$
1	$\frac{1}{2} \cdot 2^1$	1	$(1, 1)$
2	$\frac{1}{2} \cdot 2^2$	2	$(2, 2)$
3	$\frac{1}{2} \cdot 2^3$	4	$(3, 4)$
4	$\frac{1}{2} \cdot 2^4$	8	$(4, 8)$

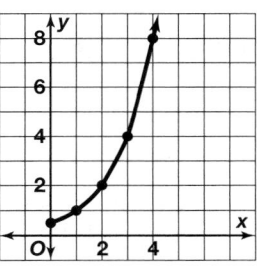

33.

x	3^x	y	(x, y)
0	3^0	1	$(0, 1)$
1	3^1	3	$(1, 3)$
2	3^2	9	$(2, 9)$
3	3^3	27	$(3, 27)$
4	3^4	81	$(4, 81)$

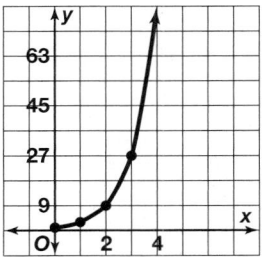

34.

x	$\left(\frac{1}{2}\right)^x$	y	(x, y)
0	$\left(\frac{1}{2}\right)^0$	1	$(0, 1)$
1	$\left(\frac{1}{2}\right)^1$	$\frac{1}{2}$	$\left(1, \frac{1}{2}\right)$
2	$\left(\frac{1}{2}\right)^2$	$\frac{1}{4}$	$\left(2, \frac{1}{4}\right)$
3	$\left(\frac{1}{2}\right)^3$	$\frac{1}{8}$	$\left(3, \frac{1}{8}\right)$
4	$\left(\frac{1}{2}\right)^4$	$\frac{1}{16}$	$\left(4, \frac{1}{16}\right)$

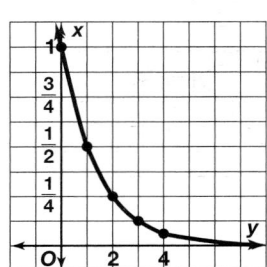

35. monomial **36.** binomial **37.** monomial
38. trinomial **39.** monomial **40.** monomial
41. binomial **42.** binomial **43.** binomial
44. trinomial **45.** 32 **46.** 7 **47.** 6 **48.** -12 **49.** 9
50. $3a^2 + 2a + 8$ **51.** $4m^2 - 2m - 12$
52. $4x^2 - 2x + 2$ **53.** $4p - 7q - 2$
54. $3w^2 + 9w - 5$ **55.** $6x + 6y$ **56.** $2a^2 + 5a$
57. $12c^2 - 28c$ **58.** $-30y^2 - 18y$
59. $3x^3 - 3x^2 - 15x$ **60.** $x^3 + 7x^2$
61. $2x^4 - 6x^3 - 12x^2$ **62.** $x^2 + 7x + 12$
63. $x^2 - 4x - 5$ **64.** $x^2 - 6x + 8$ **65.** $x(x - 1)$
66. $9(p^2 + 3)$ **67.** $3x(x^2 - 3x + 2)$
68. $5(b^5 + 4b^3 - 6)$ **69.** $2x(4x^2 + x + 2)$
70. $4a(7a - b)$ **71.** 2,401 ft^2 **72.** Answers may
vary. Sample: A diagram gives a visual picture
of the problem. A table organizes possible
dimensions and their related areas. Looking
for a pattern leads to the answer.

Extra Practice

Chapter 1 p. 744

1. $x - 6$ **5.** $8p$ **9.** 9 **11.** 5 **13.** 42 **15.** 11
19. $=$ **21.** $>$ **23.** -7 **27.** -32 **31.** Start with -12,
and add 9 to the previous term. 33, 42, 51
33. Add the two previous terms. 21, 34, 55 **37.** 24
41. 9 **42–50.**

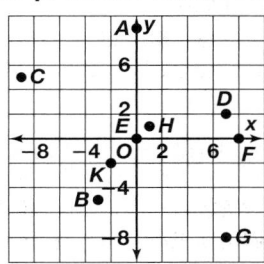

Chapter 2 p. 745

1. $99 + (-99) + 45 + (-46)$
Commutative Property of Addition
$0 + 45 + (-46)$
additive inverse
-1
5. $2 \cdot 50 \cdot 58$
Commutative Property of Multiplication
$100 \cdot 58$
Multiply from left to right.
5,800

7. 20 **13.** $-17y + 38$ **17.** $\frac{-3}{-1} = 3$; true **21.** -24
25. 24 **33.**

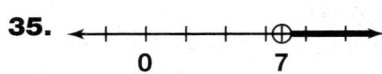

35.

39. $x > -13$ **43.** $c \leq -15$

Chapter 3   p. 746

1. about 13; rounding **5.** about 120; clustering
7. about 120 **11.** about 18 **13.** mean: 12.9;
median: 12; modes: 10 and 12; outlier: 19
15. mean: $27.30; median: $29; mode: $30; outlier:
$15 **17.** 130 yd **19.** 175 mi **25.** 63.6 **33.** 3
37. 0.25 **45.** 0.036

Chapter 4   p. 747

3. 1, 2, 4, 8, 16, 32, 64 **5.** 1, 2, 3, 4, 6, 9, 12, 18, 36
7. 64 **11.** 48 **13.** composite; 5^2 **15.** prime **19.** 10
21. $5x$ **25.** $\frac{7}{16}$ **31.** $\frac{x}{15}$

35–39.

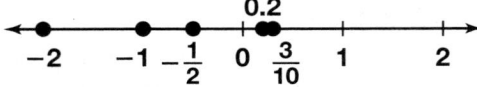

41. $-\frac{2}{5}$ **43.** $\frac{4}{25}$ **45.** $6y^5$ **49.** $3t^{15}$ **53.** 6.6×10^{16}

Chapter 5   p. 748

1. 30 **3.** $24xy$ **5.** > **7.** = **11.** $0.\overline{27}$ **13.** -0.7
15. $1\frac{3}{10}$ **19.** $\frac{7}{20}$ **23.** $-\frac{3}{8}$ **27.** $\frac{20 + 3t}{4t}$ **31.** -1
37. -2 **39.** 5 ft **41.** 64 oz **43.** $8\frac{1}{2}$ **47.** $1\frac{13}{24}$
51. $a^5b^5c^{15}$ **55.** $\frac{4c^2}{d^6}$

Chapter 6   p. 749

1. $\frac{1}{2}$ **3.** $\frac{1}{4}$ **5.** $58.\overline{6}$ ft/s **7.** 82.5 gal/h **9.** 84 **13.** 26.7
17. 34.4 mi **19.** 18.8 mi **21.** 0; 0 to 6 **23.** $\frac{2}{6}$, or $\frac{1}{3}$;
1 to 2 **25.** $\frac{2}{1}$; 2 **27.** $\frac{7}{400}$; 0.0175 **29.** 15% **31.** 41.7%
35. 40 **37.** 36.3 **39.** 150% increase
41. 12.5% decrease **43.** $45

Chapter 7   p. 750

9. $-5\frac{1}{3}$ **17.** -5
23. $a \geq -3$

27. $t \leq 50$

31. $p = s - c$ **33.** $a = c + b$
37. $4,500 **41.** $1,480.24

Chapter 8   p. 751

1. No; there are two range values for the domain
value 4. **3.** Yes; there is one range value for each
domain value. **5.** $(-3, -11)$, $(0, -2)$, $(2, 4)$
9. $(-3, -4)$, $(0, -4)$, $(2, -4)$ **13.** 5, -4 **17.** $\frac{3}{5}$, -1

21.

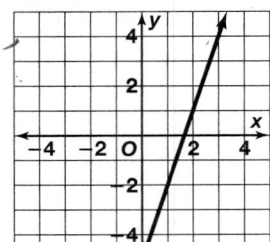

23.

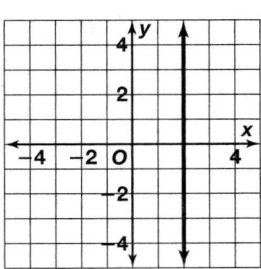

27. $y = 3x - 1$ **29.** $y = 5x + y$ **31.** $y = 2x + 3$
34. Positive correlation; as you move to the right,
most scores increase.
35. $(-3, -4)$ **37.**

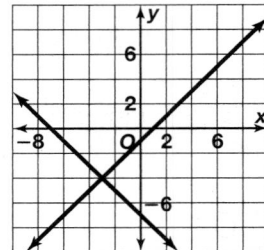
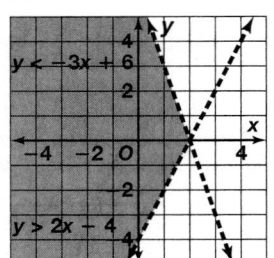

Chapter 9   p. 752

1. $\overleftrightarrow{AB}$, $\overleftrightarrow{AC}$, $\overleftrightarrow{BC}$ **3.** $\overline{RS}$, $\overline{MQ}$, $\overline{MN}$, $\overline{UR}$ **5.** $\overline{UT}$, $\overline{NP}$,
$\overline{ST}$ **7.** $m\angle 7 = 67°$; $m\angle 4 = 67°$; $m\angle 1 = 67°$;
$m\angle 8 = 113°$; $m\angle 6 = 113°$; $m\angle 2 = 113°$;
$m\angle 3 = 113°$ **9.** rectangle **11.** A **13.** 78.5 ft
15. 314 m
17.

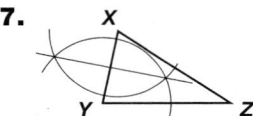

19.

Chapter 10   p. 753

3. 75 m^2 **5.** 20 ft^2 **7.** 676π m^2, 2,122.6 m^2
9. 75π yd^2, 235.5 yd^2 **13.** 803.8 cm^2, 2,143.6 cm^3
17. 35.2 yd^2, 12.6 yd^3

Chapter 11   p. 754

3. -6 **5.** 5 **7.** 3 **9.** 10 **11.** rational
15. irrational **17.** 7.5 yd **19.** 5.7 **21.** 10.4
23. $\left(\frac{1}{2}, -\frac{3}{2}\right)$ **25.** $x = 32\sqrt{2}$ cm   45.3 cm,
$y = 32$ cm **27.** $x = 15$ mi, $y = 15\sqrt{2}$ mi   21.2 mi
29. 11.4301 **33.** 0.4226

Chapter 12   p. 755

1. range = 3

Number	Frequency
20	2
21	5
22	2
23	1

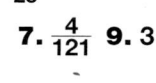

3.
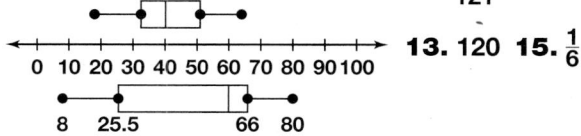

7. $\frac{4}{121}$ **9.** 3

13. 120   **15.** $\frac{1}{6}$

Chapter 13   p. 756

1. 20, 0, −20; start with 100 and add −20 repeatedly **5.** −3,125, 15,625, −78,125; start with −5 and multiply by −5 repeatedly.

9. 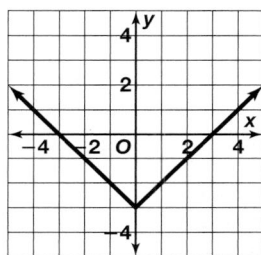   **13.**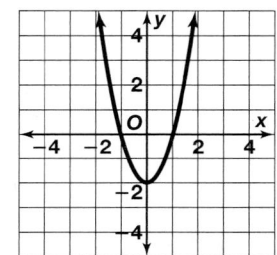

15.

x	y
0	1
1	4
2	16
3	64
4	256

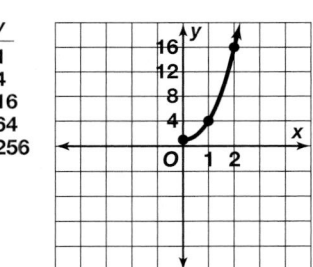

17.

x	y
0	10
1	5
2	2.5
3	1.25
4	0.625

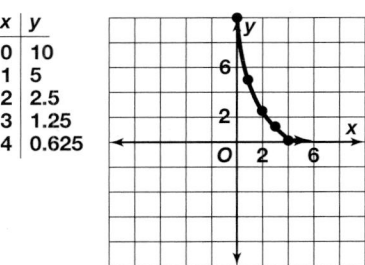

19. trinomial **23.** monomial **27.** $7y - 2$
31. $6x^2 + 5x - 12$ **35.** $10x^3 + 12x$
39. $2y^2 + 16y + 24$ **43.** $2(a^2b - 2a + 3b)$
45. $w(5w^2 + 6w - 3)$

Skills Handbook

PAGE 757 1. > **3.** > **11.** 3,347; 3,474; 3,734; 3,747; 3,774 **13.** 30,256,403; 30,265,403; 32,056,403; 302,056,403

PAGE 758 3. 670 **5.** 7,030 **15.** 82,000 **17.** 35,000 **23.** 71,230,000 **25.** 400,000

PAGE 759 17. 9,214 **19.** 492

PAGE 760 37. 26 R 8 **39.** 7 R 32

PAGE 761 1. 9 hundred-thousandths **3.** 5 hundredths **9.** 0.000008 **11.** 0.012 **15.** eleven hundred-thousandths **17.** twelve thousandths

PAGE 762 1. < **3.** > **13.** 0.23, 0.231, 2.31, 3.21, 23.1 **15.** 0.002, 0.02, 0.22, 0.222, 2.22

PAGE 763 1. 105,000 **5.** 4,312,000 **7.** 3 **9.** 101 **11.** 82.0 **13.** 20.4 **17.** 96.40 **19.** 4.23 **33.** 2.58 **35.** 19

PAGE 764 41. 12.403 **43.** 747.1109

PAGE 765 9. 1.1424 **11.** 2.07828

PAGE 766 31. 0.01812 **33.** 0.007

PAGE 767 23. 2.551 **25.** 3.9

PAGE 768 15. 0.47 **17.** 0.236

PAGE 769 15. 16 **17.** 44

PAGE 770 1. 0.046 **3.** 0.075

PAGE 771 9. 3 **11.** 16 **17.** $\frac{5}{6}$ **19.** $\frac{3}{4}$

PAGE 772 9. $3\frac{2}{5}$ **11.** $4\frac{1}{4}$ **39.** $\frac{24}{7}$ **41.** $\frac{31}{10}$

PAGE 773 7. $\frac{3}{8}$ **9.** $\frac{3}{5}$

PAGE 774 13. $7\frac{1}{2}$ **15.** $43\frac{3}{4}$ **19.** $\frac{7}{8}$ **21.** $1\frac{3}{8}$

PAGE 775 5. 3 **7.** 12 **11.** < **15.** >

Index

F

Face, of a space figure, 539–543, 545–550, 551–555, 556–559, 563
Factor, 223
  binomial, of a trinomial, 723
  common, 187, 269
  divisibility tests and, 178–179
  fractions, exponents, and, 177–229
  greatest common, 187–193, 224
  of polynomials, 716
  prime factorization, 187–190, 224
  properties of, 179
Factor tree, 187
Fahrenheit–Celsius formula, 379
Fair game, 668
Fibonacci sequence, 692
Flip, 503–506. *See also* Reflection.
FOIL method for multiplying binomials, 728
Formulas
  area of figures, 522, 780
  area of circle, 532, 780
  batting average, 379
  brick laying, 380
  circumference of circle, 487–489, 780
  compound interest, 384, 386, 391–392
  consecutive integers, 353, 355–356
  defined, 143, 170
  distance, 592
  experimental probability, 665–668, 681, 682
  lateral area, 545–555
  in math and science, 143
  midpoint, 594
  parallelogram, area of, 523, 571, 780
  perimeter, 144–146, 170, 780
  perimeter of rectangle, 144
  polygon, sum of angles of, 475
  probability, 305–306, 308–309
    of dependent events, 656–658
    of independent events, 654–658
  Pythagorean theorem, 780
  pyramid, surface area of, 780
  radio signal, 203
  rate, time, distance, 376, 379
  reading, 551
  rectangle, area of, 522–525, 780
  rectangular prism, 780
  simple interest, 382–383, 391–392
  for solving problems, 143–146, 379
  solving, for variables, 378–381, 391, 392
  in spreadsheets, 147
  square, area of, 275, 522–525, 780
  substituting into, 143–144
  sum of angles of polygon, 475
  surface area
    of cone, 553–555, 560, 780
    of cube, 780
    of cylinder, 547–550, 780
    of prism, 545–546, 548–549, 551
    of pyramid, 552–553, 555, 780
    of rectangular prism, 780
    of sphere, 553–555, 560, 780
    of triangular prism, 551

  temperature, 143–145, 379
  theoretical probability, 650–652, 680
  trapezoid, area of, 529–530, 571, 780
  triangle, area of, 527–528, 530, 571, 780
  triangle angle sum, 780
  trigonometric ratios, 780
  transforming, 378–381, 391, 392
  volume
    of cone, 566, 568–569, 780
    of cube, 277, 557–560
    of cylinder, 558–560, 780
    of prism, 557–560, 780
    of pyramid, 567, 568–569, 780
    of square pyramid, 567–568
    of sphere, 567–569, 780
Four-step plan. *See* Problem-Solving Strategies; Tools for Problem Solving.
Fraction bar, 9, 46, 202, 212, 213
Fractions
  adding, 243–247, 252, 256, 280, 282, 773
  commonly used, 241, 242
  comparing, 233–234
  decimals and, 238–242
  denominator of. *See* Denominator.
  dividing, 774
  equivalent, 192–195, 201, 224
  evaluating, with variables, 202–203
  improper, 242, 772
  least common denominator, 234–235, 279
  least common multiple (LCM), 232–233
  like denominators, 244
  mental math and, 235
  mixed numbers and, estimating with, 242
  multiplying, 248–252, 774
  multi-step equations with, 357–358
  number line and, 233–234
  numerators of. *See* Numerator.
  operations with, 231–235
  ordering, 202, 232–236, 238
  prime factorization, 232–233
  reciprocal of, 250, 280
  rounding in estimation, 242
  simplifying, 192–195, 224
  solving equations
    by adding fractions, 265–268, 282, 283
    by inverse operations, 264–267
    by multiplying fractions, 268–272, 281, 282
    by subtracting fractions, 264–267, 281, 282
  subtracting, 243–247, 252, 256, 280, 282, 773
  writing
    decimals as fractions, 239, 241, 261, 267, 270
    fractions as decimals, 237–241, 280, 282, 303, 309
    fractions as percents, 311–314, 339
    fractions in simplest form, 192–193, 224

    fractions as mixed numbers, 239–241
    percents as fractions, 310–314, 339
    ratios as fractions, 288–290, 339
  See also Decimals; Improper fractions; Percents.
Frequency tables, 630–631, 679
Front-end estimate, 128–131, 167, 214
Function
  absolute value, 695, 730
  cubing, 696
  defined, 400, 449
  domain of, 400, 449
  identifying, 400–401
  graphing, 401–404, 694–703
  linear, 411–422, 450
  nonlinear, 694–697, 703, 730
  quadratic, 694, 697, 730
  range of, 400, 449
  writing rules for, 418–422, 450
Function notation, 418
Function rule, 418
  input-output, 34, 418
  using, 418–422
  writing
    from graph or table, 419–421, 450
    from words, 418, 420–422

G

GCF. *See* Greatest common factor.
Geometric formulas, table of, 780. *See also* Formulas.
Geometric constructions, 491–496, 515
Geometric sequence, 689–690, 729
Geometry
  acute angle, 464
  angle. *See* Angle.
  area. *See* Area.
  base. *See* Base.
  basic figures, 458
  circle. *See* Circle.
  circle graph, 487–488
  circumference, 486–487, 489–490, 515, 520, 692, 780
  classifying polygons in, 470–474, 514
  complementary angles, 465, 468
  cone. *See* Cone.
  congruence, 465, 468, 480–481
  congruent triangles, 465–468, 481
  constructing congruent angles, 492
  constructing congruent segments, 491
  constructing congruent triangles, 481
  constructions, 491, 496
  coordinate plane. *See* Coordinate plane.
  coordinates. *See* Coordinates.
  corresponding angles, 299, 466–468, 514
  cosine, 608–612, 623
  cube, 277, 542, 545–550, 557–560, 780
  cylinder. *See* Cylinder.
  diagonal, 475–477
  diameter, 486

dilation, 304, 500
drawing diagrams, 476–479, 512
drawing lines, 460
early, 625
endpoint, 491–495, 506
equilateral triangle, 470–474
exercises that use, 42, 53, 98, 166, 185,
    199, 200, 207, 236, 249, 258, 261, 275,
    276, 277, 297, 309, 336, 356, 361, 364,
    404, 420, 438, 439, 478, 502, 583, 588,
    595, 596, 606, 612, 647, 668, 672, 676,
    677, 696, 706, 707, 713, 714, 718, 721,
    726, 727
face. *See* Face, of a space figure.
flip. *See* Reflection.
formulas. *See* Formulas.
geometric figures, naming, 459
geometric patterns, 467, 482
geometric sequence, 689, 729
height. *See* Height.
hexagon, 472, 606
hypotenuse, 584, 603, 622
intersecting, parallel, and skew lines,
    459–460
isosceles triangle, 470
line of symmetry, 503, 505–506
line. *See* line.
measuring angles, 475
net. *See* Net.
obtuse angle, 464, 492, 516
octagon, 472, 475
ordered pair, 50, 59
origin, 50, 507
pairs of angles, 465–469
parallel lines, 459–460
parallelogram. *See* Parallelogram.
pentagon, 472
perimeter. *See* Perimeter.
perpendicular bisector, 492–496, 515
perpendicular lines, 492
pi (π), 486
plane, 458
point, 458, 513
prism. *See* Prism.
pyramid. *See* Pyramid.
Pythagorean theorem, 584–589, 622, 625
quadrilateral, 471–472
quadrant, 50–54, 59, 60
radius. *See* Radius.
ray, 458, 464, 513
rectangle. *See* Rectangle.
reflection. *See* Reflection.
regular polygon, 472, 475–479
rhombus, 471
right angle, 464
right triangle. *See* Right triangle.
rotation, 507–510
scalene triangle, 470, 473
segment, 458, 470, 491, 513
similar figures. *See* Similar figures.
similarity. *See* Similarity.
sine, 608–612, 623
skew line, 459–460
slant height, 552
slide. *See* Translation.
software, 304, 496
solid. *See* Space figure.
space figure. *See* Space figure.

sphere, 539, 553–554, 567, 780
square. *See* Square.
supplementary angles, 465
surface area. *See* Surface area.
symbols. *See* Symbols.
tangent, 490
tessellation, 511
transformation. *See* Transformation.
translation, 497–500, 515
transversal, 466–469, 514
trapezoid, 471, 528–529, 571
three-dimensional figure. *See* Space
    figure.
triangle. *See* Triangle.
trigonometric ratios, 608–612, 613, 623,
    779, 780
turn. *See* Rotation.
vertex. *See* Vertex.
vertical angle, 465, 514
volume. *See* Volume.

Glossary, 784–827

Graph
bar, 642, 644, 648
box-and-whisker plot, 635–637, 680
break symbols in, 642
circle, 487–488, 501
choosing appropriate, 642–647
critical reading of, 36, 642–647
data and, 100–101, 630–647
describing, by writing inequalities, 103
finding slope from, 411–416
function rules from, 419
histogram, 634
line, 406–409, 417, 642–647
line plot, 630–635
misleading, 642–647
multiple line, 100
persuading with, 642–647
reading, 429, 698
relating to events, 398–399
scale for, 642–647
scatter plot, 423–429
shapes of, 411–416
sketching, 399
solutions to equations with two
    variables on, 406–409
Solve by Graphing problem-solving
    strategy, 430–434
solving problems with, 695
stem-and-leaf plot, 640–641
step, 398–399
writing rules from, 419

Graphing
absolute value, 695–697, 730
absolute value functions, 695, 697, 730
compound inequalities, 377
coordinates. *See* Coordinate plane;
    Coordinates.
data, 694–698, 100–101
dilations, 304
equations in slope-intercept form,
    413–415
equations with two variables, 406–407
exponential decay, 700–702, 730
exponential growth, 699–702, 730
functions, 401–402
horizontal lines, 412

inequalities, 102, 447
integers on number line, 17–21
linear equations, 406–409, 413
linear inequalities, 441–443
lines, 417
nonlinear functions, 694–697, 730
on number line, 19
ordered pairs, 55–59
points, 51–54
in quadrants, 50–54, 58
quadratic functions, 694
rational numbers, 202
reflections, 503–506
relations, 401–402
rotations, 507–508
solving problems by, 430–433
systems of linear equations, 435–436
systems of linear inequalities, 443
translations, 497–501
vertical line test, 402
writing rules from, 419–421
See also Linear functions.

Graphing calculator
degree mode, 613
evaluating expressions with, 209
evaluating permutations, 660
generating random numbers, 673
Graph feature of, 634
hints, 609, 661
histograms, 634
graphing inequalities, 447
Math PRB menu, 661
mean and median, finding, 142
graphing nonlinear functions, 703
one-variable equations, solving, 372
ordered pairs, 55
right triangles, finding angles of, 613
sequences, displaying, 693
graphing equations in slope-intercept
    form, 417
solution of a system of linear
    equations, 436
Stat feature of, 634
Table function, 333, 372, 417
table that displays repeated
    operations, 333
trigonometry ratio on, 609
Zoom feature of, 417, 447, 634
See also Calculator.

Greatest common factor (GCF), 187–188,
    224, 226, 228, 716–717

Greatest possible error, 258

Gridded Response exercises, 56, 90, 121,
    227, 257, 319, 343, 361, 416, 453, 490,
    569, 575, 596, 668, 683, 702, 735

Group Activity, working on, 23, 44, 71, 84,
    110, 126, 127, 186, 215, 242, 243, 248,
    305, 325, 352, 367, 398, 411, 423, 480,
    486, 522, 532, 584, 608, 630, 649, 654,
    688, 694

Grouping symbols, 9, 13, 46

H

Height
of cone, 553
of cylinder, 545, 547

Index

Acknowledgments

Staff Credits

The people who made up the Pre-Algebra team—representing editorial, editorial services, education technology, design services, market research, marketing, marketing services, project office, production services, and publishing processes—are listed below. Bold type denotes the core team members.

Leora Adler, Carolyn Artin, Peter Brooks, Judith D. Buice, Justin Collins, Sheila DeFazio, Marian DeLollis, **Emily Ellen,** Jayne Holman, Karen Holtzman, Kate House, Lisa LaVallee, **James Lonergan,** Cheryl Mahan, Constance McCarty, Eve Melnechuk, Terri Mitchell, Janet Morris, Cindy Noftle, Michael Oster, Rashid Ross, Dennis Slattery, Lisa Smith-Ruvalcaba, Nancy Smith, Deborah Sommer, Mark Tricca, **Joe Will,** Mathew Wilson, Helen Young

Cover Design
Brainworx Studio

Cover Image
Peacock, Charles Philip/Corbis; Ferris wheel, PhotoDisc, Inc./Getty Images, Inc.

Technical Illustration
Nesbitt Graphics, Inc.

Illustration
Suzanne Biron: 42, 256, 482, 738t, 739t, 740t, 741t, 742t, 743t, 743b; photocompositing—6, 51, 128, 162, 258, 260, 460, 464, 467, 473, 480, 481, 483, 498, 503, 508t
DLF Group: 613
Ortelius Design, Inc.: 31, 53, 145, 158, 218, 241, 244, 249, 300b, 349, 379, 529, 598t
Pat Packer-Williams: 300b, 738b, 739b, 740b, 741b, 742b, 743m; photocompositing—87, 289, 300b, 411, 426, 635, 642, 643
Wendy Simpson: photocompositing—300b, 411, 508b, 635
J/B Woolsey Associates: 33, 36, 46, 51, 68, 72, 75, 92, 129, 130, 137, 138, 148, 199, 245, 247, 248, 253, 261, 300t, 312, 317, 321, 326, 355, 375, 421, 462, 469, 472, 488, 498, 511, 532, 534, 535, 568, 586, 588, 598b, 600, 601, 610, 614, 616, 617, 624, 640, 642, 644, 645, 646, 667, 715

Photo Research
Sharon Donahue

Photography
Picture Research: Toni Michaels
Front Matter: Page v, ©Royal Tyrrell Museum of Palaeontology/Alberta Community Development; **vi,** Jose L./Palaez; **vii,** Stone/Doug Armand; **viii,** Russell C. Hansen/Peter Arnold, Inc.; **ix,** Stone/Jason Hawkes; **x,** Stone/Renee Lynn; **xi,** Jose Carillo/PhotoEdit; **xii,** Joe Sohm/The Image Works; **xiii,** Alfred Pasteka/Science Photo Library/Photo Researchers; **xiv,** Sara Krulwich/NYT Pictures; **xv,** Stone/Hideo Kurihara; **xvi,** Marilyn Kazmers/Peter Arnold, Inc.; **xvii,** Bob Burch/Bruce Coleman; **xxviii, xix, xx, xxi,** Richard Haynes.

Chapter One: Pages 2–3, Stephen Frink/Index Stock Imagery Inc.; **5,** ©Royal Tyrrell Museum of Palaeontology/Alberta Community Development; **6,** PhotoDisc, Inc.; **10 tl,** Minnesota Dept. of Natural Resources; **10 bl,** Richard Haynes; **10 mr,** Richard Haynes; **15,** Russ Lappa; **16,** Stone/Stuart Westmorland; **26,** Albuquerque Seismological Lab, USGS; **29,** Patrick Somelet/DIAF/The Stock Market; **31,** ©Sowers/Penn State University; **33,** Index Stock Imagery; 40, Michael Simpson/FPG International; **42 t,** PhotoDisc, Inc.; **42 b,** Russ Lappa; **44,** OAR/National Undersea Research Program (NURP); **51,** Tom Van Sant/The Stock Market; **62 bl,** Dorling Kindersley/Charlestown Shipwreck Heritage Centre; **62 tr,** Corbis Digital Stock; **62 br,** EyeWire/Getty Images, Inc.; **63 tl,** AP/Wide World Photos; **63 r,** Stephen Frink/Getty Images, Inc.

Chapter Two: Pages 64–65, Mark Richards/PhotoEdit; **68,** Russ Lappa; **70,** Mark Kelley/Stock Boston; **72,** Tony Freeman/PhotoEdit; **81,** Stone/Chris Simpson; **84 all,** Ken O'Donoghue; **86 both,** Anthony Neste; **87,** David R. Frazier Photolibrary; **96,** Superstock; **99,** Jose L./Palaez; **103 l,** D. & J. Heaton/Stock Boston; **103 m,** Superstock; **103 r,** Spencer Grant/PhotoEdit; **107,** Russ Lappa; **111,** Andrew Yates/Image Bank; **112 both,** Richard Haynes; **122 t,** Dennis Galante/Getty Images, Inc.; **122 bl,** Arthur Tilley/Getty Images, Inc.; **122 m,** Davies & Starr/Getty Images, Inc.; **123 tl,** www.Merlin-Net.com; **123,** Doug Menuez/Getty Images, Inc.

Chapter Three: Pages 124–125, Alan Goldsmith/Corbis; **128,** Russ Lappa; **129 both,** Richard Haynes; **132,** Russ Lappa; **133,** G. Cigolini/Image Bank; **143,** Alvin Staffan/Photo Researchers; **148,** Corel Corp.; **150,** Kevin Schafer/Peter Arnold, Inc.; **151,** Dilbert reprinted by permission of United Features Syndicate, Inc.; **153,** Corbis/Bettmann; **158,** Stone/Ed Simpson; **160,** Stone/Doug Armand; **162 both,** Russ Lappa; **164,** Stone/I. Burgum/P. Boorman; **167,** Bob Daemmrich/Stock Boston; **174 t,** Smithsonian Institution/National Numismatic Collection/Douglas Mudd; **174 ml,** Equity Management, Inc.; **174 l,** Stamp from the private collection of Professor C.M. Lang, photography by Gary J. Shulfer, University of Wisconsin, Stevens Point; **174 mr,** U.S. Postal Service; **174 b,** Eric Meola/Getty Images, Inc.; **175 tl,** Getty Images, Inc.-Hulton Archive Photos; **175 mr,** Phil Banko/Getty Images, Inc.

Chapter Four: Pages 176–177, John Mitchell/Photo Researchers, Inc.; **179,** Russ Lappa; **183 all,** ©Bruce Iverson; **186,** Russ Lappa; **188 both,** Richard Haynes; **193,** Bob Daemmrich/Stock Boston; **197,** Russ Lappa; **202,** AP/Dusan Vranic/Wide World Photos; **208,** Peggy Yoram Kahana/Peter Arnold, Inc.; **212,** Russell C. Hansen/Peter Arnold, Inc.; **213,** Mark Downey/Liaison Agency; **216,** Tim Barnwell/Stock Boston; **218,** K & G Photo/FPG International; **228 t,** Breck P Kent/Animals Animals/Earth Scenes; **228 b,** Colin Keates/Dorling Kindersley; **229 br,** Gary C. Will/Visuals Unlimited.

Chapter Five: Pages 230–231, Gary Noland/Seeley Swan/Pathfinder; **234,** Monkmeyer/Grant Pix; **237 both,** Ken Karp; **244,** Mark Gibson/Corbis; **245 both,** Richard Haynes; **249,** Alan Schen; **250,** Russ Lappa; **257,** Photri/The Stock Market; **258,** Russ Lappa; **259,** Stone/Jason Hawkes; **260 all,** Russ Lappa; **266,** Jim Corwim/Photo Researchers; **270,** Daniel Lyons/Bruce Coleman; **275,** Dirk Weisheit/DDB Stock Photo; **284 t,** ROBERT KIRKHAM/Buffalo News; **284 b,** New England

Quilt Museum. Gift of The Brinney Family, 1995.20. Photo by Greg Heins.; **285 br,** Pilgrim/Roy Quilt Collection Warner, NH.

Chapter Six: Pages 286–287, Michael Paras/Image State; **289,** Russ Lappa; **291,** Stone/Kindra Clineff; **295,** NASA; **297,** REAL LIFE ADVENTURES ©1999 GarLanco. Reprinted with permission of Universal Press Syndicate. All rights reserved.; **302,** Richard Haynes; **304, 305,** Russ Lappa; **307 all,** The United States Mint; **311,** Stone/Renee Lynn; **313,** Jay Syverson/Stock Boston; **317,** Cincinnati Zoo; **330 both,** Richard Haynes; **334,** Joseph Sohm/Stock Boston; **336,** Tek Image/Science Photo Library/Photo Researchers; **337,** Spencer Grant/Stock Boston; **344 tr,** Rafael Macia/Photo Researchers, Inc.; **344 b,** 1997 ChromoSohm/Sohm; **345 tr,** Charles Thatcher/Getty Images, Inc.; **345 m,** Bruno Joachim/Index Stock Imagery/PictureQuest.

Chapter Seven: Pages 346–347, Marc Romanelli/Getty Images, Inc.; **349,** Stone/Mark Lewis; **359 both,** Richard Haynes; **360,** Tim Barnell/Stock Boston; **362,** The Granger Collection, New York; **368,** James Frank/Stock Connection/PNI; **371,** Michael Heron/The Stock Market; **374,** Jose Carrillo/PhotoEdit; **379,** Stone/David Schultz; **394 tl,** Russ Lappa; **394 tl,** Dieceland Technologies Corp; **394 tr,** Bob Mitchell/Corbis; **394 br,** Dieceland Technologies Corp; **395 bl,** The Boston Globe via www.Merlin-Net.com; **395 br,** The Boston Globe via www.Merlin-Net.com.

Chapter Eight: Pages 396–397, Dana White/PhotoEdit; **401,** David Young Wolff; **402,** Corel Corp.; **405,** Lester Lefkowitz/The Stock Market; **411,** Stone/Jess Stock; **415 t,** Bob Daemmrich/The Image Works; **415 b,** Donald Dietz/Stock Boston; **416,** Stone/Don Smetzer; **426,** Russ Lappa; **430,** Erwin & Peggy Bauer/Bruce Coleman Inc.; **437 both,** Richard Haynes; **442,** Joe Sohm/The Image Works; **454 t,** Haruyoshi Yamaguchi/Corbis; **454–455 b,** Raoul Minsart/Corbis; **455 tl,** Yoshida-Fujifotos/The Image Works; **455 tr,** Lester Lefkowitz/Getty Images, Inc.

Chapter Nine: Pages 456–457, Jim Corwin/Stock Boston; **458,** Photo Researchers; **460,** James Marshall/The Stock Market; **463,** AP/Paul Warner/Wide World Photos; **464,** Jon Chomitz; **467 r,** Courtesy of J.C. Guillois/Santa Fe Stained Glass; **467 mr,** Richard Haynes; **467 br,** Richard Haynes; **472,** Peter Gridley/FPG International; **473,** Gianalberto Cigolini/Image Bank; **476,** Alfred Pasteka/Science Photo Library/Photo Researchers; **480,** Georg Gerster/Photo Researchers; **481,** John Heiney/Sportschrome; **483,** R. Wahhlstrom/Image Bank; **486, 491,** Russ Lappa; **492,** Jon Chomitz; **498, 503 tl,** Russ Lappa; **503 bl,** Patti Murray/Animals Animals; **503 tr,** Russ Lappa; **503 br,** C. Zeiss/Bruce Coleman; **508 t,** Russ Lappa; **508 b,** Danilo G. Donadoni/Bruce Coleman; **509 tl,** Steve Solum/Bruce Coleman; **509 tr,**

Adam Peiperl/The Stock Market; **509 bl,** Larry West/Bruce Coleman; **509 br,** John Gerlach/Tom Stack & Associates; **518 tr,** C. Kropp, Publ. Milwaukee No 331; **518–519 b,** Ray Juno/Corbis; **518 l,** B.W. Kilburn/Corbis; **519 tr,** Kyodo News International, Inc.

Chapter Ten: Pages 520–521, Barth Falkenberg/Stock Boston; **522,** Leslye Borden/PhotoEdit; **526,** Ken Chernus/FPG/PNI; **528,** Pascal Quittemelle/Stock Boston; **529,** Corbis-Bettmann; **533,** Alan Carey/Photo Researchers, Inc.; **540,** Ellis Herwig/Stock Boston; **542 all, 544, 547,** Russ Lappa; **554 tl,** Russ Lappa; **554 ml,** J. Sapinsky/The Stock Market; **554 bl,** Richard Haynes; **554 mr,** Richard Haynes; **556,** Sara Krulwich/NYT Pictures; **558, 560,** Russ Lappa; **562,** Stone/Steven Peters; **567,** Jeff Foott/Bruce Coleman; **576 l,** Jim Cummins/Getty Images, Inc.; **576–577 b,** Eyewire/Getty Images, Inc.; **577 tl,** Bill Sikes AP Wide World Photo; **577 tm,** Steve Lipofsky/Index Stock Imagery; **577 tr,** Jamie Squire/Getty Images News & Sport.

Chapter Eleven: Pages 578–579, Steve Casimiro/Getty Images, Inc.; **581,** Alese/Mort PECHTER/The Stock Market; **582,** Telegraph Colour Library/FPG International; **589,** Stone/Chad Slattery; **598,** Stone/Hideo Kurihara; **601,** H.P. Merten/The Stock Market; **603,** Landslides; **610 all,** Richard Haynes; **612,** Lance Nelson/The Stock Market; **626 b,** Ping Amranand/ Superstock; **627 tl,** Sydney McGinley, credit: Collection of the Artist; **627 tr,** ©ARS, NY Anthony Scibilia/Art Resource, NY.

Chapter Twelve: Pages 628–629, Zoran Milich/Getty Images, Inc.; **635,** Stone; **636 t,** Marilyn Kazmers/Peter Arnold, Inc.; **636 b,** David Madison/Bruce Coleman; **642 l,** Brent Jones/Stock Boston; **642 r,** Nik Wheeler/Corbis; **643,** Gerard Lacz/Peter Arnold, Inc.; **650,** Russ Lappa; **655,** John Lemker/Earth Scenes; **660,** Corel Corp.; **663,** Lynn Rogers/Peter Arnold, Inc.; **666 both,** Richard Haynes; **674,** Stone/Greg Pease; **684 tr,** AFP/Corbis; **684 b,** Al Bello/Getty Images News & Sport; **685 tm,** Andy Crawford/Dorling Kindersley; **685 tl,** AP/Wide World Photos/FIFA; **685 tr,** AFP/Corbis.

Chapter Thirteen: Pages 686–687, Tannen Maury/The Image Works; **689,** Marc Romanelli/Image Bank; **695,** Sydney Thompson/Animals Animals; **697,** Bob Daemmrich/Stock Boston; **699,** Andrew Henley/Auscape; **700,** Peter Berndt, M.D., P.A.; **705,** Bob Burch/Bruce Coleman; **720 both,** Richard Haynes; **724,** John Davenport/Liaison Agency; **736 tr,** SuperStock, Inc.; **736 bl,** Dorling Kindersley/Royal British Columbia Museum; **736 l,** James King-Holmes/Photo Researchers, Inc.; **737,** Malcolm Macgregor/Dorling Kindersley.